NTA UGC NET/JRF/SET

PAPER - 2

Human Resource Management, Labour Welfare, Industrial Relations, Labour & Social Welfare and Personnel Management

Author

Bharti Sharma *(Masters in Commerce)*

Bhavana Chopra *(MBA)*

ARIHANT PUBLICATION (INDIA) LIMITED

卐 **Administrative & Production Offices**

Regd. Office

'Ramchhaya' 4577/15, Agarwal Road, Darya Ganj, New Delhi -110002
Tele: 011- 47630600, 43518550

卐 **Head Office**

Kalindi, TP Nagar, Meerut (UP) - 250002
Tel: 0121-7156203, 7156204

卐 **Sales & Support Offices**

Agra, Ahmedabad, Bengaluru, Bareilly, Chennai, Delhi, Guwahati, Hyderabad, Jaipur, Jhansi, Kolkata, Lucknow, Nagpur & Pune.

卐 **PRICE** ₹ 635.00

卐 PO No. : TXT-59-T065729-06-25

Published by Arihant Publications (India) Ltd.

For further information about the books published by Arihant, log on to www.arihantbooks.com or e-mail at info@arihantbooks.com

CONTENTS

Human Resource Management (Paper-2)

Solved Paper, September 2024

General Instructions

1. There are total one hundred questions in this paper. Each question carries 2 marks.
2. All questions are compulsory.

1. Select the authorities covered under the provision of the Employees Provident Fund and Miscellaneous Provisions Act, 1952 from the followings.

A. Central Board
B. Board of Trustees
C. State Board
D. Advisory Committee
E. Executive Committee

Choose the correct answer from the options given below:

(1) A, C, D, E only (2) A, B, C, E only
(3) A, B, C, D only (4) B, C, D, E only

2. Match the List-I with List-II.

List-I (Principles of labour welfare)		List-II (Explanation)	
A.	Adequacy of wages	I.	Development of human personality
B.	Social responsibility of industry	II.	Coordinated effort will promote a healthy development of worker
C.	Re-personalisation	III.	Workers have a right to adequate wages
D.	Co-ordination	IV.	Industry has an obligation towards its employees to look after their welfare

Choose the correct answer from the options given below.

(1) A-I, B-II, C-III, D-IV (2) A-IV, B-II, C-III, D-I
(3) A-IV, B-I, C-III, D-II (4) A-III, B-IV, C-I, D-II

3. In economy, the trade cycle revolves around the phases of boom, recession, depression and recovery. The unemployment caused due to effects of recession and depression is called

(1) Structural unemployment
(2) Frictional unemployment
(3) Cyclical unemployment
(4) Seasonal unemployment

4. The displacement allowance equal to which of the following to be paid by a contractor to every Inter-state Migrant Workmen at the time of recruitment as per the provisions of the Inter-state Migrant Workmen (Regulation of Employment and Conditions of Service) Act, 1979?

(1) Seventy-five percent of monthly wage payable to him or one hundred rupees whichever is higher.
(2) Fifty percent of monthly wage payable to him or one hundred rupees whichever, is higher.
(3) Fifty percent of monthly wage payable to him or seventy five rupees whichever is higher.
(4) One month wage to be payable to him or two hundred and fifty rupees whichever is higher.

5. Which among the following are classical theories of wages?

A. The Subsistence theory
B. The Standard of Living theory
C. The Marginal Productivity theory
D. The Wage Fund theory
E. The Bargaining theory

Choose the correct answer from the options given below.

(1) A, B, C only (2) A, B, D only
(3) B, C, E only (4) A, C, D only

6. Which among the following are process of staffing?

A. Division of activities
B. Manpower planning
C. Selection
D. Training and development
E. Defining authority and responsibility

Choose the correct answer from the options given below.

(1) A, B, C only (2) C, D, E only
(3) B, C, D only (4) A, C, E only

7. In which of the following stages an expatriate suffers from the phenomenon of cultural shock?

(1) During the period of recruitment and selection.
(2) During the period of assignment abroad.
(3) During the period of repatriation.
(4) During the period of training.

8. The Certificate of fitness issued by the certifying surgeon to an adolescent worker shall remain valid for which period under the Factories Act, 1948?

(1) Six months (2) Twelve months
(3) One year (4) Two year

9. As per the provisions of the Minimum Wages Act, 1948 a worker is required to present his application for less payment of wages before the claim authority within which time from the date on which minimum wage become payable to which he is eligible?

(1) Three months (2) Six months
(3) Sixty days (4) Ninety days

10. Which of the following culture are associated with OCTAPACE culture of HRD style?

A. Openness B. Collaboration
C. Technology D. Authenticity
E. Confrontation

Choose the correct answer from the options given below.

(1) A, B, C only (2) A, B, D, E only
(3) A, C, D, E only (4) A, B, C, D, E only

11. Who has started the Bengali weekly 'Janawani' in Calcutta?

(1) S.A. Dange (2) Muzzaffar Ahmed
(3) M.N. Lokhandey (4) M.N. Roy

12. Which among the following is not summerised under three C^s^ Model of Human Resource Development?

(1) Competence (2) Communication
(3) Commitment (4) Culture

13. Who was the founder of 'Madras workers' union?

(1) B.P. Wadia
(2) N.M. Joshi
(3) N.M. Lokhandey
(4) Cowasji Nanabhoy Davar

14. In process by which people group stimuli into recognisable pattern so that meaning can be assigned to them, is known is

(1) Stereotyping
(2) Perceptual organisation
(3) Perceptual constancy
(4) Perceptual intigration

15. Which approach of management emphasises that "the task of managers is to identify which technique will, in a praticular situation, under particular circumstances, and at a particular time, best contribute to the attainment of management goals"?

(1) Behavioural approach
(2) System approach
(3) Quantitative approach
(4) Contingency approach

16. The 5 S technique is mainly associated with which of the following?

(1) Quality control
(2) Compensation management
(3) Performance appraisal
(4) Shop-floor housekeeping

17. Which among the following are theories relating to accidents and risk taking behaviour?

A. Psychological theories
B. Economic theories
C. Structural theories
D. Psycho-sociological theories
E. Anthropological theories

Choose the correct answer from the options given below.

(1) A, B, C only
(2) C, D, E only
(3) A, C, D only
(4) B, C, E only

18. **Match the List-I with List-II.**

List-I (Theories of Motivation)	List-II (Propagator)
A. Equity Theory	I. Victor Vroom
B. ERG Theory	II. David C. Mc Clelland
C. Achievement Theory	III. Clay Alderfer
D. Expectancy Theory	IV. Adams

Choose the correct answer from the options given below.

(1) A-I, B-III, C-II, D-IV
(2) A-IV, B-III, C-II, D-I
(3) A-III, B-I, C-IV, D-II
(4) A-II, B-IV, C-I, D-III

19. **Arrange the following poverty elimination/ alleviation programmes according to the year of their launching in earlier to later order.**

A. Swarna Jayanti Gram Swarojgar Yojana
B. Swarna Jayanti Shahri Rojgar Yojana
C. National Rural Employment Guarantee Act
D. Sampoorna Grameen Rojgar Yojana
E. Pradhan Mantri Kaushal Vikas Yojana

Choose the correct answer from the options given below.

(1) B, A, D, C, E (2) B, C, D, A, E
(3) A, B, C, E, D (4) A, C, B, E, D

20. **Under which section of the Trade Union Act, 1926 the formation of seperate political fund for promotion of civil and political interest of Trade Union has been provided?**

(1) Section 6 (2) Section 12
(3) Section 16 (4) Section 18

21. **What are the minimum and maximum number of 'Protected workmen' prescribed under the Industrial Disputes Act, 1947?**

(1) Minimum 20 and Maximum 100
(2) Minimum 15 and Maximum 75
(3) Minimum 10 and Maximum 50
(4) Minimum 5 and Maximum 100

22. **Under the provisions of the Inter-state Migrant Worker (Regulation of Employment and Conditions of Services) Act, 1979 other facilities to be provided to the migrant workmen by his employer includes**

A. To ensure suitable conditions of work.
B. To provide and maintain suitable residential accomodation.
C. To provide education facilities to the children of migrant workmen.
D. To provide the prescribed medical facilities to workmen.
E. To provide such protective clothing to workmen.

Choose the correct answer from the options given below.

(1) A, B, C, and D only
(2) B, C, D and E only
(3) A, B, D and E only
(4) A, B, C, D, E

23. **Who has developed/outlined the 'Human Capital Appraisal Approach?**

(1) T.V. Rao
(2) Udai Pareek
(3) Friedman
(4) Yeung and Berman

24. **Who has defined social security as "It is a controversial and dynamic subject with various facets-philosophical, theoretical, humanitarian, financial, administrative, social, economic, political, statistical, acturial, medical and legal"?**

(1) Fridlander
(2) Lord Beveridge
(3) Weber and Cohen
(4) ILO

25. **Arrange the following provisions in ascending order from the year of enactment or amendment under the Employees Provident Fund and Miscellaneous Provision Act, 1952.**

A. Employees Provident Fund Scheme
B. Employees' Deposit-linked Insurance Scheme
C. Employees' Pension Scheme
D. Family Pension Scheme

Choose the correct answer from the options given below.

(1) A, B, C, D (2) A, D, B, C
(3) A, C, D, B (4) D, C, B, A

26. **Match the List-I with List-II.**

List-I (HRD Framework)	List-II (Developer/Formulator)
A. The strategic framework approach	I. Yeung and Berman
B. The integrative framework approach	II. Ulrich and Lake
C. HRD scorecard approach	III. Curtis and Team
D. The People Capabillity Matuarity Model (P-CMM) approach	IV. T.V. Rao

Choose the correct answer from the options given below.
(1) A-II, B-I, C-IV, D-III
(2) A-II, B-III, C-I, D-IV
(3) A-I, B-III, C-IV, D-II
(4) A-III, B-II, C-I, D-IV

27. Arrange the following in the sequence as mentioned under the Minimum Wages Act, 1948 with regard to fixing and revising minimum rate of wages by the appropriate government.

A. For different localities.

B. For different classes of work in the same schedule employment.

C. For different schedule employment.

D. For adults, adolescent, children and apprentice.

Choose the correct answer from the options given below.

(1) A, B, C, D (2) C, B, D, A
(3) D, C, B, A (4) B, C, D, A

28. Arrange the following four types of firms as identified by Bolwijn and Kumpe, in terms of their emergence starting from the earliest to the latest.

A. The quality firm

B. The innovative firm

C. The efficient firm

D. The flexible firm

Choose the correct answer from the options given below.

(1) A, C, B, D (2) C, A, D, B
(3) B, D, C, A (4) D, B, A, C

29. When welfare work is used as a means to secure, preserve and develop the efficiency and productivity of labour, it is called

(1) Philanthropic Theory
(2) Trusteeship Theory
(3) Functional Theory
(4) Placating Theory

30. Match the List-I with List-II.

List-I (Laws)	List-II (Underlying Principle)
A. The Factories Act	I. To promote social security
B. The Equal Remuneration Act	II. To regulate the relation
C. The Employees Provident Fund and Miscellaneous Provisions Act	III. To promote welfare and protect from exploitation
D. The Industrial Employment (Standing Orders) Act	IV. To promote social justice

Choose the correct answer from the options given below.

(1) A-III, B-IV, C-I, D-II
(2) A-IV, B-III, C-II, D-I
(3) A-II, B-I, C-III, D-IV
(4) A-I, B-II, C-IV, D-III

31. The Committee of Experts on Welfare facilities for industrial workers constituted by ILO in 1963 has divided the welfare services in two groups-intra-mural and extra-mural. What service is not included in extra-mural services?

(1) Maternity benefit
(2) Health service including occupational safety
(3) Library and reading room
(4) Transport to and from the place of work

32. Which among the following are theories of Labour Welfare?

A. Efficiency **B. The Police**
C. Responsibility **D. The Placating**
E. The Functional

Choose the correct answer from the options given below.

(1) B, D, E only (2) A, C, D only
(3) B, C, D only (4) A, C, E only

33. Which of the following factors had played their legitimate part in building up of the Madras Labour Union?

A. The status of the labourer as labourer in relation to his employer, affecting the economic and industrial life of the country.

B. The status of the labourer as citizen affected by the political movement and their result.

C. The status of the labourer in their international world of labour due to Russian Revolution.

D. The status of the Indian Crony Capitalism that forces the labour to be associated.

Choose the correct answer from the options given below.

(1) A, B, C only (2) A, B, D only
(3) B, C, D only (4) A, C, D only

34. Arrange the steps in the process of controlling in proper order from earlier to later.

A. Setting standard

B. Determination of areas of control

C. Comparison of performance against standard

D. Measurement of performance

E. Correction of deviation

Choose the correct answer from the options given below.

(1) A, B, C, D, E (2) A, C, D, B, E
(3) B, A, D, C, E (4) B, C, D, A, E

35. Arrange the following processes involved in reference of dispute to Voluntary Labour Arbitration from beginning to end.

A. Arbitration agreement
B. Submission of an Award
C. Signing of an Award
D. Choice of Dispute settlement
E. Selection of Arbitrator

Choose the correct answer from the options given below.

(1) A, E, D, B, C (2) D, E, A, C, B
(3) C, B, A, D, E (4) A, B, C, D, E

36. Arrange the following steps of performance appraisal process from begining to end.

A. Communicate performance expectations to employees.
B. Establish performance standards
C. Compare actual performance with standards.
D. Measure actual performance.
E. Discuss the appraisal with the employees and, if necessary, initiate corrective actions.

Choose the correct answer from the options given below.

(1) A, B, D, C, E (2) B, A, D, C, E
(3) B, C, A, D, E (4) C, B, A, E, D

37. Labour welfare has been defined as "efforts to make life worth living for workers" by

(1) Oxford Dictionary
(2) Chamber's Dictionary
(3) R.R. Hopkins
(4) James Todd

38. Combining of functional and project or product patterns of departmentation in the same organisation structure is

(1) Departmentation by time
(2) Customer departmentation
(3) Matrix organisation
(4) Equipment departmentation

39. The theory of personality which is based on physical attributes or psychological factors for categorisation of personalities is known as

(1) Type theory
(2) Trait theory
(3) Psychometric theory
(4) Social Learning theory

40. The supply curve of a commodity slops

(1) upward in right
(2) downward in right
(3) in straight line
(4) is perpendicular to y-axis

41. Arrange the following Trade Unions in proper sequence according to their formation from earlier to later.

A. Hind Mazdoor Sabha
B. The Hindustan Mazdoor Sevak Sangh
C. The Red Trade Union Congress
D. The Textile Labour Association, Ahmedabad
E. Bhartiya Mazdoor Sangh

Choose the correct answer from the options given below.

(1) A, C, B, D, E
(2) B, C, A, D, E
(3) D, C, B, A, E
(4) E, A, B, C, D

42. Match the List-I with List-II.

List-I (Functional classification of trade unions)	List-II (Suitable examples)
A. Business unionism	I. The knights of labour
B. Friendly unionism	II. American federation of labour
C. Revolutionary unionism	III. The brotherhood of teamsters
D. Predatory unionism	IV. Industrial workers of the world

Choose the correct answer from the options given below.

(1) A-II, B-I, C-III, D-IV
(2) A-II, B-I, C-IV, D-III
(3) A-I, B-III, C-IV, D-II
(4) A-III, B-IV, C-I, D-II

43. Match the List-I with List-II.

List-I (Methods)	List-II (Application)
A. Assessment centre	I. Recruitment
B. Application blank	II. Performance appraisal
C. Job rotation	III. Selection
D. Employment exchange	IV. Training and development

Choose the correct answer from the options given below.

(1) A-II, B-III, C-IV, D-I
(2) A-I, B-II, C-III, D-IV
(3) A-III, B-I, C-II, D-IV
(4) A-IV, B-III, C-II, D-I

44. Which among the following are traditional techniques of controlling?

A. Personal observation
B. Management audit
C. Budgeting

D. Responsibility accounting
E. Break-even analysis

Choose the correct answer from the options given below.

(1) A, B, C only (2) B, C, D only
(3) C, D, E only (4) A, C, E only

45. Arrange the following five career stages starting from the earliest to the latest.

A. Exploration B. Decline
C. Late-career D. Mid-career
E. Establishment

Choose the correct answer from the options given below.

(1) A, E, D, C, B (2) A, D, E, C, B
(3) A, C, D, E, B (4) A, B, D, C, E

46. Which of the following statements are not true relating to grapevine?

A. Information usually travels relatively more slow through grapevine.
B. Grapevines are found in every organisation.
C. The grapevine is a more spontaneous form of communication.
D. The number of people who serve as actual links in the grapevine are generally large.

Choose the correct answer from the options given below.

(1) C and D only (2) B and C only
(3) A and D only (4) A and C only

47. Which of the following were recommended by the study group set-up by Union Ministry of Labour in order to investigate and report the working of the Joint Management Council in 1962?

A. Workers Education and Development
B. Involvement of the middle management personnel.
C. Information sharing
D. 35 percent outsides should be workers representatives in Joint Management Council.

Choose the correct answer from the options given below.

(1) A, B and C only (2) A, C and D only
(3) B, C and D only (4) A, B and D only

48. Arrange the steps in the process of planning in proper order from earlier to later.

A. Setting objectives
B. Identifying alternative
C. Being aware of the opportunity
D. Choosing an alternative
E. Comparison of alternatives in the light of goals sought.

Choose the correct answer from the options given below.

(1) C, A, B, E, D (2) C, B, E, A, D
(3) A, B, C, D, E (4) B, A, C, D, E

49. Match the List-I with List-II.

List-I (Business Games)	List-II (Utility)
A. Case Study	I. Encountering Skills
B. Role Play	II. Situational judgement and problem-solving skill
C. In-basket method	III. Analytical judgemental and decision-making skill
D. Simulation	IV. Human Relation Skill

Choose the correct answer from the options given below.

(1) A-I, B-II, C-III, D-IV
(2) A-II, B-III, C-IV, D-I
(3) A-III, B-IV, C-II, D-I
(4) A-IV, B-I, C-III, D-II

50. The core of planning is

(1) Objective (2) Decision-making
(3) Strategy (4) Forecasting

51. Match the List-I with List-II.

List-I (Authorities)	List-II (Acts)
A. Advisory Committee	I. The Payment of Gratuity Act, 1972
B. Controlling Authority	II. The Minimum Wages Act, 1948
C. Advisory Board	III. The Equal Remuneration Act, 1976
D. Central Board	IV. The Employees Provident Fund and Miscellaneous Act, 1952

Choose the correct answer from the options given below.

(1) A-III, B-I, C-II, D-V
(2) A-II, B-III, C-IV, D-I
(3) A-IV, B-II, C-III, D-I
(4) A-IV, B-I, C-II, D-III

52. Arrange the following provisions of the Industrial Disputes Act, 1947 in ascending order in accordance with their years of enactment/ amendment.

A. Dismissal etc, of an individual workman to be deemed to be an industrial dispute.
B. Setting up Grievance Redressal Machinery.
C. Voluntary reference of dispute of arbitration.
D. Payment of full wages of workman pending proceeding in higher courts.
E. Definition of continuous service.

Choose the correct answer from the options given below.

(1) E, D, A, B, C (2) A, B, D, E, C
(3) C, E, A, D, B (4) B, C, E, D, A

53. Which of the following are the on-the job training methods?

A. Job rotation
B. Vestibule training
C. Role playing
D. Committee assignments
E. Coaching

Choose the correct answer from the options given below.

(1) A, B, C only (2) A, D, E only
(3) C, D, E only (4) A, B, D only

54. Match the List-I with List-II.

List-I (Sources of power)	List-II (Features)
A. Reward power	I. Ability to influence others as a result of being liked and respected
B. Legitimate power	II. Ability to influence other by recognised competencies
C. Expert power	III. Ability to influence others by one's formal position
D. Referrent power	IV. Ability to influence others by giving rewards

Choose the correct answer from the options given below.

(1) A-I, B-II, C-III, D-IV
(2) A-II, B-I, C-IV, D-III
(3) A-III, B-IV, C-I, D-II
(4) A-IV, B-III, C-II, D-I

55. Arrange the main provisions of the Trade Unions Act, 1926 according to their sections from earlier to later.

A. Rights and Privileges of a Registered Trade Union.
B. Registration of Trade Union.
C. Incorporation of a registered Trade Union.
D. Power to make regulation.
E. Amalgamation and dissolution of a Trade Union.

Choose the correct answer from the options given below.

(1) B, C, A, E, D (2) B, A, E, C, D
(3) A, B, C, D, E (4) C, B, A, D, E

56. Arrange the provisions of the Maternity Benefit Act, 1961 according to their section in earlier to later order.

A. Notice of claim for maternity benefits and payment there of.
B. Employment of or work by, women prohibited during certain period.
C. No deduction of wages in certain cases.
D. Right to payment of maternity benefit.
E. Dismissal during absence of pregnancy.

Choose the correct answer from the options given below.

(1) A, B, C, D, E (2) B, D, A, E, C
(3) B, A, E, C, D (4) A, C, D, B, E

57. The provision for constituting various committees under the Building and Other Construction Worker (Regulation of Employment and Conditions of Service) Act, 1996 are

A. Technical Advisory Committee
B. Central Advisory Committee
C. State Advisory Committee
D. Safety Committee
E. Expert Committee

Choose the correct answer from the options given below.

(1) A, B and C only
(2) A, B and E only
(3) B, C, D and E only
(4) A, B, C, D, E

58. Which among the following are the characteristics of Indian Labour Market?

A. Diversity in workplace
B. Existence of perfect mobility
C. Monopoly in labour market
D. Monopsony in labour market
E. Highly competitive in character

Choose the correct answer from the options given below.

(1) A, D, E only (2) A, B, C only
(3) B, C, E only (4) C, D, E only

59. Reich distinguished three professional categories of the labour force in a global terms. Which of the following does not belong to the categories identified by Reich?

(1) Routine production services
(2) In-person services
(3) Symbolic-analytic services
(4) High tech services

60. Match the List-I with List-II.

List-I (Forms/Types of strikes)	List-II (Appropriate meaning)
A. Lightning strike	I. Physical blockade caused by a conflict and organised mostly by employees
B. Gherao	II. Strike suddenly announced without proper notice
C. Picketing	III. An act of posting pickets and implies marching of workmen in front of the premises of the employer
D. Stay in strike	IV. A group of employees take possession of property of the business and stop production and refuse access to the owners desiring to work

Choose the correct answer from the options given below.

(1) A-II, B-III, C-I, D-IV (2) A-II, B-I, C-III, D-IV
(3) A-III, B-I, C-IV, D-II (4) A-II, B-I, C-IV, D-III

61. An event, repeated several times, evoking desired responses is known as

(1) Operant conditioning
(2) Instrumental conditioning
(3) Classical conditioning
(4) Cognitive conditioning

62. Which of the following are core elements of the System Framework of Industrial Relations described by John T. Dunlop?

A. Certain actors B. Certain context
C. Certain habits D. Certain ideology
E. Technological context.

Choose the correct answer from the options given below.

(1) A, B, C only (2) A, B, C, E only
(3) A, B, D, E only (4) B, C, D, E only

63. Who has concluded that non-financial incentive are more important than financial incentives?

(1) F.W. Taylor (2) Henri Fayol
(3) Elton Mayo (4) Mary Parker Follet

64. Match the List-I with List-II.

List-I (Provisions)	List-II (Acts)
A. Committees	I. The Contract Labour (Regulation and Abolition) Act, 1970
B. Workers Participation in Safety Management	II. The Child and Adolescent Labour (Prohibition and Regulation) Act, 1986
C. State Advisory Board	III. The Factories Act, 1984
D. Technical Advisory Committee	IV. The Mines Act, 1952

Choose the correct answer from the options given below.

(1) A-IV, B-III, C-II, D-I (2) A-III, B-IV, C-II, D-I
(3) A-IV, B-III, C-I, D-II (4) A-I, B-II, C-IV, D-III

65. Arrange the following five states of personality development given by Freud, starting from the earliest to the latest.

A. Phallic stage B. Genital stage
C. Oval stage D. Anal stage
E. Latency period

Choose the correct answer from the options given below.

(1) C, D, A, E, B (2) D, C, A, B, E
(3) A, B, D, C, E (4) B, D, A, E, C

66. Match the List-I with List-II.

List-I (Formats of organisation)	List-II (Explanation)
A. Project organisation	I. Structured to accomplish specific task within the constraints of time, money and quality.
B. Functional organisation	II. Personnel manager ensures appointment of right people at the right time and place.
C. Matrix organisation	III. A hybrid organisational structure which is a combination of functional and project structure.
D. Networking organisation	IV. A multinational structural arrangement that combines elements of function, product and geographic design to link worldwide subsidiaries.

Choose the correct answer from the options given below.

(1) A-IV, B-III, C-II, D-I
(2) A-II, B-I, C-IV, D-III
(3) A-IV, B-II, C-III, D-I
(4) A-I, B-II, C-III, D-IV

67. The process of identifying and uncovering of candidates through a proactive recruitment technique is known as

(1) Head hunting
(2) Poaching
(3) Candidate sourcing
(4) HR stock taking

68. According to Herzberg's Two Factor Theory which of the following come under the category of motivater?

A. Achievement B. Supervision
C. Responsibility D. Salary
E. Advancement

Choose the correct answer from the options given below.

(1) A, B and D only (2) B, C and D only
(3) A, C and D only (4) A, B and C only

69. A leader who is concerned for High Task and High Relationship exhibits which of the following type of leadership?

(1) Supportive style (2) Autocratic style
(3) Free - Rein style (4) Participative style

70. In which Convention Number of International Labour Organisation, 'the right to organise and collective bargaining' has been declared as Fundamental Rights?

(1) Convention No. 19 (2) Convention No. 87
(3) Convention No. 98 (4) Convention No. 103

71. In which of the following organisations the scheme of workers participation in management-1983 was made applicable?

(1) Public sector undertaking
(2) Private sector undertaking
(3) Central Public sector undertaking
(4) State Public sector undertaking

72. As per the provision of the Payment of Bonus Act, 1965, bonus payable to an employee shall be paid with in how many months from the close of the accounting year?

(1) Two months (2) Three months
(3) Six months (4) Eight months

73. Under the provisions of the Employee Provident Fund and Miscellaneous Provisions Act, 1952, a Tribunal may within which period of time from the date of its order can rectify any mistake apparent from record and amend the order?

(1) Within One year (2) Within Three year
(3) Within Five year (4) Within Seven year

74. Arrange the following steps of human resource planning in proper sequence starting from the begining.

A. Plan to modify or adjust the organisational plan.
B. Analysing the organisational plan.
C. Forecasting the demand and supply aspects of human resource.
D. Estimating the net human resource requirements.
E. Plan to manage deficit surplus of human resources.

Choose the correct answer from the options given below.

(1) D, A, E, C, B (2) A, C, B, D, E
(3) B, C, D, A, E (4) C, D, A, B, E

75. As per the provisions for the Mines Act, 1952, if any owner agent or manager fails to submit within which period a draft bye-law after being called upon by the Chief Inspector or Inspector, the Chief Inspector or Inspector on his own may propose a draft of such bye-law as appear to him as sufficient?

(1) One month (2) Two months
(3) Six months (4) Twelve months

76. As per the provisions of the Payment of Wages Act, 1936 for which of the following industries, the appropriate government is the Central Government?

A. Railways B. Ports and Docks
C. Mines D. Oilfields

Choose the correct answer from the options given below.

(1) A, B, C only (2) A, C, D only
(3) A, B, D only (4) B, C, D only

77. "If a strike is resorted to for a short period such as a day or two to give the employer a warning of the likely wider form of confrontation if their demands are not prompty conceded" is called?

(1) General strike (2) Particular strike
(3) Token strike (4) Jurisdictional strike

78. Who has developed the Technological Theory of Traded Unionism?

(1) Robert F. Hoxie (2) Frank Tannenbaum
(3) Selig Perlman (4) John. R. Commons

79. The Advisory Committee constituted under the Equal Remuneration Act, 1976 shall consist of how many person nominated by the appropriate government of which one-half shall be women?

(1) Six persons (2) Eight persons
(3) Ten persons (4) Fourteen persons

80. Match the List-I with List-II.

List-I (Types of unemployment)	List-II (Explanation)
A. Technological	I. When economy faces structural changes like decline in export trade, it occurs.
B. Structural	II. Trade cycle revolves around boom and recession. In periods of depression and recession, demand decreases and leads to this type of unemployment
C. Frictional	III. Changes in the techniques of production leads to unemployment
D. Cyclical	IV. Immobility of labour, shortage of raw materials, breakdown of machinery etc cause it

Choose the correct answer from the options given below.
(1) A-III, B-IV, C-II, D-I
(2) A-III, B-I, C-IV, D-II
(3) A-II, B-I, C-III, D-IV
(4) A-IV, B-III, C-II, D-I

81. The doctrine of conspicuous consumption was propounded by
(1) Throstein Veblen (2) Robert Giffin
(3) Paul A. Samuelson (4) Alfred Marshall

82. What is not a characteristics of competitive market?
(1) There are many buyer and many sellers in the market.
(2) Goods offered by the various sellers are largely the same.
(3) Buyers and sellers are said to be price takers.
(4) Firms can freely enter the market but cannot exit.

83. Match the List-I with List-II.

List-I (Propounders of management thought)	List-II (Explanation)
A. Charles Babbage	I. Development of personnel
B. Robert Owen	II. Running organisation in more rational manner instead of traditional authority or charismatic authority
C. Max Weber	III. A system view point may provide the impetus to unify management theory
D. Fred Luthans	IV. Work specialisation

Choose the correct answer from the options given below:
(1) A-IV, B-III, C-II, D-I
(2) A-IV, B-I, C-II, D-III
(3) A-I, B-II, C-III, D-IV
(4) A-I, B-III, C-II, D-IV

84. Which of the following statements relating to transactional analysis are true?
A. There are three different types of transactions namely complimentary, crossed and ulterior occur between the egos.
B. In the crossed transaction, there is no scope for conflict.
C. In the ulterior transaction, there is high scope of conflict.
D. In the complimentary transction, there is no scope of conflict.

Choose the correct answer from the options given below.
(1) A, B and C only (2) B, C and D only
(3) A, B and D only (4) A, C and D only

85. As per the provisions of the Mines Act, 1952 the special officers after giving not less than how many days notice to the manager of the mine, enter the mine for survey, level or measure the mine?
(1) Thirty days (2) Fifteen days
(3) Seven days (4) Three days

86. Which of the following is the correct expansion of PERT?
(1) Programme Evaluation and Review Technique
(2) Performance Evaluation and Report Technique
(3) Progress Evaluation and Review Trend
(4) Programme Evaluation and Research Technique

87. Which of the following organisational issues are examined closely in HRD Audit?
A. Long term and short-term plans and vision to assess competency requirements.
B. Identification of broad competency requirements for future business goals and objectives.
C. Physical and mental conditions, diseases of worker and his family.
D. Examination of adequacies and inadequacies HRD.

Choose the correct answer from the options given below.
(1) A, B, D only (2) A, B, C only
(3) B, C, D only (4) A, C, D only

88. Match the List-I with List-II.

List-I (Provision)	List-II (Laws/Act)
A. Subsistence Allowance	I. The Industrial Disputes Act, 1947
B. Disability Allowance	II. The Inter-state Migrant Workmen (Regulation of Employment and Conditions of Service) Act, 1979
C. Journey Allowance	III. The Industrial Employment (Standing Orders) Act, 1946
D. Notice of Change	IV. The Mines Act, 1952

Choose the correct answer from the options given below.
(1) A-IV, B-III, C-I, D-II
(2) A-I, B-II, C-IV, D-III
(3) A-III, B-IV, C-II, D-I
(4) A-II, B-I, C-III, D-IV

89. Which of the following organisations are autonomous organisations under Ministry of Labour?

A. Employees State Insurance Corporation
B. Employees Provident Fund Organisation
C. Dattopant Thengadi Board for Workers Education and Development.
D. Labour Bureau
E. V.V. Giri National Labour Institute.

Choose the correct answer from the options given below:

(1) A, B, C, D only (2) A, B, C, E only
(3) B, C, D, E only (4) A, B, D, E only

90. Who among the following is the proponent of Theory Z in HRM?

(1) John Storey (2) William G. Ouchi
(3) Vladimir Puick (4) Michael Beer

Directions (Q. Nos 90-95) *Read the passage carefully and answer the question.*

In the Indian context, the social evils suffered by laboures such as, exploitation, illiteracy, lack of skill training, substance abuse, among many others, are reduced to a greater or lesser extent by the country's welfare policies. During the pre-independence period, the industrial relations policy of the British government was generally based on laissez faire and selective intervention.

There were hardly any labour welfare schemes. After Independence, labour legislation has been introduced which has shaped industrial relations and social security in contemporary India. The legislation have also provided for the machinery for bipartite and tripartite consultations for the settlement of labour-management disputes.

Soon after independence, the government at a tripartite conference in December, 1947 adopted an industrial truce resolution. The following laws were enacted to maintain industrial peace and harmonious labour-management relations: the Factories Act of 1948, the Employees State Insuraance Act of 1948 and the Minimum Wages Act of 1948. Later, the Bonus Act was passed in 1965.

The Constitution of India also spells out of the underlying principles of state policy which place an emphasis on labour welfare, especially Articles 38 to 43 of the Constitution. Labour welfare in India is aimed at getting the best out of the worker in the production process by creating the worker conditions required for this outcome.

In the early 1990s, the neoliberal economic reforms that were introduced by the government set in motion a series of measures to reduce state regulation of industries, particulary the larger industries.

In general, the country's worker have opposed these economic liberalisation policies out of fear of unemployment while the country's enterpreneurs have welcomed it in hope of obtaining new opportunities to improve India's industries. These new economic policies have directly affected industrial relations in the country.

91. How did labour generally react to the neoliberal economic reform in early 1990s?

(1) With concern over potential job loss.
(2) With widespread support and enthusiasm.
(3) With increased demand of higher wage.
(4) With calls for stricter government regulations.

92. What was the predominant industrial relations policy of the Birtish Government in per-independence India?

(1) Socialist welfare state
(2) Total state control
(3) Laissez faire and selective intervention
(4) Free market capitalism

93. What was the primary goal of Labour Welfare Policies in India as stated in the passage?

(1) To promote international trade agreements.
(2) To increase corporate profits.
(3) To enhance worker productivity through improved conditions.
(4) To encourage privatisation of industries.

94. Which legislation aimed to provide social security benefits to workers in India?

(1) Minimum Wages Act, 1948
(2) Payment of Bonus Act, 1965
(3) Factories Act, 1948
(4) Employees State Insurance Act, 1948

95. The Tripartite Conference of 1947 adopted which resolution?

(1) Socialist revolution resolution
(2) Industrial truce resolution
(3) Labour strike resolution
(4) Industrial democracy resolution

Directions (Q. Nos 96-100) *Read the passage carefully and answer the question.*

The Labour Force Participation Rate (LFPR) and Unemployment Rate (UR) reflect a combination of whether an individual is looking for job and actually able to get one. The UR is defined as the percentage of unemployed individuals in the labour force as a share of the employed and the unemployed— the term unemployed itself referring to those who are willing and/or able to work but have not been able to find work. The LFPR, in turn, is the percentage of the employed and the unemployed as a share of the working age population in the labour force.

A major misconception about the labour market is that a low UR is unambiguously a positive indicator of the health of the labour market. The reason is that a fall in unemployment does not necessarily imply a rise in employment. Both can move in the same direction because of the presence of third category, the Out of Labour Force (OLF). In other words, the total working age population of the economy is divided into three, not two, categories.

The OLF consist of individuals who are either not willing to of not looking for work. If there is a rise in the share of the OLF because individuals get discouraged by job prospects and stop looking for jobs, it can still lead to a fail in UR without the creation of any jobs. The unemployment measure in itself thus is not a fair indicator of the health of the labour market. More importantly, even if the fall in unemployment is due to an actual rise in unemployment and not the PLF, the rise in the broad category of employment itself need not be a sufficient cause for cheer. It would indeed be a positive development if it being driven by an increase in high- wage jobs, including salaried ones, or people setting up flourishing businesses and generating employment. On the contrary, it may be driven by rise in forms of employment that are not particularly remunerative, such as some form of low-return informal sector self-employment activity just to eke out a living or as a helper in household enterprises, a subcategory of the self-employed because they cannot find anything better to do.

96. What does the term 'Out of labour Force' (OLF) refer to?
(1) Individuals not looking for work
(2) Individuals not willing to work
(3) Individuals not able to work.
(4) Individuals neither looking nor willing to work.

97. What type of increase in employment does the passage suggests as positive for the labour market?
(1) Increase in informal sector jobs.
(2) Rise in household enterprises.
(3) Growth in high-wage jobs and salaried positions.
(4) Expansion of low-wage jobs and salaried positions.

98. What does the Unemployment Rate (UR) measure?
(1) Percentage of individuals out of the labour force
(2) Percentage of unemployed individual in the labour force
(3) Percentage of employed individual in the labour force
(4) Percentage of the working age population

99. How has the Labour Force Participation Rate (LFPR) been interpreted in the passage?
(1) Percentage of unemployed in Labour Force.
(2) Percentage of employed individual in the Labour Force.
(3) Percentage of employed and unemployed individuals in the working age population.
(4) Percentage of the working age population.

100. Why might a decrease in the unemployment rate (UR) not necessarily indicate a healthier labour market?
(1) Because it may coincide with an increase in the out of labour force
(2) Because it directly correlates with a rise in high-wage job
(3) Because it indicates a decrease in low-employment
(4) Because it suggests an increase in government assistance programmes

ANSWERS

1	(2)	2	(4)	3	(3)	4	(1)	5	(2)	6	(3)	7	(2)	8	(2)	9	(2)	10	(2)
11	(2)	12	(2)	13	(1)	14	(2)	15	(4)	16	(4)	17	(3)	18	(2)	19	(1)	20	(3)
21	(4)	22	(3)	23	(3)	24	(3)	25	(2)	26	(1)	27	(2)	28	(2)	29	(3)	30	(1)
31	(2)	32	(1)	33	(1)	34	(3)	35	(2)	36	(2)	37	(1)	38	(3)	39	(1)	40	(1)
41	(3)	42	(2)	43	(1)	44	(4)	45	(1)	46	(3)	47	(1)	48	(1)	49	(3)	50	(2)
51	(1)	52	(3)	53	(2)	54	(4)	55	(1)	56	(2)	57	(3)	58	(1)	59	(4)	60	(2)
61	(3)	62	(3)	63	(3)	64	(3)	65	(1)	66	(4)	67	(3)	68	(*)	69	(4)	70	(3)
71	(3)	72	(4)	73	(3)	74	(3)	75	(2)	76	(2)	77	(3)	78	(2)	79	(3)	80	(2)
81	(1)	82	(4)	83	(2)	84	(4)	85	(4)	86	(1)	87	(1)	88	(3)	89	(2)	90	(2)
91	(1)	92	(3)	93	(3)	94	(4)	95	(2)	96	(4)	97	(3)	98	(2)	99	(3)	100	(1)

** Indicates dropped question.*

Human Resource Management (Paper-2)

Solved Paper, December 2023

General Instructions

1. There are total one hundred questions in this paper. Each question carries 2 marks.
2. All questions are compulsory.

1. Who authored the book 'The Nature of Managerial Work'?

(1) Peter Drucker (2) Henry Mintzberg
(3) Chester I. Barnard (4) Henri Fayol

2. According to whom, 'management is the art of getting things done through people'?

(1) Mary Parker Follet (2) Peter F. Drucker
(3) Elton Mayo (4) Chester I. Barnard

3. Which of the following is a single use plan?

(1) Programme (2) Procedure
(3) Policy (4) Rules

4. Who developed an approach that incorporates the organisation environment into organisational design?

(1) Joan Woodward
(2) David H. Burnham
(3) Tom Burns and GM Stalken
(4) Chester I. Barnard

5. The Concept of 'Hard HRM' and 'Soft HRM' has been developed by

(1) John Storey (2) Vladmir Pucik
(3) Nina Hatvany (4) Michael Beer

6. The online systems that help employers attracts, gather, screen, compile and manage applicants is called

(1) Application Service Provider
(2) Application Screening Device
(3) Applicant Tracking Systems
(4) Applicant Recruiting Systems

7. Which of the following is not a method of HR Demand Forecasting?

(1) Managerial Judgement
(2) Markov Analysis
(3) Scatter Plot
(4) Ratio Analysis

8. A group of jobs having similarities in comparable factors or those considered as existing at the same level in terms of their values is called

(1) pay grade
(2) pay range
(3) pay scale
(4) pay standard

9. Hofstede making a study an national culture identified four dimensions along with managers and employees appear to vary. Which one of the following is not a dimensions identified by him?

(1) Power distance
(2) Relationship to authority
(3) Uncertainty avoidance
(4) Masculinity versus femininity

10. A performance appraisal method which keeps a record of uncommonly good or undesirable and reviewing it with the employee at predetermined times is known as

(1) Critical incident method
(2) Behaviourally anchored rating scale
(3) Alteration ranking method
(4) Management by objectives

11. **If the top management of a multi-national corporation, allows the national subsidiaries to fill management posts by themselves with host country national, then the attitude of the management is characterised by**
(1) Polycentricity (2) Ethnocentricity
(3) Regiocentricity (4) Geocentricity

12. **Which of the following is vestibule training?**
(1) On the job training (2) Apprenticeship training
(3) Job rotation training (4) Off the job training

13. **The linking pin model given by Rensis Likert is associated with**
(1) intra-individual behaviour and conflict.
(2) interpersonal behaviour and conflict.
(3) intergroup behaviour and conflict.
(4) interorganisational behaviour and conflict.

14. **Which one of the following is identified as the third dimension in the Reddin's Three Dimensional Model of Leadership?**
(1) Effectiveness (2) Environments
(3) Motivation (4) Conflict

15. **Who among the following had identified the three different skills namely, conceptual skills, human relation skills and technical skills for effective management?**
(1) Robert Blake (2) Robert J. House
(3) Robert Katz (4) Robert Hoxie

16. **The S-O-B-C model of organisational behaviour identifies four major variables, which are related to another. Which of the following stands for letter 's'?**
(1) Structure (2) Stimulus
(3) System (4) Social

17. **Who was the main architect of the legislation 'the Bombay Industrial Disputes Act, 1938' being the Parliamentary Secretary in the Bombay Congress Ministry?**
(1) Gulzarilal Nanda (2) Jaiprakash Narayan
(3) NM Joshi (4) Balgangadhar Tilak

18. **'Every class struggle is a political struggle' who said this?**
(1) Lenin (2) Karl Marx
(3) G.D.H Cole (4) Fedrick Engele

19. **The criteria for the recognition of trade Unions have been laid down under**
(1) the Industrial Disputes Act, 1947
(2) the Trade Unions Act, 1926
(3) Code of Discipline
(4) Industrial Employment (Standing Orders) Act, 1946

20. **Which pair of scheme of workers participation and the year of its establishment is inconsistent?**
(1) Works Committee, 1947
(2) Joint Management Council, 1958
(3) Shop Council, 1972
(4) Joint Council in Commercial and Service Organisation in the Public Sector, 1977

21. **'A strike called by proper authority in a Union and in conforming with the requirement of law' is called**
(1) wild cat strike
(2) authorised strike
(3) juristicational strike
(4) general strike

22. **Who has developed the 'Hot-Stove Rule' for handling discipline?**
(1) Donglas McGregor
(2) Michael J. Jucius
(3) Charles A. Myers
(4) Henri Fayol

23. **What are the minimum and maximum numbers prescribed under the Industrial Disputes Act, 1947 for 'Protected workmen'?**
(1) Minimum 20 and maximum 100
(2) Minimum 15 and maximum 75
(3) Minimum 10 and maximum 50
(4) Minimum 5 and maximum 100

24. **Which method of settling industrial disputes does not include direct state intervention?**
(1) Statutory Establishment of Bipartite Committee
(2) Adjudication
(3) Collective Bargaining
(4) Compulsory Conciliation

25. **The Right of Children to Free and Compulsory Education Act, 2009 was enacted in accordance with which of the following Article of Constitution in India?**
(1) Article 41 (2) Article 38
(3) Article 19 (4) Article 47

26. **Which of the Constitution of India provide for the participation of workers in management of industries?**
(1) Article 39A (2) Article 41
(3) Article 43A (4) Article 43B

27. **The Site Appraisal Committee is required to submit the report to the State Government after how many days of the receipt of an application for establishment of a factory involving a hazardous process under the Factories Act, 1948?**
(1) Thirty days
(2) Sixty days
(3) Ninety days
(4) One hundred twenty days

28. **The term 'Wages' under the Contract Labour (Regulation and Abolition) Act, 1970 has the same meaning assigned to it under which of the following legislations?**
(1) The Industrial Disputes Act
(2) The Payment of Wages Act
(3) The Industrial Employment (Standing Orders) Act
(4) The Minimum Wages Act

29. **The Advisory Board constituted under the Minimum Wages Act, 1948 is to**
(1) advise the employers to pay minimum wages as fixed under the act.
(2) coordinate the works of committees and sub-committees.
(3) coordinate the work of the advisory committees.
(4) coordinate between the employer and employees to fix minimum wages.

30. **Under the provisions of the Minimum Wages Act, 1948, the representation of independent members in the Central Advisory Board shall not exceed.**
(1) One-fourth of the total members
(2) One-half of the total members
(3) One-third of the total members
(4) Two-third of the total members

31. **What is the minimum number of persons to be nominated by the appropriate Government to the Advisory Committee constructed under the provisions of the Equal Remuneration Act, 1976?**
(1) Five (2) Seven
(3) Ten (4) Twelve

32. **An exempted establishment formed under the provisions of the Employees Provident Fund and Miscellaneous Provisions Act, 1952 required to establish, which of the following for the administration of the fund?**
(1) Exempted Provident Fund Board
(2) Board of Trustees
(3) An Executive Committee
(4) An Establishment Level Committee

33. **Who defined Social Welfare as:**
"The organised system of social services and institutions designed to aid individuals and groups to attain satisfying standards of life and health, and personal and social relationship which permit them to develop their full capacities and to promote their well being in harmony with the needs of their families and community".
Choose the correct options.
(1) RR Hopkins
(2) Friedlender
(3) Arther James Todd
(4) ES Proud

34. **Which welfare amenity is not included in intra-mural amenity by the committee of exports on welfare facilities for industrial workers constituted by the International Labour Organisation in the year 1963?**
(1) Washing and bathing facilities
(2) Latrines and urinals
(3) Leave travel facilities
(4) Health services including occupational safety

35. **Access to social security has become a fundamental human right to which every individual is entitled as a member of the society. This right has been embodied in the Universal Declaration of Human Rights adopted by United Nations General Assembly. In which years, it was adopted?**
(1) In the year 1948 (2) In the year 1946
(3) In the year 1950 (4) In the year 1952

36. **When was the Royal Commission on Labour was appointed under the Chairmanship of JH Whitley?**
(1) In the year 1919 (2) In the year 1929
(3) In the year 1938 (4) In the year 1944

37. **The shape of supply curve of Individual Labour is**
(1) backward bending
(2) straight line
(3) negatively sloped
(4) perpendicular to the X axis

38. **Advanced capitalist economies generally suffer from which type of unemployment?**
(1) Structural unemployment
(2) Classical unemployment
(3) Disguised unemployment
(4) Cyclical unemployment

39. **Which of the following is true as per modern economists?**
(1) Cut in money wage is the best way to increase labour demand and bring full employment.
(2) Expansionary monetary policy is effective in increasing employment.
(3) Flexible wage policy is instrumental in achieving full employment.
(4) Money illusion does not affect labour union.

40. **In an income leisure diagram, the wages rate is graphically represented by the**
(1) slope of indifference curve
(2) curvature of indifference curve
(3) slope of the budget line
(4) tangency of budget line with indifference curve

41. **Which of the following is/are correct relating to the system approach to management?**
A. A system is an interrelated set of elements punching as a whole.
B. Each system has a boundary that separates it from its environment.
C. Each system interacts with its environment.
D. Feedback is not the key to control the system.
Choose the correct answer from the options given below.
(1) A and B (2) B and C
(3) A, B and C (4) A, C and D

42. Which of the following is/are not the functions of management according to Henri Fayol?

A. Staffing B. Organisation
C. Controlling D. Commanding
E. Coordinating

Choose the correct answer from the options given below.

(1) Only A (2) Only D
(3) Only E (4) D and E

43. Which of the following are the advantages of group decision making?

A. More information and knowledge are available
B. Enhanced communication of decision may result
C. Undesirable compromises may happen
D. Groupthink may occur
E. It is costlier

Choose the correct answer from the options given below.

(1) A and B (2) A and D
(3) A, B and D (4) A, B and C

44. Which of the following is/are not form of simulation?

A. Role playing B. Coaching
C. Business game D. Conference
E. In basket exercise

Choose the correct answer from the options given below.

(1) B and C (2) B and D
(3) A, B and D (4) B, C and D

45. Which of the following is/are not the components of direct compensation?

A. House rent allowance
B. Pay for vacations
C. Employer's contribution towards PF
D. Incentives
E. Bonus

Choose the correct answer from the options given below.

(1) B and C (2) B and D
(3) B, C and D (4) C, D and E

46. Which of the following statements are true relating to human personality?

A. The word personality can be traces to the latin words 'persona'.
B. The meaning of the word 'persona' when translated into english is 'to look through'.
C. Human personality includes the external appearance and behaviour.
D. Human personality includes inner awareness of self as a permanent organising force.

Choose the correct answer from the options given below.

(1) A, B and D (2) A, C and D
(3) A, B and C (4) B, C and D

47. Which of the following are the decisional roles of the managers as identified by Henry Mintzberg?

A. Figurehead role
B. Leadership role
C. Negotiator role
D. Entrepreneurs role
E. Disturbance handler role

Choose the correct answer from the options given below.

(1) C, D and E (2) A, B and D
(3) B, C and D (4) A, B and C

48. As per Herzberg's two factor theory of motivation, which of the following are the motivators?

A. Interpersonal relations
B. Achievement
C. Advancement
D. Supervision
E. Responsibility

Choose the correct answer from the options given below.

(1) A, B and D (2) B, C and E
(3) B, C and D (4) A, D and E

49. Which of the following statements can contribution for developing HRD climats in an organisation?

A. Strong belief of the top management on the capabilities of the employees.
B. HRD policies showing high concern for employees.
C. Good HRD sub-systems for increasing effectiveness.
D. Presence of strong trade unions in the organisation.

Choose the correct answer from the options given below.

(1) B, C and D
(2) A, C and D
(3) A, B and C
(4) A, B and D

50. Which of the following factors influence the multi-national corporations to recruit host country nationals?

A. They are familiar with the culture.
B. To maintain and facilitate organisational coordination and control.
C. To develop good public relations.
D. The company's conviction that it must maintain a foreign image in the host country.

Choose the correct answer from the options given below.

(1) A and D only (2) B and C only
(3) A and C only (4) B and D only

51. Which of the following factors had played legitimate part in the formation of the Madras Labour Union?

A. The status of the labourer as labourer in relation to his employer, affecting the economic and industrial life of the country.

B. The status of the labourer as a citizen affected by and affecting the political movement and their result.

C. The status of the labourer in the international world of labour which has been emerging into great importance ever since the Russian revolution.

D. The status of the Indian crony capitalism that forces the labour to be associated and form trade union.

Choose the correct answer from the options given below.

(1) A and B (2) A, B and C
(3) A, C and D (4) B, C and D

52. Which of the following three-tier system of participation was recommended by a Tripartite Committee on Worker's Participation in 1977 under the Chairmanship of Shri Ravindra Verma?

A. Unit Level B. Shop Floor Level
C. Plant Level D. Corporate Level

Choose the correct answer from the options given below.

(1) A, B and C (2) A, C and D
(3) B, C and D (4) A, B and D

53. Which of the following All India Trade Union organisations were in existence by the end of 1933?

A. All India Trade Union Congress
B. The Red Trade Union Congress
C. National Trade Union Federation
D. Indian Trade Union Federation

Choose the correct answer from the options given below.

(1) A and B (2) B and C
(3) A, B and C (4) B, C and D

54. Which of the following statements are correct relating to lockout?

A. A lockout is the closure of a place of business or employment or the suspension of work.

B. A lockout is an antithesis of a strike.

C. A lockout is the closure of an industrial undertaking because of the existence of or apprehension of an industrial dispute, violence and damage.

D. A lockout means termination of employment by retrenchment.

Choose the correct answer from the options given below.

(1) A, B and C
(2) B, C and D
(3) A, C and D
(4) C and D

55. Which of the following are the role of inspectors appointed by the government under respective labour legislations?

A. Enforce the labour law and related regulations.

B. Advice employers and workers on how to comply with the laws and regulations.

C. Issue show cause notice to offending employers for not complying with provisions of the law.

D. File prosecution in the concerned court if despite show cause notice compliance is not secured in time.

E. To investigate the dispute as arbitrator and submit the report before the appropriate authority.

Choose the correct answer from the options given below.

(1) A, B, C and D
(2) B, C, D and E
(3) A, C, D and E
(4) A, B, D and E

56. As per the provisions of the Inter-State Migrant Workmen (Regulation of Employment and Conditions of Service) Act, 1979, the duties of the contractor includes

A. to furnish such particulars in the form prescribed to the specified authority in the state from which, the inter-state migrant workman is recruited.

B. to issue every inter-state migrant workman, a passbook affixed with a passport size photograph indicating the details of employment, payment of wages, working hours, etc.

C. to provide retention allowance to the inter-state migrant workman when not in employment.

D. to furnish in respect of every inter-state migrant workman who ceases to be employed, a return in such form and in such manner as prescribed to the specified authority in the state form which, he is recruited.

Choose the correct answer from the options given below.

(1) A, B and C (2) A and C
(3) B, C and D (4) A, B and D

57. The certifying surgeon appointed under the provisions of the Mines Act, 1952 shall perform which of the following duties?

A. The examination of person engaged in a mine in such dangerous occupation or process.

B. To conduct medical supervision as may be prescribed for any mine where cases of illness have occurred.

C. To conduct enquiry into any accident happened in the mine.

D. For payment of disability allowances to the persons confit to work in the mine.

Choose the correct answer from the options given below.

(1) A, B and D (2) A and B
(3) A and D (4) A, B, C and D

58. As per the provisions of the Building and Other Construction Workers (Regulation of Employment and Conditions of Service) Act, 1996, the appropriate Government may make rules to

A. fix the number of hours of work which shall constitute a normal working day.

B. provide for a day of rest in every period of seven days.

C. providing for payment of work on a day of rest not less than the average daily wage.

D. fix the number of hours of work for a normal working day inclusive of one or more specified intervals.

E. payment of full remuneration in respect of such days of rest.

Choose the correct answer from the options given below.

(1) A and C
(2) A, B and C
(3) A, B, D and E
(4) A, B, C and E

59. Which of the following statement is/are not correct with regard to the applicability of the Employees Provident Fund and Miscellaneous Provisions Act, 1952?

A. To every establishment which is a factory engaged in manufacture specified in Schedule-I of the Act.

B. To any establishment registered under the Cooperative Societies Act, 1912 employing less than 50 person working without the aid of power.

C. To an establishment belonging to or under the control of the Central Government or a State Government whose employees are entitled to the benefit of contributory provident fund.

D. To any other establishment set-up under any Central, Provinicial or State Act and where employees are entitled to contributory provident fund and old age pension.

Choose the correct answer from the options given below.

(1) Only A (2) A and B
(3) A and C (4) B, C and D

60. As per the provisions of the Employees Provident Fund and Miscellaneous Provisions Act, 1952, a pension fund to be created with which of the followings?

A. Such sum from the employers contribution not exceeding eight and one-third percent of the basic wage, dearness allowance and retaining allowances, of any of the concerned employee.

B. Such sum as are payable by the employers of the exempted establishments.

C. The net assets of the Employees Family Pension Fund as on the date of the establishment of the Pension Fund.

D. Such sum from the employees contribution not exceeding one and one-third percent of the basic wage and dearness allowance or retaining allowances, if any.

E. Such sum as the Central Government may, after due appropriation by the parliament by law.

Choose the correct answer from the options given below.

(1) A, B and C (2) A, B, C and D
(3) A, B, C and E (4) A, B, C, D and E

61. Which is not a principle of Labour Welfare?

A. Principle of Social Responsibility of Industry

B. Principle of Re-personalisation

C. Principle of Trusteeship

D. Principle of Public Relation

E. Principle of Totality of Welfare

Choose the correct answer from the options given below.

(1) A and E (2) B and C
(3) C and E (4) C and D

62. Which among the following is not included under Statutory Welfare measure pertaining to canteen facility?

A. Section 46 of Factories Act, 1948

B. Section 11 of Plantation Labour Act, 1951

C. Section 44 of Factories Act,1948

D. Section 12 of Plantation Labour Act, 1951

E. Section 16 of Contract Labour (Regulation and Abolition) Act, 1970

Choose the correct answer from the options given below.

(1) A and B (2) C and D
(3) A and E (4) B and D

63. Which is not a theory of Labour Welfare?

A. The Police Theory of Labour Welfare
B. The Theory of Adequacy of Wage
C. The Philanthropic Theory
D. The Theory of Efficiency
E. The Placating Theory

Choose the correct answer from the options given below.

(1) A and C (2) C and E
(3) B and D (4) D and E

64. Wage-goods strategy of development was propounded by

A. CN Vakil
B. PR Brahmananda
C. Amartya Sen
D. Abhijit Sen
E. AR Desai

Choose the correct answer from the options given below.

(1) A and E (2) C and D
(3) A and B (4) B and D

65. What are the economic causes of migration?

A. Better employment opportunities
B. Marriage
C. Higher wage
D. Social discrimination
E. Attraction of better facilities and infrastructure

Choose the correct answer from the options given below.

(1) A, B and C
(2) C, D and E
(3) A, C and E
(4) B, C and D

66. Arrange the following management concepts in terms of period of evolution from earliest to latest.

A. Informal organisation
B. Time and motion study
C. Six sigma
D. Need hierarchy model
E. Management by objectives

Choose the correct answer from the options given below.

(1) B → D → A → E → C
(2) B → D → A → C → E
(3) B → A → D → E → C
(4) A → B → D → C → E

67. Arrange the following steps in sequential order for designing a structured interview.

A. Create interview questions
B. Appoint the interview panel
C. Analyse the job
D. Rate the job's main duties
E. Create benchmark answer

Choose the correct answer from the options given below.

(1) B → A → E → C → D
(2) C → D → A → E → B
(3) C → D → E → A → B
(4) A → E → B → C → D

68. Arrange the following phases of development of multinational corporations as identified by Alder and Ghadar starting from Phase-I.

A. Global B. Domestic
C. Multinational D. International

Choose the correct answer from the options given below.

(1) B, C, A, D
(2) C, B, A, D
(3) C, B, D, A
(4) B, D, C, A

69. Arrange the following steps of OB modification in the right sequence starting from the beginning.

A. Identification of critical behaviours
B. Measurement of the behaviours
C. Evaluation to ensure performance improvement
D. Functional analysis of the behaviour
E. Development of an intervention strategy

Choose the correct answer from the options given below.

(1) A, B, E, D, C
(2) A, D, B, C, E
(3) A, B, D, E, C
(4) A, B, C, D, E

70. Arrange the main government sponsored schemes of Worker's Participation in Management in India From earlier to latest.

A. Institutions of employees participation in management for public sector undertakings
B. Shop councils and unit councils under the 20-points programme
C. Board-Level Participation
D. Works Committee
E. Joint Management Councils

Choose the correct answer from the options given below.

(1) A, B, C, E, D (2) D, E, C, B, A
(3) B, C, D, E, A (4) C, D, E, A, B

71. **Arrange the process of disciplinary action is an industrial undertaking in proper sequence.**

A. Domestic enquiry
B. Framing of charges
C. Charge-sheeting
D. Inflicting punishment

Choose the correct answer from the options given below.

(1) A, B, C, D (2) B, C, A, D
(3) B, A, D, C (4) D, C, A, B

72. **Arrange in a sequence the Committees/ Commissions set-up by the Central Government in the country with regard to the matters concerning labour from the earliest to latest.**

A. Bombay Textile Labour Enquiry Committee
B. Royal Commission on Labour
C. Health Survey and Development Committee
D. First National Commission on Labour

Choose the correct answer from the options given below.

(1) A, B, C, D
(2) B, A, C, D
(3) C, A, B, D
(4) B, A, D, C

73. **Arrange the following provisions in the ascending order as mentioned under the Payment of Gratuity Act, 1972.**

A. Determination of the Amount of Gratuity
B. Compulsory Insurance
C. Nomination
D. Payment of Gratuity
E. Recovery of Gratuity

Choose the correct answer from the options given below.

(1) A, B, C, D, E
(2) D, B, C, A, E
(3) B, C, D, A, E
(4) D, A, C, B, E

74. **Arrange the following welfare facilities provided under the Factories Act, 1948 in ascending order as per their sections.**

A. Creche
B. Canteen
C. Washing
D. First-aid appliances
E. Facilities for sitting

Choose the correct answer from the options given below.

(1) A, C, E, B, D
(2) C, E, D, B, A
(3) B, A, C, E, D
(4) D, C, B, A, E

75. **Given below are two statements.**

Statement (I) 'Wages form the pivot round which most of the Labour problems revolve'.

Statement (II) Problems concerning the economic social conditions of wage earners have become topical.'

In the light of the above statements, choose the correct answer from the options given below.

(1) Both Statement I and Statement II are correct.
(2) Both Statement I and Statement II are incorrect.
(3) Statement I is correct, but Statement II is incorrect.
(4) Statement I is incorrect, but Statement II is correct.

76. **Match List-I with List-II.**

	List-I (Names)		List-II (Concepts)
A.	Max Weber	I.	Social systems approach
B.	Chester I. Barnard	II.	Hierarchy
C.	Vilfre Pareto	III.	Unit production
D.	Joan Woodward	IV.	Informal structure

Codes

	A	B	C	D
(1)	II	I	IV	III
(2)	II	IV	I	III
(3)	III	I	IV	II
(4)	II	I	III	IV

77. **Match List-I with List-II.**

	List-I (Types of Interview)		List-II (Meanings)
A.	Situational Interview	I.	A series of job-related questions that focus on how the candidate reacted to actual situation in the past.
B.	Behavioural Interview	II.	A series of job-related questions that focus on how the candidate would behave in a given situation.
C.	Job-related Interview	III.	A series of often rude questions that make the candidate uncomfortable.
D.	Stress Interview	IV.	A series of job-related questions that focus on relevant past job-related behaviour.

Codes

	A	B	C	D
(1)	I	II	IV	III
(2)	I	III	IV	II
(3)	II	I	IV	III
(4)	II	IV	I	III

78. **Match List-I with List-II.**

	List-I (HRD Frameworks)		List-II (Development Formulaters)
A.	The Integrative Framework Approach	I.	TV Rao
B.	The Strategic Framework Approach	II.	Friedman
C.	The HRD Scorecard Approach	III.	Ulrich and Lake
D.	The Human Capital Approach	IV.	Young and Berman

Codes

	A	B	C	D		A	B	C	D
(1)	IV	III	I	II	(2)	I	II	IV	III
(3)	III	II	I	IV	(4)	II	I	III	IV

79. **Match List-I with List-II.**

List-I (Theories of Motivation)	List-II (Propagators)
A. Expectency Theory	I. J. Stacy Adams
B. Equity Theory	II. Victor Vroom
C. ERG Theory	III. Fritz Heider
D. Attribution Theory	IV. Clayton P. Alderfer

Codes

	A	B	C	D		A	B	C	D
(1)	IV	III	II	I	(2)	III	IV	I	II
(3)	I	II	III	IV	(4)	II	I	IV	III

80. **Match List-I with List-II.**

List-I (Authors)	List-II (Books)
A. Karl Marx	I. A Theory of the Labour Movement
B. Selig Perlman	II. The Poverty of Philosophy
C. Robert F. Hoxie	III. The World of Labour
D. GDH Cole	IV. Trade Unionism in the United States

Codes

	A	B	C	D		A	B	C	D
(1)	II	I	IV	III	(2)	II	IV	III	I
(3)	IV	III	I	II	(4)	III	IV	II	I

81. **Match List-I with List-II.**

List-I (Form of Strikes)	List-II (Basic Features)
A. Authorised strike	I. Restored for a short period such as day or two to give the employer a warning of the likely wider form of consideration if their demands are not promptly conceded.
B. Wildcat strike	II. Such a strike is usefully resorted to in offence, to put pressure on the management.
C. Sit-down strike	III. When a section of workmen without authorisation from the union and often in defiance of the direction of the competent authority in a union.
D. Token strike	IV. Called by proper authority in a union and in confirmity with the requirements of law.

Codes

	A	B	C	D
(1)	III	IV	II	I
(2)	IV	III	II	I
(3)	I	III	II	IV
(4)	IV	II	III	I

82. **Match List-I with List-II.**

List-I (Authorities)	List-II (Legislations)
A. Technical Advisory Committee	I. The Contract Labour (Regulation and Abolition) Act, 1970
B. Central Advisory Board	II. The Factories Act, 1948
C. Export Committee	III. The Child and Adolescent Labour (Prohibition and Regulation) Act, 1986
D. Site Appraisal Committee	IV. The Building and other Construction Workers (Regulation of Employment and Conditions of Service) Act, 1996

Codes

	A	B	C	D		A	B	C	D
(1)	III	I	IV	II	(2)	IV	III	II	I
(3)	I	II	III	IV	(4)	II	IV	I	III

83. **Match List-I with List-II.**

List-I (Legislations)	List-II (Authorities)
A. The Minimum Wages Act	I. Advisory Committee
B. The Equal Remuneration Act	II. Controlling Authority
C. The Employees Provident Fund and Miscellaneous Provision Act	III. Central Advisory Board
D. The Payment of Gratuity Act	IV. Board of Trustees

Codes

	A	B	C	D		A	B	C	D
(1)	II	III	IV	I	(2)	I	III	IV	II
(3)	III	I	IV	II	(4)	IV	II	III	I

84. **Match List-I with List-II.**

List-I (Occupational Diseases)	List-II (Particulars)
A. Anthrax	I. Degree of accuracy, speed of work and concentration required for the job
B. Silicosis	II. Making of asbestos mattresses
C. Asbestosis	III. Caused by inhaling dust containing silica
D. Telegraphic Cramp	IV. Disease of animals

Codes

	A	B	C	D		A	B	C	D
(1)	III	IV	I	II	(2)	IV	III	I	II
(3)	IV	III	II	I	(4)	I	II	III	IV

85. **Match List-I with List-II.**

List-I (Name of Theories)	List-II (Propounders)
A. Wage Fund Theory	I. Ricardo
B. Residual Claimant Theory	II. JB Clark
C. Marginal Productivity Theory	III. JS Mill
D. Subsistence Theory	IV. Walker

Codes

	A	B	C	D		A	B	C	D
(1)	III	IV	II	I	(2)	III	II	I	IV
(3)	I	II	III	IV	(4)	II	III	IV	I

86. Given below are two statement, one is labelled as Assertion (A) and the other is labelled as Reason (R).

Assertion (A) It is argued that the best way to motivate workers is through job enrichment, which comprises of increasing opportunities for worker to experience feelings of responsibility, achievement growth and recognition.

Reason (R) Empowered employees would do their jobs well because they realise their responsibilities for providing quality service and towards other dimensions of their work.

In the light of the above statements, choose the correct answer from the options given below.

(1) Both A and R are true and R is the correct explanation of A.
(2) Both A and R are true, but R is not the correct explanation of A.
(3) A is true, but R is false.
(4) A is false, but R is true.

87. Given below are two statements, one is labelled as Assertion (A) and the other is labelled as Reason (R).

Assertion (A) It is the employee's perception of a situation that becomes the basis for his/her behaviour.

Reason (R) Individuals behave in a given manner based not on the way their external environment is but, rather on what they see or believe it to be.

In the light of the above statements, choose the correct answer from the options given below.

(1) Both A and R are true and R is the correct explanation of A.
(2) Both A and R are true, but R is not the correct explanation of A.
(3) A is true, but R is false.
(4) A is false, but R is true.

88. Given below are two statements.

Statement (I) Closed shop is an industrial or business establishment in which the union security clause in collective agreement provides that a job seeker must become the member of the union at the time of his employment and continue to do so in order to retain his job.

Statement (II) Closed shop agreements were widely prevalent in the USA and India following the enactment of the Wagner Act (National Labour Relation Act) in 1935 and the Trade Union Act, 1926 respectively.

In the light of the above statements, choose the correct answer from the options given below.

(1) Both Statement I and Statement II are correct.
(2) Both Statement I and Statement II are incorrect.
(3) Statement I is correct, but Statement II is incorrect.
(4) Statement I is incorrect, but Statement II is correct.

89. Given below are two statements, one is labelled as Assertion (A) and the other is labelled as Reason (R).

Assertion (A) The Factories Act, 1948 is meant to regulate the working conditions and meant to protects workers from exploitation and unhygenic working conditions within the factory premises.

Reason (R) In the absence of regulated health, safety and welfare provisions along with working hours, leave and restrictions on employment, certain category of workers are likely to be exploited by the greedy business establishment.

In the light of the above statements, choose the correct answer from the options given below.

(1) Both A and R are true and R is the correct explanation of A.
(2) Both A and R are true, but R is not the correct explanation of A.
(3) A is true, but R false.
(4) A is false, but R true.

90. Given below are two statements, one is labelled as Assertion (A) and the other is labelled as Reason (R).

Assertion (A) The main determinants of the general level of wages are the value of the marginal net product of labour, the degree of competition in the markets for the products of industry and the relative bargaining power of the workers and employers.

Reason (R) Most economists now confine their explanation of the determination of wage in the modern free labour market to a combination of marginal productivity theory and bargaining theory.

In the light of the above statements, choose the correcr answer from the options given below.

(1) Both A and R are true and R is the correct explanation of A.
(2) Both A and R are true, but R is not the correct explanation of A.
(3) A is true, but R is false.
(4) A is false, but R is true.

Directions (Q.Nos. 91-95) *Read the passage carefully and answer to the questions that follows.*

According to recent survey, India's economic growth in FY23 has been principally led by private consumption and capital formation and they have helped generate employment as seen in the declining urban unemployment rate and in the faster net registration in Employee Provident Fund. Moreover, world's second-largest vaccination drive involving more than 2 billion doses also served to lift consumer sentiments that may prolong the rebound in consumption. Still, private capex soon needs to take up the leadership role to put job creation on a fast track.

It also points out that the upside to India's growth outlook arises from (i) limited health and economic fallout for the rest of the world from the current surge in Covid-19 infections in China and therefore, continued normalisation of supply chains; (ii) inflationary impulses from the reopening of China's economy turning out to be neither significant nor persistent; (iii) recessionary tendencies in major Advanced Economies (AEs) triggering a cessation of monetary tightening and a return of capital flows to India amidst a stable domestic inflation rate below 6% and (iv) this leading to an improvements in animal spirits and providing further impetus to private sector investment.

The survey says, the credit growth to the Micro, Small and Medium Enterprises (MSME) sector has been remarkably high, over 30.6 %, on average during January-November 2022, supported by the extended Emergency Credit Linked Guarantee Scheme (ECLGS) of the Union Government. It adds that the recovery of MSMEs is proceeding apace, as is evident in the amounts of Goods and Services Tax (GST) they pay, while the Emergency Credit Linked Guarantee Scheme (ECGLS) is easing their debt servicing concerns.

Apart from this, increase in the overall bank credit has also been influenced by the shift in borrower's funding choices from volatile bond markets, where yields have increased and external commercial borrowings, where interest and hedging costs have increased, towards banks. If inflation declines in FY24 and if real cost of credit does not rise, then credit growth is likely to be brisk in FY24.

91. What factor has contributed to the recovery of Micro, Small and Medium Enterprises (MSME) sector?

(1) Liberalising government policies
(2) External Emergency Credit Linked Guarantee Scheme (ECLGS)
(3) Credit creation by the RBI
(4) Boost in industrial export

92. What need to take a leadership role to accelerate Job Creation, according to the survey?

(1) Private capital expenditure (capex)
(2) Foreign Direct Investment (FDI)
(3) Public expenditure
(4) Maintaining GPD growth rate

93. What played a role in boosting consumer sentiments and consumption rebound in India?

(1) Indo-US relationship
(2) GDP Growth Rate
(3) World second largest vaccination drive
(4) Implementation of the government policies

94. Given below are two statements.

Statement (I) India's economic growth in FY23 has been principally led by boost in agriculture export.

Statement (II) Inflationary impulses from reopening of China's economy turned out to be neither significant nor persistent.

In the light of the above statements, choose the correct answer from the options given below.

(1) Both Statement I and Statement II are correct.
(2) Both Statement I and Statement II are incorrect.
(3) Statement I is correct, but Statement II is incorrect.
(4) Statement I is incorrect, but Statement II is correct.

95. What were the two main factors contributing to India's economic growth in Financial Year 2023?

(1) Public healthcare initiatives and agriculture reforms
(2) Export growth and technological advancement
(3) FDI and credit formation
(4) Private consumption and capital formation

Directions (Q.Nos. 96-100) *Read the passage carefully and answer to the questions that follows.*

During the last couple of decades, with the expansion of technology, internet, urbanisation and more recently the COVID-19 pandemic, the debate on 'what is the future of work' has been rife among employers.

In the 2019 report of the World Bank Group on the 'Changing Nature of Work', it was estimated that less and than 0.5% of the active labour force participates in the gig economy globally, with less than 0.3% in developing countries. As per the 2022 report by India's public policy think tank, NITI Aayog, on 'India's Booming Gig and platform Economy' (NITI Report), the share of gig workers in total workers increased from 0.54%in 2011-12 to 133% in 2019-20. The advancement of technology has also enabled the emergence of temporary workers using online platforms thereby amplifying the focus on gig work.

The NITI Report considers 'gig workers' as those engaged in work outside the traditional employer-employee arrangement. There are two subsets to gig workers i.e., platform workers and non-platform workers. When these gig workers use online algorithmic matching platforms i.e., websites or apps like Amazon or Uber to connect with customers, they are known as platform workers.

The workers who work outside of these platforms are non-platform workers. These mainly include construction workers, day-job workers and non-technology based temporary workers.

96. Given below are two statement, one is labelled as Assertion (A) and the other is labelled as Reason (R).

Assertion (A) There are two subsets to gig workers, i.e., platform workers and non-platform workers.

Reason (R) The NITI Reports considers 'gig workers' as those engaged in work outside the traditionally employer-employee arrangement.

In the light of the above statements, choose the correct answer from the options given below.

(1) Both A and R are true and R is the correct explanation of A.
(2) Both A and R are true, but R is not the correct explanation of A.
(3) A is true; but R is false.
(4) A is false, but R is true.

97. What factors have contributed to the ongoing debate about the future of work?

(1) Changing demographics, labour strikes and government policies
(2) Natural disasters, labour unions and globalisation
(3) Economic recession, political instability and social changes
(4) Technological expansion, urbanisation and COVID-19 pandemic

98. According to the 2019 report of the World Band Group, what percentage of the global active labour force participates in the gig economy?

(1) Less than 0.5% (2) Around 1%
(3) About 5% (4) Over 10%

99. In the context of gig work, what are the platform workers?

(1) Workers who work exclusively offline
(2) Workers who have traditional employer-employee arrangements
(3) Workers who use online platforms to connect with customers
(4) Workers who engage in temporary

100. Given below are two statements, one is labelled as Assertion (A) and the other is labelled as Reason (R).

Assertion (A) Recently, the world has experienced a rise in the number of gig workers.

Reason (R) During the last couple of decades, with the expansion of technology, internet, urbanisation and more recently the COVID-19 pandemic, the debate on 'what is the future of work' has been rife among employers.

In the light of the above statements, choose the correct answer from the options given below.

(1) Both A and R are true and R is the correct explanation of A.
(2) Both A and R are true, but R is not the correct explanation of A.
(3) A is true, but R is false.
(4) A is false, but R is true.

ANSWERS

1	(2)	2	(1)	3	(1)	4	(3)	5	(1)	6	(3)	7	(2)	8	(1)	9	(2)	10	(1)
11	(1)	12	(4)	13	(3)	14	(1)	15	(3)	16	(2)	17	(1)	18	(2)	19	(3)	20	(3)
21	(2)	22	(1)	23	(4)	24	(3)	25	(1)	26	(3)	27	(3)	28	(2)	29	(2)	30	(3)
31	(3)	32	(2)	33	(2)	34	(3)	35	(1)	36	(2)	37	(1)	38	(4)	39	(2)	40	(3)
41	(1)	42	(1)	43	(1)	44	(2)	45	(1)	46	(2)	47	(1)	48	(2)	49	(3)	50	(3)
51	(2)	52	(3)	53	(3)	54	(1)	55	(1)	56	(4)	57	(2)	58	(3)	59	(1)	60	(3)
61	(4)	62	(2)	63	(3)	64	(3)	65	(3)	66	(3)	67	(2)	68	(4)	69	(3)	70	(2)
71	(2)	72	(2)	73	(2)	74	(2)	75	(1)	76	(2)	77	(3)	78	(1)	79	(4)	80	(1)
81	(2)	82	(1)	83	(3)	84	(3)	85	(1)	86	(1)	87	(1)	88	(3)	89	(1)	90	(2)
91	(2)	92	(1)	93	(3)	94	(4)	[illegible]	(4)	96	(2)	97	(4)	98	(1)	99	(3)	100	(1)

Solved Paper

2022

Human Resource Management & Labour Welfare (Paper-2)

Solved Paper, October 2022

General Instructions

1. There are total one hundred questions in this paper. Each question carries 2 marks.
2. All questions are compulsory.

---

1. Who among the following is associated with the idea that "The human personality progresses along a continuum from immaturity as an infant to maturity as an adult"?

(1) Sigmund Freud
(2) Erik Erikson
(3) Chris Argyris
(4) Daniel Levinson

2. Gagne-Briggs Theory of training is otherwise called as

(1) Instructional Design theory
(2) Component Display theory
(3) Elaboration theory
(4) KSA theory

3. One of the assumptions of Theory Y is as follows

(1) the normal human being intrinsically dislikes work and attempts of avoid it if the can do so.
(2) human beings have a hierarchy of needs.
(3) people are governed by self-direction and self-control.
(4) None of the above

4. Managerial Officers associations are registered under which of the following Act?

(1) Societies Registration Act, 1860
(2) Trade Union Act, 1926
(3) Either 1 or 2
(4) Neither 1 nor 2

5. The set of processes developed in an organisation to create, gather, store, transfer and apply knowledge describes

(1) Organisational memory
(2) Knowledge processes
(3) Knowledge management
(4) Knowledge assets

6. Matrix organisation is the combination of

(1) project and line organisation.
(2) line and staff organisation.
(3) project and functional organisation.
(4) functional organisation and product organisation.

7. Selecting the best possible objects, policies, procedures and programmes out of available alternatives comes under

(1) coordination (2) organisation
(3) planning (4) controlling

8. Questionnaire, personal interviews and observations are which part of HR audit?

(1) Setting benchmarks (2) Giving feedback
(3) Creating action plans (4) Data gathering

9. Which of the following strategy options will use data from the knowledge audit to develop employee profiles?

(1) E-learning (2) Expertise database
(3) Intranet (4) Corporate portal

10. In which types of strike, some of the union workers are posted at the factory gate for the purpose of watching and dissuading those who go to work?
(1) Picketing (2) Stay away strike
(3) Protest strike (4) Cat-call strike

11. "Press the right button but convincingly, to get a desired reaction". For which function of management this statement is quoted?
(1) Organisation (2) Motivation
(3) Control (4) Direction

12. Which of the following is not the advantage of delegation?
(1) It causes lack of trust in subordinates
(2) It improves managerial effectiveness
(3) It facilitates organisational growth
(4) It motivates subordinates

13. Who said action research is a process of systematically collecting research data about an ongoing system relative to some objective, goal or need of that system?
(1) Kurt Lewin (2) D Conback
(3) Henry Fayol (4) JC Collins

14. Selecting the best possible objects, policies, procedures and programmes out of available alternatives comes under
(1) coordination (2) organisation
(3) planning (4) controlling

15. The preferred method for achieving total quality in process is to
(1) build and install an error-proof process and maintain it.
(2) rely on operator self-inspection and self-correction.
(3) rely on a team of highly trained and dedicated inspectors.
(4) perform inspection at the next process.

16. What is meant by Kaizen?
(1) Card signal
(2) To avoid inadvertent errors
(3) Change for better quality
(4) None of the above

17. The 'carrot and stick' theory of motivation is related to
(1) Theory X
(2) Theory Y
(3) Maslow's recent assumptions about human motivation
(4) None of the above

18. Which of the following is responsible for establishing an entity's internal controls?
(1) Management (2) Auditors
(3) Committee of sponsoring organisations
(4) Management and auditors

19. R Likert believed which of the following types of leaders to be more effective?
(1) Production oriented (2) Task oriented
(3) People oriented (4) Job centered

20. Healthy people show the behaviour of maturity, while unhealthy people tend to demonstrate child like immature behaviour. Who among the following behavioural scientists said this?
(1) John Berry (2) Blake and Mouton
(3) FW Taylor (4) Chris Argyris

21. Who suggested that changes in organisations occur in three phases called unfreezing, changing and refreezing?
(1) David Nadler (2) Kurt Lewin
(3) Gary Hamel (4) Noel Tichy

22. Taylor's differential piecework plan provides that
(1) all labourers should be assigned work according to their capacity.
(2) all labourers should be put in different shifts.
(3) those who produce above standard should receive higher wages than those producing below standard .
(4) payment should be the same on fixed standard.

23. Consider the following statements and select which is/are true using the codes given below.
I. The amount sufficient to enable a worker to line is reasonable comfort, having regard to all obligations to which an average worker would ordinarily be subject to is called living wage.
II. The PDCA Cycle of quality management was given by W Edwards Deming.
III. Bedeaun point plan focuses on group incentive.

Codes
(1) I and II (2) Only I
(3) I and III (4) Only II

24. 5 'S' japanese model is accociated with
(1) quality management
(2) cost effective activities
(3) housekeeping
(4) All of the above

25. Successful career planning and development requires action from
(1) the organisation, the employees immediate manager and the employee himself.
(2) the employee and his/her immediate manager.
(3) a variety of source both internal and external to the organisation.
(4) the employee with some assistance/guidance from his or her immediate manager.

26. Which is not normally an essential condition for an effective HRIS?
(1) Changing the HR manager.
(2) Sustained enhancement of HRIS capabilities.
(3) Ensuring clarity of goals related to HRIS.
(4) Strengthening infrastructure and support systems.

27. On the basis of our understanding about human resource development, which of the following is most important for HRD?
(1) To be clearly related to the organisation's objectives.
(2) To be clearly related to the expertise in the department.
(3) To be flexible to be able to respond to sudden crisis.
(4) To operate as an extension of the HRM department.

28. Its basic premise is that the behaviour of human beings is determined by the sum of external environmental factors and not by internal needs, desires and wants. The reference is to
(1) Vroom's contingency Model of Motivation
(2) Skinner's Operant Theory of Motivation
(3) Adam's Equity Theory of Motivation
(4) All of the above

29. What is quality assurance?
(1) Quality assurance deals with activities which prove that products and services meet the required quality standard.
(2) Quality assurance deals with activities which aim at customers satisfaction.
(3) Quality assurance deals with controlling the quality of products by inspection.
(4) All of the above

30. What is the correct order of the following phases of training?
I. Development Phase
II. Design Phase
III. Need Analysis Phase
IV. Implementation Phase
V. Evaluation Phase

Codes
(1) III, II, I, IV, V (2) II, I, III, V, IV
(3) III, IV, I, II, V (4) IV, II, I, III, V

31. In a way Alderfer's ERG Theory is an extension of Maslow's Theory. Alderfer suggested three categories of needs rather than five. The needs suggested by Alderfer are
(1) Emotion, Rationality, Growth
(2) Efficacy,Reasoning, Giving
(3) Existence, Relatedness, Growth
(4) Exclusion, Relevance, Giving

32. "An agreement between an employee and the employer stating that the employer will neither join nor participate in union activities as a condition of employment" is called
(1) Union Shop Contract (2) Employment Contract
(3) Yellow-dog Contract (4) Business Contract

33. Which of the following statement is incorrect?
(1) Management audit signifies evaluation of the effectiveness of the management and its functional performance.
(2) Ratio analysis is a synonym for cost profit volume analysis.
(3) Budgetary control helps in delegation.
(4) None of the above

34. Select the right sequence of Kurt Lewin's planned change.
I. Unfreezing, changing, refreezing
II. Refreezing, moving, unfreezing
III. Changing, refreezing, unfreezing

Codes
(1) II, III, I (2) I, II, III
(3) III, II, I (4) None of these

35. Who said, "Management Development concerns the means by which a person cultivates those skills application of which will improve the efficiency and effectiveness with which the anticipated results of particular segment are achieved
(1) Flippo (2) Dale Yoder
(3) Koontz and O' Donnell (4) Robert Owen

36. Which of the following is not the advantage of delegation?
(1) It causes lack of trust in subordinates.
(2) It improves managerial effectiveness.
(3) It facilitates organisational growth.
(4) It motivates subordinates.

37. A leadership theory which proposed that effective group performance, depended on the proper match between a leader's style and degree to which the situation allowed the leader to control and influence is called
(1) Trait theory
(2) Situational theory
(3) Fiedler's contingency model
(4) Path goal theory

38. Which of the following is not the main objective of human resource development?
(1) To provide suitable need based tranining programmes.
(2) To evaluate the job and set the weges/salary.
(3) To contribute towards the excellence of technical and management education.
(4) To motivate the employees in order to show better performance.

39. Which of the following statement(s) is/are correct?

I. Potential appraisal and performance management are HRD mechanisms.

II. Personnel function is maintenance oriented while HRD is development oriented.

Codes

(1) Neither I nor II (2) Only I
(3) Both I and II (4) Only II

40. ...... is not a unilary concept incorporated only with hierarchy of perspectives such as job satisfaction, pay structure etc but also factors that broadly reflect life satisfaction and general feelings of well being.

(1) Quality of person
(2) Quality of work life
(3) Quality of human
(4) None of the above

41. The managers did not like scientific management theory because

(1) they felt that the workers were given undue importance in the theory.
(2) it reduced managerial remuneration.
(3) they felt that it had the effect of giving away more wages to the worker.
(4) they felt that the rigid scientific methods will take away their managerial freedom in decision making.

42. Which of these is/are the consequence(s) of inequity as per Adam's Equity theory?

(1) The person can alter inputs i.e people who feel they are underpaid for their efforts may tend to reduce their efforts, and people who feel they are overpaid might want to increase their effort
(2) The person can cognitively distort input or outcomes
(3) The person might quit the job
(4) All of the above

43. Quality of work life is a combination of employee's welfare, working conditions and workplace democracy. Who highlighted the concept of workplace democracy?

I. Eric Tryst
II. Udai Pareek
III. Einar Thorsrud
IV. Fred Emery

Codes

(1) I and II (2) I, III and IV
(3) I and IV (4) All of these

44. Consider the following for the different type of strikes. Which of the following statement(s) is/are correct?

I. Workmen involved in Gherao are considered guilty under Section 339 or 340 of Indian Penal Code.

II. Boycotting is a form of strike and protest under which workers stand in front of the premises of employers with flash cards, banners and playcards.

III. In sympathetic strikes, workers are not having any issues with their employers.

Codes

(1) I and II (2) II and III
(3) I and III (4) All of these

45. Which of the following is not an objective of workers education in India?

(1) To strengthen among all section of the working class including rural workers, a sense of patriotism, national integrity unity, communal harmony, secularism and pride in being an Indian.
(2) To equip all section of workers including rural workers for their intelligent participation in asserting their right through strike.
(3) To develop leadership among the rank and file of workers themselves.
(4) To enable trade union themselves to take over ultimately the functions of workers education.

46. According to the Mines Act, 1952, which of the following is incorrect?

(1) No person shall be allowed to work in a mine who has already been working in any other mine within the preceding twelve hours.
(2) No adult employed above ground in a mine shall be required or allowed to work for more than forty-eight hours in any week.
(3) No adult employed above ground in a mine shall be required or allowed to work for more than ten hours in any day.
(4) A person will not work for more than five hours, continuously before he has had an interval for rest of atleast half an hour.

47. Which of the following is an important feature of 'Autonomous Working Group'?

(1) The group reports directly to the senior management by passing their immediate bosses.
(2) The creation of teams which have a high level of autonomy and control over their immediate working environment.

(3) The bringing together of various individuals who have a common interest in solving certain problems.

(4) A group of experts brought into research new ways of producing a product.

48. Arrange the following sentences related to the process of succession planning in proper sequence.

I. Identification of areas where development is necessary.

II. Assessment of individuals who have potential for filing the position.

III. Identification of the KSAs or competencies required for the CEO position.

IV. A plan to provide individual with opportunities to develop improvement requiring areas.

Codes

(1) III, II, I, IV (2) I, II, III, IV
(3) II, I, III, IV (4) IV, III, I, II

49. Which of the following statements about 'housekeeping' are true?

I. It believes in a place for everything and everything in its place principle.

II. It is a culture of maintaining cleanliness.

III. It is a system of arranging materials in order of their importance and frequency of use.

IV. It talks about the infrastructural facilities provided by the organisation.

Select the correct answer using the codes given below.

(1) I and III (2) I and II
(3) I, II and III (4) All of these

50. Match List I with List II.

List I	List II
A. Frank B Gilbreth	I. Theory of bureaucracy
B. Max Weber	II. Time and Motion studies
C. F W Taylor	III. Application of psychology to industry and management
D. Hugomunsterberg	IV. Scientific management

Codes

	A	B	C	D
(1)	I	II	IV	III
(2)	II	I	IV	III
(3)	II	I	III	IV
(4)	I	III	II	IV

51. Apart from legislations which of the following institutions operate in controlling and directing individual actions into desirable channels?

I. Religious prescriptions

II. Social customs, traditions and conventions

III. Socialist and revolutionary ideas

IV. Political freedom and extension of franchise

Codes

(1) I, II and III (2) II and III
(3) I and II (4) I, II and IV

52. Which of the following is not considered as 'Wage' under the provisions of Payment of Wages Act?

(1) Any sum paid to the employed person to defray special expenses entailed by him by the nature of his employment.

(2) Any remuneration to which the person is entitled in respect of overtime work.

(3) Any sum to which the person employed under any scheme framed under any law in force.

(4) All of the above

53. Which of the following statements are true?

I. Speed boss maintains the planned speed of production.

II. Gang boss makes the arrangement of men, material and machines for the job.

III. Inspector determines the process of job.

IV. Route clerk maintains proper discipline.

Codes

(1) I and III (2) II and IV
(3) I and II (4) I and IV

54. Match List I with List II.

List I	List II
A. Fayol	I. Grapevine
B. Simon	II. Shared understanding
C. Shannon	III. Cybernetics
D. Weiner	IV. Gang Plank
E. Millet	V. Noise

Codes

	A	B	C	D	E
(1)	I	II	III	IV	V
(2)	I	IV	II	III	V
(3)	IV	I	V	III	II
(4)	IV	II	I	V	III

55. Given below are two statements, one is labelled as Assertion (A) and the other labelled as Reason (R). Select the correct option from the codes given below.

Assertion (A) Scientific management is also called the physiological organisational theory.

Reason (R) Scientific management is concerned with only that range of human behaviour which relates to production.

Codes

(1) Both A and R are true and R is the correct explanation of A
(2) Both A and R are true, but R is not the correct explanation of A
(3) A is true, but R is false
(4) A is false, but R is true

56. Which of the following statements are true?

I. Henry Fayol was the first person to recognise the different qualities of manager.
II. Chester Barnard, Douglas McGregor, Abraham Maslow, Elton Mayo are classical theorists.
III. The classical scientific branch arose because of need to increase productivity and efficiency

Codes

(1) I and II (2) I and III
(3) II and III (4) Only III

57. Out of the following activities of trade unions, which are considered as social activities?

I. Initiating and developing workers education scheme.
II. Running cooperatives
III. Organising welfare and recreational activities such as mutual insurance, providing monetary and other help during periods of strikes and economic distress.

Codes

(1) II and III (2) I and II
(3) I, II and III (4) I and III

58. Which of the following characteristics of transactional and transformational leaders are not correctly matched?

	Leader	Characteristic
I.	Transaction leader	Idealised influence
II.	Transformational leader	management by exception
III.	Transformational leader	Laissez Faire
IV.	Transactional leader	Contingent reward
V.	Transformational leader	Intellectual stimulation

Codes

(1) I, II and IV (2) III, IV and V
(3) I, II and III (4) I, IV and V

59. Which of the following are examples of compensable factors?

I. Technical skills conceptual skills, inter personal skills.
II. Experience or length of working years.
III. Efforts and initiative.
IV. Responsibilities to be undertaken.
V. Supervision required.
VI. Working environment in which job is to be performed.
VII. Gender of the employee.

Codes

(1) II, III, IV and VII
(2) I, IV, V and VI
(3) I, II, III, IV and VII
(4) I, II, III, IV, V and VI

60. Identify the correct statements.

I. In MMPI model, the applicant is requested to answer 495 items as either 'True', 'False' and 'Cannot Say'. They meausre ten different personality dimensions such as depression, hysteria, paranoia etc
II. The big five personality model gives the five basic traits that reflect human personalities. These 5 traits are extraversion, agreeableness, conscientiousness, emotional stability neuroticism and openness to experience.
III. TAT, regarded to be the most well known formal interest test, comprise of pictures.

Codes

(1) Only I (2) I and II
(3) II and III (4) All of these

61. Which of the following correctly explains a recruiting yield pyramid?

(1) Company records showing present performance and promotability of inside candidates for the most important positions.
(2) A forecasting technique for determining future staff needs by using ratios between, for example, sales volume and number of employees needed.
(3) The historical arithmetic relationships between recruitment leads and invites, invitees and interviews, interviews and offers made, and offers made and offers accepted.
(4) Finding and/or attracting applicants for the employer's open positions.

62. An ideal wage system should fulfil certain characteristics. Which among the following is not a characteristic of an ideal wage system?

(1) It should develop harmonious relationship between parties
(2) It should be conducive to the interests of both the parties-the employer and the employees
(3) It should be capable of providing certain incentives to workers necessary to accelerate production
(4) It should be fairly complex and rigid

63. Given below are two statements, one is labelled as Assertion (A) and the other labelled as Reason (R). Select the correct option from the codes given below.

Assertion (A) Structural unemployment creates a great deal of concern and dominates the policy discussions.

Reason (R) Structural unemployment arises because of mismatch between the skills 'that workers are supplying and the skills that firms are demanding.

Codes
(1) R is wrong and therefore A cannot be said to be a correct assumption
(2) A is correct and R is not a proper explanation of A
(3) A is correct, but R is wrong
(4) A is correct and R explains A

64. Which of the following statements are true?

I. The first industrial policy resolution in India was introduced in 1948.
II. The Indian Parliament accepted the 'socialist pattern of society' as the national objective of its social and economic policy in December 1955.
III. The second industrial policy resolution in India was made in 1956.
IV. Under the second industrial policy resolution, industries were classified into three categories on the basis of the role the state would play in each of them.

Codes
(1) III and IV
(2) I, III and IV
(3) I and II
(4) I, II and III

65. Match List I with List II.

List I	List II
A. Achievement Test	I. Testing about verbal comprehension, word fluency, memory reasoning etc
B. Intelligence Test	II. Testing the knowledge about his claims
C. Personality Test	III. Testing one's level of interest in particular area
D. Aptitude Test	IV. Testing about his inter personal competence, leadership confidence etc
E. Interest Test	V. Testing the ability to do a specific job

Codes

	A	B	C	D	E		A	B	C	D	E
(1)	II	I	IV	V	III	(2)	V	IV	III	II	I
(3)	I	II	III	IV	V	(4)	III	II	IV	V	I

66. Given below are two statements, one is labelled as Assertion (A) and the other labelled as Reason (R). Select the correct option from the codes given below.

Assertion (A) The basic planning process always involves setting objectives, forecasting and assessing basic planning "premises" or assumptions, determining alternatives causes of actions, evaluating which options are best and then choosing and implementing plan.

Reason (R) There is usually a hierarchical aspect to managerial planning. Top' management approves a long-term or strategic-plan. Then each department creates its own budgets and other plans to fit and to contribute to company's long-term plan.

Codes
(1) A is right, but R is wrong.
(2) A is wrong, but R is right.
(3) A and R both are right, R explains A.
(4) A and R both are right, R does not explain A.

67. Which of the following statements about the Marxist approach to 'industrial relations is not correct?

(1) It see's industrial conflict as synonymous with political and social conflicts.
(2) It consideres pluralism as a mere illusion.
(3) It believes that capitalism cannot continue to maintain itself only by lowering the standard of living of the working class.
(4) It favours transformation of trade unions into revolutionary organisations.

68. Match the contents of different schedules given in List I with their respective schedules given in List II under the provisions of the Factories Act, 1948.

List I	List II
A. Permissible levels of certain chemical substances in work environment	I. First Schedule
B. List of notifiable disease	II. Second Schedule
C. List of industries involving hazardous processes	III. Third Schedule

Codes

	A	B	C		A	B	C
(1)	II	III	I	(2)	III	I	II
(3)	I	II	III	(4)	II	I	III

69. Indifference curves relating to supply of labour have a number of properties some of which are mentioned below

I. Indifference curves are downward slopping.
II. Indifference curves are upward slopping.
III. Higher indifference curves indicate lower levels of utility.
IV. Higher indifference curves indicate higher levels of utility.
V. Indifference curves do not intersect.
VI. Indifference curves intersect.
VII. Indifference curves are concave to.the origin.
VIII. Indifference curves are convex to the origin.

Which among the following properties are not true?

(1) I, II, III and IV
(2) II, VI, VII and VIII
(3) I, III, V and VII
(4) II, III, VI and VII

70. Which one of the following statements is correct about the Rajiv Gandhi Shramik Kalyan Yojana scheme provided under the Employees State Insurance Act, 1948?

(1) The unemployed person should have contributed to the scheme for atleast five years prior to loss of employment.
(2) The rate of unemployment allowance is at the rate of 50% of the daily wages.
(3) The minimum period of unemployment in a spell should be fifteen days for entitlement of the benefit.
(4) The allowance is payable for a maximum period of six months in one spell or different spells.

71. Match List I management functions with their possible explanation List II.

List I	List II
A. Controlling/ monitoring	I. Making optimum use of the resources required to enable successfully carrying out the plans.
B. Leading/ motivating	II. Deciding what needs to happen in future and generating plans for action.
C. Organising	III. Checking progress against plans, which may need modification based on feedback.
D. Planning	IV. Getting others to play an effective part in achieving plans.

Codes

	A	B	C	D		A	B	C	D
(1)	I	II	III	IV	(2)	IV	I	III	II
(3)	III	IV	II	I	(4)	III	IV	I	II

72. Which of the following statements are true?

I. Societal objectives of HRM deals with compliance with natural laws, human right laws and labour laws.
II. The personnel objectives entails manpower planning.
III. The functional objectives comprise of recruitment, selection, training, appraisal and others.

Codes

(1) Only I
(2) Only II
(3) I and III
(4) Only III

73. Which of the following statement is incorrect?

(1) Management audit signifies evaluation of the effectiveness of the management and its functional performance.
(2) Ratio analysis is a synonym for cost profit volume analysis.
(3) Budgetary control helps in delegation.
(4) None of the above

74. Which of the statements relating to the protected workman is not correct under the Industrial Disputes Act, 1947?

(1) The maximum number of protected workmen is limited to one hundred.
(2) The minimum number of protected workmen is limited to ten.
(3) It shall be limited to one percent of the total number of workmen employed.
(4) It is limited to the executives or office bearers of registered trade unions connected with the establishment.

75. Given below are two statements, one is labelled as Assertion (A) and the other labelled as Reason (R). Select the correct option from the codes given below.

Assertion (A) The hard boiled business man's approach is that 'labour' is an inevitable nuisance constancy asking for more.

Reason (R) Unlike West, in India it was hardly realised that labour is important for the social and economic processes of an egalitarian society.

Codes

(1) A is false if considered by its basic philosophy and R validate A
(2) A is true, but R is false
(3) Both A and R are false
(4) A is true, but R does not validate A

76. Given below are two statements, one is labelled as Assertion (A) and the other labelled as Reason (R). Select the correct option from the codes given below.

Assertion (A) Wage boards are set up by the Government of India for fixation and revision of wages.

Reason (R) Wage boards are not governed by any legislation but are appointed on an adhoc basis by the government.

Codes

(1) Both A and R are true
(2) Both A and R are false
(3) A is true, but R is false
(4) A is false, but R is true

77. Match List I with List II.

List I	List II
A. Markov Analysis	I. Files of personnel education, experience, interest skill etc that allow managers to quickly match job opening with employee backgrounds.
B. Replacement Chart	II. Study of firm's past employment needs over a period of years to predict future needs.
C. Skill Inventories	III. Method for tracking the pattern of employee movements through various jobs.
D. Trend Analysis	IV. A profile of job holders department wise and orders a snapshot of who will replace, of there is a job opening.

Codes

	A	B	C	D		A	B	C	D
(1)	II	III	IV	I	(2)	III	IV	I	II
(3)	I	II	III	IV	(4)	I	III	II	IV

78. Total Quality Management (TQM) programmes are more likely to remain effective, if a number of prescriptions are followed, which of the following prescrptions should not be followed?

(1) TQM does not become a separate 'bolt-on' set of activities.
(2) Slogans and exhortations about TQM's effectiveness are avoided.
(3) TQM should become a substitute for normal managerial leadership.
(4) Quality improvement relates to an operation's performance objectives.

79. Following steps are undertaken for developing a workforce score card.

I. Identify critical and carefully defined outcome measures.
II. Translate the measures into specific actions and outcomes.
III. Identify high and low performing employees.
IV. Develop and communicate detailed description of what is expected.
V. Develop supporting HRM and measurement systems.

What is the correct chronological order of these steps?

(1) I, II, III, IV
(2) I, II, IV, III
(3) I, II, IV, V
(4) I, III, IV, V

80. Performance management is a system that

I. ensures that employee's performance is supporting company's aims.
II. starts with fixing performance standards and ends with comparing results with those standards.
III. includes daily or weekly interactions to ensure continuous improvement in employee's performance.
IV. ensures that employee has requisite training to perform the job.

Codes

(1) Only I
(2) I and IV
(3) I, III and IV
(4) All of these

81. Match the following in relation to staffing approaches adopted by MNCs.

List I	List II
A. Ethnocentric Approach	I. Requires host county nationals to be hired to manage subsidaries whereas parent country nationals occupy key positions at corporate headquarters.
B. Polycentric Approach	II. Seeks the best people for key jobs regardless of nationality.
C. Geocentric Approach	III. Requires parent-country nationals on all the key positions.

Codes

	A	B	C		A	B	C
(1)	III	I	II	(2)	I	II	III
(3)	II	III	I	(4)	III	II	I

82. Given below are two statements, one is labelled as Assertion (A) and the other labelled as Reason (R). Select the correct option from the codes given below.

Assertion (A) Globalisation has opened up opportunities like open markets, free flow of goods, services and people as well as has posed threats like jobless economic growth, and cultural erosion and environmental degradation.

Reason (R) There has been an uneven competition between the developed and developing countries resulting in issues like dumping, privatisation of primary services like health and education, thereby remaining beyond the reach of millions of poor and unemployed.

Codes

(1) Both A and R are not correct
(2) A is correct, But R is not correct
(3) A is not correct, but R is correct
(4) A is correct, R is also correct, but does not fully explain the A

83. Benchmarking involves employees learning and adopting so called best practices by comparing their HRM practices with those of other (more successful) organisations. Identify the correct sequential steps of benchmarking.

I. Indentify HR practices for benchmarking
II. Identify benchmarking partners
III. Constitute a core or a project team to handle the benchmarking process
IV. Develop action plans to improve HR strategy and practices
V. Collect data from each of the benchmarking partners
VI. Analyse and interpret the data
VII. Prepare a comprehensive report based on the data analysis and interpretation

Codes

(1) I, III, IV, II, VII, V, VI
(2) IV, V, VI, III, I, II, VII
(3) I, III, II, V, VI, VII, IV
(4) IV, III, I, II, V, VI, VII

84. Arrange the steps in manpower planning in the order in which they occur

I. Identifying sources of manpower supply
II. Manpower forecasting
III. Determining manpower requirements
IV. Manpower inventory
V. Selection
VI. Recruitment
VII. Placement

Codes

(1) III, II, IV, I, VI, V, VII
(2) I, III, II, IV, V, VI, VII
(3) IV, I, II, III, VI, V, VII
(4) III, IV, I, II, VI, V, VII

85. Which of the following statements are true?

I. Training is a short term educational process and utilising systematic and organised procedures by which employees learn technical knowledge and skills for a definite purpose.
II. Training bridges the difference between job requirements and employee's present skills and abilities.
III. Training facilitates manpower planning.

Codes

(1) I and II (2) I and III
(3) II and III (4) Only I

86. The steps of motivation process as proposed by Keith Davis are as follows

I. Finding out objective
II. Observing the feelings of employees
III. Team spirit
IV. Communication
V. Integrate personal interest with organisation's interest
VI. Provide auxiliary condition

Which is the correct sequence of motivational process?

(1) I, II, IV, V, VI, III
(2) I, II, III, IV, V, VI
(3) I, III, IV, VI, II, V
(4) VI, IV, II, I, V, III

87. Following are the probable errors committed during organisational processes.

A. Leniency or severity error
B. Primacy and recency effects
C. Halo effect
D. Spill over effect
E. Status effect
F. Perceptual set

Which of the following statement(s) given above is/are true?

I. A, B, C are rectuitment errors
II. A, B, C are recruitment errors and D, E and F are rating errors
III. All are rating errors
IV. None are recruitment errors.

Codes

(1) II is true, IV is false
(2) I is false, III is true
(3) III is true, I is false
(4) III and IV are true, I and II are false

88. **Given below are two statements, one is labelled as Assertion (A) and the other labelled as Reason (R). Select the correct option from the codes given below.**

Assertion (A) **Quality circles in India was an imported idea from Japan without proper cultural changes in the organisations.**

Reason (R) **The corporate culture assimilating learning, empowerment and participation as equals could not be developed due to obsolete mindset of both employers and employees.**

Codes

(1) A is false and R is not the correct explanation of A
(2) Both A and R are false
(3) A is true, but R is not the correct explanation of A
(4) Both A and R are true and R validates A

89. **List I refers to the six key elements encountered by managers in designing their organisation structure.**

List II provides possible answer to address the key elements encountered in organisation designing.

List I		List II	
A.	To what degree are activities subdivided into separate jobs?	I.	Span of Control
B.	On what basis will jobs be grouped together?	II.	Centralisation and Decentralisation
C.	To whom do individuals and groups report?	III.	Departmentalisation
D.	How many individuals can a manager efficiently and effectively direct?	IV.	Work specialisation
E.	Where does decision-making authority lie?	V.	Chain of Command
F.	To what degree will there be rules and regulations to direct employees and managers?	VI.	Formalisation

Codes

	A	B	C	D	E	F
(1)	III	IV	V	II	I	VI
(2)	IV	III	V	I	II	VI
(3)	I	II	III	IV	VI	V
(4)	II	II	IV	VI	V	I

90. **In the 'Kirkpatrick Model', which level of training evaluation helps in knowing that trainees have applied their gained learning to the job?**

(1) Learning
(2) Reaction
(3) Job behaviour
(4) Ultimate value/results

Direction ***(Q. Nos 91-95) Read the following passage and answer the questions that follows.***

Peole differ in their abilities and their aptitudes. There is always some difference between the quality and of the same work on the same job being done by two different people. Performance appraisals of employees are necessary to understand each employees's abilities competencies and relative merit and work for the organisation. Performance appraisal rates the employees in term of their performance.

Performance appraisals are widely used in the society. The history can be dated back to the 20th century and then to the Second World War when the merit rating was used for the first time.

An employer evaluating their employees is a very old concept. It is an indispensable part of performance measurement. Performance appraisal is necessary to measure the performance of the employees and the organisation to check the progress towards the desired goals and aims.

The latest mantra being followed by organisations across the world being "get paid according to what you contribute" the focus of the organisation is turning to performance management and specifically to individual performance. Performance appraisal helps to rate the performance of the employees and evaluate their contribution towards the organisation goals.

If the process of performance appraisals is formal and properly structured, it helps the employees to clearly understand their roles and responsibilities and give direction to the individuals performance. It helps to align the individuals performance with the organisational goals and also review their performance.

Performance appraisal takes into account the past performance of the employees and focuses on the improvement of the future performance of the employees.

91. **According to this passage,**

(1) there is always some difference between the quality and quantity of the same work on the same job being done by two different people.

(2) there is no difference between the quality and quantity of the same work on the same job being done by two different people.
(3) there is always some similarities between the quality and quantity of the same work on the same job being done by two different people.
(4) there is sometime difference between the quality and quantity of the same work on the same job being done by two different people.

92. Performance appraisal is necessary
(1) to measure the deficiencies of the employees and organisation to check the points where a blame can be imposed upon the employees on their improper performance.
(2) to keep the employee under strict control according to the objective of the organisation.
(3) to enhance the performance of the employees and the organisation to check the progrees towards the desired goals and aims.
(4) to measure the performance of the employees and the organisation to check the progress towards the desired goals and aims.

93. The latest mantra being followed by organisation across the world
(1) "get paid according to what you contribute".
(2) "get paid according to your power and connections with superiors".
(3) "get paid according to the recommendation of political leaders".
(4) "get paid according to the prescriptions give by the government".

94. Performance appraisal takes into account
(1) the expected performance of the employees and focuses on the improvement of the future performance of the employees.
(2) the past performance of the employees and focuses on the improvement of the future performance of the employees.
(3) the desired performance of the employees and focuses on the improvement of the future performance of the employees.
(4) the past performance of the employees and focuses on the deficiencies of the performance of the employees.

95. If the process of performance appraisal is formal and properly structured
(1) it helps the employees to clearly understand their roles and responsibilities and give direction to the individual's performance.
(2) it helps the employers to clearly understand their roles and responsibilities of the employees and give direction for their performance.
(3) it helps the government to clearly understand the rule and policies applied in the organisation.
(4) it helps the organisation to understand the policies and rules and regulations for industries adopted by the Government.

Direction (*Q. Nos. 96-100) Read the following passage and answer the questions that follows.*

Labour market issues include employment, unemployment, participation rates and wages.In particular, in recent times,demographic changes have resulted in an increasingly ageing workforce. Labour markets provide the structure through which workers and employers interact in relation to jobs,working conditions and pay. Labour market outcomes are influenced by the institutions and processes of collective, including the roles played by employers' organisations and trade unions.

Eurofound monitors developments in pay, working time and quality of work and employment in the EU. It reports on labour market policies and conducts research on new forms of work organisation and employment, labour flexibility and trends in job creation and labour market mobility.

In the context of an ageing population and increasing demand for care services in the EU, there is growing concern about the supply of suitably qualified care workers. Eurofound researches strategies for employment in social care to meet current demands and future needs are researched.

One area of employment that is playing an increasingly important role in European social policy is childcare. Eurofound research has taken an in-depth look at childcare for schoolchildren.It details developments in employment, demonstrates good practices in the childcare sector and takes a 'look at the future of the sector.

96. Which of the following is not an issue of labour market?
(1) Employment
(2) Unemployment
(3) Participation rates and wages
(4) Competition in market

97. What does the labour market provide?
(1) The structure of interaction between workers and employers in relation to jobs, working conditions and pay.
(2) The structure of able management to increase the productivity of the organisation.

(3) The structure of interaction between workers and employers in relation to social gathering or out of the work relations.
(4) None of the above

98. Which of the following area of employment playing an increasingly important role in European social policy?
(1) Participatory management in the organisation
(2) Childcare
(3) Strikes and riots
(4) None of the above

99. Which among the following is correct?
(1) Labour market outcomes are influenced by the institutions.
(2) Labour market outcomes are influenced by the effect of the multinational companies.
(3) Labour market outcomes are influenced by the effect of the government policies.
(4) None of the above

100. According to this passage,
(1) there is growing concern about the supply of suitably qualified care workers.
(2) there is diminishing concern about the supply of suitably qualified care workers.
(3) there is no concern about the supply of suitably qualified care workers.
(4) None of the above

ANSWERS

1	(3)	2	(4)	3	(3)	4	(4)	5	(1)	6	(3)	7	(3)	8	(4)	9	(2)	10	(1)
11	(2)	12	(1)	13	(1)	14	(3)	15	(1)	16	(2)	17	(1)	18	(1)	19	(3)	20	(4)
21	(2)	22	(3)	23	(2)	24	(3)	25	(1)	26	(1)	27	(1)	28	(2)	29	(1)	30	(1)
31	(3)	32	(3)	33	(2)	34	(2)	35	(3)	36	(1)	37	(3)	38	(2)	39	(3)	40	(1)
41	(4)	42	(4)	43	(2)	44	(3)	45	(1)	46	(3)	47	(2)	48	(1)	49	(3)	50	(2)
51	(3)	52	(2)	53	(3)	54	(3)	55	(1)	56	(2)	57	(3)	58	(3)	59	(3)	60	(2)
61	(3)	62	(4)	63	(4)	64	(2)	65	(1)	66	(3)	67	(3)	68	(1)	69	(4)	70	(3)
71	(4)	72	(3)	73	(2)	74	(2)	75	(3)	76	(1)	77	(2)	78	(3)	79	(2)	80	(3)
81	(1)	82	(4)	83	(3)	84	(1)	85	(1)	86	(1)	87	(4)	88	(2)	89	(2)	90	(4)
91	(1)	92	(4)	93	(1)	94	(2)	95	(1)	96	(4)	97	(1)	98	(2)	99	(1)	100	(1)

Solved Paper

2021

Labour Welfare (Paper-2)
Solved Paper, November 2021

General Instructions

1. There are total one hundred questions in this paper. Each question carries 2 marks.
2. All questions are compulsory.

---

1. Explaining a relationship between satisfaction and performance, which of the following implicitly assumes that 'satisfaction leads to improved performance and dissatisfaction detracts from performance'?
(a) Attribution theory of motivation
(b) Content theories of motivation
(c) Vroom's Expectancy theory
(d) Adam's Equity theory

2. The belief that 'conflict is not only a positive force in a group but that it is absolutely necessary for a group to perform effectively' is associated with which of the following?
(a) Unitarist view
(b) Traditional view
(c) Interactionist view
(d) Human Relations view

3. OCTAPACE is an acronym developed by Udai Pareek which identifies eight important values relevant to an organisation's culture. Which one of the following gives the correct expansion of the term OCTAPACE?
(a) Openness, Cooperation, Trust, Authenticity, Proaction, Autonomy, Collaboration, Experimentation
(b) Openness, Confrontation, Trust, Authenticity, Proaction, Autonomy, Collaboration, Experimentation
(c) Openness, Confrontation, Trust, Autonomy, Proaction, Avoidance, Cooperation, Experimentation
(d) Openness, Cooperation, Truthful, Authenticity, Proaction, Authority, Collaboration, Experimentation

4. Consideration and Initiating Structure as the dimensions of leadership were identified by which of the following?
(a) The Iowa leadership studies
(b) Michigan leadership studies
(c) The Ohio State leadership studies
(d) The Harvard leadership studies

5. Who developed the Warwick Model of HRM?
(a) David Guest
(b) Hendry and Pettigrew
(c) Dave Ulrich
(d) Harvard

6. Which one of the following is related to on- the- job training?
(a) Committee assignments
(b) Special classes
(c) Case study
(d) Role playing

7. The process of estimating the quantity and quality of people required to meet future needs of the organisation is called
(a) Managerial Judgement
(b) Human Resource audit
(c) Supply forecasting
(d) Demand forecasting

8. Job analysis is the procedure for
(a) Describing about the remuneration
(b) Determining the duties and skill requirements
(c) Fixing the responsibility
(d) Allotment the duties

9. What should be the maximum number of representatives in the Joint Management Council?
(a) Six only (b) Twelve only
(c) Sixteen only (d) Twenty only

10. Under which section of the Industrial Disputes Act 1947, both the Central and State Government have the power to constitute a Court of Inquiry?
(a) Section 6 (b) Section 10
(c) Section 7 (d) Section 5

11. Which country is called 'Home of Collective Bargaining'?
(a) Japan (b) Great Britain
(c) United States of America (d) Canada

12. An unauthorised strike that is called for without the approval of the union, is commonly known as
(a) Bandh (b) Quickie strike
(c) Wild-cat strike (d) Sit-down strike

13. Excluding provisions of Section 22 of the Payment of Bonus Act, 1965, what is the maximum time limit, within which the bonus should be paid by the employer with sufficient reasons?
(a) One year (b) Two years
(c) Three years (d) Five years

14. Which one of the following Articles of Fundamental Rights includes Equality of Opportunities for all citizens in matters relating to employment or appointment to any office under the state?
(a) Article 16 (1) (b) Article 17 (1)
(c) Article 19 (1) (d) Article 18

15. Which one of the following authorities has the power to prescribe the certificate of fitness to workers in a factory under the provisions of the Factories Act, 1948?
(a) The Certifying Surgeon
(b) The Owner or Occupier of the Factory
(c) The Chief Inspector
(d) The State Government

16. When an employer asks employees to sign a type of loyalty oath stating that "the employee would neither join nor participate in the activities of a union" is known as
(a) The Conspiracy Doctrine
(b) The Yellow-Dog Contract
(c) Unfair Labour Practices
(d) Collective Bargaining Agreement

17. Under the provisions of the Building and Other Construction Workers' (Regulation of Employment and Conditions of Service) Act 1996, at least how many days before the commencement of the building work is an employer required to send a written notice regarding the construction of building?
(a) Ninety days (b) Sixty days
(c) Thirty days (d) Two months

18. "Labour is not a commodity" is the assertion made in which of the following?
(a) The Magna Carta
(b) The Philadelphia Declaration of ILO
(c) The Constitution of India
(d) The Universal Declaration of Human Rights

19. If any question arises as to the application or interpretation of standing orders certified under the provisions of the Industrial Employment (Standing Orders) Act, 1946, either the employer or workmen can refer the same to which one of the following authorities?
(a) Appropriate government
(b) Industrial tribunal
(c) Labour court
(d) Civil court

20. Who viewed 'trade unions as a means of representing the interests of workers through the strategies of mutual insurance, collective bargaining and legal enactments'?
(a) John R. Commons
(b) Sidney and Beatrice Webb
(c) Neil W. Chamberlain
(d) Karl Marx

21. As per the provisions of the Payment of Wages Act, 1936, no fine shall be imposed on any employed person under the age of
(a) Twenty one years (b) Eighteen years
(c) Sixteen years (d) Fifteen years

22. "We believe that if these committees (Works Committees) are given proper encouragement and the past errors are avoided, they can play a useful role in the Indian Industrial System".
This statement was given by
(a) The Whitley Committee of 1916
(b) The Royal Commission on Labour, 1929
(c) The First National Commission on Labour, 1969
(d) The Second National Commission on Labour, 2002

23. As per the provisions of the Payment of Wages Act, 1936, the registers, records relating to the payment of wages shall be preserved for at least how many years after the date of last entry?
(a) Three years (b) Ten years
(c) Five years (d) Seven years

24. Which one of the following statements is correct with respect to the Minimum Wages Act?
(a) Only one Schedule covers different types of seasonal industries
(b) Only one Schedule covers different shops and commercial establishments
(c) Three Schedules cover Factories, Plantations and Mines
(d) One Schedule having two parts covers industries and agriculture

25. Which among the following is not a major type of Safety Audits?
(a) Scheduled Audit
(b) Unannounced Audit
(c) Compliance with standards
(d) Promotion of safe behaviour

26. Social Insurance is described as 'giving in return for contribution' and benefits up to the level of
(a) Luxurious living
(b) Fair living
(c) Subsistence living
(d) Descent living

27. Due to the operation of the law of diminishing returns, the demand curve oflabour
(a) Slopes down
(b) Moves upward
(c) Remains static
(d) Slopes downward and then moves upward

28. Usual Status (US) unemployment is calculated with reference to the date of the survey to a preceding period of
(a) One day
(b) Seven days
(c) Thirty days
(d) Three hundred sixty five days

29. Full Employment is said to exist, if
(a) The actual rate of unemployment does not exceed the natural rate
(b) The actual rate of unemployment exceeds its natural rate
(c) The actual rate of unemployment is equal to natural rate
(d) All of the above

30. Which one of the following is not concerned with a Job Description?
(a) Job summary (b) Experience
(c) Working condition (d) Supervision given

31. Explaining to understand human behaviour which one of the following emphasises that, "the person and the environmental situation do not function as independent units but, in conjunction with the behaviour itself, reciprocally interact to determine human behaviour".
(a) Social learning Framework
(b) Behaviouristic Framework
(c) Cognitive Framework
(d) Organisational Development Framework

32. "The labour movement prepares the ground wherein the seed of trade unionism grows." Who said this?
(a) G. D. H. Cole (b) S. D. Punekar
(c) Karl Marx (d) Frank Tannenbaum

33. The determination of basic long term objectives of an enterprise and the adoption of courses of action and allocation of resources necessary to achieve these goals is known as
(a) Strategies (b) Policies
(c) Procedures (d) Rules

34. Which one of the following is not a principle of coordination laid down by Mary Parker Follett?
(a) Principle of direct contact
(b) Principle of early start
(c) Principle of reciprocal relationship
(d) Principle of completeness

35. Who is also known as 'the father of social system school' of management thought?
(a) Herbert A. Simon
(b) Henri Fayol
(c) Elton Mayo
(d) Chester Barnard

36. In an attempt to integrate individual and organisational goals, who developed the concept of Linking Pin?
(a) Elton Mayo
(b) Rensis Likert
(c) Max Weber
(d) Mary Parker Follett

37. A set of human resource management policies and practices that promote organisational effectiveness is known as
(a) Human Resource Information System
(b) Human Resource Management System
(c) Human Resource Audit System
(d) High Performance Work System

38. Taking into account the characteristics of transnational managers, the three core roles and responsibilities: worldwide, business strategist, architect of an asset and resource configuration and cross- border coordinator and controller are associated with which of the following forms of transnational management?
(a) Worldwide functional management
(b) Geographic subsidiary management
(c) Global business management
(d) Top-level corporate management

39. Who among the following focussed on the soft side of an organisation as a sequel to globalisation comprising adhocracy, simple structure, the divisionalised form, the machine bureaucracy and the professional bureaucracy?
(a) Burns and Stalker
(b) Henry Mintzberg
(c) J. S. Black
(d) Bartlett and Ghoshal

40. The quantitative gauge of a human resource management activity, such as employee turnover, hours of training per employee, or qualified applicants per position is known as
(a) Human Resource Benchmarking
(b) Human Resource Data Analytics
(c) Human Resource Metrics
(d) Human Resource Appraisal

41. Which of the following are the internal factors of recruitment?
1. Recruitment Policy
2. Sons of the soil
3. Image
4. Human Resource Planning
Choose the correct answer from the options given below:
(a) 1, 2 and 3 (b) 1 and 2
(c) 1 and 4 (d) 1, 3 and 4

42. Which among the following are the determinants of the supply of labour?
1. Product demand
2. Preference for Work versus Leisure
3. Number of firms
4. Number of qualified suppliers
Choose the correct answer from the options given below:
(a) 1 and 2 (b) 2 and 3
(c) 3 and 4 (d) 2 and 4

43. Which among the following are theories of labour welfare?
1. Social Responsibility theory
2. Placating theory
3. Public Relations theory
4. Coordination theory
5. Accountability theory
Choose the correct answer from the options given below:
(a) 1 and 2 (b) 2 and 4
(c) 2 and 3 (d) 4 and 5

44. Which among the following are the indirect costs of industrial accidents?
1. Loss of earning power
2. Loss of production
3. Paperwork
4. Legal issues
5. Equipment
Choose the correct answer from the options given below:
(a) 1 and 2 (b) 1 and 3
(c) 2 and 4 (d) 4 and 5

45. Who among the following are Classical Economists?
1. J. B. Say
2. Marshall
3. Pigou
4. David Ricardo
Choose the correct answer from the options given below:
(a) 1 and 2 (b) 2 and 3
(c) 1 and 4 (d) 3 and 4

46. Who among the following were the founder members of the Red Trade Union Congress?
1. S. V. Deshpandey
2. G. L. Khandelkar
3. B. T. Ranadiv
4. R. R. Bhalla
Choose the correct answer from the options given below:
(a) 1, 3 and 4 (b) 1, 2 and 3
(c) 2, 3 and 4 (d) 1, 2 and 4

47. Which of the following are the ways of determining a representative union for the purpose of Collective Bargaining in India?
1. Code of Discipline
2. Secret Ballot
3. Check-off System
4. Membership Verification
Choose the correct answer from the options given below :
(a) 1 and 2 (b) 1, 2 and 3
(c) 2, 3 and 4 (d) 1, 2, 3 and 4

48. Which three welfare schemes for unorganised workers, the Central Government shall formulate and notify time-to-time under the Unorganised Worker's Social Security Act, 2008?
1. Life and Disability Cover
2. Protection of Employment Cover
3. Health and Maternity Benefit
4. Old Age Protection
Choose the correct answer from the options given below :
(a) 1, 2 and 3 (b) 1, 3 and 4
(c) 1, 2 and 4 (d) 2, 3 and 4

49. By end of 1933, which three all India Trade Union organisations were in existence?
1. All India Trade Union Congress
2. The Red Trade Union Congress
3. National Trade Union Federation
4. Indian Trade Union Federation

Choose the correct answer from the options given below:

(a) 1, 2 and 4
(b) 1, 2 and 3
(c) 2, 3 and 4
(d) 1, 3 and 4

50. Who among the following took the lead in organising the Federation of Indian Chamber of Commerce?

1. Sri Purshottamdas Thakurdas
2. Lala Shriram
3. G. D. Birla
4. Dhirubhai Ambani

Choose the correct answer from the options given below:

(a) 1, 2 and 4 (b) 1, 2 and 3
(c) 2, 3 and 4 (d) 1, 3 and 4

51. Which of the following are the key components of a third-generation balanced scorecard?

1. Destination Statement
2. Strategic Objectives
3. Strategic Linkage Model and Perspective
4. Measures and Initiatives

Choose the correct answer from the options given below:

(a) 1 and 2 (b) 3 and 4
(c) 1, 2 and 3 (d) 1, 2, 3 and 4

52. Which two of the following organisations conducted a joint workshop on the subject of defining the informal sector in 1997?

1. The National Commission on Labour
2. National Council for Applied Economic Research (NCAER)
3. The Self-Employed Women's Association (SEWA)
4. The National Commission on Rural Labour

Choose the correct answer from the options given below:

(a) 1 and 2 (b) 2 and 3
(c) 3 and 4 (d) 1 and 4

53. As per the approved list of Indian Labour Conference, in which of the following three items should the Works Committee not normally deal with?

1. Wages and Allowances
2. Administration of welfare and funds
3. Bonus and profit-sharing schemes
4. Matters connected with the fixation of the standard labour force

Choose the correct answer from the options given below:

(a) 1, 2 and 3 (b) 1, 3 and 4
(c) 2, 3 and 4 (d) 1, 2 and 4

54. Choose the correct options regarding the theories of Motivation.

1. Theory 'X' and 'Y' are similar to each other
2. Two factor theory is derived by McGregor
3. The concept of ERG theory is similar to Maslow's hierarchy of needs theory
4. McClelland has identified the need for power, need for achievement and need for affiliation as the motivating needs

Choose the correct answer from the options given below:

(a) 1 and 3 (b) 2 and 3 (c) 3 and 4 (d) 1 and 2

55. By which three of the following ways can an individual performance be planned?

1. Task analysis or activities analysis
2. Key Result Areas and Goal settin
3. Key Performance Area
4. Key Description Area

Choose the correct answer from the options given below:

(a) 1, 2 and 3 (b) 2, 3 and 4
(c) 1, 3 and 4 (d) 1, 2 and 4

56. Consider the statements relating to the fines under the Payment of Wages Act, 1936.

1. No fine shall be imposed on any employed person until he has been given an opportunity of showing cause against the fine.
2. The total amount of fine which may be imposed in any one wage period on any employed person shall not exceed an amount equal to three per cent of wages.
3. Every fine shall not be deemed to have been imposed on the day of the act or omission in respect of which it was imposed.
4. Fine shall not be imposed on any employed person who is under the age of fifteen years.
5. All fines and all realisations shall be recorded in a register to be kept by the person responsible for the payment of wages

Choose the correct answer from the options given below:

(a) 1, 2, 3 and 4
(b) 1, 2, 3, 4 and 5
(c) 1, 2, 4 and 5
(d) 1, 2, 3 and 5

57. Consider the statements with respect to the minimum rate of wages fixed or revised, under the Minimum Wages Act, 1948.

1. Basic rate of wages with or without the cost of living allowances
2. Basic rate of wages and a special allowance at a rate to be adjusted at such intervals by the appropriate government
3. An all-inclusive rate allowing for the basic rate
4. Basic rate inclusive of house rent allowances and travelling allowances
5. Cash value of concessions, if any

Choose the correct answer from the options given below:

(a) 1, 2, 3 and 5
(b) 2, 3, 4 and 5
(c) 1, 2, 3, 4 and 5
(d) 1, 3, 4 and 5

58. Consider the statements in connection with the Nomination under the provisions of the Payment of Gratuity Act, 1972.

1. An employee who has completed one year of service shall require to make the nomination in the prescribed form
2. An employee may, in his nomination, distribute the amount of gratuity payable to him, against more than one nominee
3. An employee is required to make a nomination in favour of one or more member of his family if having family at the time of making the nomination
4. If a nominee predeceases the employee, the interest of the nominee shall not revert to the employee
5. A nomination once made by an employee can be modified by the employee at any time with written notice to the employer

Choose the correct answer from the options given below:

(a) 1, 2, 3 and 4 (b) 2, 3, 4 and 5
(c) 1, 2, 4 and 5 (d) 1, 2, 3 and 5

59. Which of the following are the advantages of group activities in accordance with the functions of an enterprise?

1. Logical reflection of functions
2. Maintain power and prestige of major functions
3. Follows principle of occupational specialisation
4. Responsibility for profit is at the top only

Choose the correct answer from the options given below:

(a) 1, 2 and 3 (b) 1 and 3
(c) 1, 2 and 4 (d) 1, 3 and 4

60. Which of the following factors are given in Porter's Diamond?

1. Factor conditions
2. Related and supporting industries
3. Market conditions
4. Demand conditions
5. Firm strategy and rivalry

Choose the correct answer from the options given below:

(a) 1, 2, 3 and 4 (b) 2, 3 and 4
(c) 1, 3, 4 and 5 (d) 1, 2, 4 and 5

61. The facilities covered under the welfare and health of contract labour as per provisions of the Contract Labour (Regulation and Abolition) Act, 1970 are

1. Canteens
2. Drinking water facilities
3. Creches
4. Restrooms
5. First-aid facilities

Choose the correct answer from the options given below:

(a) 1, 2, 3, 4 and 5
(b) 1, 2, 4 and 5
(c) 1, 2, 3 and 4
(d) 1, 2, 3 and 5

62. Which two of the following conventions of ILO related to Freedom of Association, Right to Organise and Collective Bargaining have not been ratified by India?

1. Convention No 11
2. Convention No 87
3. Convention No 98
4. Convention No 100

Choose the correct answer from the options given below:

(a) 1 and 2 (b) 2 and 3
(c) 3 and 4 (d) 1 and 4

63. Consider the following statements under the Building and other Construction Workers' (Regulation of Employment and Conditions of Service) Act, 1996.

1. A building worker who has been registered as a beneficiary under the Act shall cease to be beneficiary when he attains the age of sixty years.

2. A building worker shall cease to be a beneficiary if he has not worked for at least ninety days in a year.
3. If the building worker had been a beneficiary for at least three years continuously immediately before attaining the age of sixty years, shall be eligible to get benefits.
4. While computing the period of ninety days, the period of absence from the building or other construction work due to any personal injury caused to him by accident arising out of and in the course of his employment shall be included.

Choose the correct answer from the options given below:

(a) 1, 2 and 3 (b) 1, 2, 3 and 4
(c) 2, 3 and 4 (d) 1, 2 and 4

64. Which of the following are true relating to Potential Appraisals?

1. Inform employees about their future prospects
2. Help the organisation to chalk out a suitable succession plan
3. Update training efforts from time to time
4. Advise employees about what they must do to improve their career prospects

Choose the correct answer from the options given below:

(a) 1 and 2 (b) 2 and 3
(c) 1, 2 and 3 (d) 1, 2, 3 and 4

65. Consider the statements in connection with the liability for payment of wages to an inter-state migrant workman under the provisions of the Inter-State Migrant Workmen (Regulation and Employment and Conditions of Service) Act, 1979.

1. The contractor shall be responsible for payment of wages to each inter-state migrant workman
2. The principal employer shall nominate a representative duly authorised by him to be present at the time of disbursement of wages by the contractor
3. It shall be the duty of the contractor to ensure the disbursement of wages in presence of the employers representative
4. In case the contractor fails to make payment of wages, the principal employer shall not be liable to pay wages to the inter-state migrant workman

Choose the correct answer from the options given below:

(a) 1, 2 and 3 (b) 2, 3 and 4
(c) 1, 2 and 4 (d) 1, 3 and 4

66. Match List I with List II.

	List I (Trade Unions)		List II (Founder President)
A.	Madras Workers Union	1.	B. P. Wadia
B.	All India Trade Union Congress	2.	V. V. Giri
C.	Indian Trade Union Federation	3.	Lala Lajpat Rai
D.	Indian National Trade Union Congress	4.	Suresh Chandra Bannerjee

Choose the correct answer from the options given below:

	A	B	C	D
(a)	1	3	2	4
(b)	1	2	3	4
(c)	2	1	3	4
(d)	1	4	2	3

67. Match List I with List II.

	List I (Provisions given in the schedule)		List II (Schedule of Industrial Disputes Act)
A.	Illegality or otherwise of a strike or lock-out	1.	Schedule III
B.	Shift working otherwise than in accordance with standing orders	2.	Schedule V
C.	Any changes in contribution paid or payable by the employer to any provident fund or pension fund	3.	Schedule II
D.	Failure to implement award, settlement, or agreement	4.	Schedule IV

Choose the correct answer from the options given below:

	A	B	C	D
(a)	3	2	1	4
(b)	3	1	4	2
(c)	4	2	3	1
(d)	1	4	2	3

68. Match List I with List II.

List I	List II
A. Job analysis	1. A list of human requirements of a job
B. Job specification	2. Assigning workers additional activities at the same level
C. Job description	3. Procedure for determining the duties and skill requirements of the job
D. Job enlargement	4. A list of duties and responsibilities of a job

Choose the correct answer from the options given below:

	A	B	C	D
(a)	3	1	4	2
(b)	1	2	3	4
(c)	4	3	2	1
(d)	2	4	1	3

69. Match List I with List II.

List I (Type of MNC)	List II (Focus)
A. Multinational	1. Home market and export
B. Global	2. Local responsiveness and transfer of learning
C. Domestic	3. Global strategy, low cost and price competition
D. International	4. Local responsiveness and global integration

Choose the correct answer from the options given below:

	A	B	C	D
(a)	1	2	3	4
(b)	3	4	1	2
(c)	4	3	2	1
(d)	2	1	4	3

70. Match List I with List II.

List I	List II
A. Committees	1. The Building and Other Construction Worker's (Regulation of Employment and Conditions of Service) Act, 1996
B. Expert Committees	2. The Child and Adolescent Labour (Prohibition and Regulation) Act, 1986
C. Safety Committee	3. The Mines Act, 1952
D. Technical Advisory Committee	4. The Factories Act, 1948

Choose the correct answer from the options given below:

	A	B	C	D
(a)	1	3	4	2
(b)	2	4	3	1
(c)	3	1	4	2
(d)	4	3	2	1

71. Match List I with List II.

List I	List II
A. Ivan Pavlov	1. Social Learning Theory
B. B. F. Skinner	2. S-O-B-C Model
C. Alberta Bandura	3. Classical Conditioning
D. Fred Luthans	4. Operant Conditioning

Choose the correct answer from the options given below:

	A	B	C	D
(a)	4	3	2	1
(b)	1	2	4	3
(c)	3	4	1	2
(d)	2	1	3	4

72. Match List I with List II.

List I	List II
A. Product life cycle theory	1. David Ricardo
B. Transaction cost theory	2. R. G. Vernon
C. Comparative Cost Difference theory	3. Dunning
D. Relative Comparative Cost Advantages theory	4. Heckscher-Ohlin

Choose the correct answer from the options given below:

	A	B	C	D
(a)	2	3	4	1
(b)	1	2	3	4
(c)	3	1	2	4
(d)	2	4	1	3

73. Match List I with List II.

List I (Training techniques)	List II (Descriptions)
A. Monodrama	1. Training with an external perspective
B. Mirroring	2. Insight into a given interaction
C. Skill games	3. Games to test ability to plan ahead
D. Strategic Planners	4. Test to develop analytical skills

Choose the correct answer from the options given below:

	A	B	C	D
(a)	2	1	4	3
(b)	3	4	2	1
(c)	4	3	1	2
(d)	2	4	1	3

74. Match List I with List II.

List I (Theory of group formation)	List II (Characteristics)
A. Propinquity theory	1. Activities interactions and sentiments
B. Balance theory	2. Similar attitudes towards commonly relevant objects and goals
C. Exchange theory	3. Reward-cost outcomes of interaction
D. George Homans' theory	4. Spatial or geographical proximity

Choose the correct answer from the options given below:

	A	B	C	D		A	B	C	D
(a)	1	2	3	4	(b)	2	4	1	3
(c)	4	2	3	1	(d)	3	1	4	2

75. Match List I with List II.

List I	List II
A. Elton Mayo	1. Father of Modern Management Theory
B. F. W. Taylor	2. Hawthorne effect
C. Henri Fayol	3. Comprehensive social system approach
D. Chester Barnard	4. Principles of scientific management

Choose the correct answer from the options given below:

	A	B	C	D
(a)	2	4	1	3
(b)	2	4	3	1
(c)	3	4	2	1
(d)	3	1	4	2

76. Arrange the following in sequential order from the beginning to the end so far as the procedure for implementation of Certified Standing Orders under the provisions of the Industrial Employment (Standing orders) Act, 1941

1. Draft Standing Orders submitted by the Employer to the Certifying Officer
2. Modified copies of the Standing Order submitted before the Certifying Officer if required
3. Copies of the Standing Orders communicated to the Employer and representatives of workmen
4. Implementation of Certified Standing Orders
5. Application of model Standing Orders

Choose the correct answer from the options given below :

(a) 4, 1, 3, 2, 5 (b) 5, 1, 3, 2, 4
(c) 1, 3, 2, 5, 4 (d) 3, 2, 1, 5, 4

77. Given below are the different steps of process of learning. Arrange these from beginning of the process to the end.

1. Assimilation or retention
2. Acquiring knowledge
3. Internalisation of new knowledge
4. Application of new learning
5. Self-monitored learning

Choose the correct answer from the options given below :

(a) 1, 2, 3, 4, 5 (b) 2, 1, 3, 4, 5
(c) 2, 1, 4, 3, 5 (d) 5, 1, 4, 3, 2

78. The career management process can be sequenced in five stages. Arrange these stages from the beginning to the end

1. Strategy
2. Assessment
3. Planning
4. Development
5. Evaluation

Choose the correct answer from the options given below:

(a) 1, 3, 2, 4, 5 (b) 1, 2, 3, 4, 5
(c) 2, 1, 4, 5, 3 (d) 1, 3, 5, 4, 2

79. Arrange the four levels of training evaluation from the first to the last as given by Kirkpatrick.

1. Reaction 2. Results
3. Job behaviour 4. Learning

Choose the correct answer from the options given below:

(a) 2, 3, 4, 1 (b) 3, 2, 1, 4
(c) 4, 1, 2, 3 (d) 1, 4, 3, 2

80. Arrange the different phases of strategic planning in multinational firms starting from the beginning to the end.

1. Strategic business units
2. Entry and participation strategy
3. External and internal analysis
4. Organisational structure, control and coordination mechanism

Choose the correct answer from the options given below :

(a) 3, 1, 2, 4
(b) 1, 3, 4, 2
(c) 2, 4, 1, 3
(d) 4, 2, 3, 1

81. Arrange the following Indian Trade Union/Organisations on the basis of their founding year from the earliest to the latest

1. United Trade Union Congress
2. The Red Trade Union Congress
3. The Textile Labour Association of Ahmedabad
4. Hind Mazdoor Sabha
5. Self Employed Woman's Association

Choose the correct answer from the options given below :

(a) 3, 2, 4, 1, 5 (b) 1, 3, 4, 5, 2
(c) 2, 3, 1, 4, 5 (d) 5, 4, 3, 1, 2

82. Arrange the following phases of internationalisation from the first to the fourth phase as identified by Adler and Ghadar.

1. Domestic
2. Multinational
3. Global
4. International

Choose the correct answer from the options given below:

(a) 3, 4, 2, 1 (b) 1, 3, 4, 2
(c) 1, 4, 2, 3 (d) 1, 2, 3, 4

83. Arrange the main schemes of Workers Participation in Management according to their year of formation from the earliest to the latest.

1. Joint Management Councils
2. Shop Councils
3. Board-Level Participation
4. Institution of Employees' Participation in Management for Public Sector Undertakings
5. Works Committee

Choose the correct answer from the options given below :

(a) 5, 1, 3, 2, 4 (b) 5, 2, 4, 3, 1
(c) 5, 3, 1, 2, 4 (d) 5, 4, 3, 2, 1

84. Arrange in sequence the following legislations in order of their years of enactment from the earliest to the latest.

1. The Minimum Wages Act
2. The Payment of Wages Act
3. The Payment of Gratuity Act
4. The Payment of Bonus Act
5. The Equal Remuneration Act

Choose the correct answer from the options given below :

(a) 1, 2, 5, 4, 3
(b) 2, 1, 4, 3, 5
(c) 2, 1, 5, 4, 3
(d) 5, 3, 4, 1, 2

85. Arrange the committees/commission in sequence from the latest to the earliest, as per the year they were set up.

1. Royal Commission on Labour
2. National Commission on Labour
3. Standing Labour Committee
4. Labour Investigation Committee
5. Bihar Labour Enquiry Committee

Choose the correct answer from the options given below :

(a) 3, 2, 4, 5, 1 (b) 2, 4, 3, 5, 1
(c) 5, 2, 3, 4, 1 (d) 1, 5, 4, 2, 3

86. Given below are two statements, one is labelled as Assertion (A) and the other is labelled as Reason (R).

Assertion (A) Financial inclusion is desirable to help the weaker sections of the society in the country.

Reason (R) Investment activity needs to be promoted to facilitate access to development benefits.

In light of the above statements, choose the most appropriate answer from the options given below

(a) Both (A) and (R) are correct and (R) is the correct explanation of (A)
(b) Both (A) and (R) are correct, but (R) is not the correct explanation of (A)
(c) (A) is correct, but (R) is not correct
(d) (A) is not correct, but (R) is correct

87. Given below are two statements, one is labelled as Assertion (A) and the other is labelled as Reason (R)

Assertion (A) Intra-mural and extra-mural welfare facilities in organisations are mutually complimentary

Reason (R) The work-life balance needs to be ensured in order to get the best output from an employee.

In light of the above statements, choose the most appropriate answer from the options given below

(a) Both (A) and (R) are correct and (R) is the correct explanation of (A)
(b) Both (A) and (R) are correct but (R) is not the correct explanation of (A)
(c) (A) is correct, but (R) is not correct
(d) (A) is not correct, but (R) is correct

88. Given below are two statements, one is labelled as Assertion (A) and the other is labelled as Reason (R)

Assertion (A) Structural inertia is an organisational resistance process to change because organisations have a built in mechanism to produce stability.

Reason (R) People with a high need for security are likely to resist change because it threatens their feeling of safety.

In light of the above statements, choose the most appropriate answer from the options given below

(a) Both (A) and (R) are correct and (R) is the correct explanation of (A)
(b) Both (A) and (R) are correct, but (R) is not the correct explanation of (A)
(c) (A) is correct, but (R) is not correct
(d) (A) is not correct, but (R) is correct

89. Given below are two statements, one is labelled as Assertion (A) and the other is labelled as Reason (R).

Assertion (A) It is one thing to hold that the role of the state should be minimal, and quite another to hold that industrial relations should be based only on bilateralism.

Reason (R) Bilateralism is an essential ingredient of industrial relations and both parties should rely on it as far as possible. But it cannot be denied that there is a role that mediation, arbitration, adjudication or third party intervention can play to ensure industrial peace with justice to both sides and to the society.

In light of the above statements, choose the most appropriate answer from the options given below

(a) Both (A) and (R) are correct and (R) is the correct explanation of (A)
(b) Both (A) and (R) are correct, but (R) is not the correct explanation of (A)
(c) (A) is correct, but (R) is not correct
(d) (A) is not correct, but (R) is correct

90. Given below are two statements, one is labelled as Assertion (A) and the other is labelled as Reason (R)

Assertion (A) Attitudes of confrontation must give place to an attitude of genuine partnership

Reason (R) Organisations of workers as well as employers, and the state itself, should identify and create the conditions on which harmonious relations that we need can be created and maintained.

In light of the above statements, choose the most appropriate answer from the options given below

(a) Both (A) and (R) are correct and (R) is the correct explanation of (A)
(b) Both (A) and (R) are correct, but (R) is not the correct explanation of (A)
(c) (A) is correct, but (R) is not correct
(d) (A) is not correct, but (R) is correct

Directions (Q. Nos. 91-95) *Read the passage carefully and answer the question that follows :*

Following the latest trends and being fashionable is the 'in thing' these days. This fad is not only prevalent in clothes, accessories, home decor and every conceivable thing, but also in attitudes and behaviours. These days being rude, loud, intolerant and aggressive is 'COOL'. Anyone who is quiet, polite and keeps a low profile is labelled a sissy, simple and regressive.

Increasingly, the world is becoming 'I' centric. Everyone believes and follows the principle of 'ME' and 'MYSELF' above 'YOU' and 'YOURS'. Checking the phone repeatedly when in company, not listening to others, interrupting a conversation, talking loudly on the phone in a public place, parking the car in the middle of the road and being unmindful of the traffic chaos, being nasty on social media, aggression on the road is all a part of normal behaviour these days. A 2013 survey found that as social media usage surged over the years, it has given rise to increasing cases of incivility; with 78 per cent of 2698 people reporting an increase in rudeness online.

Social media has brought about an increase in bad manners and loss of courtesies, decency and etiquette in society. Perhaps, it is easier to be mean, and rude when one is not in a face to face interaction with somebody. Sadly, appaling behaviour, intolerant views, a good dose of abuse, aggression and expletives thrown in, have become fodder for the soul.

91. In order to be fashionable and cool these days, one has to be

(a) dressed in latest fashion
(b) intolerant, ill-mannered and aggressive
(c) knowledgeable
(d) funny and friendly

92. We are becoming increasingly rude because

(a) We like being rude
(b) Social media encourages such behaviour
(c) We are subjected to modern day stresses
(d) We are not concerned about others' feelings

93. What is not included in identification of a low profile individual?

(a) Regressive
(b) Sissy
(c) Attractive
(d) Simple

94. What is not considered as a part of normal behaviour these days?

(a) Following the traffic rules
(b) Talking loudly over phone in public place
(c) Being nasty on social media
(d) Not listening to others

95. When is it easier to be nasty?

(a) When one meets the other person
(b) When one is not face to face
(c) When one talks in a group
(d) When one is in a public place

Directions (Q.Nos. 96-100) *Read the passage carefully and answer questions that follow :*

'Chanakya Neeti' is synonymous with efficient statecraft around the world, and Chanakya is India's face of political statecraft and the rich political understanding of its ancient heritage. No political efficiency is devoid of understanding Chanakya and his ways of statecraft. In fact, he showed the world that political theory is in practice. Ancient Indian history is incomplete without a reference to his ways of statecraft and politics.

Chanakya amazes any scholar with his multifaceted character, but it had a distinct focused aim. He was more about philosophy and thoughts put into action. He does not bore you with his philosophical theory but engages you to think, act and achieve what you dream of. He overthrew a mighty empire and put in the throne a humble man like Chandragupta Maurya.

He identified the potential ruler from a group of children, thus gave the world a great sovereign who united the Indian subcontinent into a political and administrative unit. For sure, Chanakya's mental capabilities were superb. The modern global diplomacy revolves around his principle of 'saam, daam, dand, bhed' (persuade, purchase/set a price upon, punish, exploit the weakness).

His *Arthashastra* elevates the state to a position where service to it entails imperatives unknown to morality. Chanakya would have been identified as a professor of political science and economics at Takshila. He was an economic, political and royal adviser and a think tank, and can be credited to have given India its complex united empire.

96. 'Chanakya Neeti' is
(a) an individual
(b) a political treatise
(c) a philosophy
(d) a complex way of thinking

97. Chanakya amazes scholars because of
(a) his character
(b) his focused aim
(c) boring political philosophy
(d) ability to get people to think, act and achieve their dreams

98. In *Arthashastra*, Chanakya places the interest of the state
(a) Below moral responsibility
(b) At par with moral responsibility
(c) Above any moral responsibility
(d) The state has nothing to do with moral responsibility

99. The modern day global diplomacy follows the principle of
(a) Reward, request, entreaty and punishment
(b) Request, cajole, threaten and persuade
(c) Purchase, punish, request and accept
(d) Persuasion, exploitation, punishment and purchase

100. Chanakya identified the potential ruler from among which one of the following?
(a) Politicians
(b) Kings
(c) Teachers
(d) Children

ANSWERS

1	(b)	2	(c)	3	(b)	4	(c)	5	(b)	6	(a)	7	(d)	8	(b)	9	(b)	10	(a)
11	(b)	12	(c)	13	(b)	14	(a)	15	(d)	16	(b)	17	(c)	18	(b)	19	(c)	20	(b)
21	(d)	22	(b)	23	(a)	24	(d)	25	(d)	26	(c)	27	(a)	28	(d)	29	(c)	30	(b)
31	(a)	32	(b)	33	(a)	34	(d)	35	(d)	36	(b)	37	(d)	38	(c)	39	(b)	40	(c)
41	(c)	42	(d)	43	(c)	44	(a)	45	(c)	46	(b)	47	(d)	48	(b)	49	(b)	50	(b)
51	(d)	52	(b)	53	(b)	54	(c)	55	(a)	56	(c)	57	(a)	58	(d)	59	(a)	60	(d)
61	(b)	62	(b)	63	(a)	64	(d)	65	(a)	66	(a)	67	(b)	68	(a)	69	(b)	70	(c)
71	(c)	72	(a)	73	(a)	74	(c)	75	(a)	76	(b)	77	(b)	78	(b)	79	(d)	80	(a)
81	(a)	82	(c)	83	(a)	84	(b)	85	(b)	86	(a)	87	(a)	88	(b)	89	(a)	90	(a)
91	(b)	92	(b)	93	(c)	94	(a)	95	(b)	96	(b)	97	(d)	98	(c)	99	(d)	100	(d)

SOLVED PAPER

2020 & 2019

Labour Welfare (Paper-2)
Solved Paper, November 2020

General Instructions

1. There are total one hundred questions in this paper. Each question carries 2 marks.
2. All questions are compulsory.

---

1. The statement "I love the company, I am working for, I love my job, I am a learning state and I am growing because of my organisation and so I will give my company the best in return" is associated with

(a) The Eiffel Tower Culture
(b) The Family Culture
(c) The Incubator Culture
(d) The Guided Missile Culture

2. "Minimum requirement about membership of a Trade Union," as Section 9A, inserted by way of an amendment in the Trade Unions Act, 1926, came into force from

(a) 9th January, 2020 (b) 9th January, 2002
(c) 1st April, 2002 (d) 1st July, 2001

3. Which of the following human resource forecasting techniques is considered as the 'quickest' forecasting technique?

(a) Managerial Judgement
(b) Ratio-Trend Analysis
(c) Delphi Technique
(d) Regression Analysis

4. Selection criteria for selection of staff for international assignment are broadly categories under two categories namely; individual and situation. Which of the following is covered under the situation criteria?

(a) Language
(b) Family requirements
(c) Technical ability
(d) Cross-Cultural suitability

5. The provision relating to 'Subsistence allowance' finds place under which one of the following legislations?

(a) The Industrial Disputes Act, 1947
(b) The Industrial Employment (Standing Orders) Act, 1946
(c) The Trade Unions Act, 1926
(d) The Plantation Labour Act, 1951

6. Based on the statement given below, choose the correct option.
'Changes in product demand that increase the product price will raise the marginal revenue product of labour and therefore, increase the demand for labour.'

(a) The statement is wrong
(b) the statement is correct
(c) The demand for product has nothing to do with marginal revenue product of labour.
(d) Even if the demand for product increases, the marginal physical product of labour shall remain constant.

7. Which among the following is left out while calculating natural rate of Unemployment?

(a) Seasonal Unemployment (b) Frictional Unemployment
(c) Structural Unemployment (d) Cyclical Unemployment

8. Under the provisions of the Industrial Employment (Standing Orders) Act, 1946, a certified standing order shall not be modified until the expiry of which period from the date, the certified standing order came into operation?

(a) Two months (b) Three months
(c) Six months (d) Twelve months

9. Which one of the following subjects is not enumerated in the 'Concurrent List of Indian Constitution?

(a) Oil fields
(b) Trade Unions
(c) Factories
(d) Vocational and Technical Training of Labour.

10. Which of the following statement is correct to define 'child' as per the provisions of the Child and Adolescent Labour (Prohibition and Regulation) Act, 1986?

(a) A person who has not completed his fourteenth year of age;
(b) A person who has not completed such age as may be specified in the Right of Children to Free and Compulsory Education Act, 2009;
(c) A person who has not completed his fourteenth year of age or such age as may be specified in the Right of Children to Free and Compulsory Education Act, 2009; whichever is more;
(d) A person who has not completed his fourteenth year of age or such age as may be specified in the Right of Children to Free and Compulsory Education Act, 2009, whichever is less.

11. As per the provisions of the Minimum Wages Act, 1948. Which of the following authority advises the appropriate government for fixing and revising minimum wages and coordinating the work of the committees and sub-committees constituted under the Act?

(a) The Advisory Committee
(b) The Central Advisory Board
(c) Advisory Board
(d) The Central Government

12. Shops and Commercial Establishment Legislation comes under which one of the categories of Labour Legislations?

(a) Welfare Legislations
(b) Social Security Legislations
(c) Protective Labour Legislations
(d) Wage Legislations

13. Under the provisions of the Payment of Bonus Act, 1965, an employee of an establishment, shall be entitled for bonus to be paid by the employer provided the employee has worked for a minimum period of how many days in the establishment in a financial year?

(a) Thirty Days (b) Sixty Days
(c) Ninety Days (d) Two hundred forty Days

14. Ranking employees from the best to worst on a particular trait, choosing highest then lowest, until all are ranked is termed as

(a) Graphic Rating Scale
(b) Alternation Ranking Method
(c) Paired Comparison Method
(d) Forced Distribution Method

15. The process for enabling employees to better understand and develop their career skills and interests and to use these skills and interest more effectively is called as

(a) Career Development (b) Career Management
(c) Career Planning (d) Career Counselling

16. What percentage of the net profit of the company, the top managers are entitled for their compensation under the Companies Act, 2013?

(a) 4 Per cent (b) 11 Per cent
(c) 20 Per cent (d) 10 Per cent

17. Which approach suggests that there is no best way to handle any of the management problems and there is no best organisational structure to suit all situations?

(a) Operational Approach (b) Contingency Approach
(c) Case/empirical Approach (d) System Approach

18. Who among the following is called "the father of brainstorming"?

(a) AlexOsborn
(b) W Edwards Deming
(c) Frank and William Gilbreth
(d) Thomas Peters

19. A Leader who guide or motivate their followers in the direction of established goals by clarifying role and task requirements is

(a) Transformational Leader
(b) Charismatic Leader
(c) Transactional Leader
(d) Facilitative Leader

20. Giving employees more authority to make decisions is known as

(a) Authority (b) Responsibility
(c) Employee Empowerment (d) Decentralisation

21. As per Vroom's Expectancy Theory of Motivation 'Instrumentality' relates?

(a) Efforts to Performance
(b) Efforts with first level outcome
(c) Performance with first level outcome
(d) First level outcome to second level outcome

22. Based on the statement given below, choose the correct option.

'In the case of decrease in product demand, marginal revenue product of labour will decline'.

(a) The statement is wrong
(b) The statement is correct
(c) The demand for product has nothing to do with marginal revenue product of labour
(d) Even if the demand for product decreases, the marginal physical product of labour shall remain constant.

23. 'System Theory of Organisation' was given by

(a) Max Weber (b) Chester Barnard
(c) Robert Owen (d) FW Taylor

46. Given below are some of the conventions adopted by ILO. Arrange those conventions in a sequence from the earliest to latest according to the years of adoption.

1. The Protection of Wage Convention
2. The Minimum Wage Fixing Machinery Convention
3. The Holidays with Pay Convention
4. The Minimum Wage Fixing Machinery (Agriculture) Convention

Choose the correct answer from the options given below.

(a) 1, 3, 2, 4 (b) 2, 3, 1, 4
(c) 2, 4, 1, 3 (d) 1, 2, 4, 3

47. Arrange the following steps in proper sequence relating to HR Planning.

1. Forecast of Personnel needs and supplies
2. Defining organisational objectives and policies
3. Control and evaluation
4. HR Programming
5. HRP implementation

Choose the correct answer from the options given below.

(a) 1, 2, 4, 5, 3
(b) 4, 5, 2, 3, 1
(c) 2, 4, 1, 3, 5
(d) 2, 1, 4, 5, 3

48. Given below are the matters provided in different schedules of the Employee's Provident Fund and Miscellaneous Provisions Act, 1952. Arrange them in a sequence from Schedule I to IV as provided in the Act.

1. Matters for which provision may be made in the Pension Scheme.
2. Matters for which provision may be made in a Scheme
3. Matters to be provided for in the Employees' Deposit-linked Insurance Scheme.
4. List of Industry notified

Choose the correct answer from the options given below.

(a) 2, 4, 3, 1 (b) 4, 2, 1, 3
(c) 2, 1, 3, 4 (d) 3, 1, 4, 2

49. Arrange the folowing components of Guest Model of HRM in proper sequence.

1. Behavioural outcomes
2. HRM practices
3. HR outcomes
4. Performance outcomes
5. HRM strategies

Choose the correct answer from the options given below.

(a) 2, 3, 5 4, 1 (b) 5, 2, 3, 1, 4
(c) 1, 2, 3, 5, 4 (d) 3, 1, 4, 5, 2

50. Given below the ILO Conventions ratified by the Government of India Arrange them in a chronological order according to the year of ratification starting from the earliest to the latest.

1. Hours of work (Industry) Convention.
2. Underground work (Women) Convention.
3. Prevention of Major Industrial Accidents Convention.
4. Labour Inspection Convention.

Choose the correct answer from the options given below.

(a) 1, 2, 3, 4 (b) 1, 2, 4, 3
(c) 3, 1, 2, 4 (d) 1, 4, 3, 4

51. Identify the correct sequence of the following from options in the light of the lowest to the highest level.

1. Living Wage
2. Minimum Wage
3. Fair Wage

Choose the correct answer from the options given below.

(a) 3, 1, 2 (b) 2, 3, 1
(c) 3, 2, 1 (d) 2, 1, 3

52. The schemes under the Provident Fund Act, 1952 enacted at different years. Arrange those schemes according to their year of enactment from the earliest to the latest.

1. Employees Pension Scheme
2. Family Pension Scheme
3. Employees Deposit-linked Insurance Scheme
4. Employees Provident Fund Scheme

Choose the correct answer from the options given below.

(a) 1, 4, 3, 2 (b) 1, 3, 2, 4
(c) 4, 2, 3, 1 (d) 2, 4, 3, 1

53. Appreciative Inquiry Process was developed by David Cooperrider and Suresh Srivastava giving four phases. Arrange the four phases from one to four.

1. Dream
2. Design
3. Discovery
4. Delivery

Choose the correct answer from the options given below.

(a) 2, 3, 1, 4 (b) 3, 1, 2, 4
(c) 2, 1, 4, 3 (d) 4, 1, 3, 2

54. Given below is a list of organisations. Arrange them in a chronological order starting from the earliest to the latest, on the basis of the years of their formation.
1. Bombay Mill Hands Association
2. Amalgamated Society of Railway Servants in India and Burma
3. Madras Labour Union
4. Indian Federation of Labour

Choose the correct answer from the options given below.
(a) 1, 2, 3, 4 (b) 1, 3, 2, 4
(c) 2, 3, 4, 1 (d) 3, 2, 1, 4

55. The four steps of frustration cycle is given below. Arrange the correct sequence of frustration cycle.
1. Adaptive deterioration
2. Isolation
3. Defensive Behaviour
4. Distorted Perception

Choose the correct answer from the options given below.
(a) 1, 3, 4, 2
(b) 1, 2, 4, 3
(c) 3, 1, 2, 4
(d) 2, 1, 4, 3

56. Choose the correct options regarding theories of Motivation.
1. The concept of ERG theory is similar to Maslow's hierarchy of needs.
2. Theory 'X' has positive assumptions while theory 'Y' has negative assumptions.
3. Two factor theory is derived by Mc gregor.

Choose the correct answer from the options given below.
(a) 1 only
(b) 1 and 2 only
(c) 2 and 3 only
(d) 1, 2 and 3 only

57. TV Rao has described four indicators, which can be used to arrive at a comprehensive score for HRD maturity. Identify the four indicators from the following.
1. HRD System Maturity Score
2. HRD Competence Score
3. The HRD Innovation Score
4. Business Linkage Score
5. The HRD Culture

Choose the correct answer from the options given below.
(a) 1, 2, 3, 4 only (b) 1, 2, 4, 5 only
(c) 1, 2, 3, 5 only (d) 1, 3, 4, 5 only

58. Contigency Theories of leadership were developed by.
1. Blake and Mouton
2. Fiedler
3. Hickson
4. Vroom and Yetton

Choose the correct answer from the options given below.
(a) 1, 2 and 3 only (b) 1, 3 and 4 only
(c) 2, 3 and 4 only (d) 1, 3 and 4 only

59. Trait Theories of Leadership were developed by.
1. Stogdill
2. Mc call and Lombardo
3. Bennis and Thomas
4. Kurt Lewin

Choose the correct answer from the options given below.
(a) 1 and 2 only (b) 1, 2 and 3 only
(c) 1, 3 and 4 only (d) 1, 2, 3 and 4 only

60. Given below are some of the matters within the jurisdiction of the Industrial Tribunals. As per the provisions of the Industrial Disputes Act, 1947, which option is correct?
1. Hourse of work and rest intervals
2. Leave with wages and holidays
3. The application and interpretation of standing orders
4. Rules of Discipline

Choose the correct answer from the options given below.
(a) 1, 2, 3 only
(b) 2, 3, 4 only
(c) 1, 2, 4 only
(d) 1, 3, 4 only

61. Given below are some of the provisions relating to Strikes and Lockouts in Public Utility services under the I.D. Act, 1947. No person employed in a public utility service shall go on strike.
1. Without giving to the employer notice of strike within six weeks before striking.
2. Within Forty Five days of giving such notice.
3. Before the expiry of the date of strike specified in any such notice as aforesaid.
4. During the pendency of any conciliation proceeding before a conciliation officer and fifteen days after the conclusion of such proceedings.

Choose the correct answer from the options given below.
(a) 1 and 3 only (b) 1, 2 and 3 only
(c) 1, 3 and 4 only (d) 1, 2, 3, 4 only

62.* Given below are some incentive schemes. Find out the schemes which are covered under the category "Earnings very less proportionately than output"?

1. Hasley Plan
2. Emerson's Efficiency Plan
3. Bath Scheme
4. Rowan Plan

Choose the correct answer from the options given below.

(a) 1, 2, 3 only (b) 2, 3, 4 only
(c) 1, 3, 4 only (d) 1, 2, 4 only

63. Given below are some of the training methods for the executives. Choose the methods which are covered under off-the-job methods.

1. Special Projects
2. Programmed Instructions
3. Committee Assignment
4. Conference Training

Choose the correct answer from the options given below.

(a) 2 and 3 only (b) 1, 2 and 3 only
(c) 1 and 4 only (d) 2 and 4 only

64.* As per the provisions of the Payment of Gratuity Act, 1972, the definition of 'family' in relation to an employee includes

1. In case of male employee, himself, his wife, his children whether married or unmarried his dependant parents and children of his predeceased son, if any
2. In case of female employee, herself, her husband, her children whether married or unmarried, her dependant parents and dependant parents of her husband and the widow and children of her predeceased son, if any.
3. In case of male employee, himself, his wife, his children, whether married or unmarried, his dependants parents and the dependant parents of his wife and children of his predeceased son, if any.
4. In case of a male employee, himself, his wife, his children whether married or unmarried and his dependant parents.

Choose the correct answer from the options given below.

(a) 1, 2, 4 only (b) 1, 2, 3 only
(c) 1, 3, 4 only (d) 2, 3, 4 only

65.* Given below are some of the items, which are normally covered under 'Wages'. From these items, which of them are included under the definition 'basic wages' as per the Employees' Provident Fund and Miscellaneous Provisions Act, 1952?

1. Cash value of any food concession
2. Any dearness allowance
3. House rent allowance
4. Leave travel concession

Choose the correct answer from the options given below.

(a) 1, 2, 4 only (b) 1, 2, 3 only
(c) 2, 3, 4 only (d) 1, 3, 4 only

66. As per the provisions of the Employees' Provident Fund and Miscellaneous Provisions Act, 1952. Who among the following officers are to be appointed by the Central Government?

1. Central Provident Fund Commissioner
2. Chief Acounts Officer
3. Insurance Commissioner
4. Financial Adviser

Choose the correct answer from the options given below.

(a) 1, 2, 3 only (b) 1, 2, 3 only
(c) 1, 3, 4 only (d) 2, 3, 4 only

67. As per the provisions of the Payment of Gratuity Act, 1972, an employee on termination of employment after continuous period of five years, shall be eligible to receive the Gratuity from employer under which of the following conditions?

1. On his superannuation
2. On his retirement or resignation
3. On his death or disablement due to accident
4. On dismissal from the employment for gross misconduct

Choose the correct answer from the options given below.

(a) 1, 2, 4 only (b) 1, 3, 4 only
(c) 1, 2, 3 only (d) 2, 3, 4 only

68. Given below are some statements relating to payment of wages/incentives. Choose the statements which are correct?

1. Time rate system is more suitable where strict supervision is possible.
2. In Halsey's premium plan, time wages are guaranteed.
3. Under the Rowan Plan, incentive paid is fixed.
4. Under the Emerson's Efficiency Plan, the worker gets a normal wage upto 67 per cent of efficiency.

Choose the correct answer from the options given below.

(a) 2, 3 and 4 only (b) 1, 2 and 4 only
(c) 1, 3 and 4 only (d) 1, 2 and 3 only

* Answer not given in official answer key.

69. Which of the following statements relating to the Sachar Committee are true?

1. It was appointed in 1977.
2. It submitted its report in 1979.
3. One of the terms of reference for the Committee was to suggest measures by which workers' participation in the share capital and management of companies can be brought about.
4. The Committee did not recommend any "mandatory participation in equity by the workers."

Choose the correct answer from the options given below:

(a) 1, 2, 3 only (b) 2, 3, 4 only
(c) 1, 3, 4 only (d) 1, 2, 4 only

70. Which of the followings are related to steps of Job Analysis?

1. Gather Information 2. Questionnaire
3. Job description 4. Job specification

Choose the correct answer from the options given below.

(a) 1, 2 and 3 only (b) 2, 3 and 4 only
(c) 3 and 4 only (d) 1, 3 and 4 only

71. As per the provisions of the Industrial Disputes Act, 1947, workman who is not a member of the trade union, but is a party to dispute, shall be entitled to be represented by whom?

1. By any other workman employed in the industry
2. By any member of the executive of the trade union.
3. By any member of the executive or office bearer of a Federation of Trade Unions.
4. By a Legal Practioner

Choose the correct answer from the options given below.

(a) 1, 2, 3 only (b) 1, 2, 4 only
(c) 2, 3, 4 only (d) 1, 3, 4 only

72. Which of the following statements relating to the criteria for Recognition of Unions described in the code of Discipline are true?

1. Where there is more than one union, a union claiming recognition should have been functioning for atleast one year after registration; where there is only one union, this condition would not apply.
2. A union may claim to be recognised as a representative union for an industry in a local area if it has a membership of atleast 25 per cent of the workers of that industry in that area.
3. When a union has been recognised, there should be no change in its position for a period of three years.
4. Where there are several unions in an industry or establishment, the one with the largest membership be recognised.

Choose the correct answer from the options given below.

(a) 1, 2, 3 only (b) 2, 3, 4 only
(c) 1, 3, 4 only (d) 1, 2, 4 only

73. Which of the following statements relating to the Trade Union Movement in India are true?

1. The Indian National Trade Union Congress was formed by Hindustan Mazdoor Sevak Sangh.
2. There was a rift in the All India Trade Union Congress in 1970.
3. The first President of the All India Trade Union Congress was Chaman Lal.
4. The Indian Trade Union Federation was formed in 1930.

Choose the correct answer from the options given below.

(a) 1, 2, 3 only (b) 2, 3, 4 only
(c) 1, 2, 4 only (d) 1, 3, 4 only

74. Which among the factors mentioned below are the hidden cost of accident?

1. Legal issues
2. Loss of morale
3. Spoiled work
4. Training cost of replaced worker
5. Lost time by fellow employers

Choose the correct answer from the options given below.

(a) 1, 2 and 3 only (b) 1, 3 and 5 only
(c) 3, 4 and 5 only (d) 1, 2, and 4 only

75. An employee after completion of one year of service is required to give nomination under the provisions of the Payment of Gratuity Act, 1972. From the statements given below, which are the correct options for nomination by the employee?

1. If having family, in favour of one or more members of his family.
2. If the employee at the time of nomination, has no family, infavour of any person or persons of his choice.
3. If having family, giving nomination in favour of a person, who is not a member of his family.
4. If the nominee predeceases the employee, giving fresh nomination in favour of a member of the family.

Choose the correct answer from the options given below.

(a) 1, 2, 3 only (b) 1, 2, 4 only
(c) 2, 3, 4 only (d) 1, 3, 4 only

76. Which among the following services are offered by National Safety Council, a voluntary non-profit making body governed by a Board of Directors representing the Government, Employers and Trade Union representatives?

1. Publication Service
2. Ambulance Service
3. Mobile Clinic Service
4. Safety Training Service

Choose the correct answer from the options given below:

(a) 1 and 4 only
(b) 1 and 2 only
(c) 2 and 3 only
(d) 3 and 4 only

77. The main function of the shop council is to increase production and overall efficiency of the shop or department. Which of the following are the functions of the shop council?

1. Improvement of physical conditions of working.
2. To study absenteeism in the shops.
3. The preparation of schedule of working hours and holidays.
4. Awarding rewards for valuable and creative suggestions.

Choose the correct answer from the options given below.

(a) 1, 2 and 3 only
(b) 1 and 2 only
(c) 1 and 3 only
(d) 1, 3 and 4 only

78. Which of the following statements relating to the Trade Union Movement in India are true?

1. The Ahmedabad Textile Labour Association was established in 1920.
2. The AITUC was established in 1920.
3. Lala Lajpat Rai was the first General Secretary of the AITUC.
4. There was a split in the AITUC in 1929.

Choose the correct answer from the options given below.

(a) 1, 2, 3 only (b) 2, 3, 4 only
(c) 1, 3, 4 only (d) 1, 2, 4 only

79. Turner and Hodge has proposed four areas of concern in the study of professionalism. They are

1. Degree of Substantive Theory and Technique
2. Degree of Monopoly
3. Degree of External Recognition
4. Degree of Organisation
5. Degree of Philosophy

Choose the correct answer from the options given below.

(a) 1, 2, 3, 4 only (b) 1, 2, 3, 5 only
(c) 1, 2, 3, 5 only (d) 2, 3, 4, 5 only

80. Which among the following are the essential elements of Social Insurance?

1. Contributory finance
2. Benefits prescribed in law
3. Person's other income and resources are taken into account.
4. Benefits are paid without contribution as legal right in prescribed categories of need.

Choose the correct answer from the options given below.

(a) 1 and 4 only (b) 1 and 3 only
(c) 2 and 4 only (d) 1 and 2 only

81. Match List I and List II.

List I	List II
A. Reformist Unions	1. Industrial Workers of the World (IWW)
B. Revolutionary Unions	2. Unions affiliated to the American Federation of Labour and Congress for Industrial Organisation (AFL-CIO)
C. Craft Unions	3. Rashtriya Mill Mazdoor Sangh, Bombay
D. Industrial Unions	4. The Ahmedabad Weavers Union

Choose the correct answer from the options given below.

	A	B	C	D
(a)	2	1	4	3
(b)	3	2	1	4
(c)	1	3	2	4
(d)	4	3	1	2

82. Match List I and List II.

List I	List II
A. Kaizen	1. focuses on meeting the customer requirement on time
B. Value Stream Mapping	2. focuses on continuous improvements in manufacturing, engineeringor management
C. 20-Point Programme	3. Focuses onintense and regular scrutiny of every step in the work processes in an organisation
D. Total Quality Management	4. Focuses on specific socio-economic measures

Choose the correct answer from the options given below.

	A	B	C	D
(a)	1	2	3	4
(b)	2	1	4	3
(c)	3	1	2	4
(d)	4	3	1	2

83. Match List I and List II.

List I	List II
A. Subsistence Theory	1. JB Clark
B. Wage Fund Theory	2. Walker
C. Residual Claimant Theory	3. JS Mill
D. Marginal Productivity Theory	4. Ricardo

Choose the correct answer from the options given below.

	A	B	C	D
(a)	4	3	2	1
(b)	1	2	3	4
(c)	4	2	1	3
(d)	2	4	1	3

84. Match List I and List II.

List I (Training Description)	List II (Training Technique)
A. Providing a common focus of discussion	1. Shadowing
B. Insight into a given interaction	2. Multiple role playing
C. Brings out ideas that are not often expressed.	3. Monodrama
D. Working under a senior to watch and learn	4. Doubling

Choose the correct answer from the options given below.

	A	B	C	D
(a)	2	3	4	1
(b)	3	2	4	1
(c)	4	3	1	2
(d)	2	1	4	3

85. Match List I and List II.

List I	List II
A. Discipline	1. The Payment of Wages Act, 1936
B. Regulation of Employer-Employees Relations	2. the Industrial Employment (Standing Orders) Act, 1946
C. Wage Revision	3. The Industrial Disputes Act, 1947
D. Mode and Time of Payment of Wages	4. The Minimum Wages Act, 1948

Choose the correct answer from the options given below.

	A	B	C	D
(a)	2	3	4	1
(b)	3	4	1	2
(c)	3	4	2	1
(d)	3	2	4	1

86. Match List I and List II.

List I	List II
A. Frictional Unemployment	1. Unemployment that varies predictably with season.
B. Seasonal Unemployment	2. When people are in transition from one job to another or when they first enter the labour market.
C. Cyclical Unemployment	3. In periods of economic change when new jobs being created have requirements different from the old jobs being lost.
D. Structural Unemployment	4. Associated with a reduction in real outputs during periods of recession.

Choose the correct answer from the options given below.

	A	B	C	D
(a)	2	3	1	4
(b)	2	1	4	3
(c)	2	3	4	1
(d)	4	1	3	2

87. Match List I and List II.

List I (Commission Committee)	List II (Chairman)
A. Royal Commission on Labour	1. Ravindra Verma
B. First national Commission on Labour	2. DV Rege
C. Labour Investigation Committee	3. JH Whitley
D. Second National Commission on Labour	4. PB Gajendra Gadkar

Choose the correct answer from the options given below.

	A	B	C	D
(a)	2	1	4	3
(b)	4	3	1	2
(c)	3	4	2	
(d)	1	2	3	4

88. Match List I and List II.

List I	List II
A. Group influences in the work place	1. Max Weber
B. Administrative Theory-Rules of Management	2. Chester Barnard
C. Father of Modern Management Theory	3. Mary Parker Follet
D. Systems Theory	4. Henri Fayol

Choose the correct answer from the options given below.

	A	B	C	D
(a)	2	4	1	3
(b)	4	1	2	3
(c)	3	1	4	2
(d)	2	3	4	1

89. Match List I and List II.

List I	List II
A. The other fellow is to be conquered and put at my service	1. Paternalism
B. The other fellow should be helped up when down, without too much concern for what got him down	2. Participation
C. The other fellow has something to contribute to my efforts and can help me	3. Welfare
D. The other person should be cared for, and I will decide to what extent	4. Slavery

Choose the correct answer from the options given below.

	A	B	C	D
(a)	2	1	4	3
(b)	4	3	2	1
(c)	3	4	1	2
(d)	1	2	4	3

90. Match List I and List II.

List I (Legislations)	List II (Provisions)
A. The Trade Unions Act, 1926	1. Retrenched and Protected Workman
B. The Code of Discipline	2. Collection of forms for Political Participation
C. The Industrial Disputes Act, 1947	3. Recognition of Trade Unions
D. The Industrial Employment (Standing Orders) Act.	4. Disciplinary action for misconduct

Choose the correct answer from the options given below.

	A	B	C	D
(a)	1	2	3	4
(b)	2	3	1	4
(c)	4	1	2	3
(d)	3	4	1	2

Directions *(Q. Nos. 91-95) Read the following paragraph and answer the five questions which as follows :*

An organisation which is keen to retain good talent must have systems to inform employees that the organisation cares for them, belongs to them and it is they who can make it prosper and grow. In other words, people are empowered to consider the organisation as their own.

This, to a large extent can be achieved if the employer is sensitive and caring and makes effort to develop proper systems. This has to be demonstrated through efforts and actions, not merely words. It is important to have systems which seek employees involvement in deciding policy matters, technological upgradation, improving general administration and productivity etc, instead of thrusting decisions on them. When employees are consulted, two benefits clearly accrue. The first being employees who are well entrenched in operation will normally know the intricacies and will be able to offer valuable suggestions for its improvement.

Secondly, once they have participated in the decision making process, acceptance and implementation become much esier since the staff members are in a position to explain to others who may not have participated. Most importantly, seeking participation makes people feel wanted and cater to their esteem needs. They feel respected and recognised. They are empowered to think that they are responsible partners in the process of development and contributing to growth.

91. How can an organisation retain good talent?
(a) By caring of them
(b) By belonging to them
(c) By making the prosper
(d) By making them to feel that the organisation is their own

92. How can the objective of retaining good talent be achieved?
(a) If proper systems are suggested.
(b) If the employer is caring and sensitive.
(c) If the demands of the employees are met.
(d) By imposing decisions on them.

93. Which of the following statement is not correct?
(a) Proper systems can be demonstrated through actions.
(b) Systems can be made to work through efforts.
(c) Systems can become effective through powerful words and dramatic gestures.
(d) Systems are needed for employees involvement.

94. The benefits of consultation are.
(a) Operation and implementation become easier
(b) Production cost goes down
(c) Employees feel proud and superior
(d) Employees do not insist on their rights

95. Participation makes the employees feel that
(a) their demands are looked into favourably
(b) they are respected and recognised
(c) they have become indispensable
(d) they are saviours of the organisation

Directions *(Q. Nos. 96-100) Read the following paragraph and answer the five questions which as follow :*

When we look around we see glaring inequalities between man and man. While the constitution and law ensure an ordered society, it is only our hard work and disciplined conduct that will enable us to achieve our social objectives and economic goals that we have set before us.

Bapu rightly stressed "Democracy is the art and science of mobilising the entire physical, economic and spiritual resources of all sections of the people in the service of the common good for all." The purpose of the Government is to achieve this.

Our people possess intelligence in abundance, have immense capacity for hard work and they feel for the country. All this is to be mobilised to the best advantage of the nation. Again to quote Gandhi, "Swaraj of a people means the sum total of the Swaraj (Self-rule) of individuals. And such Swaraj comes only by performance of individuals, of their duty as citizens. They come when they are needed for better performance of duty." It is but proper that we remind ourselves of these teachings of the father of the nation.

96. Which of the following will help us to achieve our social goals?

(a) Scientific attitude
(b) Intelligent understanding
(c) Disciplined behaviour
(d) Mobilising the physical resources

97. According to the passage, the Indians are praised for which of the qualities?

1. Intelligence
2. Hard work
3. Patriotism
4. Service for all

Choose the correct answer from the options given below.

(a) 1, 2 and 3 only
(b) 1, 2 and 4 only
(c) 2, 3 and 4 only
(d) 1, 3 and 4 only

98. According to Gandhiji, people are required to do their duties.

(a) without thinking of their rights.
(b) without bothering about others.
(c) without thinking of the type of govenment.
(d) without bothering about the inequalities.

99. Which of the following statement is not correct according to the passage?

(a) There are inequalities among the people.
(b) We can achieve our economic objective with hard work.
(c) Democracy is the art of mobilising all resources.
(d) Indians do not have the capacity for hard work.

100. As per the passage, what should be the purpose of the govenment?

(a) To educate people for their betterment.
(b) To provide people adequate source of living.
(c) To mobilise the entire physical, economic and spiritual resources of all sections of people in the service of common good for all.
(d) To mobilise the financial resources of the country for its all round development.

ANSWERS

1	(c)	2	(b)	3	(b)	4	(a)	5	(b)	6	(b)	7	(d)	8	(c)	9	(a)	10	(c)
11	(c)	12	(c)	13	(a)	14	(b)	15	(b)	16	(b)	17	(b)	18	(a)	19	(c)	20	(c)
21	(d)	22	(b)	23	(b)	24	(c)	25	(c)	26	(d)	27	(d)	28	(a)	29	(a)	30	(a)
31	(c)	32	(b)	33	(c)	34	(b)	35	(d)	36	(b)	37	(d)	38	(b)	39	(c)	40	(c)
41	(a)	42	(a)	43	(a)	44	(b)	45	(a)	46	(b)	47	(d)	48	(b)	49	(b)	50	(b)
51	(b)	52	(c)	53	(b)	54	(a)	55	(b)	56	(a)	57	(b)	58	(c)	59	(b)	60	(c)
61	(a)	62	(*)	63	(d)	64	(*)	65	(*)	66	(a)	67	(c)	68	(b)	69	(c)	70	(d)
71	(a)	72	(d)	73	(c)	74	(d)	75	(b)	76	(a)	77	(b)	78	(d)	79	(a)	80	(d)
81	(a)	82	(b)	83	(a)	84	(a)	85	(a)	86	(b)	87	(c)	88	(c)	89	(b)	90	(b)
91	(d)	92	(b)	93	(c)	94	(a)	95	(b)	96	(c)	97	(a)	98	(a)	99	(d)	100	(c)

Labour Welfare (Paper-2)

Solved Paper, June 2019

General Instructions

1. There are total one hundred questions in this paper. Each question carries 2 marks.
2. All questions are compulsory.

Directions *(Q. No. 1-5) Read the passage given below carefully, and answer the following question which as follows:*

Biased appraisals have a variety of causes. One study of bias (the tendency for individual differences to affect judgements) focused on rater personality. Raters who scored higher on 'conscientiousness' tended to give their peers lower ratings-they were stricter, in other words; those more 'agreeable' gave higher ratings-they were more lenient. Managers also tend to be more lenient when appraising subordinates for administrative purposes like pay raises than for development purposes. Furthermore, "performance ratings amplify the quality of the personal relationship between boss and employee. Good relationships tender to create good (appraisal) experiences, bad relationships bad ones."

Unfortunately, subordinates' demographic traits (age, race, gender and so on) also affect ratings. A 36-year-old supervisor ranked a 62-year-old subordinate at the bottom of the department's rankings and then fired him. The court held that the younger boss's discriminatory motives might have prejudiced the dismissal decision. In one study, promoted women had to have received higher performance ratings than promoted men to be promoted, "suggesting that women were held to stricter standards for promotion." In another study, raters penalised successful women for their success. The point is that the appraisal often says more about the appraiser than about the appraisee. (Or, as one researcher said, "Rater idiosyncratic biases account for the largest percentage of the observed variances in performance ratings") Potential bias is one reason to use multiple raters, have the supervisor's boss review the rating and/or have 'calibration' meetings where supervisors discuss their reasons for the appraisals they gave each of their subordinates.

1. Two statements are given below. First statement will be called Assertion (A) and the second will be called Reason (R).

Assertion **(A) Rater's idiosyncratic biases account for the largest percentage of the observed variance in performance rating.**

Reason **(R) Potential bias is one reason to use multiple raters.**

Select the alternative that best establishes relationship between Assertion and Reason:

(a) Assertion is not true
(b) Reason is not correct
(c) Reason explains Assertion
(d) Assertion and Reason have no relationship

2. Who are likely to give lower rating to their peer?

(a) Agreeable rater
(b) Liberal rater
(c) Conscientiousness rater
(d) Aged rater

3. A rater has to rate an employee for the purpose of pay increase. The rater will
(a) have liberal approach
(b) have stricter approach
(c) have unchanged approach without being affected by the purpose
(d) refuse the job

4. Choose the correct statement.
(a) Relationship plays no role in rating.
(b) Good relationship leads to lower rating.
(c) Better the relationship, higher is the rating.
(d) Strained relationship leads to higher rating.

5. Which one is the correct statement?
(a) Age of the rater and ratee has nothing to do in rating.
(b) Gender of the ratee is not taken into consideration while rating.
(c) Age of the rater and ratee have bearing on rating.
(d) Demographic traits do not influence rating.

6. Two statements, namely Assertion and Reason, are given below:
Assertion (A) Organisation involves the grouping of activities necessary to accomplish goals and plans, the assignment of these activities to appropriate departments and the provision for authority delegation and coordination.
Reason (R) Organisation is an executive function that consists of breaking up the entire work into different segments, assigning each segment to the qualified individuals and coordinating the efforts of job holders to attain the organisational goals.
Which alternative is most appropriate among the one' given below which exhibits their relationship?
(a) Assertion is incorrect and has no relationship with Reason.
(b) Reason is incorrect and has no relationship with Assertion.
(c) No inter-relationship can be established between the two statements.
(d) Reason appropriately explains Assertion.

7. The function of the management which is associated with measuring results against pre-established standards and taking corrective action for maintaining the system is known as
(a) controlling
(b) planning
(c) coordinating
(d) directing

8. List-I below gives some names who have contributed for development of different management functions/activities and List-II gives the specific functions they are associated with.

	List I		List II
A.	Robert Owen	1.	Scientific Management
B.	Henry Fayol	2.	Modern Personnel Management
C.	FW Taylor	3.	Work Study
D.	HL Gantt	4.	Modern Management Theory

Which of the following gives right match between items of List-I and List-II?

Codes

	A	B	C	D
(a)	2	3	4	1
(b)	1	2	3	4
(c)	2	4	1	3
(d)	3	1	2	4

9. Process orientation concept of management was developed by numerous authors. Who among the following is not associated with this concept?
(a) McFarland
(b) E. F. L. Breech
(c) Lawrence A. Appley
(d) George R Terry

10. The Behavioural School of Management has developed many behavioural theories. Arrange the correct sequence of the major contributors to the behavioural school from the earliest to the latest.
1. Mary Parker Follet
2. Abraham Maslow
3. Elton Mayo
4. Douglas McGregor
5. Chris Argyris

Select the correct options.
(a) 1 2 3 4 5
(b) 1 3 2 4 5
(c) 1 3 4 2 5
(d) 2 3 4 1 5

11. Given below are the major contributors in List-I and their contributors in List-II of Behavioural School of Management.

	List I		List II
A.	Mary Parker Follet	1.	Group influences in the workplace.
B.	Elton Mayo	2.	Relates human motivation to a hierarchy of needs.
C.	Abraham Maslow	3.	Effects of human motivation on productivity and output.
D.	Douglas McGregor	4.	Emphasises human characteristics theory X and theory Y and the corresponding style of leadership

Match List-I with List-II and choose the correct match.

Codes

	A	B	C	D
(a)	1	3	2	4
(b)	1	2	4	3
(c)	1	4	3	2
(d)	2	1	3	4

12. "A horizontal set of divisional reporting relationship is superimposed on a hierarchical functional structure. This is known as Grid organisation or Project management organisation." What type of structure it has? Choose the correct one from the alternatives given below.

(a) Hybrid structure
(b) Functional structure
(c) Matrix structure
(d) Divisional structure

13. "If the leadership style allows substantial participation by members of the group in the management . and decision-making process, subordinates are frequently consulted by the manager on wide-ranging problems and are allowed sufficient freedom to communicate with the leader and also with their fellow subordinates." It is called

(a) autocratic style of leadership
(b) democratic style of leadership
(c) laissez fair style of leadership
(d) paternalistic style of leadership

14. Harvard model of Human Resource Management centered on four C's of Human Resource Practices. Which among the following has not been described as the HR Practices under Havard model?

(a) Commitment
(b) Competitiveness
(c) Competence
(d) Cost effectiveness

15. Professor J Barney and Prof. Patrick Wright have developed a comprehensive model in 1997 to establish Human Resources as a competitive advantage of the firm, which is known as

(a) VRIO Framework
(b) Soft Model of HRM
(c) Multiple Stakeholder Model
(d) Business Process Model

16. Which one of the following is not a Human Resource Planning technique?

(a) Predictor variables
(b) Zero-base techniques
(c) Simulation techniques
(d) Managerial Grid Techniques

17. "Take my physical assets, leave my people and in five years I will have it all back." Who said this?

(a) Alfred Sloan
(b) Peter F Drucker
(c) Bill Gates
(d) Rensis Likert

18. Placement aims at placing right man at the right job at right time. It is an attempt to correlate job requirement and individual characteristics. In this context, placement, being a continuous process should come after

(a) recruitment (b) selection
(c) training (d) development

19. Talent management starts with understanding what jobs need to be filled and the human traits and competencies employee need to do those jobs effectively. Two lists are given below. List-I is term and List-II is their appropriate meaning.

List I		List II	
A.	Job analysis	1.	A list of job's 'human requirements' that is the requisite education, skills, personality and so on.
B.	Job description	2.	A list of job's duties, responsibilities, reporting relationships, working conditions and supervisory responsibilities.
C.	Job specification	3.	The procedure for determining the duties and skill requirements of a job and the kind of person who should be hired for it.
D.	Work Flow analysis	4.	A detailed study of the flow of work from job to job in a work process.

Which of the following alternatives gives the correct match between List-I and List-II?

Codes

	A	B	C	D
(a)	2	3	1	4
(b)	3	2	1	4
(c)	4	2	3	1
(d)	1	2	3	4

20. "A technique by which a new employee is adjusted into the changed surroundings and introduced to the practices, policies and purpose of the organisation" is called

(a) placement (b) induction
(c) training (d) development

21.* On-the-job training is based on the principle of 'learning by doing'. Which one of the following is not an on-the-job training method?

(a) Coaching (b) Understanding
(c) Role playing (d) job rotation

22. Performance appraisal means evaluating an employee's current and/or past performance relative to his or her performance standards. Performance appraisal always involves the three steps. Which one of the following is not a step of performances appraisal process?

(a) Setting work standards.
(b) Assessing the employee's actual performance relating to those standards.

* Answer not given in official answer key.

(c) Providing feedback to the employee with the aim of helping him or her to eliminate performance deficiencies or to continue to perform above par.
(d) Grading on a curve predetermined percentages of rates are placed in various performance categories.

23. Two lists are given below, List-I is related to terms of managing career and List-II is related to their appropriate meaning.

List I	List II
A. Career planning	1. The process for enabling employees to better understanding and develop their career skills and interests and to use these skills and interests more effectively.
B. Career management	2. The deliberate process through which some one becomes aware of personal skills, interest, knowledge, motivations and other characteristics and establishes action plan to attain specific goals.
C. Career development	3. The lifelong series of activities that contribute to a person's career exploration, establishment, success and fulfilment.
D. Career coaching	4. Focuses on teaching, educating, instructing and training subordinates.

Choose the alternative which gives the right match of List-I with List-II.

Codes

	A	B	C	D		A	B	C	D
(a)	2	1	3	4	(b)	1	2	3	4
(c)	2	1	4	3	(d)	4	2	3	1

24. There are four new approaches to compensation rewards. Two lists are given below. List-I relates with approach and List-II relates to appropriate benefits and features.

List I	List II
A. Skill-based pay	1. Support for participative organisational structures and improved effectiveness of work teams.
B. Broad banding	2. Greater scope for recognising individual differences in employee performance
C. Variable pay	3. Motivation of sustained high performance and better linkages between individual and organisational goals.
D. Team rewards	4. Multi-skilled workforce, job assignment, flexibility and higher employee satisfaction and commitment.

Match List-I with List-II and choose the correct answer.

Codes

	A	B	C	D		A	B	C	D
(a)	1	3	2	4	(b)	4	2	3	1
(c)	4	1	3	2	(d)	1	2	3	4

25. Human Capital Appraisal Approach of HRD function was outlined in 1998. Who among the following has developed the Human Capital Appraisal Approach?
(a) TV Rao
(b) Udai Pareek
(c) Friedman
(d) Ulrich and Lake

26. Values are core of the culture. Both values and belief provide guidelines for employee to follow in their work. Some organisations have created their own value. Two lists are given below. List-I indicates the name of organisation and List-II indicates their value:

List I	List II
A. Caterpillar (USA)	1. "In 24 hours parts services anywhere in the world."
B. Larsen and Tubro (India)	2. "Faith in youth and tap the youth."
C. Microsoft (USA)	3. "Computer on every desk and every house."
D. TERI (India)	4. 'People are prime movers."

Match List-I with List-II and choose the correct answer.

Codes

	A	B	C	D
(a)	1	2	3	4
(b)	1	4	3	2
(c)	2	3	4	1
(d)	3	2	1	4

27. There are different techniques to Human Resource Accounting. Which one of the following is not human resource accounting technique?
(a) Historical Cost Method
(b) Replacement Cost Method
(c) Quality Cost Method
(d) Opportunity Cost Method

28. Which one of the following is not associated with the three facets of career motivation?
(a) Career resilience
(b) Career insight
(c) Career counselling
(d) Career identity

29. **The goal of training is that the trainees learn the task or material presented and the same are retained by them. Which of the following issues influences the retention process?**

(a) Contiguity, the law of effect and practice.
(b) Task analysis, task achievement and task sequencing.
(c) Meaningfulness of material, degree of original learning and interference.
(d) Active practice, mental practice and over learning.

30. **Who among the following have suggested that learning outcomes can be three types, namely, cognitive, skill based and affective?**

(a) Kirkpatrick and Ford
(b) Kraiger, Ford and Salas
(c) Holton and Galvin
(d) Phillips and Brinkerhoff

31. **Which of the following factors identified by Dunning in his Eclectic Theory are to be simultaneously met by a company that wishes to set up production unit in a foreign country and wants to operate as a multinational?**

(a) Advantages relating to labour, land and capital.
(b) Advantages relating to ownership, location and internationalisation.
(c) Advantages relating to capital, technology and products.
(d) Advantages relating to cost, capital and labour.

32. **Based upon a study on cultural diversity in multinational corporations, the following four dimensions emerged that differentiated national cultures in terms of their managerial ideologies.**

1. Organisation as a political system
2. Organisation as an authority system
3. Organisation as role formalisation system
4. Organisation as hierarchical-relation system

Who among the following is associated with the study?

(a) Hofstede
(b) Triandris
(c) Laurent
(d) Maurice

33. **A multinational company appointing a person in a subsidiary, belonging to the country where its subsidiary is located reflects, which of the following approaches?**

(a) Ethnocentrism
(b) Geocentrism
(c) Regiocentrism
(d) Polycentrism

34. **The competitive strategies for multinational corporations are given in List-I and their features in List-II as below.**

List I	List II
A. Multidomestic strategy	1. Gives prime importance to efficiency.
B. Global strategy	2. Gives prime importance to development and diffusion of innovations worldwide
C. International strategy	3. Gives prime importance to global efficiency, national responsiveness and worldwide learning at the same time
D. Transnational strategy	4. Gives prime importance to national responsiveness

From among the following which one gives the right combination between the strategies and their features?

Codes

	A	B	C	D		A	B	C	D
(a)	4	1	2	3	(b)	1	2	3	4
(c)	3	4	1	2	(d)	2	3	4	1

35. **According to Henry Mintzberg managers perform ten different highly interrelated roles, which are grouped under three broad roles, namely, Interpersonal roles, Information roles and Decisional roles. From among the following which one is associated with the Interpersonal role?**

(a) Monitor and Disseminator
(b) Leader and Figurehead
(c) Spokesperson and Entrepreneur
(d) Negotiator and Resource allocator

36. **Three theories of learning are given in List-I and their characteristics in List-II below.**

List I	List II
A. Classical conditioning	1. People can learn through observation and direct experience.
B. Operant conditioning	2. A type of conditioning in which an individual responds to some stimulus that would not ordinarily produce such a response.
C. Social learning theory	3. A type of conditioning in which desired voluntary behaviour leads to a reward or prevents a punishment.

Which one of the following gives the correct combination between the theories and their characteristics?

Codes

	A	B	C		A	B	C
(a)	1	2	3	(b)	3	1	2
(c)	1	3	2	(d)	2	3	1

37. As per 'Johari window,' the 'closed area' is explained by which one of the following?

(a) An individual's behaviour is known to himself or herself and to those with whom the individual interacts.

(b) Those aspects of the person's behaviour and style that others know, but not known to the person himself or herself.

(c) The aspects of the person's behaviour and style which are known to the person but not revealed to others.

(d) The aspects of behaviour and style neither known to the person nor others.

38. A group consisting of members working together to attain a specific objective with which each is concerned, is known as

(a) informal group
(b) task group
(c) friendship group
(d) interest group

39. As per the managerial grid given by Blake and Mouton, the leadership style focussing on low task and high concern for the people is known as

(a) impoverished management
(b) club country management
(c) team management
(d) middle of the road management

40. According to Vroom's expectancy theory of motivation, which of the following refers to the term 'valence'?

(a) Subjective probability of achieving an outcome.

(b) Efforts made by an individual for the first level outcome.

(c) Relation between the first level and second level outcomes to each other.

(d) Strength to an individual's preference for a particular outcome.

41. Which one of the following statements are true relating to the Myers-Briggs Type Indicator of personality?

(a) There are sixteen personality types generated on the basis of four basic elements.

(b) There are twenty personality types generated on the basis of five basic elements.

(c) There are ten personality types generated on the basis of four basic elements.

(d) There are eighteen personality types generated on the basis of six basic elements.

42. The term 'grapevine' is associated with which one of the following communication networks of an organisation?

(a) Formal communication
(b) Horizontal communication
(c) Informal communication
(d) Vertical communication

43. The dynamic balance of the driving force and restraining force of change is associated with which of the following?

(a) Force field analysis model
(b) Force analytical model
(c) Force field balancing model
(d) Force field contingent model

44. The process of change namely coercive, mimetic and normative isomorphisms are associated with which of the following perspectives on organisational change?

(a) Resource dependence perspective
(b) Contingency perspective
(c) Population-ecology perspective
(d) Institutional perspective

45. Which of the following statements relating to Dunlop's industrial relations framework is not correct?

(a) Dunlop's framework was designed to broaden the industrial relations horizon from collective bargaining to the full spectrum of present-day industrial relations.

(b) This framework cannot be used for a study of industrial relations within a country as a whole.

(c) Dunlop's industrial relations framework puts emphasis on rule-making by management, workers and specialised government agencies concerned with workers, enterprises and their relationships.

(d) Dunlop's framework focuses on the ideology of the industrial relations system.

46. Which of the following perspectives concerning industrial relations is based on the assumption that conflict is irrational in an organisation?

(a) Unitary perspective
(b) Pluralistic perspective
(c) Trusteeship perspective
(d) Radical perspective

47. Who among the following is associated with the Human Relations approach to industrial relations?

(a) Charles A. Myers (b) Dale Yoder
(c) Michael Poole (d) Elton Mayo

48. Who is called Sidney Webb in the United States?

(a) John R. Commons
(b) Noel Arnold Levin
(c) Robert F. Hoxie
(d) Frank Tannenbaum

49. The Bombay Mill Hands Association was established under the presidentship of

(a) Bal Gangadhar Tilak (b) CF Andrews
(c) NM Joshi (d) NM Lokhande

50. The Bharatiya Mazdoor Sangh was formed under the leadership of

(a) SA Dange (b) SV Ghate
(c) Dattopant Thengadi (d) KN Joglekar

51. As per the recommendations of the Second National Commission on Labour, what should be the percentage of support of workers, a union should have in an establishment for claiming recognition as a single negotiating agent on the basis of check-off system?

(a) 25 per cent (b) 33 per cent
(c) 50 per cent (d) 66 per cent

52. Which of the following statements relating to the 'Participation of Workers in Management Bill' is wrong?

(a) The Bill was introduced in the Rajya Sabha on 30th May, 1990.
(b) The Bill was the first comprehensive legislative effort towards promotion of workers' participation in management in the country.
(c) It has a provision for constitution of Shop-floor Councils in every establishment.
(d) The Bill does not have any provision regarding the representation of the workers on the Board of Management.

53. The Indian Labour Conference approved 'illustrative lists' of items which the Works Committees should normally deal with and those which they should not. Which of the following items figures in the list of items to be dealt with by the Works Committee?

(a) Bonus and profit-sharing
(b) Rationalisation and matters connected with the fixation of workload.
(c) Adjustment of festival and national holidays.
(d) Housing and transport services

54. Given below are different statements, some of which are only relevant to productivity bargaining:

1. Productivity bargaining is a management-initiated process.
2. It has an element of input-output relationship.
3. It is based on the principle of mutuality.
4. It is not a continuous process.

From among the following, which alternative presents the relevant features of productivity bargaining?

(a) Only 1 and 2
(b) Only 2 and 3
(c) 1, 2 and 3 only
(d) 1, 2, 3 and 4

55. Which of the following statements relating to the Model Grievance Procedure is correct?

(a) According to the Model Grievance Procedure, an aggrieved worker who is not satisfied with the decision of the departmental head in respect of his grievance, may directly present his grievance to the grievance committee.
(b) The Model Grievance Procedure has a provision regarding reference of a grievance to voluntary arbitration.
(c) According to the Model Grievance Procedure, an aggrieved worker shall have the right to leave the department during working hours without obtaining the prior permission of his superior.
(d) The procedure laid down for the redressal of grievances has to be followed even in the case of any grievance arising out of the dismissal of a worker.

56. The Office of the Director General of Mines Safety is located at

(a) New Delhi
(b) Asansol
(c) Dhanbad
(d) Kolkata

57. Which of the following is not an attached office of the Ministry of Labour, Government of India?

(a) Office of the Chief Labour Commissioner
(b) Labour Bureau
(c) VV Giri National Labour Institute
(d) Office of the Director General, Factory Advice Service and Labour Institutes

58. There are two sets, that are given below. List-I gives the list of terms and List-II indicates their meanings.

List I		List II	
A.	Orbiter dictum	1.	A cursory remark
B.	Puisne	2.	Subordinate
C.	Mens rea	3.	Guilty mind
D.	Ultra vires	4.	Beyond one's powers

Which of the following gives the correct match between the terms and their meanings?

Codes

	A	B	C	D
(a)	1	2	3	4
(b)	2	3	4	1
(c)	4	1	2	3
(d)	3	4	1	2

59. The ILO's Tripartite Consultation (International Labour Standards) Convention, 1976 was ratified by India in the year

(a) 1978 (b) 1982
(c) 1996 (d) 2016

60. A registered trade union of workmen functioning in an industry having five hundred workmen should have to maintain a minimum of what number of workmen as members in order to continue the registration of the trade union?

(a) Seven (b) Fifty
(c) One hundred (d) Twenty

61. As per the provisions of the Trade Unions Act, 1926, who among the following shall not be eligible to be the executive or office bearer of the trade union?
(a) A member of the Legislative Assembly
(b) A member of the Parliament
(c) An elected representative of local body
(d) A minister in the Union Cabinet

62. Under the provisions of the Industrial Disputes Act, 1947, the employer of any industry declares lay-off, is required to provide alternate employment to the workmen laid-off in any other industry belongs to him and located at a distance not more than
(a) eight miles
(b) six miles
(c) five miles
(d) seven miles

63. How many days advance notice is to be given to the affected workmen for change in the conditions of service of workmen, when no proceeding is pending before any adjudicative authorities under the provisions of the Industrial Disputes Act, 1947?
(a) Thirty days
(b) Fourteen days
(c) Twenty-one days
(d) Seven days

64. Under the provisions of the Industrial Disputes Act, 1947, the total members of the Grievance Redressal Committee shall not exceed
(a) ten (b) six
(c) eight (d) twelve

65. Under the provisions of the Industrial Employment (Standing Orders) Act, 1946 who among the following can apply for modifications in the standing orders?
(a) Any employer or the workmen
(b) Any workmen, trade union or representative of workmen
(c) Any employer, workmen, trade union or representative of workmen on agreement
(d) Only trade union

66. As per the provisions of the Industrial Employment (Standing Orders) Act, 1946 the Certifying Officer is required to send copies of the modified standing orders to the employer and the trade union with in how many days from the date of notifications?
(a) Five days
(b) Seven days
(c) Twelve days
(d) Fifteen days

67. As per the provisions of the Factories Act, 1948 a worker of a factory, who quits the employment, shall be paid his wages for the days of unavailed leave before
(a) the expiry of two months from the date of quitting the employment.
(b) the expiry of the second working day from the date of quitting.
(c) the expiry of one month from the date of quitting.
(d) the expiry of his wage period.

68. As per provisions of the Factories Act, 1948 under power to make exempting orders, the total number of hours of work in any day for a worker shall not exceed:
(a) Eleven hours (b) Twelve hours
(c) Thirteen hours (d) Ten hours

69. As per the provisions of the Mines Act, 1952 the special officer duly authorised in writing by the Chief Inspector, shall enter into any mine for the purpose of surveying, levelling and measuring after giving notice to the manager of the mine for not less than
(a) Three days
(b) Seven days
(c) Ten days
(d) Thirty days

70. Who among the following is authorised by the Chief Inspector by a special order in writing to enter the mine for the purpose of surveying, levelling and measuring the mine or part there of as per the provisions of the Mines Act, 1952?
(a) Surveyor
(b) Special Officer
(c) Analyst
(d) Survey Inspector

71. As per the provisions of the Inter-State Migrant Workmen (Regulation of Employment and Conditions of Service) Act 1979, who is required to issue the passbook duly affixed with a passport size photograph of the workman to the migrant workman?
(a) The Licensing Officer
(b) The Registering Officer
(c) The Contractor
(d) The Inspector

72. The Inter-State Migrant Workmen (Regulation of Employment and Conditions of Service) Act, 1979 will apply to the establishments employing a minimum of
(a) twenty or more migrant workmen
(b) fifteen or more migrant workmen
(c) ten or more migrant workmen
(d) five or more migrant workmen

73. An employer of an establishment can only employ contract labour, under which one of the following provisions of the Contract Labour (Regulation and Abolition) Act, 1970?

(a) Obtaining a licence from the licensing officer.
(b) Obtaining a certificate of registration from the registering officer.
(c) Obtaining a written permission from the inspector.
(d) Obtaining the permission from the appropriate government.

74. Under the provisions of the Building and Other Construction Workers (Regulation of Employment and Conditions of Service) Act, 1996 is order to apply for registration as a beneficiary under the Act, a construction worker must have worked for a minimum period of how many days in the preceding twelve months?

(a) Not less than two hundred forty days
(b) Not less than one hundred twenty days
(c) Not less than one hundred eighty days
(d) Not less than ninety days

75. As per the provisions of the Building and Other Construction Workers (Regulation of Employment and Conditions of Service) Act, 1996, because of financial hardship, if a beneficiary under the Act has not paid his contribution, the Board may waive the contribution at a time for a period

(a) not exceeding three months
(b) not exceeding six months
(c) not exceeding nine months
(d) not exceeding twelve months

76. Child labour shall not be employed or permitted to work in any of the processes in any workshop set forth in which part of the schedule attached to the Child Labour (Prohibition and Regulation) Act, 1986?

(a) Part A (b) Part B
(c) Part C (d) Part D

77. "State to secure a social order for the promotion of welfare of the people" is mentioned in which Article of the Directive Principles of State Policy of the Constitution of India?

(a) Article 43A
(b) Article 43
(c) Article 38
(d) Article 42

78. Under the provisions of the Payment of Wages Act, 1936 establishments which are not covered under the Act, the tate government after giving how many months notice may extend the provisions of the Act to such establishments?

(a) One month (b) Two months
(c) Three months (d) Six months

79. As per the provisions of the Payment of Wages Act, 1936 'fine' imposed on any employed person cannot be recovered after expiry of how many days from the day the fine was imposed?

(a) Ninety days
(b) One hundred days
(c) One hundred twenty days
(d) One hundred eighty days

80. The appropriate government is empowered under Sec 7 of the Equal Remuneration Act, 1976 to appoint authorities for hearing and deciding claims and complaints, persons not below the rank of

(a) Labour Commissioner
(b) Asst Labour Commissioner
(c) Labour Inspector
(d) Labour Officer

81. Under the provisions of the Payment of Bonus Act, 1965 in order to determine the bonus of an employee, who is not covered under the Scheduled Employment under the Minimum Wages Act, what amount of monthly wage from the following to be taken into consideration?

(a) Two thousand five hundred rupees
(b) Three thousand five hundred rupees
(c) Five thousand rupees
(d) Seven thousand rupees

82. The representation of the independent members in the Central Advisory Board constituted under the Minimum Wages Act, 1948 shall not exceed what portion of its total members?

(a) One-fourth
(b) One-third
(c) One-half
(d) Two-third

83. The authority constituted by the Central Government under the Provident Fund and Miscellaneous Provisions Act, 1952 to decide the cases regarding the determination of money due to be recovered from the employers is

(a) Employee's Provident Funds Tribunal
(b) Employee's Provident Fund Organisation
(c) Employees' Provident Fund Court
(d) Employees' Provident Funds Appellate Tribunal

84. As per the provisions of the Employees' Provident Fund and Miscellaneous Provisions Act, 1952 the determination of the escaped amount to be recovered from the employer shall be made within which period from the date of communication of the order passed by the authorised officer?

(a) Three years
(b) Five years
(c) Seven years
(d) Ten years

85. **As per the provisions of the Payment of Gratuity Act, 1972 an employee working in a seasonal establishment, shall get his gratuity after superannuation from the employment at the rate for how many days wages for each season, he had worked in that establishment?**

(a) Fifteen days
(b) Ten days
(c) Eight days
(d) Seven days

86. **'Compulsory Insurance' provision finding its due place under which of the following legislations?**

(a) The Employee's Provident Fund Act, 1952
(b) The Employee's Compensation Act, 1923
(c) The Payment of Gratuity Act, 1972
(d) The Employees' State Insurance Act, 1948

87. **In order to hear and decide any claims arising out of payment of less than the minimum rate of wages, under the provisions of the Minimum Wages Act, 1948, the State Governments shall appoint any officer not below the rank of**

(a) Chief Inspector under the Minimum Wages Act
(b) Asst. Labour Commissioner
(c) Labour Commissioner
(d) Dy. Labour Commissioner

88. **Personal causes of industrial accident is one of the important causes of accident.**

Among the cause given below, which one is not a personal cause of industrial accident?

(a) Neglect in housekeeping
(b) Carelessness, ignorance and inadequate skill
(c) Relationship with supervisor
(d) Improper supervision

89. **Labour welfare is dependant on certain basic principles. Each of these principles has its own content. Two lists are given below. In List-I, principles are given and in List-II, content of the principles are given:**

List I	List II
A. Principles of adequacy of wages	1. Welfare is a total concept, coordinated approach will promote healthy development
B. Principle of re-presonalisation	2. Employer should not bargain labour welfare as substitute to wages.
C. Principle of democratic value	3. Consultation with and the agreement of workers in formulation and implementation of welfare services.
D. Principle of integration	4. Development of human personality should be the goal of labour welfare.

Match the principles with their contents.

Codes

	A	B	C	D
(a)	2	4	3	1
(b)	2	1	4	3
(c)	4	2	1	3
(d)	4	3	2	1

90. **Provisions for ensuring occupational health and safety for workers are contained in Articles 24, 39(e), 39(f) and 42 of the Directive Principles of State Policy of the Constitution of India. Based on the spirit of these, rules have been framed. The subject matter of the rules are both in Union List and Concurrent List. Which among the following is not in Concurrent List?**

(a) Conditions of work
(b) Safety in mines
(c) Provident funds
(d) Maternity benefits

91. **Industrial safety is primarily whose responsibility under the Factories Act, 1948?**

(a) Central Government
(b) State Government
(c) Occupier/Management
(d) Safety Committee

92. **Occupational diseases are those which arise out of and in the course of employment. Industrial workers fall prey of these occupational diseases.**

Two lists are given below. List-I contains the names of the diseases, while List-II contains the type of workers who are likely to suffer from these diseases.

List I (Name of the disease)	List II (Type of workers)
A. Mercury poisoning	1. Barometer worker, refiners of gold and silver
B. Anthrax	2. Workers likely to inhale bagasse or sugarcane dust
C. Bagassois	3. Textile workers
D. Byssionosis	4. Workers engaged in handling wood, hair bristles

Codes

	A	B	C	D
(a)	1	3	2	4
(b)	1	4	2	3
(c)	4	1	3	2
(d)	4	3	2	1

93. **Two statements are given below. We will consider the first statement as Assertion (A) and the second one as Reason (R).**

Assertion **(A) Social security has wider aims than prevention or relief of poverty.**

Reason **(R) The fundamental purpose of social security is to give individuals and families the confidence that their level of living and quality of life will not be eroded, as far as possible, by any social or economic eventuality.**

On the basis of the above given statements, choose the correct answer:

(a) Assertion is wrong
(b) Reason is wrong
(c) Individuals or their families cannot be given confidence
(d) The Reason given justifies Assertion

94. An indifference curve between income and leisure shows

(a) various combinations of income and leisure which give different levels of satisfaction.
(b) various combinations of income and leisure which give equal satisfaction.
(c) same amount of income and leisure at each point on it which give different levels of satisfaction.
(d) same amount of income and leisure which give same amount of satisfaction.

95. Whether an individual will supply more work effort or less as a result of the rise in the wage rate depends on

(a) income effect only
(b) substitution effect only
(c) the relative strength of income and substitution effects
(d) neither income effect nor substitution effect

96. The term 'management exploitation' was given by

(a) Mrs John Robinson (b) Prof Chamberlin
(c) JB Clark (d) JM Keynes

97. The demand curve of labour of the monopsonist is given by

(a) the curve of value of the marginal product.
(b) the curve of marginal revenue productivity.
(c) the average factor cost curve.
(d) average wage curve.

98. In rural India, which type of unemployment is common?

(a) Educated unemployment
(b) Cyclical unemployment
(c) Disguised unemployment
(d) Voluntary unemployment

99. What is true about weekly status unemployment?

1. It is measured in number of persons and shows chronic unemployment.
2. It shows both open and chronic unemployment.
3. It is measured in person, days or years and shows underemployment.
4. It shows only open unemployment.

Choose the correct answer

(a) Only 1
(b) 1, 2 and 3
(c) Only 2
(d) Only 4

100. According to Lord Keynes, unemployment in advanced economies was due to

(a) lack of supply
(b) deficiency of effective demand
(c) business cycle
(d) lack of both demand and supply

ANSWERS

1	(d)	2	(c)	3	(a)	4	(c)	5	(c)	6	(d)	7	(a)	8	(c)	9	(c)	10	(b)
11	(a)	12	(c)	13	(b)	14	(b)	15	(a)	16	(d)	17	(a)	18	(b)	19	(b)	20	(b)
21	(*)	22	(d)	23	(a)	24	(b)	25	(c)	26	(b)	27	(c)	28	(c)	29	(c)	30	(b)
31	(b)	32	(c)	33	(d)	34	(a)	35	(b)	36	(d)	37	(c)	[illegible]	(d)	39	(b)	40	(d)
41	(a)	42	(c)	43	(a)	44	(d)	45	(b)	46	(a)	47	(d)	[illegible]	(a)	49	(d)	50	(c)
51	(d)	52	(d)	53	(c)	54	(c)	55	(b)	56	(c)	57	(c)	[illegible]	(a)	59	(a)	60	(b)
61	(d)	62	(c)	63	(c)	64	(b)	65	(c)	66	(b)	67	(b)	[illegible]	(b)	69	(a)	70	(b)
71	(c)	72	(d)	73	(b)	74	(d)	75	(a)	76	(b)	77	(c)	78	(c)	79	(a)	80	(d)
81	(d)	82	(b)	83	(d)	84	(b)	85	(d)	86	(c)	87	(c)	88	(a)	89	(a)	90	(b)
91	(c)	92	(b)	93	(d)	94	(b)	95	(c)	96	(a)	97	(b)	98	(c)	99	(a)	100	(b)

SOLVED PAPERS

LABOUR WELFARE (Paper-2)

Solved Paper, December 2018

General Instructions

1. There are total one hundred questions in this paper. Each question carries 2 marks.
2. All questions are compulsory.

Directions *Read the passage carefully and answer the questions that follow (1-5)*

Ethics refer to the principles of conduct governing an individual or a group; specifically, the standard one uses to decide what one's conduct should be. Making ethical decisions always involves normative judgements. Ethical decisions always involve questions of morality which is society's highest accepted standards of behaviour. Moral standards guide behaviours of the most serious consequence to society's well being. Authoritative bodies like legislatures cannot change what morality means. Moral judgements also trigger strong emotions. Violating moral standards may therefore make someone feel ashamed or remorseful. Asking 'Is what I am doing legal?' would not necessarily reveal if it is ethical. Firing a 39-year-old employee with 20 years' tenure without cause may be legal but some would view it as unethical. Ethics means making decisions that represent what you stand for, not just what the laws are.

1. Which among the following is not a characteristic of ethical decision?

(a) It should involve question of morality
(b) It evokes strong emotions
(c) It should lead to most serious consequences to make society's well being
(d) It can be change by legislatures

2. Which among the following cannot be a parameter of being called ethical?

(a) Standard one uses to decide what one's conduct should be
(b) Decisions involving normative judgements
(c) Conduct governing an individual or group
(d) Decisions involving authoritative judgements

3. Consider the following

1. Supportive leadership behaviour.
2. Participative leadership behaviour.
3. Instrumental leadership behaviour.
4. Achievement-oriented leadership behaviour.

The above leadership behaviours are related to which of the following?

(a) Path-goal approach of leadership
(b) Situational theory of leadership
(c) Managerial grid approach of leadership
(d) Fiedler's contingency model of leadership

4. "A process by which an organisation responds to employee needs for developing mechanisms to allow them to share fully in making decisions that design their lives at work" is called

(a) Social security
(b) Performance management
(c) Quality of work life
(d) Career planning

5. What is the minimum number of days an employee should have served in an accounting year to be entitled for receiving bonus under the Payment of Bonus Act, 1965?

(a) Ninety days
(b) One hundred days
(c) Sixty days
(d) Thirty days

6. Assertion (A) Structural unemployment creates a great deal of concern and dominates the policy discussions.

Reason (R) Structural unemployment arises because of mismatch between the skills that workers are supplying and the skills that firms are demanding.

Codes

(a) (R) is wrong and therefore (A) cannot be said to be a correct assumption
(b) (A) is correct and (R) is not a proper explanation of A
(c) (A) is correct, but (R) is wrong
(d) (A) is correct and (R) explains (A)

7. Who said, "Management Development concerns the means by which a person cultivates those skills application of which will improve the efficiency and effectiveness with which the anticipated results of particular segment are achieved"?

(a) Flippo (b) Dale Yoder
(c) Koontz and O'Donnell (d) Robert Owen

8. Assertion (A) Trade unions have to change their own attitudes and activities to sustain themselves in future.

Reason (R) Trade unions have to change their attitude from antagonism to understanding and from militancy to mutual cooperation.

Codes

(a) Both (A) and (R) are wrong
(b) (A) is correct, but (R) is wrong
(c) Both (A) and (R) are correct, but (R) is not an interpretation of (A)
(d) (A) is correct and (R) interprets (A)

9. The directive principles of state policy as contained in the Constitution of India provide for a number of articles.

Provision for just and human conditions of work and maternity relief is contained under which article of the constitution?

(a) Article 40 (b) Article 41
(c) Article 42 (d) Article 43

10. Which of the following core conventions of the International Labour Organisation has not been ratified by India?

(a) Minimum Age Convention No. 138
(b) Equal Remuneration Convention No. 100
(c) Abolition of Forced Labour Convention No. 105
(d) Freedom of Association and Right to Organise Convention No. 87

11. What is the time period within which a complaint relating to an offence has to be made before a court from the date on which the alleged commission of the offence came to the knowledge of the inspector or authorised person concerned under the provisions of the Inter-State Migrant Workmen (Regulation of Employment and Conditions of Service) Act, 1979?

(a) Two months (b) Six months
(c) One month (d) Three months

12. Which of the following statements relating to the model standing orders are correct?

1. The model standing orders classify workers into six categories.
2. According to the model standing orders, in order to terminate the employment of a permanent monthly rated worker, the employer has to give one month's notice in writing or pay in lieu thereof.
3. The model standing orders provide a list of acts and omissions, which are to be treated as misconducts.
4. The model standing orders provide that every permanent workers shall be entitled to a service certificate at the time of dismissal, discharge or retirement from service.

Codes

(a) 1, 3, and 4 (b) 2, 3 and 4
(c) 1, 2, 3 and 4 (d) 1, 2 and 3

13. Match the following.

List I (Labour Law Term)	List II (Meaning)
A. Puisne	1. Junior or subordinate
B. Ratio decidendi	2. The ground decision
C. Res judicata	3. A thing decided

Codes

	A	B	C		A	B	C
(a)	3	2	1	(b)	2	1	3
(c)	1	2	3	(d)	1	3	2

14. Matrix organisation is the combination of

(a) Project and line organisation
(b) Line and staff organisation
(c) Project and functional organisation
(d) Functional organisation and product organisation

15. Assertion (A) In India, inequality between contracting parties in employment relationship have warranted third party intervention.

Reason (R) As a custodian of the broader social interest, the government has to ensure that the economic needs of the community are satisfied by an uninterrupted flow of goods and services.

Codes

(a) Both (A) and (R) are true and (R) is the correct explanation of (A)

(b) (A) is wrong, but (R) is correct

(c) Both (A) and (R) are true, but (R) is not the correct explanation of (A)

(d) (A) is correct, but (R) is wrong

16. A situation in which the parties to a conflict, each desire to satisfy fully the concern of all parties is known as

(a) Competing (b) Collaborating

(c) Accommodating (d) Compromising

17. If there is a dispute regarding the subsistence allowance payable to a workman under the provisions of the Industrial Employment (Standing Orders) Act, 1946, then workman or the employer concerned may refer the dispute to

(a) The Labour Court Consitituted under the Industrial Disputes Act, 1947

(b) Industrial Tribunal Constituted under the Industrial Disputes Act, 1947

(c) The Labour Commissioner

(d) The Certifying Officer

18. The Directive Principles of state policy as contained in the Constitution of India provide for a number of articles.

"Securing and protecting effectively a social order in which justice shall inform all institutions of national life" is contained under which Article of the Constitution?

(a) Article 43 (A) (b) Article 38

(c) Article 41 (d) Article 37

19. Which of the following approaches of leadership focuses on 'personal competence' and 'social competence'?

(a) Situational approach of leadership

(b) Trait theory of leadership

(c) Emotional intelligence approach

(d) Charismatic leadership approach

20. Which one of the following authorities is a subordinate office under the ministry of labour in India?

(a) Directorate General of Mines Safety

(b) Labour Bureau

(c) Directorate General, Factory Advice Service and Labour Institutes

(d) Directorate General, Employment and Training

21. Who among the following was the Founder President of the International Trade Union Confederation (ITUC)?

(a) Sharan Burrow

(b) Guy Ryder

(c) Jeremy Bentham

(d) Pascal Lamy

22. Provisions relating to rehabilitation and re-employment schemes for employees are provided under which of the following legislations?

(a) The Contract Labour (Regulation and Abolition) Act, 1970

(b) The Employees' Compensation Act, 1923

(c) The Inter-State Migrant Workmen (Regulation of Employment and Conditions of Service) Act, 1979

(d) The Employees' State Insurance Act, 1948

23. Under the provisions of the Contract Labour (Regulation and Abolition) Act, 1970, what is the time period within which a case in to be filed for an offence punishable under the Act from the date on which the alleged commission of offence came to be knowledge of an inspector?

(a) Six months (b) Four months

(c) Two months (d) Three months

24. In which types of strike, some of the union workers are posted at the factory gate for the purpose of watching and dissuading those who go to work?

(a) Picketing

(b) Stay away strike

(c) Protest strike

(d) Cat-call strike

25. Related to group, when the tendency for individuals to expend less effort when working collectively than when working individually is called

(a) Group think

(b) Group cohesiveness

(c) Social loafing

(d) Group conflict

26. What is the maximum percent of its total expenses for the 'building and other construction workers' welfare fund during a financial year that shall be met towards salaries, allowances and other remuneration to its members and other employees?

(a) Five percent

(b) Ten percent

(c) Six and one-fourth percent

(d) Eight percent

27. An ideal wage system should fulfil certain characteristics. Which among the following is not a characteristic of an ideal wage system?

(a) It should develop harmonious relationship between parties

(b) It should be conducive to the interests of both the parties-the employer and the employees

(c) It should be capable of providing certain incentives to workers necessary to accelerate production

(d) It should be fairly complex and rigid

28. Match the provisions given under List I with the respective legislations under which they are covered as given under List II.

List I	List II
A. Subsistence allowance	1. The Payment of Gratuity Act, 1972
B. Compulsory insurance	2. The Minimum Wages Act, 1948
C. Scheduled employment	3. The Industrial Employment (Standing Orders) Act, 1946
D. Recovery officer	4. The Employees Provident Fund and Miscellaneous Provisions Act, 1952

Codes

	A	B	C	D
(a)	4	3	1	2
(b)	3	1	2	4
(c)	2	4	3	1
(d)	1	2	4	3

29. Match the theories given in List I with its propounders given in List II.

List I	List II
A. Subsistence theory of wage	1. Walker
B. The wage fund theory	2. Karl Marx
C. Residual claimant theory	3. Ricardo
D. Theory of exploitation	4. J.S. Mill

Code

	A	B	C	D
(a)	1	3	2	4
(b)	1	4	2	3
(c)	3	4	1	2
(d)	3	2	1	4

30. Which of the following is not correctly matched?

(a) Job classification - Grouping of job on some specified basis
(b) Job enlargement - Horizonatal expansion of job
(c) Job enrichment - Vertical loading of job
(d) Jobanalysis - Deciding the content of job and relationship

31. Any person aggrieved by the decision of the apprenticeship advisor, relating to a dispute between an employer and an apprentice arising out of contract of apprenticeship, may perfer an appeal against the decision to which of the following under the Apprenticeship Act, 1961?

(a) The National Council to Technical Education
(b) The Apprenticeship Council
(c) The All India Council
(d) The National Council

32. The determination of the basic long-term objectives of an organisation/enterprise and the adoption of courses of action and allocation of resources necessary to achieve goals is called

(a) Gol (b) Strategy
(c) Procedure (d) Policy

33. In the context of human resource management 'head hunting' refers to which of the following?

(a) Training (b) Compensation
(c) Recruitment (d) Retrenchment

34. Assertion (A) Labour welfare is a relative concept.

Reason (R) This is so because it is related to time and space.

Codes

(a) (A) is correct, but (R) is worng
(b) Both (A) and (R) are correct and (R) is the correct explanation of A
(c) (A) is wrong, but (R) is correct
(d) Both (A) and (R) are correct, but (R) is not the correct explanation of (A)

35. Who among the following can be appointed as the authority to hear and decide any claims arising out of deductions form wages or delay in payment of wages under the Payment of Wages Act, 1936?

1. Any Commissioner for Employees Compensation Act.
2. Any regional labour commissioner appointed by the Central Government.
3. Any assistant labour commissioner appointed by the Central Government.
4. Any assistant labour commissioner appointed by the State Government with atleast two years of experinece.
5. A Judge of a Civil Court.

Codes

(a) 2, 3, 4 and 5 (b) 1, 3, 4 and 5
(c) 1, 2, 4 and 5 (d) 1, 2, 3 and 4

36. Which one of the following in not a quantitative method for forecasting supply of human resource?

(a) Markov Analysis (b) Regression Analysis
(c) Goal Programming (d) Turnover Analysis

37. Arrange the following unions in a chronological order, on the basis of the years of their establishment in USA, starting from the oldest.

1. International Brotherhood of Electrical Workers, USA.
2. United Auto Workers, USA.
3. Transport Workers Union of America.

Codes

(a) 1, 2, 3 (b) 1, 3, 2 (c) 2, 1, 3 (d) 3, 1, 2

38. Who among the following are eligible for appointment as presiding officers of the employees provident fund appellate tribunal?

1. A Judge of a High Court.
2. A District Judge.
3. An additional District Judge with atleast three years of experience in the grade.
4. An Officer of Indian Legal Service with five years of experience in grade III.

Codes

(a) 1, 2 and 4 (b) 1 and 2
(c) 1, 2 and 3 (d) 1, 2, 3 and 4

39. Which of the following features relating to the participation of workers in management bill introduced in the year 1990 are correct?

1. This was the first comprehensive legislative effort towards promotion of workers' participation in management.
2. The Bill envisaged a two-tier system of participation in management.
3. It proposed to delete Section 3 of the Industrial Disputes Act concerning the works committee.
4. It proposed for appointment of inspectors.

Codes

(a) 1, 2 and 4 (b) 1, 2 and 3
(c) 1, 3 and 4 (d) 2, 3 and 4

40. Which of the following statement are true/false?

1. The first industrial policy resolution in India was introduced in 1948.
2. The Indian Parliament accepted the 'socialist pattern of society' as the national objective of its social and economic policy in December 1955.
3. The second industrial policy resolution in India was made in 1956.
4. Under the second industrial policy resolution, industries, industries were classified into three categories on the basis of the role the state would play in each of them.

Codes

(a) 3 and 4 and the true and 1 and 2 are false
(b) 1, 3, 4 are true and 2 is false
(c) 1 and 2 are true and 3 and 4 are false
(d) 1, 2, 3 are true and 4 is false

41. Among the following statements, which one is not true?

(a) Ethical decisions represent what one stands for.
(b) Ethical decisions involve questions of morality
(c) Ethical decisions are always legal.
(d) A decision may be legal, but may not be ethical.

42. The Building and Other Construction Workers (Regulation of Employment and Conditions of Service) Act, 1996 shall become applicable to an establishment engaged in building and construction work employing a minimum number of

(a) ten building workers
(b) thirty building workers
(c) twenty building workers
(d) fifty building workers

43. An adolescent worker employed in a factory who has not attained the age of seventeen years but has been granted a certificate of fitness shall not be allowed to work between

(a) 8 pm to 5 am (b) 8 pm to 6 am
(c) 7 pm to 6 am (d) 9 pm to 5 am

44. In which of the following establishments was the Equal Remuneration Act, 1976 fi[illegible] enforced?

(a) Mines covered under the Mines Act, 1952
(b) Plantations covered under the Plantation Labour Act, 1951
(c) Hospitals, nursing homes and dispensaries
(d) Local authorities

45. Who suggested that changes in organisations occur in three phases called unfreezing, changing and refreezing?

(a) David Nadler
(b) Kurt Lewin
(c) Gary Hamel
(d) Noel Tichy

46. Which of the following statements relating to the All India Manufacturers' Organisation are correct?

1. It was set up in 1942.
2. It was set up under the leadership of M. Vishweswarayya.
3. It was established to represent the trade and labour interests of the member firms in the medium and small sectors.

Choose the correct answer from the code given below

Codes

(a) Both 1 and 3 (b) Both 1 and 2
(c) 1, 2 and 3 (d) Both 2 and 3

47. A leadership theory which proposed that effective group performance depended on the proper match between a leader's style and degree to which the situation allowed the leader to control and influence is called

(a) Trait theory
(b) Situational theory
(c) Fiedler's contingency model
(d) Path goal theory

48. The Traders Union Congress, U.K. is affiliated to

(a) International Confederation of Free Trade Unions
(b) World Federation of Trade Unions
(c) International Trade Union Confederation
(d) International Federation of Christian Unions

49. Who among the following introduced quality control in Japan?

(a) Thomas Peters
(b) W. Edwards Deming
(c) Robert R. Blake
(d) Laurence Peter

50. The provisions relating to 'continuous service' (Section 2-A) was inserted in the Payment of Gratuity Act, 1972 by a amendment in the year

(a) 1981
(b) 1984
(c) 1987
(d) 1980

51. Which one of the following statements in correct to the 'Rajiv Gandhi Shramik Kalyan Yojana' scheme provided under the Employees' State Insurance Act, 1948?

(a) The unemployed person should have contributed to the scheme for atleast five years prior to loss of employment.
(b) The rate of unemployment allowance is at the rate of 50% of the dary wages.
(c) The minimum period of unemployment in a spell should be fifteen days for entitlement of the benefit.
(d) The allowance is payable for a maximum period of six months in one spell or different spells.

52. A general impression of an individual that is influenced by single characteristic is called

(a) Personal prejudice (b) Stereotyping
(c) Halo effect (d) Group effectiveness

53. Out of the following activities of trade unions, which are considered as social activities?

1. Initiating and developing workers' education scheme.
2. Running cooperatives.
3. Organising welfare and recreational activities such as mutual insurance, providing monetary and other help during periods of strikes and economic distress.

Codes

(a) 2 and 3 (b) 1 and 2
(c) 1, 2 and 3 (d) 1 and 3

54. Which among the following is not an objective of labour welfare?

(a) To further the political interests of employers
(b) To combat the influence of outside agencies on employees
(c) Desire to show-off and advertise concern for labour
(d) Avoiding payment of taxes on surplus

55. Match the following.

	List I (Type of Unions)		List II (Example)
A.	Craft Unions	1.	The International Woodcarvers, Association
B.	Industrial Unions	2.	Tata Workers' Union
C.	General Unions	3.	Jamshedpur Labour Union

Codes

	A	B	C		A	B	C
(a)	2	1	3	(b)	1	2	3
(c)	1	3	2	(d)	3	2	1

56. Information relating to which one of the following is not covered under job specification?

(a) Training (b) Job identification
(c) Education (d) Experience

57. The six stages of training evaluation model suggested by Brinkerhoff given below are jumbled up. Choose the alternative which gives the correct sequence from the codes given below

1. Programme Design
2. Goal Setting
3. Immediate Outcomes
4. Impact and Worth
5. Intermediate on usage Outcomes
6. Programme Implementation

Codes

(a) 2, 1, 3, 5, 4, 6 (b) 1, 2, 4, 3, 5, 6
(c) 2, 1, 5, 3, 6, 4 (d) 2, 1, 6, 3, 5, 4

58. Which of the statements relating to the protected workman is not correct under the Industial Disputes Act, 1947?

(a) The maximum number of protected workmen is limited to one hundred.
(b) The minimum number of protected workmen is limited to ten.
(c) It shall be limited to one percent of the total number of workmen employed.
(d) It is limited to the executives or office bearers of registered trade unions connected with the establishment.

59. Assertion (A) Violation of moral standards makes someone feel remorseful.

Reason (R) In the event of violation of moral standards, inner sense of guilt starts haunting.

Codes

(a) (A) is wrong, but (R) is correct
(b) (A) is correct, but (R) is wrong
(c) Both (A) and (R) are correct, but (R) is not the correct explanation of (A)
(d) Both (A) and (R) are correct and (R) is the correct explanation of (A)

60. Which of the following statements relating to representation of parties under the provisions of The Industrial Disputes Act, 1947 is not correct?

(a) Any of the parties can be represented by legal practioner in any conciliation proceedings.
(b) A party to a dispute may be represented by a legal practioner with the consent of the other parties in any proceeding before a labour court or tribunal.
(c) A workman who is a party to a dispute shall be represented in any proceeding under the Act by any office bearer of a registered trade union of which he is a member.
(d) Any employer who is a party to a dispute shall be entitled to be represented in any proceeding under the Act by an officer of an association of employers of which he is a member.

61. Under the provisions of the Trade Union Act, 1926, what is the maximum amount of fine to be imposed for supplying false information regarding Trade Unions?

(a) One hundred rupees
(b) Two hundred fifty rupees
(c) One hundred fifty rupees
(d) Two hundred rupees

62. An order issued to public officials and public bodies to carry out their legal duties in known as

(a) Mandamus (b) Quo warranto
(c) Res judicata (d) Certiorari

63. Assertion (A) Principle of compulsory arbitration leads to an authoritarian imposition of terms and conditions of employment and supresses the possible self-governance in industries.

Reason (R) In a democratic society, industrial democracy, implying collective and joint determination of the terms and conditions of employment and settlement of their disputes, should prevail without any oútside interference

Codes

(a) (A) is wrong, but (R) is correct
(b) Both (A) and (R) are correct and (R) is the correct explanation of (A)
(c) Both (A) and (R) are correct, but (R) presents only one-sided view to justify (A)
(d) Is correct, but (R) is wrong

64. A conscious change that occurs as a result of logic is called

(a) Subsystem change
(b) Emergent change
(c) Remedial change
(d) Planned change

65. The first wage board in India was established for which of the following industries?

(a) Iron and steel (b) Cement
(c) Textile (d) Coal

66. Theory 'Y' of motivation assumes that

(a) People do not hate work
(b) A person has inherent dislike for work
(c) A person works only when coerced
(d) An average employee cannot be motivated

67. Which of the following conventions of the ILO was ratified by the Government of India in the year 2017?

(a) Freedom of association and right to organise (Convention No. 87)
(b) Force labour covention (No. 29)
(c) Discrimination (Employment/Occupation) Convention (No. 111)
(d) The minimum age for admission to employment (Convention No. 138)

68. Which of the following schedules of the Constitution of India has provided the three lists namely Union list, State list and Concurrent list for making laws by the Parliament and by the legislatures of the states?

(a) Sixth Schedule
(b) Eighth Schedule
(c) Seventh Schedule
(d) Fourth Schedule

69. The right delegated to an individual or a department to control specified processes, practices, policies or other matters relating to activities undertaken by persons in other departments in called

(a) Functional authority delegation
(b) Empowerment of employees
(c) Delegation of power
(d) Centralisation of power

70. The distinct patterns of self-perceived talents, attitudes, motives and values that direct and stabilise an individual's career are called

(a) Career goals
(b) Career paths
(c) Career anchors
(d) Career planning

71. The American Federation of Labour was established in the year

(a) 1885 (b) 1884
(c) 1886 (d) 1887

72. What is the minimum amount of compensation payable to an employee who is permanently and totally disabled from an injury by accident arising out of and in course of employment under the Employees' Compensation Act, 1923?

(a) ₹ 1,40,000 (b) ₹ 1,20,000
(c) ₹ 1,50,000 (d) ₹ 1,60,000

73. The Kochan, Katz and McKersie's framework of industrial relations proposes a three-tier structure of industrial relations activities.

Match the three categories of the actvities with the respective levels where they take place, as given below

List I (Level/Tier)	List II (Category of activity)
A. Top-tier	1. Collective bargaining and persdnnel policy
B. Middle-tier	2. Workplace, individual and organisational relationship
C. Bottom-tier	3. Long-term strategy and policy-making

Codes

	A	B	C		A	B	C
(a)	1	3	2	(b)	1	2	3
(c)	3	1	2	(d)	2	1	3

74. An organisation that provides autonomy to its business units operating in other countries, is called

(a) Global corporation
(b) International corporation
(c) Multinational corporation
(d) Transnational corporation

75. Which among the following is not a determinant of supply of labour?
(a) Non-wage aspects of the job
(b) Number of firms
(c) Other wage rates
(d) Non-wage income

76. The committee of experts on welfare facilities for Industrial Workers constituted by ILO in 1963 had divided labour welfare services in two groups, intra-mural and extra-mural.
Which among the following is not an extra-mural welfare amenity?
(a) Occupational safety
(b) Social insurance measures including sports
(c) Maternity benefit
(d) Leave travel facilities

77. Under the provisions of the Bonded Labour System (Abolition) Act, 1976, what is the extent of punishment for a person, who compels any person to render any bonded labour?
(a) Imprisonment for a maximum period of three years and also with fine which may extend to four thousand rupees
(b) Imprisonment for a maximum term of five years and also with fine which may extend to five thousand rupees
(c) Imprisonment for a maximum period of two years and also with fine which may extend to three thousand rupees
(d) Imprisonment for a maximum term of three years and also with fine which may extend to two thousand rupees

78. Who has given the system theory of organisation?
(a) Laurence Peter
(b) Frank and Lillian
(c) Elton Mayo
(d) Chester Barnard

79. A strike that is conducted with a view to force an employer to recogise or bargain with a particular trade union instead of another is known as
(a) Jurisdictional strike
(b) Political strike
(c) General strike
(d) Ordinary strike

80. Who is the present leader of the Labour Party, UK?
(a) Ed Miliband
(b) Jeremy Bernard Corbyn
(c) Mary Bousted
(d) Sally Hunt

81. Who among the following made significant contributions to early unions of Great Britain?
1. Francis Blake
2. Robert Owen
3. Sidney and Beatrice Webb
4. Pelloutier

Codes
(a) 1, 2 and 3 (b) 2, 3 and 4
(c) 1, 2 and 4 (d) 1, 3 and 4

82. Which of the following statements relating to the second industrial truce resolution are correct?
1. It was passed in 1962.
2. It emphasised that all disputes should be settled through adjudication, especially those relating to dismissal, discharge and retrenchment of workers.
3. It emphasised that all disputes should be settled by voluntary arbitration, especially those relating to dismissal, discharge and retrenchment of workers.

Choose the correct answer from the code given below
Codes
(a) 1 and 3 (b) 2 and 3
(c) 1 and 2 (d) 1, 2 and 3

83. A firm engaging in social actions in response to some popular social needs is called
(a) Social obligations
(b) Social responsibility
(c) Social action
(d) Social responsiveness

84. Arrange the following participative schemes in a chronological order starting from the latest to the earliest.
1. The scheme which was introduced and made applicable to all central public sector enterprises.
2. The scheme that was extended to commercial and services organisation employing 100 or employees
3. The scheme which was meant for the manufacturing and mining industries employing 500 or more workers.

Codes
(a) 1, 3 and 2 (b) 1, 2 and 3
(c) 3, 2 and 1 (d) 2, 1 and 3

85. The behaviour of a person under the Adult ego state under transactional analysis is
(a) Evaluative and judgemental
(b) Protective and critical
(c) Impulsive and emotional
(d) Rational and logical

86. Who is the President of the Trades Union Congress, UK for the year 2018?
(a) Mary Bousted
(b) Sally Hunt
(c) Liz Snape
(d) William Henry Wood

87. Under the provisions of the Maternity Benefits Act, 1961 every woman employee who joins duty after delivery of a child shall be entitled to nursing breaks until the child attains the age of
(a) Twenty-four months
(b) Twelve months
(c) Fifteen months
(d) Eighteen months

88. Under the provisions of the Minimum Wages Act, 1948, what is maximum amount of fine that can be imposed on an employer of contravenation of any of the provisions of the Act?

(a) One thousand rupees
(b) Seven hundred rupees
(c) Two hundred fifty rupees
(d) Five hundred rupees

89. Assertion (A) Imperfections existing in the employment markets are the causative factor for wage differentials.

Reason (R) In developed countries, inter-industry wage differentials are narrowing.

Codes

(a) (A) is correct, but (R) is wrong
(b) Both (A) and (R) are correct and (R) is the correct explanation of (A)
(c) Both (A) and (R) are wrong
(d) Both (A) and (R) are correct, but (R) is not the correct explanation of (A)

90. Match the contents of different schedules given in List I with their respective schedules given in List II under the provisions of the Factories Act, 1948.

List I	List II
A. Permissible levels of certain chemical substances in work environment	1. First Schedule
B. List of notifiable disease	2. Second Schedule
C. List of industries involving hazardous processes	3. Third Schedule

Codes

	A	B	C
(a)	2	3	1
(b)	3	1	2
(c)	1	2	3
(d)	2	1	3

91. Who among the following is associated with the idea that "The human personality progresses along a continuum from immaturity as an infant to maturity as an adult?"

(a) Sigmund Freud
(b) Erik Erikson
(c) Chris Argyris
(d) Daniel Levinson

92. The British Trades Union Congress was formed in the year

(a) 1878
(b) 1858
(c) 1888
(d) 1868

93. Who have coined the term 'strategic intent' to refer to the determination of an organisation to achieve goals that are out of all proportion to their resources and capabilities?

(a) Gary Hamel and C.K. Prahalad
(b) David Nadler and Micheal
(c) John W. Meyer and W.Richard Scott
(d) Tom Burns and G.M. Stalker

94. Which of the following statements relating to the recommendations of the Second National Commission on Labour are correct?

1. The commission recommended that the ITIs need to run market-driven courses, review, and if necessary, revise curriculum every 5 years to keep them contemporary.
2. The commission recommended for a skill development fund.
3. The commission recommended the some ITIs may be selected, on a pilot basis, for development into institutes of excellence.

Codes

(a) 2 and 3
(b) 1 and 2
(c) 1, 2 and 3
(d) 1 and 3

95. Match the provisions provided under the Directive Principles of State Policy given in List I with the respective Articles under which they are covered given in List II.

List I	List II
A. Equal pay for equal work for both men and women	1. Article 39
B. Participation of workers in management of industries	2. Article 42
C. Public assistance in cases of unemployment, old age, sickness and disablement	3. Article 43 A
D. Just and human conditions of work	4. Article 41

Codes

	A	B	C	D
(a)	1	3	4	2
(b)	4	2	1	3
(c)	2	1	3	4
(d)	3	4	1	2

96. Assertion (A) Some of the earliest pieces of legislation in India appear to have been enacted to protect the interest of the employers.

Reason (R) The policy of the government was to protect the social system rather than to protect the workmen.

Codes

(a) (A) is correct, but (R) is wrong and (R) is the correct explanation of (A)
(b) (A) is correct, but (R) is wrong
(c) Both (A) and (R) are correct
(d) Both (A) and (R) are wrong

97. Who has been referred to as the 'Father of Personal Management'?

(a) Max Weber
(b) Robert Owen
(c) Peter Drucker
(d) Louis A. Allen

98. Which one of the following is not a modern method of performance appraisal?

(a) Ranking method
(b) 360
(c) M.B.O.
(d) BARS

99. Which of the following trade union federations was formed with the objective of "dictatorship of the proletariat"?

(a) All India Trade Union Congress
(b) All India Railwaymen's Federation
(c) All India Trade Union Federation
(d) Red Trade Union Congress

100. Two lists are given below. Match both the lists and choose the correct answer from the code given below.

	List I		List II
A.	Programme Evaluation and Review Technique (PERT)	1.	F.W. Taylor
B.	Managerial Role Approach	2.	Hugo Munsterberg
C.	Application of Psychology to Industry and Management	3.	Mintzberg
D.	Principles of Scientific Management	4.	Henry L. Gantt

Codes

	A	B	C	D		A	B	C	D
(a)	3	1	4	2	(b)	4	1	2	3
(c)	4	3	2	1	(d)	2	3	4	1

ANSWERS

1 *(d)*	2 *(d)*	3 *(a)*	4 *(c)*	5 *(d)*	6 *(d)*	7 *(c)*	8 *(c)*	9 *(c)*	10 *(d)*
11 *(d)*	12 *(c)*	13 *(c)*	14 *(c)*	15 *(a)*	16 *(b)*	17 *(a)*	18 *(b)*	19 *(c)*	20 *(a)*
21 *(a)*	22 *(d)*	23 *(d)*	24 *(a)*	25 *(c)*	26 *(a)*	27 *(d)*	28 *(b)*	29 *(c)*	30 *(d)*
31 *(b)*	32 *(b)*	33 *(c)*	34 *(b)*	35 *(c)*	36 *(b)*	37 *(b)*	38 *(b)*	39 *(c)*	40 *(b)*
41 *(c)*	42 *(a)*	43 *(c)*	44 *(b)*	45 *(b)*	46 *(d)*	47 *(c)*	48 *(c)*	49 *(b)*	50 *(b)*
51 *(c)*	52 *(c)*	53 *(c)*	54 *(a)*	55 *(b)*	56 *(b)*	57 *(d)*	58 *(b)*	59 *(d)*	60 *(a)*
61 *(d)*	62 *(a)*	63 *(c)*	64 *(d)*	65 *(c)*	66 *(a)*	67 *(d)*	68 *(c)*	69 *(d)*	70 *(c)*
71 *(c)*	72 *(a)*	73 *(c)*	74 *(d)*	75 *(b)*	76 *(a)*	77 *(d)*	78 *(d)*	79 *(a)*	80 *(b)*
81 *(a)*	82 *(a)*	83 *(d)*	84 *(b)*	85 *(d)*	86 *(b)*	87 *(c)*	88 *(d)*	89 *(d)*	90 *(a)*
91 *(c)*	92 *(d)*	93 *(a)*	94 *(c)*	95 *(a)*	96 *(c)*	97 *(b)*	98 *(a)*	99 *(d)*	100 *(c)*

NTA

UGC

NET/JRF/SET

HUMAN RESOURCE MANAGEMENT, LABOUR WELFARE, INDUSTRIAL RELATIONS, LABOUR & SOCIAL WELFARE, PERSONNEL MANAGEMENT

Principles and Practices of Management

Management is a discipline of managing resources to the fullest and achieving optimum results. This chapter emphasises on various theories and principles that have evolved to lay the foundation of management as a discipline.

Concept of Management

Management is the art of getting things done through the people. Management is a process and not merely a body of individuals. Those who perform this process are called managers. The managers exercise leadership by assuming authority and direct others to act within the organisation. Managers can transform organisations and it can create new ways of making and distributing goods and services by the people and through the people. Management is a discipline of getting individuals together to achieve a desired common goal, by efficiently deploying resources.

According to **Harold Koontz**, "Management is the art of getting things done through and with people in formally organised groups."

According to **O'Donnell**, "Management is the creation and maintenance of an internal environment in an enterprise where the individuals working in groups, can perform efficiently and effectively towards the attainment of group goals."

According to **Henry Fayol**, "To manage is to forecast and to plan, to organise, to command, to coordinate and to control."

According to **Peter Drucker**, "Management is a multi-purpose organ that manages business and manages managers and manages workers and work."

Nature of Management

Management is Innovative

Techniques of management are dynamic and innovative. They need to be attuned to the situations. Also, another manager need not replicate the decisions of one manager. Similarly, a manager has to modify his judgements under different circumstances.

In this Chapter

- *Concept of Management*
- *Development of Management Thought*
- *Theories and Approaches in Management*

Management Aims at Coordination of Activities

Coordination is the spirit of management. It stretches one clear direction to the entire organisation and brings accord and agreement in the whole business unit. For such coordination, effective communication at all levels is vital.

Management is Universal and all Pervasive

Management is complete and covers all departments, activities and employees. Managers operate at diverse levels but their functions are alike. This specifies that management is a universal and all pervasive process.

Management involves Achieving Results through the Efforts of Others

Management is the art of getting the things done through others. Managers are expected to guide and motivate subordinates and get the expected performance from them. Management acts as an activating factor.

Management is Dynamic

Organisations are affected by variations in economic, social, political, technological and human resource. Management alters itself to the varying atmosphere making appropriate forecasts and changes in the policies. Hence, management is treated as a vibrant and dynamic activity.

Management is Science as well as an Art

Management comprises of standardised tools and techniques and a systematic procedure. Thus, it is considered as a science. However, the principles of management can be creatively crafted and applied according to the situation. Thus, it is also considered as an art.

Management Targets at Attaining Prearranged Objectives

Management is a significant activity. All organisations are essentially groups of individuals formed for achieving common objectives. An organisation exists for the accomplishment of specific objectives.

Management is a Group Activity

It is not an isolated individual activity but a shared activity or an activity performed by a group. It objects at using group efforts for accomplishing purposes. Managers manage the groups and organise the activities of groups working in an organisation.

Functions of Management

- Management performs various functions which have been described differently by various authors. **Fayol** has given six managerial functions which are forecasting, planning, organising, commanding, coordinating and controlling.
- On the other hand, **Luther Gullick** has given a keyword 'POSDCORB' where P stands for Planning, O stands for Organising, S stands for Staffing, D stands for Directing, Co stands for Coordination, R stands for Reporting and B stands for Budgeting.
- **George and Jerry** have given only four functions namely planning, organising, actuating and controlling.
- But the most extensively acknowledged are the functions of management given by **Koontz** and **O'Donnel**, *i.e.* planning, organising, staffing, directing and controlling. These are explained in the next chapter.

Significance of Management

- It helps the institution in working in a volatile environment. This is done with the help of planning in advance and preparing strategies for this volatility.
- It prevents conflict in the organisation and promotes harmony among the workers. The various posts are filled with competent individuals who have apt knowledge, qualification and skills.
- It helps the management in achieving the organisational goals effectively. This is done with the help of coordination among various levels in the organisation.
- It helps in yielding quality output while minimising costs.
- It fosters coordination thus reduces duplication of work. This also saves time, money and efforts. It also minimises wastage of physical and human resources.

Management Skills

Their are various abilities and traits which an ideal manager must possess so as to accomplish the tasks of the company.

Prof Robert Katz has bifurcated managerial skills into three sub-parts.

They are as follows

1. **Conceptual Skills** These skills induce the person to have vision about the organisation as a whole. Conceptual skills are amalgamation of initiative, creative and analytical skills. Such skills help in identifying the source or cause of problem, thus enabling the managers to solve the problem for the entire organisation.
2. **Human Relation Skills** These skills are otherwise known as inter-personal skills. It deals with an ability of the manager to effectively and efficiently work with humans. Such skills enhance communication and working with others. This skill is required at all the hierarchies of management, as management works with people.

3. **Technical Skills** These are skills which enhance the worker in executing or performing the job. It enables the manager to use various tools and machines in order to perform the desired activity.

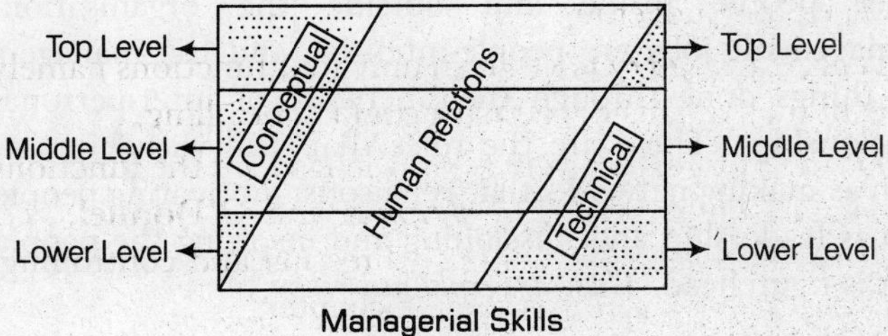

Apart from these skills, there are various other skills that managers at all levels must possess

1. **Administrative Skills** They deals with running an organisation and keeping the firm organised such as experts in policy formulations, getting their work done effectively, coordinate various functions of organisation.
2. **Leadership Skills** Managers must be able to influence people. Motivational skills are key component of leadership skills.
3. **Problem Solving Skills** A manager must possess these skills as the business works in a dynamic environment. This results in various hindrances during the operations. Hence, a manager must be able to solve problems by analysing the situation and identifying the cause. Such skill requires up-to-date knowledge, intelligence and experience.
4. **Decision-making Skills** Management requires decision- making. This skill is vital for the managers of all levels. *These are as follows*
   - It encompasses quick decision-making alongwith making appropriate decision.
   - This skill determines the gain or loss for the organisation.
5. **Analytical Skills** The managers must be competent enough to collect the information and analyse it. On the basis of this analysed information, he must be able to take effective decisions that solve the problem of the business. *e.g.* Data analysis, business analysis and operation analysis.
6. **Communicational Skills** This skill is required at all the managerial levels. *It is as follows*
   - The manager should be able to pass on, explain the policies to lower level.
   - He must avoid technical jargons to make the communication process smooth and effective. Such manager must concentrate on free flow of communication.
7. **Listening Skills** Alongwith communicating skills, manager must possess listening skills.

   These are as follows
   - It deals with the readiness of the manager to receive the message accurately and interpret the information precisely.
   - If the managers lack listening skills, then the message will be wrongly interpreted and implemented.
8. **Time Management Skills** A manager is required to drive the organisation and reach the destination in a stipulated time. Managers at all levels often utilise their time in performing various activities simultaneously such as planning, organising, controlling, directing etc.

   These are as follows
   - Time management skills include setting aims, analysing time required to accomplish the given task, alloting and organising.
   - Time management skills prohibit the manager and has team from wasting time on unnecessary activities.
9. **Conflict Management Skills** A key manager is a good referee during the time of conflicts.

   These are as follows
   - Conflict management skills give solutions to the problems and build harmonious relationship with the stakeholders.
   - Managers with conflict management skills are able to lead successful organisations.

Significance of Managerial Skills for Organisation

- Easy administration.
- Cordial relationship between various levels of management.
- Optimum utilisation of resources.
- Achievement of organisational goals due to effective communication, motivation and leadership skills.
- Attract high performing employees.
- Retention of quality and competent resources. Managers having inter-personal skills build amicable relation with the workers, thus it enhances the productivity of the organisation.

Levels of Management

Operational Level Management

They have following responsibilities

- They assign tasks to employees.
- Guide and supervise subordinates on daily basis.
- Responsible for quality and quantity of production.
- Give suggestions to the middle level managers.
- Help in execution of various policies and programmes formulated at higher levels.

- Lower level managers are the actual executors, hence they must acquire **technical** skills, having incharge of operations and executions, they must know how to make their subordinates work on technical grounds.

Middle Level Management

They have following responsibilities

- They are subordinate to the top level management, however they are superior to the lower level management.
- Accountable to higher level managers.
- They guide and lead supervisory level (lower level) managers.
- Communicate the policies formulated at the upper level to the lower level managers.
- They form a link between upper level and lower level managers.
- Middle level manager must possess **human relation skills** as he is a communicator between the top level and lower level management. He discloses top level strategies to lower level and gives feedback to the top level.

Top Level Management

They have following responsibilities

- Responsible for organising, strategising and controlling the entire firm.
- Policy formulation, setting-up of goals.
- Making decisions on long-term issues.
- Answerable to various stakeholders such as general public, shareholders, government etc.
- Top level management require **conceptual skills** as they devote their time in problem solving, organising and planning.

Managerial Role Model

According to **Hill**, "Managerial roles are specific behaviours associated with the task of management. Managers adopt these roles to accomplish the basic functions of management, *i.e.* planning and strategising, organising, controlling and leading and developing employees."

Henry Mintzberg developed a list of 10 roles that he grouped into three categories, *i.e.* inter-personal roles, informational roles and decisional roles.

This was given in the book "Mintzberg on Management: Inside our Strange World of Organisations" in 1990. Here, he emphasised that managing is an integrated activity, so these roles are rarely distinct. An event relates to two or more roles simultaneously.

These roles are explained below

1. Inter-personal Roles

Inter-personal roles are roles that include interacting with other people inside and outside the organisation. Management jobs are people-intensive and the managers get things done through their network of inter-personal relationships. These are the roles that deal with humans such as making networks that is liaisons, motivating people that is leadership and missioning and inspiring the people that is figurehead. *These are explained below*

(i) Figurehead

- Managers at all levels are figureheads. They greet visitors, represent the company at community events, serve as spokespeople and function as emissaries for the organisation.
- The figurehead role aims at inspiring workers in the organisation and makes them feel connected with the organisation and each other. They play the role of an individual who is available to help the worker and support them.
- The variety of figurehead roles are performed when managers accompany senior executives or outside visitors on tours through the work area, help their teams celebrate performance milestones, welcome new staff, give performance awards to employees etc.

(ii) Leader

- It is known that leadership is one function of management. Managers also take on a leadership role to get things done within organisations. A central task of leaders is to give their organisations a sense of direction and purpose. They do this by identifying and pronouncing strategic visions for the organisations (by strategising) and then by motivating others to work toward this vision.
- Manager leads his team with motivation and support and focus on achieving organisational objectives. This role includes guiding the workers about their work and how they can accomplish set targets. The leader then rewards the worker for fulfilling the task. Managers act as leaders to inspire, motivate and direct others within organisations and to strategise, plan, organise, control, and develop.

(iii) Liaison

- In their liaison role, managers connect with people outside their immediate units. The manager works as a good communicator and communicates with a variety of people both inside and outside the organisation.

- These roles can include communication with the managers of other units within the organisation or individuals outside the organisation, such as suppliers, buyers and strategic partners. An important purpose of such liaisons is to build a network of relationships. Thus, this role is purely based on the communication skill of the manager.
- Managers can use their networks to help coordinate the work of their units with others, to gain access to valuable information and more generally to get things done and further their own agendas within the organisation.
- This also facilitates smooth function of the company because there is harmonious communication between the outsiders that is suppliers, customers, stakeholders and insiders that is the employees and superiors.

2. Informational Roles

Informational roles are concerned with collecting, processing and circulating information. Managers collect information from various sources both internal and external to the organisation, process that information and distribute it to others who need it. Mintzberg found that managers spend 40 per cent of their time in these tasks. Mintzberg divided the information roles of management into three types spokesperson, monitor and disseminator.

These are as follows

(i) Monitor

- The monitoring role of management is part of the controlling function. In addition, the information collected from monitoring can help managers think more clearly about the company's strategy. This is the key role as the prime job of a manager is to manage the situation. He administers as well as monitors the changes occurring in the environment and preparing well in advance.
- He also responds quickly to the changes. By monitoring the external competitive and internal organisational environment for information, managers try to gain knowledge about how well the organisation is performing and whether any changes in strategy or operational processes are required.

(ii) Disseminator

- In their dissemination role, managers repeatedly inform staff about the company's direction and sometimes about specific technical matters. At the supervisory level, the disseminator role often takes the form of one-to-one informal conversations with specific employees about particular matters.
- This role enables the manager in sharing the knowledge and information with his team. It is the process of gathering information from external as well as internal sources and disseminating relevant information with the team mates. Thus, it is a crucial part of interpersonal role.

(iii) Spokesperson

- As a spokesperson, the manager transmits the information to the individual outside the organisation, such as experts and stakeholders. He performs the role of a representative of his team. He speaks about the achievement of his team or the problems faced by it.
- If the manager is not a good spokesperson then the outsiders will not be able to learn about the accomplishment of the team. In their spokesperson role, managers deliver specific information to individuals and groups located outside their department or organisation. Sales managers communicate with business partners regarding new sales strategies.
- They communicate valuable information to important constituencies and in doing so they can help to shape their perception of the organisation and the way they interact with it.

3. Decisional Roles

In the words of **Peter Drucker**, "whatever managers do, they do through making decisions." The information collected through monitoring is directed toward discovering problems or opportunities, weighing options, making decisions and ensuring that those decisions are put into action.

These roles deal with taking decisions for the betterment of the organisation, whereas inter-personal roles deal with people and informational roles deal with knowledge, decisional roles deal with action. They translate the people and information into processes with the purpose of moving the organisation toward its strategic goals. Mintzberg identified four decision roles, *i.e.* resource allocator, disturbance handler, entrepreneur and negotiator,

which are as follows

(i) Disturbance Handler

- Disturbance handling includes addressing unanticipated complications as they arise and solving them expeditiously. In managerial work, unanticipated problems arise often. Disturbances are unavoidable in the business environment, hence this role enables the manager in getting the team return to the track after the disturbance has occurred.
- Managers must decide what to do about these unexpected glitches often quickly. Thus, he aims at resolving conflicts and tackling any problem outside the business.

(ii) Entrepreneur

- In their role as entrepreneurs, managers must ensure that their organisations innovate and change whenever necessary, developing or adopting new ideas and technologies and improving their own products and processes. They must make decisions that are consistent with such entrepreneurial behaviour. If they do not, their organisations will be quickly outwitted by more agile competitors.
- Thus, managers work like an entrepreneur where he runs his small business. Though he has various superiors, but often he had to make decisions on his own. This reflects the role of an entrepreneur, where he finds the solution to the problem quickly, takes decisions, constantly thinks about new methods through which the team will move forward.

(iii) Resource Allocator

- Resources are scarce and can be used in many different ways. Organisations never have enough money, time, facilities or people to satisfy all their needs. As a resource allocator, a manager approves rejects and makes important decisions. The manager is expected to get the work done by managing and allocating resources judiciously.
- Thus, it is a crucial role to manage within given resources. A crucial decision responsibility of managers is to decide how best to allocate the scarce resources under their control between competing claims in order to meet the organisation's goals.

(iv) Negotiator

- Managers who are successful when making negotiation decisions can lower input costs, strike better deals with customers, gain access to more high-quality resources within the organisation and better organise their own subordinates. Managers negotiate with suppliers for better delivery, lower prices and higher quality inputs.
- They negotiate with customers over the pricing, delivery and design of products and services. They negotiate with peers in their own organisation over shared resources and cooperative efforts. They negotiate with their superiors for access to scarce resources, including capital, personnel and facilities.
- They even negotiate with subordinates in their own work unit, trying to allocate employees between tasks to meet the goals of both the organisation and individual employees. Thus, skilled negotiators are more likely to successfully implement strategy and raise the performance of their organisations guided by the strategy of the organisation.

Development of Management Thought

Industrial revolution encompassed the period when the world began to shift from an almost totally farming based society to an industrialised society. Once industrialisation began, it continued at a rapid pace. By the end of the nineteenth century, the economies had shifted from being mainly agricultural to being heavily involved with manufactured goods and industrial markets. This led to evolution of new methods of production and management. The period of evolution has been broadly classified into three phases namely, classical approach, neo-classical approach and modern approach.

This has been shown in different phases

Approach	Period-approximately	Propounders
I. The Classical Approach		
Bureaucratic Model	1905	Max Weber
Administrative and Functional Theory	1910	Henry Fayol
Scientific Management	1911	Frederick Winslow Taylor, Gilbreths, Gantt, MP Follett
II. The Neo-classical /Human Relations/Behavioural Approach		
Human Relations Approach	1924	George Elton Mayo and Roethlisberger
Behavioural Sciences Approach	1940s-60s	McGregor, Abraham Maslow etc
III. Modern Approach		
System Approach	1950	Chester Barnard, L. Bertalanffy David Easton, Fred Riggs, Chris Agryis
Operation Research/ Quantitative Approach	1960s	Harold Koontz
Situational or Contingency Approach	1960s	JW Lorsch and PR Lawrence, Fiedler
Qualitative Approach	1980s	Deming, Shewhart and Juran

Thoughts on Scientific Management

Production methods were rough and worker training was almost non-existent. There were no methods or standards for measuring work. Work had not been studied to determine the most desirable way to complete a task. The psychological and physical aspects of a job such as boredom, repetitiveness and fatigue were not studied or even considered in the design of most jobs.

At this point in the development of management, the engineering profession made significant contributions. The development of specialised tasks and of departments within organisations had come with the rapid industrial growth and the creation of big business. One person no longer performed every task but specialised in performing only a few tasks.

Some of the propounders are as follows

- **Taylor**

  Timekeeping was fundamental to Frederick Winslow Taylor's theories on management. Taylor worked with and observed production workers at all levels. It did not take him long to figure out that many workers put forth less than 100 per cent effort.

  Taylor referred to this tendency to restrict output as soldiering. Taylor's efforts became the true beginning of what would become known as scientific management.

- **Gantt**

  Several followers and colleagues of Taylor helped to promote scientific management. Henry Lawrence Gantt worked with Taylor. Gantt was also one of the first management pioneers to state publicly the social responsibility of management and business.

  Gantt is best known for his work in production control and his invention of the Gantt chart which graphically depicts both expected and completed production.

- **Frank and Lillian Gilbreth**

  They were inspired by Taylor and scientific research and were among the first to use motion picture films to study hand and body movements to eliminate wasted motion. Frank Gilbreth's major area of interest was the study of motions and work methods, while Lillian Gilbreth's area was psychology.

  Lillian Gilbreth became known as the First Lady of Management. By combining time and motion study and psychology, the Gilbreths contributed greatly to research in the areas of fatigue, boredom and morale.

Thoughts on Administration

Various theorist had emerged who emphasised on the management of organisation as a whole. Administrative theories are the general principles that have been designed specially for upper level management.

Some of the contributors are

- **Henry Fayol**

  A Frenchman, was the first to issue a complete statement on a theory of general management. FW Taylor focussed on standardisation of processes and focussed on management principles that can be followed at operational levels or for executor level. Henry Fayol developed principles for the top level management and middle level management in order to facilitate administration of subordinates.

  Today, Fayol's greatest contribution is considered to be his theory of management principles and their 14 elements which will be explained in the upcoming sections. Fayol was probably the first to outline what today are called the functions of management. In essence, he recognised planning, organising, commanding, coordinating and controlling as elements of management.

  The works of Taylor and Fayol are essentially complementary. Both believed proper management of personnel and other resources is the key to organisational success. Both used a scientific approach to management. The major difference is in their orientation. Taylor stressed the management of work, whereas Fayol emphasised the management of organisation.

- **Weber**

  Max Weber propounded the theory of bureaucracy. Bureaucracy is an administrative system intended to achieve a large scale administrative tasks by methodically coordinating the work of many persons.

- **Mooney and Reiley**

  In their book, 'Onward Industry' 1931 they provided an elaborated historical account of management thought for them 'principles' are set of statements showing importance of leadership, coordination and leadership. Mooney, in his article 'Papers on science of administration' maintained that it was coordination which is the fundamental principle of any human organisation. They also discussed the functional principles of management. They defined three functions that define a job.

  They are

  (a) determinative function (setting goals),
  (b) the interpretative function (decision-making) and
  (c) the application function.

- **Gullick and Urwick**

  Luther Gullick and Lyndall Urwick had a great experience in the working of military, civil service and industrial organisation. They focused on rationalise the work process by bringing work together in a centralised area.

  They are the key contributer towards the development of classical theory of organisation, called administrative theory. They gave various principles of organisation. Gullick gave principles such as decentralisation, span of control etc while Urwick gave eight principles of administration. Gullick also coined the term PODSCORB.

All of these thinkers were classical administrators. However, up till here, the employees and workers were regarded as machines and the only objective of the organisation was to extract maximum output per worker. This led to another series of evolution of management thoughts that revolved around the human element in the organisation. Thus, began the period of neo-classical era.

Thoughts on Human Relations and Behaviourism

The neo-classical era shifted its focus from management of work to conditions of workers. The Great Depression of 1929-32 saw unemployment in excess of 25 per cent. Afterward, unions sought and gained major advantages for the working class.

In this period, known as the Golden Age of Unionism, legislatures and courts actively supported organised labour and the worker. The general climate tended to emphasise understanding employees and their needs (as opposed to focusing on the methods used to conduct work).

A major research project, known as the Hawthorne studies, is generally recognised as igniting the interest of business in the human element of the workplace. This was followed by various studies under Behavioural approach.

Some of the propounders are as follows

- **George Elton Mayo**

  The Hawthorne studies began in 1924 when the National Research Council of the National Academy of Sciences began a project to define the relationship between physical working conditions and worker productivity. The Hawthorne plant of Western Electric in Cicero, Illinois, was the study site.

  In early 1927, the researchers called in a team of psychologists from Harvard University led by Elton Mayo. Hawthorne researchers have been questioned but they did create great interest in the human problems in the workplace and focused attention on the human factor.

- **Mary Parker Follett**

  MP Follett was not a businesswoman in the sense that she managed her own business. However, through her writings and lectures, she had a great impact on many business and government leaders. She was an administrator.

  While concerned with many aspects of the management process, her basic theory was that the fundamental problem of any organisation is to build and maintain dynamic yet harmonious human relations within the organisation.

Thoughts on System Approach

Many management theorists sought to use a systems approach to assimilate the various management schools. A system is a set of connected elements that function as a whole. The systems approach to management was viewed as "a way of thinking about the job of managing that provides a framework for visualising internal and external environmental factors as an integrated whole."

Under this approach, the organisation can be seen as either an open system where it interacts with its external environment or a closed system where it has no interaction with its external environment. Most organisations are run as open systems, but even then they can make the mistake of ignoring their environment and acting as though they can operate independently of the world around them.

Chester Barnard and **David Easton** was a prominent theorist who grounded his theory on the basis of system approach.

Thoughts on Quantitative Approach

Mathematicians, physicists and other scientists joined forces during World War II to solve military issues. The quantitative approach is the result of study conducted during World War II. To enhance decision-making, the quantitative management approach involves the use of quantitative techniques such as statistical data, information models, figures and computer simulations.

Supervisors, administrators can use computational models to find the best way to do something while saving money as well as time. Managers use a number of applications for science. Mathematical projections enable the planning process that makes projections useful. Modelling inventory helps to regulate inventories by determining quantitatively how and when to order a product.

Some of the models are explained below

- **Operations Management** Management of operations is a narrow branch of the quantitative management approach. It focuses on controlling the process of transforming materials, labour and capital in and out of services or goods that are useful.
- **Management Information Systems** (MIS) It is the quantitative school's latest sub-field. A MIS arranges and processes past, present and estimated data from internal and external sources into usable information, which is then made available to supervisors at all levels of the organisation.
- **Linear Programming** This was developed by **George Danlzig** which was used to determine the optimal allocation of scarce resources.

- **Operations Research** Other techniques about like capacity planning, transportation problems, sequencing, six-sigma, facility location, queuing theory, determining the location, quality control etc were also developed under quantitative approach.

Thus, quantitative management though developed out of statistical and mathematical advancements which gave solutions to complex managerial problems. Today, it directly help in making crucial decisions for the organisation.

Thoughts on Contingency Approach

In the contingency approach to management, different situations and conditions require different management approaches. Proponents believe there is no one best way to manage, the best way depends on the specific circumstances. This theory is based on the premise that situations dictate managerial actions. Management is continuously affected by different and changing situations that require managers to use different approaches and techniques.

Managing an entrepreneurial set-up might vary from running a departmental set-up in a large corporate setting. Contingency approach is often regarded as situational approach because the management uses different techniques in different situations. Thus, according to this approach, the management values and concepts have no universal applications. There are various contingency theorists such as Selznick, Burns and Stalker, Woodward, Lawrence and Lorsch, James Thompson.

As per this approach, organisational efforts should be based on the behaviour of actions outside the system so that organisations easily get integrated with the environment. There is no one best way of management of employees. This is totally contradictory to the scientific management given by **Taylor**.

Different situations call for different approaches. The choice of a particular method of managing largely depends on the nature of the job, the people involved and the situation.

Implications of Contingency Approach

- **Professor Koontz**, described contingency approach as the best approach to solve all the problems in his book "Management Theory Jungle".
- **Kast and Rosenzweig** have rightly said that the contingency theory "falls somewhere between simplistic specific principles and complex vague notions."
- **Robert Albanese** highlights two important features of contingency approach, *which are as follows*
  (a) It focuses on specific situational factors that influence the appropriateness of one managerial strategy over another.
  (b) It highlights the importance of developing skills by managers in analysing situation and finding out contingency factors that influence their approach. A manager trained in the contingency approach may offer solution to the problem that is responsive to the characteristics of the total situation being faced.

  The system approach takes a general view of organisational variables that is personal, social, technical structural and external variables.

  The contingency approach, on the other hand is concerned with achieving, a fit between the organisation and its environment. It considers each organisation to be unique. It is more pragmatic and action oriented approach.

Thoughts on Qualitative Approach

The recent developments in management are emphasising on quality and not quantity in the production process. Contributors like Taylor, Gilberth etc developed theories that had improved the production process and output was maximised.

The sole objective was to produce maximum number of units, per work, per period, however, the quality of the produce was overlooked. However, recent developers such as Walter A. Shewhart, William E. Deming, Joseph Juran focused on quality management, where they gave the principle of 'do it right the first time'.

Deming is known for his '14 points on Quality'. Various concepts such as Kaizen, Total Quality Management six sigma, bench marking etc have emerged.

This approach is customer oriented, employee oriented and quality oriented. Though, the early writers began exploring the qualitative aspect of management in 1920s and 50s it became popular in 1980s.

Theories and Approaches in Management

There are the set of inter-related concepts, definitions and principles that present a systematic view of various interactions among people in the organisation. Following are some of the prominent theories of classical, neo-classical and modern era.

Classical Theories

These are the long established and traditional theories which became the foundation stones of systematic study of the organisation. These theories prescribe that an organisation is built around the work to be done and believes that incentives motivates the employees.

Following are the two important theories given by FW Taylor and Henry Fayol

1. Taylor's Scientific Management

With industrialisation, one person no longer performed every task but specialised in performing only a few tasks. This created a need to coordinate, integrate and systematise the workflow.

The time spent on each item could be significant, if a company was producing several thousand items. Increased production plus the new need for integrating and systematising the workflow led engineers to begin studying workflows and job content.

Scientific management is the philosophy of Frederick W Taylor that sought to increase productivity and make the work easier by scientifically studying work methods and establishing standards. Taylor wanted to use scientific and empirical methods rather than tradition and custom for setting work standards.

Taylor's efforts became the true beginning of Scientific Management. He is known as the Father of Scientific Management.

This approach emphasises the scientific study of work in order to improve worker's efficiency. He tried to find out effective work standards and developed scientific method to improve productivity of the workers. He called his workers as Schmidt.

Principles of Scientific Management

Scientific management, as developed by Taylor, was based on four main principles which are

(i) Science not Rule of Thumb

This aimed at the development of a scientific method of designing jobs to replace the old rule of thumb methods. This involved gathering, classifying and tabulating data to arrive at the 'one best way' to perform a task or a series of tasks. Taylor has given that the management is a science and the decisions should be based on facts. Thus, he suggests the manager must not stick to an old rule of thumb rather try to find out the one best way of work after discussing it with his workers.

The work allocated to any worker should be examined and evaluated with regard to each element or part of it and the time involved in it in order to identify the best way to execute that work and to determine the standard output for it.

(ii) Harmony not Discord

He also propagated that the workers must practice harmony while working and avoid any dispute. He also saw the value of matching the job to the worker.

He also emphasised the need to study worker strengths and weaknesses and to provide training to improve employee performance.

On the part of both managers and workers, Taylor suggested complete mental revolution. Here, he calls for mental revolution where the management and worker should not pull each other rather support each other. Mental revolution is an important concept given by **Taylor**.

(iii) Cooperation not Individualism

Workers must be counted as part of the management and be invited to participate in the management decision-making process. Management must always welcome and recompense their suggestions if their recommendations prove beneficial to the organisation with respect to cost reduction or production increase etc.

There should be a division of work resulting in interdependence between management and workers. Taylor believed if they were truly dependent on each other, cooperation would naturally follow. At the same moment, staff should also withstand striking or making unnecessary management demands.

Employees must be regarded as an integral part of the company and all major decisions must be taken after proper employee consultation.

(iv) Development of Each and Every Person to his or her Greatest Efficiency and Prosperity

Taylor held that new and scientific methods of job design should not merely be put before a worker but they should also be fully clarified by management. He also believed that the management and the workers are complementary to each other.

He said that every worker can be made efficient and expert by properly identifying his talent and giving him opportunities. He assumed that the workers would show little resistance to changes in methods if they understood the reasons for the changes and saw a chance for greater earnings for themselves.

He also proposed that there should be a match between the skills and abilities of the employees with their jobs. Thus, he proposed concept of scientific training and selection.

Techniques of Scientific Management

It emphasised maximum output with minimum effort through the elimination of waste and inefficiency at the operational level of the organisation. A methodological approach was used to study job tasks. This approach included research and experimentation methods (scientific methods).

Standards were set in the areas of personnel, working conditions, equipment, output and procedures. The managers planned the work; the employees performed it. The result was closer cooperation between managers and employees.

The basic six techniques are explained below

(i) Scientific Work Study

It implies conducting an in-depth analysis of all operations undertaken within the organisation with the objective of producing the highest possible quality output at minimal cost. *Taylor has showed the following studies*

- **Motion Study** It aims at reducing the unnecessary motions of the workers during the work so that they can generate more output in lesser time. It relates to conducting the study of employee and machine motions while doing the job. This study is conducted using the film camera. Thus, the study's main goal is to eliminate unwanted motions.
- **Method Study** The main goal of this study is to minimise production costs and maximise client satisfaction and quality. All the factors affecting a job performance are identified and studied. Process chart and operation research techniques are used for steering this study. Thus, it relates to identifying the most appropriate way of performing a specific activity.
- **Time Study** This is the method to find the optimum time or the standard time to be taken to perform a given task or to complete an activity. This is very significant for the management because of the performance appraisal of the worker is possible only after learning the total and standard time taken for completing a task. Using a stopwatch, this study is conducted. The study's primary goals are to obtain the estimated labour cost figure, to calculate the number of workers required and to determine the right incentive plan.
- **Fatigue Study** This helps the manager in learning about the duration and frequency of interval given to the worker between the work schedules. The primary goal of this study is to maintain a certain level of worker efficiency. There might be so many factors of fatigue, such as long hours of work, bad working conditions, inappropriate work, unhappy boss relationships etc. Thus, fatigue study relates to determining the rest interval duration and frequency to finish a specific job. The rest are refreshing the employees. With their full capacity, they are working again.

(ii) Differential Piece Rate /Wage System

To encourage employees, Taylor has advised the adoption of differential wage systems. As per this system, payment of wages is based on the work done and not on hours spent doing the work. Two different salary rates are used in this system one is the high salary rate and the other is the low salary rate.

Those employees who are capable of producing the standard number of units in a fixed period of time are paid according to the high rate of pay and all those workers who are unable to produce the standard number of units within the same period are paid according to the lower rate of pay.

This is explained with the following example. In a company, there can be two piece rates ₹ 20 and ₹ 25. Every worker has to achieve a target of producing 8 units in a day and the worker who produces beyond 8 units is entitled to a wage rate of ₹ 25 while the employees missing the target will be paid ₹ 20 per unit.

Thus, Taylor suggested that higher piece rate and differential piece rate will attract the workers in producing more and more output. As an outcome, the less competent workers will be driven to work more and efficient workers will be inspired to maintain their efficiency.

(iii) Standardisation of Work

Standardisation means, after due deliberation, setting a standard for various factors. The worker is supposed to do the standard amount of work each day.

The standards are required to be set in advance for deciding the work procedures, quality parameters, time schedules, working conditions. Thus, standardisation increases the efficiency of the employees as well as organisation. *Standards can be set in the following manner*

- **Standardised Material** By standardising material, it implies that the supplied raw material should be in accordance with the required quality of finished goods. This can be done by standardising that for a particular quality of output, a particular quantity of input is required. This standard is to be followed for the rest of the production.

- **Standardisation of Machines and Tools** Standardisa- tion of machines and instruments will decrease workers' mistakes as to which tools or machines are to use and work can therefore proceed much faster. Thus, standardisation of machinery requires telling in advance what tools and machines are required to produce a given output. This also results in consistency and uniform outputs.
- **Standardised Method** It can move ahead at a faster pace albeit with greater ease by standardising the optimum working techniques. When such work is performed, the method determined to perform a particular activity is used uniformly.
- **Standard Working Conditions** Working environment has a profound impact on workers' efficiency. It is observed in standardised working conditions how much heat, ventilation, illumination, sanitation and safety at the workplace is required.

  The working conditions are standardised after proper studies and attempts are made to keep them in the workplace.

(iv) Simplification

Simplification implies ending needless types, characteristics, weights, sizes etc. A company must aim at manufacturing simple and few variants of its products. *e.g.* A company producing shoes can have sizes ranging in whole numbers such as 0, 1,2,3,4 etc and not 0, 0.25,0.5,0.75 etc.

This is because for each size new machinery is to be installed and there will be a reduction in the productivity. Thus, the organisation must follow simplified methods of productions and simple standards.

(v) Functional Foremanship

This type of organisation is entirely based on the specialisation concept and makes full use of the knowledge of different experts. Work is divided into several small parts within a functional organisation so each part is assigned to an expert. In this way, it takes advantage of all the benefits of specialisation.

Taylor suggested dividing the factory manager's work into two sub-departments

(i) Department of Planning
(ii) Department of Production.

In each department, four experts are appointed. The planning department experts do planning and the manufacturing department experts help in manufacturing.

These are

(a) Planning Department

This comprises of the following specialists

- **Route Clerk** This clerk makes sure the completion series of a particular work, meaning the stages that must be completed before finalisation. He also determines what work is to be done for the day and where to do it. He instructs and defines about the timing and the procedure of doing the work.
- **Instruction Card Clerk** This clerk arranges the workers' instruction cards and hands them over to the gang boss. Such card contains information on the nature of work, how to do it, the material being used and the equipment details. He gives the necessary instructions to the workers that are required to carry out the task.
- **Time and Cost Clerk** This clerk determines when to start and end a particular work, which means when the entire work will take place. At the same time it is also decided at what cost the item will be manufactured. He sets the standard time to complete the given task and the cost involved in completing the task.
- **Disciplinarian** The discipline officer helps ensure disciplined performance of all work. He is responsible for the overall planning function and ensures that all work is done properly.

(b) Production Department

This department comprises of the following specialists

- **Gang Boss** From the control point of view, the workers are divided into different groups. A group leader who is known as the boss of the gang is selected. He is responsible for the activities of the group as he represents his group. It is anticipated that he will make sure that both the employees and the machines are sufficiently fit for manufacturing and that they will have access to the material required for their use.
- **Speed Boss** The speed boss' primary function is to guarantee that all employees perform their work at the right speed or expected. If not, the speed boss will try to find out the cause of slow speed and thus come up with a solution for it.
- **Repair Boss** He is responsible for maintaining all machines and tools in proper working condition so that there is no hindrance in the production process. Thus, the main purpose of the repair boss is to keep the machines and tools in operational condition.
- **Inspector** He examines the products produced and relates their quality to their standard and tries to determine the difference. He undertakes corrective action in the event of an unfavourable outcome.

(vi) Mental Revolution

As discussed earlier, mental revolution calls for both employers and workers to change their mind-set. According to **Taylor**, both managers and workers need a revolution as it will foster a sense of cooperation and benefit both groups.

He propagated that instead of focussing more on division of surplus they should together turn their attention towards increasing the size of their surplus until this surplus or profit becomes so large that is becomes necessary to quarrel over how it should be divided.

Instead of battling over profit division, both groups should make efforts to raise profits, according to Taylor. Such a situation will lead to increased production and as such a high increase in profits that will make any talk about surplus hollow.

Criticism of Taylorism

While it is accepted that scientific management allows managers to put resources to their best use and ways, severe criticism has not been spared. It has been criticised for exploitation of workers, monotony, over speeding, weakening of trade union, deterioration of quality etc.

Also, it is criticised that scientific management is limited to shop management and lower level employees and does not highlight managerial functioning. This drawback has been combated by Henry Fayol with his theory of administration.

2. Administrative Theory by Henry Fayol

Henry Fayol, a Frenchman, was the first to issue a complete statement on a theory of general management. Fayol developed his list of principles from the practices he had used most often in his own work. He used them as general guidelines for effective management but stressed flexibility in their application to allow for different and changing circumstances. *Fayol identified the 14 principles of management which have been explained below*

(i) Authority and Responsibility

Authority and responsibility are coexisting. If authority is given to a person, he should also be made a responsible. In a same way, if anyone is made responsible for any job, he should also have concerned authority.

Authority refers to the right of superiors to get exactness from their subordinates, whereas responsibility means obligation for the performance of the job assigned. Thus, he gave difference between formal (positional) authorities versus personal authority.

(ii) Division of Work

Henry Fayol has stressed on the specialisation of jobs. He gave the concept of specialisation of work. He recommended that work of all kinds must be divided and sub-divided and allotted to various persons according to their expertise in a particular area. Sub-division of work makes it simpler and results in efficiency which also leads to specialisation.

(iii) Principle of One Boss/Unity of Command

He proposed that each employee should receive orders from only one superior. He said that a subordinate must receive orders and should be accountable to one and only boss at a time. In other words, a subordinate should not receive instructions from more than one person because this weakens discipline, delays and creates chaos at the work place.

It also overlaps the efforts and divides the loyalty of the subordinate. There can be confusion and the subordinate may escape responsibility. Thus, dual subordination should be avoided unless and until it is absolutely essential.

(iv) Initiative

He called for individual zeal and energy in all efforts. He propounded that the workers should be encouraged to take initiative in the work assigned to the, without being asked to do so. Fayol advised that management should provide opportunity to its employees to suggest ideas, experiences and new method of work, as it builds an environment of trust and boosts morale. They can be encouraged with the monetary and non-monetary incentives.

(v) Discipline

It is based on obedience and respect. According to him, discipline means sincerity, obedience, respect of authority and observance of rules and regulations of the enterprise.

This principle states that subordinate should respect their superior and obey their order, this ensures smooth functioning. Discipline can be enforced if there are competent superiors, fair agreement alongwith adequate punishment.

(vi) Order

He insisted on ensuring there is a place for everything. This principle is concerned with proper and systematic arrangement of things and people in an organisation. Arrangement of things is called material order and placement of people is called social order. *These can be*

(a) material order which states that there should be a safe, appropriate and specific place for every article and every place to be effectively used for specific activity and commodity.

(b) social order which means the selection and appointment of appropriate people.

(vii) Remuneration of Employees

He proposed that the mode of payment of wages was dependent on many factors. The quantum and method of remuneration to be paid to the workers should be fair, reasonable, satisfactory and rewarding of the efforts. As far as possible, it should accord satisfaction to both employer and the employees.

Wages should be determined on the basis of cost of living, work assigned, financial position of the business, wage rate prevailing etc. Logical and appropriate wage rates and methods of their payment reduce tension and differences between workers. Fayol also recommended provision of other benefits such as free education, medical and residential facilities to workers.

(viii) Unity of Direction

He suggested there should be one boss and one plan for a group of activities having the same objective. He advocates one head one plan policy. This means that there should be one plan for a group of activities having similar objectives. Related activities should be grouped together.

There should be one plan of action for them and they should be under the charge of a particular manager. All the efforts of employees should be directed towards in the common organisational goals because it leads to unity of action.

(ix) Equity

Here, he proposed a theory which contradicts theory of differential piece rate. He states that equity results from justice and kindness. This entails that the organisation should encourage an atmosphere which is based on equity. This should also be equipped with a climate of trust, friendliness and justice in employee and employer relationship, to enable the employees to fulfill their duties with devotion.

(x) Stability of Tenure

He called for orderly personnel planning. Fayol emphasised that employees should not be moved frequently from one job position to another that is the period of service in a job should be fixed.

According to him, time is required for an employee to get used to new work and succeed doing it well but if he is removed before that he will not be able to render worthwhile services.

As a result the time, effort and money spent on training the worker will go waste. Stability of job creates team spirit and sense of belongingness among workers which ultimately increase the quality as well as quantity of work.

(xi) Scalar Chain

It shows the line of authority. He shows the routing of the line of authority and formal communication channels. He defines a scalar chain as the chain of superiors ranging from the ultimate authority to the lowest. Every orders, instructions, messages, requests, explanations etc has to pass through scalar chain. But for the sake of convenience and urgency, this path can be cut short and this short cut is known as Gang Plank.

It is a temporary arrangement between the two different points to facilitate quick and easy communication as explained below. In the figure below, if D has to communicate with G, he will first send the communication upwards with the help of C, B to A and then downwards with the help of E and F to G, which will consume time. Thus, in case of emergency, he can use a gang plank which can be DE and GB.

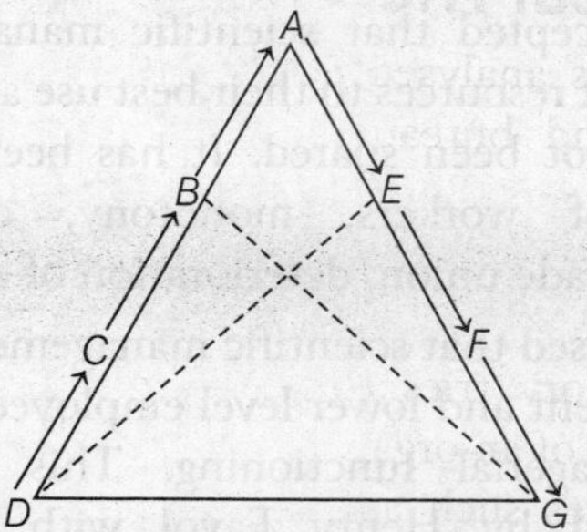

Gang plank clarifies that management principles are not rigid rather they are very flexible. They can be moulded and modified as per the requirements of the situations.

(xii) Centralisation and Decentralisation

According to **Fayol**, "Degree of centralisation and decentralisation depends on number of factors like the size of business, experience of superiors, dependability and ability of the subordinate."

An organisation must balance between centralisation and decentralisation. Centralisation refers to concentration of authority at the top level. Decentralisation means disposal of decision-making authority to all the levels of the organisation.

(xiii) Subordination of Individual Interests to General Interest

He proposed a plea to abolish the tendency to place individual interest ahead of the group interest. An organisation is much bigger than the individual it constitutes, thus, the interest of the undertaking should prevail in all circumstances.

As far as possible, reconciliation should be achieved between the group interests and individual interests, but in case of conflict, individual must sacrifice for bigger interests.

(xiv) Espirit De Corps

This principle stressed the building of harmony and unity within the organisation. It refers to team spirit that is harmony in the work groups and mutual understanding among the members promotes hard work.

He cautioned the managers against dividing the employees into competing groups. Because this might damage the moral of the workers and interest of the undertaking in the long run. He also cautioned against the more use of Britain communication to the subordinates, which is face-to-face communi- cation should be developed.

The managers should infuse team spirit and belongingness. There should be no place for misunderstanding. People then enjoy working in the organisation and offer their best towards the organisation.

Neo-classical Theories

Scientific theories analysed activities of workers whereas administrative and bureaucratic theory focused on the activities of managers. Both theories forgot the importance of individual as well as group relationships in an organisation.

Neo-classical theory tries to find out the social factors affecting working of an organisation. This theory comprises of various theories such as Hawthorne Experiments and other Behavioural Approaches. These studies discovered that the real cause of human behaviour was more than mere physiological variables.

Since, behavioural approach or human relation approach has suggested only modification in the basic postulates of classical theory, it is referred as neo-classical theory.

Certain principles that distinguish human relation theories/neo-classical theories from classical theories are given below

- Social factors affect the people more than the organisational factors. Informal groups exist in the organisation in which the employees fulfil their social needs of entertainment, mutual cooperation for fulfilling personal needs etc. These informal groups have direct impact on formal organisation.
- A conflict between personal and organisational goals exists for an employee. Man is motivated not only by economic factors but he wants to fulfil different needs and sometimes he can behave irrationally.
- Leadership is important for directing group behaviour. However, leadership cannot come from direct positions. There must be informal leaders who can identify themselves with the group by way of human relation approach.
- Communication is the way for better understanding between the management and workers by identifying their attitudes, opinions and methods of working and taking suitable actions.
- Friendly supervision with concern for employees ensures good results, better morale and healthy organisational climate.

Thus, neo-classical or human relations approach believes that man is a social animal and led to formation of flat and informal structures.

Behavioural Approach

The behavioural approach to management developed mainly because the practitioners discovered that it was not possible to achieve total efficiency and workplace coexistence by adopting the ideas of the classical approach.

Some of the main behavioural researchers who made considerable contributions to the progression of the behavioural approach to management are Mary Parker Follett, Douglas McGregor, Kurt Lewin, Chester Barnard, Abraham Maslow, George Romans etc.

This approach considered an organisation as a socio-technical system. Individuals working together tend to form their own informed groups. It is an advanced theory as compared to human relations approach.

Human relation approach focussed on individual's inter-personal interaction, whereas behavioural approach lays stress on group or organisation behaviour. It draws its roots from various sciences such as psychology, sociology, which study human behaviour.

The behavioural approach has been divided into two branches the human relations approach and the behavioural science approach. We will study them in two different sections.

1. Human Relation Approach

The term 'relationships between people' means the way managers connect with subordinates. Supervisors face many challenges because employees don't usually adhere to preordained and balanced behaviour patterns. Human relations advocates are of the opinion that administrators should acknowledge the need for recognition and social acceptance of employees.

The work group should be viewed by management as a positive force that can be used productively. Managers must therefore be knowledgeable with technical skills in human relationships. This proposition was furthered by Hawthorne Experiments.

Hawthorne Experiments

The Hawthorne studies began in 1924 when the National Research Council of the National Academy of Sciences began a project to define the relationship between physical working conditions and worker productivity. The Hawthorne plant of Western Electric in Cicero, Illinois, was the study site.

First, the researchers lowered the level of lighting, expecting productivity to decrease. To their astonishment, productivity increased.

Over the next several months, the researchers repeated the experiment by testing many different levels of lighting and other variables. These experiments were called 'Hawthorne experiments' by **Henry A Landsberger.**

The different stages of these experiments have been explained below

(i) Experiments on Illumination (1924-27)

The illumination experiments were conducted by **George A Pennock**. Experiments on illumination were conducted to discover how different levels of illumination (amount of light at the workplace, a physical factor) affected productivity. The hypothesis was that efficiency will increase with higher lighting.

These were conducted in five phases, *which are as follows*

- **First Experiment**

  Here three departments were selected for the execution of this experiment. Inspection of small parts was done in the first department, assembly of relays in the second department and winding of coils was done in the third department. Production was assessed with all employees working under the existing illumination conditions to maintain a 'Control' for the experiment.

  These workers working in the existing and consistent level of illumination were called control groups while the groups which faced varying, illumination were called the 'test groups'.

  The control group had constant light, while the test group had varying lights. In the first department, where the levels of average illumination intensity were 3, 6, 14 and 23 foot candles, the production of the workers varied without any direct relation to the amount of illumination. There was increase in production. In the second and third department, also the results were the same.

- **Second Experiment**

  To set up this experiment, a single department with two test groups of participating workers was used. Test group was the group that worked under different levels of illumination. Better methods were used in this experiment included the same number of participating workers with the same experience and average production.

  The production was then measured under the current relatively constant lighting or illumination to maintain a control for the experiments. In the second department, where the levels of average illumination intensities were 5, 12, 25 and 44 foot candles, the production increased but not merely as a result of illumination variation.

  By separating their workplace, the spirit of competition among test groups was denied. Then both test groups were subjected to three different intensities of illumination. The results of this experiment revealed an identical and appreciable increase in production in both test groups.

- **Third Experiment**

  The third lighting experiment was done because the second experiment failed to show exactly what production increase could be attributed to lighting. Daylight was entirely replaced this time by artificial light, beginning with 10 foot candle intensity and gradually reducing intensity by 1 foot candle per period until the test group ended up working under 3 foot candle intensity.

- **Fourth Experiment**

  Here, two females volunteered to work in a room that received gradually reducing light. Lastly the light intensity was lowered to become equivalent to that of moonlight. The two girls not only continued production but also described lack of eyestrain and fatigue compared to conditions of working under bright light.

- **Fifth Experiment**

  At the start of test, the concentration of light was increased day-by-day. Later, even when the lights remained constant or were reduced, the production was unchanged. Thus, the researchers concluded that the employees reacted probably not to the changes in illumination but some other factor.

Conclusion The main goal was to study the connection between illumination intensity and output, but those were disappointing to the researchers as the workers had not responded to actual changes in illumination but to some other variable and therefore no real change in production had been recorded. Thus, in 1927, the researchers called in a team of psychologists from Harvard University led by **Elton Mayo**.

(ii) Relay Assembly Test Room Experiment (1927-32)

- Relay assembly test room tests were designed to identify the effect on group productivity of changes in different working situations, as the illumination experiments could not build a relationship between illumination intensity and production. To this end, two girls were chosen to set up a relay assembly test room.

- The work attributed to telephone relay assembly. Each relay comprised of several parts assembled into finished products by girls. Output depended on how quickly and continuously girls worked with.
- The experiments began with the introduction of numerous sequence changes ranging from **four to twelve weeks** in duration of each change.
- These changes comprised of change in incentive system, Two five- minute rests, the rest time period was reduced however, its frequency was increased, changes in working hours and work day were introduced and productivity was seen to be increased with reduction in working hours for females.
- As each change was implemented, absenteeism fell, morality improved and less supervision was needed. It was thought that because of the different factors being measured and making them more positive, these positive factors were present. The psychologists decided at this time to return to their original situation, with no rest and other advantages. But, surprisingly, there was no reduction in output.
- This development triggered a considerable amount of redirection in thought process and the result implied that productivity increased not due to positive changes in physical factors but due to changes in the attitudes of females towards work and their working group.
- They developed a sense of stability and belongings. They developed a sense of responsibility because there was more freedom of job and the association between supervisor and workers became close and friendly.

(iii) Mass Interviewing (1928-31)/Human Attitudes and Sentiments

- Approximately 20,000 interviews were conducted between 1928 and 1930 during the course of tests to determine the perceptions of employees towards business, management, insurance plans, supervision, promotion and wages. Here, the organisation was seen as a social structure.
- These interviews were initially conducted through direct interviews such as "do you like your supervisor? Is he fair in his judgements" etc. The interview programme gave valuable insights about the human behaviour in the company such as a grievance is not simply an objective recital of factual information rather it is a symptom of personal disturbance, the cause of which may be deeply rooted. The company's social organisation represents a system of values from which the worker derives satisfaction or dissatisfaction in accordance with his social perception.
- It was discovered that workers' behaviour was being influenced by group behaviour and the workers' social demands are based on social experience within and outside the workplace in groups. Now, a detailed study of the shop condition began to determine the behaviour of small groups of workers.

(iv) Bank Wiring Observation Room Experiment (1931-32)/Social Organisation

This study was conducted by **W Lloyd Warner** and **Elton Mayo**. These experiments were conducted to determine the impact on individuals of small groups and group incentive system. A group of 14 male workers were formed into 3 small working groups in this experiment. The men were involved in assembling terminal banks for use in exchanges of telephones.

For certain equipment used in telephone changes, the work involved connecting wire with switche The hourly wage was fixed for each labourer on the basis of each worker's average output.

Here, the wages were paid on the basis of group incentives and each member received his share on the basis of the total output of the group. Bonus was payable by group effort as well. Highly efficient workers were expected to put pressure on less efficient employees to increase output and benefit from group incentive plan.

The research team found that the workers defined their own group norms for standard output, which was kept lower to the management target. The work group formulated a highly integrated social structure and used the informal pressure to set right the deviant member.

Following code of conduct was given for the group activity

(a) One should not turn out too little work, if he does, then he is a **chester**.

(b) One should not turn out too much work, if he does, then he is a **Rate buster**.

(c) One should not tell a supervisor anything negative about the group, if he does, then he is a '**Squealer**'.

(d) One should not maintain social distance or act officious, otherwise he is an **inspector**, and should not act like one.

However, this strategy did not work and the labourers set their own production standards and this was rigorously enforced by different methods of social pressure. The workers quoted numero motives for this behaviour, *i.e.* fear of increase in output, fear of unemployment, desire to protect slow workers etc.

Principal Conclusions

- The findings of Hawthorne experiments were that the administrators should acknowledge that people are basically social beings, not just economic beings. They are members of a group as a social being and management should seek to understand group perceptions and group psychology.
- The researchers also discovered that the employees responded positively to the attention paid to them by the researchers. This phenomenon has since become known as the Hawthorne. Another finding was the significance of effective supervision to both productivity and employee morale.
- While the methods used and the conclusions reached by the Hawthorne researchers have been questioned, they did generate great interest in the human problems in the workplace and focused attention on the human factor.
- They suggested a new mix of managerial skills. In addition to complex and technical aspects, managers must manage human aspects. They also evolved that group standards are a major influence on the behaviour of individuals in organisation. Instead of economic incentives, non-economic rewards for instance group sanctions and social rewards must be given. Mayo also encouraged democratic participation.

2. Behavioural Science Approach

It states that an employee may behave differently when in group and in isolation. Individuals are different from other on the basis of value systems, perceptions and attitudes. Inter-personal relations are affected by wide range of factors. It also propagates that conflict cannot be avoided when dealing with groups. Sometimes, conflict is required and it should be faced with determination and understanding.

Hence, the behavioural science approaches in an improved version of human relation approach and Hawthorne experiments. It gave importance to people and groups' attitudes, actions and performance within the organisations.

The proponents of the approach to behavioural science consider human beings to be much more complex than the description of the classical approach by economic man and the explanation of the approach to human relations by social man.

This approach concentrates on the nature of work and how satisfactory it will be. Behavioural approach has allowed various theories to propagate. These theories are generally based on the behaviour of an individual.

Some of these theories are

(i) **Abraham Maslow** He was a practitioner of psychology, developed one of the theories of need most widely regarded, a theory of motivation based on human needs consideration.

(ii) **Douglas McGregor** He gave theory X and theory Y, and proposed a simple division of management styles that took what he argued were basically different ways of managing people.

(iii) **Dr. William Ouchi** He propounded Theory Z that tries to integrate American and Japanese management practices. It focused on improving worker loyalty to the company by offering a lifetime job with a strong emphasise on staff well being, both on and off-the-job.

Views of Mary Parker Follett

M.P. Follett's notions on negotiation, power and employee involvement were extremely influential in the advancement of organisational and administrative studies fields. Follett built on the tenets of classical management to lay the groundwork for many of the modern thinking of management in use today.

Follett is often revered as one of the precursors of feminist organisational theory, which proposed defining notions of organisation and management through the knowledge and navigation of the social world by women.

Her key concepts, including constructive conflict, coordination, integration and power with regard to relationships with individual people, are all concerned with ways to foster creative dynamics in those relations based on feelings.

Elements of Mary Parker's View

1. Constructive Conflict

Follett argues that conflict is a natural and unavoidable part of organisation; however it does not have to lead to harmful results necessarily.

Conflict resolution, as described by Follett, was an alternative dispute settlement strategy aimed at reframing the issue so the result is a healthy and balanced outcome of the interests of all involved parties. She contends that dissimilarities or conflict of interest in itself does not result into a conflict.

According to Follett, there are three ways to respond to conflict

(i) **Dominance** Dominance implies victory of one party over the other. Thus, this works in short-term but is not useful in the long run. Mary referred to the example of The World War I.

(ii) **Compromise** It implies that both the party has to give up something for the sake of a meaningful reduction of friction. Thus, far be it from the ideal, the compromise often leaves the parties unsatisfied because they have given up something of value.

(iii) **Integration** This is the option which has been fostered by Follett. It means creatively and artistically incorporating the fundamental desires and interests of the parties into the solution. She states when the two interests are integrated then this implies that a solution has been devised in which both desires have found a place and no one has to sacrifice anything.

Thus, there is higher satisfaction in this method of resolving conflict. Thus, she called for 'integration of conflicts'. Conflict resolution through integration implies identifying and meeting the fundamental and often consistent needs of each party, (as opposed to trying to satisfy each party's often conflicting expressed desire), often leads to a mutually beneficial situation.

2. Coordination

It is done to achieve the goals of an institution. It is a process which is not rigid and fixed. Coordination implies integrating the functions of management. Follett has given four principles of coordination which are called Follett's principles of coordination. *They are as follows*

- **Principle of Early Stage** Here, the coordination must begin at an early stage in the management process. This implies that it should start at the planning stage. This will ensure that best plans are built and successfully implemented.

  The management can perform rest of the functions successfully only when events are well coordinated in the beginning which will result in quick achievement of objectives.
- **Principle of Continuity** As per this principle, coordination should be continuous process and not a single time activity. The process of coordination must start when the organisation starts and should continue till the cessation of the company. It should be followed while performing all the managerial functions, *i.e.* planning, organising, controlling, directing etc.
- **Principle of Direct Contact** This implies that all the managers and superiors should establish direct contact with their subordinates. This will nurture good relations between the subordinates and their bosses.

  This will also eliminate any misunderstanding, disputes and misrepresentation. Thus, there will be perfect coordination between various activities.
- **Principle of Reciprocal Relations** This implies that the actions and decisions of all individuals (employees and managers) and the departments are inter-related. Thus, the action and decision of one department will affect all other individuals and departments in the institution.

  Hence, prior making any decision, all the managers must learn the resulting effect on all the individuals and departments of the organisation. This is termed as principle of reciprocal relations.

3. Power

Follett lays special attention to the problems of power. She defines power as the ability to make things happen, to be a causal agent, to initiate change. Power is termed as the capacity to produce the intended effect. It is an inborn urge or characteristic in all human beings.

She has made a distinction between 'Power Over' and 'Power With' where the former is termed as 'coercive-power' while the latter is the 'coactive power.' Coercive power is one group or individual's power over another, while coactive power involves sharing obligations and benefits within a power structure.

Follett has said that coactive power is superior to coercive power because it reduces conflict and friction. She suggests that it is not necessary to remove coercive power, but it should be substantially reduced to promote harmony in the organisation.

4. Control

She has also developed principles and concepts about control. She postulated that control should be dependent on conditions and should not be rigid. She thus suggests that control mechanisms should be connected at several levels in the organisational structure.

If the companies are to be well integrated, coordinated, unified then the control should be developed and defines as a part of joining or unifying process. Such organisations are self-directing and self-regulating. Thus, Mary felt control becomes self-control.

5. Authority

She has defined authority as the vested power or the right to develop and exercise power. Authority in terms of status and the subordination of one to another, insults dignity of a human being and may result into undesirable friction and reactions. Thus, it should not be the basis of the organisation.

According to **Follett**, the authority stems from the tasks that are being performed. Hence, it is derived from the circumstances and situations. She suggests that function is the true basis from which the authority should be derived.

She says that central authority deriving from the top management (CEO) should be swapped by authority of function where each person has final authority within the allotted functions. Follett expresses clearly that delegate of authority should become an obsolete expression and similar to authority, the responsibility also stems from situations and functions. She believes in pluralistic concept of authority and responsibility.

6. Democracy

Follett described democracy as a social world process, instead of simply a political activity or civil liberties set. Follett related her idea of democracy to community participation and cooperative group effort, suggesting that her concept of democracy was more social than individualistic.

7. Leadership

Follett lays emphasise on the length of the process of leadership. She believes that the old idea of leadership is evolving because of the changes in the concept of human relations and various developments in management.

According to her, a leader is, "the man who can energise his group, who knows how to encourage initiative, how to draw from all what each has to give." Thus, she believes that such people are found not only at the top of the organisation but at various levels of the organisation.

She also distinguished between three different types of leaderships

(a) **Leadership of Position** Here, the leader holds the position of formal authority.
(b) **Leadership of Personality** Here, the person becomes a leader because of his forceful personality.
(c) **Leadership of Function** This type of leadership is inherent in the job and its tasks.

Modern Theories of Management

Modern organisation theories are of recent origin developed in early 1950s which combines various features of classical and behavioural models to evolve a systematic view applicable in today's period. Modern theory studies the organisation as an open system, having sub-parts interacting with each other. MOT has a number of features which differentiate it from early organisational theories.

Some of the approaches and theories are explained below

1. System Approach

Systems approach is grounded on the generality that everything is inter-related and interdependent. A system is simply an accumulation or combination of things or parts forming a complex whole. A system is composed of related and dependent element which when in interaction, forms a unitary whole.

It includes

Open System

Under the systems approach to management, the organisation is seen as an open system that is influenced by its internal and external environmental factors. The organisation then, in turn, influences these same internal and external environmental factors and as a result, a dynamic relationship is created.

Systems theory is useful to management because it aims at achieving the objectives and it views administration as an open system. Chester Barnard was the first person to apply the systems approach in the field of management. Other theorists such as Herbert Simon viewed organisation as a complex system of decision-making process.

Closed System

By contrast closed systems do not interact with their external environments. These are visible in classical theories such as scientific management, bureaucracy etc.

Sub-systems of an Organisation

The parts that make up the whole of a system are called sub-system. Each sub-system can be a part of bigger sub-system. Thus, a department can be a sub-system of a plant, a plant can be a sub-system of a company and a company can be a sub-system of an industry and an industry can be a sub-system of an economy.

Thus, Carzo and Yanuazas have identified three sub-systems in an organisation, which are as follows

- **Power Sub-system** The power can be defined as the capacity to induce others to produce an intended result through the presentation of force. People in the organisation use power from official authority, location job importance, tenure and experience.

  As such formal structure plays a significant role in power distribution in the organisation. Beside this, individuals also acquire power by way of their skills, knowledge, competency in taking right decision and transforming them into effective actions with successful results.
- **Technical Sub-System** It includes knowledge and techniques of transforming inputs into outputs, tools and equipments, employee skills, jobs. Technical sub-system constitutes formal arrangement of the functions.
- **Social Sub-system** It includes individuals, informal groups, social or group norms, status, role norms and values. This subsystem arises spontaneously from social interaction and shared values of people interacting in an organisation. Values and implicitly accepted norms govern social sub-system.

Linking Process of Social Sub-systems

- Scott has identified three linking processes, *i.e.* communication, decision and balance.
- Likert proposed linking pin model for connecting various parts of the organisations. It is based on the assumption that every individual functions as a linking pin for interlocking groups and he is the group leader of the lower unit and a group member of the upper unit. Thus, there is a group to group relationship.

Characteristics of System Approach

- Instead of isolating each other, the different sub- systems should be studied in their inter-relationships.
- It is set of inter-related and interdependent parts organised in a way that creates a integrated whole. A system is made up of elements that interact.
- An institutional system shall have a boundary which shall determine the internal and external parts.
- There's no system in a void. It gets inputs from other structures for information, material and energy. Such inputs undergo a process of change within a system and leave the system to other systems as output.
- An organisation, as it responds to its environment, is a dynamic system. In its environment, it is vulnerable to change.
- In the systems approach, consideration is paid towards the total efficiency of the system rather than the efficiency of the sub-systems.

Chester Barnard's Social System Approach

In 1938, Chester Barnard, president of New Jersey Bell Telephone for many years, published a book that combined a thorough understanding of organisational theory and sociology. Barnard viewed the organisation as a social structure and stressed the behavioural aspects of organisations.

Effectively integrating traditional manage- ment and the behavioural sciences, Barnard's work had a great effect on managers and teachers of management.

The earlier studies of systems approach was a closed system approach such as scientific management by Taylor, administrative management, Weberian Bureaucracy etc. Later, with onset of human relation movement, the system approach resulted into open system approach.

Chester Barnard is a prominent theorist in the modern administrative thought. He defines an organisation as "a system of consciously coordinated activities or forces of two or more persons."

The three elements according to Chester Barnard are

(a) common purpose
(b) willingness to serve
(c) communication.

Barnard considers an organisation as a cooperative system. Cooperative system needs to be understood in terms of relationship between individual and organisation. Barnard felt that the study of the forces underlying social action had been neglected by social scientists.

Principles by Chester Barnard

At two levels, Barnard tries to understand human beings one from within the organisation and two from outside the organisation. They are treated from the inside, as 'participants in a particular cooperative system.' In their purely functional aspects, they are considered here. They are depersonalised in their efforts and have to fit in with the formalised roles.

Elements of Barnard's Theory

Organisation Concept According to Barnard, when the following three conditions are met, an organisation exists. (a) Persons are able to communicate with each other (b) able to contribute to the action (c) willing to achieve a common purpose.

Organisational Essentials Barnard proposed four components of a formal organisation, *i.e.* a fictionalisa- tion (specialisation) system, a system of effective and effective rewards and incentives, a system of power to accept executive decision and a system of rational decision-making.

Formal and Informal Organisations Two types of organisations may exist which are both formal and informal. There is a coordinated interaction in the formal organisation that is deliberate and has a common object. The informal organisation, on the other hand, pertains to those social interactions that don't have a purposeful joint object.

Informal organisations solve formal organisation problems. Barnard has laid special emphasise on role of informal organisation. He has proposed that both formal and informal organisations depend on each other and the two interact on an on-going basis.

Concept of Authority Which is referred to as 'Acceptance Theory of Authority' or 'Bottom-up Authority' Person should, in his opinion, obey an order, not because it was given by the superior, but as communication.

This is only feasible if

- He can understand the communication.
- He considers that the organisational purpose is not contradictory.
- It is consistent with the totality of his self-interest and
- He can follow it mentally and physically.

Thus, he said that authority is surrounded by a '**Zone of Indifference**' which implies that employees' nature to agree to authority within a sphere of action.

Executive Functions There are three types of functions that an executive performs, according to Barnard, *i.e.* maintaining organisational communication through an organisational system, obtaining basic services from people in organisations in order to achieve organisational purpose and formulating and defining organisational purpose.

Organisational Balance This implies matching individual efforts and organisational efforts to satisfy individuals. The organisation has to provide individuals with satisfaction. This requires the organisation's balance.

Motivation Barnard has proposed a number of non-financial techniques to motivate people in addition to financial incentives.

They are power and distinction opportunities, workmanship pride, relaxing participation in the organisation, mutual support of personal attitudes, sense of belongings etc.

Effectiveness of the Executive Liable and accountable leadership is necessary to make the executive effective. Leadership is also the most strategic factor to secure people's cooperation. Executive leadership requires high level of talent, skills in technology and social skills. It should be above bias and personal preference.

EXAM BASED QUESTIONS

1 Which of the following are features of management?
(a) It is an art
(b) It is a science
(c) It is based on coordination among various resources
(d) All of the above

2 Which level of management deals with formulation of policies?
(a) Lower level (b) Middle level
(c) Top level (d) All of these

3 Prof Robert Katz has divided managerial skills into
(a) conceptual, analytical, technical
(b) conceptual, analytical, human relations
(c) technical, human relation, conceptual
(d) technical, analytical, social

4 The top level management possesses .... skills.
(a) technical
(b) conceptual
(c) administrative
(d) None of the above

5 The lower level management possess .... skills.
(a) conceptual (b) technical
(c) interpersonal (d) None of these

6 Management has become more complex because
(a) there is less time to react to competitive actions
(b) the equipments used in many of the firm's activities have become more complex
(c) both formal and informal communication
(d) this term is not related to communication

7 Which one of the following theory of organisation can be regarded as first coherent theory of organisation?
(a) Human Relation theory
(b) Scientific Management
(c) System Approach theory
(d) Classical theory

8 In the view of classical theorists, an organisation is
(a) closed system
(b) open system
(c) Both (a) and (b)
(d) completely connected and influenced by its external environment

9 The most important concern of .... is the formulation of organisation.
(a) neo-classical theories
(b) classical theories
(c) human relation theories
(d) scientific management

10 Which of the following books provides the most comprehensive enunciation of classical theory?
(a) Principles on organisation
(b) Papers on science of administration
(c) Principle of scientific management
(d) General and industrial management

11 The overall goal of scientific management is
(a) maximisation of productivity
(b) maximisation of employment
(c) higher industrial efficiency
(d) greater profit to producer

12 The managers did not like scientific management theory because
(a) they felt that the workers were given undue importance in the theory
(b) it reduced managerial remuneration
(c) they felt that it had the effect of giving away more wages to the worker
(d) they felt that the rigid scientific methods will take away their managerial freedom in decision-making

13 Which of the following is not the main concern of scientific management?
(a) Production
(b) Efficiency
(c) Mechanistic Methods
(d) Rationality

14 Taylor's differential piecework plan provides that
(a) all labourers should be assigned work according to their capacity
(b) all labourers should be put in different shifts
(c) those who produce above standard should receive higher wages than those producing below standard
(d) payment should be the same on fixed standard

15 Scientific management addressed itself to the problem of
(a) bottom part of the organisation
(b) top management
(c) middle level management
(d) All of the above

16 Taylorism
(a) viewed man as an adjunct of man
(b) ignored the psychological aspects
(c) did not emphasise on human motivation
(d) emphasised only on a limited number of psychological variables

17 Taylor recommends
(a) line organisation
(b) functional organisation
(c) military organisation
(d) None of the above

18 The mechanistic theory of organisation is also referred to as the
(a) classical theory
(b) bureaucratic theory
(c) scientific management theory
(d) behaviouralistic theory

19 In which of the following way, scientific management theory is criticised?
(a) It ignores social environment
(b) It dehumanises the workers
(c) It makes wrong assumption that money is the main motivator
(d) All of the above

20 Which of these were not an integral part of scientific management?
(a) Differential piece wage system
(b) Worker control of production
(c) Systematic selection of worker
(d) Work specialisation

21 Which of the following was an early key management idea, pre-dating the work of FW Taylor & Max Weber?
(a) Differential pay rates
(b) Rule-by-the office
(c) Work specialisation
(d) Classical management theory

22 Which of the following is not a key concept associated with scientific management?
(a) One best way (b) Formalisation
(c) Time and motion studies (d) Systematic selection

23 Which of the following is not true of the concept of scientific management?
(a) It raises questions as to how rewards from increased productivity should be distributed
(b) It gave rise to the modern operation research
(c) It is outdated as a theory and cannot be applied in today's modern organisation
(d) None of the above

24 Which of the following is considered as the first principle of management?
(a) Coordination
(b) Delegation
(c) Line, staff, auxiliary agencies
(d) Supervision

25 According to American School of thought, the difference between administration and management is that
(a) administration is largely deterministic while management is essentially executive
(b) management is largely deterministic while management essentially executive
(c) management is performed at higher level of management while administration is performed at lower levels of management
(d) administration and management are same

26 Which of the following is not the classical theorist?
(a) Winslow Taylor
(b) Fayol, Crulik and Urwick
(c) Elton Mayo
(d) Max Weber

27 Which one of the following is not the principle of Taylor's scientific theory?
(a) Harmony and not discord
(b) Differential piece rate system
(c) Functional foremanship
(d) Remuneration of personal

28 Which of these are the elements of bureaucracy?
(a) Impersonal relationships
(b) Records, rules and regulations
(c) Administrative class
(d) All of the above

29 Which of the following is/are the features of neo-classical theory?
(a) Flat structure with wide span of control
(b) Decentralised management
(c) Delegation of authority
(d) All of the above

30 Why is the classical theory of organisation known as mechanistic theory?
(a) Because it has formal declared pattern of relationship established by law
(b) Because it does not explain the dynamics of organisational behaviours
(c) Because it underestimated human factor and oversimplified human motivation
(d) Because it treats organisation as a closed system unconcerned with and uninfluenced by its external environment

31 Gang plank theory of communication advanced by Henry Fayol is an example of
(a) downward communication
(b) lateral communication
(c) upward communication
(d) network communication

32 The Father of modern management theory is
(a) Henry Fayol (b) Taylor
(c) Elton Mayo (d) None of these

33 According to Fayol the terms 'Management' and 'Administration' are
(a) same (b) different
(c) he did not consider it all (d) could not conclude

34 Human relations is worth studying because it contributes towards
(a) 'people skills' building (b) mass conformity
(c) weakening of unions (d) None of these

35 Human relation theory focuses on
(a) individuals (b) role of individuals
(c) system (d) informal organisation

36 Hawthorne studies lead to the development of
(a) scientific management
(b) one best method of doing the work
(c) specialisation
(d) human relations

37 The delegation of authority depends on the subordinate's
(a) training
(b) educational qualifications
(c) ability and potential
(d) personal appearance

38 Which of the following can be a criticism against human relations theory?
(a) Sentimentality and unrealistic desire to make everyone happy
(b) Most significantly ignoring economic variables
(c) Tender –mindedness
(d) All of the above

39 The main focus of human relations theory is on
(a) formal organisation
(b) informal organisation
(c) individuals
(d) participatory decision-making

40 The behavioural scientists have been making contribution since the days of
(a) Hawthorne experiment
(b) scientific management
(c) classical theory
(d) bureaucratic theory

41 In which of the following way the bureaucratic theory is criticised?
(a) That it takes too much mechanistic view of human nature
(b) That it ignores the effect of human feelings, emotions group loyalties etc on organisations
(c) That it makes wrong assumptions about human motivation
(d) All of the above

42 .... theory is the formulation of universal principles of organisation.
(a) Classical (b) Human relations
(c) Bureaucratic (d) Scientific management

43 Henry Fayol supports
(a) humanistic approach (b) mechanistic approach
(c) organic approach (d) scientific approach

44 "Focus on social environment" is related to the
(a) human relations (b) unity of direction
(c) unity of command (d) None of these

45 According to neo-classical theory, an organisation is
(a) a structure with well-defined functions
(b) a structure with well-defined objectives
(c) a group of people with a common objectives
(d) a structure with order and objective rationality

46 Who coined the term 'POSDCORB'?
(a) L Urwick (b) L Gulick
(c) Both combined (d) H Fayol

47 Neo-classical theory of organisation is characterised by
(a) decentralisation
(b) non-formal organisation
(c) human oriented management
(d) All of the above

48 Which of the following statements are true about human relations theory of organisations?
(a) It rejects formal institutionalisation
(b) It considers the informal structure more effective
(c) It assumes organisational behaviour is a complex phenomenon
(d) All of the above

49 Accent of human relations theory is
(a) action-oriented (b) hierarchy-oriented
(c) organisation-oriented (d) None of these

50 Hawthorne experiments were carried out in
(a) the USA (b) the UK
(c) Japan (d) France

51 Hawthorne experiments were carried out at
(a) Honda Motor Co (b) General Motors
(c) Western Electric Co (d) Suzuki International

52 Hawthorne experiments were conducted under the leadership of
(a) D Bright (b) T Ford
(c) Elton Mayo (d) K Tanaka

53 "Too often we try to solve human problem with non-human tools and in terms of non-human data. It is my simple thesis that a human problem requires a human solution. First we have to learn to recognise a human problem when we see one; and second, upon recognising it, we have to learn to deal with it as such and not as it were something else. A human problem to be brought to a human solution requires human data and human tools". Who said this?
(a) Max Weber (b) FJ Roethlisberger
(c) Taylor (d) LD White

54 Who popularised the behavioural approach to organisation?
(a) Chester Barnard (b) Cart Roger
(c) H Simon (d) JD Mooney

55 Behavioural approach in the study of organisation meant
(a) study of system in organisational context
(b) study of the behaviour of individual public servants only
(c) use of behaviour science in the study of all aspects of organisation behaviour
(d) study of the organisational structure on the basis of behaviour of the groups only

56 The human relations theory can be termed as
(a) humanistic theory (b) social economic theory
(c) Either (a) or (b) (d) Both (a) and (b)

57 Which of the following is/are the features of neo-classical theory?
(a) Flat structure with wide span of control
(b) Decentralised management
(c) Informal organisation
(d) All of the above

58 In the implications of the Hawthorne studies, which of the following reasons are given by the workers?
(a) Small group (b) Type of supervision
(c) Incentive (d) All of these

59 Modern theory of organisation includes
(a) the genetic societal system involving the level of a cell society, characterised by a division of labour among cells
(b) the open system characterised by the ability of rejuvenation, growth and reproduction
(c) the simple dynamic system involving the level of a clock having predetermined motions
(d) All of the above

60 Which one is/are the outcomes of the modern management theory?
(a) There should be links between sub-systems in an organisation
(b) These sub-systems are interdependent
(c) A system is made-up of certain strategic elements
(d) All of the above

61 Carzo and Yanaozas identifies three sub-systems in an organisation as a systems approach. Which one is not the sub-system?
(a) Technical sub-system
(b) Economic sub-system
(c) Social sub-system
(d) Power sub-system

62 The .... to management was viewed as "a way of thinking about the job of managing that provides a framework for visualising internal and external environmental factors as an integrated whole."
(a) contingency approach (b) systems approach
(c) quantitative approach (d) None of these

63 Here, the organisation can be seen as either an .... where it interacts with its external environment or a .... system where it has no interaction with its external environment.
(a) closed, open (b) internal, open
(c) open, closed (d) external, closed

64 Identify the social scientist, whose notions on negotiation, power and employee involvement were extremely influential in the advancement of organisational and administrative studies fields.
(a) FW Taylor (b) MP Follett
(c) Henry Fayol (d) Mintzberg

65 Which of the following are not the elements of MP Follett's theory?
(a) Consultative conflict
(b) Theory of integration
(c) Coactive power
(d) Piecemeal wage distribution

66 Which of the following statements are true with regard to theory propounded by MP Follett?
(a) Follett described democracy as a social world process, instead of simply a political activity or civil liberties set
(b) Follett expresses clearly that delegate of authority should become an obsolete expression
(c) Mary felt control becomes self-control
(d) All of the above

67 Which of the following is not a type of leadership under theory propounded by MP Follett?
(a) Leadership by Position
(b) Leadership by Personality
(c) Leadership by Role
(d) Leadership by Function

68 The concept of "Zone of acceptance or indifference" is given by
(a) MP Follett (b) Chester I Barnard
(c) FW Taylor (d) Weber

69 Which of the following statement(s) is/are true about the social system theory?
(a) Barnard also laid a lot of emphasis on clear and formal as well as informal channels of communication as it was the life of a smooth functioning organisation
(b) He defines an organisation as "a system of consciously coordinated activities or forces of two or more persons"
(c) Barnard tries to understand human beings: one from within the organisation and two from outside the organisation
(d) All of the above

70 The quantitative approach to management has also been referred to by which of the following names?
(a) Sales optimisation
(b) Management science
(c) Managerial theory
(d) Statistical reformulation

71 Which school of thought had been developed on the idea that there is no single best method to find solutions to managerial problems?
(a) System approach (b) Empirical approach
(c) Contingency approach (d) Operational approach

72 Professor Koontz, described contingency approach as the best approach to solve all the problems in his book "..........".
(a) Management Theory Jungle
(b) Management Theory Planet
(c) Jungle of Management Thoughts
(d) None of the above

73 Operation research, facility layout, MIS are outcome of
(a) contingency approach
(b) quantitative approach
(c) system approach
(d) process approach

74 Which of the following are correctly matched?
(a) Administrative management: Taylor
(b) Administrative theory: Fayol
(c) Scientific management theory: Fayol
(d) Scientific management theory: Webber

75 Which of the following are not correctly matched?
(a) Lower level managers: Supervisors
(b) Middle level managers: Foreman
(c) Top level managers: CEO
(d) Middle level managers: Production Manager

76 According to Douglas and Massie, " Management is the process by which a .... group directs action of others towards common goals."
(a) cooperative (b) small
(c) social (d) large

77 According to Henry Fayol, which one of the following combinations of qualities are required in a manager?
(a) Physical, mental, experience, educational and conceptual
(b) Technical, human, conceptual, mental and moral
(c) Physical, mental, moral, educational, technical and experiences
(d) Mental, moral, conceptual, educational, technical and experience

78 Neo-classical organisation theory emphasises on which one of the following?
(a) Flat structure of organisation
(b) Tall structure of organisation
(c) Co-ordination by hierarchy
(d) Unity of command

79 "Hierarchy consists in the universal application of the superior-subordinate relationship through a number of levels of responsibility reaching from the top to the bottom of the structure." This observation is attributed to
(a) L Gulick (b) LD White
(c) TD Moonev (d) Lyndal Urns CR

80 The term 'General system theory' owes its origin to
(a) Max Weber
(b) Taylor
(c) Lundurg Von Bertalanffy
(d) Mary Parker Follett

81 "Papers on the Science of Administration" is written by
(a) L Urwick (b) L Gullick
(c) Both (a) and (b) (d) MP Follett

82 "Increased output per unit of human effort through the use of right method, right tool and right procedures" refers to which of the following theory/approach?
(a) Human relation approach
(b) Scientific management approach
(c) Classical theory
(d) Bureaucratic theory

83 The overall goal of scientific management is
(a) higher industrial efficiency
(b) maximisation of employment
(c) maximisation of social welfare
(d) All of the above

84 Consider the following statements.
1. There is a clear hierarchy of offices.
2. The functions are clearly specified.
3. There is a career structure.
4. There is money as great motivator.
The above are the characteristics of
(a) the Administration
(b) the Government
(c) the Bureaucracy
(d) All of the above

85 The main drawback of functional organisation developed by Taylor is that it fails to recognise the
(a) scalar principle
(b) principle of equity
(c) principle of unity of command
(d) principle of Espirit de Corps

86 Who is the author of 'The Function of the Executive'?
(a) Chester Barnard (b) Cart Rogers
(c) AH Maslow (d) E Mayo

87 According to E Mayo output apart from the physical conditions of work which of the following factor is responsible for the output of the worker?
(a) Objective
(b) Treatment of the worker as a human being
(c) Technique
(d) Attitude of supervisor

88 What are the facts regarding system theory approach?
(a) System theory provides a useful framework for looking at the whole spectrum of factors and considering them in searching for solutions
(b) Its importance to organisation is that organisations are systems comprising, technical, economic and social sub-system
(c) The application of system theory to practice is known as contingency administration or management
(d) All of the above

89 Three necessary and sufficient conditions that must be satisfied if traits should be unique determinants of the Leadership Index are

1. The trail quality should follow a descending order as one traverse from the highest to the lowest levels.
2. There must be a high correlation between the level of traits and the level of success.
3. The achievement trait curve should be convex to the trait axis as one travels from the low to the high trait terminals.

The above conditions have been suggested by

(a) FW Taylor (b) Elton Mayo
(c) Edwin E Ghiselli (d) Dorwin Cartwright

90 Which approach emerged from findings of Hawthrone experiments?

(a) System approach
(b) Human behaviour approach
(c) Human relation approach
(d) Process approach

91 Following are the statements with regard to management and its functions. Select the appropriate code.

1. Management can be considered as a profession because it has a well-defined structure of knowledge.
2. Management is considered to be an art because it depends on the creativity of the manager.
3. It is a science because it has certain standard principles to be followed.

(a) Only 1 (b) Both 1 and 2
(c) 1, 2 and 3 (d) Both 2 and 3

92 Top management of the company comprises of

1. Clerks 2. BOD
3. CEO 4. Managing Directors
5. Foreman

(a) 1, 3, 5 (b) Both 1 and 5
(c) 2, 3, 4 (d) 2, 4, 5

93 Which of the following statements are correct?

1. Genenral Manager is in top level management.
2. General Manager is in middle level management.
3. General Manager formulates policies.

(a) Only 1 (b) Only 2
(c) Both 1 and 3 (d) 1, 2, 3

94 Which one of the following concepts are not associated with scientific management?

1. Rule of Thumb 2. Mental Revolution
3. Unity of Command 4. Time and Motion Study
5. Differential Piece Rate System

Codes

(a) Both 1 and 3 (b) Both 1 and 3
(c) 3, 4 and 5 (d) 1, 2, 3 and 5

95 According to system approach, Carzo and Yanouzas identify which of the following elements as sub-systems?

1. Technical sub-system
2. Goals and value sub-system
3. Power sub-system
4. Structural sub-system
5. Social sub-system

Codes

(a) 1, 2 and 4 (c) 1, 2, 3, 4 and 5
(b) 1, 3 and 5 (d) 2, 4 and 5

96 Which of the following concepts are not associated with scientific management?

1. Standardisation of tools
2. Unity of Direction
3. Equity
4. Scientific Selection
5. Differentiate Piece Rate Plan

Select the correct answer by using the codes given below

(a) 1, 2 and 4 (b) 2, 3 and 4
(c) Both 2 and 3 (d) 1, 4 and 3

97 What does 'Hierarchy of Authority' means?

1. The lower levels have to pursue the goals laid down by higher levels.
2. The upper levels of hierarchy set the goals to be pursued.
3. The upper level cannot take disciplinary action against subordinates.
4. The lower levels have freedom to carry out the operations.

Select the correct answer by using the codes given below

(a) Both 1 and 2
(b) Both 2 and 3
(c) Both 3 and 4
(d) Both 1 and 4

98 Taylor whose thoughts go under the name of scientific management made two assumptions

1. The application of the methods of science to organisational problems leads to higher industrial efficiency.
2. The incentive of high wage will promote the mutuality of interest between workers and managers which, in its turn, will lead to higher productivity.
3. The staff members are personally free, observing only the impersonal duties of their offices.
4. There is a clear hierarchy of offices.

Select the correct answer by using the codes given below

(a) Both 1 and 2
(b) Both 1 and 3
(c) Both 2 and 3
(d) All of the above

99 The scientific management is based upon which of the following assumption?

1. Application of the scientific methods to organisational problems leads to efficiency.
2. The good worker is one who accepts orders, but does not initiate actions.
3. Worker is more important than the work.
4. Each worker is interested in maximising his monetary rewards.

Select the correct answer by using the codes given below

(a) 1, 2 and 3 (b) 1, 2 and 4
(c) 2, 3 and 4 (d) All of these

100 Arrange the following experiments conducted by Elton Mayo in the chronological order.

1. Bank Wiring Experiment
2. Textile Mill Experiment
3. Illumination Experiment
4. Mass Interviewing Programme

Select the correct answer by using the codes given below

(a) 2, 1, 3 and 4 (b) 2, 3, 4 and 1
(c) 1, 2, 3 and 4 (d) 2, 3, 1 and 4

101 Which of the following are the principles of 'Scientific Management'?

1. Development of a science of work.
2. Different piece rate.
3. Standardisation of tools and equipments.
4. Scientific selection of workman.
5. Co-operation between managers and workers.

Select the correct answer by using the codes given below

(a) 1, 3, 4 and 5 (b) 1, 4 and 5
(c) 1, 2, 3 and 4 (d) All of these

102 Which of the following are associated with the scientific management movement?

1. Functional Foremanship
2. Centralisation
3. Time and motion study
4. Unity of command

Select the correct answer by using the codes given below

(a) Both 1 and 3 (b) Both 2 and 4
(c) 1, 2 and 3 (d) 2, 3 and 4

103 The three main objectives of scientific management are

1. Standardisation of working conditions.
2. Standardisation of work methods.
3. Planning of large daily tasks.
4. Maximisation of output.

Select the correct answer by using the codes given below

(a) 1, 2 and 4 (b) 1, 2 and 3
(c) 2, 3 and 4 (d) 1, 3 and 4

104 The three methods of science are

1. Observation and measurement
2. Experiment
3. Analysis and tabulation
4. Representation

Select the correct answer by using the codes given below

(a) Both 1 and 2 (b) Both 2 and 3
(c) Both 3 and 4 (d) 1, 2 and 3

105 Find out correct answer regarding classical theory of organisation?

1. It throws focus on human beings as such.
2. It throws focus not on human beings as such but on the role.
3. It is normally the dominant set of work relationship.
4. All of the above

Select the correct answer by using the codes given below

(a) Both 1 and 2 (b) Both 2 and 3
(c) Both 1 and 3 (d) Only 4

106 The classical theory of organisation manifests following certain features, which are

1. Impersonality 2. Division of work
3. Hierarchy 4. Efficiency

Select the correct answer by using the codes given below

(a) Both 1 and 2 (b) Both 3 and 4
(c) 1, 3 and 4 (d) 1, 2, 3 and 4

107 Important names associated with the classical theory are those of

1. Henry Fayol 2. Max Weber
3. Luther Gulick 4. FW Taylor

Select the correct answer by using the codes given below

(a) Both 1 and 2 (b) 4, 3 and 1
(c) Both 1 and 4 (d) Both 2 and 3

108 Mooney and Reiley enunciated the following principles of organisation

1. The co-coordinative 2. The scalar
3. The functional 4. The staff line principle

Select the correct answer by using the codes given below

(a) 1, 2 and 3 (b) 1, 2 and 4
(c) Only 1 (d) All of these

109 Who among the following writers are included in the classical school?

1. Taylor 3. Fayol
2. Barnard 4. Luther Gulick

Select the correct answer by using the codes given below

(a) 1, 2 and 3 (b) 1, 3 and 4
(c) 2, 3 and 4 (d) 1, 2 and 4

110 Hawthorne experiments brought out the fact that

1. Individuals crave for self-interest and have no regard for social norms.
2. Workers constituted a small, well-knit social group.
3. Men are not isolated creatures.
4. An organisation was a social system, a group of people behaving with each other.

Select the correct answer by using the codes given below

(a) 1, 2, 3 and 4 (b) 2, 3 and 4
(c) Both 3 and 4 (d) Only 4

111 Which of the following are the principles of scientific management?
1. Different piece rate plan
2. Equal pay for all
3. Cooperation between managers and workers
4. Standardisation of tools and machines
5. Scientific selection of workman

Codes
(a) 1, 2 and 5 (b) 2 3 and 5
(c) 1, 3, 4 and 5 (d) 1, 2 and 3

112 Hawthorne studies have proved that
1. wherever the supervisors are employee centered, the output of the employees is high.
2. wherever the supervisors are production centered, the output of the employees is more.
3. wherever the supervisors are employee centered, the output of the employees is less.
4. wherever the supervisor are production centered, the output of the employees is less.

Codes
(a) Both 1 and 2 (b) Both 2 and 3
(c) Both 1 and 4 (d) Both 1 and 3

113 The scientific management stressed upon
1. rationality 2. predictibility 3. specialisation
4. technical competence

Codes
(a) Both 3 and 4 (b) 1, 2, 3 and 4
(c) 1, 3 and 4 (d) Both 3 and 4

114 Which of the following are essence of human relations theory?
1. Dominant emphasis on people
2. Complete ignorance of human
3. Rejection of formal institutionalisation

Select the correct answer by using the codes given below
(a) Both 1 and 2 (b) Both 1 and 3
(c) Only 3 (d) All of these

115 Which of the following statement(s) is/are correct?
I. Lack of proper management results in wastage of time and resources.
II. Management establishes a sound organisation by allocating the work to individuals.
III. Management is a science but not art.

Codes
(a) Only statement I (b) Only statement II
(c) Both statements I and II (d) All of these

116 Which of the following statements are correct?
I. Human relation approach was started by Taylor.
II. Scientific management was given by Fayol.
(a) Both statements are correct
(b) Both statements are incorrect
(c) Statement I is correct and Statement II is incorrect
(d) Statement II is incorrect and Statement I is correct

117 Which of the following statements are correct?
I. Fayol's principle order indicates the authority to given orders to subordinates.
II. Equity principle of Fayol indicates that all persons in the organisation should be treated equally.
(a) Both statements are correct
(b) Both statements are incorrect
(c) Statement I is correct and Statement II is incorrect
(d) Statement II is correct and Statement I is incorrect

118 Which of the following statement(s) is/are correct?
I. Coactive power involves sharing obligations and benefits within a power structure.
II. Coercive power is one group or individual's power over another.
(a) Both statements are correct
(b) Both statements are incorrect
(c) Statement I is correct and Statement II is incorrect
(d) Statement II is correct and Statement I is incorrect

119 **Assertion** (A) Management is a set of principles relating to its functions.

Reason (R) Management is essential to run all types of organisations.

Codes
(a) Both (A) and (R) are correct and (R) is the right explanation of (A)
(b) Both (A) and (R) are correct, but (R) is not the right explanation of (A)
(c) Both (A) and (R) are incorrect
(d) (A) is correct, but (R) is incorrect

120 **Assertion** (A) Managerial roles are dynamic in nature.

Reason (R) Managerial skills define managerial roles.

Codes
(a) Both (A) and (R) are correct and (R) is the correct explanation of (A)
(b) Both (A) and (R) are correct, but (R) is not the correct explanation of (A)
(c) (A) is correct, but (R) is incorrect
(d) (A) is incorrect, but (R) is correct

121 **Assertion** (A) Negotiator is a decisive role.

Reason (R) Decisive roles involve taking decisions about various business aspects.

Codes
(a) Both (A) and (R) are correct and (R) is the correct explanation of (A)
(b) Both (A) and (R) are correct, but (R) is not the correct explanation of (A)
(c) (A) is correct, but (R) is incorrect
(d) (A) is incorrect, but (R) is correet

122 **Assertion** (A) Coordination is an integral function of management.

Reason (R) Coordination is done through planning, organising, staffing and controlling.

Codes

(a) (A) is correct and (R) is the right explanation to it
(b) (A) is correct, but (R) is not the right explanation to it
(c) (A) is not correct while (R) is a correct statement
(d) Both (A) and (R) are incorrect

123 **Assertion** (A) Management is a continuous process involving the integration of all functions.

Reason (R) Management first plan, then organise and finally perform the function of controlling.

Codes

(a) Both (A) and (R) are correct and (R) is the correct explanation of (A)
(b) Both (A)and (R) are correct, but (R) is not the correct explanation of (A)
(c) (A) is correct, but (R) is incorrect
(d) (A) is incorrect, but (R) is correct

Directions (Q. Nos. 124-129) *In the question given below are two statements labelled as Assertion (A) and Reason (R). In the context of two statements, which of the following is correct?*

Codes

(a) (A) and (R) are true and (R) is the correct explanation of (A)
(b) (A) and (R) are true, but (R) is not the correct explanation of (A)
(c) (A) is false, but (R) is true
(d) (A) is true, but (R) is false

124 **Assertion** (A) Scientific management is also called the physiological organisation theory.

Reason (R) Scientific management is concerned with only that range of human behaviour which relates to production.

125 **Assertion** (A) Functional aspects shows leaders as a manager.

Reason (R) A leader does all the management functions.

126 **Assertion** (A) C Barnard identified communication channels with channels of authority.

Reason (R) C Barnard thinks that a communication that cannot be understood can have no authority.

127 **Assertion** (A) Scientific management believes in cooperation and harmony between workers and managers.

Reason (R) Taylor believed in participative management.

128 **Assertion** (A) The neglect of the human side of the organisation has been one of the major criticism of Taylorism.

Reason (R) Taylor and his followers had viewed organisation mechanistically.

129 **Assertion** (A) Scientific management believes in cooperation and harmony between workers and managers.

Reason (R) Taylor believed in participative management.

130 **Assertion** (A) Scientific management is also called the physiological organisational theory.

Reason (R) Scientific management is concerned with only that range of human behaviour which relates to production.

Codes

(a) (A) and (R) are true and (R) is the correct explanation of (A)
(b) (A) and (R) is true, but (R) is not the correct explanation of (A)
(c) (A) is true, but (R) is false
(d) (A) is false, but (R) is true

131 Which of the following statements are true/false?

1. Speed boss maintains the planned speed of production.
2. Gang boss makes the arrangement of men, material and machines for the job.
3. Inspector determines the process of job.
4. Route clerk maintains proper discipline.

(a) 1 and 3 are true, 2 and 4 are false.
(b) 2 and 4 are true, 1 and 3 are false.
(c) 1 and 2 are true, 3 and 4 are false.
(d) 1 and 4 are true, 2 and 3 are false.

132 Which of the following statements are true/false?

1. Henry Fayol was the first person to recognise the different qualities of manager.
2. Chester Barnard, Douglas McGregor, Abraham Maslow, Elton Mayo are classical theorists.
3. The classical scientific branch arose because of need to increase productivity and efficiency.

(a) 1 and 2 are true, 3 is false.
(b) 1 and 3 are true, 2 is false.
(c) 2 and 3 are true, 1 is false.
(d) 3 is true, 1 and 2 are false.

133 Arrange the following events in the descending order of their evolution.

1. Scientific management
2. Operation research
3. Hawthorne experiments
4. System approach
5. Contingency approach

(a) 2, 5, 4, 3, 1
(b) 1, 3, 2, 4, 5
(c) 5, 2, 4, 3, 1
(d) 4, 5, 2, 3, 1

134 Which of the following statements are true/false?

1. The behavioural approach developed as the results of Hawthorne experiment.
2. The behavioural management theory is often called the human relations movement because it addresses the human demension of work.
3. Chester Barnard introduced the idea of informal organisation.
4. Fayol's administration principles are for shop management.

(a) 1, 2 are true, 3 and 4 are false.
(b) 1, 2, 3 are true, 4 is false.
(c) 2 and 4 are true, 1 and 3 are false.
(d) 1 and 4 are true, 2 and 3 are false.

135 Which of the following statements are true/false?

1. Ludwig von Bertalaffy is called the father of system approach.
2. System approach comprises of sub-system, synergy, a feedback mechanism and defined boundaries.
3. The management science school emerged as a quantitative approach to solve managerial problems.
4. Operation management, management information system are theories under system approach.

(a) 1, 2, 3 are true, 4 is false.
(b) 1, 4 are true, 2 and 3 are false.
(c) 2, and 4 are true, 1 and 3 are false.
(d) 3 and 4 are true, 1 and 2 are false.

136 Match the items of List I with List II and choose the correct code of combination.

List I	List II
A. The Fundamentals of Top Management	1. Peter F Drucker
B. Middle Management	2. RC Davis
C. The Essence of Management	3. ELF Brech
D. Principles and Practice of Management	4. Mary Caushing Nile

Code

	A	B	C	D		A	B	C	D
(a)	2	4	3	1	(b)	2	4	1	3
(c)	2	3	1	4	(d)	3	4	1	2

137 Match the items of List II with List I and choose the correct code.

List I	List II
A. Sales Executive	1. Top-middle Management
B. Branch Manager	2. Middle Management
C. Foreman	3. Lower Management
D. Production Manager	4. Operating Force

Codes

	A	B	C	D		A	B	C	D
(a)	4	2	3	1	(b)	2	3	4	1
(c)	3	4	2	1	(d)	1	2	3	4

138 Match the following.

List I	List II
A. Decision-making	1. Management
B. Execution	2. The CEO
C. Lower level management	3. Administration
D. Top level management	4. Foreman

Codes

	A	B	C	D		A	B	C	D
(a)	4	2	3	1	(b)	2	3	4	1
(c)	3	1	4	2	(d)	1	2	3	4

139. Match the following.

List I	List II
A. Newman & Summer	1. Organising, planning and controlling
B. Henry Fayol	2. Planning, organising, commanding, coordinating and controlling
C. Luther Gullick	3. Planning, organising, staffing, directing, controlling
D. Koontz & O Donnell	4. PODSCORB

Codes

	A	B	C	D		A	B	C	D
(a)	4	2	3	1	(b)	2	3	4	1
(c)	3	1	4	2	(d)	1	2	4	3

140 Match the following.

List I (School of Theories)	List II (Period of Development)
A. Classical Theory	1. 1890-1930
B. Behavioural Theory	2. 1930-1960
C. System Theory	3. 1965
D. Contingency Theory	4. 1960 onwards

Codes

	A	B	C	D		A	B	C	D
(a)	1	2	4	3	(b)	1	4	2	3
(c)	1	2	3	4	(d)	2	3	2	4

141 Match the following.

List I (Theories)	List II (Developers)
A. General principles of management	1. Max Weber
B. Neo-classical theory	2. Fayol
C. Classical theory	3. Elton Mayo
D. Western electric company	4. Hawthorne studies

Codes

	A	B	C	D		A	B	C	D
(a)	1	2	3	4	(b)	2	3	1	4
(c)	4	3	2	1	(d)	1	3	2	4

142 Match the following.

List I	List II
A. Fayol	1. Grapevine
B. Simon	2. Shared understanding
C. Shannon	3. Cybernetics
D. Weiner	4. Gang Plank
E. Millet	5. Noise

Codes

	A	B	C	D	E		A	B	C	D	E
(a)	1	2	3	4	5	(b)	1	4	2	3	5
(c)	4	1	5	3	2	(d)	4	2	1	5	3

143 Match the following.

List I (Theories)	List II (Elements)
A. Classical	1. Incentives for performance
B. Behavioural	2. Fact-orientation
C. Human relations	3. Structure
D. Systems	4. Informal organisation
	5. Environment

Codes

	A	B	C	D		A	B	C	D
(a)	1	3	2	4	(b)	2	4	3	5
(c)	3	4	1	5	(d)	2	3	4	5

144 Match the following lists and select the correct code of matching.

List I	List II
A. FW Taylor	1. Fair day's pay for fair day's work
B. Henry L Gantt	2. Motion study
C. Frank and Lillian Gilbreth	3. Graphic scheduling for planning and controlling of work
D. Max Weber	4. Bureaucratic organisation

Codes

	A	B	C	D		A	B	C	D
(a)	1	2	3	4	(b)	1	3	2	4
(c)	4	3	2	1	(d)	4	1	2	3

145 Match the following.

List I (Management Thinkers)	List II (Contributions)
A. FW Taylor	1. Application of psychology to management
B. Henry Fayol	2. Sociological concept of group behaviour
C. Elton Mayo	3. Time and motion study
D. Hugo Munsterberg	4. 14 principles of management

Codes

	A	B	C	D
(a)	2	3	1	4
(b)	3	4	2	1
(c)	4	2	3	1
(d)	3	1	2	4

146 Match the following.

List I	List II
A. Schemidt	1. Type of technique for controlling
B. Espirit de Corps	2. Element of control
C. Monitoring	3. Taylor
D. Activator	4. Henry Fayol

Codes

	A	B	C	D		A	B	C	D
(a)	1	2	3	4	(b)	2	1	3	4
(c)	4	2	3	1	(d)	3	4	1	2

Directions (Q. Nos. 147-149) **Blue Heavens Ltd. purchased a new hi-tech machine from Germany for manufacturing high quality auto components in a cost effective manner. But during the production process, the manager observed that the quality of production was not as per standard. On investigation, it was found that there was lack of knowledge amongst the employees of suing these hi-tech machines. So, frequent visit of engineers was required form Germany. This resulted in high overhead charges.**

147 What can be done to develop the skills and abilities of employees for producing high quality products by using these hi-tech machines?

(a) Selection of new employees
(b) Training of employees
(c) Developing new plans
(d) Firing of employees

148 Training of the employees will help the organisation by

(a) obtaining effective response to fact changing environment
(b) improving skills and knowledge of the individual
(c) increasing employee morals and reduces absenteeism
(d) All of the above

149 Which of the following function of management was not correctly performed in Blue Heaven's Ltd?

(a) Planning (b) Controlling
(c) Staffing (d) Organising

Directions (Q. Nos. 150-154) *Read the following passage and answer the questions that follow.*

For years the managerial philosophers had called management's attention to its total responsibility. The indication of a moral oughtness was there, they stressed. As stewards for stockholders, managers had a prime to the employees, the customers, and the community - along with their well-recognised responsibility to the owners. By and large, these early pronouncements apparently fell on deaf ears. By the mid-thirties, however, heartening signs began to appear. In 1937, for example, Raymond Moley declared that while management remained legally and ethically a primary agent of the investor, its secondary responsibility to the public and labour had become relatively greater. Four years later, Roger D Lapham asserted that in the narrow sense of the past, management had been considered solely responsible to its ownership - its stockholders - but there was a growing conviction that in the broader sense management's duty to its customers, to the public, and to its employees came first. By 1951, this view was well established, and Frank Abraham's writing in the Harvard Business Review enunciated the new philosophy when he indicated that the job of management was to conduct the affairs of the enterprise in such a way as to maintain an equitable balance among the claims of the variously interested groups. In the mid-sixties and early seventies, we have again recognised changes in philosophy that reflect management's gradual assumption of its moral and social obligation of good corporate citizenship. We see it, for example, in management's assuming its social responsibility by cooperating with the federal government in withholding goods from countries if those goods would jeopardise our national security; in maintaining prices at a level consistent with a healthy economy, not raising them to a point considered critically inflationary; in training the unemployed; in cleaning up city ghettos; and in recognising and acting upon pollution problems. More examples could be cited, but the point of the broadened view taken by management of its total responsibility has been made.

150 **Raymond Moley advocated management's responsibility to**
(a) owners of organisation only
(b) owners and employees only
(c) owners, public and labour
(d) owners, public, labour and customers

151 **Which of the following is not a part of corporate social responsibility?**
(a) Controlling prices to prevent inflation
(b) Training of employees
(c) Acting upon pollution related problems
(d) Jeopardising the security of nation

152 **Corporate social responsibility comprises of the following**
(a) Moral obligations of an organisation
(b) Social obligations of an organisation
(c) Moral and social obligations of an organisation
(d) None of the above

153 **Abraham is of the opinion that**
(a) it is difficult to satisfy variously interested groups
(b) job management is to conduct affairs of enterprise
(c) there should be a balance among the interested groups
(d) None of the above

154 **In view of Lapham, management must take care of**
(a) investors only
(b) stockholders and employees only
(c) stockholders, public and customers only
(d) stockholders, customers, public and employees

Directions (Q. Nos. 155-159) *Read the paragraph and answer the following questions.*

Taylorism is a variation on the theme of efficiency; it is a late-19th-and-early-20th-century instance of the larger recurring theme in human life of increasing efficiency, decreasing waste, and using empirical methods to decide what matters, rather than uncritically accepting pre-existing ideas of what matters. Taylor system is a theory of management that analyses and synthesises workflows, improving labour productivity. The core ideas of the theory were developed by Frederick Winslow Taylor in the 1880s and 1890s, and were first published in his monographs, Shop Management (1905) and The Principles of Scientific Management (1911). Frederick Taylor believed that decisions based upon tradition and rules of thumb should be replaced by precise procedures developed after careful study of an individual at work. Its application is contingent on a high level of managerial control over employee work practices. Thus, it is a chapter in the larger narrative that also includes, for example, the folk wisdom of thrift, time and motion study, Fordism, and lean manufacturing. In management literature today, the greatest use of the concept of Scientific Management (or Taylorism) is as a contrast to a new, improved way of doing business. It overlapped considerably with the Efficiency Movement, which was the broader cultural echo of scientific management's impact on business managers specifically. In political and sociological terms, Taylorism can be seen as the division of labour pushed to its logical extreme, with a consequent de-skilling of the worker and dehumanisation of the workplace.

155 **Scientific management is a theory of management**
(a) that promotes the rule of thumb
(b) that promotes the democratic pattern in industrial organisation
(c) that analyses and synthesises workflows, improving labour productivity
(d) that promotes the unity of command within the organisation

156 **Frederick Taylor believed that**
(a) decisions based upon tradition and rules of thumb should be replaced by precise procedures developed after careful study of an individual at work
(b) decisions based upon precise procedures developed after careful study of an individual at work should be replaced by tradition and rules of thumb
(c) Strict discipline should be applied at the workplace
(d) Workers should be treated as a means of productivity like machine

157 Taylorism is based on
(a) decreasing efficiency, increasing waste, and using empirical methods to decide what matters, rather than uncritically accepting pre-existing ideas of what matters
(b) increasing efficiency, decreasing waste, and using empirical methods to decide what matters, rather than uncritically accepting pre-existing ideas of what matters
(c) decreasing efficiency, increasing waste, and using traditional methods for day-to-day decision
(d) decreasing efficiency, increasing waste, and applying completely democratic pattern within the organisation

158 Scientific management
(a) overlapped considerably with the efficiency movement, which was the broader cultural echo of scientific management's impact on business managers specifically
(b) overlapped considerably with the effectiveness movement, which was the broader cultural echo of scientific management's impact on business managers specifically
(c) overlapped considerably with the democatic movement, which was the broader cultural echo of scientific management's impact on business managers specifically
(d) overlapped considerably with the autocratic pattern, which was the broader cultural echo of scientific management's impact on business managers specifically

159 In political and sociological terms,
(a) Taylorism can be seen as the division of labour pushed to its socialistic pattern, with a consequent de-skilling of the worker and dehumanisation of the workplace
(b) Taylorism can be seen as the division of labour pushed to its democratic pattern, with a consequent de-skilling of the worker and dehumanisation of the workplace
(c) Taylorism can be seen as the division of labour pushed to its democratic pattern, with a perfect skilling of the worker and humanisation of the workplace
(d) Taylorism can be seen as the division of labour pushed to its logical extreme, with a consequent de-skilling of the worker and dehumanisation of the workplace

PREVIOUS YEARS' QUESTIONS

2018

1 Who has given the system theory of organisation?
(a) Laurence Peter (b) Frank and Lillian
(c) Elton Mayo (d) Chester Barnard

2 Two lists are given below. Match both the lists and choose the correct answer from the code given below.

	List I		List II
A.	Programme Evaluation and Review Technique (PERT)	1.	FW Taylor
B.	Managerial Role Approach	2.	Hugo Munsterberg
C.	Application of Psychology to Industry and Management	3.	Mintzberg
D.	Principles of Scientific Management	4.	Henry L Gantt

Codes

	A	B	C	D		A	B	C	D
(a)	3	1	4	2	(b)	4	1	2	3
(c)	4	3	2	1	(d)	2	3	4	1

3 Match List I with List II and select the correct answer codes given below.

	List I		List II
A.	Frank B Gilbreth	1.	Theory of bureaucracy
B.	Max Weber	2.	Time and motion studies
C.	FW Taylor	3.	Application of psychology to industry and management
D.	Hugomunsterberg	4.	Scientific management

Codes

	A	B	C	D		A	B	C	D
(a)	1	2	4	3	(b)	2	1	4	3
(c)	2	1	3	4	(d)	1	3	2	4

4 Among the following who is known for scientific selection of workers and "Harmonious Co-operation between labour and management."
(a) Gilbreth
(b) Elton Mayo
(c) Max Weber
(d) Henry L Gantt

2017

5 Who among the following are known for study of work arrangements to eliminate wasteful hand and body motions?
(a) Henry Gantt and CI Barnard
(b) Frank and Lillian Gilbreth
(c) Elton Mayo and H Emerson
(d) FW Taylor and Henry Gantt

6 Match the following.

List I	List II
A. Robert Owen	1. Organisations based on group ethics rather than individualism
B. Hugo Munsterberg	2. Social norms and standards of group
C. Mary Parker Follett	3. Employers treat their machines better than workers
D. Elton Mayo	4. Scientific study of human behaviour to identify

Codes

	A	B	C	D		A	B	C	D
(a)	1	2	3	4	(b)	3	4	1	2
(c)	4	3	1	2	(d)	4	3	2	1

7 Assertion (A) Both Weber's Bureaucracy and Taylor's scientific management emphasise on rationality, predictability, impresonality, technical competence and authoritarianism.

Reason (R) Though Weber's writings were less operational than Taylor's, yet 'ideal bureaucracy' describes many contemporary organisations.

Codes

(a) (A) is right and (R) is wrong
(b) (A) is wrong and (R) is right
(c) Both (A) and (R) are right
(d) Both (A) and (R) are wrong

8 Match List I with List II and select correct answer by using the codes given below.

List I	List II
A. Application of psychology to industry and management	1. Henry L Gantt
B. Program evaluation and review technique	2. Walter Dill Scott
C. Widely acclaimed first lady of management	3. Lillian Gilbreth
D. Application of psychology to advertising marketing and personnel	4. Hugo Munsterberg

Codes

	A	B	C	D		A	B	C	D
(a)	2	1	4	3	(b)	4	1	3	2
(c)	3	4	1	2	(d)	3	1	2	4

9 Examine the following statements about scientific management and identify those which are true and false.

1. The term 'Scientific Management' was not coined by Frederick Winslow Taylor.
2. Henry R. Towne's 'Engineer as a economist' influenced Taylor's ideas.
3. 'Shop Management' embodies 'Therbligs'.
4. Louis D Brandies heard the case filed against Taylor's Scientific Management by Trade Unions.

Codes

(a) 1, 2, 3 are true and 4 is false
(b) 1, 2, 4 are true and 3 is false
(c) 1, 2 are true and 3, 4 are false
(d) 1, 3 are true and 2, 4 are false

10 Match the following.

List I (Themes)	List II (Propagators)
A. POSDCORB	1. Henry Fayol
B. Espirit de Corps	2. George A Pennock
C. Integration theory	3. Mary Parker Follette
D. The illumination experiment	4. Luther Gullick

Codes

	A	B	C	D		A	B	C	D
(a)	4	1	2	3	(b)	4	1	3	2
(c)	3	1	2	4	(d)	4	2	3	1

11 Which of the following statements about open systems as given by Daniel Katz and Robert Khan are true?

1. The exportation of energic inputs into the environment.
2. Transformation of available energy as through put, so that work is done.
3. The importation of the output from the environment.
4. A cycle of events in which the product exported to the environment provides the energy for repetition of the cycle.

Codes

(a) 1, 2 (b) 2, 3 (c) 2, 4 (d) 1, 4

12 According to which one of the following approaches, management is the function of planning, organising, leading and controlling?

(a) Process approach
(b) Systems approach
(c) Quantitative approach
(d) Human behaviour approach

2016

13 Which of the following pair is correctly matched?

(a) FW Taylor – Human Relations Approach
(b) Henry Fayol – Universality of Management
(c) Elton Mayo – Psychological Approach
(d) M Parker Follet – Scientific Management

14 Match the following experiments List I with the pioneers who are associated List II with them.

List I	List II
A. Case of Schimdt	1. George A Pennock
B. Ahmedabad Experiment	2. FJ Roethlisberger
C. Illumination Experiment	3. AK Rice
D. Bank Wiring Observation Test Room Experiment	4. FW Taylor

Codes

	A	B	C	D		A	B	C	D
(a)	4	3	2	1	(b)	4	1	3	2
(c)	3	1	4	2	(d)	4	3	1	2

15 Arrange the following phases of Hawthorne experiments in the right order.

1. Mica Splitting Test Room
2. Bank Wiring Observation Test Room
3. Experiments on Illumination
4. Relay Assembly Test Room
5. Personnel Counselling
6. Mass Interviewing Programme

Codes

(a) 3, 4, 1, 6, 2, 5 (b) 3, 2, 1, 6, 4, 5
(c) 3, 1, 2, 6, 5, 4 (d) 3, 4, 6, 2, 1, 5

16 Who corrected the difficulties of Taylor's differential piece rate system of wages?

(a) Henry Towne
(b) HL Gantt
(c) Frank and Lillian Gilbreths
(d) Newmann and Summer

17 Assertion (A) Each role must have enough stressers which may help the role occupant to stretch himself/herself to meet the challenge. In the role, where the scope is limited to routine work, the role occupants do not perceive any challenge.

Reason (R) While every role has some routine elements, challenge can also be incorporated into every role. However, the challenge should not exceed an optimal limit, otherwise it may produce dysfunctional stress, resulting in poor performance or damage to the health of the employee in the long-run.

Codes

(a) (A) and (R) both are true, (R) does not explains (A)
(b) (A) and (R) both are true, (R) explains (A)
(c) (A) is true, (R) does not explain (A)
(d) (A) is not true, (R) explains (A)

2015

18 Match the following.

List I (Statements)	List II (Approaches)
A. Organisation has interconnected and interrelated elements	1. Decision theory approach
B. Organisations work through motivation, leadership communication and participative management	2. Systems approach
C. Management is essentially decision-making	3. Human behaviour approach
D. Appropriate managerial action depends on external environment, internal states and needs	4. Contingency approach

Codes

	A	B	C	D		A	B	C	D
(a)	2	3	4	1	(b)	2	3	1	4
(c)	1	2	3	4	(d)	2	4	1	3

19 Which of the following are the principles of co-ordination according to Mary Parker Follett?

1. Principle of Direct Contact
2. Principle of Reciprocal Relationship
3. Principle of Timing
4. Principle of Dynamism
5. Principle of Continuity
6. Principle of Co-ordination at early stages

Select the correct answer by using the codes given below

(a) 1, 3, 5 and 6 (b) 1, 2, 3 and 4
(c) 1, 3, 4 and 5 (d) 1, 4, 5 and 6

20 Match the following.

List I	List II
A. Henry L Gnatt	1. Theory of Bureaucracy
B. Max Weber	2. Father of Modern/Administrative Management Theory
C. Alex F Osborm	3. Graphic methods of describing plans and harmonious cooperation
D. Henry Fayol	4. Father of brainstorming

Codes

	A	B	C	D		A	B	C	D
(a)	4	3	2	1	(b)	3	1	4	2
(c)	4	1	3	2	(d)	1	2	4	3

21 In which year, the book entitled 'Principles of Scientific Management' was published?

(a) 1901 (b) 1903
(c) 1911 (d) 1912

22 The scalar principle of organisation implies

(a) all authority must vest in one single person
(b) manager should directly supervise only a limited number of subordinates
(c) line of authority must be clearly defined
(d) a subordinate should have only one superior

23 Which of the following is/are not feature(s) of bureaucracy as advocated by Weber?

1. Administrative class is responsible for maintaining coordinative activities in the organisation.
2. Division of labour is based on specialisation.
3. Organisation structure is adhoc and represents unstable relations.
4. Decisions and activities are formally recorded.

Select the correct answer by using the codes given below

(a) Both 1 and 2 (b) Both 3 and 4
(c) Only 3 (d) Only 4

24 Which of the following approaches to management is a reactive approach instead of being proactive?

(a) Systems approach (b) Quantitative approach
(c) Decision theory approach (d) Contingency approach

2014

25 Match the following.

List I (Books)	List II (Authors)
A. Competitive Advantage	1. Peter Senge
B. Competing for Future	2. Douglas Murray McGregor
C. The Fifth Discipline	3. Michael E Porter
D. The Human Side of Enterprise	4. CK Prahallad and Gary Hamel

Codes

	A	B	C	D		A	B	C	D
(a)	3	4	1	2	(b)	1	2	3	4
(c)	4	3	2	1	(d)	3	4	2	1

26 According to Henry Fayol, which of the following statements is correct?

(a) Management is a part of administration

(b) Administration is a part of management

(c) There is no difference between management and administration

(d) There is great difference between management and administration

27 Which of the following is/are not a part of classical approach to management ?

(a) Scientific management

(b) Administrative management

(c) Decision theory

(d) Bureaucratic organisation

28 Match the following.

List I (Thinker)	List II (Principle)
A. Henry Fayol	1. Careful design of jobs with ten efficient work methods
B. Elton Mayo	2. Unity of direction
C. FW Taylor	3. Organisational equilibrium
D. Chester I Barnard	4. Social factors and group norms

Codes

	A	B	C	D		A	B	C	D
(a)	2	4	1	3	(b)	2	4	3	1
(c)	1	2	3	4	(d)	1	3	2	4

29 Who identified the basic elements of work known as 'therbligs'?

(a) Henry L Gantt (b) Frank B Gilbreth

(c) FW Taylor (d) All of these

30 Who among the following concluded that the factory was a social system and informal groups at work place play a vital role in industrial affairs?

(a) Elton Mayo (b) Henry Fayol

(c) Blake and Mouton (d) Herzberg

31 Formulation of policies, programmes and procedures is the primary concern of

(a) top management (b) middle management

(c) operating management (d) Both (b) and (c)

ANSWERS

Exam Based Questions

1 (d)	2 (c)	3 (c)	4 (b)	5 (b)	6 (a)	7 (b)	8 (a)	9 (b)	10 (b)
11 (a)	12 (d)	13 (c)	14 (c)	15 (a)	16 (b)	17 (b)	18 (a)	19 (d)	20 (b)
21 (c)	22 (b)	23 (c)	24 (a)	25 (a)	26 (c)	27 (d)	28 (d)	29 (d)	30 (b)
31 (d)	32 (a)	33 (a)	34 (a)	35 (b)	36 (d)	37 (c)	38 (d)	39 (c)	40 (a)
41 (d)	42 (a)	43 (b)	44 (a)	45 (c)	46 (b)	47 (d)	48 (d)	49 (a)	50 (d)
51 (c)	52 (c)	53 (d)	54 (c)	55 (c)	56 (c)	57 (d)	58 (d)	59 (d)	60 (d)
61 (b)	62 (b)	63 (c)	64 (b)	65 (d)	66 (d)	67 (c)	68 (b)	69 (d)	70 (b)
71 (c)	72 (a)	73 (b)	74 (b)	75 (b)	76 (a)	77 (c)	78 (a)	79 (b)	80 (c)
81 (c)	82 (b)	83 (a)	84 (c)	85 (c)	86 (a)	87 (b)	88 (d)	89 (c)	90 (c)
91 (c)	92 (c)	93 (a)	94 (a)	95 (d)	96 (c)	97 (a)	98 (a)	99 (b)	100 (b)
101 (d)	102 (a)	103 (c)	104 (a)	105 (b)	106 (d)	107 (c)	108 (d)	109 (b)	110 (b)
111 (c)	112 (c)	113 (b)	114 (b)	115 (d)	116 (b)	117 (d)	118 (a)	119 (b)	120 (d)
121 (c)	122 (d)	123 (c)	124 (a)	125 (c)	126 (b)	127 (c)	128 (a)	129 (c)	130 (a)
131 (c)	132 (b)	133 (c)	134 (b)	135 (d)	136 (a)	137 (a)	138 (c)	139 (d)	140 (a)
141 (b)	142 (c)	143 (c)	144 (b)	145 (b)	146 (d)	147 (b)	148 (d)	149 (c)	150 (c)
151 (b)	152 (c)	153 (c)	154 (d)	155 (c)	156 (a)	157 (b)	158 (a)	159 (d)	

Previous Years' Questions

1 (d)	2 (c)	3 (b)	4 (d)	5 (b)	6 (b)	7 (c)	8 (b)	9 (b)	10 (b)
11 (c)	12 (a)	13 (b)	14 (d)	15 (a)	16 (b)	17 (b)	18 (b)	19 (*)	20 (b)
21 (c)	22 (c)	23 (c)	24 (d)	25 (a)	26 (c)	27 (c)	28 (a)	29 (b)	30 (a)
31 (b)									

Note (*) No option is correct

Functions of Management

The functions of management are the operational activities performed to meet the organisational objectives. This chapter highlights the prominent functions of management.

In this Chapter

- *Planning*
- *Decision-making*
- *Organising*
- *Staffing*
- *Direction*
- *Controlling*
- *Coordination*

Managerial functions are the series of activities that are performed by the managers in the business. Many authors have bifurcated the functions on the basis of different characteristics.

GR Terry has defined management as, "a distinct process consisting of planning, organising, actuating and controlling, performed to determine and accomplish stated objectives by the use of human beings and other resources."

Fred Luthans alongwith his co-workers have segregated managerial functions into four categories. *These are as follows*

1. **Traditional Management** Comprising of planning, directing and controlling.
2. **Communication** Exchange of relevant and regular information and handling paperwork.
3. **Human Resource Management** Staffing, training, motivating, discipline and managing conflict.
4. **Networking** Interaction with external people, socialising and building networks which are useful for the organisation in future.

Managerial functions are broadly classified into eight categories.

These are

1. Planning	2. Organising	3. Staffing
4. Controlling	5. Motivating	6. Controlling
7. Coordinating	8. Communication	

Planning

It involves the determination of future course of action. Planning is deciding in advance what to do and how to do. It is one of the basic managerial functions.

According to **Koontz** and **O' Donnell**, "Planning is deciding in advance what to do, how to do and who is to do it. Planning bridges the gap from where we are to where we want to go. It makes it possible for things to occur which would not otherwise happen."

According to **McFarland**, "Planning may be broadly defined as a concept of executive action that embodies the skills of anticipating, influencing and controlling the nature and direction of change."

According to **Terry** and **Franklin**, "Planning is selecting the information and making assumptions regarding the future to formulate activities necessary to active organisation objectives."

In short, planning is preparing today for tomorrow. Planning helps in focussing on the effective goals of the company. Managers use various techniques to identify and define their goals. On such technique is setting 'SMART' goals. This is an acronym for Specific, Measurable, Attainable, Relevant and Timely. It is the activity that allows managers to determine what they want and how they will achieve it.

Features of Planning

Futuristic It focuses on attaining pre-set goal by looking into the future.

Prime Activity It is the first step in management.

Pervasive It is done at all managerial levels. Top level management indulge in strategic planning, middle level management does administrative planning and the lower level management is responsible for planning the operations.

Coordination It builds coordination between the why, how, where, who and when aspects of planning.

Considers Limiting Factors Planning takes care of limited resources (manpower, money) before hand and plans are formulated in accordance to it.

Flexibility It is flexible as it can be changed according to different environmental conditions.

Intellectual Process The quality of mind and the intellect of the manager describes the quality of planning.

Advantages of Planning

- It focuses on objectives and goals.
- The resources are used optimally and there is reduction in uncertainities by measuring risk and preparing in advance.
- Also, there reduction in duplication of work which promotes economical operations, new ideas, innovations and creativity is promoted to tackle with emerging risks.
- It helps in controlling and promotes management by exception which emphasises that managers need not intervene all the time. The lower level will follow the plan themselves.
- Promotes delegation of work as the objectives are pre-defined in plans which helps in execution.
- It involves constant screening of the environment and selecting the best plan, hence it tackles uncertainty effectively.

Disadvantages of Planning

- It is costly and consumes time.
- There is a risk of human error and danger of under targeting and over targeting.
- It indulges into paperwork and is rigid.
- Sometimes lack of reliable information and delay in action.
- It is inflexible in the time of emergency.
- It promotes false sense of immunity against risk.

Process of Planning

Step 1 Analysing exterior business environment.

Step 2 Analysing interior business environment.

Step 3 Determining the mission, *i.e.* the fundamental cause for which the organisation exists.

Step 4 Determining the objectives in operational areas, departments and various sections.

Step 5 Forecasting by probing into the future, based on historical data and relevant tools and techniques.

Step 6 Determination of different course of action, thus this step focuses on identifying various options or methods that are available before the management.

Step 7 Evaluation of alternative course of action. Among the various alternatives determined before, the managers examine their weak or strong aspects.

Step 8 Selection of the best alternative. This is the step where real decision-making takes place.

Step 9 Establishment of sequence of action plan.

Step 10 Formulating the final action plan which comprises of three constituents.

These are as follows

- Time limit
- Task of individual worker
- Schedule of work or time table

Types of Planning

On the basis of Activity Covered

On the basis of activity covered planning can be classified into

Corporate Planning

Planning activities at the top level with long-term orientation. It includes setting of objectives, organising the work, making people and systems to enable to attain those objectives, motivating through the planning process and through the plans, measuring performance, controlling progress of the plan and developing people through better decision-making, clearer objectives, more involvement and awareness progress, strategic planning, long range planning and operational planning comes after corporate planning.

Functional Planning

Not integrated but segmental, it is derived out of corporate planning. It is under taken for sub-functions within each major function.

On the basis of Importance

On the basis of importance, it can be classified as

Strategic Planning

It helps in determining the long-term direction of the organisation in which it wants to proceed in future. Strategic planning is the process of deciding the objectives of the organisation, changes in the objectives, the resources used to attain these objectives and the policies that are to govern the acquisition, use and disposition of these resources. It encompasses all functional areas of business and involves analysis of environments factors. It is done for longer period, *i.e.* 3-5 years.

Operational Planning

Operational planning is done for short-term and is generally formulated at middle level. It focuses on effectively utilising the resources for 1 year and planning accordingly.

On the basis of Action

Pro-active Planning

It involves designing suitable courses of action in anticipation of likely changes in the relevant environment. It uses broad planning approaches, broad environmental scanning and decentralised control. It reserves resources before environmental changes.

Reactive Planning

It is a plan that is made after a certain event has occured. The plan is the 'response' or 'reaction' to the change in the environment. There is no choice left in this form of planning.

On the basis of Formalisation

Formal planning

It is a well structured process involving different steps. It is done by separate corporate cell, *i.e.* the high level in the organisation. The professionals go for detailed study of the impact. It is systematic, rational, documented and formal.

Informal Planning

It is done by small organisations, where plans are formulated on the basis of gut feeling, memory of events and intuitions. It is successful for small companies.

Types of Plan

Plans are broadly classified into tactical, contingency, single use and standing plans. *These are as follows*

Tactical Plan

- It is concerned with what and how the lower level units within each division must do.
- It is concerned with shorter time frames and narrower scopes than strategic plans.
- Short-term goals are considered by tactical plan and their time of span is not more than one year.
- It is the responsibility of middle level manager to identify specific tactical actions.

Contingency Plan

- It is the plan to cope up the unpredictable changes of environment and uncertainty.
- These plans are the result of intelligence of managers. It generally comprises of scenario plans and crisis management plans.
- An intelligent manager always remain ready to face the challenges and keeps other options also open.

Single Use Plan

They are formulated for a single goal. Hence, they cannot be put to use repeatedly. They are based on repeat use or standing plans of the organisation. They are non-recurring in nature.

These plans includes the following

Programmes They are part of single use plans. They help in coordination as they are the schedule of action. It facilitates step-by-step performance of various tasks. Instead of guiding about how the work is to be done, (*i.e.* done by procedure) it focuses on what work is to be done.

Hence, it is an arrangement which focuses on what work is to be performed and when it is to be performed.

Budget It states what the company expects in the near future. The expectations are stated in quantified manner. The period for which budgeting is done is limited and pre-defined.

According to **Brown and Howard of Management Accountant**, "A budget is a pre-determined statement of managerial policy during the given period which provides a standard for comparison with the result actually achieved."

Repeat Use/Standing Plans

They act as guideline and are formulated for long-term use. They are recurrent in nature. Hence, decisions are made based on knowledge and past data hence it involves informed decision. They focus on the main objective of the organisation and include objectives, procedures, strategies, rules, policies and methods. These plans have to be changed repeatedly.

These plans includes the following

1. Objectives

They are the goals desired by an organisaton. They give direction to the activities of the organisation. They serve as benchmark for gauging the effectiveness and efficiency of the organisation. Planning without objectives is meaningless.

According to **Koontz** and **O'Donnell**, "An objective is a term commonly used to indicate the end point of a management programme."

Features of objective are as follows

- They are pre-determined.
- They should be quantifiable and measurable.
- They should be clear and specific, any ambiguous term should be removed.
- They ought to be feasible and realistic.
- The objectives should be mutually supportive and there must be an interconnection among various objectives.
- The objectives can be of long range, medium range or short range.
- The management must set objectives in each area.

2. Strategies

It is a special form of plan which is made to combat the challenge possessed by competitor's strategy. It is based on competitor's plan of action. It is shaped by the forces in the external environment of the business. The scenario in the industry and the forces in economy assist in formulating the strategies.

According to **Haimann**, "Strategy is a policy that has been formulated by the top level management for the purpose of interpreting and shaping the meaning of other policies."

Hence, strategies are those plans which are based on the plans practiced by the firm's competitors.

Features of strategies are as follows

- Appropriate combination of various components.
- It forms a bridge between the organisation and its environment. It is an action to combat a specific challenge.
- Unlike objective, strategy is the way to achieve an end result, it is not the goal or end in itself.
- Top level management formulates strategy and it is based on assumed and estimated risk.

3. Policies

This kind of plan acts as a directive force which aims at providing a stable and endless framework for executing the actions on repeated managerial problems. They are the plans that guide the organisation in making decisions.

Policies can exist at all the levels, chiefly departmental and divisional of corporate level. It empowers the lower levels employees to solve the managerial problems on their own without depending on the upper level management.

Features of a policy are as follows

- It is clear, positive and definite.
- It should be able to be translated while practicing.
- Flexible as well as high degree of durability.
- It should be comprehensive and must encompass all anticipatable scenarios.
- It should be based on sound judgement and reliable facts.
- It should be communicated to everyone in the organisation.

4. Rules

They are the most uncomplicated type of plan. They help in controlling the business. They are also used to alter or influence the altitude of the workers and the organisation.

According to **Koontz** and **O'Donnell**, "A rule requires that a specific and definite action with respect to a situation."

Features of rules are as follows

- Rule is basically a statement which explain what a person is expected to do and what he is not.
- It demarcates, clarifies and is an interpretation of a policy. It sets the standards and forms the basis of norms essential for guiding the organisation, its workers and their conduct. They are specific and concise in nature.
- Non-compliance results in punishment.

Types of rules are as follows

- **Folklore** They are the rules which are not published and are communicated by behaviour and are understood implicitly.

- **Guidelines** They are the generally published and suggested practices which give some place of discretion with regards to their use and interpretation.
- **Mandates** They are also published regulations and orders which are to be strictly followed. They cannot be ignored in any situation. Violation of mandates will leads to punishment.

5. Procedures

It implies a sequence of activities which are required to be followed by the managers in order to achieve the desired future goals. They give the series of steps to be followed.

According to **Allen**, "Procedure prescribes the manner or methods through which work is to be performed."

Hence, it is a determined, fixed and bit-by-bit sequence of activities where the starting point and ending point are clearly mentioned. These steps have to be followed correctly in the same order in order to accomplish the task.

Features of procedures are as follows

- It gives the definite way in which the task is to be executed. They are designed generally for the internal workers.
- The procedures are performed in chronological order. They ensure high quality uniform level of execution because the steps are pre-determined and published.
- Procedures eliminate overlapping and duplication of work because each task is to be performed one after another.
- Like policies help in thinking about the actions, procedures guide actual execution in order to achieve stipulated goals.

6. Method

They are standardised, habitual and established manner or way to perform a particular task. It is logical and a systematic way of accomplishing ends with certainty, efficiency and accuracy.

Features of method are as follows

- They are standardised ways of performing a task which are flexible in nature.
- Violation of methods does not result into penalty or fine.
- When the manager selects apt method, then the organisation saves time, efforts and also money.
- Methods increase efficiency and productivity. They are fixed steps in nature.

Decision-making

The origin of word 'decision' lies with Latin word 'decido/deciso' meaning 'cutting off'. Hence, the process of making decisions deals with the cutting of various alternatives and choice of the desirable alternative.

According to **George R Terry**, "Decision-making is the selection based on some criteria from two or more possible alternatives."

According to **Felix M Lopez**, "A decision represents a judgement, a final resolution of a conflict of needs, means or goals and a commitment to action made in face of uncertainty, complexity and even irrationally."

According to **PF Drucker**, "Whatever a manager does he does through making decisions."

According to **RC Davis**, "Decision-making is an intellectual process which involves selection of one course of action out of many alternatives. Decision-making will be followed by the second function of management called planning."

Decision-making as Management Function

It is an integral part of modern management. Decision-making is the basic and key element of management. The function of a manager is to make rational and sound decisions. It involves choosing a course of action in order to choose among various options and alternatives to get the preferred outcome.

Decision-making bridges the ends with the means of achieving the outcomes. The efficiency of the manager is directly linked with the judgments and decisions made by him. **PF Drucker** has said, "whatever a manager does, he does through decision-making."

Characteristics of Decision-making

- Decision-making can be based on rationale, judgemental, critical and emotional.
- It chooses the best option that aligns the outcomes with organisational goals. Hence, it focuses on a pre-determined goal.
- It relies on dependable and true information, data and feedback. The value of the decision is dependent on the quality of information. Hence, generally, management uses different software to gather and keep relevant organisational information.

- It is an intellectual process and requires mental judgement. Decision-making needs maturity, skills and knowledge.
- They can be articulated through words or can be inferred from certain behaviour.
- This process involves time. The process encompasses a collection of information and searches for various alternatives. Various steps are required to be completed in order to make decisions.
- It is a continuous process. Managers daily have to make decisions. It encompasses all the organisational processes. It never ends in the business management process as the decisions relate to various policies and tasks.
- It deals with uncertainty as the outcome of each course of action is unknown.

Advantages of Decision-making

- It is the primary function and precedes all the other functions of the organisation. This is because unless the top management takes important decisions, key activities cannot be performed. Resources cannot be allocated to various departments unless there is strategic decision-making at the top level.
- Decision-making helps in planning, organising controlling and directing. Hence, it facilitates the management process. The decisions taken by the top level management in the form of planning are implemented and help in coordination and control.
- Decision-making makes manager competent enough to face problems and challenges. Hence, decision-making serves as an armour against uncertainty. In decision-making, the management strives for searching new alternatives and plans that help in combating the changing environment.

Types of Decisions

1. **Routine Decisions**

   These are the day-to-day decisions taken by the low level and middle level managers. They are taken after analysing the already laid procedures, rules and policies.

   The middle level managers use the standard policies set by the top level management as a benchmark to derive at a certain choice.

   They are also known as tactical decisions. They can be easily delegated to the subordinates as they are mostly programmed. The results or outcomes of routine decisions or tactical decisions only affect a small portion of the organisation.

2. **Strategic Decisions**

   These decisions taken by the managers which are very crucial for the growth of the organisation. They deal with policy formulation, developing new business models, analysing the environment and various alternatives in order to derive one outcome.

   Strategic decisions are generally taken by the top level managers. The outcomes of such decisions affect the health of the entire organisation. They cannot be delegated to the subordinates.

3. **Programmed Decisions**

   These are the day-to-day decisions taken by the manager after considering rules of the organisation. Various rules and procedures are laid down beforehand in order to guide the manager while making decisions. It defines how the manager is programmed to take decisions.

4. **Non-programmed Decisions**

   These are the decisions to combat the non-recurrent problems of the company. They are undertaken to resolve exclusive and uncommon problems of the company. Such problems are complex and options cannot be ascertained in advance. There are no handy solutions. These decisions are highly significant for the growth of the company. Top level management engages in non-programmed decisions.

5. **Irreversible Decisions**

   These decisions which cannot be upturned or changed.

6. **Reversible Decisions**

   These decisions that can be changed after their implementation. When McDonald faced criticism for selling beef in India, it quickly discontinued its sales.

7. **Individual Decisions**

   When the decision maker makes a decision on his own then it is called individual decision-making. In case of sole proprietorship or where the subject matter is not very complex, the decisions are made by the owner of the company only.

8. **Group Decisions**

   Here, the decisions are made by a group of managers and persons. This type of decision-making is done when the problem is complex and vast and it also requires specialist knowledge of different individuals. The decisions of the committee, task force or board of director are part of group decision-making. They generally comprise of relevant problems which require specialised and mutual discussion.

9. **Authoritative Decisions**

   It is a style of making decisions which are derived at the top. The president or CEO makes a decision which is to be followed by all the subordinates it is called authoritative decision-making.

10. **Facilitative Decisions**
Here, the superior and the subordinate jointly collaborate and come to a single outcome. The head of the departments, workers and employees have primary information about customers, processes and market trends, whereas the top level management has expertise and knowledge. This amalgamation of facts and knowledge leads to better decision-making.

11. **Consultative Decisions**
This is a form of facilitative decision-making. However, here the final decision is made by the higher authority only. The manager/decision-maker will ask for the advice from the employees and various departmental heads but the decision will be made by him individually.

Decision-making Process

The process was designed by **Herbert Simon**.

The model comprises three distinct elements which are as follows

Intelligence This refers to the raw data which is gathered and probed. This data helps in identifying the problem which requires decision-making. It helps in knowing the problem is about.

Design This element focuses on developing, designing, inventing and examining various alternatives which can result in decision-making. Once, these alternates are identified, they are testified for feasibility and implementation. Probing is done to calculate the value of the outcome of the decision.

Choice After the manager has developed various substitutes, the final element is to select the best alternative. This selection is done on the basis of pre-determined criteria.

Following steps are involved in decision-making

1. **Identify the Decision** This deals with the identification of the decision to be made. It also defines what outcomes are desired to be achieved. Whether it is a strategic decision or routine decisions and what will be the impact of this decision on the organisation. It encompasses identifying the nature of a decision to be made, which can be short-term or long-term or reversible or irreversible.
2. **Gather Information** This step deals with the collection of information from various sources. The various decision can be with regard to what type of information is required and from where the data will be collected. After identifying the sources of input, the manager has to identify how he can reach to the sources.
In this step, the manager has to deal with the internal(reports, internal surveys, facts, documents etc) as well as external(published articles, internet, libraries, government agencies etc) environment to collect the data.
3. **Identify Alternatives** The third step is to identify various alternatives for decision-making. On the basis of the data collected, the manager lays down all the possible course of action. Sometimes, he uses past knowledge or information to build new alternatives. Hence, all the desirable and feasible alternatives are identified here.
4. **Weigh the Evidence** As the manager is equipped with all the possible action plans, he then weighs each of them. Keeping the requirement of *Step* 1 (Indentify the decision) in mind, he judges whether the stated plan will give the desired results. The decision-maker uses his emotions and intelligence while evaluating the course of actions. He will rank the alternatives on the basis of priority and desirability.
5. **Select Among Alternatives** In this step, the manager will choose among the ranked action plans. This choice is based on cost benefit analysis. Various pros and cons are looked upon before selecting the said alternative. The decision-maker can choose a blend of one or two alternates.
6. **Take Actions** Here, the decision-maker actually takes the action and implements the chosen alternative in the organisation.
7. **Review Decision** After the decision is made, the manager must review the decision and see whether the desired consequences have been achieved or not. If the decision lacks certain consequences then the decision-maker should repeat *Step* 1 (Identify the decision).

Errors and Common Biases in Decision-making

Sometimes managers fall back on heuristics or general rule of thumb while making decisions. These are called decision heuristics and congnitive biases. They are used to understand complex situations while making decisions. *e.g.* 80-20 rule which states that 80% of the consequences of a phenomenon stem from 20% of the causes. However, sometimes these heuristics lead to some biases which adversely affect the decision-making.

These are known as cognitive biases. These are the decision-making errors that we are all prone to making and that have been recurrently verified in laboratory setting or controlled experiments with human decision-makers.

Some of them are explained below

1. **Availability Bias** Under this bias, the decision maker makes his decisions and judgements on the basis of information, data and facts that are freely and easily available. If any piece of information is easily available, then it can be remembered easily which helps in decision-making.

2. **Overconfidence Bias/Illusion of Control** This bias arises when the decision-maker is given factual data and is asked to evaluate the probability that his choice is correct. In this case, the decision-maker overestimates his accuracy and is overconfident about his decision.
3. **Anchoring Bias** The manager relies on first-hand information rather than the entire information. Hence, he fixes his attention to the information received first and the decisions are made on the basis of this information only. The subsequent information is ignored.
4. **Hindsight Bias** This bias makes the decision- maker believe that he had accurately anticipated the outcome, even when the outcome is known.
5. **Representative Bias** The decision-maker assesses the probability of occurrence of an outcome by linking it with a preceding outcome.
6. **Randomness Error Bias** Here, the decision-maker takes a decision on the basis of random thoughts, facts and information. He tries to find meaning in randomness and imaginarily links the events with superstitions.
7. **Escalation of Commitment Bias** This is the most challenging bias for a decision-maker. The decision-maker stays and continues with the decisions made by him, even when there is clear evidence that it is incorrect. This is because the decision-maker feels he has devoted his efforts, time and energy in taking the decision and convinces himself that this decision is right.
8. **Confirmation Bias** This is also a personal bias where the decision-maker focuses on seeking out information that restates his decisions from the past. Similarly, if any information contradicts his preconceived notions, then such information is rejected in the first place.
9. **Risk Aversion Bias** Many decision-makers try to play safe by not indulging into risky decision-making. They select only those course of actions where the outcome is cent per cent known. Hence, they avoid risk by preferring a certain thing over an uncertain outcome.
10. **Indecisiveness Bias** If the manager is fearful about the outcome, then he may become indecisive. The nervousness in making a decision may lead to a delay in decision-making. Many managers postpone the decision- making process which leads to making decisions under stress of lack of time. This hampers thorough analysis of alternatives and may lead to poor decision.
11. **Others** The decision-maker sometimes focuses on the symptoms of the problem rather than the root cause. He should be capable of separating causes and their symptoms. The method used in analysing and quantifying the problem may also be inappropriate as per the situation.

Theories of Decision-making

1. Normative Decision Theory

It is a classical approach to decision-making. This theory identifies the best decisions by selecting one perfect decision-maker who has perfect knowledge, rational and accuracy in taking the best decisions. This theory also focuses on practical application and deals with how managers should make decisions. It forms the basis for decision analysis.

This theory aims at identifying and developing various techniques, methods and tools that support people in making better decisions. It is also known as the prescriptive theory of management.

The theory was generally propounded by **PF Drucker** and **Ansoff.** This theory is generally used where decisions are to be made with regard to quantitative data, numbers such as economics and finance. The key focus of the theory is on how managers should make decisions if they want to maximise their productivity.

The theory is based on various assumptions such as there is perfect information about the decision to be made, there is certainty and the aim is to maximise the behaviour. Various decision-makers have a consensus over the values of the input variables.

It also assumés that the decision-maker fully relies on computed values which in return help him in making decisions. He knows what he desires to reach(ends) and how he can reach them(means) in advance. Here, the decision-maker is neutral, he abstains from biases, disliking or liking and judgement and relies on logic reasoning.

This theory is apt for decisions that are to be made repeatedly. Thus, the decision-maker is economical and focuses on programming the decisions so that there is maximum output with minimum efforts and time input.

However, this theory face criticism as there is a scope of ignorance and uncertainty. Due to lack of time, resources and knowledge, the decision-maker sometimes act as satisfier rather than a maximiser.

This implies he makes decisions that are just sufficient and not maximising. Rationality is an idyllic theory however it is impractical because organisations deal with human behaviour which is dynamic and complex.

Another limitation of this theory is the assumption that there is consent over values. Various decision-makers do not affirm to certain values of the inputs. This creates disharmony in the process of decision-making.

It is also known as rational theory or economic man theory.

*The steps in making rational decisions are defined by **Stephen Robbins** as*

- Describing the problem.
- Identification of the criteria for making decisions.
- Assigning a value to the decision-making criteria.
- Developing various options or alternatives.
- Assessing the options.
- Selecting the finest alternate.

2. Descriptive Theory

It is also known as a positive theory. This theory was propounded by **March** and **Ceyart**. This is opposite to rational theory in the sense that it focuses on identifying the decisions that people actually make rather than what they are supposed to make.

It explains and characterises the consistencies in various choices made by different people in the same situation. Thus, it focuses on the real decisions made and not what ought to be made. It is dependent on observed behaviours of individuals and groups under certain assumptions and situations.

This decision-making theory helps in better coalitions as the decisions are made on the basis of human behaviour and not numbers. The key focus here is how the superiors actually make decisions. It is also known as behavioural decision theory.

However, the theory faces limitation as the term coalition means a compromise between various stakeholders, *i.e.* the government, customers, shareholders, employees etc.

3. Bounded Rationality Theory

In rational decision theory, the decision-maker aims at optimising the decision by selecting the best alternative. However, bounded rationality theory states that the decision-maker is bounded by various constraints such as time constraints, intellectual limitations or the information possessed by them. Hence, his rationality is bounded. In these circumstances, he cannot make optimal decisions but satisfying decisions.

It was proposed by **Herbert A Simon**. He propounds that attainment of rationality is unrealistic. It is rare to achieve rationality. It is based on the principle that the human mind cannot perceive retain and retrieve all the information(future, present or past) and data given to him. The manager, being a human will not be able to identify all the alternatives available to solve the problem even with the help of machines and computers.

Hence, because of this limitation and foundations, the decision-maker will take decisions that are just satisfactory and not optimal. The term satisfactory implies that a course of action which is just good enough in solving the said problem.

The person making a decision has his own soft emotions, hence he cannot make unbiased decisions. His preferences and experiences will alter the decisions. Hence, bounded rationality is associated with 'satisficing' rather than 'optimising'.

4. Practical Approach

This theory to decision-making is based on both behavioural and rational approach. It focuses on giving a more realistic decision-making process for the organisation.

The theory postulates that the manager should generate all alternatives(taken from a rational approach) but he should identify all the alternatives within the stipulated period of time and financial resources(taken from a behavioural approach). Thus, it amalgamates the two theories, *i.e.* finding all the possible plans but within the resources.

This theory uses the analytical framework of the normative approach and moderating influence of the behavioural approach. It is appropriate for the managers who take impulsive and rushed decisions or who keep changing their decisions rapidly, as they do not use much data or rationality to identify all possible alternatives and derive at the decision.

5. Personal Approach

It was given by **Janis** and **Mann.** This theory focuses on how the individuals actually make a decision when they are agitated, worried, nervous or anxious be it in the personal or organisational atmosphere.

It is also known as the 'conflict model'. This theory deals with the conflicts personally faced by the decision maker especially in difficult decision-making conditions. However, this approach deals with life decisions such as education, career; job marriage etc.

It also focuses on aspects of postponement and reasoning are the devices through which individuals evade from taking decisions and undergoing stress related to decision-making. The decision-maker, as per this approach, judges the situation as per his moral standards. If any decision confronts his ethics, then such a decision is not taken.

Tools and Techniques in Decision-making

Decision Tree It is a chart, graph or a model that focuses on each event and its outcomes. It also focuses on the likelihood of occurrence of these events. They are used in quantitative decision-making. The diagram consists of a tree shaped figure which shows a course of action.

The branch of the tree represents various outcomes. It also presents if a certain course of action is selected then what outcomes will follow it. These outcomes are mutually exclusive.

Delphi Technique It helps in estimating the probability of the occurrence of future happenings. It involves a written process where a group of people fill their responses in multiple questionnaires. There is no physical meetings and discussion.

Every new questionnaire is based on the information collected from the previous questionnaire. The process ceases when the group agrees to a single decision. The responses of the members are kept anonymous.

Decision Matrix All the options of a decision are presented in the form of a table or matrix. All the options are listed in the first column. The factors affecting the decisions are presented in the first row. The manager then scores and weighs the options on the basis of the factor of decision. More score is awarded to more important factors. The sum of the scores reveals the best alternative.

Cost Benefit Analysis Under this, the manager weighs the various options on the basis of financial constraints. He identifies what will be the cost of exercising the option and what will be the monetary benefit derived out of it. The alternative that gives maximum cost-benefit, *i.e* lower cost resulting into higher benefits, will be selected.

T Chart It is a technique where the manager writes minuses (negative points) and plusses (positive points) of each alternative. This decision helps in judging the pros and cons of each alternative.

PEST Analysis It is one of the techniques to look into the external environment and decide in accordance with it. It stands for political, economic, social and technological. This decision-making technique helps in identifying the current trend in the outside environment and making decisions accordingly.

SWOT Analysis It stands for Strengths, Weaknesses, Opportunities and Threats. It is an effective decision-making tool that helps in strategic planning. The top level manager uses this technique to gauge the internal as well as external environment.

Conjoint Analysis This decision-making method is generally used by the leaders of the business to learn about the preferences of the consumers. It generally helps in pricing the product.

Pareto Analysis This method is used in the circumstances where the manager is overloaded with a variety of decisions. He is required to make numerous decisions simultaneously. In this, the manager prioritises and arranges the tasks. This is done by determining which activity will have a great impact on the organisation. *e.g.* It provides most common sources of defect, highest occuring type of defects and frequent reasons for customer complaints.

Multivoting It is a decision-making process where a group of people are involved in decision-making. This helps in jotting down a huge list of options which is filtered over and over again until a final decision is obtained.

Linear Programming It is a technique of depicting complex relations between different variable through a linear function. This is followed by finding the optimum points that will either maximise the profits or minimise the costs. Thus, this methods establishes a relationship between a different variable and identifying the feasible outcomes.

Monte-Carlo Simulation/Simulation Technique It is a technique where the manager replaces and amplifies the real experiences on the basis of some guided techniques. It is done on the basis of random sampling so that there is true variability. It is generally used in social care and health information system, supply chain management and logistics.

Payback Analysis It is a technique used in the financial analysis of a project. This technique helps in ascertaining the time required by the project to cover the investment cost. Various alternatives are ranked according to the number of years in which the invested amount will be yielded back. The alternative with the lowest payback is selected.

Experiences The past experiences of the manager helps in taking new decisions.

Facts The primitive tool in decision-making is the facts and data gathered by the manager. Reliable and qualitative data is the core of effective decision-making.

Intuition The manager takes the decision on the basis of inner conscience and gut feelings. However, often managers use quantitative techniques, they rely on intuitions for making judgements.

Intuitions are an amalgamation of experiences, past training and acquired knowledge. It is made by the sub-conscious mind. Generally, it is considered irrational, but it not necessarily incorrect.

Organising

It is the second step of the management process. The organisation encompasses various decisions regarding the structure of an organisation and its design in order to promote coordination in the organisation. It also aims at providing the right things(tools, human resource, financial resource and physical resources) at right time.

Meaning and Definition of Organising

It is that function of management which deals with the development of organisational structure and allocation of various resources to accomplish the pre-determined goals. It deals with variety of process and coordinates them to yield effective results and helps in transforming plans into actions.

According to **Theo Haimann**, "Organising is the process of defining and grouping the activities of the enterprise and establishing authority relationships among them."

According to **Koontz** and **O'Donnell**, "The establishment of authority relationship with provision for coordination between them both vertically and horizontally in the enterprise structure."

Process of Organising

Organising is also a process as it establishes relationship among various units, sub-units, people, process and systems. The relationship among people are created on the basis of responsibility and authority. Organising leads to emergence of a structure where several roles are designed, to be filled by competent, suitable and skilled workers and the inter-relationship of such roles is defined. *The process is as follows*

1. **Determination of Objectives** Without setting objectives, the firm cannot organise itself. It is the first step. Identification of prime objectives is important because the structure of the organisation is built on the basis of set objective. By determining the objective, the firm will enable, the firm in ascertaining why the proposed structure of the organisation is to be set-up.
2. **Identification of Total Work** Organisation comprises of people. Since, various individuals and departments pool in their knowledge, work and efforts, there ought to be a clear division of activities. The total work is identified and divided into important activities. This will remove any ambiguity and workers will learn about their respective work.
3. **Classification of Activities** This step is also called division of work. Here, the work is further classified on the basis of commonality of function and purpose, similarity and the type of physical and human resource required. Activities that are intimately related are grouped and divisions and departments are formed. Activities in the department are further bifurcated into sections. It includes departmentalisation or departmentation.
4. **Assigning of Duties** Once the classification of job is done, jobs are assigned to competent and different subordinates so that the work is performed.

   Kimball and **Kimball** defined this aspect as, "Organisation embraces the duties of designating the departments and the personnel that are to carry on the work, defining their functions and specifying the relations that are to exist between department and individuals."

   Hence, this step deals with assignment of work according to the competencies of the workforce.
5. **Delegation of Authority** Allocation of work will not suffice. There is a need to establish reporting relationship in the organisation because of numerous people simultaneously work in an organisation. Thus, there should be clarity between authority and responsibility.
6. **Authority and Responsibility**
   - This enables smooth functioning as each individual get clarity about whom he should approach, who is the boss and who is the subordinate.
   - This also promotes delegation of authority.
   - No organisation can function without authority and responsibility.
   - Hence, the final step of the process of organisation is to establish reporting relationships.

Significance of Organising

- Promotes specialisation by systematically allocating jobs.
- Effective administration clarity in job descriptions and superior subordinate relationship.
- Easy adaptation to change. This occurs by changing the organisational structure according to the situation.
- By eliminating duplication of work, organising promotes judicious use of resources.
- Boosts morale of the personnel. Delegation empowers the subordinate and assists him in learning new challenging work. This leads to the development of the employee.
- Transparency and certainty in working relationship.
- Growth and expansion of the organisation.

Organisational Structure

Organisational structure refers to a system where the work is divided formally. These smaller tasks are gathered and synchronised in order to promote coordination in the organisation. It refers to an outline of groups, individuals, operation systems and job putting efforts to attain stipulated goals. It is the arrangement of jobs which is formally defined.

According to **Mintzberg** (1972), "Organisational structure is the framework of the relations on jobs, systems, operating process, people and groups making efforts to achieve the goals. Organisational structure is a set of methods dividing the task to determined duties and coordinates them."

According to **Hold** and **Antony** (1991), "Structure is not a coordination mechanism and it affects all organisational process. Organisational structure refers to the models of internal relations of organisation, power and relations and reporting, formal communication channels, responsibility and decision-making delegation is clarified."

Importance of Organisational Structure

Organisational structure is a mechanism through which management directs, coordinates and controls the business.

A sound organisational structure

- facilitates management process and overall operations of the organisation and provides better coordination.
- encourages growth by increasing the efficiency and gives clarity about roles and responsibilities.
- builds relationship across various managerial levels and encourages human beings to attain psychological satisfaction from his work, his position and his working environment.
- defines organisational relationships and stimulates creativity in the organisation by initiating new and improved ways of work processes.

Factors affecting Organisational Structure

According to **Peter F Drucker**, "Structure is a tool to achieve short and long-term goals of the organisation. Thus, any discussion should be regarding goals and strategy in structure."

The factors are as follows

1. **Interaction with the Customer** If the interaction of the lower level management is more with the customers, then there is need of independent decision-making, hence, a decentralised structure is appropriate. If the lower management seldom interacts with the customers, then the highly centralised structure is best.
2. **The Sensitivity of Data** If the company deals with sensitive and personal data, then the decentralised structure is best suited as the personal information can be accessed by only selective managers. Where the information is insensitive, then there can be a centralised structure where the information is centrally stored.
3. **Innovation** If the company is based on innovations and creativity, then the lower the levels of management, the better it is for the company. In this case, flat organisations are best suited as they remove the delay in approval from different layers.
4. **Marketing Consideration** If the company sells differentiated products, then the divisional structure is beneficial as there will be separate divisions for each market, on the other hand, is the product, *i.e.* alike then functional structures are best suited.
5. **Size of the Organisation** If the organisation is large in size, then there will be higher managerial levels. Smaller organisations will have 0-1 levels of management.
6. **Business Cycle of the Organisation**

   There are namely four stages

   - **Birth** There are no levels or delegation of authority, no formal structure.
   - **Youth** The formal structure is introduced in this stage as the customers begin to increase.
   - **Middle Life** Here, the operations attain zenith hence the organisational structure is large, complex and various layers are introduced.
   - **Maturity** The firm attains maturity and turns into a lesser innovating and expanding the organisation. Hence, with an increase in profits, the organisations spend fewer resources in experimenting with the organisational structure. There are no new inventions in the organisational structure. They remain stable and are continued in future.
7. **Strategy** When the organisation wants to attain first mover advantage, then the organisation must use organic structures. Firms which aim at producing already existing products must follow mechanistic structure.
8. **Environment** It comprises of legal, socio-political and economic environment. *It includes*
   - **Stable Environment** Mechanistic structure is apt as it increases productivity.
   - **Unstable/Dynamic Environment** Organic structure is beneficial as helps in tackling the changing environment aggressively.
9. **Technology** Organisational structure depends on the technology and the production of the organisation.

   It includes

   - **Small Batch Production** They produce customised and a smaller quantity of goods, hence the organisational structure are more flexible.
   - **Mass Production** They indulge in bulky production, hence there organisational structure is more rigid.
10. **Routine Activities** When the organisation performs more routine activities, then the structure is standardised, while non-routine activities need repeated upgradation hence decentralised and flexible structure is appropriate.

Types of Organisational Structures and Chart

An organisational chart (or organogram) is a figure depicting the arrangement of an institution and defines the associations of jobs/positions and various ranks.

It shows the internal structure of the organisation.

The various types of chart are as follows

1. Line Organisational Structure

- It is simplest type of structure which is based on the vertical line of responsibility and authority. It is establishes clear subordinate superior relationships based on the scalar principle.
- Chain of command is followed and it simplifies and explains the relationship between boss and worker.
- There is quick decision-making, because the management and workers share close relations as there are no complex levels of management.
- However, it lack specialisation. A key limitation is it becomes ineffective when the scale of the company increases.
- It promotes dependence on only key managers, who get overloaded with responsibilities.

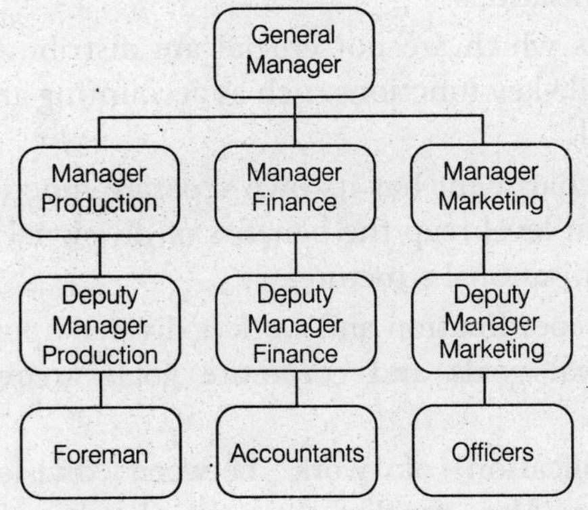

Organisational Structure Chart Under Line Organisational

2. Functional or Staff Organisational Structure

- It is the most widely used structure and the activities are grouped according to similar work and functions. It comprises two elements, *i.e.* line organisation and staff organisation.
- Line organisation serves the purpose of the shortest chain of command while staff organisation deals with providing expert opinions which assist the line organisation in making decisions. Marketing activities are clubbed together and financing activities are grouped in another department.
- It is suitable for medium to small institutions and is apt for the organisations having a lesser variety of product.
- There is specialisation of function also. This structure helps in coordinating and using the specialised knowledge of the functional managers.
- In line organisation, the manager at the top has general knowledge hence he cannot impart specialised knowledge, while in functional authority the management is competent in the said function. It is also known as staff organisation.
- However, it promotes sectional interest as one department sees its objectives from a narrower perspective. There is a violation of the unity of command under this structure as a single employee receives a command from the line authority and staff authority. It conflicts in the organisation.

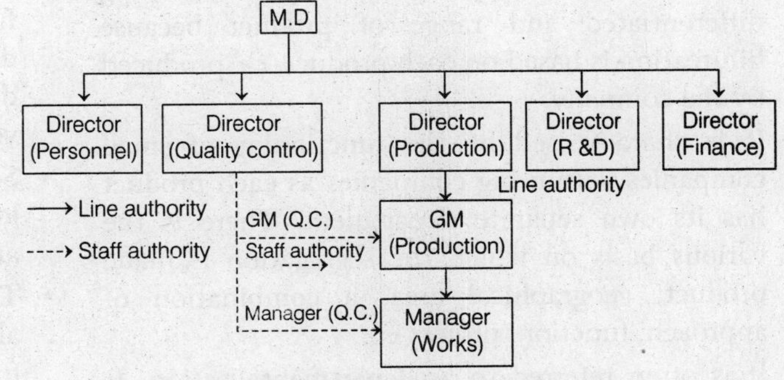

Functional Organisational Structure

3. Line and Staff Organisational Structure

- It is followed by large organisations. These institutions follow both line as well as staff organisational structures. Straight up the (vertical) association is comprehended by special knowledge of the staff organisation.
- Major functions are performed by line executives (a feature of line organisation), however the staff executives help the line executives with their expert knowledge. It is traditionally related to personnel management.
- The staff executives are mere supports and do not have any right or power of command. There are three types of staff executives, *i.e.* control, service and advisory.

- Staff executives/functionaries are not held answerable, thus, they may become insincere in their work and advice. It is highly flexible and it increases span of control.

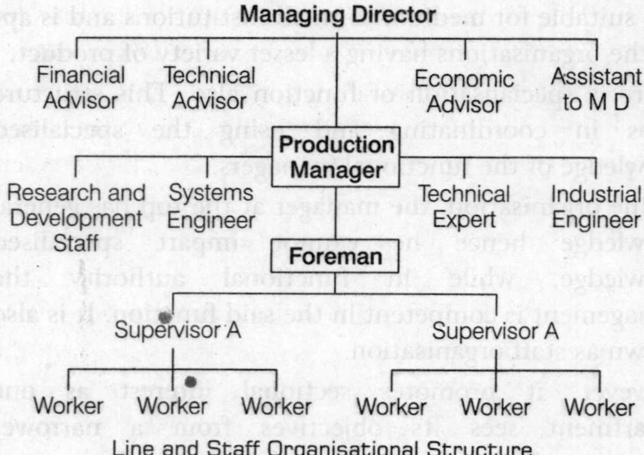

Line and Staff Organisational Structure

4. Divisional Organisational Structure

- It is also known as product organisational structure. It is apt for companies selling differentiated and range of product because bifurcation is based on each product, *i.e.* produced by the company.
- It is characterised by the functioning of small companies within big companies as each product has its own separate department. There is the various basis on which the segregation is made product, geographical area, a combination of approach, function, project etc.
- It is often referred to as departmentalisation. It encourages diversification for the company. The company is able to manage a variety of products. As each product is independent of other, there is minimum risk.
- One major unit comprises of all the technical experts from various fields(finance, marketing etc). Hence, their specialised knowledge is grouped together for one particular unit.
- This micro bifurcation shifts the focus from common organisational goals to departmental goals. Each unit strives to endorse its own product. However, there can be internal unhealthy competition within the organisation which may lead to conflicts.

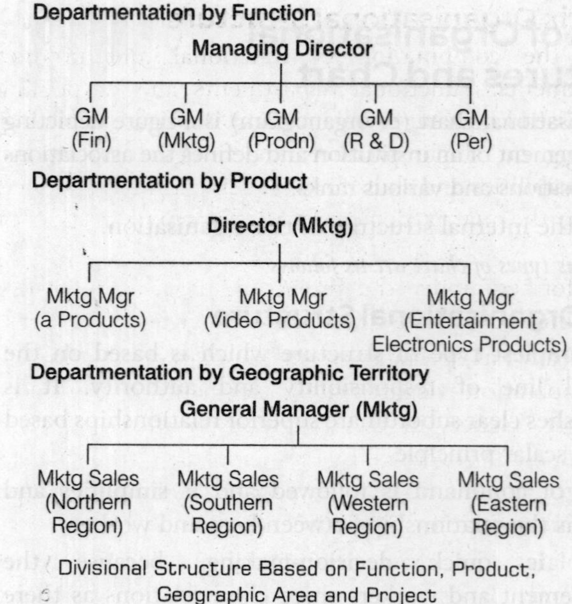

Divisional Structure Based on Function, Product, Geographic Area and Project

5. Hybrid Organisational Structure

- It is based on the characteristics of both divisional as well as functional organisational structures. The World Bank has defined it as the organisation where several organisational designs are used. There is less rigidity, hence it is suitable for very large organisations.
- Some functions which are not crucial are distributed among lower levels while key functions such as accounting and finance are kept central.
- The product department has its own separate function. Thus, all the units and level reap the benefits of divisional as well as functional organisational structures.
- There is better coordination and work is divided appropriately as the divisional goals and corporate goals are effectively aligned.
- However, duplication of work between divisional and functional areas. Also, conflict may arise between divisional head office and main headquarters. There is an excessive cost of administration.

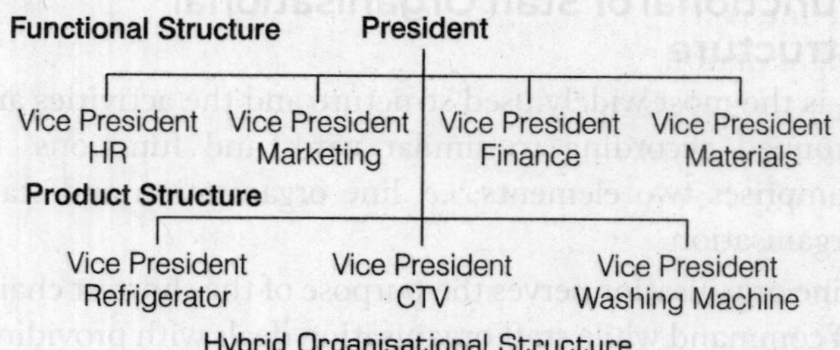

Hybrid Organisational Structure

6. Matrix Organisational Structure

- It is the combination of functional and product departments. Functional departments aim at pooling specialised knowledge while product department aims at focusing on single product and brings together the responsibilities and skills for producing a single product. Hence, the matrix department is an amalgamation of both.
- It is formed under the project manager who is also sometimes referred to the product manager.
- This team has specialists from the marketing, finance and operation departments, alongwith the project manager. Hence, in this organisation structure, each individual is governed by two superiors, the project manager and the functional manager(Finance manager, HR manager etc.)
- It violates the management principle of unity of command. It is a permanent and fixed type of organisational structure. The decisions made are highly decentralised. There is solid coordination between the process, project and the product.
- It leads to costly administration, greater probability of conflicts and confusion and ambiguity about responsibility and authority relationships.

7. Formal Organisational Structure

- It clearly defines the jobs and the amount of authority and responsibility associated with it and gives the rules and procedure, instructions, guidelines and processes that help in managing the work and behaviour of the worker.
- It is given in the office's formal documents which gives hierarchical arrangements of the organisation.

8. Informal Organisational Structure

- When the workers of a formal organisation interact with each other, they form social connections or groups. These clusters together are known as informal organisations. It occurs because of physical vicinity, their common work or interests. It is unstructured in comparison to formal organisation.
- It is not given by the organisation as it has procedures, processes and rules of its own. These structures evolve during the process as they are not formally written in the organisation.
- There are no fixed patterns of communication and anybody can communicate with anyone. Thus, it helps in quick completion of work and effective communication.
- It gives emotional support, increases span of control and fosters better management. However, reduces control and is less reliable.

9. Project Organisational Structure

- Most of the traditional organisational structure focus on vertical relations between the various levels of management. However, under certain complex projects, there is a need for other modes of communication also, such as horizontal and diagonal, downward or upward.
- Hence, project organisations are formed that give means to define authority responsibility relation- ships especially when there are interconnected, independent and interdependent activities.
- They are formed for a shorter duration, hence are temporary. They are specific in nature.
- They are built by accommodating various specialists of the organisation. It has its own project manager. The resources and vigour are divulged into the functioning of one single project.
- They are suitable for time bound projects and those projects which require highly specialised knowledge. Such organisation dissolves after the completion of the specific project, *i.e.* each functionary specialist go back to his permanent department.
- It provides better and speedy communication between the experts from various departments. It is highly motivating as it causes synergy and achieves the project's goal and gives adaptability to the managers in managing various tasks together. *e.g.* R & D projects, bridges, shopping complex etc.

10. Committee/Task Force Organisational Structure

- It was experimented by Ford Motors in1980. They are temporary in nature and are built to solve specific common issues.
- A single committee comprises of various heads from different departments. *e.g.* Finance committee will comprise of heads from various other departments to ascertain the financial needs of each department.
- The decisions and advice are followed by line authorities. It follows the principle of participative management.
- It gives new ideas and generally, all the departments are willing to follow them because they are being mutually devised.
- This organisation structure relieves the top management from catering to irrelevant issues. The decisions made as a committee are superior to the decisions made individually.
- It enhances creative thinking and promotes stability. It promotes flexibility and dynamic. It can be formed as per the requirement.

- However, aggressive nature of few managers may distort cordial relations which sometimes it leads to delayed decision and buck passing.

11. Mechanistic Organisational Structure

- The term mechanistic symbolises the formal and a strict structure. There is a clear division of labour. This leads to specialisation in jobs.
- The organisation is treated as a machine and there are stringent procedures, rules and command. The company aims at achieving predictable output and standardised production.
- It is similar to the bureaucratic structure as it is vertically oriented and has greater control.
- It is also known as tall organisations(different levels).
- It has promoted economy and productivity but it curbs creativity and treats employees as machines.
- There is centralised decision-making and clear authority responsibility relationship.

12. Organic Organisational Structure

- It is given by **Burns and Stalker**, which is opposite to mechanistic.
- There focus was on becoming horizontal organisations with lesser rules and regulations. Thus, they are highly flexible.
- There is minimal managerial layers and no direct administration. However, there is lesser specialisation in job.
- It is flat structured and promotes quick communication because of lesser complexity.
- It is similar to boundary less organisations.

13. Vertical Organisational Structure/Tall Organisation

- It is traditional structure with many levels of management.
- There are additional levels of communication. The goals and mission values are clearly communicated with the subordinates.
- There is top notch specialisation and it can be sustained in such organisation structure. There is delay in communication as it has to pass through various layers which leads to delay in decision-making.
- The lower level management does not take risks and initiative. Thus, it is also known as top-down management because it is characterised by central decision-making and lower level managers generally do not participate in decision-making.

14. Horizontal Organisational Structure/Flat Organisation

- It is propounded by **Douglas Smith** and **Frank Ostroff.** Rather than promoting functionality flat structure aims at promoting cooperation, teamwork and orientation towards customers. There are 3-5 core processes.
- This is achieved by removing unproductive work, merging disjointed activities and tasks and reducing the activities within each procedure. Multidisciplinary and cross functional groups are formed who do not need constant supervision.
- The aim of the organisation is earning profits and satisfying the customers. The employees directly interact with the customers, suppliers.
- The lower level management is equiped with data in order to promote decision-making at lower levels also. It focuses on training and empowering lower level employees. It also promotes skill development, collaboration, cooperation and openness among the employees to boost creativity. Employees are rewarded for developing multiple skills.
- It enhances quick decision-making. There is no accountability and responsibility and reporting by subordinates.

15. No Boundary Organisational Structure

- It is a contemporary model which was introduced by **GE Motors** Chairman, **Jack Welch**. It is best suited for a multinational organisation.
- It aims at eliminating horizontal and vertical boundaries present in the institution and reducing or breaking down the external barriers between the company and its stakeholders like suppliers and customers.
- *Various measures are taken to remove vertical barriers such as*
  (a) Participative decision-making.
  (b) Cross hierarchical teams comprising of lower level managers, top level managers and middle level managers.
  (c) 360 degree performance appraisal.
- *Various actions are taken to eradicate horizontal barriers such as*
  (a) Making cross functional teams encouraging team building on the basis of process and not functions.
  (b) Horizontal or lateral transfers.
  (c) Rotation of employees to and from different functions.
- Removal of external boundaries takes place by the formulation of a strategic alliance with the consumers and suppliers. Thus, this organisation helps in achieving a global advantage.

16. Virtual Organisational Structure

- It is also known as network structures. It is a small organisation in comparison to traditional organisational structures. It depends on outsourcing key business tasks.
- There is no departmentalisation and it focuses on building relationships *via* a network with other organisation of the world located in different geographical areas.
- It enters into various contracts such as marketing, distribution, research and development.
- It is based on the internet and electronic technology which deals with other virtual organisations and brick and mortar companies as well.
- It is flexible, impermanent and opportunistic which focuses on core capabilities and coordination is done with the help of networking. *e.g.* IBM, Reebok, Nike etc.

17. Inverted Pyramid Organisational Structure

- The customers are prioritised and kept at the top as they have the key role in driving business.
- The lower level management or front line workers who directly deal with the customers are also given top position. The top level management such as the CEO remains at the lower level and takes back seat.
- Hence, in this organisation, lower management supports upper management rather than receiving commands from upper management.
- It enables communication without any barrier. Policies are framed in accordance with the actual environment, *i.e.* the customer's demand.

18. Linking Pin Organisational Structure

- It is the model developed by **Rensis Likert.**
- It is based on the fact that each individual in the organisation works as a linking pin. It links the lower divisions with the upper division, thus there is overlapping of work and responsibilities. Therefore, a single individual is a key member in two distinct groups.

Organisational Design

It is the process that aligns the aims and objectives of the organisation with the structure with the aim of increasing effectiveness. An organisational structure defines the formal relations and roles of employees.

It is a step-by-step process in which the organisation focuses on defective procedures, systems, structures and work flow, restructures them according to the new business requirements and then formulates plans to incorporate the new moderations.

Elements of Organisational Design

Work Specialisation How the activities should be divided and to what extent?

Chain of Command Groups and individual should report to whom?

Formalisation What should be the number of regulations?

Departmental How the grouping of jobs should be done?

The Span of Control A manager can manage how many subordinates effectively?

Centralisation and Decentralisation Where does the authority of making decision lie?

Work Specialisation

It is the process of splitting up the work into a smaller and single task and it is done as a single process but cannot be handled by a single worker individually. It is also known as the division of labour.

When an individual does a task continuously, he gains specialisation in. It is done by a large organisation where there are elongated processes of performing a specific job.

The complicated jobs are broken into various segments and experts are hired to perform the jobs. Thus, it is a crucial element in the organisational design. The more complex job, the more division of labour, the more positions are to be filled with competent labour.

This element promotes excellence in work, good payment for the expertise, increases productivity and fosters upward growth for the company. The work is done without supervision because the job performers are experts in their fields. There is minimum wastage of resources.

Limitations of work specialisation are

- The workers are not suitable for the managerial position.
- The worker may get bored doing performing the same activity again and again.
- There are no socialising opportunities available to the worker and he cannot take breaks and curbs creativity which results into absenteeism.

Chain of Command

It is the continuous line of authority which starts from the top level management and runs down to the lower level management. It specifies who will command whom and who should report to whom. It is based on the principle of unity of command and authority.

Authority is the power exercised by the higher levels over lower levels. These are the rights to command, direct orders and believe these commands to be followed. Each person is given a special place in the command chain, hence each superior has authority to a certain extent. Unity of command states that a worker should be headed by only one boss. This element prevents conflicts and confusion in the organisation.

Formalisation

It is the extent to which the tasks are standardised within an institution. It is associated with set standards, rules, techniques and procedures that are laid by the top management. The focus is more on setting standards rather than the people in the organisation.

This element aims at promoting standardisation and clarity in the work of the organisation. There is negligible choice or opinion about what work is to be done, how it is to be done and when is it to be done? The subordinate has no option to do the work according to his creativity.

The result of formalisation is constant and identical output. The rules, techniques and procedures are explicitly mentioned in the rules and job descriptions. It aims are justifying and rationalising the decision-making in the organisation.

Departmentation

It is a process of dividing a large and complex organisation into smaller, flexible administrative units called departments or divisions. It is the organisation wide division of work into various departments. It refers to horizontal differentiation in an organisation. It is also known as departmentalisation.

The divisions of work on the basis of specialisation of the department. It is found in private and public organisations. According to **Louis A Allen**, "Divisionalisation is a means of the large and monolithic functional organisation into smaller flexible administrative units."

Significance of Departmentation

- It facilitates/organisation's structure supports.
- It describes responsibility and provides flexibility.
- It is the scope of diversification and growth.
- It promotes specialisation and increases efficiency.
- It facilitates control and promotes coordination.
- It shares organisation's resources.

Departmentation by Function

Functional department is the most widely used basis for organising activities at different levels of the management hierarchy. These basic functions are determined on the basis of their necessity and importance to the achievement of organisational objectives. It promotes centralisation at top level.

Departmentation by Product

It is also called as divisionalisation, is adopted in the case of a multi-product enterprise where the products are relatively complex and a great deal of capital and manpower is required for the plant. Here, product lines become diversified and volume of production is large, *e.g.* automobile and electronic industries. The contribution of each product line to organisational profit can be evaluated easily.

Departmentation by Territory

Large companies that distribute products or services on a massive scale nationally, often cannot coordinate all regions from the headquarters. Each region of the country has distinct needs, tastes and facilities that demand coordination.

Geographic departmentation helps in exploiting local advantages. Decisions regarding product design, pricing and marketing may be left to the discretion of territorial managers who know the needs of local people better. Here, all the activities in a given area is divided into zones, regions, sections and branches.

Departmentation by Customer

The basic idea behind departmentation on the basis of customer is to provide service to clearly identified group of customers. Such an organisation helps managers to satisfy the customer's requirements more efficiently and successfully. Such forms of departmentation are more common in banking, book publishing and food industry.

Departmentation by Process/Equipment

Under the departmentation by process or equipment, activities are grouped on the basis of various manufacturing processes. This is generally done in production department, at floor level, in manufacturing process. *e.g.* Departments for drilling, grinding, welding, assembling, finishing, packaging etc. Similar types of labour and equipments are brought together in one department.

Departmentation by Time

In some organisations, where the work is performed round the clock like in railway, post and telegraph offices, hospitals, BPOs etc the departmentation is based on time and work is divided into shifts.

Span of Control

It is also called as span of management. It refers to the number of subordinates that report to one supervisor. In other words, it can be defined as the number of subordinates that a manager can control or supervise. But, there is a limitation on the number of people that a manager can effectively manage because of certain constraints like time, energy, skills and so on.

To overcome these limitations, every manager has to delegate work to as many subordinates as he can properly manage.

It has two types

Narrow When a single supervisor controls very few number of subordinates, then it is termed as narrow span. It results into multiple hierarchical levels, *i.e.* tall structure.

Wider Span When a single supervisor controls, instructs or check more number of subordinates (1:20), then it is wider span of management, the wider the control, the flatter is the structure.

Factors Determining Span of Control

1. **Physiological Capacity of a Manager** Psychological factors like attitude, personality, decision-making, leadership determine the span of management. Managers with these qualities can control wider span.
2. **Capacity of Subordinates** Subordinates with high trainability knowledge and skills can be easily managed and do not require much supervision. Hence, the manager can have wider span. In case, subordinates are efficient in doing their duties, manager can control wider span.
3. **Nature of Work** Unskilled, routine and simple work requires less supervision, hence under span of management, while complex and technical work requires lesser span. It is also affects the span of control. If the tasks are of routine nature with less changes in functioning, the manger can cover wider span of management.
4. **Availability of Time for Supervision** If the top level management invests time in planning, organising, directing, then it will have narrower span. However, the lower level management will practice wider span.
5. **Planning Quality** If rules and policy are free from confusion, then there is no requirement of constant supervision, hence there can be wider span. Unclear plans require narrower span.
6. **Physical Dispersion** If more workers are located in a single place, then there can be effective management, facilitating wider span.
7. **Control** If the organisation wants supervisors to personally monitor the subordinates then it will lead to narrower span. If the management works with the principle of MBO, then it can practice wider span.
8. **Dynamism** If organisation's policies are stable, then there is lesser requirement of close supervision, hence, wider span. If policies change rapidly, then narrower span.
9. **Degree of Decentralisation** Higher is the degree of decentralisation, wider is the span of management. A manager with clear authority can deflagrate responsibility clearly on the subordinates.
10. **Communication Techniques** If one uses advance techniques of communication like email, voice mail, video conferencing, he can supervise more number of people, thus wider span of management can be controlled.

Span of Management in Vertical and Horizontal Structure

A narrow span throughout an organisation causes vertical structure with large number of levels in hierarchy. This creates problems both in terms of cost and efficiency as extra cost is incurred on various managers sitting at different levels in hierarchy. Also, the communication has to travel through scalar chain which not only delays it to reach appropriate points, but it also gets distorted or manipulated. Also, the vertical structure presents problems in coordination.

A wider span of management results in flat horizontal structure with few levels of hierarchy. Communication chain is shorter, though there is more cross communication. In flat structures, people feel more autonomy and develop independent spirit. It also reduces cost of managing organisation.

To take advantage of flat structure, many large MNCs are following wide span of management. It leads to decentralisation and allows for increasing size of organisation. A span of 8 to 10 is considered best.

Graicunas Theory

V.A. Graicunas has described in each organisation three specific types of superior-subordinate relationships, leading to the question of the total count of subordinates that a superior can properly manage. *They are the following*

1. **Direct Single Relationship** This refers to relations that are identified easily and clearly by the individuals who are his immediate subordinate. They are equal to the administered number of subordinates. For instance, if X has three subordinates, three direct single relationships would exist. This is identified as Direct Relationship Number = n.
2. **Direct Group Relationships** This implies group relationships between the top and every possible subordinate combination. A manager has opportunities to counsel, confer advice, inform or discuss with any or all of the subordinates present.

   This kind of relationship occurs in all possible combinations between the superior and his group of subordinates. A manager having three subordinates would have three direct group relationships. The formula for the same will be $n(2^{n-1} - 1)$, where n is the subordinate number.
3. **Cross Relationships** They are shared relationships between subordinates that are needed to work under the same boss. This results from the need for a common superior's subordinates to consult with each other.

Graicunas created the formula as a result of this analysis of the three types of relationships to give the total number of all three types of relationships. The formula is $n(2^{n/2} + n + 1)$ where n is the number of subordinates.

Centralisation

According to **Louis A Allen**, "Centralisation is the systematic and consistent reservation of authority at central points within the organisation."

Power and authority are concentrated at the top levels only. It facilitates in early stages of organisational growth to provide for integration among all departments to achieve a common goal.

The top management is responsible for making key decisions and subordinates and lower departments are only into the implementation of the rules. The lower department does not have any authority over their functions. However, they are accountable to the higher management. The top level formulates policies, middle level managers operate the policies and lower level management performs the work in reality.

Advantages of Centralisation

- It provides opportunity for new managers to develop personal leadership.
- It facilitates integration of efforts of all parts of the organisation.
- Duplication of efforts and activities are avoided.
- Emergencies can be handled fastly by quick decisions and prompt actions.
- It helps in reducing wastage of efforts, hence bring economy in operation.
- It facilitates product growth and diversification. Proportionate and balanced emphasis can be given to all products.

Disadvantages of Centralisation

- It is not appropriate for the organisations where there a large scale of operations, with various branches, locations and departments.
- The top level manager is overburdened and overloaded with responsibilities as he does micro management.
- The subordinates will be less motivated as they do not participate in decision-making.
- The organisation will not be able to adjust to the changing environment as there are less flexibility and more control in decision-making.
- The manager is not able to focus on core activities and spends time performing non-programmed activities.

Decentralisation

It is an extension of the concept of delegation. It actually refers to the degree to which authority is delegated to lower levels. It gives added responsibility to managers at all level below the top. Only those responsibilities are left which can be exercised centrally only or by top management.

The centres of decision-making are dispersed throughout the organisation. It is considered as 'Golden Calf' of management philosophy of new era.

Decentralisation can be comprehended as the logical and systematised assignment of power and authority, all over managerial levels in the institution. It presents how the power is distributed at various managerial levels.

It is opposite to centralisation where the power is concentrated at the centre. Hence, it includes disseminating the authority and function from the centre of the organisation to various levels.

According to **Louis A Allen**, "Decentralisation refers to tire systematic effort to delegate to the lowest levels all authority except that which can only be exercised at central points".

Factors affecting Degree of Decentralisation

- The cost involved in decision-making and decentralisation. It also depends on the background and history of the enterprise, its size, change in environment.
- It checks if the organisation have many managers.
- It checks whether the subunits desire independence and whether the subordinates are able to cope up with the change.

Advantages of Decentralisation

- It reduces the workload of overburdened senior executives.
- It brings the decision-making process closer to the actions without any delays.
- It facilitates product diversification. Each product division has a separate management.
- It gives individuals an opportunity to learn by doing through the freedom of decision-making and better control.
- It often results in effective controls and performance measurements at lower levels.
- Most advantage is of profit center principle for large multi-product firms.
- It facilitates quick decision-making and better control.
- It developes managerial skill of the subordinate.

Disadvantages of Decentralisation

- Conflicts between divisional heads.
- Costs increases due to large group of managerial staff for each division.
- Decentralisation demands training programmes that may be time consuming and highly expensive.
- Increases risk as tasks are delegated.
- It is not suitable for services that require specialist knowledge.

Delegation of Authority

Delegation is the process by which manager assigns as many operating tasks as possible to subordinates by virtue of his authority and concentrates his efforts on managerial tasks. Manager grants certain duties on others in the form of work and authority.

According to **Allen**, "The entrustment of a part or responsibility and authority to another and the creation of accountability for performance."

Characteristics of Delegation

- It is two sided relationship between a senior and a subordinate in granting and accepting authority based on act of trust and confidence.
- It gives freedom to think, decide and manage on his own. It creates dependency relationship between senior and subordinate.
- The manager delegating the task should have authority of the task himself. However, the entire authority cannot be delegated.
- There is no delegation of responsibility and the superior can exercise his power over the subordinate even after delegation.

Types of Delegation

Specific Delegation Assigning particular function or single task, generally done by middle level manager.

General Delegation Tasks such as planning, staffing, directing etc are delegated. It is done by top level manager.

Formal Delegation When duties are delegated according to the formal structure of delegation.

Informal Delegation It occurs because of situations and not formal organisation's structure.

Lateral Delegation When the subordinate does not follow formal verticle hierarchy and seeks any other superior for guidance, it is called lateral delegation.

Reserved Authority The authority which is not delegated by the superior.

Delegated Authority The authority is given by the superior to his subordinate is delegated authority.

Effective Delegation

The following guidelines helps managers to delegate effectively

- Select subordinates according to their skills, experience and past results.
- Provide guidance, training, advice as and when required, to delegates.
- Define goals, responsibilities and expected results to the subordinate and motivate them to perform their delegated tasks.
- Provide complete freedom to act on his own. Allow the subordinates to see the big picture and create an atmosphere of trust, confidence and cooperation.
- Establish adequate standards against which the subordinate can measure and evaluate his own performance. Self-control is more effective than a system of external control imposed from superiors.

Difference between Decentralisation and Delegation

Basis	Delegation	Decentralisation
Definition	It means handing over an authority from superior to subordinate	When delegation of authority is performed systematically and to the lowest level, the final outcome is decentralisation
Nature	Technique of Management	Philosophy of Management
Accountability	Superiors are accountable for the acts done by subordinates	Department heads are accountable for the acts of the concerned department
Relationship	Creates superior subordinate relationship	A step towards creation of semi-autonomou s units
Control	The ultimate control in the hands of superior	The overall control vests with top management and delegates authority for day-to-day control to departmental heads
Liberty of work	Subordinates do not have full freedom	A substantial amount of freedom is there

Staffing

It is a managerial function which aims at putting persons to work. It aims to find right person for the right work. It forms a part of HRM.

According to **Dalton E McFarland**, "Staffing is the function by which manager builds an organisation through the recruitment, selection, development of individuals as capable employees."

According to **Koontz** and **O'Donnell**, "The managerial function of staffing involves managing the organisational structure through the proper and effective selection appraisal and development of personnel to fit the roles designed into the structure."

Features of Staffing

- It is a crucial managerial function because human resource runs the organisation, thus the selection and retention of competent human resource is crucial and critical.
- The process is never ending which starts with recruitment, training, transfers, promotions, appraisals etc. These functions are continuous in nature.
- The basic resource here is human.
- It is a complex function as it deals with humans. Each person has different behaviour and attitude. This dynamism creates complexity in staff.

Significance of Staffing

- It helps in obtaining suitable candidates for the organisation.
- High performance, when the right person is hired for the right job, the organisation experiences high productivity.
- With effective staffing, the organisation can attain high growth rate and may continue to survive in long run.
- Proper staffing also helps in improving job satisfaction of employees. This boosts the morale of the employee and they become content with their work and organisation.
- Staffing forms basis of other managerial functions. All the functions of the organisation are performed by humans and humans are introduced to the organisation through staffing.
- Efficient staffing also helps in optimum utilisation of resources. Staffing ensures that adequate number of people are staffed. This saves high amount of funds from being wasted on unnecessary remuneration.

Process of Staffing

1. **Human Resource Planning** (HRP) It deals with estimating the manpower requirements as this encompasses estimating and deciding how many people are required and what kind of skills are required in the firm.

   There are two techniques which helps in manpower estimation, *which are as follows*
   - **Workload Analysis** It assesses the quantity of human resource required alongwith determining the type of people required.
   - **Workforce Analysis** It deals with determination of type of workforce already available in the organisation. This helps in ascertaining how many employees are working, what are their skills, is the organisation overly staffed or understaffed etc.
2. **Recruitment** This process probes and searches for prospective and potential candidates and prompting them to apply for the said job.

   According to **Edwin Flippo**, "Recruitment is the process of searching for prospective employees and stimulating them to apply for jobs in the organisation. Recruitment is done before selection or employment of workers."

   There are various sources through which employees are recruited. There are internal sources and external sources of recruitment.
3. **Selection** This process deals with screening the potential candidates. The candidates have to take various tests such as analytical test, aptitude test, IQ test, which enable the firm in deciding and selecting the best candidate. Only those candidates who have cleared previous stages are sent to next stages and for the interview as well.

   It is negative process because it involves rejection of incompetent candidates and selection of one best candidate for each post.
4. **Placement and Induction** On the day of joining, the employee is supposed to be placed on the position for which he has been selected and is best suited. Induction is the process where the employee is introduced or oriented towards the new organisation, its procedures, rules and objectives.
5. **Training and Development** Once the employee reports on duty and is introduced to the work, it is the duty of the manager to train the candidate for performing the said job. The existing capacities of the newly recruited staff have to be developed and channelised to attain the organisation's objectives.

6. **Appraisal** It is a process where there is a discussion between the employee and the manager. The employee is rated on the basis of his performance and other criterias set by the organisation. It is structured and standardised for all employees. It helps in taking decision about the requirement of training, transfer, demotion, promotion or simply removal from the job.
7. **Promotion** The next step is promotion. If the appraisal shows that the employee has developed various skills and he is capable of holding higher and challenging situations, then he is promoted to the next level of the hierarchy. Promotion gives increased salary and greater prestige and authority to the employee.
8. **Compensation and Remuneration** Human resources are to be remunerated or compensated for the services rendered by them. The final step is making equal and fair remuneration to the person. This step is important because a just remuneration system will make the employee satisfied and will keep him motivated for longer run.

Direction

It is the process in which the managers instruct, guide and oversee the performance of the workers to achieve pre-determined goals.

It takes place after planning, organising and staffing. Directing can either lead to success or failure.

Haimann defines "Direction as the process and technique of issuing instructions and making certain that operations are carried out as planned".

Newman and Warren defined "Direction actively dealing with the steps a manager takes to get subordinates and others to carry out plans".

According to **Marshall**, "Directing involve determining the course, giving order and instruction and providing dynamic leadership".

According to **GR Terry**, "Directins means activating and moving into action supplying simulative power to the group."

Features of Direction

- Performed at every level of management that means it is all pervasive and the manager at every level provides guidance and inspiration to his subordinates.
- A continuous process as it is required through out the left of the organisation.
- Is initiated at the top level and followed to bottom through hierarchy.
- Serves dual purpose (a) aims at getting things done by subordinates (b) to free superiors for other important work.
- Directing deals with an objective of change in human behaviour by way of leading, motivating or communicating. Thus, apart from rules and legislations, the religion, customs and beliefs of the employee also affect directing.

Importance of Direction

Direction plays an important role as every action is initiated through direction, *which can be seen as follows*

- It helps in initiating action and it is the first function where the execution of work begins.
- It integrates the efforts of individuals in the organisation. No department can function in isolation, thus various elements of direction helps in integrating all the levels of organisation.
- Direction enhances the morale and performance of the employee by way of motivation, leadership and effective communication.
- Direction helps in bringing stability in the organisation as with effective leadership, the conflicts can be minimised. It also helps in bringing change.

Principles of Direction

- It provides adequate satisfaction.
- Facilitates harmony of objective.
- Facilitates effective supervision.
- It promotes effective leadership.
- It works on the system of effective feedback.

Elements of Directing

Supervision It means to carry out managerial functions of planning, organising etc at various levels of management. Top managers supervise activities of middle managers who further 'supervise' activities of lower managers. The term 'supervisor' is generally associated with managers at the lowest level who look over activities of workers. They interact face-to-face with the company's employees and act as a link between managers and workforce.

Motivation It is a force that drives a person into action that leads to accomplishing goals of the organisation. Every employee is driven towards his own needs, emotions and other factors. Manager use motivation to direct human behaviour towards organisation's goals. A good motivator change the perception of employees and directs their behaviour towards appropriate rewards.

Leadership It is the ability of an individual to influence others to accomplish an objective and direct the organisation to make it more effective. It is the process to build confidence and zeal among people and attain specified goals. A leader conducts and guides others and is followed by disciplines in any profession.

Communication It is the systematic process of transfer of ideas, opinions, information, feelings etc to a receiver who gives feedback. Effective communication involves sending messages at a minimum cost, in the most impactful way. Communication can be done formally as well as informally by managers to create a good relationship with subordinates and lead them to achievement of their goals.

Controlling

Controlling is one of the managerial functions like planning, organising, directing and staffing. It is an important function because it helps to check the errors and to take the corrective action so that deviation from standards are minimised and stated goals of the organisation are achieved in desired manner.

Some important definitions of controlling are given below

According to **Terry** and **Franklin**, "Controlling is determining; what is being accomplished that is evaluating performance and if necessary applying corrective measures so that the performance takes place according to plans."

According to **Henry Fayol**, "Control of an undertaking consists of seeing that everything is being carried out in accordance with the plan which has been adopted, the orders which have been given and the principles which have been laid down. Its object is to point out mistakes in order that they may be rectified and prevented from recurring."

According to **EFL Breach**, "Control is checking current performance against pre-determined standards contained in the plans, with a view to ensure adequate progress and satisfactory performance."

According to **Harold Koontz**, "Controlling is the measurement and correction of performance in order to make sure that enterprise objectives and plans devised to attain them are accomplished."

Features of Controlling

- Control looks forward as it aims at controlling what will happen in the future.
- It is also a backward looking process because it constantly looks at the past performance.
- It is a continuous process. The manager is able to control the action. There is a specific time table which is to revised and followed on daily, monthly and yearly basis.
- It is an integrated and well coordinated system.
- It is exercised at all the managerial levels from bottom till the top.
- The dominant function of any manager is to control the activities in their departments.
- Control is an affirmative process because it effectively uses various resources. It is a negative process because it cuts down the misuse of resources.
- Controlling goes hand-in-hand with planning. Controlling is based on certain pre-defined standards which are used as benchmarks to measure the performance. These standards are set in the process of planning only. Contrarily, if the management does not measure and compare the actual performance, then plans cannot be revised or altered.

Significance of Controlling

1. **Accomplishment of Organisational Goals** This function concentrates on execution of plans and their performance. Due to this close and careful watch, the organisation is able to reach its goals.
2. **Promotes Better Coordination** It gives direction to various activities and facilitates coordination. Various departments and activities are controlled by pre-set standards. Thus, work is done in an orderly fashion.
3. **Efficient Use of Resources** As controlling promotes effective use of human resource, physical alongwith financial resources, there is minimum wastage because their use is predefined.
4. **Employee's Motivation is Enhanced** Standards are set well in advance, this assists the employee in understanding what is expected from them. He himself keeps an eye on the standards and performs accordingly.
5. **Discipline and Order** Controlling reduces the probability of corrupt behaviour because the goals are pre-determined and the manager keeps a close watch over the performance and activities of the employee. Thus, it promotes order and discipline.
6. **Enhances Delegation** Control focuses on defining the duties and authorities. It also facilitates delegation of authority as it promotes sense of relationship with the organisation.

Process of Controlling

1. **Establishing Performance Standard** Performance standards are the benchmark which are used for measuring the performance. They can be prescribed in

qualitative as well as quantitative terms. They should be capable of modification so that they can be changed whenever required.

2. **Measuring Actual Performance** Measurement should be done with reliable tools and techniques. The objective of measurement should be clearly defined. The measurement of performance should be done in the same units which are described in the standards. Performance should be measured frequently and repeatedly. Techniques to measure includes personal observation, performance reports, sample checking and accounting ratios.
3. **Comparison of Standards and Actual Performance** It is done to figure out any 'deviation'. Deviation is the gap between what was expected and what is actually achieved by the organisation.
4. **Analysing Deviations** If there are any deviations then the control manager identifies the cause of such deviation. There is an acceptable range in which the range or degree of deviation is pre-defined, alongwith some key result areas. *It includes*
    - **Critical Point Control** (CPC) It focuses on 'Key Result Areas' (KRAs). These are the activities or range which are important or crucial for the success of the institution. It is impossible and uneconomical to keep an eye on all the activities, hence only critical areas are monitored.
    - **Management by Exception** (MBE) It is rightly said, when a manager focuses on controlling all the activities, he is unable to control anyone of them. Hence, the concept of MBE has emerged, where only significant deviations are focused upon. Those deviations which are under acceptable range are avoided.
    - **Taking Corrective Actions** Once the deviations are analysed and the causes are identified, the managers take remedial acts to curtail the deviation. If the deviations are within permissible range then such deviations are ignored.

    e.g.

Causes	Corrective Action
(i) Outdated machinery	Up gradation of outdated technology
(ii) Defects in manufacturing process	Modify specification standards
(iii) Defects in material used	Modify the quality benchmark for material
(iv) Abnormal physical conditions	Modify and improve the environment

Types of Organisational Controls

Control can focus on the activities, events before, during or after the process. They are formally called feedforward, concurrent and feedback control system respectively.

These are as follows

1. **Feed Forward** This is also known as preventive control or preliminary control which aims at identifying and preventing deviations in the standards before they actually occur. They focus on the financial resources human and material resources in the organisation such as selection of right candidates.
2. **Concurrent Controls** They monitor ongoing employee activity to ensure consistency with the quality standards, regulations, rules for guiding employee behaviours and tasks. They aim at ensuring that the work activities give desired results. Thus, in concurrent control employees monitor the activities during the process.
3. **Feedback Control** This involves visiting back, or reviewing information to determine whether performance meets established standards. Thus, it looks back after the event has finished.

Techniques of Controlling

1. **Direct Observation and Surveillance** It is the traditional technique which is done by supervisor himself. He remains in immediate contact with the worker. He gets first hand message, knowledge and information. This is best suited for small scale enterprises.
2. **Financial Statements** Various financial statements are prepared which give quantitative analysis. *e.g.* Balance sheet, profit and loss account, cash flow statement. They keep in comparison with organisation's standards alongwith industrys' standards. Ratio analysis is a popular technique used that helps in measuring liquidity, profitability and activity.
3. **Budgetary Control** A budget is an instrument that assists in both planning as well as controlling. It is the essence of controlling the finances of the organisation. It is done for various financial aspects such as production, cash, sales etc.
4. **Break-even Analysis** BE means a situation where there is no profit or no loss. It helps in determining the company's performance thus it is an effective control device.
5. **Return on Investment** (RoI) It is an important technique that ascertains how much return is generated on the investment made. The financial manager pre-defines a set target of RoI to be achieved. Then the actual RoI is calculated and compared with the desired RoI.

6. **Management by Objectives** (MBO) It is again a technique based on planning and controlling. Various objectives are set by the superior boss for individuals. The manager undertakes periodic evaluation. He also practices regular feedback in order to perform evaluation of the performance. If the individual has achieved his objective, then he is rewarded.
7. **Management Audit** This audit is done to evaluate the work of the management as one single body. All the underlying processes of management starting from planning till controlling are critically examined and evaluated. Data is gathered from past records, employees and clients, this information is then interpreted and results are obtained.
8. **Management Information System** (MIS) It is a system that gathers and arranges various information required by the management. This information can be external or internal. It helps in identifying the problems and ascertaining remedy for such solutions, because of prompt, relevant and reliable database of information.
9. **PERT/CPM Techniques** It is a significant technique which aims at examining the total time required to complete one activity and total cash outlay required to do the specific job. Critical activities are identified and importance is given to these activities. The time of completion of critical activity is controlled.
10. **Self-control** The individual is given liberty to formulate his individual targets, measure his own performance and take remedial measure on his own as per his individual requirement. Self-control is the best control technique because it frees the boss from micro management.

Coordination

By now, we have seen various functions that are performed in an organisations. These functions are planning, directing, staffing, organising etc. However, there is another function which coordinates among all these functions. It is coordination.

The objectives of all the aforementioned functions are supposed to be in harmony with the overall goals of the institution. Thus, coordination is important to synchronise the working of these individual functions to attain one common objective.

Coordination promotes unity of activities and efforts of different groups, individuals and departments; and promotes harmony in performing different activities simultaneously.

According to **Henry Fayol**, "Coordination harmonises, synchronises and unifies individual efforts for better action and for the achievement of the business objectives."

According to **McFarland**, "Coordination is the process whereby an executive develops an orderly pattern of group efforts among his subordinates and secures unity of action in the pursuit of common purpose."

Features of Coordination

- Inter relates various parts of work and job.
- Promotes good relationship between employees especially those belonging to different departments.
- Develops cordial relationship with outsiders including stakeholders, government and investors.
- It plays significant role in large organisations as there are numerous employees and departments. Hence, there is a high probability of conflicts, effective coordination reduces the chances of disharmony.
- It is also called the essence of management because it's functions spreads to all the levels of management, all the departments and all the branches as well.
- It eventually reconciles the objectives, aims and goals of different organisational groups.

Need of Coordination

Growth in Size As the size of the firm grows, there is greater need of coordination to integrate the work of various organisational departments.

Functional Differentiation There are separate wings in each organisations. These departments have distinct objectives, strategies and policies. Hence, to avoid any disharmony coordination among all is required.

Specialisation Specialists are hired in order to perform specified task such as HR manager, finance manager, operation manager etc. Each specialist perceives his work to be superior to another, which usually results in conflict. Here, coordination again plays the role of umpire and promotes harmony in organisation.

Coordination is an Integral Function

Coordination through Planning Planning helps in coordinating by encompassing various plans and strategies through mutual exchange of thoughts and discussion.

Coordination through Organisation While organising resources, the primary thought of the manager is coordination. He assigns the work and groups the activities and synches them with other activities of the organisation.

Coordination through Staffing Coordinating helps in pre-determination of the new staff and where will it be placed. Managers ensure coordination between the jobs and the personnel recruited for it.

Coordination through Directing It is a part of direction. Coordination aims at giving clarity to the manager. The orders, guidance, motivation is done in synchronisation (coordination) with other organisational goals and activities.

Coordination through Controlling Coordination forms part of the reporting process. The focus of the manager is to coordinate and ensure that there is no difference between the desired results and actual results.

Types of Coordination

1. Internal Coordination

- **Vertical and Horizontal Coordination** It is very important to have healthy communication channel and synchronisation of both vertically and horizontally means among the peer groups of different departments, *e.g.* production, marketing, personal, finance etc.
- **Substantive and Procedural Coordination** Every organisational work is comprised of two dimensions substantive dimension and procedure dimension. Substantive dimension involves deciding 'what to do' and procedural dimension involves 'how to do'. Both the functions in every organisation are equally important and high degree of coordination is required to get the desired results.

2. External Coordination

It refer to coordination between an organisation and its external environment, *e.g.* investors and financers, customers, suppliers, government agencies, media, public etc. Every organisation works as input-output mediator.

So, we may say that higher the degree of coordination with all the outside agencies, higher the output in terms of organisational goals.

Principles of Coordination

The classical management thinker **Mary Parker Follett** suggested four basic principles of co-ordination and two were added later on, *which are as follows*

Principle of Direct Contact It is based on the theme that coordination can never be achieved by freedom, authority, power, order, instruction, coercion but by mutual understanding, good relationship, better communication skills, open discussions and informal gatherings where direct contact with the others is facilitated.

Coordination at Early Stage Conflict, disagreement, hospitality, indifference will be reduced if coordination has been tried at the early stage of work cycles that is at the planning stage. If the members have been involved in decision-making process, then they will realise the problems and will not create the hurdles.

Principle of Continuity Coordination is a continuous, perpetual, never ending process and should be done on regular basis; it emerges with the organisation and ends with it.

Principle of Dynamics Change is the only factor which is constant and changes in the organisation occur externally as well as internally. Many organisational practices do get out-of-date when organisational changes take place. Coordination work on dynamic basis rather than rigid and fixed basis.

Principle of Timing It states that timing of various organisational performances should synchronise with each other so that no wastage of time and others resources is there.

Principle of Reciprocal Relationship In every organisation, all the departments are correlated with each other affect each others' performance, though the amount of reciprocity may not be equal. The principle of reciprocal relationship states that the way of performing such functions should be altered in such a way that these affect each other positively.

EXAM BASED QUESTIONS

1 Planning function in any enterprise is
(a) a short-term
(b) a continuous process
(c) done in emergencies
(d) top management's will

2 Examination of alternative courses of action is an activity which falls under
(a) planning function (b) organisation function
(c) direction function (d) control function

3 Planning function of management is primarily performed by
(a) top management (b) middle management
(c) lower management (d) All of these

4 Policy making is an important part of the process of
(a) planning (b) coordinating
(c) organising (d) motivating

5 A special kind of plan formulated in order to meet the challenge of competitors is called
(a) single use plan (b) programme
(c) strategy (d) projects

6 The necessity of planning arises because of the fact that business organisation have to
(a) operate (b) survive
(c) progress (d) All of these

7 Which is not a step in planning?
(a) Determination of objectives for the organisation
(b) Forecasting
(c) Decision-making
(d) Welfare activities

8 Arrange the following activities in correct sequence.
1. Organising 2. Planning
3. Directing 4. Staffing
5. Controlling
Codes
(a) 1,2,3,4,5 (b) 2, 1,4,3,5
(c) 2,4,1,5,3 (d) 2, 4,1,3,5

9 Corporate planning encompasses
(a) strategic planning (b) selection
(c) automation (d) defamation

10 .... are rigid and their violation leads to punishment.
(a) Procedures (b) Methods
(c) Rules (d) Objectives

11 Which among the following is a planning as well as controlling technique?
(a) Procedure (b) Method
(c) Budget (d) Policy

12 The statement "management planning involves the development of forecasts, objectives, policies, programmes, procedures, schedules and budgets" is given by
(a) Henry Fayol (b) Koontz O' Donnell
(c) Louis A Allen (d) Theo Haimann

13 Which of the following statement about planning is correct?
(a) Planning does not involve control of activities
(b) Planning does not identify alternatives
(c) Planning does not result into selection of correct alternative
(d) Planning does not set goals

14 Which of the following is not a part of strategic planning?
(a) Social responsibility (b) Objectives
(c) Choice of business (d) Purpose and mission

15 Strategic planning in service organisations is all about
(a) where the organisation is heading
(b) where the organisation should be heading
(c) how the organisation needs to change in order to be more effective
(d) what the organisation intends to accomplish for the community

16 The most effective way to plan for the future is
(a) appoint a long range planning committee
(b) develop solid relationships throughout your organisation
(c) hold a retreat
(d) engage in strategic planning

17 The biggest challenge in planning for change is
(a) who will be affected by the change
(b) anticipating its unintended, unexpected outcomes
(c) deciding who should implement the change
(d) communicating why the change is needed

18 The overall process of decision-making in staff selection includes which of these stages?
(a) Deciding which candidate to appoint
(b) Identifying the need for a new member of staff
(c) Agreeing the job specification
(d) All of the above

19 Which of the factors listed below is not a reason for decision-making in organisations being a complex process?
(a) People have to make decisions in a historical context
(b) Several stakeholders will have an interest in the decision
(c) Factors in the current context of the organisation affect the decision
(d) Modern information systems enable people to evaluate a range of possible outcomes

20 A solution to a problem that is arrived at through an unstructured process of decision-making is called a

(a) bounded rationality (b) programmed decision
(c) non-programmed decision (d) uncertainty

21 As a manager moves to higher positions in an organisation, the ability to make .... becomes .... important.

(a) programmed, less (b) non-programmed, more
(c) non-programmed, less (d) programmed, much more

22 Which of the following is not a benefit of informal organisation to employees?

(a) Security (b) Status
(c) Self-actualisation (d) Social satisfaction

23 Advantages of participative decision-making include

(a) employees set higher goals for themselves
(b) more points of view are offered
(c) participants buy into the final decision
(d) All of the above

24 A/An .... organisation is a network of personal and social relations not established or required by the formal organisation and arising spontaneously as people associate with one another.

(a) informal (b) formal
(c) partly formal (d) strategic

25 Decision-making situations can be categorised along a scale which ranges from

(a) certainty to risk to uncertainty to ambiguity
(b) certainty to uncertainty to risk
(c) certainty to risk to uncertainty
(d) uncertainty to certainty to risk

26 Decision-making step, which consists of organisation goals, predicting alternatives and communicating goals is called

(a) organisation (b) alternation
(c) planning (d) valuing

27 What are the characteristics of a programmed decision?

(a) Routine and non-complex
(b) Low risk and certain
(c) Uncertain and non-routine
(d) Complex and risky

28 What is not an assumption underpinning the rational decision-making model?

(a) High level of certainty regarding the environment
(b) A structured problem
(c) An agreed goal
(d) Incomplete information

29 Simon (1960) is associated with what type of decision-making model?

(a) Programmed (b) Administrative
(c) Classical (d) Rational

30 .... decisions are non-repetitive in nature.

(a) Programmed (b) Non-programmed
(c) Operative (d) All of these

31 For planning and decision-making, the method that consists in analysing and stimulating is known as

(a) the model
(b) the marginal analysis
(c) the experiment
(d) All of the above

32 In which type of decision, the information system plays a critical role?

(a) Unprogrammed decisions
(b) Programmed decisions
(c) Experience decisions
(d) Top-level management decisions

33 Simon observes that serious blockades may occur at three levels of communication.

Which of the following is not one of them?

(a) Initiation (b) Transmission
(c) Reception (d) Noise

34 Almost all decisions need to be preceded by the same set of logical analyses. This is known as

(a) decision-making process
(b) logic of decision-making
(c) process of logic
(d) universality of decision-making process

35 For planning and decision-making, the method that consists in consulting the past, is known as

(a) experience (b) experiment
(c) the model (d) None of these

36 For planning and decision-making, the method that consists in trying out alternatives, is known as

(a) experience (b) experiment
(c) the model (d) None of these

37 Which of the following is not an important factor in decision-making?

(a) The name of the organisation
(b) Relevant facts gathered by the staff agencies
(c) Attitude of superiors and subordinates
(d) Competence and morale of the decision-making

38 The ability to follow a systematical, logical and thorough approach in decision-making is called

(a) Rationality (b) Feasibility
(c) Self-efficacy (d) Bounded rationality

39 Organisation is a process of

(a) identifying and grouping of work to be performed
(b) defining and delegating the responsibility and authority
(c) Both (a) and (b)
(d) None of the above

40 Organisation establishes relationship between
(a) people, work and resources
(b) customer, work and resources
(c) people, work and management
(d) customer, work and management

41 The organisational charts are used
(a) for giving the plan of action and the responsibilities of all employees
(b) for formulating things apart from social legitimacy
(c) for providing a picture of the organisation at a glance
(d) as manuals and statutes that define relationship between various offices

42 Responsibility always flows from
(a) superior to subordinate (b) subordinate to superior
(c) Both (a) and (b) (d) None of these

43 "No one on the organisation should have more than one boss" is a statement of
(a) principle of specialisation
(b) principle of authority
(c) principle of unity of command
(d) principle of span of control

44 The effective number of individuals to be supervised by a single superior or departmental head should be limited to .... in an average firm.
(a) six (b) ten
(c) fourteen (d) twenty

45 The following is not a type of organisational structure.
(a) Line organisation
(b) Functional organisation
(c) Line and staff organisation
(d) Flexible organisation

46 Organising aims to serve
(a) common purpose (b) co-operation
(c) authority structure (d) All of these

47 In which of the following organisational structure, each specialist is supposed to give his functional advice to all other foremen and workers?
(a) Line organisation
(b) Functional organisation
(c) Line and staff organisation
(d) All of the above

48 In hospitals, the following type of departmentation is common
(a) by function (b) by committee
(c) by geographical region (d) All of these

49 The following is also known as military organisation.
(a) Line organisation
(b) Functional organisation
(c) Line and staff organisation
(d) None of the above

50 In line organisation, the business activities are divided into following three types.
(a) Accounts, production, sales
(b) Production, quality, sales
(c) Production, quality, maintenance
(d) Production, maintenance, sales

51 The process of dividing the work and then grouping them into units and sub-units for the purpose of administration is known as
(a) departmentation
(b) organisational structure
(c) committee
(d) All of the above

52 Linking pin structure of the organisation was proposed by
(a) Scott (b) Kahn (c) Sherwood (d) Likert

53 The following is not a principle of organisation.
(a) Principle of exception (b) Principle of balance
(c) Principle of complexity (d) Principle of coordination

54 Which organisation structure is generally followed by big steel plants?
(a) Line organisation
(b) Functional organisation
(c) Line and staff organisation
(d) All of the above

55 A reporting relationship in which an employee receives orders from and reports to, only one supervisor is known as
(a) line of authority (b) centralisation
(c) unity of direction (d) unity of command

56 Organisation structure is primarily concerned with .... and .... of tasks and authority.
(a) allocation, delegation
(b) allocation, apportionment
(c) reporting, delegating
(d) setting standards, delegation

57 Authority always flows from
(a) superior to subordinate
(b) subordinate to superior
(c) Both (a) and (b)
(d) None of the above

58 As per the principle of balance, there should be balance between
(a) the activities
(b) authority and responsibility
(c) standardisation of procedures and flexibility
(d) All of the above

59 Departmentation is a process where
(a) tasks are grouped into jobs
(b) jobs are grouped into effective work groups
(c) work groups are grouped into identifiable segments
(d) All of the above

60 The department can be created
(a) by function (b) by product
(c) by process (d) All of these

61 Departmentation leads to grouping of
(a) activities (b) personnel
(c) Both (a) and (b) (d) None of these

62 The .... refers to the assignment of formal authority and responsibility to another person for carrying out specific activities.
(a) decentralisation of authority
(b) delegation of responsibility
(c) centralisation of authority
(d) delegation of authority

63 Why is decentralisation a significant tool in management?
(a) It helps you to dump your work on someone else
(b) It allows you to get rid of the distasteful tasks and assign to someone else
(c) It is a tool to help you achieve more and develop your people at the same time
(d) It allows you to punish the smart alecks with so much work they will never dig out

64 Decentralisation is a disadvantage due to
(a) growth and diversification
(b) lack of uniformity
(c) executive development
(d) All of the above

65 In a formal organisation, 'power' is associated with
(a) an individual (b) position
(c) relationship (d) control

66 The structure of organisation includes
(a) identification and classification of required activities
(b) informal organisation
(c) establishing enterprise objectives
(d) authority relationships

67 The degree to which an organisation relies on rules and procedures to direct the behaviour of employees is
(a) complexity
(b) formalisation
(c) centralisation
(d) motivation

68 One of the advantage of matrix structure is that
(a) it is easily understood by the people involved
(b) improved lateral communications
(c) product lines can be recognised as cost centres, it eases financial control
(d) top management has more time to devote to long-term strategic issues

69 Unity of command means
(a) parity of authority and responsibility
(b) flow of command from subordinate to superior
(c) flow of command from superior to subordinate
(d) parity in controlling

70 Which of the following activities should be performed by the superior in the process of delegation?
(a) Commensurate authority
(b) Clear responsibility
(c) Development the subordinates
(d) All of the above

71 Which of the following give rise to authority?
(a) Traditions (b) Legal positions
(c) Charisma in personality (d) All of these

72 Which of the following is a limitation of decentralisation?
(a) Does not aid organisation in adapting to the environment
(b) Gives managers more freedom
(c) Considerable expense for training managers
(d) Adds to burden on top management

73 Indicate which of the following is not among the six main types of organisational structure?
(a) Line organisation (b) Functional organisation
(c) Committees (d) Department

74 The willingness of subordinates to take on additional responsibilities is a factor that affects the degree of ....
(a) centralisation (b) decision-making
(c) decentralisation (d) controlling

75 .... is the unbroken line of authority linking each employee with the top most position in the organisation through a series of management posts.
(a) Unity of command (b) Chain of command
(c) Degree of command (d) Unity of direction

76 Restricted view of organisational goals is represented by deploying a
(a) vertical structure (b) divisional structure
(c) horizontal structure (d) functional structure

77 Shared task divisioning is encouraged at
(a) linear structure (b) vertical structure
(c) horizontal structure (d) compound structure

78 Managers not having control over many activities is a drawback of
(a) matrix structure (b) network structure
(c) vertical structure (d) horizontal structure

79 Managerial decision-making refers to
(a) programmed decisions (b) unprogrammed decisions
(c) information system (d) operational research

80 These decisions are original and the product of managerial wisdom. These decisions are known as
(a) programmed decisions (b) unprogrammed decisions
(c) middle-level system (d) top-level decision

81 A manager multiples himself through
(a) delegation (b) coordination
(c) cooperation (d) influence

82 The delegation of authority depends on the sub-ordinate's
(a) training (b) educational qualifications
(c) ability and potential (d) personal appearance

83 Which managerial function deals with placing right things at right places?
(a) Planning (b) Organising
(c) Staffing (d) Directing

84 Decentralisation, delegation of authority forms part of which of the following managerial functions?
(a) Staffing (b) Planning
(c) Organising (d) Budgeting

85 A management step which is already systematised, predetermined by rules, regulations or procedures is better known as
(a) a management decision
(b) an unprogrammed decision
(c) a programmed decision
(d) an act of management

86 The mechanistic theory of organisation is also known as
(a) Bureaucratic theory (b) Scientific management
(c) Behaviourist theory (d) Classical theory

87 'Grapevine' is a term used in relation to
(a) formal communication
(b) informal communication
(c) Both (a) and (b)
(d) this term is not used in relation to communication

88 The greatest weakness of the informal organisation is
(a) its utter instability
(b) its behaviour can be predicted
(c) it does not change
(d) All of the above

89 To achieve vertical linkages, first vertical device is
(a) management information system
(b) plans
(c) rules
(d) hierarchical referral

90 Specialised task divisioning takes place at
(a) computed structure
(b) vertical structure
(c) complex structure
(d) horizontal structure

91 The procedure of removing inappropriate applicants is called ....
(a) selection (b) recruitment
(c) training (d) aptitude test

92 Recruitment and selection are part of which of the following managerial function?
(a) Planning (b) Organising
(c) Staffing (d) Controlling

93 Among the following alternatives which of the managerial function deals with filling and keeping the organisation structure filled?
(a) Planning (b) Organising
(c) Directing (d) Staffing

94 Which of the following activities focus on estimating how many workers are currently employed in the organisation?
(a) Job analysis (b) Workforce analysis
(c) Workload analysis (d) Job dpecification

95 One cannot perform control function without
(a) staffing (b) planning
(c) organising (d) All of these

96 Which of the following is the meaning of human resource planning?
(a) Evaluation of job
(b) Satisfaction of the employees on the job
(c) Appraising the performance of employees
(d) It is the process by which an organisation ensures that it has the right number and kind of people at the right place, at the right time

97 The management of personnel is also called
(a) staffing (b) controlling
(c) co-ordinating (d) communication

98 Directing comprises of the following activities.
(a) Issuance of commands to the juniors and their supervision
(b) Guidance to the subordinate
(c) Leading and motivating the subordinate
(d) All of the above

99 To guide and oversee the efforts of assistants in order to attain administration's objectives is a function of
(a) planning (b) organising
(c) directing (d) controlling

100 Which of the following statement is not correct?
(a) Staffing does not involve recruitment
(b) Controlling is looking backward as well as forward
(c) Directing is all pervasive
(d) Orientation and appraisal is a part of staffing

101 Which of the managerial function is the essence of management?
(a) Planning (b) Coordination
(c) Communication (d) Directing

102 An organisation designed for efficiency, emphasises on
(a) centralisation
(b) horizontal communication
(c) decentralisation
(d) vertical communication

103 An organisation that emphasises horizontal communication and coordination, is designed for
(a) adaptation (b) efficiency
(c) quality (d) return on share

104 **Which one of the following is considered as the first principle of organisation?**
(a) Delegation (b) Coordination
(c) Unity of command (d) Supervision

105 **Who gave this definition of control, "Management is the profession of control"?**
(a) Harold Koontz (b) Stafford Beer
(c) Adam Jr Elbert (d) Mckenna

106 **Some of the ancient control techniques used for controlling are**
(a) break-even analysis (b) unity of policies
(c) budgetary control (d) All of these

107 **Which of the following is a type of coordination?**
(a) External (b) Internal
(c) Vertical and Horizontal (d) All of these

108 **Which of the following statement is correct?**
(a) Techniques of managerial control are useful in conducting shareholder's meetings
(b) Control techniques help in planning for profit
(c) Control techniques identify appropriate technology
(d) Techniques of control helps in selecting plant location

109 **Which of the following statement is incorrect?**
(a) Management audit signifies evaluation of the effectiveness of the management and its functional performance
(b) Ratio analysis is a synonym for cost profit volume analysis
(c) Budgetary control helps in delegation
(d) None of the above

110 **The function of attracting, acquiring, retaining and developing human resource is**
(a) recruitment
(b) training and development
(c) selection
(d) staffing

111 **Personnel management is not possible**
(a) where the workforce is too less
(b) large-sized concern
(c) number of workers so large
(d) None of the above

112 **Hierarchy has been described as the 'scalar process' by**
(a) LD White (b) Mooney and Reiley
(c) PH Appleby (d) Gullick and Urwick

113 **Effective supervision is an activity of**
(a) organisation function
(b) staffing function
(c) direction function
(d) control function

114 **Which of the following is not non-monetary?**
(a) Job security
(b) Effective communication
(c) Bonus
(d) Motivation

115 **The managerial function of guiding, overseeing and leading people is**
(a) planning
(b) directing
(c) motivating
(d) coordinating

116 **Which of the following activities is associated with coordination of work in the business organisation?**
(a) Planning (b) Organising
(c) Staffing (d) Directing

117 **Selecting the best possible objects, policies, procedures and programmes out of available alternatives comes under**
(a) coordination (b) organisation
(c) planning (d) controlling

118 **You are the manager of a firm. Which of the following activities do you initiate first?**
(a) Planning (b) Organising
(c) Staffing (d) Directing

119 **Forecasting helps the management in**
(a) developing a business
(b) providing adequate information for exercising effective control
(c) helping the management executives in effective coordination
(d) All of the above

120 **Which of the following is not the advantage of delegation?**
(a) It causes lack of trust in subordinates
(b) It improves managerial effectiveness
(c) It facilitates organisational growth
(d) It motivates subordinates

121 **Which of the following is not related to staffing?**
(a) Human resource planning
(b) Managerial appraisal
(c) Decision-making
(d) Job definition

122 **To channelise the activities of the workers and to induce them to work is**
(a) control (b) coordination
(c) motivation (d) organisation

123 **"Press the right button but convincingly; to get a desired reaction." For which function of management this statement is quoted?**
(a) Organisation
(b) Motivation
(c) Control
(d) Direction

124 **Management by exception means**
(a) only important problems are looked after by the top management
(b) rewarding the efficient and punishing the inefficient
(c) Neither of the above
(d) Either of the above

125 Arrange the following activities to form the process of planning.

1. Identifying a problem
2. Identification of decision criteria
3. Allocating weights to different criteria
4. Developing alternatives
5. Analysing various alternatives
6. Selecting alternative
7. Implementation of the alternative

Codes

(a) 2, 3, 1, 4, 6, 5, 7 (b) 4, 3, 2, 1, 6, 5, 7
(c) 1, 2, 3, 4, 5, 6, 7 (d) 1, 3, 2, 4, 5, 6, 7

126 Arrange the following activities in the correct sequence to describe the process of staffing.

1. Human resource planning
2. Recruitment
3. Placement and Induction
4. Selection
5. Training and Development
6. Promotion
7. Appraisal
8. Remuneration

Codes

(a) 1, 2, 3, 4, 5, 6, 7, 8 (b) 1, 2, 4, 3, 5, 7, 6, 8
(c) 2, 1, 4, 3, 5, 7, 6, 8 (d) 2, 1, 3, 4, 5, 7, 6, 8

127 Which of the following statement(s) is/are correct?

1. Budgetry control facilitates control by exception.
2. Budgetary control deals with numerical data.
3. Budget is a control device.

Codes

(a) Only 1 (b) Both 1 and 3
(c) Both 1 and 2 (d) All of the above

128 Which of the following statement(s) is/are true?

1. The essence of communication is in sharing information.
2. The main purpose of communication is to share understanding.
3. Communication emphasises on sharing ideas and views.

Select the correct answer by using the codes given below

Codes

(a) Both 1 and 3 (b) Both 1 and 2
(c) Both 2 and 3 (d) All of the above

129 The main difference between delegation and decentralisation are

1. Delegation involves transfer of authority and not responsibility; where as decentralisation involves transfer of authority and responsibility.
2. Decentralisation is by the will of the superior; while delegation is done legally.
3. Distributing authority can take place at will while in decentralisation it requires a legal action.

Select the correct answer by using the codes given below

(a) Both 1 and 2 (b) Both 1 and 3
(c) Both 2 and 3 (d) All of the above

130 What does 'Hierarchy of Authority' means?

1. The lower levels have to pursue the goals laid down by higher levels.
2. The upper levels of hierarchy set the goals to be pursued.
3. The upper level can not take disciplinary action against subordinates.
4. The lower levels have freedom to carry out the operations.

Select the correct answer by using the codes given below

(a) Both 1 and 2 (b) Both 2 and 3
(c) Both 3 and 4 (d) Both 1 and 4

131 The main drawback of functional organisation developed by Taylor is that it falls to recognise the

1. scalar principle 2. principle of equity
3. principle of unity of command
4. principle of Espirit de Corps

Which of the following statements are true/false?

Codes

(a) 1 and 2 are true, 3 and 4 are false
(b) 2 and 3 are true, 1 and 4 are false
(c) 1 and 4 are true, 2 and 3 are false
(d) 1, 2, 3 are true, 4 is false

132 Below are given some points.

1. It is automatic and uniform given identical situations.
2. It can be assigned to clerical or routine managerial levels.
3. The more of an organisation's decision-making areas are programmed, the more it leaves the senior management free to concentrate on larger decision areas.
4. It helps the communication process as everybody seems to know the outcome of a certain set of conditions or situation.
5. It minimises eroticism or the subjective element in management decision.

These all are the qualities of

(a) a programmed decision
(b) an unprogrammed decision
(c) a top-level management
(d) a middle-level management

133 Which of the following statements are correct? Coordination in the organisation means

1. removal of redundancy in the tasks and roles in the organisation.
2. removal of any conflict within the organisation.
3. securing the harmony in operations and different units in the organisation.
4. complete control of the activities of the employees.

Select the correct answer by using the codes given below

Codes

(a) Both 1 and 4 (b) 1, 2 and 3
(c) 2, 3 and 4 (d) All of the above

Directions (Q. Nos. 134-136) *In the questions given below are two statements labelled as Statement I and Statement II. You have to examine these two statements carefully and select the correct code.*

Codes

(a) Statement I is correct, but Statement II is incorrect
(b) Statement II is correct, but Statement I is incorrect
(c) Both statements are correct
(d) Both statements are incorrect

134 Which of the following statements are correct?
I. It is a significant feature of human that he plans.
II. A plan is a trap to capture the future.

135 Which of the following statements are correct?
I. Planning helps in optimum utilisation of resources.
II. Planning limits the use of resources beforehand.

136 Which of the following statements are correct?
I. Bounded rationality states that the decision maker is bounded by various constraints such as time constraints, intellectual limitations etc.
II. Bounded Rationality was given by P.F. Drucker.

137 Which of the following statements are correct?
I. Organisation promotes specialisation.
II. Organisation promotes judicious use of resources.

138 **Assertion** (A) Staffing promotes higher performance.
Reason (R) It enables the firm in obtaining suitable candidates for the institution.

Codes

(a) Both (A) and (R) are correct and (R) is the correct explanation of (A)
(b) Both (A) and (R) are correct, but (R) is not the correct explanation of (A)
(c) Both (A) and (R) are incorrect
(d) (A) is correct, but (R) is incorrect

139 **Assertion** (A) Coordination is an integral function of management.
Reason (R) Coordination is done through planning, organising, staffing and controlling.

Codes

(a) (A) is correct and (R) is the correct explanation to it
(b) (A) is correct, but (R) is not the correct explanation to it
(c) (A) is not correct while (R) is a correct statement
(d) Both (A) and (R) are incorrect

Directions (Q. Nos. 140-148) *In the questions given below are two statements labelled as Assertion (A) and Reason (R). In the context of the two statements, which one of the following is correct?*

Codes

(a) Both (A) and (R) are true and (R) is the correct explanation of (A)
(b) Both (A) and (R) are true, but (R) is not the correct explanation of (A)
(c) (A) is false, but (R) is true
(d) (A) is true, but (R) is false

140 **Assertion** (A) Planning is necessary at all levels of management alongwith all the departments.
Reason (R) Planning does not involve mental contemplation.

141 **Assertion** (A) Directing must promote effective leadership.
Reason (R) Manager should direct the employee through effective communication and facilitate free and quick transmission of information between the superior and subordinate.

142 **Assertion** (A) Staffing causes reduction in frequency of failure and avoids wrong actions.
Reason (R) Staffing enhances job satisfaction.

143 **Assertion** (A) Control looks backward.
Reason (R) It is related to future because past cannot be controlled but future can be controlled.

144 **Assertion** (A) Budgets give benchmarks against which the performance is measured.
Reason (R) Budgets assist the managers in taking corrective actions.

145 **Assertion** (A) Staffing motivates the human resource of the organisation.
Reason (R) It is a very gentle function of the organisation because it deals with humans.

146 **Assertion** (A) Planning is the first step in management, hence it is a primary function.
Reason (R) It proceeds logically the enactment of all the other management activities.

147 **Assertion** (A) Job creation and departmentalisation is the third step in organising.
Reason (R) Jobs are created and specified on the basis of similarities.

148 **Assertion** (A) One of the key component of management process is directing.
Reason (R) Directing initiates all the other actions of the management process.

149 Which of the following statements are true/false?
1. Directing provides adequate satisfaction.
2. Directing comprises of delegation, authority and departmentalisation.
3. Directing ensures proper feedback.
4. Directing entails maximum contribution.

Codes

(a) 1, 2, 4 are true and 3 is false
(b) 1, 3, 4 are true and 2 is false
(c) 2, 3, 4 are true and 1 is false
(d) 1 and 3 are correct, 2 and 4 are false

150 Which of the following statements are true/false?

1. Organisation structure refers to a system where the work is divided formally.
2. The smaller tasks are gathered and divided formally.
3. Organising helps in looking into the future.
4. Organising promotes order in the organisation.

Codes

(a) 1, 2, 3 are true, 4 is false
(b) 1 and 2 are true, 3 and 4 are false
(c) 2 and 4 are true, 1 and 3 are false
(d) 1, 2 and 4 are true, 3 is false

151 Which of the following statements are true/false?

1. Communication is the systematic process of transfer of ideas, opinions and organisational values.
2. Henry Fayol coined the term PODSCORB.
3. Delegation is a two sided relationship between a superior and subordinate.

Codes

(a) 1 is true, 2 and 3 are false
(b) 2 is true, 1 and 3 are false
(c) 1 and 3 are true, 2 is false
(d) 1 and 2 are true, 3 is false

152 Which of the following statements are true/false?

1. Control helps to monitor environment changes and their effects on organisation's process.
2. Delegation of authority in participative management does not change the nature of control process.
3. Staffing function deals with human capital.

Codes

(a) 1 and 2 are correct, 3 is false
(b) 2 and 3 are correct, 1 is false
(c) 1 and 3 are correct, 2 is false
(d) 2 is correct, 1 and 2 are false

153 Match the following.

List I	List II
A. Decision-making	1. Management
B. Execution	2. The CEO
C. Lower level management	3. Administration
D. Top level management	4. Foreman

Codes

	A	B	C	D		A	B	C	D
(a)	2	4	3	1	(b)	2	3	4	1
(c)	3	1	4	2	(d)	1	2	3	4

154 Match the following.

List I	List II
A. Newman and Summer	1. Organising, planning and controlling
B. Henry Fayol	2. Planning, organising, commanding, coordinating and controlling
C. Luther Gullick	3. Planning, organising, staffing, directing and controlling
D. Koontz and O' Donnell	4. PODSCORB

Codes

	A	B	C	D		A	B	C.	D
(a)	4	2	3	1	(b)	2	3	4	1
(c)	3	1	4	2	(d)	1	2	4	3

155 Match the following.

List I	List II
A. Planning	1. Training
B. Staffing	2. Forecasting
C. Directing	3. Evaluating
D. Controlling	4. Motivating

Codes

	A	B	C	D		A	B	C	D
(a)	2	1	4	3	(b)	2	1	3	4
(c)	1	2	4	3	(d)	4	1	3	2

156 Match the following.

List I	List II
A. Staffing	1. Manpower planning
B. Planning	2. Selection of best alternative
C. Directing	3. Initiation of action
D. Organising	4. Departmentalisation

Codes

	A	B	C	D		A	B	C	D
(a)	1	2	3	4	(b)	3	4	1	2
(c)	2	1	4	3	(d)	4	1	2	3

157 Match the following.

List I	List II
A. Controlling	1. Clarity in working relationships
B. Planning	2. Integration employees' efforts
C. Directing	3. Promotion of innovative ideas
D. Organising	4. Ensuring discipline and order

Codes

	A	B	C	D		A	B	C	D
(a)	4	2	1	3	(b)	1	4	2	3
(c)	2	3	4	1	(d)	4	3	2	1

158 Match the following.

List I	List II
A. Staffing	1. Helps in the reduction of uncertainty
B. Planning	2. Optimal utilisation of resources
C. Directing	3. Vacant positions are filled
D. Organising	4. Integrates human efforts

Codes

	A	B	C	D		A	B	C	D
(a)	3	1	4	2	(b)	1	4	2	3
(c)	2	3	4	1	(d)	4	3	2	1

159 Match the following.

List I	List II
A. Management audit	1. Calculation of profits at different activity levels
B. Ratio analysis	2. Estimate for one time is prepared
C. Break-even analysis	3. It is not bounded by any law
D. Critical point control	4. Computation of ratios for further analysis

Codes

	A	B	C	D		A	B	C	D
(a)	3	1	4	2	(b)	3	4	2	1
(c)	2	3	4	1	(d)	4	3	2	1

160 Match the following.

List I	List II
A. Planning	1. Primary function
B. Directing	2. Supervision
C. Controlling	3. Manpower planning
D. Staffing	4. Break-even analysis

Codes

	A	B	C	D		A	B	C	D
(a)	3	1	4	2	(b)	3	4	2	1
(c)	1	2	4	3	(d)	4	3	2	1

161 Match the following.

List I	List II
A. Network organisation	1. Traditional structure with many levels of management
B. Boundary less organisation	2. Virtual organisation
C. Vertical structure	3. Free movement of information
D. Horizontal structure	4. It is also known as a flat organisational structure

Codes

	A	B	C	D		A	B	C	D
(a)	1	3	2	4	(b)	2	3	1	4
(c)	4	1	3	2	(d)	2	3	4	1

162 Match the following.

List I	List II
A. Normative theory	1. Simon
B. Bounded rationality	2. Taylor, Drucker
C. Practical theory	3. Combination of normative and administrative theory
D. Personal Theory	4. Individual behaviour

Codes

	A	B	C	D
(a)	1	2	3	4
(b)	3	4	1	2
(c)	2	1	3	4
(d)	4	1	2	3

163 Match the following.

List I (Organisational Structure)	List II (Advantages)
A. Functional structure	1. Clarity of project objectives
B. Divisional structure	2. Smooth delegation of authority and responsibility
C. Matrix structure	3. Simple and inexpensive
D. Strategic Business Unit (SBU)	4. Ease of fixing accountability

Codes

	A	B	C	D
(a)	1	2	3	4
(b)	3	4	1	2
(c)	3	1	2	4
(d)	4	1	2	3

Directions (Q.Nos. 164-168) *Read the following passage and answer the questions that follows.*

Perhaps the most powerful model for coordination systems is the 'game'. The players make up a 'society' where players follow rules and strategies and use resources in ways that contribute to the common objective. The players can be humans, computational agents or both. The elements of a game are:

Players are the agents (including people) who interact in the system. There can be one or many. There can be rules of eligibility: only certain types of people or levels of skill are allowed in the game.

Objectives are the goals that the players are collectively trying to achieve. There are two types of game, finite and infinite. The objective of a finite game is for someone to win. The objective of an infinite game is to continue the play. For example, a ball game or video game is finite; the players seek to have someone declared the winner by scoring the most points. The market economy is an infinite game; the players come and go and their objective is to keep the economy going and growing. The internet is likewise an infinite game.

Resources of the game are the various tools and items of equipment that the players need for their moves. For example, the resources of chess are a board, black pieces and white pieces. The resources of a baseball game are the playing field, the bases, the balls and the bats. The resources of the market economy are communication systems including internet, banks, transportation systems and offices.

A rule is a statement that authorises or limits actions. An authorising rule can be expressed C:M, where C is a Condition and M is a Move (action); the move is allowed whenever the condition holds. A limiting rule can be expressed M:C; the move is allowed except when C is true. In the game of driving, "turn right on red after stop" is authorising and "do not cut someone off" is limiting.

A strategy is a guideline for series of actions that are known by experience to help attain the objectives of the game. In chess, exchanging pieces of similar point values is a good strategy. In driving, watching the brake lights of cars two or three lengths ahead is a good strategy.

164 According to this passage,
(a) the players make up a 'society' where players do not follow rules and strategies and use resources in ways that contribute to the common objective
(b) the players make up a 'society' where players follow rules and strategies and use resources in ways that contribute to the common objective
(c) the players make up a 'society' where players makes there own rules and strategies and use resources in ways that contribute to the common objective
(d) the players make up a 'society' where players follow rules and strategies and use resources in ways that contribute to the personal objective

165 According to this passage, the resources refers to
(a) the various tools and items of equipment that the players need for their moves
(b) the various facilities that players should be given
(c) the various resources like man, material, machinery, money etc
(d) the various incentives that the players need for their moves

166 The objective of a finite game and infinite game are
(a) not to make any difference in winning and losing
(b) to continue the play and to win respectively
(c) to win and to continue the play respectively
(d) to win the game in both cases

167 An authorising rule can be expressed C:M,
(a) where C is a cancellation and M is a management
(b) where C is a criteria and M is a motivation (action)
(c) where C is a creativity and M is a move (action)
(d) where C is a condition and M is a move (action)

168 A strategy is
(a) a guideline for individual actions that are known by chance to help attain the objectives of the game
(b) a guideline for series of actions that are known by experience to help attain the objectives of the game
(c) a guideline for series of actions that are known by chance to help attain the objectives of the game
(d) a disciplinary actions that are used to forbid or discourage unwanted actions

PREVIOUS YEARS' QUESTIONS

2018

1 Matrix organisation is the combination of
(a) project and line organisation
(b) line and staff organisation
(c) project and functional organisation
(d) functional and product organisation

2 The determination of the basic long-term objectives of an organisation/enterprise and the adoption of courses of action and allocation of resources necessary to achieve goals is called
(a) goal (b) strategy
(c) procedure (d) policy

3 The right delegated to an individual or a department to control specified processes, practices, policies or other matters relating to activities under taken by persons in other departments is called
(a) functional authority delegation
(b) delegation of power
(c) empowerment of employees
(d) centralisation of power

4 Apart from legislations which of the following institutions operate in controlling and directing individual actions into desirable channels ?
1. Religious prescriptions
2. Social customs, traditions and conventions
3. Socialist and revolutionary ideas
4. Political freedom and extension of franchise

Codes
(a) 1, 2 and 3 (b) Both 2 and 3
(c) Both 1 and 2 (d) 1, 2 and 4

5 Experienced managers have a simple and effective way to check whether their goals are good or not they use the acronym 'SMART', which stands for
(a) Specific, Manageable, Attainable, Reasonable and Timely
(b) Sophisticated, Measurable, Attainable, Relevant and Targeted
(c) Simple, Measurable, Ambitious, Relative and Target-oriented
(d) Specific, Measurable, Attainable, Relevant and Timely

6 **Assertion** (A) The basic planning process always involves setting objectives, forecasting and assessing basic planning 'premises' or assumptions, determining alternatives causes of actions, evaluating which options are best and then choosing and implementing plan.

Reason (R) There is usually a hierarchical aspect to managerial planning. Top management approves a long-term or strategic plan. Then each department creates its own budgets and other plans to fit and to contribute to company's long term plan.

Codes
(a) (A) is right and (R) is wrong
(b) (A) is wrong and (R) is right
(c) (A) and (R) both are right and (R) explains (A)
(d) (A) and (R) both are right, but (R) does not explain (A)

7 Match List I management functions with their possible explanation List II.

List I	List II
A. Controlling/ Monitoring	1. Making optimum use of the resources required to enable successfully carrying out the plans
B. Leading/ Motivating	2. Deciding what needs to happen in future and generating plans for action
C. Organising	3. Checking progress against plans, which may need modification based on feedback
D. Planning	4. Getting others to play an effective part in achieving plans

Codes

	A	B	C	D
(a)	1	2	3	4
(b)	4	1	3	2
(c)	3	4	2	1
(d)	3	4	1	2

8 Assertion (A) It has been suggested that while roles answer the question 'how to be interfaced with other people to reach our goals' ? Functions answer the question 'what do you do to accomplish our goals'?

Reason (R) Roles are more relational while functions go beyond inter-personal relations. Functions such as planning, decision-making etc may not necessarily involve working with others and several managerial functions can be performed without communication with people.

Codes
(a) (A) and (R) both are right, (R) explains (A)
(b) (A) is true, (R) is not true
(c) (A) and (R) both are not true
(d) (A) is wrong, hence (R) is not an explanation of (A)

9 An organisation structure defines how job, tasks are formally divided, grouped and coordinated. Managers need to address six key elements when they design their organisation's structure.

Match List I with List II given below.

List I Refers to the six key elements encountered by managers in designing their organisation structure.

List II Provides possible answer to address the key elements encountered in organisation designing.

List I	List II
A. To what degree are activities sub-divided into separate jobs?	1. Span of Control
B. On what basis will jobs be grouped together?	2. Centralisation and Decentralisation
C. To whom do individuals and groups report?	3. Departmentalisation
D. How many individuals can a manager efficiently and effectively direct?	4. Work specialisation
E. Where does decision-making authority lie?	5. Chain of Command
F. To what degree will there be rules and regulations to direct employees and managers?	6. Formalisation

Codes

	A	B	C	D	E	F
(a)	3	4	5	2	1	6
(b)	4	3	5	1	2	6
(c)	1	2	3	4	6	5
(d)	2	3	4	6	5	1

2017

10 Which of the following has specialists from different functional departments working on one or more projects that are led by a project manager?
(a) Functional organisation (b) Cross-Functional team
(c) Matrix organisation (d) Product organisation

11 According to which one of the following approaches, management is the function of planning, organising, leading and controlling?
(a) Process approach
(b) Systems approach
(c) Quantitative approach
(d) Human behaviour approach

12 The steps in planning process are jumbled up. Arrange them in correct sequence.
1. Specifying alternatives
2. Analysing alternatives
3. Goal setting
4. Elaborating plans and specifying details
5. Establishing standards for measurement
6. Maintaining communication
7. Maintaining a time perspective
8. Planning for unpredictable contingencies
9. Organising
10. Implementing
11. Ensuring participation
12. Follow-up, providing for flexibility

Codes
(a) 3, 5, 7, 1, 2, 4, 11, 6, 9, 10, 12, 8
(b) 3, 1, 7, 2, 4, 11, 6, 10, 9, 8, 12, 5
(c) 4, 3, 1, 6, 7, 9, 2, 5, 12, 8, 10
(d) 3, 7, 5, 2, 1, 11, 4, 9, 6, 10, 12, 8

13 Read the following statements about 'staffing' as a strategy formation. Identify the ones which are true.

1. Organisations need to hire 'best' people emphasising person-organisation fit over person-job fit.
2. Organisations need to hire people with unique as well as complementary KSAs in order to have the capability to implement flexible and focused business strategies in a fast changing environment.
3. Organisation need to hire people with talent and creativity to contribute to business strategies in a manner that will take any possible course of action in any direction.

Codes

(a) Only 1 (b) Both 1 and 2
(c) Both 2 and 3 (d) All of the above

14 Match the type of managerial decisions List I with the examples given in List II.

List I	List II
A. Judgemental decisions	1. Daily routines and scheduled activities
B. Adaptive decisions	2. Complex production and engineering problems
C. Mechanistic decisions	3. Marketing, investment and personnel problems
D. Analytical decisions	4. Research and development and long-term corporate planning

Codes

	A	B	C	D		A	B	C	D
(a)	3	1	4	2	(b)	2	4	1	3
(c)	3	4	1	2	(d)	1	2	3	4

15 Which of the following is not a characteristic of 'spaghetti organisation structure' adopted by MNCs?

(a) Paperless organisation
(b) Smart office design
(c) 'Meat Balls' or knowledge centres
(d) Formal communication between people

16 Examine the following statements about span of control and identify the ones which are true?

1. More task complexity requires narrower span of control.
2. Routine tasks can have greater span of control than exceptional tasks.
3. When tasks are dissimilar, then span of control can be larger.
4. Spans of control are generally narrower at the top and broader at the bottom of the hierarchy.

Codes

(a) Both 1 and 2 (b) 1, 3 and 4
(c) Both 2 and 4 (d) 1, 2 and 4

17 Which of the following represents the rights inherent in a managerial position to give orders and expect them to be obeyed?

(a) Power (b) Authority
(c) Influence (d) Responsibility

2016

18 Which of the following is the correct formula for calculating the direct group relations of 'span of control' as given by VA Graicunas?

(a) $r = n\left(\frac{2^n}{n} + (n-1)\right)$ (b) $r = n\left(\frac{2^n}{n} - (n+1)\right)$

(c) $r = n\left(\frac{2^n}{n} - 1\right)$ (d) $r = n\left(\frac{2^n}{n} + 1\right)$

19 Match List I with List II and choose the right answer by using the codes given below.

List I	List II
A. Staffing	1. Motivation
B. Planning	2. Training
C. Directing	3. Forecasting
D. Controlling	4. Comparison of performance

Codes

	A	B	C	D		A	B	C	D
(a)	1	2	3	4	(b)	2	3	1	4
(c)	3	2	4	1	(d)	4	2	3	1

20 Which of the following statements are true about Herbert A Simon's decision-making process?

1. Decision-making process involves intelligence, design and choice activities.
2. Decision-making involves choice between alternative plans of action.
3. Bounded rationality has no significance in decision-making process.
4. Satisficing model brings about a balance between individual and organisational value judgement in decision-making process.

Codes

(a) Both 1 and 2 are true
(b) Both 1 and 4 are true
(c) 1, 2 and 3 are true
(d) 1, 2 and 4 are true

21 Examine the following statements on the line and staff and identify the ones which are true.

1. Line and staff concept originated from Military.
2. Line decides and staff assists.
3. Personnel role is performed both by line and staff.
4. The Personnel Department's role is a staff function.

Codes

(a) Both 2 and 4 (b) 1, 2 and 4
(c) 2, 3 and 4 (d) All of the above

22 Which of the following statements are true about Herbert A Simon's decision-making process?

1. Decision-making process involves intelligence, design and choice activities.
2. Decision-making involves choice between alternative plans of action.
3. Bounded rationality has no significance in decision-making process.
4. Satisficing model brings about a balance between individual and organisational value judgement in decision-making process.

Codes

(a) 1 and 2 are true (b) 1 and 4 are true
(c) 1, 2 and 3 are true (d) 1, 2 and 4 are true

2015

23 Which of the following interpretations is true based on the statements I and II?

Statement I Staff can make an advise to a line manager.

Statement II A line manager may or may not accept the advice.

Codes

(a) Both statements are correct
(b) Statement I is correct, but Statement II is incorrect
(c) Statement I is incorrect, but Statement II is correct
(d) Both statement are incorrect

24 Which of the following is a general statement that guides or channels thinking in decision-making?

(a) Strategy
(b) Policy
(c) Rule
(d) Procedure

25 Which of the following is not an element of planning?

(a) Establishing leadership qualities
(b) Finalising objectives
(c) Evaluating alternatives
(d) Establishing sequence of action

26 According to classical theorists, the four pillars of organising are

(a) division of labour, scalar and functional processes, structures and span of control
(b) division of labour, identity, structures and cooperation
(c) identity, structures, scalar chain and span of control
(d) structures, scalar chain, span of control and specialisation

27 Consider the following statements.

1. Coordination means synchronisation of efforts with respect to time and direction.
2. The basic principles of coordination are direct contact and continuity of efforts.
3. In a given situation, cooperation may exist without coordination.

Which of the statement(s) given above is/are correct?

(a) Only 1 (b) Only 2
(c) Both 1 and 2 (d) All of the above

28 'The scalar principle of organisation' implies

(a) all authority must vest in one single person
(b) manager should directly supervise only a limited number of subordinates
(c) line of authority must be clearly defined
(d) a subordinate should have only one superior

29 Which of the following represents the general statements that guide or channel thinking in decision-making?

(a) Strategies (b) Policies
(c) Procedures (d) Programmes

30 The on-going process of identifying, assessing and developing organisational leadership to enhance performance is called

(a) strategic planning (b) succession planning
(c) organisational planning (d) career planning

31 Which of the following is/are not the method(s) of financial control?

1. Break-even analysis
2. ABC analysis
3. Internal audit
4. Quality circles

Select the correct answer using the codes given below

(a) Only 4 (b) Both 2 and 4
(c) 1, 2 and 3 (d) 1, 2 and 4

32 'X' organisation has a Personnel/HR Department, whose head reports to the General Administrative Manager, under whom there are other departments like public relations, security, estate etc. Under the head of Personnel/HR Department, there is one Personnel Manager looking after personnel functions and an Industrial Relations Manager to deal with unions. Such a Personnel/HR Department is called

(a) independent split-function department
(b) independent integrated department
(c) staff coordinated integrated department
(d) staff coordinated split function department

2014

33 Arrange the steps of decision-making process in the correct sequence.

1. Analysis of alternatives
2. Identification of decision criteria
3. Implementation of alternative
4. Identification of problem
5. Selection of alternative

Codes

(a) 4, 2, 1, 5, 3 (b) 4, 1, 2, 5, 3
(c) 4, 1, 2, 3, 5 (d) 4, 1, 5, 2, 3

34 The function of attracting, acquiring and inducting human resources in an organisation is called
(a) selection
(b) recruitment
(c) staffing
(d) training and placement

35 Formulation of policies, programmes and procedures is the primary concern of
(a) top management
(b) middle management
(c) operating management
(d) Both (a) and (b)

36 Which of the following comes under the scope of line and staff relationship?
(a) The relationship between works manager and maintenance engineer
(b) The relationship between works manager and personnel manager
(c) The relationship between personnel manager and development engineer
(d) The relationship between the public relation officer and the public

37 The first step in control process is to
(a) measure actual performance
(b) establish objectives and standards
(c) compare results with objectives
(d) take corrective action

38 Which of the following is a long-term plan regarding enterprise objectives, course of action and allocation of resources?
(a) Mission (b) Strategy
(c) Policy (d) Programme

39 Which of the following is not a barrier to effective planning ?
(a) Difficulty of accurate premising
(b) Environmental changes
(c) Flexibilities in management
(d) Time and cost factors

40 In line and staff organisation,
(a) lines of authority and instructions are vertical
(b) unity of command is maintained
(c) staff specialists advise line managers to perform their duties
(d) staff decides without consulting line authority

41 Graicuna's formula suggests that
(a) the number of subordinates and relations both increase in arithmetic progression
(b) the number of subordinates increases in geometric progression and number of relations increases in arithmetic progression
(c) the number of subordinates and relations both increase in geometric progression
(d) the number of subordinates increases in arithmetic progression while the number of relations increase in geometric progression

42 A virtual organisation has which of the following elements?
1. E-mail integration and office systems integration
2. Information technology
3. Mobile data
4. Voice mail alert

Codes
(a) Only 1 (b) Both 1 and 2
(c) 1, 2 and 3 (d) All of these

43 Departmentation is
1. Structuring work to accomplish organisational goals.
2. Visual display of organisation structure.
3. Grouping of jobs on some basis.
4. Arranging jobs in a hierarchy.

Select the correct answer using the codes given below
(a) Both 1 and 2 (b) Both 2 and 3
(c) Only 1 (d) Only 3

44 Personnel management is essentially a
(a) matrix function
(b) line function
(c) staff function
(d) line and staff function

45 Which of the following types of control is applied when the work is in progress?
(a) Feed forward control (b) Feedback control
(c) Concurrent control (d) Regular control

46 Pareto chart represents
1. most common sources of defects
2. highest occurring type of defects
3. most frequent reason for customer complaints

Select the correct answer using the codes given below
(a) Both 1 and 3 (b) Both 1 and 2
(c) Both 2 and 3 (d) 1, 2 and 3

ANSWERS

Exam Based Questions

1 (b)	2 (a)	3 (a)	4 (a)	5 (c)	6 (c)	7 (d)	8 (b)	9 (a)	10 (c)
11 (c)	12 (c)	13 (a)	14 (a)	15 (b)	16 (d)	17 (b)	18 (d)	19 (d)	20 (c)
21 (b)	22 (b)	23 (d)	24 (a)	25 (a)	26 (c)	27 (a)	28 (c)	29 (b)	30 (b)
31 (a)	32 (c)	33 (a)	34 (d)	35 (a)	36 (b)	37 (a)	38 (a)	39 (c)	40 (a)
41 (d)	42 (b)	43 (c)	44 (a)	45 (a)	46 (b)	47 (b)	48 (a)	49 (a)	50 (a)
51 (a)	52 (d)	53 (c)	54 (c)	55 (d)	56 (a)	57 (d)	58 (d)	59 (d)	60 (d)
61 (c)	62 (d)	63 (c)	64 (b)	65 (b)	66 (a)	67 (b)	68 (b)	69 (c)	70 (d)
71 (d)	72 (c)	73 (d)	74 (c)	75 (b)	76 (d)	77 (c)	78 (b)	79 (b)	80 (b)
81 (a)	82 (c)	83 (b)	84 (c)	85 (c)	86 (b)	87 (b)	88 (a)	89 (d)	90 (b)
91 (a)	92 (c)	93 (d)	94 (b)	95 (b)	96 (d)	97 (a)	98 (d)	99 (d)	100 (d)
101 (b)	102 (d)	103 (a)	104 (b)	105 (b)	106 (d)	107 (d)	108 (a)	109 (b)	110 (d)
111 (b)	112 (d)	113 (c)	114 (c)	115 (b)	116 (b)	117 (c)	118 (a)	119 (d)	120 (a)
121 (c)	122 (b)	123 (b)	124 (a)	125 (c)	126 (d)	127 (d)	128 (a)	129 (b)	130 (a)
131 (b)	132 (d)	133 (b)	134 (c)	135 (c)	136 (a)	137 (c)	138 (a)	139 (b)	140 (d)
141 (b)	142 (a)	143 (d)	144 (a)	145 (b)	146 (a)	147 (a)	148 (a)	149 (b)	150 (d)
151 (c)	152 (c)	153 (a)	154 (d)	155 (a)	156 (a)	157 (d)	158 (a)	159 (b)	160 (c)
161 (b)	162 (c)	163 (b)	164 (b)	165 (a)	166 (c)	167 (d)	168 (b)		

Previous Years' Questions

1 (c)	2 (b)	3 (a)	4 (c)	5 (d)	6 (c)	7 (d)	8 (a)	9 (b)	10 (c)
11 (a)	12 (a)	13 (d)	14 (c)	15 (d)	16 (d)	17 (b)	18 (a)	19 (b)	20 (d)
21 (d)	22 (d)	23 (a)	24 (b)	25 (a)	26 (a)	27 (d)	28 (c)	29 (b)	30 (b)
31 (a)	32 (d)	33 (a)	34 (c)	35 (a)	36 (d)	37 (b)	38 (b)	39 (c)	40 (c)
41 (d)	42 (d)	43 (d)	44 (d)	45 (c)	46 (d)				

Fundamentals of Human Resource Management

In today's era of globalisation and development, the management of man is a very significant and challenging profession. This is so because two individuals are not alike in mental abilities, sentiments and behaviours. They therefore, need a tactful handling by management personnel.

Conceptual Framework of Human Resource

People generate, retain and utilise knowledge and skills which is the 'human capital' and create intellectual capital also. Their knowledge is enhanced by their interactions which is nothing but the social capital and generates an organisation's systemic knowledge which is the organisational capital.

Human capital is the knowledge, skills and abilities of the people employed in an organisation and this term was originated by **Schultz**. He states that these are the qualities which are valuable and can be enlarged by suitable investment will be human capital. **Scarborough** and **Elias** believe that human capital is to a large extent 'non-standardised, tacit, dynamic, context dependent and embodied in people'. *Human capital resource comprises of the following*

Intellectual Capital It is the stocks and flows of knowledge that is available to an organisation. These can be regarded as the intangible resources associated with people which, together with tangible resources that is money and physical assets, comprise the market or total value of a business.

Social Capital This concept was given by **Putnam** as it comprises of the knowledge derived from networks of relationships within and outside the organisation. These are the social life features such as networks, standards and trust that enable individuals to act more efficiently together to pursue shared goals.

In this Chapter

- *Conceptual Framework of Human Resource*
- *Human Resource Planning*
- *Job Analysis*
- *Recruitment*
- *Selection*
- *Placement*

Organisational Capital Organisational capital is the institutionalised knowledge possessed by an organisation that is stored in the databases, manuals etc.

Thus, approaching human workers as a capital allows managers to view people as an important asset. It is the stance by which the organisation can use the manpower, not only for the organisation's advantages, but also for the concerned people and their development, growth and self-satisfaction.

Concept of Human Resource Management

The Human Resource Management (HRM) is the use of measures to guide a way of managing people that views them as resources and exemplifies that strategic investments in those assets to achieve competitive edge through employee engagement and retention, talent management and programs for learning and development.

HRM helps in bridging the human resource strategy with the business strategy. It can be defined as the total knowledge, skills, competencies, intelligence, values, attitudes and aptitudes of the employees working in an organisation.

With the growing importance of manpower in the organisation, its management is also crucial to retain good skill and talent. Thus, simply put, it is a management function that helps managers to recruit, select, train and develop manpower for an organisation. HRM also includes employee's remuneration, motivation and career growth.

There is a marginal difference between personnel management and HRM. Personnel management deals with the effective control and use of manpower. HRM varies from personnel management in considering people as 'resource'. In HRM, people are considered as human capital and that their tangible and intangible benefits flow from their utilisation. Thus, according to HRM, the organisations have to effectively harness this resource in order to be productive.

According to **Armstrong**," Human capital management is concerned with obtaining, analysing and reporting on data that inform the direction of value adding people management, strategic, investment and operational decisions at corporate level and at the level of front line management."

According to **Dunn** and **Stephens**, "The HRM is the process of attracting, holding and motivating all manager line and staff."

According to **Invancevich** and **Glueck**, "HRM is concerned with most effective use of people to achieve organisational and individual goals. It is a way of managing people at work, so that they give their best to the organisation."

Versions and Perspectives of HRM

1. Hard HRM

Human resources have to be acquired, developed and deployed in ways that maximise their utility. Thus, here the focus is on calculative and strategic aspect of managing human resource. The approach is based on facts and the objective is maximising benefit and minimising cost.

The emphasis of hard HRM is on the interest of management as opposed to workers. Thus, hard HRM deals with quantitative output, superiors and bosses, managers, employee's obedience, discipline, development of organisation and tasks given to the employee. It is short-term in nature.

2. Soft HRM

Soft HRM is dependent on the behavioural approach of management. It treats its employees as co-contributors rather than helpers in organisational culture. It stresses on the need to gain constant commitment of employees through democratic means such as participative management, meaningful involvement in policy formulation and other methods of developing high-commitment and highly trusted culture in the organisation.

Employees are treated as valued assets and a source of competitive advantage which needs to be optimised by showing ethical qualities such as commitment, adaptability and high quality performance. Thus, Soft HRM deals with quality, recognition, flexibility, performance of rights and environments in the employee relations. Soft HRM has long-term impact and it is strategic.

3. Critical Perspective of HRM

This is the result of normative perception. It states that institutions follow 'soft HRM' approach only to manifest in the policies, *i.e.* the soft HRM is present in the documents, whereas hard HRM is exercised in reality, so as to control the organisation. Thus, it is criticism to normative approach.

It criticises that the organisations only make others believe that they are people oriented, however they actually exploit workers through downsizing and work intensification.

4. Strategic Perspective of HRM

Here, the employees are treated as an important resource to achieve the organisational targets. Thus, they are treated as strategic/key resources to improve organisational efficiency. This approach gives the strategic plan that supports the objectives and long-term business goals. It is more future oriented and deals with long-term HR planning.

It matches the future concerns with the culture, values, skills, quality, structure and commitment required for attaining future goals. It develops steady policies and programmes that can be carried even in future.

5. System Perspective of HRM

Here, the organisation is treated as a system comprising of inputs, processes and outputs accompanied by their surroundings. Employees are treated as inputs, and the product and services are the output. HRM in this perspective ensures that the workforce has required abilities and skills to work as an input for the organisation. Also, they focus more on managing behaviour and performance evaluation, compensation systems to boost productivity of the labour.

6. Behavioural Perspective of HRM

This perspective believes that the behaviour of the employee must be controlled and moulded in order to get the desired results from him. This can happen by focussing on identifying the desired behaviour, development of the required skills and motivation of the employees to act in the specified manner. This is generally done with the help of organisational practices which increases the efficiency.

Role of Human Resource Function

- It plays a major part in the creation of an environment that enables people to make the best use of their capacities, to recognise their potential to the benefit of both the organisation and themselves.
- The function ensures that HR strategies, policies and practices are introduced and maintained that cater for everything concerning the employment, development and well-being of people and the relationships that exist between management and the workforce.
- The function is to maintain employees by encouraging value system and creating environment of trust by way of rewards, incentives, and facilities and to appraise their performance in order to reward them or to take corrective actions, so that stability of employment can be ensured.
- The role of the HR function is to take initiatives and provide guidance, support and services on all matters relating to the organisation's employees. This also includes working as a counsellor and mediator at the time of conflict.

Role of HR Manager

1. **Karen Legge** (1978)

   There are two types of HR managers which are
   - Conformist innovators, who go alongwith their organisation's ends and adjust their means to achieve them and
   - Deviant innovators who attempt to change this means or ends relationship by gaining acceptance for a different set of criteria for the evaluation of organisational success and their contribution to it.
2. **The Tyson and Fell** (1986) There are three types of roles, *i.e.*
   - clerk of works, where the authority is entrusted to the line managers and HR activities are largely routine employment and daily administration;
   - contract managers, where the HR manager uses a sophisticated systems especially in the field of employee relations and
   - the Architect, where the head of the HR department helps in formulating corporate strategies.

Nature of HRM

1. **Action Oriented** HRM is an action oriented as it focuses attention on action, rather than record keeping, written procedures or rules.
2. **Continuous** HRM is continuous activity because it requires continuous awareness of human capital needs of the organisation.
3. **Facilitates Coordination** HRM is an integrating mechanism as it attempts to build and maintain coordination between all operative levels in an organisation.
4. **Comprehensive Function** HRM is a comprehensive function, because it is concerned directly or indirectly with every decision that is related to human resource irrespective the managerial level or other department.
5. **Pervasive** HRM is a pervasive function as it permeates all levels of decision-making in an organisation.
6. **Human Oriented** HRM is people oriented and focuses on deploying right person at right place at right time.
7. **Employee Benefit** HRM seeks to maximise employee motivation to make them contribute to their maximum potential.
8. **Multi-disciplinary Approach** HRM derives its meaning and philosophies from various disciplines such as anthropology, sociology, psychology, economics etc.

Objectives of HRM

The objectives of HRM are broadly classified into four categories which are presented below

1. **Societal** The social laws and societies can modify the objectives of HRM. This is because, HRM deals with management of humans which requires adherence to labour laws, basic human rights and other laws prevalent in the society.

Some of the societal objectives are

- **Legal Compliance** A company aims at meeting the laws and regulations which can be with regard to reservation, remuneration, working conditions or unionisation.
- **Benefits** The ultimate objective of a company is to provide benefits to the society which can be in the form of goods, products, services or even by following just and fair procedures in the company. It also aim at focusing on societal concerns and focusing on quality.
- **Union-management Relations** Another societal objective is to foster cordial relations between the management and labour unions.

2. **Organisational Objectives** This is from the perspective of the organisation and focuses on its strategies, coordinating and harmonising organisation wide efforts and emphasising the role of HRM in contributing towards effectiveness and efficiency in the organisation.

Some of the organisational objectives are

- **Human Resource Planning** It comprises of analysing the need of human resource, its types and skills required.
- **Employee Relations** Establishing human standards and fostering better employee relations in the organisation. This can be done by promoting participative leadership, effective communication, motivation and effective redressal mechanism.
- **Talent Management** Another organisational objective is to manage the human capital to the fullest, focus on their individual needs such as quality of work life, work-life balance.

3. **Functional Objectives** These objectives have been chiefly adopted from personnel management. It represents the functional or operational goals that are to be achieved by the organisation.

Functional goals generally comprise of the following

- **Recruitment and Selection** The primary objective here is to invite potential candidates and select the best fit.
- **Training and Development** Another functional objective is to mould, train and equip the candidate with necessary skills and knowledge to perform the task. It also aims at building the capacity of the employee for future endeavours. This is called development.
- **Appraisal** A key functional objective is to gauge and appraise the trained personnel, evaluate his performance according to the predetermined standards. This is called performance appraisal. Thus, the objective is to ascertain the efficiency and effectiveness of an employee.
- **Remuneration** This entails aiming at just and fair compensation policies. The organisation focuses on building competitive yet equitable remuneration policies that reward the performer and motivate the underperformer.

4. **Personal Objectives** This implies how the employees are assisted in achieving their personal goals. This is important because the fulfillment of personal objectives help in achievement of organisational goals. If they want to retain the employees, then personal objectives must be met.

Some of them are

- **Training and Development** This is done from the perspective and capabilities of the employee. *e.g.* assisting him in defining his career path and then aiding him in achieving his career goals.
- **Appraisal** The objective is to promote fair dialogue between the appraisor and the employee and constructively providing him with the feedback.
- **Compensation** Employee aim at better wages and perks, hence the organisation aims at compensating the individual according to his goals. *e.g.* Various companies provide house rent allowance to the expatriates residing in a rented house.

Functions of HRM

1. **Employment** It deals with obtaining and employing individuals with key skills and knowledge to perform specific tasks.
2. **Job Analysis** It identifies the skills, knowledge and aptitude required to perform the job.
3. **HR Planning** It estimates the requirement of personnel of the organisation.
4. **Recruitment** It is the process of looking for competent prospective employees against the vacant position.
5. **Selection** It is the process of choosing right individual for right job.
6. **Placement** It comprises of placing the selected employee in the right position/department of the organisation.
7. **Induction** This implies introducing the employee with the organisation, its policies and procedures and his colleagues.
8. **Training** It aims at providing the skills and knowledge required to perform specific tasks.
9. **Performance Appraisal** It deals with evaluating the performance of employees and rating then accordingly.
10. **Management Development** It is an important function dealing with developing the employees in order to meet future challenges and changes.

11. **Career Planning and Development** It comprises of helping the employee in the identification of his career objectives and formulation of strategies to achieve them.
12. **Compensation** It is the process of formulating fair and just remuneration for the employees. It includes benefits, salary, job assessment and employee relations.
13. **Grievance Handling and Discipline** It ensures that there is discipline in the organisation and also focuses on providing a mechanism to handle and redress employee grievances.
14. **Industrial Relations** It is an important function to understand the employment relationship between various employers and employees, trade unions and the state or the government. It helps in running an organisation on the basis of various rules and laws present in the state.

Human Resource Planning

Human Resource Planning (HRP) is the strategy for acquisition, utilisation, improvement and preservation of the human resources of an enterprise. The objective is to provide right personnel for the right work and optimum utilisation of the existing human resources.

It puts the objectives of the organisation on paper and plans into the number and kind of personnel needed to accomplish those objectives. Thus, HRP involves determination of future manpower needs to help management in being upbeat. It is a proactive process.

It aids the management to anticipate deficiencies or surpluses of human resource in future and correct these imbalances, before they become uncontrollable and expensive. Through HRP tool, the management strives to have the right number and the right kind of people at the right places, at the right time for maximum benefit of both employees and organisations.

According to **Coleman**, " Human resource planning is the process of determining objectives, policies and programmes that will procure, develop and utilise human resource so as to achieve the goals of the organisation."

According to **Geisler**, "Manpower planning is the process including forecasting, developing, implementing and controlling by which a firm ensures that it has the right number of people and right kind of people, at the right place, at the right time, doing things for which they are economically most suitable."

According to **Decenzo** and **Robbins**, "Human resource planning is the process by which an organisation ensures that it has the right number and kind of people, at the right place, at the right time, capable of effectively and efficiently completing those tasks that will help the organisation to achieve its overall objectives."

Significance of HRP at Micro Level

- It helps in the creation of a reservoir of talent in the organisation for all times.
- It assists in the preparation of people for future by training and motivational techniques.
- It helps in developing talents as in today's competitive world, the rate of movement of personnel is quite high.
- It helps in adjusting personnel with the expanding or contracting scales of operations.
- It helps in cutting costs by maintaining appropriate manpower budget for each division and reduces overall cost.
- It helps in succession planning by preparing promising candidates in advance for senior positions.
- It helps in coping up with the changes in the external environment by strategically planning, the human resource requirement of the organisation to the corresponding change.

Significance of HRP at Macro Level

Technological Changes There have been intensive and rapid reforms in production technologies, marketing methodologies and management techniques. Their impact on job content and job contexts was profound.

These changes cause redundancy, reskilling and redeployment problems. All of these indicate the need for intensive and systematic planning of manpower needs.

Employment-Unemployment Situation Although the amount of educated unemployed in general is on the rise, for a variety of skills, there is an acute shortage. This stresses the need to recruit and retain people more effectively.

Governmental Influences Government control and legislative changes regarding affirmative action for socially disadvantaged, working conditions and working hours, limitations on women and child employment, casual and contract work etc encouraged organisations to participate in systematic HRP.

Organisational Changes In a dynamic environment represented by cyclical fluctuations and discontinuities, the nature and pace of changes in the organisational environment, activities and structures affect the needs of manpower and require strategic considerations.

Skill Shortages Joblessness does not mean that the labour market is the market of a buyer. Organisations have become more complex in general and require a wide range of rare and scarce specialist skills. When such employees leave, problems arise.

Demographic Changes The altering profile of the workforce has implications for HRP in terms of age, sex, literacy, technical inputs and social background.

Human Resource Planning Process

1. Corporate Analysis

- This comprises of setting strategies and objective of the business. This step is to see clearly about the objectives of any organisation out of which plans and policies are generated and it is very important to identify and incorporate organisational policies with regard to effective utilisation of human resources in planning process.
- HR manager then develops its organisational plans and ascertain whether the vacancies are to be filled by promotions or by hiring from outside or how are the training and development models going to meet the human resource planning objectives. Thus, various plans are built at the organisational levels.
- Corporate analysis also deals with preparing the production and sales targets of each department which helps in estimating the number of employees required in each department. This is accompanied by estimating the cost of recruitment and training, which is done by preparing financial plans.

2. Demand Forecasting

- The manpower needs are forecasted which are aligned to organisational objectives. Manpower needs depends upon the scale of operations of the organisation over that period of time and some other factors like machine-man ratio, change in productivity etc.
- It makes us clear about the amount of services required to produce a given number of goods. It does a complete survey of staffing levels in different parts of the organisation.
- It helps in avoiding unnecessary panic due to non-availability of people when and where required. It helps in monitoring legal requirements related to reservation of jobs and maintaining compliance to them.

3. Supply Forecasting

- This comprises of creating and studying manpower inventory. Manpower inventory means putting together information related to person's skills, abilities and potentials.
- Manpower inventory can be classified as managerial and non-managerial skills inventory. Since non-managerial personnel differ from managerial personnel, different types of information are required for preparing their inventories.
- In skills inventory, information about the employee's personal data, education, job experience training etc is collected. Information about his special achievements, salary and potentials of the employee is also implored.
- In management inventory, alongwith the above mentioned information some other things are to be known, *e.g.* strength, weaknesses, career plan, communication skills, overall personality, ability to work in a team, co-ordination etc.
- Through this inventory, the existing and future gaps in personnel and their abilities can be identified which becomes the basis for suitable managerial actions. The techniques of demand and supply forecasting are discussed in upcoming section.

4. Identifying Manpower Gap

- It is very important to forecast manpower gap to have the smooth functioning of any organisation. Manpower gap is the difference between manpower required at a particular time and the personnel being available at that particular time.
- This gap may be either in the form of having surplus human resources or having shortage of human resources. Only calculating the number of personnel will not serve the purpose rather it has to be measured in respect of various types of personnel.
- How to deal with both the cases of surplus as well as shortage of personnel is going to be explained in the next step of action plans.

5. Preparing Action Plan

- In case of surplus manpower, actions such as voluntary retirement scheme, layoff retrenchment, reduced working hours can be taken, considering legal problems. In case of shortage of human resources, actions, such as recruitment and selection, promoting personnel developing personnel, motivating and integrating them with the organisation can be implemented.
- Some of the labour shortage tactics are employee overtime, outsourcing and contingent labour, employee retention, employee promotion, transfers or demotions and recruitment. While, some of the labour surplus tactics are layoffs, attrition and hiring freeze, early retirements etc.

Demand Forecasting

It is the process of estimating the requirement of different kinds of personnel in future on the basis of annual budget and long-term corporate plan of action.

There are four basic demand forecasting methods

1. Qualitative Techniques

These are the techniques that are based on qualitative aspects and do not require dealing with data. Forecasting is also an art apart from science, hence it can be done with qualitative techniques also.

These are as follows

- **Managerial Judgement** These are used in smaller companies, it simply requires the functional managers to sit and think about their future workloads and decide manpower required. It can use the two forecasts by 'bottom-up' and 'top-down' approach, then the personnel department also prepares its forecasts.

  He compares the two forecasts and submit the final approved forecast which is the combination of the two, this is called 'right angle method'.
- **Delphi Technique** It relies on group discussion about demand forecasting. Here, the experts are individually asked about the human resource demand until a consensus is derived. It is cost effective because number of experts is consulted in a short time.

  It attempts to limit the subjectivity of forecasts by summarising the judgements of all these experts. Expert never meet face-to-face, but rather communicate through the facilitator. Thus, this technique is dependent on greater sense of coordination and cooperation.

2. Work Study Techniques

They are used to measure the length of activities and the amount of work required when it is possible to apply work measurement. Various techniques like motion study, work study, time study and method study studied alongwith other techniques. *Work study technique tries to assess the workload of an organisation in coming years and uses three types of analysis which are*

- **Workforce Analysis** In this analysis, the average loss of manpower due to leave, retirement, death, transfer, discharge etc during the last five years is taken into account. The rate of absenteeism and labour turnover should also be considered in order to arrive at the manpower inventory and learn about current workforce.
- **Workload Analysis** The companies try to calculate the number of man hours required for various jobs with reference to a planned output.
- **Job Analysis** It helps in finding out the skills and talent required to do the jobs efficiently.

3. Statistical Techniques

Managerial judgement and work study techniques can be applied to smaller organisations with few operations for short-term demand forecasting. Long range forecasting of big organisations required statistical and mathematical techniques.

These are as follows

- **Ratio Analysis** Ratio of number of workers to productions volume can be used to project the manpower requirement of future. Ratio analysis implies making forecasts based on the past or historical ratio between a causal factor such as quantity of goods sold and the number of human resource required such as sales executives.
- **Trend Analysis** It means studying variations in the firm's employment levels over the last few years. HR needs can be estimated by projecting past trends. It uses some organisational index to forecast the manpower requirement.

  It is done by first analysing the business factor annual volume of sales and then estimating the total number of employees, then a comparison of the productivity ratio is done. Then calculation of human resources demand is done and the human resource requirements are forecasted.
- **Scatter Plot** It graphically shows how two variables such as the company's staffing levels and sales are related. If they are related, whether negatively or positively, then the manager can forecast the business activity such as sales, then he should also be able to approximate the human resource requirement.
- **Nominal Group Technique** The nominal group technique is a decision-making method for use among groups of many sizes, who want to make their decision quickly, as by a vote, but want everyone's opinions taken into traditional voting.
- **Bureks Smith Model** To find estimated level of personnel, on the basis of total lag (volume of business in rupees) and total growth in business. *The formula is*

$$E_n = [(\text{Lag}+\text{G})\,\text{I}/\text{X}]/\text{Y}$$

where, E_n is the estimated demand of employees in 'n' planning period, Lag is overall turnover of business, G is total growth of business, X is the average productivity improvement, Y is conversion figure relating today's overall activity to personnel required.

4. Econometric Models

These are the models that are used by estimating on the basis of sales, revenue and profits. Econometric models for estimation of manpower requirement differ from the statistical methods.

Past statistical data are analysed in the hope that it will prove possible to describe precisely the relationships between a number of variables in mathematical and statistical terms. *They are*

- **Regression Method** Here, the demand for manpower is treated as dependent variable and various factors that affect the demand of human resource are considered as independent variable. This is done on the basis of past data. Thus, by using past data, the future needs are forecasted. If there are more than one variable, then multiple regression is used.
- **Simultaneous Equation Method** The model is based on exogenous variable (outside the model) and endogenous variable(input determined within the model). The model is solved for each endogenous variable in terms of exogenous variable and final prediction is made.

Supply Forecasting

It is concerned with the estimate of size and quality of personnel available within the organisation to occupy various positions. It can be termed as preparing manpower inventory. Every organisation will have two major sources of supply of manpower.

These are as follows

Internal Sources

Requirements in terms of internal movement due to transfer, promotions, retirements etc must be assessed in advance. Manpower audits may be carried out to find out inventory of skills with organisations. It comprises of replacement chart.

The various methods of supply forecasting for internal sources are

- **Succession Planning** It is a longer-term process of grooming a successor, who is selected from a pool of candidates on the basis of perceived competency for management or critical positions.

  This comprises of determining the internal labour supply calls for a detailed analysis of how many people are currently in various job categories or have specific skills within the organisation.

  The planner then modifies this analysis to reflect changes expected in the near future as a result of retirements, promotions, transfers, voluntary turnover and terminations.
- **Replacement Chart** A chart is [illegible] posts in higher level jobs and identify how potential [illegible] supply can fill these vacancies by way of internal movements from lower levels jobs. Thus, replacement charts provide identification of potential replac[illegible] for vacancies within an organisation.

  A comprehensive replacement chart will include information regarding possible replacements for vertical or horizontal movement. Generally, a replacement chart includes information about employees' performance, readiness to fill the position and education.
- **Markov Analysis** This analysis helps in predicting the internal employee movement from one year to another by identifying percentages of employees who remain in their jobs, get promoted or demoted, transfer and exit out of the organisation.

  By tracking and predicting employment movement within an organisation, the Markov analysis permits for the development of a transition matrix to forecast internal labor supply.

  A transition matrix, or Markov matrix, can be used to model the internal flow of human resources. These matrices simply show as probabilities the average rate of historical movement from one job to another.
- **Skill Inventories** These are the list of employee's education, past work experience, vocational, interests, specific abilities and skills, compensation history and job tenure. Generally, software's like Human Resource Information System and SAP etc are used.

External Sources

Organisations look on employment agencies, professional colleges to replenish the exhausted personnel. Organisations growth and diversification require the use of external sources to obtain young and fresh talent. These are elaborated in upcoming sections.

Job Analysis

A job is an organisational unit which consists of a group of defined tasks or activities to be carried out or duties to be performed. Job analysis is a formal and detailed examination of jobs in order to understand the tasks that needs to be done and the skills required to do these tasks under this job. It is a significant HR activity.

Job analysis provides the analyst with basic data related to specific jobs in terms of duties, responsibilities, skills, knowledge, degree of risk etc. It investigates into the responsibilities and duties that are necessary to perform a job. It tells what individuals do in their job and what their requirement for performing the job satisfactorily is.

Job analysis gives information that helps in writing job descriptions (what work is to be performed) and job specification (what kind of skill, talent and knowledge is required, what kind of workforce is to be hired).

Job analysis is the process of collecting job related information. Such information helps in the preparation of job description and job specification. Job analysis was conceptualised by two of the founders of industrial or organisational psychology, **Federick Taylor and Lillian Moller Gilberth**. It provides the information which helps to determine which employees are best fit for specific job.

A job analysis is a systematic process for gathering, documenting and analysing data about the work required for a job. The data collected in a job analysis and reflected through a job description, includes a description of the context and principal duties of the job and information about the skills, responsibilities, mental models and techniques for job analysis.

According to **Armstrong**, "Job analysis is the process of collecting, analysing and setting out information about the content of jobs in order to provide the basis for a job description and data for recruitment, training, job evaluation and performance management. Job analysis concentrates on what job holders are expected to do."

According to **Flippo**, "Job analysis is the process of studying and collecting information relating to the operations and responsibilities of a specific job. The immediate products of this analysis are job descriptions and job specifications."

According to **Dessler**, "Job analysis is the procedure through which one determines the duties of the positions and the characteristics of the people to hire for them. Job analysis produces information for writing job descriptions (a list of what the job entails) and job (or person) specifications (what kind of people to hire for the job).

Virtually every personnel related action , take interviewing applicants and training and appraising employees, for instance depends on knowing what the job entails and what human traits one needs to do the job well."

Significance of Job Analysis

- Job analysis produces information about a job, such as what is the overall purpose, why the job exists and what the job holder is expected to do.
- It also gives the information about to whom the job holder reports and who reports to the job holder.
- It also describes the content of the job which explains the nature and scope of the job in terms of the tasks and operations to be performed.
- It helps in human resource planning in determining the number and kinds of jobs and qualifications needed to fill these jobs.
- It makes recruitment and selection process easier by way of job description and job specification. Placement, orientation, training and development programmes can be directed towards helping the employee learn activities that are required to perform a given job.
- Job analysis establishes standards of performance that helps in evaluating performance appraisal. Job specification, as a part of job analysis, helps in vocational guidance and counselling of employees. Job analysis makes organisation re-designing possible through time and motion study, job specifications and work measurement.
- Job analysis provides opportunity to trace out health hazards related with the job. This helps in minimising the chance of risks to health and safety of employees.
- The modern job analysis addresses development through the provision of tools for employees that address
  (a) what it takes to do a job,
  (b) what an individual brings to the job and
  (c) what the gaps (learning and development needs).

Role of Job Analysis

- **Provide Base for Different Jobs** Job analysis provides the base for identifying the contents of different jobs, their inter-relationship and interdependence, responsibility involved in a job and authority that may be required to perform the job.
- **Human Resource Planning** Job analysis proves to be of great help in case of human resource planning by providing information for forecasting human resource needs in terms of knowledge, skills and experience. Job analysis also helps in planning for promotions and transfers by showing relationships among different jobs laterally as well as vertically.
- **Recruitment and Selection** Job analysis provides the basic ingredient required for recruitment and selection. It is well understood that recruitment and selection, taken together, is a process of identifying the source from where the personnel can be hired, motivating them, analysing them and selecting the ones who match the concerned job.

We can say that matching jobs and individuals is the whole process of recruitment and selection. Moreover, both the types of information in the form of job description and job specification are provided through job analysis.

- **Orientation and Placement** Job analysis also helps in orientation and placement by providing complete information about job requirements. It further helps when an individual is selected to perform number of jobs and not a specific job.
- **Career Planning** Job analysis helps in career planning by providing information about the opportunities in terms of career paths and jobs availability in the organisation. With the help of this information, both individuals and organisation are able to chart out their plan for career planning and development.
- **Employee Safety** Job analysis helps in taking precautions to save the employees from the hazardous environmental and operational conditions in various jobs. It is obvious that all such kind of information related to a particular job will be provided by job analysis.
- **Counselling** Job analysis also helps in providing counselling to employees in different areas. Sometimes, employees are unable to bear the stress of a particular job, then they are advised to opt for another job, but this is only possible with the information provided by job analysis.
- **Helps in Organisational Design** Job analysis provides all the required information to get the framework of organisational design. Organisational design is building a network of relationships among various functions and positions.

  In organisational design, various jobs to be perform are identified and grouped together on the basis of similarity. This process can only be done with the help of job analysis.

Process of Job Analysis

1. Understanding the Relevance of Job Analysis

This implies decide how one will use the information. This will determine the data one shall collect. Some data collection techniques like interviewing the employee are good for writing job descriptions. Other techniques, like the Position Analysis Questionnaire (PAQ) give numerical ratings for each job which can be used to compare jobs for compensation purposes.

Job analysis is undertaken more comprehensively, systematic and in written form in large organisations. In this case, information is collected from various sources in various forms. In smaller organisations, job analysis is used for limited purposes and job analysis process is mostly informal based on limited amount of information.

2. Design the Job

This is done on the basis of meeting production goals, promoting job mobility and career ladders, creating entry level jobs and removing artificial barriers to employment of special groups.

3. Collecting the Information

Here, the important information is collected to formulate the various characteristics of job. The information is collected in terms of activities involved in the job, responsibilities associated with the job, the type of environment in which the job is performed and the requirements in the person who will perform the job. This can be done on the basis of various process charts and organisational charts.

Organisational charts show the organisation-wide division of work and where the job fits in the overall organisation. A process chart provides a more detailed picture of the work flow. The various sources from where the relevant information can be gathered are personal observation, checklist prepared for analysing the job, questionnaire interview of the present employees performing similar job etc.

4. Processing the Information

After the information is collected, it becomes important to process the information by editing and keeping them under relevant categories. Job description and job specifications are prepared based on this exercise.

5. Writing Job Description

Then the job content is written in the job description and the identification of critical job requirements is done. Also, the assessment of job in relation to others to determine salary is conducted.

Techniques of Job Analysis

There are different approaches to deal with figures of job description. Some method designed to study jobs include the Position Analysis Questionnaire (McCormick, Jeanneret, and Mecham, 1972), Functional Job Analysis (Fine, 1974), Critical Incidents (Flanagan, 1954), Job Elements (Primoff, 1975) and the Physical Abilities Requirement Approach (Fleishman, 1975) and others.

1. Functional Job Analysis (FJA)

FJA was postulated by **Sidney A Fine**. The foundation behind FJA is that jobs must be well defined in terms of the interaction between the task, the individuals responsible for accomplishing the task and the environment in which the task is to be performed. In FJA, the experts make judgments about the content of job.

According to **Fine**, "These analysis study jobs in terms of five components. First, the purpose, goals and objectives of a specific job need to be identified and second, analysis must identify and describe the tasks necessary to accomplish a job. Thirdly, the analysts determine the specific abilities necessary to perform the job successfully. For this the job is evaluated on the basis of 7 dimensions, *i.e.* things, people, data, language, reasoning, mathematics and amount. Fourth, from this information, performance standards are set and then, fifth, training needs are identified in the final stages of functional job analysis."

The benefits of FJA are that FJA yields an extremely detailed picture of what tasks constitute a specific job. This detailed information can be used to identify wrong and possibly damaging suppositions about job task.

However, the drawback includes cost. This is because studying jobs, identifying tasks, developing performance standards and testing operators involves large numbers of personnel in a major effort.

2. Critical Incident Technique (CIT)

CIT asks employees for specific examples of on-the-job behaviour that demonstrates both high and low levels of performance. The CIT gathers data and analysis it to recognise job specific behaviours which affect the failure or victory of an individual or collective group performing a definite job.

Data about distinct critical events, such as unique instances of accomplishment or failure is gathered through questionnaires or interviews immediately after the occurrence of the event. These events are then classified according to related job behaviours to disclose patterns performance strengths or performance gaps.

Flangan has defined 'critical incidents' as "extreme behaviour, either outstandingly effective or ineffective with respect to attaining the general aims of the activity." Critical incident sources include employees, supervisors, managers and others.

The job analyst will typically ask informants to think about the latest example of a very high level worker performing. Informants will define what led to the event, what precisely the employee did and the perceived effects of the behaviour and whether or not these consequences were within the scope of the incident.

The advantage includes that it can be used to collect large amounts of figures in a short period of time. Labours are convened in groups and asked to come up with incidents. The disadvantage includes adverse effect on productivity of employees as the information is being derived from them.

3. Job Elements Approach

Ernest Primoff at the Federal Office of Personnel Management developed this method of job analysis and uses the elements that a worker uses in performing a specific job as his focus. He said that the elements of the job include Knowledge, Skills and Abilities (KSAs) and willingness, interest and personal characteristics.

Employment elements are based on the knowledge and experience of superiors and employees. These SMEs engage in a brainstorming session where they identify as many of the elements of a specific job as possible.

Then, they rate the elements on four factors which are

- Barely acceptable, *i.e.* what relative portion of even barely acceptable workers is good in the element?
- Superior, *i.e.* how important is the element in picking out the superior worker?
- Trouble, *i.e.* how much trouble is likely if the element is ignored when choosing among applicants?
- Practical, *i.e.* element practical and to what extent can we fill our job openings if we demand it?

On the basis of the statistical procedure developed by Primoff, ratings on the above mentioned four factors are analysed to decide what elements are most vital in selecting superior workers.

This method provides a detailed analysis of a particular job. The advantage is that recognises the tasks that constitute a particular job and thus, it is particularly useful for developing training programs. The drawbacks include that job elements are time consuming and costly to operationalise. Also, the analysts must be well versed with computer software.

4. Position Analysis Questionnaire (PAQ) Method

It was developed by **McCormick** in 1972. It is a questionnaire that is used to collect quantifiable data concerning the duties and responsibilities of various jobs. The PAQ approach centres on broad categories communal to all jobs rather than on distinct elements of specific jobs.

In this method, the analysis of job is done by personnel officers, methods analysts and job analysts or supervisors. Although job officials may use the PAQ form, this is usually restricted to managers and white-collar workers.

In the words of **McCormick**, Given the thousands of tasks for one job that the other methods may identify, PAQ attempts to put this data into a more manageable form. PAQ reduces all jobs to 194 elements, which are classified in terms of six broader dimensions.

These six dimensions are

- information input with 35 elements
- mental processes with 14 elements
- work output with 49 elements
- inter-personal activities with 36 elements
- work situation and job context with 19 elements
- miscellaneous aspects with 41 elements.

The final PAQ score shows the jobs rating on each of these six activities. The job analyst decides if each of the 194 items plays a role and, if so then to what extent.

The advantage of PAQ is in assigning jobs to job classes for pay purposes .With ratings for each jobs decision-making, skilled activity, physical activity, operation and information processing characteristics, one can quantitatively compare jobs relative to one another, 19 and then classify jobs for pay purpose.

Also, it can be applied in a wide variety of situations without modifications. However, Levine found that PAQ was not favoured because its language was not specific to particular jobs.

5. Physical Ability Requirements Approach

All of the aforementioned methods identify those tasks that a worker is expected to accomplish but not the information about the physical requirements. For numerous jobs, qualities such as reaction time, manual skill or trunk strength may be critical to successful job performance.

Uncertainty about physical requirements can also result in turnover or attrition that can be quite costly to the employer.

Fleishman and **Quittance** had developed a categorisation of physical and cognitive abilities that is designed to describe the performance standards of any job.'

According to Fleishman, abilities are the foundation on which skills are built. Whereas, operating heavy equipment is a skill, some of coordination and rate control.

The advantage of this approach is that it focuses on the physical abilities which are important Lecause poor match between applicant skills and physical requirements can result into a higher accident rate. However, the disadvantage is analysis of jobs with regard to this approach has not been widely explored in industrial and organisational psychology.

6. Others

Other methods include

- **Participation** The job analyst himself performs the job to perceive it first hand. He is able to understand the characteristics of jobs himself. However, this method cannot be used in technical and complex jobs.
- **Technical Conference** The information about the task is gathered from the supervisors who are the experts, instead of the actual performers *i.e* job incumbents.
- **Management Position Analysis Questionnaire** (MPAQ) This is designed with 208 elements, which are specially designed for describing, classifying, comparing and evaluating 'manager' or 'white-collar jobs.'

Hence, it is concluded that job analysis consists of examining a job, its component parts, and the circumstances under which it is performed. It results into a job description that sets out a job's purpose, scope, duties and responsibilities. A job specification can be derived from job analysis and job description, which is a statement of the abilities, expertise and other personal attributes required to perform the job.

Job Description

Job description is a list containing tasks or functions and responsibility of a position which are to be performed. Job description is a written statement mentioning the job title, tasks to be performed, duties and responsibilities involved in a job. It also mentions the working conditions, hazards, stress and other problems involved in a job and 'the relationship with other jobs. It is also called 'the duty statement.'

According to **Flippo**, "A job description is an organised, factual statement of duties and responsibilities of a specific job. In brief, it should tell what is to be done, how it is done, and why. It is a standard of function, in that it defines the appropriate and authorised content of a job."

Techniques of Writing Job Description

Job descriptions are based on the detailed job analysis and should be as brief and as factual as possible.

Techniques of writing a job description are explained below

Job Title The existing or proposed job title indicates as clearly as possible the function in which the job is carried out and the level of the job within that function.

Reporting to The job title of the manger or superior to whom the job holder is directly responsible is given under this heading.

Overall Responsibilities This part concisely defines the overall purpose of the job. The aim is to convey in no more than two or three sentences a broad picture of the job which will clearly differentiate it from other jobs and establish the role of job holder.

Main Task *The steps taken to define the main tasks of the job are as follows*

- Identify and list the tasks that have to be carried out. No attempt is made to describe in detail how they are carried out, but some indications is given of the purpose or objectives of each task.

- Analyse the initial list of tasks and so far as possible, simplify the list by grouping related tasks together so that no more than, say, seven or eight main activity areas remain. Decide on the order in which tasks should be described like their chronological order, order of importance, frequency with which they are carried out etc.
- Describe each main task separately in short numbered paragraphs. No more than one or at most two sentences are used for the description.

Advantages of Job Description

Role Clarity Role ambiguity is avoided and organisational procedures and processes become simpler.

Work Clarity Apart from describing the role, it helps the employee in understanding their work better.

Job Outcome It helps in focusing on the outcome of the job and lays down what is expected of the job.

Job Evaluation Job description help in maintaining a stable salary structure and facilitates compensation administration.

Job Specification

The job specification takes the job description and identifies the human traits and experience that are required to do the job effectively. It shows what kind of person to recruit and for what qualities one should test that person.

Job specification is useful in the selection process because it offers a clear set of qualifications for an individual to be hired for a specific job.

A job specification describes the knowledge, skills, education experience and abilities which are essential to performing a particular job. Job specification is developed from job analysis.

It is a written statement of minimum acceptable qualities required to complete a job and perform it effectively. It specifies various features of job holder, whereas job description provides various features of the job and follows job description or it is based on the job description.

Elements of Job Specification

Physical Specifications There are certain jobs where some special physical features may be required. These specific physical aptitudes and skills essential for a given job have to be specified. These may refer to height, weight, vision, finger dexterity, voice, poise, hand and foot coordination, motor coordination, colour discrimination, age-range etc.

Behavioural Specifications Certain management personnel at higher levels of management are expected to behave in a particular manner. These are not officially listed but have to be kept in mind during the process of recruitment, selection and placement. Some of them are general intelligence, memory, judgement, foresight, ability to concentrate etc.

Emotional and Social Specifications These include features which will affect his working with others, like personal appearance, manners, emotional stability, aggressiveness or submissiveness, extroversion or introversion, leadership, cooperativeness, initiative and drive, skill in dealing with others, social adaptability etc.

Mental Specifications These include intelligence, memory, judgement, ability-plan, ability to estimate, , to think and concentrate, to read, to write, arithmetical abilities etc. Different jobs require different degrees of such abilities and the more important ones should be specified.

Guidelines for Writing Job Specification

It may be a section of the job description or a separate document and generally follows these guidelines

- Writing job specifications for trained employees is comparatively forthright in comparison to untrained professionals. A job specification for trained employees focuses mostly on qualities like length of previous service, quality of relevant training and previous job performance.
- For untrained employees, this process is complex. Here, one must specify qualities such as interest, personality, physical traits or sensory skills that suggest some potential for performing or for being trained to do the job. Use task statements for writing job specifications. Each of a jobs task statements shows what the worker does on one particular job task, how the worker does it and for what purpose.

Difference between Job Description and Job Specification

Basis	Job Description	Job Specification
Concept	It is a written statement that explains the major requirements of a particular job.	This is a written statement that gives the minimum eligibility requirements, *i.e.* qualification skills etc to perform the given work.
Content	It provides the list of task, duties and the responsibilities involved in a job.	It provides the list of attributes, qualification, skill, abilities, age, domicile etc of the employee.
Objective	It describes what an employee is expected to do when he gets employed.	It describes what the applicant must possess to get selected and employed.
Prepared from	Job Analysis	Job Description
Describes	Jobs	Jobholders
Explain	Designation, place of work, scope, authority, responsibility, working hour, salary range etc.	Educational qualification age, work experience, skill, work orientation, interest, training factors, knowledge, education etc.

Job Design

Job design is the way tasks are combined to form a complete job. In this process, the work content (tasks, functions, relationships), the reward (extrinsic and intrinsic) and the qualifications required (skills, knowledge, abilities) for each job are integrated in a manner that statisfies the employees and the organisation. Some jobs are routine because the tasks are standardised and repetitive whereas others are non-routine. Some require a large number of varied and diverse skills; others are narrow in scope.

Some jobs limit employee behaviour by putting constraints and requires them to follow very precise procedures; other allow employees substantial freedom in how they do their work. Some jobs are better accomplished by giving substantial freedom in how they do their work, whereas some are best done by groups of employees working as a team.

Job design generally comprises of job content (work to be performed) and organisational responsibilities complying with rules and regulations. Thus, job design is a process of determining the specific tasks and responsibilities to be carried out by each member of the organisation.

Techniques for Designing Jobs

Basically, there are four techniques used in the design of jobs. These include job simplification, job enlargement, job enrichment and job rotation.

These are as follows

Job Simplification

Job simplification is a design method whereby jobs are divided into smaller components and subsequently assigned to workers as whole jobs. Simplification of work requires that jobs be broken down into their smallest units and then analysed.

Each resulting sub-unit typically consists of relatively few operation. These sub-units are then assigned to the workers as their total job.

These appears to be two major advantages in using job simplification. First, since the job requires very little training, they can be completed by less costly unskilled labour. Second, job speed increases because each worker is performing only a small portion of the previously large job and thus is able to master a smaller, less complicated job unit.

On the negative side, job simplification results in workers experiencing boredom, frustration, alienation, lack of motivation and low job satisfaction. This, in turn, leads to lower productivity and increased cost.

Job Enlargement

Job enlargement expands job horizontally. It is also called horizontal loading. It increases job scope, *i.e.* it increases the number of different operations required in a job and the frequency with which the job cycle is repeated.

By increasing the number of tasks an individual performs, job enlargement, increases the job scope or diversity. Instead of only sorting the incoming mail by department, for instance, a mail sorter's job could be enlarged to include physically delivering the mail to the various departments or running outgoing letters through the postage meter.

Efforts at job enlargement have met with less than enthusiastic results. As one employee who experienced such a redesign on his job remarked, "Before i had one lousy job. Now, through enlargement, I have three!" So, while job enlargement attacks the lack of diversity in over specialised jobs, it has done little to provide challenge or meaningfulness to a workers' activities.

Job Rotation

Job rotation refers to the movement of an employee from one job to another. Jobs themselves are not actually changed, only the employee are rotated among various jobs. An employee who works on a routine job moves to work on another job for some hours/days/months and returns back to the first job.

This measure relieves the employee from the boredom and monotony, improves the employee's skills regarding various jobs and prepares worker's self-image and provides personal growth. However, frequent job rotations are not advisable in view of their negative impact on the organisation and the employee.

Job Enrichment

This is called vertical loading. Job enrichment as currently practiced in industry, is a direct outgrowth of Herzberg's Two Factor Theory of Motivation. The assumption is to motivate personnel, the job itself must provide opportunities for achievement recognition, responsibility, advancement and growth.

The basic idea is to restore to jobs the elements of interest that were taken away under intensive specialisation. Job enrichment tries to embellish the job with factors that Herzberg characterised as motivators achievement, recognition, increased responsibilities, opportunities for growth, advancement and increased competence.

There is an attempt to build into jobs, a higher sense of challenge and achievement, through vertical job loading. "Enrichment means building challenge and achievement into workers' jobs by changing their jobs' content-letting them order and inspect their own goods, schedule their own day and so forth."

Difference between Job Enlargement and Job Enrichment

Basis	Job Enlargement	Job Enrichment
Definition	A technique of job design in which the task is related to a single job are enhanced and increased.	It is a method of job design, which is used as a tool to motivate the employee by adding responsibilities in the job.
Nature	It leads to quantitative expansion of job.	It leads to qualitative expansion of job.
Aim	To remove or lessen the boredom in performing a redundant task.	To make the nature of work more challenging, creative and interesting.
Result	It may or may not be positive.	It leads to the development of the employee, hence it is always positive.
Expansion	Horizontal loading	Vertical loading
Supervision	More	Comparatively less
Requirement of additional skills	No	Yes

Recruitment

Once the company conducts the company analysis and describes the qualities, skills required for filling the vacant job, they seek for potential candidates. Thus, the next step is recruitment followed by selection. Employee recruiting implies discovering and attracting candidates for the employers open positions.

It is the process of searching prospective candidates for employment and stimulating them to apply for jobs in the organisation. It is also known as 'Head Hunting'. It is the linking activity that brings together employer and seeking employees. To be effective, the recruitment process should attract qualified applicants and provide enough information for unqualified persons to screen themselves out.

According to **Taylor**, "Recruitment is the process of locating, identifying and attracting capable applicants."

According to **Flippo**, "Recruitment is a process of searching for prospective employees and stimulating and encouraging them to apply for jobs in an organisation."

According to **Dale S. Breach**, "Recruitment is the development and maintenance of adequate manpower resources. It involves creation of a pool of available labour upon whom the organisation can draw when it needs additional employees."

According to **Dale Yoder**, "Recruitment is a process to discover the sources of manpower to meet the requirements of the staffing schedule and to employ effective measures for attracting that manpower in adequate numbers to facilitate effective selection of an effective working force."

Features of Recruitment

- It aims at building an inventory of eligible persons from amongst whom proper selection of the most suitable person can be made.
- It is a positive action as it involves inviting people to apply.
- It involves location of such personnel motivating them to offer their candidature.

Process of Recruitment

Defining Requirements

The manager must decide what type of persons are to be invited and what their characteristics should be. This generally comprises of preparing role profiles and person specifications and also deciding terms and conditions of employment. The number and categories of people required must be set in formal workforce plans from which recruitment plans are derived.

Requirements are set out in the form of job descriptions or role profiles and person specifications. *i.e.* KSA etc. It should define the knowledge, skills, abilities and role of the person. It should also comprise of person specification, for example, Seven-point plan given by **Rodger** and Five-fold grading scheme given by **Munro-Frase**.

Planning for Sources of Recruitment

Recruitment can be done internally or externally. A manager must decide whether the position has to be filled from within or outside the organisation. There are various internal sources and external sources to choose from.

Recruitment planning will comprise of the number and types of employees required to cater for expansion or new developments and make up for any deficits and the sources of such candidates. It will also give details about plans for selecting alternative sources and finally tell how the recruitment programme will be conducted.

Selecting the Method

This comprises of reviewing and evaluating various sources of applicants, inside and outside the company. These methods can be transfers, promotions, advertising, online recruiting and consultancies. This generally comprises of analysing the recruitment strengths and weaknesses of each source and then deploying the best method. The sources of recruitment are explained in the upcoming sections.

Sources of Recruitment

There are two major sources which are explained below

1. Internal Sources

It comprises of filling job positions by present workforce by way of promotion, transfer and rehiring ex-employees. These include personnel already on the payroll of the organisation as also those who were once on the payroll of the company but who plan to return or whom the company, would like to rehire. Such candidates are those who quit voluntarily or those on production layoffs.

Advantages of Internal Sources

- Morale of employees is increased which increases their performance.
- Cheaper as compared to external source selection; as there is no cost of advertisement and interview expenses.
- The company can already assess the strength and weakness of the employee.
- Transfer or job rotation is a tool of training the employees to prepare them for higher jobs.
- The company needs to spend less on induction and orientation.

Disadvantages of Internal Resources

- There is reduction in scope of fresh talent.
- The employees who are not promoted may be discontented and dejected.
- It sometimes hampers spirit of competition because the candidates feel confident that he will be promoted in future.

Methods of Internal Recruitment

Job Posting Internal source of recruitment heavily relies on job posting which means publishing jobs to employees by posting on bulletin boards or intranets. This is called as Internal Job Posting (IJP). It is the most common method used to find qualified applicants from inside the organisation.

Transfers Transfers are horizontal transfers/lateral transfers, where the employee is shifted on the same level, *i.e.* to a department or a branch. There is no change in authority or responsibility with horizontal transfers.

Promotions Promotions are vertical movement in the position of and increased pay. He also gets more power and command. There is higher authority and responsibility accompanied with increased compensation and remuneration. It is similar to walking one step up in the organisational ladder.

However, organisations offer promote employees with additional responsibility without increasing their 'pay'. This is called dry promotion.

Rehiring Former employees are also an internal source of applicants. Some retired employee may be willing to come back to work on a part-time basis or may recommend someone who would be interested in working for the company.

Employee Recommendations Personnel may be employed on some special recommendations from employee side. A team leader may be given a liberty to form his team of his choice. It can be said that juniors are employed in the recommendations of their seniors.

2. External Sources

These sources lie outside the organisation, such as the new entrants to the labour force without experience technically known as freshers. These include college students, the unemployed with a wider range of skills and abilities, the retired experienced persons and others not in the labour force, such as married women.

Advantages of External Recruitment

- There is availability of well qualified and trained people in the market.
- The company as a wider choice to select right people.
- It allows for getting fresh talent with creative ideas, thus there is an experienced and talented work.
- There is a competitive spirit between new and old employees ensures better performance.

Disadvantages of External Recruitment

- It is a lengthy and costly process.
- It may leads old employees to feel anxious of promotions and face direct competition from young employees.

Methods of External Recruitment

Virtual Job Fairs It is similar to regular fair, however it is fully digitised. Employees or the candidates leave their resumes, interact with live chats and communicate with recruiters.

Waiting Lists Many firms lean heavily on their own application files. These accounts list individuals who have specified their interest in jobs, either after visiting the organisation's employment office or making queries by mail or phone. Such records prove a very useful source if they are kept up-to-date.

Dot Jobs These are internet portals that give employees a way to visit the website of the recruiter and directly submit their resume on its official website.

Trade Unions These are often called on by the employers to supply whatever extra employees may be needed. Unions may be asked for recommendations largely as a matter of courtesy and an evidence of goodwill and cooperation.

Advertisements The employees can give ads in different media such as newspapers, TV, radio or bill boards, to attract potential candidates. Telecasting is also a part of advertisement.

Casual Callers The applicants visit the prominent institutions and 'drop' their resumes. This is a cost effective method of recruitment.

Manned Exhibits The associations send recruiters to conventions and seminars, setting up exhibition at fairs, and using mobile offices to go to the desired centres.

Employment Agencies These are employment exchange, which are run by the government. They provide data of skilled, semi-skilled labour. In certain cases, it is mandatory to post vacancies.

Management Consultancies These are the firms that help the organisations to acquire technical, managerial and professional candidates. *e.g.* Manatee consultants, AF Ferguson.

Campus Recruitment Prominent organisations maintain relations with prestigious colleges and business schools/ engineering colleges for recruitment to various profiles.

Professional Societies They may provide indications and clues in providing talented candidates for engineering, technical and management positions. Some of these maintain mail order placement services.

Recruitment Pyramid

Various employers use a recruiting yield pyramid to calculate the number of applicants, they must generate to hire the required number of new employees. They are generally carried on the basis of certain assumptions which have been derived from the past experiences.

For this, various recruitment yield ratios are calculated which measure how many candidates were hired from a total number of applications. It shows 'the percentage of candidates pass from one stage of the hiring process to another. *The formulae for calculating yield ratio*

$$\text{Yield Ratio Stage } n = \frac{\text{No. of Hirable Candidates Resulting from Stage } n}{\text{Total no. of Candidates who came in Stage } n}$$

Example

A firm needs 100 employees and from the past experience it know that

(i) The ratio of offers made to actual new hires is 2 : 1.
(ii) The ratio of candidates interviewed to offers made is 3 : 2.
(iii) The ratio of candidates invited for interviews to candidates interviewed is 4 : 3. Hence, the pyramid will look like

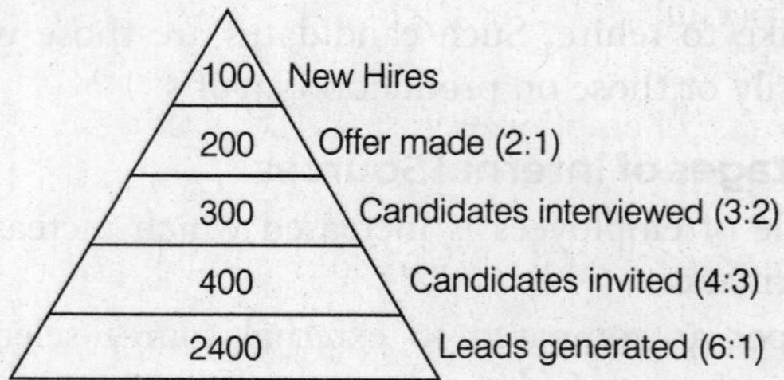

Thus, 2400 leads must be generated in order to finally select 100 candidates. Therefore, it is seen recruitment yield pyramids gives a historical arithmetic regression between leads, invites, interviews, offers and selection.

Selection

It is the process of picking individuals who have relevant qualifications and experience to fill jobs in an organisation. Selection is a negative process in contrast to the positive nature of recruitment because the selection involves rejection of applicants who are unfit for the job. This process establishes a contractual relationship between the employer and the worker.

According to **Decenzo** and **Robbins**, "Selection activities follow a standard pattern, beginning with an initial screening interview and concluding with final employment decision."

According to **Dale Yoder**, "Selection is the process by which candidates for employment are divided into two classes those who will be offered employment and those who will not."

MJ Jucious has defined, "The selection procedure is the system of functions and devices adopted in a given company for the purpose of ascertaining whether or not candidate possess the qualifications called for by, a specific job."

Heinz Weihrich and **Harold Koontz** have defined, "Selection is the process of choosing form the candidates, from within the organisation or from outside, the most suitable person for the current position or for the future positions."

Importance of Selection

- Selection of employee helps in achieving the organisational goals.
- Selection of employees with right kind of aptitude and attitude will reduce the absenteeism and employee turnover to a great extent.
- Competent employees will prove effective and efficient to organisation.
- Right person for the right job induces higher job satisfaction.
- The morale of employees who are satisfied with their jobs is often high.

Factors of Selection

Physiological Features Physique, height, weight, sight and endurance.

Personal Characteristics Marital status, size of family and economic position.

Proficiency Qualification, training and experience.

Competency Potential for learning and performing.

Temperament Mental and emotional stability, honesty, loyalty and social skills.

Aptitude and Attitude Finding out the interest of person in job.

Selection Process

Selection process may be different for various organisation and different positions. The main objective of selection process is to extract the maximum information from the candidate which helps in analysing the suitability of a candidate for a particular job.

It involves rejection of unsuitable or less suitable applicants. This can be done at any of the successive hurdles which an applicant must cross. These obstacles act as screens intended to eliminate an unqualified applicant at any point in the process. This technique is known as the 'successive hurdles technique' and Yoder calls these hurdles 'go, no-go' gauges. *Selection process includes following steps*

1. Preliminary Interview or Interview Screening

This is a sorting process in which prospective applicants are given the necessary information about the nature of the job and also, necessary information is elicited from the candidates about their education, experience, skill, salary expected etc.

Job applications are written by the candidates; mentioning about their qualifications, experience, interests and other credentials. On the basis of this information, applicants are screened out and considered for employment.

The candidates who are found to be meeting the job standards or the candidates, whose credentials are matching the job requirement, are called for an interview. The organisations decide a suitable number of candidates to be called for the next step.

2. Receipt and Scrutiny of Application

By way of advertisement or at the reception, it helps in giving the basic idea about the candidates. The candidate is asked to give details about age, marital status, educational qualifications, work experience and references.

Then various types of application forms may be used by the same organisation for different types of employees, for example, one for peon, one for supervisor and another for manager.

The application forms are utilised in two ways: First, they assist in finding out the basis of information given as to the chances of success of the candidate in the job for which he is applying, and second to give a starting point for the interview.

3. Screening Interview

It is also called as courtesy interview. A junior executive from personnel department may conduct a brief interview to eliminate unsuitable candidates in initial stages so as to save time and efforts of interviewers' panel.

4. Employment Tests

A test is an illustration of an characteristic of an individual's behaviour, performance or attitude. It can also be an efficient process for comparing the behaviour of two or more persons. The employer uses tests in personnel selection in order to learn that individuals are different in their job related abilities and skills and that these skills are adequately and accurately measured.

In order to decide that a particular individual has the level of ability, knowledge, interest and aptitude for the job, certain employment tests were conducted, such as intelligence tests, aptitude tests, personality tests, simulation tests, assessment centre/ trade/proficiency tests which are explained in detail in upcoming section.

5. Employment Interview

An interview is a discussion with an objective between two individuals. An employment interview helps in obtaining information, giving information and giving motivation. It is the oral examination of candidates for employment.

Interview gives the recruiter an opportunity to ask questions that are not covered in tests and to judge his personality, temperament and to brief applicant about job. It can be structured (pre-determined questions) or unstructured (random questions).

There are various types of interviews which are discussed here

- **Informal Interview** Here, employer or a manager in the HR department may ask a few questions, like name, place of birth, previous experience etc.
- **Formal Interview** This held in a more official atmosphere in the employment office by the employment officer with the assistance of well-structured queries.
- **Planned Interview** Here, the examiner has a plan of action with regard to the time to be devoted to each applicant, what kind of information to be sought, information to be given to him etc.
- **Patterned Interview** This is also a planned interview but pre-arranged to a higher degree of accuracy, precision and exactitude. A list of questions and areas are carefully prepared in advance.
- **Panel Interview** This is done by members of the interview board or a selection committee. This is done generally for supervisory and managerial positions.
- **Group Interview** This is designed to see how the candidates react to and against each other. All the candidates may be brought together in the office and they may be interviewed.
- **Depth Interview** This is considered the best method to intensively examine the candidate's background and thinking and to go into considerable detail on a particular subject to special interest to the candidate.
- **Stress Interview** This is intended to test the applicant and his conduct and behaviour by putting him under conditions of stress and strain.
- **Non-directive Interview** This is designed to let the interviewee speak his mind freely. The interviewer is a careful and patient listener, prodding whenever the candidate is silent.

6. Reference Checks

The personnel department engages in checking references. This will fetch reliable information about candidate's regularity at work, character and progress from his previous employers.

The interviewee is requested to remark in his application, the names and addresses of three such persons who generally know him well. These can be his previous employers, friends or professional co-workers.

These individuals are approached by mail or phone and requested to supply their frank opinion, without incurring any liability, about the candidate either on stated points or in general. They are guaranteed that all information given by them will be kept confidential.

7. Physical or Medical Examination

Certain jobs require certain physical qualities like clear vision, perfect hearing, stamina and tolerance for long work hours, clear voice etc. It is important because it gives an signal regarding fitness of a applicant for the job concerned. It also helps in preventing employment of those suffering from some type of contagious diseases.

It generally comprises of the applicant's medical history, his special senses such as visual and auditory activity, his physical measurements such as height, weight etc and other general examination such as skin, musculature and joints.

8. Final Decision and Hiring

Applicants who cross all the hurdles are finally considered. If there are more persons than the number required for a job the best ones that is those with the highest scores are finally selected.

A true understanding between line managers and personnel managers should be established so as to make a right selection of right people. Once the decision to hire is taken, organisation has to intimate this decision to successful as well as unsuccessful candidates. Organisation will send appointment letter to selected candidates.

Employment Tests

As discussed in the aforementioned section, there are various tests that are used in the process of selection.

Some of the formal definitions of a test are given by following authors

According to **Lee J. Groonbach**, "A test is a systematic procedure for comparing the behaviour of two or more persons".

According to **Milton M. Blum**, "A sample of an aspect of an individual's behaviour, performance and attitude is called a test."

Thus, the employer can use various tests to evaluate the capability of the prospective candidates by deploying suitable tests.

Selection Tests

There are different types of tests conducted by different organisations with different objectives to measure different attributes. *These can be bifurcated into various categories such as*

1. Achievement or Intelligence Tests

These are also called tests of performance or proficiency tests. These assess the skills or knowledge obtained through a training program and the work experience. It measures the potential of an individual in a specified area/job.

Such tests, in other words, gauge what a individual can do based on the skill or experience that he/she has already acquired.

Achievement tests are typically used in educational institutions for admission to specific courses. Intelligence tests assess the general aptitude for intelligent presentation.

The various tests under intelligence tests are

- **Work Sample Tests** This measures the ability with which equipment can be handled by the applicant. This is done by giving him a portion of work to judge, how professionally he does it.
- **Trade Test** These are the tests that are done to ascertain the job knowledge. These are overseen to determine information of typing, shorthand and in operating calculators, adding machines, dictating and transcribing machines or simple mechanical equipment. These are generally oral tests and are believed to be satisfactorily answered only by those who know the job and work.

2. Aptitude or Potential Ability Tests

These tests of aptitude assess the testee's ability and strengths. These tests gauge and indicate how well after training a person could perform and not what he/she did. Aptitude tests are therefore used to predict a person's future ability/performance.

There are two aptitude testing goals. One to recommend young people or jobseekers on the field of operations they are likely to be successful in. This is known as 'vocational guidance'. Second, selecting the best people where they can succeed for jobs. This test is known as 'vocational selection'.

The various tools under these tests are

- **Psychomotor or Skill Tests** These measure a person's ability to do a specific job. These are run to determine mental ability or motor capacity and similar attributes involving muscular movement, control and coordination.
- **Mechanical Aptitude Tests** These ascertain the capacity of a person to learn a particular type of mechanical work. These are useful when apprentices, machinists, mechanics, maintenance workers and mechanical technicians are to be selected.
- **Mental Tests** These tests measure the overall intellectual ability or the intelligence quotient. IQ is obtained by dividing mental age by the actual age. An IQ of an individual can allow the manager to know whether he has the mental capacity to deal with new problems or not. These determine an employee's fluency in language, his memory, interaction level, his reasoning and speed of perception alongwith spatial visualisation.

3. Interest Tests

It is constructed on the mind-set that people having interest in an area will perform better in that as compared to the ones who have no interest. So, it becomes very important to locate the area of interest and to find what gives him satisfaction. These are also known as interest inventories. Interest inventories equate ones interests with those of people in several occupations. These tests are designed to discover a person's areas of interest and to identify the kind of work that will satisfy him.

*A prominent interest test is **Kuder Reference Record** which comprises of three forms which are elaborated below*

- The first form analyses the interest in vocations such as electrical, computational, artistic, literary, musical and clerical, mechanical.
- The second element of interest tests measures interest in private and personal areas such as group activities, conflict avoidance etc.
- The third form of interest test analyses preference responses to specific professions such as accountants, sellers, farmers etc.

4. Personality Tests

These tests are designed to assess personality dimensions, *i.e.* characteristics such as interpersonal expertise, dominance-submission, extroversion-introversion, self-confidence, leadership ability and aspiration. These learn signs to an individual's value system, his emotional reactions, maturity and his typical mood.

The tests help in measuring a person's motivation, his ability to adjust himself to the strains of everyday life and his capacity for social relations and for projecting an impressive image of himself. There are various tools to assess the personality of the person. These will be elaborated in the further units.

Some of the common tests are explained here

- **MBTI Model** (Myers-Briggs Type Indicator) It is a personally assessment tool with 100 questions. The respondents are classified as J or P (Judging or Perceiving), T or F(Thinking or Feeling), S or N(Sensing or Intuitive) and E or I(Extraverted or Introverted).
- **Type A and Type B** Mryer Friedman and Ray Rosenman have identified the type A and type B behaviours and have identified different traits in each category.
- **The Big Five Model** It gives the five basic traits that reflect human personalities. They predict how people behave in the real life situations. These five traits are extraversion, agreeableness, conscientiousness, emotional stability/neuroticism and openness to experience.
- **Minnesota Multiphasic Personality Inventory** (MMPI) It was developed by Morgan and King where they have requested to answer 495 items as either 'True', 'False' and 'Cannot Say'. They measure ten different personality dimensions such as depression, hysteria, paranoia etc.

- **Situation Tests** These measure an applicant's response and reaction when he is placed in a peculiar situation, his ability to undergo stress and his demonstration of ingenuity under pressure.

5. Projective Test

Here, an applicant is requested to project his own analysis onto certain standard stimuli. The way in which he replies to these stimuli depends on his own values, motives and personality. Such tests are premised on images or items that are incomplete.

The testee is required to tell or project on such stimuli, his own interpretation. The response of the testee represents its own principles, motivations, attitude, apprehensions, character etc. These tests are referred to as projective as they stimulate the testee to show or narrate the test situation into the scenario.

The popular tools for projective tests are

- **Thematic Apperception Test** (TAT) It is regarded to be the most well-known formal projective test, comprise of pictures. These images are shown to the respondent and a story based on the images is then asked to be compiled.
- **Rosenzweig Test** It is formally called Rosenzweig Picture-Frustration study and measures the latent hostility. It comprises of 24 cartoon pictures that shows two people in frustrating situations and each picture contains two "speech ballons".
- **Holtzman Ink Blot Test** HIT aims at detecting the personality of the candidate and has been developed in an effort to eliminate some of the statistical problems that beset Rorschach test. There are series of 45 inkblots and the candidate has to pick only one response.
- **Tomkins-Horn Picture Arrangement Test** (PAT) Developed by Tomkines, it comprises of strip like comic pictures that are presented in a random order. The candidate is required to quickly arrange the pictures in a desired sequence to give a meaningful and reasonable story. This generally comprises of 25 platee where each plate comprises of 3 sketches. The subject arranges the plates and his intelligence and personality is assessed.
- **Rorschach Blot Test** (RBT) It entails of 10 cards with ink blot and the respondent is asked to define what he/she sees in it.
- **House-Tree-Person Test** Developed by Buck, it comprises of 60 questions to ask the respondent. The subject is asked to draw a picture of house, tree and person. After completion of the drawing, the examiner asks few questions and then answers are analysed. *e.g.* Who resides here? Its the occupant happy? etc.
- **Draw a Person Test** The candidate is required to draw a person according to his imagination. The examiner then analyses the factor such as size of particular parts of body, overall shape of image and details given to the figure.

6. Pseudo-Scientific Tests and Methods

There are some stereotyped impressions of personality and characteristics that are still used as a basis of selection.

Some of them are

- **Polygraph** Polygraph is a lie detector test and it is done to confirm the exactness of information given in the application form.
- **Graphology** This test is conducted by some organisations to learn the level of energy, anxieties and spontaneity found in the writer, revealing idiosyncrasies, peculiarities and elements of balance and control to understand the testee's personality.
- **Physiognomy Tests** These evaluations indicate a distinct correlation between facial characteristics and behavioural and physiological functions. The structures of features reflect personality traits and characteristics according to these tests.

Precautions While Conducting Tests

Tests are useful when the number of candidates is big. Furthermore, tests will be not useful if they are not properly built or selected or administered. *Following are certain guidelines that must be followed while using various selection tests*

- It is very important to use the instrument which is valid and reliable to get the desirable results. Validity of a test refers to the content of measurement, *i.e.* it is measuring the relevant qualities of the candidates. Reliability refers to the consistency with which a test yields the same results throughout a series of measurements.
- Each test used should be assigned a weightage in the selection and the test scoring, administration and interpretation should be completed by persons having technical aptitude and training in testing.
- The standardised instrument has to be used which refers to the uniformity of procedure in administrating and scoring the test, testing conditions like the time limit, instructions, tester's state of mind and health and other facilities while administering the test.

Selection Criteria

To minimise the selection error, a technique formally called 'confusion matrix' is used by the organisations.

This is represented below

	Cut off	
FALSE NEGATIVE (right candidate not selected; error)	TRUE POSITIVE (Rightly selected) (High Hit)	Cut off
TRUE NEGATIVE Rightly rejected 'Low Hit'	FALSE POSITIVE (Wrong candidate selected)	Error

Performance Criteria ↑ Selection Criteria →

1. **False Negative** An applicant who would have succeeded is rejected because failure was predicted. Generally, these errors go unnoticed. This means that the selection score is low, though the performance score is high.
2. **False Positive** This is opposite to false negative where even the performance score is low, the selection score is high. An organisation that makes false positive error incurs three kinds of cost.
   (a) Cost associated with employing the candidate, *i.e.* absenteeism, damaged public relation, image.
   (b) Cost associated with training, termination, transfer etc.
   (c) Cost of recruitment, selection and training of the employee replacing the previous one.

➠ **Note** False positive and false negative are kind of selection error as a wrong candidate is selected or right candidate is rejected.

3. **True Negative** These represent a right decision where a wrong candidate is rejected. The examiner predicts the failure and it happens. It is called 'low hit'.
4. **True Positive** It is called 'high hit' and is the best criteria where the company selects the right candidate. True positive results when a candidate is hired expecting success and the success results.

Thus, the organisation must carefully select the employee to abstain from future costs.

Placement

Placement is the next process after selection. After selection the candidate is placed on the job for which he has been selected and this is known as placement.

Placement is the method of allocating a particular job to each of the chosen candidates. The newly employed individual is sent for work to some department. It also means that and person is assigned a specific rank and responsibility.

Placement refers to the allocation of people to jobs. It includes initial assignment of new employees and promotion, transfer or demotion of present employees. The essence of the positioning is to match the job requirements with a candidate's qualifications.

According to **Pigors** and **Myers**, "Placement is the determination of the job to which an accepted candidate is to be assigned and his assignment to that job. It is a matching of what the supervisor has reason to think he can do with the job demands.

It is a matching of what he imposes (in strain, working conditions etc) and what he offers (in the form of payroll, companionship with others, promotional possibilities etc)."

It is the actual posting of an employee to a specific job. It is very important and necessary for an employee that the departmental head or supervisor accepts him and has faith in his abilities and potentials that he will be able to fulfil the job requirements.

Due to all these reasons of the new employee's compatibility and his/her acceptance by the line/personnel, he/she is usually put on probation for a specified period during which he/she is on trial, which may vary from few weeks, months or even years as in government.

Benefits of Placement

There are numerous benefits of placement which are enlisted below

- Employees show good result on the job because the work assigned to them is according to their calibre and skills.
- Employees can easily build inter-personal and professional relations as they are comfortable with their job position.
- Placement helps in increasing the morale of the employees and they have high spirits.
- A rightly placed employee is comfortable and confident, thus he will avoid mistakes and accidents.

Conclusion

Hence, we can conclude that placement is the last step before welcoming the employee in the organisation which is known as induction. It is the welcoming process to make new employee feel at home and generate in him a feeling of belongingness.

Placement position the employee in the 'ready to go' mode, whereas induction welcomes the employees and prepares them for training and development. They are elaborated in upcoming chapter.

EXAM BASED QUESTIONS

1 The ultimate responsibility for HRM activities rests with the

(a) every manager (b) sales manager
(c) personal manager (d) All of these

2 Which of these activities are not included in the scope of Human Resource Management?

(a) Job analysis and design
(b) Motivation and communication
(c) Safety and health
(d) Organisational structure and design

3 People generate, retain and utilise knowledge and skills which is the ....

(a) human knowledge (b) human capital
(c) human competencies (d) None of these

4 Human capital comprises of which of the following?

(a) Social capital (b) Intellectual capital
(c) Organisational capital (d) All of these

5 Who has given the statement, "The HRM is the process of attracting, holding and motivating all manager line and staff."

(a) Dunn and Stephens (b) Armstrong
(c) Dessler (d) None of these

6 Personnel management cover the

(a) lower (b) top
(c) middle (d) All of these

7 Which of the following are the managerial functions of human resource manager?

(a) Plannning and organising
(b) Directing
(c) Both (a) and (b)
(d) None of the above

8 Do HR activities have an effect on employee and managerial behaviour?

(a) Yes, but these effects can be negative as well as positive
(b) HR has limited impact on either employee behaviour or managerial
(c) HR impacts on employee behaviour but not on managerial
(d) No, it is managerial behaviour which impact on HR

9 Human relation consists

(a) motivation (b) morale
(c) communication (d) All of these

10 Which of the following statements are correct?

(a) HRM has replaced the traditional concept of labour welfare and personnel management
(b) Human resource personnel do not recruit the personnel
(c) The role of labour welfare officer was not limited to welfare activities of employees
(d) None of the above

11 In this cut-throat competition, many organisations are undergoing the process of retrenchment in order to minimise the cost. Who of the following play an important role in preserving the reputation of the employer?

(a) Senior Management Personnel
(b) Media Personnel
(c) HR Specialists
(d) Close relatives of the owners'

12 Which one of the following statement is not true in the case of Human Resource Management?

(a) It performs developmental function
(b) Employees are motivated by salary
(c) It is proactive in nature
(d) It consists of various sub-systems

13 In which of the following aspect of HR it is very important for HR Department to depict its fairness and non-discrimination?

(a) Recruitment and selection
(b) Grievance and discipline
(c) Reward management
(d) All of the above

14 Why is it important to ensure that HR plans are flexible?

(a) To adapt the fast changing environments in which most organisations operate
(b) To accomodate the changes arising because of high attrition rate
(c) To ensure the availability of labour force at all times
(d) To adapt the changing skills and qualifications of all the professions

15 Which one of the following is not considered as the main function of Human Resource Management?

(a) Attracting applicants
(b) Separating employees
(c) Retaining employees
(d) Motivating employees

16 What is that which creates demand for human resources in the organisations at large?

(a) Expansion of industry and new ventures
(b) Shifting of plant location
(c) Population explosion
(d) All of the above

17 .... is the process of forecasting an organisations future demand for and supply of, the right type of people in the right number.

(a) Human Resource Planning
(b) Recruitments
(c) Human Resource Management
(d) Human Capital Management

18 **Which of the following factors state the importance of the Human Resource Planning?**
(a) Creating highly talented personnel
(b) International strategies
(c) Resistance to change and move
(d) All of the above

19 **......... is the process of estimating the quantity and quality of people required to meet future needs of the organisation.**
(a) Demand forecasting
(b) Supply forecasting
(c) Environmental forecasting
(d) None of the above

20 **Which of the forecasting technique is the fastest?**
(a) Work study technique
(b) Flow models
(c) Ratio trend analysis
(d) HR demand forecast

21 **......... is a systematic procedure for collecting, storing, maintaining, retrieving and validating data needed by an organisation about its human resources.**
(a) Data collection
(b) Human Resource Information System
(c) Management Information System
(d) Maintenance of records

22 **Which of the following is a barrier while doing human resource planning?**
(a) HR information often is incompatible with the information used in strategy formulation
(b) Implementing human resource information system
(c) Managing inventories
(d) Supply forecast

23 **What technique(s) is/are used while analysing the internal supply?**
(a) Inflows and outflows
(b) Turnover rate
(c) Conditions of work and absenteeism
(d) All of the above

24 **Choose the correct option, where Human Resource Information System can be used.**
(a) Succession planning (b) Retirement
(c) Designing jobs (d) Inducting new hires

25 **Which is/are the function(s) of human relations?**
(a) Minimise dissatisfaction
(b) Moral building programmes
(c) Personal contacts
(d) All of the above

26 **Which is/are the principle(s) of human relations?**
(a) Principle of work recognition
(b) Principle of participation
(c) Principle of motivation
(d) All of the above

27 **Which of the following strategies adopted by HR to attract potential candidates to apply in the process of recruitment, may result in indirect discrimination?**
(a) Advertisement on the web portals
(b) Word of mouth
(c) Through HR agencies and job centres
(d) Advertisement in the Employment Bulletin

28 **Are the best and most productive employees likely to be**
(a) quite expensive in terms of recruitment and selection
(b) a matter of just luck in terms of recruitment and selection
(c) quite cheap in terms of recruitment and selection
(d) no effect on cost in terms of recruitment and selection

29 **Which of the following is a barrier while doing human resource planning?**
(a) HR information often is incompatible with the information used in strategy formulation
(b) Implementing human resource information system
(c) Managing inventories
(d) Supply forecast

30 **Which of the following is not a quantitative demand forecasting method under HRP?**
(a) Regression Model
(b) Ratio and Trend Analysis
(c) Delphi Technique
(d) Bureks Smith Model

31 **Which of the following is not a method of supply forecasting?**
(a) Markov Analysis (b) Replacement Chart
(c) Succession Planning (d) Scatter Plot

32 **Which of the following statements are correct with regard to trend analysis?**
(a) Trend analysis means studying variations in the firm's employment levels over the last few years
(b) HR needs can be estimated by projecting past trends
(c) It uses some organisational index to forecast the manpower requirement
(d) All of the above

33 **Human resource planning not only fulfills the demand for labour but also involve**
(a) the cost incurred in employing given number of people
(b) the cost incurred in directing line managers
(c) the cost incurred in developing line managers
(d) All of the above

34 **A process that is used for identifying and developing internal people with the potential to fill key business leadership positions is called ....**
(a) succession planning
(b) investment in hunan resource
(c) highly talented personnel creation
(d) None of the above

35 The Delphi technique uses

(a) mathematical models as input to the decision-making process
(b) a panel of experts making a series of independent decisions
(c) a 'top-down' approach
(d) None of the above

36 Which is the scope of HRM as per Dale Yoder and Robert?

(a) Departmental administration
(b) Collective bargaining
(c) Training
(d) All of the above

37 Manpower planning can also be called as

(a) human resource planning
(b) human resource management
(c) human resource information system
(d) succession planning

38 Which of the following option is not the factor that hinders with the HRP process?

(a) Time horizons
(b) Environmental uncertainties
(c) Type and quality of forecasting information
(d) Unite the perspective of line and staff managers

39 The primary purpose of skill inventors is to

(a) determine salary classification
(b) make promotion and transfer decisions
(c) consolidate information about human resources
(d) predict human resource requirements

40 Which of the following is the simplest flow model used for forecasting?

(a) Markov model (b) Resource Based model
(c) Semi-Markov model (d) Vacancy model

41 Which of the following is the fastest technique of demand forecasting?

(a) Work study techniques (b) Flow models
(c) Ratio and trend analysis (d) Delphi technique

42 What are the pre-requisites for successful HRP?

(a) Backing of top management
(b) Personal records must be complete
(c) Techniques of planning should be the best
(d) All of the above

43 One of the major issues faced while performing the process of personnel planning is

(a) type of people to be hired
(b) multiple positions to be held
(c) type of information which should be used in making forecasting
(d) All of the above

44 In regard to staffing function, which combination activities in sequential order is correct?

(a) Job analysis, recruitment, selection, placement
(b) Recruitment, selection, placement, job analysis
(c) Selection, job analysis, placement, recruitment
(d) Placement, recruitment, selection, job analysis

45 The Delphi technique which is used for HR forecasting makes use of which of the following aspects?

(a) Social needs (b) Personal needs
(c) Emotional needs (d) All of these

46 The purpose of .... is to establish and document the 'job relatedness' of employment procedures such as training, selection, compensation and performance appraisal.

(a) induction (b) job description
(c) job specification (d) job analysis

47 The process of establishing the value of jobs in a job hierarchy is known as

(a) job analysis (b) job requirement
(c) job evaluation (d) performance evaluation

48 Which of the following is not offered in a job analysis?

(a) Candidate's attributes
(b) Working conditions
(c) Performance appraisal
(d) Job specifications

49 To review job description is the major function of

(a) supervisors (b) employees
(c) HR department (d) All of these

50 Job analysis is a process of gathering information about the

(a) job holder (b) job
(c) Both (a) and (b) (d) organisation

51 The final process of a job analysis is the preparation of two statements, namely,

(a) job observation and job description
(b) job specification and job observation
(c) job description and job specification
(d) None of the above

52 Which of the following is the key objective of job analysis?

(a) What it takes to do a job
(b) What an individual brings to the job
(c) What the gaps (learning and development needs)
(d) All of the above

53 Which of the following terms is not associated with job analysis?

(a) Task (b) Duty
(c) Position (d) Competitor

54 The process of bringing together different tasks to build a job is called

(a) job evaluation (b) job design
(c) job classification (d) job description

55 The written statement of the findings of job analysis is called

(a) job design (b) job classification
(c) job description (d) job evaluation

56 Which of the following may be termed as a scientific and systematic effort to modify the characteristics of an employee's job?
(a) Job redesign (b) Job enlargement
(c) Job enrichment (d) Job description

57 A structured questionnaire method for collecting data about the personal qualities of employees is called
(a) functional job analysis
(b) management position description questionnaire
(c) work profiling system
(d) None of the above

58 The process of grouping of similar types of works together is known as
(a) job classification (b) job design
(c) job evaluation (d) job description

59 Which of the following statements are correct with regard to job analysis?
(a) Job analysis is a list which containing tasks or functions and responsibility of a position which are to be performed
(b) It also mentions the working conditions, hazards, stress and other problems involved in a job and the relationship with other jobs
(c) Both (a) and (b)
(d) Neither (a) nor (b)

60 Job descriptions are based on the detailed .... and should be as brief and as factual as possible.
(a) human resource planning
(b) job analysis
(c) job evaluation
(d) job specification

61 Most job descriptions contain sections that cover
(a) responsibilities and duties
(b) job summary
(c) working conditions
(d) All of the above

62 Steps of job enrichment involves
(a) increasing the responsibility of the activity
(b) providing wider scope, more authority
(c) allowing employers to set their own targets
(d) All of the above

63 Which of the following statement is true?
(a) Job analysis is the process of examining a job to identify its component parts and the circumstances in which it is performed
(b) Job analysis is the process of critically evaluating the task, duties and job relationships
(c) Job is a group of position involving substantially the same duties, skins, knowledge and responsibilities
(d) All of the above

64 Who has given the definition of recruitment as "Recruitment is a process of searching for prospective employees and stimulating and encouraging them to apply for jobs in an organisation."
(a) Dale (b) Flippo (c) Taylor (d) Koontz

65 Which of the following statement is incorrect about recruitment?
(a) It aims at building an inventory of eligible persons from amongst whom proper selection of the most suitable person can be made
(b) It involves location of such personnel motivating them to offer their candidature
(c) It is a positive action
(d) It is a negative process

66 Which of these is/ are late the purpose(s) of recruitment?
(a) Make sure that there is match between cost and benefit
(b) Helps in increase the success rate of the selection process by reducing the number of visibly under qualified or over qualified job applicants
(c) Help the firm to create more culturally diverse workforce
(d) None of the above

67 Which of the following are the decisions to be made while devising the strategies to hire?
(a) Geographic distribution of labour markets comprising job seekers
(b) Make or buy employees
(c) Sequencing the activities in the recruitment process
(d) All of the above

68 Which one is the source of recruitment in India?
(a) Employment exchange (b) College campus
(c) Employee reference (d) All of these

69 Choose the method which is not a type of external recruitment technique?
(a) Acquisitions and mergers (b) Radio and television
(c) Former employees (d) Advertisements

70 Which of these is the most important external factor governing recruitments?
(a) Sons of soil (b) Labour market
(c) Unemployment rate (d) Supply and demand

71 Too much reliance on internal recruitment can result in
(a) restricted talent pool
(b) poor team work
(c) internal conflict
(d) more burded on HR Department

72 A major internal factor that can determine the success of the recruiting programme is whether or not the company engages in ....
(a) HRP (b) selection
(c) Induction (d) None of these

73 Which is the least expensive method for recruitments?
(a) Walk-ins and casual callers
(b) Campus placements
(c) Employment exchanges
(d) Consultants

74 While recruiting for non-managerial, supervisory and middle-management positions which external factor is of prime importance?
(a) Political-Legal (b) Unemployment rate
(c) Labour market (d) Growth and Expansion

75 What is the natural perception of people on the process of recruitment and selection?
(a) Positive
(b) Negative
(c) Both (a) and (b)
(d) None of the above

76 .... refers to the process of identifying and attracting job seekers so as to build a pool of qualified job applicants.
(a) Selection (b) Training
(c) Recruitments (d) Induction

77 Which mode of recruitment is through advertisements, newspapers and want ads?
(a) Direct (b) Indirect
(c) On payroll (d) None of these

78 Which of the following are general costs incurred in the recruitment process?
(a) Costs of material
(b) Costs of overtime and outsourcing while the vacancies remain unfilled
(c) Costs of property
(d) None of the above

79 What is the main objective of the recruitment and selection process?
(a) Recruit the right candidates
(b) Meet the high labour turnover
(c) To reduce the costs of recruiting
(d) None of the above

80 Recommendation of an employee is included as
(a) internal source (b) external source
(c) Both (a) and (b) (d) None of these

81 Identifying the right people in rival companies, offering them better terms and luring them away is popularly called as ....
(a) competition (b) acquisition
(c) poaching (d) None of these

82 Which of these is an alternative to recruitments?
(a) Employee leasing
(b) Contractors
(c) Trade associations
(d) None of the above

83 An interviewer must be skilled enough in asking which of the following category of questions to know about the opinions the interviewee on a particular issue?
(a) Questions that can be answered in yes or no
(b) Open ended questions
(c) Neither open ended nor close ended
(d) Either open ended or close ended

84 Which of the following are the major sources of recruitment of educated manpower?
(a) Local employment exchange
(b) On-campus interview
(c) Web portals
(d) All of the above

85 Selection is .... in its application as much as it seeks to eliminate as many unqualified applications as possible in order to identify the right candidates.
(a) positive (b) negative
(c) Both (a) and (b) (d) None of these

86 Which of the following is matched incorrectly?
(a) Job posting: Done within the organisation
(b) Transfers: Vertical movements with rise in authority
(c) Rehiring: Former employees
(d) Lateral transfers: No change in position

87 "Establish rapport and get ready to show your best" is the mantra of
(a) recruitment procedure (b) interview procedure
(c) orientation procedure (d) None of these

88 .... is the process of differentiating between applicants in order to identify and hire those with a greater likelihood of success in a job.
(a) False negative error (b) Training
(c) Selection (d) None of these

89 Rejection of an applicant who would have succeeded is ....
(a) false positive error (b) true positive
(c) true negative (d) false negative error

90 Selection is now .... and is handled by the human resource department.
(a) unplanned (b) outsourced
(c) centralised (d) None of these

91 .... occurs when an interviewer judges an applicant's entire potential for job performance on the basis of a single trait, such as how the applicant dresses or talks.
(a) Stress producing (b) Halo effect
(c) Unstructured (d) None of these

92 Which tests are designed to ensure accuracy of the information given in the applications?
(a) Graphology test (b) Interest test
(c) Grammatology test (d) Polygraph test

93 Which of the following is not a significance of selection process?
(a) Selection requires time, effort and money to get right type of people
(b) Selection of employees with right kind of aptitude and attitude will reduce the absenteeism and employee turnover to a great extent
(c) It is a negative process and results into rejection of candidates
(d) Competent employees will prove effective and efficient to organisation

94 **Which one of the following is a type of interview where a series of job related questions are asked that focus on how the candidate would behave in a given situation?**
(a) Behavioural interview (b) Job related interview
(c) Situational interview (d) Structured interview

95 **Which of the selection steps is the most critical?**
(a) Physical examination
(b) Selection decision
(c) Reference and background checks
(d) Employment interviews

96 **A test that seeks to predict success or failure through one's handwriting is ....**
(a) polygraph (b) graphology
(c) grammatologist (d) None of these

97 **In ...., the interviewer uses pre-set standardised questions which are put to all applicants.**
(a) unstructured interview
(b) structured interview
(c) behavioural interview
(d) mixed interview

98 **Which test assesses an individual's achievement and motivational levels?**
(a) Thurstone Temperament Survey
(b) Minnesota Multiphasic Personality
(c) Thematic Apperception Test
(d) Guilford - Zimmerman Temperament Survey

99 **Who has given the following statement of selection "Selection is the process by which candidates for employment are divided into two classes those who will be offered employment and those who will not."**
(a) Yoder (b) Jucious
(c) Robbins (d) Koontz

100 **Screening interview is also known as**
(a) courtesy interview (b) rejection interview
(c) casual interview (d) final interview

101 **Which of the following is also known as the Ink Blot test?**
(a) TAT (b) TBT (c) RBT (d) SAT

102 **Procedure of fitting right person into right job is classified as**
(a) placement of employees (b) interviewing applicants
(c) maintaining records (d) administering tests

103 **Identify the odd one out.**
(a) Physiological Features: Physique, height, weight, sight and endurance
(b) Personal Characteristics: Marital status, size of family and economic position
(c) Proficiency: Qualification, training and experience
(d) Competency: Mental and emotional stability, honesty, loyalty and social skills

104 **Purpose of selection for an organisation is**
(a) maintain records
(b) administering tests
(c) placement of employees
(d) interviewing applicants

105 **Which type of information is conveyed by orientation?**
(a) Training and education benefit
(b) Job location
(c) Job safety requirements
(d) General information about the daily work routine

106 **.......... is a systematic and planned introduction of employees to their jobs, their co-workers and the organisation.**
(a) Job evaluation (b) Investiture orientation
(c) Orientation (d) Placement

107 **Which of the following statements are correct?**
I. Manpower planning helps the organisation to realise the importance of manpower management which ultimately helps in the stability of a concern.
II. Manpower planning helps in reducing the overall cost of production by making optimum use of physical resources in an organisation.
(a) Both statements are correct
(b) Statement I is correct and Statement II is incorrect
(c) Both statements are incorrect
(d) Statement II is correct and Statement I is incorrect

108 **Which of the following statements are correct?**
I. It is the basic function of the top management to perform various activities of the organisation.
II. Personnel management and HRD are included in HRM.
(a) Both statements are correct
(b) Statement I is correct and Statement II is incorrect
(c) Both statements are incorrect
(d) Statement II is correct and Statement I is incorrect

109 **According to which of the following techniques of job analysis, the analysis reduces all jobs to 194 elements?**
(a) PAQ
(b) Critical incident technique
(c) Functional job analysis
(d) Job element approach

110 **Which of the following statements are correct?**
1. Human resource management is a strategic management function.
2. Under HRM, employee is treated as a resource.
3. HRM is the management of employee's skills, talents and abilities.
Codes
(a) Only 2 (b) Both 1 and 2
(c) All of the above (d) None of the above

111 Arrange the following in the process of job analysis.
1. Understanding the relevance of job analysis
2. Collecting the information
3. Design the job
4. Processing the information
5. Writing job description

Codes
(a) 5, 1, 2, 3, 4 (b) 1, 2, 3, 4, 5
(c) 1, 3, 2, 4, 5 (d) 5, 3, 1, 2, 4

112 Which of the following statements are correct with regard to FJA?
1. FJA was postulated by Sidney A Fine.
2. The foundation behind FJA is that jobs must be well defined in terms of the interaction between the task, the individuals responsible for accomplishing the task and the environment in which the task is to be performed.
3. FJA asks employees for specific examples of on-the-job behaviour that demonstrates both high and low levels of performance.
4. In FJA, the experts make judgements about the content of job.

Codes
(a) 1, 2 and 3 (b) 1, 2 and 4
(c) Both 1 and 4 (d) Both 2 and 3

113 Which of the following statements are true?
1. HRP facilitates international expansion strategies.
2. Job analysis helps in understanding duties and responsibilities of a job by drawing attention to a unit of work and its linkage with other units of work.
3. Job description is developed from job specification.
4. Job description describes the knowledge, skills and education experience which is essential to perform a job.

Codes
(a) Only 4 (b) Only 2
(c) Both 1 and 2 (d) Both 2 and 4

114 Which of the following options are used as forecasting techniques?
1. Ratio Analysis
2. Delphi Technique
3. Staffing Projections

Codes
(a) Both 1 and 3 (b) Both 2 and 3
(c) 1, 2 and 3 (d) Both 1 and 2

115 Rearrange the following steps of recruitment.
1. Searching
2. Evaluation and control
3. Planning
4. Screening
5. Strategy development

Codes
(a) 3, 2, 1, 5, 4 (b) 3, 5, 1, 4, 2
(c) 4, 5, 3, 1, 2 (d) 2, 1, 4, 5, 3

116 Rearrange the following steps involved in the human resource planning process in proper order.
1. HR programming
2. HR demand forecast
3. Environmental scanning
4. Control and evaluation of programme
5. Surplus restricted hiring
6. HRP implementation
7. HR supply forecast
8. Organisational objectives and policies
9. Shortage recruitments and selection

Codes
(a) 1, 2, 3, 4, 5, 6, 7, 8, 9 (b) 3, 8, 2, 7, 1, 6, 4, 5, 9
(c) 8, 9, 4, 5, 2, 3, 1, 6, 7 (d) 9, 8, 7, 6, 5, 4, 3, 2, 1

117 Which of the following statements are correct?
1. Polygraph is a lie detector test and it is done to confirm the exactness of information given in the application form.
2. Physiognomy tests: These evaluations indicate a distinct correlation between facial characteristics and behavioural and physiological functions.
3. Graphology test is conducted by some organisations to learn the level of energy, anxieties, and spontaneity found in the writer and analyse his writing.

Codes
(a) Both 1 and 2
(b) Both 2 and 3
(c) Both 1 and 3
(d) All of the above

118 Rearrange the following steps involved in the selection process.
1. External environment
2. Internal environment
3. Preliminary interview
4. Selection test
5. Employment interview
6. Reference and background analysis
7. Selection decision
8. Physical examination
9. Job offer
10. Employment contract
11. Evaluation

Codes
(a) 11, 10, 9, 8, 7, 6, 5, 4, 3, 2, 1
(b) 1, 2, 3, 4, 5, 6, 7, 8, 9, 10, 11
(c) 1, 2, 3, 4, 5, 6, 8, 7, 9, 10, 11
(d) 1, 3, 4, 5, 7, 9, 11, 2, 6, 8, 10

119 Which of the following statements are correct?

I. The employer uses tests in personnel selection in order to learn that individuals are different in their job related abilities and skills and that these skills are adequately and accurately measured.

II. An interview is a discussion with an objective, between two individuals. An employment interview helps in obtaining information, giving information and giving motivation.

(a) Both statements are correct
(b) Both statements are incorrect
(c) Statement I is correct and Statement II is incorrect
(d) Statement II is correct and Statement I is incorrect

120 The difference between job enrichment and job enlargement is that

(a) enlarged jobs include some of the planning and control systems whereas enrichment means getting more money for the same job
(b) enlarged jobs contain a large number of similar tasks, while enriched jobs include some of the planning and control in the hands of job holder
(c) enriched jobs include performing number of boring jobs as well alongwith the one he is performing
(d) All of the above

121 Do HR activities have an effect on employee and managerial behaviour?

(a) Yes, but these effects can be negative as well as positive
(b) HR has limited impact on either employee behaviour or managerial
(c) HR impacts on employee behaviour but not on managerial
(d) No, it is managerial behaviour which impact on HR

122 Which of the following statements are correct?

I. The immediate products of job analysis are job descriptions and job evaluation.

II. The basic purpose of recruitment is to create a talent pool of candidates to enable the selection of best candidates for the organisation.

(a) Both statements are correct
(b) Both statements are incorrect
(c) Statement I is correct and Statement II is incorrect
(d) Statement II is correct and Statement I is incorrect

123 Which of the following statements are correct?

I. Job ranking method and job classification method are usually used for the purpose of job description.

II. Personnel management is an extension to general management and concerned with promoting and stimulating competent workforce to make their fullest contribution to the concern.

(a) Both statements are correct
(b) Both statements are incorrect
(c) Statement I is correct and Statement II is incorrect
(d) Statement II is correct and Statement I is incorrect

124 Which of the following statements are correct?

I. Job evaluation evaluates the job and not the job holder.

II. Job specification is prepared on the basis of job description.

(a) Both statements are correct
(b) Both statements are incorrect
(c) Statement I is correct and Statement II is incorrect
(d) Statement II is correct and Statement I is incorrect

125 Which of the following statements are correct?

I. Job enrichment is a part of job analysis.
II. Job enlargement is a part of job design.
III. Job design is a part of job description.

(a) Only I
(b) Only II
(c) All of these
(d) None of these

126 Which of the following statements are correct?

I. Graphology entails study of candidates hand writing.
II. Ink blot test is a projective test.
III. Recruitment pyramid comprises of calculation of arithmetic relations.

(a) Both I and II
(b) Both II and III
(c) All of these
(d) None of these

127 Which of the following statements are incorrect?

I. Job description describe the education and experience required.
II. Position analysis questionnaire is a method to evaluate candidate's intelligence and personality.

(a) Only I
(b) Only II
(c) Both I and II
(d) None of these

128 Which of the following statements are incorrect?

I. Markov analysis is a method to conduct supply forecast.
II. Burek-Smith model is a method to conduct demand forecast.

(a) Only I
(b) Only II
(c) Both of these
(d) None of these

129 Which of the following statements are correct?

I. Casual callers are the applicants that drop their CVs at reception.
II. Dot jobs is a selection method.

(a) Only I
(b) Only II
(c) Both of these
(d) None of these

130 Identify the correct statement.

1. The experience, education, skills and knowledge are the main components of job specification, which need to be specified.
2. The process of establishing the value of jobs in a job hierarchy is known as job analysis.
3. Certain management personnel at higher levels of management are expected to behave in a particular manner, thus they write behavioural specifications while preparing job specification statement.

Codes

(a) Only 1
(b) Both 1 and 3
(c) Both 2 and 3
(d) All of the above

131 Identify the correct statements.

1. In MMPI model, the applicant is requested to answer 495 items as either 'True', 'False' and 'Cannot Say'. They measure ten different personality dimensions such as depression, hysteria, paranoia etc.
2. The big five personality model gives the five basic traits that reflect human personalities. These 5 traits are extraversion, agreeableness, conscientiousness, emotional stability/ neuroticism and openness to experience.
3. TAT, regarded to be the most well-known formal interest test, comprise of pictures.

Codes

(a) Only 1
(b) Both 1 and 2
(c) Both 2 and 3
(d) All of the above

132 Consider the following statements and state which of these are correct?

1. External sources of recruitment offer wider choice of candidate.
2. Advertisement is an external source of recruitment.
3. Transfer is an international source of recruitment.

Codes

(a) Both 2 and 3 (b) Only 3
(c) Both 1 and 3 (d) All of the above

133 Which of the following is correctly paired?

(a) Blank application form is supplied after: Preliminary interview
(b) Dexterity is used to judge: Intelligence
(c) Psychological test: Aptitude test
(d) External source of recruitment : Transfer of employees

134 Assertion (A) Human resource helps the organisation in reaching its goals.

Reason (R) Human resource manager need to get the right people in to right place at right time.

(a) Both (A) and (R) are correct
(b) Both (A) and (R) are incorrect
(c) Both (A) and (R) are correct and (R) is the correct explanation of (A)
(d) (A) is correct and (R) is incorrect

135 Assertion (A) Human resource planning is essential to determine the future manpower needs in an organisation.

Reason (R) It would be difficult to have the services of right kind of people at the right time in absence of HR planning.

(a) Both (A) and (R) are correct
(b) Both (A) and (R) are incorrect
(c) (R) is correct and (A) is incorrect
(d) (A) is correct and (R) is incorrect

Directions (Q. Nos. 136-143) *In the questions given below are two statements labelled as Assertion (A) and Reason (R). You have to examine these two statements carefully and select the correct code.*

Codes

(a) Both (A) and (R) are correct and (R) is the correct explanation of (A)
(b) Both (A) and (R) are correct, but (R) is not the incorrect explanation of (A)
(c) (A) is correct and (R) is incorrect
(d) (A) is incorrect and (R) is correct

136 Assertion (A) Competency based job analysis describes jobs in terms of measurable, observable and behavioural competencies.

Reason (R) Re-engineering re-designs the business process in such a manner that small multi-disciplinary self-managing teams get the task done together multi-skilled competencies.

137 Assertion (A) Job analysis information provides the foundations of an organisations human resource information system.

Reason (R) Job analysis information can be collected through interviews, expert juries advice, observation, mail questionnaires.

138 Assertion (A) Promotion is a move ment within the organisation to a higher position that has greater responsibilities and requires more advanced skills.

Reason (R) Promotion may not involve a raise in status but a bike in salary is a must.

139 Assertion (A) TAT is a projective test.

Reason (R) TAT comprises of analysing the personality of the candidate by his interelations about the pictures.

140 Assertion (A) True positive is high hit.

Reason (R) This is so because true positive means rejecting wrong candidate.

141 Assertion (A) External sources of recruitment may lead to demotivation of old employees.

Reason (R) External sources are costly and time consuming.

142 Assertion (A) Job specification is useful in selection process.

Reason (R) It helps in identifying the jobs and duties that are to be performed by the candidate.

143 Assertion (A) Job enrichment is horizontal loading.

Reason (R) The employee is given several tasks related to specific/single job.

144 Which of the following statements are true/false?

1. Training is a short-term educational process and utilising systematic and arganised procedures by which employees learn technical knowledge and skills for a definite purpose.
2. Training bridges the difference between job requirements and employee's present skills and abilities.
3. Training facilitates manpower planning.

Codes

(a) 1 and 2 are true, 3 is false
(b) 1 and 3 are true, 2 is false
(c) 2 and 3 are true, 1 is false
(d) 1 is true, 2 and 3 are false

145 Which of the following statements are true/false?

1. Corporate analysis focuses on the objectives and strategies of the organisation during HRP process.
2. Supply forecasting means the quantum of manpower required in the organisation.
3. Demand forecasting implies creating and studying manpower inventory.

(a) 1 and 2 are true, 3 is false
(b) 1 is true, 2 and 3 are false
(c) 2 is true, 1 and 3 are false
(d) 2 and 3 are true, 1 is false

146 Which of the following statements are true/false?

1. Informal interview comprises of an interviewer or a manager from HR Department asking casual questions such as name, previous experience etc.
2. Stress interview is intended to test the applicant and his conduct, behaviour in a stressful situation.
3. Depth interview is conducted to examine the candidates background and thinking and to go in detail about his special interest.
4. Planned interview is also informal in nature.

Codes

(a) 1 and 2 are true, 3 and 4 are false
(b) 1, 2 and 3 are true, 4 is false
(c) 1 and 4 are true, 2 and 3 are false
(d) 2 and 4 are true, 1 and 3 are false

147 Which of the following statements are true/false?

1. Societal objectives of HRM deals with compliance with natural laws, human right lows and labour laws.
2. The personnel objectives entails manpower planning.
3. The functional objectives comprise of recruitment, selection, training, appraisal and others.

(a) 1 is true, 2 and 3 are false
(b) 2 is true, 1 and 3 are false
(c) 1 and 3 are true, 2 is false
(d) 3 is true, 1 and 2 are false

148 Match the following.

List I	List II
A. Markov Analysis	1. Files of personnel education, experience, interest, skill etc that allow managers to quickly match job opening with employee backgrounds
B. Replacement Chart	2. Study of firm's past employment needs over a period of years to predict future needs
C. Skill Inventories	3. Method for tracking the pattern of employee movements through various jobs
D. Trend Analysis	4. A profile of job holders department wise and orders a snapshot of who will replace, of there is a job opening

Codes

	A	B	C	D		A	B	C	D
(a)	2	3	4	1	(b)	3	4	1	2
(c)	1	2	3	4	(d)	1	3	2	4

149 Match the following.

List I	List II
A. Union Management Relations	1. Functional
B. Compensation	2. Organisational
C. Employee Relations	3. Societal
D. Assessment	4. Personal

Codes

	A	B	C	D		A	B	C	D
(a)	4	3	1	2	(b)	3	2	4	1
(c)	2	3	1	4	(d)	4	1	3	2

150 Match the following.

List I (Terms)	List II (Features)
A. Job analysis	1. Job classification
B. Wage administration	2. Merit rating
C. HRM	3. HR planning
D. Labour turnover	4. Termination

Codes

	A	B	C	D		A	B	C	D
(a)	1	3	2	4	(b)	1	2	3	4
(c)	1	4	2	3	(d)	4	2	1	3

151 Match the following.

List I	List II
A. Industrial relations	1. Collective bargaining
B. Employee services	2. Recreation facility
C. Planning and development	3. Training
D. Wage and salary administration	4. Rating

Codes

	A	B	C	D		A	B	C	D
(a)	1	3	2	4	(b)	1	2	3	4
(c)	4	1	2	3	(d)	1	4	2	3

152 Match the following.

List I (Steps in Selection)	List II (Elements)
A. Application form	1. Encoding
B. Preliminary interview	2. Aptitude test
C. Employment test	3. Experience
D. Appointment interview	4. Bio-data

Codes

	A	B	C	D
(a)	1	2	3	4
(b)	4	2	3	1
(c)	4	3	2	1
(d)	1	3	2	4

153 Match the following.

List I	List II
A. Dot com jobs	1. Cheapest method
B. Casual callers	2. Freshers
C. Advertisements	3. Expensive method
D. Campus Recruitment	4. Monster and Naukri. com

Codes

	A	B	C	D
(a)	1	2	4	3
(b)	1	3	2	4
(c)	2	4	3	1
(d)	4	1	3	2

154 Match the following.

List I	List II
A. Personnel replacement chart	1. A chart prepared for each position in a company to show possible replacement candidates and their qualifications
B. Job posting	2. The on-going process of systematically identifying, assessing and developing organisational leadership to enhance performance
C. Succession planning	3. Company records showing present performance and promotability of inside candidates for the most important positions
D. Position replacement card	4. Publicising an open job to employees and listing Its attributes. like qualifications, supervisor, working, schedule etc.

Codes

	A	B	C	D
(a)	2	1	3	4
(b)	3	1	4	2
(c)	4	2	1	3
(d)	3	4	2	1

155 Match the following.

List I	List II
A. Predictive analytics to help anticipate the result of HR strategy	1. Job specification
B. Statement of purpose, scope, duties, task and responsibilities of job	2. Ernest J MC Cormick
C. Position analysis questionnaire	3. Job description
D. Statement of qualification and qualities required of an employee to be successful	4. Workforce analytics

Codes

	A	B	C	D
(a)	4	3	2	1
(b)	1	2	3	4
(c)	1	4	2	3
(d)	2	4	1	3

156 Match the following.

List I (Authors)	List II (Books)
A. Brech	1. Personnel- The Management of People at Work
B. RP Calhoon	2. Managing Personnel
C. Powel R	3. Management and Executive Needs
D. Hamblin	4. Evaluation and Control of Training

Codes

	A	B	C	D
(a)	1	3	2	4
(b)	1	4	3	2
(c)	1	2	3	4
(d)	1	3	4	2

157 Match the following.

List I	List II
A. Planned Interview	1. Here, the examiner has a plan of action with regard to the time to be devoted to each applicant, what kind of information to be sought, information to be given to him etc
B. Patterned Interview	2. Here, a list of questions and areas are carefully prepared in advance
C. Panel Interview	3. This is done by members of the interview board or a selection committee. This is done generally for supervisory and managerial positions
D. Group Interview	4. This is designed to see how the candidates react to and against each other

Codes

	A	B	C	D
(a)	2	3	4	1
(b)	3	4	1	2
(c)	1	2	3	4
(d)	1	3	2	4

158 Match the following and select the code of correct matching.

List I	List II
A. Identification of leadership potential	1. Vocational tests
B. Finding most suitable area of working	2. Aptitude tests
C. Discovering interest and potential for acquiring skills	3. Intelligence tests
D. Measuring capacity to think, learn and draw relationships	4. Personality tests

Codes

	A	B	C	D
(a)	4	3	2	1
(b)	1	2	3	4
(c)	4	1	2	3
(d)	1	3	2	4

159 Match the following.

List I	List II
A. The process of examining how work creates and adds value to the on-going processes in a business	1. Job enrichment
B. A fundamental re-thinking and radical re-design of business processes to achieve dramatic improvements in cost quality service and speed	2. Job design
C. The process of organising work into the tasks required to perform a specific task	3. Work flow analysis
D. The process of putting specialised tasks back together so that one person is responsible for producing a whole product or an entire service	4. Business Process Re-engineering (BPR)

Codes

	A	B	C	D
(a)	1	2	3	4
(b)	2	1	4	3
(c)	3	4	1	2
(d)	3	4	2	1

160 Match the following.

List I	List II
A. Aptitude Test	1. Psychomotor or Skill Tests
B. Achievement Test	2. Trade Test
C. Personality Test	3. Big Five Model
D. Projective Test	4. Thematic Apperception Test

Codes

	A	B	C	D
(a)	2	3	4	1
(b)	3	4	1	2
(c)	1	3	2	4
(d)	1	2	3	4

161 Match the following.

List I	List II
A. Achievement Test	1. Testing about verbal comprehension, word fluency, memory reasoning etc
B. Intelligence Test	2. Testing the knowledge about his claims
C. Personality Test	3. Testing one's level of interest in particular area
D. Aptitude Test	4. Testing about his inter-personal competence, leadership confidence etc
E. Interest Test	5. Testing the ability to do a specific job

Codes

	A	B	C	D	E
(a)	2	1	4	5	3
(b)	5	4	3	2	1
(c)	1	2	3	4	5
(d)	3	2	4	5	1

Directions (Q. Nos. 162-166) *Read the following passage and answer the questions the follows.*

Human resource planning is the strategy for acquisition, utilisation, improvement and preservation of the human resources of an enterprise. The objective is to provide right personnel for the right work and optimum utilisation of the existing human resources. It puts the objectives of the organisation on paper and plans into the number and kind of personnel needed to accomplish those objectives.

Thus, HRP involves determination of future manpower needs to help management in being upbeat. Manpower planning starts with examining the overall objectives of the organisation. In fact, manpower plan should be integrated into the overall objectives. The number of employees required to perform various operations will be derived from the objectives of the organisation. Overall objectives of the organisation have to be understood in order to draw a good manpower plan. Manpower demand is the number of people required to handle the present jobs.

Forecasting the demand for manpower is the process of estimating the future quantity and quality of employees required. For instance, in a retail organisation, the manpower demand is forecasted based on the work to be performed in every retail stores. Obviously the long-term corporate plans, budgets and annual plans would become basis for forecasting the demand for labour. Supply forecast is also known as manpower inventory.

The objective of preparing manpower inventory is to find out the number and quality of manpower available within the organisation to employee in various jobs identified in the organisation. Development of supply of manpower data relating to present human resources in terms of components, number, designations and department wise should be developed. Here potential losses in the existing manpower should be considered.

The loss of manpower arises out of voluntary retirements, deaths, retirements, dismissals, layoffs, disablement due to ill health, accidents and other losses occurring due to poor attitude and low commitment to the organisation. Gap analysis is the process of identifying the difference in the estimated number of employees and actual number of employees available in the organisation. This enables to determine the quantity and quality of manpower needed. This gap reveals the number of personnel to be recruited to fill the gaps.

162 Forecasting the demand for manpower
(a) is the process of estimating the future quantity and quality of employees required
(b) is the process of calculating current workforce engaged in different operations in the organisation
(c) is the process of estimating the critical situations, that may occur during the production process
(d) is the process of analysing the performance of the workers engaged in the organisation in past years

163 According to this passage,
(a) the number of employees required to perform various operations will be determined by the government
(b) the number of employees required to perform various operations will be derived from the objectives of the organisation
(c) the number of employees required to perform various operations will be derived from the market forces
(d) the number of employees required to perform various operations will be determined by the Trade Unions

164 Supply forecast is also known as
(a) manpower inventory (b) manpower analysis
(c) manpower planning (d) manpower forecasting

165 The objective of preparing manpower inventory is
(a) to find out the number and quality of manpower prescribed by government and other industrial regulating agencies
(b) to find out the number and quality of manpower required for future operations in the organisation
(c) to find out the number and quality of manpower available in the market
(d) to find out the number and quality of manpower available within the organisation to employee in various jobs identified in the organisation

166 Gap analysis is the process of
(a) identifying the total of the estimated number of employees and actual number of employees available in the organisation
(b) identifying the difference in the estimated number of employees and actual number of employees available in the labour market
(c) identifying the difference in the estimated number of employees and actual number of employees available in the organisation
(d) identifying the required number of employees and actual number of employees available in the organisation

PREVIOUS YEARS' QUESTIONS

2018

1 Which of the following is not correctly matched?
(a) Job classification - Grouping of job on some specified basis
(b) Job enlargement - Horizontal expansion of job
(c) Job enrichment - Vertical loading
(d) Job analysis - Deciding the content of job and relationship

2 In the context of HRM 'Head hunting' refers to which of the following?
(a) Training (b) Compensation
(c) Recruitment (d) Retrenchment

3 Which of the following is not a quantitative method for forecasting supply human resource?
(a) Markov analysis (b) Regression analysis
(c) Goal programming (d) Turnover analysis

4 Information relating to which of the following is not covered under job specification?
(a) Training (b) Job identification
(c) Education (d) Experience

5 Which one of the following falls under 'Dry promotion' category?
(a) Responsibilities remain the same but pay increases
(b) Responsibilities increase but there is no increase in the pay
(c) Responsibilities reduce but pay remains the same
(d) Responsibilities reduce but pay increases

6 A human resource specialist normally collects which of the following information via the Job analysis?
1. Work activities
2. Human behaviours
3. Machines, tools, equipments and work aids
4. Performance standards
5. Job context
6. Human requirements

Codes
(a) 1, 2, 4 and 5 (b) 1, 2, 3 and 6
(c) 1, 2, 3, 4, 5 and 6 (d) Both 1 and 5

7 Identify the correct sequence of procedure in creating 'Structured Situational Interview'.
1. Analyse the job
2. Appoint the interview panel and conduct interviews
3. Create interview questions
4. Create benchmark answers
5. Rate the job's main duties

Codes
(a) 1, 2, 3, 4, 5
(b) 1, 3, 2, 5, 4
(c) 1, 5, 3, 4, 2
(d) 1, 5, 4, 2, 3

8 Which of the following correctly explains a 'recruiting yield pyramid'?

(a) Company records showing present performance and promotability of inside candidates for the most important positions
(b) A forecasting technique for determining future staff needs by using ratios between, for example, sales volume and number of employees needed
(c) The historical arithmetic relationships between recruitment leads and invitees, invitees and interviews, interviews and offers made and offers made and offers accepted
(d) Finding and/or attracting applicants for the employer's open positions

2017

9 Job description implies

(a) identification of the qualities required in the job holder
(b) performance of job in a methodical way
(c) laying down systematically the duties and responsibilities of the job
(d) determination of the performance standards of the job

10 The human resource planning is a

(a) positive process (b) negative process
(c) reactive process (d) pro-active process

11 Match the following HRM models List I with their themes List II.

List I	List II
A. Long-term Labour Purchase Model	1. Seeks to minimise wage and benefit costs; and Employment levels within organisational boundaries. Outsourcing and externalisation of employment are encouraged
B. Workforce Commitment Model	2. Different employment models for core and non-core work are adopted
C. Labour Transactional Model	3. Firms would employ workers, for as long as they performed well and the company has the capacity to pay
D. Mixed Model	4. Employers provide job security in order to elicit long-term commitment and organisation can develop social and intellectual capital within the boundaries of the firm

Codes

	A	B	C	D		A	B	C	D
(a)	3	1	4	2	(b)	3	4	1	2
(c)	2	4	1	3	(d)	3	2	4	1

12 **Assertion** (A) The unilateral HR decision-making process partly gave way to negotiated decision-making.

Reason (R) Government norms and market forces imposed HR decisions.

(a) Both (A) and (R) are wrong
(b) Both (A) and (R) are right, but (R) does not explain (A)
(c) (A) is right, but (R) is wrong
(d) Both (A) and (R) are right and (R) explains (A)

13 Match the following tests (List I) with the tools used (List II) for carrying out these tests.

List I	List II
A. Thematic Apperception Test	1. Ten cards having prints of ink blots
B. Rosenzweig Test	2. 45 inkblot cards
C. Rorschach Test	3. 25 plates, each consisting 3 sketches
D. Holtzman Ink Blot Test	4. Pictures
E. Tomkins-Horn Picture Arrangement Test	5. Cartoons with balloons above

Codes

	A	B	C	D	E		A	B	C	D	E
(a)	4	2	1	3	5	(b)	5	3	2	1	4
(c)	4	5	1	2	3	(d)	4	3	1	2	5

14 The following three types of tests namely objective tests, projective tests and situation tests are basically used as tools of

(a) Intelligence tests (b) Personality tests
(c) Cognitive ability test (d) Competency mapping

2016

15 Examine the following statements relating to induction and identify those which are either true or false.

1. Induction today is renamed as employee orientation programme.
2. It is also known by the term 'on boarding'.
3. It is for the purpose of socialising the new employees.
4. Informal induction is better than formal induction.

Codes

(a) 1, 2 are true, 3, 4 are false
(b) 2, 3 are true, 1, 4 are false
(c) 1, 2 and 3 are true, 4 is false
(d) 1, 2 and 4 are true, 3 is false

16 A company wants to determine the staffing level required to sustain and improve its sales volume. Out of the following methods which will be used for forecasting the personnel required for the purpose?

1. Trend analysis 2. Ratio analysis 3. Scatter plot

Codes

(a) Only 2 (b) Only 3
(c) Both 2 and 3 (d) All of the above

17 Which model of HRM propagates that, "if integrated set of HRM practices is applied in a coherent fashion, with a view to achieving the normative goals of high commitment, high quality and task flexibility, then superior individual performance will result, which would lead to superior organisational performance."

(a) Harvard Model (b) Warwick Model
(c) David Guest Model (d) John M Storey Model

18 **Match the following selection errors (List I) with their descriptions (List II).**

List I	List II
A. True negative	1. Selection score is high, performance score is low
B. True positive	2. Both selection and performance scores are low
C. False negative	3. Selection score is low, performance score is high
D. False positive	4. Both selection and performance scores are high

Codes

	A	B	C	D		A	B	C	D
(a)	2	3	4	1	(b)	2	4	3	1
(c)	4	1	2	3	(d)	3	2	4	1

2015

19 **Five phases constitute the strategic HRM process, they are**
1. Identify Source of Competitive Advantage
2. Implementing HR Strategies
3. Environmental Scanning
4. Monitoring and Evaluating HR Strategies
5. HR Strategy Formulation

Codes
(a) 3, 1, 4, 2, 5 (b) 1, 3, 4, 2, 5
(c) 3, 1, 5, 2, 4 (d) 3, 2, 4, 5, 1

20 **Which of the following is not an HR Demand Forecasting Technique?**
(a) Managerial Judgement (b) Ratio Trend Analysis
(c) Merrick Differential Plan (d) Work Study Techniques

21 **Which of the following methods of forecasting is based on the principle that decisions from a structured group of individuals are more accurate than those from unstructured groups?**
(a) Opinion poll (b) Delphi technique
(c) Extrapolation (d) Input-output analysis

22 **What is the correct sequence of following stages in manpower acquisition process?**
1. HR need forecast
2. Assessing existing manpower
3. Net manpower needed
4. Organisational objectives and policies
5. Recruitment process

Codes
(a) 2, 1, 4, 3, 5 (b) 4, 1, 2, 3, 5
(c) 4, 1, 3, 2, 5 (d) 1, 2, 5, 4, 3

23 **Match the following.**

List I	List II
A. Reference checking	1. To predict success and failure through one's handwriting
B. Graphology test	2. To determine how well an individual can perform tasks related to job
C. Aptitude test	3. To ensure accuracy of the Information given in the application
D. Ability test	4. To determine a person's potential to learn in a given area

Codes

	A	B	C	D		A	B	C	D
(a)	3	1	4	2	(b)	4	2	1	3
(c)	2	3	4	1	(d)	3	4	1	2

24 **Which of the following statement(s) is/are correct?**
1. Job enrichment does not need a motive to perform.
2. Job enlargement is the expansion of number of different tasks performed by an employee in a single job.
3. Moving employee from one job to other adds variety and reduces boredom.
4. Participation cannot affect the enrichment process.

Select the correct answer by using the codes given below

Codes
(a) Both 1 and 3
(b) Both 2 and 3
(c) Only 3
(d) All of the above

25 **Which one of the following is an immediate product of job analysis?**
(a) Job description
(b) Job rotation
(c) Job enrichment
(d) Job enlargement

26 **The basic objective of manpower planning in organisation is**
(a) to ensure the skilled manpower
(b) to ensure the supply of manpower for future requirement
(c) to ensure the supply of right number and right type of manpower at the right time
(d) to ensure the increased productivity of manpower

27 **The ongoing process of identifying, assessing and developing organisational leadership to enhance performance is called**
(a) Strategic planning
(b) Succession planning
(c) Organisational planning
(d) Career planning

28 **Human capital refers to**
(a) total salaries of the employees in an organisation
(b) collective expenses incurred by employees in an organisation
(c) capital consumed in recruiting manpower in an organisation
(d) collective skills and knowledge of the total workforce of an organisation

2014

29 The broad statement of the duties and responsibilities of a job or position is called

(a) job description (b) job specification
(c) job analysis (d) job evaluation

30 Which of the following is not correct?

(a) Recruitment is first and selection is second step
(b) Selection is first and recruitment is second step
(c) Recruitment is positive process
(d) Selection is negative process

31 Which of the following pairs is correctly matched

(a) Job Analysis method : Observation method
(b) Job Description : Necessary qualifications required
(c) Job specification : Relationship of a job with other jobs in the organisation
(d) Transfer : Lateral shifting of employees

32 Which of the following models is popular for its comparison of personnel management and human resource management on the basis of 'Hard' and 'Soft' approach?

(a) David Guest's model (b) John M Storey's Model
(c) CJ Formburn's Model (d) Karen Legge's Model

33 The procedure for determining duties, responsibilities, working conditions and reporting relationships is known as

(a) job design (b) job description
(c) job specification (d) job evaluation

34 Test reliability is

1. ability of the test to measure the variable under study.
2. consistency of scores obtained by the same person when retested with the same test.
3. ability of the test to measure large number of variables.

Select the correct answer using the codes given below

(a) Only 1 (b) Only 2
(c) Only 3 (d) Both 1 and 2

35 TAT stands for

(a) Thematic Application Test
(b) Thematic Apperception Test
(c) Training Aptitude Test
(d) Thematic Attitude Test

36 Being a manager in an organisation, if you are asked to enrich the job of your subordinate, you will be consider which of the following?

(a) Remove some controls while retaining accountability
(b) Increase the accountability of individuals to their work
(c) Introduce new and more difficult tasks compared to those handled previously
(d) Assign general tasks to people to make them experts in those tasks

37 The tests to assess a person's ability to undertake a particular type of work or to learn particular skills are called

(a) aptitude tests (b) knowledge tests
(c) intelligence tests (d) attitude tests

ANSWERS

Exam Based Questions

1 (c)	2 (a)	3 (b)	4 (d)	5 (a)	6 (d)	7 (c)	8 (a)	9 (d)	10 (a)
11 (b)	12 (b)	13 (d)	14 (a)	15 (b)	16 (a)	17 (a)	18 (d)	19 (a)	20 (c)
21 (b)	22 (a)	23 (d)	24 (a)	25 (d)	26 (d)	27 (b)	28 (a)	29 (a)	30 (c)
31 (d)	32 (d)	33 (a)	34 (a)	35 (b)	36 (d)	37 (a)	38 (d)	39 (c)	40 (a)
41 (c)	42 (d)	43 (c)	44 (a)	45 (b)	46 (d)	47 (a)	48 (c)	49 (c)	50 (c)
51 (c)	52 (d)	53 (d)	54 (b)	55 (c)	56 (a)	57 (c)	58 (a)	59 (d)	60 (b)
61 (d)	62 (d)	63 (d)	64 (b)	65 (d)	66 (b)	67 (d)	68 (d)	69 (c)	70 (d)
71 (a)	72 (a)	73 (a)	74 (c)	75 (a)	76 (c)	77 (b)	78 (b)	79 (a)	80 (a)
81 (c)	82 (a)	83 (b)	84 (d)	85 (b)	86 (b)	87 (b)	88 (c)	89 (d)	90 (c)
91 (b)	92 (d)	93 (c)	94 (c)	95 (b)	96 (b)	97 (b)	98 (c)	99 (a)	100 (a)
101 (c)	102 (a)	103 (d)	104 (c)	105 (d)	106 (c)	107 (b)	108 (d)	109 (a)	110 (b)
111 (c)	112 (b)	113 (c)	114 (d)	115 (b)	116 (b)	117 (d)	118 (c)	119 (a)	120 (b)
121 (a)	122 (d)	123 (d)	124 (a)	125 (b)	126 (c)	127 (c)	128 (d)	129 (a)	130 (a)
131 (b)	132 (d)	133 (c)	134 (a)	135 (a)	136 (a)	137 (b)	138 (c)	139 (a)	140 (c)
141 (b)	142 (c)	143 (d)	144 (a)	145 (b)	146 (b)	147 (c)	148 (b)	149 (b)	150 (b)
151 (b)	152 (c)	153 (d)	154 (d)	155 (a)	156 (c)	157 (c)	158 (c)	159 (d)	160 (d)
161 (a)	162 (a)	163 (b)	164 (a)	165 (d)	166 (c)				

Previous Years' Questions

1 (d)	2 (c)	3 (b)	4 (b)	5 (b)	6 (c)	7 (c)	8 (c)	9 (c)	10 (d)
11 (b)	12 (b)	13 (c)	14 (b)	15 (c)	16 (c)	17 (c)	18 (b)	19 (c)	20 (c)
21 (b)	22 (b)	23 (a)	24 (b)	25 (a)	26 (c)	27 (b)	28 (d)	29 (a)	30 (b)
31 (d)	32 (b)	33 (b)	34 (c)	35 (b)	36 (d)	37 (a)			

Induction and Performance Management

This chapter highlights the functions that are performed after the individual is selected and placed in the organisation. It begins with induction programme and followed by training and development. The chapter also highlights various measures that assist in measuring the performance of the employee.

Induction

As we have studied, placement is regarded as sending the selected candidate to a particular department. However, induction or orientation is a process of socialisation of a new employee or organisational member. The term 'induction' means 'installation' or 'initiation'.

The activities covered in induction include introducing an employee to his new department and not merely place him. It is also marked as a beginning of the blending process that assists in fusing the organisational goal with the personal goals of the organisation.

Planned induction welcomes the employee and creates a favourable attitude which results into reduced labour turnover. It also increases the commitment and productivity of the employee. Induction is a technique in which a new employee is introduced to the purposes, policies and practices of the organisation, nature of work, working conditions, norms and ethos of the organisation.

It is basically the process to develop the level of comfort between the new joinee and the work, he is supposed to perform. It involves providing him the basic information, he needs to settle down quickly and happily and start his work in comfortable ways.

In this Chapter

- *Induction*
- *Training*
- *Management Development*
- *Performance Management*

According to **Flippo**, "Induction is the welcoming process to make the new employee feel at home and generate in him a feeling of belongingness to the organisation." Thus, induction is the welcoming process to make new employee feel at home and generate in him a feeling of belongingness.

Objectives of Induction

- To orient a new employee to his work group and the organisation.
- To promote a feeling of belonging and loyalty to the organisation among new-corners that increases his confidences as a result.
- To give new employee, an information about services and facilities and provide rules, regulations and HR policies to new employees.
- To remove fears, adjust and adapt to new job requirements which reduce the likelihood of the employee leaving quickly.

Essentials of An Induction Programme

A good induction curriculum must include the following aspects

- It must introduce the company, its past and products, process of production and major operations that are involved in his job.
- The importance of the job with all essential information about it including job training and job hazards alongwith the terms and conditions of service, conveniences and welfare facilities.
- It must explain the opportunities, promotions, transfer, suggestion schemes and job satisfaction and the structure of the organisation and the functions of various departments.
- It must include employee's own department and job, and how he fits into the organisation.
- It should state the social benefits and recreation services and personnel policy and sources of information and the company policies, practices, objectives and regulations.
- The rules and regulations governing hours of work and over-time, safety and accident prevention, holidays and leave, methods of reportage, lateness and absenteeism should also be stated.
- Finally, the policies with regard to counselling services, grievances procedure and discipline handling should be reported.

Induction Programmes

Induction programmes are conducted by the organisation in order to make the employee comfortable with the organisation, its structures, and its rules and about his job. This is done with the assistance of both, *i.e.* formal and informal induction programmes. They both are complementary to each other and not the substitutes of each other. *They are explained below*

Informal Induction Programme

Following are the steps in informal induction programme

Reception

This deals with receiving the employee. **Fowler** has given various characteristics that must be followed during the reception process. Some of them include ensuring that the person who has to receive the candidate is aware about their pending arrival, training the reception staff and guiding the new trainee, if he has to go to another location in the organisation, avoiding keeping the new starter waiting.

Documentation

A variety of documents may then be issued to employees, including safety rules and safety literature, a company rule book or an employee handbook. The employee handbook must contain a brief description of the organisation.

Some details of basic terms and conditions of employment such as hours of work, holidays organisation's pension scheme, insurance, payment arrangements, company rules, medical first aid etc.

Company Induction

The member of the HR department or other individual who is looking after new employees should run through the main points with each individual or, when larger numbers are being taken on, with groups of people. Thus, a more personal touch is delivered and queries can be answered. The formal induction programme begins from here.

Formal Induction Programme

A formal course is a chance to deliver messages about the business, its products and services, its values, missions and visions, by deploying a range of media such visual aids, documentaries, presentations that would not be available within sub-divisions.

The procedure of formal programme is as follows

General Orientation by the Staff

In this, general information regarding the history and code of conduct of the firm is given. The main purpose is to build up the positive image of the organisation in the eyes of an employee and fill the employee with a sense of pride that he is part of such reputed organisations.

In this, the detail of achievements, ranks, awards, certification and recognitions from different authentic and relevant bodies is given to the employee.

Specific Orientation by the Job Supervisor

It is usually done in his or her department where the person is supposed to work. The employee is shown the department and place of the work, the location and the facilities provided to him.

He is also explained about the other necessary departments and personnel with whom he needs to coordinate to get the work done. The purpose is to enable the employee to adjust with his job and work environment.

Follow up Orientation by the Personnel Department

It is basically the activity in which feedback of new entrant is taken. This is conducted within one week to six months of the initial induction. It is usually taken by an expert or a senior to find out whether the employee is reasonably satisfied with the organisation and the kind of facilities being provided to him.

If there is any difficulty experienced by the new comer which may become a bottleneck while fulfilling the work assigned to him, then the efforts are made to solve them or suggest him some alternatives through personal talks, guidance and counselling.

Enhancing Effectiveness of Induction Programme

- Training the supervisors is the art of orienting new workers.
- Orientation should be systematic and thoroughly planned.
- The responsibility of HR manager and the immediate superior must be clearly defined.

Training

It means providing new or current employees, the skills that they require to perform their jobs. Training can involve having the current job holder explain the job to the new hire or multi-week classroom or internet classes etc.

Training is the act of increasing the knowledge and skills of employees in improving their performance. The major outcome of training is learning how to perform jobs in most effective manner. It is a planned programme to bring measurable changes in skills, aptitude and social behaviour of employees.

The strategic plans of the employer should govern its training goals. This is done to identify the employee's behaviour, the company will require to execute its strategy and then infer what competencies, for instance, skills and knowledge employees will need.

Thus, training is an essential part of HRM as it links the competencies required by the company with the competencies possessed by the individual.

According to **Steinmez**, "Training is a short-term process utilising a systematic and organised procedure by which non-managerial personnel learn technical knowledge and skill."

According to **Robeeins**, "Training is a learning process, which seeks a relatively permanent change in behaviour that occurs as a result of experience."

Need of Training

Due to changing technology, quality conscious customers, greater productivity and better management, every organisation needs training.

It can be understood with the help of following needs

- To impart new skills and increasing knowledge of workers in doing specific jobs.
- To bring changes in the attitudes, building confidence and providing security to employees at the workplace.
- To improve performance, this leads to promotion and self-growth, higher earnings.
- To make the workers handle machine, material and equipment's more safely, so as to be less prone to accidents.
- Training develops adaptability among workers to changing work conditions and new technology.

Thus, it is seen that training is a crucial management process which is significant at both, the organisational level and individual level.

Importance of Training to Organisation

Best Development of Human Resource It aids in providing a prospect and broad structure for the development of technical and behavioural skills of the human resources in an institute. It also helps the worker in attaining personal growth.

By providing training to the workers, there is an increase in the skill, knowledge and talent in them. Thus, they can make themselves proficient of occupying positions at higher levels.

Development of Skills It also leads to an increasing in the job knowledge and skills of employee at each level. It aids in expanding the horizons of human intelligence and an overall personality of the workers.

Training increases the skills of staffs and they perform the job better than before which increases their productivity and overall effectiveness of the company.

Enhanced Utilisation of Human Resources It helps in augmenting the utilisation of human resource that further helps the worker to attain harmony between the organisational goals as well as their personal goals.

Tool for Effective Management Training helps the employee in learning new and challenging work which can help him in attaining higher positions. Also, a superior can delegate the work to his subordinate only when he is trained and willing to do it.

Less Supervision A well trained employee requires less supervision and thus, saves time and cost for the company.

Improves Organisational Climate It helps in building positive view and feeling about the organisation. The employees get these outlooks from leaders, subordinates and peers.

Importance of Training for Employees

Increased Safety A trained employee knows how to handle the machine and thus, this ensures his safety.

Higher Earnings There is quick chance of being promoted to higher positions, thus training helps in self-development and increased income.

Confidence Training also boosts the morale and confidence of the employee and gives a feeling of security and safety at the workplace.

New Skills The employee learns new skills which work as a valuable asset to him.

Adaptability A trained employee can easily adapt to the working environment and his job requirement.

Building an Effective Training Programme

The company must use a rational training process. There is a standard model that is used for building an effective training programme. It is the 'Analysis-Design-Develop- Implement-Evaluate' which is popularly called the ADDIE Model.

It comprises of five steps that are

Analysing the training need by conducting Training Need Analysis (TNA).

Designing the overall training programme.

Develop the course, *i.e.* assembling or creating the material for training.

Implementing the training methods, by actually training the targeted employee.

Evaluating the effectiveness of the course.

These steps are elaborated in five different sections.

Step 1 Training Need Analysis (TNA)

TNA is the method of assessing the gap between training of employees and training needs. Evaluation of the training needs is the first stage of the training process and includes a series of steps revealing whether training would help to solve identified problems.

It identifies the gap between present and essential levels of knowledge, skills and attitude. It makes the most of use of scarce resources. It confirms that appropriate and relevant training is delivered. Thus, a TNA delivers information on the training and skills development requirements of all members of the company.

Models of Training Need Assessment

A training need shows a gap in results and training can fill that gap. There is a lack of Knowledge, Skills and Attitudes (KSAs) when the worker does not know-how to do the job. **McGhee** and **Thayer's** have developed a 'Three Level Analysis' for conducting training need assessment.

These three layers are the organisational level (strategic need analysis), operational level(task analysis) and individual level (performance analysis). *These are explained below*

Strategic Training Need Analysis

Strategic goals which can be entering new business lines or expanding abroad often mean that the company would need to fill new jobs. Strategic training needs analysis describes the training workers will need to fill these jobs in the future. It comprises of conducting organisational analysis.

Organisational analysis is the analysis conducted to ascertain the progress of the company towards attainment of its objectives and goals.

This comprises of scanning the environment for opportunities and threats and evaluating the strengths and weakness internally. The prime consideration here is to see whether the proposed training will be compatible with the strategy, culture and goals of the organisation.

Similarly, an internal organisational analysis can be conducted in order to learn about the employee grievances, turnover absenteeism so as to see whether training is required or not.

Analysis of Current Training Needs

Most training efforts are aimed at improving current performance which includes specifically training new workers and those whose performance is inadequate. Examining the training needs of existing staff is more complicated, because one also needs to determine if training is the answer.

Performance can be low due to poor motivation, *e.g.* it is generally done by conducting task analysis (operational analysis) and performance analysis (individual analysis). Task analysis is a comprehensive study of the work to define what specific skills, *e.g.* like preparing spread sheets, reading diagrams, are needed to perform the job.

The goal here is to give these workers the skills and knowledge that they need to do the job. Job descriptions and job specifications are essential for conducting task analysis. It helps in learning about the gap between the KSAs (Knowledge, Skills and Abilities).

This is followed by competency model. The competency model combines, a detailed overview of the aptitudes an employee needs to do the job well. Hence, task analysis is used by supervisors to define the training needs of staff.

Conducting Analysis at Individual Level

Sometime, training is not the only solution for underperforming current employees, thus performance analysis is required at the individual level. This basically confirms a performance insufficiency and helps the supervisor in identifying its cause.

Administrators also identify training needs by evaluating performance standards by performing the job and asking existing employees and their supervisors. Performance analysis begins with relating the person's actual performance to what it should be. This decides which employee actually needs training programmes.

Performance analysis is the cycle of ascertaining that there is a performance defect and deciding whether by training or some other means, for example, transfer, the boss should correct such shortcomings. Here, the analysis must differentiate between can't do and won't do problems.

Can't do problems reflect problem in the organisational/job structure, whereas won't do problems reflect problem in the attitude of the individual. Hence, performance analysis is conducted to identify the training needs of existing employees.

Step 2 Designing the Training Programme

Design means preparing the overall training system including goals of training, methods of delivery and assessment of the programme. The information gathered in need analysis tells the managers where training is required most in the organisation, what training should focus on and which employees should participate in the training programmes.

Thus, it gives a clear understanding of the goals of the programmes. It generally includes various sub-steps such as identifying the performance objectives, constructing a thorough training outline from the start to end, selecting a program delivery method like internet or lectures and finally corroborating the overall programme design with management. *The process of designing the programme is as follows*

Setting Learning Objectives

Training, development, learning or instructional objectives must specify what the trainee must be able to do after completing the training programme. This must be done in the measurable terms. The learning objective should be practical and with a given training budget.

Here, the other constraints include the time constraint. It should also address to all the performance deficiencies identified during TNA. Also, a clear understanding of the goals of the programme should be set to ensure that it is a result oriented and supports the mission of the organisation.

Making a Motivational Learning Atmosphere

Learning requires both ability and motivation and thus, they have a prominent role while developing a design plan. First, in terms of ability, the learner who is the trainee needs various abilities, such as the reading, writing and mathematics skills. The manager must be attentive while developing a training programme because different individuals have different levels of skills.

Second, in terms of motivation, the trainee or the learner should also be motivated. This is because no supervisor should waste his time in presentation a disinterested worker how to do the job.

Make the Learning Substantial

The learners are motivated only when they can attach some meaning to it. Hence, while developing the training plan, the organisation must provide a bird's-eye view of the material, use familiar examples and visual aids, organise the information and use terms and concepts that are already familiar to trainees.

Make Skills Transfer Obvious and Easy

The design should be such that makes it easy to handover new skills and behaviours from the training site to the job site. For this, the manager must provide adequate practice, maximise the similarity between the training condition and the work condition, label or identify each feature of the step in process or machine.

Reinforce the Learning

Finally, the plan must ensure the learner gets plenty of feedback. When the trainer uses phases such as "well done, very good", the trainee easily reinforces the learning. The manager must conduct partial day training rather than full day training. He must also incentivise and offer learners' incentives of outdoor trip for completing each step of training programme.

Ensure Transfer of Learning to the Job

This step is required while design the programme because often trainees are not able to transfer what they have learnt to the actual situation. Thus, the programme must ensure that prior to training he must get learner and supervisor input in designing the programme and encourage employees to participate.

During training, he must provide apprentices with training experiences and conditions that look like the actual work environment. After training, reinforce what trainees learned by giving them rewards for the new skill acquired and executed.

Step 3 Developing the Programme

On the basis of above two steps, the manager must develop the programme. Development of the programme means designing the training content and materials of the programme. It means selecting the unique and specific content to be presented by the programme as well as developing/selecting the specific instructional methods, such as readings, cases, web-based etc.

It must mention various training equipment that will be used, such as workbooks, lectures, computer based activities, course activities, trainer manuals. Various employers build their own training content, while others use general content available online/offline. Thus, once the manager designs, approves and develops the programme, management can implement and then evaluate it.

Before the training, the manager must send announcements in advance, give directions alongwith a point of contact and ensure that applicants have materials required before training. Ensure that all attendees have a point of contact during training, if they have queries or need advice. Keep in mind that training does not end when the programme ends. Instead, check whether those trainees convert their learning to the job on a regular basis or not.

Step 4 Implementing the Training Programme

Aforementioned steps dealt with analysing, designing and developing the content for training. The fourth stage is to implement this content to the focused group. There are different training methods available for different categories of personnel in the organisation relevant for its training needs.

This step focuses on how the content will be delivered to the audience because there are various ways through which the training can be imparted to the trainees such as on-the-job-training and off-the-job training,

which are as follows

On-the-Job Training

OJT involves allowing the person to learn the job by doing it in real work situation. The new employee follows the orders, carriers out instruction and adopts the right technique while doing this job under supervision of an experienced employee. This method is popularly known as learning by doing and here the trainee is given an opportunity to handle and observe the job by being its literal part.

He learns under the guidance and supervision of the superior or an instructor. These on-the-job engagements can be complemented by self-managed learning arrangements by offering access to flexible learning packages and by providing advice on learning opportunities.

Advantages of On-the-Job Training

- It is an adaptable method because learning when one can see how a project is being carried out is better. Also, there is no need for a lot of training arrangement.
- It is a cheaper method because there are no demands for training associated with on-the-job training. To train the new trainers or staff, one doesn't need instructors from outside the organisation.
- It boosts quick learning because it helps the trainee to quickly learn by becoming part of the implementation, so no extra time is spent in explaining how the system works.

Disadvantages of On-the-Job Training

- Teaching is an art and not everybody can best explain the work because it requires clear communication, patience to hear the queries and abilities to answer them.
- Employers generally rush into the training process. Rushing into the training process to complete it as soon as possible can lead to new errors and less efficient trainee, creating a lot of doubts and confusion right from day one.
- Discussions between superiors and apprentices can lead to unwanted disruptions on their concentration at the job, for the individual alongwith his co-workers.
- When the instructors are directly involved in the process of production and also have no expertise, then there is a very high likelihood of a mishap and accident.

Methods of On-the-Job Training

Coaching or Understudy Method The employee is trained by an experienced worker or a trainee supervisor. This may include simply observing the supervisor or showing the steps to the new hire, step-by-step, by the boss or job expert.

It is a one-to-one training given by one senior worker to one junior worker on a personal basis. Mentoring is extension of coaching for a period of several years until the individual is capable of replacing the mentor.

Job Rotation Another OJT method is job rotation, where a worker goes from work-to-work at scheduled intervals. This training technique involves moving the apprentice from one job to another from different job assignments to gain experience and knowledge.

It makes flexibility possible in the department. It is common for training managers and non-technical workers. It makes a manager to know different operations procedures and practices in a department. It is also known as cross training.

Refresher Training Rapid changes in technology for the companies to go in for such training so that employees may be kept up-to-date and ready to face challenges is changing future environment.

Orientation Training Orientation or induction training try to accommodate the new employees to the organisation's rules and regulations and facilities.

Job Instruction Training (JIT) Many jobs consist of a sequence of steps best learned step-by-step. Thus, this step-by-step training is called job instruction training. It is the most common method where the trainee is prepared by giving instructions, the trainee is put at work site, checking whether the instructions have been well understood or not. This is succeeded by follow up the training to identify and correct the deficiencies.

Apprenticeship Training It is used to train in some skilled trades, such as electronics, mechanics, tailors, bricklayers for long time from two to five years. Trainee work for a very small salary in exchange for a specified number of formal training hours. It is a combination of on-the-job and off-job-training.

A formal process through which individuals become skilled professionals through a confluence of classroom teaching and on-the-job training. This technique provides the apprentices with instructions through theoretical and practical facets.

Informal Training Generally workers learn on-the-job through informal means which includes performing their jobs while interacting every day with their colleagues. Also, the employers can expedite informal learning, for example, by installing whiteboards with markers in the cafeteria area.

Cross Training Training workers to do diverse tasks or jobs than their own which helps in facilitating flexibility and job rotation.

Ice Breaking Sessions Ice breakers, energizers and engrossing activities increase the efficiency of training sessions when directed at the topic of training, speech or dissemination and needs of the participants and trainees.

Vestibule Training Trainees learn about the actual or simulated equipment with vestibule training but are trained off-the-job that is either in a separate room or vestibule. A method of skills training where educational facilities approximate actual working conditions and are fitted with actual equipment and machineries for manufacturing. Thus, here a duplicate machinery or complete infrastructure is fitted which is called the vestibule.

Since, the trainee is given a separate place, this method does not create much disturbance for the co-workers and also, a large number of employees can be effectively trained at the same time. Here, the trainee does not feel frightened or embarrassed. Vestibule training is needed when it is too expensive or unsafe to train employees on-the-job. It is middle path of on-the-job and off-the-job training methods.

Off-the-Job Training

Under this method, trainee is separated from the job situation and his attention is focused upon learning the job. There is an opportunity for freedom of expression to ask any questions.

Advantages of Off-the-Job Training

- It helps in increasing the productivity because it is conducted exteriorly and the business or workplace and apprentices are not involved in the production process.

- It helps in minimising the errors because the trainee does not form part of the production process and only trained skilled employees perform the task. Thus, errors are minimised.
- It helps in avoiding disturbance because the apprentices are not permitted to work in the actual workstation. Thus, existing employees can do their jobs effortlessly and efficiently.
- It is economical because a huge number of workers can be involved in this technique and guidance can be provided at the same time. It significantly reduces the costs of training.

Disadvantages of Off-the-Job Training

- Sometimes it can be more expensive due to extra space, experts' fees and accommodation and transportation costs.
- Sometimes it becomes less effective as it is steered outside the working environment. And the trainees may need extra induction training to handle their job.
- Also, it stagnates the production process because the trainees cannot take part in the production process. Thus, the possible yield and time is lost here.

Methods of Off-the-Job Training

Conference Training Conference means consultation. Here, individuals share information with the audience of a large number of people. It is an effective training method for both the instructor and the audience. The trainee learns to respect the viewpoints of other individuals.

Lectures Lecturing is a fast and simple technique to present information to large groups of apprentices. This is also known as classroom training. Thus, here the key focus is more on imparting knowledge rather than sills. This method is less costly because the cost per trainee is low. Generally, teachers use lecture-cum-discussion methods in order to reinforce the learning.

Incident Method Events and instances are prepared based on actual situations that have occurred in different organisations and each worker in the training group is expected to make judgements as if it were an actual-life situation.

Later, the entire group examines and describes the event on the rationale of individual and group decisions and takes decisions related to the case.

Case study Generally, case study deals with any issue faced by a company that a worker can fix. The trainee has a chance to analyse the case and come out with all possible alternatives. This technique can improve an employee's analytical and critical thought.

Role Playing This technique is generally used for human relations and leadership training. This increases the inter-personal skills. It is also known as 'psychodrama' or socio-drama'. Here, trainees are given diverse roles to be played and both interact with each other. Thus, this method helps the apprentices in learning how to behave in a conflicting role.

Step 5 Evaluating Training Effort

The final step in the AIDDE model is evaluation of the training programme. There are many things the HR can measure such as, the emotional responses of the participants to the programme, what the trainees discovered from the curriculum and to what extent the curriculum changed their on-the-job behaviour or outcomes.

Various models have been developed to assess the effectiveness of training programme. The prominent method is Kirkpatrick model alongwith **Brinkerhoff's Success Case Method (SCM) and Phillips model for learning.**

***Kirkpatrick** has given the following four methods in order to measure the effectiveness of training*

Reaction The reaction of trainees' must be studied, as they indicate the effectiveness of training programme. The relevant information can be gathered by constructing a questionnaire and getting it filled by them. If the response is positive then it can be concluded that the programme was effective, otherwise not.

Learning This measures the extent to which the skills and knowledge have been learnt by the employees. Thus, it aims at knowing the extent to which the trainees have greater knowledge or skill after the training programme they did before. Thus, the instructor can conduct a three step examination, *i.e.*

- by conducting written tests
- by testing their performance
- by graded simulations.

Behaviour The job behaviour of the employees reflect whether the acquired skills and knowledge have been applied and adapted or not. It is putting learning into practice.

It is to check the kind of change in the behaviour of trainee after training and to check whether the skills and knowledge learnt during training are being used by them or not.

All this information can be collected from the performance data which is prepared by the superior, peer, client and subordinate.

Result It aims at measuring quality improvement, productivity improvement, reduction in accidents absenteeism and labour turnover of the desired results are achieved then the training programme is considered to be effective.

They are the major contributors towards training effectiveness. The ultimate results in terms of productivity improvement, quality improvement, cost reduction, accident reduction, reduction in labour turnover and absenteeism are few of the criteria for evaluating training effectiveness.

Brinkerhoff's Model

This model involves identifying the most and the least successful cases within the learning or training programme and then studying them in detail.

This is generally done by comparing success to failures, which further helps in identifying what is to be changed to ensure success in future.

It is also known as **six stage model** and helps the evaluator in learning the effectiveness of training programme.

Management Development

Development of management is an effort to improve the performance of management by educating the administrators, changing attitudes or increasing skills. It therefore involves in-house programmes such as coaching, courses and rotational assignments, professional degrees such as SHRM programmes, certificate and online programmes from multiple sources and university programmes such as executive MBAs, leadership programmes.

It is important specially for promotion because promotion from within is a major source of management talent and nearly all promoted managers require some development to prepare them for their new jobs.

It is the process where manager not only acquires skills and competencies, but also capabilities for future managerial tasks. Management development denotes planned efforts to improve current and future performance of executives to prepare them for higher jobs in organisation.

According to **Mumford**, "Management development is an attempt to improve managerial effectiveness through a planned and deliberate learning process."

According to **Dale S Beach**, "Management development is a systematic process of training and growth by which individual gain and applies knowledge, skills, insights and attitudes to manage work of organisation effectively."

According to **Michael Armstrong**, "Management development is a systematic process which aims to ensure that the organisation has the effective managers it required to meet its present and future needs."

Role of Management Development

- It aims at increasing the knowledge alongwith enhancement of decision-making and conceptual skills.
- It also fosters creation of reserve of capable, competent and well trained managers.
- It aims at influencing the long-term behaviour of the employees.
- It also strives to bring change in the organisation by working as agent to change.
- It prevents obsolescence of employees by giving them adequate opportunities to exchange their knowledge and learn from challenges.

Nature of Management Development

Education Process It is an education process and broader than training. Management development implies development of people of different aptitudes, aspirations, talents, motivations and needs.

Behavioural Changes It is a process of learning and growth which is designed to bring behavioural change among the executives.

Continuous Process It is a continuous process and continues throughout the career of the executive because there is no end to learning.

Self-Development The managers aim at developing themselves by engaging in development programmes. The experiences earned during actual job can also add to self-development. It is an important principle of self-development.

Significance of Management Development

- The manager must enhance his knowledge due to rapid change in the environment and up gradation in the technology.
- The manager must also update his socio-cultural knowledge in order to understand the behaviour of employees, suppliers, customers and other clients.
- The workers in the present scenario are more aware and educated, hence the management must also update its knowledge about various laws and regulations with regard to worker's participation, wages etc prevailing in the country.
- There is an increased recognition of social responsibility by modern business houses has increased the need of management development.

Difference between Training and Development

Basis	Training	Development
Meaning	Training is a learning process in which workers get an opportunity to improve skill, competency and knowledge as per the requirement of the job.	Development is an educational practice which is concerned with the complete growth of the workers.
Objective	It aims at improving the work performances of the workers.	It aims are preparing the workers for future challenges.
Focus on	Present	Future
Managerial Level	It is given to the lower level employees.	It is provided to the higher level employees.
Duration	It has a fixed tenure.	It is a continuous process.
Term	Short-term	Long-term
Number of Individuals	Many	Only one
Orientation	Job oriented	Career oriented
Aim	Specific job related	Conceptual and general knowledge
Motivation	It comes from the trainer.	It comes from within.

Conditions for Management Development

- The individual should be interested in developing himself.
- The individual should know the areas of his potential development.
- A positive emotional and professional climate should be created in the workplace for the employee to progress and review himself.
- He should identify mechanisms of using these opportunities and get the support he needs from his superiors and the organisation.
- The individual should make a clear choice about the direction in which he would like to grow and develop.
- He should make efforts to develop.
- He should take outside help to periodically review his progress.

Skills to be Developed by a Manager

A manager must possess skills in order to effectively manage the dynamic organisational situations. *Some of the skills required by the managers alongwith their methods are enlisted below*

Decision-making Skills These skills can be learned by methods like in-basket, business game and case study.

Inter-personal Skills These skills are generally acquired through role play, sensitivity training.

Job Knowledge These skills are obtained through on-the-job training, coaching, understudy etc.

Organisational Knowledge These skills are acquired by job rotation, succession planning etc.

Methods of Management Development

On-the-Job Method

These methods are generally followed in the real environment where the supervisor has to work actually. They are most suitable when the objective is to improve the on-the-job behaviour of the executive.

There is high level of comfort level and motivation when the employee learns in the real life situation. However, in this the trainee is not free from the routine job responsibilities and pressure of their respective jobs.

Some of the on-the-job development methods are enlisted below

Coaching Here, the direct superior guides the junior about various ways and methods to perform a particular work. The objective of coaching is not only to impart the necessary skills for doing his task (which is training) but also provide him with differentiated knowledge so that he may grow and advance in future (which is development).

Brain Storming A method that brings together a group of five to eight supervisors to fix a problem. So as the name suggests, the brain storms to cultivate originality in thought. It creates new ideas.

The concept is that every idea, plan and thought presented at a group meeting must be assessed critically. It makes the assumption that everybody has a sharp mind and the ability to create fresh ideas.

Position Rotation This is also known as 'job rotation' as learnt under training methods. This method injects new ideas in to the different departments of the organisation. This stimulates a more co-operative attitude by exposing man to the problems and viewpoints of others. This is crucial for a person working at managerial level. This method broadens the outlook of the worker.

Understudy An understudy is a person who is under training by a superior to assume his position in future. The superior involves him in decision-making by discussing the daily operating issues to be tackled.

It is similar to coaching but the difference is that the manager can pick any one individual from his unit to become his understudy. Normally, the understudy relieves the executive of certain responsibilities, giving the trainee a chance to learn the job.

Multiple-Management It is a system in which permanent advisory committees of managers study problems of the company and makes recommendations to higher management. The technique was developed by **Charles P McCormick**. It is also called as 'Junior-board of executives'.

The junior board discusses various subjects with the senior board and make recommendations. However, the senior board is not compelled to accept the recommendations made by the junior board. This is the cheapest way of finding the hidden talent in the organisation.

Action Learning It is a training technique by which management trainees are allowed to work full-time analysing and solving problems in other departments.

Its comprises of carefully selecting teams of 5 to 25 members and then assigning them real-world business problems that spread beyond their normal areas of proficiency and structured learning through coaching and feedback. The senior managers of the employee choose the projects and decide whether to accept the recommendation of the team.

Special/Committee Assignments It gives lower-level executives immediate experience in working on actual problems. This is often done in groups. A group of recruits are requested by discussing the issue to fix a given organisational problem.

This improves the work of the team. Here, an ad-hoc committee is formed and is given a subject to discuss and make recommendations. It is a significant device of teaching the managers to acquire general background and to modify their behaviour towards the selected problem.

Succession Planning It includes developing workforce plans for the business's top managerial positions. It is the continuing process of methodically identifying, evaluating and developing managerial leadership to enhance the performance of the employee and the organisational as a whole.

Off-the-Job Method

Sensitivity Training This is a method of changing behaviour through unstructured group (comprising of 10-15 people) interaction. Sensitivity training is sought to help managers towards building better relations with others. The primary focus is on reducing inter-personal conflicts.

The actual technique employed in this training is T-Group (T stands for Training.) It is a small group of ten to twelve people assisted by a professional behavioural scientist who merely creates the opportunity for group members to express their ideas and to feeling freely. Group will work out its own methods of proceeding. A leader-less and agenda-free session is on. Focus is on behaviour rather than task.

Outside Seminars Numerous companies and universities offer online-based and traditional classroom management development seminars and conferences which help the managers in enhancing their knowledge and skills.

In-house Developmental Centres These are known as corporate universities. Companies can team up with academic institutions, and with training and development program providers and web-based educational portals, to create packages of programmes and materials for their centres.

Executive Coach He is an outside adviser who interrogates the executive's associates in order to find the executive's strong point and flaws, and then counsels and advises the manager, so he or she can exploit on those strengths and overcome the weaknesses.

Grid Training It is a six-year on-going and phased programme. It involves the development, enactment and appraisal stages of planning. The grid takes into account parameter such as people's concern.

Electronic Performance Support Systems (EPSS) These are electronic tools and displays that automate training, documentation and phone support. It integrates this automation into applications and then provides support that is quicker, inexpensive and more operative than traditional methods.

This method is generally used by customer care services. They are also called job aids. Job aids are sets of directions, illustrations, commands or similar methods available at the job site to guide the employee.

Computer Based Training (CBT) It is the method that boosts knowledge or skills using interactive computer-based systems. The system provides trainees to preview the lessons and answer questions and is particularly useful when combined with the watchful eye of an instructor with actual practice. It can be interactive or virtual.

The interactive multimedia training assimilates the use of graphics, audio-visual, photographs, text, animation and sound to generate a complex training atmosphere with which the trainee interacts, whereas virtual reality training puts the trainees into a simulated environment.

Programmed Learning It is a systematic method for educating job skills, containing presenting questions or facts, enabling the individual to respond and providing instant feedback to the trainee on the accuracy of their answers.

Programmed learning decreases the amount of time required for training. It also makes learning easier by allowing apprentices to learn at their own pace, receive instant feedback and reduce their chances of error.

Simulation Method It is the most well-known and heart of all methods of job training. Trainees are taught on the specially built equipment or machine in the simulation training method, which seems to be used for the field or in the job. *It comprises of three techniques*

- **Case Study Method** It is an off-the-job development method in which the manager is offered with a written description of an administrative problem to diagnose and resolve.
- **In-basket Method** This method was developed by **Kurt Levin**. The workers are provided with data about an fictional company, its practices and products, employees, HR and all the company related data.

  The trainee is given multiple papers like memorandum, reports and emails that a manager usually handles. These papers call for actions ranging from routine task to urgent situation. Trainee managers learn to assign priority to each particular matter.

  The apprentice must take notes, delegate tasks and arrange schedules within a specified period. These can develop workers' circumstance judgements and rapid decision-making skills.
- **Management Games** The interns are split into groups according to this technique and each group has to talk about specific activities and processes of an imaginary organisation.

  They explore and make a decision on different topics, such as production, publicity, pricing etc. This results in the process of cooperative decision-making.

  It is a development technique in which team members of managers compete for realistic but recreated situations by making automated decisions.

Behaviour Modelling A training method that first shows good management techniques to trainees in a film, asks them to play characters in a simulated situation and then their supervisor gives feedback and applaud.

First, trainees watch live or video instances showing models behaving effectively in a problem situation, this is known as modelling. Then, the learners get roles to play in an imitated situation, here they have to practice the real behaviours demonstrated by the models, which is called the role-play.

Then, the trainer offers reinforcement in the form of praise and constructive feedback, which is called social reinforcement. Finally, learners are encouraged to apply their new skills when they are back on their jobs.

Organising an Executive Development Programme

In order to organise an executive development programme, *following steps are need to be followed which are similar to those of training process*

- Analysis of present and future needs of managerial and executive man power.
- Preparing inventory of management talent in terms of skills, experience, education, age etc.
- Appraisal of performance of the executives in terms of their decision-making and its resultant outcome.
- Planning for a well-planned training programme, identifying its key objectives. Types of methods to be employed are selected.
- Execution and evaluation of executive development programme.

Performance Management

Performance management is an important HRM process that provides the basis for improving and developing performance and is part of the reward system in its most general sense.

Performance management is a process through which employees and managers work together to strategies, observe and review the work goals and overall contribution of an worker to the organisation.

Performance management is a much broader and deeper and complex function of human resources, since it includes activities such as setting common goals, constant review of significant progress and regular communication, feedback and mentoring for better performance, execution of employee development programmes and successful achievements. It is different from performance appraisal.

According to **Weiss and Hartle**, "A process for establishing a shared understanding about what is to be achieved and how it is to be achieved and an approach to managing people that increases the probability of achieving success is called performance management."

According to **Dessler**, "Performance management is a continuous process of identifying, measuring and developing the performance of individuals and teams and aligning their performance with the organisations' goal."

According to **Armstrong** and **Baron**, "Performance management is both a strategic and an integrated approach to delivering successful results in organisations by improving the performance and developing the capabilities of teams and individuals."

Objectives of Performance Management

- To encourage employees to achieve higher job performance standards.
- To help workers in identifying the knowledge and skills desired to carry out the task efficiently, as this would lead to the right task being carried out.
- To boost employee productivity by promoting employee motivation and empowerment alongwith implementation of an effective reward system.
- To promote a two-way conversation system between managers and employees to clarify expectations about roles and accountabilities, communicate functional and organisational aims and deliver regular and transparent feedback to increase employee performance and on-going coaching.

Features of Performance Management

- It is different from merit-rating as it is wider than merit-rating.
- It focuses on the performance and future potential whereas merit rating is detrimental to decide salary increment. It aims to develop rational bases for personnel decisions.
- It measures what the person does (performance) whereas merit rating measures what the person is (traits). It is a process consisting of a series of steps.
- It is the systematic and scientific analysis of an employee's strengths and weaknesses in terms of the job. It is completely objective, rational, formal and scientific study.
- It is a continuous and perpetual process and the employee is evaluated time-to-time under a definite plan. It is done to collect information necessary for reaching an objective and correct decisions on employees.

A Shift towards Performance Management

Contemporary organisations are experiencing a transformation to address changing environmental needs and excellence in the company by proactively developing their adaptive abilities to manage change. Earlier appraisal system was termed as merit-rating.

The conventional performance assessment system was not sufficient to meet the needs of the constantly changing scenario, as it was mainly used as a mechanism for the assessment of employees, in which supervisors were urged to subjectively assess the performance behaviour of employees against the pre-determined employment standards.

Performance assessments or appraisals were often carried out yearly to measure an individual's degree of achievement and were simply carried out on the top-down basis in which managers played an important role in assessing an employee's performance without requiring the employee's active involvement.

However, in the current scenario, the organisations have turned their attention from performance assessments to performance management, as a result of HR internationalisation and business globalisation.

Performance Appraisal

Performance appraisal is the method of evaluating the behaviour of employees in the workplace, evaluating the quantitative and qualitative aspects of job performance in terms of output.

According to **Dale Yoder**, "Performance appraisal includes all formal procedures used to evaluate contributions of group members in a working organisation. It is a continuous process to secure information necessary for making correct and objective decisions on employees."

Objectives of Performance Appraisal

Compensation Decisions It can serve as a basis for pay raises. Performance appraisal helps managers to identify employees who are performing at or above expected levels to compensate for merit.

Promotion Decisions Individuals performing at their best are rewarded with promotion.

Training and Development Programmes Perfor- mance appraisal can help employees to self-assess their skills, any training required to improve skills for better performance.

Transfers Unsatisfactory performance calls for transfer, demotions and discharges due to economic conditions of organisation. It is greatly influenced by appraisals.

Feedback Performance appraisal enables the employee and the employer to know how well the individual is performing.

Self-improvement Through discussions with individual employees, a line manager can find out why they perform at lower levels, which steps can be initiated to improve their performance. The discussion between the senior and the subordinate gives a chance to the employees for introspection and to enhance his output to organisation.

Performance Management Appraisals play a central role in the employer's performance management process.

Parties Conducting Appraisals

The appraiser or evaluator can be a person who has complete knowledge about job content, parameters to be judged, standards of the job contents and also a person who observes the employee while performing a job. He should prepare reports and make judgements without any bias.

These appraisers can be

Supervisors Boss, departmental head, line managers, etc who are senior in position to the employee being appraised. Generally, immediate senior is the appraiser.

Peers Peer appraiser may be reliable if the work group is stable over a long period of time and the peers are matured enough to appraise without personal prejudices.

Subordinates Such kind of appraisal is done in educational institutes where teachers are evaluated by students. Now this concept is introduced in MNCs also, provided the relationships between superiors and subordinates are cordial.

Self-appraisal If the individuals understand their job expectations, their responsibilities and the parameters on which they are to be evaluated, they are in best position to appraise their performance. Such employees are highly motivated.

Rating Committees A rating committee typically comprises of the employee's immediate supervisor and three or four other supervisors.

Users of Services In case of service industries, employees are evaluated by customers relating to behaviour, promptness in handling customer query, speed of delivery service and the accuracy of performance.

Consultants When the organisation do not trust his employees for supervisory appraisal, peer appraisal or even the self-appraisal, such cases, organisations hire external consulting agencies. Consultants are trained and they observe the employee at work for sufficiently long periods for the purpose of appraisal.

Process of Performance Appraisal

Setting Work Standards

The performance appraisal should compare 'what should be' with 'what is'. Hence, the first step here should be to define how the employee must perform and let him know the performance standards that he is expected to meet. Executives use one or more of three bases, *i.e.*

- goals
- job dimensions or traits
- behaviours or competencies

Administrators often say that effective goals should be 'SMART,' *i.e.* they must be specific, measurable, attainable relevant and are timely.

Assessing the Employee's Actual Performance Related to those Standards

The next step is to measure the employees performance. This can be conducted by any of the aforementioned parties individually or in a combined manner. This step also entails using choosing the best performance appraisal method. These methods are discussed in detail in a separate section.

Providing Feedback to the Employee

This aims at helping the employee in eliminating the performance deficiencies in case of lower ratings, or to continue to perform above par in case of excellent performance.

Methods of Performance Appraisal

1. Individual Evaluation Techniques

Here, the employee is rated solely only the basis of his performance. Generally, these are the traditional methods, *which are as follows*

Confidential Report

It is created by immediate superior at the end of year in subjective form. It is quite a subjective method to analyse rather than objective as the assessment is entirely based upon the impressions rather than data.

It is a descriptive method and used for promotions and transfers of employees. The apraisee does not get any kind of feedback about his performance therefore its credibility is very low.

Essay Evaluation

Rater is asked to express strong as well as weak points of the employee's behaviour, his general planning, organising abilities and attitudes towards job. It is unstructured appraisal. The evaluator is expected to be honest, factual, concrete and objective in his approach.

It provides a detailed description of appraisee which is the basis of his increment and promotion. However, it suffers from the danger of evaluator being biased as there are no specific dimensions given related to the job performance.

Critical Incident Technique

Manager prepares a list of events which are critical representing the outstanding or poor behaviour of the employees on the job. The boss keeps a record of positive and negative critical incidents (examples) of a junior's work-related behaviours. The supervisor and junior meet half yearly or annually, to discuss the performance of the subordinate, by using these instances.

Checklists

It represents a simplest form of list of descriptive statements about the employee's behaviour on job. A rating score from the weighted checklist helps the manager in evaluating the performance to be good or bad or moderate.

Graphic Rating Scale

Under this method, scales are established in form of very good, good, average, poor and very poor. It can be either 'Competency/behaviour/skill based' or 'job dimensions or trait based'. Then, a number of specific job related factors are ranked on these scales.

Factors to be rated are personal characteristics like initiative, leadership etc and contributions such as quantity and quality of work. In continuous scale, the degrees of a trait are measured in numbers ranging from 0 to 5 whereas in a discrete or discontinuous scale appropriate boxes are used. There is heavy burden on the rater as he has to evaluate performance on several factors each having five degrees.

Forced Choice Method

This method requires the rater to select the most descriptive statement in each pair of statements about the employee, who is being evaluated.

Narrative Forms

All or part of the written appraisal may be in narrative form, the individual's supervisor evaluates the employee's past performance and required areas of improvement. The supervisor's narrative assessment helps the employee in understanding where his or her performance was good or bad and how to improve that performance.

Behaviourally Anchored Rating Scale (BARS)

It is also known as the behavioural expectations sale. It is a combination of the rating scale and critical incident techniques. The critical incidents serve as anchor statements on a scale and the rating form usually contains six to eight defined performance dimensions.

Evaluator rates each statement on a 1 to 7 or 1 to 9. A rating of 1 presents ineffective performance; the top scale value reflects effective performance. Means and standard deviations are calculated on these scale value assigned to each incident.

Mixed Standard Scales

They are slightly similar to BARS. They are named mixed scales because the employer 'mixes' together successively the good and poor behavioral example statements when listing them. This is done to minimise the rating measures.

2. Multi-person Evaluation Techniques

In these types of techniques, one employee is evaluated in comparison to another. These are also the modern methods of appraisal. *They include*

Alternation Ranking Method

The ranking of each employee in a work group is done against that of other employees. Employees are ranked according to their performance in a group. Under this method, evaluator is asked to rate employees from highest to lowest on some overall criterion.

Different ranks are set ranging from the extra ordinary performer to the poorest performer and then the employees are fit into those ranks based on their performance. It is the oldest and simplest and time-saving method.

Paired Comparisons

In this method, each worker is compared with all other employees in the group for each and every trait. If there are 'n' employees, then 'n(n – 2) comparisons' are made. It generally comprises of '+' and '–' where, '+' means 'better than' and '–' means 'worse than'. Then, the number of '+'s added in each column to get the highest ranked employee.

Management by Objective (MBO)

It is also termed as goal setting approach. Essential feature of this method is mutual establishment of job goals. Superior discusses Key Result Areas (KRAs) with the subordinates, checkpoints are established for the evaluation, superior and subordinates meet the target mutually at say half yearly or yearly.

Field Review Method

A trained, skilled representative of the HR department goes into the field and assists line supervisors with their ratings of their respective subordinates. HR specialist requests the supervisor to provide information about employee's performance.

Based on this information, HR expert prepares a report which is sent to the supervisor for review, changes, approval and discussion with the employee who is being rated on standardised objective forms.

Electronic Performance Monitoring (EPM)

This allows the bosses monitor electronically the amount of computerised data, that a worker is processing per day and then evaluating his or her performance.

Forced Distribution Method

The rater is asked to rate the employee on a pre-determined distribution scale between two extremes 'good' or 'bad'. The two criteria used for rating are job performance and promotability. There are no descriptive statements.

This method assumes that all top grade workers should go to the highest 10 % grade, 20% employees should go to the next highest grade and so on. The forced distribution method is similar to grading on a curve. In this method, employees are placed under some category but are not ranked within a category. Bell shaped curve is there to distribute employees in anyone of the category.

Promotional Scale

It consists of three points likely promotional, may be/may not be promotional and quite unlikely promotional material.

Web Based and Computerised Performance Appraisal

Companies are now using high-tech computersied or internet-based appraisal systems. These methods allow the executives to compile computerised notes on subordinates during the year and then to merge these with ratings for the employee on several performance traits.

HR Audits

A human resource audit involves systematically reviewing all aspects of human resources usually in a checklist fashion. It is to recognise strengths and identify any needs for improvement in the human resources function. A properly executed audit will reveal problem areas and provide recommendations and suggestions for the remedy of these problems.

Some of the reasons to conduct such as review include ensuring the effective utilisation of the organisation's human resources and reviewing compliance concerns with a myriad of administrative regulations.

360 Degree Appraisal and Feedback

The 360 degree of appraisal is a kind of appraisal in which rating of an employee is given by all personnel above, alongside and below the employee. It tries to include as many sources as possible. Supervisors, peers, subordinates and even customers.

Since it is a very comprehensive method, it is considered to be more accurate. Hence, the 360 degree feedback uses multiple raters often including self-ratings as well.

It is the best method to conduct appraisal because it gives a total overview about the employee and his performance. There is a multiple feedback which helps in reconfirming the appraisal from different angles.

Conducting Appraisal Interview

It is an interview where supervisor and subordinate review the appraisal and make plans to remedy, deficiencies and reinforce strengths. These interviews are difficult because they entail negative feedback as well. Hence, *the managers generally face four types of appraisal situations which are as follows*

Satisfactory-Promotable The performance of the individual is satisfactory and promotion becomes visible. Thus, the manager must develop specific developmental plans.

Satisfactory-Not Promotable This is for those individuals whose performance is acceptable but for whom promotion is not conceivable. Here, the manager must focus on incentives which are significant to the individual and sufficient to maintain performance.

Unsatisfactory-Correctable This entails when the performance is not up to the standard, however it can be corrected and improved. Here, the manager must the lay out an action plan for correcting the inadequate performance.

Unsatisfactory-Uncorrectable This is not the worst situation where the performance is satisfactory, nor it can be improved. Hence, generally managers prefer dismissing the employee.

Problems with Performance Appraisal

Judgement Errors

Managers commit mistakes while appraising the employee's performance due to certain basis and errors which distort the measurement. *These are as follows*

- **First Impression** The appraiser's first impression of a candidate may decide his evaluation of all subsequent behaviour. This is called as 'primary effect'.
- **Halo Effect** It occurs when one aspect or trait of the employee affects the rater's evaluation of other performance attributes.
- **Horn Effect** The rater's bias is directed towards one negative quality of the rate, he is being rated harshly for his one negative trait.
- **Leniency** Depending on rater's own mood at the time of evaluation, he can rate very strictly or very leniently.
- **Central Tendency** Rater rates all employees moderately at average point.
- **Stereotyping** Generalising behaviour of a person on the basis of mental picture already set in the mind of appraiser.
- **Recency Effect** The rater gives greater weightage to recent incidents than earlier performance.

Poor Appraisal Forms

Rating scale may be quite vague and unclear form ignores important performance parameters, the form is too lengthy, difficult and confusing.

Lack of Rater's Preparedness

Appraiser in not properly trained to carry out appraisal. Insufficient time, lack of skills, lack of self-confidence, unclear fundamental thought process can be some reasons.

Ineffective Organisational Policies

Rater gets influenced by other senior managers who will review his ratings. This causes him to manipulate the evaluation process in order to build his good image. As a result, rater goes off the track and cause significant damage to the rating process.

Essentials of an Effective Appraisal System

- A good appraisal system should provide reliable valid data which can be used to rate the employee on specified parameters. It must measure only job related aspects.
- Appraisal forms, procedures, ratings, data analysis techniques etc should be standardised so as to rate all employees equally.
- They must comply with the provisions of various acts relating to labour and should be easy to understand.
- It should be ensured that the appraisers are honest and rational in their judgement and behaviour.
- Appraisers should be given training to get insights and ideas on rating and to document the appraisals.
- The appraisal system should fit in the structure and operations of the organisation.
- The top management must build trust among employees on the appraisal system to be a fair and error free process.

Difference between Performance Appraisal and Performance Management

Basis	Performance Appraisal	Performance Management
Recency	It is a conventional term.	It is a recent term.
Purpose	The main purpose of is to determine wage increase, promotion, transfer and layoff.	The main purpose of performance managemert is to consider the development of the individual and improve his competencies.
Application	It is usually applied to rank and file workers.	It is applied on managerial and technical personnel.
Nature	Operational	Strategic
Assessment	Top-down assessment	More likely to involve dialogue between the appraiser and apraisee
Orientation	Retrospective for corrections	Future-oriented for growth
Frequency	Typically once or twice per year	On-going or continuous review, interspersed with formal reviews
Tools	Often uses ratings or rankings and usually takes a quantitative approach	Less likely to involve ratings but combines quantitative and qualitative approaches
Adaptability	Rigid structure or the system	Flexible process
Perspective	Not linked to business needs	Linked to business needs
Purpose and Rigidity	Often linked to compensation and is often very bureaucratic with a focus on paperwork/documents	Not usually linked to compensation and less concerned with documentation
Conducted by	Usually done by the human resource department	Conducted by managers and supervisors

EXAM BASED QUESTIONS

1 **The statement "induction is the welcoming process to make the new employee feel at home and generate in him a feeling of belongingness to the organisation"is given by**

(a) Flippo (b) Drucker
(c) Mayo (d) Armstrong

2 **......... is a systematic and planned introduction of employees to their jobs, their co-workers and the organisation.**

(a) Job evaluation (b) Investiture orientation
(c) Induction (d) Placement

3 **Which type of information is conveyed by orientation?**

(a) Training and education benefit
(b) Job location
(c) Job safety requirements
(d) General information about the daily work routine

4 **Which of the below options are the topics covered in employee orientation programme?**

(a) Training and education benefit
(b) To employee counsellor and the relationship to other jobs
(c) Disciplinary regulations
(d) All of the above

5 **Which of the following is not an objective of employee orientation?**

(a) Preventing employee alienation
(b) Developing team spirit
(c) Acclimatising the employees
(d) Raising the salary of the employees

6 **Induction refers to**

(a) giving training to the employee
(b) giving incentive to the employee
(c) introducing employees to the culture and situation of the organisation
(d) increasing the morale of the employees

7 **Which of the following is not the objective of induction?**

(a) To orient a new employee to his work group and the organisation
(b) To train the employee how to perform his work
(c) To promote a feeling of belonging and loyalty to the organisation among new corners that increases his confidences as a result
(d) To give new employee, an information about services and facilities and provide rules, regulations and HR policies to new employees

8 **Which of the following is a step in the process of informal induction?**

(a) Reception (b) Documentation
(c) Company Induction (d) All of these

9 **Off-the-job training method consists of**

(a) role playing method (b) case study
(c) programmed training (d) All of these

10 **Which one is the conventional method of HR training?**

(a) Conference training
(b) Case study method
(c) Incident method
(d) All of the above

11 **The main objective of training method is**

(a) introduction of new technology
(b) to earn money
(c) to obtain position and fame
(d) to make accounting

12 **'On-the-job' training can be provided through**

(a) non-formal education (b) mobile teacher
(c) distance education (d) All of these

13 **Training and development refers to the total structure of on-the-job and off-the-job training systems used by the**

(a) organisation (b) experts
(c) candidates (d) consultants

14 **......... refers to the learning opportunities designed to help employees grow.**

(a) Training (b) Development
(c) Education (d) All of these

15 **Which of the following is a benefit of employee training?**

(a) Improves morale
(b) Helps people identify with organisational goals
(c) Provides a good climate for learning, growth and coordination
(d) None of the above

16 **Which of these is the benefit of needs assessment?**

(a) Assessment makes training department more accountable
(b) Higher training costs
(c) Loss of business
(d) Increased overtime working

17 **......... seeks to examine the goals of the organisation and the trends that are likely to affect these goals.**

(a) Organisational support
(b) Organisational analysis
(c) Person analysis
(d) Key skill abilities analysis

18 **Which of these is an off-the-job training method?**

(a) Television
(b) Job rotation
(c) Orientation training
(d) Coaching

19 Which of this is a step in training process?
(a) KSA deficiency
(b) Provide proper feedback
(c) Obstacles in the system
(d) Use of evaluation models

20 Training information system includes
(a) training aids
(b) internal and external faculty
(c) training resources
(d) training needs

21 Which of the following is a method used in group or organisational training needs assessment?
(a) Consideration of current and projected changes
(b) Rating scales
(c) Interviews
(d) Questionnaires

22 Which of the following is not the significance of training?
(a) Development of skills
(b) Improves organisational climate
(c) More supervision
(d) Best development of human resource

23 Choose which of the following is a benefit to the individual while receiving training?
(a) Creates an appropriate climate for growth, communication
(b) Aids in increasing productivity and/or quality of work
(c) Satisfies a personal needs of the trainer
(d) None of the above

24 ADDIE is with reference to
(a) job evaluation process
(b) training programme process
(c) development programme process
(d) performance management

25 In the term ADDIE, the letter I stands for
(a) innovating (b) implementing
(c) inducting (d) None of these

26 Which of the following statements are correct with TNA?
(a) It is the method of assessing the gap between training of employees and training needs
(b) It identifies the gap between present and essential levels of knowledge, skills and attitude. It makes the most of use of scarce resources
(c) It confirms that appropriate and relevant training is delivered
(d) All of the above

27 McGhee and Thayer's have developed a 'Three Level Analysis' for conducting training need assessment. Which of the following is not one of these layers?
(a) Organisational Level
(b) Operational Level
(c) Individual Level
(d) Supervisor Level

28 Another term for company level analysis is
(a) task analysis (b) organisational analysis
(c) individual analysis (d) industry analysis

29 Another term used for performance analysis in TNA assessment is
(a) individual analysis (b) organisational analysis
(c) strategic analysis (d) task analysis

30 Which of the following statement is not correct with regard to organisational analysis?
(a) It is the analysis conducted to ascertain the progress of the company towards attainment of its objectives and goals
(b) This comprises of scanning the environment for opportunities and threats and evaluating the strengths and weakness internally
(c) It aims at improving current performance which includes specifically training new workers and those whose performance is inadequate
(d) Strategic training needs analysis describes the training workers will need to fill these jobs in the future which is done by organisational analysis

31 Which of the following statements are correct with reference to task analysis?
(a) Task analysis is a comprehensive study of the work to define what specific skills, *e.g.* like preparing spread sheets, reading diagrams, are needed to perform the job
(b) The goal here is to give these workers the skills and knowledge they need to do the job
(c) Job descriptions and job specifications are essential for conducting task analysis
(d) All of the above

32 Which of the following is the correct sequence of evaluating training efforts?
(a) Reaction, Learning, Behaviour, Result
(b) Reaction, Behaviour, Learning, Result
(c) Reaction, Behaviour, Result, Learning
(d) Learning, Reaction, Behaviour, Result

33 The model for evaluating training efforts given by........ .
(a) Drucker (b) Mayo (c) Kirkpatrick (d) Shein

34 Which of these is a hindrance to effective training?
(a) Career planning workshop
(b) Aggregate spending on training is inadequate
(c) Mentoring
(d) Career counselling

35 The following training aims to provide broad training to enable the trainee to take up a wide variety of tasks within his field of specialisation.
(a) Demonstration (b) On-the-job training
(c) Apprenticeship (d) All of these

36 Demonstration type of training method is used to train
(a) workers (b) supervision
(c) managers (d) All of these

37 The following is vertical expansion of the
(a) Job rotation
(b) Job enrichment
(c) Management by Objectives (MBO)
(d) All of the above

38 The following is not a on-the-job training method
(a) Understudies
(b) Job rotation
(c) Management by Objectives (MBO)
(d) Case study method

39 .... is widely used for human relations and leadership training.
(a) Business games (b) Role playing
(c) Case study method (d) Job rotation

40 Training Within the Industry (TWI) scheme imparts training in
(a) job instructions (b) job rotation
(c) job method (d) All of these

41 How does training and development offer competitive advantage to an organisation?
(a) Removing performance decencies
(b) Deficiency is caused by a lack of ability
(c) Individuals have the aptitude and motivation to learn
(d) None of the above

42 Which of the following is not a method of group training need identification?
(a) Quality Circle (b) Work sample
(c) Exit interview (d) MBO

43 Which of the following is not true about training?
(a) It is a short duration exercise
(b) It is technical in nature
(c) It is primarily for managers and executives
(d) It is concerned with specific job skills

44 In which type of analysis are corporate goals and plans compared with the existing manpower inventory to determine the training needs?
(a) Organisation analysis (b) Operation analysis
(c) Individual analysis (d) None of these

45 Training concentrates on
(a) coaching the members of an organisation how to perform effectively in their current jobs
(b) expansion of the knowledge and skills of the members of an organisation
(c) preparing the employees to take on new responsibilities
(d) None of the above

46 Who has given the following statement, "Management development is an attempt to improve managerial effectiveness through a planned and deliberate learning process"?
(a) Mumford
(b) Dale
(c) Molander
(d) None of the above

47 Development provides .... and .... which will be helpful to employees in higher positions.
(a) general knowledge, behaviour
(b) general knowledge, specific skills
(c) general knowledge, attitudes
(d) specific skills, attitudes

48 A homogenous group of .... men from the plant constitutes an ideal conference group.
(a) 8-10 (b) 12-15
(c) 18-20 (d) 22-25

49 The following method is used to give to trainees the important information in permanent form for immediate of future use.
(a) Lecture methods
(b) Conference
(c) Written instructional method
(d) Training Within the Industry (TWI)

50 Which of the following is not a feature of development?
(a) It is an education process
(b) It is a process for a specific period of time
(c) It causes behavioural changes
(d) It leads to self-development

51 In employee training, third stage for trainee's on-the-job training is to
(a) do the follow up
(b) practice of trainees
(c) present the information
(d) prepare the learners

52 Which of these is an advantage of the critical incidents methods while performing performance appraisal?
(a) Minimise inventory costs
(b) Negative incidents are generally more noticeable than positive ones
(c) Evaluation is based on actual job behaviour
(d) None of the above

53 To be effective a point based rating system requires
(a) close management control
(b) comprehensive reliable and consistent information
(c) objectivity in assessments
(d) 360 degree assessments

54 Steps involves in employer's movement for performance management is
(a) total quality (b) appraisal issues
(c) strategic planning (d) All of these

55 An equal rating of all employees such as 'good', where the manager gives an average rating to all the members is called
(a) lenient tendency
(b) strict tendency
(c) biasing tendency
(d) central tendency

56 An advantage of Management by Objectives (MBO) is
(a) avoids central tendency and biases
(b) jointly agreed performance objectives
(c) provides behavioural anchors
(d) on-going basis evaluation

57 Basic approach in employee's performance compares with their current performance to
(a) set standards
(b) performance in previous years
(c) performance in last job
(d) None of the above

58 Main disadvantage of critical incident method is
(a) It is difficult to develop
(b) It causes of disagreements
(c) It is time consuming
(d) difficult to rate

59 Gender discrimination, lower appraisal rating is an example of which of the following rating methods?
(a) Lenient/Strict tendency
(b) Bias
(c) Central tendency
(d) Different tendencies

60 Situation, subordinates collude to rate high with each other, known as
(a) logrolling (b) dialog rolling
(c) up rating (d) lenient/strict tendency

61 Which of the following is an advantage of 'BARS' system in performance appraisal?
(a) Simple to use
(b) Avoids central tendency and biases
(c) Ends up with pre-determined rating figures
(d) Providing behavioural anchors

62 Which of the following is the key objective of performance management?
(a) Goal oriented
(b) Performance oriented
(c) Sales oriented
(d) None of the above

63 An alternation ranking method is often classified as
(a) "what you are measuring?"
(b) "how you are measuring performance?"
(c) "what are the set standards?"
(d) "the rules of performance appraisals"

64 Easiest performance appraisal interview is
(a) satisfactory-promotable interview
(b) satisfactory-not promotable interview
(c) unsatisfactory-correctable interview
(d) unsatisfactory-uncorrectable interview

65 Performance development plan is set for the employee by his
(a) employer (b) department head
(c) immediate boss (d) Any of these

66 An appraisal interview which results in occasional 'well-done' technique is said to be
(a) satisfactory-promotable interview
(b) satisfactory-not promotable interview
(c) unsatisfactory-correctable interview
(d) unsatisfactory-uncorrectable interview

67 Edward Deming argues that employee's performance is result of
(a) training communication (b) quality management
(c) own motivation (d) Both (a) and (b)

68 The whole process of conducting 360 degree feedback process in any organisation can last about
(a) 1 to 3 months (b) 3 to 6 months
(c) 6 to 9 months (d) 9 to 12 months

69 Advantage of 'graphic rating scale method' is that; it is
(a) simple to use
(b) avoids central tendency and biases
(c) ends up with predetermined rating figures
(d) an on-going basis evaluation

70 In performance management, main feature of performance management is to
(a) estimate whether there should be an increase in salary
(b) developing planning incentives
(c) comparing performance with goals
(d) comparing sales figures from last year

71 Forced distribution and ranking are considered as methods of
(a) comparative methods
(b) narrative methods
(c) behavioural methods
(d) category rating methods

72 Ranking of all employees, measuring a specific trait such as communicating is measured in
(a) graphic rating scale method
(b) management by objectives
(c) alternation ranking method
(d) paired comparison method

73 Enabling employees to link company's and his own departmental goals is the key characteristic of which of the following?
(a) Direction sharing
(b) Goal alignment
(c) On-going performance monitoring
(d) On-going feedback

74 Which of the following statement best describes '360 degree feedback'. It is
(a) a method used to appraise employees
(b) a system where managers give feedback to all their staff
(c) a system where feedback on any individual is derived from peers, subordinates supervisors and occasionally customers
(d) a development tool

75 An interview, in which you discuss person's career plans and plan professional development, it is said to be
(a) a satisfactory-promotable interview
(b) a satisfactory-not promotable interview
(c) an unsatisfactory-correctable interview
(d) an unsatisfactory-uncorrectable interview

76 'Performance' appraisal feedback always includes
(a) assessment of employee performance
(b) setting work standards
(c) providing feedback to the employees
(d) All of the above

77 An employee is rated high in performance appraisal because of 'religion', is an example of
(a) lenient/strict tendency
(b) bias
(c) central tendency
(d) different tendencies

78 In which of the following step an employer and employee discuss performance and plans for future?
(a) Defining the job
(b) Training session
(c) Feedback session
(d) Interview session

79 A rating scale which enlists traits and performance values is called
(a) graphic rating scale method
(b) management by objectives
(c) alternation ranking method
(d) in-house development

80 Online and face-to-face feedback about goal's progress is
(a) direction sharing
(b) goal alignment
(c) on-going performance monitoring
(d) on-going feedback

81 Mostly employees' promotion decision is based on
(a) performance appraisal
(b) training results
(c) hiring tests
(d) in-house development

82 To keep on track employees' performance, building block to be used is
(a) direction sharing
(b) goal alignment
(c) rewards and recognition
(d) coaching and development support

83 Accessing employees' telephones and computers for monitoring employees' rate and accuracy is
(a) critical incident method
(b) forced distribution method
(c) behaviourally anchored rating scale
(d) electronic performance monitoring

84 When rating of employee trait biases its performance on other traits, it is called
(a) Halo effect
(b) Deja vu effect
(c) Narrow effect
(d) Placebo effect

85 An advantage of 'alternation ranking method' is that it
(a) is simple to use
(b) avoids central tendency and biases
(c) ends up with pre-determined rating figures
(d) provides behavioral anchors

86 Performance management includes
(a) daily and weekly interactions
(b) meeting semi-annually
(c) yearly meetings
(d) never having meeting with subordinates

87 Aligning and evaluating employee's performance with company's set goals is called
(a) appraisal management
(b) performance management
(c) hierarchy of management
(d) off-the-job training

88 Disadvantage of graphic rating scale is
(a) It leads to halo effect
(b) It causes bias
(c) It is a measure of central tendency in rating
(d) All of the above

89 When ratings are collected from supervisors, customers and peers, considered as
(a) 350 degree feedback
(b) 320 degree feedback
(c) 360 degree feedback
(d) 380 degree feedback

90 Which of the following is a learning principle?
(a) Recognition of individual differences
(b) Schedules of learning
(c) Transfer of learning
(d) All of the above

91 Which of the following pairs are not correctly matched?
(a) In such type of training, a master worker or trainer is appointed who guides the worker or learner regarding the skill of job-Apprenticeship programme
(b) Training is conducted away from the actual work place-Vestibule training
(c) This kind of training involves shifting the trainee from one department to another or from one job to another-Internship
(d) None of the above

92 Which of the following are not correctly matched?
(a) It involves growth of an employee in all respects-Development
(b) It is tied to the goals of organisations more than to the goals of the individual-Training
(c) It is work centred-Education
(d) None of the above

93 Rearrange the steps in training programme.
1. What should be the level of training?
2. What principles of learning?
3. Who are the trainees?
4. What methods and techniques?
5. Where to conduct the programme?
6. Who are the trainers?

Codes
(a) 1, 2, 3, 4, 5, 6 (b) 4, 5, 3, 1, 6, 2
(c) 3, 1, 4, 6, 2, 5 (d) 3, 6, 4, 1, 2, 5

94 Which of the following is not a method of on-the-job development?
1. Understudy 2. Coaching
3. Brain Storming 4. Committee Assignment
5. Vestibule Training 6. Succession Planning

Select the correct answer by using the codes given below
Codes
(a) 1, 2, 3, 4, 5 (b) 1, 3, 4, 5
(c) 1, 3, 5, 6 (d) 1, 2, 3, 4, 6

95 Which of the following points is not important for training?
1. Reduction in supervision
2. Reduction in cost
3. Increased stability
4. Easy coordination
5. Improvement in industrial relations

Select the correct answer by using the codes given below
Codes
(a) 1, 3, 5 (b) 1, 2, 3
(c) All of the above (d) None of the above

96 Which of the following are the methods of off-the-job development method?
1. Outside seminars
2. Programmed learning
3. Vestibule training
4. Simulation
5. Multiple management
6. Grid training
7. Sensitivity training

Select the correct answer by using the codes given below
Codes
(a) 1, 2, 5, 6 (b) 1, 3, 5, 6, 7
(c) 1, 2, 4, 6, 7 (d) 1, 4, 5, 6

97 Which of the following statements are true/false?
(i) ADDIE is an effective model for building a training programme.
(ii) TNA evaluates a training programme.
(iii) On-the-job training allows the person to learn the job by doing it in real work situation.

(a) (i), (ii) are true and (iii) is false
(b) (i) is true and (ii), (iii) are false
(c) (i), (iii) are true and (ii) is false
(d) (iii) is true and (i), (ii) are false

98 Which of the statements are true/false?
(i) Action learning and special committee assignments are methods of on-the-job development.
(ii) Sensitivity training aims at changing the behaviour of trainees.
(iii) Critical incident method entails rating the individual on the basis of pre-set qualities.
(iv) BARS is also called behavioural expectation scale.

(a) (i), (ii) are true and (iii), (iv) are false
(b) (i), (iii) are true and (ii), (iv) are false
(c) (i), (ii), (iv) are true and (iii) is false
(d) (iii), (iv) are true and (i), (ii) are false

99 Which of the following statements are the conditions required for management development?
1. The individual should be interested in developing himself.
2. The individual should know the areas of his potential development.
3. A positive emotional and professional climate should be created in the workplace for the employee to progress and review himself.
4. He should identify mechanisms of using these opportunities and get the support he needs from his superiors and the organisation.
5. The individual should have basic working knowledge.

Codes
(a) 1, 2, 3 and 4 (b) 2, 3 and 5
(c) Both 1 and 4 (d) All of the above

100 Which of the following statements are correct about performance management?
1. It aims at promote a two-way conversation system between managers and employees to clarify expectations about roles.
2. Encourage employees to achieve higher job performance standards.
3. Boost employee productivity by promoting employee motivation

Codes
(a) Only 1 (b) Both 1 and 2
(c) Both 2 and 3 (d) All of the above

101 Which of the following statements are true?
1. Some organisations develop specific materials for the development of their employees The content developed corresponds to the needs of the institutions. It is a part of career development.
2. Some organisations offer their employees seminars and workshops that last two or more days so that they can develop their careers within the organisation. It is a part of career planning.

3. PDP plan summarises the needs of workers' personal development and the specified effort and action plan for achievement.

Codes
(a) Both 1 and 2 (b) Both 2 and 3
(c) Both 1 and 3 (d) None of the above

102 Consider the following statements.

1. Sensitivity training was developed by Kurt Lewin
2. In-basket excercise is a simulated training method
3. Depth interview is also known as directive interview
4. Job evalution is carried out for promoting job satisfaction

Which of the following statements given above are true?

(a) Both 1 and 3 (b) Both 1 and 2
(c) 1, 2 and 3 (d) 2, 3 and 4

103 Arrange the following steps of training and development process in the right sequence.

1. Need analysis
2. Validation
3. Evaluation
4. Implement the programme
5. Instructional design

Codes
(a) 1, 5, 4, 3, 2 (b) 1, 5, 3, 2, 4
(c) 1, 5, 2, 4, 3 (d) 1, 2, 5, 3, 4

104 Which of the following is part of management development?

1. SHRM programmes
2. Vestibule training
3. Certificate and online programmes from multiple sources
4. MBAs and leadership programmes
5. Coaching

Codes
(a) 1, 2, 3, 4 (b) 1, 3, 4, 5
(c) 2, 3, 4, 5 (d) 1, 3, 4, 5

105 Consider the following statements.

1. Training is required at different levels namely, for unskilled worker, semi-skilled workers, skilled workers, office, staff, supervisory staff and managerial.
2. Semi-skilled workers are selected amongst the unskilled wokers who have made themselves convergent with the handling of machine.
3. Management training has become an essential activity of every firm.
4. Training programmes should be periodically evaluated to determine its effectiveness.

Which of the following statements given above are correct?

(a) Both 1 and 2 (b) 1, 2 and 3
(c) All of the above (d) Both 2 and 3

106 Which of the following are considered as development function of human resource management?

1. Training
2. Executive Development
3. Career Planning and Development
4. Pay and Allowance

Codes
(a) 1, 2, 3 (b) 1, 3, 5
(c) 2, 3, 4 (d) Both 2 and 3

107 Arrange the following steps of performance appraisal process in the correct order.

1. Measuring the actual performance.
2. Establishing performance standards.
3. Comparing the actual performance with the desired performance.
4. Communicating the standards.

Codes
(a) 4, 3, 2, 1 (b) 2, 4, 3, 1
(c) 3, 1, 4, 2 (d) 2, 4, 1, 3

108 Consider the following statements.

1. Using multiple raters improves evaluations.
2. Rating scales are particularly subject to bias.
3. Objective appraisal measures are always popular with employees.

Which of the following statements given above are correct?

Codes
(a) Both 3 and 1 (b) Both 1 and 2
(c) All of the above (d) None of the above

109 Which of the following statement is correct?

I. Induction is designed to give new comer necessary information about the latest trends in fashion and to discuss current politcal issues.
II. Induction helps to build up a two-way channel of communication between management and workers.

(a) Both statements are correct
(b) Statement I is correct and Statement II is incorrect
(c) Statement II is correct and Statement I is incorrect
(d) Both statements are incorrect

110 Which of the following statement is true?

I. Vestibule training utilises equipment which closely resemble the actual ones used on the job.
II. Job Ranking method and job classification method are usually used for the purpose of job description.

(a) Both statements are correct
(b) Statement I is correct and Statement II is incorrect
(c) Statement II is correct and Statement I is incorrect
(d) Both statements are incorrect

111 Which of the following statements are correct?
I. Assessment centre includes observation for a particular situation to evaluate performance of the employee alongwith his growth potential with regard to specific job characteristics.
II. The situations under assessment method of competency mapping, does not aim at revealing the capacity, aptitude and skills of the individuals.
(a) Both statements are correct
(b) Both statements are incorrect
(c) Statement I is correct and Statement II is incorrect
(d) Statement I is incorrect and Statement II is correct

112 Which of the following statement(s) is/are true?
I. Brain storming creates new ideas. The concept is that every idea, plan and thought presented at a group meeting must be assessed critically.
II. MBO is a technique oriented towards results.
(a) Both statements are correct
(b) Both statements are incorrect
(c) Statement I is correct and Statement II is incorrect
(d) Statement I is incorrect and Statement II is correct

Directions (Q. Nos. 113-118) *In the questions given below are two statements labelled as Assertion (A) and Reason (R). In the context of the two statements, which one of the following is correct?*

Codes
(a) Both (A) and (R) are true and (R) is the correct explanation of (A)
(b) Both (A) and (R) are true, but (R) is not the correct explanation of (A)
(c) (A) is true and (R) is false
(d) (A) is false and (R) is true

113 **Assertion** (A) Development means mental growth of an employee.
Reason (R) Development is described as non-executive development.

114 **Assertion** (A) Training programme are organised for long-terms.
Reason (R) Training is job centred in nature.

115 **Assertion** (A) Performance appraisal cannot be done in isolation.
Reason (R) Performance appraisal is linked to job analysis.

116 **Assertion** (A) Demonstration method of training is generally used for workers.
Reason (R) Demonstration are very effect in teaching because it is much easier to show a person how to do job than to tell him to gather instructions from the reading material.

117 **Assertion** (A) Induction is to rehabilitate the employee into his surroundings.
Reason (R) The purpose of induction is to introduce the new employee and organisation to each other.

118 **Assertion** (A) Paired comparison method is an improvised version of critical incident method.
Reason (R) Paired comparison method compares each employee with all the persons in pairs one at a time.

119 Match the following.

List I	List II
A. Reaction	1. Conducting written tests
B. Learning	2. Reduction in absenteeism
C. Behaviour	3. Putting learning into practice
D. Result	4. Filling questionnaires

Codes

	A	B	C	D		A	B	C	D
(a)	1	2	4	3	(b)	1	3	2	4
(c)	2	4	3	1	(d)	2	1	4	3

120 Match the following.

List I	List II
A. Tag teams	1. Games to get team members know each other
B. Outward-bound training	2. Games to test ability to plan ahead
C. Mirroring	3. Training with an external perspective
D. Strategic planners	4. Adventure sports for teams
E. Ice breakers	5. One role played alternately by two participants

Codes

	A	B	C	D	E		A	B	C	D	E
(a)	5	4	3	2	1	(b)	1	4	5	3	2
(c)	4	1	3	5	2	(d)	3	4	2	1	5

121 Match the following.

List I (Specific training methods)	List II (Qualities)
A. On-the-job training	1. Under this method, trainee is separatly focussed on learning the material related to is future performance.
B. Off-the-job training	2. Mostly, the executive training is done on the job. An executive is expected to learn his work while working.
C. Understudy method	3. The executive under this method is assigned an understudy or an assistant who in addition to his regular duties is expected to acquire some familiarity with the tasks and practices of his supervisor.
D. Role playing method	4. Under this method, an employee learns by playing role in drammatic setting which corresponds to his work.

Codes

	A	B	C	D		A	B	C	D
(a)	1	2	3	4	(b)	2	1	3	4
(c)	2	3	4	1	(d)	4	2	3	1

122 Match the following.

List I (Authors)	List II (Definitions)
A. Dale Yoder	1. The process by which management determines how the organsiation should move from its current manpower position to its desired manpower position
B. Beach	2. Training is the process by which manpower is filled for the particular jobs it is to perform
C. Flippo	3. Training is the organised procedure by which people learn knowledge and skills for definite purpose
D. Vetter	4. Training is the act of increasing the knowledge and skill of an employee for doing a particular job

Codes

	A	B	C	D		A	B	C	D
(a)	1	2	3	4	(b)	3	1	4	2
(c)	2	3	4	1	(d)	4	2	3	1

123 Match the following.

List I (Methods of training)	List II (Features)
A. Job rotation	1. Instead of using original machinery employees are trained on dummy model
B. Vestibule training	2. It is well adopted to convey specific information
C. Apprenticeship programmes	3. It allowes trainees to interact with other employees facilitating future cooperation among departments
D. Lectures	4. After completion of training, the master worker goes and the trainee gets full charge of the job position

Codes

	A	B	C	D		A	B	C	D
(a)	1	2	3	4	(b)	3	1	4	2
(c)	2	3	4	1	(d)	4	2	3	1

124 Match the following.

List I (Methods)	List II (Definitions)
A. Narrative Essay	1. Evaluation by boss, peers and subordinates
B. 360 degree feedback	2. A candid statement from a rater
C. Assessment centres	3. Assessment based on response to a battery of tests
D. Graphic rating scales	4. A scale that lists a number of traits and range of performance for each

Codes

	A	B	C	D		A	B	C	D
(a)	1	2	3	4	(b)	2	1	3	4
(c)	2	3	4	1	(d)	4	2	3	1

125 Match the following.

List I (Methods)	List II (Definitions)
A. Graphic rating scale	1. Order of ranking from best to worst
B. BARS	2. Evaluation based on key incidents
C. Simple ranking	3. It lists a number of traits and a range of performance for each
D. Critical incident method	4. Rating in behaviour[illegible] terms

Codes

	A	B	C	D		A	B	C	D
(a)	1	2	3	4	(b)	2	1	3	4
(c)	3	4	1	2	(d)	4	2	3	1

126 Match the following.

List I	List II
A. Satisfactory-promotable	1. Performance is satisfactory but promotion is not conceivable.
B. Satisfactory-not promotable	2. Performance is sub-standard but can be improved or corrected.
C. Unsatisfactory correctable	3. Dismissal of employee
D. Unsatisfactory uncorrectable	4. Promotion is visible as the performance is satisfactory.

Codes

	A	B	C	D		A	B	C	D
(a)	3	4	2	1	(b)	4	1	2	3
(c)	4	3	2	1	(d)	4	2	1	3

PREVIOUS YEARS' QUESTIONS

2018

1 Who said, "Management development concerns the means by which a person cultivates those skills application of which will improve the efficiency and effectiveness with which the anticipated results of particular segment are achieved"?

(a) Flippo (b) Dale Yoder
(c) Koontz and O'Donnell (d) Robert Owen

2 A general impression of an individual that is influenced by single characteristic is called

(a) Personal prejudice (b) Stereo typing
(c) Halo effect (d) Group effectiveness

3 The six stages of training evaluation model suggested by Brinkerhoff given below are gumbled up. Choose the alternative which gives the correct sequence from the codes given below.

(i) Programme design
(ii) Goal setting
(iii) Immediate outcomes
(iv) Impact and worth
(v) Intermediate on usage outcomes
(vi) Programme implementation

Codes

(a) (ii), (i), (iii), (v), (iv), (vi)
(b) (i), (ii), (iv), (iii), (v), (vi)
(c) (ii), (i), (v), (iii), (vi), (iv)
(d) (ii), (i), (vi), (iii), (v), (iv)

4 Which one of the following is not a modern method of performance appraisal?

(a) Ranking method (b) 360
(c) M.B.O (d) BARS

5 Identify the correct sequence of steps in developing a BARS (Behaviourally Anchored Rating Scales) as suggested by Gray Dessler

(i) Scale the incidents
(ii) Reallocate incidents
(iii) Develop performance dimensions
(iv) Write critical incidents
(v) Develop a final instrument

Codes

(a) (iii), (ii), (iv), (i), (v) (b) (ii), (i), (iv), (iii), (v)
(c) (iv), (iii), (ii), (i), (v) (d) (i), (ii), (iii), (iv), (v)

6 Which one of the following methods is not a behavioural method of performance appraisal?

(a) Balanced scorecard method
(b) Critical incident method
(c) Assessment centre method
(d) Behavioural check list method

7 **Assertion** (A) While all programming strategies need to provide for all three phases of individual and organisational learning, they differ according to the training modalities chosen for implementing them.

Reason (R) The chosen modality provides the frame for designing and sequencing training inputs and selecting methods to produce the desired results.

Codes

(a) (A) is not correct, (R) is correct
(b) Both (A) and (R) are not correct
(c) Both (A) and (R) are correct, but (R) does not explain (A)
(d) Both (A) and (R) are correct, (R) explains (A)

8 Match the Techniques of Training (List I) with the Possible Discriptions thereof (List II) given below

List I	List II
A. Ice Breakers	1. One role played alternatively by two participants
B. Tag Teams	2. Listing of alternative solutions to problems
C. Morphological Analysis	3. Games to get team members know each other
D. Gordon Teahnique	4. Steering a discussion to crytallise solutions

Codes

	A	B	C	D		A	B	C	D
(a)	1	4	2	3	(b)	2	3	4	1
(c)	1	3	4	2	(d)	3	1	2	4

2017

9 The degree to which a particular selection device accurately predicts the level of performance is known as

(a) construct validity (b) criterion related validity
(c) logical validity (d) concurrent validity

10 'Bell curve' is represented by which of the traditional methods of performance appraisal?

(a) Forced choice method
(b) Free from essay method
(c) Critical incidence method
(d) Forced distribution method

11 Which of the following is/are not a commonly used method of training?

1. Buzzing 2. Regression
3. Role playing 4. Rationalisation
5. Brain Storming 6. Persuasion

Codes

(a) 2, 4 and 6 (b) 1, 3 and 5
(c) 4, 5 and 6 (d) 1, 3 and 6

2016

12 Following are the probable errors committed during organisational processes.
(i) Leniency or severity error
(ii) Primacy and recency effects
(iii) Halo effect
(iv) Spill over effect
(v) Status effect
(vi) Perceptual set
Which of the following statement(s) given above is/are true/false ?
1. (i), (ii), (iii) are recruitment errors
2. (i), (ii), (iii) are recruitment errors and (iv), (v) and (vi) are rating errors
3. All are rating errors
4. None are recruitment errors

Codes
(a) 2 is true, 4 is false
(b) 1 is false, 3 is true
(c) 3 is true, 1 is false
(d) 3 and 4 are true, 1 and 2 are false

13 Which of the following methods of training is also known as 'socio-drama' or 'psychodrama' ?
(a) Strategic planner (b) Mirroring
(c) Apprenticeship (d) Role playing

2015

14 Which of the following are the errors, an appraiser is likely to commit during performance appraisal process?
1. Rigor Martis Syndrome
2. Central Tendency
3. Recency *vs* Primacy Effect
4. Halo Effect

Select the correct answer by using the codes given below

Codes
(a) 1, 2 and 3 (b) 2, 3 and 4
(c) 1, 3 and 4 (d) 1, 2 and 4

15 In the 'Kirkpatrick Model', which level of training evaluation helps in knowing that trainees have applied their gained learning to the job?
(a) Learning
(b) Reaction
(c) Job behaviour
(d) Ultimate value/results

16 'BARS', a scale constructed to measure the effectiveness of organisational process with particular reference to behaviours exhibited, stands for
(a) Behaviour Analysis Rating Scale
(b) Behaviourally Anchored Ranking Scale
(c) Behaviourally Anchored Rating Scale
(d) Behaviour Analysis Ranking Scale

17 Sensitivity training is usually provided to
1. individual employee.
2. small group of 10-12 people.
3. large group at organisational level.
4. the employees for increased awareness of their own behaviour and how others perceive them.
Which of the following statements given above are correct?
(a) 1, 2 and 4 (b) Both 2 and 3
(c) Both 2 and 4 (d) 1, 2, 3 and 4

18 Which of the following explanations refer to 'Problem Clinic' method of training?
(a) To analyse performance is simulated exercise to reveal individual and/or group training needs
(b) To self-evaluate and know what additional knowledge, skill or insight is needed
(c) To meet and talk informally with people for finding clues to training needs
(d) To arrange meetings of a homogeneous group to discuss a common problem and develop a solution

19 Which of the following methods of performance appraisal places pre-determined percentages of ratees into several performance categories?
(a) Alternation ranking method
(b) Paired comparison method
(c) Graphic rating scale
(d) Forced distribution method

20 Match the following.

List I (Training Techniques)	List II (Descriptions)
A. Ice Breakers	1. Isolation, selection and evaluation of a problem
B. Monodrama	2. Role play with pre-determined objectives
C. Structured Role Playing	3. Games to get team members know each other
D. Attribute Listening	4. Insight into a given interaction

Codes

	A	B	C	D		A	B	C	D
(a)	1	2	3	4	(b)	3	4	2	1
(c)	4	3	2	1	(d)	1	3	2	4

21 The primary and recency effects, perceptual set, spill over effect and status effect refer to
(a) common recruitment errors
(b) common selection errors
(c) common rating errors
(d) common planning errors

22 Which method of training utilises equipments that closely resemble the actual ones used on the job?
(a) Role playing
(b) Vestibule training
(c) Sensitivity training
(d) Programmed instruction

2014

23 The BARS constructed by Charles L Hulin and Milton R Blood, for appraising the performance of a clerk in a grocery store, had how many anchors of job performance?

(a) 6 (b) 8 (c) 10 (d) 12

24 Performance management is a system that

1. ensures that employee's performance is supporting company's aims.
2. starts with fixing performance standards and ends with comparing results with those standards.
3. includes daily or weekly interactions to ensure continuous improvement in employee's performance.
4. ensures that employee has requisite training to perform the job.

Codes

(a) Only 1
(b) Both 1 and 4
(c) 1, 3 and 4
(d) All of the above

25 Which of the following is not a method of performance appraisal?

(a) Forced distribution method
(b) Factor comparison method
(c) Forced choice method
(d) Critical incident method

26 Gagne-Briggs Theory of training is otherwise called as

(a) Instructional Design theory
(b) Component Display theory
(c) Elaboration theory
(d) KSA theory

27 Which of the following is not a method of job evaluation?

(a) Ranking method
(b) Grading method
(c) Paired comparison method
(d) Point method

28 Which of the following is not a simulation technique of development?

(a) In-basket (b) Case study
(c) Sensitivity training (d) Management games

ANSWERS

Exam Based Questions

1 (a)	2 (c)	3 (d)	4 (d)	5 (d)	6 (c)	7 (b)	8 (d)	9 (d)	10 (d)
11 (a)	12 (d)	13 (c)	14 (b)	15 (b)	16 (a)	17 (b)	18 (a)	19 (d)	20 (a)
21 (a)	22 (c)	23 (c)	24 (b)	25 (b)	26 (d)	27 (d)	28 (b)	29 (a)	30 (c)
31 (d)	32 (a)	33 (c)	34 (b)	35 (c)	36 (a)	37 (b)	38 (d)	39 (b)	40 (d)
41 (a)	42 (b)	43 (c)	44 (a)	45 (a)	46 (a)	47 (c)	48 (b)	49 (c)	50 (b)
51 (b)	52 (c)	53 (b)	54 (d)	55 (d)	56 (b)	57 (a)	58 (d)	59 (b)	60 (a)
61 (d)	62 (a)	63 (b)	64 (a)	65 (c)	66 (b)	67 (d)	68 (a)	69 (a)	70 (c)
71 (a)	72 (c)	73 (b)	74 (c)	75 (a)	76 (d)	77 (b)	78 (c)	79 (a)	80 (d)
81 (a)	82 (c)	83 (d)	84 (a)	85 (b)	86 (a)	87 (b)	88 (d)	89 (c)	90 (d)
91 (c)	92 (c)	93 (d)	94 (d)	95 (c)	96 (c)	97 (a)	98 (c)	99 (a)	100 (d)
101 (c)	102 (b)	103 (d)	104 (b)	105 (c)	106 (a)	107 (d)	108 (b)	109 (c)	110 (b)
111 (c)	112 (a)	113 (c)	114 (d)	115 (a)	116 (a)	117 (b)	118 (d)	119 (b)	120 (a)
121 (b)	122 (c)	123 (b)	124 (b)	125 (c)	126 (b)				

Previous Years' Questions

1 (c)	2 (c)	3 (d)	4 (a)	5 (c)	6 (a)	7 (d)	8 (d)	9 (b)	10 (d)
11 (a)	12 (d)	13 (d)	14 (b)	15 (d)	16 (c)	17 (c)	18 (d)	19 (d)	20 (b)
21 (c)	22 (b)	23 (b)	24 (c)	25 (d)	26 (d)	27 (c)	28 (c)		

Job Evaluation, Compensation Management and Emerging Trends

This chapter deals with determining the worth of his job, *i.e.* job evaluation and how he should be compensated alongwith the benefits. This is followed by the emerging concepts in managing human resource.

Job Evaluation

Certain jobs contribute more to organisational effectiveness and success than others, are worth more than others and should be paid more than others. Thus, an evaluation is important to ascertain the true worth of a job. Job evaluation is an orderly and systematic technique to find out the relative worth of the jobs. It tries to make systematic comparison between jobs to assess their relative worth for the purpose of establishing a rational pay structure.

Job evaluation methods involve assigning values to each of the company's jobs. This process helps produce a pay plan in which each job's pay is equitable based on what other employers are paying for these jobs and based on each job's value to the employer.

The basic notion of job evaluation is that jobs requiring greater qualifications and comparatively additional responsibilities and more complex job duties must receive more pay than jobs with lesser requirements.

According to **The International Labour Organisation** (ILO), "Job evaluation is an attempt to determine and compare the demands which the normal performance of particular jobs makes on normal workers without taking into account of the individual abilities or performance of the workers concerned."

According to **Dessler**, "Job evaluation is a formal and systematic comparison of jobs to determine the worth of one job relative to another. Job evaluation eventually results in a wage or salary structure or hierarchy (this shows the pay rate for various jobs or groups of jobs)."

In this Chapter

- *Job Evaluation*
- *Compensation Management*
- *Employee Incentives and Benefits*
- *Managing Career*
- *Changing Environment of HRM*
- *Emerging Concepts in HRM*

According to **Miller**, "The purpose of job evaluation is the establishment of rates of pay for various jobs on an equitable basis. It is intended to eliminate chance, favouritism and individual bargaining in determining wage rates and for establishment of fair and equitable wages."

Objectives of Job Evaluation

- Job evaluation seeks to determine the relative worth of each job so that salary differentials can be established.
- Jobs are evaluated on the basis of their content in order to rank their importance.
- Job evaluation is done in order to match firm's overall wage structure with that of the industry in which the firm operates.
- It helps to maintain consistent wage policy and periodic review of salary structure.
- It serves as a basis for negotiation with the trade unions or employees union.
- It enables management to administer and control its payroll costs more accurately.
- Job evaluation covers only hourly rated jobs.
- It ensures that the institute meets equal pay for work of equal value obligations.
- It reduces grievances and labour turnover, in turn increases employee morale and improves management employee relationships.

Significance of Job Evaluation

Job evaluation serves the purpose of removing the evils in the hierarchy or wages and salary, if being done regularly and objectively. Knowles and Thomson have traced few irregularities which may develop in an organisation, if job evaluation is not done properly. *These are as follows*

- There is a possibility that higher salaries are being paid to jobs which do not require any special skill, knowledge, hard work and responsibility.
- Objective, unbiased and impersonal mind set is required to have the smooth functioning of the organisation. Therefore, job evaluation will find out if any injustice is being done on the basis of race, sex, religion, background etc.
- It is also very important to maintain salaries on the basis of seniority and job evaluation is an effective tester. It is only possible through job evaluation to maintain proper balance between specialised jobs and salaries. Because of division of labour, enterprises have got hundreds of jobs and many employees to perform them.
- It also helps in the selection of candidates as the factors determined for job evaluation can be taken into account.
- There will be harmonious relationship between employees and employers through proper job evaluation method and all kinds of salaries controversies can be minimised.
- It also needs to be seen that people with same knowledge, skills, abilities are enjoying same positions and same salaries.
- It has to be kept in mind that fresher's salary should not be less than what one person needs to lead a respectable life.

Approaches of Job Evaluation

There are two approaches to determine the worth of a job, which are as follows

Formal Job Evaluation

- They use standardised methods to evaluate jobs that can be analytical or non-analytical.
- Another way is basing the evaluation at the market rate. It is called the 'extreme market pricing' where the formal pay structures and individual rates of pay are entirely based on thoroughly collected and analysed information on market rates and no importance is given to internal relativities.

Informal Job Evalutaion

- Informal methodologies price jobs either on the basis of expectations about internal and external relativity or just by referring the market rates while recruiting people, one must note that here this reference is unsupported by any systematic analysis.
- Sometimes, a semi-formal approach may need some companies evidence to support a market pricing decision and also the use of role profiles to deliver greater accuracy to the matching process.

Steps in Job Evaluation Process

The steps includes in job evaluation process are as follows

- Setting the objectives of job evaluation to establish satisfactory wage and salary differentials.
- Job analysis thorough examinations of jobs by collecting data.
- Preparing job description and job specification to find out the importance of job to the organisation.
- Comparison of one job with another on the basis of job rating.
- Arranging jobs according to rating in terms of value to firm.
- Assigning wage rate to each job as per its ranking.
- Job classification grading jobs according to scale of pay.

Selection of Job Factors in Job Evaluation

The job evaluation committee usually includes atleast several workers and has the important task of evaluating the worth of each job using compensable factors.

Compensable factor is a fundamental compensable element of a job, which can be know-how, problem solving and accountability, knowledge, problem-solving skills and working conditions. Compensable factors have key role in job evaluation.

Job evaluation involves the evaluation of various jobs in terms of certain factors like

- Technical skills, conceptual skills, inter-personal skills etc.
- Experience or length of working years
- Efforts and initiative
- Responsibilities to be undertaken
- Supervision required
- Working environment in which job is to be performed

Methods of Job Evaluation

There are various quantitative and non-quantitative methods of job evaluation which are presented below

Non-quantitative Methods

They are also termed as non-analytical methods which form grade hierarchy but are non-quantitative. Generally, small organisations prefer non-analytical. This comprises of ranking method and classification/grading method, *which are as follows*

Ranking Method

- Each job is rated by different experts. It is done to see whether jobs comprises of same level of skills, duties and responsibilities. Experts rank jobs on the basis of relevance. It is quite a simple method of comparing the whole job with others and ranking them on the basis of comparison.
- It begins with job analysis followed by selection of groups and jobs. Thereafter, the compensable factors are selected. Then each member of the job evaluation committee ranks the job independently either in comparison to the other jobs or the benchmark job.

  If major differences are there in the opinion of all members, then either the average is calculated or the mutual consultation is done to reach the consensus.
- Job ranking also may not indicate the degree of difference between jobs. In some cases, it might be too noticeable whereas in others, it can be negligible which is one of its drawbacks. For instance, 2 and 3 may be relatively closer than 3 and 4. Rank does not bring out the measure of difference.

Job Classification Method

- This is also known as the 'grading method'. It is a method for categorising jobs into groups and classes. Under this method, jobs are categorised and given various grades by the committee members.
- 'Forming classes' means grouping jobs based on a set of rules for each group or class, such as amount of independent judgement, skill, physical effort and the classes usually contain similar jobs.
- Selection is made of one of two jobs from each level of the grading structure and standard descriptions of duties, responsibilities and requirements of these jobs are prepared. These jobs are known as benchmark or key jobs.
- Grading system is a job classification system like the class system, although grades often contain dissimilar jobs, such as secretaries, mechanics and firefighters. Grade descriptions are written based on compensable factors listed in classification systems.
- *Job grades can be determined in either of the way, i.e.*

  (a) All the jobs are ranked and their obvious classes may be determined.

  (b) A series of job class description in advance may be prepared by the evaluation committee on the basis of which various jobs may be graded.
- After the job grades have been decided by adopting either way, different characteristics of each job are matched with description of job class and is placed in the class with which it matches best.

Quantitative Methods

They are also called the analytical methods. They can be expressed in some numerical form. They are generally preferred by the larger companies. These comprise of the point method and factor comparison method, *which are as follows*

Point Method

- It is most widely used method. It is analytical and gives quantitative results. Each job value factor is assigned points. The compensation for each job is fixed on the basis of points earned by each job.
- Points are allotted to each specific factor of a job which determines the relative worth of a job. These allotted points to various job factors are summed up to find the worth of the job. Relative worth of various jobs is determined by comparing this total with the sum of other jobs.
- In this method, it is important to divide jobs into difference components; which are very important contributing factors towards organisational effectiveness, *e.g.* knowledge, skill, responsibility etc. Each major component is further broken into sub-factors to go into minute details of it.

- The points allotted to the major component are also sub-divided into points to different minor job factors. After the identification of major components and minor factors contributing towards organisational effective- ness scaling of each minor factor is done on the basis of degrees.
  Each degree is assigned a particular point keeping in mind, the importance of the degree is minor factor. *For example,* Taking education as a minor factor, scaling will be based on the degrees ranging from metric pass to doctorate degree or above in a particular stream.
  Now, the total points assigned to major component will be divided into minor factors and the points allotted to minor factors again will be further distributed to different degrees of education. All these points are then summed up to the total points scored by a job.
- It is more objective and free from personal biases as compared to the above two methods. It is more convincing and understandable as the job factors, components and degrees on the basis of which the points have been given are well-defined.
- Since, it is a quantitative method and numerical points have been assigned to each contributing factor, so wages and salary fixation is more easy and objective process.

Factor Comparison Method or Key Job Method

- This method was developed by **Eugene J Benge** in 1926 to overcome the demerits of point method of job evaluation. Benge identified five factors *viz* mental effort, skill, physical effort, responsibility and working conditions instead of determining the relative importance of factors and describing their degrees; as per point method of job evaluation.
- In this method, 15-20 key jobs from various departments are selected at the initial stage. These key jobs should represent all levels of wages and salaries which are acceptable to all and in line to all internal as well as external agencies.
- The above identified five factors are to be compared with the same factor of the key job and ranking is given to each factor. The same is done with all other factors as well. All ranks obtained by different factors of a job are summed up to determine the relative worth of the job.
- To make it more easy, objective and convincing to the trade union leaders, ranks are expressed in terms of monetary values and these values are added to get the wages directly and correctly.

Limitations of Job Evaluation

- Job evaluation is not exactly scientific.
- The modes operand of most of the techniques is difficult to understand, even for supervisions.
- The factor taken by the programme is not exhaustive.
- There may be wide fluctuations in compensable factors in view of change in technology, value and aspirations of employers etc.

Compensation Management

Compensation can be described as a wide range of financial and non-financial rewards to employees, for rendering their services to the organisation. They can be paid vacations, insurance, wages, salaries, retirement benefits, maternity leaves etc.

As money is the prime need for human beings to meet their basic needs, everyone tries to earn as much money as possible. Wage and salary administration is the group of activities involved in the development, implementation and maintenance of pay system.

According to **Dale Yoder**, "Compensation is paying people for work."

According to **Edwin B Flippo**, "The function of compensation is defined as the adequate and equitable remuneration of personnel for their contributions to the organisational objectives."

According to **Benham**, "Compensation is the value of work of the employees according to the agreement between employer and employee".

According to **Dessler**, "Employee compensation includes all forms of pay going to employees and arising from their employment."

The phrase 'all forms of pay' in the definition does not include non-financial benefits, but all the direct and indirect financial compensations. It has two main components, direct financial payments (wages, salaries, incentives, commissions and bonuses) and indirect financial payments (financial benefits like employer paid insurance and vacations).

Objectives of Compensation Management

- To establish a fair and equal proportion of remuneration and job responsibilities and to establish internal equity as well as external equity.
- Internal equity means similar pay for similar work. External equity within the organisation means remunerations compatible with the employees working with same job responsibilities outside the organisation.
- To get the best talent out of available talent pool with the sound and competent wage and salary administration and to pose a good image of the company in public and alleviate, it is important to have sound and competent wage and salary administration.
- To enhance productivity and morale of the employees in any organisation, it is very important to have effective wage and salary administration. It is obvious that highly paid employees would like to work more effectively and efficiently.
- To establish job hierarchy and lines of promotion, it is again important to have sound and full proof wages and salary administration. It will be the basis of all other decisions.
- To have cordial relationship between management and union, it is important to have sound and competitive wage and salary administration so that they don't feel exploited and their level of satisfaction is high.
- To retain the employees, it is very important to have competent wage and salary administration; otherwise the rate of change of employees will be quite high.

Advantages of Compensation Management

A well designed compensation plan will benefit your organisation in the following ways

Job Satisfaction Your employees would be happy with their jobs and would love to work for you if they.

Motivation We all have different kinds of needs. Some of us want money so they work for the company which gives them higher pay.

Some value achievement more than money, they would associate themselves with firms which offer greater chances of promotion, learning and development. A compensation plan that hits workers' needs is more likely to motivate them to act in the desired way.

Low Absenteeism Why would anyone want to skip the day and watch not so favourite TV programme at home, if they enjoy the office environment and are happy with their salaries and get what they need and want.

Low Turnover Would your employees want to work for any other boutique if you offer them fair rewards. Rewards which they thought they deserved.

Factors Affecting Wage and Salary Administration

- Demand and supply factors are the major factors which affects wage and salary administration process. Number of available talent determines the wages rate. If number of talented people available is more than required, wages will be low and vice-versa.
- Attitude and ability of employers will also affect the wages and salary structure and obviously, they will pay according to their returns and profits.
- Labour unions also play an important role in determining the wages. They exert pressure on the employers to be competitive with their competitors outside. The pressure may be exerted through collective bargaining, strikes and other methods.
- It has become very difficult to beat inflation as it is increasing at high speed and therefore, the value of real wages decline. Dearness allowance is given to maintain the balance and there is a clause in labour agreements also, according to which pay increases with the increase in cost of living automatically.
- Wages and salary also depends upon the inputs given by job evaluation. Job evaluation actually determines the worth of job keeping in mind the job requirements.
- Major determining factor is that what others are paying in the same industry to the individual with same qualifications. Every employer has to pay according to that.
- Wages and salary are basically determined by the performance of an individual as it affects the efficiency and productivity of any organisation. The more they get, the more they would like to give it back.

Principles of Wage Administration

It is guided by following principles

- Wage policies should be wisely formulated while having keeping the interest of all the individuals within and outside the company(community, employees, consents and management).
- Wage policies should be clearly expressed in writing so that there is uniformity and stability.
- Wage policies should incorporate the differences in the jobs. There must exist a definite plan.
- They should carefully make distinction between jobs and employees.

- They should be based on the principle of equal pay and should not be based.
- Wage policies should be communicated to the employees.

Determination of Wages and Salary

The following are the steps to determine wages and salary

Job Analysis to Determine Wages It is very important to analyse the job and then get prepared with the content of job description and job specification. The data collected through job analysis is the major determinant of wages and salary.

Job Evaluation Job evaluation is also done through the data provided by job description. Hierarchy is also made by job evaluation and in this way, the relative fixation of wages and salary is done. The relative job value is then converted into money value.

Wage Survey The major factor which any employer would consider while fixing wages and salary is that what is the wage/salary level in that particular region in the same industry for similar jobs. Other facilities being provided by their competitors would also be considered.

Developing Wage Structure After undergoing through survey and confirming about their competitors, a wage structure compatible to the competitors is prepared, keeping in mind few things like rules and norms prescribed by regulatory bodies, legislation relating to wages, width of pay-grades, inflation, provision for performance increase, coordination between job evaluation and salaries amount etc.

Formulating Rules It is very necessary to formulate norms and rules that will govern hike in payments, promotions from one grade to another. How much time period and the kind of meritorious performance is required to get the promotions.

After the rules are formulated, they need to be communicated formally to all the employees wi... ... any ambiguity.

Performance Evaluation The performance of each and every individual is evaluated adopting various methods of performance evaluation and the hike in the salary and promotion will depend upon the results obtained after performance evaluation.

It is feasible that the employee working for many years may earn more on the lower pay scale than a fresher working on the higher scale due to continuous increments.

Thus, this is how the fixation of wages and salary of any individual can be done. The effective, proper and authentic administration of wages and salary is done, provided all the steps are followed properly.

Wage Theories

There are various theories of wages that assist the manager in defining the pay. These are given by different authors, *which are as follows*

- Subsistence Theory
- The Surplus Value Theory of Wages
- Wages Fund Theory
- Marginal Productivity Theory
- Reinforcement Theory
- Residual Claimant Theory
- Wage Behavioural Theories
- The Bargaining Theory of Wages
- Equity Theory

➠ **Note** *These are elaborated in unit 8.*

Wage Policy in India

In India, the question of wages assumes paramount importance because of acute poverty, larger scale unemployment and high population. No fixed norms and means are followed in fixing wages and salary. So, lots of expediencies are found in fixing wage.

Following are the main objectives of wage policy in India

- To ensure the fulfilment of their basic needs atleast in every sector, whether in agriculture, industry or service sector.
- To create a highly objective, impersonal and unbiased system so that disparities related to occupation, industry, region or regional are reduced to minimum level.
- To beat inflation and compensate employees equitable to the rise in prices.
- To ensure no disparity between the wages and salary of private and public sector.
- To maintain proper balance between high profitability units and others to avoid stress and frustration.
- To maintain proper coordination with the outside agencies and other regulatory bodies so that there is no conflict with the trade unions.
- To motivate and encourage employees by providing them with proper incentive systems of payment.

Methods of Wage Payments

There are two methods of payment

Time Wage System

Wages are paid on the basis of time spent irrespective of the work done. In the past, workers were paid on the daily basis. In this method, workers feel secure, confident and assured of being paid at the end of the day. It is one of the oldest method.

There is no need to maintain any record in this case and therefore, no hassle of appointing special staff for all this. A worker can work skilfully in this case as there is no hurry of finishing in stipulated time.

Every worker is being paid equally and therefore, a sense of equality and solidarity is created among them. This method is more convenient and suitable where work done of an intangible nature and not feasible to measure the output. It is suitable in continuous or assembly line production, where the output is not dependent upon individual worker.

The wages are calculated as

Wages = Number of hours worked × Rate per hour

Piece Wage System

In this method, compensation is based on the amount of work done or output of a worker. Reward is in proportion to the effort, so people tend to work hard to gain more incentives. Efficient workers get an opportunity to showcase their talent and earn more, if ambitious. Promotions become more objective as they are dependent upon the performances instead of anyone's whims and fancies.

This method will be more advantageous as will lead to reduction in the overall labour cost and increase in productivity.

This reduction in labour cost will ultimately benefit the consumer in the form of lower prices or better quality, the society as a whole stands to gain. Low supervision will be required in this case as workers themselves are keen to increase their efficiency level.

Worker cooperate more in this method with innovative schemes of rationalisation designed to improve efficiency of operations.

The wages are calculated as

Wages= Number of units produced × Rate per unit

Components of Compensation

Compensation can be bifurcated into base compensation and supplementary compensation, which are as follows

1. Base Compensation

The term base compensation means the monetary benefits that are given to the employees in the form of wages and salaries. Wages means the remuneration to workers doing the manual or physical work and salary means compensation to the office employees, foreman, managers and professional and technical staff.

Following are the major components of base compensation package

(i) Base Pay/Guaranteed Pay

This is the monetary (cash) reward paid by an employer to an employee based on employee/employer relations. The most common form of guaranteed pay is the basic salary. It is the first and foremost part of pay, package, which is determined through job evaluation. Pay differentials are to be in proportionate with the worth of job.

There are few determinants of basic pay, *i.e.* demand and supply of expertise, competitor's policy of wages and salary administration, statutory requirements, employer's attitude etc.

The fair wage committee gave three concepts relations to basic wages

- **Minimum Wage** The amount of money which is sufficient to fulfil the basic needs of any individual, *i.e.* Roti, Kapra aur Makaan irrespective of the capacity of the industry to pay.
- **Fair Wage** It is more than just fulfilling the basic needs of an employee but little bit more depending upon the capacity of an industry to pay and other factors like the performance of an employee, the prevailing wages in the market, the contribution of industry towards GDP etc.
- **Living Wage** It is the amount that not only fulfils the basic needs but in addition provides certain amenities necessary for the well being of the worker.

(ii) Allowance

- Dearness allowance is given to protect the salary from inflation, as inflation rate keeps on increasing day-by-day.
- Under Section 3 of the Minimum Wages Act, it is described as cost of living allowance. There are different methods used to calculate dearness allowance.
- Same amount is paid as dearness allowance to all the employees irrespective of their basic pay and grades at flat rate. Earlier it was used in jute, cotton and engineering industries in Paschim Banga.

- Dearness allowance differs in different slabs, *i.e.* graduated scale. It increases with the increase in basic pay and decreases with the decrease in basic pay.
- Index based dearness allowance method is applicable in the cotton mills of Mumbai and Chennai as well as many Central Government undertakings. In this method, a flat rate per point of index is prescribed irrespective of pay scale, in this way, all the employees get the same amount.
- Dearness allowance linked to index and pay scale method is used to pay dearness allowance to government employees and central public sector undertakings. In this method, amount is controlled by both index as well as pay scale.
- Under this method, dearness allowance is inversely proportional to basic pay as a higher rate of dearness allowance is prescribed for lower pay scales and a lower rate for higher pay scales.
- House rent allowance is given as a percentage of basic pay, *i.e.* 30% of basic pay in case of government employees. This allowance is given by the employers who do not provide living house accommodation.
- City compensatory allowance is given to the employees in metros and other big cities where cost of living is comparatively high in order to compensate expenditure.
- Conveyance allowance is given by the employer in order to manage the travelling expenses. It varies from organisation-to-organisation and different for different designations.

2. Supplementary Compensation

Supplementary compensation involves the fringe benefits that are offered through several employee services and benefits such as crèche, medical aid, subsidised food housing etc. They are also known as employee benefits, non-wage payments and service programmes.

They chiefly comprise of the following two

(i) Incentives

Bonus, profit sharing, commission on sales etc are the various forms of incentives and basically they are performance based. Star performers are found out and incentives are given to them.

(ii) Fringe Benefits

These benefits are usually paid to the senior officers. Provident funds, pensions, gratuity, encashment of earned leave, company house, company car, leave travel concession, medical aid, interest free loan, holiday homes, entertainment, stock options etc are the examples of such benefits.

There is a wide variety of employee benefits, such as paid time-off, insurances (life insurance, medical/dental insurance and work disability insurance), pension plan, company car and more. A benefit plan is designed to address a specific need and is often provided not in the form of cash.

Many countries dictate different minimum benefits, such as minimum paid time-off, employer's pension contribution, sick pay and more. These incentives and benefits are elaborated in the upcoming sections.

Executive Compensation

Salaries of managerial posts come under this category and depends on the following factors

- The more complex the job, the more is the compensation. These jobs require creativity, innovation, decision-making, leadership, communication skill, higher skills and greater responsibilities. These things differ from industry to industry.
- It varies with the capacity of the company to pay. High profit making companies pay more than small houses.
- It also depends upon the kind of education and experience, one possesses. Sometimes more experienced professionals are paid lower than the fresher's because of their latest knowledge and dynamic attitude.
- Performance and efficiency definitely play an important role in the fixation of salaries of executives. Obviously, people showing good performances are given more salaries.
- With an advent of globalisation and liberalisation many multinational have come up and in this competition other local companies also have to pay relatively high to retain good employees.
- Managerial compensation is subject to government control under the Companies Act and therefore, controlled by legislation also. *e.g.* it is pre-defined that total remuneration payable to managerial personnel should be 11% of the maximum percentage of annual net profit. 5% of the total profit should be paid to the director and 5% to the manager.

  All these mandates given in the various acts are necessary to be followed by the companies while deciding managerial fixation.

Elements of Executive Compensation

The components of executive's compensation are

Basic Salary It is the key component in the compensation but not the major portion of package. The areas of focus are performance based pay and incentives.

Annual Bonus Plans Any profit-making organisation offers bonus schemes to its managers which is considered to be a short-term performance linked incentive scheme. It is computed and paid on the basis of the performance in a single year.

Bonus schemes can be classified on the basis of performance measure, performance standards and pay performance relationship structure. Organisations may use one or more measures like accounting profits (like EBIT, revenue growth and operating income) or non-financial performances like goal accomplishments by the managers.

Bonus can be computed on various forms of performance standards like budget standards, past year performance standards, discretionary standards (subjective standards set by the management), peer group standards and timeless standards.

Employee's Stock Option Plan (ESOP) In this unique type of plan, the managerial personnel get the right to buy the stocks (mostly equity shares) of their company in the future at a price which may be equal or less than the price prevailing at the time of purchase.

The stock option is normally a non-tradable long-term incentive available to the managers. However, the option to buy stock would normally lapse when the executive leaves the organisation for any reasons.

This option encourages the executive to accept increased responsibility for their decisions involving the future of the organisation. The main advantage of this scheme is that there is no direct or immediate cash outflow for the company when the manager exercises this stock option.

Additional Long-term Incentive Plans (LTIP) The aim of this option is to enhance the performance pay relationship by computing the basis of the cumulative performance of managers on a multi-year cycle. Performance unit or share is one of the popular forms of the long-term incentive plan.

According to this incentive scheme, a manager would be entitled to get specific cash or shares as the reward in the event of completing the performance targets successfully. Though long-term incentives are generally tied to the overall organisational performance, they may also be linked to group performance within the organisation.

Managerial Commission Commission pay is one of the important components of executive compensation packages. It is an annual performance based incentive scheme, computed in two ways commission payable on profit before charging such a commission and commission payable on profits after charging such a commission.

Executive Perks It is a different type of benefit payable to the top managers as recognition for their contribution to the growth of the organisation based on the job worth. It is given to a selected group of key executives.

It involves, luxurious residential apartments, company cars, special parking space at office, private dining rooms, membership in country clubs, sponsored vacation trips, interest free loans, insurance schemes and annual health examination.

Sometimes, these facilities are also extended to their family members like reimbursement of children's educational expenses and spouse travel.

Employee Incentives and Benefits

Recently, organisations are focusing on compensating the employees for their personal needs such as career breaks, child care, financial planning. Merely compensating the employee in terms of money is not sufficient. Thus, various incentives and benefits are provided to the employee to enhance job satisfaction and loyalty. They are explained in different sections.

Employee Incentives

It is a stimulus or a reason to do. It can be anxiety, worries, fear, hope, prestige, money, security and so on and generally focuses more on what the organisation can do to foster employee career development.

According to **George R Terry**, "Incentives means that which incites or has a tendency to incite action." Career plans can be implemented, atleast in part, through an organisation's training programmes.

The basic objective of incentive plans is to increase the production by giving an inducement to workers in the form of higher wages.

Types of Incentives

There are two types of incentives

Positive Incentives

It includes

- Praise and encouragement
- Participation and cooperation
- Corrections
- Confidence and faith
- Rivalry and competition

Negative Incentives

It includes

- Threat, criticism, rebuke
- Punishment
- Neglect and dogtrick
- Fine

Incentive Wage Plans

There are various incentive plans which are generally classified into individual incentive plans and group incentive plans which are further bifurcated into various activities. *There are as follows*

Individual Plans

The individual wage incentive plan is the extra payment paid to an individual over a specified amount for his production effort. They are based upon certain norms which are established by work measurement techniques such as past performance, bargaining between union and the management, time study, standard data, pre-determined elemental times and work sampling.

The individual plans are further divided into time based and work based. *These are as follows*

Time Based Plans

Here, a standard time is determined for doing a job. A standard time serves as the basis of giving bonus to the workers if they meet the standard or exceed the standard time. If a worker finishes his task in less time, then he is termed as efficient.

There are four plans under this head which are

1. Halsey Premium Plan

- A standard time is set for the completion of the job in this technique. Every employee is guaranteed a minimum base salary. If an employee finishes his job in the standard time, no incentive will be given to him.
- If, in less than standard time, a employee executes his job, he is given incentive. The incentive is equal to 50% of the worker's time saved. The slow worker is paid the time wages and the efficient worker is paid some bonus in addition.
- *The total wages are calculated by using the following formula*

$$W = T \times R + 50\% \text{ of } (S - T) \times R$$

Where, W is total wages, T is time taken by the worker, R is rate of wages and S is standard time.

2. Rowan Plan

- This scheme is very similar to the plan of Halsey. It only differs in terms of the time saved while calculating the incentive. The worker receives the minimum guaranteed wages. There is no penalty for the slow worker.
- A standard time is fixed for completion of a job and bonus is paid to a worker on the basis of time saved by him. Thus, bonus is that proportion of wages for the time taken which the time saved bears to the time.

As the time saved increases, time taken will be reduced and bonus will increase in diminishing rate. Thus, it checks the over speeding which is not done by the Halsey Plan.

- Thus, in Halsey plan, the bonus is a fixed percentage of time, while in Rowan it keeps on varying.
- The incentive to complete the job in less than standard time is paid based on a ratio that saves time over standard time per standard unit time.
- *The formula for the same is slightly different as it considers efficiency as the ratio of time saved and standard time*

$$\text{Total Wages} = T \times R + \left[T \times R \times \frac{\text{Time Saved}}{\text{Standard Time}} \right]$$

3. Emerson's Efficiency Plan

- In this proposal, every employee is paid a fixed wage on a timely basis and incentives are given on the productivity basis.
- The ratio of time taken to standard time determines efficiency. Bonus or incentive payment is related to employee efficiency.
- Those employees who achieve more than 2/3rd, *i.e.* 66.67 per cent of efficiency, will be given incentive. At 66.67 per cent efficiency, no incentive will be given. The hourly rate is 20 per cent at a 100 per cent efficiency incentive. For efficiency exceeding 100 per cent, for every 1 per cent increase in efficiency, 1 per cent incentive or bonus is paid.

4. Bedeaux Plan

It is also known as units or point system. The Bedeaux system guarantees a minimum base wage. The standard time and time taken for each job is reduced to minutes under this plan. It is referred to every minute as 'B', *i.e.* one hour is the same as 60B.

- Workers completing the job in standard time will be paid at a normal rate of time. Bonus will be paid to those who complete the job in less time. The bonus paid to the worker is 75% of the time saved wages. The time saved is split between managers and employees.
- *The formula for the same is*

$$W = TR + 75\% \text{ of } (S - T)R$$

Work Based Plans

It is also known as production based plans where the standard of output is determined on scientific basis and the payments are made on the basis of the number of units produced by the worker. A higher rate per unit is paid to the worker who is more efficient.

It comprises of following three plans

1. **Taylor's Differential Piece Rate Plan**

- This was given by **FW Taylor**. The main features of this scheme are two lower and one higher wage rates being fixed.
- It suggests a low rate for that workforce who are unable to achieve the standard production within the standard time and a higher rate for those capable of producing the standard production within or below the standard time.
- Thus, it provides incentives to efficient worker and the inefficient worker is penalised. Also, this system is simple and easy to implement.

2. **Merrick's Multiple Piece Rate Plan**

- To remove the drawbacks of differential piece rate system, Merrick advocated a modified plan in which, three piece rates are applied for workers with different levels of performance. *These were*
  - (a) Workers producing less than 83% of the standard output are paid at basic rate.
  - (b) Workers producing between 83% and 100% of standard output will be paid 110% of basic piece rate.
  - (c) Those producing more than 100% of the standard output will be paid 120% of basic piece rate.
- Thus, Merrick's plan is liberal for the efficient workers but it does not guarantee minimum wages.

3. **Gantt's Task and Bonus Wage Plan**

- This strategy is based on studying a job carefully. This plan's main characteristic is that it incorporates time, piece rate and bonus. To do a specific job, a standard time is fixed.

  The actual performance of the labourer is contrasted to the standard time and its effectiveness is defined.
- If a labourer does not finish the work within the standard time, *i.e.* it takes longer than the standard time (efficiency below 100 per cent), **no bonus** will be given, but wages will be provided for the time taken by him.
- If a labourer completes the job within the standard time (efficiency of 100 per cent), wages will be given for the standard time and **bonus of 20 per cent of wages earned.**
- If the worker finishes the job in less than the standard time (*i.e.* efficiency more than 100%), wages are paid according to piece rate.

Performance Based Incentive Plans

Traditionally there were only group and time based incentive plans. However, now incentives are also paid on the basis of performance of the employee. They are called performance linked compensation.

Some of the examples are

- **Piece Rate Pay** It offers incentive for higher productivity.
- **Merit Pay** It is an annual increment tied to the employee's performance during the preceding year.
- **Lumpsum Merit Pay** This is also called re-earnable bonus and the employee gets a single amount which is not added to his base salary.
- **Commission** It is generally found in sales jobs which can be based on straight commission or base salary plus commission.

Group Plans

The group or area incentive scheme delivers for the payment of a bonus either equally or proportionately to individuals within a group or area. The bonus is related to the output achieved over an agreed standard or to the time saved on the job. This is the difference between allowed time and actual time.

Such schemes may be most appropriate where individuals have to work together and teamwork has to be encouraged and high levels of production depend on the cooperation existing among a team of workers as compared with the individual efforts of team members.

It generally comprises of

Profit Sharing

- It is an agreement between the management and the employees under which the employees receive a share, fixed in advance, of profits.
- According to Geneva Report (1948), "Profit sharing is a method of industrial remuneration under which an employer undertakes to pay his employees a share in the net profit of the enterprise in addition to their regular wages."
- The profit on compensation can be in the form of stocks, bonds or cash and can be paid immediately or on retirement. Profit sharing is an agreement freely entered into, by which the employees receive a share in advance of the profits.

Priestman's Plan

- Under this plan, a standard production is set for the entire enterprise. If productivity surpasses the standard, the bonus will be paid according to the increase. If production fails to reach the standard, workers will only receive minimum wages.
- Workers get enough incentives to increase their performance. A team spirit is visible among the employees because with the combined efforts of the organisation's various limbs, production will increase.

- However, this technique does not provide incentives for individual employees. Inefficient employees share efficient workers' attempts because higher production benefits all the institution's workforce.

Scalon Plan

- The name of this method is Joseph Scalon. According to this plan, there is indeed a one per cent participating bonus payment for each per cent increase in productivity.
- Except for top management, the bonus is available to all employees. The sum or bonus of the entitlement is not paid each month.
- To offset any change in labour costs, a reserve fund of one-half of the first fifteen per cent is created.
- This reserve will remain unused at the end of the year, this amount will also be spread to workers in the last month of the year and a fresh reserve will be created in the year.

Co-partnership

- The workers are given shares of the company at lower rates in this plan. The fee is also collected in instalments. The employees share profits of the enterprise as its members.
- The fundamental notion of this method is to make workforces feel as a part of the organisation and recognise view point of the administration. As co-partners they will act in a responsible manner and will try to make the concern more and more profitable and successful.

Employee Benefits

Employee benefits are the components of remuneration given in addition to the various forms of cash pay. They generally comprise of elements which are not part of remuneration such as leaves and holidays.

Objectives of Employee Benefits

- Provide a tax-efficient method of compensation or remuneration.
- Boost the morale and increase the commitment of employees to the organisation.
- Look after the personal needs of employees.
- Provide a competitive and holistic remuneration package that both attracts and retains high-quality employees.

Key Types of Employee Benefits

Pension They are the most important employee benefits and are designed to support the employee after he retires. It provides an income to employee when they retire and to their surviving dependent on the death of the employee.

Personal Security These are the benefits that enhance the individuals personal and family security with regard to illness, health, life insurance and accident.

Personal Needs This generally comprises of entitlements that recognise the interface between the work as well as domestic responsibilities of the employee. These generally comprises of earned leaves, career breaks, financial counselling, retirement counselling, child care fitness and recreational activities.

Financial Needs Companies and public institutions provide financial assistance with regard to relocation assistance, house purchase scheme, loan assistance, employee stock ownership plan, pension or saving plan, profit sharing scheme etc. They also aid in financial growth of the employee.

Company Cars and Petrol Various institutions also provide discounted transport facilities to the employees.

Others There are various other incentives and benefits of gratuity, leave with pay, housing allowance, meals, vouchers, refund of telephone costs, overtime allowance, credit card facilities etc.

Flexible Benefits It is also called 'cafeteria system', allow the employees to decide on the make-up of their benefit package, however this is done within certain limits. Thus, employee benefits are additional benefits that are provided to the employees in addition to their basic remuneration.

Managing Career

Career is defined as the occupational position a person has had over many years. It is an appropriate sequence of activities related to work. Such work related activities in relation to experience also include role experiences at an individual's different hierarchical levels that leads to an increasing level of responsibilities, status, power, achievements and rewards.

According to **David A Decenzo** and **Stephen P Robbins,** "Career is a sequence of positions occupied by a person during the course of life time."

Career management is the process for enabling workers to better comprehend and improve their career skills and interests and to use these talents and interests more effectively. It is a process by which people can steer their careers, direct them and influence them.

Career management is concerned with the provision of opportunities for people to develop their abilities and their careers in order to safeguard that the institute has the flow of talent it needs and to satisfy their own goals. It is about integrating the needs of the organisation with the needs of the individual. It comprise of career planning and career development.

Key Concepts of Career Management

Career Perspective

Career can be regarded from the perspective of individuals and organisations. With his own aspiration, an employee will plan his career. He might leave the organisation and join the other where he still locates better opportunities than the previous. She/he may leave the organisation and join the other where he still locates better opportunities than the previous.

The employer may consider career management as a process which involves moving through hierarchical career paths. The interest of the organisation is to seek managerial talents and ensure impartial opportunity to every talented person to go along who accomplishes the organisation's need.

Self-managed Careers (Career Anchors)

The organisation may need to manage careers as part of its talent management and management succession programmes and can provide support and guidance to people with potential.

Edgar Schein invented the idea of career anchors. According to him, "it is the self-concept of people consisting of self-perceived talents and abilities, basic values and a sense of motives and needs relating to their careers."

For instance, when individuals gain work experience, career anchors grow and function as alleviating forces, hence the metaphor of 'anchor'. Career anchors are the pivots around which a person's career swings, a person becomes conscious of them because of learning through experience, about his or her talents and abilities, motives and needs and attitudes and values.

Career anchors mean the basic motivations that create the urge to take up a certain type of career.

These are as follows

S.No.	Drives	Examples
1	Creativity	Opportunities for risk taking and innovation
2	Autonomy	Freedom to perform/take actions, autonomy or independence
3	Security	Following organisational norms to feel secure
4	Managerial Competence	Opportunities for higher responsibility, control influence, decision-making
5	Technical Competence	Professional satisfaction, continuous learning, public relations etc

Career Stages

This means how careers progress the ways in which people move through their careers *i.e.* upwards when they are promoted or by enlarging or enriching their roles to take on greater responsibilities or make more use of their skills and abilities. There are generally stages in the career of any employee which is given by DT Hall. *These are as follows*

Exploration

This stage is generally not done by the individual himself but by the parents. Parents start exploring career choices, the day their child is born. The individual himself starts exploring after 10th class and this exploration ends when one makes transition from college to work.

In this stage, an individual have lots of self-exploration to know what does he want and what kind of jobs are available in the market?

Initial Stage

This stage is also known as establishment period. This stage begins when exploration stage ends and the individual starts working on his first job. The quality of this stage depends upon what the person has learnt during student life and exploration stage.

It is very important in this stage that one learns to cooperate with others and feels accepted by others. There are more chances of mistakes at this stage, but performance is loaded by zeal and enthusiasm.

Growth Stage

This is the mid-career stage. At this stage, people work very hard to climb the ladder of success very fast. By this time, every individual is quite clear about his/her career goals and strive harder to achieve it.

In this stage, an individual is mature enough to understand his emotions and the ways to channelise them and move towards career goals with clarity.

Late Career

This is the maturity stage. It is the most pleasant stage where an individual can enjoy the ripened juicy fruit which is the resultant of his hardwork during the upper three stages. At this stage, an individual has big and competent force to follow and regard them. Young employees respect them for their maturity and experience.

On the contrary, the people who could not reach the level they wished for, they deserved or they wanted; they feel stagnated and start realising that they cannot change the world. Such people may feel little bit depressed and frustrated. They wait for their retirement and wish to go out of scene calmly.

Decline

It is the final stage of anyone's career which is quite painful and depressing because it is the stage of retirement, when organisation gives clear indication that one's services are not at all required in the organisation. It is difficult to bear this movement after decades of continuous achievement. However, dynamic, meticulous, outstanding and methodical one was in his working, one has to face this last of his career.

The aforementioned stages are briefly explained by the following career curves in the diagram

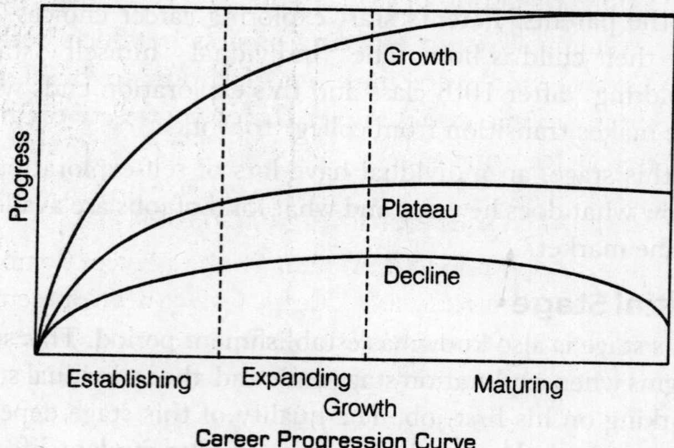

Career Progression Curve

However, sometimes, at a certain stage, the upward mobility stops for many employees. This is known as career plateau. This cannot be avoided in many pyramidal organisation structures. This generally occurs at the age of 40s.

This has been represented by the middle arrow. This leads to stagnation in growth and the possibility to rise in the organisation is less. Managers can use various tactics such as mentoring, providing additional career ladders to support such candidates.

Career Path

Career path is understood as a line, a track or a course along which an employee ascends or move upward in business's hierarchical structure. This concept has been given by Mondy *et al*. The career paths are generally influenced by the policy of the strategy of the company.

Some of the types of career paths are defined below

- **Traditional** Traditional career paths were generally depicted with straight lines where an employee generally entered the organisation at a lower level and retired at the top position.
- **Spiral** Modern organisation is dynamic in nature which entails change in size of organisation. This means new positions are opened at middle and top levels also which means a new employee can join the organisation at that level also. Similarly, there can be transfers, promotions or demotions. Hence, modern career paths are spiral in nature.

Career Planning

Career planning is a lifelong process, which includes choosing an occupation, getting a job, growing in our job, possibly changing careers and eventually retiring. This may happen once in our lifetimes, but it is more likely to happen several times as we first define and then redefine ourselves and our goals.

Career planning is a conscious, deliberate process through which a person becomes aware of his individual skills, knowledge, interests, motivations and other attributes; acquires information, opportunities, options, recognises and identifies career related goals and builds action plans to attain these goals.

Career planning helps in assisting the employee to plan his career in terms of their capacities within the context of organisational needs. It is devising an organisational system of career management and growth opportunities from the point of entity of an individual in employment till his retirement.

Characteristics of Career Planning

- Its main characteristic is to develop human beings.
- It is a way to manage people to get maximum out of them.
- It is an on-going perpetual process without any stop due to ever changing environment.
- Career planning is thought to be a person aspect and therefore, individual's own responsibility. But, employees are the integral part of every organisation, therefore, it is the responsibility of an organisation to provide guidance and counselling to plan their careers, develop themselves and make use of their knowledge and skills up to maximum.
- Both the personal career goals of an individual should be streamlined with the organisational goals.

Objectives of Career Planning

- To retain and provide job satisfaction to the talented and competent people and to explore the willingness of employees in terms of training and development.
- To provide job satisfaction to the employees and ensure higher productivity and to reduce labour turnover and absenteeism and make better use of human resources.
- To utilise each and every manager in the organisation to its fullest and to raise the level of motivation and employee morale by providing opportunities for promotion.
- To make an employee significant in the organisation by opening the channel of communication and help him in realising that one day the promising persons will get what they deserve.

- To know about their suitability to be promoted for higher positions and to persuade employees to fulfil their goals and mentoring them to reach there.
- To achieve higher productivity and organisational development.

Steps in Career Planning

Step 1 The very first key step in career planning is to collect information about yourself to help make a career decision. This includes learning about the development needs, skills aptitudes, values, your realities, preferred environments, roles and interest.

Step 2 The second step in career planning is to explore your choices and investigate them. Your self-assessment takes you one step even further by looking at your self-interests, abilities, values and work life needs and narrowing it down to areas of opportunity.

This comprises of researching about the industries in which the individual would like to work, exploring about the occupations in which he is interested and also researching about the labour market.

Step 3 After completing your self-assessment and exploring your options, you should be ready to make some career decisions. Now, the question is how you decide. This is done with the help of aligning the needs and opportunities of oneself.

The person should identify possible outcomes, evaluate these outcomes, explore the alternatives and choose both a short-term and long-term option.

Step 4 Getting experience connected with your career can help you in creating knowledge and skills to strengthen your career objectives. This contains developing a job search strategy, investigating sources of additional training and education, writing the resume, gathering information about companies, composing cover letter, preparing job interviews.

Step 5 Implementation is the last step in the process of implementing what you have learned and moving towards a new job or further education. You should also continue to assess your choices and make alterations, if necessary.

Career Development

Individuals need to really develop newer and better skills to promote and achieve a higher organisational level. Organisations must also be diligent in the design and development of their employees' career advancement programs.

Though employees are responsible for planning their careers, it is the responsibility of employers to provide them with prospects to achieve their desires in today's turbulent and terribly ambiguous world of work.

Career development is an on-going process in which both employees and employers must make efforts to build a favourable environment so that even their own objectives can be achieved at the same time.

Significance of Career Development

- It is a way to prevent job burnouts. The employees do not lose interest in their jobs and careers. Career development enriches their job experience alongwith providing success, which enhances their performance.
- The employees are provided with career information. It can be a learning experience for the employees where they will learn about recent trends and opportunities in their career.
- It ensures improved quality of working life as it helps in removing monotony of work.

Methods of Career Development

There are several methods widely used for the development of careers. But, these are mostly used in unique combination with more than one method.

The commonly used career development methods are as follows

Discussion with Experienced People The subordinate is paired with his superior in this method, in order to agree on the best career development activities. In some cases, this service is provided by counsellors and psychologists.

Material by Company Some organisations have created specific materials for the development of their employees. The content developed corresponds to the needs of the institutions.

In addition, job descriptions can be regarded as good content that shows workers to decide whether their strengths and weaknesses correspond to the requirements of any job offering within their own organisation.

Workshops Some organisations offer their employees seminars and workshops that last two or more days, so that they can develop their careers within the organisation. The career goals are described and matched by the workers with the organisations' needs.

Personal Development Plans (PDP) Some organisations encourage their employees to submit their own personal growth plans. This plan summarises the needs of workers' personal development and the specified effort and action plan for achievement. The upper management therefore encourages staff to examine their weaknesses and strengths.

Others In addition to these career development methods, there are other ways to develop careers, such as specialised software packages and special websites, lifelong learning budgets where both employee and employer provide money, career centres, career libraries etc.

Thus, career management is concerned with the provision of opportunities for people to develop their abilities and their careers in order to safeguard that the institute has the flow of talent it needs and to satisfy their own goals.

Changing Environment of HRM

There is a constant change in the business environment which is affecting the competitiveness of firms. Changing environment is bringing new challenges for the managers. The traditional HR and management policies are not working effectively in handling these contemporary challenges.

Contemporary Challenges

Managers are using new ways to provide transactional analysis. *New policies and practices have been developed to cater to recent challenges are given below*

Globalisation

It has led to the expansion of business. This sometimes means that production takes place in the host country instead of home countries. It becomes difficult for the employees as the jobs become hard and less secure.

Hence, there is a change in HRM, as concepts of job offshoring are emerging. Job offshoring means getting work done outside the home country which was previously done in the home country.

Slower Economic Growth in many Countries

HRM is now fiscally conservative and the organisation spends its resources only on obtaining competent employees. Thus, there are various new and extensive tests taken before hiring a new employee. They are becoming more cost conscious. Thus, HRM not only deals with humans, but also there must be a command on financial budgeting and strategic management.

Technological Innovation

HRM is becoming more competitive as there is always a dilemma between human capital and machines. HRM is now focussing on making workforce competitive so that they can deal with technological innovations.

Now, they focus on scientific decisions in order to make efficient decisions. Also, HRM is now depending on various social sites for recruiting candidates.

Increased Competition

Because of global integration, companies are facing higher competitions. Each companies aims at attaining first mover advantage. Also, key attention is given to reactions of the competitors.

Thus, HRM practices focuses on recruiting and sustaining workforce which are more responsive and faster. Adequate training programmes must be developed to the employee for tackling challenges.

Deregulation and Increased Indebtedness

Many countries opened-up their economies and financing avenues. There are lesser regulations because of which companies and individuals are in debt. Rather, many countries such as US, India have negative balance of payment. This leads to cost cutting. Hence, HRM practices have now become more cost effective and competitive.

Challenges in Nature of Work

It includes the following

- **More Knowledge Work** Now, HRM revolves around more empowered teams as organisations deal with more of intellectual work. Hence, alongwith technical requirements, human resource manager also pays equal attention to the knowledge and its application by the candidate. HRM must focus on creating high performance work systems.
- **Hi-tech Work** With technological advancements and upgradations, employees are required to perform hi-tech functions in the organisations. This is especially in case of computer industries, aviation's, pharmaceuticals, electronic companies etc. The processes and devices are becoming complex which requires special training by HRM for performing these new hi-tech operations.
- **More Service Jobs** Production jobs are transferred to developing or under developing nations. Thus, generally companies are producing services and not products. Thus, there is a shift in trends from product jobs to service jobs. Hence, HRM policies and practices are also witnessing change.

Demographic Trends and Work Force Diversity

The workforce of the nation also changes with time. India has more of young people working while US and Japan are working with ageing generation. Alongwith this, there are individuals belonging to different cultures and ideologies.

Thus, changing demographic trends are making recruitment difficult for companies. HRM polices are witnessing changes because they have to encompass cross cultural employees, retires and non-traditional workers in the organisations.

Thus, new human resource managers are focussing on bigger picture apart from traditional functions like recruitment, selection, training and compensation. They now strategically plan the workforce requirement and the environment in the future in order to combat aforementioned challenges. For this, various new concepts have been emerging in HRM. They are discussed in the next section.

Emerging Concepts in HRM

Human Resource Development

Human Resource Development (HRD) is a positive humanistic concept in human resource management based on the belief that an investment in human beings is necessary and will invariably bring in substantial benefits to the organisation in the long run. HRD seeks to show people as assets on the credit side of balance sheets.

Nature of HRD

- People can do better if they get chance of grow. Thus, it focuses on involving them and trusting them.
- Focus on the strengths of people and help them overcome their weaknesses.
- Integrate the needs and aspirations of individuals into the strategic goals and the mission of an organisation for better results.
- Encourage individual initiative and response by providing a fostering culture.

Features of HRD

- HRD is a system having interdependent sub-systems such as procurement, appraisal, development etc.
- HRD is a planned and systematic way of nurturing workforce, which is a continuous process.
- HRD involves development of competencies at personal level, inter-personal level, group level and organisational level.
- HRD is an inter-disciplinary concept like sociology, psychology and aims at improving quality of life of employees.
- It comprises of various concepts, such as HRD matrix, HRD culture, HRD climate, OCTAPCE culture etc.

Total Quality Management

Total Quality Management (TQM) believes in company wide responsibility towards quality.

According to **Edward Deming**, "TQM is a way of creating an organisational culture committed towards continuous improvement of skills, teamwork, processes and product service quality and customer satisfaction."

According to **Kiser** and **Sashkin**, "TQM may be defines as creating an organisational culture committed to the continuous improvement of skills, teamwork, processes, product and service quality and customer satisfaction."

The TQM is built around four main ideas

- **Do it Right the First Time** It emphasise on identifying and eliminating causes of quality issues in the beginning of the process. So, that product produced will be defect free.
- **Be Customer Centered** Anticipating the customer's needs, knowing what they want and how they can be satisfied and responding appropriately to the customer.
- **Make Continuous Improvement a Way of Life** Kaizen practitioners look at quality as endless journey, in order to improvise. They experiment, measure and improve continuously. It implies lower costs, less waste and faster cycle times.
- **Build Teamwork and Empowerment** TQM is built around employees, their needs, aspirations and expectations. Empowerment takes place when employees are properly trained, provided with all relevant results.

TQM aims at embedding awareness about quality in all the organisational procedures. It aims at maintaining the quality standards, while performing various management functions, such as planning, organising, controlling etc.

Thus, for enhancing quality, it is necessary to establish that the activities are performed rightly for the first time and that wastage and defects in the activities are removed from the operations.

TQM is a recent development in quality management. Initially, there were foreman and inspectors to ensure the quality. This was replaced by SQC. Now, the latest concept to study quality management is TQM.

It helps in developing the product which the consumer actually requires and desires. *e.g.* Toyota's SQCDM model, *i.e.* Safety, Quality, Cost, Delivery, Morale, focuses on the holistic development of the company alongwith enabling employees to design their procedures and have autonomy.

Implementation of Total Quality Management

WE Deming known as the father of TQM has given a PDCA cycle which stands for Plan-Do-Check-Act Cycle for implementing TQM. *Following are the steps of PDCA cycle*

Step 1 Lay down the objectives and policies of TQM and determine what the customer should be receiving and what is he actually receiving.

Step 2 Chalk out the methods that will help in achieving TQM goals.

Step 3 Educate and train the employees alongwith workers to understand and meet the requirement of TQM.

Step 4 Start executing the operations of TQM by introducing the new method, new product, new procedure or new machinery.

Step 5 Observe the results from the operations and probe into the causes that lead to non-conformance of quality standard.

Step 6 Analyse the results and see the results of non-conformity.

Step 7 Suggest measures for improvement.

Techniques and Standards under TQM

There are various techniques and standards under TQM, *which are as follows*

1. Kaizen

Kaizen refers to a Japanese word which means 'improvement'. It is a continuous effort put in by each and every individual in the organisation, right from the top level management till the lower level management, to ensure that the systems and processes are improved in the organisation.

Japanese companies heavily rely on this technique to outshine all the other rivalries in the market. Kaizen is based on a basic principle of 'Every change results in good'. Thus, Kaizen depicts a continuous improvement of processes and function of a company through change.

There are endless improvements in the procedures, policies and methods which aim at achieving organisation's success. Thus, the base is 'regular, small, changes'. The improvements are not only required to be done in the production or manufacturing process, but in all the other departments.

Working : The 5 'S'

Kaizen technique works with 5 'S' that stand for Sort, Set in order, Shine, Standardise and Sustain. These 'S' describe how the work should be organised in order to attain effectiveness and efficiency.

Kaizen technique was initially developed for housekeeping, which was later adopted to management. This is done by identification and storage of items that are used, maintaining the items and areas and sustaining new orders.

These 5'S' are as follows

(i) **Seiri** (Sort) It comprises of various improvements, *such as*
- Removing unnecessary items and disposing them properly, *i.e.* clearing.
- Removing waste from the area.
- Reducing chance of being disturbed by irrelevant forces.
- Removing obstacles to facilitate working.
- Prevention of accumulation of irrelevant items.
- Segregation of unnecessary items from workplace.

(ii) **Seiton** (Set in order) This comprises of activities, *such as*
- Arranging the necessary items so that they can be picked up easily, *i.e.* orderliness.
- Preventing loss and wastage of time by keeping the workstation arranged in a way that all the equipments and tools are within the reach of the worker.
- Ensuring that the order of first come first served basis is followed.

(iii) **Seiso** (Shine)
- The individuals must keep their workplace tidy and clean.
- This can be done with sweeping or washing.
- Prevention of machinery deterioration.
- Keeping workplace safe and keeping away any element that can be hazardous to the workplace or the information carried near the workstation.

(iv) **Seiketsu** (Standardise)
- This is considered as the best practice in the work area, *i.e.* it focuses on standardisation and cleanliness.
- In this, the workers must set higher standards.
- There must be orderliness and everything must be placed in its right place.

(v) **Shitsuke** (Discipline and Sustainability)
- This ensures that all the previous 'S' are followed. It focuses on keep working in a systematised order.
- It also means that the worker must be able to perform the job without being directed constantly.
- Training and maintaining **discipline** about orderliness.

2. Benchmarking

Benchmarking in TQM is the process of measuring a company's internal proceses by identifying, understanding and adapting outstanding practices from other organisations which are considered to be best in class. It measures a company's performance against a 'benchmark' or performance of best in class companies.

This helps in the determination of how the best in class organisations achieve those high quality standards and using the information as a basis for the company's own strategies, targets and procedures. Thus, benchmarking is based on 'moving from where we are to where we want to be'.

According to **Baker**, "It is the practice of identifying, studying and building upon the best practices in the industry or in the world."

Objectives of Benchmarking

- To achieve quality awards in the industry.
- To improve the morale of the employees.
- To facilitate reduction in cost while performing various tasks.
- To acquire an external view or perspective about what is possible.
- To improve the performance.
- To build a competitive edge in the market.
- To aid in setting the strategic goals for the organisation.

Principles of Benchmarking

Benchmarking in context of TQM is based on the principles of TQM, *which are as follows*

- There must be a comparison with the best practice in the industry.
- There must be a strong emphasise on fulfilling the desires and need of customers.
- Benchmarking lays down stress on effectiveness and efficiency in business processes.
- There is a constant need for improvement.
- Benchmarking must enhance TQM programme.

Levels of Benchmarking

- **Internal Benchmarking** Within one's company.
- **Competitive Benchmarking** With one's own competitors or analysing the practices followed by the best in the market.
- **Non-competitive Benchmarking** Learning about various methods that help in increasing the productivity.
- **World Class Benchmarking** Adopting the global practices and looking towards a well established and recognised leader.

Types of Benchmarking

Benchmarking can be classified as strategic, functional and operational. *These are as follows*

Strategic Benchmarking

This probes into and learns from various companies. It closely examines how other organisations calculate and look upto the winning strategies which have enabled them to attain competitive advantage.

Functional/Process Benchmarking

It deals with identifying the best class practices with regard to various functions and processes in the organisation. This generally comprises of methods for employee training, billing, entering the order and fulfilling it.

Operational/Performance Benchmarking

This deals with acknowledging best practices with regard to operations such as, technical quality of operations, pricing and other quality features.

Thus under benchmarking, the organisation aims at identifying the best practice which is prevalent outside the organisation.

Phases of Benchmarking

The various phases of benchmarking can be summarised in five heads

Planning Identifying the process, service or product which is to matched or attained.

Analysing Identifying the gap between company's current performance and the performance of the best in class firm. It also aims on identifying the reasons for these gaps.

Integration Establishing objectives and obtaining assistance from the employees who aid the management with required resources to attain the goals.

Action Developing plan of action and assigning work to the teams, implementation of plans and monitoring progress with regard to the benchmark.

Maturity When the company achieves the leadership position in the market, then it means that benchmark practices are fully integrated.

3. Quality Circles

Quality Circles (QC) are small group of individuals where the employees work in a same area and frequently meet in breaks. They voluntarily meet and discuss the relevant information or problems related to their job.

Quality Circles emerged in Japan, under the guidance of W.Edward Deming (1900-1993), while this concept was first introduced by BHEL, Ramachandrapuram Hyderabad in 1981, under the leadership of Mr S.R. Udpa.

They together identify, probe into the situation, learn about the causes of distortion and resolve the problems that are related to work. This concept is based on the notion of 'respect for the individual'.

Traditional management styles were based on mistrust and suspicion between the individuals and the higher authority. But, QC focuses on empowering the individuals by allowing them to resolve the issues themselves.

Objectives of QC

- It aims at improving the safety, productivity, quality and reduction in costs.
- It also focuses on giving an opportunity to the workers to deploy their creative and thinking skills.
- Another aim is to foster cooperative and cohesive culture among the members.
- It focuses on promoting self alongwith mutual development of leadership attribute.
- The key objective is to improve the working conditions and work life of the employees.

Characteristics of QC

- QC generally comprises of 5-8 individual who perform similar kind of work and they voluntarily decide to meet often in order to ascertain the reasons causing issues in their job.
- It aims at enhancing and helping the individuals, grow and develop as an individual and in the organisation also.
- It gives a chance to the members to deploy and share their acquired knowledge, skills wisdom, experience and creativity in solving the organisational problems related to their jobs.
- It helps in conversion of difficulties of the job into opportunities, which in return assist in employees' development.
- It encourages the sense of belonging as the employees are not closely monitored, rather they are given certain decision-making authority with regard to their jobs.
- Another key characteristic include that each member of the circle must participate in the discussion and decision-making and the motive of QC or the objective must be known.
- The most relevant attribute of QC is that all the members of the QC must be willing to openly communicate and listen to each other.
- In case of disagreements, the circle must not feel uncomfortable. The decisions must be arrived at after the consent of other members.

Thus, it is concluded that QC helps in solving the chronic problems of the organisation. The leader ensures that every member participate and a common solution to the work related issue is arrived at.

Fish Bone Analysis

Quality circles specifically use various TQM techniques and tools such as Pareto charts, control charts etc. to enhance the quality. Dr. Kaoru Ishikawa, similarly provided with 'Fishbone' chart which is another name for cause and effect diagram which focuses on cause of quality defects and problems.

4. Six Sigma

It is an operations management strategy which focuses on enhancing the quality of procedures by minimising the variations and errors. It was given by **Jack Welch** (1995) and he incorporated this strategy at GE motors. Six sigma assures that high quality of products is maintains.

Bill Smith is known as 'father of six sigma' (1986) when he introduced it to Motorola.

The term 'sigma' is a mathematical term which is used to measure deviation or quality variation. Hence, it has been adopted in management, where it focuses on reducing defects in the manufacturing procedure, as this ensures high level of quality. The concept is based on an underlying concept of variation.

Variation implies that two products will never be perfectly identical. Thus, six sigma uses statistical and mathematical techniques to focus on identifying the variations and minimising them so that the standards of production are maintained.

A procedure which has achieved the capability of six sigma, is the one where the deviation is very small. A process is said to be six sigma, when 99.999966 per cent of the total goods manufactured are expected to be free from defects. This means only 3.4 defects out of 1 million products.

Thus, six sigma is a quality measure, hence it is regarded a technique to ensure TQM.

Characteristics of Six Sigma

Statistical Quality Control It is a statical concept and is often denoted as 'σ' standard deviation. SD measures variance, hence it is used in production process also to identify and reduce variance.

Methodical Approach Six sigma comprises of various clearly defined methods and steps. It has two approaches, *i.e.* Design-Measure-Analyse-Improve-Control (DMAIC) and Design-Measure-Analyse-Design-Verify (DMADV).

Based on Database and Facts This method of six sigma can only be applied on various data and facts. Thus, it requires quantitative data.

Project Based This technique is objective based and can be tailored as per the need of organistaion. The process can be altered to suit the requirement and conditions of the project.

Customer Focus This approach focuses on improving the quality of product and ensuring there is less variability, so that customers get standardised products.

Significance of Six Sigma

Improvement in Overall Business This methodology aims at improving the overall quality of the business as desired under TQM.

Curtails Variability Six sigma helps in removing defects and leads to standardisation of products by minimising variance in output.

Cost Reduction A company using six sigma aims at improving quality, reducing defects and reducing costs wherever possible.

Cycle Time Improvement When a process is optimised, defects and delay are removed, then there is improvement in the cycle time. Money gets saved as there is lesser breakdown, which saves time also.

Customer Satisfaction Increases When the other aforemention objectives of six sigma are achieved, customer satisfaction is achieved automatically.

Methodologies of Six Sigma

Six sigma comprises of following two methods, i.e. DMAIC and DMADAV, which are as follows

DMAIC

It is used for the operations where projects aim at enhancing the already existing business procedures.

This methodology has five phases

Define It comprises of defining the system or the desire of the customer, their expectations and requirements from the company or any other project good.

Measure It comprises of measuring various aspects of the procedures that are currently being used and collection of relevant data.

Analyse The data is analysed to arrive at the cause and effect relation. It aims at determining what are the relationships between various factors. The key reason for deviation is analysed here.

Improve It comprises of optimising the current procedures on the basis of analysis of data. Various techniques like proofing, poka-yoke, future state process are used. Various pilot tests are also run to assure that the improvements have been incorporated.

Control This step aims at controlling future state processes to ensure that any variation from the target, before they affect the productivity and result in defects. Various control systems can be established such as production boards, visual workplaces, statistical process control etc.

DMADV

This method also comprises of the following five phase

Define This is similar to defining customer desires, needs and requirements from the company alongwith the strategy of the enterprise is defined.

Measure The characteristics that are Critical to Quality (CTQs) are measured and identified alongwith risks and production process capabilities.

Analyse The data obtained is analysed to formulate and design the alternatives.

Design This step distinguishes DMAIC and DMADV. DMADV is used for the projects that aim at building a new product or a process design. Thus, this step helps in designing an improved version or alternative which is best suited for the analysis done.

Verify This means running pilot tests and verifying the newly designed process before handing it over to the manager of the process.

Roles in Six Sigma

Executive Leadership It comprises of top management like CEO and other who are responsible for visualising set-up of six sigma.

Champions They take the duty of implementing six sigma in an integrated manner.

Master Black Belts They are identified by the champions and are the coaches on six sigma. Their time gets fully devoted into establishing and developing six sigma practices.

Black Belts These individuals operate under masters black belt to apply the methodology to particular project.

Green Belts They are the lower level employees who actually perform the six sigma methods alongwith their job responsibilities.

Hence, it is concluded that six sigma ensures that any defects are removed from the procedure and quality is ensured. There are various softwares that are used for six sigma such as Arena, STATA, MATLAB, JMP etc.

Employee Engagement

Employee engagement refers designing the workplace to improve employee's emotional attachment towards the corporation. Various companies are shifting to this concept and usually term it as building employee relations. It ensures that the employee's well being is enhanced. This is done to improve their feelings about their position, duties, companions and organisation's culture.

It ensures that employees are fully committed towards their organisational goals and motivated to add to the organisation's performance. It is an emotional state where the individual feels passionate, energetic and committed towards his work. They fully invest their best selves, spirits, minds and hands, the work they do.

According to **Michael Shuck** and **Karen Wallard**, "An emergent and working condition as a positive cognitive, emotional and behavioural state directed towards organisational outcomes."

The psychological contract is the expectation of the employee from the organisation. These are hidden inside him and comprises of hopes, dreams and ideas that define his performance in the organisation.

Satisfied employees are different from engaged employee as satisfied worker will work hard for the compensation being paid to him and not beyond that. They only perform those activities which are expected from them.

An engaged employee will align his goals alongwith organisational goals and work hard to attain them. Employee engagement is a broader concept that employee retention.

Types of Employee Engagement

Depending on the level of commitment, the employees can be classified into three categories, *which are as follows*

Not Engaged Such workers put their time in the work, but they do not perform their work with passion and vigour. They are the ones who do only what is asked of them.

These employees can hold either positive or negative attitude towards the association. They believe that they work only for money and nothing beyond that.

Actively Engaged The engaged staffs work with full vigour and are emotionally attached to the institution. They provide new ideas and are innovative. They also give consistent performance to accelerate the business.

They personalise the company's goals and objectives and always work above and beyond their job requests for the improvement of the business.

Actively Disengaged These employees spread negativity within the organisation and are unhappy and resentful. Though, despite doing less than the minimum, these personnel last longer in the organisation by eliminating employees whom they perceive will reach top positions.

Strategies for Employee Engagement

It consists of 10 C's of engagement, which are explained below

- **Credibility** Every worker should be ethical and truthful, where the leader is trustworthy for the employees. Hence, the leader must build ethical environment.
- **Collaborate** Trust binds and helps to collaborate all the employees together for attaining the aims for themselves and for the institute.
- **Control** The management must be in control as it assists in executing a task in a stable way and give positive outputs. Hence, the head should always inspire his teams to be in control while taking formal decisions.
- **Confidence** Self-confidence among workers is very significant for the improvement of the business. Hence, it is the chief duty of a head to implant confidence among the personnel.
- **Career** The manager must provide opportunities to the employees to accomplish challenging jobs in their respective areas.
- **Convey** Effective communication must be maintained transparent to minimise and avoid any confusion. Clearly conveying information is an extremely important purpose.
- **Connect** All the employees must be valued and these morals come with a good association which is only possible through decent connections.
- **Clarity** The visions and mission of the corporation must be clearly expressed to every employee so that they can design their objectives with respect to their career development.
- **Contribute** Manager must contribute and support their subordinates in attaining their personal aims.
- **Congratulate** Every worker must be acknowledged and respected, whenever they give astonishing and applaud able output as it makes them motivated.

Measurement of Employee Engagement Survey Method

Employee engagement is generally measured using an 'employee engagement survey'. Engagement can be precisely measured through surveys containing few questions. But these surveys provide only a hint of whether workers are involved or engaged in their work.

The survey comprises of the following steps

Define a Goal for Employee Engagement Creation of high performing organisation, improving organisational culture, effectively managing the talent of the organisation.

Establishing Measurement and Key Metrics Engagement can be measured by future goals, level of satisfaction and alignment of individual goals with organisational goals. Also, it will be decided whether it will be a structured or open ended survey.

Communicating Effectively The purpose of the survey must be clearly communicated with the organisation in order to increase the affectivity of survey. The results should also be communicated.

Overcoming Roadblocks The finding of the survey should not be procrastinated. The leaders must arrange for necessary resourced to bring the suggested changes.

Building Action Plan It comprises of revisiting strategies, following established procedures, quickly working on deviations, listening to feedback and expressing gratitude towards employee, alongwith focussing on long-term success.

Quality of Work Life (QWL)

It is defined as the overall quality of a person's working life. QWL is a concept which talks about the overall focus on worker as an individual rather than just the work done by him. A good work life balance motivates an employee the most to do his job and also devote quality time with his family. QWL is a combination of employee's welfare, working conditions and workplace democracy.

American society of training and development defines it as "QWL is a process of work organisations which enables its members at all levels to participate actively and efficiently in shaping the organisation's environment methods, outcomes."

It is a value based process which is aimed towards meeting the twin goals of enhanced effectiveness of the organisation and improved quality of life at work for the employees. QWL is the degree to which the employees are able to satisfy their personal needs through their experience in the institution. Various social scientists such as Eric Tryst, Einar Thorsrud and Fred Emerry gave the concept of workplace democracy.

Scope and Areas of Quality of Work Life

Respect for Non-work Activities The activities performed outside the organisation and personal achievements should also be recognised.

Social Relevance of Work The employee's role in the attaining organisational goals must be communicated.

Protection of Individual Rights The management can introduce specific procedures which guarantee the rights of workers.

Social Integration Any kind of individualism and discrimination must be removed and formation of social groups should be encouraged.

Job Design The needs of the organisation and employees both should be kept in view before designing the job. The work must be satisfying and interesting.

Job Security The workers must not work under constant threat of losing jobs. The workplace must give security to the employee. Employees' retrenchment and layoffs must be avoided. Job insecurity builds tension and uncertainty in the life of the employee which hampers his productivity.

Health and Safety QWL also focuses on ensuring healthy and safe working environment to the employee. *e.g.* Factories Act, 1948 and other labour laws. The environment can adversely affect the emotional, mental and physical state of mind.

Compensation QWL encompasses that the employees must be paid fairly for their share in the prosperity and progress of the firm. The remuneration should be enough to meet his personal and family needs and minimum standard of life.

Work Life Balance

- It implies securing balance between an individual's work and personal life. The problem of work life balance is observed when there is a case of dual career couples.
- A dual career couple is the one where both the individuals working have occupational responsibilities. These result into depression, stress and anxiety for both the people which leads to stress and lower productivity.
- Thus, new HRM practices are focussing on ass1stmg employees in balancing their personal and professional life in order to reduce the stress. Studies have shown that a company providing balance to the employees outperform in comparison to others.
- This is because employees give back increased loyalty, energy and productivity in exchange for the institute's real support with managing work life strains.

Methods of Encouraging Work Life Balance

Compressed Work Week

The organisations must try to reduce or condense the work week such as 4 ten hours days, 4 nine hour days, 3 twelve hour days or 5 eight hour days. With this, the employee gets enough space to balance professional and personal responsibilities.

This method reduces labour turnover, absenteeism and enhances, job satisfaction, productivity. Compressed workweek gives space for leisure time, lessens commuting time and gives more time to spend on personal work.

Employee Counselling

A company may arrange special counselling services for the members to deal with the stress either related to family or office. Professional counsellors can help the employees in distressing and balancing their lives. They give various strategies to manage tensions arising in office and at home.

Flexitime

It implies workers are given flexible work schedule or flexible work hours. This theory believes that employees are paid on the basis of work performed by them and not on the basis of fixed number of hours spent. The employees are given freedom to choose the time to arrive and leave the organisation.

Such work schedules enable the employees in managing their personal tasks alongwith organisational tasks. The employees work for specific number of hours for the entire week, however, they can vary hours spent each day as per their discretion.

Telecommuting

This arrangement implies that workers can perform work from their home. Employees performing most of the work with the help of computers and internet are allowed to perform their duties from home rather than visiting the workplace. The communication takes place electronically or through phones. It is cost effective as it saves money and time in commuting.

Adequate Leaves

Apart from flexitime and compressed workweek, employers must give adequate leaves to the employees. Employees feel motivated when they are given paid leaves. Leaves like sick leave, maternity leave, child/dependent care leaves are highly welcomed.

Green HRM

Green HRM is the use of HRM strategies to endorse the sustainable use of resources within organisations and supports the cause of environmental sustainability. The HR function will become the driver of environmental sustainability inside the institute by arranging its policies and practices in a line with sustainability aims at reflecting a focus on the environment.

HRM policies can be used to motivate the employees about sustainable use of assets and resources within the organisation and produce green culture through charting strategies and rules to increase employee's consciousness and commitment towards environment.

It spreads and reinforces sustainable business activities that boost the morale of the workers by working in an environmental friendly manner. Green HRM practices are visible from recruitment to exit.

HR strategy must reflect and inspire the ambitions of the HR team and other employees and aligning with the strategy of the business culture and values so that it delivers sustainable returns to the investors . Alongwith this, it focuses on sustainably delivering services to the customers and responding to new environmental and societal trends. Green initiatives within HRM form part of wider programs of corporate social responsibility.

Significance of Green HRM

Green Workforce Green organisations are the most preferred choices for people who are aware about the eco-friendly problems. Thus, it helps in getting competent as well as eco-friendly workforce.

Increase in Sales Such organisations are recognised by the customers increases brand loyalty.

Wider Perspective The firm makes green business decisions that help in its long-term survival. By following environmental friendly practices, the business gets a wider perspective. They are acknowledged by the government for their green practices which gives them an edge over others.

Green HRM Practices

It includes undertaking environment friendly HR initiatives that result in lower costs, greater efficiencies and better employee retention and engagement.

Some of the Green HRM practices are

Green Recruitment

Firms are now beginning to recognise the fact that gaining reputation as a green employer is an effective way to attract new talent. Many firms are now adopting environmental actions and a green appearance to draw high quality candidates.

Recruiting applicants with green bend of mind make it easy for companies to welcome professionals who are aware with ecological procedures and processes and are already acquainted with basics like conservation, reusing, recycling and creating a more sustainable and rational world.

Green Training and Development

It deals in educating staffs about the value of environmental management, training them in operational methods that reduce waste, preserve energy and provide opportunity to engage workers in environmental problem solving and spreading environmental awareness within the institution. Thus, organisations are training their employees about the finest business practices inspired by green initiatives.

Green Performance Management

It contains issues connected to environmental issues and guidelines of the company. It also focuses on environmental responsibilities of the individual and the organisation as a whole.

Today, some firms deal with the issue of performance management by installing corporate wide environmental performance standards and green information systems/ audits to gain useful data on environmental performance (Marcus and Fremeth).

Green Compensation

Modern organisations are modifying their reward systems to inspire the employee about eco-friendly initiatives. It is generally witnessed that employee commitment to EM programmes increased when they were offered rewards to take up responsibilities with regard to environmental responsibilities.

Apart from these, managers are focussing on paperless office, conservation of energy, recycling waste disposal, rewarding employees for coming up with sustainable green ideas and strategies reusing materials, online training, teleconferences and virtual interviews carpooling, e-filing, reducing the use of energy, water and raw materials, treating bio-medical waste and electronic waste, planting trees and conducting green awareness for employees, implementing a smoking free office policy.

Business Process Re-engineering (BPR)

It involves the fundamental reshaping of core business activities and processes to attain dramatic developments and improvements in quality, cycle times and productivity. Organisation starts from scratch and reconsider the existing procedures to deliver more value to the clients.

They usually accept a new value system which places importance on client's requirements. Corporations reduce structural layers and also remove fruitless activities in two aspects, *i.e.* they redesign functional organisations into cross functional groups and they focus on using technology to enhance and improve data distribution that facilitates decision-making.

Features of BPR

- It is primarily meant for introducing the planned change, meeting competition and total customer satisfaction. Re-engineering focuses on empowering the workers where they make more decisions.
- Re-engineering should not be confused with restructuring as restructuring involves determining the core competencies and identifying the areas which need the changes. However, re-engineering is a broader concept and restructurings are an outcome of re-engineering.
- Re-engineering comprises of rewriting the rules of the organisation, alongwith process improvement and cost reduction.
- BPR affects HRM practices as it reorganises the teams with personnel from different departments. It focuses on building multi skilled workers, for these changes are made in the recruitment and selection policies. It also leads to creation of empowered jobs and shifting of focus from activities to results.

EXAM BASED QUESTIONS

1 The purpose of job evaluation is to determine
(a) worth of a job in relation to other jobs
(b) time duration of a job
(c) expenses incurred to make a job
(d) None of the above

2 Job evaluation tries to make a systematic comparison between
(a) workers (b) jobs
(c) machines (d) departments

3 Basis of job evaluation is
(a) job design (b) job ranking
(c) job analysis (d) Any of these

4 The important objectives of a job evaluation programme
(a) establishment of sound wage differentials between jobs
(b) maintenance of a consistent wage policy
(c) installation of an effective means of wage control
(d) All of the above

5 The .... provides the essential information on which each job is evaluated.
(a) job ranking (b) job enrichment
(c) job description (d) job enlargement

6 Which of the following is not a job evaluation method?
(a) Factor comparison method
(b) Point method
(c) Ranking method
(d) Assessment method

7 Job evaluation is carried on by
(a) groups (b) individuals
(c) Both (a) and (b) (d) None of these

8 In which of the following methods jobs can be arranged according to the relative difficulty in performing them?
(a) Ranking method
(b) Point method
(c) Factor comparison method
(d) Classification method

9 A quantitative process of job evaluation does not include
(a) classifying jobs (b) grading jobs
(c) ranking jobs (d) None of these

10 Second step in ranking method of job evaluation is to
(a) combine ratings
(b) rank jobs
(c) selecting compensable factors
(d) grouping jobs

11 Job evaluation process, in which raters categorise jobs into groups is called
(a) point method (b) job classification
(c) job grading (d) aligned reward strategy

12 The ranking method is best suited for
(a) complex organisations
(b) large organisations
(c) small organisations
(d) Any of the above

13 A 'quantitative technique' in job evaluation processes is
(a) job classification
(b) alternative ranking method
(c) aligned reward strategy
(d) point method

14 Point method is suitable for
(a) small size organisation
(b) mid size organisation
(c) large organisation
(d) Both (b) and (c)

15 In factor comparison method, each factor is recognised with a
(a) money value (b) ranking
(c) scale (d) None of these

16 The simplest method for job evaluation is method in which jobs are arranged from highest to lowest order in terms of their value or merit to the organisation.
(a) Paired comparison method
(b) Ranking method
(c) BARS
(d) MBO

17 Analysis of job such as job specification and job description leads to
(a) job evaluation (b) garnishment laws
(c) pay surveys (d) Both (a) and (c)

18 Which of the following statements are correct with regard to factor comparison method?
(a) Factor comparison is systematic and scientific method designed to carry out job evaluation which instead of ranking job as a whole, ranks according to a series of factors
(b) The aim of factor comparison is to assign financial value to the relative parts of each job role
(c) Both (a) and (b) are correct
(d) Both (a) an (b) are incorrect

19 Which of the following statement is correct with regard to job evaluation?
(a) It also helps in the selection of candidates as the factors determined for job evaluation can be taken into account
(b) It takes precautions to save the employees from the hazardous environmental and operational conditions in various jobs
(c) It provides all the required information to get the framework of organisational design
(d) It helps in orientation and placement by providing complete information about job requirements

20 Which of the following is not the objective of job evaluation?
(a) It seeks to determine the relative worth of each job so that salary differentials can be established
(b) Jobs are evaluated on the basis of their content in order to rank their importance
(c) It is a systematic process for gathering, documenting and analysing date about the work required for a job
(d) It is done in order to match firm's overall wage structure with that of the industry in which the firm operates

21 The statement "The purpose of job evaluation is the establishment of rates of pay for various jobs on an equitable basis. It is intended to eliminate chance, favoritism and individual bargaining in determining wage rates and for establishment of fair and equitable wages" is given by
(a) Miller (b) Dessler
(c) Armstrong (d) Flippo

22 Type of rewards employees get in form of praise for successfully accomplishing goals or completing project is classified as
(a) primacy rewards (b) intrinsic rewards
(c) extrinsic rewards (d) leniency rewards

23 Compensation management consists
(a) job evaluation
(b) wage and salary administration
(c) fringe benefits
(d) All of the above

24 Compensation can be .... benefits.
(a) monetary (b) non-monetary
(c) Both (a) and (b) (d) None of these

25 The following is paid only at the time of employees exit after serving more than five years
(a) perquisites (b) claims
(c) gratuity (d) allowances

26 Incentives depends upon
(a) productivity (b) sales
(c) profits (d) All of these

27 Which of the following factor influence(s) employee compensation?
(a) Labour market (b) Cost of living
(c) Labour unions (d) All of these

28 The remuneration system needs to meet the following type(s) of equity.
(a) Internal (b) External
(c) Individual (d) All of these

29 .... are also called 'payments by results'.
(a) Allowances (b) Claims
(c) Incentives (d) Fringe benefits

30 Which of the following is a perquisite?
(a) Club membership (b) Provident fund
(c) Medical allowance (d) Group insurance

31 Wages represents .... rates of pay.
(a) hourly (b) daily (c) weekly (d) monthly

32 'A fair day work for fair day pay' denotes a sense of .... felt by employees.
(a) responsibility (b) equity
(c) happiness (d) respect

33 Any compensation plan must be
(a) understandable, workable, acceptable
(b) reasonable, workable, acceptable
(c) understandable, feasible, acceptable
(d) understandable, workable, compensable

34 Which of the following is not a part of remuneration model?
(a) Job description (b) Job evaluation
(c) Job hierarchy (d) Job analysis

35 Which of the following is not a concept of wage?
(a) Daily wages (b) Minimum wages
(c) Fair wages (d) Living wages

36 A .... must be fixed considering the general economic conditions of the country.
(a) minimum wages (b) fair wages
(c) living wages (d) All of these

37 Factors must be considered to price jobs in any organisation includes
(a) job importance
(c) difficulty of job
(c) skills and abilities required
(d) All of the above

38 Direct compensation includes which of the following?
(a) Flexible benefits
(b) Long-term incentive pay
(c) Workers' compensation
(d) Unpaid leave

39 Concept in which whole or part of yearly pay increase is paid as single payment, is called?
(a) Consumer price index adjustment
(b) Lumpsum increase
(c) Cost of living adjustment
(d) All of the above

40 Perceived fairness between what person receives and what person did is classified as
(a) procedural justice (b) distributive justice
(c) recency justice (d) equity

41 Indirect compensation is represented by which of the following?
(a) Social security benefits (b) Short-term incentive pay
(c) Differential pay (d) Merit pay

42 Primary benefits of most organisation include
(a) Worker's compensation
(b) Severance pay
(c) Unemployment compensation
(d) All of the above

43 **Which one of the following is not a labour law related to wages?**
(a) The Workmen's Compensation Act, 1923
(b) The Payment of Bonus Act, 1965
(c) The Payment of Wages Act, 1936
(d) The Minimum Wages Act, 1948

44 **Time spent in organisation while performing particular job is classified as**
(a) seniority (b) career maturity
(c) career equity (d) non-equity

45 **Most common and usual form of direct compensation paid in organisations is**
(a) base pay and benefits
(b) base and variable pay
(c) variable pay and benefits
(d) All of the above

46 **Benefits offered in traditional compensation approach are usually**
(a) fixed and tied to tenure
(b) variable and tied to tenure
(c) benchmarked to other companies
(d) None of the above

47 **A pay system that rewards employees for developing knowledge or skill is a**
(a) time motion system
(b) measured hours work system
(c) knowledge based system
(d) profit sharing system

48 **In which of the following situations it won't be suitable to pay a monthly salary to the employee?**
(a) When people are employed on a part-time basis
(b) When people are employed on regular fixed incomes
(c) When people are employed on temporary basis
(d) When overtime is large part remuneration

49 **A fixed salary which is decided as mutual understanding between the employer and employee; is an expression of what type of rewards?**
(a) Rewards as rights
(b) Rewards as those which are contingent
(c) Rewards as those which are incentives
(d) All of the above

50 **Which of the following is not an objective of wage incentive programmers?**
(a) Developing ownership interest
(b) Improving employee retention
(c) Reducing labour cost
(d) Facilitating the separation of employees

51 **Evaluating the relative worth of the employees in the organisation and then deciding the awards for them is called**
(a) Merit rating
(b) Differential piece rate
(c) Task and time bonuses
(d) Straight piece rate

52 **Which of the following incentive systems recommends a two-piece rate for wage determination?**
(a) Merrick multiple piece rate plan
(b) Taylor's differential piece rate plan
(c) Emerson efficiency plan
(d) Gantt task and bonus system

53 **In which of the following methods is the standard time stated as minutes and points?**
(a) Bedeaux system
(b) Barth variable incentive plan
(c) Task and time bonus
(d) None of the above

54 **Which of the following incentive plans has the following equation for computing the earnings of employees? (Actual hours worked × Time rate) + (Actual time worked/Standard time) × Time saved × Time rate**
(a) Emerson efficiency plan
(b) Rowan incentive plan
(c) Halsey incentive plan
(d) Barth variable incentive plan

55 **Achieving cost saving not only on labour cost but also on overheads is the crux of**
(a) Towne's incentive plan (b) Priestman bonus plan
(c) Rucker incentive plan (d) Halsey incentive plan

56 **Which of the following methods discourages too much speed in the production by the employees?**
(a) Straight piece rate
(b) Differential piece rate
(c) Task and time bonuses
(d) None of the above

57 **Which of the following is not usually a group incentive plan?**
(a) Halsey incentive plan
(b) Priestman bonus plan
(c) Rucker incentive plan
(d) Towne's incentive plan

58 **In which method is the standard time expressed in terms of man-minutes called 'MANT'?**
(a) Hayne's incentive plan
(b) Rowan incentive plan
(c) Barth variable incentive plan
(d) Bedeaux system

59 **Which of the following is an example of fringe benefits?**
(a) Health and accident insurance
(b) Contribution to superannuation funds
(c) Leave facilities
(d) All of the above

60 **When the same rate of incentives is paid to the employees for each unit of goods produced by them, it is called**
(a) Straight piece rate (b) Differential piece rate
(c) Task and time bonuses (d) None of these

61 When more than one piece rate is offered to the individuals for goods produced by them, it is called
(a) Straight piece rate
(b) Differential piece rate
(c) Priestman bonus plan
(d) None of these

62 .... is that wage which must invariably by paid whether the company, big or small, makes profit or not.
(a) Fair wage (b) Minimum wage
(c) Living wage (d) None of these

63 Minimum Wages Act, 1948 provides for setting up a tripartite body consisting of
(a) employees (b) union
(c) government (d) All of these

64 Wages and allowances of Central and State Government employees are determined through the
(a) pay commission (b) wage boards
(c) wage committee (d) None of these

65 An employee's perception that compensation received is equal to the value of work performed.
(a) Incentive (b) Pay grades
(c) Pay equity (d) None of these

66 A job that is used to anchor the employee's pay scale and around, which other jobs are arranged in order of relative worth?
(a) Benchmark job (b) Job equity
(c) Job policy (d) None of these

67 Factors influencing compensation levels include
(a) job needs
(b) productivity
(c) unions
(d) All of the above

68 Employee compensation is classified into
(a) base compensation
(b) supplementary compensation
(c) Both (a) and (b)
(d) Neither (a) nor (b)

69 Wage which must invariably be paid whether the company, big or small, makes profit or not is called
(a) minimum wage (b) fair wage
(c) living wage (d) None of these

70 .... serve as a cushion or sort of insurance against increase in price level of commodities.
(a) Compensatory allowance
(b) Dearness allowance
(c) Supplementary compensation
(d) None of the above

71 Institutions involved in payment of wages are
(a) employer
(b) collective bargaining
(c) legislation, wage board and pay commission
(d) All of the above

72 Rewards, one gets from the employer usually money, a promotion or benefits
(a) extrinsic rewards
(b) intrinsic rewards
(c) employee stock option plan
(d) None of the above

73 Job security would fall under which of the following needs?
(a) Safety (b) Social
(c) Ego (d) Self actualisation

74 Which of the following statements is/are incorrect?
(a) Under incentive systems, worker pay is determined by performance
(b) Subjective evaluation is a problem with merit pay systems
(c) Both (a) and (b)
(d) None of the above

75 Which of the following pairs is/are not correctly matched?
(a) It must invariably be paid whether the company big or small, makes profits or not—Minimum wage
(b) It is a dynamic concept, which grows in line with the growth of the national economy—Fair wage
(c) Both (a) and (b)
(d) None of the above

76 Which of the following statements is/are incorrect?
(a) Living wage is the highest wage
(b) Minimum wage is a dynamic concept which grows in line with the growth of the national economy
(c) Fair wage is that which is above the minimum wage, but below the living wage
(d) All of the above

77 Group incentives would work best among
(a) assembly line workers (b) lawyers
(c) accountants (d) car sales people

78 Unions oppose incentive schemes because
(a) it dilutes union power
(b) standards may go up
(c) it reduces union membership
(d) None of the above

79 Which of the following statements is/are incorrect?
(a) Fringe benefits helps to create and improve sound industrial relations
(b) Welfare and recreational facilities include canteens, consumer societies etc
(c) Provident fund is meant for social welfare of the employees
(d) All of the above

80 Which of the following pairs is/are correctly matched?
(a) Adding more responsibilities, autonomy and control to a job— Job enrichment
(b) Adding more tasks to a job to increase the job cycle— Job enlargement
(c) Both (a) and (b)
(d) None of the above

81 Which of the following statements is/are correct?
(a) Salary survey aimed at finding prevailing wages rates
(b) Motivational devices used to encourage special work effort is called an incentive
(c) Both (a) and (b)
(d) None of the above

82 Indirect rewards given to employees of organisation for being member of organisation are called
(a) productivity compensation
(b) effectivity compensation
(c) benefits
(d) philosophical compensation

83 According to compensation programs, benefits such as retirement pensions and life insurances are classified in category of
(a) direct compensation (b) primacy compensation
(c) indirect compensation (d) recency compensation

84 According to compensation programs designed for employee, variable pay other than base pay is classified as part of
(a) indirect compensation (b) recency compensation
(c) direct compensation (d) primacy compensation

85 Types of compensation employees get from organisation after timely completion of work includes
(a) intrinsic rewards (b) extrinsic rewards
(c) strictness reward (d) Both (a) and (b)

86 Which of the following is not a fringe benefit?
(a) Transport facility
(b) Subsidised canteen facility
(c) Free education to the children
(d) Dearness allowance

87 The statement "Career is a sequence of positions occupied by a person during the course of life time" is given by
(a) Stephen P Robbins (b) Flippo
(c) Ricardo (d) Mayo

88 In a career development, offering and discussing variety of paths for career development, included
(a) individual role (b) manager role
(c) employer role (d) line manager

89 Career progress largely depends on
(a) performance (b) experience
(c) qualifications (d) All of these

90 All employees have .... career goals.
(a) similar (b) dissimilar
(c) no (d) None of these

91 An example of a career development ability would be
(a) scaling a maintain
(b) getting another degree
(c) working hard
(d) All of the above

92 It is a deliberate attempt by an individual to become more aware of his or her skills, values choices and opportunity.
(a) Transition planning (b) Career planning
(c) Succession planning (d) HR planning

93 A concern or value that employee will not give up, if a choice has to be made is called
(a) career path (b) career anchors
(c) career survival (d) career dynamics

94 The less of employees, who quit an organisation for various reasons.
(a) Downsising (b) Retrenchment
(c) Attrition (d) None of these

95 The sequential pattern of one's job that form career is called
(a) career (b) career path
(c) career planning (d) mid-career phase

96 Which one of the following represents a state of a career development cycle?
(a) Freedom and independence
(b) Decline stage
(c) Three time frames
(d) Growth and development of employees

97 A condition of stagnating in one's current job is called
(a) mid-career crisis (b) plateuing
(c) reality shock (d) None of these

98 People pursue careers to satisfy deeply
(a) individual needs (b) organisational needs
(c) leadership skills (d) None of these

99 In career development, focused individual goal setting is part of
(a) training and development
(b) performance appraisal
(c) recruitment and placement
(d) human resource planning

100 Making progress in one's career through a series of right moves in called
(a) career progression (b) career development
(c) career planning (d) None of these

101 Career development is the process by which employees' progress through a series of stages, each characterised by a different set of development tasks activities and relationships. Which of the following is not true regarding maintenance stage of career development?
(a) Employees at this stage try to update his/her knowledge and skills
(b) The employee at this stage like others to perceive him as one who is a major contributor to the organisation
(c) The employee at this stage strives to maintain a reputation
(d) Employees at this stage try to identify their likes and dislikes

102 A programme that encourages young managers with high potential to remain within an organisation by enabling them to advance more rapidly than those with less potential.
(a) Fast track programme
(b) Career development workshop
(c) Career mentoring
(d) None of the above

103 Which of the following is a challenge for HRM?
(a) Work force analysis (b) Work load analysis
(c) Work force diversity (d) All of these

104 Which of the following statement represents recent trends in HRM?
(a) HRM not only deals with humans, but also there must be a command on financial budgeting and strategic management
(b) HRM focuses on focus on scientific decisions
(c) Recently HRM has led emphasis on employee's health benefits
(d) Both (a) and (b)

105 HRD is a .... concept.
(a) pluralistic (b) humanistic
(c) materialistic (d) All of these

106 Which of the following statement is not correct with regard to HRD?
(a) HRD is a system having interdependent sub-systems such as procurement, appraisal, development etc
(b) HRD involves development of competencies at personal level, inter-personal level, group level and organisational level
(c) HRD deals with procurement and retention of best resources
(d) HRD is a planned and systematic way of nurturing workforce, which is a continuous process

107 Which of the following is not a new concept of HRD?
(a) HRD Matrix (b) HRD Grid
(c) HRD Culture (d) HRD Climate

108 The most important indicators of HRD
(a) those which measure a country's stock of human capital
(b) those which measure the additions to this stock
(c) Both (a) and (b)
(d) None of the above

109 First step of Human Resource development in any organisation is
(a) determining development approaches
(b) assessing the needs for development
(b) identifying capabilities
(d) formulate HR plans

110 The following are the factors which come under 'work planning' that is component systems of HRD?
(a) Contextual analysis (b) Role analysis
(c) Performance appraisal (d) All of these

111 Process of improving ability of employees regarding handling of assignments is classified as
(a) workforce staffing
(b) career identification
(b) Human resource development
(d) career planning

112 Promotion are made available from within and competitive advantages based on human resources are focuses of
(a) regression planning
(b) aggressive planning
(b) development
(d) training

113 HRD process variable include
(a) role clarity
(b) work planning
(c) better communication
(d) All of the above

114 Which of the following is chief idea about TQM?
(a) Do it right the first time
(b) Make continuous improvement a way of life
(c) Be product centric
(d) Both (a) and (b)

115 Which of the following statements are correct with regard to TQM?
(a) TQM is built around employees, their needs, aspirations and expectations
(b) Empowerment takes place when employees are properly trained, provided with all relevant results
(c) It implies lower costs, less waste and faster cycle times
(d) All of the above

116 The statement "TQM is a way of creating an organisational culture committed towards continuous improvement of skills, teamwork, processes and product service quality and customer satisfaction." Has been given by
(a) Edward Deming (b) Sashkin
(c) Edward Flippo (d) None of these

117 The PDCA cycle of TQM is given by
(a) Flippo (b) Mayo
(c) WE Deming (d) Drucker

118 Improving quality through small, incremental improvements is a characteristic of what type of quality management system?
(a) Just-in-time
(b) Six Sigma
(c) Total Quality Management
(d) Kaizen

119 What is the term for the monitoring of events both internal and external to the organisation that affects strategy?
(a) Operational control
(b) Strategic surveillance
(c) Strategic control
(d) Environmental scanning

120 The preferred method for achieving total quality in process is to
(a) build and install an error-proof process and maintain it
(b) rely on operator self-inspection and self-correction
(c) rely on a team of highly trained and dedicated inspectors
(d) perform inspection at the next process

121 Which of the following are key components of a Total Quality Management system?
(a) Individual responsibility, incremental improvement, use of raw data
(b) Collective responsibility, continual improvement, use of raw data
(c) Group responsibility, staged improvement, knowledge
(d) Involves everyone, continual improvement, use of data and knowledge

122 Which one of the following is not a typical feature of TQM?
(a) Customer driven quality
(b) Continuous improvement
(c) Action based on facts, data and analysis
(d) Strong inspection oriented establishment

123 Quality means that at a ...., all production must be within specification limits and the .... variation from the nominal, the better the quality.
(a) minimum, less (b) minimum, more
(b) maximum, less (d) maximum, more

124 In order to achieve quality, organisations must consider
(a) product policy
(b) product design and manufacturing
(c) final use of the product
(d) All of the above

125 Total Quality Management (TQM) programmes are more likely to remain effective, if a number of prescriptions are followed. Which of the following prescriptions should not be followed?
(a) TQM does not become a separate 'bolt-on' set of activities
(b) Slogans and exhortations about TQM's effectiveness are avoided
(c) TQM should become a substitute for normal managerial leadership
(d) Quality improvement relates to an operation's performance objectives

126 TQM expands on earlier approaches to quality management. Which of the following is ordered correctly from earlier to later ideas?
(a) Quality Control, Inspection, Quality Assurance, Total Quality Management
(b) Inspection, Quality Control, Quality Assurance, Total Quality Management
(b) Quality Assurance, Inspection, Quality Control, Total Quality Management
(d) Quality Assurance, Quality Control, Inspection, Total Quality Management

127 What is quality assurance?
(a) Quality assurance deals with activities which prove that products and services meet the required quality standard
(b) Quality assurance deals with activities which aim at customers satisfaction
(b) Quality assurance deals with controlling the quality of products by inspection
(d) All of the above

128 Which quality management programme is related to the maintenance of plants and equipments?
(a) Environmental management systems
(b) Fault tree analysis
(b) Failure mode effect analysis
(d) Total productive maintenance

129 Which of the following is responsible for quality objective?
(a) Top level management
(b) Middle level management
(c) Frontline management
(d) All of the above

130 TQM and ISO both focuses on
(a) customer (b) employee
(c) supplier (d) All of these

131 In total quality perspective, quality planning and strategic business planning are treated as which of the following?
(a) Different (b) Consistent
(c) Indistinguishable (d) Dissimilar

132 While setting quality objective, ... to be considered.
(a) material quality
(b) customer need
(c) market demand
(d) All of the above

133 What is meant by Kaizen?
(a) Card signal
(b) To avoid inadvertent errors
(b) Change for better quality
(d) None of the above

134 What does Kaizen mean, when translated from Japanese into English?
(a) Change good (b) Change slow
(c) Process change (d) Process slow

135 Which is the best description of Kaizen?
(a) A slow process of continuous improvement
(b) A quick process of continuous improvement
(c) A process to re-engineer all company processes
(d) A process to have outside consultants implement improved methods of production

136 Significant feature of Kaizen Budgeting is
(a) employee suggestion
(b) customer suggestion
(c) cost suggestion
(d) price suggestion

137 Which of the following statements is not true about benchmarking strategy?
(a) It is related to the efforts of Kaizen
(b) It is related to the raising of criteria for selection
(c) It is raising the performance standards of the organisation
(d) It is a people driven activity

138 Which of the following is not an external driver for benchmarking?
(a) Customers continually demand better quality, lower prices, shorter lead times
(b) Competitors are constantly trying to get ahead and steal markets
(c) Legislation
(d) None of the above

139 The process of identifying other organisations that are best at some facet of operations and then modeling organisation after them is known as
(a) continuous improvement (b) employee empowerment
(c) benchmarking (d) patent infringement

140 Which category of benchmarking, involves specific competitor to competitor comparisons for a product, service or function of interest?
(a) Internal (b) Functional
(c) Generic (d) Competitive

141 What approach is used to compare organisation operations with those of other companies?
(a) Competitor performance assessment
(b) SWOT analysis
(c) Benchmarking
(d) PERT analysis

142 The origins of benchmarking as it is used today go back to which company?
(a) Toyota (b) McDonald's
(c) Microsoft (d) Xerox

143 Benchmarking against external organisations that do not compete directly in the same markets is called
(a) non-assault benchmarking
(b) non-competitive benchmarking
(c) practice benchmarking
(d) collaborative benchmarking

144 Which of the following is regarded as a fundamental flaw in the whole concept of benchmarking?
(a) It is not a continuous process
(b) It limits critical thinking
(c) It limits improvements to currently accepted methods of operating
(d) It does not involve learning

145 What is the primary objective of Quality Circle?
(a) Keep employees occupied
(b) Higher profit
(c) Self and mutual development of employees
(d) To solve the problem

146 Quality Circle concept was started in India in the year
(a) 1984 (b) 1992
(c) 1980 (d) 1986

147 Six-Sigma quality indicates
(a) 2.4 defects per thousand
(b) 2.7 defects per thousand
(c) 3.4 defects per thousand
(d) 3.7 defects per thousand

148 Which of the following represents the DMADV approach?
(a) Kaizen (b) Six-sigma
(c) TQM (d) QC

149 Which of the following statement is not correct about six-sigma?
(a) Six-sigma achieves minimum defects
(b) Six-sigma reduces variance
(c) Six-sigma shorterns the cycle time
(d) Six-sigma directly fulfills the customer needs

150 Which of the following reflect the key focus of six-sigma?
(a) Reduction in the cycle time
(b) Analysing and minimising the standard deviation in output
(c) Improving the quality of product
(d) Defining the layout of production facility

151 What does 'A' stand for in the six-sigma technique of DMAIC?
(a) Assurance
(b) Analysis
(c) Arrangement
(d) Ascending

152 Which of the following statements are correct with regard to employee engagement?
(a) Employee engagement refers designing the workplace to improve employee's emotional attachment towards the corporation
(b) It ensures that the employee's well being is enhanced
(c) This is done to improve their feelings about their position, duties, companions and organisation's culture
(d) All of the above

153 The .... is the expectation of the employee from the organisation.
(a) written contract
(b) psychological contract
(c) expectancy contract
(d) psychosomatic contract

154 Which of the following is not a reason for labour turnover?
(a) Feeling undervalued (b) No growth opportunities
(c) Worklife imbalance (d) Adequate leaves

155 Which of the following is not a type of employee engagement?
(a) Not engaged (b) Actively engaged
(c) Actively disengaged (d) Engaged

156 It is defines as the overall quality of a person's working life.

(a) Work life balance (b) Quality of Life
(c) Both (a) and (b) (d) Neither (a) nor (b)

157 A .... couple is the one where both the individuals working have occupational responsibilities.

(a) dual-career (b) double career
(c) single career (d) None of these

158 Which of the following is not a methods to provide work life balance?

(a) Compressed workweek (b) Promotion
(c) Flexitime (d) Adequate leaves

159 This arrangement implies that workers can perform work from their home.

(a) Flexitime (b) Telecommuting
(c) Office-home integration (d) All of these

160 Firms are now beginning to recognise the fact that gaining reputation as a green employer is an effective way to attract new talent. Many firms are now adopting environmental actions and a green appearance to draw high-quality candidates. The statement is referring to which one of the following?

(a) Green selection (b) Green recruitment
(c) Green training (d) Green compensation

161 Which one of the following are the practices followed under GHRM?

(a) Paperless office (b) Recycling waste disposal
(c) Conservation of energy (d) All of these

162 Educating staffs about the value of environmental management, comprises of

(a) Green education
(b) Green development
(c) Green training
(d) Green selection

163 What is the term for incremental changes to processes in an organisation using information technology?

(a) Business Process Improvement
(b) Business Process Re-engineering
(c) Business Process Change
(d) Business Process Advance

164 The principles of the Business Process Re-engineering (BPR) approach do not include

(a) checking that all internal customers act as their own suppliers to identify problems
(b) scrapping any process line over two years old and starting again from scratch
(c) re-thinking business processes cross-functionally to organise work around natural information flows
(d) striving for improvements in performance by radical rethinking and redesigning the process

165 Which of the following pairs is/are not correctly matched?

(a) It is an incentive payment that is given to an employee beyond one's normal standard wage—Bonuses
(b) These are extra payments given for superior performance—Fringe benefits
(c) Both (a) and (b)
(d) None of the above

166 Which of the following statements are not correct?

1. Pay of an employee includes actual money that employee receives in exchange of his work.
2. Job evaluation provides a basis for measuring individual performance.
3. Human relation theory respects formal institutionalisation.
4. Minimum wages are not guaranteed under incentive plan.
5. Job enrichment amounts to expanding vertical and horizontal dimensions of a job.

Codes

(a) Both 1 and 2 (b) Both 3 and 4
(c) Both 4 and 5 (d) Both 1 and 5

167 Which of the following are examples of compensable factors?

1. Technical skills conceptual skills, inter-personal skills.
2. Experience or length of working years.
3. Efforts and initiative.
4. Responsibilities to be undertaken.
5. Supervision required.
6. Working environment in which job is to be performed.
7. Gender of the employee.

(a) 2, 3, 4, 7 (b) 1, 4, 5, 6
(c) 1, 2, 3, 4, 7 (d) 1, 2, 3, 4, 5, 6

168 Following steps are undertaken for developing a workforce score card.

1. Identify critical and carefully defined outcome measures.
2. Translate the measures into specific actions and outcomes.
3. Identify high and low performing employees.
4. Develop and communicate detailed description of what is expected.
5. Develop supporting HRM and measurement systems.

What is the correct chronological order of these steps?

(a) 1, 2, 3, 4 (b) 1, 2, 4, 3
(c) 1, 2, 4, 5 (d) 1, 3, 4, 5

169 Which of the following statements are not correct?

1. Pay of an employee includes actual money that employee receives in exchange of his work.
2. Job evaluation provides a basis for measuring individual performance.
3. Human relations theory respects formal institutionalisation.

4. Minimum wages are not guaranteed under incentive plan.
5. Job enrichment amounts to expanding vertical and horizontal dimensions of a job.

(a) Both 1 and 4 (b) Both 3 and 4
(c) Both 4 and 5 (d) Both 1 and 5

170 Arrange the following steps in the process of job evaluation.

1. Setting the objectives of job evaluation to establish satisfactory wage and salary differentials.
2. Job analysis thorough examinations of jobs by collecting data.
3. Preparing job description and job specification to find out the importance of job to the organisation.
4. Comparison of one job with another on the basis of job rating.
5. Arranging jobs according to rating in terms of value to firm.
6. Assigning wage rate to each job as per its ranking.
7. Job classification grading jobs according to scale of pay.

(a) 1, 3, 2, 4, 5, 6, 7 (b) 1, 2, 3, 4, 5, 6, 7
(c) 1, 4, 2, 3, 5, 6, 7 (d) 2, 1, 3, 4, 5, 6, 7

171 Consider the following statements. Which of the statements given is/are correct?

1. Employees only have themselves to blame for stalled careers.
2. All employees have similar career goals.
3. Career development aims at tracking career sponsors.

(a) Only 2 (b) Both 1 and 2
(c) All of false (d) None of the above

172 Consider the following statements. Which of the statement(s) given is/are correct?

1. Unions oppose job enrichment.
2. Increased variety in the job adds to self-esteem.
3. The time needed to complete every task in the job is called 'job cycle'.

(a) Only 1 (b) Only 2
(c) Both 1 and 3 (d) Both 1 and 2

173 Consider the following statements. Which of the following statement(s) given is/are correct?

1. Career planning helps the management of a diverse workforce.
2. All employees have similar career goals.

(a) Only 1 (b) Both 1 and 2
(c) Only 2 (d) None of the above

174 Arrange the following in which TQM is implemented.

1. Lay down the objectives and policies of TQM and determine what the customer should be receiving and what is he actually receiving.
2. Chalk out the methods that will help in achieving TQM goals.
3. Educate and train the employees alongwith workers to understand and meet the requirement of TQM.
4. Start executing the operations of TQM by introducing the new method, new product, new procedure or new machinery.
5. Observe the results from the operations and probe into the causes that lead to non-conformance of quality standard.
6. Analyse the results and see the results of non-conformity.
7. Suggest measures for improvement.

Codes
(a) 1, 3, 2, 4, 5, 6, 7 (b) 1, 2, 3, 4, 5, 6, 7
(c) 1, 4, 2, 3, 5, 6, 7 (d) 1, 2, 4, 3, 5, 6, 7

175 Which of the following are individual challenges of HRM?

1. Job Insecurity 2. Brain Drain
3. Restructuring

Codes
(a) Both 1 and 2 (b) Both 2 and 3
(c) Both 1 and 3 (d) None of the above

176 Which of the following are organisational challenges of HRM?

1. Restructuring 2. Improving quality
3. Cost control and reduction

Codes
(a) Both 1 and 2 (b) Both 2 and 3
(c) Both 1 and 3 (d) All of the above

177 Which of the following are environmental challengers of HRM?

1. Globalisation
2. Rapid change in technology
3. Legislation
4. Job and family roles
5. Workforce diversity
6. Job security

Codes
(a) 1, 3, 4, 5, 6 (b) 1, 2, 3, 4, 5
(c) 2, 3, 4, 5, 6 (d) All of the above

178 Arrange the following in the sequence of measuring employee engagement.

1. Overcoming roadblocks
2. Communicating effectively
3. Defining goal
4. Establishing measurement keys
5. Establishing action plans

Codes
(a) 3, 4, 1, 2, 5 (b) 3, 1, 2, 4, 5
(c) 3, 4, 2, 1, 5 (d) 1, 3, 2, 4, 5

179 Which of the following statements are correct?

I. As per marginal productivity theory of wage determination, the salaries or wages are determined on the basis of the production contributed by the last employee, *i.e.* marginal worker. His or her output is called 'marginal output.'

II. As per residual claimant theory proposed by Walker, what remains is compensated as wages to workers once all the other three factors are rewarded. Thus, the employee or the laborer is the residual claimant according to this theory.
(a) Both statements are correct
(b) Both statements are incorrect
(c) Statement I is correct and Statement II is incorrect
(d) Statement II is correct and Statement I is incorrect

180 Which of the following statement is correct?
I. A job evaluation is a systematic way of determining the value/worth of a job in relation to other jobs in an organisation. It tries to make a systematic comparison between jobs to assess their relative worth for the purpose of establishing a rational pay structure.
II. Compensable factor is a fundamental, compensable element of a job, which can be know-how, problem solving and accountability, knowledge, problem-solving skills and working conditions.
(a) Both statements are correct
(b) Statement I is correct and Statement II is incorrect
(c) Statement II is correct and Statement I is incorrect
(d) Both statements are incorrect

181 Which of the following statements are correct?
I. In ranking method, experts rank jobs on the basis of relevance. It is quite a simple method of comparing the whole job with others and ranking them on the basis of comparison.
II. This is also known as the grading method. It is a method for categorising jobs into groups and classes.
III. In factor comparison method, points are allotted to each specific factor of a job which determines the relative worth of a job. These allotted points to various job factors are summed up to find the worth of the job.
(a) Both statement I and II (b) Both statement II and III
(c) Both statement I and III (d) All of the above

182 Which of the following is correct?
I. Time wage system is suitable when workers are new and learning the job.
II. Piece wage system is suitable where quality and workmanship are not very important.
(a) Both statements are correct
(b) Both statements are incorrect
(c) Statement I is correct, but Statement II is incorrect
(d) Statement I incorrect, but Statement II is correct

183 Which of the following statements are correct?
I. Fringe benefits, now a days are a significant component of 'compensation'.
II. Under piece rate plan, employees are paid at a stipulated rate per hour of work done by the employee.
(a) Both statements are correct
(b) Both statements are incorrect
(c) Statement I is correct, but Statement II in incorrect
(d) Statement I is incorrect, but Statement II is correct

184 Which of the following statement is correct?
I. Total quality management implies an organisation is dedicated to delighting the customer by meeting or exceeding customer expectations.
II. The objective of TQM is to provide a quality product to customers at a lower price.
(a) Both statements are correct
(b) Both statements are incorrect
(c) Statement I is correct and Statement II is incorrect
(d) Statement I is incorrect and Statement II is correct

Directions (Q. Nos. 185-188) *In the questions given below are two statements labelled as Assertion (A) and Reason (R). In the context of the two statements, which one of the following is correct?*

Codes
(a) Both (A) and (R) are true and (R) is correct explanation of (A)
(b) Both (A) and (R) are true, but (R) is not the correct explanation of (A)
(c) (A) is true, but (R) is false
(d) (A) is false, but (R) is true

185 **Assertion** (A) HRM is becoming more competitive as there is always a dilemma between human capital and machines.

Reason (R) HRM now focus on scientific decisions in order to make efficient decisions which is due to technology changes.

186 **Assertion** (A) Job offshoring means getting work done outside the home country which was previously done in the home country; this is a result of globalisation.

Reason (R) This is because production takes place in the host country instead of home count rises. It becomes difficult for the employees as the jobs become hard and less secure.

187 **Assertion** (A) QWL is a concept which talks about the overall focus on worker as an individual rather than just the work done by him.

Reason (R) A good work life balance motivates an employee the most to do his job and also devote quality time with his family.

188 **Assertion** (A) New HRM practices are focusing on assisting employees in balancing their personal and professional life in order to reduce the stress. Studies have shown that a company providing balance to the employees outperform in comparison to others.

Reason (R) Employees give back increased loyalty, energy and productivity in exchange for the institute's real support with managing work-life strains.

Directions (Q. Nos. 189-192) *In the questions given below are two statements labelled as Assertion (A) and Reason (R). In the context of the two statements, which one of the following is correct?*

(a) Both (A) and (R) are true and (R) is the correct explanation of (A)
(b) Both (A) and (R) are true but (R) is incorrect explanation of (A)
(c) (A) is false, but (R) is true
(d) (A) is true, but (R) is false

189 **Assertion** (A) An engaged employee will align his goals along with organisational goals and work hard to attain them.

Reason (R) The Psychological Contract is the expectations of the employee from the organisation.

190 **Assertion** (A) QWL encompasses that the employees must be paid fairly for their share in the prosperity and progress of the firm.

Reason (R) The remuneration should be enough to meet his personal and family needs and minimum standard of life.

191 **Assertion** (A) Green HR is the use of HRM strategies to endorse the sustainable use of resources within organisations and supports the cause of environmental sustainability.

Reason (R) It spreads and reinforces sustainable business activities that boost the morale of the workers by working in an environmental friendly manner.

192 **Assertion** (A) Firms are now beginning to recognise the fact that gaining reputation as a green employer is an effective way to attract new talent. Many firms are now adopting environmental actions and a green appearance to draw high-quality candidates.

Reason (R) Recruiting applicants with green bend of mind make it easy for companies to welcome professionals who are aware with ecological procedures.

193 **Assertion** (A) Wage boards are set up by the Government of India for fixation and revision of wages.

Reason (R) Wage boards are not governed by any legislation but are appointed on an adhoc basis by the government.

Codes
(a) Both (A) and (R) are true
(b) Both (A) and (R) are false
(c) (A) is true, but (R) is false
(d) (A) is false, but (R) is true

194 **Assertion** (A) Under performance base incentives performance that is rewarded is likely to be repeated.

Reason (R) People tend to do things that are rewarded.

Codes
(a) Both (A) and (R) are true
(b) Both (A) and (R) are true and (R) is the correct explantion of (A)
(c) Both (A) and (R) are false
(d) (A) is true, but (R) is false

195 **Assertion** (A) Incentives should not be a costly affair.

Reason (R) The benefits must not exceed the cost.

Codes
(a) (A) and (R) are correct and (R) is the correct explanation of (A)
(b) (A) and (R) are correct, but (R) is not the correct explanation of (A)
(c) (A) is true, but (R) is false
(d) (A) is false, but (R) is true

196 On which of the following statements are true/false?

(i) The amount sufficient to enable a worker to live is reasonable comfort, having regard to all obligations to which an average worker would ordinarily be subject to is called living wage.
(ii) The PDCA cycle of quality management was given by W.Edwards Deming.
(iii) Bedeaux point plan focuses on group incentive.

(a) (i) and (ii) are true, (iii) is false
(b) (i) is true, (ii) and (iii) is false
(c) (i) and (iii) are true, (ii) is false
(d) (ii) is true, (i) and (iii) are false

197 On which of the following statements are true/false?

(i) Managerial compensation is influenced by various factors such as capacity to pay, education and experience, economic environment etc.
(ii) Payment for time not worked is a fringe benefit.
(iii) Gantt's Task plan is a group plan.

(a) (i) and (ii) are true, (iii) is false
(b) (ii) and (iii) are true, (i) is false
(c) (i) and (iii) are true, (ii) is false
(d) (iii) is true, (i) and (ii) are false

198 On which of the following statements are true/false?

(i) Career planning is an integral part of human resource planning.
(ii) Career progression is the progress in one's career.
(iii) Career cycles are the flexible paths/lines of progression
(iv) Career paths are the stages through which a person's career evolves.

(a) (i) and (ii) are true, (iii) and (iv) are false
(b) (i) and (iv) are true, (ii) and (iii) are false
(c) (i) and (iii) are true, (ii) and (iv) are false
(d) (ii) and (iv) are true, (i) and (iii) are false

199 On which of the following statements are ture/false?

(i) Gratuity is a form of incentive plan.
(ii) Pension is a form of employee benefit.
(iii) Job evaluation rates the job holder.
(iv) Kaizen is associated with housekeeping.

Codes
(a) (i), (ii) and (iv) are true, while (iii) is false
(b) (ii) and (iv) are true, while (i) and (iii) are false
(c) (i) and (ii) are true, while (iii) and (iv) are false
(d) (i) and (iii) are true, (ii) and (iv) are false

200 Match the following.

List I		List II
A. Claims	1.	Medical allowance, internet allowance, telephone allowance
B. Perquisites	2.	Canteen, uniform, accident relief
C. Fringe benefits	3.	Club membership furnished house, paid holidays, company car

Codes

	A	B	C
(a)	3	1	2
(b)	1	2	3
(c)	1	3	2
(d)	2	1	3

201 On which of the following statements are true?

(i) NQ Herrick and M Maccoby have given four principles which humanise work and improve QWL.
(ii) Exploration stage of career planning is a stage where the individual builds expectation about his career.
(iii) Nominal wage is the wage expressed in terms of money.

(a) (i) and (ii) are true, (iii) is false
(b) (i) and (iii) are true, (ii) is false
(c) (i), (ii), (iii) are true
(d) (i), (ii), (iii) are false

202 Match the following.

List I		List II
A. The process of examining how work creates or adds value to the on-going processes in a business	1.	Job enrichment
B. A fundamental rethinking and radical redesign of business processes to achieve dramatic improvements in cost quality, service and speed	2.	Job design
C. The process of organising work into the tasks required to perform a specific task	3.	Work flow analysis
D. The process of putting specialised tasks back together so that one person is responsible for producing a whole product or an entire service	4.	Business Process Re-engineering (BPR)

Codes

	A	B	C	D
(a)	1	2	3	4
(b)	2	1	4	3
(c)	3	4	1	2
(d)	3	4	2	1

203 Match the items given in List I with the items of List II.

List I		List II
A. Career management	1.	The lifelong series of activities that contribute to a person's career exploration, establishment, success and fulfilment
B. Career development	2.	The deliberate process through which someone becomes aware of personal skills, interests, knowledge, motivations and other characteristics and establishes action plans to attain specific goals
C. Career planning	3.	The process for enabling employees to better understand and develop their career skills and interests and to use these skills and interests more effectively

Codes

	A	B	C
(a)	3	2	1
(b)	3	1	2
(c)	1	2	3
(d)	2	1	3

204 Match the items given in List I with the items of List II.

List I		List II
A. Plateauing	1.	A situation in which both husband and wife have distinct careers outside the home
B. Dual career couple	2.	A sequence of positions occupied by a person during a cause of a life time
C. Mid career phase	3.	A career stage marked by a continuous improvement in performance, levelling off in performance or the beginning of deterioration of performance
D. Career	4.	A condition of stagnating in one's job

Codes

	A	B	C	D
(a)	4	1	3	2
(b)	1	2	3	4
(c)	2	1	3	4
(d)	4	3	2	1

205 Match the following.

List I (Incentive Plans)	List II (Concerned Formulaes)
A. Halsey plan	1. $\frac{\text{Time saved}}{\text{Standard time or time allowed}} \times$ Time taken × Hourly rate = Bonus
B. Rowan plan	2. Bonus = 50% of time saved
C. Barth variable sharing plan	3. Bonus = 50% as against 75% of the Bedeaux plan
D. Haynes manit plan	4. $\sqrt{\text{Standard hours} \times \text{actual hours}} \times$ rate per hour

Codes

	A	B	C	D		A	B	C	D
(a)	3	1	2	4	(b)	2	1	4	3
(c)	4	3	2	1	(d)	1	2	3	4

206 Match the following.

List I (Individual Incentive Plans)	List II (Features)
A. Halsey plan	1. If the worker exceeds the standards, he is paid a higher price rate
B. Rowan plan	2. Every operation or job is expressed in terms of so many standard minutes
C. Gantt task plan	3. It recognises individual efficiency and pays bonus on the basis of time saved
D. Bedeaux plan	4. Bonus is paid on the basis of time saved

Codes

	A	B	C	D		A	B	C	D
(a)	4	3	2	1	(b)	3	4	1	2
(c)	2	1	4	3	(d)	4	3	1	2

207 Match the following.

List I (Concepts)	List II (Merits)
A. Time wage system	1. It offers the necessary incentive to the high class labour, which is important for obtaining high production level.
B. Piece wage system	2. The rate of bonus increases gradually from 67% to 100% efficiency
C. Modified time rate	3. Workers do not suffer from temporary loss of efficiency
D. Emerson's efficiency plan	4. This method is just and fair to all

Codes

	A	B	C	D		A	B	C	D
(a)	4	1	2	3	(b)	3	4	1	2
(c)	2	3	4	1	(d)	2	1	4	3

208 Match the following.

List I (Types of Fringe Benefit)	List II (Features)
A. Safety and health	1. When the employee's services get confirmed, his job becomes secure
B. Voluntary arrangements	2. Dependents of the employee are eligible for compensation in case of death of the employee
C. Workmen's compensation	3. The Factories Act, 1948 stipulated certain requirements regarding working conditions with a view to provide safe working environment
D. Employee security	4. Medical benefits are extended to employee family members

Codes

	A	B	C	D		A	B	C	D
(a)	4	3	2	1	(b)	3	4	2	1
(c)	2	3	4	1	(d)	4	1	2	3

209 Match the following.

List I (Type of Incentive Plans)	List II (Examples)
A. Individual incentive plans	1. Profit sharing
B. Group incentive plans	2. Rucker plan
C. Organisation wide incentive plans	3. Rowan plan
D. Individual incentive plans	4. Gantt task and Bonus plan

Codes

	A	B	C	D		A	B	C	D
(a)	4	2	1	3	(b)	2	1	4	3
(c)	3	1	4	2	(d)	4	3	2	1

210 Match the following.

List I (Group Incentives Plans)	List II (Features)
A. Priestman's production bonus	1. Employees receive a constant proportion of the 'added value'
B. Scanlon plan	2. A standard is fixed in terms of units or points
C. Co-partnership	3. Constant proportion of added value of output is paid to the workers, who are responsible for the addition of the value
D. Rucker plan	4. Employees share the capital as well as profits

Codes

	A	B	C	D		A	B	C	D
(a)	4	1	2	3	(b)	2	3	4	1
(c)	3	4	1	2	(d)	4	3	2	1

211 Match the following.

	List I (Concepts)		List II (Features)
A.	Succession planning	1.	It may take the form of bonus of premium
B.	Incentive rates	2.	It provides no incentive for better performance
C.	Fringe benefits	3.	It ensures the continuity of leadership in organisation
D.	Time wage system	4.	It may be statutory or voluntary

Codes

	A	B	C	D		A	B	C	D
(a)	3	1	4	2	(b)	2	1	4	3
(c)	4	3	2	1	(d)	1	2	3	4

212 Match the following.

	List I (Individual incentive Plans)		List II (Features)
A.	Taylor's differential piece rate system	1.	Day wages are guaranteed
B.	Merrick's differential piece rate system	2.	It penalises the slow worker by paying low rate
C.	Halsey plan	3.	Under this, there are three piece rates instead of two
D.	Gantt task plan	4.	Standard time is fixed for each job or operation

Codes

	A	B	C	D		A	B	C	D
(a)	4	3	2	1	(b)	3	4	1	2
(c)	2	3	4	1	(d)	4	3	1	2

213 Match the following.

	List I (Concepts)		List II (Meanings)
A.	Merit pay	1.	Extra benefits provided to employees in addition to the normal compensation paid in the form of wage or salary
B.	Fringe benefits	2.	Financial and non-financial rewards to the employees for their services rendered to the company
C.	Compensation	3.	Compensation plan where all team members receive an incentive bonus payment when production or services standards are met or exceeded
D.	Team incentive plan	4.	Any salary increase awarded to an employee based on his or her individual performance

Codes

	A	B	C	D		A	B	C	D
(a)	4	3	2	1	(b)	2	1	4	3
(c)	3	1	4	2	(d)	4	1	2	3

214 Match the following.

	List I		List II
A.	Sort	1.	Seiton
B.	Set in order	2.	Seiketsu
C.	Shine	3.	Seiri
D.	Standardise	4.	Seiso

Codes

	A	B	C	D		A	B	C	D
(a)	4	1	2	3	(b)	3	1	4	2
(c)	2	3	1	4	(d)	1	3	4	2

215 Match the following.

	List I		List II
A.	TQM promotes	1.	Small change
B.	Kaizen is	2.	Continuous improvement
C.	Quality circle can solve problem related to	3.	Employee participation
D.	Quality circle benefit to	4.	Employee

Codes

	A	B	C	D		A	B	C	D
(a)	3	1	2	4	(b)	1	3	2	4
(c)	3	1	4	2	(d)	3	2	1	4

216 Match the following.

	List I		List I
A.	Telecommuting	1.	Ways to manage stress
B.	Compressed week	2.	No work schedule
C.	Employee counselling	3.	Work from home
D.	Flexitime	4.	Lesser number of working hours

Codes

	A	B	C	D		A	B	C	D
(a)	1	4	3	2	(b)	3	4	2	1
(c)	3	4	1	2	(d)	3	2	1	4

217 Match the following 'S' with their correct explanation under Kaizen.

	List I		List II
A.	Sustain	1.	Removing obstacles
B.	Set in order	2.	Keeping workstation clean
C.	Sort	3.	Prevention of wastage of time
D.	Shine	4.	Performance without being supervised

Codes

	A	B	C	D
(a)	4	3	1	2
(b)	4	3	2	1
(c)	3	4	1	2
(d)	1	3	2	4

218 Match the following.

List I	List II
A. Digital dashboards	1. It is Japanese technique comprising of circle of groups
B. Quality circle	2. It is an information management tool which is used for tracking metrics, Key Performance Indicators (KPIs)
C. BPR	3. It involves the fundamental reshaping of core business activities and processes to attain dramatic developments and improvements in quality
D. Empowerment	4. It means allowing the individuals and encouraging them to take personal responsibilities for improving their capabilities

Codes

	A	B	C	D		A	B	C	D
(a)	2	1	3	4	(b)	3	4	1	2
(c)	3	1	2	4	(d)	4	1	2	3

219 Match the following 10' C of engagement.

List I	List II
A. Confidence	1. Being ethical
B. Collaborate	2. Inspiring teams to be in control
C. Control	3. Leader infusing confidence
D. Credibility	4. Trusting and binding employees

Codes

	A	B	C	D		A	B	C	D
(a)	4	2	1	3	(b)	2	3	1	4
(c)	4	3	1	2	(d)	1	3	2	4

PREVIOUS YEARS' QUESTIONS

2018

1 **A process by which an organisation responds to employee needs for developing mechanisms to allow them to share fully in making decisions that design their lives at work is called**

(a) Social security
(b) Performance management
(c) Quality of work life
(d) Career planning

2 **Who among the following introduced quality control in Japan?**

(a) Thomas Peters (b) W. Edwards Deming
(c) Robert R. Blake (d) Laurence Peter

3 **The distinct patterns of self-perceived talents, attitudes motives and values that direct and stablise an individual's career are called**

(a) Career goals (b) Career paths
(c) Career anchors (d) Career planning

4 **Match the following**

List I (Japanese word under 55 Concept)	List II (English Equivalent)
A. Shitsuko	1. Clearing
B. Seiton	2. Cleanliness
C. Seiketsu	3. Sweeping/washing
D. Seiri	4. Orderliness
E. Seiso	5. Discipline

Codes

	A	B	C	D	E		A	B	C	D	E
(a)	5	4	2	1	3	(b)	4	3	5	2	1
(c)	1	2	3	4	5	(d)	2	1	4	5	3

5 **Which of the following is a group incentive plan?**

(a) Barth Variable Incentive Plan
(b) Hayne's Incentive Plan
(c) Rowan Incentive Plan
(d) Scanlon Incentive Plan

2017

6 **Assertion** (A) **Workforce diversity requires employers to be more sensitive to the differences that each group brings to the work setting.**
Reason (R) **Employees need to be responsive to the values, needs, interests and expectations of fellow employees.**

Codes

(a) (A) is right, but (R) is wrong
(b) (A) is wrong, but (R) is right
(c) Both (A) and (R) are right, but (R) does not explain (A)
(d) Both (A) and (R) are right and (R) explain (A)

7 **Knowledge workers are**

A. The workers whose man capital is knowledge.
B. The workers whose jobs are designed around the acquisition and application of informaiton.
C. The workers whose jobs concentrate on routine problems.

Codes

(a) Only A (b) A and B
(c) B and C (d) A, B and C

8 **In which year, in which factory and by whom the first quality circle in India ws introduced?**

(a) 1982 : Bharat Electronics Ltd, SR Udpa
(b) 1981 : Hindustan Aeronautics Ltd, SR Udpa
(c) 1982 : Hindustan Machine Tools, RS Tarneja
(d) 1982 : Bharat Heavy Electricals Ltd, SR Udpa

9 Match the following concepts of career planning List I with their propagators List II.

List I	List II
A. Career Anchor Model	1. Mondy *et al*
B. Career Stage Model	2. John Holland
C. Career Path Model	3. Edgar Schein
D. Career Choice Model	4. DT Hall

Codes

	A	B	C	D		A	B	C	D
(a)	3	2	4	1	(b)	3	1	2	4
(c)	3	2	1	4	(d)	3	4	1	2

10 Quality of work life is a combination of employee's welfare, working conditions and workplace democracy. Who highlighted the concept of workplace democracy?

1. Eric Tryst
2. Udai Pareek
3. Einar Thorsrud
4. Fred Emery

Codes

(a) Both 1 and 2 (b) 1, 3 and 4
(c) Both 1 and 4 (d) All of the above

11 Which one of the following is not a benefit of Total Quality Management?

(a) Maximising cost
(b) Providing greater satisfaction to all concerned
(c) Creating quality consciousness
(d) Creating good public image

12 What is TQM 'Kitemarks'?

(a) It is a set of TQM techniques
(b) It is a set of TQM objectives
(c) It is a set of TQM philosophies
(d) It is a set of TQM awards

13 Which of the following are the four key HR challenges, identified by Deloitte, in its 'Compensation Trends Survey Report' for 2012-2013?

1. Reducing operating cost
2. Retaining critical talent
3. Reducing capital investment
4. Hiring of skilled talent
5. Increasing productivity
6. Engaging the employees
7. Restructuring
8. Training and Developing potential leaders

Codes

(a) 1, 3, 5 and 7 (b) 2, 4, 6 and 8
(c) 3, 5, 1 and 7 (d) 4, 6, 7 and 8

2016

14 Social security provided by a 'means test' is called

(a) Need based assistance (b) Social assistance
(c) Social assurance (d) Mutual assistance

15 Who corrected the difficulties of Taylor's differential piece rate system of wages?

(a) Henry Towne
(b) HL Gantt
(c) Frank and Lillian Gilberhts
(d) Newmann and Summer

16 The foundation stone for union-management cooperation is said to have been laid in India in

(a) Oil Industry in 1977 (b) Textile industry in 1982
(c) Jute Industry in 1957 (d) TISCO in 1938

17 Which of the following statements about quality is not true?

(a) Quality is all about meeting or exceeding customer expectation
(b) Performance, durability, services available and ease of repair are attributes of quality
(c) W Edwards Deming and Joseph M Juran are quality gurus who taught the Japanese on quality issues
(d) Statistical analyses has no place in Total Quality Management

18 Which set of strategies do not come under the TQM?

(a) Customer Orientation and Strategic Leadership
(b) Business Process Re-engineering and Lean Thinking
(c) Corporate Governance and Corporate Social Responsibility
(d) Learning, Experimentation and Continuous Improvement

19 Benchmarking involves employees learning and adopting so called 'best practices' by comparing their HRM practices with those of other (more successful) organisations. Identify the correct sequential steps of benchmarking.

1. Indentify HR practices for benchmarking
2. Identify benchmarking partners
3. Constitute a core or a project team to handle the benchmarking process
4. Develop action plans to improve HR strategy and practices
5. Collect data from each of the benchmarking partners
6. Analyse and interpret the data
7. Prepare a comprehensive report based on the data analysis and interpretation

Codes

(a) 1, 3, 4, 2, 7, 4, 6 (b) 4, 5, 6, 3, 1, 2, 7
(c) 1, 3, 2, 5, 6, 7, 4 (d) 4, 3, 1, 2, 5, 6, 7

2015

20 Which of the following is a job grading structure that falls between using spot salaries versus many job grades to determine what to pay to particular positions and incumbents within those positions?

(a) Broadbanding (b) Variable compensation
(c) Executive compensation (d) Team base pay

21 Match the following.

List I	List II
A. Outsourcing	1. Achieving large cost savings by eliminating unneeded activities and consolidating work
B. Open-book management	2. Broad based approach for achieving high levels of performance
C. Total quality management	3. Sharing financial and performance information with employees
D. Re-engineering	4. Contracting out of activities that were previously performed in-house

Codes

	A	B	C	D		A	B	C	D
(a)	3	4	2	1	(b)	4	1	2	3
(c)	4	3	2	1	(d)	1	2	3	4

22 Quality of work life as a socio-technical concept was advanced by

(a) Fred Luthans (b) Eric Trist
(c) AK Rise (d) Peter F Drucker

23 **Assertion** (A) Total Quality Management aims at delighting customers, both external and internal, on a continuous basis.

Reason (R) Quality process involves the understanding of who the customers are, what are their needs and how these needs can be satisfied.

Codes
(a) Both (A) and (R) are wrong
(b) (A) is wrong and (R) is correct
(c) Both (A) and (R) are correct, but (R) does not explain (A)
(d) Both (A) and (R) are correct and (R) explains (A)

24 The deliberate process through which someone becomes aware of personal skills, interests, knowledge, motivations and other characteristics, and establishes action plans to attain career specific goals is called

(a) Career management (b) Career development
(c) Career counselling (d) Career planning

25 Which of the following is/are organisation wide incentive plan(s)?

1. Commission Plan
2. Employee Stock Option Plan
3. Gain Sharing Plan

Select the correct answer by using the codes given below

Codes
(a) 1, 2 and 3 (b) Both 1 and 2
(c) Both 2 and 3 (d) Only 1

26 Arrange the following phases of quality circles in the correct sequence.

1. Start up
2. Approval of initial suggestions
3. Initial problem-solving
4. Expansion of problem-solving
5. Implementation
6. Decline

Codes
(a) 1, 2, 4, 3, 6, 5 (b) 1, 2, 3, 4, 5, 6
(c) 1, 3, 2, 5, 4, 6 (d) 6, 5, 4, 3, 2, 1

27 The early formed attitudes consisting of values, needs and talents of a person which make a person hold to a particular type of carrer are called

(a) career anchors
(b) career drives
(c) career needs
(d) career aspirations

2014

28 Which of the following is the correct sequence of career development stages in Evan's Model of Stages in Career Development?

1. Establishment
2. Mid Career
3. Exploration
4. Late Career
5. Decline

Codes
(a) 1, 2, 4, 3, 5 (b) 3, 1, 2, 4, 5
(c) 1, 2, 3, 4, 5 (d) 2, 3, 4, 1, 5

29 Which of the following is the correct sequence of the stages of emergence of TQM process beginning from 1910?

1. Creativity and Innovation
2. Product Design Improvement
3. Detection and Rectification of Defects
4. Prevention of Defects

Codes
(a) 3, 4, 2, 1 (b) 1, 2, 3, 4
(c) 4, 3, 2, 1 (d) 1, 4, 3, 2

30 In which of the following pay plans, employer divides the value added for the period by the total payroll expenses?

(a) Scanlon Plan (b) Rucker Plan
(c) Improshare Plan (d) All of these

31 Total quality management is a

(a) responsibility of quality management staff to identify and solve quality related problems
(b) commitment to quality that goes beyond internal company issues to suppliers and customers
(c) system where top management takes decisions
(d) procedure which involves quantitative tools exclusively for quality improvements

32 Quality circle members are

(a) paid by management for participation in quality circles
(b) formally trained for participation in quality circles
(c) external consultants who improve quality
(d) led by active trade union leaders

33 What is the full form of SQCDM, which characterises Toyota Perfection?

(a) Systematic, Questioning, Comparing, Discussing, Measurement
(b) Statistical, Qualitative, Comprehensive, Directive, Measurement
(c) Systematic, Qualitative, Collaborative, Diversifying, Monitoring
(d) Safety, Quality, Cost, Delivery, Morale

34 Who popularised quality of work life as a global phenomena?

(a) TV Rao, Biju Varkkey and Hasmukh Adhia
(b) James Austin, Peter Villanova and Hugh Hindwar
(c) Einar Thorsrud, Fred Emery and Eric Tryst
(d) Richard Reilly, James Smithy and Nicholas Vasilopolous

35 How many defects per million products or services are permitted under Six Sigma Technique?

(a) 3.4 (b) 4.3
(c) 2.3 (d) 3.2

36 **Assertion** (A) Quality circles in India was an imported idea from Japan without proper cultural changes in the organisations.

Reason (R) The corporate culture assimilating learning, empowerment and participation as equals could not be developed due to absolete mindset of both employers and employees.

Codes

(a) (A) is false and (R) is not the correct explanation of (A)
(b) Both (A) and (R) are false
(c) (A) is true, but (R) is not the correct explanation of (A)
(d) Both (A) and (R) are true and (R) validates (A)

37 Which of the following does not help in meeting the needs of dual-career couples?

(a) Flexitime
(b) Compressed work week
(c) Job sharing
(d) Life-cycle accounts

38 5 'S' Japanese model is accociated with

(a) quality management
(b) cost effective activities
(c) housekeeping
(d) All of the above

39 In making fish bone diagram, causes of problems are identified through

(a) synetics
(b) brainstorming
(c) nominal grouping
(d) creative thinking

40 I. Time wage system is suitable when workers are new and learning the jobs.

II. Piece wage system is suitable where quality and workmanship are not very important.

Codes

(a) Both statements I and II are correct
(b) Both statements I and II are incorrect
(c) Statement I is correct, but statement II is incorrect
(d) Statement II is correct, but statement I is incorrect

41 Which of the following is not a method of Job Evaluation?

(a) Ranking method
(b) Grading method
(c) Paired comparison method
(d) Point method

42 Which of the following statements about 'housekeeping' are true?

1. It believes in 'a place for everything and everything in its place' principle.
2. It is a culture of maintaining cleanliness.
3. It is a system of arranging materials in order of their importance and frequency of use.
4. It talks about the infrastructural facilities provided by the organisation.

Select the correct answer using the codes given below

(a) Both 1 and 3 (b) Both 1 and 2
(c) 1, 2 and 3 (d) All of these

43 Which of the following trends are currently seen in the employment front in India?

1. Increased women labour force participation.
2. Underemployment.
3. Growing employment in informal sector.
4. Increasing demand for unskilled manpower.

Codes

(a) 1, 2 and 4 (b) 1, 2 and 3
(c) 2, 3 and 4 (d) 1, 3 and 4

44 In which of the following systems, minimum wage is guaranteed, but beyond a certain efficiency level, bonus is given in addition to minimum day wages?

(a) Straight piece rate system
(b) Differential piece rate system
(c) Gantt task and Bonus system
(d) Emerson's Efficiency system

45 'A place for everything and everything in its place' is the basic underlying principle of

(a) Safety (b) Housekeeping
(c) Workplace governance (d) None of these

ANSWERS

Exam Based Questions

1 (a)	2 (b)	3 (c)	4 (d)	5 (c)	6 (d)	7 (a)	8 (a)	9 (d)	10 (d)
11 (c)	12 (c)	13 (d)	14 (d)	15 (a)	16 (b)	17 (d)	18 (c)	19 (a)	20 (c)
21 (a)	22 (b)	23 (d)	24 (c)	25 (c)	26 (d)	27 (d)	28 (d)	29 (c)	30 (a)
31 (a)	32 (b)	33 (a)	34 (d)	35 (a)	36 (c)	37 (d)	38 (b)	39 (b)	40 (d)
41 (a)	42 (d)	43 (a)	44 (a)	45 (b)	46 (a)	47 (c)	48 (d)	49 (a)	50 (d)
51 (a)	52 (b)	53 (a)	54 (b)	55 (c)	56 (b)	57 (a)	58 (a)	59 (d)	60 (a)
61 (b)	62 (b)	63 (d)	64 (a)	65 (c)	66 (a)	67 (d)	68 (c)	69 (a)	70 (b)
71 (d)	72 (a)	73 (a)	74 (b)	75 (b)	76 (b)	77 (a)	78 (b)	79 (c)	80 (c)
81 (b)	82 (c)	83 (c)	84 (c)	85 (d)	86 (d)	87 (a)	88 (c)	89 (a)	90 (b)
91 (b)	92 (b)	93 (b)	94 (c)	95 (b)	96 (b)	97 (b)	98 (a)	99 (b)	100 (a)
101 (d)	102 (a)	103 (c)	104 (d)	105 (b)	106 (c)	107 (b)	108 (c)	109 (d)	110 (d)
111 (d)	112 (b)	113 (d)	114 (d)	115 (d)	116 (a)	117 (c)	118 (d)	119 (b)	120 (a)
121 (d)	122 (d)	123 (a)	124 (d)	125 (c)	126 (b)	127 (a)	128 (d)	129 (a)	130 (a)
131 (b)	132 (b)	133 (b)	134 (a)	135 (a)	136 (a)	137 (b)	138 (d)	139 (c)	140 (d)
141 (c)	142 (d)	143 (b)	144 (c)	145 (c)	146 (c)	147 (c)	148 (b)	149 (d)	150 (b)
151 (b)	152 (d)	153 (b)	154 (d)	155 (d)	156 (b)	157 (a)	158 (b)	159 (b)	160 (b)
161 (d)	162 (c)	163 (b)	164 (b)	165 (b)	166 (b)	167 (c)	168 (b)	169 (b)	170 (b)
171 (d)	172 (d)	173 (a)	174 (b)	175 (a)	176 (a)	177 (d)	178 (c)	179 (a)	180 (a)
181 (a)	182 (a)	183 (d)	184 (a)	185 (a)	186 (a)	187 (a)	188 (a)	189 (b)	190 (a)
191 (b)	192 (a)	193 (a)	194 (b)	195 (c)	196 (a)	197 (a)	198 (a)	199 (b)	200 (b)
201 (d)	202 (d)	203 (b)	204 (a)	205 (b)	206 (b)	207 (b)	208 (b)	209 (a)	210 (b)
211 (a)	212 (c)	213 (d)	214 (b)	215 (a)	216 (c)	217 (a)	218 (a)	219 (c)	

Previous Years' Questions

1 (c)	2 (b)	3 (c)	4 (a)	5 (d)	6 (c)	7 (b)	8 (d)	9 (d)	10 (b)
11 (a)	12 (d)	13 (b)	14 (b)	15 (b)	16 (b)	17 (d)	18 (c)	19 (c)	20 (a)
21 (c)	22 (b)	23 (d)	24 (d)	25 (c)	26 (c)	27 (a)	28 (b)	29 (a)	30 (b)
31 (b)	32 (b)	33 (d)	34 (c)	35 (a)	36 (b)	37 (d)	38 (c)	39 (b)	40 (b)
41 (c)	42 (c)	43 (b)	44 (d)	45 (b)					

UNIT 3

Human Resource Development

HRD is a positive humanistic concept in HRM which is based on the belief that an investment in human beings is necessary and will invariably bring in substantial benefits to the organisation in the long run.

Concept of Human Resource Development

Human resource refers to the people who make up the workforce of a particular organisation. Because of their education, skill and training, combined with the capacity to work, human are considered as an important resource. They have the ability to develop the other resources also. Human resource development is the development of human absorbed in an organisation, a sector or in an economy.

Human Resource Development (HRD) is a fundamental concept in generating and implementing employee competencies. HRD can give the tools needed to manage and operate the organisation right from production management, marketing, sales to research and development in order to be more productive.

Leonard Nadler introduced the term 'HRD' in 1969. He defined HRD as "Those learning experiences which are organised for a specific time and designed to bring about the possibility of behavioural change".

According to **TV Rao** "HRD is a process in which the employees of an organisation are continually helped in a planned way to

- acquire or sharpen capabilities required to perform various functions associated with their present or expected future roles.
- develop their general capabilities so that they may be able to discover their own inner potentialities and explore them to full for their own and organisational development purpose.

In this Chapter

- develop an organisational culture where superior-subordinate relationships, teamwork and collaboration among different sub-units are strong and contribute to organisational wealth and motivation and pride of the employees".

Features of HRD

- It is a planned and systematic approach to the development of the people.
- It is a continuous process of developing the competencies of the people, motivating them to continuous improvement in their efficiencies.
- It is based on the belief system that the development of an individual is a never-ending process.
- It is an inter-disciplinary concept and involves confluence of ideas from many sciences. Different streams contribute differently towards the human resource development.
- At the micro level, it is concerned with improving the skills, attitudes and behaviours of employees to benefit both the individual as well as organisation.
- At the macro level, it is concerned with the development of people by providing them the right environment to grow and realise his fullest potential. It is the part of educational and developmental planning for nation's welfare.

Importance of HRD

- Empowers and strengthens executive skills. It enhances the capabilities of people by exploring their hidden potentials and shaping them to achieve organisational goals.
- Improves the communication system to open the channel of communication, so that every one understands the other person in a better way and there is no chance of ambiguity.
- Helps the organisation in keeping the right person at the right place for the right time and making its effective use.
- Enhances the employee morale as well as develops the sense of belongingness as proper rewards are being given to the star performer.
- Improves co-ordination and co-operation which leads to cohesive groups and teams.
- Provides a concrete raw material to facilitate human resource planning and control.
- Creates trust and openness among employees and develops analytical and rational skills among employees which helps them in becoming more innovative, proactive and risk taking.
- Makes employees ready to change and undergo transformation and relearn after unlearning what they had already learnt.
- Ultimately leads to overall growth and development of the employee.

Objectives of HRD

- To develop the capabilities of each employee as an individual.
- To develop the professional and technical skills of an individual.
- To develop team-spirit and functioning in every department and to develop the sense of co-ordination and co-operation among different departments.
- To develop a cordial and harmonious relationship between the subordinate and supervisor. Thus, increasing the overall efficiency of the total organisation.

Functions of HRD

- To develop the specific and clear HR policies and to monitor its implementation.
- To motivate all the employees to develop a desire to learn and develop consistently.
- To design innovative ways and systems to develop and strengthen the HRD.
- To be aware of the organisational objectives and focus all HRD effort to achieve these goals.
- To develop perfect co-ordination between trade unions and other regulatory bodies.
- To develop research development centres and motivate people to undergo research processes and come out with new ideas and concepts.

Evolution of HRD in India

The concept of HRD came into picture only in 1970's. Larsen and Toubro was the pioneer in India to design and implement an integrated HRD system in the 1970's. Slowly other companies also started establishing it. The first workshop of HRD was held in 1979. Xavier Labour Relations Institute, Jamshedpur was the first to establish a centre for HRD.

A survey conducted in 1982 by TV Rao revealed that the organisations started implementing HR policies with a positive approach and the techniques like open appraisal system, training and development, grievance handling etc were also used in the developed organisations. It was concluded after survey that only 17 of 53 companies had formal policy focusing on HRD.

To analyse HRD climate in Indian organisations another survey was carried out and it was found that there were indifferences among employees due to which the general climate was not very conducive.

The top management's commitment and devotion towards effective implementation of HRD was also not satisfactory. Slowly the need and importance of HRD evolved and the Indian Government also started realising its importance.

A separate ministry of human resource was created on 26th September, 1985, through the 174th amendment to the Government of India (allocation of business) Rules 1961. Government is also making a valuable contribution by formulating new policies to develop appropriate linkages between education, public health, adult literacy and other social programmes so as to ensure the overall development of people in the country.

The HRD also develops various vocational education programmes and apprenticeship programmes.

Following diagram shows the evaluation of HRD

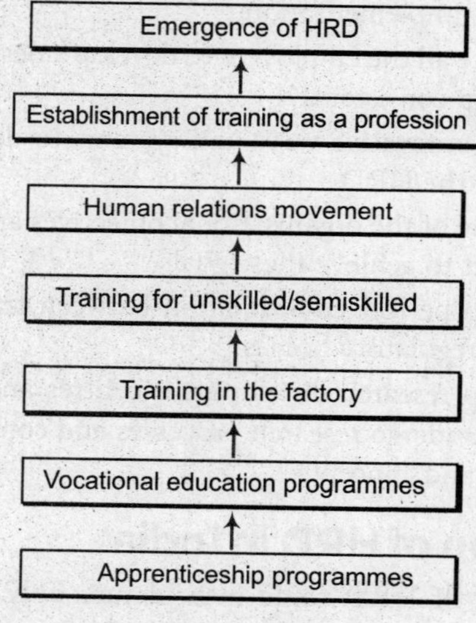

Evolution of HRD

Assumptions of HRD

HRD has emerged as a complex field serving diverse purposes. *Some assumptions of HRD are as follows*

- HRD involves the drive to enhance organisational performance and shareholder value.
- HRD is concerned with issues of resource maximisation, skill development and productivity enhancement.
- In the field of HRD, humanism is perceived as central, so employees are co-contributors and co-recipients.
- HRD is distinct from HRM as the former accompanies the latter.
- HRD function involves management and investment in labour for the benefit of the organisation.
- HRD is effective in the creation of positive organisational and learning cultures.
- HRD is required to both creating and changing the organisational culture and climate.
- HRD is effective in the inculcation of organisational norms and values.

Values related to HRD

The values promoted by the organisation help in the overall development of the human resource which is considered to be the most important resource in an organisation.

Values promoted by HRD are

Integrity and Commitment The values of honesty, sincerity and trust is promoted to facilitate integrity and a sense of commitment towards the organisation.

Teamwork HRD promotes teamwork to develop cooperation and encourages equal participation of people from diverse cultures and backgrounds.

Encourage Communication HRD encourages two way communication to facilitate greater transparency.

Continuous Improvement HRD embraces change and innovations to faster creativity and support continuous improvements.

Healthy Work Environment HRD believes in giving a safe, productive work environment in order to produce quality results.

Maximising Potential HRD helps in realising the potential of each employee by supporting and encouraging the efforts made.

Instrument/Mechanism of HRD

Human resource is the most important resource and needs to be developed to achieve the organisational goals. It has to be developed in a way that is beneficial both to the individual and the organisation. It is necessary to have a healthy and open climate to implement the process of human resource development.

Trust and mutual collaboration will lead to employee commitment. If organisation is able to develop the sense of belongingness, then the effectiveness will be higher in the organisation as it will boost the morale of the employee. The human resource development instruments are the skills required to perform a job effectively.

To achieve this objective, following techniques are to be adopted

- Performance appraisal
- Potential appraisal and development
- Career planning
- Training
- Rewards
- Organisational development
- Quality of work life
- Recruitment and selection
- Job rotation
- Quality circles
- HR planning
- HRD Matrix

Performance Appraisal

Performance appraisal is a process that provides an analysis of a person's overall capabilities and potential, allowing informed decisions to be made for particular purpose.

According to **Flippo**, "Performance appraisal is the systematic, periodic and an impartial rating of an employee's excellence in matters pertaining to his present job and his potential for a better job".

It is beneficial for the managers as the performance appraisal helps them to place the right employees for the right jobs depending on their skills.

Characteristics of Performance Appraisal

- It is different from merit-rating as it is wider than merit-rating.
- It focuses on the performance and future potential whereas, merit-rating is detrimental to decide salary increment.
- It aims to develop a rational bases for personnel decisions.
- It measures what the person does (performance) whereas merit-rating measures what the person is (traits).
- It is a process consisting of a series of steps.
- It is the systematic and scientific analysis of an employee's strengths and weaknesses in terms of the job.
- It is completely objective, rational, formal and scientific study.
- It is a continuous and perpetual process and the employee is evaluated time-to-time under a definite plan.
- It is done to collect information necessary for reaching an objective and correct decisions on employees.

Potential Appraisal

It refers to the identification of hidden talents and skills of a person. It is future oriented, where the main objective is to evaluate the potential of the employees to place them in higher position in organisational hierarchy. It can also be used as a part of performance appraisal processes.

However, it is different from performance appraisal in the way that performance appraisal is based on current appraisal while potential appraisal is based on future appraisal possibilities. Many organisations combine performance and potential appraisal systems while many keep it differently.

Characteristics of Potential Appraisal

- It's main aim is to identify the future prospects of a company.
- It identifies hidden skills and abilities.
- It has no fixed period.
- It may or may not be part of performance appraisal.
- It does not guarantee of promotion.
- It uses the power of analysis based on observations, experiences and speculations about the future.
- It is also based on the results of performance appraisal.
- It stimulates growth.

Difference between Performance and Potential Appraisal

Performance Appraisal	Potential Appraisal
Evaluating the performance so it represents current time period.	Evaluating the potential future time period.
Here, the performance targets are set.	Here, the latent targets are explored.
The actual performance is measured objectively and accurately.	The future roles are assigned and assessed.
The picture of current and part performances are taken into consideration through appropriate methods.	The picture of abilities to assume challenging responsibilities through appropriate methods are considered.

Career Planning

According to **Flippo**, "Career is a sequence of separate but related work activities that provide continuity, order and meaning to a person's life."

It is a path followed by an individual across time and space over the span of his life. Heredity, parents, culture, age level, job experiences etc are the factors, which are determinental in shaping the person's career.

There may be a conflict because of changing expectations of employees and organisation's inability to meet these expectations due to their own constraint. People join any organisation not for job but for career. So, it is very important to have career planning.

It is the construction of a careerpath designed for the employees in which growth opportunities are provided from the stage of employment to the retirement.

Characteristics of Career Planning

- Its main characteristic is to develop human beings.
- It is a way to manage people to get maximum out of them.
- It is an ongoing perpetual process without any stop due to ever changing environment.
- Career planning is thought to be a person aspect and therefore, individual's own responsibility. But, employees are the integral part of every organisation, therefore, it is the responsibility of an organisation to provide guidance and counselling to plan their careers, develop themselves and make use of their knowledge and skills up to maximum.
- Both the personal career goals of an individual should be streamlined with the organisational goals.
- It accesses the suitability of employees to be promoted to higher position.
- It strives for achieving higher productivity and organisational development.

Training

Training is a process of learning designed to achieve a relatively permanent change in an individual that improves one's ability to perform a specific task. It modifies the aptitudes, skills and abilities to accomplish certain tasks.

The aim of training is to fill the gap between the present competence of an employee and the needs to fulfill organisational objectives. It is a continuous process that helps in improving the behaviour and performance of a person. Training is related to a specific job requirement and looks at the present job.

Significance of Training

- It helps in raising the level of performance of the employees which further increase productivity of the organisation.
- It improves the quality of work as it is obvious that trained and skilled people will commit less operational mistakes as compared to untrained people.
- Proper training schedule will save time and employees will not be trapped in the process of trial and error.
- Definitely, it will help the employees to learn more quickly and reach the acceptable level of performance.
- Well trained people will make economical use of raw materials and no wastage will be there, which will subsequently reduce the manufacturing as well as maintenance cost.

Rewards

Rewards are a way of recognising the efforts of an employee. It is a way to acknowledge the contribution or the value of expertise and the level of experience of an employee or a team. Reward is a return on an employees' effort, dedication and the results.

It gives dignity and worth to an employee and is governed by mutual respect. It is expressed through gestures, kind words, behaviours and monetary benefits. Certificates and awards are also forms of rewards. It is an important part of instrument mechanism of development of human resource.

Characteristics of Rewards

- Rewards are fairly distributed in an equitable manner.
- Rewards should be visible so that the employees know that they are rewarded for their efforts.
- Rewards should hold a degree of importance to the person receiving the reward.
- Rewards are to be carefully accessed before giving them.
- Rewards are based on performances, efforts, skills, difficulty of the job etc.
- Rewards help in deciding which employee deserves promotion.
- Rewards are used by the selection committee to judge the employees on a set criteria.
- Rewards should be low in cost but high in value. *e.g.* Certificates, shields, awards etc.

Organisational Development

Organisational development is an organisation improvement strategy. The term 'Organisational Development' (OD) refers to a broad range of behavioural science based strategies used to diagnose the need for change in organisations and to implement changes when necessary. It is relatively a new field of study of around 60's.

Organisational development can be defined as a technique for bringing change in the entire organisation, rather than focusing attention on individuals to bring change easily in the entire organisation. It is basically about how organisations and people function and how to get them function better. Organisation development consultants are experts in organisational change.

According to **Cummings** and **Worley**, "Organisational development is a systematic application of behavioural science knowledge to the planned development and reinforcement of organisational strategies, structures and processes for improving an organisation is effectiveness."

According to **Burke**, "Organisation development is a planned process of change in an organisation in culture through the utilisation of behavioural science technologies, research and theory."

Nature of Organisational Development

Organisational development is a general strategy or approach to organisational change that is employed to analyse and diagnose the sources of organisational problems and to develop and implement action plans for their solution.

According to Bennis, OD has the following characteristics

- It is an education strategy for bringing planned change.
- It relates to real problems of an organisation.
- Laboratory training methods based on experienced behaviour are primarily used to bring the change.
- Change agents applying OD technique for change is external to the forms of consultants.
- There is a close working relationship between change agents and the people who are being changed. The relationships involve mutual trust, joint goals, means and mutual influence.

Quality of Work Life

The term 'QWL' is gaining importance and has evolved in recent years because of increase in education level, increase in job aspirations, association of workers, significance of human resource management, widespread industrial unrest and evolved knowledge in human behaviour.

It has been researched and confirmed that QWL has a significant influence on productivity of employees as well as physical and psychological aspects of employees.

According to **American Society of Training and Development**, "Quality of working life is a process of work organisation which enables its members at all levels to actively participate in shaping the organisation's environment, methods and outcomes. This value based process is aimed towards meeting the twin goals of enhanced effectiveness of organisation and improved quality of life at work for employees."

Recruitment and Selection

Recruitment

After identifying the number and type of personnel required in any organisation by the process of manpower planning and job analysis, next comes the process of recruitment and selection. Both recruitment and selection are integrated and interrelated terms.

Recruitment involves location of such personnel motivating them to offer their candidature and selection involves selecting the suitable candidates and rejecting the unfit ones.

According to **Taylor**, "Recruitment is the process of locating, identifying and attracting capable applicants."

According to **Flippo**, "Recruitment is a process of searching for prospective employees and stimulating and encouraging them to apply for jobs in an organisation."

According to **Dale Yoder**, "Recruitment is a process to discover the sources of manpower to meet the requirements of the staffing schedule and to employ effective measures for attracting that manpower in adequate numbers to facilitate effective selection of an effective working force."

Selection

Selection is the process of putting right men on right job. It is a procedure of matching organisational requirement with skills and qualified people.

According to **Dale Yoder**, "Selection is the process by which candidates for employment are divided into class-those who will be offered employment and those who will not."

According to **David** and **Robbins**, "Managerial decision-making process as to predict which job applicants will be successful if hired."

Job Rotation

It refers to a specific strategy where employees rotate between different jobs within the same organisation or business. Employees take on new tasks for a period of time and then rotate back to their original position.

It is a management approach where the employees are tested for various skills to match their competitiveness. It is a management tool to look for new dimesions in an employee in order to place that employee at an appropriate position.

Objectives of Job Rotation

- To create right employee job fit in order to enhance productivity and to derive maximum benefit.
- To test the skills and competencies of the employees for the purpose of assiging them proper work.
- To develop a wider range of work experiences by changing the area of operations.
- To reduce the monotony of doing a routine job where repetitivenes is involved.
- To develop a pool of employees who can be placed at a senior level.
- To develop higher competencies and motivate employees to deal with new challenges.

- To help managers in exploring the hidden talents of the people working in an organisation.
- To align the competencies needed in a job with the job requirements thus created.

Quality Circles

Quality circle is a group of employees belonging to the same area, who continuously work towards the improvement and the development of the organisation.

Objectives of Quality Circles

- To identify, analyse and solve the quality work related problems.
- To make everybody understand the importance of human relations.
- To make everybody understand the contribution of job satisfaction, job involvement, career planning and other HR related policies in the total efficiency of the organisation.
- To develop the necessity of exploration of hidden potentials of every individual and facilitating them to make maximum use to improve the efficiency of the organisation.

Human Resource Planning

Human resource planning is a process through which an organisation ensures that right people, at right place and at right time are available. It involves determination of future, manpower needs to help management in being proactive.

It also help the management in understanding the gap between available manpower and the future needs. This understanding plays an important role in bridging the gap.

It is primacy in nature and all other staffing functions follow it. It puts the objectives of the organisation on paper and plans into the number and kind of personnel needed to accomplish those objectives.

According to **Decenzo** and **Robbins**, "Human resource planning is the process by which an organisation ensures that it has the right number and kind of people, at the right place, at the right time, capable of effectively and efficiently completing those tasks that will help the organisation achieve its overall objectives."

HRD Matrix

HRD matrix shows the interrelationships between HRD instruments, processes, outcomes and organisational effectiveness.

These are as follows

HRD Instruments

These include performance appraisal, counselling, role analysis, potential development, training, communication policies, job rotations, rewards, job enrichment programmes etc.

These instruments may vary depending on the size of the organisation, the internal environment, the support and commitment of the top management, the competitive policies etc.

HRD Processes

The HRD instruments lead to the generation of HRD processes like role clarity, performance planning, development climate, risk-taking, dynamism in employees. Such HRD processes should result in more competent, satisfied and committed people that would make the organisation grow by contributing their best to it.

HRD Outcomes

HRD instruments and processes make people more committed and satisfied, where they tend to give their best to the organisation enthusiastically.

Organisational Effectiveness

HRD outcomes influence the organisational effectiveness, which in turn, depends on a number of variables like environment, technology, competitors etc.

Action-Research Model

The action-research model is a model adopted in human resource development in which an initial research about the organisation provides information to plan the subsequent action. After the action is taken, then the results of the action are accessed to provide further information to guide for further action.

This model focusses on planned change as a cyclical process to frame subsequent action plan. It involves active participation in a changed situation set within the framework of an organisation.

The action refers to programmes and interventions which are framed by undertaking proper research to solve various problems.

According to **Kurt Lewin**, "Action-research is a process of systematically collecting research data about an ongoing system relative to some objective, goal or need of that system".

Cummings and **Worley** have summarised the action-research model, which is actually a problem-solving method in eight steps.

The Cummings and Worley (2001) portrayal of the action-research process and their description of each process as follows

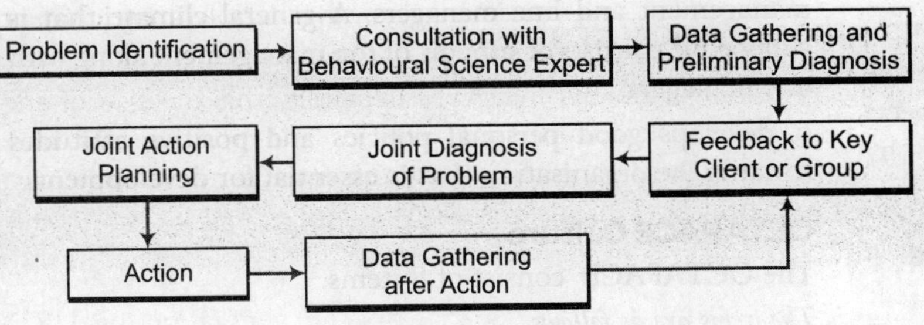

Problem Identification

This stage begins with a key executive in the organisation or someone with power and influence who senses that the organisation has one or more problems that might be solved with the help of an OD practitioner.

Consultation with a Behavioural Science Expert

During the initial contact, the HRD/OD practitioner and the client carefully assess each other. The practitioner has his or her own normative, developmental theory or frame of reference and must be conscious of those assumptions and values. Sharing them with the client from the beginning establishes an open and collaborative atmosphere.

Data Gathering and Preliminary Diagnosis

This step is usually completed by the HRD/OD practitioner, often in conjunction with organisation members. It involves gathering appropriate information and analysing it to determine the underlying causes of organisational problems. The four basic methods of gathering data are interviews, process observation, questionnaires and organisational performance data.

Feedback to a Key Client or Group

As action research is a collaborative activity, the diagnostic data are feedback to the client, usually in a group or work team meeting. The feedback step, in which members are given the information gathered by the HRD/OD practitioner, helps them determine the strengths and weaknesses of the organisation or the department under study. The consultant provides the client with all relevant and useful data.

Joint Diagnosis of the Problem

At this point, members discuss the feedback and explore with the HRD practitioner whether they want to work on identified problems. A close interrelationship exists among data gathering, feedback and diagnosis because the consultant summarizes the basic data from the client members and presents the data to them for validation and further diagnosis.

Joint Action Planning

Next, the HRD practitioner and the client members jointly agree on further actions to be taken. This is the beginning of the moving process (as described in Lewin's change model), as the organisation decides how best to reach a different quasi-stationary equilibrium.

At this stage, the specific action to be taken depends on the culture, technology and environment of the organisation, the diagnosis of the problem and the time and expense of the intervention.

Action

This stage involves actual change from one organisational state to another. It may include installing new methods and procedures, reorganising structures and work designs and reinforcing new behaviours.

Such actions typically cannot be implemented immediately but require a period as the organisation moves from the present to a desired future state.

Data Gathering after Action

Because action research is a cyclical process, data must also be gathered after the action has been taken to measure and determine the effects of the action and to feed the results back to the organisation. This leads to re-diagnosis and new action.

HRD Culture and Climate

The culture and climate of HRD in an organisation results in the performance of that organisation. If the HRD culture is good, then the performance of the organisation will be good and *vice-versa*.

HRD Climate

According to **Abraham**, "Organisational climate is a set of characteristics of an organisation which are referred in the descriptions employees make of the policies, practices and conditions which exist in the working environment".

HRD climate is the perception that the employees have about the policies, procedures, practices and conditions which exist in the environment.

It is the way employees interact and members conduct themselves with the other members of the organisation and outsiders. It conveys the physical layout.

By proper selection of people, nurturing their dynamism and other competencies, an organisation can make its employees proactive and growth oriented.

An organisation must prepare its employees to meet the challenges. Therefore, HRD climate refers to those aspects of the environment that are consciously perceived by organisational members.

Factors Needed to Develop HRD Climate

The following factors are needed to develop HRD Climate

Top to Bottom Effort Effort is needed at both, top and bottom levels. Top management should emphasise on proper implementation of decisions by adopting various controlling technique. Bottom level workers should have a loyal mind set and they should work with dedication.

Role of Motivator Managers and supervisors have to play the role of motivators to help employees develop their competencies and expertise. This prepares the human resource to different situations.

Free Expression of Feelings The favourable HRD climate is when, there is freedom of expression of feelings from top to bottom and *vice-versa*. Clear communication establishes good HR practices.

Feedback Feedback helps to idetify the drawbacks and other loose areas. Employee feedback is good for the manager. It also builds trust in the organisation.

Discouraging Favouritism Management should avoid favouritism and give equal importance to everyone. It should appreciate people who are working performing good and guide those who needs improvement.

Risk Taking Experimentation Experimentation should be done in the organisation even if it involves risk. Tackling risky areas will bring expertise to handle difficult situations and develop confidence.

Instruments and Systems Instruments to bring change and open systems of appraisal, councelling, career development, training contribute in generating a good HRD climate.

Elements of HRD Climate

The elements/dimensions of HRD climate are grouped into three broad categories. They are general climate, OCTAPACE culture and HRD mechanism.

These are as follows

General Climate

The general climate deals with the importance given to development of human resources in general by the top management and line managers. A general climate that is supportive consists of support of top management along with line managers.

It develops good personal policies and positive attitudes towards the organisation that is essential for development.

OCTAPACE Culture

The OCTAPACE consist of 8 items.

The items are as follows

Openness It is the openness where employees feel free to discuss their ideas, activities and feelings related to the organisation.

Confrontation It refers to bringing out the problems and issues with a view to solve them instead of hiding them for fear of hurting or getting hurt.

Trust It stands for taking people at their face value and beleiving what they say.

Autonomy It shows giving freedom to people so that they work independently with responsibility.

Pro-Activity It refers to encouraging employees to take initiative and risks.

Authencity It is the tendency on the part of people to do what they say.

Collaboration It stands for acceptance of interdependencies to be helpful to each other and to work as teams.

Experimenting It involves the use of innovative approaches to solve problems or in other words, new ways of dealing with organisational problems.

HRD Mechanism

HRD mechanism is a set of mechanisms and techniques concerned with the present and future performance of the employees by increasing their ability, knowledge, attitude and skill. They improve the overall organisational climate.

The major ones are performance appraisal, potential appraisal, career planning, training and employee development, organisation development, rewardş, employee welfare, job rotation and quality of work life.

The implementation of HRD mechanisms is an integrated approach where all the aspects of HRD will be looked upon. The organisation makes an effort to use as many mechanisms as possible. The mechanism should be implemented seriously to derive maximum gain to HRD.

HRD Climate and Organisational Climate

HRD is a part of organisational climate. It is defined as the perception an employee may have on the developmental environment of an organisation.

The development climate have the following features

- A tendency at all levels to treat people as the most important resource from top management to lowest level.
- A perception that developing the competencies of the employee by the manger/supervisors.
- Faith in the abilities of the employees to acquire new skills and competencies at any stage of life.
- Encouraging experimentation and risk taking ability.
- A tendency to be open in communications and discussions rather than being secretive.
- Prevailing a general climate of trust.
- Supportive personal policies, HRD practices.
- Making efforts to help employees realise their strengths and weaknesses.
- Developing team spirit.
- A tendency to discourage stereotypes and favouritism.
- A tendency on the part of the employee to be generally helpful to each other and to collaborate with each other.

Culture

Culture refers to the structure of the organisation that is deep rooted in the values, beliefs and assumptions held by organisational members.

Organisational Culture

It is the pattern of beliefs, customs, attitutes, knowledge, way and mode of conduct in an organisation. It is also an integral part of an organisation and unique to it. It may result in part or seen as a whole. Oganisational culture can be supportive or unsupportive. It can be negative or positive.

Organisational culture can also be correlated to work culture. The work culture is most effective when it supports the organisations HR strategies. This is mostly done by aligning the behaviour, processes and methods to read to the desired results. The methods to achieve to the desired results are equally important. Having a sound and supportive organisation culture is critical to long-term success of the organisation.

An ideal organisational culture is when there is good relationship between the supervisor and subordinate, collaboration, team work and professional well being.

The employees should be motivated to reach to their excellence which adds to the pride of the employees.

HRD Culture

HRD culture facilitates development of an enabling culture in an organisation. The HRD culture enables an organisation to go through frequent restructuring and redesigning. It develops on enabling culture. The elements of HRD culture are similar as that of HRD climate.

They are as follows

- Openness
- Trust
- Proactiveness
- Collaboration
- Confrontation
- Autonomy
- Authenticity

Characteristics of HRD Culture

- HRD culture varies from one organisation to other as it is specific to each organisation.
- It is multidimensional as there are different components of HRD culture at different levels.
- It takes time to be established as there is no fixed period of establishment.
- It is more or less fixed and is not ever changing.
- Changing a corporate culture takes time.
- HRD culture is established and influenced by the management. It does so by way of communication, assistance and general behaviour towards employees.
- HRD culture presents a clear cut picture of the organisation.
- It is influenced by organisation's environment and also influences the organisation.
- HRD culture is greatly influenced by the values, norms and management style of an organisation.
- The style of working in an organisation provide an understanding of its culture.

HRD Interventions

An intervention is referred as a set of sequenced and planned actions or events that are intended to help on organisation to increase its effectiveness.

The interventions in human resource development are defined as the role of organisations and the employees in respect to the work participation. It relates to what can be done or what measures can be taken at the workplace to prevent the early retirement.

Human resource interventions are referred as a sequence of planned actions that intend to develop the human resource of an organisation to increase its effectiveness. It caters to improve the performance and effectiveness of HRD and consist of drawing up plans and strategies.

Intervention Cycle

The intervention cycle of HRD consists of the following steps

- Desire to bring changes to improve the existing practices
- Investigation of the problem that needs to be changed
- Explore the possible solutions and bench marks
- Design interventions and draw results
- Implement the interventions
- Evaluate the performing of interventions and learning.

Features of HRD Interventions

- They are specific to the needs of the organisation.
- They help in providing informed choices to the organisation in their decision-making process.
- The interventions are based on knowledge of intended outcomes that can actually be produced.
- It takes into consideration the individual differences as well as the organisational goals.
- The members of HR, accept the ownership of the interventions.
- HR interventions are result of strategic planning after accessing all the strengths and weaknesses.

Types of HR Interventions

There are different ways through which HR interventions takes place. *They are as follows*

Leadership Development Programs

This program aims to develop a leadership and managerial effectiveness tool. Feedback profiles are made that are called 360 degree feedback profiles as it cosiders each and every aspect of HR.

The assessments are based on the assessments made by juniors, seniors and top management also. The trends of the feedback are shared and development activities are undertaken by the HR department individual coaching is also done.

Performance Management System

Performance management system are treated as a management tool to manage people, estimate the value of each employee. A managers time is required to plan, review and develop performance, competencies and culture of individuals and teams.

Assessment and Development Centers

ADCs are powerful assessment tools that are used as competency building tools. They are used to identify succession plans and people who have the potential and ability to be successful.

The higher goals consist of creating a competency culture, high performance culture, leadership culture etc. Aditya Birla Group, NTPC, HPCL have brought HR interventions through this technique.

Team Building

This intervention can take the form of interviews, offsite sessions, prework etc. The idea is to work as a single unit and apply coordination and cooperation plans. The intervention can also be derived by drawing up plans on problem solving within the framework of a team.

Interventions to Standardise

Activities framed to automate the processes and standardise the tasks, tools, equipments, materials, components and measures applied in the HR department. For example, setting the standards for adopting the ISO 2000. Special kind of interventions are designed to reach upto that level.

Competency Mapping Exercise

Use of participative processes to map the competencies and use of facilitators to initiate the exercise. The facilitator to initiate the interventions should have skills in identifying knowledge, attitudes, skills and competency of mapping techniques.

The linkage of HR with different systems is a whole system and through it mapping can be done with entire organisation.

HR Accounting and Audit

HR Accounting

Human resource accounting is an important part of the Human resource management. HRA is the process to recognise the investment reports made in this sphere. It takes care of those accounting practices that are non-conventional and that may not be included in general accounting.

It is an expansion of the accounting principles of matching revenue and costs. HRA engages in accounting for the organisations management and sees employees as human capital that provides benefits.

According to **M.N. Baker**, "It is an accounting profession to quantify cost and value of employee employing in the organisation".

According to **American Accounting Association**, "HR accounting is the process of identifying and measuring data about human resources and communicating this information to interested parties".

According to **Flameouts**, "HR accounting is the measurement of costs and values of the people for the organisation".

Approach of HRA

In the human resource accounting approach, the balance sheet is made by taking human resource into consideration. The expenditures associated with the human resource are regarded as assets. This is because human resource is reported as an asset and any expenditure on it becomes an asset.

On the contrary, the conventional accounting treats costs associated with human resource as an expenditure and treated as expenses on the income statement which reduces profit. Human resource yields benefits which is quantifiable in financial terms.

It involves the costs incurred to recruit, select, employ, train and develop employees and to judge their economic value to the organisation.

Historical Review of HRA

The American Accounting Association Committee, yields Human Resource Accounting as the process of identifying and measuring data about human resource and communicating this to the interested parties.

Likert (1917) explains that several purposes in an organisation is served by Human Resource Accounting. For example, it provides cost/value information to management for taking decisions on acquiring, allocating, developing and maintaining human resource to maintain cost effectiveness.

Jasrotie (2007) strengthened the need for human resource accounting in India because in the Indian economy, the success of organisation depends on the knowledge and intellectual capabilities of personnel.

The suggestion was that Indian Government should make the accounting and reporting of human resources mandatory for every organisation in the way similar to Denmark from the year 2015.

Flamholtz (1979) explains the Human Resource Accounting model as 'psycho-technical systems' approach to organisational measurement. The approach indicates two functions of measurement, *i.e.* process function in the process of measurement and numerical information from the numbers.

The HRA process increases the recognition that human capital is vital to the short and long-term productivity and expansion of an organisation.

Objectives of HR Accounting

HR accounting is an integral part of any organisation. *The objectives of HRA are as follows*

- It provides information related to costs, revenues, acquiring and developing human resource.
- It provides the necessity to bring changes in the allocation and maintenance of resources for HR.
- It enables management to effectively monitor the use of HR practices.
- An objectives of HR accounting is to find out whether human asset appreciating or depreciating over a period of time.
- HR accounting is very essential in planning the physical resource of an organisation by giving valuable information about it.
- HR accounting task is to motivate individual persons working in an organisation to increase their worth by training.

Uses of HRA

- It is like a political tool to demonstrate the management practices adopted in human resource.
- It is like a pedagogical instrument for analysing and structuring.
- It is used as an aid to decision-making model to know about the HR practices.
- It provides cost value information about acquiring, developing, allocating, reallocating, monitoring and managing the HR.
- It acts as a measure to know about the appreciation or depreciation of HR.
- It deems to know about the financial consequences of various practices and helps to know whether they should be continued or discontinued.

Benefits of HRA

The benefits or advantages of using HRA are as following

- It is helpful in gathering the information related to manpower planning.
- Various policies of the organisation related to planning, human resource development, training etc are taken in accordance with the accounting.
- It helps in foreseeing the changes needed in the human resource of an organisation.
- It provides valueable information to investors which helps them in judging about a company.
- It helps individual employer to aspire and do better.
- It is also used as a motivational tool as it increases morale.
- It calculates returns on investment, *i.e.* know about the financial cost and revenue of human resource.
- It helps an organisation in attracting the best human resource as it tells about how much an organisation can spare on acquiring new talents.

Limitations of HRA

There are certain limitations of HRA. *These are as follows*

- HRA assumes that employer are stable for a specific period but this assumption is wrong as employee mobility is very high.
- If the valuation of human resource is not done properly, then it may lead to dehumanising of human resource.
- There are no specific standards of HRA, therefore, it becomes extremely difficult to draw comparisons between two organisations.
- There are no specific and clear-cut guidelines for cost and value of human resources in an organisation.
- The exact value of human resource is uncertain because the exact capability of a resource remains unknown since they are intangible assets.

HR Accounting Techniques

There are different viewpoints to HRA, regarding components of costs, investment and value related to employees of an organisation. *There are various approaches and methods to assign monetary values to these aspects which are explained below*

1. The Cost Approach

This approach comprises of historical cost, opportunity cost and replacement cost method. *These are as follows*

Historical Cost Method All the costs incurred in recruitment, selection, placement, training and development of employees are taken into account while evaluating the value of human resources. Some of these costs are direct costs like salaries while costs in terms of time spent in training and development are indirect costs.

Opportunity Cost Method It was Hekimian and Jones who had advocated this method and it is also known as the market value method. This method calculates what would have been the returns if the money spent on HR was spent on something else.

Replacement Cost Method Replacement cost refers to the costs that would have to be incurred if the existing employees were to be replaced by identical ones. When an employee leaves the organisation, costs of recruiting, selecting, placing and training the new employee would have to be incurred in order to replace him.

2. Non-Monetary Methods

The value of human resources can be measured by non-monetary methods as well. These methods may be used to supplement monetary methods. *It includes*

Skills Inventory This is a simple listing of the education, knowledge, experience, skills of the organisation's human resources.

Performance Evaluation Method This includes methods like simple ranking method, paired comparison, check lists, graphic rating scales etc.

Potential Assessment It refers to the identification of hidden skills, talents and abilities in a person which even he may be unaware of. It determines an employee's capacity for promotion and advancement.

Attitude Measurements These measurements assess employees' attitudes towards their jobs, remuneration, work environment etc in order to determine their levels of satisfaction or dissatisfaction.

3. The Economic Value Approach

It includes

Flamholtz's Model of Determinants of Individual Value to Formal Organisations

According to Flamholtz, the value of an individual to an organisation is determined by the services he is expected to render. The current value of an employee is the present worth of the services that he is likely to render to the organisation in future.

As an employee moves from one position to another within the organisation, the set of services provided by him changes. While calculating the current value of the individual, the present cumulative value of all the possible services that may be rendered by him during his tenure with the organisation is taken. *There are two dimensions to this value*

- **Expected Conditional Value** This is the worth that could be possibly realised from the services of an individual over the period of his productive work life in the organisation.
- **Expected Realisable Value** The expected realisable value depends upon the expected conditional value of an employee and the probability that the individual will remain in the organisation for the duration of his productive work life.

  Since, the employees may leave the organisation any time they wish, it is important to ascertain the chances of their turnover.

Flamholtz's Stochastic Rewards Valuation Model

This model considers the movement of employees in an organisation through various roles. This process of progressing through organisational states is called a stochastic process. The stochastic rewards valuation model measures a person's expected conditional value and expected realisable value.

In any organisation, employees generate value as they move along organisational roles and render a set of services in different capacities. It is presumed that any employee would move from one state to another over a duration of time, in this model the separation of an employee from his workplace is also considered a state.

This is a very sophisticated and complex model that requires extensive information for determining the value of individuals.

The Lev and Schwartz Model

According to this model, the value of human resources is calculated as the present value of estimated future earnings discounted by the rate of return on investment (cost of capital). This is the most commonly used method for HRA used by most companies in India.

The mathematical formula for calculation of value of human resources is as follows

$$V_y = \frac{I(t)}{(1+r)^{t-y}}$$

Where,

V = the value of an individual '*y*' years old

$I(t)$ = the individual's annual earnings up to retirement.

t = retirement age

r = a discount rate specific to the cost of capital to the company

Hekimian and Jones Competitive Bidding Model

In this method, the managers bid against each other for the human resources already available in an organisation. The highest bid is taken as the value of the employee. This is a highly subjective method as there are no set criteria to evaluate the employees. The value of an employee is based solely on the judgement of the managers.

4. Discounted Present Value of Future Earnings Method

This is the widely used method which is used for valuation of human capital. The model of measurement of human capital suggested by Brauch Lev and Aba Schwartz is based on the economic concept of human capital. Capital is defined as a source of income over a period of time and its worth is the present value of future incomes discounted by a certain rate.

According to **Lev** and **Schwartz**, the value of human capital represented by a person of age is the present value of his remaining future earnings from his employment.

They have given the following formula for calculating the value of an individual

$$V_r = \frac{T}{\sum_{t-r}} \frac{I(t)}{(1+r)^{m \quad t-1}}$$

Where,

V_r = the value of an individual '*r*' years old

$I(t)$ = the individual's annual earnings up to the retirement

T = retirement age

r = discount rate specific to the person

t = active service (in years)

Lev and Schwartz are of the opinion that "the determinations of the total value of a firm's labour/human force is a straightforward extension" of the measurement of the value of individual. They have divided the whole labour force into certain groups as unskilled, skilled, semi-skilled, technical staff, managerial staff etc, and in accordance with different age groups.

Average earning profiles for different classes and age-groups are prepared for each group of personnel separately and present value of human capital is calculated in accordance with the above formula. The aggregate present value of the different groups of personnel will represent the capitalised future earnings of the firm as a whole.

They have advocated the use of "cost of capital" rate for the purpose of discounting the future earnings of the employees for arriving at their present value.

Human Resource Audit

Human resource audit is a comprehensive method that reviews the current human resources, policies, procedures etc. HR audit identifies the need for improvement and enhancement of the HR practices to compliance with the ever changing rules and regulations.

Auditing is a formal process and used as a diagnostic tool to view the current status of things. It also studies the gaps between the current status and the desired status in the area where auditing is done. It is a routine exercise which goes on in every organisation.

However, human resource auditing is not mandatory to continue in an organisation, so it may or may not be in practice. The companies prefer this type of auditing to know about the exact status of human resource.

According to **Flamholtz**, "Human resource audit is the measurement and reporting of the cost and value of people in organisational resources".

According to **Amercian Accounting Association**, "The process of identifying and measuring data about human resources and communicating this information to interested parties".

Need for HR Audit

- It is designed to investigate the policies, strategies, procedures, structure, systems and practices of an organisation.
- It systematically evaluates the strengths, constraints and developmental needs of the human resource.
- The human resource processes must be constantly redirected and revived to make it responsive to the changing needs.
- HR audits are directed to find solutions to various ongoing problems in the organisation.
- It is needed to increasing the dependency of the organisation on the prevailing HR systems.
- It is needed to change the philosophy of management towards various HR practices.

Scope of HR Audit

The scope of HR audit is within the organisational structure. It's scope can be seen in making corporate strategy for human resource management. To make a consistent strategy, HR audit provides detailed review and analysis of the past, present and future requirements related to HR.

It also provides valueable cues to the managers about the result of implementing policies, procedures and legal requirements. HR audit is also beneficial in knowing about the employee satisfaction level in an organisation. It helps to formulate various practices regarding satisfaction of the employees, knowing about absenteeism, employee turnover and safety records.

Types of HR Audit

HR audit can be classified into two types. *They are as follows*

Internal Audit

As the name suggests, internal audit is conducted by an organisation to know about the internal matters of the company such as to know about their staff, to know about the value of resources, process of resource allocation etc.

It tells about the internal matters and is used as a supervising tool to control the activities going on in an organisation. The managerial level is involved in the auditing process. Staff, employees are audited in internal audit.

External Audit

External audit refers to auditing done by the outsiders. An organisation specially appoints a person or a group to carry on auditing of the human resource. The external audit is unbiased and presents a true picture of the people working in an organisation.

The unbiased evaluation is helpful in formulating manpower policies by the management. However, external audit may be costlier as special people from outside the organisation have to be hired for this purpose.

Approach to HR Audit

These are a set of five approaches designed for the purpose of evaluation of human resource in any organisation.

These approaches are as follows

Comparative Approach In this approach, the auditors identify a company and take it as a model. The audit is done based on the model of the competitor company. The results are then compared.

Outside Authority Approach In this approach, the auditors use a standard model that is set as a benchmark for the purpose of comparison.

Statistical Approach In this, the statistical measures are adopted to measure the performance that is developed considering the company's existing information.

Compliance Approach In this approach, the authors review part actions to calculate whether those activities comply with legal requirements, industry policies and procedures.

Management by Objective Approach In this approach, performance is measured against specific goals to arrive at a final decision about organisation's actual performance with the set objectives.

Preparation for an Audit

There are various steps that needs to be followed for the process of auditing to begin.

The steps are as follows

Auditor Engagement

The first step is to select the person who will do the auditing process. That person should be competent to understand the value and importance of audit. The person should be non- political.

In case of internal audit, the person should not be high on authority or hierarchy level. They should be told about scope, process of audit and should be provided appropriate training.

Data Gathering

The second way is to collect data. For this, several ways of gathering data can be used like questionnaire, personal interview, observation etc. Audit members use audit questionnaire as a tool to review the areas within the range of audit. Audit questionnaire consists of a list of specific questions.

Setting Benchmarks

To complete the audit process, the auditors have to set benchmarks, so that they can compare the results of the audit. The comparison offers insight into the audit results. Benchmarking should include the number of days to fill a position, absenteeism rates, cost of employee benefits etc. Benchmarking also includes audit of general and administrative costs, cost of acquiring new employee.

Create Action Plans

The organisation must generate action plans for the implementation of the action plans proposed by the audit. The findings are separated according to the order of importance into high, medium and low. The importance of audit can be seen only when an action plan is drawn to implement the results.

Provide Feedback

In this step, the audit team must give a feedback to the organisation. The feedback will be in the form of findings, recommendations and the plans for the future. This is done by analysing the findings and developing a framework to determine the action plan.

A formal report is written that contain the findings alongwith the recommendations. Thus, the audit report will faster the changes needed in the human resource department.

Continuous Improvement

At the end of audit, it is essential to observe and improve the company's policies, procedures and practices. This will greatly help in increasing an organisations efficiency.

Similarly, it is important to record the audit findings, changes made, turnovers, employee surveys etc. Identifying problematic issues, growth areas that can assist in the decision-making process where measures are taken regarding allocation of time and money.

Benefits of HR Audit

- HR audit helps to find out the proper contribution of the HR department towards an organisation.
- It enhances the image of the HR department within the organisation.
- It motivates the HR manager to find out the problems and solve them effectively.
- It reduces the HR cost and motivates the HR personnel.
- It helps the organisation to achieve its objectives, apply processes for efficient working and in ensuring a smooth working environment.
- It helps an organisation to identify its strengths and weaknesses and guides the company in many ways.

Limitations of HR Audit

- It is not possible to find out the solutions to various employee related problems, where employee mobility is very high.
- The specific standards may not be applicable in all organisations as the conditions of HR are different in each organisation.
- A competitior firm model may not give proper results which may lead to confusion. This ultimately results in misleading of information.

Consultant-Client Relationship

The relationship of consultant-client in an organisation is very important.

Consultant

Consultant is like an advisor who is under a contract to help an organisation to realise its objectives in independent manner.

According to **Canback**, "Those who provide general management analysis and advice within strategic, organisational or operational context and who are institutionally organised in firms are consultants".

Role of Consultant

The role of consultant in an organisation is as follows

- As a strategic navigator, the consultant recommends courses of action with an understanding of the market and competitive dynamics.
- As a management physician, the consultant gives a realistic perspective of the organisation arising out of deep understanding of the market and competitive dynamics.
- As a mental adventurer, the consultant applies rigorous economic methods and experience base for the benefit of the organisation.
- As a system architect, it helps to redesign processes, routines and systems.
- As a friendly co-pilot, the consultant guides as a facilitator rather than an expert.

Client

Client is the management body or person who hires the consultant to audit and bring changes in the management practices. The client receives information, feedback, report and recommendation from the consultants regarding various issues.

Initially, a single person designated in the post of manager acts as a client but further interaction may initiate whereby the subordinates and the organisation also acts as a client.

Type of Clients

The different type of clients are as follows

Primary Client The person who owns the problem or issue that is being worked upon by the consultant. They approve the budget needed to hire a consultant.

Contact Ctient The person who contacts the consultant and *vice-versa*. They also answer the queries of the consultant and become the single point of contact initially.

Intermediate Client The people or groups who get involved in interaction with the consultant.

Unwitting Client People who are above, below or laterally related to the primary client and are affected by interventions.

Indirect Client People who are aware that they will be affected by the interventions but who are unknown to the consultants.

The Consultant-Client Relationship

The relationship between a consultant and a client is of a professional, formal type where both parties mutually benefit from each other. If the consultant is for enhancing the clients' system abilities in the sphere of problem solving, then the consultant is in the business of assisting the managerial skills and insights.

However, the relationship is not prolonged as it fully need based relationship. The ongoing relationship can be retained in an organisation by appointing internal auditors. External auditors may also be put into a long-term relationship whereby they remain involved with various processes of an organisation.

The Code of Conduct

The code of conduct says that consultants are expected to maintain professional and ethical standards while dealing with their clients. This can take the form of maintaining an arm's length relationship not intervening too much in the internal matters of the organisation or the politics of the organisation.

Keeping confidential information away from the concerned parties is violation of the code of conduct. The consultants are needed to report any violation in the conduct whether it is of financial, operational and behavioural nature by the client's organisation.

This is the code of conduct that is usually prescribed for all the consultants when they take on work from client organisations.

Realities of C-C Relations

The code of conduct is prescribed to the consultants and clients to adhere to the issues so that the end result is beneficial for both the parties. But the reality is different as the conduct is not followed. As an evidence, there are large number of corporate scandals that have emerged in the last few decades. There are a number of situations where the consultant was found to be aiding and even assisting the wrong doings conducted by the client.

For example, the **Enron Scandal**-The scandal manifested into itself because the consulting firm was secretly conspiring with the client in changing the account books. It was found in this case, that the consulting firm's partners went beyond collaboration and were indeed one of the culprits.

The **Satyam Scandal** in India was also found to be a case in which some of the consultants knew about the goings-on in the company and also were in breach of the code of conduct and legal aspects as they did not report the matter after anquiry to the regulators.

The saving grace in this case was that when the conspiracy become too big, then it was the new consulting firm that had been roped in for another purpose that blew the whistle on the ongoing Satyam Scan.

Scandals

The example of **Enron** and **Satyam** indicate the consultants have to walk a thin line to fulfill professional obligations and report unethical behaviour. As they are paid by the client, most often the consultants are reluctant to reveal the matter to the regulators. Considering the extremely competitive nature of the market where there are several consulting firms competing for the same client, consultants are often found to go along with the likes of the client.

There are no easy answers when one considers all the aspects and it would indeed be a brave and conscientious consultant who would dare to act against the wishes of the client.

However, some solutions have emerged in recent years for the course of action that can be taken by the consultants. After the Enron Scandal, the Securities and Exchange Commission as well as other regulators ensured that new rules are made to separate consulting and investment banking. So that there will be two different firms advising on financial matters and for consulting.

This was intended to reduce the conflict of interest since consultants and investment bankers will now represent two new firms. Their way of work and procedure will be different. Still it is debatable as to how for this law has succeeded given the global crises on the economic front in 2008 where several other scams came to light.

Conflict of Interest

The real issue is the conflict of interest of the consultant and the client. It is upto the interest of the consultant to see how far it can go to report unethical behavior to the regulators. This is expected from the consultant as this is the very core for which a client hires a consultant. Many consultants are often embroiled in clients internal politics. The taking of sides in that scenario may end up in corporate and boardroom battles.

This shows the tricky nature of the problem of the relation between consultant and client. There is a lot of tempetation to use confidential and insider information to one's advantage that is motivated by greed and power.

Normative Consultant-Client Relations

The maintenance of normative consultant-client relation depends on the institutional structures, the incentives for good behaviour and the incentives for moral hazards.

The role of the regulators and how strictly they enforce the laws is also important here. The individuals themselves consider that they are the ones who are either benefiting or losing out when the scandal breaks out. This factor is a self-governing factor where the consultant decides upon the course of action.

It is also human nature to find it hard to resist the temptations of money and power, but at the same time, it is essential to be true to the professional obligations and the observane of the code of conduct.

Knowledge Management

Knowledge Management (KM) in the field of Human Resource Development is the process of creating, sharing, using and managing the knowledge and information of an organisation.

It is a systematic arrangement and presentation of processes and strategies that enhance the management related to human resource. It is a way to achieve organisational objectives by using and channelising knowledge. It takes into consideration various strategies that improves the organisational set-up.

Knowledge management tells about where and in what form the knowledge exists, what the organisation needs to know, how to generate and acquire knowledge, how to enhance performance, how to allocate work and resources and so on.

According to **JP Girard**, "Knowledge management is the process of creating, sharing, using and managing the knowledge and information of an organisation".

According to **Sunny Liu**, "Knowledge management refers to a multi-disciplined approach to achieving organisational objectives by making the best use of knowledge".

Evolution of KM

The discipline of knowledge management was initiated in 1990s. It is a multi-disciplinary concept that is used in IT, business administration, information systems, management, library and information sciences, media, resarch and Human Resource Management.

Knowledge management his specially developed in the second half of the 20th century with the advent of computers. Specific adaptations of information systems via internet, group decision support system, expert systems, knowledge bases, intranets, computer supported work have been possible through the use of knowledge management.

The emergence of KM was supported by individual practitioners in 1990s. **Leij Edvinsson** of Sweedon was the world's first Chief Knowledge Officer (CKO), who was hired by Skandia. Other important names in this field are Hubert-Saint-Onge, Ikujiro Nonaka and Hirotaka Takeuchi of Hitotsubashi University, Thomas Davenport of Babson College and Baruch Lev of New York University.

Thomas A Stewart is credited with popularising the discipline of knowledge management by publishing a cover story "Intellectual Capitals in Organisations" in 2001, in Fortune magazine. From then onwards, the number of academic journals have increased. At present, there are about 27 outlets of knowledge management journals.

Objectives of KM

Knowledge management is a part of an organisation's strategy. It ensures that an organisation retrieve the knowledge assets whenever it is needed. It is useful to maintain a competitive advantage. *The objectives are as follows*

- To enable an organisation to be more effective in its functions and processes.
- To ensure that the goals of the organisation are realised properly.
- To ensure that all employees have clear and common understanding of the processes in which they are working.
- To provide complete and accurate information whenever needed at any given point of time.
- To provide information from reliable sources and make it available throughout the organisation.
- To maintain an effective and updated knowledge base that can be easily assesssed.
- To enable the organisation in order to maintain a competitive advantage in its structure of knowledge.

- To keep employees informed and encourage innovation wherever possible.
- To ensure that the right kind of information is available to the right kind of people.

Four Stages of KM

The structure of knowledge management can be displayed through four stages, *which are as follows*

Data The first stage of KM is data which is the raw data. The raw form of data is the information that is collected and processed. This data in first stage of KM as it is readily changed to information that can be distributed to team members.

Information Information is the second stage of KM and it is the outcome of the processed raw data. The information must be able to answer the five W's *i.e.* who, what, where, when and why.

Knowledge This is the third stage where information is analysed while considering own experiences into account. The information after analysis becomes knowledge which can be used to make decisions.

Wisdom The acquiring of knowledge which is in conjunction with your experiences, expertise and judgement is transformed into wisdom. Thus, personal judgements form wisdom.

Types of the Knowledge

Understanding different forms of knowledge can help in the process of understanding knowledge management.

These are as follows

Explicit Knowledge This kind of K is formalised, codified and assembled. It is easy to identify, store and retrieve. This knowledge is reviewed, updated and part of it or whole may also be discarded depending upon the need. This knowledge is found in databases, memos, notes and documents. It is also called as know-what.

Tacit Knowledge This kind of K is context dependant, personal in nature and deeply rooted in action. It is largely experience based and is the most valuable source of K. It is also referred as know-how. It is found in the values, attitudes, cultural beliefs, mental models, skills and capabilities.

Embedded Knowledge It refers to the knowledge that is locked in processes, routines, artifacts, structures and cultures. It is embedded either formally through a management initiative or informally by the organisation. The challenges in mapping embedded knowledge varies considerably. The organisation that is able to manage it successfully also enjoys a competitive advantage.

Propositional Knowledge It is also called descriptive or declarative knowledge. It refers to knowing something or having the knowledge of something. For eg-after reading the steps, you know-how to program a computer.

Benefits of KM

KM has become the need of the hour. It reduces costs and enhances productivity. *The benefits of KM are*

Standardise the Processes KM sets standards for an organisation. All the processes going on in human resource management when documented and processed properly than a standard is set. Therefore, it becomes easier to work according to the set standards.

Make Informed Decisions When employees share their experiences about accomplishing a task in an organisation, then other employees can also benefit from it. Access to other experiences and processes helps in smoothening out the present processes which in turn helps to take the right decisions.

Make Fewer Mistakes Sharing the information through proper channels within the organisation will help the employees in many ways. They will make fewer mistakes as they can reap benefits from the experience of others. Mistakes can be learnt which gives greater advantage.

Reduces Time Knowledge management reduces the time taken to accomplish a task. The experiences and information given by coworkers make up the database which can be accessed by everyone. Thus, existing knowledge can help the other people. They can use it without having the need to recreate some related aspects.

Strategies of KM

The strategies for implementing a successful knowledge management program are as follows

Motivate

All actions related to acquiring and managing of knowledge is initiated by providing motivation through incentives, rewards to targeted users.

The first step is to align the organisation with the change in management programs. Second is to establish goals that individuals must strive to achieve and third is motivation to achieve those goals.

Employees can be motivated by opening channels of communication, evaluating performance, close monitoring, providing incentives for meeting objectives, rewarding performances and modeling behav urs to see the expected behaviours. For example, manager can take coffee talk sessions to standardise performance goals, know about monthly reports etc.

Network

KM can be applied by setting-up connections, by sharing, by direct contact and opening all the channels of communication. Network establishes a common link in an organisation to share ideas and experiences. It also improves collaboration within communities that enables people to learn, exchange ideas and discuss views of others.

Building network helps in expanding social circles, builds trust, gains insight and spark new ideas. It facilitates better understanding, collaboration and committment.

Supply Side KM

The supply side of knowledge management includes collection of document and files, capturing information and storing the information into ways that are easily accessible. The supply strategy also includes project databases, skills, documents etc.

They are raw forms of data which are stored for future use. They are expandable, *i.e.* they can be put to various uses after changes. They can be analysed, codified, disseminated, queried, searched, retrieved and reused.

Taking relevant information to be reused reduces the time taken to complete a particular task.

Analyse

Analyse is a strategy of applying the captured knowledge in different ways. The content collected either through supply strategy or processed on their own can be analysed for future use. If can be lengthened, shortened, condensed or summarised depending on the need.

Analysing current data can also be used in new ways, *e.g.* to identify the trends, patterns, practices, relationships and connections between groups. This helps to form newer strategies that suit the present needs of the organisation.

Codify

Codify refers to consolidation of the content that can be collated and processed which can be integrated to yield improve results. The codified materials can be produced to have standard methodologies, reusable materials and repeatable processes.

Codification of data is very helpful as data can be easily found them, tagging content can be useful for discovering connections and collections. Producing a catalogue of official materials, refining knowledge and identifying processes are the examples of codification.

Disseminate

A strategy of knowledge management is to disseminate the information to the targeted sectors and all potential users. To disseminate the knowledge, various ways can be adopted such as publishing of newsletters, sending information via emails, web sites etc. The content can be dispersed through syndication. On the other hand, content can be collected through aggregation by visiting blogs, wikis and podcasts. Personalising of websites is also possible to display relevant information. A knowledge management corner on the intranet page of the organisation, monthly podcasts featuring important issues, interviews, conversations are the examples of dissemination.

Demand

Demand involves searching for people, content, asking questions, retrieving information and submitting queries. Demand driven knowledge management is stimulated by dissemination and is enabled by different resources. It takes advantage of networks, supply, analysis and codification.

Demand driven strategies examples can be located in use of search engines, e-learning systems, threaded discussions and other user specific tools that provide support.

Act

Knowledge management comprises of taking effective actions. Therefore, this strategy works best in situation where action is involved such as making decisions. This is supported by network and analysis. Implementation of change to replicate proven practices and processes that are based on previous experiences.

The action also includes incorporation of knowledge into routine workflow and procedures is a part of the action initiative. Responding to requests, answering questions, using and reusing content are also part of action strategy. Thus, this strategy closely relates to all the previous strategies and associates with each one of it.

Invent

This strategy of knowledge management relates to invention of new products and/or services. It is associated with conceptualising and creation of a new idea. The examples of invent in context of KM is generating new sources of customer demand, stimulating organisational as well as personal growth, rethinking the rules, guidelines etc. This will help an organisation to develop, thrive and endure.

Triggering of imagination to create new processes or new ways to look at things is also part of invent strategy. This facilitates development of new ideas, thoughts, patterns and processes.

Augment

This strategy refers to augmenting the power of observation, analysis, decision-making, processing and responding. The augmentation process can be done to new or to routine tasks and even in challenging situations.

The augmentation strategy is used to extend the ability of humans to understand, decide, act, learn and to avoid problems. Various tools can be used for augmentation such as IBM artificial intelligence tools that are designed for individual use like Google Now, Microsoft Cortona etc. Augmentation stimulates human thought processes as it acts upon the way human brain works.

These ten strategies work best in the situation where knowledge management is applied. The objectives of a company can be realised properly and in the best possible manner by applying knowledge management strategies. These are becoming an essential part of HRM.

These strategies are used for better collaboration between sales services, back office functions, flow of ideas for new products and services and reusing matter, content, old ideas, concepts, in selecting of best practices, analysis of information, reusing wherever applicable, building now products etc.

Human Resource Information System

The Human Resource Information System (HRIS) is a software or online solution provider that is used for data entry, tracking of data, gathering of the data information needed in human resource management, payroll and book keeping related operations of an organisation.

It is a useful tool to collect, track and process the purposeful data. An able HRIS system is required in every organisation.

Reasons for Introducing an HRIS

The CIPD (2007) survey established that the top 10 reasons for introducing an HRIS were

- To improve quality of information available.
- To produce HR metrics.
- To aid human capital reporting.
- To improve productivity.
- To reduce operational costs.
- To reduce administrative burden on the HR department.
- To improve speed at which information is available.
- To improve fexibility of information to support business planning.
- To improve services to employees.
- To manage people's working time more effectively.

Features of HRIS

Use of Software

It is customary to buy software from an external supplier. There is a choice between buying a 'vanilla system' (i.e. an 'off-the-shelf' system without any upgrades) or customize the supplier's system to meet specified business requirements.

Extensive customisation can make future upgrades problematic and expensive, so it is important to limit it to what is absolutely necessary.

Integration

Enterprise Resource Planning (ERP) systems integrate all data and processes of an organisation into a unified system with the same database. HR systems are not frequently integrated to this extent, although they often link payroll administration with other HR functions.

Intranet

An intranet system is one where computer terminals are linked so that they can share information within an organisation or within part of an organisation.

The scope of the information that can be shared across terminals can be limited to preserve confidentiality and this security can be enhanced by using passwords.

Human Resource Self-Service System (HRSS)

It allows managers and employees to access information and the facility to interact with the system to input information or make choices of their own.

This can operate through an HR portal (a site that functions as a point of access to information on the intranet) that may be specially designed to produce a brand image of the HR function. This is sometimes referred to as a Business to Employees (B2E) portal.

HRIS enhancing HR Management

HRIS is geared towards enriching the human resource management systems in an organisation.

It enriches the HR in the following ways

- It simplifies the workflow of the human resource management system by organising it.
- It simplifies the collection of data process which is otherwise a very exhaustive process.
- It absorbs new technology with ease and assimilates it with the existing technologies.
- It optimises precision, brings stability and credibility of the workforce data.
- HRIS is an efficient tool to report, evaluate and administer all staff data.

- HRIS is able to keep an account of company records, staff handbooks and disaster evacuation methods.
- HRIS can also be used as a comprehensive payroll in addition to other accounting system and financial softwares.
- An efficient HRIS helps an organisation to track attendance, pay scale history, personal staff data etc.
- It also helps in the formation of development strategies, disciplinary actions and key succession plans.

Key Considerations for Selecting the Best HRIS

There are many different types of HRIS softwares available. It is important to look for the features that will greatly help in selecting the best HRIS.

An HRIS is a major undertaking for a business. It's selection is challenging as often there are misleading informations are available in the net that greatly influences the choice of an organisation.

The best solution for the business depends upon the specific organisational needs that consist the type of industry, payroll, budget, type of employee etc. *The list of features that needs to be considered to make the right choice of HRIS*

Staff Size

It refers to the workforce, *i.e.* large, small or small to medium workforce. Depending upon the workforce, the appropriate software is chosen. The HRIS eliminates the need of keeping track of spreadsheets or sending emails.

Recruiting and Tracking

An organisation that needs to post job applications is numerous sites and also keep a track of applicants, their corrospondence with the organisation can purchase an HRIS software that has built in applicant tracking system.

The software should be capable of storing and managing of candidates applications and evaluation reports related to questionnaire, aptitude test results, comments of the interviewer, screening of the application and verification of results. HRIS will be able to standardise and automate the process.

Reporting

Organisation should look for a particular HRIS programme that is able to generate reports that can be used to analyse key workforce metrics such as turnovers, compensation history, compliance and training history and performance data.

HRIS provides a central point of management and a consolidate database of employee information. The reports range from individual or personnel data to high level organisational views.

Payroll and Benefits

HRIS automates that various aspects of employee compensation which includes managing salaries, wages, bonuses and superannuation payments based on time, performance reviews, paid time off (sick leave, maternity leave) of the employees responsibilities.

Training and Development

HRIS software schedules, delivers and records each employees' related to the companys' training and compliance programs. HRIS software also ensure new updates, include new curriculum with existing ones and generate specific reports on employee progress. Therefore, the particular HRIS software selected by the organisation should be able to formalise the staff training programs.

Employee Interface

HRIS package selected by the organisation should give employees and managers a basic level of access to HR information. This can be used to update personal information, enter performance review data, download payslips, populate timesheets, apply for leave etc. This is far better than applying in paper forms.

Analytics

The particular HRIS package should be able to deliver a wide range of benefits starting from identifying ways to retain high value employees to helping managers make more strategic decisions during the time of assigning rules and responsibilities. The analytical ability of HRIS is a driving force for its selection.

Inclusions in HRIS

A computerised HRIS software is an integrated system that makes use of computers in exercising control, movement, noting and regulating down all the procedures connected to HR. *It includes the following items*

- Employee name, contact information
- Department, job title
- Grade, salary
- Salary history, position history
- Special qualifications and trainings
- Ethnicity, veteran status
- Benefits, bonuses
- Attendance
- Management and key employee succession plans
- Applicant tracking, interviewing, selection
- Pay hikes and history
- Performance development plans
- Disciplinary actions
- Suspensions, demotions or other negative actions
- Hiring and rehiring details.

EXAM BASED QUESTIONS

1 **HRD can be**

(a) a platform for organisational transformation
(b) a vehicle for global knowledge transfer
(c) Both (a) and (b)
(d) Neither (a) nor (b)

2 **HRD systems or processes may include the following process mechanisms or sub-systems**

(a) career planning, manpower planning and collective bargaining
(b) performance appraisal, motivation and grievance handling
(c) performance appraisal, career planning, organisation development
(d) training and development, communication and quality of work life

3 **In which of the following processes HRD is not needed?**

(a) Implementing a new policy
(b) Deciding to buy the latest machinery
(c) Meeting changes in the organisational development
(d) Changing an organisation's culture

4 **Which of the following can be considered as HRD functions?**

(a) Identifying and imparting training needs
(b) Identifying and selecting the best candidate
(c) Mapping the competency and encouraging the employee
(d) All of the above

5 **On the basis of our understanding about human resource development, which of the following is most important for HRD?**

(a) To be clearly related to the organisation's objectives
(b) To be clearly related to the expertise in the department
(c) To be flexible to be able to respond to sudden crisis
(d) To operate as an extension of the HRM department

6 **Which of the following is not the main objective of human resource development?**

(a) To provide suitable need based training programmes
(b) To evaluate the job and set the wages/salary
(c) To contribute towards the excellence of technical and management education
(d) To motivate the employees in order to show better performance

7 **Modern approach of HR accounting treats human resource as**

(a) expenditure
(b) physical assets
(c) physical liabilities
(d) capital investment

8 **Process of forecasting, developing and controlling human resource in an enterprise, is called as**

(a) HR audit (b) HR control
(c) HR planning (d) HR process

9 **Which of the following term is used to describe the process of helping a new employee to settle quickly into their job so they become efficient and productive workers?**

(a) Job rotation (b) Induction (c) Training (d) [illegible]tion

10 **Which of the following managerial functions contribute to human resource management?**

(a) Recruitment and selection
(b) Performance management, training and development
(c) Retention, industrial relations
(d) All of the above

11 **........ are involved with efforts to improve productivity through changes in employee relations.**

(a) Human resource department
(b) Cultural department
(c) Social awareness department
(d) None of the above

12 **Social attitudes, legal requirements, industrial relations, technological and environmental changes generate the need of ....**

(a) scientific management
(b) social management
(c) human resource development
(d) infrastructure development

13 **........ can be defined as the set of systematic set of activities designed by an organisation to provide its members with the necessary skills to meet current and future job depends.**

(a) Human resource development
(b) Scientific management
(c) Social management
(d) None of the above

14 **Which of the following are the main objectives under which all the outcomes of the efforts done by training and development process can be put under**

(a) individual and organisational objectives
(b) functional and societal objectives
(c) Both (a) and (b)
(d) Neither (a) nor (b)

15 **Planned Development Programmes will return values to the organisation in terms of**

(a) increased productivity (b) reduced costs
(c) high morale (d) All of these

16 Who does not play a key role in the process of training and not entrusted with any responsibility in the entire process?
(a) Top Management Personnel
(b) HR Department/Supervisors
(c) Supervisors/Employees
(d) Customers/Vendors

17 Which of the following are the components or parts of an effective performance management system?
(a) Performance planning
(b) Data gathering, observation and documentation
(c) Performance diagnosis and coaching
(d) All of the above

18 Common uses of information generated *via* performance appraisal include all of the following except
(a) administrative/personal decisions
(b) organisational training and development programme
(c) input to job content evaluation
(d) feedback to individuals performance

19 Successful career planning and development requires action from
(a) the organisation, the employees immediate manager and the employee himself
(b) the employee and his/her immediate manager
(c) a variety of source both internal and external to the organisation
(d) the employee with some assistance/guidance from his or her immediate manager

20 A frequently used method for determining training needs involves
(a) observation analysis conducted by training experts
(b) group discussions with employee groups
(c) individual skill assessment by supervisors
(d) All of the above

21 The ultimate goal of organisational development is to
(a) structure the organisational environment so that managers and employers can use their developed skills and abilities to the fullest
(b) reduce the levels of uncertainty in managerial decision-making throughout the organisation
(c) create an internal environment which is conducive to self expression
(d) change the traditional relationship between the supervisors and subordinates

22 A set of actual data are tried with the model: the result obtained is then checked with what happens in reality. If the result from the model does not conform to be actual situation, the model is adjusted to secure a close resemblance to the actual situation. The procedure described above related to
(a) formulation of a model (b) testing a model
(c) monitoring a model (d) application of a model

23 An experienced employee offering guidance and support to a junior employee so that the latter learns and advances in the organisation is called
(a) mentoring (b) counselling
(c) coaching (d) job instruction training

24 The test, which samples and measures an applicant's knowledge and skills for the purpose of employee selection is termed as
(a) achievement test (b) aptitude test
(c) personality test (d) emotional intelligence

25 Which of the following is not a typically used procedure to reduce the total number of employees?
(a) Layoff
(b) Terminations
(c) Downsizing
(d) Early retirement inducements

26 In which of the following kinds of interview, the questions are predetermined?
(a) Panel (b) Stress
(c) Group (d) Structured

27 Which of the following is the formal rewards provided by organisations that lends itself to being related to performance?
(a) Insurance plans (b) Merit plans
(c) Paid holidays (d) Paid vacations

28 Which of the following can be referred as the best description of learning organisation?
(a) An organisation which helps the managers to get promotions
(b) An organisation which does lots of training sessions on an adhoc basis
(c) An organisation which facilitates the learning of all its members and continuously transfoms itself
(d) An organisation which encourages all its member to learn

29 The method of performance appraisal required to correct the tendency of a rater to give consistently high or low ratings to all the employees is
(a) critical incident technique
(b) behaviourally anchored rating scale
(c) forced choice method
(d) graphic rating scale

30 Which of the following performance appraisal method, rates the appraisee on various parameters on a point scale?
(a) Critical Incident method (b) MBO method
(c) Graphic Rating scale (d) Bell Curve method

31 Which one of the following is not an important feature of effective training plan?
(a) Shorter learning time
(b) Lower costs per participant
(c) Reduced travel cost
(d) Going far-flung places

32 Which of the following is not an important characteristic of an effective trainer?

(a) Having good diagnostic skills
(b) Having good physical features
(c) Having good range of technical skills
(d) Having good interpersonal and judgemental skills

33 Total training cost include

(a) participants ongoing salaries
(b) overheads during training
(c) cost of R and D in training needs analysis
(d) All of the above

34 A retrenchment strategy is used to reduce

(a) technical losses
(b) financial losses
(c) the scale and scope of the business operation
(d) All of the above

35 Which of the following is not an objective of modern performance appraisal system?

(a) Salary increase (b) Identifying training needs
(c) Punishing the employees (d) Promotion decision

36 The work performed, responsibility involved and the skill and training required is present with

(a) development plans (b) marketing plans
(c) financial plans (d) None of these

37 Task analysis is a component of

(a) selection procedure
(b) human resource planning
(c) training process
(d) None of the above

38 A performance rating system is

(a) a grade or score relating to overall performance
(b) financial targets accomplished during the year
(c) attendance of the individual during the year
(d) None of the above

39 Performance management should be seen as a process which is a

(a) once a year task
(b) twice a year activity
(c) ongoing process or cycle
(d) engaged in when the appraisals are carried out

40 Which of the following provides a set of rights, responsibilities and obligations that structure the behaviour of the employer and the employee?

(a) The employment contract
(b) The financial contract
(c) The ethical contract
(d) Any of the above

41 Many a times in the organisations, the schemes that reward employees for their better performance, fail because

(a) management does not take timely action
(b) the link between extra pay and performance is unclear
(c) undue politics prevail
(d) they do not compliance with trade union agreements

42 The time scale for performance appraisals are

(a) annually
(b) biannually
(c) monthly
(d) weekly

43 Training and development helps to achieve

(a) personal goals
(b) group goals
(c) organisational goals
(d) All of the above

44 Which of the following statement clearly denotes the meaning of the word 'Appraisal'?

(a) A system used to improve the performance of personnel
(b) The main way in which employees wages are determined
(c) The evaluation of an individual employee's performance over a given period of time
(d) None of the above

45 Sensitivity training is a part of

(a) in-house development
(b) behaviour modeling
(c) organisational development
(d) None of the above

46 In house development centres usually

(a) combine class-room learning with, in-basket exercises
(b) combine class-room training with behaviour modeling
(c) combine behaviour modeling with in-basket exercises
(d) None of the above

47 Which of the following strategy, the managing director of the company will adopt in order to cope up with the problem of quitting the job by an employee after being trained as one gets lucrative offer from the competitors of the present employer?

(a) Increase the recruitment and training budgets
(b) Stop training the employees
(c) Increase the salary comparable to competitors
(d) Redesign jobs to make skills and training more specific to the needs of the firm

48 Which of the following is responsible to make some organisations more successful than others?

(a) Creating vibrant organisational culture
(b) Recruiting highly qualified and experienced people
(c) Spending lots of money on training and development
(d) Creating management systems to ensure high performance from everyone

49 In which of the following ways organisations are benefitted through training and development?

(a) It leads to profitability
(b) It improves relationship between employer and employee
(c) It improves the job knowledge and skills at all levels of the organisaton
(d) All of the above

50 **Which of the following is not a way of benefit to an individual working in an organisation through training and development?**
(a) It helps the individual in making better decisions and effective problem solving
(b) It aids in achieving self-development and self-confidence
(c) It helps in increasing the bank deposit of an individual
(d) It helps in improving leadership and communication skills

51 **Who of the following has defined performance appraisal as follows: "It is the process of evaluating the performance of employees, sharing that information with them and searching for ways to improve their performance."**
(a) Newstrom (b) Keith and Davis
(c) Flippo (d) TV Rao

52 **Which of the following cannot be considered as the objective of performance appraisal?**
(a) To provide feedback to the employees regarding their past performance
(b) To take decisions related to increments
(c) To take decisions related to overall objectives of the organisation
(d) To judge the effectiveness of the other human resource functions such as recruitment, selection, training and development

53 **Which of the following are the main reasons for re-designing jobs to have better quality of work life?**
(a) Classical design originally gave inadequate attention to human needs
(b) The needs and aspirations of workers themselves were changing
(c) Both (a) and (b)
(d) Neither (a) nor (b)

54 **Which of the following is not an advantage of quality circles?**
(a) Rise organisational morale
(b) Promote job involvement
(c) Help and provide information to determine job analysis
(d) Improve communication within the organisation

55 **Which of the following are the principles of quality circles?**
(a) Employees want to show excellent performance and want to be recognised
(b) Employees want to be well informed about organisational goals and problems
(c) Both (a) and (b)
(d) Neither (a) nor (b)

56 **Which of the following are the most determinant of quality of work life?**
(a) Career achievement
(b) Career satisfaction
(c) Career balance
(d) All of the above

57 **Which of the following aspect of job cannot be considered under quality of work life?**
(a) Freedom and autonomy to make decisions on the job
(b) Freedom and autonomy to leave work place without taking permission from the superiors
(c) Satisfactory physical surroundings
(d) Job satisfaction and job safety

58 **Which of the following psychological growth needs were described by Hackman and Oldham to the consideration of quality of working life?**
(a) Skill variety and task variety
(b) Task significance
(c) Autonomy and feedback
(d) All of the above

59 **Career planning is**
(a) leaving the decisions to seniors and parents
(b) getting information and not taking timely decision
(c) going along with peers and other personal relations
(d) exploring and taking decision in congruence with one's own self

60 **Which of the following is not a part of basic seven quality control tools?**
(a) Check sheets and pareto chart
(b) Ishikawa diagram, scatter, plot
(c) Flow diagram, histogram, control chart
(d) Correlation and regression

61 **Which of the following factors need to be considered while designing a training programme?**
(a) Purpose of the training
(b) Identification of employee and trainer
(c) Physical features of employee selected
(d) Method of training

62 **........ is the another name of performance appraisal.**
(a) Performance evaluation
(b) Motivation
(c) Performance controlling
(d) None of the above

63 **Which of the following are the sources of knowledge/skill acquisition?**
(a) Organisation itself
(b) Combination of internal and external sources
(c) Special training schools and corporate universities
(d) All of the above

64 **The older name for performance appraisal is also described as .... in which one individual is ranked in comparison to others.**
(a) number method (b) task method
(c) ranking method (d) None of these

65 **........ is the most common and the oldest method of training in crafts, trades and technical areas.**
(a) Tradesmanship (b) Training
(c) Apprenticeship (d) None of these

66 **Which of the following is not a limitation of career planning?**
(a) Is not relevant due to rapid changes in government policies
(b) Is not effective in small organisations
(c) Is not useful in taking decisions related to filling the vacancies well in time
(d) Lots of other economical, political factors intervene

67 **......... refers to a permanent team that normally meets from time to time to uncover as well as solve problems in work place.**
(a) Quality aspect (b) Total quality
(c) Quality circle (d) None of these

68 **In .... type of performance appraisal, the various sources of inputs are from the superiors, peers, customers vendor and the employee himself.**
(a) 360 degrees (b) 180 degrees
(c) 270 degrees (d) 90 degrees

69 **......... developed BARS (Behaviourally Anchored Rating Scales) one of the kinds of performance appraisal.**
(a) Adam Smith (b) Smith Kendall
(c) Charles Beffage (d) None of these

70 **......... identified more programmatically few basic extrinsic as well as intrinsic essential components of quality of working life.**
(a) Taylor (b) Henry Fayol
(c) William Wordsworth (d) Charles Babbage

71 **......... is not a unilary concept incorporated only with hierarchy of perspectives such as job satisfaction, pay structure etc but also factors that broadly reflect life satisfaction and general feelings of well-being.**
(a) Quality of person
(b) Quality of work life
(c) Quality of human
(d) None of these

72 **The major focus of .... is to match personal goals and opportunities that are realistically available.**
(a) carrer planning (b) controlling
(c) settlement of dispute (d) None of these

73 **......... is the process of managing, coaching, developing and evaluating employees.**
(a) Performance appraisal (b) Motivation
(c) Back up (d) None of these

74 **Which of the following ways contribute towards improving quality of work life?**
(a) Quality circles
(b) Management by objectives
(c) Suggestion system
(d) All of the above

75 **......... is the best method to improve interpersonal skills, ability to comprehend and present himself effectively in short period of time.**
(a) Group discussion (b) Seminar
(c) Coaching (d) None of these

76 **......... gave the different aspects to quality of work life.**
(a) Richard Walton (b) Charles Baffage
(c) Bill Gates (d) None of these

77 **The .... gives an opportunity to an employee to showcase his talent to the fullest and make his reach to the other departments also.**
(a) job rotation (b) vestibule training
(c) coaching (d) None of these

78 **The main advantage of .... is that they help in the generation of creative ideas as the happy and contented person can only be creative.**
(a) quality circle
(b) quality improvement programme
(c) quaility management
(d) None of the above

79 **......... must find out the ways to satisfy worker's needs at least through non-monetary benefits, if monetary benefits are not in their hands.**
(a) Union leader (b) Government
(c) Management (d) None of these

80 **The multiple management technique of management development programme was developed by ....**
(a) Charles PMC Cormick
(b) Charles Babbage
(c) Mike Thompson
(d) None of these

81 **Which of the following is a characteristic of action research?**
(a) Results are generalised
(b) Data is usually qualitative
(c) Variables are tightly controlled
(d) Results show cause effect relationship

82 **Who said "action research is a process of systematically collecting research data about an ongoing system relative to some objective, goal or need of that system"?**
(a) Kurt Lewin
(b) D Conback
(c) Henry Fayol
(d) JC Collins

83 **Which is not an assumption of action-research?**
(a) Results enable to evaluate performance of others
(b) Researchers have basic research skills to analyse data
(c) Professionals need and want feedback on their performance
(d) People are capable of assuming responsibility for their own professional growth

84 All are true statements about action research except
(a) results are generalised
(b) data systematically organised
(c) data collected systematically
(d) results are used to improve practice

85 Which phase of action research model is also called input phase?
(a) Changing phase (b) Refreezing phase
(c) Unfreezing phase (d) None of these

86 The prevailing atmosphere that exists in the HR department of an organisation and its impact is termed as
(a) performance appraisals
(b) HR climate
(c) corporate culture
(d) job restructuring

87 Reflex Inc. decides to allow its front line workers to take decisions related to ordering of certain supplies that were initially done by managers. This initiative is an example of what?
(a) A change in organisational climate
(b) Workplace incentives
(c) Employee empowerment
(d) Management development

88 Influences of external environment having direct/ indirect influence on HRM includes which among the following?
(a) Labour market conditions
(b) HR culture
(c) HR climate
(d) Decreasing workforce diversity

89 In the OCTAPACE culture the letter 'C' denotes what?
(a) Climate (b) Culture
(c) Communication (d) Confrontation

90 Which is not a characteristic of an organisation culture?
(a) Attention to detail (b) Innovation
(c) Assertiveness (d) Risk taking

91 Which is not a function of organisation culture?
(a) A sense of identity
(b) Stable social system
(c) Generation of commitment
(d) Acceptance of diversity

92 Which is not associated with organisation with high ethical standards?
(a) High in risk tolerance (b) High aggressiveness
(c) High in innovation (d) Focus on means

93 Employees view the behaviour of ...... as a benchmark for defining appropriate behaviour.
(a) new employees (b) top management
(c) immediate supervisor (d) old employees

94 The conditions essential for an effective HR audit is/are
(a) clarity of HR objectives
(b) top managements commitment
(c) regularity and continuity
(d) All of the above

95 Which among the following is normally not considered for HR audit?
(a) Details about exit and other interviews
(b) Job specification and job description
(c) Hiring policies and practices
(d) None of the above

96 What is not true about HR audit?
(a) It is done by internal employees
(b) It is done by external consultants
(c) It is statuary requirement
(d) It establishes a benchmark for performance measuring

97 Which of the following is responsible for establishing an entity's internal controls?
(a) Management
(b) Auditors
(c) Committee of sponsoring organisations
(d) Management and auditors

98 Which is not one main reason, why the auditor should properly plan engagements?
(a) To enable the auditor to obtain sufficient competent evidence
(b) To avoid misunderstandings with the client
(c) To keep audit costs reasonable
(d) To enable proper on-the-job training of employees

99 Questionnaire, personal interviews and observations are which part of HR audit?
(a) Setting benchmarks (b) Giving feedback
(c) Creating action plans (d) Data gathering

100 The expectation of consultants and clients from each other are taken into consideration in which stage of action-research model?
(a) Diagnosis (b) Consulting
(c) Entering (d) Contracting

101 Practitioners of organisational development need to gain clarity about the relevance of change effort to the client system in order to prevent
(a) coercion
(b) technical ineptness
(c) misrepresentation of problem
(d) value and goals conflict

102 Which of the following is most suitable for different place, same time conditions in knowledge sharing process ?
(a) Face-to-face meeting
(b) Peer-to-peer shared computer
(c) Video confrencing
(d) Emailing and chatting

103 Which of the following is a feature of knowledge capturing?
(a) Choosing the right expert (b) Taping knowledge
(c) Determining feasibility (d) All of these

104 .... is the relevant group involved in the change program of degree to which the client system is organised.
(a) Indentification (b) Evaluation
(c) Organisation (d) Covention

105 Knowledge stored in the form of manuals indicates which characteristic of knowledge?
(a) Codify (b) Analyse
(c) Diffusible (d) Expandable

106 Which is not a component of KM ?
(a) Technology (b) Currency
(c) Internal portal (d) Processes

107 Which of the following donot includes a dimension of knowledge management?
(a) Price (b) People
(c) Processes (d) Products

108 Which of the following strategy options will use data from the knowledge audit to develop employee profiles ?
(a) E-learning (b) Expertise database
(c) Intranet (d) Corporate portal

109 All are parts of European knowledge management framework except
(a) develop knowledge (b) create knowledge
(c) share knowledge (d) capture knowledge

110 Knowledge workers require which of the following?
(a) Powerful graphics (b) Analytical tools
(c) External databases (d) All of these

111 The set of processes developed in an organisation to create, gather, store, transfer and apply knowledge describes
(a) Organisational memory (b) Knowledge processes
(c) Knowledge management (d) Knowledge assets

112 Information systems can also provide knowledge networks for linking people so that .... knowledge can be shared.
(a) explicit knowledge (b) embedded knowledge
(c) tacit knowledge (d) propositional knowledge

113 Which is not normally an essential condition for an effective HRIS?
(a) Changing the HR manager
(b) Sustained enhancement of HRIS capabilities
(c) Ensuring clarity of goals related to HRIS
(d) Strengthening infrastructure and support systems

114 Which is not an advantage of HRIS?
(a) Better supervision (b) Control over HR
(c) Manage voluminous data (d) None of these

115 Which among the following is a subsystem of HRIS?
(a) Budgeting system
(b) Compensation management system
(c) Performance management system
(d) All of the above

116 The purpose of selection of employees is influenced by
(a) Principles and programmes
(b) Rules and regulations
(c) Strategies and objectives
(d) None of the above

117 The purpose of any human resource information system is to
(a) replace human decision making with computerised decision making
(b) provide data and data summarises (statistical analysis) that are error free
(c) assist management in decision-making
(d) reduce the number of low-level support staff

118 System designed to provide useful information while making decisions regarding HR is classified as
(a) HRIS
(b) KM
(c) HR Planning
(d) Decisional informational system

119 Which test acts as an instrument to discover the inherent ability of the candidate?
(a) Physical test (b) Psychological test
(c) Attitude test (d) Aptitude test

120 The automation of the processes of attendance keeping, applicant tracking and payroll preparation are activities that are carried out at
(a) decision support system
(b) electronic data processing
(c) management information system
(d) None of the above

121 Which is the best explanation of HRIS?
(a) An information management system that allows employees to access their personnel information
(b) A database used to store information for HR purposes
(c) A system to acquire, store, retrive and analyse HR
(d) A computer system to manage information relevant to HR

122 The flow of management information system is
(a) need dependent (b) management dependent
(c) organisation dependent (d) information dependent

123 The components of information system should be made-up only of information units that enhance effective ....
(a) project management
(b) human resource decision
(c) personnel management decision
(d) None of the above

124 Arrange the following sentences related to the process of succession planning in proper sequence.

1. Identification of areas where development is necessary.
2. Assessment of individuals who have potential for filing the position.
3. Identification of the KSAs or competencies required for the CEO position.
4. A plan to provide individual with opportunities to develop improvement requing areas.

Codes

(a) 3, 2, 1, 4 (b) 1, 2, 3, 4
(c) 2, 1, 3, 4 (d) 4, 3, 1, 2

125 Arrange the steps in manpower planning in the order in which they occur

1. identifying sources of manpower supply
2. manpower forecasting
3. determining manpower requirements
4. manpower invently
5. selection
6. recruitment
7. placement

Codes

(a) 3, 2, 4, 1, 6, 5, 7 (b) 1, 3, 2, 4.5, 6, 7
(c) 4, 1, 2, 3, 6, 5, 7 (d) 3, 4, 1, 2, 6, 5, 7

126 What is the correct order of the following phases of training?

1. Development Phase 2. Design Phase
3. Need Analysis Phase 4. Implementation Phase
5. Evaluation Phase

Codes

(a) 3, 2, 1, 4, 5 (b) 2, 1, 3, 5, 4
(c) 3, 4, 1, 2, 5 (d) 4, 2, 1, 3, 5

127 Find the right sequence of Kurt Lewin's planned change

1. Unfreezing, changing, refreezing
2. Refreezing, moving, unfreezing
3. Changing, refreezing, unfreezing

Codes

(a) 2, 3, 1 (b) 1, 2, 3
(c) 3, 2, 1 (d) None of these

128 Which of the following statement(s) is/are correct?

I Potential appraisal and performance management are HRD mechanisms.

II Personnel function is maintenance oriented while HRD is development oriented.

(a) Both are incorrect
(b) I is correct, II is incorrect
(c) Both are correct
(d) I is incorrect, II is correct

129 Which of the following statement(s) is/are correct?

I knowledge management is the process of creating, sharing, using and managing the knowledge and information of an organisation.

II OCTAPACE is a technique of knowledge management.

(a) Both are incorrect
(b) I is correct, II is incorrect
(c) Both are correct
(d) I is incorrect, II is correct

130 Which of the following statement(s) is/are correct?

I HRD instruments : Lead to the generation of HRD process like role clarity, performance planning etc.

II HRD outcome : These include performance appraisal, counselling, role analysis etc.

(a) Both are incorrect
(b) I is correct, II is incorrect
(c) Both are correct
(d) I is incorrect, II is correct

131 Which of the following statement(s) is/are correct?

I HRA measurement process facilitates to increase recognition that human capital is vital to the organisation's short-term and long-term productivity and expansion.

II Consultants are expected to maintain professional and ethical standards when dealing with their clients.

(a) Both are incorrect (b) I is correct, II is incorrect
(c) Both are correct (d) I is incorrect, II is correct

132 Which of the following statements are true/false?

1. Leadership development programmes, assessment and development centres are types of potential appraisal methods.
2. Top management style and personnel policies affect the HRD climate.
3. HRD system must try to develop a habit of the team work among human resource.

Codes

(a) 1 is true, 2 and 3 are false
(b) 1 and 2 are true, 3 is false
(c) 2 is true, 1 and 3 are false
(d) All are true

133 Which of the following statements are true?

1. Digital dashboards, empowerment are methods of HRD.
2. It is believed that human supply are heterogeneous as each human is different from one another.
3. The Lev and Schwartz model calculates the present value of estimated future earnings.
4. The economic value approach of HRA has been given by Schwartz.

Codes

(a) 1, 2 and 3 are true, 4 is false
(b) 1 and 2 are true, 3 and 4 are false
(c) 3 is true, 1, 2 and 4 are false
(d) 2 and 3 are true, 1 and 4 are false

134 Assertion (A) HRD provides a comprehensive framework for the overall personality of each and every person in the organisation.

Reason (R) A better trained and educated workforce is well aware of its rights and is better able to protect against human right violation.

(a) Both (A) and (R) are correct and (R) explains (A)
(b) Both (A) and (R) are correct, but (R) does not explain (A)
(c) (A) is true, (R) is false
(d) (A) is false, (R) is true

135 Assertion (A) HRD climate of an organisation plays a very important role in ensuring the competency, motivation and development of its employees.

Reason (R) The elements of HRD climate can be grouped into OCTAPAC culture, HRD mechanism and general climate.

(a) Both (A) and (R) are correct and (R) explains (A)
(b) Both (A) and (R) are correct, but (R) does not explain (A)
(c) (A) is true, (R) is false
(d) (A) is false, (R) is true

136 Assertion (A) HRIS can be used for training received, pay grades, performance development plans, attendance etc.

Reason (R) HRIS is a software and offline solution for the data entry, data tracking and data information needs of HR payroll etc.

(a) Both (A) and (R) are correct and (R) explains (A)
(b) Both (A) and (R) are correct, but (R) does not explain (A)
(c) (A) is true, (R) is false
(d) (A) is false, (R) is true

Directions (Q. Nos. 137 and 138) *In the questions given below are two statements labelled as Assertion (A) and Reason (R). In the context of two statements, which of the following is correct?*

Codes
(a) (R) is correct, but (A) is not correct
(b) (A) is correct, but (R) is not correct
(c) Both (A) and (R) are correct
(d) Both (A) and (R) are not correct

137 Assertion (A) One cannot be sure that the quality of appraisal is related on the basis of length of service.

Reason (R) Initial appraisal and promotion appraisal are done separately and differently since length of service is different.

138 Assertion (A) Recruitment is positive while selection is negative in its application.

Reason (R) Recruitment aims at increasing the job seekers while selection rejects a large number of unqualified applicants.

139 Match the following.

List I	List II
A. Achievement test	1. Testing verbal comprehension, word fluency, memory
B. Intelligence test	2. Testing the knowledge about the claims
C. Personality test	3. Testing one's level of interest in an area
D. Aptitude test	4. Testing about inter-personal competence, leadership, confidence
E. Interest test	5. Testing the ability to do a specific job

Codes

	A	B	C	D	E
(a)	2	1	4	5	3
(b)	5	4	3	2	1
(c)	1	2	3	4	5
(d)	3	2	4	5	1

140 Match the following.

List I	List II
A. Training	1. Indentification of hidden talents and skills for future possibilities
B. Career planning	2. Process of learning skills and abilities
C. Potential appraisal	3. Sequence of related work activities to provide continuity
D. Rewards	4. Way of recognising the efforts

Codes

	A	B	C	D		A	B	C	D
(a)	3	4	2	1	(b)	2	1	4	3
(c)	2	3	1	4	(d)	1	2	4	3

Directions (Q. Nos. 141-145) *Read the following passage and answer the questions that follow.*

People differ in their abilities and their aptitudes. There is always some difference between the quality and of the same work on the same job being done by two different people. Performance appraisals of employess are necessary to understand each employee's abilities, competencies and relative merit and worth for the organisation. Performance appraisal rates the employees in terms of their performance.

Performance appraisals are widely used in the society. The history can be dated back to the 20th century and then to the Second World War when the merit rating was used for the first time. An employer evaluating their employees is a very old concept. It is an indispensable part of performance measurement. Performance appraisal is necessary to measure the performance of the employees and the organisation to check the progress towards the desired goals and aims.

The latest mantra being followed by organisations across the world being–"get paid according to what you contribute"–the focus of the organisation is turning to performance management and specifically to individual performance. Performance appraisal helps to rate the performance of the employees and evaluate their contribution towards the organisation goals. If the process of performance appraisals is formal and properly structured, it helps the employees to clearly understand their roles and responsibilities and give direction to the individual's performance. It helps to align the individual performance with the organisational goals and also review their performance.

Performance appraisal takes into account the past performance of the employees and focuses on the improvement of the future performance of the employees.

141 According to this passage,

(a) there is always some difference between the quality and quantity of the same work on the same job being done by two different people
(b) there is no difference between the quality and quantity of the same work on the same job being done by two different people
(c) there is always some similarities between the quality and quantity of the same work on the same job being done by two different people
(d) there is sometime difference between the quality and quantity of the same work on the same job being done by two different people

142 Performance appraisal is necessary

(a) to measure the deficiencies of the employees and the organisation to check the points where a blame can be imposed upon the employees on their improper performance
(b) to keep the employees under strict control according to the objectives of the organisation
(c) to enhance the performance of the employees and the organisation to check the progress towards the desired goals and aims
(d) to measure the performance of the employees and the organisation to check the progress towards the desired goals and aims

143 The latest mantra being followed by organisation across the world

(a) "get paid according to what you contribute."
(b) "get paid according to your power and connections with superiors."
(c) "get paid according to the recommendations of political leaders."
(d) "get paid according to the prescriptions given by the government."

144 Performance appraisal takes into account

(a) the expected performance of the employees and focuses on the improvement of the future performance of the employees
(b) the past performance of the employees and focuses on the improvement of the future performance of the employees
(c) the desired performance of the employees and focuses on the improvement of the future performance of the employees
(d) the past performance of the employees and focuses on the deficiencies of the performance of the employees

145 If the process of performance appraisal is formal and properly structured

(a) it helps the employees to clearly understand their roles and responsibilities and give direction to the individual's performance
(d) it helps the employers to clearly understand their roles and responsibilities of the employees and give direction for their performance
(c) it helps the government to clearly understand the rule and policies applied in the organisation
(d) it helps the organisation to understand the policies and rules and regulations for industries adopted by the Government

PREVIOUS YEARS' QUESTIONS

2018

1 **The general pattern of behaviour, shared beliefs and values that organisation members have in common is called**

(a) Organisational Climate
(b) Organisational Culture
(c) Organisational Effectiveness
(d) Organisational Structure

2 **According to which of the following methods of human resource accounting present value of future earning of human resources is taken into account?**

(a) Standard cost method
(b) Economic value method
(c) Opportunity cost method
(d) Replacement cost method

2017

3 **Read this small passage on HRD and answer questions at the end by choosing appropriate answer from the given alternatives.**

HRD is a competence building exercise through which people everywhere (of the world, of the nation, and of the organisation) are enabled to recognise their potential so as to utilise their capabilities and available resources and opportunities equitably for not only their own development, but also development of their organisations, Nations and the world on a sustainable basis.

Which of the following statements picked up from the passage is/are true or false?

A. It talks about Macro and Micro level HRD.
B. At macro level, it encompasses world and national development.
C. It highlights the contents of HRD vividly.
D. At all levels, HRD aims at sustainable development.

Codes

(a) A, B are true, C, D are false
(b) A, B, D are true, C is false
(c) A, B, C are true, D is false
(d) All the statements are true

4 **Which of the following statements about HR scorecard are true?**

A. Measurement is central to HR score-card.
B. HR architecture inclusive of sum of HR function; the broader HR system and the resulting employee behaviour is crucial to HR score-card.
C. Measurements generally include total compensation, cost per hire, employer, job satisfaction levels, appraisal categories etc.
D. Capability, commitment, competencies, learning outcomes are difficult to be measured resulting into a difference between 'what is measured' and 'what is important' in HR.

Codes

(a) A and D (b) A, C and D
(c) A, B and D (d) A, B, C and D

5 **The HRD matrix linking HRD subsystems to development dimensions has been advanced by**

(a) Dharani P Sinha (b) DM Pestonjee
(c) Udai Pareek (d) TV Rao

6 **Which of the following statement (s) is/are true ?**

A. Configurational or bundle theorists propose that there are ideal types of configurations of HR practices that promote synergies.
B. High performance work systems combining information sharing, decentralised decision-making via teams, participative management at operational, tactical and strategic levels are, however not part of the configurational framework.

Codes

(a) Only A (b) Only B
(c) Both A and B (d) Neither A nor B

Directions (Q. Nos. 7-14) *Read the following passage and answer the questions that follow.*

The past decade has upset many preconceptions about development and this, more than anything else, makes it difficult to be overly definite about what the next decade has in store. But there are a few things that one can assert with some confidence. First, education, health and productive employment are crucial both for growth and for equity. We have tended to assume that all of these are the consequences of rapid economic growth and that only growth can generate the resources required for these purposes. But, increasingly, it appears that these are better seen as the causes rather than as consequences of development.

Virtually every case of successful development involves a prior improvement in literacy, technical skills, health status and access to productive work. Second, technological competence is the most important resource endowment and it explains a far large proportion of growth in output and trade than more conventional factors like natural resources or capital accumulation.

The competence required is not just in research. In fact technological dynamism in the factory and the farm is more important than the presence of large research establishment. Third, the environmental imperative can no longer be ignored. Today, as an international issue, it is second only to disarmament. Nationally, the developmental consequences of environmental neglect are increasingly obvious. In the Indian context, there are atleast two further factors which reinforce the above propositions. The first is population growth. Given the pace of expansion of the population and the work force, human resource development acquires an added urgency. Population growth is also one, but not necessarily the most important factor, which underlines environmental stress in rural and urban areas. The second factor is that as a large country, we cannot carve out an independent position in the global system without building up a substantial capacity for self-reliant growth.

The acquisition of technical competence is crucial for this purpose. Until now we have tended to treat human resource development, technology and environment as subsidiary to the main task of planning. The thrust has been on-quantitative expansion of infrastructure and production with a focus on targets like tonnes of steel, KWH of electricity etc, capacity targets like road length, rail kilometres; and coverage targets like number of schools and students, number of villages electrified etc, catching up with known technologies-fuller use of natural resources – maximum mobilisation of financial resources.

7 What seems to be the purpose of the author in writing this passage?

(a) To appreciate the steps taken by our Government in the past and doubts about the future
(b) To show how the policy makers have failed
(c) A review of world affairs with special emphasis on developed countries
(d) To prove how his predictions have turned out to be correct

8 According to the author, at the national level, with passage of time, the effects of which of the following are being felt?

(a) Lack of attention and action for protecting environmental wealth
(b) Reduction in growth rate of population
(c) Progressive degradation of technological competence in urban areas
(d) Emphasis on slow rate of disarmament as compared to other nations

9 What seems to be the approach of the author regarding present status of research?

A. He desires that more research establishments should come up.
B. Application of new technologies in factories and field is more vital than setting up of research laboratories.

Codes

(a) Only A (b) Only B
(c) Neither A nor B (d) Both A and B

10 According to the author, which of the following is a less important factor resulting in environmental stress in rural and urban areas?

(a) Rapid economic growth
(b) Availability of productive employment
(c) Rate of growth of population
(d) Continued environmental neglect

11 According to the passage, we have so far placed more emphasis on which of the following?

(a) More use of available natural resources
(b) Increased number of basic facilities and meeting number targets
(c) Maximum utilisation of available finances
(d) Following known technologies

12 Which of the following statements is not true in the context of the passage?

(a) We have to now emphasise on aspects of human resource development
(b) Technological competence has to be given due priority over more conventional factors
(c) We cannot afford to ignore the importance of environment
(d) We will have bright future by only catching up with known technologies

13 According to the passage, which is not viewed as cause of development?

(a) Betterment in health services
(b) Increase in underdevelopment
(c) Enhancement in technical skills
(d) Improvement in literacy

14 In his book "The Time Bind : When Home becomes work and work becomes Home", Arlie Hochschild highlights the danger of total integration between work and home leading to either 'workholics' or 'work busters'. The first neglecting the family and realising it too late. The second 'soldering' on work compromising with efficiency.

From the above observation, which of the following inferences can be drawn?

A. Home becoming work and work becoming home is an ideal condition.
B. Home becoming work and work becoming home may create 'workholics' who are good employees and bad home-makers resulting into family break-down.
C. Employee 'soldering' means taking the job easy leading to inadequate performance.
D. The passage advocates for work-life balance.

Codes

(a) B, C and D (b) A, B and C
(c) A, C and D (d) A, B, C and D

2015

15 **Knowledge management refers to**
(a) providing the best skills to employees through planned training programmes
(b) capturing, developing, sharing and using organisational knowledge
(c) creating data bank of information about employees and customers
(d) gathering information from employees for bringing planned change

16 **Assertion** (A) Culture refers to a set of values, rules and standards among generations and are aimed at modelling behaviours so that they fall within acceptable limits.

Reason (R) Cultural norms play important role in determining values because individuals anchor their conduct in the culture of the group to which they belong.

Codes
(a) Both (A) and (R) are not correct
(b) Both (A) and (R) are correct, but (R) does not explain (A)
(c) Both (A) and (R) are correct, but (R) explains (A)
(d) (A) is wrong and (R) is correct

2014

17 **Who is the propagator of Human Capital Approach to Human Resource Development?**
(a) Lim Teck Ghee
(b) Lorraine Corner
(c) TW Schultz
(d) FD Lawrence

18 **Potential effectiveness of a person in both personal and interpersonal situations while in performance in a position is known as**
(a) role effectiveness
(b) role efficacy
(c) role making
(d) role linking

19 **Which of the following statements about Human Resource Development is not true?**
(a) It is an enabling process
(b) It is a competence building exercise
(c) It shall be implemented in an incremental way with geographical, vertical, functional and sophisticating phasing
(d) It does not cover the global and country level Human Resource Development practices

ANSWERS

Exam Based Questions

1 (c)	2 (c)	3 (b)	4 (d)	5 (a)	6 (b)	7 (b)	8 (c)	9 (b)	10 (d)
11 (a)	12 (c)	13 (a)	14 (c)	15 (d)	16 (d)	17 (d)	18 (c)	19 (a)	20 (c)
21 (a)	22 (b)	23 (c)	24 (b)	25 (c)	26 (d)	27 (b)	28 (c)	29 (c)	30 (c)
31 (d)	32 (b)	33 (d)	34 (c)	35 (c)	36 (a)	37 (c)	38 (a)	39 (c)	40 (a)
41 (b)	42 (a)	43 (d)	44 (c)	45 (c)	46 (a)	47 (d)	48 (d)	49 (d)	50 (c)
51 (a)	52 (c)	53 (c)	54 (c)	55 (c)	56 (d)	57 (b)	58 (d)	59 (d)	60 (d)
61 (c)	62 (a)	63 (d)	64 (c)	65 (c)	66 (c)	67 (c)	68 (a)	69 (b)	70 (a)
71 (a)	72 (a)	73 (a)	74 (d)	75 (a)	76 (a)	77 (a)	78 (a)	79 (a)	80 (a)
81 (b)	82 (a)	83 (a)	84 (a)	85 (c)	86 (b)	87 (a)	88 (a)	89 (d)	90 (c)
91 (d)	92 (b)	93 (d)	94 (b)	95 (d)	96 (c)	97 (a)	98 (d)	99 (d)	100 (d)
101 (c)	102 (c)	103 (d)	104 (a)	105 (d)	106 (b)	107 (a)	108 (b)	109 (a)	110 (d)
111 (a)	112 (c)	113 (a)	114 (d)	115 (d)	116 (c)	117 (c)	118 (a)	119 (b)	120 (b)
121 (d)	122 (a)	123 (b)	124 (a)	125 (a)	126 (a)	127 (b)	128 (c)	129 (b)	130 (a)
131 (c)	132 (d)	133 (a)	134 (b)	135 (a)	136 (a)	137 (d)	138 (c)	139 (a)	140 (c)
141 (a)	142 (d)	143 (a)	144 (b)	145 (a)					

Previous Years' Questions

1 (b)	2 (b)	3 (b)	4 (d)	5 (d)	6 (a)	7 (b)	8 (a)	9 (b)	10 (c)
11 (b)	12 (d)	13 (b)	14 (a)	15 (b)	16 (c)	17 (b)	18 (b)	19 (d)	

International Human Resource Management

Companies rely on IHRM to deal with golbal HR challenges. This chapter highlights various methods and models used by multinationals for managing their employees effectively.

Globalisation

Recently, globalisation has led to integration of economies and the businesses have realised that without attention to foreign markets and competitors their prosperity and very survival may be at stake. Thus, organisations are going international to capitalise on the opportunities in terms of wider market, cheaper resources and favourable policies. There are various types of organisations that work at international level. *They are as follows*

International Company

Such company transports its business outside home country and each of its operations is a replication of the company's domestic experience. It is geographically structured and involves subsidiary general managers. International companies have no Foreign Direct Investments (FDI) and make their product or service only in their home country.

In other words, they're exporters and importers. They have no staff, warehouses or sales offices in foreign countries. The best examples of international companies, in the strict sense, are exotic retail shops that sell imported products, or small local manufacturers that export to neighbouring countries. Most of them evolve to become multinational companies.

Thus, they are domestic firms that build on its existing capabilities to penetrate overseas market. *e.g.* Honda, General Electric, P&G.

In this Chapter

- *Globalisation*
- *International Human Resource Management*
- *Organisational Context of IHRM*
- *IHRM and Sustainable Business*
- *Cross Cultural Issues in IHRM*
- *Cultural Diversity*
- *Transnational Organisations*
- *IHRM Models*

Multinational Company

It grows and defines its business on a worldwide basis, but continues to allocate its resources among national or regional areas to maximise the total. MNCs have operating units (subsidiaries) located in foreign countries and the subsidiaries function as autonomous units. Multinational companies cross the FDI threshold.

They invest directly in foreign assets, whether it's a lease contract on a building to house service operations, a plant on foreign soil, or a foreign marketing campaign. Generally, though, multinational companies have FDI only in a limited number of countries, and they do not attempt to homogenize their product offering throughout the countries they operate in.

They focus much more on being responsive to local preferences than a global company would. *e.g.* Shell, Philips, Xerox.

Global Organisations

They treat the entire world as though it were one large country, may be the entire company or one or more of its product lines, may operate with a mixture of two or more organisational structure simultaneously. They maintain control over their worldwide operations (subsidiaries) through a centralised home office. They treat the entire world as a single market.

Global companies have investments in dozens of countries but maintain a strong headquarters in one, usually their home country. Their mantra is economies of scale, and they'll homogenize products as much as the market will allow in order keeping costs low. Their marketing campaigns often span the globe with one message (though in different languages) in an attempt to smooth out differences in local tastes and preferences. *e.g.* Matsushita.

Transnational Organisation

They use specialised facilities to permit local responsiveness, more complex coordination mechanism to provide global integration. They provide autonomy to independent country operations but bring these operations together into an integrated whole through networked structure. They combine the local responsiveness of an MNC and the efficiency of a global corporation.

Transnational companies are often very complex and extremely difficult to manage. They invest directly in dozens of countries and experience strong pressures both for cost reduction and local responsiveness. These companies may have a global headquarters, but they also distribute decision-making power to various national headquarters, and they have dedicated R&D activities for different national markets. *e.g.* Ford & Unilever.

International Human Resource Management

International Human Resource Management (IHRM) is a set of management activities that are aimed at organising human resources at the international level. These activities are set within the organisational structure. It includes HRM functions like selection, recruitment, training, appraisals, dismissals and so on.

In multinational companies, IHRM plays a very vital role in smoothening out the relationship between organisation and employees. Sometimes, the top management and employees, ground staff may belong to different cultural values and traditions. In that case, it is the task of IHRM to equate the two parties and bring them to a common ground for the purpose of the welfare of organisation.

According to **P Boxall (1992),** "International human resource management is concerned with the human resource problems of multinational firms in foreign subsidiaries or more broadly with the unfolding HRM issues that are associated with the various stages of internationalisation process."

According to **Mark Mendenhall (2000),** "IHRM is concerned with HRM issues that cross national boundaries or are conducted in locations other than the home country headquarters."

Dimensions of IHRM

According to **P.V. Morgan,** IHRM is the interplay among 3 dimensions *i.e.,* HR activities, types of countries and types of employees.

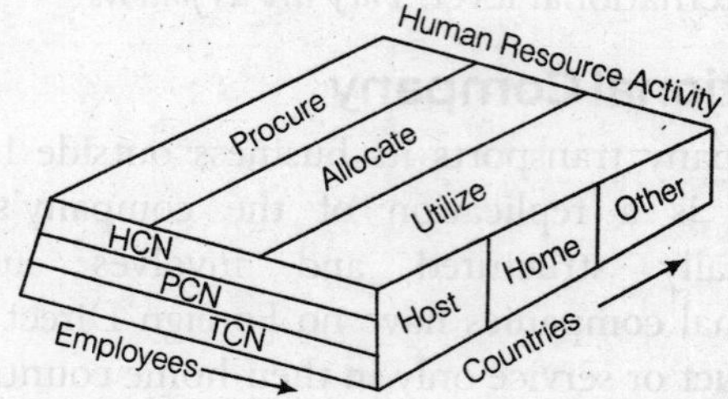

International HR Activities

The activities in IHRM includes major operative human resource function of procurement. This relates to planning of human resource and its induction. It seeks and procures skilled people. The second activity is to allocate the talent and skills according to the ongoing projects and needs of the organisation. Third activity is effective utilisation of all the resources and maximising efficiency and productivity.

Types of Countries

The IHRM operates in three type of countries. First is the home country where the company's headquarters are located. Second is the host country where the subsidiary or branch is located and third is the third country that has sources of finance and several other resources.

Types of Employees

IHRM manages employees at international level. It achieves the control of three kinds of employees that are working in a multinational company. A multinational company is a large corporation that have branches in various countries.

Due to its worldwide activities, it employs various kinds of employees. They are home country employee, host country employee and third country employee. IHRM manages all three kind of employees. *These are as follows*

Home Country National (Parent Company National) (PCN) They are the employees that belong to the home country, where the headquarter of a firm, company or organisation is situated. It is easy to manage these employees as there will be little or no cultural difference.

Host Country National (HCN) They are the employees where an MNC has opened its branch *i.e.* a country other than the home country. There may be cultural differences between the top management and the employees, so IHRM has no active role in it.

Third Country National (TCN) These are the employees that neither belong to home country nor to host country. For example, if a Japanese company that opens a factory in India and employees a French CEO, the French person will be a third country employee.

Difference between HRM and IHRM

Domestic HRM	International HRM
Done within the national boundaries.	Practiced beyond national boundaries.
Manages employees from one (domestic) nation.	Manages employees from different nations and cultures.
Concerned with managing limited number of HRM activities at national level.	Concerned with managing additional activities such as expatriate management.
It is less complex due to minimum influence from external environment, e.g. risk exposure, political risk etc.	It is highly complicated as it is affected heavily by external factors such as institutional factors, cultural differences and risk.
HR managers can frame programme for employees belonging to single nationality.	HR managers here face problems in addressing HR issues of employees belonging to more than one rationality.
There are less risks involved in HRM.	There are greater risk involved in IHRM such as golbal economic crisis, host countries policies etc.

Needs of IHRM

- To respect cultural values and traditions.
- To adhere to governmental policies and legal formalities of the host country.
- To review the present education system and match it with skills needed for operation modes in the organisation.
- To fulfill the host country demands of compensations, allowances, products and services.
- To regularise the flow and volume of information.
- To apply control mechanisms in order to keep a strict vigil over industrial relations.
- To know the exact size and structure of an organisation.

IHRM Functions

Global human resource managers have to perform a number of functions within the organisational set up. The arena of tasks may be even outside the boundaries of the host country.

The functions done by HR on a global scale are as follows

Recruitment

An important function is attracting, hiring and retaining the workforce that aptly suits the needs of the organisation. This task is broken down into small steps *i.e.* developing a job description, interviewing candidates, making offers, negotiating salaries and parks.

Unlike home-country, a multinational has four categories of potential labour that can be hired. These are expatriates, loculs, home-country nationals and third-country nationals

Selection

This process becomes complex in the international arena due to various differences in the educational systems, language of instruction, course of study etc. Therefore, selection is a time consuming and tiring process also subjected to careful monitoring and scrutiny.

Expatriates

They are people living outside the native country. The skill set of these people may be different, so it is the work of IHRM to match the skills with the requirements of the job. IHRM also takes care of compensation of expatriates.

Training and Development

In spite of hiring skilled people, every firm has to provide some sort of on-the-job training. This is because, the style of working of every company is different. Therefore, training and development of human resource to suit the requirements of the job is necessary.

Continuous Professional Development

It is about providing growth opportunities on individual basis and motivating employees to develop skills in multiple areas. IHRM may also mean moving employees across boundaries from one branch to another. Organising conferences, trade shows, employee contact programs are part of this exercise.

Benefits

IHRM also decides upon the benefits in the form of monetary and non-monetary benefits according to prevailing norms of the country in which it is operating.

It is mostly seen that the benefits offered are slightly higher than other firms operating in the host country to attract skilled and talented people. IHRM also tries to minimise the differences in pay between host, home and third country employees.

Legal Compliance

IHRM ensures legal compliance of the organisation in relation to the policies of the host country. It ensures compliance with labour laws, taxation policy and other business operations related to working hours, wages, salaries, working conditions and policies on appraisal, dismissal etc.

Administrative Tasks

IHRM also does various administrative tasks related to working with a global workforce. They communicate company policies to the employees and strive to attain a good relationship between the both. IHRM administers various processes like payroll enrollment, expense reports etc.

Cultural Training

Another important function of IHRM is to lay emphasis on cultural training. It is the responsibility of IHRM to train the expatriates to the culture and tradition of the host country and to train the employee of host country to the norms of the organisation. It also lay emphasis on language training, training in manner and mannerisms.

Industrial Relations

It is a function of IHRM to manage a smooth working environment by handling the industrial relations in an efficient manner. It also maintains a cordial relation with trade unions and other subsidiaries.

At the same time, IHRM also takes care of the international industrial relations and match it with the industrial relations and norms prevailing in the host country.

Compensating Policy

This challenge deals with estimating the remuneration for the workforce working abroad. Many firms have there choices infront of them, i.e. pay, so that person's home-country standard of living stays the same, pay based on what locals in the new country are paid or continue paying based on the person's current home-country pay.

Companies pay numerous incentives to inspire the worker to take the job overseas, like foreign service premiums, which are financial payments over and above regular base pay (typically ranging between 10% and 30% of base pay).

Hardship allowances pay expatriates for hard living and working conditions at certain foreign locations.

Organisational Context of IHRM

In context of an organisation, the size as well as structure keeps on changing. When an organisation which is successfully operating in one country, opens its branch/ subsidiary in another country, then various changes have to be made. These changes occur due to various reasons.

They are as follows

- Growth objectives and geographical disperses encounter greater pressure to change.
- Develop greater coordination and control access business units.
- Cultural and language parameters of the host country.
- Regulations an ownership and equity as well as constraints imposed by host government.

Stages of Internationalisation

The stages of internationalisation relates to the steps involved in the process of an organisation while changing its set up from national to international operations.

These stages are

First Stage is Exporting which refers to the initial stage of international operations. It is handled by intermediaries, foreign agent or distributors. Role of HR is not clear here.

Second Stage is Scales Subsidiary that replaces foreign agents/distributors with own people through sales or branch offices. This step gives greater control to an organisation. HR involvement arises in this step.

Third Stage is International Division which is closely related to foreign productivity. Here, a separate division is created where all the activities of the group overseas are combined. Staffing of key positions takes place.

HR plays a lead role here as it selects expatriates from the home country who would work or given training in host country. Licensing and other related issues are solved by the management in collaboration with the HR department.

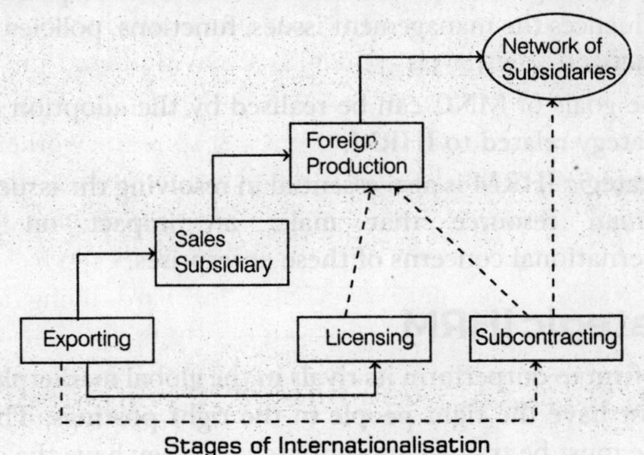

Stages of Internationalisation

Export Department Structure

The export department is purposefully made to formally channelise the process of setting-up international units. They are first built into the regular domestic unit or in other words, the home country unit. The built in export unit operates alongwith other departments in the home country.

The HR manager writes about the roles and responsibilities of the built in export department and appoints an international manager for the same purpose. The built in export department works in the area of international marketing and looks after the overseas business at the initial stage.

Later on, when the export department grows in size and structure, then an overseas unit/branch/subsidiary is established .

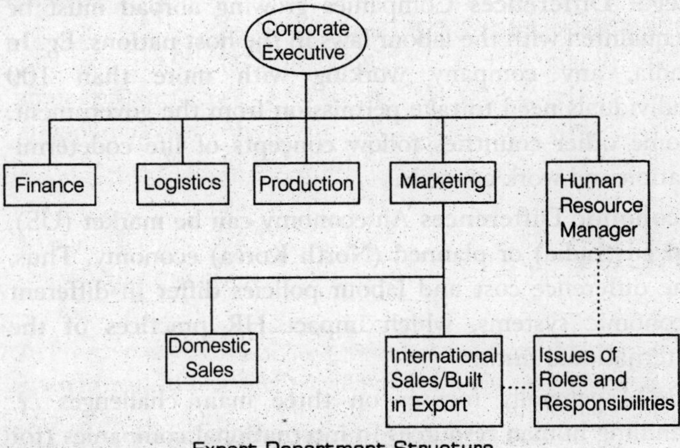

Export Department Structure

International Product Division Structure

The international product division structure takes care of the necessary functions to open a subsidiary in a different country. The subsidiaries produce a particular product or a service like that of the headquarter. However, it may make its area and country specific. The production process is broken down into many small steps.

The international product division structure increases responsiveness to competitive opportunities, efficiency, innovation and quality. These divisions may operate in clusters or separately. They are closely linked to the headquarters that are the head of all type of operations.

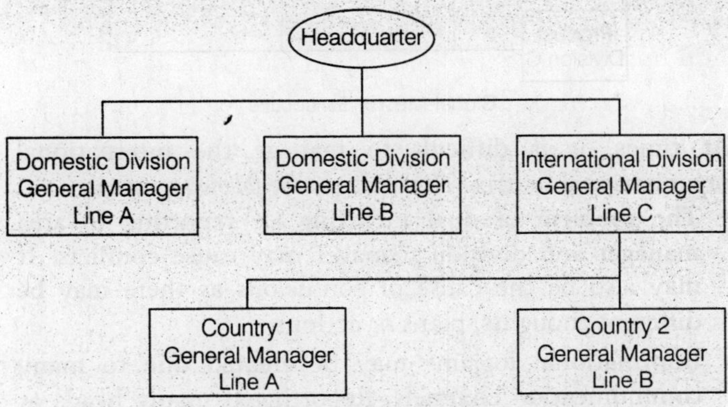

Intermational Product Divison Structure

International Matrix Organisation Structure

Matrix structure is a combination of two or more structures. In an international matrix organisation structure, a foreign subsidiary. reports to one or more than one group. Multinational corporations usually combine product groups with geographic units.

For example, product managers have responsibility for the development, manufacturing and distribution of their products or service while the managers of different geographic units have responsibility for the success of business in their region. Each group shares responsibility.

The groups try to simultaneously deal with competing pressures for global integration as well as local responsiveness.

Matrix structure makes each group more responsible for foreign operations and enables greater exchange of information and resources.

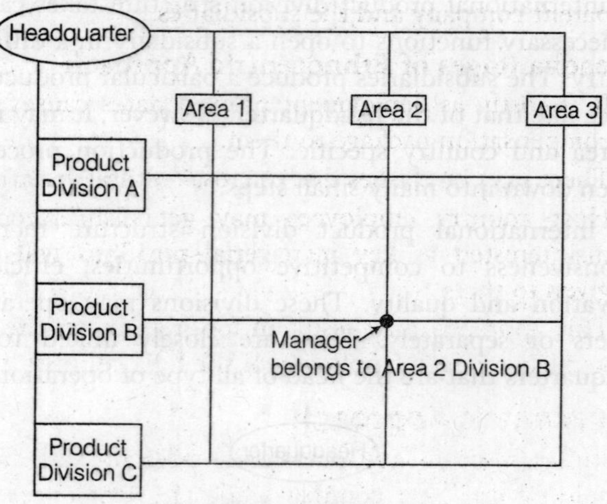

Global Matrix Structure

At times, it is difficult to manage the international organisational matrix. *This is due to the following reasons*

- The problem of dual reporting *i.e.* reporting to area manager and division manager may cause conflicts. It may also be the cause of confusions as there may be different thoughts, plans or actions.
- Informational logjams may be created due to many communication channels. Reporting to many heads at various levels or phases may cause large amount of exchange of information that may cause logjam.
- The overlapping of responsibilities may result in field battles (sustained fight between departments) and loss of accountability.
- It becomes very difficult for the managers to resolve the conflicts and confusions created due to distance, language, time and cultural barriers.

IHRM and Sustainable Business

It is important to understand the operations of multinational corporations in the global context. Multinational corporations have subsidiary units operating in different countries. Integration of these units with the parent unit is essential to maintain a sustainable business model. This is called internationalisation.

The internationalisation is important to form a multinational corporation that has strong business links. There are several ways or strategies to develop the global links.

The reasons to develop IHRM strategy are as follows

- The IHRM strategy is needed to all the levels of human resource management process.
- The strategic components of multinational corporations influences the management issues, functions, policies and practices.
- The goals of MNC can be realised by the adoption of a strategy related to IHRM.
- Strategic IHRM is also essential in resolving the issues of human resource that make an impact on the international concerns of these enterprises.

Strategic IHRM

For a firm to outperform its rivals in the global marketplace, it must have the right people in the right postings. Those people must be trained appropriately, so they have the skill sets required to perform their jobs effectively and so they behave in a manner that is congruent with the desired culture of the firm.

Their compensation packages must motivate them to take actions that are consistent with the strategy of the firm, similarly, the performance appraisal systems of the firm uses must measure the behaviour that the firm wants to encourage.

Factors affecting international human resource practices are as follows

Cultural Differences Cultural differences show themselves in differences in how people from different nations act, think, and expect others to respond or act. Hofstede helps the managers in learning about various cultures and their implications.

Legal Differences Companies growing abroad must be acquainted with the labour laws in the host nations. Eg. In India, any company working with more than 100 individuals need to take permission from the government. Some other countries follow concepts of life codetermination and work councils.

Economic Differences An economy can be market (US), mixed (India) or planned (North Korea) economy. Thus, the difference cost and labour policies differ in different economic systems, which impact HR practices of the international firms.

IHRM generally focuses on three main challenges *i.e.* handling human resources in international companies (for example, staffing, training, and compensating employees who work abroad), managing expatriate workers (those the employer sends abroad) and comparing HRM practices in different countries.

Components influencing Strategic IHRM

There are two major strategic components of the multinational corporations that influence strategic IHRM.

They are as follows

Inter Unit Linkages

Inter unit linkages means to bond together the otherwise separate units. The multinational enterprises are concerned with how to operate the worldwide units effectively. Therefore, they hire general managers and other staff with knowledge, skills, expertise and vision so as to implement cross border strategies.

The different units operate differently as per the specifications and requirements. At the same time, they also integrate the best practices, control and coordinate the activities.

Internal Operations

It refers to the procedures that are carried within MNC. The operations should make the work smooth and fulfill the organisational goals. Each unit is to be operated in order to maintain MNC effectiveness and competitive advantage over other competitors.

If the internal operations are upto the mark, then the business is also sustainable for a long period of time.

Approaches of IHRM

There are basically three approaches that describes how multinational companies manage the human resources. The success of IHRM strategies depend upon the quality of human resource and how efficiently they are allocated the best jobs according to their capabilities.

The approaches to IHRM are as follows

Ethnocentric Approach

This approach goes with the mindset that employees of home country can perform better to fulfill the organisation's mission, vision and objectives. Therefore, the strategic positions of subsidiaries are filled by nationals of the parent company. Expatriates are deployed in host countries and they keep a tight control.

Strategic decisions are taken by headquarter while the management practices are transferred to the subsidiaries. This practice is usually seen in the early stage of a firm's internationalisation process and where a firm wants to maintain a unified corporate culture.

Advantages of Ethnocentric Approach

- The vision, mission and objectives of the parent organisation can be easily adopted by the subsidiaries.
- With this approach, proper control is possible.
- The operations of the subsidiaries can be monitored easily by this method.
- Greater level of coordination is possible between the parent company and the subsidiaries.

Disadvantages of Ethnocentric Approach

- It is costly as deployment of expatriates causes greater compensation package to them.
- There may be clashes due to cross-cultural variations.
- Host country employees may get disheartened and disinterested as key managerial positions will not be given to them.
- This approach may result in loosing out on the skilled and experienced employees of the host country.

Polycentric Approach

In this approach, key managerial positions are filled by people of the host country while the employees of the parent company do the roles of communication and coordination. The number of private country nationals declines and expatriates may not be sent.

The employees of host country are aware and keep a greater understanding of local cultures, beliefs and value systems. Therefore, many multinational corporations adopt the polycentric approach.

The local managers are given greater autonomy and they are encouraged to adopt or develop their management practices. This approach is closure to adopting local business ethics readily and formulate new management practices. Subsidiaries enjoy a greater degree of freedom to form strategies in this method. The vision and mission is also formulated accordingly.

Advantages of Polycentric Approach

- There is greater coordination with the prevailing business environment.
- There is no difficulty in adopting to cultural issues since the managers are aware of the value and beliefs.
- It is cheaper as hiring host country employees is less expensive than hiring expatriates.
- It gives greater job satisfaction to the employees of host country which ultimately reflects positively in their work.

Disadvantages of Polycentric Approach

- There may not be better coordination between headquarter and subsidiaries of an MNC.
- The host country managers may not equate with the vision and mission of the parent organisation.
- A gap develops between the management of host and parent company.
- Quick application of operations may not be possible by the parent organisation.

Geocentric Approach

This approach is the combination of other two approaches. Organisations neither hire the employees of parent company nor the employees of the host company. The criteria of selection is placed on the level of competency of the people *i.e.* finding the right match to the required needs of the job.

Organisations hire people according to the set criteria of selection *i.e.* qualifications, experience, competency which is irrespective of the nationality. This type of approach facilitates competitive advantage as talented and skilled people are hired. The best of headquarter and subsidiary are combined to come up with a global implemented HR strategy.

Advantages of Geocentric Approach

- This approach enables the firms to make the best use of human resource.
- Hiring best people without any biases or prejudices facilitates the firms to fulfil its objectives in a better way.
- It helps in reducing the clashes or unfair treatments.
- It results in greater intermixing of cultures.

Disadvantages of Geocentric Approach

- Hiring is a tedious process in geocentric approach as it involves greater searching.
- It may not always facilitate better coordination or control.
- At times, it becomes difficult to monitor and control the operations.
- Sometimes, cross cultural variations may arise.
- It is also an expensive process due to the greater selection process involved.

Cross Cultural Issues in IHRM

International human resource management is gaining steady popularity due to the rapid globalisation. There is greater movement of workforce from one country to another. Workforce is becoming increasingly diverse and multicultural in nature. It gives rise to cultural differences across countries. The cultural differences reflect in the manner of work done by the employees.

Hofstede puts it that it is important to understand different cultural backgrounds to be able to identify the consequences for international management.

The complexities of culture is represented by the way of talking, food eaten, selection of dress, body language, values and assumptions. Thoughts on religion and philosophy are also reflected by culture of a person. The cross-culture issues are more in a globalisation of business enterprises. This poses a challenge for the organisation. These challenges are tackled by human resource management systems.

Increasing competition in national and international front have given way to focus deeper upon effective human resource management policies. The IHRM is gaining its importance in organisational set up as it is their task to perceive and react to different cultural beliefs and practices for smooth functioning of the organisation.

Culture-Introduction

Culture is said to be a set of ideas, concepts or notions that are shared by the members of a community, a society, a religion or even a country. Culture can also said as a set of ideas that are transferred from one generation to another through anecdotes, symbols etc.

Culture is always learned and passed on from one generation to the other. It exists from the past actions of members of a group. Culture can be seen in almost everything a person does. It gets reflected in the language, religious beliefs, traditions, social habits, cuisine, music, fine arts, clothes etc.

Therefore, it can be rightly said that culture moulds a person's behaviour and changes one's perception of the world.

Cultural Conditioning

Cultural conditioning is about how people acquire their culture, learn about behaviours, accept different values and the overall framework of living in a society. Cultural conditioning is reflected through the way a person thinks, speaks, acts, religious beliefs, considers wrong and right, way of eating, dressing etc. It is just like a wind that shapes a sand dune.

The process of cultural conditioning varies significantly from culture to culture. It starts to develop in early childhood and continues throughout the life. New values and behaviours are acquired continuously. This keeps on shaping the behaviour of a person. The cultural conditioning gets reflected through individual behaviour, emotional reactivity, preconceptions, thoughts and actions.

The role of human resource management is to see the cultural backgrounds of the employees. HRM should be mindful and aware to pay attention to the feelings, thoughts and actions of people coming from different cultures.

Layers of Culture Model

Culture is present in various layers in the personality of a person. The culture model represents culture in a series of layers where each layer represents different values and assumptions. The outermost layer corresponds to assumptions which get reflected through dress, food and body language.

The middle layer corresponds to religion, values and philosophies and gets reflected through the thinking like what is right and what is wrong. The layer at the core is invisible layer that represents culture's universal truth. This layer is most difficult to understand.

Organisational Culture Model

American management professor **Edgar Schein** developed an organisational culture model in 1980. This model is present in every organisation and is indicated through different ways. There are three different layers or levels of this model. The organisational culture model is also called 'Onion Model' as it is based on different layers. The outer layer is easy to adopt and change. The inner layers are harder and takes time to adjust.

These layers are as follows

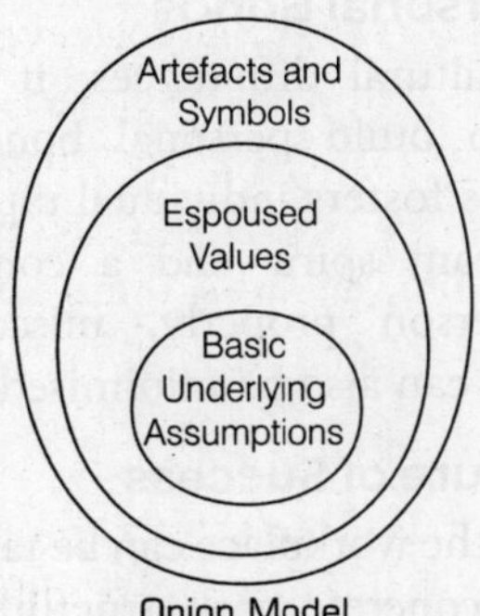

Onion Model

Artefacts and Symbols

This is the outermost layer. They are the visible elements in an organisation such as structure, architecture, logo, processes etc. This culture is easily visible and recognisable to external parties also.

Espoused Values

These are the rules of conduct, values and standards maintained in an organisation. They are expressed in strategies, objectives and philosophies. They are conveyed by top management to their subordinates. Problem arises when the ideas are not in line with the basic assumption of the organisation.

Basic Underlying Assumptions

These are assumptions that are deeply embedded in the organisational culture. They are experienced as basic underlying assumptions are hard to recognise. They are experienced as self evident and unconscious behaviour.

The IHRM's role is of great value in coordinating the cross-cultural issues to the organisational culture.

Cultural Comparison

Hofstede in 1980 studied the employees working in IBM. They were from 40 different countries which later expanded to include 50 countries. By undergoing attitude surveys, **Hofstede** presented a classic study of work values to compare cultures across different countries.

He presented four dimensions for which each country could be classified in. These four dimensions are individualism-collectivism, power distance, uncertainty avoidance and masculinity- feminity.

These are as follows

Individualism-Collectivism

Individualism or individualist refers to the extent to which an individual identifies one's self. It refers to the degree where people prefer to make their own decisions, take care of themselves and are not bound or dependent on their groups or families.

The success of an individual is independent of the success of the group. A highly individualist society consists of impersonal and loose relationships between people while a low individualist society consists of tight relationships between people.

Collectivism or Collectivist refers to an individual who associates himself with a large group, team, family or organisation. Collectivism means having a collective identity, it has more tight relationships.

In collectivism, the success and survival of an individual is dependent on the teams' success. Cooperation and integrity is the prerequisite of collectivism. The emotional and psychological orientation are somewhat similar in collectivism but it may also vary with members of other groups.

Power Distance

Power distance denotes the attitude of society towards power differences and towards reaching the level of equality. It relates to how cultures perceive the notion of power and status in organisation and societies. Large power distance in organisations is characterised by formal hierarchies.

There subordinates have little influence in the organisation and boss have the total authority. Low power distance is where there is more of equality in the organisational hierarchy. Power distance plays significant role in workplace relationships.

Depending upon power differences, there can be a high power and low power distance. The power distance can be seen in community, society and country even.

Uncertainty Avoidance

This model refers to the interpretation of uncertainty in various cultures. It focuses on the level which a country tolerate uncertainty and ambiguity within the society. All societies are affected by uncertainty but the level avoidance of uncertainty varies from culture-to-culture.

High uncertainty means that the country/society has low tolerance towards uncertainty avoidance. Low uncertainty means that the society/country has high tolerance towards uncertainty avoidance. They are more tolerant towards threats and anxieties.

Masculinity–Feminity

This dimension describes if a culture is bound towards values that are seen as more similar to women's or men's values. Masculinity or male orientations are characterised by ambition, assertiveness, competition and excellence while feminity is characterised by sensitivity, modesty, harmony and propensity for quality of life. High masculinity indicates a high degree of gender differences, usually favouring men rather than women.

Cross-Cultural Management

Cross-cultural management refers to managing work teams in a way that considers the differences in cultures, practices and preferences in the context of international or global business. It describes organisational behaviour and seeks to understand how to improve the interaction of coworkers, managers, executives, clients, suppliers and partners.

Cross-cultural management gains all the importance in multinational companies where employees come from various cultures. Therefore, each employees comes with different attitude, practices, behaviour and values. It is the work of the manager to manage his subordinates who are coming from diverse cultures. This in turn helps in keeping the employees integrated with organisational goals and to keep them cooperative towards management.

Thus, it is the most important task of the manager to solve problems that appear at encountering individual company and national cultures.

Strategies for Successful Cross-Cultural Management

A crucial feature of an effective team is to reduce the cultural barriers of people working in an organisation by channelising their thoughts towards acquiring a composite culture in an organisation. The multi-cultural issues pose challenges which is needed to be resolved.

The strategies for resolving cross-cultural differences are as follows

Good Knowledge of Foreign Culture

The managers should be somewhat aware of the cultural beliefs and values of the people. This is specially true with managers working with host country employees. Prior knowledge helps to gain insight about the customs, traditions and mannerisms. This creates amaible environment in the organisation.

Not only knowledge of foreign culture but also respect for that culture is important so that it shows in the behaviours and mannerisms. Knowing and respecting a culture helps in understanding the cultural differences. This includes knowing about the language, food, dressing style etc.

Create Clear Norms and Maintain Them

The manager acts as a team leader who establishes norms about the working style. The style of work should be similar for everyone and not biased towards any form of cultural ethics.

Once the manager creates a style, it can be imposed to every member of the team. The manager can also implement a work style by taking inspiration from other cultures.

Work to Build Personal Bonds

To reduce cross cultural differences, it is essential for the team leader to build personal bonds. Establishing personal connections fosters individual rapport. This helps in developing a team spirit and a composite culture. By knowing a person properly, misconceptions and miscommunications can also be minimised.

Creating a Structure of Success

Multiculturalism at the workplace can be tackled effectively by way of building a concrete work structure. In the absence of a definite structure, there will be complete chaos. Therefore, the work of HRM is to establish a structure and all the employees irrespective of their culture, are to follow its mechanism.

Managing Differences

People from different cultures grow up differently. They have different idea of even the related concepts such as team, time or schedule. Americans are more individualistic while Asians are more collective. The concept of office time, break time, over time is also different. The work schedule is also different.

For example for Muslims, Friday is the day of prayer. Chinese celebrate their own new year which is different from the normal calender dates. These differences need to be managed tactfully without hurting the sentiments of others.

Work Environment

The work atmosphere should be friendly, so that cultural differences become a seamless part of the workplace. The work environment should be adaptive, open and cooperative.

Employees should be motivated to work for the organisation by eliminating their personal and cultural differences. They should work to achieve excellence and realise the organisations mission.

Cultural Diversity

Cultural diversity refers to a system of beliefs and behaviours that recognises the presence of all diverse groups in an organisation or society. Cultural diversity can be used interchangeably with multiculturalism.

The important actions that defines cultural diversity are respect for differences, valuing other cultures, encouraging diversity, recognition of abundant diversity, empowering people to achieve their potential without any biases and celebrating the differences instead of tolerating.

Cultural diversity is important as a community, society or a country consist of people coming from various cultures, racial and ethnic groups. Having a certain level of understanding about other cultures brings respect for the cultures.

This helps in facilitating collaboration and cooperation among the people. Learning about different cultures also helps in understanding different perspectives and helps dispel negative stereotypes and personal biases about different groups.

Cultural diversity helps us to recognise and respect others which in turn aids in building bridges to inculcate trust, respect and understanding across different cultures. Diversity also makes the country more interesting and usher in new ways of thinking, knowledge and experiences.

Examples of Cultural Diversity

- Language differences by hiring multi-lingual staff.
- Age differences by ranging a wide age group.
- Religious diversity by hiring people with different religious beliefs.
- Race diversity by hiring people from different races.

Cultural Diversity at the Workplace

Cultural diversity at the workplace takes place when the organisations hire employees from different backgrounds, regardless of race, religion or culture. This generally happens with organisations that have became multi national organisations. But now-a-days, many national companies also recruit and retain diverse pool of resources.

Benefits of Cultural Diversity at the Workplace

There are positive benefits of having a cultural diversity at the workplace. *They are as follows*

Increase Creativity among teams as diversity gives the ability to have a more diverse set of solutions to specific problems.

Greater Insight into Business comes from diversity as people from different cultures add their skills and experiences into the ongoing processes.

Local Market Knowledge *i.e.* the knowledge about the ongoing trends and marketing strategies can be had from people coming from diverse cultures.

Positive Reputation of a company is established by recruiting people from diverse cultures. It is seen as a rational step.

Better Performance and Productivity prevails due to diversity of people with different skills are absorbed.

Valuing Diversity Enhances Employee Engagements by showing that the company understands and respects different cultures.

Transnational Organisations

Transnational Organisations (TNO) refer to international organisations that are beyond the state boundaries. There are contracts, coalitions and interactions that are directed by international laws which govern these organisations. Transnational organisations are multinational business enterprises.

Examples of transnational organisation are international air transport cartels, international non- governmental organisations etc. Amnesty International is a transnational organisation that is inspired to bring social change, so it is a transnational social movement as its working is spread across many countries.

These organisations carry a significantly centrally directed operations in the territory of two or more nations. Transnational organisations operates beyond national boundaries with the support of atleast one nation. Transnational organisation refers to international organisations that transcends the idea of a nation-state.

Difference between MNC and TNO

The differences are as follows

Definition MNC owns or controls production of goods and services in one or more countries other than their home country.

TNO does business in many countries and does not consider any particular country its home.

Home Country MNC has a separate identity belonging and headquartered at a particular country. TNO is borderless and does not consider any particular country as its headquarter.

Products MNC is more focussed on adapting their products and service specific to the area of operation.

TNO gives decision-making, research and development, marketing powers to each of the foreign market where it is operating.

Management MNCs have a centralised management system. They face a greater barrier in decision-making due to its centralised management systems. TNOs do not have a centralised management system. They are able to gain more interest in the local markets since they maintain their own systems.

Advantages of Transnational Organisations

The advantages of these type of organisations are as follows

Expanded Business New markets and new customers can be gained. This opens up a whole new kind of opportunities as well as employment benefits. The scale of operations also increases.

Different Regulatory Regimes Transnational organisations benefit from the different type of rules and regulations in different countries. The production of a product or a component may be highly regulated in one country but the situation may be different in other places.

Deeper Cultural Understanding Having locations in multiple countries, gives the opportunity to transnational organisations to know about cultural differences. This helps in diversifying the production and work force.

Favourable Taxation Transnational companies are able to organise their productive activities in such as way so that they earn profits by paying lower taxes and shifting expenses.

IHRM Models

Models of IHRM have been developed by using various HRM models. They have been explained below and are used interchangeably.

The defining features of HRM are popularly known as models. These models provide analytical framework for studying HRM. They provide characterisation of HRM that establishes variables and relationship to be researched. They help in explaining the nature of HR practices.

They study various management issues in detail, for example situational factors, stakeholders, strategic choices and level of competency.

Four most common models are

The Forbrum Model

This is the first model of HRM. It was developed in 1984. It emphasises four functions of management and their interrelatedness.

These are **Selection, Appraisal, Development** and **Rewards**. These four factors are expected to contribute to **organisational effectiveness.**

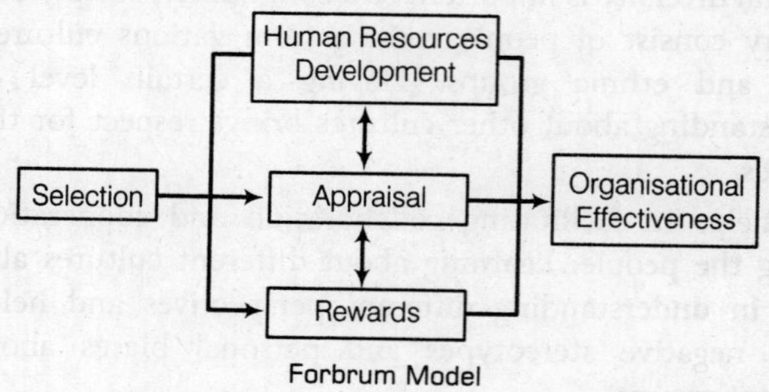

Forbrum Model

This model focuses on only four functions and ignore all other environmental once contingency factors. But, this model is simple and can serve as a heuristic frame work for explaining the nature and significance of HR activities.

The Harvard Model

This model consists five components namely **stakeholders, interests, situational factors, HRM policy choices, HR outcomes** and **long-term consequences.**

The model can be understood with the help of following diagram

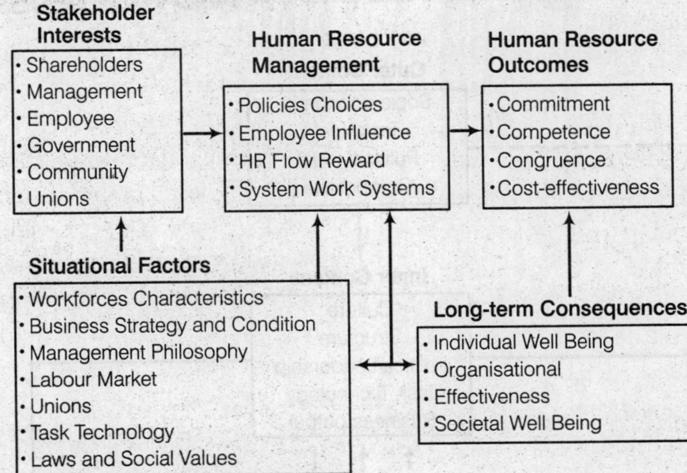

Harvard Model

The Guest Model

This model was developed by **David Guest** in 1997. This model emphasises on the assumption that HR manager has specific strategies to begin with, which demand certain practices and when executed will result in outcomes. These outcomes include behavioural performance related and financial rewards.

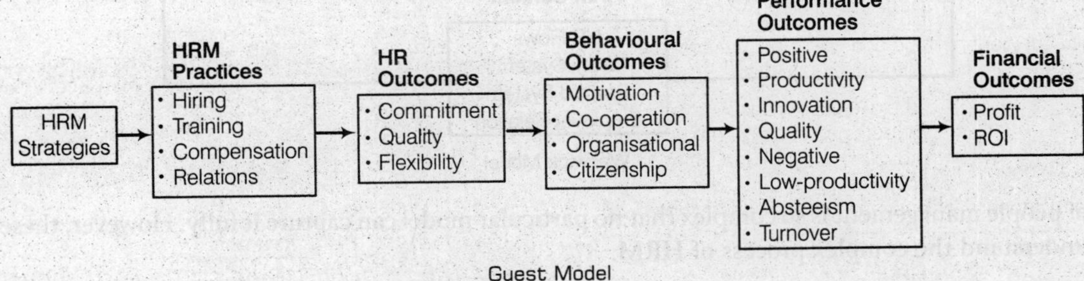

Guest Model

The Guest model clearly maps out the field of HRM and indicates the exact position of income and outcomes.

The Warwick Model

This model was developed by Hendry and Pettigrew of University of Warwick.

This model was concentrated or five elements

(a) Outer content

(b) Inner content

(c) Business strategy content

(d) HRM content (role, definition, etc)

(e) HRM content (HR flows, work system, etc)

The strength of this model is that it identifies and classifies important environmental influences on HRM.

This model takes knowledge of business strategy and HR practices, the external and internal content, in which these activities take place and process by which such changes take place including transactions between changes in both external content and internal content.

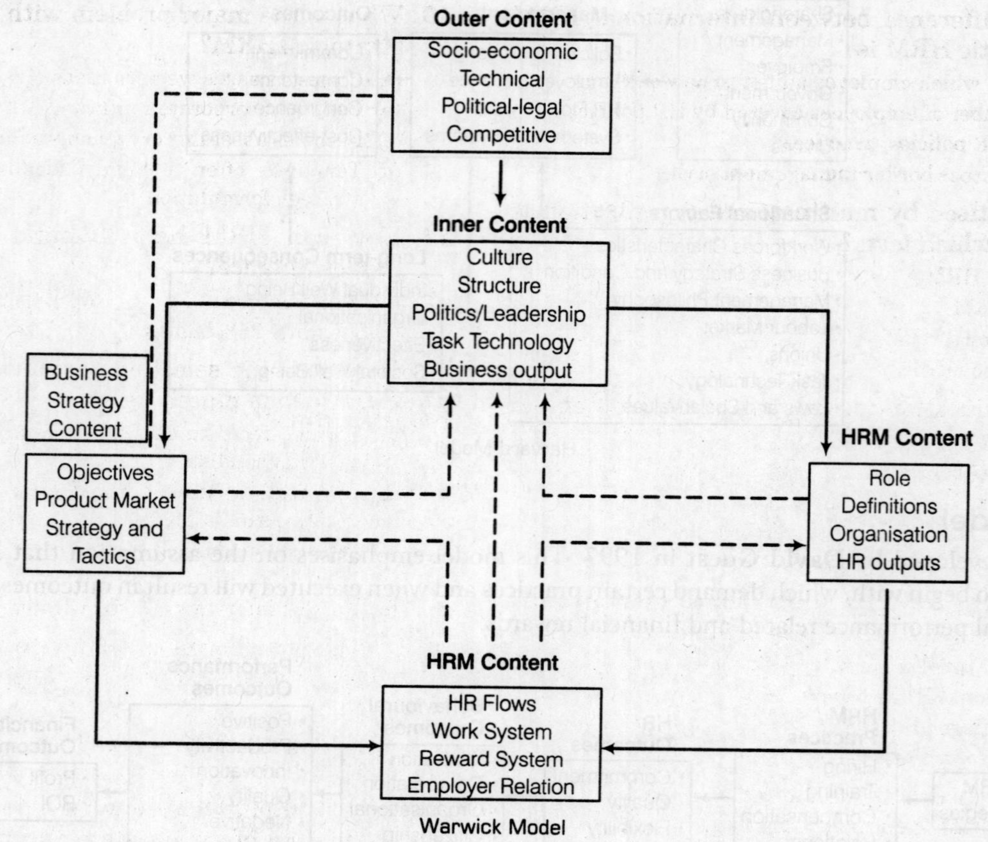

Warwick Model

The dynamics of people management is so complex that no particular model can capture it fully. However, these four models are studied to understand the complex process of HRM.

EXAM BASED QUESTIONS

1 A major difference between international HRM and domestic HRM is

(a) ease with which employee adjust to new cultures
(b) total number of employees covered by HR policies
(c) foreign HR policies, practices
(d) effective cross border management styles

2 HRM practised by multinational organisation is known by which term?

(a) Domestic HRM
(b) Global HRM
(c) International HRM
(d) Multinational HRM

3 The key question asked while developing on IHRM policy is

(a) what cross-border training is to be given
(b) who will be the CEO of new branch
(c) when will HR policies be developed
(d) what kind of organisation is desired

4 If a company uses its performance management system worldwide, then it is example of what?

(a) Extended management
(b) International HRM policy
(c) Global village philosophy
(d) Attempt to increase productivity

5 The difference between good and bad, right or wrong is greatly reflected through what?

(a) One's responsibilities (b) Social expectations
(c) Culture and ethics (d) All of these

6 The headquarters of a multinational company where it is situated is known as

(a) Host country (b) Third country
(c) Subsidiary country (d) Home country

7 Which among the following is not directly related to the success fo expatriate assignments?

(a) Intextions of expatriate employees
(b) Nature of products produced by the company
(c) Spouse of expatriate not adjusting to new situation
(d) Personality of expatriate employees

8 Understanding behaviour and culture of host country's market by a manager from host country is .... policy.

(a) expat-centric (b) ethnocentric
(c) polycentric (d) geocentric

9 TCN is related with

(a) Expatriates
(b) Nationals of third country
(c) Nationals of host country
(d) Nationals of the main branch

10 What is the major problem with the theorising of strategic IHRM?

(a) Biased towards western ideas
(b) Fails to incorporate conflict
(c) Becomes absolute very quickly as change occurs so fast
(d) Tends to offer a highly idealised perspective on strategy formulation

11 How can HRM help to build successful cross border alliance?

(a) Joint venture (b) Exporting ideas
(c) Spending 25% budget (d) All of these

12 How does the selection of international assignee usually take place?

(a) Formal recruitment process including internal and external candidates
(b) Informal discussion based on chance conversations with internal staff
(c) Informal discussion between each member of a specie-team
(d) Formal interview process with internal staff

13 The ability of forms to succeed in the face of growing international competition depends increasingly on

(a) good infrastructure (b) work culture
(c) skilled labour (d) relaxed legal system

14 Which among the following is not a criteria for the evaluation of expatriate performance?

(a) Technical skills (b) Personality
(c) Work performance (d) Language proficiency

15 The executives working in Australian branch of United Kingdom multinational bank citizen of US are an example of

(a) Second country nationals
(b) Home country nationals
(c) Host country nationals
(d) Third country nationals

16 Lumpsum payments given to employees who move from one branch to another as the need arises are

(a) Mobility premium (b) Trip premium
(c) Ethnocentric premium (d) Extra service premium

17 Non-citizen employees of a country in which they are working are known as what?

(a) Coordinates (b) Expatriates
(c) Subordinates (d) None of these

18 Human Resource Management aims at maximising employees as well as organisational

(a) effectiveness (b) efficiency
(c) economy (d) performance

19 A distinction can be made between hard and soft types of HRM. Soft HRM can be characterised by
(a) seeing people as organisational assets
(b) a quantitative approach to HRM
(c) a mutual commitment of employees and employers to the goals of the organisation
(d) being driven by costs

20 The best and beneficial view of the firm is one that, believes the key human resources are
(a) the employees, not the members of trade unions
(b) knowledge workers
(c) used to create new capabilities that help to achieve organisational success
(d) those willing to work overtime

21 In the 'Global Village' kind of scenario, HR is facing lots of challenges due to
(a) diversified cultures and backgrounds of the employees
(b) two many people working together
(c) large size of the organisation
(d) too many work stations

22 IHRM is an area of academic study which focuses on
(a) the International level research
(b) the movement of individuals across national boundaries
(c) the exchange of ideas and practices
(d) the policies and practices of MNC's

23 Cultural shock which is often the outcome of the negative experience of moving from a familiar culture to that of unfamiliar is important to understand in the context of globalisation because
(a) it can effect the international economy
(b) it can effect the bureaucrats of the country
(c) it can impact on individuals taking overseas assignments
(d) it can effect the tourism industry

24 Why is it important to ensure that HR plans are flexible?
(a) To adapt the fast changing environments in which most organisations operate
(b) To accomodate the changes arising because of high attrition rate
(c) To ensure the availability of labour force at all times
(d) To adapt the changing skills and qualifications of all the professions

25 Key to successful management of HR practices in IHRM is the ability of manager to
(a) travel abroad
(b) have good contacts
(c) have appropriate training systems
(d) have the ability to identify key potential of all the individuals and make maximum utilisation of that

26 In retrospect, when today's HR researcher look at the practices being followed in 1980's and 90's one finds them overly prescriptive and inflexible because
(a) they were underdeveloped
(b) they were not carried out by experts
(c) they were very rigid and directive
(d) All of the above

27 In which of the following aspect of HR it is very important for HR Department to depict its fairness and non-discrimination?
(a) Recruitment and selection
(b) Grievance and discipline
(c) Ward management
(d) All of the above

28 What approach is the firm employing when it follows a strategy of choosing only from the nationals of the parent company?
(a) Geocentric Approach (b) Polycentric Approach
(c) Ethnocentric Approach (d) None of these

29 The strategy of limiting recruitment to the nationalities of the host country where the branch is located as ....
(a) polycentric approach (b) ethnocentric approach
(c) geocentric approach (d) All of these

30 What is the strategy adopted by a firm of recruiting the most suitable person for the job position irrespective of nationality?
(a) Ethnocentric Approach (b) Geocentric Approach
(c) Polycentric Approach (d) None of these

31 Values of top executives will be included in which of the following?
(a) Polycentric (b) Ethnocentric
(c) Geocentric (d) All of these

32 Ethnocentric orientation is a predisposition towards
(a) the global economy
(b) regionalism
(c) the home country
(d) geographically proximate regions

33 Understanding behaviour and culture of host country's market by a manager from home country is ....
(a) expat centric (b) ethnocentric
(c) geocentric (d) polycentric

34 Hofstede's five variables: Power distance; individualism masculinity/feminity, uncertainty avoidance and long term versus short term-orientation, were terms used to describe
(a) Leadership traits (b) HR strategies
(c) National differences (d) Family traits

35 Special assistance is provided by centers of expertise in which of the following?
(a) Long-term strategic plan
(b) Production department
(c) Organisational Change
(d) Updates regarding appraisal

36 Cultures where indirect language and non-verbal communication are used to transfer ideas
(a) high context cultures
(b) low context cultures
(c) medium context cultures
(d) context cultures

37 When a person from one culture exchanges ideas from a person from other culture, then it is
(a) multi cultural link
(b) two way communication
(c) verbal communication
(d) cross Cultural communication

38 In high power distance organisations, employees expect what?
(a) Managers giving decision making power to subordinates
(b) Managers taking decision and telling then what to do.
(c) Managers asking for opinion of the employees
(d) Employees making the decision on their own

39 If employees expect to have a greater say in decision making and more autonomy in their work, then these cultures have which of the following?
(a) High Power distance (b) Equality
(c) Low Power distance (d) Cooperation

40 Cultures valuing hierarchy and status differentials will frame compensation strategies to
(a) reinforce differentials
(b) minimise differentials
(c) initiate individual achievements
(d) initiate group performance

41 "Integration is managed differently for different groups"– Which among the following term defines the above phrase?
(a) Integration (b) Multiculturalism
(c) Assimilation (d) Cultural diversity

42 Which is not a benefit of multiculturalism?
(a) Equal opportunities for everyone
(b) Valuing of ethnicity, diversity and cultural variations
(c) Reduction of stereotypes that are negative in nature
(d) Enforcing beliefs and behaviours of dominant ethnic group

43 Which among the following are the factors under diversity?
(a) Gender (b) Cultural background
(c) Social status (d) All of these

44 Dimension of culture which defines extent of people how they act as individuals instead of groups is classified as
(a) collectivism (b) certainty avoidance
(c) power distance (d) individualism

45 The process of training, planning and reassigning of employees to their belonging countries is classified as
(a) expatriation (b) repatriation
(c) distant assignments (d) foreign advancement

46 Assistance to top level management for the purpose of drawing strategic plans is provided by which group?
(a) Embedded HR (b) Corporate HR
(c) Center of expertise (d) Transactional HR

47 Which is not one of the layers of cultural influence?
(a) Company (b) Organisation (c) Business (d) Social

48 Why are transnational organisations becoming increasingly important?
(a) They are increasing in interdependencies
(b) Operations are facilitated by recent technical changes
(c) Increases employment of resources
(d) All of the above

49 One of the major issues concerning the political impact of transnational corporations is that they
(a) are eager to cooperate with international organisations
(b) strengthen the political independence of countries
(c) major supports of spread of democracy
(d) effectively erode state sovereignity

50 Which among the following is not a part of Schein's model of cultural formation?
(a) Shared Values (b) Shared beliefs
(c) Pre-Conceptions (d) Norms

51 The overall goal of .... is to achieve global competitiveness through recognising cross-border market similarities and differences and to link the capabilities of the organisation across national boundaries.
(a) global organisation
(b) transnational organisation
(c) multinational organisation
(d) joint venture

52 Kochan and Barooci's (1985) model of HRM includes which elements?
(a) HRM/IR Systems effectiveness, extend and internal environment
(b) External environment, HRM/IR System, internal environment
(c) HRM, internal environment, HRM/IR system effectiveness
(d) External environment, HRM, HRM/IR system effectiveness

53 Which company produces, markets and operates across the world?
(a) Transnational (b) Multinational
(c) International (d) Global

54 The important components in aligning business strategy with HR practices include which of the following?
(a) Marketing strategy
(b) Business strategy
(c) Human resource practices
(d) Both (b) and (c)

55 Which of the following is not a dimension of global strategy?
(a) Standardisation
(b) Integration
(c) Localisation
(d) Coordination and configuration

56 Treating employees as a precious resource is the basis of which type of human resource management?
(a) Hard HRM (b) Self HRM
(c) Medium HRM (d) All of these

57 Creating an environment that facilitates a continuous and two way exchange of information between the superiors and the subordinates represents which model?
(a) High performance management model
(b) High involvement management model
(c) High commitment management model
(d) None of the above

58 Top management is interested in knowing how human resource management is contributing to
(a) profit making
(b) training of employees
(c) value of organisation
(d) None of the above

59 Which of the following is a new challenge in the field of IHRM?
(a) Outsourcing (b) Diversity management
(c) Right sizing (d) All of these

60 Which of the following is not a traditional model of outsourcing?
(a) Transactional outsourcing
(b) Functional outsourcing
(c) Operational outsourcing
(d) Utility outsourcing

61 Which is the right sequence of a stages of internationalisation?
1. Global 2. Transnational
3. Multinational 4. Domestic
5. International
(a) 4, 2, 1, 5, 3 (b) 4, 5, 3, 1, 2
(c) 4, 3, 5, 2, 1 (d) 4, 5, 2, 3, 1

62 The country where the headquarters of a multinational company is located is known as
(a) host-country (b) home-country
(c) third-country (d) None of these

63 When an international firm follows a strategy of choosing only from the nationals of the parent country, it is called
(a) polycentric approach (b) geocentric approach
(c) ethnocentric approach (d) None of these

64 When the firms adopt a strategy of limiting recruitment to the nationalities of the host country where the branch is located, it is called
(a) polycentric approach (b) geocentric approach
(c) ethnocentric approach (d) None of these

65 When the firms choose a strategy of recruiting the most suitable persons for the positions available in the firm, irrespective of their nationalities, it is called
(a) polycentric approach
(b) geocentric approach
(c) ethnocentric approach
(d) None of the above

66 Which of the following factors is not related directly to the success of expatriate assignments?
(a) The personality of expatriate employees
(b) The intentions of expatriate employees
(c) The incapability of the spouse to adjust to the new situation
(d) The nature of products produced by the company

67 Financial payments, above and over a regular base pay for employees are called
(a) ethnocentric allowances (b) mobility premiums
(c) hardship allowances (d) foreign service premiums

68 Understanding behaviour and culture of host country's market by host manager in corporation orientation is known to be
(a) ethnocentric (b) polycentric
(c) geocentric (d) expat-centric

69 Non-citizen employees of a country in which they are working is classified as
(a) expatriates (b) subordinates
(c) coordinates (d) None of these

70 Specific procedure according to which 'employees of company has legal rights to take part in policy designing' is classified as
(a) sub-determination (b) subordination
(c) coordination (d) co-determination

71 In corporation orientation, management style and evaluation criteria of home country is superior to anything that host country offers, known as
(a) polycentric (b) geocentric
(c) ethnocentric (d) expat-centric

72 **Procedure that aims to assess probable success of assignees, in handling of a foreign transfer is classified as**

(a) adaptability screening (b) ethnocentric screening
(c) polycentric screening (d) geocentric screening

73 **Lumpsum payments given to employees, who move from one assignment to another are classified as**

(a) ethnocentric allowances (b) mobility premiums
(c) hardship allowances (d) foreign service premiums

74 **Indian executives, who are working in Australian branch of United Kingdom multinational bank are an example of**

(a) third-country nationals (b) second-country nationals
(c) home-country nationals (d) None of these

75 **Indian citizen work in China, in subsidiary of company whose headquarter is located in India, an example of**

(a) expatriates (b) second-country nationals
(c) home-country nationals (d) Both (a) and (c)

76 **Compensation given to expatriates for exceptionally hard working and living conditions at certain locations is classified as**

(a) ethnocentric allowances
(b) mobility premiums
(c) hardship allowances
(d) foreign service premiums

77 **Values of top executives include**

(a) polycentric (b) geocentric
(c) ethnocentric (d) All of these

78 **There are a number of criticisms against the current literature on International Human Resource Management (IHRM). Which of the following is not one of these criticisms?**

(a) The field is not clearly defined
(b) It is influenced by a discussion of concepts and issues with little backing systematic research
(c) The field should be built around a broader set of questions
(d) It lacks appropriate theoretical structures

79 **The main focus on IHRM is the**

(a) management of expatriates
(b) worldwide management of people
(c) management of small businesses internationally
(d) management of international organisations

80 **Two groups of factors influence the choice of 'global *vs* local' HR practices and policies in multinational enterprises. These factors are known as**

(a) exogenous and endogenous
(b) ancillary and accessory
(c) interactive and inter-personal
(d) concessionary and cooperation

81 **The use of Third Country Nationals (TCNs) provides a number of advantages. Which of the following is not one of these advantages?**

(a) They take the organisation away from criticism as ethnocentric
(b) They are usually considerably cheaper
(c) They often have a cultural awareness which can be beneficial
(d) They have an adequate knowledge of home office goals and procedures

82 **International organisations normally employ expatriates in the following roles, except**

(a) country manager
(b) technical specialist
(c) financial controller
(d) union leader

83 **In international human resource management, communication in ethnocentric organisations are ....**

(a) totally connected in a network of subsidiaries and subsidiaries with headquarters
(b) little among subsidiaries and little between the subsidiary and headquarters
(c) from headquarters to local subsidiaries
(d) little between the subsidiary and headquarters, medium to high among subsidiaries in regions

84 **In international human resource management, communication in geocentric organisations are ....**

(a) totally connected in a network of subsidiaries and subsidiaries with headquarters
(b) little among subsidiaries and little between the subsidiary and headquarters
(c) from headquarters to local subsidiaries
(d) little between the subsidiary and headquarters, medium to high among subsidiaries in regions

85 **In international human resource management, communication in polycentric organisations are ....**

(a) totally connected in a network of subsidiaries and subsidiaries with headquarters
(b) little among subsidiaries and little between the subsidiary and headquarters
(c) from headquarters to local subsidiaries
(d) little between the subsidiary and headquarters, medium to high among subsidiaries in regions

86 **In international human resource management, geocentric organisations are usually staffed with ....**

(a) home country managers
(b) the best people where they can be utilised the best
(c) host country managers
(d) managers that may come from nations within the region

87 **In international human resource management, polycentric organisations are usually staffed with ....**

(a) home country managers
(b) the best people where they can be utilised the best
(c) host country managers
(d) managers that may come from nations within the region

88 **In international human resource management, ethnocentric organisations are usually staffed with ....**

(a) home country managers
(b) the best people where they can be utilised the best
(c) host country managers
(d) managers that may come from nations within the region

89 **Which one of the following statements regarding international transfers is incorrect?**

(a) International organisations are increasingly employing expatriates on local terms and conditions
(b) Expatriation is relatively inexpensive
(c) The development of Information and Communication Technology (ICT) will not render international transfers and international travelling redundant
(d) Short-term assignees, international commuters, the frequent flyers and the international project teams share in many ways the same stresses as expatriates in terms of their social lives and family pressures

90 **Factors creating the global marketplace include all of the following except**

(a) lowering of costs of doing business globally
(b) privatisation and globalisation of government services
(c) growth in domestic businesses
(d) satellites and computer technology

91 **Someone who lives and works in a foreign country is an**

(a) expatriate
(b) holiday maker
(c) international jet-setter
(d) immigrant

92 **HRM as practised by multinational organisations is called**

(a) global HRM
(b) personnel management practices
(c) domestic HRM
(d) international HRM

93 **The key questions to be asked when developing an international HRM policy is**

(a) who is going to coordinate the HRM functions?
(b) what type of organisation is desired?
(c) how can cross boarder training be designed?
(d) when should the HR manager begin developing HR policies?

94 **Whirlpool's user of a performance management system worldwide is an example of**

(a) extended management control over employees
(b) attempts to increase productivity in all its branches
(c) an international HRM policy
(d) a policy that has adopted a global village philosophy

95 **To be effective in the international environment HRM policies must**

(a) reflect an international view
(b) focus on domestic issues
(c) accommodate differences in management styles
(d) effectively transplant HRM policies and practices from the home country to all other offices

96 **Organisations that do not adopt a strategic HRM approach and a global vision**

(a) develop effective two way communication
(b) are virtually guaranteed to fail
(c) find it easier to implement traditional HRM activities
(d) have much more flexibility in responding to environmental changes

97 **When a person from one culture communicates with a person from another culture they are engaging in**

(a) cross-cultural communication
(b) two way communication
(c) multi-focus communication
(d) verbal communication

98 **HR issues that will require adaptation to fit different cultures include all of the following except**

(a) training and development
(b) performance appraisal
(c) compensation
(d) job analysis

99 **Which of the following was not suggested by stone as a suitable criteria for the evaluation of expatriate performance**

(a) technical skills
(b) language proficiency
(c) work performed
(d) personality variables

100 **All aspects of training and development in international organisations are affected by all of the following except**

(a) cultural differences
(b) diversity of the workforce
(c) financial costs
(d) language differences

101 **Japanese firms stress the importance of what type of training?**

(a) Leadership (b) Communication
(c) Inter-personal skills (d) Technical knowledge

102 When an organisation enters the international training and development area, the HR manager needs to
(a) be sensitive to local customs and expectations
(b) identify costs of developing cross boarded programs
(c) develop programs that focus on enhancing technical skills and knowledge
(d) ensure that training and development programs are clearly linked to compensation management

103 Compensation strategies that reward individual performance and the acquisition of individual skills and know-how are common in
(a) individualistic cultures (b) egalitarian cultures
(c) collectivist cultures (d) risk-averse cultures

104 Bureaucratic reward systems that emphasise fixed pay are preferred in
(a) individualistic cultures
(b) group oriented cultures
(c) risk-averse cultures
(d) egalitarian cultures

105 When building employees working near a Chinese restaurant were paid an allowance because the cooking aromas made them hungry it was called
(a) hardship allowance
(b) stress pay
(c) danger pay
(d) dim sim allowance

106 When implementing industrial relations practices overseas, an Indian head office should ensure coordination so that
(a) policies are the same as in India
(b) practices adhere to and reinforce strategic HRM philosophies and policies and are in harmony with the desired corporate culture
(c) all employees belong to key trade unions in the industry
(d) concessions are made in each country so that operations can run smoothly

107 IHRM is an area of academic study which focuses on
(a) comparative research
(b) the movement of individuals across national boundaries
(c) the exchange of ideas and practices
(d) the policies and practices of MNC's

108 A global economy means
(a) greater convergence of national economic and social identities
(b) greater divergence
(c) unrestricted movement of people across national boundaries
(d) a global culture

109 Often the reason why expatriate assignments fail and why some immigrants and migrant workers in the UK find difficulty in assimilating into the British way of life is because of
(a) cultural differences
(b) homesickness
(c) climate
(d) reduction in remuneration in pay and conditions

110 Hofstede's five variables power distance; individualism, masculinity/femininity; uncertainty avoidance and long-term *v/s* short-term orientation; were terms used to describe
(a) family traits (b) HR strategy
(c) national differences (d) globalisation

111 International HRM originally consisted of three major clusters on inquiry, namely
1. the conduct of people management in internationally operating companies.
2. the international transfer of staff, focused on expatriation.
3. comparing HRM policies and practices across different countries.
4. comparing different culture with each other.

Codes
(a) 1, 2 and 3 (b) 2, 3 and 4
(c) 1, 3 and 4 (d) All of these

112 Which of the following statements are true?
1. When an organisation enters the international training and development area the HR manager must consider issues of ethnocentricity
2. National culture does not have any impact on compensation strategies.
3. Effective managers use one consistent style of management in all situations.

Codes
(a) Only 1 (b) Both 2 and 3
(c) Both 1 and 3 (d) All of these

113 Which of the following statements are true/false?
(i) Domestic HRM is restricted within the national boundaries.
(ii) IHRM is less complicated as it can be customised as per country's need.
(iii) Organisational structures of IHRM change due to constrains imposed by host government regulations and ownership equally.
(iv) Individualism *vs* collectivism refers to the level in which people in a certain country tolerate uncertainity.

Codes
(a) (i) and (ii) are true, (iii) and (iv) are false
(b) (i) and (iii) are true, (ii) and (iv) are false
(c) (i) and (iv) are true, (iii) and (i) are false
(d) (i), (ii) and (iii) are true, (iv) are false

114 **Which of the following statements are true/false?**

(i) When a person from one culture communicates with a person from another culture they are engaging in cross cultural communication.

(ii) The development of the global marketplace and global organisation has been influenced by workforce mobility.

(iii) The employee easily adapts to the new environment due to cultural difference.

Codes

(a) (i) is true, (ii) and (iii) are false
(b) (ii) is true, (i) and (iii) are false
(c) (i) and (ii) are true, (iii) is false
(d) (iii) is true, (i) and (ii) are false

115 **Which of the following statements are true/false?**

(i) International companies donot have direct foreign investment.

(ii) MNCs have localised subsidiaries.

(iii) Global organisations treat the entire world as one single country.

(iv) TNCs combine the local responsiveness of an MNC and the efficiency of a global corporation.

Codes

(a) (i) and (ii) are true, (iii) and (iv) are false
(b) (i), (ii) and (iii) are true, (iv) is false
(c) (i), (iii) and (iv) are true, (ii) is false
(d) (iii) and (iv) are true, (i) and (ii) are false

116 **I. Expatriates are non-citizens of the countries in which they are working.**

II. Third Country Nationals (TCN) are citizens of a country other than the parent or the host country.

Codes

(a) Both statements are correct
(b) Both statements are incorrect
(c) Statement I is correct, II is incorrect
(d) Statements I is incorrect, II is correct

117 **I. Codetermination is the rule where employees have the legal right to voice in setting company policies.**

II. Work councils are formal, employee elected groups of worker representatives.

Codes

(a) Both statements are correct
(b) Both statements are incorrect
(c) Statement I is correct, II is incorrect
(d) Statements I is incorrect, II is correct

118 **Assertion (A) Performance appraisal cannot be error free and unbiased.**

Reason (R) The appraisal methods are covertly influenced by human judgement, which may be vitiated by inter-personal discriminatory impulses.

Codes

(a) (A) is true, but (R) is false
(b) (A) is false, but (R) is true
(c) (R) does not subscribe to the (A)
(d) Both (A) and (R) are true and (R) validate (A)

119 **Assertion (A) Ethnocentric approach is easily adaptable.**

Reason (R) The vision, mission and objective of the parent company can be easily adopted by the subsidiaries.

Codes

(a) (A) is true, but (R) is false
(b) (A) is false, but (R) is true
(c) (R) does not subscribe to the (A)
(d) Both (A) and (R) are true and (R) validate (A)

120 **Assertion (A) Hofstede have identified five cultural dimensions for which each coutnry could be classified in.**

Reason (R) The five dimensions are power distance, uncertainity avoidance, masculinity versus feminity, individualism versus collectivism and time constraint.

Codes

(a) (A) is true, but (R) is false
(b) (A) is false, but (R) is true
(c) (R) does not subscribe to the (A)
(d) Both (A) and (R) are true and (R) validate (A)

121 **Assertion (A) The most common approach to formulating expatriate pay is balance sheet approach.**

Reason (R) Balance sheet approach equalises the purchasing power across countries.

Codes

(a) (A) is true, but (R) is false
(b) (A) is false, but (R) is true
(c) (R) does not subscribe to the (A)
(d) Both (A) and (R) are true and (R) validate (A)

122 **Match the following.**

List I	List II
1. Split pay approach	A. Equalising purchasing power
2. Balance sheet approach	B. Half a person's pay in home currency and other half in local currency.
3. Hardship allowance	C. Compensation for hard living and working conditions.
4. Mobility premiums	D. Lumpsum payments to reward employees for moving from one assignment to other.

	A	B	C	D
(a)	1	2	4	3
(b)	2	1	3	4
(c)	1	2	3	4
(d)	2	3	4	1

123 Match the following.

List I	List II
A. Polycentric approach	1. Hiring employees throughout the world.
B. Ethnocentric	2. Home country employees are better performers.
C. Geocentric	3. Host country employees are better performers.

	A	B	C
(a)	1	2	3
(b)	2	1	3
(c)	3	2	1
(d)	1	3	2

124 Match the following.

List I	List II
1. Functional structure	A. Specialised jobs are grouped according to traditional business functions.
2. International division structure	B. Grouping each international business activity into its own division local currency.
3. Matrix division	C. Similar products are grouped under one product head.
4. Product division structure	D. Simultaneously deals with competing pressure for global integration and local responsiveness.

	A	B	C	D
(a)	1	2	3	4
(b)	1	4	2	3
(c)	1	2	4	3
(d)	1	3	4	2

PREVIOUS YEARS' QUESTIONS

2018

1 An organisation that provides autonomy to its business units operating in other countries is called

(a) Global corporation
(b) International corporation
(c) Multinational corporation
(d) Transnational corporation

2 Multinational corporations are categorised into four categories namely multidomestic, global, international, and transnational on the basis of their response to two factors namely; global integration and national responsiveness. Keeping this in view match the type of Multinationals given in List I with their respective characteristics given in List II.

List I	List II
A. Multidomestic	1. High national responsiveness, and high global integration
B. Global	2. High national responsiveness and low global integration
C. International	3. High global integration and low national responsiveness
D. Transnational	4. Low to moderate global integration and low to moderate national responsiveness

Codes

	A	B	C	D
(a)	2	3	4	1
(b)	1	2	3	4
(c)	3	4	2	1
(d)	4	1	3	2

3 Which of the following are the trends in International Industrial Relations System ?

1. MNCs try to cultivate centralised ethnocentric approach to the extent of pressurising the National Governments to bring out unprecedented economic and labour reforms.
2. MNCs aspire for hassle free business climate and for this, adopt the practice of replacing expensive labour with cheap labour through outsourcing.
3. MNCs promote individual centric human resource policies to keep trade unions at bay.
4. MNCs act like 'octopus'. Nations, trade unions and other actors of industrial relations only grapple with the unfathomable strength of MNCs.

Codes

(a) 1 and 3 (b) 2, 3 and 4
(c) 1, 3 and 4 (d) 1, 2, 3 and 4

4 From among the following, who focused on the 'soft side of organisation' as a sequel to globalisation comprising adhocracy, simple structure, the divisionalised form, the machine and professional bureaucracy ?

(a) Henry Mintzberg
(b) Barlett and Ghosal
(c) Galbraith and Kazanjaam
(d) Burns and Stalker

5 Match the following.

List I	List II
A. Ethnocentric Approach	1. Primary positions held by nationals from host country
B. Polycentric Approach	2. Qualified people are hired at home and from abroad irrespective of nationality

List I	List II
C. Regiocentric Approach	3. Primary positions are held by citizens of home country
D. Geocentric Approach	4. Primary positions are held by people from same region with similar cultures, experiences and management practices

Codes

	A	B	C	D		A	B	C	D
(a)	4	1	3	2	(b)	2	4	1	3
(c)	3	2	1	4	(d)	3	1	4	2

6 Which of the following is not a characteristic of culture according to Hofstede?

(a) Power distance
(b) Person's relationship with natural world
(c) Masculinity and femininity
(d) Individualism *vs* collectivism

7 Match the following.

List I	List II
A. Human Capital Approach	1. Human Development Report
B. Socio/Psychological Approach	2. TU Schultz
C. Poverty Alleviation Approach	3. David MC Clelland
D. World Human Development Approach	4. Mahbub-Ul-Haq

Codes

	A	B	C	D
(a)	2	3	4	1
(b)	2	1	4	3
(c)	2	3	1	4
(d)	2	4	1	3

8 Match the following.

List I (HRM Models)	List II (Themes)
A. Long-term Labour Purchase Model	1. Seeks to minimise wage and benefit costs; and Employment levels within organisational boundaries. Outsourcing and externalisation of employment are encouraged.
B. Work-force Commitment Model	2. Different employment models for core and non-core work are adopted.
C. Labour Transactional Model	3. Firms would employ workers, for as long as they performed well and the company has the capacity to pay.
D. Mixed Model	4. Employers provide job security in order to elicit long term commitment and organisation can develop social and intellectual capital within the boundaries of the firm.

Codes

	A	B	C	D		A	B	C	D
(a)	3	1	4	2	(b)	3	4	1	2
(c)	2	4	1	3	(d)	3	2	4	1

9 Which of the following are the trends in International Industrial Relations System?

1. MNCs try to cultivate centralised ethnocentric approach to bring extent of pressurising the National Governments to bring out unprecedented economic and labour reforms.
2. MNCs aspire for hassle free business climate and for this, adopt the practice of replacing expensive labour with cheap labour through outsourcing.
3. MNCs promote individual centric human resource policies to keep trade unions at bay.
4. MNCs act like 'octopus'. Nations, trade unions and other actors of industrial relations only grapple with the unfathomable strength of MNCs.

Codes

(a) 1 and 3
(b) 2, 3 and 4
(c) 1, 3 and 4
(d) 1, 2, 3 and 4

2016

10 Which model of HRM propagates that, "if integrated set of HRM practices is applied in a coherent fashion, with a view to achieving the normative goals of high commitment, high quality and task flexibility, then superior individual performance will result, which would lead to superior organisational performance"?

(a) Harvard Model
(b) Warwick Model
(c) David Guest Model
(d) John M Storey Model

11 Perlmutter (1969) has proposed and distinguished three attitudes of top management with respect to internationalisation, which influence the organisational structure, lines of communication and information, and approach to HRM activities etc.
Match the attitude List I with their descriptions given in List II.

List I	List II
A. Ethnocentric	1. Personnel management is based largely on the view that values, norms, and customs differ from country to country, and local markets can therefore best be reached by local managers (host country nationals).
B. Polycentric	2. Personnel management focuses to a great extent on recruiting and training parent country nationals for key positions, regardless of location.
C. Geocentric	3. Approach is to utilise the best managers throughout the world, regardless of their nationality.

Codes

	A	B	C		A	B	C
(a)	1	2	3	(b)	3	1	2
(c)	1	3	2	(d)	2	1	3

2015

12 Match the followings in relation to staffing approaches adopted by MNCs.

List I	List II
A. Ethnocentric Approach	1. Requires host country nationals to be hired to manage subsidiaries whereas parent-country nationals occupy key positions at corporate headquarters.
B. Polycentric Approach	2. Seeks the best people for key jobs regardless of nationality.
C. Geocentric Approach	3. Requires parent-country nationals on all the key positions

Codes

	A	B	C		A	B	C
(a)	3	1	2	(b)	1	2	3
(c)	2	3	1	(d)	3	2	1

13 When an international company followed a strategy of choosing employees only from the nationals of the parent country, it is called

(a) Geocentric approach (b) Ethnocentric approach
(c) Polycentric approach (d) Both (a) and (b)

14 When a new employee's high expectations and enthusiasm confront the reality of a boring and unchallenging job, it is called

(a) Expectancy shock (b) Future shock
(c) Reality shock (d) Cultural shock

15 The person whose nationality is the same as that of the country in which the corporate office of the MNC is located, but differs from the country in which he is working, is called

(a) Parent Country National
(b) Host Country National
(c) Third Country National
(d) Home Country National

16 Which of the following is not a cultural dimension of Hofstede's model?

(a) Power distance
(b) Uncertainity avoidance
(c) Time orientation
(d)Individualism collectivism

17 Which of the following approaches aims at payments so as to maintain home-country living standards plus some financial incentive?

(a) Balance sheet approach (b) Going rate approach
(c) Host based approach (d) Global market approach

18 Hofstede's cultural variable of 'Power Distance' means

1. the extent to which less powerful members of organisation accept and expect that power is distributed unequally.
2. that the society's level of inequity of power is endorsed by followers as much as by leaders.
3. that power and inequity are fundamental facts of any society.

Select the correct answer using the codes given below

Codes

(a) Only 1 (b) Only 2 (c) 1 and 2 (d) 1,2 and 3

19 Assertion (A) Globalisation has opened up opportunities like open markets, free flow of goods, services and people as well as has posed threats like jobless economic growth, and cultural erosion and environmental degradation.

Reason (R) There has been an uneven competition between the develped and developing countries resulting in issues like dumping, privatisation of primary services like health and education, thereby remaining beyond the reach of millions of poor and unemployed.

Codes

(a) Both A and R are not correct
(b) A is correct, but R is not correct
(c) A is not correct, but R is correct
(d) A is correct, R is also correct, but does not fully explain the A

20 Match the following.

List I	List II
A. Outsourcing	1. Specialists are invited at client location to perform specific tasks for which there is no internal resource
B. Insourcing	2. Disciplined provisioning and blending of business and IT services from both internal and external providers
C. Multi-sourcing	3. Regular use of external agency for non-core functions
D. Open sourcing	4. Act of releasing free software license containing knowledge and information by professional and scientific groups

Codes

	A	B	C	D		A	B	C	D
(a)	3	1	2	4	(b)	1	4	3	2
(c)	4	2	3	1	(d)	2	3	1	4

2014

21 The country, where the headquater of a multinational company is located is knows as

(a) Host country (b) Home country
(c) Third country (d) None of these

22 In which of the following approaches, a multinational company treats each subsidiary as a distinct national entity with some decision-making autonomy?

(a) Ethnocentric approach
(b) Geocentric approach
(c) Polycentric approach
(d) Regiocentric approach

23 Which of the following factors is not related directly to the success of expatriation?

1. The nature of product produced by the company.

2. The personality of expatriate employees.

3. The intensions of expatriate employees.

4. The incapability of the spouse of expatriate employees to adjust to the new situation.

Select the correct answer using the codes given below

Codes

(a) Only 1 (b) Only 2 (c) Only 3 (d) 1 and 4

24 Being a manager in an organsation, if you are asked to enrich the job of your subordinate, you will not consider which of the following?

(a) Remove some controls while retaining accountability

(b) Increase the accountability-of individuals to their work

(c) Introduce new and more difficult tasks compared to those handled previously

(d) Assign general tasks to people to make them experts in those tasks

25 A polycentric organisation has

(a) parent country oriented approach

(b) host country oriented approach

(c) global approach

(d) third country oriented approach

26 Which of the following models is popular for its comparison of personnel management and human resource management on the basis of 'Hard' and 'Soft' approach?

(a) David Guest's Model (b) John M Story's Model

(c) CJ Fomburn's Model (d) Karen Legge's Model

27 A multicultural organisation

(a) reflects interests of diverse socio-cultural groups in its mission and operations

(b) is committed to eradicate social oppression in all forms within the organisation

(c) includes members of diverse cultural and social groups in decision-making

(d) All of the above

28 Globalisation refers to

1. the process of growing interdependence among elements of global economy.

2. worldwide interdependence of resource flows, product markets and business competition.

3. interdependence of product markets only.

4. interdependence for resources only.

Codes

(a) Only 4 (b) Both 1 and 2

(c) Only 3 (d) All of these

29 Which of the following characteristics of an economy is a barrier to globalisation of business?

(a) Shift of labour intensive Industry to low cost technology and advanced process

(b) Surplus labour

(c) Flexible production chains.

(d) Global production chains and integrated supply chain

ANSWERS

Exam Based Questions

1 *(c)*	2 *(c)*	3 *(d)*	4 *(b)*	5 *(c)*	6 *(d)*	7 *(b)*	8 *(c)*	9 *(b)*	10 *(d)*
11 *(d)*	12 *(b)*	13 *(c)*	14 *(d)*	15 *(d)*	16 *(a)*	17 *(b)*	18 *(a)*	19 *(c)*	20 *(c)*
21 *(a)*	22 *(c)*	23 *(c)*	24 *(a)*	25 *(d)*	26 *(d)*	27 *(d)*	28 *(c)*	29 *(a)*	30 *(b)*
31 *(d)*	32 *(c)*	33 *(b)*	34 *(b)*	35 *(c)*	36 *(b)*	37 *(d)*	38 *(b)*	39 *(c)*	40 *(a)*
41 *(b)*	42 *(d)*	43 *(d)*	44 *(d)*	45 *(b)*	46 *(b)*	47 *(a)*	48 *(d)*	49 *(d)*	50 *(c)*
51 *(b)*	52 *(d)*	53 *(a)*	54 *(a)*	55 *(c)*	56 *(d)*	57 *(a)*	58 *(c)*	59 *(d)*	60 *(b)*
61 *(b)*	62 *(b)*	63 *(c)*	64 *(a)*	65 *(b)*	66 *(d)*	67 *(d)*	68 *(b)*	69 *(a)*	70 *(d)*
71 *(c)*	72 *(a)*	73 *(b)*	74 *(a)*	75 *(c)*	76 *(c)*	77 *(d)*	78 *(d)*	79 *(b)*	80 *(a)*
81 *(b)*	82 *(a)*	83 *(c)*	84 *(a)*	85 *(d)*	86 *(b)*	87 *(c)*	88 *(a)*	89 *(b)*	90 *(c)*
91 *(a)*	92 *(d)*	93 *(b)*	94 *(c)*	95 *(a)*	96 *(b)*	97 *(b)*	98 *(d)*	99 *(b)*	100 *(c)*
101 *(d)*	102 *(a)*	103 *(a)*	104 *(c)*	105 *(d)*	106 *(b)*	107 *(d)*	108 *(a)*	109 *(a)*	110 *(c)*
111 *(a)*	112 *(d)*	113 *(b)*	114 *(c)*	115 *(c)*	116 *(a)*	117 *(a)*	118 *(d)*	119 *(d)*	120 *(a)*
121 *()*	122 *(b)*	123 *(c)*	124 *(b)*						

Previous Years' Questions

1 *(d)*	2 *(a)*	3 *(d)*	4 *(a)*	5 *(d)*	6 *(b)*	7 *(a)*	8 *(b)*	9 *(d)*	10 *(d)*
11 *(d)*	12 *(a)*	13 *(b)*	14 *(c)*	15 *(a)*	16 *(c)*	17 *(a)*	18 *(d)*	19 *(d)*	20 *(a)*
21 *(b)*	22 *(c)*	23 *(a)*	24 *(d)*	25 *(b)*	26 *(b)*	27 *(d)*	28 *(b)*	29 *(b)*	

UNIT 4

Organisational Behaviour

Organisational behaviour is a discipline that studies individual as well as the group behaviour in the organisation. This chapter highlights various theories related to leadership, motivation alongwith managing organisational changes.

Concept of Organisational Behaviour

Organisational Behaviour (OB) relates to the behaviour of people working in an organisation towards their organisation. An organisation is a unit or an association of people that come together for a definite purpose. The purpose of organisation is to work towards achieving a common goal.

It relates to what people think and feel about their institution. Studying of the human behaviour helps to understand the people. This kind of knowledge and understanding helps in improving the relationships between people working in an organisation and overall working of an organisation.

Organisational behaviour is concerned with understanding human behaviour, predicting certain actions or behavioural changes in the employees and moulding it at the same time for the betterment of the organisation.

Organisations have to adopt a winning attitude to stand 'different' from others. For this, they have to successfully manage people.

When people are the key, then innovative managing skills need to be adopted to manage people which will help the managers make a transition to the new paradigm.

According to **Robbins**, "Organisational behaviour is a field of study that investigate the impact that individuals, groups and structure have on behaviour within organisation for the purpose of applying such knowledge towards improving organisation's effectiveness".

According to **Keith Davis**, "Organisational behaviour is the study and application at knowledge about how people (as individuals and group) act within organisation. It strives to identify ways in which people can act more effectively."

In this Chapter

According to **Luthans**, "Organisational behaviour can be defined as the understanding, prediction and management of the human behaviour that affect the performance of the organisations."

Thus, organisational behaviour is concerned with the study of the behaviour, attitudes and performance of workers in an organisational settings and the effects of workers on the organisation and its effectiveness.

Elements of Organisational Behaviour

The key elements in the organisational behaviour are individual, group, structure, technology and the environment in which the organisation operates.

These are as follows

Individuals

People make up the internal and social system of the organisation. They consist of individuals and groups. Individual employees work in the organisation to satisfy their needs, ego, aspirations and experiences.

The work behaviour of every individual is influenced by his heredity characters, family relationships, social set up, racial background, religious beliefs, technological innovations and so on. The desires, needs, wants, attitudes drives goals and experiences are also instrumental in framing anyone's behaviour.

Groups

In every organisation, human beings either work individually or in a group. The groups may be large or small, formal or informal, official or unofficial. Groups are dynamic and they work in the organisation to achieve their objectives.

The main function of groups is to set goal, behave and think and act accordingly, to accomplish the set objectives and show outstanding performance.

Structure

Structure defines the formal relationships of the people in organisations. These formal and structured relationship are instrumental in shaping the behaviour of employees at work.

Technology

Technology such as machines and work processes provide the resources with which people work and it affects the tasks performed by people in the organisation.

The technology used has a significant influence on working relationships. It allows people to do more and work better but it also restricts' people in various ways.

Environment

All organisations operate within an external environment. The environment consists of government policies, social systems, religious beliefs, family and economic conditions, national philosophies, employee's psychology which have their own behaviour and influence mutually on each other.

Scope of Organisational Behaviour

In the Field of Psychology Psychology is the science that seeks to measure, explain and some times change the behaviour of human. Psychologists concern themselves with studying and attempting to understand individual behaviour.

Their contribution have been expanded to include learning, perception, personality, emotions, training, leadership effectiveness, job satisfaction, performance appraisals, attitude measurement, employee selection work design etc.

In the Field of Sociology Sociology is the study of people in relation to their fellow human beings. It has made its greatest contribution to organisational behaviour through the study of group behaviour in organisation.

Group dynamics, design of work teams, organisational cuture, communications etc help to know more about social behaviour and how to maintain harmony within different departments of the organisation.

Social Psychology Social psychologists make significant contribution in the area of measuring, understanding and changing attitude, communication pattern, the way in which groups activities can satisfy individual needs and groups decision-making process. This subjects help in understanding human as well as social behaviour, needs and aspirations.

Anthropology Anthropologists work on culture and environment has helped us to understand difference in fundamental values, attitudes and behaviour between people in different countries and within different organisation. Knowledge of this subject gives an overall information about the type of people working in an organisation.

Political Science It studies the behaviour of individuals and groups within a political environment. This helps in understanding the dynamics of power centres, individual interests, allocation of power. The knowledge of this subject can be used to understand the behaviour of employees under different conditions.

Economics The study of this subject helps to understand various aspects of the organisation which are related to costs, transactions, internal coordination and market trends. This helps in avoiding market failures and better understanding of the human resource and the environment of the organisation.

Significance of Organisational Behaviour

To get the productive work from employees, managers must know how the people in the organisation behave.

Thus, the significance of OB is explained in three heads

Understanding Human Behaviour

A human behaviour is a complex phenomenon and is affected by a large number of factors *i.e.* psychological, social, cultural etc. *OB studies individual behaviour in respect of these factors at four levels, which are as follows*

Individual Level Individual behaviour of each person.

Interpersonal Level Behaviour with other people.

Group Level Behaviour in a group.

Intergroup Level Interaction between two groups.

Controlling and Directing Behaviour

Once the manager understands that why a person is behaving in a particular manner, he should also know the technique of controlling his employees' behaviour, so that the organisational goals can be achieved. For this purpose, OB helps managers to use any one of these tools to control employees, *which are as follows*

Use of Power and Sanctions Power is the capacity of an individual to take certain actions only under given authority. Sanctions are certain restrictions on the actions of employees which can be employed using power.

Leadership It is the managerial trait inherent in the manager which can greatly influence the behaviour of employees. A manager can adopt different leadership styles keeping in view the kind of people, an organisation is having and the situations.

Communication Managers spend considerable time in communicating with internal as well as external world. Communication is a tool by which anyone can influence the behaviour of other person. It is through counselling and advice that various personal problems of employees can be sorted out.

Organisational Climate A climate conducive to the growth and well being of people makes the organisation more efficient. Climate does not mean only physiological conditions and facilities.

A good organisational climate is made up of effective supervision, opportunity for realisation of personal goals, congenial relations with peers and subordinates at work place and a sense of our organisation. Such climate can make the employees behave confirming to organisational norms.

Organisational Adaptation

An organisation never works in isolation. It will continually interact with environmental changes *i.e.* changing standards of living, way of thinking, technological changes, etc. An organisation has to adapt itself to such changes. A manager has to find out the need for changes, than he has to face resistance from employees to these changes.

Features of Organisational Behaviour

- OB uses scientific research to know and understand the functioning of an organisation.
- This knowledge and understanding helps to predict the human behaviour under different conditions.
- It helps organisation in the field of marketing, management, human resources, organising events, maintaining cordial industrial relations etc.

Approaches to Organisational Behaviour

There are mainly four approaches to organisational behaviour. *They are*

Human Resource Approach

The human resource approach is concerned with the growth and development of people towards higher levels of competency, creativity and fulfillment, because people are the central resource in any organisation.

This approach helps employees become better in terms of work and responsibility and then it tries to create a climate in which they can contribute to the best of their improved abilities.

Contingency Approach

A contingency approach to organisational behaviour implies that different situations require different behavioural practices for effectiveness instead of following a traditional approach for all situations. Each situation must be analysed carefully to determine the significant variables that exist in order to establish the more effective practices.

This approach encourages analysis of each situation prior to action. Thus, it helps to use all the current knowledge about people in the organisation in the most appropriate manner.

Productivity Approach

Productivity is a ratio that compares units of output with units of input. It is often measured in terms of economic inputs and outputs.

Productivity is considered to be improved, if more outputs can be produced from the same amount of inputs. Besides economic inputs and outputs, human and social inputs and outputs are also very important and cannot be ignored for holistic and sustainable development.

Systems Approach

As discussed earlier, a system is an interrelated part of an organisation or a society that interacts with everyone related to that organisation or society and functions as a whole.

Within the organisation, 'people' employ 'technology' in performing the 'task' that they are responsible for, while the 'structure' of the organisation serves as a basis for co-ordinating all their different activities.

The systems view emphasises the interdependence of each of these elements within the organisation, if the organisation as a whole is to function effectively.

Organisations must also recognise their interdependence with the broader environments within which they exists. So, there is dependency on each other for achieving organisational effectiveness.

Contemporary Organisational Behaviour

Organisational behaviour is now considered as a separate field of study. Still it is not considered as a perfect science. Now, efforts have been made to synthesize principles, concepts and processes. *OB in contemporary business and management practices is considered as*

An Interdisciplinary Approach

Organisational behaviour is basically an interdisciplinary approach. It draws from other disciplines like Psychology, Sociology and Anthropology, Economics, Political Science, Law and History etc. It assimilates the elements of various disciplines.

Organisational behaviour addresses the issues related to perception, attitudes, behaviour, personality, belief systems, idelogies etc and looking forward to get the answers of pertinent questions which belong to all these above mentioned disciplines.

An Applied Science

The basic objective of organisational behaviour is to make application of various researches to solve the organisational problems, particularly related to the human behavioural aspect.

Normative and Value Centered

Organisational behaviour is a normative science. A normative science prescribes how the various findings of researches can be applied to get organisational results, which are acceptable to the society.

Thus, what is acceptable by the society or individuals engaged in an organisation is a matter of values of the society and people concerned.

Humanistic and Optimistic

Organisational behaviour focuses on people from humanistic point of view. It is based on the belief that needs and motivation of people are of high concern.

Further, there is optimism about the innate potential of man to be independent, creative, predictive and capable of contributing positively to the objectives of the organisation.

Oriented towards Organisational Objectives

Organisational behaviour is oriented towards organisational objectives. Infact, organisational behaviour tries to integrate both individual and organisational objectives so that both are achieved simultaneously.

A Total System Approach

An individual's behaviour can be analysed keeping in view his psychological framework, interpersonal-orientation, group influence and social and cultural factors. Thus, individual's nature is quite complex and organisational behaviour by applying systems approach tries to find solutions for this complexity.

Objectives of Organisational Behaviour

Scope of organisational behaviour can be understood from the following points

- To find out the determinants which constitute behaviour.
- To find out the particular cause and effect relationship and learn which can be modified and which is beyond control.
- To develop more refined and workable sets of assumption that are directly relevant to the tasks at hand.
- Predict human behaviour in the organisational setting by drawing a clear distinction between individual behaviour and group behaviour.
- Organisational behaviour assists in making judgements, assumptions about a particular situation explicitly taking into consideration the goals, motives, blind spots and weaknesses associated with the organisation.

Different Perspectives to View Organisational Behaviour

Organisational behaviour can be viewed from the perspective of three levels of analysis. The first level of analysis is from the perspective of individuals. The second is from the interaction of team members or groups and the third level is from the view point of the organisation as a whole.

These are as follows

Organisation at the Individual Level

Organisational behaviour can be studied with the perspective of individual members of the organisation. This approach to organisational behaviour draws heavily on the discipline of psychology and explains why individuals behave and react the way they do to different organisational policies, practices and procedures.

Within this perspective, theories of learning, motivation, satisfaction and leadership are brought to bear upon the behaviour and performance of individual members of an organisation.

Factors such as attitudes, beliefs, perceptions and personalities are taken into account and their impact upon individuals' behaviour and performance on the job is studied.

Organisation at the Group or Inter-personal Level

Under this perspective, it is studied how do people work together in groups? What factors determine whether group will be cohesive and productive? What types of tasks could be assigned to groups? These are some of the questions that can be asked about the effective functioning of groups in organisations.

An important component of organisational behaviour involves the application of knowledge and theories from social psychology to the study of groups in organisations.

Organisation at the Organisational Level

The analysis of organisation as a whole is a macro perspective that draws heavily on concepts and theories from Sociology. It studies the implications of the relationship between the organisation and its environ- ment.

Emphasis is laid on understanding how effectiveness of an organisation is influenced by organisational structure and design. These are several other factors that are studied as they affect the organisation in a big way, such as technology employed, size and age of the organisation. The functioning of each entity is examined in detail in context of organisational structure.

Model of Organisational Behaviour

The following four models of organisational behaviour are as follows

Autocratic Model

In an autocratic model, the manager has the power to command his subordinates to do a specific job. Management believes that it knows what is best for an organisation and therefore, employees are required to follow their orders.

The psychological result of this model on employees is their increasing dependence on their boss. Its main weakness is its high human cost.

Custodial Model/Paternity Model

This model focuses on better employee satisfaction and security. Under this model, organisations satisfy the security and welfare needs of employees. Hence, it is known as custodial model.

This model leads to employee dependence on an organisation rather than on boss. As a result of economic rewards and benefits, employees are happy and contented but they are not strongly motivated.

Supportive Model

This model assumes that employees will take responsibility, develop a drive to contribute and improve them if management will give them a chance.

Therefore, management's direction is to 'support' the employee's job performance rather than to 'support' employee benefit payments, as in the custodial approach. Since, management supports employees in their work, the psychological result is a feeling of participation and task involvement in an organisation.

Collegial Model

The term 'Collegial' relates to a body of persons having a common purpose. It is a team concept, *i.e.* management is the coach that builds a better team.

The management is seen as joint contributor rather than as a boss. The employee response to this situation is responsibility. The psychological result of the collegial approach for the employee is 'self-discipline'.

In this kind of environment, employees normally feel some degree of fulfillment and worthwhile contribution towards their work. This results in enthusiasm in employees' performance.

Comparison Between four Models of Organisational Behaviour

Organisational Behaviour	Autocratic	Custodial	Supportive	Collegial
Basis of model	Power	Economic Resources	Leadership	Partnership
Managerial-orientation	Authority	Money	Support	Team work
Employee psychological result	Dependence on boss	Dependence on organisation	Participation	Self-discipline
Employee needs met	Subsistence	Security	Status and Recognition	Self-actualisation
Performance result	Minimum	Passive cooperation	Awakened drives	Moderate enthusiasm

Motivation

Motivation refers to the willingness to strive towards predetermined goals. The word 'motivation' is derived from 'motive', which means an active form of a desire, craving or need that must be satisfied.

Motivation is the key to organisational effectiveness. The manager in general has to get the work done through others. These 'others' are human resources who need to be motivated to attain organisational objectives.

Motivation is referred as a driving force that initiates and directs behaviour. It is simply a desire or passion to achieve the particular goals.

According to **George R. Terry**, "Motivation is the desire within an individual that stimulates him or her to action."

According to **Viteles**, "An unsatisfied need which creates a state of tension or disequilibrium, causing the individual to move in a goal directed pattern towards restoring a state of equilibrium, by satisfying the need."

According to **Robert Dubin**, "It is the complex of forces starting and keeping a person at work in an organisation."

Characteristics of Motivation

- Motivation is an intrinsic drive, which activates and compels the person to behave in a particular manner.
- It originates from the needs and wants of an individual. It is a strong desire to achieve something, which forces him to work more efficiently.
- The motivation process is channelised by personality traits, learning abilities, perception and competence of an individual.
- Motivation is a way of stimulating and channelising the energy of an individual for achieving set goals.
- Motivation also plays a crucial role in determining the level of performance. Highly motivated employees get higher satisfaction, which may lead to higher efficiency.
- Motivating force and its degree, may differ from individual to individual depending on his personality, needs, competence and other factors.
- Motivation may be positive as well as negative. Positive motivation includes incentives, rewards and other benefits while negative motivation implies some punishment, fear, use of force etc.

Nature of Motivation

- It is related to personal feelings and thinking.
- It produces goal oriented behaviour.
- It is a continuous process.
- It follows a complex, system oriented approach.
- It can be positive or negative.
- It varies from person-to-person.

Importance of Motivation

- Motivation puts human resources into action. It creates willingness in the employees to work and helps in improving the productivity and thereby, increasing the level of efficiency and reduction in cost of operations.
- Motivation makes it possible to have optimum utilisation of resources and to live in a co-operative work environment.
- Motivation will ultimately bring stability in work force which will prove to be extremely effective in building up a good repution on the firm. It will enforce loyalty and sense of belongingness among employees.

Need-Based Theories to Motivation

Need-based theories try to answer the question, "what factor(s) motivate people to choose certain behaviours?"

Some of the widely known need-based theories are as follows

1. Maslow's Hierarchy of Needs

Maslow Abraham proposed his theory in the 1940s. This theory is popularly known as the Hierarchy of Needs. It assumes that people are motivated to satisfy five levels of needs *i.e* Physiological, Security, Social, Esteem and Self-actualisation needs.

The following figure shows Maslow's hierarchy of needs

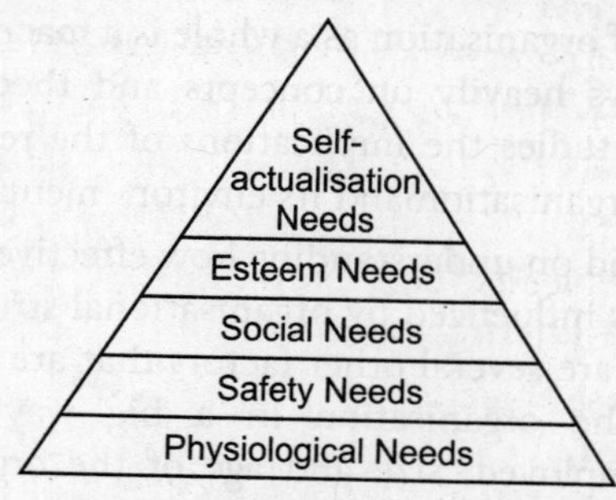

Maslow's Hierarchy of Needs

Maslow suggested that the five levels of needs are arranged in accordance with their importance, starting from the bottom of the hierarchy. *These are as follows*

- **Physiological Needs** represent the basic issues of survival such as food, sex, water and air.
- **Security or safety Needs** refer to the requirements for a secure physical and emotional environment. Examples include the desire for adequate housing and clothing, job security and the desire for safe working conditions.

- **Belonging or Social Needs** are related to the social aspect of human life. They include the need for love and affection and the need to be accepted by one's peers. For most people, these needs are satisfied by a combination of family and community relationships and friendships on the job.
- **Esteem Needs** *actually comprise of two different sets of needs*
  (a) The need for a positive self-image and self-respect.
  (b) The need for recognition and respect from others.
  Organisations can help address esteem needs by providing a variety of external symbols of accomplishment such as job titles and spacious offices.
- **Self-actualisation** is the top most need according to Maslow which is the challenging job for a manager to address. Self- actualisation needs involve knowing about his own potentials, abilities, skills and aptitudes. Self-exploration and self-awareness are very necessary exercises to be done to realise one's own potential.

2. ERG Theory of Motivation

Clayton Alderfer has proposed an alternative hierarchy of needs called the ERG Theory of Motivation. The letters E, R and G stand for Existence, Relatedness and Growth.

The following figure shows ERG theory

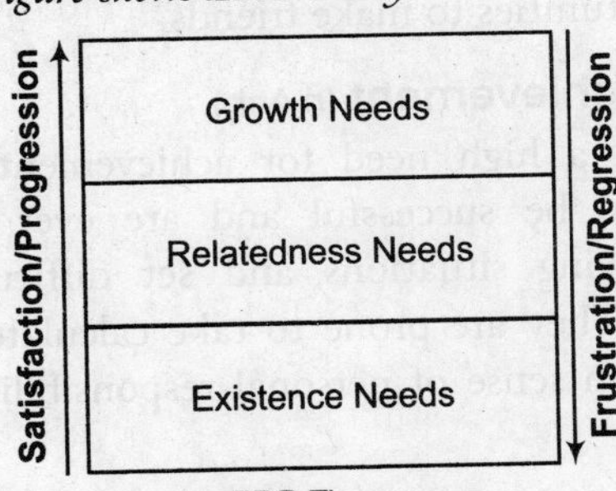

ERG Theory

- **Existence Needs** The existence needs in this theory refers to the physiological and security needs of Maslow.
- **Relatedness Needs** It refers to belongingness and esteem needs.
- **Growth Needs** It refers to both self-esteem and self-actualisation needs.

Although, ERG theory assumes that motivated behaviour follows a hierarchy in somewhat the same manner as suggested by Maslow, there are two important differences, *which are as follows*

- ERG theory suggests that more than one kind of need may be operative at the same time. *e.g.*, it allows for the possibility that people can be motivated by a desire for money (existence), friendship (relatedness) and an opportunity to learn new skills (growth) all at time. It is not essential that after being satisfied by one need, an individual will be shifted to other need.
- ERG theory has an element of frustrations/regression that is missing from Maslow's need hierarchy. Maslow maintained that one need must be satisfied before an individual can progress to needs at a higher level.

'Frustration/Regression' process given in ERG theory says that if needs remain unsatisfied at some higher level, then the person may become frustrated and regret to a lower level needs and will start pursuing with lower level needs.

3. Herzberg's Two Factor Theory

Another popular need-based approach to motivation is the dual-structure approach developed by Frederick Herzberg. This is also known as Two-factor Theory or hygiene factor theory.

Frederick Herzberg conducted a research study to know the feelings of 200 engineers and accountants in nine different companies in Pittsburgh, USA. During structured interview, they were asked to describe a few job conditions in which they felt 'exceptionally good or bad' about jobs.

On analysing the information collected by interviews, Herzberg concluded that there are two categories of needs essentially independent of each other affecting behaviour in different ways. *These are as follows*

Hygiene Factors These are job conditions which operate primarily to dissatisfy employees when the conditions are absent. However their presence does not motivate them in a strong way. These factors are also termed as maintenance factors as they are required to maintain minimum level of productivity of employees. *These are*

- Company policy and administration
- Relationship with subordinates
- Salary
- Relationship with supervisor
- Status
- Relationship with peers
- Security
- Personal life
- Supervision
- Work conditions

These factors produce no growth in a worker's output, they only prevent losses in worker's performance. Any decrease in these factors will dissatisfy employees. So, they are also called dissatisfiers.

Motivational Factors These factors have a positive effect on job satisfaction often resulting in one's total output. Most of these factors are intrinsic to the job. *These are*

- Achievement
- Advancement
- Growth
- Recognition
- Work itself
- Responsibility

Any increase in these factors will act as motivators for satisfying the employees, however any decrease will not affect their satisfaction level. Herzberg maintains that it also depends upon the personality characteristics of individuals, how they seek these factors.

Job enrichment is one of the applications of Herzberg theory. Job enrichment seeks to bring more motivation to the job by attaching more responsibility, more power and more work to the position or job.

4. 'X' and 'Y' Theories of Motivation

Douglas McGregor observed two contradictory viewpoints of managers about their employees, one is negative called "Theory of *X*" and another is positive called "Theory of *Y*".

These are as follows

(i) Theory of 'X'

Following are the assumptions of managers who believe in the "Theory of X" regarding their employees

- Employees dislike work.
- Employees must be coerced, controlled or threatened to do the work.
- Employees avoid responsibilities and seek formal direction.
- Most employees consider security of job, most important of all other factors in the job and have very little ambition.

Theory '*X*' in its applicability, places exclusive reliance upon external control of human behaviour, while theory '*Y*' relies heavily on self-control and self-direction.

Theory '*X*' is tuned to the traditional approach of management. Literally, this theory of behaviour is related to organisations that lay rigid standards of work behaviour.

Some examples of such organisations are, organisations that have stringent rules and policies, establish targets of production, design equipment to control worker's pace of work, and employees are severely punished in case of disobedience. The concept of autocracy and coerciveness and dominancy are quite consistent with theory *X*.

(ii) Theory of 'Y'

Following are the assumptions of managers who believe in the "Theory of Y" regarding their employees

- Employees love work as play or rest.
- Employees are self-directed and self-controlled and committed to the organisational objectives.
- Employees accept and seek responsibilities.
- Innovative spirit is not confined to managers alone, some employees also possess it.

Theory '*Y*' on other hand, secures the commitment of employees to organisational objectives. This motivational theory places emphasis on satisfaction of employees. While applying this theory, the use of authority, as an instrument of command and control is minimal. Employees exercise self-direction and self-control.

5. McClelland's Need Theory of Motivation

David C. McClelland and his associate **Atkinson** have contributed to an understanding of motivation by identifying three types of basic motivating needs.

These needs have been classified as

Need for Power (*n* Pow)

According to this theory, the need for power, which might be defined as the desire to be influential in a group and to control one's environment, is an important motivation factor.

Research suggests that people with a strong need for power are likely to be superior performers and occupy supervisory positions. Such types of individuals generally look for positions of leadership, they act effectively, are outspoken, have a stubborn character and exert authority.

Need for Affiliation (*n* Aff)

The need for affiliation means the desire for human companionship and acceptance. Those with a high need for affiliation often behave the way they think other people want them to, in an effort to maintain friendship. They prefer a job that entails a good deal of social interaction and offers opportunities to make friends.

Need for Achievement (*n* Ach)

People with a high need for achievement always feel ambitious to be successful and are ever prepared to face challenging situations and set difficult goals for themselves. They are prone to take calculated risks, and possess a high sense of personal responsibility in getting jobs done.

These people are concerned with their progress and feel inclined to put in longer hours of work. Failures never dishearten them and they are always ready to put in their best efforts for excellent performance.

Process-Based Theories to Motivation

Process-based theories to motivation are concerned with how motivation occurs. They focus on why people choose to enact certain behavioural options to fulfill their needs and how they evaluate their satisfaction after they have attained these goals. Two of the most useful process-based approaches to motivation are expectancy theory and equity theory.

These are follows

1. Expectancy Theory of Motivation

Expectancy theory of motivation was developed by **Victor Vroom**. Basically, Vroom's expectancy theory views motivation as a process of governing choices. This theory postulates that rewards lead to motivation. The expectancy theory tries to explain 'how' and 'why' people choose a particular behaviour over an alternative.

The theory suggests that motivation depends on two things *i.e.* how much an individual desires a particular goal and how likely he thinks he can get it. The theory aims at reducing pair or maximising pleasure. This is the only motivational theory based on a cognitive model, *i.e.* it is based on the conscious thoughts about the situation.

When people are faced with a number of behavioural options leading to need satisfaction, they will evaluate the potential outcomes of these options and select the one that promises most important outcomes.

Expectancy Model

People are motivated by rewards as a result of the outcome or performance.

Victor Vroom expressed motivation as
Motivation (force)
= Valence × Expectancy × Instrumentality

Valence The value a person places on the rewards that he expects to receive from his performance. *It can have values*

- positive, if rewards encourages behaviour
- negative, if rewards or outcomes result in dissatisfaction and
- zero, if reward has no effect on behaviour.

Expectancy The perceived relationship between a given level of efforts and an expected performance. It is the belief that efforts leads to performance. *It can have values*

- zero, if efforts are unsuccessful.
- one, if efforts are rewarding.

Instrumentality It refers to the degree to which a first level outcome will lead to a desired second level outcome. It is a belief that performance is instrumental in giving rewards. High performance (first level outcome) lead to promotion (second level outcome).

Implications of Vroom's Theory

- It emphasises performance payoffs.
- Rewards should be tied to performance and be equitable.
- It emphasises expected behaviours.

Limitations of Expectancy Theory

- It is difficult to apply because it needs to identify all the potential outcomes for each employee, to determine all relevant expectancies and then to balance everything to maximise employee motivation.
- Expectancy theory also assumes that people are rational, therefore, they will systematically consider all the potential outcomes and their associated expectancies before selecting a particular behaviour.
- However, few people actually make decisions in such a precise and rational manner.

2. Porter and Lawler's Expectancy Theory

Porter and Lawler have proposed an extension to the expectancy theory. *This is as follows*

- First, an individual's initial effort is influenced by his perception regarding the value of reward and the likelihood that the effort will yield a reward.
- The probability that increased effort will lead to improved performance is affected by an individual's traits, abilities and perception of his role in an organisation.
- The model also distinguishes between intrinsic and extrinsic rewards.
- The Porter-Lawler model borrows the idea from equity theory that the employee's satisfaction depends on the perceived equity of the rewards relative to the effort expended and the level of performance attained.

Implications of Managers

Expectancy theory can be useful for organisations attempting to improve the motivation of their employees. Porter and Lawler suggest a series of steps for managers in applying the basic ideas of the theory. *These are as follows*

- They should determine the primary outcomes that each employee likely desires.
- They should decide what kind and levels of performance are needed to meet organisational goals.
- They should ascertain that the desired levels of performance are attainable.
- They should ensure that desired outcomes and performance are linked.
- They should also analyse the complete work situation for conflicting expectancies.
- They should ensure that the rewards are large enough.
- They should ensure that the overall system is equitable for everyone.

3. Equity Theory

This theory was developed by **J. Stacy Adams**. The equity theory argues that motivations arise out of simple desire to be treated fairly. Equity can be defined as an individual's belief that he is being treated fairly relative to the treatment of others.

A person's perception of equity develops through a four-step process as shown below

- First an individual evaluates the way he is being treated by an organisation.
- The next step is for an individual to choose a co-worker who seems to be in a roughly similar situation and to observe how an organisation treats him.
- In the crucial step of equity theory, an individual 'compares' the two treatments.
- In the fourth step, he evaluates a sense of equity to see if the two treatments seem similar or they are different.

Adam suggests, that employees make these comparisons by focusing on input and outcome ratios. An employee's contributions or input to an organisation include time, education, effort, experience and loyalty.

Outcomes are what an individual receives from an organisation such as, pay, recognition and social relationships. The theory suggests that people view their outcomes and inputs as ratio and then compare their ratio to the ratio of someone else. There may be exceptions of benevolent types who do not compare themselves with others.

This other 'person' may be someone in the work group.

The comparison may result in three types of attitudes

- The individual may feel equitably rewarded
- Under-rewarded
- Over-rewarded

An individual will experience a feeling of equity when the two ratios are equal. If an individual has the feeling of equity, then he should maintain the status. If he has a feeling of inequity, then he is likely to change the input.

Thus, if rewards are to motivate employees, they must be perceived as being equitable and fair. However, managers must remember that different employees have different sense towards basis for a reward and this may result in problems. Hence, the best way to avoid such problems is to make all employees aware of the basis for rewards.

Reinforcement Theory of Motivation

The theory was proposed by **BF Skinner**. The reinforcement theory states that an individual's behaviour is a function of its consequences. The theory is based on the fairly simple assumption that behaviours that result in rewarding consequences are more likely to be repeated, whereas behaviour that results in punishing consequences are less likely to be repeated.

This theory focuses on the consequences that follow after an individual has taken an action. It is deeply related to extrinsic form of motivation. The theory helps in devising of mechanisms for the moulding of an individuals behaviour. The theory overlooks the internal feelings and individual drives.

Reinforcement theory can be applied for motivating people by giving positive reinforcement, *e.g.* praising an employee for the timely completion of a job.

Negative reinforcements can be given to remove undesirable consequences, *e.g.* close monitoring of an employee if he/she is often coming late and noting the time of entry and exit.

New Approaches to Motivation in Organisations

New approaches are emerging to supplement the established models and theories of motivation. Two of the most promising are Goal-Setting Theory and the Japanese Approach. *These are as follows*

Goal-Setting Theory

This approach to motivation has been pioneered in the USA by **Edwin Locke** and his associates in 1960s and refined in 1980s. Goal-setting theory suggests that managers and subordinates should set goals for an individual on a regular basis, as suggested by MBO.

These goals should be SMART *i.e.* Specific, Measurable, Attainable, Realistic and Timely and of type that an employee will accept and make a commitment to accomplishing them.

Rewards should be directly related to accomplished goals. When involved in goal-settings, employees see how their effort will lead to performance, rewards and personal satisfaction. *Some of the elements are explained below*

Goal Specificity

Goals must be stated in specific terms if they are to motivate effective performance. Goals must be set in terms of measurable criteria of work performance, instead of being vague, *i.e.,* number of units produced, fixed sales target and must specify a time period within which the goal is to be attained.

Goal Difficulty/Challenge

There exists a relationship between goal difficulty and work motivation. More challenging the goal, the harder an individual works to accomplish it. The more difficult and challenging the goal is, the higher the level of motivation and performance.

Goal Acceptance

It is very important that an individual accepts the goal. In order to influence motivation and performance, a goal must be internalised by an individual. Once he takes it completely then he will start putting his best into it.

Goal Setting in Practice

The most obvious implication of goal-setting theory is that managers should be helping subordinates to set goals that are specific and reasonably difficult, so that subordinates accept and internalise them as their own goals. Besides this, there are a number of issues that arise in implementing goal setting in practice.

The manager can stimulate goal acceptance in atleast three ways

- By involving subordinates in goal-setting process.
- By demonstrating a supportive attitude and approach toward his subordinates.
- By assigning various rewards to the achievement of goals.

Management By Objectives (MBO) is a managerial technique for improving motivation and performance using goal-setting principles.

Japanese Approach to Motivation

The basic concept of the Japanese approach is that managers and workers should perform together as partners. Since both of them see themselves as one group, all members are committed and motivated to work in the best interests of an organisation.

In this concept, no one is called an employee, instead everyone is a team member, team leader or coach and everyone owns the 'share' of an organisation. Like goal-setting the Japanese approach is likely to become more common in businesses throughout the world.

One of the prominent Japanese theory is Theory '*Z*'.

Theory Z

This theory was given by **Dr. William Ouchi** takes into account the strengths of Japanese Management (Social cohesion, job security, concern for employees) as well as American Management (Speedy decision-making, risk taking, skills, individual autonomy, innovation and creativity) and proposed a mixed system.

Characteristics of theory Z are as follows

- Trust, integrity and openness.
- Strong-long-lasting relationship between organisation and employee.
- Employee participation.
- Structureless organisation.
- Holistic concern for employees.

Integration of Motivation Theories

It is important to integrate the various theories of motivation so as to maintain inter and intra-relation of an establishment. Integrating all the theories will help to improve the understanding of motivation. By greater understanding, more amount of positive motivation can be generated.

Enhancing Motivation in Organisations

The organisation can enhance motivation by adopting the following ways

Incentives Giving various incentives to people mostly in non-monetary form.

Morale Boosting the morale of the people by praising on the virtues and individual qualities.

Humanise Promote an atmosphere of friendliness and look at things with a humanistic approach.

Personal Interest Show a personal interest in the daily or routine proceedings of the organisation along with preparation of special occassions also.

Short and Long Goals Be clear in explaining the short and long term goals of the organisation to encourge people working in the organisation.

Admit Mistakes Instead of hiding, admitting one's mistake enhances respect and concern.

Promote A person showing good work and dedication needs to be promoted by giving monetary benefits.

Quality Circles Quality Circles (QC) are small groups of workers who meet regularly with their supervisor as their 'circle leader' to solve work-related problems.

Alternative Work Schedule Flexibility in working hours brings a lot of comfort to an employee. Many organisations use the modified 'work-week' as a way to increase employee motivation.

Job-Redesign Job-Redesign or changing the nature of people's job is also being used more as a motivational technique.

Pay and Job Performance Motivate employees through revising their pay by creating a belief that good performance certainly leads to high levels of pay.

Leadership

Leadership is the process of influencing other's behaviour towards the fulfillment of a definite objective or a goal in a given situation. It is the ability of an individual to guide others, teams or organisations.

Leadership is an integral part of management and plays a vital role in managerial operations. It influences behaviour of the individuals. It has an ability to attract others and potential to make them follow the instructions. Individuals can be induced to contribute their optimum towards the attainment of organisational goals through effective leadership.

According to **Katz** and **Kahn**, "Leadership is the influential increment over and above mechanical compliance with the routine directives of the organisation."

According to **Hemphill** and **Coons**, "Leadership is the behaviour of an individual directing the activities of a group towards a shared goal."

Thus, leaders are people who are able to influence the behaviour of others without recourse to threats or other forms of force towards the individuals. Leaders are the people who are accepted by the other individuals, as a superior person to them. It is necessary to be an effective leader to become an effective manager.

Features of Leadership

- Leadership is to facilitate accomplishment common objectives by influencing others.
- Leadership is to direct the individuals to attain the tasks assigned to them by following the instructions of their leaders.
- Leadership is to get acceptance from others and to give the individuals, a vision for future.
- Leadership is the continuous process of influencing behaviour. It encourages liveliness in the group by stimulating and persuading others.

Importance of Leadership

- Good leadership motivates people to become followers and to achieve their goals.
- Able leadership builds team spirit and keeps the team members together.
- Leadership helps to maximise efficiency to achieve organisational objectives.
- Leadership focuses more on group objectives rather than individual goals.
- Leadership in able hands handles daily life challenges easily and efficiently.

Types of Leadership

Autocratic or Authoritarian

In this type of leadership, there is a complete centralisation of authority with the leader, *i.e.* authority is centered in the leader himself. He has all the powers to make decisions. He uses coercive measures and adopts strict ways to get the work done.

He wants immediate obedience of his orders and instructions. Any negligence on the part of subordinates results in punishment. There is no participation from the subordinates in decision-making. An autocratic leader never gives weightage to the views of his subordinates.

It can be divided into following categories

- **Strict Autocrat** They use negative influence and expects that the employees should obey their orders immediately. Non-compliance of their orders results in punishment. He makes all decisions and does not disclose anything to anyone. He is quite rigid on performance.
- **Benevolent Autocrat** Benevolent autocrat leader uses positive influences and develops effective human relations. He is known as paternalistic leader. He praises his employees if they follow his orders and invites them to get the solutions of the problems from him. He feels happy in controlling all the actions of his subordinates.
- **Manipulative Autocrat** Leader under such type, is manipulative in nature. He creates a feeling in the minds of his subordinates and workers that they are participating in decision-making processes. But, he makes all decisions by himself. Non-compliance of his orders also results in punishment.

Democratic or Participative

Participative leadership aims at encouraging participation from the subordinates. Democratic or participative leadership is also known as group centered or consultative leadership. In this type of leadership, leaders consult their groups and consider their opinion in the decision-making process.

Leaders encourage discussion among the group members on the problem under consideration and arrive at a decision depending on their consent. Leaders give more freedom to their group members, who feel that, their opinions are honored and given importance.

Laissez-Faire or Free Rein

Here there is virtual absence of direct leadership. It is, therefore, known as "no leadership at all". There is complete delegation of authority to subordinates, so that they can make decisions by themselves.

Absence of leadership may have both positive and negative effects. Members may feel insecure and develop frustration for lack of decision-making authority.

Theories of Leadership

There are a number of theories to know and apply leadership. *They are classified as below*

1. Great Man Theory

This theory is also known as the Charismatic Leadership Theory. This theory is based on the belief that leaders are exceptional people born with innate qualities destined to lead and imbibed with divine power.

According to this theory, leadership qualities are-commanding, charm, courage, intelligence, persuasiveness and aggresiveness which cannot be taught. Also the leadership qualities cannot be acquired through formal education and are sufficient to be successful.

2. Trait Theory

This theory was given by **Ralph Stogdill** in 1940. This theory of studying leadership is taken into consideration to analyse the personal, psychological and physical traits of strong leaders. The lists of traits or qualities associated with leadership exist is abundance and continue to be produced.

The assumption made in this theory was that some basic traits or set of traits differentiates leaders from non-leaders. *e.g.*, the leadership traits might include intelligence, assertiveness, above average height, self-confidence, initiative and understanding of interpersonal human relations. The existence of these traits determines the importance of leadership.

Possession of these traits helps the individuals to gain possession of leadership. Since all individuals do not have these qualities, only those who have them would be considered potential leaders.

3. Behaviour Theory

This theory concentrated on what leaders actually do rather than on their qualities. The behavioural theory assumed that effective leaders behaved differently from ineffective leaders. Different pattern of behaviour are observed and categorised as '**Styles of Leadership**'. It also identified the need of consistency of behaviour of good leaders.

4. Contingency Theory

This leadership approach was applied for the first time in 1920 in the armed forces of Germany with the objective to get good generals under different situations.

This theory was given by **Fiedler**. This is a refinement of the situational view point and focuses upon identifying the situational variables which best fit the situation. The main assumption of contingency theory is that the behaviour of an appropriate leader varies from one situation to another.

The motive of a contingency theory is to identify key situational factors and to specify how they interact to determine appropriate behaviour of a leader. Fiedler grouped situational variables into three areas of concern-Leader member relations, Task sturcture and Position of the Leader.

The LPC (Least Preferred Co-worker) Scale

Fred Fiedler developed a least preferred co-worker scale to measure the two basic styles of leadership. Fiedler identified two types of leadership-task-oriented and relationship-oriented.

Fiedler used the Least Preferred Co-worker (LPC) scale to measure the type of leadership. A leader is asked to describe characteristics of the person with whom he or she is least comfortable while working.

Leader-Member Relations

A leader-member relation refers to the nature of relationship between the leader and his work group. These refer to the compatibility between group members and managers.

If the leader and the group enjoy mutual trust, respect, confidence and they like one another, relations will remain good. Fred Fiedler believed leader-member relations to be the most important situational variable.

Task-Structure

We know that the nature of jobs and how tasks are structured influence leadership. Task-structure is the degree to which the group's task is clearly defined. If the tasks are highly structured, with formal guidelines and well-defined expectations, it will be directive style.

Position-Power

The position-power of leaders is influenced by organisation culture, the hierarchy of management and the style or work environment.

Position-power is the power vested in the position of a leader in an organisation.

If the leader has the power to assign work, administer rewards and punishment, recommend employees for promotion or demotion, position-power is assumed to be strong.

5. The Path-Goal Theory

The path-goal theory of leadership was introduced by **Martin Evans** and **Robert House**. The given model emphasises that the leader behaviour should be such as to complement the group work setting and aspirations.

Path-Goal theory says that a leader can motivate subordinates by influencing their expectations. This approach is based upon the expectancy theory of motivation.

The path-goal model assumes that leaders can change their style or behaviour to meet the demands of a particular situation. *The main propositions of the path-goal model are*

- Leaders behaviour is acceptable to the extent of subordinate's source of satisfaction.
- Leader's behaviour is motivational as it complements the environment of subordinates.

This model identifies four kinds of leader behaviour, which are directive, supportive, participated and achievement oriented.

6. Vertical Dyad Linkage Model

This model stresses the fact that leaders actually have different kinds of working relationship with different subordinates. Each manager-subordinate relationship represents one vertical dyad.

The vertical dyad linkage model suggests that leaders establish special working relationships with some subordinates based on some combination of respect, trust and liking. These people constitute the 'in-group'. Other subordinates remain in the 'out-groups, who receive less of leader's time and attention.

Those in the 'in-group' receive more of the manager's time and attention and are better performers.

Research shows that people in the 'in-group' are more productive and more satisfied with their work than 'out-group' members.

7. Transactional *vs* Transformational Leadership

According to **Burns**, "The more traditional transactional leadership involves an exchange relationship between leaders and followers, but tranformational leadership is based more on leaders' shifting the values, beliefs and needs of their followers."

The Transactional Leaders

Transactional leaders value order and structure of an organisation and focus on results. Such types of leaders motivate followers by appealing to their self interest. Their focus is on exchange of rewards for efforts and try to maintain the principle of equity in that.

They watch carefully and are highly vigilant in checking deviations from rules and standards. They take very prompt and speedy action in taking corrective measures. They focus on man's needs to get a job done. They are pre-occupied with power, position, politics and encourage to perform individuals within a structured environment.

The Transformational Leaders

These leaders show performance beyond expectations. They expand the follower's self interest, his portfolio of needs, capable enough to elevate the follower needs. They create an environment that enables followers to recognise and realise an organisational goal that exceeds past accomplishments.

They try to bring change, innovations and entrepreneurship among team members. They relate to people in more intuitive and empathetic ways.

Such leaders lead by inspiring a shared vision, enable others to act by encouraging and modelling their way. They make use of conflict and economic cruses positively to raise their follower's consciousness and transform them.

They induce followers to transcend their self-interest for the higher purpose of the group and provide vision and sense of mission to their followers.

Transformational leaders are charismatic and inspire the followers. They give personal attention, counsel and coach individuals.

8. Leadership Continuum

Tannenbaum and Schmidt have depicted a broad range of leadership styles between two extremes, *i.e.* Autocratic and Free-rein.

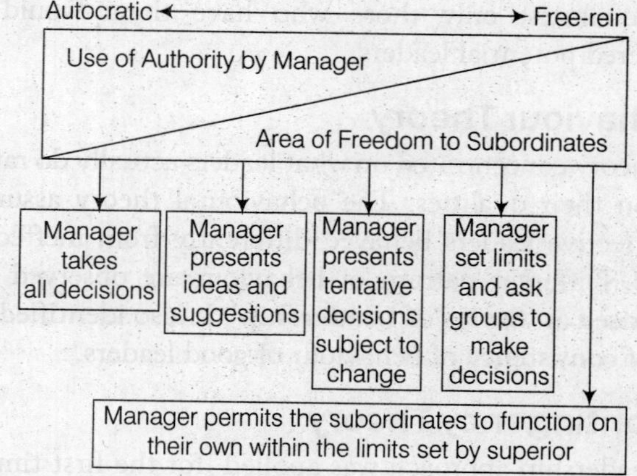

Managers who are production oriented use autocratic style of leadership to get the work done. They treat employees as tools for accomplishing the jobs and focus on output.

Managers who are employee-oriented use participative or free-rein style of leadership. They emphasises that every individual is important and take interest in views and suggestions of employees. They work with the team.

9. Managerial Grid

Managerial grid is most effective practical contribution made by 'Blake and Mouton' which assumes that a manager shows either task-oriented behaviour or relation-oriented behaviour. Managers are concerned for people or production or a balance of two.

Managerial grid identifies five leadership styles which are as follows

(1,1) **Impoverished** Manager put little efforts to get work done and sustain morale of employees.

(1,9) **Country Club** Manager show great concern for employees and make good organisational climate for work.

(9,1) **Task** Manager gets little involvement of employees in setting work, he is more structural and technical in approach.

(5,5) **Middle Road** A good balance of work requirements and maintaining satisfactory morale leads to adequate performance.

(9,9) **Team** Work is accomplished by a team or committed people with interdependence through a common stake in organisation, gaining trust, respect and resulting productivity.

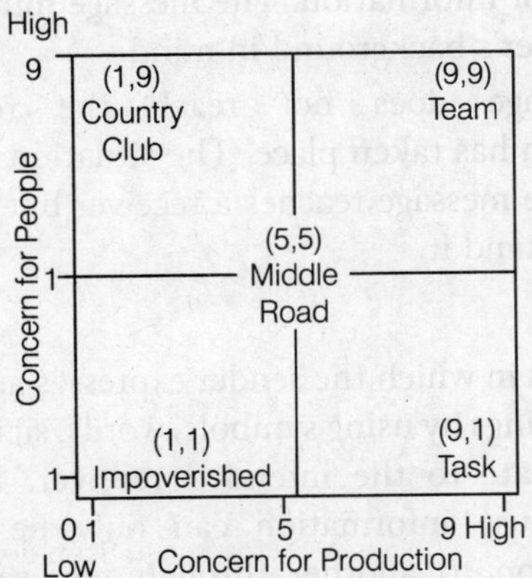

10. Life Cycle Theory of Leadership or Situational Model

The theory, proposed by **Hursey** and **Blanchard** assert that the leader has to match his leadership style according to the needs of maturity of subordinates which moves in a life-cycle.

Maturity in this model has been used in the context of ability and willingness of the people for directing their own behaviour.

The four leadership styles attached to different levels of maturity are

Telling High task directive behaviour, people have low ability and low willingness.

Selling Supportive and directive behaviour.

Participating Participative leadership style.

Delegating Subordinates have high maturity. Delegation behaviour involving low task behaviour and low relationship behaviour.

11. Three Dimensional Grid

'William Reddin' is the first to introduce Effectiveness Dimension(ED), Task Orientation (TO) and Relationship Orientation (RO) as the 3 dimensions to exhibits the leadership styles to become 'Effective Leader' or 'Ineffective Leader'.

Effectiveness is defined as the extent to which a manager is successful in his position. When style is appropriate to a given situation, it is termed as effective.

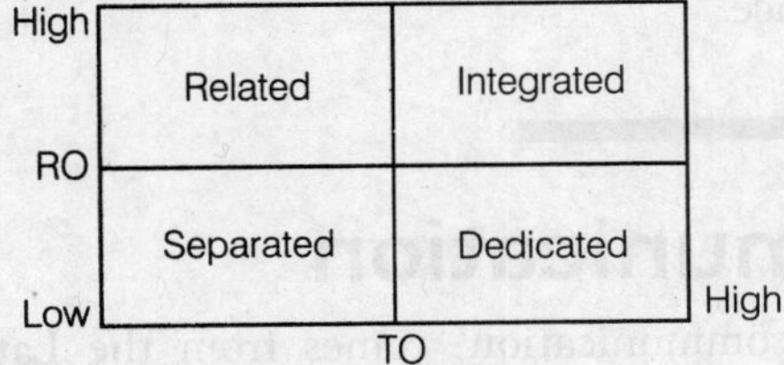

The grid of RO and TO shows four basics styles-related, dedicated, integrated and integrated.

These four basic styles when integrated with effectiveness dimension generates; 8 styles

4 Less Effective styles	4 More Effective Styles
Missionary	Developer
Compromiser	Benevolent Autocrat
Deserter	Bureaucrat
Autocrat	Executive

3-D approach is a combination of managerial-grid and contingency theory.

12. Emotional Intelligence Approach

Daniel Goleman popularised the concept of emotional intelligence EI is the ability to understand and manage your own emotions and those of the people around you. For leaders having emotional intelligence is essential for success.

EI in leadership can be understood with following five elements

- **Self Awareness** Being self aware helps in having a clear picture of your strength and weakness and it means behaving with humility. Thus, this theory aims at personal competence.

- **Self Regulation** Leaders who regulate themselves effectively rarely verbally attack others make rushed or emotional decisions, sterecotype people or compromise their values. This element covers leaders's flexibility and commitment to personal accountability.
- **Motivation** Self motivated leaders work consistently towards their goals and they have extremely high standards for the quality of their work.
- **Empathy** For leaders having empathy is critical to managing a successful team or organisation. Leaders with empathy have the ability to put themselves in other's shoes.
- **Social Skills** Leaders who do well in social skills elements of emotional intelligence are great communicators. They're just as open to hearing bad news and good news, and they're expert at getting their team to support them and be excited about new project and mission. Thus, this theory also focuses on social competence.

Communication

The term 'communication' comes from the Latin word 'communis', which means 'to share'. Communication refers to the commonness or sharing of information, ideas, facts, opinions, attitudes and understanding. Communication essentially means transmission of commonly meaningful information.

Miller (1951) puts it this way, "Communication takes place when there is information at one place or person and we want to get it to another place or person."

According to **Redfield**, "Communication is the broad field of human interchange of facts and opinions."

According to **Revesz**, "Communication encompasses all forms of expression which serves the purpose of mutual understanding."

Features of Communication

- Communication consists of a two way process, *i.e.* giving/sending and getting/receiving.
- Communication is a continuous process that keeps on running.
- It dispels the misunderstandings, misinterpretations and permits greater understanding.
- It conveys a definite message to the people concerned.
- It consists of exchange of ideas between two or more than two people.
- Communication can be both direct *i.e* through face-to-face or indirect *i.e.* through other means such as ringing of bell for closing of a school.
- Communication requires a medium to convey the message. Therefore, it can be oral, written or symbolic.

Communication Process

The cycle of communication involves the following elements, *which demonstrate the basic concept of communication process*

Communication Process

Sender → Message → Encoding → Channel → Receiver → Decoding → Feedback

Sender/Communicator

Communication process begins with the sender. The person who conveys the message is known as sender or communicator. The sender initiates the message by encoding a thought and attempts to achieve understanding and change in the behaviour of the receiver. Four conditions usually affect the encoded message-skill, attitude, knowledge and socio- cultural system.

Message/Ideation

The next element of communication process is message. It is the subject matter of any communication. It may involve any fact, idea or information. The message must be crafted with the receiver's background in mind.

If the message does not reach the receiver, no communication has taken place. The situation is not much improved if the message reaches a receiver but the receiver doesn't understand it.

Encoding

It is the process in which the sender expresses and organises his ideas or feelings by using symbols, words, signs etc which will communicate to the intended receiver. Encoding is necessary because information can only be transferred from one person to another through representations or symbols. The manager must have linguistic competence as well as organisational competence to encode the message properly.

Linguistic competence refers to language skills, analysis of facts and informations, usage of appropriate rhetorical devices, graphs, charts and diagrams. Organisational competence refers to the ability to organise the entire message in a logical and structured way. It is also the ability to sequence thoughts in a sentence and paragraph according to the need of the topic.

Medium/Channel

Communication channel is the media through which the sender passes the message. The choice of channel depends on the nature of the message. It is very important to choose proper time, proper place and a proper way for effective communication. It could be oral or written.

When the message is long, formal in nature, the written channel (letters, reports, memos, faxes, proposals, notices etc.) should be preferred but when the message is personal or when the immediate feedback is important, oral channel (staff meeting, discussions, presentations, seminars, conferences etc.) should be selected. While selecting a channel, the receiver background must be kept in mind.

Receiver

The receiver is the person who receives the message. The communication process is incomplete without the existence of the receiver. It is the receiver who receives and tries to understand the message.

Decoding

Decoding is the process by which the receiver interprets the message and translates it into meaningful words for the purpose of understanding. Decoding helps the receiver to derive meaning from the message.

Decoding in oral communication is in the form of listening and understanding. Decoding in written communication is in the form of reports, instructions, manuals, professional messages etc.

Feedback

Feedback is the last stage in the communication process. When the sender transmits a message, he expects a response. The reaction and response of the receiver is known as feedback.

It may be immediate or deferred, written or oral, favourable or unfavourable. It helps in evaluation of what is right and what is wrong in a particular communication.

Business Communication

"Business communication is a multi-dimensional, dynamic and interactive process that involves the effective transmission of facts, ideas, thoughts and systematic understanding of scientific theories and practical aspects." Defined by **Newstrom** and **Keith Davis**.

Business communication always has specialised content, specific audience, specific purpose, specific time and specific place.

7C's of Business Communication

- **Completeness** means the message has to be complete, it bring desired results, no chance of lawsuits, it provides necessary information and answer all the question give something extra, when required.
- **Conciseness** means to be brief, fewest possible words, benefits-saves time and expense, more interesting.
- **Clarity** The message has to be crystal clear which can be achieved through appropriate length of sentences.
- **Correctness** Accuracy of facts, figures and words otherwise no credibility will be there, no outdated information should be given in business communication.
- **Concreteness** Specific, definite and vivid rather than vague and general. *e.g.* Goods are soon being dispatched. Goods will be dispatched on 2nd July.

Passive	Active
Your savings would earn a high rate of interest	Your savings would earn 8% interest compounded quarterly
Your efforts are appreciated by all of us	All of us appreciate your efforts

- **Consideration** A message with the intended receiver in mind, focus on 'you' instead of 'I' and 'we', show audience benefit, emphasise positive pleasant facts, show empathy.
- **Courtesy** Thank, generousity, apologies for a mistake, avoid irritating expressions, use non-discriminatory expressions, equal treatment- regardless of gender, race, ethnic origin and physical features.

Importance of Business Communication

The importance of business communication is better understood from the following points

Helps to Present the Knowledge related to Business World Effectively Business communication helps the managers to present and receive technical and professional information effectively. In this modern world when flow of information is very fast, it becomes important to communicate effectively and efficiently.

Best Medium for Technological Advancement Success in the modern world depends on the rapid changes in the technology. Only an effective system of communication can help to bring the latest technology.

Important Means of Interaction Modern society is based on a wide platform. The whole world has become a global market. To unite the world, a continuous interaction among various components is needed. Communication is one of the important means of interaction.

Unified Individual Activities Business communi- cation helps in unifying the activities of individual as a work team by facilitating the managerial function of leadership, motivation, training and development etc.

Types of Communication

Oral Communication

Oral communication refers to the spoken words and understood in the form of sounds. It is the most commonly used method for communication mostly in informal situations inside and outside business entities.

It is also referred as verbal communication and usage of non-verbal communication deftly makes it more impressive and effective. Oral communication takes place in many ways casual and serious, formal and informal, structured and unstructured. It is instantaneous two way process in which prompt response is there.

Oral communication can be readily used, persuasive, cost effective and facilitates effective and fruitful conversation. It works very well in small groups where there is informal and friendly environment.

Oral communication is not effective in very large groups and rigid and closed environment. It has it own constraints of hesitation, not having full command on the language, accent and vocabulary.

Oral communication may not be effective in the presence of various physical and psychological barriers. Oral communication does not work in extremely formal conditions where record keeping and documentation is quite important.

Written Communication

Written communication may take the form of letters, memorandum, instruction bulletins, suggestion box etc. No business can exist without writing. Written words become a record of things planned, carried out and acknowledged. Effective writing includes proper choice of words, proper organisation of words in correct order to make meaningful sentences which effectively convey the meaning.

Written communication is well structured and quite useful in formal situations. It includes good vocabulary and collection of all relevant facts and figures to make the communication effective, concrete and well-structured. It helps in maintaining records and documents that can be preserved over a period of time.

Written communication has the facility of making amendments, if any error has occurred. The scope of written communication is wide and facilitates repeated reference.

Written communication does not depends on the memory of the listeners since records can be referred again, whenever required. It is more time consuming and requires conscious effort. It is left interactive and is constrained by vocabulary, writing skills, handwriting and efficiency of the tools used.

Non-verbal Communication

Non-verbal communication is the actions that creates or represents some specific meaning. It is reflected in the mannerisms and behaviours. It is not expressed in words. It includes facial expressions that are very specific and reflects certain emotions.

Non-verbal communication is also expressed through body movements, gestures and behaviours. It is considered a very effective means of communication.

In business communication, non-verbal expressions tell a lot about an organisation. Facial expressions, eye contact or even architecture, symbols, graphics help in understanding the type of organisation. These are considered silent speakers and reflect the overall perspective of an organisation.

Non-verbal communication in speech includes para language, voice quality, voice intonation, emotion, style of speaking, rhythm and stress on certain words. Non-verbal communication in written form consists of style of writing, handwriting, spatial arrangements of words etc.

Levels of Communication

Communication is a universal activity. There are so many levels at which people or organisations can communicate. *These are*

Interpersonal Communication

All communication, which takes place between persons or among people, is interpersonal communication. It can be both formal and informal.

This form of communication is very advantageous because direct and immediate feedback is possible. If there is a doubt, it can be easily removed.

Organisational Communication

An organisation is a composite of many individuals working together, towards its growth. They are constantly interacting with each other and with people outside the company. On this basis, communication can be categorised into internal, mass and external communication.

Interaction among members of the same organisation is called internal communication.

All the communication that takes place between one organisation and other organisation is known as external communication.

Mass communication is the message sent from person/group through a transmitting device (a medium, such as radio, television newspaper etc.) to a large number of audiences. It is rewarding and give you brand and name recognition and increase your credibility.

It occurs when a small number of people send message to a large anonymous and usually heterogeneous audience through the use of specialised communication media.

Flow of Communication

On the basis of the flow of information, communication may be classified into four types

Downward Communication

When information passes from the higher level to the lower levels, downward communication takes place. The communication from the manager to the employees shows the downward flow of information.

Notices, letters, circulars, memos, emails, face-to-face conversation, telephonic conversation are the different modes of downward communication. This is required to pass orders, advices and instructions.

Upward Communication

In upward communication, the flow of information goes from the lower levels to the higher levels. The communication from the employees to the manager, shows upwards communication reports, proposals, suggestion box grievance committee etc are the different forms of upward communication. This is required to communicate grievances, keep the superior informed and to suggest improvement.

Horizontal or Lateral Communication

Horizontal communication shows the transfer of information among persons working at the same level. The forms of horizontal communication may include letters, memos, meetings, telephonic conversations, gossips, conferences and face-to-face contacts. This is required to enhance team spirit and coordination among differnt departments.

Diagonal Communication

Diagonal communication is also known as 'cross communication'. It flows in all directions and cuts across different levels in an organisation. When a supervisor in the marketing department communicates directly with the managing director of the production, who is not only in a different department but also at a higher level in an organisation, diagonal communication takes place.

Letters, emails, telephone calls, face-to-face contacts are included in the forms of diagonal communication. This is required to increase the efficiency and quick decision-making in the organisation.

Barriers to Communication

The problem of communication arises because there are various obstacles, hindrances which may distort the meaning of communication by way of filtering certain part of communication. These obstacles are known as the barriers to communication.

The barriers to communication are as follows

Semantic Barriers

Semantics is the study of meaning in language. In English, one word can have different meanings. Semantic barriers arise from limitations in the use of symbols with which we communicate. When two individuals attach different meanings to a word, a breakdown in communication can occur.

Types of semantic errors are as follows

- Symbols with different meanings.
- Badly constructed messages.
- Faulty translations.
- Unclarified assumption.
- Use of specialist's language like jargons.

Mechanical Physical Barriers

It result from defects in devices that are used in the process of communication. Physical barriers appear because of noises and distance between receiver and sender.

They chiefly occur because of the following reasons

- Outdated equipment
- Physical distance
- Time lag
- Overloaded information
- Inadequate sound or light
- Noise

Psychological Barriers

These are emotional or interpersonal barriers.

These are as follows

- Premature evaluation introduced by "Rogers and Roethlisberger". This can be removed by empathy.
- Inattention preoccupied mind of a receiver.
- Loss by transmission and poor retention and undue reliance on the written word.
- Failure to communicate in right sense, time pressure due to deadlines, information overload, resistance to change, perceptual distortion, closed mind, inattention, prejudice, attitude and premature evaluation.

Organisational or Structural Barriers

They arise because of organisational rules, regulations and policies, status relationships, specialisation elongated chain of command, complexity in organisational structure, poor layout of institution and unsuitable medium.

Personal Barriers

They arise out of individual perception such as feeling of jealousy, attitudes of people, fear of challenging job, lack of confidence perceptual differences and lack of awareness.

Informal Communication: Grapevine

Grapevine is the informal way of communication. In this type of communication, the official news is transmitted through informal interactions. It includes tea time gossip, casual gathering, lunch-time meetings and personal parties etc. It has its own benefits and limitations.

Top managers rely heavily on informal contact with outsiders to exchange information that might be useful to their company. Channels like grapevine are more active in organisations better that are not transparent.

However, they not very reliable as they may be just rumor or time pass. But it can be helpful in team building and useful in relieving the pent-up emotion of the grievance holders.

Advantages of Informal Communication

Following are the few benefits which a company can achieve through grapevine

- Less expensive than formal channels.
- May give some information that one may find otherwise difficult to collect through formal channels.
- An outlet for employees to share their anxieties, worries and frustrations.
- Used voluntarily by many employees.
- Fastest means of spreading information.

Limitations of Informal Communication

- Fast spreading nature can cause damage to the organisation.
- If unverified, may cause troubles.
- May lead to misunderstanding, if incomplete.
- May not be reliable as it is oral only and also nobody owns the responsibility for the information.

Guidelines of Informal Communication

- To be used as a supplementary to formal channel.
- Information should be verified for facts and also the source should not be ignored.
- Employees using this channel should not be threatened or encouraged too much.

Group Dynamics

A group is a two or more individual who interact regularly with each other to accomplish a common purpose or goal.

A group consists of a number of individuals working together for a common objective. Groups have significant influence on an organisation and are inseparable from an organisation. They are useful for the organisation as they form foundation of human resources.

Dynamics is a word that has Greek origin. It means force. Therefore, group dynamics relates to the study of different forces that are operating within an organisation or a group. It takes into consideration the social interaction that takes place within each group and gives it the group a dynamic form.

Group dynamics studies the interaction taking place within a group (intragroup). It also considers the interaction taking place within different social groups (intergroup).

Group dynamics is also identified as a set of behavioural and psychological processes that takes place between different groups, between large groups and between large institutions. The social interaction gives way to certain behaviour that changes the organisational structure.

Basic Assumptions of Group Dynamics

- Groups are inevitable and ubiquitous.
- Groups influence the behaviours and performance.
- Groups determine organisational effectiveness.
- Group dynamics is essential for the managers in order to obtain desirable results from the groups.
- Groups act as the primary tools used by managers to coordinate individual behaviour to reach the organisational goals.
- Groups make a manager's job easier. The tasks are explained to the groups and not to each and every individual.

Importance of a Group

The reasons for the need of groups are as follows

- Groups are needed to introduce industrial democracy at workplace. Where work committees are formed, there workers get due recognition. They willingly participate in decision-making.
- Groups help in making participative management more effective.
- Groups of all kinds and types help by cooperating in all the matters related to production and human relations.
- An individual cannot perform each and every task. Group efforts are required for its completion.

- While accomplishing tasks, all members of a group together use their creative and innovative ideas than a single individual.
- In a group, individuals communicate with each other, discuss their work performances and take suggestions from each other to make it better.
- Group dynamics help in managing social loafing, where an individual demostrates less efforts while working in group, than working individually.

Types of Groups

In an organisation, there are three types of groups, *which are as follows*

1. Formal Groups

These groups are permanent in nature. They have to follow rules, regulations and policy of the organisation. *e.g.* HR department, purchase department, accounts department etc.

According to **AL Stencombe**, "A formal group is said to be any social arrangement in which the activities of some persons are planned by others to achieve a common purpose".

Formal groups comprise of team groups and task groups.

Team Groups/Committees These groups have no specific roles to its members and each individual works as a team. Often they take shape of committees such as planning committee or budget committee which are often permanent in nature.

Task Group Task groups are the groups formed by an organisation to accomplish a narrow range of purposes or specific tasks within a specified time. These groups are temporary in nature. They also develop a solution to a problem or complete its purpose. Informal committees, task forces and work teams are included in task groups.

Command Group These are the sections of formal groups, departments in the organisation.

2. Informal Group

Informal groups are the groups formed for the purposes other than the organisational goals. Informal groups form when individuals are drawn together by friendship, by mutual interests or both. These groups are spontaneous.

These are the groups formed by the employees themselves at the workplace while working together. The organisation does not take any active interest in their formation.

Informal groups are very effective and powerful. These groups work as an informal communication network forming a part of the grapevine to the organisations.

Types of Informal Group

Group Based on Same Interest

Interest groups are the groups formed to attain a common purpose. Employees coming together for payment of bonus, increase in salary, medical benefit and other facilities are the examples of interest groups.

Group Based on Similar Mindsets

Friendship groups are the groups of individuals belonging to same age group, having similar views, tastes and opinions. These groups can also be formed outside the plant or office and can be in the form of clubs and associations.

Group Based on Reference

Reference groups are the groups where individuals shape their ideas, beliefs, values etc. They want support from the group.

Groups Based on Cliques

Cliques comprise of smaller number of members who have similar standards and social norms. Cliques comprises of associates and colleagues closely intimated to each other. M.Dalton has given three types of cliques. *They are*

- **Horizontal Clique** Comprises of people of similar rank who work more or less in the same area. The members are able to find commonness among each other.
- **Vertical Clique** Comprises of members working in the same department regardless of their levels. These groups cut across hiearachical lines.
- **Mixed/Random Clique** This group comprises of members from different departments, ranks and physical location.
- **Group Based on Pressure Tactics**
  They have been described by L.R Sayles as
  (a) **Erractic Group** They are easily pacified and easily inflamed and lak consistency in thei behaviour.
  (b) **Apathetic Group** This group has few grievances and seldom use pressure tactics. There is lack of clearly defined leadership.
  (c) **Strategic Group** The members are able to prepare strategy for putting pressure on the group and management. These people are highly united and actively participate in union activity.
  (d) **Conservative Group** This comprises of highly skilled employees and professionals such groups are often found at top levels, and exercise restrained pressure for highly specified goal.

Theories of Group Formation

Propinquity Theory

This theory states that individuals and groups can affiliate with one another because of spatial or geographic proximity. The more near people are at the workplace, the more probability they have to be in groups.

Homan's Theory

It is also known as interaction theory of group formation. According to this theory, more the involvement through activities, more the interactions and more the emotions and therefore more the probability to be in groups.

Balance Theory

This theory was proposed by **Theodore Newcomb**. According to this theory, persons are attracted to one another on the basis of similar attitudes towards commonly relevant objects and goals. The given theory is the additive of above two theories and balance between Propinquity and Homan's theory.

Exchange Theory

This theory was proposed by **Thaibaut and Kelly**. According to this theory, the outcome of a relationship must be rewarding in order to have attraction or affliation among the members of a group.

Stages of Group Development

The five stages of group development are givn by **Bruce Tuckman**. *They are as follows*

Forming (Getting Familiar)

The very first stage of a group development is to form a group by becoming familiar with each other. During this stage, the members of the group get acquainted with one another and check, which inter-personal behaviour is acceptable and which is unacceptable by the other members of the group.

Storming (Conflicts and Learning)

The second stage of group development is communicating, sharing their thoughts and making decision. Group members seek out similar individuals and pairing takes place. Sometimes there are instances of conflicts as they don't consider the restrictions imposed by it on their individuality. During this stage, group members share their opinions and formulate the group's goals.

Norming (Understanding One's Role and Other's Role)

Each person recognises and accepts his role as well as accepts and understands the roles of others. Members also become more comfortable with each other and develop a sense of group identity and unity. At this stage, members establish norms to perform the tasks properly. The group structure solidifies and leadership emerges.

Performing (Achieving the Set Goals)

The fourth stage is to achieve the set goals by controlling and organising, in which the members perform the roles they have accepted and direct their group efforts towards goal attainment.

Adjourning (Break-off)

The fifth stage takes place in case of temporary groups when after completion of the task, the groups decide to disband. There may be mixed reactions or feelings related to adjourning. In case of permanent groups, the fifth stage do not takes place.

Characteristics of Mature Groups

Mature groups are groups that are well functioning groups. They are permanent groups that perform tasks effectively. Initially, they are teams working together, then a team become well functioning to convert into a mature group. *There are following characteristics of a mature group*

Role Structures

Role structure is the set of defined roles and interrelationships among those roles that the group members define and accept.

Behavioural Norms

The mature groups must be indicating certain behavioural norms. They are well defined in case of formal groups but not in case of informal groups. Over a period of time, these informal groups also show particular behavioural norms although they are temporary groups.

Informal Leadership

Each informal group has one or more leaders. These leaders come forward on the basis of acceptance of all the group members. Every informal group has one primary leader apart from the secondary leaders.

The primary leader has more influence on the group members than the secondary leaders. These leaders are not nominated by any authority and the leaders are made on the basis of their own potentials.

Cohesiveness

Cohesiveness is defined as the attractiveness of group members towards the group. It also emphasises on the group's ability to satisfy its members needs. It, therefore, helps the group members to work more consistently and make greater contribution to the achievement of the organisational goals. It is also psychologically more satisfying to all of its members.

Cohesiveness can be determined by the following factors

- Ability of a group to retain its members.
- Power of the group to influence its members.
- Degree of participation and loyalty of members.
- Feeling of security on the part of the members.

Group Norms

Norms refer to group behaviour standard, beliefs, attitudes, traditions and expectations shared by group members. Group norms can be defined as the set of rules or guidelines of accepted behaviour which have automatically been established by a group and now monitoring the behaviour of its members.

They are framed to achieve objectives of the group. They can be social and fair in nature. Norms define boundaries between acceptable and unacceptable behaviour.

Types of Group Norms

There are two types of group norms, which are as follows

Behaviour Norms Behaviour norms are rules that standardise how individuals act while working on a day-to-day basis. These norms tend to reflect motivation, commitment to the organisation and therefore results in high level of performance.

Performance Norms Performance norms are rules that standardise employee output and number of hours worked.

Norms Conformity

Group norms enforces a particular trait. It has been observed that norms have the power to force a certain degree of conformity. It depends on the personality of group members that how much pressure, they can sustain.

They may exert for conformity than others. The history of the group and its members also plays a part in conformity, *e.g.* if the group has always been successful by following certain behaviours, new group members are also asked to follow the same.

If the group was not successful in the past, a new group member may have greater freedom to exhibit other behaviours. It can be said a tested behaviour is repeated.

Group Cohesiveness

According to **Rensis Likert**, "Cohesiveness is the attractiveness of the members towards the group or resistance of the members leaving it". It refers to the attachment of members with the group.

Attractiveness is the key to cohesiveness. Cohesiveness is the extent to which group members are loyal and committed to the group and to each other.

Advantages of Group Cohesiveness

- High morale of the group members.
- No conflicting views, which decreases the chances of confrontation/conflict/clashes among members at the workplace or elsewhere.
- Regularity at the work and increased productivity.
- Better communication among workers because of harmonious relationship.

Organisational Change

Change simply refers to alteration in the existing conditions of an organisation. Even in most stable organisations, change is necessary to maintain stability. The reason being that daily new researches bring new concepts, new technology which force to bring change.

The economic and social environment is so dynamic that without adapting to such change even the most successful organisations cannot survive in the changed environment. It becomes necessary to cope up with the environmental change to face the challenges brought up due to these changes.

Thus, organisational change refers to the social and economic changes in nature that the organisation brings in from time-to-time.

Organisational change is all about the process of upgrading the strategies and tactics, procedures, processes, innovations and cultural identity of an organisation and the effects on the organisation of such changes.

Organisational change is the system through which organisations move from their current state to a preferred future state in order to increase their efficiency.

According to **Cambridge Dictionary**, "A process in which a large company or organisation changes its working methods or aims, for example in order to develop and deal with new situations or markets".

According to **N.Greenman**, "Any change in the distribution of power, skills and information or in the lines of communication thus constitutes an organisational change."

Factors Forcing for Organisational Change

External Forces

External forces originate outside an organisation. There are four key external forces for change. *These are as follows*

- **Demographic Characteristics** These include age, education, skill level and gender of employees.
- **Technological Advancements** Adoption of new technology requires massive changes in the organisational structure.
- **Market Changes** The emergence of a global economy is force organisations to change the way they do business. Organisations are entering into new partnerships with their suppliers in order to deliver higher quality products at lower prices.
- **Political Pressure** Government regulations, their policies, trade practices, laws and agreements are some of the causes which compel an organisation to make changes in their present structure.
- **Social Pressure** Changes in the social outlook, composition of the society, social norms are forces that affect the needs, priorities, goals and working of an organisation.

Internal Forces

Internal forces for change come from inside the organisation. This may come from both human resource problems and managerial behaviour. *These are as follows*

- **Human Resource Problems** Human beings are unique with their own mindsets, so the conflict between them is inevitable. Organisations might respond to these problems by using the various approaches to job design by implementing realistic job previews and by reducing employees' role conflict, stress, work overload and ambiguity.
- **Managerial Behaviour** It is said that people change people, not the organisation. The clashes between managers and subordinates may lead the organisation to disasters. Inappropriate behaviour of the leaders such as inadequate direction and support are the cause of conflict between managers and their subordinates.
- **Structural Change** Internal changes such as change in the administration, restructuring of the overall organisational design, issues with profitability, downsizing, human resource planning strategy, reorientation of the employees etc result in the massive change in organisational processes.

Nature of Organisational Change

- All Organisational Change (OC) are introduced through people. Unless the people are willing to accept the need and responsibility for organisational change, intended changes can never be translated into reality.
- Individuals have to learn to adapt their attitudes and behavioural patterns to constantly changing environments.
- Management of organisational change involves both individual and organisation. Individual change is behavioural change, which is determined by individual characteristics such as knowledge, attitudes, beliefs, needs, expectations. While OC is stategic changes in different aspects related to the organisation.
- It is possible to bring about a total change in an organisation by changing behaviours of individual members through participative and educative strategies.
- Bringing total behavioural change in all the groups and members of an organisation involves difficult long-range effort. More often than not, it is a slow painful process to usher a total cultural change in an organisation.
- It is possible to change total organisation without focusing at the level of individual's change of knowledge, attitude and behaviour.
- Modification in the organisation's structures, policies, procedures and techniques leads to total organisational change.

Process of Change

These are the eight steps into which the entire process of change can be broken down.

Following is the process of change showing how one step glides to another step

1. Recognise the Basic Dynamics Change

The first step in this model is recognising need for change. For marketing managers, who anticipate needed change, recognition is likely to come much earlier, as a result of marketing forecasts indicating new market potential, expert indications about impending socio-economic change or a perceived opportunity to capitalise on a key technological breakthrough.

These managers tend to initiate change because they expect it to be necessary in the near future in any case.

2. Identify Challenges and Goals for Change

The manager must then set goals for the proposed change. It is important for the manager to specify goals that the change is supposed to accomplish.

The goals can be set to maintain or increase the market standing, to enter new markets, to restore employee morale, to reduce employee's turnover, to settle a strike and to identify good investment opportunities.

3. Understand People's Natural Resistance to Change

An important next step is diagnosing organisational variables that have brought about the need for change. It is also very important to understand and get the feel of people's resistance to change. To carry out this diagnosis, the manager may discuss the situation with employees and other managers.

4. Select Right Opportunity to Foster Change

After the manager has developed an understanding of the problem and its causes, then he must select a change intervention that will accomplish the intended goal. It is important to strike the iron when it is not so, finding a right opportunity is again important.

An intervention is a specific change induced in an organisation with the intention of solving a particular problem or accomplishing a specific objective.

5. Generate an Action Plan

The manager must then carefully plan the implementation of change. Planning the implementation of change involves consideration of the cost of the change, how the change will affect other areas of the organisation and the degree to which employees should participate in bringing about the change.

Hastily implemented change can result in more harm than benefit. Moreover, if change is thrust upon the employees too quickly, their resistance may stiffen.

6. Enhance your Skills at Dealing with Change

The manager needs to equip himself/herself with the required skills needed to implement change in a proper way, *e.g.* if some new technology is to be adopted by an organisation to run the organisational work smoothly like the concept of SAP had come few years back. Then, it is mandatory for the manager to learn SAP and be confident, if he wants SAP to be adopted by all the individuals of a particular organisation.

7. Implement Change and Monitor the Change

It is necessary to change smoothly, slowly and coolly. A systematically implemented change is more likely to proceed smoothly and to encounter fewer obstacles than is a change that is implemented too quickly and without adequate preparation. An abrubt, quick change will not at all be successful because of resistance of people.

8. Evaluate the Change

Finally, after the change has been implemented, the manager should verify that it has accomplished its intended goals.

A change may fail to bring about the intended results.

This may be due to inappropriate goals or inaccurate diagnosis of the situation or wrong selection of intervention.

Models of Planned Change

Researchers and managers have tried to identify effective ways to manage the change process.

The following models have been developed to effectively manage change

1. Kurt Lewin's Unfreezing, Changing and Refreezing Model

Lewin's model is based on the idea that until a change organisation is actually introduced, it must be fully prepared for change, inspired to change, established and incorporated into the behaviour of the organisation.

The following is a brief description of these phases

Unfreezing There is no change in a closed system from which there is no prior viewpoint. To the extent that the new view deviates from the old perspective, the old one indicates doubt about its own existence. To learn new things, this requires an unlearning of old things. It is known as unfreezing.

It means actively encouraging people to reject old behaviours by shaking the balance that maintains the things on the same ground (status quo). Unfreezing therefore means creating the need for radical change, inspiring people to change and minimising change resistance.

Changing The individual is ready for new behaviour and a change in viewpoint after he has unlearned his past experience. Efforts are being made to replace old attitudes, ideals and behaviours. This implies the transformation from old behaviour to new behaviour experimentation.

Refreezing In this third and the last step, the new status quo is formed with new mind-sets, ideas, behaviours and attitudes. The new ways of functioning are therefore cemented and strengthened. This means strengthening and incorporating change by strengthening and adding new behaviours into formalised and interpersonal relationships as well as personality.

2. Larry Griener's Model

Change occurs in some sequential stages, according to **Griener**. The external power or stimulus pressurises the organisation's management to undertake the process of change. The management is motivated to take action to introduce organisational change in response to this external stimulus.

Following the actions, the different stages of change arise in a synchronous way, such as the diagnosis of the issue, the discovery of a different solution, the improvisation with a new solution and the strengthening of positive outcomes.

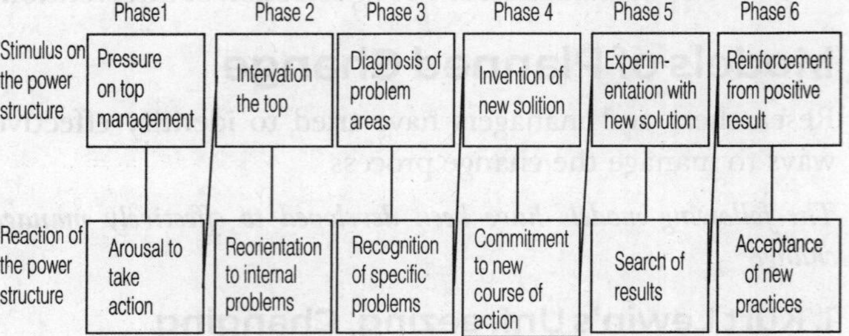

Greiner's Equential Models

The OD model of Leavitt is based on the interactive nature of the different subsystems in the process of transition or change. Four subsystems *i.e* tasks, structure, people and technology interact in an organisational system.

Change in any of the subsystems appears to have implications for the other subsystems because of their interactive nature. Depending on the situation, changes can be made in any of the subsystems. According to Leavitt, how different subsystems interact with one another in a process of change.

3. Lewin's Force Field Model

A classic model of OD, commonly referred to as the 'force field' model, was proposed by Kurt Lewin in 1951. He described organisations as systems which are held in a constant state of 'equilibrium' by equal and opposing forces.

The model suggests that a range of 'driving forces', which exert a pressure for change, are balanced by a number of opposing 'resisting forces'. Driving forces urging change might include the availability of new technology, economic pressure from competitors or even changes in local or national legislation.

Conversely, resisting forces might include a firmly established organisational culture and climate or industry-specific customs. Lewin proposed that any process of organisational change can be thought of as implementing a move in the equilibrium position towards a desired or newly established position.

4. Seven Stage Model by E. Huse

In 1980, Edgar Huse proposed a seven-stage OD model based upon the original three stage model of Lewin.

It includes

- **Scouting** Where representatives from the organisation meet with the OD consultant to identify and discuss the need for change. The change agent and client jointly explore issues to elicit the problems in need of attention.
- **Entry** This stage involves the development of, and mutual agreement upon, both business and psychological contracts. Expectations of the change process are also established.
- **Diagnosis** Here, the consultant diagnoses the underlying organisational problems based upon their previous knowledge and training. This stage involves the identification of specific improvement goals and a planned intervention strategy.
- **Planning** A detailed series of intervention techniques and actions are brought together into a timetable or project plan for the change process. This step also involves the identification of areas of resistance from employees and steps possible to counteract it.
- **Action** The intervention is carried out according to the agreed plans. Previously established action steps are implemented.
- **Stabilisation and Evaluation** The stage of 'refreezing' the system. Newly implemented codes of action, practices and systems are absorbed into everyday routines. Evaluation is conducted to determine the success of the change process and any need for further action is established.
- **Termination** The OD consultant or change agent leaves the organisation and moves on to another client or begins an entirely different project within the same organisation.

5. Edgar Schein's Model of Change

Kurt Lewin gave a three-stage model of change that has come to be known as the unfreezing-change-refreeze model that requires prior learning to be rejected and replaced. Edgar Schein provided further detail for a more comprehensive model of change calling this approach "cognitive redefinition.

Stage 1 This comprises of becoming motivated to change (unfreezing). This unfreezing process has three sub-processes that relate to a readiness and motivation to change. *These are*

- Disconfirmation where present conditions lead to dissatisfaction, such as not meeting personal goals.

- Previous beliefs now being seen as invalid creates "survival anxiety." However, this may not be sufficient to prompt change if learning anxiety is present.
- Learning anxiety triggers defensiveness and resistance due to the pain of having to unlearn what had been previously accepted. Three stages occur in response to learning anxiety denial; scapegoating and passing the buck; and manoeuvring and bargaining.

Stage 2 Change what needs to be changed (unfrozen and moving to a new state). Three possible impacts from processing new information are: words take on new or expanded meaning, concepts are interpreted within a broader context, and there is an adjustment in the scale used in evaluating new input.

Stage 3 Making the change permanent (refreezing) Refreezing is the final stage where new behaviour becomes habitual, which includes developing a new self-concept and identity and establishing new interpersonal relationships.

6. Carnall's Change Management Model

Colin Carnall (1990) has produced a useful model that brings together a number of perspectives on change. *He says that the effective management of change depends on the level of management skill in the following areas*

- managing transitions effectively,
- dealing with organisational cultures,
- managing organisational politics.

A manager who is skilled in managing transitions is able to help people to learn as they change, and create an atmosphere of openness and risk-taking.

A manager who deals with organisational cultures examines the current organisational culture and starts to develop what Carnall calls 'a more adaptable culture'. This means for example developing better information flow, more openness, and greater local autonomy.

A manager who is able to manage organisational politics can understand and recognise different factions and different agendas. He or she develops skills in utilising and recognising various political tactics such as building coalitions, using outside experts and controlling the agenda.

7. John P Kotter's Model

John Kotter introduced the "Kotter's Eight Step Change Model" to improve an organisation's ability to change and to increase its chances of success. *These are as follows*

- **Establish a Sense of Urgency** Discussing today's competitive realities, looking at potential future scenarios. Increasing the 'felt-need' for change.
- **Form a Powerful Guiding Coalition** Assembling a powerful group of people who can work well together.
- **Create a Vision** Building a vision to guide the change effort together with strategies for achieving this.
- **Communicate the Vision** Kotter emphasises the need to communicate atleast 10 times the amount you expect to have to communicate. The vision and accompanying strategies and new behaviours need to be communicated in a variety of different ways. The guiding coalition should be the first to role model new behaviours.
- **Empower Others to Act on the Vision** This step includes getting rid of obstacles to change such as unhelpful structures or systems. Allow people to experiment.
- **Plan for and Create Short-term Wins** Look for and advertise short-term visible improvements. Plan these in and reward people publicly for improvements.
- **Consolidate Improvements and Produce still more Change** Promote and reward those able to promote and work towards the vision. Energise the process of change with new projects, resources, change agents.
- **Institutionalise New Approaches** Ensure that everyone understands that the new behaviours lead to corporate success.

8. Nadler and Tushman's Congruence Model

This model views the organisation as a system that draws inputs from both internal and external sources (strategy, resources, environment) and transforms them into outputs (activities, behaviour and performance of the system at three levels: individual, group and total). In this model of the transformation process, the organisation is composed of four components, or sub-systems, which are all dependent on each other. *These are*

- **The Work** This is the actual day-to-day activities carried out by individuals. Process design, pressures on the individual and available rewards must all be considered under this element.
- **The People** This is about the skills and characteristics of the people who work in an organisation. What are their expectations, what are their backgrounds?
- **The Formal Organisation** This refers to the structure, systems and policies in place. How things are formally organised?
- **The Informal Organisation** This consists of all the unplanned, unwritten activities that emerge overtime such as power, influence, values and norms.

This model proposes that effective management of change means attending to all four components, not just one or two components.

9. Bullock and Batten's Model of Change

Bullock and Batten's (1985) phases of planned change draw on the disciplines of project management. There are many similar 'steps to changing your organisation' models to choose from. They analysed over 30 models of change management and arrived at their own 4-phase model of programmed change management, *which are as follows*

- **Exploration** It involves verifying the need for change, and acquiring any specific resources (such as expertise) necessary for the change to go ahead.
- **Planning** It is an activity involving key decision makers and technical experts. A diagnosis is completed and actions are sequenced in a change plan. The plan is signed off by management before moving into the action phase.
- **Action** They are completed according to plan, with feedback mechanisms which allow some replanting if things go off track. The final integration phase is started once the change plan has been fully actioned.
- **Integration** It involves aligning the change with other areas in the organisation, and formalising them in some way via established mechanisms such as policies, rewards and company updates.

10. Beckhard and Harris Formula

Beckhard and Harris developed their change formula from some original work by Gelicher in 1987. The change formula is a concise way of capturing the process of change, and identifying the factors that need to be strongly in place for change to happen. *The formula is*

$$C = [ABD] > X$$

Where, C = Change
A = Level of dissatisfaction with the status quo
B = Desirability of the proposed change or and state
D = Practicality of the change (minimal risk and disruption)
X = 'Cost' of changing

Implication Factors A, B, and D must outwe… the perceived costs [X] for the change to occur. If any person or group whose commitment is needed is not sufficiently dissatisfied with the present state of affairs [A], eager to achieve the proposed end state [B] and convinced of the feasibility of the change [D], then the cost [X] of changing is too high, and that person will resist the change. Beckhard and Harris emphasised the need to design interventions that allow these three factors to surface in the organisation.

11. The Six Box Model

The six-box model is a framework developed by the American analyst Marvin Weisbord to assess the functioning of organisations. It is a generic framework and is intended for use across a wide variety of organisations. It is based mainly on the techniques and assumptions of the field of organisational development.

The model represents a particular way of looking at organisational structure and design. It gives attention to issues such as planning, incentives and rewards, the role of support functions such as personnel, internal competitions among organisational units, standards for remuneration, partnerships, hierarchies and the delegation of authority, organisational control, accountability and performance assessment.

The model also follows the basic 'systems' approach to organisational functioning including the well-known inputs and 'outputs' categories.

The six-box model is comprised of the following components (boxes)

1. **Purposes** What 'businesses' are we in?
2. **Structure** How do we divide up the work?
3. **Relationships** How do we manage conflict (coordinate) among people? With our technologies?
4. **Rewards** Is there an incentive for doing all that needs doing?
5. **Leadership** Is someone keeping the boxes in balance?
6. **Helpful Mechanisms** Have we adequate coordinating technologies?

12. McKinsey 7S Framework

It is a **Value Based Management** (VBM) model developed by well-known business consultants **Waterman** and **Peters** (who also developed the MBWA—"Management By Walking Around'', and authored "In Search of Excellence"). This was a strategic vision for groups to include businesses, business units, and teams. The 7S are structure, strategy, systems, skills, style, staff and shared values.

The theory also defines hard and soft elements which are as follows

Hard Elements

They are easier to define or identify and management can directly influence them. These are strategy statements, organisation charts and reporting lines and formal processes and IT systems. *These are*

S1-Strategy Plans for the allocation of firm's scarce resources to reach identified goals in time.

S2-Structure The way the organisation's units relate to each other. Centralised, functional divisions (top-down), decentralised (large holdings), matrix, network.

S3-System Procedures, processes and routines that characterises how work is to be done, financial systems, hiring procedure, information systems, performance appraisal.

Soft Elements

It can be more difficult to describe and are less tangible and more influenced by culture. However, these soft elements are as important as the hard elements, if the organisation to be successful. *These are*

S4-Shared Values What does the organisation stands for and what it believes in central beliefs and attitudes.

S5-Staff Numbers and types of personnel within the organisation.

S6-Style Cultural style of organisation and how key managers behave in achieving goals.

S7-Skill Distinctive capabilities of personnel or of the organisation as a whole.

Resistance to Change

Law of Inertia works and people resist to change. They want to be in the state where they are.

Therefore, managers need to recognise the manifestations of resistance both in themselves and in others, if they want to be more effective in supporting change.

The sources of resistance to change within organisations are classified into organisational sources of resistance and individual sources of resistance.

Overcoming Resistance to Change

It is basically manager's responsibility to find the solutions of overcoming resistance to change. An effective manager is the one who can get the change done smoothly. So, the managers need not abandon planned change because of the fear of resistance.

Few suggestions have deduced out of the extensive research done by various scholars.

First, an organisation must be ready for change.

Second, the top management should inform the employees about the process of change.

Third, the employees perceptions or interpretations of a change should be considered.

Few methods of overcoming resistance to change are as follows

Participation

Participation is generally considered the most effective technique for overcoming resistance to change. Participation from the stage of planning is more effecting in overcoming resistance. Employees who have the opportunity to express their own ideas and to understand the perspectives of others are likely to accept change gracefully.

Communicate about the Advantages

Educating employees about the need for and the expected results of an impending change help reduce their resistance. Managers should maintain an open channel of communication while planning and implementing change. However, it is also a time-consuming process.

No Haste in Implementing Change

Introducing change gradually, making only necessary changes, announcing changes in advance and allowing time for people to adjust to new ways of doing things can help reduce resistance.

Give Weightage to Other's Opinions

Listen to all the voices being raised against change. In almost any situation, where a change is being planned, there are forces acting for and against the change. They may improyise or facilitate the process.

Confrontation

It is important to sit together and comfront with their own view points. It is necessary to convince others if some wrong notion is there. Where someone or some group will clearly lose out in a change and where that group has considerable power to resist, there confrontation is required.

Manipulation and Cooperation

This is followed when other tactics will not work or are too expensive. It can be quick and inexpensive; however, it can lead to further problems if people feel manipulated.

Use of Authority, Power and Influence

The most powerful and extensively used tool to overcome resistance to change. This is adopted where speed is essential and where the change initiators possess considerable power. It is speedy and can overcome resistance. It is direct way and therefore does not waste time at all.

Organisational Development

Organisational Development is an organisation improvement strategy. The term Organisational Development (OD) refers to a broad range of behavioural science based strategies used to diagnose the need for change in organisations and to implement changes when necessary. It is relatively a new field of study of around 60's.

Organisational Development can be referred as a technique for bringing change in the entire organisation, rather than focusing attention on individuals to bring change easily in the organisation. It is basically about how organisations and people function and how to get them function better.

According to **Cummings** and **Worley**, "Organisational development is a systematic application of behavioural science knowledge to the planned development and reinforcement of organisational strategies, structures and processes for improving an organisation's is effectiveness."

According to **Burke**, "Organisation development is a planned process of change in an organisational culture through the utilisation of behavioural science technologies, research and theory."

Nature of Organisational Development

Organisational development is a general strategy or approach to organisational change that is employed to analyse and diagnose the sources of organisational problems and to develop and implement action plans for their solution.

According to Bennis, OD has the following characteristics

- It is an educational strategy for bringing planned change.
- It relates to real problems of an organisation.
- Laboratory training methods based on experienced behaviour are primarily used to bring the change.
- There is a close working relationship between change agents and the people who are being changed. The relationships involve mutual trust, joint goals, means, and mutual influence.

Features of Organisational Development

Planned OD is a strategy that is planned. It is an educational strategy that requires careful study, research, analysis and drawing-up plans to develop the organisation according to the emerging needs.

Long-term Process The process of OD is a long-term process as the time period involving the development may range from a few months to an year or more. This is because each and every aspect of the organisation needs to be planned.

Systems Orientation OD studies the various groups and their interactions within the organisation. It is related to all the systems and structures operating in an institution.

Organisation as a Whole OD sees the organisation as a whole. Even if development of a part of process takes place, then also its implications are studied on that entire organisation and changes are monitored.

Individuals from the Top OD flows from top to bottom *i.e* from the managerial level to the employees. It is the work of the organisation to push the vision and mission of the organisation to its employees by various developmental processes.

Organisational Culture OD closely relates to the culture of on organisation. Therefore, OD is special and unique to every institution since every institution has a distinct culture. OD is done according to the particular situation. It is consistent with the culture of the organisation.

Organisational Development Interventions

Organisational Development (OD) interventions are organised to address a problem, enabling an organisation to accomplish the goals.

Such intervention activities are also meant to improve the functioning of the organisation and allow mangers and leaders to handle their team and organisational cultures better. *It includes*

Survey Feedback

Information is collected using the survey method. This is the most popularly used and successful data collection method. This information collected by survey is used by managers to make decisions.

The broad range of information is obtained on employment conditions, quality of the work, work hours, salaries and employee attitudes. The managers' team then analyses these informations. They identify the problem, assess the outcomes and come up with solutions.

All members of the organisation collect information. Supervisors meet with their juniors and examine the data, and allow the data to be interpreted by subordinates. After these plans are prepared, necessary changes will be made.

Team Building

Team building is also another way of developing the organisation. This technique is designed specifically to enhance employees' abilities and motivate them to work effectively together.

It is the OD method that prioritises the creation or formation of teams to improve organisational efficiency. All these teams comprise of same rank of workers and supervisors. Even this technique applies sensitivity training to completely different departmental teams.

The teams or working groups comprised of 10 to 15 people are quite small. Under the supervision of an expert trainer, they usually have group discussions with a supervisor.

Sensitivity Training

It is also recognised as training in the laboratory. This technique asks employees to communicate in groups. The purpose of sensitivity training is to make people understand and gain knowledge so that then they also feel free and fearless.

This technique allows different groups of workers to mix and speak freely and build interpersonal relationships. This technique enables workers to know the thoughts and behaviour of others and the effect of their behaviour on others.

It creates acceptance, improves communication skills, and tolerates individual differences and the art of conflict resolution is built. It helps in reducing organisational personal and social conflicts.

Grid Organisation Development

It is a comprehensive model of people, organisation and group together. Grid organisation development, developed by **Blake** and **Mounton**, is a comprehensive and systematic organisational development programme.

The programme aims at individuals, groups and the organisation as a whole. In this, the idea of synergy was also given according to which abilities of individuals complement each other.

It utilises a considerable number of instruments, enabling individuals and groups to assess their own strength and weaknesses. '**Synergogy**' defined by Blake and Mouton describes a systematic approach to learning that leads to team members to learn from each other.

It also focuses on skills, knowledge and processes necessary for effectiveness at the individual, group and inter-group and total organisation levels.

Barriers to Organisational Development

- No consideration of optical standards
- Poor team work
- Inappropriate leadership style
- No compliance with authorities
- Unclear goal
- Poor quality production
- Clashes and conflicts within group
- No alignment to organisational strategies
- Inappropriate organisation structure
- Communication gap

Process of Organisational Development

The organisational development is a long drawn process that needs to be done very carefully. The development process should not hamper the day-to-day activity of the organisation. The process should bring in subtle changes that goes with the flow of the organisation.

The entire process of OD is broken down into seven steps beginning from initial diagnosis to team building

Initial Diagnosis It refers to the identification of the inadequacies in an organisation. After indentifying the problematic areas, the organisation can take the decision to bring developmental changes.

For this, it can employ professionals or consultants who prepare the step by step process of bringing organisational development.

Data Collection After identification of the problematic areas, the next step isto collect the data. The data collection process is related to the development of the problematic areas as identified in step one.

For this, survey method, direct observation, analysis of documents and reports is undertaken to know about the organisational climate.

Data Feedback After the collection of the data, it is analysed by people or committee specially hired or selected from within the organisation for the purpose of organisational development.

After careful reviewing and analysis, the areas of disagreement and/or confrontation of ideas and/or different opinions are discussed. Then the areas that needs priority are selected.

Selection and Design of Interventions The activities that needs to be changed and developed are called interventions. These are planned in advance and introduced simultaneously into the system to accomplish the improvements and desires changes one needs to see.

Implementation of Interventions The way to implement the interventions into the system of the organisation is planned and the process of development by means of interventions take place.

Interventions take various forms like on-the-job activities, feedback form, group discussion, formation of workshops etc. The process may be a quick process or it may be slow. But the target is to implement the intervention as smoothly as possible.

Problem Solving The preparation and implementation of interventions within the targeted areas or specific areas of the organisation should solve the problems that were identified in the beginning. The task is to prepare recommendations that can be used in future and tasks can be planned accordingly.

Team Building The consultants/professionals encourage the formation of teams so that people develop a team spirit and put their combined efforts to achieve different tasks successfully. After the formation of groups, intergroup activities are planned and executed to achieve the set goals. The joint meetings between the managers of different departments and between managers and subordinates also increases team building. This is an integral part of an organisation.

EXAM BASED QUESTIONS

1 The manifestations of OB relate to
(a) organisational structure, management processes and technology
(b) biological-physiological, structure, and personality
(c) organisationl dynamics, conflict, change and adaptation
(d) None of the above

2 Which of the following are core disciplines contributing to HR and OB?
(a) Economics, Semantics and Physiology
(b) Psychology, Sociology and Anthropology
(c) Political Science, Economics and History
(d) None of the above

3 Human relations is worth studying because it contributes towards
(a) "people skills" building (b) mass conformity
(c) weakening of unions (d) None of these

4 Formal organisation variable consists of
(a) organisational structure, management process and technology
(b) people, structure, technology and external social system
(c) productivity, absenteeism, turnover and job satisfaction
(d) None of the above

5 One of the assumptions of Theory Y is as follows
(a) the normal human being intrinsically dislikes work and attempts of avoid it if the can do so
(b) human beings have a hierarchy of needs
(c) people are governed by self-direction and self-control
(d) None of the above

6 Success of management is largely a matter of
(a) effective direction and leadership
(b) proper planning
(c) effective communication
(d) All of the above

7 Behavioural factors affecting an individual consist
(a) personal attitudes
(b) behaviour patterns and work habits
(c) physical fitness
(d) None of the above

8 Weber contribution is crystallisation of thinking on
(a) organisation structure
(b) organisational behaviour
(c) organisational development
(d) All of the above

9 Who of the followings are supporter of behaviouralist theory of organisation?
(a) A H Maslow (b) Kurt Lewis
(c) Chester Bernard (d) All of these

10 Who popularised the behavioural approach to organisation?
(a) Chester Bernard (b) H Simon
(c) Cart Roger (d) J D Mooney

11 The understanding, prediction, management of human behaviour in organisations is referred to as............
(a) organisational design
(b) organisational development
(c) organisational behaviour
(d) organisational culture

12 In the .... model of organisational behaviour, employees cease to depend on managers, but their dependence on the organisation increases.
(a) custodial (b) supportive
(c) collegial (d) autocratic

13 Which of the following forms the basis for autocratic model of OB?
(a) Obedience (b) Authority
(c) Power (d) Dependence on boss

14 Motivation is an element of
(a) planning function
(b) organisation function
(c) direction function
(d) coordination function

15 "Motivation" is a branch of
(a) planning (b) organising
(c) controlling (d) staffing

16 The 'carrot and stick' theory of motivation is related to
(a) Theory X
(b) Theory Y
(c) Maslow's recent assumptions about human motivation
(d) None of the above

17 According to behavioural approach, situation includes the following
(a) immediate stimulus and environment
(b) physiological, cognitive and psychological processes
(c) responses and patterns of behaviour
(d) None of the above

18 The basis of influence in informal organisations is
(a) position (b) person
(c) authority (d) None of these

19 The major goal of informal organisation is
(a) satisfaction of their members
(b) profitability of the enterprise
(c) service to the society
(d) None of the above

20 The top ranking incentives for Indian managers as identified by Laxmi Narain include
(a) feeling of worthwhile accomplishment, recognition, and decision-making authority
(b) opportunity for promotion, job security and prestige
(c) pay, allowances and other benefits
(d) None of the above

21 **As suggested by Pareek, one of the strategies for improving motivation at individual level is**
(a) performance as.a cause of work satisfaction and an outcome of effort
(b) promotion as a function of merit and competence
(c) encouragement of open communication
(d) None of the above

22 **As suggested by Pareek, one of the organisation level strategies to improve motivation is**
(a) differing reinforcement of motivations
(b) dynamic nature of individual's motivation
(c) successful experience with challenging tasks
(d) None of the above

23 **Decision-making process can be optimised by trust by**
(a) brainstorming
(b) development of cohesive, versatile work teams
(c) line pin systems
(d) None of the above

24 **Which of the following asserts that people tend to affiliate with one another because of spatial or geographical closeness?**
(a) Balance theory (b) Exchange theory
(c) Propinquity theory (d) None of these

25 **Schein has identified a number of environmental, membership and dynamic factors for**
(a) satisfaction of individual needs
(b) attainment of organisational goals
(c) integration of individual needs and organisational goals
(d) None of the above

26 **'Theory Y' states that**
(a) workers prefer to be directed
(b) workers exercise self-direction and self-control
(c) workers have inherent disliking for work and will avoid it if they can
(d) workers do not work on their own

27 **'Theory X' states that**
(a) workers prefer to be directed
(b) workers exercise self-direction and self-control
(c) workers have inherent liking for work
(d) worker do not work on their own

28 **McGregor's Theory 'X' approximates to**
(a) employee orientation (b) employment orientation
(c) production orientation (d) input orientation

29 **X and Y theory was propounded by**
(a) Herzberg (b) Maslow
(c) Porter and Lawler (d) McGregor

30 **Theory 'Y' approximates to**
(a) employee orientation (b) employment orientation
(c) production orientation (d) input orientation

31 **Expectancy theory of motivation is given by**
(a) Herzberg (b) Vroom
(c) Porter and Lawler (d) Maslow

32 **The need-hierarchy theory of motivation is given by**
(a) Maslow (b) Herzberg
(c) Vroom (d) McGregor

33 **Maslow's need-hierarchy theory of motivation has classified the human needs into five categories as follows. Arrange the following needs in ascending order given by Maslow**
1. Safety needs 2. Esteem needs
3. Social needs 4. Physiological needs
5. Self-actualisation needs
What is the sequence of domtion of these needs?
(a) 1, 4, 3, 2, 5 (b) 4, 1, 3, 2, 5
(c) 5, 3, 2, 4, 1 (d) None of these

34 **According to Maslow's need-hierarchy theory of motivation**
(a) an unsatisfied need is a motivator of behaviour
(b) a satisfied need is a motivator of behaviour
(c) depends upon the situation
(d) None of the above

35 **Two factor theory is related to**
(a) leadership (b) motivation
(c) communication (d) None of these

36 **Under expectancy theory of motivation, increase in motivation results when**
(a) valence increases (b) valence decreases
(c) no effect of valence (d) both ways

37 **According to Maslow's need-hierarchy theory, the low level needs are**
(a) physiological (b) security
(c) self-esteem (d) All of these

38 **According to McGregor, what contributes towards the leadership**
(a) knowledge
(b) consistent discipline
(c) atmosphere of approval
(d) All of the above

39 **The ERG theory is related to**
(a) Herzberg (b) Maslow
(c) Adam (d) Alderfer

40 **Its basic premise is that the behaviour of human beings is determined by the sum of external environmental factors and not by internal needs, desires and wants. The reference is to**
(a) Vroom's Contingency Model of Motivation
(b) Skinner's Operant Theory of Motivation
(c) Adam's Equity Theory of Motivation
(d) All of the above

41 **Which one of the following theories is not a process theory of motivation?**
(a) Maslow's need-hierarchy theory
(b) Vroom's expectancy theory
(c) Expectancy theory-The Porter and Lawler model
(d) Equity theory

42 In equity theory, the employees are not motivated when
(a) the reward is proportionate to the work
(b) the reward is not proportionate to the work
(c) reward is more than the expectation
(d) Anyone of the above

43 According to Herzberg's motivation hygiene theory, which one of the following is a motivating factor?
(a) Job security
(b) Work itself
(c) Company policy
(d) Interpersonal relations characteristic

44 In Maslow's need-hierarchy theory, which of the following cannot be considered as high order needs?
(a) Safety needs (b) Social needs
(c) Self-esteem needs (d) Self-actualisation needs

45 Which of the following statement implies motivation correctly?
(a) Exert more effort to accomplish the desired goals of the organisation
(b) Exert more efforts to accomplish the individual goals
(c) Exert more effort to accomplish the common goals of employees
(d) Exert more effort to accomplish the desired goals of the employer, employees and the government

46 Which of the following factors can have a lasting impairment on a person's motivation to learn?
(a) A negative experience of learning in childhood
(b) Learning for achievement
(c) Learning which is challenging
(d) Learning which is interesting

47 The significance of leadership stems from
(a) existence of informal groups in organisation
(b) incompleteness of organisational design
(c) need for decision-making in organisation
(d) None of the above

48 If the followers are able and unwilling, then leader will have to use the
(a) authoritarian style
(b) participative style
(c) situational style
(d) strategic style

49 Acoording to situational leadership approach, the style that denotes a high-task and a low-relationship style is
(a) selling style (b) delegating style
(c) participating style (d) telling style

50 Which one of the following is a characteristic of autocratic leader?
(a) Strict
(b) Incompetent
(c) Benevolent
(d) Free-rein

51 Which of the following type of leader encourages the participation of team members in the formulation of policies and decision-making?
(a) Autocratic leader
(b) Democratic leader
(c) Laissez-Faire leader
(d) Benevolent leader

52 It incorporates the relationship between perception, effort, expected reward and satisfaction. This is model of motivation
(a) Porter and Lawler Expectancy model
(b) Fiedler's contingency model
(c) Vroom's contingency model
(d) None of the above

53 Managerial-Grid model of leadership was developed by
(a) Blake and Mouton (b) Evans and House
(c) Fayol and Taylor (d) Vroom and Fiedler

54 R Likert believed which of the following types of leaders to be more effective?
(a) Production-oriented (b) Task-oriented
(c) People-oriented (d) Job-centered

55 Ohio State Model suggests the following as the best leader behaviour.
(a) Low structure and low consideration
(b) High concerns both for production and people
(c) Low concern both for production and people
(d) High structure and high consideration

56 Which one of the following is the external dimension to the leaders?
(a) Task (b) Relations
(c) Style (d) Attitude

57 It is a desire to maximise one's potential and to become what one is capable of becoming. The reference is to
(a) self-esteem needs (b) self-actualisation needs
(c) physiological needs (d) security needs

58 Who concluded that in a structured situation with 'oriented followers' style, and identified goal paths the desirable leader style is high on relations and low on task?
(a) L P Bradford (b) Fred E Fiedler
(c) R Likert (d) Robert J House

59 Ohio state, leadership model identified two leader-behaviour variables. These are.
(i) Drive (ii) Consideration
(iii) Intelligence (iv) Initiating structure
(a) i + ii (b) ii + iv
(c) ii + iii (d) i + ii + iii + iv

60 Who of the following is related to path-goal theory of leadership?
(a) R Likert (b) Chester Bernard
(c) Douglas McGregor (d) Abraham Maslow

61 **A leader who possess special and unique skill and experience is said to have**
(a) Monopoly power
(b) Coercive power
(c) Autocratic power
(d) Dominant power

62 **In Likert's system approach, which of the following characteristics is not there in system?**
(a) The leader does not trust the subordinates and closely supervises them
(b) The leader defines the work in great detail
(c) Fear is the main motivator
(d) There is free communication between the leader and the subordinates

63 **A leader uses the following methods.**
(i) Uses criticism
(ii) Encourages growth
(iii) Sets objectives
(iv) Gives orders and directions
(a) (i) and (ii) (b) (iii) and (iv)
(c) (ii) and (iii) (d) (i), (ii) and (iv)

64 **This type of power largely stems from personalised leader qualities.**
(a) Coercive power
(b) Coercive negative power
(c) Coercive positive power
(d) Persuasive power

65 **"Leadership is the activity of influencing people to strive willingly for group objectives." The definition of leadership has been given by**
(a) Carry O'Donnel (b) George R Terry
(c) Irving R Weschler (d) Fred Massarik

66 **The leadership theory given by G.R Terry emphasised on**
(a) willingness to accept
(b) force to influence people
(c) compulsion to influence people
(d) All of the above

67 **Indeed I have never observed any leader who was able to state adequately or intelligently, why he was able to be a leader, nor any statement of followers that expressed why they followed him. The statement is given by**
(a) Chester Barnard (b) Henry Fayol
(c) George Terry (d) None of these

68 **"In this style, the leader consults his team and drive them to the goal which is well defined and set with common consent". The reference is to**
(a) low-low management style
(b) low-high management style
(c) high-high management style
(d) high-low management style

69 **Which one of the following leadership is based on organisational status?**
(a) Informal leadership (b) Diplomatic leadership
(c) Charismatic leadership (d) Bureaucratic leadership

70 **The Greatman theory of leadership led to the rise of**
(a) the behavioural theory of leadership
(b) the trait theory of leadership
(c) the situational theory of leadership
(d) None of the above

71 **Given the following variables that determine leadership**
(i) Followers (F)
(ii) The goal (G)
(iii) A measure of willingness (W)
(iv) A given situation (S)
(v) Leadership (L)
The leadership function may be desecrated as
(a) $F = f(L, G, W, S)$ (b) $L = f(F, G, W, S)$
(c) $G = f(F, L, W, S)$ (d) $S = f(F, L, W, G)$

72 **In this style, the leader is authoritarian, "task-oriented, derives power from his authority position and levels his team with instructions and discipline." The leadership style is known as**
(a) high-low management style
(b) high-high management style
(c) low-high management style
(d) low-low management style

73 **Two factor theory was prepared by**
(a) Herzberg (b) Porter and Lawler
(c) Maslow (d) McGregor

74 **Below are given four different theories**
(i) Trait approach (ii) Attitude criterion
(iii) Behaviour approach (iv) Situational approach
These are identified with
(a) administrative behaviour
(b) organisational behaviour
(c) leadership index
(d) administrative approaches

75 **In this style, the leader keeps his team in good humour, underplays problems, often pleases followers to get things done.**
(a) high-low management style
(b) low-high management style
(c) high-high management style
(d) high-low management style

76 **The motion of men implicit in the classical theory leads to generate a kind of employee psyche, which may be described as**
(a) self-development oriented
(b) aggressive
(c) submissive
(d) deficiency-oriented

77 Effective leadership behaviour is a result of following variable
(a) structure (b) consideration
(c) environment (d) All of these

78 Structure variable is synonymous with
(a) task (b) relations
(c) style (d) attitude

79 Environment is synonymous with
(a) task (b) relations
(c) people (d) situational variables

80 Which of the following is an important dynamic variable?
(a) Superior's style and behaviour
(b) Organisational nature
(c) The task structure
(d) Cultural variables

81 The democratic leadership style goes with
(a) Theory X (b) Theory Y
(c) Theory Z (d) None of these

82 The authoritarian leadership style goes with
(a) Theory X (b) Theory Y
(c) Theory Z (c) None of these

83 Likert believed the following types of leaders to be more effective
(a) job-centered
(b) production-oriented
(c) task-oriented
(d) people-centered

84 Managerial Grid suggests the following as the best leader-behaviour
(a) low structure and low consideration
(b) high concern both for production and people
(c) low concern both for production and people
(d) high structure and high consideration

85 "Superiors with the best records of performance focus their primary attention on the human aspects of their subordinates problems and on endeavoring to build effective work-groups with high performance goals." The observation has been made by
(a) Andrew W Halpin
(b) Ohio State University
(c) Rensis Likert
(d) Michigan Model

86 Which of the following statement about the basic characteristics of the phenomenon of motivation is not correct?
(a) It derives people's behaviour towards goals that are pay-offs or incentives
(b) Like needs, the goals also originate within the individual only
(c) An internal need within the individual creates a desire or drive
(d) Achievement of goals creates satisfaction which in turn reinforce perpetuation of the needs

87 Which of the following leadership style permits substantial delegation of authority to subordinates and allows them to set objectives and solve problems themselves?
(a) Autocratic (b) Democratic
(c) Permissive (d) None of these

88 Who has asserted that management skill is a must, while technical competence is highly desirable but not essential?
(a) Fayol (b) Appley
(c) Goode (d) None of these

89 Who has provided four systems of management?
(a) Blake and Mouton (b) Hersey and Blanchard
(c) Likert (d) None of these

90 Who has (have) formulated 'Life Cycle Theory' of leadership?
(a) Reddin (b) Fiedler
(c) Hersey and Blanchard (d) None of these

91 The ultimate aim of all leadership theories and model is to build
(a) a cause and effect relationship
(b) a leadership model
(c) a process that leads to optimisation
(d) postulate for maximising benefits

92 A leader is seen to possess certain traits, his leadership index can be read-off a leadership meter. This statement relates to
(a) the administrative approach
(b) attitude approach
(c) trait approach
(d) criterion approach

93 Michigan leadership studies are based on the following approach to the study of leadership
(a) trait approaeh (b) attitude criterion
(c) behaviour approach (d) situational approach

94 Michigan leadership studied two variables. These were
(i) Employee orientation (ii) Employment orientation
(iii) Input orientation (iv) Production orientation
The correct code is given above
(a) (i) and (ii) (b) (ii) and (iv)
(c) (i) and (iv) (d) (i) and (iii)

95 One who tries to bring discipline and order through formal structures, plans and processes and tries to monitor performance against plans is a
(a) leader (b) manager
(c) coordinator (d) team-player

96 Which of the following is not considered as a leadership style?
(a) Task oriented leadership style
(b) Society oriented leadership style
(c) Employee oriented leadership style
(d) Autocratic leadership style

97 Who has stressed the group theory (behavioural) of organisation?
(a) Likert (b) Simon
(c) Woodward (d) None of these

98 Which of the following cause the least resentment and the highest satisfaction among workers?
(a) Situational initiation (b) Authority initiation
(c) Procedural initiation (d) None of these

99 Which of the following group of traits is perceived to the most important for Indian managers?
(a) Aggressive, dominant and conforming
(b) Cooperative, intelligent and energetic
(c) Sociable, self-controlled and flexible
(d) None of the above

100 The traditional view relating to informal organisation is as follows
(a) they can exert powerful positive influence upon productivity and job satisfaction provided their cooperation is sought by the management
(b) they obstruct the attainment of organisational goals
(c) they facilitate as well as hamper organisational goals
(d) None of the above

101 Which of the following are characterised by a relatively consistent antagonism, continuous pressures, well planned and consistent grievance activity, high degree of internal unity, sustained union participation and usually good production record in the long-run?
(a) 'Family' informal groups
(b) 'Strategic' informal groups
(c) 'Conservative' informal groups
(b) None of the above

102 The tendency for individuals to put less effort when working collectively than when working individually is
(a) group inequity
(b) group dynamics
(c) group shift
(d) social loafing

103 Decision-making, heavily depends on the individual
(a) understanding (b) creativity
(c) perception (d) ability

104 In formal groups and organisations, an individual has maximum access to
(a) referent power (b) reward power
(c) legitimate power (d) coercive power

105 In which of the following kind of group discussion, the members are encouraged to generate as many imaginative and creative ideas as they can in a short period of time?
(a) Simulation method
(b) Case-study method
(c) Role play method
(d) None of the above

106 Which of the following is an important feature of "Autonomous Working Group"?
(a) The group reports directly to the senior management by passing their immediate bosses
(b) The creation of teams which have a high level of autonomy and control over their immediate working environment
(c) The bringing together of various individuals who have a common interest in solving certain problems
(d) A group of experts brought into research new ways of producing a product

107 Who has defined communication as the transmission and reception of ideas, feelings and attitudes, both verbally and non-verbally, which give rise to a response?
(a) Kelly
(b) Stewart
(c) Sigband
(d) None of the above

108 What are the basic units of communication?
(a) Consumatory and instrumental
(b) Media and channel
(c) Meaning and message
(d) None of the above

109 Which of the following communication networks is more effective vis-a-vis speed and accuracy of performance?
(a) Circle (b) Wheel
(c) Chan (d) None of these

110 Which of the following is more relevant in determining ability of individuals to remember communication over time?
(a) Non-verbal communication
(b) Feedback
(c) Presentation
(d) None of the above

111 The major obstacle in the part of an Indian top executive's open contacts with the worker is
(a) his own official position
(b) trade union
(c) attitude of workers
(d) None of the above

112 The motives which are unlearned but not physiologically based are called
(a) primary motives
(b) secondary motives
(c) general motives- competence, manipulation, activity's curiosity
(d) None of the above

113 Which is true about grapevine?
(a) It is result of social forces at workplace
(b) It is common in times of high organisational commitment
(c) It exists when member of formal group know each other
(d) All of the above

114 Cluster is a type of

(a) grapevine (b) informal communication
(c) formal communication (d) None of the above

115 The ultimate goal of organisational development is to

(a) structure the organisational environment so that managers and employees can use their developed skills and abilities to the fullest
(b) reduce the levels of uncertainty in managerial decision-making throughout the organisation
(c) create an internal environment which is conducive to self expression
(d) None of the above

116 Who has defined OD as a planned, organisation-wide and managed from the top effort aiming to increase an organisation's effectiveness and health through planned interventions in the organisational process employing behavioural science knowledge?

(a) Bennis (b) Beckhard
(c) French (d) None of these

117 One of the objectives of organisational change is

(a) changes in an organisation's level of adaptation to its environment
(b) increased motivation
(c) greater innovation
(d) None of the above

118 The developmental branch of MBO is developed by

(a) Drucker (b) Odiome
(c) McGregor (d) None of these

119 Which level of change in OD is concerned with development of skills and improvement of value systems required for effective teamwork and personal development?

(a) Intra-team (b) Inter-personal
(c) Intra-personal (d) None of these

120 Who has (have) provided five OD steps (processes) comprising diagnosis, strategy planning, education, consulting and training and evaluation?

(a) Beckhard (b) Blake and Mouton
(c) Lippitt (d) None of these

121 Who has (have) defined QWL as a process by which an organisation responds to employee needs for developing mechanisms to allow them to share fully in making the decisions that design their lives at work?

(a) Hackman and Suttle (b) Walton
(c) Lehrer (d) None of these

122 The groups to which an individual aspires to belong, *i.e.* the one with which he or she identifies is called

(a) coalitions (b) committees
(c) reference groups (d) task groups

123 Individual employees can be converted into team players through

(a) appropriate feedback
(b) training
(c) monitoring
(d) demonstration

124 Which of the following has advocated that as there is no single way of organise, the organisational design must be matched with the prevailing environmental situations?

(a) Behavioural theory (b) Systems theory
(c) Contingency theory (d) None of these

125 Who has (have) shown that organisational design and management process are the functions of environmental uncertainties?

(a) Bums and Stalker
(b) Lawrence and Lorsch
(c) Galbraith
(d) None of the above

126 Who has (have) concluded that his (their) OD experiences at International Services were rewarding?

(a) Chattopadhyay and Pareek
(b) Appley
(c) Pillai
(d) None of the above

127 In Vroom's expectancy theory, which of the following statements is/are true?

(a) Valency can be positive or negative
(b) Expectancy can be zero or one
(c) Valency can have value zero
(d) All of the above

128 Which of these is/are the consequences of inequity as per Adam's Equity theory?

(a) The person can alter inputs. *i.e.* people who feel they are underpaid for their efforts may tend to reduce their efforts, and people who feel they are overpaid might want to increase their effort
(b) The person can cognitively distort input or outcomes
(c) The person might quit the job
(d) All of the above

129 Which statements is/are true?

(a) Leadership is that aspect of the managerial role which integrates individual efforts and organisational objectives
(b) Management involves coordinating resources in an organisation
(c) Leadership is influenced by situation
(d) All of the above

130 The Greatman theory of leadership led to the rise of

(a) the behavioural theory of leadership
(b) the trait theory
(c) the situational theory
(d) None of the above

131 Group dynamics are
(a) the way group members interact and respond change
(b) the way group members determine their roles
(c) the measured level of group participation
(d) the way group chooses leader

132 What is the normative team model?
(a) An approach that defines a team in terms of a set of shared values
(b) An approach that puts values at heart of teamwork
(c) A model that has norms as the key of teamwork
(d) A model that suggests individual decision-making cannot be permitted in a team

133 What is group think?
(a) An approach to group decision-making that explains how decisions are made in a team
(b) An idea that shows why dictator are inevitably overthrown
(c) A model that suggests team change with time
(d) An attempt to explain why groups occasionally reach erroneous conclusions even when the prevailing data would give alternative end

134 What is the phase based, model of team building?
(a) An idea that values, norms, and behaviour of individuals in team settings changes over time
(b) An approach that shows how an individual's emotions change over time
(c) A model that suggests team change with time
(d) A model that shows a leader how to behave in a team

135 Which of the following statements is/are true?
(a) The difference between punishment and negative reinforcement is that in the former case, a noxious consequence is applied to decrease the frequency or strength of an undesired behaviour, whereas in the latter, a noxious consequence is with held when a desired behaviour is exhibited
(b) Punishment can have undesirable side effects if administered too frequently
(c) Negative reinforcement increases the frequency and strength of a desired behaviour by making it contingent upon the avoidance of undesirable consequences for the employee
(d) All of the above

136 Which of the following statements are true/false?
(i) Clayton Alderfer has proposed an alternative hierarchy of needs called ERG theory of motivation.
(ii) Maslow's model comprises of growth needs.
(iii) The dual structure approach to motivation is also called Herzberg's two factor model.

Codes
(a) (i) is true, (ii) and (iii) are false
(b) (i) and (ii) are true, (iii) is false
(c) (i) and (iii) are true, (ii) is false
(d) (ii) and (iii) are true, (i) is false

137 Which of the following statements are correct?
(i) The growth needs in ERG model are similar to self actualisation and self esteem needs of need hierarchy model.
(ii) Absence of hygiene factor leads to dissatisfaction.
(iii) Presence of hygience factors leads to satisfaction.
(iv) Presence of motivators leads to satisfaction.

Codes
(a) (i) and (ii) are true, (iii) and (iv) are false
(b) (i), (ii), (iv) are true, and (iii) is false
(c) (ii) and (iii) are true (i) and (iv) are false
(d) (i) and (iv) are true, (ii) and (iii) are false

138 On which of the following statements are true/false?
(i) Goal setting theory focuses on establishing SMART goals.
(ii) Reinforcement theory is proposed bef BF Skinner.
(iii) According to great man theory, leadership skills can be acquired through formal education and training.

Codes
(a) (i) is true, (ii) and (iii) are false
(b) (i) and (ii) are true, (iii) is false
(c) (ii) is true, (i) and (iii) are false
(d) (iii) is true, (i) and (ii) are false

139 Arrange the elements of Maslow's hierarchy of needs according to their arrangement of importance starting from the bottom of hierarchy.
(i) Need for positive self image and recognition
(ii) Needs related to security, money, workplace
(iii) Psychological needs and basic needs
(iv) Needs of realising one's potential, continued growth
(v) Needs related to love, affection, belongingness, acceptance

(a) (v), (i), (iii), (iv), (ii)
(b) (iii), (v), (iv), (i), (ii)
(c) (ii), (v), (iv), (i), (iii)
(d) (iii), (ii), (v), (i), (iv)

140 Arrange the four stages of group formation into the correct sequence of their development.
(i) Members develop a sense of group identity and unity
(ii) People get acquainted with each other to form the acceptable behaviour
(iii) Composite membership and teams strive to achieve the set goals
(iv) People share their thoughts and formulate goals

(a) (iv), (iii), (i), (ii)
(b) (ii), (iv), (i), (iii)
(c) (ii), (i), (iv), (iii)
(d) (i), (ii), (iii), (iv)

Directions (Q. Nos 141-145) *In the questions given below are two statements. In the context of the two statements, which one of the following is correct?*

(a) Both are correct
(b) Both are incorrect
(c) I is correct II is incorrect
(d) I is incorrect and II is correct

141 I. Coordination is the central principle of theory *X*.
II. Theory *X* was developed by Blake.

142 I. Managers must use colloquial and ambigous words.
II. Communication is a two way process.

143 I. Cohesiveness is the extent to which group members are loyal and committed to the group and two each other.
II. Group norms are the set of rules and guidelines of accepted behaviour which have automatically been established by a group and now monitoring the behaviour of its memers.

144 I. All organisational change are introduced through people.
II. It is easy to bring total behavioural change in all the groups and members in the organisation.

145 I. A participative leader focuses on authority and power.
II. An autocratic leader focuses and applies effective managerial leadership techniques to boost the morale of subordinates.

146 **Assertion** (A) Organisational behaviour is concerned with control processes and interactions within an organisation.

Reason (R) It deals with the behaviour or individuals and groups operating in an organisation.

Codes
(a) Both (A) and (R) are correct and (R) is correct explanation of (A)
(b) Both (A) and (R) are correct, but (R) is not the correct explanation of (A)
(c) (A) is correct, but (R) is incorrect
(d) (R) is correct, but (A) is incorrect

147 **Assertion** (A) Some basic set of traits differentiate leaders from non-leaders.

Reason (R) The existence of self-confidence, intelligence, understanding of interpersonal human relations leadership.

Codes
(a) Both (A) and (R) are correct and (R) is correct explanation of (A)
(b) Both (A) and (R) and correct, but (R) is not the correct explanation of A
(c) (A) is correct, but (R) is incorrect
(d) (R) is correct, but (A) is incorrect

Directions (Q. Nos. 148-154) *In the questions given below are two statements labelled as Assertion (A) and Reason (R). In the context of the two statements, which one of the following is correct?*

Codes
(a) (A) and (R) are true and (R) is the correct explanation of (A)
(b) (A) and (R) are true, but (R) is not the correct explanation of A
(c) (A) is false, but (R) is true
(d) (A) is true, but (R) is false

148 **Assertion** (A) Functional aspects shows leaders as a manager.

Reason (R) A leader does all the management functions.

149 **Assertion** (A) The Maslow's hierarchy of needs are not watertight compartments.

Reason (R) Emergence of particular need after satisfaction of a lower order need is a sudden phenomenon.

150 **Assertion** (A) C Bernard identified communication channels with channels of authority.

Reason (R) C Bernard thinks that a communication that cannot be understood can have no authority.

151 **Assertion** (A) The theory and hypothesis of Argyris suggest no relationship between personal development of the individual and the organisational situation.

Reason (R) The principles and the characteristics of a formal organisation, in the opinion of Argyris, are incongruent to the needs of adult human beings.

152 **Assertion** (A) The Laissez-faire style of leadership depends on the leader to provide external motivation.

Reason (R) The leader principally assumes the role of group member and supply material inputs when asked.

153 **Assertion** (A) Herzberg's hygiene factors prevent dissatisfaction.

Reason (R) They are associated with the job context.

154 **Assertion** (A) Equity theory of work motivation is based on social exchange process, in which individuals make contribution (inputs) and accept certain rewards (outcomes).

Reason (R) Individuals decide whether or not a particular exchange is satisfactory by comparing their inputs and outcomes with those of others and thy to rectify inequality.

155 The steps of motivation process as proposed by Keith Davis are as follows
1. Finding out objective
2. Observing the feelings of employees
3. Team spirit
4. Communication
5. Integrate personal interest with organisation's interest
6. Provide auxiliary condition

Which is the correct sequence of motivational process?

Codes
(a) 1, 2, 4, 5, 6, 3 (b) 1, 2, 3, 4, 5, 6
(c) 1, 3, 4, 6, 2, 5 (d) 6, 4, 2, 1, 5, 3

156 Match the following.

List I (OB Theory)	List II (Developer)
A. Comparative theory	1. Bernard
B. Systems theory	2. Backkey and Kricks
C. Decision theory	3. Arnest Del
D. Fusion Process theory	4. Herbert Siamon

Codes

	A	B	C	D		A	B	C	D
(a)	1	2	3	4	(b)	4	1	3	2
(c)	3	1	4	2	(d)	1	4	2	3

157 Match the following.

List I (Motivators)	List II (Factors)
A. Abrahm Maslow	1. Personality
B. Herzberg	2. Working conditions
C. Victor Vroom	3. Work
D. Lawler	4. Motivation in work organisation

Codes

	A	B	C	D		A	B	C	D
(a)	1	4	2	3	(b)	1	3	2	4
(c)	1	2	3	4	(d)	4	2	3	1

158 Match the following.

List I (Theories)	List II (Developers)
A. X-Y Theory	1. McClelland
B. Hygiene Theory	2. F Herzberg
C. ERG Theory	3. Alderfer
D. Three Needs Theory	4. McGregor

Codes

	A	B	C	D		A	B	C	D
(a)	1	2	3	4	(b)	4	3	2	1
(c)	4	2	3	1	(d)	1	4	2	3

159 Match the following.

List I (Types of Motivation)	List II (Elements)
A. Positive motivation	1. Bonus
B. Negative motivation	2. Job-security
C. Financial motivation	3. Termination
D. Non-financial motivation	4. Award

Codes

	A	B	C	D
(a)	1	2	3	4
(b)	1	3	4	2
(c)	4	3	1	2
(d)	2	3	1	4

160 Match the following.

List I (Theories)	List II (Developers)
A. 3-D theory	1. VJ Reddin
B. Life Cycle theory	2. Paul Hersey and Blanchard
C. Continuum approach	3. Tannenbaum and Schmidt
D. Managerial grid	4. Mountain and Blake

Codes

	A	B	C	D		A	B	C	D
(a)	1	2	3	4	(b)	1	3	2	4
(c)	1	4	3	2	(d)	1	3	4	2

161 Match the following.

List I (Maslow's needs)	List II (Examples)
A. Physiological	1. Love
B. Safety	2. Food
C. Social	3. Autonomy
D. Self-esteem	4. Job security

Codes

	A	B	C	D		A	B	C	D
(a)	1	2	3	4	(b)	2	4	1	3
(c)	4	1	2	3	(d)	2	1	3	4

162 Match the following.

List I (Needs)	List II (Factors)
A. Safety	1. Appreciation
B. Self-actualisation	2. Member in a group
C. Self-esteem	3. Provident fund
D. Social	4. Potential control

Codes

	A	B	C	D		A	B	C	D
(a)	3	4	1	2	(b)	2	3	4	1
(c)	1	3	2	4	(d)	3	1	4	2

163 Match the following.

List I (Leadership Styles)	List II (Factors)
A. Emulation	1. Excel
B. Suggestion	2. Plan
C. Persuasion	3. Advise
D. Coercion	4. Compel

Codes

	A	B	C	D
(a)	1	3	2	4
(b)	1	2	3	4
(c)	4	2	3	1
(d)	1	3	4	2

164 Match the items of list II with the items of List I.

	List I (Model of OB)	List II (Employee Orientation)
A.	Collegial	1. Job performance
B.	Autocratic	2. Responsible behaviour
C.	Supportive	3. Obedience
D.	Custodial	4. Security and benefits

Codes

	A	B	C	D		A	B	C	D
(a)	1	4	3	2	(b)	2	3	1	4
(c)	4	1	2	3	(d)	3	2	4	1

165 Match the items of list II with the items of list I.

	List I (Theories of Motivation)	List II (Proposed by)
A.	Two factor theory of motivation	1. J Stacy Adams
B.	Expectancy theory of motivation	2. Victor Vroom
C.	Need theory of motivation	3. Herzberg
D.	Equity theory of motivation	4. McClelland

Codes

	A	B	C	D		A	B	C	D
(a)	4	3	2	1	(b)	1	4	3	2
(c)	3	2	4	1	(d)	2	1	3	4

Directions (Q. Nos. 166-168) *Read the following passage and answer the questions that follows.*

Organisational effectiveness is the concept of how effective an organisation is in achieving the outcomes the organisation intends to produce. The idea of organisational effectiveness is especially important for non-profit organisations as most people who donate money to non-profit organisations ad charities are interested in knowing weather the organisation is effective in accomplishing its goals.

However, scholars of non-profit organisational effectiveness acknowledge that the concept has multiple dimensions and multiple definitions. e.g. while most non-profit leaders define organisational effectiveness as 'outcome accountability,' or the extent to which an organisation achieves specified levels of progress toward its own goals, a minority of non-profit leaders define effectiveness as 'overhead minimisation,' or the minimisation of fund-raising and administrative costs.

According to **Richard Et Al** (2009), organisational effectiveness captures organisational performance plus the myriad internal performance outcomes normally associated with more efficient or effective operations and other external measures that relate to considerations that are broader than those simply associated with economic valuation (either by shareholders, managers or customers), such as corporate social responsibility.

An organisation's effectiveness is also dependent on its communicative competence and ethics. The relationship between these three are simultaneous. Ethics is a foundation found within organisational effectiveness. An organisation must exemplify respect, honesty, integrity and equity to allow communicative competence with the participating members. Alongwith ethics and communicative competence, members in that particular group can finally achieve their intended goals.

Foundations and other sources of grants and other types of funds are interested in organisational effectiveness of those people who seek funds from the foundations. Foundations always have more request for funds or funding proposals and treat funding as an investment using the same care as venture capitalist would in picking a company in which to invest.

Organisational effectiveness is an abstract concept and is difficult for many organisations to directly measure. Instead of measuring organisational effectiveness directly, the organisation selects proxy measures to represent effectiveness. Proxy measures may include such things as number of people served, types and sizes of population segments served, and the demand within those segments for the services the organisation supplies.

166 According to this passage,

(a) the idea of organisational effectiveness is especially important for profit seeking business organisations
(b) the idea of organisational effectiveness is not important for profit seeking business organisations
(c) the idea of organisational effectiveness is especially not important for not-for-profit organisations
(d) None of the above

167 An organisation's effectiveness

(a) does not dependent on its communicative competence and ethics
(b) partially dependent on its communicative competence and ethics
(c) dependent on its communicative competence and ethics
(d) rarely dependent on its communicative competence and ethics

168 An organisation must exemplify

(a) respect, honesty, integrity and equity to allow communicative competence with the participating members
(b) only equity to allow communicative competence with the participating members
(c) strict discipline and not to allow communicative with the participating members
(d) respect, honesty, integrity and equity to allow communicative competence with the participating members

PREVIOUS YEARS' QUESTIONS

2018

1 Consider the following
(i) Supportive leadership behaviour
(ii) Participative leadership behaviour
(iii) Instrumental leadership behaviour
(iv) Achievement oriented leadership behaviour
(a) Path-goal approach of leadership
(b) Situational theory of leadership
(c) Managerial grid approach of leadership
(d) Fielder's contingency model of leadership.

2 Which of the following approaches of leadership focuses on 'personal competence' and 'social competence'?
(a) Situational approach of leadership
(b) Trait theory of leadership
(c) Emotional intelligence approach
(d) Charismatic leadership approach

3 Related to group, when the tendency for individuals to expend less effort when working collectively than when working individually is called
(a) Group think
(b) Group cohesiveness
(c) Social loafing
(d) Group conflict

4 Who suggested that changes in organisations occur in three phases called unfreezing, changing and refreezing?
(a) David Nadler (b) Kurt Lewin
(c) Gary Hamel (d) Noel Tichy

5 A leadership theory which proposed that effective group performance depended on the proper match between a leader's style and degree to which the situation allowed the leader to control and influence is called
(a) Trait theory
(b) Situational theory
(c) Fiedler's contingency model
(d) Path goal theory

6 A conscious change that occurs as a result of logic is called
(a) Subsystem change
(b) Emergent change
(c) Remedial change
(d) Planned change

7 Theory 'Y' of Motivation assumes that
(a) People do not hate work
(b) A person has inherent dislike for work
(c) A person works only when coerced
(d) An average employee cannot be motivated

8 Which of the following characteristics of transactional and transformational leaders are not correctly matched?

Leader		Characteristic
(i) Transaction leader	—	Idealised Influence
(ii) Transformational leader	—	Management by Exception
(iii) Transformational leader	—	Laissez-Faire
(iv) Transactional leader	—	Contingent Reward
(v) Transformational leader	—	Intellectual Stimulation

Codes
(a) (i), (ii) and (iv)
(b) (iii), (iv) and (v)
(c) (i), (ii) and (iii)
(d) (i), (iv) and (v)

9 Which of the following statements is/are true/false regarding modes of Conflict Management Styles?
(i) The avoidance modes of conflict management aim at avoiding or postponing conflicts.
(ii) The compromise mode involves coercion and is likely to fail to reach a solution.
(iii) The main objective of the defusion mode of conflict resolution is to buy time for dealing with a conflict.
(iv) Withdrawal is a form of approach mode that involves getting away from a conflict situation.

Codes
(a) (i) and (ii) are true, (iii) and (iv) are false
(b) (i) and (iv) are true, (ii) and (iii) are false
(c) (i) and (iii) are true, (ii) and (iv) are false
(d) (ii) and (iv) are true, (i) and (iii) are false

10 The Managerial Grid Theory was propounded by Blake and Mouton (1978), having popular application of both Task, and Person Orientation. Each leader can be rated somewhere along each of the axes from 1 to 9 depending on his/her orientation.
Which of the following descriptions given below refers to 'The Leader'?
(a) The leader reflects middle ground position.
(b) The leader is extremely concerned about the task and also the people.
(c) The leader is primarily concerned for people and only incidently concerned with production.
(d) The leader is concerned with neither production nor people.

11 Which of the following statements is/are not true about the "Grid Organisation Development" (Grid OD) Program designed by Robert R Blake and Jane S Mouton?

(i) It is a eight phase program lasting about three to five years.

(ii) Through this program, an organisation can move systematically from the stage of examining managerial behaviour and style to the development and implementation of an "ideal strategic corporate model".

(iii) Behavioural science concepts and rigerous business logic are combined in the Grid OD Program's six phases.

(iv) The single most significant premise on which Grid OD rests in that the 5, 5 way of doing business which is acknowledged universally by managers as the soundest way to manage to achieve excellence.

Codes

(a) (i) and (ii) only
(b) (ii) and (iv) only
(c) (i) and (iv) only
(d) (ii) and (iii) only

12 Match the stages of Process of Organisational Change (List I) with their possible descriptions (List II) given below.

List I	List II
A. Diagnosis	1. The stage for framing a proposal in relation to the problems or issues identified
B. Stabilisation	2. The attempt to search for the main cause underlying the symptoms encountered
C. Motivation	3. The stage where people are involved in detailed consideration of the proposed change
D. Action Proposal	4. The stage of internalising the change and making it a part of the organisation's normal life

Codes

	A	B	C	D		A	B	C	D
(a)	4	3	2	1	(b)	1	4	3	2
(c)	2	4	1	3	(d)	2	4	3	1

13 Which of the following stages of group development will witness the following trend of group member's behaviour. 'Confront the differences, feel angry or frustrated, result formal leadership, lot of competition and hostilities"?

(a) Forming
(b) Storming
(c) Norming
(d) Adjourning

Directions (Q. Nos. 14-18) *Read the passage carefully and answer the question that follow*

Change is 'alien' to an organisation, yet needs to be accepted. Unless a change in internalised and integrated, it remains 'alien'. Introduction of change in an organisation is kin to the transplantation of an organ in a body. An organism and an organisation have some common features. The transplanted part in a body has to be integrated with that body. It may be rejected, and so a watch has to be kept to ensure that it is not, and steps have to be taken to facilitate integration. The same applies to an organisation. It is necessary to ensure that the change gets integrated into the organisation, is stabilised, and becomes a part of the working of the organisation. This is a part of implementation process. Implementation starts after a decision has been taken to plan a programme of change. Several contextual factors have been found significant to the success of implementation.

Fullan and Pomfret have suggested four different dimensions of implementation. These relate to the characteristics of innovation (its explicitness and complexity, or degree and difficulty, of change), strategies and tactics (in-service training, resource-support, feedback mechanism, and participation in decision-making), characteristics of the adopting unit (the adoption process, the organisational climate, environmental support, and demographic factors), and characteristics of macro socio-political units (design issues, incentive system, evaluation and political complexity). Implementation has been treated as an issue of control versus decentralisation and felicitation of change through participation.

Implementation may be seen as a multidimensional process. Paul has proposed the concept of strategic management for the implementation of public programmes as an interaction between four dimensions environment (opportunity, needs, constraints, threat, scope, diversity, and uncertainty), strategy (service-client sequence and demand-supply, resource mobilisation), process (planning and allocation, monitority and control, human resource development, and motivation compliance), and structure (differentiation-integration of tasks, structural forms, degree of decentralisation, and degree of autonomy)

The end result of implementation is the institutionalisation and stabilisation of change. Institutionalisation implies making the change a permanent part of an organisation; internalisation means stabilisation of the change so that it becomes a natural part of an organisation's working style the former is more structural and the later more processural.

In order to achieve the end results, one starts with planning the whole process of implementation. Implementation primarily consists of monitoring the change, taking action in relation to the change, and making the necessary adjustments in programme that has been accepted for implementation. This three-phase implementation process is possible if the necessary support is provided at various stages.

14 Out of the statements given below, which one is not true?

1. Change is always unwarranted.
2. Change has to be internalised and integrated.
3. Organisations and organism have no common features.
4. It is necessary to keep continuous watch on the process.

Codes

(a) Only 1 (b) Both 1 and 3
(c) Only 3 (d) Both 2 and 3

15 Which is not a stage of implementation process?

(a) Integration into organisation
(b) Becoming stable
(c) Becoming part of the working
(d) Maintaining alien status

16 Which among the following is not a pre-requisite before starting the process of implementation?

(a) After taking a decision to plan a programme of change.
(b) After finding several contextual factors significant to the success of implementation.
(c) After finishing inservice training.
(d) After resolving political complexity.

17 Who has proposed the concept of strategic managements for the implementation of public programmes as an interaction between four dimensions?

(a) Paul (b) Fullan (c) Pomfret (d) Cooper

18 The process of implementation has various phases. The number of phases comprising the process of implementation is

(a) four phases (b) three phases
(c) two phases (d) six phases

2017

19 What is 'Neotony' as a leadership trait advanced by Bennis and Thomas?

(a) Calm, confident and predictable under stressful condition
(b) Youthful, curious, playful, fearless, warm and energetic.
(c) Encouraging dissent, empathy and obsessive communication
(d) Ambitious, morally strong and competence

20 Match the following theories of leadership (List I) with their propagator (List II).

	List I		List II
A.	Leader Member Exchange Theory	1.	Robert House
B.	Path Goal Theory	2.	Ken Blanchard
C.	Situational Theory	3.	Fred Fiedler
D.	Contingency Theory	4.	George Green

Codes

	A	B	C	D		A	B	C	D
(a)	4	1	2	3	(b)	4	2	1	3
(c)	2	1	3	4	(d)	3	2	1	4

21 Match the 'Style of leadership' with the 'numbers', as they are denoted by in Managerial Grid.

	List I		List II
A.	Task Management	1.	1,1
B.	Impoverished	2	1,9
C.	Team	3.	5,5
D.	Country Club	4.	9,1
E.	Middle of the Road	5.	9,9

Codes

	A	B	C	D	E
(a)	2	1	4	5	3
(b)	2	1	5	4	3
(c)	4	1	2	5	3
(d)	4	1	5	2	3

22 Which of the following statements is/are true and false?

(i) If motivation is low, monotony (mental fatigue) grips very early.
(ii) If motivation is high, the will and desire to work increases and both fatigue and monotony decreases.
(iii) Highly intelligent people are more susceptible to monotony if subjected to repetitive work, because their level of expectations from job towards meaningfulness is low.
(iv) The anticipation at the end of the work period tends to abolish signs of monotony.

Codes

(a) (i) and (iv) are true, (ii) and (iii) are false
(b) (i) and (iii) are true, (ii) and (iv) are false
(c) (i), (ii) and (iv) are true, and (iii) is false
(d) (ii), (iii) and (iv) are true, and (i) is false

23 Which of the following statements are true/false?

(i) Maslow's need theory considers needs to explain human behaviour.
(ii) McGregor's theory considers opposite perceptions based on managerial assumption of employee behaviour.
(iii) Vroom's theory considers force, valence, expectancy, and instrumentality to explain motivation.
(iv) Cognitive evaluation theory classifies persons as intrinsically and extrinsically motivated.

Codes
(a) (i) and (iv) are true, (iii) and (ii) are false
(b) (i), (ii) and (iv) are true, (iii) is false
(c) (i), (ii), (iii) and (iv) are true
(d) (i) and (iii) are true, (ii) and (iv) are false

24 Which of the following represents the rights inherent in a managerial position to give orders and expect them to be obeyed?
(a) Power (b) Authority
(c) Influence (d) Responsibility

25 Which of the following statements about the Organisational Behaviour (OB) system is/are true and false?
(i) OB believes in open system.
(ii) It has three sub-systems namely formal organisation system, individual system and social system.
(iii) They are no intervening mechanisms to lead organisationl behaviour towards organisational effectiveness.
(iv) OB Mod and reinforcement are outside the purview of OD system.

Codes
(a) (i), (ii), (iii) are true, (iv) is false
(b) (i), (iii), (iv) are true, (ii) is false
(c) (i), (iii) are true, (ii) and (iv) are false
(d) (i) and (ii) are true, (iii) and (iv) are false

Directions (Q. Nos. 26-31) *Read the following passage and answer the questions given at the end by picking up the appropriate answer from the given alternatives.*

In principle, a cohesive group-one whose members generally agree with one another and support one another's judgements-can do a much better job at decision-making than it could if it were non-cohesive. When cohesiveness is low or lacking entirely, compliance out of fear of recrimination is likely to be strongest. To overcome this fear, participants in the group's deliberations need to be confident that they are members in good standing and that the others will continue to value their role in the group, whether or not they agree about a particular issue under discussion. As a member of a group feel more accepted by the others, they acquire greater freedom to say what they really think, becoming less likely to use deceitful arguments or to play it safe by dancing around issues with conventional comments. Typically, then, the more cohesive a group becomes, the less its members will deliberately censor what they say out of fear of being punished socially for antagonising their fellow members. But group cohesiveness can have pitfalls as well. While the members of a highly cohesive group can feel much free to deviate from the majority, their desire for genuine concurrence on every important issue often inclines them not to use this freedom. In a highly cohesive group of decision makers, the danger is not that individuals will conceal objections they harbour regarding a proposal favoured by the majority, but that they think the proposal is a good one without attempting to carry out a critical scrutiny that could reveal grounds for strong objections. Members may then decide that any misgivings they feel are not worth pursuing- that the benefit of any doubt should be given to the group consensus. In this way, they may fall victim to a syndrome known as 'groupthink'. Collective decision making has been defined as 'a deterioration of mental efficiency, reality testing and moral judgement that results from in-group pressures: Based on analyses of major fiascos of international diplomacy and military decision-making, researchers have identified groupthink behaviour as a recurring pattern that involves several factors; over estimation of the groups power and morality, manifested, e.g. in an illusion of invulnerability, which creates excessive optimism; closemindedness to warnings of problems and to alternative view points and unwarranted pressures toward uniformity, including self-censorship with respect to doubts about the group's reasoning and a concomitant shared illusion of unanimity concerning group decisions. Cohesiveness of the decision-making group is an essential antecedent condition of this syndrome but not a sufficient one. So, it is important to work toward identifying the additional factors that determine whether group cohesiveness will deteriorate into group think or allow for effective decision-making.

26 Why the author does think that the cohesive group can do a much better job at decision-making than it could if it were non-cohesive?
(i) The members of a highly cohesive group can feel much free to deviate from the majority.
(ii) Individuals will not conceal objection they harbour regarding a proposal favoured by the majority.
(iii) Participants in the group's deliberations are confident that they are members in good standing and that the others will continue to value their role in the group, whether or not they agree about a particular issue under discussion.

Codes
(a) Only (i)
(b) Only (ii)
(c) Both (i) and (iii)
(d) (i), (ii) and (iii)

27 **Which one of the following most accurately expresses the main point of the passage?**

(a) Despite its value in encouraging frank discussions. high cohesion can lead to a debilitating type of group decision-making called groupthink.
(b) Group members can guard against group thinking if they have a good understanding of the critical role played by cohesion.
(c) Only diplomacy and military affairs would suffer if there is tendency of groupthink.
(d) Low cohesion is better than high cohesion resulting in groupthink.

28 **A group of closely associated colleagues has made a disastrous diplomatic decision after a series of meetings marked by disagreement over conflicting alternatives. It can be inferred from the passage that the author would most likely to say that this scenario.**

(a) Provides evidence of chronic in decision, thus indicating a weak level of cohesion in general.
(b) Indicates that the group's cohesiveness was coupled with some other factor to produce a groupthink fiasco.
(c) Provides no evidence that groupthink played an effective role in group decision-making.
(d) Provides evidence that groupthink can develop even in some groups that do not demonstrate an 'Illusion of Unanimity'.

29 **The passage mentions which one of the following as a component of groupthink?**

(a) Unjustified suspicions among group members regarding an adversary's intentions.
(b) Group members working under unusually high stress, leading to illusions of invulnerability.
(c) Strong belief that the group's decision are right.
(d) The deliberate use of conventional comments.

30 **What the author of the passage ultimately concludes?**

(a) Group cohesiveness is always good.
(b) It is important to work towards identifying the additional factors that determine whether group cohesiveness will deteriorate into groupthink or allow for effective decision-making.
(c) Groupthink is solely responsible for ineffective decision-making.
(d) The causal factors that transform group cohesion into groupthink are unique to each case.

31 **When driven by group cohesion, a decision is taken only to be lamented for later is called**

(a) Abilene effect (b) Placebo effect
(c) Hawthorne effect (d) Halo effect

32 **Which one of the following is not a barrier to communication?**

(a) Feedback
(b) Ambiguity
(c) Lack of trust
(d) Distortions in communication

33 **Below given and four figures (List I). Match them with the communication pattern (List II)**

List I	List II
A. [figure]	(i) Linear vertical
B. [figure]	(ii) Linear Horizontal
C. [figure]	(iii) Wheel
D. [figure]	(iv) All Channel

Codes

	A	B	C	D
(a)	(iii)	(iv)	(ii)	(i)
(b)	(iv)	(iii)	(ii)	(i)
(c)	(iv)	(iii)	(i)	(ii)
(d)	(iii)	(iv)	(i)	(ii)

34 **Match phases of change process (List I) with their propagators (List II).**

List I	List II
A. Unfreezing, changing, freezing	1. Nadler ad Tushman
B. Awakening, mobilising, reinforcing awakening, mobilising, reinforcing	2. Beckhard and Renbern Harris
C. Energisting, envisioning, and enabling	3. Kurt lewin
D. Dissatisfaction with the status quo, clear goal, awareness of practical first steps	4. Neol Tirchy and Devanna

Codes

	A	B	C	D
(a)	3	2	1	4
(b)	3	4	1	2
(c)	3	1	4	2
(d)	3	2	4	1

2016

35 **The conceptual foundation of OB are anchored in the Behavioural Sciences of Psychology, Anthropology, and Political Science. Match the Behavioural Science Source in List I of the OB Topics in List II.**

List I (OB Topics)	List II (Relevant Behavioural Science Source)
A. Interpersonal Styles	1. Political Science
B. Societal Culture	2. Anthropology
C. Power and Politics	3. Psychology

Codes

	A	B	C		A	B	C
(a)	3	2	1	(b)	1	2	3
(c)	2	1	2	(d)	1	3	2

36 Which of the following theories of motivation classifies persons as 'intrinsically motivated' and 'extrinsically motivated'?

(a) Reinforcement Theory
(b) Alderfer's ERG Theory
(c) Adam's Equity Theory
(d) Cognitive Evaluation Theory

37 Which of the following statements about communication is/are either true or false?

(i) Gang plank theory of Henry Fayol is an example of vertical communication.
(ii) Encoded messages are not always decoded effectively because of different fields of organism.
(iii) 'Filtering' is not an intervention which vitiates communication.
(iv) 'Grapevine' communication moves faster than formal communication.

Codes

(a) (i) and (iii) are true, (ii) and (iv) are false
(b) (i) and (iv) are true, (ii) and (iii) are false
(c) (ii) and (iv) are true, (i) and (iii) are false
(d) (i), (ii) and (iii) are true and (iv) is false

38 Blake and Mouton proposed famous managerial Grid with 'task orientation' and 'people orientation' as two independent dimensions. Identify the correct numerical denotions of the managerial styles given below.

A. Team management
B. Impoverished management
C. Country club management
D. Middle of the road management
E. Authority compliance

Codes

	A	B	C	D	E
(a)	9,9	1,1	1,9	5,5	9,1
(b)	9,1	1,1	1,9	9,9	5,5
(c)	1,1	5,5	9,9	1,9	9,1
(d)	9,9	1,1	5,5	1,9	9,1

39 **Assertion** (A) From its inception, the study of organisational change has noted the fact that many participants respond with dogged resistance to altering the status quo. Since the industrial revolution began, workers have at times sought, occasionally in extremely violent fashion, to block the introduction of new technology.

Reason (R) Such behaviour may be either overt or covert. Overt resistance may take the form of employees deliberately failing to do the things necessary for successful change or simply being unenthusiastic about the change. Covert resistance can be more detrimental to change than open resistance because it is harder to identify and eliminate.

Codes

(a) (A) is true, (R) is false
(b) (A) is true, (R) explain (A)
(c) Both (A) and (R) are false
(d) (A) is true, (R) does not explain (A)

2015

40 In a way Alderfer's ERG Theory is an extension of Maslow's Theory. Alderfer suggested three categories of needs rather than five. The needs suggested by Alderfer are

(a) Emotion, Rationality, Growth
(b) Efficacy, Reasoning, Giving
(c) Existence, Relatedness, Growth
(d) Exclusion, Relevance, Giving

41 The leadership theories based on the assumption that 'the leader's ability to lead is contingent upon various situational factors such as the leader's preferred style, the capabilities and behaviours of the followers etc' is known as

(a) Situational Leadership Theory
(b) Behavioural Theories
(c) Contingency Theories
(d) Trait Theories

42 Match the following.

List I (Motives)	List II (Approach Dimensions)
A. Achievement	1. Growth
B. Affiliation	2. Relevance
C. Extension	3. Inclusion
D. Influence	4. Success
E. Control	5. Impacting
F. Dependency	6. Order

Codes

	A	B	C	D	E	F
(a)	1	2	4	5	6	3
(b)	3	2	4	6	5	1
(c)	4	3	2	5	6	1
(d)	1	6	5	2	3	4

43 Which of the following describes 'Command Groups'?

(a) A group established to solve a particular problem
(b) A unit established by the organisation to accomplish specific tasks
(c) Group characterised by intimate, face-to-face association and cooperation
(d) Formal groups that consists of managers and their direct subordinates

44 Match the following.

List I (Leadership Theories)	List II (Proponents)
A. Managerial Grid Theory	1. Hollandder and Julian (1969)
B. Lower Leadership Studies	2. Albert Bandura (1977)
C. Group and Exchange Theories of Leadership	3. Lippitt and White (1939)
D. Social Learning Theories	4. Blake and Mouton (1978)

Codes

	A	B	C	D		A	B	C	D
(a)	2	3	4	1	(b)	1	2	4	3
(c)	3	2	1	4	(d)	4	3	1	2

45 Which of the following statements is not the correct distinction between role and office/ position?

(a) Role is based on mutuality, while office is based on power relations
(b) Office is non-hierarchical, while role is hierarchical in nature
(c) Role is an obligational concept, while office is a relational concept
(d) Role is descriptive, while office is evaluative

46 Herzberg proposed Two-factor Theory. According to him, the distinction between the hygiene factors and motivators is

(a) hygiene factors lead to dissatisfaction while motivators lead to satisfaction
(b) hygiene factors prevent satisfaction while motivators prevent dissatisfaction
(c) hygiene factors prevent dissatisfaction while motivators provide satisfaction
(d) hygiene factors provide satisfaction while motivators enhance satisfaction

47 Horizontal clique, vertical clique and random clique are the examples of

(a) formal group (b) informal group
(c) out-group (d) in-group

48 In Lewin's three step model of successful change in organisation, the stage which refers to "for making any change something has to be done in a planned way to disturb the status quo", is known as

(a) moving (b) unfreezing
(c) refreezing (d) intervening

49 **Assertion** (A) Organisation Development (OD) is a planned effort and therefore requires a great deal of thinking and planning on the part of the OD expert. Knowledge and skills of the applied behavioural sciences are used in OD.

Reason (R) OD cannot succeed unless the people at the top are committed to what is being done. By definition, OD has a begin form the top.

Codes

(a) (A) is correct, (R) is not correct
(b) (R) is correct, (A) is not correct
(c) Both (A) and (R) are correct, (R) explains (A)
(d) Both (A) and (R) are correct, (R) does not explain (A)

50 Alpha, Beta, Gamma A and Gamma B changes are related to which change?

1. Structural change
2. System change
3. Process change
4. Cognitive change

Select the correct answer using the codes given below

(a) Both 1 and 2 (b) Only 2
(c) Only 4 (d) Both 3 and 4

51 OD is based on certain values that are important for the development of organisations as open and proactive systems. OD fosters a set of specific values 'OCTAPACE'. 'OCTAPACE' refers to

1. Openness 2. Communication
3. Trust 4. Authority
5. Experimentation 6. Evaluation
7. Autonomy 8. Productivity
9. Proctivity 10. Collaboration
11. Commitment 12. Confrontation
13. Authenticity

Codes

(a) 1, 2, 3, 4, 9, 13, 11, 6 (b) 1, 12, 3, 13, 9, 4, 11, 6
(c) 1, 12, 3, 13, 9, 7, 10, 5 (d) 1, 2, 3, 4, 8, 7, 11, 6

52 OD Cube (Sehmuck and Miles), Consulcube (Blake and Mouton) and Four Quadrants (French and Bell) are the examples of

(a) phases of organisation development proposed by respective scientists
(b) conditions for the success of OD
(c) OD interventions
(d) operational goals of OD

53 Organisational change is a complex phenomenon. In the process, organisations have to deal with resistance from different stakeholders. Consider the following

(a) Perception of imposition
(b) Role re-definition and re-orientation
(c) Participation in diagnosis
(d) Vested interests

54 Which of the following is/are true about employee empowerment?

1. It involves increasing decision-making discretion of workers.
2. It helps in decision-making by employees who are often at lower levels.
3. It helps senior managers to cope with increased work demands.

Select the correct answer using the codes given below

(a) Only 1 (b) 1 and 2
(c) Only 2 (d) 1, 2 and 3

55 The tendency of some people to work harder or perform better when they know that they are being observed is
(a) hawthorne effect (c) attitude
(b) perceptual bias (d) halo effect

56 An informal group encompassing individuals from different levels within a given area or department, is known as
(a) horizontal clique (b) vertical clique
(c) in-group (d) out-group

57 Which of the following interventions is related to intergroup relations?
(a) Life and career planning (b) Process consultation
(c) Work redesign (d) Behaviour modeling

58 Match the following.

List I (Theories)	List II (Scientists who propounded)
A. Two-Factor Theory	1. Adolf Alderfer
B. Achievement Motivation Theory	2. Murray
C. Manifest Need Theory	3. Frederick Herzberg
D. ERG Theory	4. David McClelland

Codes

	A	B	C	D		A	B	C	D
(a)	4	3	2	1	(b)	1	2	3	4
(c)	3	4	2	1	(d)	1	4	3	2

59 Selectivity in responding to information that is in conformity with one's own feeling, is because of
(a) cognitive dissonance (b) perceptual defence
(c) filtering (d) misperception

60 When one group's performance depends on another group's performance, it may result into inter-group conflict. Such dependence is described as
(a) pooled interdependence
(b) classical interdependence
(c) reciprocal interdependence
(d) sequential interdependence

61 The tendency of people to expend less effort when working collectively than when working individually is called
(a) social loafing (b) socialising
(c) adjourning (d) social action

62 Match the following.

List I	List II
A. 1, 9	1. Impoverished Management
B. 1, 1	2. Team Management
C. 9, 1	3. Country Club Management
D. 9, 9	4. Task Management

Codes

	A	B	C	D		A	B	C	D
(a)	4	3	1	2	(b)	1	3	4	2
(c)	3	1	4	2	(d)	3	1	2	4

63 Which of the following is not the characteristic of a transformational leader?
(a) Inspiring by communicating high expectations
(b) Promoting intelligence and rationality
(c) Treating employees individually
(d) Avoiding making decisions

64 Match the following.

List I (Theory of Leadership)	List II (Propagator)
A. Contingency Theory	1. Martin Evan and Robert House
B. Path-goal Theory	2. Fred Fiedler
C. Situational Leadership Theory	3. Paul Hersey and Ken Blanchard
D. Greatman Theory	4. Gordon Alport

Codes

	A	B	C	D		A	B	C	D
(a)	2	1	3	4	(b)	1	3	4	2
(c)	3	2	1	4	(d)	4	1	3	2

65 Potential effectiveness of a person in both personal and interpersonal situations while in performance in a position is known as
(a) role effectiveness (b) role efficacy
(c) role making (d) role linking

66 The essence of exchange theory regarding formation of a group is
(a) people are attracted to one another on the basis of exchange of similar attitudes towards common objects and goals
(b) people are attracted to one another interacting with one another and cooperating to achieve the goals
(c) people are attracted to one another by having propinquity to each other
(d) people are attracted to one another by interacting through reward-cost outcomes

67 The aspect of management that is concerned with the individuals, their roles, the dyads, the teams and the entire organisation is
(a) Human Resource Management
(b) Human Resource Development
(c) Organisational Behaviour
(d) Organisational Culture

2014

68 Which of the following are the syndromes of organisational maladjustment?
1. Rigore Martis 2. Young Turk
3. Anarchy 4. Smoothing
5. Rat race
Select the correct answer using the codes given below
(a) 1, 2 and 3 (b) 1, 3 and 5
(c) 2, 4 and 5 (d) 1, 4 and 5

69 Which of the following is not a critical are of Six-Box Model of Organisational Diagnosis?
(a) Structure (b) Mechanisms
(c) Relationships (d) Learning

ANSWERS

Exam Based Questions

1 (c)	2 (b)	3 (a)	4 (b)	5 (c)	6 (d)	7 (b)	8 (b)	9 (c)	10 (b)
11 (c)	12 (c)	13 (b)	14 (c)	15 (c)	16 (a)	17 (b)	18 (b)	19 (b)	20 (a)
21 (b)	22 (a)	23 (b)	24 (c)	25 (b)	26 (b)	27 (a)	28 (c)	29 (d)	30 (a)
31 (c)	32 (a)	33 (b)	34 (a)	35 (b)	36 (a)	37 (a)	38 (d)	39 (d)	40 (b)
41 (a)	42 (b)	43 (b)	44 (a)	45 (d)	46 (a)	47 (b)	48 (b)	49 (d)	50 (a)
51 (b)	52 (a)	53 (d)	54 (c)	55 (d)	56 (d)	57 (b)	58 (d)	59 (b)	60 (a)
61 (a)	62 (d)	63 (c)	64 (d)	65 (b)	66 (a)	67 (a)	68 (c)	69 (d)	70 (b)
71 (b)	72 (a)	73 (a)	74 (c)	75 (b)	76 (c)	77 (d)	78 (a)	79 (d)	80 (a)
81 (b)	82 (a)	83 (d)	84 (b)	85 (c)	86 (b)	87 (c)	88 (c)	89 (c)	90 (c)
91 (a)	92 (c)	93 (d)	94 (c)	95 (a)	96 (b)	97 (d)	98 (c)	99 (b)	100 (a)
101 (a)	102 (a)	103 (a)	104 (b)	105 (a)	106 (b)	107 (c)	108 (a)	109 (a)	110 (a)
111 (c)	112 (c)	113 (d)	114 (c)	115 (a)	116 (a)	117 (c)	118 (c)	119 (c)	120 (a)
121 (b)	122 (c)	123 (b)	124 (a)	125 (c)	126 (a)	127 (d)	128 (d)	129 (d)	130 (b)
131 (a)	132 (a)	133 (d)	134 (a)	135 (d)	136 (c)	137 (b)	138 (b)	139 (d)	140 (b)
141 (b)	142 (d)	143 (a)	144 (c)	145 (b)	146 (b)	147 (a)	148 (c)	149 (a)	150 (b)
151 (c)	152 (c)	153 (c)	154 (a)	155 (a)	156 (c)	157 (c)	158 (c)	159 (d)	160 (a)
161 (b)	162 (a)	163 (b)	164 (b)	165 (d)	166 (b)	167 (c)	168 (a)		

Previous Years' Questions

1 (a)	2 (c)	3 (c)	4 (b)	5 (c)	6 (d)	7 (a)	8 (c)	9 (c)	10 (*)
11 (c)	12 (d)	13 (b)	14 (c)	15 (d)	16 (c)	17 (a)	18 (b)	19 (b)	20 (a)
21 (d)	22 (c)	23 (c)	24 (b)	25 (d)	26 (d)	27 (a)	28 (b)	29 (c)	30 (b)
31 (a)	32 (a)	33 (c)	34 (b)	35 (a)	36 (d)	37 (c)	38 (a)	39 (b)	40 (c)
41 (c)	42 (c)	43 (d)	44 (d)	45 (b)	46 (c)	47 (b)	48 (b)	49 (d)	50 (c)
51 (c)	52 (c)	53 (d)	54 (d)	55 (a)	56 (b)	57 (b)	58 (c)	59 (a)	60 (d)
61 (a)	62 (c)	63 (d)	64 (d)	65 (d)	66 (d)	67 (c)	68 (b)	69 (d)	

Note: (*) All are correct.

Human Behaviour

Human behaviour refers to the full range of physical and emotional behaviours that humans engage in biologically, socially, intellectually and are influenced by culture, attitudes, emotions, values etc. This chapter highlights the attitude, personality, perception and learning of an individual.

Concept of Human Behaviour

Human behaviour is a dynamic term that includes anything humans do *i.e.* physical acts, anything they say *i.e.* verbal, facial expressions, gestures and all kinds of bodily movements. Human behaviour is observable and can be seen in the way of talking of a person and in the mannerisms. It is a reflection of an individual in the form of thoughts and feelings that keep on adding into a persons's behaviour.

Some of the behaviours are common, usual and acceptable. In the general sense, human behaviour refers to the range of different type of behaviours shown by human beings. It includes the way human acts.

According to **Crowder**, "Behaviour is any activity which can be observed, recorded and measured, this includes first what living beings or organisms do-that is their movement in space."

Characteristics of Human Behaviour

Behaviour is Influenced by Many Factors

There are a number of factors that influence human behaviour. Heredity and environment are the major factors. The traits that people are born with are heredity and the traits that people acquire are through environment. Apart from this, there are several factors that influence the human behaviour.

Psychological factors like ideas, attitudes, perception influence human behaviour. Physical surroundings like house, neighbourhood school, friends, society make up the human behaviour.

In this Chapter

- *Concept of Human Behaviour*
- *Personality*
- *Perception*
- *Learning*
- *Attitude*
- *Power and Authority*
- *Stress*
- *Interpersonal Behaviour*

Behaviour varies in Complexity

Behaviour ranges in the degree of complexity i.e simple and complex behaviour. Simple and complex behaviour both are influenced by a number of factors. The factors interact in multiple ways to form complex behaviours. Taking complex decisions such as a judge deciding about the judgement is a complex decision.

Likewise complex behaviour includes accomodation of a number of emotions. Sometimes the behaviour may change from simple to complex and vice versa within a given situation.

Individual Differences

People differ in their physiological and psychological conditions, their abilities, conditions of genetic formation, their background and the environment where they grow up are different. Therefore, every person has different set of behaviours.

Individual Similarities

Behaviour differ from person-to-person. Inspite of this fact, human behaviours have lot of similarity also. Some behaviours are found universally like a mother caring for her child is similar in all the cultures, races and countries.

However, similar behaviours might show some degree of differences. *e.g.* people drinking fruit juice from the juice stalls may drink from the glass given to them or ask for disposable glasses.

Behaviour is Goal Directed

Human behaviours are directed towards achieving a goal. The simple and complex behaviours, both are directed towards a goal. Therefore, it can also be said that behaviour is always purposeful. If the goal is the result, then the behaviour is the purpose to reach the result. Finding a quiet place is the purpose and the goal is to find quiet place to study. Thus, all the behaviours are goal directed.

Behaviour is Changeable to a Large Extent

Human behaviours are changeable. Hence, they can be learnt, acquired and modified. Behaviour modification means changing the behaviour according to the need of the situation. This helps people in adjusting to new surroundings, new job, new house etc.

Behavioural change also takes place in old age, it is not confined to age. Elderly people learn to adapt to the problems of old age.

Behaviour is also Stable to a Certain Extent

All human behaviours do not undergo change, some behaviours sticks to a person. There are certain behaviours that are stable and do not show any change due to ageing, change in surroundings etc.

Some people still prefer to keep their first watch, first mobile, or stick to old ways of life. This happens when people are attached psychologically and also out of habit. Thus, just like change, stability is also a part of human behaviour.

Behaviour is Integrated

Behaviour is the result of integration of different influencing factors alongwith the goals and purposes. All the factors be it psychological, physiological, personal or social provide different learning experiences. These learning experiences help in fixing of goals.

Factors Affecting Human Behaviour

There are several factors that influence the individual behaviour of the people in many ways. These factors can be inherited or can be acquired from the environment.

The factors are discussed as follows

Ability

It refers to the individual trait that a person acquires either by birth or through environment. These traits differ from person to person. *The abilities are of three types*

- **Physical Ability** Body structure, body composition that determines the motor skills, physical strength and stamina etc. to study.
- **Intellectual Ability** A person's verbal, analytical ability, intelligence, memory, reasoning that determines the quality of work a person does.
- **Self Awareness Ability** A person's perception about his own self that determines how long a person will take to finish a task.

Race and Culture

Race is the grouping of humans on similar physical and social qualities. *e.g.* Indian, American. Race affects human behaviour drastically. Culture relates to sharing of common values, ideas, customs and traditions. Race and culture both influence the human behaviour and also makes a difference at the work place.

Perception

Perception is understood as the process of interpreting what we hear, see, feel and then think about it to give our judgement on that particular thing. It transform sensory stimuli into meaningful information. Perception is related to the sensory organs.

The senses of sound, speech, touch, taste helps us to perceive about identifying vibrations, interpreting sounds of language heard, identifying objects and detect flavours by tasting. The perception therefore influences human behaviour in a significant manner.

Attribution

It is regarded as the action of assigning a work to a person or the action of regarding something as being caused by a person or a thing. There are three criterias of attribution. The first is consensus which means similar reaction of people in similar situation.

Distinctiveness is the second criteria that means the extent to which a person's behaviour can be associated to situations. The third criteria is consistency that means how often that type of behaviour occurs.

If the behaviour keeps on changing even in similar situations, then consistency criteria is not fulfilled. Human behaviour is thus related to all the three criterias of attribution.

Attitude

It is the person's response to the entire set up over a time span. Attitude when related to organisational set up tells the way a person reacts or what cognitive processes goes in the person that is reflected through his style of work, way of talking, mannerism, respect to authority, peer response and overall socialising within the environment. A person may develop an attitude of indifference or an attitude of friendliness.

Genetics

Certain behavioural traits are passed on from one generation to other. Intelligence, shyness, politeness, cunning etc are inherited through genetics. Thus, how people behave also depends to a large extent on the genetics. Genetics heredity comprises inherited tendencies that grovern interaction of the individual with the environment.

Social Norms

Social norms are like unwritten rules. They are like guidelines that the majority of the people living in a society believe in the social norms prevailing in a society, thus play a major role in shaping up of one's behaviour. In the workplace, people follow a social norm. The social norms thus become the governing behaviours of the humans.

Attention

Attention is a behavioural process of concentration an any aspect of an information. A person may have the will to focus on a particular task which determines the behaviour of that person. The way in which humans learn to process information influences the demand of attention to different type of situations.

Memory

It means retaining information as well as producing it quickly. The memory span differs from person to person. It is subjected to individual behaviour and how much a person can remember chunks of information.

Personality

Personality tells about a person's beliefs, values, habits and nature. It is the essence of a person. It is what a person actually is. Therefore, personality can be identified with a person's behaviour, emotions and thinking patterns. It is who you are, have been and will become.

'Personality' is a pattern of relatively permanent traits and unique characteristics that give both consistency and individuality to a person's behaviour. Personality is the reasonably stable patterns of emotions, motives and behaviour that distinguish one person from another.

According to **Ramond B Cattell**, "That which permits a prediction of what a person will do in a given situation."

According to **David McClelland**, "The most adequate conceptualisation of a person's behaviour in all its detail."

According to **JP Guilford**, "A person's unique pattern of traits."

According to **Gordon W Allport**, "The dynamic organisation within the individual of those psychological system that determine his characteristic behaviour and thought."

Nature of Personality

- Personality is not just an accumulation of bits and pieces, it has organisation.
- Personality is active, it has process of some sort.
- Personality is a psychological concept, but it's tied to the physical body.
- Personality is a causal force, it helps to determine how the person relates to the world.

Features of Personality

Uniqueness of the Individual

The most essential feature of personality is that it is a unique concept in each individual. Every person has a unique personality. No two people will have same personality but there may be similar or matching traits. Uniqueness is due to interplay of various forces that goes into the making of an individual.

Consistency of Behaviour

Personality psychologist generally assume some degree of continuity in individual's personality. Features common to personality is a concern for the consistency of behaviour across the time and situation.

Dynamic

Personality is dynamic and has many dimensions. It is not static or rigid and undergoes constant change. Though the personality traits are stable, yet the traits experience certain changes in their nature.

Structure

Personality has a definite structure. The structure is made up of outer and inner qualities. These qualities are derived by the heredity and environmental factors that make the structure of a personality.

Integration

Personality is the integration of various attributes in a person. It is the sum of physical, mental and social qualities. It is a blend of simplex and complex emotions, sentiments and mental trends. Therefore, only one factor do not influences it, rather it is an integration of many factors.

Cultural and Social Influences

The culture and society in which a child grows up greatly shapes a personality. Children develop moral values, adherence to social norms and respect of cultural traditions by seeing others. This in turn affects the way a person thinks and feels thereby shaping up the personality.

Determinants of Personality

Personality does not evolved by a single factor. Some of those factors are psychological, some are physical, some are biological and some are even hereditary.

The basic factors that hold great importance about personality is as follows

Brain

It is one of the most important factors of personality determinant. Electrical Stimulation of the Brain (ESB) and Split Brain Psychology (SBP) and the outcomes of genetic transmissions and are the tools that are used by the management of any organisation to mould and amend the employee's behaviour to a more positive and proper one.

Physical Factors

One of the most important factors in determining personality is the 'Physical Characteristics' of an individual. Physical features may involve the height of a person (short or tall), his colour (white or black), his health status (fat or skinny) and his beauty (handsome or ugly).

Social Factors

They also play a vital role in determining one's personality. The things that revolve and evolve around us on a regular basis determine our personality. Relationships, coordination, cooperation interaction, environment in the family organisation works places communities, societies all contribute in way or another as personality determinants.

Cultural and Religious Factors

The culture, which one lives in, that may involve traditional practices, norms, customs procedures, rules and regulations, precedents and values, all are important determinants of personality. Moreover, the creed, religion and believes are also very important factors of personality determinants.

Heredity Factors

Everyone has certain characteristics that are present at birth (body build, hair type, eye colour and skin) Heredity characteristics also include certain aptitudes. Heredity provides you with certain biological needs, but culture determines how you meet those needs.

Theories of Personality

The theories of personality have been grouped under four categories. *They are as follows*

1. Psychoanalytic Theory

This theory is based on the notion that an individual is motivated to a great extent by the unseen forces that are controlled by the conscious and rational thought. Psychologist **Sigmund Freud** is associated with this theory. According to Freud, human behaviour is the result of interaction of **Id**, **Ego** and **Super Ego**.

Id : If it feels Good, then do it

The Id is the core of personality because it is believed to be present and fully functional at birth. It is located completely in the unconscious region of mind and therefore having no actual contract with the actual world thus, it operates within its own sense of reality.

Because of its location in the unconscious mind, it reflects as those characteristic associated with the unacceptable urges, desires, memories and impulse found in the unconscious region. The expression of this impulses and desires is based on the pleasurable principle or hedonistic principle.

Ego : The Master of Reality

To deal more effectively with a demand created by impulses and unfulfilled desires, the Id than channelised some more psychic energy into forming and developing an ego. Ego helps to meet the needs and wishes of Id by creating a buffer between it and the real world.

Ego locates in three regions of mind thats why, it connects the Id at the unconscious region of mind with the external world with the conscious region or conscious awareness of mind. Ego is the component of personality that is responsible for dealing with reality.

Therefore, ego enables to be aware of the unconscious desire of the Id and the external condition under which it must operate to meet them. Ego meets the desire of Id by operating on 'reality principle'.

Super Ego : The Moral Authority of Personality

The super-ego is the final part of personality which emerges between ages of 3 and 5. It is the moral compass of the personality, upholding a sense of right and wrong. The values are learned from one's parent, i.e. how their parents guide and influence them. The super-ego provides guidelines for making judgements.

Super-ego comprises of two components

- The ego ideal includes the rules and standards for good behaviours. These behaviours include those approved by parental and other authority figures. Obeying these rules lead to feelings of pride, value and accomplishment.
- The conscience includes information about things that are viewed as bad by parents and society. These behaviours are often forbidden and lead to bad consequences, punishments or feelings of guilt and remorse.

Characteristics of Personality Structures

Characteristics	Personality Structures		
	Id	Ego	Super Ego
Level of Location within the mind	Unconscious	Conscious preconscious unconscious	Conscious Preconscious Unconscious
Purpose	The source of psychic energy associated with basic instincts and desires.	To meet the needs of the id within the contest of reality and morality.	To maintain an acceptable standard of moral behaviour when the ego is meeting the id's needs.
Basic Processes	Pleasure principle and primary process actions.	Reality principle and secondary process actions.	Ego ideal and conscience.
Outcome of Excessive Influence on Personality	An overly impulsive individual seeking immediate gratification (*e.g.* a thief or rapist).	An individual overly concerned with reality (*e.g.* lacking the ability to fantasise).	An overly moralistic and righteous person (*e.g.* a fundamentalist preacher or political zealot).

2. Socio-psychological Theory

Erik Erikson and **Karen Horney** has developed this theory majorly. This theory is also known as **neo-freud** as it was formulated after the psychoanalytic theory formulated by Sigmund Freud. This theory asserts that the individuals are interlinked to the society.

The interlinking determines the goals of an individual and how he attains it. The individual strives to meet the needs of the society. Psychologists believe that fundamental to the formation of a personality is, the social relationships one has.

Erikson : Post Freudian Theory

Erikson's Psychosocial Viewpoint Erik Erikson's fundamental reaction to Freud was to extend the stages of personality development throughout the life span, to define the stages as more social in nature and to expand significantly the role of the ego as a component of personality.

Basic Assumptions of Erikson's Psychosocial Viewpoint

Erikson formulated certain basic assumptions of personality that were quite different from Freud's. *These are as follows*

Basic Assumptions	Example
The Nature and Function of the Ego The ego serves as the unifying core of one's experiences.	Your ego integrates the sights, sounds and emotions that allow you to experience the pleasure of your favourite movie again and again.
The Psychosocial Nature of Ego Development The ego develops by resolving a series of crises that have as their goal the person functioning more effectively in society.	By successfully resolving these psychosocial crises, children learn how to initiate activities with others, adolescents learn the fundamental skills deemed important by society (*e.g.*, reading) and young adults learn about love and intimacy.
A Life-Span Perspective of Ego Development The ego continues to grow and develop throughout life, even in the face of death.	In infancy, the ego develops a sense of basic trust in others, while in late adulthood, it acquires a sense of acceptance and fulfillment that makes facing death less threatening.
Extending, not Departing from Freudian Thought Erikson's viewpoint extended Freudian ideas by making them more social (*vs* sexual) and conscious (*vs* unconscious) in nature.	A mother makes a conscious decision to leave the office early two nights a week to serve as a mentor to a group of college students to help them make career choices, as she remembers her favourite high school teacher doing for her.

Basic Concepts of Erikson's Psychosocial Viewpoint : The Stages of Ego Development

A significant contribution made by Erikson to the study of personality was his investigation into the development of personality throughout the life span.

The following are the three characteristic/features of Erikson's psychosocial developmental stages

- **The Epigenetic Nature of Ego Development** The epigenetic principle assumes that the stages of development occur in a specific sequence and build upon each previous stage. In this manner, the development at one stage is related to development at other stage.
- **Psychosocial Crisis During Ego Development** Erikson assumed that a crisis occurs at each stage of development. For Erikson, these crisis are of a psychosocial nature, because they involve psychological needs of the individual conflicting with the expectations of society.
- **The Acquisition of Basic Virtues** With the successful resolution of each of the psychosocial crisis comes the acquisition of basic virtues. Basic virtues are characteristic strengths that the ego can use to help in resolving subsequent crisis.

The Eight Stages of Psychosocial Development

Erikson's psychosocial stages of ego development represent his most significant contribution to the study of personality, an appreciation of his view point can be best achieved by examining these eight stages.

Erikson's Eight Stages of Psychosocial Development

Stage	Psychosocial Crisis	Basic Virtue	Age
1.	Trust vs Mistrust	Hope	Infancy (0 to $1\frac{1}{2}$)
2.	Autonomy *vs* Shame and doubt	Will	Early childhood ($1\frac{1}{2}$ to 3)
3.	Initiative vs Guilt	Purpose	Play age (3 to 5)
4.	Industry vs Inferiority	Competency	School age (5 to 12)
5.	Ego identity *vs* Role confusion	Fidelity	Adolescence (12 to 18)
6.	Intimacy vs Isolation	Love	Young adult (18 to 40)
7.	Generativity *vs* Stagnation	Care	Adulthood (40 to 65)
8.	Ego integrity vs Despair	Wisdom	Maturity (65+)

➠ **Note** The ages listed are not to be taken as discrete points of development, but are estimates of when each psychosocial crisis is most likely to occur the first time.

Horney Psychoanalyst Social Theory : The Search for Social Security

Karen Horney's theoretical development was in response to what she perceived as major limitations in the traditional Freudian thinking dominant at the time. Her theoretical focus was to place more importance on interpersonal relationships. The interpersonal relationships are developed in the social context.

Basic Assumptions of Horney's Social Psychological View Point

- **Motivational Nature of Personality** Horney emphasised the individuals search for a sense of security in the world as the primary motivational force in persona- lity. Horney said, each person develops a particular personality style for coping with the world.
- **Social Nature of Early Childhood** Horney assumed that the nature of the early social relationship between parents and child was extremely important in determing personality maladjustment in adulthood.
- **Cultural Nature of Personality** Taking a more cultural perspective, Horney proposed that both men and women are motivated by the same desire to seek security. She emphasised specific cultural differences to account for personality development, not unconscious desires.

The Causes and Consequences of Seeking Security

Like Adler, Horney emphasised the influence of social interactions on the nature of personality adjustment. But her emphasis was on the causes and consequence of feeling insecure in the social environment or in other words seeking security. *It includes*

- **Basic Hostility** Horney noted that the two most powerful needs that children demonstrate are for safety and satisfaction.

  Basic hostility is the sense of anger and betrayal the child feels towards parents, who are not helping to create a secure environment. Since no parents can be entirely consistent and satisfying, basic hostility is an inevitable experience for the child.
- **Basic Anxiety** It refers to feelings of insecurity, insignificance, powerlessness, inferiority and hopelessness in a social environment that an individual feels is full of hostility, betrayal and unfaithfulness. Thus, involves an expanded sense of being generalised from the parents to other people in the individual's personal and social environment.
- **Neurotic Trends** These are irrational needs and desires developed by the individual in trying to achieve a sense of security. They are created by intense feelings of basic anxiety.

The logic is that if the specific need is fulfilled, than the individual will feel safe and secure. The trends are described as neurotic because they represent unrealistic or irrational solutions to the problem of achieving psychological security.

Strategy for Achieving Social Security Moving Towards, Against and Away from People

Horney identified three broad interpersonal coping strategies for seeking social security moving towards people, moving against people and moving away from people.

These are as follows

- **Moving towards People** As an interpersonal coping strategy, moving towards people involves believing that if you go along with people and give them what they want, they will give you love and a sense of affection.
- **Moving against People** It involves a style of interaction characterised by aggressiveness, hostility and exploitation.

  This coping strategy is founded on the belief that the world is full of people who are only looking out for themselves and as a result, will attempt to exploit others if given the chance.
- **Moving away from People** It is a coping strategy characterised by with drawing or detaching one self from others. Individual achieves a sense of self-sufficiency, independence and perfection while gaining protection against attack from others.

Horney's Social Psychological Viewpoint

Basic Concept	Definition	Illustration
Basic Hostility	Feelings of hostility toward parents experienced by children, when sensing a home environment lacking security.	The feelings of anger children have when their parents tell them they are getting a divorce.
Basic Anxiety	Feelings of anxiety the individual experiences about being vulnerable in one's environment.	A woman who stays married because she feels she can't make it on her own.
Neurotic Trends	Unrealistic beliefs an individual develops in the desire to achieve security.	Breaking the law in order to achieve status in a street gang.
Strategies for Achieving Social Security	Three interpersonal strategies for achieving social security (1) moving toward people (2) moving against people and (3) moving away from people.	(1) Always agreeing with one's lover for fear of losing this person; (2) constantly lying to cover one's mistakes (3) not falling in love out of fear of rejection.

3. Self Theory

Self theory is also known as humanistic theory or humanistic approach. The humanistic view point is characterised by a belief that people are good, active, creative individuals who live in the present and base their actions on the subjective perception of experience.

This viewpoint stresses the positive, healthy aspects of personality and the uniqueness of the individual. People are seen as active agents in the perception and modification of their own reality and are assumed to be motivated to move towards personal growth and self fulfilment. **Rogers** and **Maslow** best represent the humanistic tradition in the study of personality.

Maslow's Holistic Dynamic Theory

Abraham Maslow formulated his viewpoint of personality in reaction to the pessimistic psychodynamic explanation of the unconsciously controlled individual and to behaviouralism and its emphaise on the role of environmental factors as principal determinants of behaviour.

Maslow felt that individuals are motivated by the desire for self-enhancement and self-actualisation in a manner that goes well beyond satisfying base unconscious needs and simply reacting to external stimuli. He emphasised the creative, spontaneous and optimistic side of human nature over its dark more pessimistic side.

The Nature and Structure of Human Needs

The basic concepts of Maslow's viewpoint include his conceptualisation of the nature and structure of human needs and their motivational impact on the individual. The principal objective of these needs is the motivation of the individual to reach a state of self-actualisation.

For Maslow, the state of self-actualisation involves people's attempts to reach their full potential by using their talents and abilities to the fullest extents, while trying to achieve personal growth, satisfaction and fulfilment.

The Hierarchy of Needs: The Road to Self-Actualisation

Maslow organised human needs into five main groups in a hierarchical fashion. The logic of the hierarchy of needs is that the need at the lower end of the hierarchy exert more power in that they exert a greater sense of urgency to be satisfied that the need at the next level. Progressing up the hierarchy of needs results in the individual coming closer to achieving the state of self-actualisation.

These needs are as follows

- **Physiological Needs** The most basic need directly related to the survival of the individual, they are food, water, sleep, elimination, such needs are extremely potent and, when unfulfiled can dominate the life of individual.
- **Safety Needs** The desire for stability is like creating an enviornment for living that is free from the threat of danger. They include the need for order, predictability and structure.
- **Belongingness and Love Needs** The desire to be with others directly concerned with the basic desire to feel accepted by and have meaningful interpersonal relationship with others. Belonging to various social orgnisation, community service group as well as member of a family give one a sense of acceptance and belongingness.
- **Esteen Needs** The desire to be recognised by other have respect of other and sence of self-respect. Achieving status and recognition within significant group and being perceived as a worthy and able member of them.
- **Self-Actualisation** Developing the individual's full potential involves the individual's desire to develop his or her ability to their fullest potential. Such development involves obtaining a deeper sence of ones own desires and ability and maximising their expression in an attempt to bring them together.

  The expression of the self-actualisation aslo migh involve designing clothes, working on body building or gardening. While, the self-actualisation need is at the highest level of the hierarchy. it is also the least powerful. Indivudal must be extremely motivated from within to achieve the need.

4. Trait Theory

The theory explains the definite predisposition attributes or traits that makes up the personality of an individual. The traits are specific, distinguishable and offers specific characteristics to an individual. The theoretical perspective of Allport, Cattel and Eysenck are important.

Allport's Perspective on Personality

Allport's theory of personality is personalistic in nature. Personalism is the psychology of the person. Allport emphasised on trying to understand and explain the complexity and uniqueness of the total individual. Allport's viewpoint focused on the classification and operation to traits.

Traits the Basic Unit

Allport defined a trait as "a neuropsychic structure having the capacity to render many stimuli functionally equivalent and to initiate and guide equivalent forms of adaptive and expressive behaviour.

Thus, he assumed that traits are real within the individual's and that they constantly guide the individual's thoughts and behaviour across a variety of situations.

Common Traits and Personal Dispositions

Allport made a distinction between common traits and personal dispositions. Common traits refers to those traits possessed in varying degrees by all people. To study common traits, Allport emphasised the nomothetic approach.

The nomothetic approach to the study of personality involves making comparisons of individuals or groups of individuals on certain common traits. Thus, common trait give us information involving comparisons between people rather than information about the personality of specific persons.

Motivational and Stylistic Dispositions

All personal dispositions are dynamic in the sense that they have motivational power nevertheless, some are much more strongly felt than others and Allport called these intensely experienced dispositions motivational dispositions.

He referred to personal dispositions that are less intensely experienced as stylish disposition. They guide action, whereas motivational disposition initiate action.

The Proprium as the Core of Personality

The proprium is the core of personality for Allport. The proprium includes all aspects of the individual's personaltiy that are considerd 'personally' his or her own.

In a general sense, the propium helps the person define a sense of self. It include the vital and essential physical, psychological and social aspects of life.

Developmental Aspects of the Proprium

Aspect of Proprium Development	Specific Knowledge of the Self-Acquired
Infancy (years 1 to 3)	
Bodily self (year 1)	I am separate from the environment. (*e.g.* I won't bite my own toe).
Self-identity (years 2)	I am separate from other individuals. (*e.g.* I am John).
Self-esteem (years 3)	I can manipulate and master my environment. (*e.g.* I can turn on the TV).
Childhood (years 4 to 12)	
Self-extension (years 4 to 6)	I can exist beyond my physical self. *e.g.* This is my bike).

Aspect of Proprium Development	Specific Knowledge of the Self-Acquired
Self-image (years 4 to 6)	I see myself as being like this (*e.g.* I am good at naming my colours and afraid of the dark).
Self as a rational coper (years 6 to 12)	I can solve my problems by using my brain (I can think logically *e.g.* I'll get my kite untangled by shaking the branches of the bush).
Adolescence (years 12 and above)	
Propriate striving (years12 through adolescence)	What will be in the future? (*e.g.* I will take accounting in high school to help get my college degree in business.

Cattells' Perspective on Personality

Cattell defined personality as that, which permits a prediction of what a person will do in a given situation. Cattell's approach based firmly using empirical data-combined through a statistical formula-to predict behaviour. His trait theory relies strictly on the assessment and qualification of traits.

In defining and studying the nature of personality,

Cattell used three primary sources of empirical data

L-data It consists primarily of records of life events, located in such places as public records or archives.

Q-data It includes self-ratings on questionnaires or personality tests.

T-data It involves observation of an individual in a limited situation designed to assess some aspect of personality, example of T-data include measuring the time required to complete a complex set of hand-eye coordination tests.

Basic Concepts of Traits : Cattell's Structural Units of Personality

According to **Cattell**, "A trait may be defined as that, which defines what a person will do when faced with a defined situation". Thus, he used the individual's behaviour to define traits.

Surface traits are related elements of behaviour that when empirically measured and intercorrelated, tend to cluster together. They are also the most visible evidence of a trait. *e.g.* studying long hours, making sure all of the references in a term paper are correct and showing up early to work might be considered visible evidence of the following surface traits *i.e.* perseverance, conscientiousness and punctuality respectively.

Source traits are responsible for the diversity in the personalities of those around us. Differences in perseverance, conscientiousness and punctuality across individual students are explained by differences in the degree to which they possess the underlying source trait of ambitiousness.

Common Traits *vs* Unique Traits

- Common traits are assumed to be a part of everybody's personality. *e.g.* every body possesses self-confidence to some degree.
- Unique traits are assumed to be characteristics specific to each individual. *e.g.* Jan is inversely interested in protecting the rights of animals.

Ability *vs* Temperament *vs* Dynamic Traits

- Ability traits reflect individual's skill or ability to solve problem.
- Temperament traits reflect individual's general style of behaviour.
- Dynamic traits reflect individual's level of motivation.

Personality Assessment From Cattell's Viewpoint : Measurement of Source Traits

Cattell's passion for identifying and classifying source traits also manifests itself in the application of his viewpoint to personality assessment.

The best known of the many personality tests he developed is the Sixteen Personality Factor (16PF) Questionnaire, which is a multi dimensional personality inventory containing 185 questions designed to access sixteen different source traits.

Characteristic strengths of Cattell's viewpoint include his quantitative and rigorous approach to the study of personality. Characteristic limitations are that it is too technical and it over emphasises understanding the global personality, while losing sight of the individual.

Eysenck's Trait Theory

Hans Eysenck's contributions have been in identifying fundamental dimensions of personality and their potential biological bases.

Basic Assumptions of Eysenck's Definition of Personality

Like Cattell, Eysenck relied on factor analysis extensively to help identify the existence of the underlying dimensions of personality. But unlike Cattell, Eysenck did not rely solely on factor analysis to define the outcome of personality structure. He relied on the works of others, including Jung and the ancient Greek physicians Hippocrates and Golden, to help guide his thinking.

Eysenck began with the fundamental idea that personality could be conceptualised as on two major dimension. The following figure illustrates the nature of the two major dimensions of personality and the classification of various traits proposed by Eysenck.

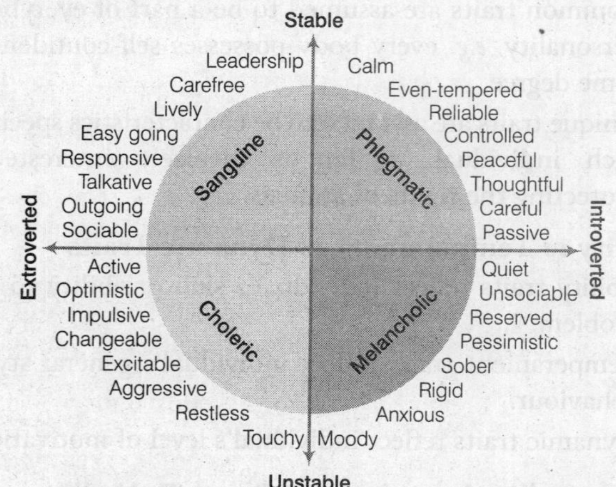

Eysenck's two major dimensions of personality and the classification of various personality traits. *Source* Eysenck and Rachman (1965)

Eysenck's Factor Theory

The personality theory of Hans Eysenck has strong psychometric and biological components. However, Eysenck contended that psychometric sophistication alone is not sufficient to measure the structure of human personality and that personality dimensions arrived at through factor analytic methods are sterile and meaningless unless they have been shown to possess a biological existence.

Criteria for Identifying Factor

Eysenck listed four criteria for identifying a factor. **First**, psychometric evidence for the factor's existence must be established. A corollary to this criterion is that the factor must be reliable and replicable.

A **Second** criterion is that the factor must also possess heritability and must fit an established genetic model. This criterion eliminates learned characteristics, such as the ability to mimic the voices of well-known people or a religious or political belief.

Third, the factor must make sense from a theoretical view. Eysenck employed the deductive method of investigation, beginning with a theory and then gathering data that are logically consistent with that theory.

The **final** criterion for the existence of a factor is that it must possess social relevance; that is, it must be demonstrated that mathematically derived factors have a relationship (not necessarily causal) with such socially relevant variables as drugt addiction, proneness to unintentional injuries, outstanding performance in sports, psychotic behaviour.

Hierarchy of Eysenck's Trait Theory

Eysenck organised traits on the basis of the nature of their expressed influence

- **Specific Responses** Action that exhibit an expressed influence in a particular situation. *e.g.* some yells when angry at work.
- **Habitual Responses** Action that exhibit an expressed influence in a number of situation. *e.g.* yelling at office and home.
- **Traits** A collection of actions that exhibit on expressed influence in a number of situations and forms. *e.g.* someone yells when angry and cries when frustrated.
- **Types** A constellation of traits that expressed an expressed influence in the form of a general style of behaviour. *e.g.* a general style of behaviour characterised by yelling and crying.

The Big Five : Ocean or Five Factor Model of Personality

The big five personality traits that are also known as five factor model or ocean model suggests five broad dimensions to describe the human personality. These five personality traits are extraversion, agreeableness, openness, conscientiousness and neuroticism.

This model of describing personality was developed by **Robert McCrae** and **Paul Costa**. It was based on the 16 item personality trait fromulated by **Raymond Cattell** in 1940.

The five personality trait are together called ocean, taking the first letter of each word in the model. These factors have been used to develop a better understanding of the individual differences in different type of personalities. A person's temperament and behaviour can be understood by the five personality traits.

The five traits are explained as follows

Openness to Experience

This can best be viewed as person's willingness to try new things and open to a new experiences. People high on openness are generally creative, imaginative, curious and liberal and have a perference for variety.

By constrast, those who score low on openness to experience are typically conventional, down-to-earth, conservative and looking in curiosity.

Conscientiousness

This trait reflects the reliability of the individual. A person scoring high points reflects that he is organised, responsible and dependable alongwith being persistent. Low scorers are disorganised and easily distracted.

Extraversion

This term was first used by **Carl Jung**, who believed that all people could be divided into personality type extraverts and introverts.

People who score high on extraversion tend to be affectionate, talkative, joiners and fun-loving. In contrast, low E scorers jovial likely to be reserved, quiet, loners, passive and lacking the ability to express strong emotion.

Agreeableness

It deals with the basic emotional type of a person. The agreeableness scale distinguishes soft-hearted people from ruthless ones. People who score in the direction of agreeableness tend to be trusting, generous, yielding, acceptant and good-natured.

Those who score in the other direction are generally suspicious, stingy, unfriendly, irritable and critical of other people.

Neuroticism

It view the person's emotional instability or stability. People who score high on neuroticism tend to be anxious, temperamental, self-pitying, self-conscious, emotional and vulnerable to stress-related disorders. Those who score low on N are usually calm, even-tempered, self-satisfied and unemotional.

The Big Five

High Scorer Characteristic	Factor (Ocean)	Low Scorer Characteristic
Creative, artistic, curious imaginative, non-conforming	Openness (O)	Conventional down-to-Earth uncreative
Organise, reliable, neat ambitious	Consciousness (C)	Unrealiable lazy, careless negligent spontaneous
Talkative, optimistic, sociable affectionate	Extraversion (E)	Reserred, comfortable being alone stay in the background
Good natured, trusting, helpful	Agreeableness (A)	Rude, uncooperative irritable aggrasive compltitive
Worrying, insecure, anxious, temperamental	Neuroticism (N)	Calm, secure, relaxed, stable

MBTI Model (Myers-Briggs Type Indicator)

It is a personally assessment tool with 100 questions. The respondents are classified as J or P(Judging or Perceiving), T or F(Thinking or Feeling), S or N(Sensing or Intuitive) and E or I(Extraverted or Introverted).

These traits are described as follows

Extraverted (E) *vs* Introverted (I) Extroverts are sociable and outgoing while introverts are shy and quiet.

Intuitive (N) *vs* Sensing (S) Intuitive rely on unconscious things while sensing people are practical and prefer order.

Thinking (T) *vs* Feeling (F) Thinking type personality depends on use of logic and reasons while handling situations. Feeling type personalities rely on their emotions and personal values.

Judging (J) *vs* Perceiving (P) Judging personality keeps their environment to be ordered and structured while perceiving types are not rigid and spontaneous. This leads to one-sided views.

Personality Types

A part from the Big Five Theory of identifying ones personality, there are many different ways of describing and categorising personality as given by psychologists. One such type of categorising personality is by classifying into personality Type A, Type B and Type C. It is given by **Maier Friedman and Ray Rosen**.

These are as follows

Type A

People having this personality trait are hard-driving and competitive. They are always in constant pressure. They strive for recognition and advancement. They undertake multiple activities with a deadline for completion.

These people always function as well-alerted man, competently and efficiently. But they are likely to become hostile, impatient, anxious and disorganised, when put under stressful conditions. They may even fume even at a slow elevator.

Type B

These people are quiet and just opposite to type 'A'. They are easy going non-competitive, placed, unflappable. They wither stress easily. They are comparable to the tortoise in the famous story of Tortoise and the Hare.

Type 'B' may be little dull, but are likely to live longer than type 'A'. Thus, type 'B' may be defined as absence of type 'A' traits. Friedman and Roseman have concluded that Type A people have a higher risk of cardiac heart disease than Type B.

Type C

Recent studies have also identified another type of personality, which is cancer prone personality, such people are cooperative, unassertive and patient. Such type of person suppress negative emotions. They comply with these in authority.

It is believed that blocking of emotions release certain neuropeptides in the brain. This causes disturbance in homeostatic mechanism and weaken the body's capacity to defend itself from cancer cells.

Friedman has also identified a self-healing personality. It can be defined in terms of enthusiasm. Such people are emotionally alert, responsive and energetic, although, they may be calm and conscientious. They are spontaneous and creative and good problem-solvers. They are also good in relationship with others and have a playful sense of hummour.

Perception

Perception is the process by which we recognise what is represented by the information provided by our sense organs. Our perception are influenced not only by the details of particular stimuli we see, but also by their relations to each other and with out expectations.

The study of perception is the attempt to understand those aspects of observation of the world of things and people that depend on the nature of observer.

It is the process where by sensory cues and relevant past experiences are organised to give more structured and meaningful picture under possible circumstances. *Hence,*

Perception = Sensation + Meaning

Perception is a complex mental congnitive process through which we have immediate and meaningful knowledge of the present stimulus in the enviornment.

According to **Forgus** and **Melamed**, "Perceptions are the processes that determine how humans interpret their surroundings".

According to **D. Scott** and **Baydon**, "Perception is a selective process as eye in **capable** of sensing more data then the brain can process."

Process of Perception

Perception involves a set of five process. *They are as follows*

Receptor Process Every sense organ has its receptor. When stimulus strikes the receptor, they get activated and sent impulse to brain for interpretation of sensation.

Selection Process Reception depends upon selection of stimuli which is governed by two factors, external factors like size, intensity, proximity, motion and internal factors like attitude, motive, interests, expectations and experiences.

Organisation Process After selection of the stimuli, it is sorted into meaningful pattern. Organisation invovles grouping of stimuli on grounds of similarity. Proximity or the closeness of stimuli affects perception.

Affective Process These give completeness to perception and form the integral part of the process of perception. Individual difference in perception are mostly guided by affective process.

Our past experiences also influence our Affective Process (AP). AP influence with what intensity we perceive the object and that whether/nor we display our readiness to perceive the same object again.

Interpretation Process It is the final presenation of the collected information after careful analysis in the mind. It refers to the process of understanding the stimuli. This process completes the perception process.

Characteristics of Perception

It has long been recognised by behavioural scientists that the interests, values and beliefs that employees entertain influence these peoples perceptions of the reality of their work places and their behaviour. An individual's perception of his or her capabilities may result in overly ambitious goals and frequent failure or under attainment. *The major characteristics of perception in organisational behaviour are follows*

Selectivity

Perception is selective. No one is capable of receiving all the stimuli with regard to a particular circumstance. As a result, people select those things that are most interesting and relevant to them, personally and factors that are most consistent with their experience.

Closure

Although, perception is selective, human beings fill in gaps and behave as if they have complete knowledge of a situation, person or event. The result is often a failure to recognise the complexity of the entire situation and the inaccurate evaluation of perceptual phenomena through such processes as stereo typing and hole effects.

Context

Perception occurs within a setting or an environment known as a context. This context is made up of physical factors, such as the amount of lighting, noise and so on. It also relates to emotional and social environments.

The perceptual context is important because through past experience, we have a point of reference. This context includes a number of elements within the environment, such as attitudes, emotions and physical properties, when distortions occur, perceptual accuracy is reduced.

Constancy

It refers to the capability of one or more perceptual systems to identify the same thing or situation. *e.g.* the perception of a coin is fixed so permanently that it can be identified even from a distance and only by touch also.

Contrast

It refers to the increase or decrease in relation to the normal intensity, degree or frequency of the other thing. *e.g.* after touching a cup with hot water, people perceive the same degree of hotness with the cup of water that is laying nearby.

Self Concept

It refers to the self constructed belief about oneself. A person with a positive self concept developes positive attributes. That person sees positive traits in other people too and vice versa.

Cognitive Structure

It refers to the individuals pattern of thinking. This affects how a person perceives various things, people and situations. Some people perceive physical traits while others see mental attributes.

Factors affecting Perception

People perceive things differently. Individual differences make up the different perception abilities in people.

The factors affecting perception are

Perceptual Learning It refers to the sensory based learning experiences that takes place in a person which helps to perceive. Education, training and past experiences influence perceptual learning.

Mental Set It refers to the presence or readiness to receive sensory inputs. The preparedness keeps the individual attentive to receive inputs.

Motives and Needs The need and motive of a person influences the perception. *e.g.* a hungry person is drain more towards food while on artistically inclined is drawn more towards appreciating work of art.

Cognitive Styles The style of receiving and the way of processing on information closely affects the perception. Strong will, rational and good attention span affect are some of the congitive indices that influence the perception of people.

Sensation and Perception

The process, through which we came to experience the stimuli present in the environment is known as sensation.

Human senses translate physical energy into electrical signals by specialised receptor cells and transmit to our brain *via* specialised sensory nerves, through which information about our environment is received. Our senses include vision, hearing, smell, taste and skin senses.

The study of sensation is related to the initial contact between organism and the physical environment focussing on different forms of sensory stimulation (*e.g.* electro-magnetic pressure, sound waves) and the input registration by the sense organs (*e.g.* the eyes, ears, nose, tongue and skin).

Perception is the process through, which we interpret and organise the received information, so as to produce our conscious experience of objects and their relationship. In this process physical energy such as light, sound waves, heat, emanating from objects is transformed by the concerned sense organs into a code and transferred to and interperted by the brain.

As conclusion, it can be inferred that sensation typically refers to the direct reception and transmission of messages, where as perception refers to the active process of integrating and organising these sensations.

Differences between Perception and Sensation

Sensation and perceptions, both are cognitive processes and serve useful purposes in knowing the world around us. For perceptual experiences to occur, sensory experience is a must. We cannot perceive any object or event unless we sense them. Hence, the two processes are interrelated to one another. However, the two processes are never alike.

They differ very minutely from each other which are as follows

Perception	Sensation
It is a complex process that provides an organised and will defined knowledge or meaning to the object (stimuli) that produces sensory experience.	It is a simple mental process of sensing the stimuli present in the environment
Perception provides a concrete meaning to the object, it is not mere apprehension.	Sensation is mere apprehension or awareness of the object or about its sensory details.
Perception is presentative as well as representative.	Sensation is only presentative
It follow sensory stimulation.	It is a primary process of cognition
Perception may differ from one individual to the other.	Sensory experience are almost uniform or similar for all individuals.
Perception is a concrete, organised, whole experience, it is reality.	Sensation is thought as a myth by many psychologists

Gestalt Law of Perceptual Organisation

How humans perceive objects was proposed by a group of researchers known as Gestalt psychologists in 1920.

The Beginning of Gestalt Psychologists

In the first decades of the 20th century, most psychologists explained perception in terms of an approach called structuralism, which stated that perceptions are created by combining tiny building blocks called **Sensations**.

However, **Max Wertheimer**, one of the founders of Gestalt psychology, disagreed with this idea. One of his arguments against structuralism is given in the figure.

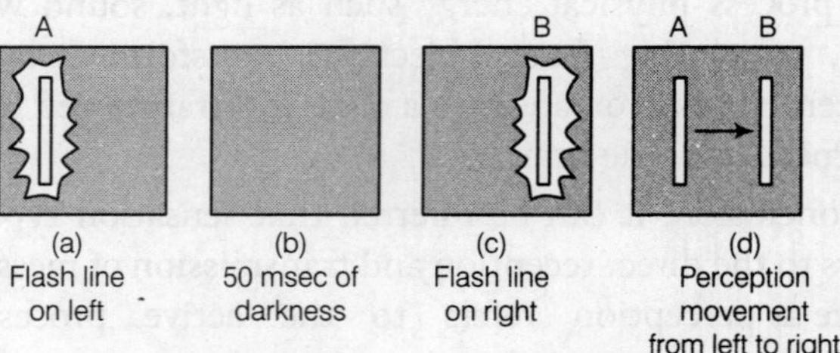

Wertheimer's 1912 Experiment in Movement Perception

When the light of A is flashed on and off and then after a dark interval of 50 msec [50/1000 sec] the light at B is flashed on and off, it appears that the light has moved through the space between A and B. This is called apparent movement-apparent because in reality there is no movement-just one light flashing on and off followed by another light flashing on and off.

Wertheimer questioned that, its possible to explain the movement that appears to occur through the dark space separating the two lights in terms of sensations?

Wertheimer and the newly formed group of researchers, who called themselves Gestalt psychologists, rejected the structuralists idea of perceptions being built from tiny sensations and in its place proposed the idea that the whole is different from the sum of its parts.

This is explained by showing two pictures

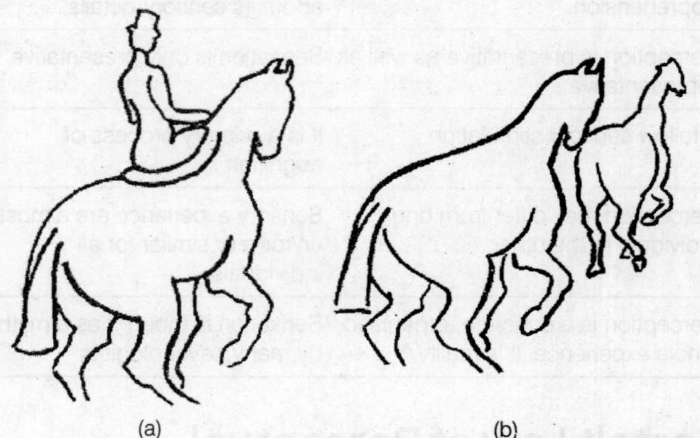

(a) A rearing horse, (b) One horse following another

We interpret the horse in the figure (a) as rearing back, but we interpret the identical horse in figure (b) as moving forward. The presence of the rider in one case and of the lead horse in the other changes our interpretation of the horse's movement.

This shows that our perception of one part of a stimulus depends on the presence of other parts of the stimulus.

The Laws of Perceptual Organisation

The laws of perceptual organisation is a series of rules that specify how we organise small parts into wholes. The Gestalt laws are simplicity, connectedness, good continuation, proximity to nearness, common fate, familarity and figure and ground.

These are as follows

Simplicity

It is formulated by **Pragnanz** and states that every stimulus pattern is seen in such a way that the resulting structure is as simple as possible. The familiar olympic symbol in this figure (a) is an example of the law of simplicity at work. We see this display as five circles and not as other, more complicated, shapes such as the ones in figure (b).

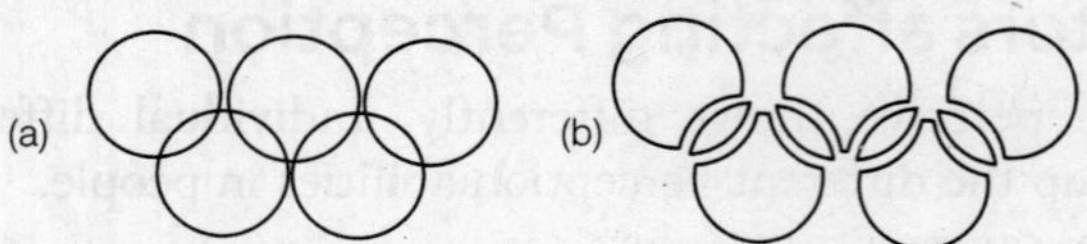

(a) This is usually perceived as five circles, and not as the nine shapes in (b)

Connectedness

In given figure, we perceive a series of dumbells rather than pairs of dots, even though the dots separated by the spaces are close together than the ones connected by the lines. This is the law of connectedness: Things that are physically connected are perceived as a unit.

Good Continuation

We see the electric cord starting at 'a' in this figure as flowing smoothly to 'b'. It does not go to 'c' or 'd', because that path would involve making sharp turns and would violate the laws of good continuation, which states; points that when connected, result in straight or smoothly curving lines are seen as belonging together and the lines tends to be seen in such a way as to follow the smoothest path.

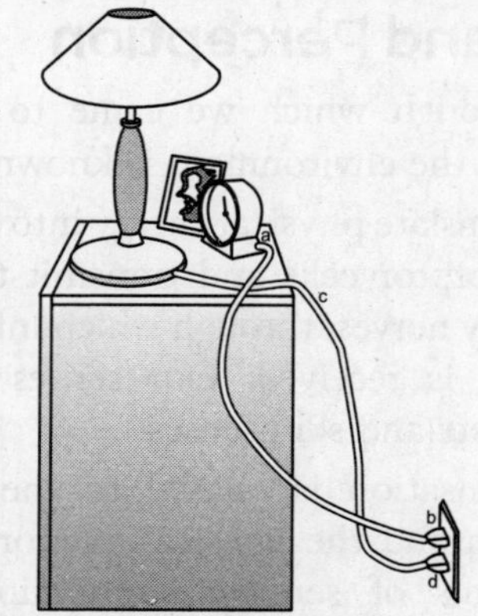

Good Continuation, Both electric cords follow a smooth plant to the electrical outlet

Proximity or Nearness

Our perception of figure (a) as horizontal rows of circles illustrates the law of proximity or nearness. Things that are near to each other appear to be grouped together. And although every other circle is changed to a square in figure (b), we still perceive horizontal rows in this case the law of proximity overpowers the law of similarity.

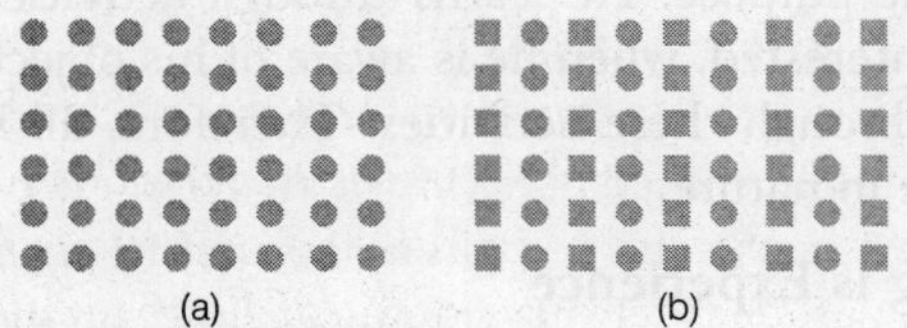

(a) (b)

Two examples of the law of nearness
(a) Perceived as horizontal rows of circles.
(b) Still perceived as horizontal rows, even though half of the circles have been changed to squares.

Common Fate

The law of common fate states that things that are moving in the same direction appear to be grouped together. Although, dance choreographers may not be familiar with the Gestalt laws, they are well aware that one way to create perceptual grouping is to choreograph groups of dancers moving together.

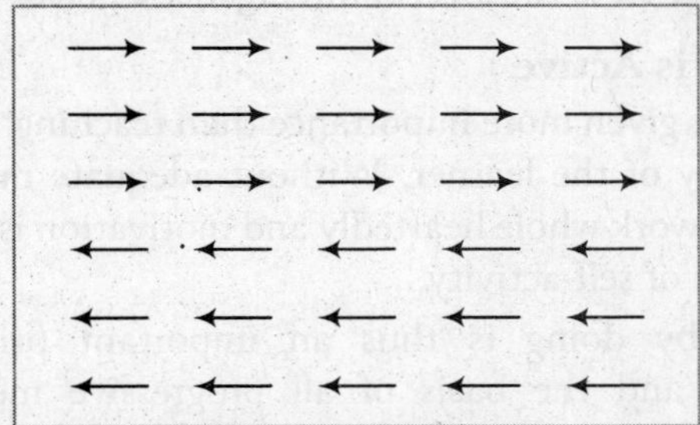

The Law of Common Fate

Meaningfulness or Familiarity

The law of familiarity states that things are more likely to form groups if the groups appear familiar or meaningful. Therefore, people in similar position or doing similar kind of job in an organisation are grouped together.

Figure and Ground

One way the Gestalt psychologists studied the properties of figure and ground was by considering patterns like in this figure, which was introduced by **Danish psychologist Edgar Rubin** in 1915.

This is called a reversible figure ground patterns, because it can be perceived either as two black faces looking at each other, in front of a white back ground or as a white case on a black background.

Some of the properties of the figure and ground are that

(a) the figure is more 'thinkable' and more memorable than ground,
(b) the figure is seen as being in front of the ground,
(c) the ground is seen as unformed material and seems to extend behind the figure and
(d) the contour separating the figure from the ground appears to belong to the figure.

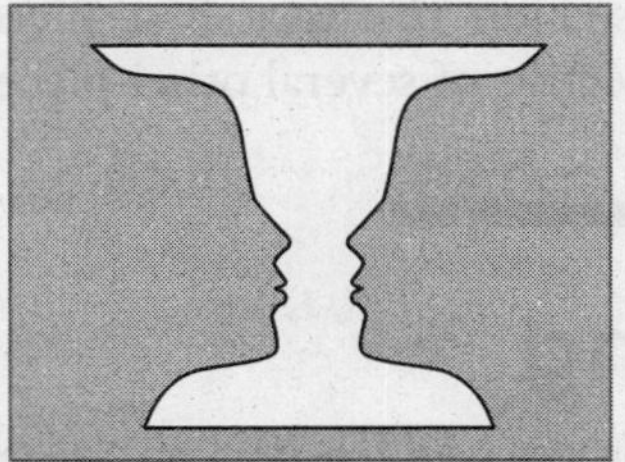

A version of Rubin's reversible face-vase figure

Perceptual Errors

Perceptual errors refers to a situation when reality is not seen. Illusion is a form of perceptual error. It is the inability to judge humans, situations or things accurately or as they really are perceptual errors may also take place in organisations and create differences with groups, departments and management. *Perceptual errors are as follows*

Stereo Typing It refers to drawing a general impression of an individual on the basis of pre-conceived notions *e.g.* girls are not good in mathematics. They are beliefs and assumptions.

Halo Effect It refers to carrying an impression (positive) created in one area over all other areas. A person good in one area or sphere of work is perceived as good in other dimensions.

Recency Effect It refers to forming an idea based upon the most recent information about a person or a situation and ignorning all the previous sources of information.

Horn Effect It is the opposite of halo effect. It refers to carrying a negative impression created in one area, over all other areas.

Similar to Me Effect It refers to favouring a person who is similar to us such as people favour the person who belong to their state, speak their mother tongue.

Self-Serving Bias It refers to the tendency of people to take the credit of success/praise to themselves and put the blame of failures/criticisms to others, which are termed as external factors.

Self-Fulfilling Prophecy It refers to a prediction or a belief or an expectation that directly or indirectly causes itself become true. It is also called pygmalion effect. *e.g.* A child labelled as stupid by a teacher starts behaving like one.

Fundamental Attribution Error It refers to the tendency to underestimate the influence of external factors and overestimate the influence of external factors while making judgements about the behaviour of others.

External factors are political, social, economic and technological effects on an organisation. Internal factors are organisational structure, leadership, communication.

Primary Effect It refers to the tendency of making judgement based on the very first piece of information recieved irrespective of several other pieces of information.

Learning

Learning is a process, which permits the organism to adopt to the changing conditions of the environment. This process determines, to a large extent, much of the observable behaviour of mammals and other complex vertebrates. It can also be acquired through experiences. People learn by experiencing which is known as experiential learning.

The goal of psychologists interested in learning has been to provide a set of general principles to account for the resulting change in behaviour."

According to **Kimble**, "Learning is a more or less permanent change in behaviour potentiality, which occurs as a result of repeated practice."

According to **Robert Gagne**, "Learning is a change in human disposition or capability that persists over a period of time and is not simply ascribable to processes of growth."

According to **Peter C. Brown**, "Acquiring knowledge and skills and having them readily available from memory, so you can make sense of future problems and opportunities is termed as learning."

Characteristics of Learning

Yoakman and Simpson have described the following nine important characteristics of learning

Learning is Growth

The individual grows as he lives. This growth implies both physical as well as mental development of the learner. The individual gains experiences through various activities. These are all sources of learning. The individual grows through living and learning.

Learning is Adjustment

Learning enables the individual to adjust himself properly with the new situations. The individual faces new problems and new situations throughout his life and learning helps him to solve the problems encountered by him. That is why, many psychologists describe learning as "a process of progressive adjustment to the ever changing conditions, which one encounters."

It is through learning that one could achieve the ability to adjust adequately to all situations of life.

Learning is Purposeful

All kinds of learning is goal-oriented. The individual acts with some purpose. He learns through activities. He gets himself interested, when he is aware of his objectives to be realised through these activities. Therefore, all learning is purposive in nature.

Learning is Experience

The individual learns through experiences. All the experiences provide new knowledge, understanding, skills and attitudes. Learning is not mere acquisition of the knowledge, skills and attitudes. It is also the reorganisation of experiences or the synthesis of the old experiences with the new.

Learning is Intelligence

Mere cramming without proper understanding does not make learning. Thus, meaningless efforts do not produce permanent results. Any work done mechanically cannot yield satisfactory learning outcomes. Learning therefore is directly related to the level of intelligence a person possess.

Learning is Active

Learning is given more importance than teaching. It implies self-activity of the learner. Without adequate motivation, he cannot work whole heartedly and motivation is therefore at the root of self-activity.

Learning by doing is thus an important principle of education and the basis of all progressive methods of education like the project, the dalton, the montessori and basic system.

Learning is both Individual and Social

Although learning is an individual activity and social, individual mind is consciously or unconsciously affected by the group activities. Individual is influenced by his peers, friends, relatives, parents and classmates and learns their ideas, feelings and attitudes in some way or others.

The social agencies like family, church, markets and clubs exert immense, influence on the individual minds. As such, learning becomes both individual as well as social.

Learning is the Product of the Environment

The individual lives in interaction of the society. Particularly, environment plays an important part in the growth and development of the individual. The physical, social, intellectual and emotional development of the child is molded and remolded by the objects and individuals in his environment.

Therefore, emphasised that child's environment should be made free from unhealthy and vicious matters to make it more effective for learning.

Learning is the Modification of Behaviour

Learning affects the learner's behaviour and conduct. Every learning experience brings about changes in the mental structure of the learner. Therefore, attempts are made to provide such learning experiences, which can mould the desired conduct and habits in the learners.

Factors affecting Learning

There are a number of factors that affect learning.

These are as follows

Intellectual Ability This refers to the mental levels of the individual. The native capacity of the individual determines the level of learning to a large extent. This is the reason why some people can do maths well while others are good at languages. Some people understand abstract concepts easily.

Physical Ability This refers to the health, physical development, growth, period of maturation and the capacity to learn. All these factors affect the learning potential of a person.

Environmental Factors It refers to the home, school, surroundings, neighbourhood where a child grows up. An overall amaible and affectionate atmosphere at home and friendly learning environment in school or office facilitates greater learning.

Social Factors Social factors such as cooperation, coordination, respect are constructive factors of learning. Society plays a major role in learning. If it gives equal opportunities to everyone for growth and development and treats every person equally, then these factors stimulate learning.

Mental Factors It refers to the factors that affect the mind. Attitude is an important mental set up, positive attitude to learning gives better results than negative aspects. Motivation also acts as an encouragement to facilitate learning.

Teaching Methods The way to teach a particular topic also affects learning. Conveying the information properly, presenting an information in an interesting way etc facilitate proper learning. Learners should be given the opportunity to learn at their own pace to make learning easy. Undue pressure do not facilitate learning.

Nature of Learning Materials The learning materials are the essential factors that make learning possible. Therefore, the meaningfulness, way of presentation, medium of presentation, shape, position, colour etc of the learning materials results in positive learning. Familiarity with the learning materials also ensures faster learning.

Theories of Learning

There are basically three basic approaches to learning. These are behaviorist, cognitive and social learning theory. The behaviorist theories are formulated by **Pavlov** and **Skinner** and focuses on learning through modification of behaviour.

Cognitive approach is propounded by **EC Tolman** and studies relationship between cognitive cues and expectations. Social learning theory states that learning takes place within social contests through interactions with a community of knowledge. *These are as follows*

1. Behaviourist Approach

This approach studies the behavioural changes that occur due to learning. The changes in behaviour occurs due to continuous exposure to stimuli *i.e.* habituation of a certain aspect that brings conditioned response. Pavlov's theory of learning relates to the behaviourist approach.

Pavlov and the Conditioned Response

Pavlov's work was greatly influenced by reflexes of the brain by Sachenov, who is supposed to be the father of Russian Physiology. The Russian Physiologist, Pavlov, while conducting his studies on digestion, observed what he called **psychic sectretion of saliva**.

This eventually led him to experiments on conditioning. He noticed that a hungry dog would salivate merely at the sight of food or event at the sound of food or event at the sound of foot steps of the person, who habitually brought him food.

Now, salivation in response to food in the mouth was a regular, natural reflex with a specific, well defined stimulus producing a definite, localised response through the mediation of a reflex arc. However, the salivary response to the sight of food is perhaps a learned reaction which Pavlov called 'Conditioned Reflex.'

Pavlov observed that the salivary response is evoked by a new stimulus like the sight of the food, only if, the animal had some previous experience with it. The sight of the food is the conditioned stimulus, whereas food in mouth is the natural or unconditioned stimulus.

Salivation in response to the novel-normal stimulus like the sight of the food is conditioned reflex, because as indicated by Pavlov, its evocation by this new stimulus was literally conditional upon the operation of repeatedly combining the originally neutral stimulus with proper stimulus food responses of the type described above are called conditioned reflexes probably because they are dependant upon certain conditions like paired presentation of the conditioned and unconditioned stimulus etc.

The value of Pavlov's contribution doesn't lie in his theorising about it, but in the precise determination of the various empirical relationship involved.

Fundamental Concepts of Conditioning

The fundamental concepts of conditioning is explained through US, UR, CS and CR. *These are as follows*

- **The Unconditioned Stimulus** (US) In the above given example, food always evoked the salivary response with complete consistency. Food is, therefore an unconditioned stimulus.

  An Unconditioned Stimulus (US) is one, which before the beginning of the experiment, elicits the response in a regular, dependable manner. Its second function is that it supplies reinforcement.

- **The Unconditioned Response** (UR) It is one which is regularly and dependably evoked by the unconditioned stimulus. The US-UR need not be a reflex as physiologically defined. All that is required is that in a given experiment, some specifiable stimulus reliably and unfailingly elicits the response in question.

- **Conditioned Stimulus** (CS) Pavlov's dog learned to salivate in response to the ticking of the metronome, originally the sound of the metronome did not evoke this response, *i.e.* it was neutral in this context. After being repeatedly paired with the US, food, it could now be definitely relied upon to elicit salivation.

  In this instance, the conditioned stimulus is the sound of the metronome.

  A stimulus is called conditional stimulus, if an account of its being paired with the unconditioned stimulus, it comes to elicit the unconditioned response.

  The distinguishing features of conditioned stimulus are

  (a) It must not evoke the same response as the US and

  (b) It must be repeatedly paired with the unconditioned stimulus.

  It is important to note that as a result of conditioning procedure, a stimulus, which did not elicit a response, finally comes to evoke it.

- **Conditioned Response** (CR) A response somewhat like the unconditioned response follows the conditioned stimulus as a consequence of the paired presentation of CS and US. Such a response is called the conditioned response. It may occur either on the test trials where the US, food is omitted entirely or it may come during the CS-US interval antedating US.

  It should be specially noted that the conditioned response only resembles the unconditioned response and is not identical with it as some early investigators mistakenly believed.

  'Saliva is Saliva' one would imagine 'whether it is elicited by the sound of the metronome or food in the mouth.' But no the salivary reaction may actually vary in the two cases in respect of the amount, the latency, with which it is elicited and so on.

Extinction

In various experimental studies, it has been observed that if Unconditioned Stimulus (UCS) is omitted, *i.e.* not presented, the Conditioned Response (CR) gradually diminishes. This is called extinction. It so happens because in conditioning procedure, the reinforcement is automic by pairing of CS with UCS.

The UCS were serves as 'reinforces' for the CS to occur. In the event of removal of UCS (unpaired presentation of CS), the reinforcement is no longer available.

Hence, the acquired CR cease or get extricated. In Pavlov's experiment, after the acquisition of CR (salivation response) associated with bell sound (IS), only CS was repeatedly presented without following the UCS reinforcement. It was found that salivation response to bell sound (CR) gradually weakened.

In 'Bechterve's experiment also, a decrease in the frequency of flexion responses (CR) was noticed. Hence, repeated presence of CS singly (without pairing with UCS) results is extinction of conditioned response. However, cessation of CR is not forgetting or erasing of what has been learnt. Extinction is rather a process of learning to 'inhibit' the acquired CR during conditioning.

It is a kind of new learning, which superimposes the old one without destroying the conditioned response acquired earlier. This fact is substantiated by two related phenomena spontaneous recovery and reconditioning.

Spontaneous Recovery

Pavlov found evidences that in extinction phenomenon, the Conditioned Response (CR) is not completely or entirely erased. Thus, all is not forgotten because the extinguished CR re-appears spontaneously after a brief rest of extinction.

Although, the re-appearance of the extincted response may not be in its original strength, but it does evidence the fact that the animals tend to retain at least some of the learning association formed by original pairing of CS with UCS. Therefore, the extinguished CR after rest of extinction spontaneously recovers, when CS alone is presented.

However, the amount of spontaneous recovery depends on the duration of lapsed time after the extinction session. The longer the duration of lapsed time, the greater is the recovery of acquired CR, such recovery occurs spontaneously.

Thus, it is obvious that experimental extinction does not cause forgetting rather, it only inhibits the response, which is weared off during rest and as such, the CR re-appears spontaneously.

Operant Conditioning

Operant conditioning is a part of the Behaviourist approach and was formulated by **BF Skinner** in 1930s. His work was published in "The Behaviour of Organisms".

Skinner's operant behaviour, a non-theoretical or descriptive approach to learning, view's behaviour as subject to the regulation of its environmental consequences. That consequences is termed reinforcement, which serves to heighten the probability or frequency of occurence of a given mode of behaviour.

If the reinforcing consequence entails the initiation or strengthening of a stimulus, then it is positive reinforcement. But, if the stimulus is aversive or negative so that the reinforcing consequence is one of stimulus termination, it is termed as negative reinforcement. The probability of the occurance of a given mode of behaviour is diminished in the presence of aversive stimuli.

Experiment of BF Skinner

By measuring or recording operant responses, Skinner can analyse animals' on going behaviours during learning. He calls this kind of learning operant conditioning, which focuses on how consequences (rewards or punishments) affect behaviours.

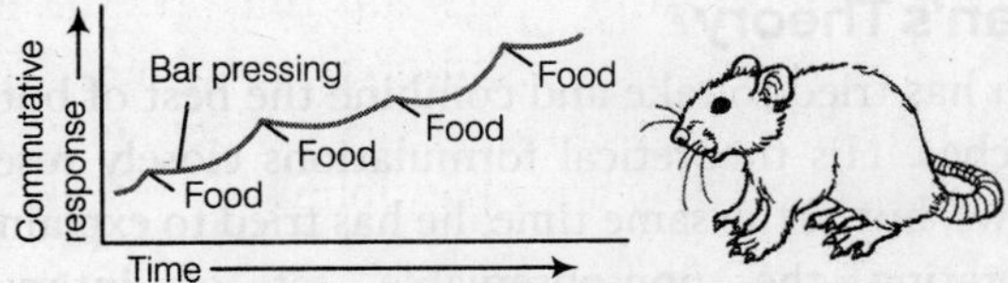

Rat learns to press a bar, which increases the chances of getting food

A simple example of operant conditioning occurs, when a rat in an experimental box accidentally presses a bar. If the bar press is followed by food, this consequence increases the chance that the rat will press the bar again.

As the rat presses the bar more times, more food follows, which in turn increases the chances that the rat will continue to press the bar (indicated by the rise of the red line in the figure above).

Using his newly developed procedure of operant conditioning, BF Skinner spent the next 50 years exploring and analysing learning in rats, pigeons, school children and adults.

A rat may initially press a bar out of curiosity and whether it presses the bar again depends on the consequences. To show how consequences can affect behaviour, imagine that you are looking over Skinner's shoulder as he places a rat into a box.

The box is empty except for a bar jutting out from one side and an empty food cup below and to the side of the bar. This box is called a Skinner box, is automated to record the animal's bar presses and deliver food pellets.

The Skinner box is an efficient way to study how an animal's ongoing behaviours may be modified by changing the consequences of what happens after a bar press. Skinner explains that the rat is a good subject for operant conditioning because it can use its front paws to manipulate objects, such as a bar and it has a tendency to explore its environment, which means that it will eventually find the bar, touch it or even press it.

Skinner goes on to explain the following three factors that are involved in operantly conditioning a rat to press a bar in the Skinner box

- The rat has not been fed for some hours so that it will be active and more likely to eat the food reward. A hungry rat tends to roam restlessly about, sniffing at whatever it finds.
- The goal is to condition the rat to press the bar. By pressing the bar, the rat operates on its environment, thus, this response is called an operant response.
- Skinner explains that a naive rat does not usually waltz over and press the bar. In conditioning a rat to press a bar, Skinner will use a procedure called shaping.

Interaction between Organism and Its Environment

Skinner informs us of three conditions of interaction between the organism and its environment *i.e.* "(a) the occasion upon which a response occurs, (b) the response itself and (c) the reinforcing consequences." Contingencies of reinforcement exist among the interrelationships of these three. A stimulus playing an unimportant role in the prevailing contingencies has little or no effect upon the organism.

Interaction between organism and environment is contingent upon positive and negative reinforcers. A reinforcer contingent upon a response, or the "class of responses upon which a reinforcer is contingent" is termed operant.

Respondent and Emitted Behaviour

Skinner made the distinction between what he called respondent behaviour and emitted behaviour. Respondent behaviour was what Pavlov has studied and it was always closely tied to a particular stimulus.

Skinner saw, as others had seen before him, that much behaviour did not appear to be tied to any particular stimulus. It seemed to be behaviour spontaneously produced, usually in certain kind of situations and Skinner referred to that form of behaviour as emitted behaviour.

Emitted Behaviour

Emitted behaviour has a relation to stimuli, but it is not the simple stimulus-response relationship that one see in the dust-sneeze example, operant behaviour is emitted behaviour, here as respondent behaviour is elicited reflexly as a reaction to stimuli, the former being instrumental conditioning and the latter classical.

The primary law of operant conditioning states that "if the occurrence of an operant is followed by presentation of a reinforcing stimulus, the strength is increased." Extinction follows or strength is decreased when the reinforcing stimulus fails to follow an operant already strengthened.

Reinforcement Schedule

Reinforcement may assume a variety of schedules continuous reinforcement or reinforcement occuring with each other response and intermittent reinforcement, where in a predetermined time schedule governs reinforcement.

Among the schedules of reinforcement, Skinner lists the fixed interval, reinforcement occuring at given time periods, fixed ratio, reinforcement following a set number of responses, variable interval or ratio, reinforcement varying within a given range, multiple schedules, shifting schedules depending upon the type of stimulus and differential reinforcement of rate of responding.

Verbal Behaviour

Verbal behaviour, as understood by **Skinner**, accords **verbal contingencies**, the same status as that maintained by laboratory equipment, except that a second organism is entailed. The prevailing contingencies in verbal societies that generate sentences account for verbal behaviour without the aid of the speaker's environment.

Teaching is viewed as the "arrangement of contingencies of reinforcement" that best expedites learning, with or without a teacher. Programmed instruction is designed so that maximal reinforcement ensures by successfully controlling the environment.

"A program is a set of contingencies, which shape topography of response and bring behaviour under the control of stimuli in an expeditious way." Teaching machines function on the principle of self-reinforced learning.

Determinants of Operant Conditioning

- **Reinforcer** It is a stimulus or event which increases the probability of the occurrence of a desired response. It can be negative or positive.

  Positive reinforcement involves stimuli that have pleasant consequences while negative reinforcements involve unpleasant and painful stimuli.
- **Frequency** Frequency of trial on which an organism has been reinforced, the amount of reinforcement *i.e.* how much food and/or water the organism (rat) receives is a determinant.
- **Quality** It relates to the type or condition of reinforcement received. This draws a comparison between what is received now and what was received earlier.

2. Cognitive Theory

Another aspect of learning theory is cognitive theory. All learning theories are categorised into two broader categories-S-R theories and S-S theories. S-S theory is also called sign theory. In the former category, the theories of Thorndike, Skinner, Hull, is studied.

The latter category includes the theories of Pavlov, Kohler and Kofka, Tolman, Adams and Zener. S-R theories strictly adheres to objectively observable behaviouristic approach and explain learning phenomenon in terms of association between stimulus and response (S-R bond).

The S-S theorist on the other hand, have explained learning by associating it with perception, which is mentalistic.

Tolman's Theory

Tolman has tried to take and combine the best of both the approaches. His theoretical formulations closely resemble S-R views, but at the same time, he has tried to explain it by incorporating the non-observable set of intervening variables such as 'demand', 'appetite', 'differentiation', 'motor skill', 'hypothesis' and 'biases'.

However, his explanation bears the behaviouristic bend of mind and he considers behaviour in terms of means-end-relationship. In other words, for him behaviour is goal-directed, *i.e.* **Purposive**. For this reason, he is characterised as Purposive behaviourist and his system is called 'purposive behaviourism'.

This bend of **Tolman**'s mind is explicitly expressed in his theory of learning, which is variously known as sign-gestalt or sign-significate or cognitive or expectancy theory.

His learning theory lays emphasis on development of cognition rather than S-R bonds. To prove it, Tolman conducted an experiment. For this purposes, a special maze was constructed.

Experiment

The maze had three paths from starting box to the goal box. Path 1 was the shortest, path 3 was longest one, while path 2 was of intermediate length.

There were 2 blocks-A and B, which the experimenter could manipulate by making them active as per planning, when block A is imposed, path 1 is blocked and when block B is made active, path 1 and 2 both are blocked as these had common segments leading to the goal box. After a preliminary acquaintance trials, experimental trials began and rats established a preference for path in order 1, 2 and 3.

Finally, results revealed that when block B imposed, rate directly ran through path 3 and secured frustrations. The finding obviously confirmed the hypothesis of 'cognitive map' of Tolman's theory.

By strengthening or confirming choices the rat develops a cognitive map of the whole maze saturation.

Tolman elaborating his theory states that while learning, we acquire large body of information from the environment, which changes our perception of the situation, depending upon the way an individual views the situation, when he is exposed to it.

New information is stored and old experience come to associate. This helps in developing an integrated cognitive map of the situation and determines—'what leads to what' and thus, the 'means-end relationship' develops.

Tolman further holds that this kind of development takes place even without any explicit manipulation of reinforcement. Development of cognitive map or means to end relationship is in fact, implicit, which is caused by sensory information processing of stimuli in the environment.

Past experience, however, has a significant role to play. This information processing and past experience enable the rat to locate food alongwith the shortest or the correct path that leads to the goal.

In essence, the cognitive learning theory proposes that the learner forms a cognitive structure in mind, it preserves and organise information about the various aspect of learning situation.

Cognitive Map

It is an internal representation of external environmental feature. By using the internal representation of physical space, people can get to the goal by knowing where it is in a complex of environmental features. Even shortcuts and changing of routes are also possible.

Tolman's Theory After 1949

Tolman later on in the year 1949, added some new learning or connections in his earlier version of the theory. These are six in number and explained them on the lines formally stated by **Freud** and **Lewin**.

These new connection or association are as follows

- **Cathexis** This refers to the attachment of specific types of goal object to basic drive. This concept has been used by Freud and is equivalent to Lewin's conception of valency.

  Here, 'Tolman' means that whatever a particular goal object satisfies a particular drive, a cathexis of that particular drive on that particular goal object is formed or associated. For this reason, perhaps a child in his early stage learns a relationship between hunger and biscuit.

- **Equivalence Beliefs** In a particular situation of reward and punishment, the situation itself is believed as equivalent to that reward and punishment. Here, the situation acquires some of the properties of goal object.

  This obviously refers to a kind of secondary reinforcement, *viz* a student receiving gold medal for his excellence at the university examination may consider it equivalent to special honour and prestige for his merit.

- **Field Expectancies** 'Field expectancies' are what Tolman earlier called sign-gestalt expectancies. When the animals learn route from one place to another or the kind of tool used for a particular purpose, a cognitive map of the field expectancy is said to be formed.

- **Field Cognition Mode** This refers to a higher order needs of expectancies and means an inclination to learn certain things more readily than the others. Such inclinations are partly innate and partly learnt our ability to use language in a variety of situations is perhaps one of the examples of field cognition mode. However, the explanation this is not much clear to define.

- **Drive Discrimination** This refers to our ability to discriminate among various types of drives. This ability is found in animals as well as men. However, this is not a very important kind of learning. This concept seems to have been derived from Hull and Leeper.

- **Motor Patterns** Following Guthrian model, Tolman here refers to the development of instrumental skill sequences and recognises this an one of the important aspects of learning. As he holds such sensory-motor associations are learned in a single trial on the basis of sheer contiguity.

3. Social Learning Theory

The social learning or modelling theory developed by **Albert Bandura** especially emphasises the important roles played by vicarious, symbolic and self-regulatory processes in psychological functioning. He agrees with the behaviorist theories of learning and adds two important ideas in it.

They are behaviour learned from the environment through observation and mediating processes occuring between stimuli and responses. Accordingly, an individual may acquire intricate response patterns simply by observing the performances of appropriate models. This is called observational learning.

Emotional responses can be conditioned observationally by witnessing the affective reactions of others undergoing painful or pleasurable experiences, fearful and avoidant behaviour can be learned through observation of modelled approach behaviour toward feared objects without any adverse consequences to the performer.

The social learning theory is therefore a mediation of behavioural and cognitive theories of learning. It states that the process of learning takes place in between the mediation of cognitive and behavior in context of social initiatives.

Persons can regulate their own behaviour to some extent by visualising self-generated consequences, with the many changes accompanying conditioning operations explained in terms of self-control processes rather than direct S-R linkages.

Observational Learning

Observational learning is primarily concerned with processes whereby observers organise response elements into the new patterns of behaviour at a symbolic level on the basis of information conveyed by modelling stimuli.

Observational learning essentially represents descriptive labeling in the guise of explanation. Like the other earlier theory of imitation developed by **Miller** and **Dollard** (1941), the operant conditioning interpretation of modelling phenomena accounts satisfactory for the control of previously learned matching response by their stimulus antecedents and their immediate consequences.

Social Learning Analysis

When a person observes a model's behaviour without simultaneously performing the responses, he can acquire the modelled responses while they are occuring only in representational forms.

The social learning analysis of observational learning therefore assigns a prominent role to representational mediators that are assumed to be acquired on the basis of a contiguity learning process.

Attitude

Attitude is an opinion about something, about some situation or about a person. The feelings attached with that thing changes into a strong opinion which then reflects in the behavioural change. An attitude is thus a strong feeling and is directed towards a definite object or a person.

It can be abstract such as positive attitude towards spirituality or it can be concrete such as attitude of acquiring new cars. The attitude either positive or negative gives a definite tendency to a person to react in a certain way. Thus, attitude greatly influences the way a person thinks and also shows in marked behavioural changes.

According to **Gordon Allport**, "An attitude is a mental and neural state of readiness, organised through experience, exerting a directive or dynamic influence upon the individual's response to all objects and situations with which it is related."

According to **P Robbins**, "Attitude is a manner, disposition, feeling and position with regard to a person or thing, tendency or orientation especially in the mind".

According to **Anastasi**, "A tendency to react favourably or unfavourably towards a designated class of stimuli, such as a national or racial group, a custom or an institution."

Characteristics of Attitude

Attitude is the tendency to react in a particular manner either negative or positive.

The characteristics that influences attitude are as follows

- Attitude is the combination of traits, behaviors, values, beliefs, motivations and personality.
- Attitude is seen in everyone irrespective of their intelligence, social and financial states.
- Attitude defines the identity of a person, guides our actions and influence the way people judge others.
- Attitude that a person carries is reflected through one's behaviour.
- Attitude helps people to see and react to different situations that come across in their life.
- Attitude can be implicit or explicit. Implicit attitudes are unconscious evaluations that occur towards an object, person or the self. Explicit attitudes are conscious evaluations that occur towards an objet, person or self.
- Attitude is influenced by past experience, so it is a summary of what the person might have faced in the past.
- Attitude has certain aspects like direction, intensity, specificity, interests and social conduct.

Types of Attitude

Attitude is a small thing, but it brings big behavioural changes in a person. It can make a person winner or loser at the same time. There are fouc basic types of attitudes.

These are as follows

Positive Attitude

It refers to keeping a positive mindset and thinking about good results, opportunities, enthusiasm no matter what the situation is. A positive attitude makes a person beleive in himself, gives strength, motivation, energy and initiative to achieve the set goals.

The problems and hurdles coming in are then seen as challenges and the mind constantly races to overcome those challenges. Thus, a person with a positive attitude is able to think positively, react to situation in a positive manner and tries to bring positivity in others also.

Positive attitude brings the following things in a person

- **Confidence** Confidence is an element that comes with positive attitude. A person who believes in his capabilities will have confidence and will be confident with self.
- **Happiness** Positive attitude brings happiness which in turn makes a person content and satisfied.
- **Sincerity** The sincerity trait comes with positive attitude. A sincere person is aware of the work that needs to be done and does it sincerely.
- **Determination** Positive attitude brings determination. Firmness helps a person to make resolutions and work hard to reach upto those resolutions.

Negative Attitude

It refers to a negative mindset. It is a feeling that is not optimistic or constructive. It is a bad feeling or a negative opinion about someone or something. It should be avoided as people with negative attitude are not able to achieve their goals. They are not able to face the problems and find solutions rather they tend to run out or away in order to avoid confrontation of the problems.

Due to negative attitude, people often ignore or neglect enjoying the good things in life. People with negative attitude often start comparing others to their self and feel jealous. At work, this attitude greatly hampers the output of an individual. *People with negative attitude face the following*

- **Anger** Anger destroys the rational thinking of a person as it is a state of intense emotional stress. It is the root cause of self-destruction.
- **Doubt** People with negative attitude doubt their abilities and due to this, they are not able to progress. This leads to low confidence.
- **Frustration** It is a negative feeling of being upset or annoyed. It blocks the path of self-achievement, progress, success and fulfilment.

Neutral Attitude

It refers to having no strongly marked attribute. Person with a neutral attitude do not stick a particular aspect. They are lazy, unemotional and often wait for others to take care of their problems. They ignore and do not want to tackle the problems in their life.

They don't want to face any challenges and in that process, often loose on any opportunities coming their way. The neutral attitude can be readily changed to positive or negative attitudes by bringing behavioural changes through attitude adjustment mental therapies.

Sikken Attitude

This is the most dangerous kind of attitude. It is more than negative attitude as it is destructive in nature. This kind of attitude is deep rooted in the personality and is difficult to change. It has the calibre to destroy every image that comes in connection with the positive attitude.

People with this kind of attitude remain angry, agitated at the smallest instance, cannot think straight and start making bad decisions. Sikken attitude reflects the mind's negativity but with time and changing the course of direction, this attitude can be changed.

Functions of Attitude

Attitudes serve four major functions of the people.

They are as follows

Adjustment Function This function of attitude pushes people to accommodate, adjust to the situations to derive pleasurable outcomes and avoid the unpleasant outcome. This function depends upon the perception of what is needed to satisfy one's needs.

Ego Defensive Function This function of attitude forms to protect the ego or self-image. The outward expressions are usually made to defend the self-position or the decision. This function is mostly related to what the person perceives to be.

Value Expression Function This function helps people to express their centrally held values. Here, certain attitudes are adopted to express something more tangibly. A conservative person may develop an attitude that does not matches with the current fashion trend.

Knowledge Function This function helps people to acquire and understand specific knowledge. It depends upon the likes and dislikes also. Suppose a person wants to learn astrology, then his attitude will be to seek, acquire and understand more on this subject.

Attitude Model

Every attitude has three components that are together called as models of attitude. The three components are affective, behavioural and cognitive. Together, they are known as the ABC Model of Attitude. *These are as follows*

Affective Component

Affective component refers to the sudden emotional reactions are shows towards an attitude object. Attitude objects are the specific things towards which, one makes a judgement or has a feeling towards.

The feelings can be negative or positive. *e.g.* If a person is afraid of snakes than by seeing a snake, that person feels extreme anxiety and fear. Here, snake is the attitude object and the feelings and judgements are anxiety, fear etc. This type of attitude is used to express our moral belief and value system.

Behavioural Component

Behavioural component is the second part of the model of attitude. It refers to the behaviour or the way one behaves towards the attitude object. In the above example, when a person is exposed to snake, then the sudden avoidance or sceam or leaving the spot suddenly is behavioural component. Anxiety and fear are affective component.

Behavioural component is also known as conative. It is the way the attitude have its influence on us or how we behave. This component is also consistent which means the behaviour of a person tends to remain inconsistent. Thus, the behaviour is consistent with the attitude.

Cognitive Component

The cognitive component is the mental set up of a person. It refers to the beliefs, thoughts, attributes and knowledge in relation to the attitude object. It is the opinion or general knowledge of a person about the attitude object.

In the above example, the knowledge that snakes are poisonous, they are dangerous are examples of cognitive component. These generally comes to light in the form of stereotypes. Such as snakes should be avoided as they are poisonous. This is the cognitive component of attitude for the person who is afraid of snakes. However, here the fact is ignored that not all snakes are poisonous.

Attitude at the Workplace

Attitude at the place of work have an effect on every person within the organisation right from the manager to the employees to the clients as well as the company owner. At the workplace, the attitude helps in developing a healthy workplace environment that greatly affects the productivity, team building and morale of the employees.

A negative attitude at the workplace creates negative atmosphere, distrust among the people, unhealthy competition and lack of enthusiasm or creativity. In such a situation, an organisation cannot function well.

A positive attitude at the workplace creates positivity. It promotes stress free work environment, increases efficiency, productivity and interpersonal relations among the people working in an organisation.

Power and Authority

Power and authority are integral parts of an organisation. Power is the capacity or the ability to influence the behaviour of others. It is the taking and implementing of decision in an organisation. It is also correlated with control. *e.g.* If A controls B and has the capability to influence B's behaviour, then it can be stated that A has the power.

According to **Cambridge English Dictionary**, "Power is the ability to control people and events."

"Power is the capability of doing or accomplishing something." Here, it do not means physical strength. Power means mental, psychological, social and structural strength that has the capacity to change a behaviour.

According to **Hague, Harrop** and **Breslin**, "In a broad sense, the power is the production of intended effects."

According to **Anthony Giddens**, "Power is the ability to make a difference, to change things from what they would otherwise have been."

Features of Power

Power is used in Relational Sense Power implies the ability to influence control over others. Therefore, it relates to interaction between two or more people. It cannot be isolated or alone. There has to be two or more elements to exhibit power.

Power is Disaggregated and Non-cumulative It is shared by many groups at the same time. It is not one whole concept. In an organisation, there may be many power centres. Similarly, many departments working together may have department heads who function as power centre. All the groups compete among themselves to capture power.

Power is not Concentrated Power cannot be accumulated or concentrated at a particular point. All the centres of power claim equal amount of power. However, there can be unequal distribution of power.

Power represents a Particular Interest Capitalist power, socialist power etc all represent a particular group. That group is derived by similar interests. Therefore, power represents a specific interest group.

Power is Conditional Concept Power depends to some extent on the conditions. If the conditions change, then the power centre can also change. *e.g.* An executive is bound to obey the manager because the latter is having legitimate power. But if he is promoted, then that condition may be changed.

Power is Complex It is difficult to understand the aspect of power in one instance. One needs to be in that situation for some time to understand the dimensions of power. Therefore, it is said that power is complex.

Sources of Power

The sources of power as identified in the sociological context of power are five.

They are as follows

Legitimate Power

This is positional power, that is given to a person due to their role in the organisation. It is determined by the structural formation that defines the hierarchy of the organisation.

Legitimate power is the legal power that is given according to the situation. It cannot be passed on. It is earned legitimately. *e.g.* A manager assigning duties to executives.

Expert Power

This is the power one can derive from possessing knowledge that is closely needed in an organisation. The expert power comes from knowledge, understanding and experience. People possessing this kind of power are highly values in an organisation.

These people remain indispensable and their opinion, ideas are also valued. A person holding expert power can be raised to the high position, where legitimate power can also be given.

Referent Power

This form of power is derived by the interpersonal relationship that a person makes in an organisation. The relation with collegues, bosses and other people in an institution results in admiration and popularity of that person.

Referent power also depends upon the personal connections that a person may have with the other important members and people in topmost positions in an organisation. These people are also very influential.

Reward Power

Reward power is derived by the allocation of incentives in an organisation. The incentives are in the form of like in salary, bonus, promotions, appraisals and other such processes.

The reward power gives fairly sense of satisfaction to the behelder. People enjoying this kind of power tend to influence the actions of the other employees. It is a great motivating power.

Coercive Power

This type of power is derived by the ability to influence others by way of punishments, threats or reprimanding. People may be demoted, suspended or fired to exhibit this type of power. The management uses this power to influence the behaviour of others, so that they adhere to the policies and norms of the organisation.

Authority

Authority is the right to exercise a certain degree of control. It is a legitimate form of power. Authority means the legal right to take decisions, allocate resources and do other functions as demanded in the position. It is formal and also written in many forms. *e.g.* The appointed manager in an organisation is given the legal right to take decisions and allocate resources. It is regarded as the power to control.

As per **Oxford Dictionary**, "The right or the capacity or both to have proposals or prescriptions or instructions accepted without recourse to persuasion, bargaining or force."

According to **MacIver**, "By authority we mean the established right within any social order to determine policies to pronounce judgements or relevant issues and to settle controversies."

According to **DD Raphael**, "To have authority to do something is to have the right to do it."

Types of Authority

Max Weber has classified authority into three types. These are traditional authority, charismatic authority and legal-rational authority. *These are explained as follows*

Traditional Authority

It is a type of authority which is established by the customs, habits and social structures prevailing in an organisation. The traditional authority goes on due to long established traditions which are not changed, stopped or violated.

The political system adopted in tribal societies or clans are examples of traditional authority. Counties like Saudi Arabia, Kuwait, Morocco are examples of traditional authority. Therefore, the son or daughter inherits the authority by their order of birth. It is a legitimate authority.

Charismatic Authority

This type of authority is based on the individual personality that in charismatic and makes a tremendous impact on the people. This type of personality naturally commands an authority. *e.g.* Hitler, Mussolini, Nepoleon.

The charismatic authority exercises power and people accept their position. In this way, the charismatic authority also become very popular leaders. This is a legitimate authority that enjoys legal power.

Legel-Rational Authority

It refers to the legal or legitimate authority which is rational or in order words authority in accordance with reason or logic. It is also backed by the constitution or the existing laws of the organisation.

The office is more important than the person, so the authority resides in the office. Examples of this type of authority is U.S. Presidency and modern British Parliament.

Characteristics of Authority

- Right to affect the behaviour of others and to mould it as per the needs is a basic feature of authority.
- Authority is legitimate as certain secured rights are given to it. The rights are based on customs, traditions, bureaucratic office or personality of the individual.
- Decision-making is a requirement of authority as the act of taking decisions is conferred to person of authority.
- Authority is influenced by the person exercising it and therefore it is subjective.
- Authority also resides in the position irrespective of the individual.
- Authority is a commanding force that binds different departments and individuals in an organisation.
- Authority is downward movement of commands.

Difference between Power and Authority

Power and authority may seem the same but there are slight differences between the two. Both are a part of the organisation.

The differences are as follows

Basis	Power	Authority
Sources	Source of power is related to individual persona, charisma and expertise. A person gains power once he is given authority.	Source of authority is related to the position or situation. A person get power automatically once he is in a position of authority.
Formality	Power can be formal such as a powerful position/designation. It can also be informal like an old employee has power in comparison to new joinee.	Authority is strictly a formal method of showing power. It is provided by the guidelines of an institution.
Legitimacy	Power may/may not be legitimate since it may not be formal.	Authority is only legitimate as it is formal and has a written code.
Ability to be Lost	Power is not easily lost as it is dependant on the individual. Charismatic personality commands a certain degree of power even without authority.	Authority is easily lost as it is a formal presentation. Removing the person from the position, taking away powers, reducing the role are ways of reducing or removing authority.
Use of Violence	Exercising power often resort to violence in order to draw support or show power.	Authority is not violent, it is authoritative. The moment one tries to use violence, it loses the support.
Specific Field	Power is not restricted or confined to a specific field. A powerful leader of the opposition may also have followers from the other side also.	Authority is confined to a specific field and it is contained within the boundaries of an institution.

Stress

Stress can be viewed as a response to a stimulus or as the stimulus itself. It is a reaction to a situation that may be giving unpleasant reactions, conditions or consequences. It is the pressure one feels mentally which then affects the physical self and also transforms the behavior of a person. It is synonyms to emotional strain, tension or pressure. It is the result of adverse situations.

Medical definition of stress, "Stress is a physical, mental or emotional factor that causes bodily or mental tension."

According to **Holyroyd** and **Lazarus**, "Psychological stress requires a judgement that environmental factor and/or internal demands exceed the individuals resource for managing them."

According to **Skinner**, "A reaction of a particular individual to a stimulus event."

Stress can be dangerous if it is prolonged or severe, but it is not always bad. As Canadian stress research pioneer **Hans Selye** observed, 'To be totally without stress is to be dead'. That's why because stress in the mental and physical condition that occurs when we adjust or adapt to the environment.

A stress reaction begins with the same automatic nervous system arousal that occurs during emotion. Imagine you are standing at the top of a wind-whipped ski jump for the first time. Internally, you would experience a rapid surge in your heart rate, blood pressure, respiration muscle tension and other ANS response. Short-term stresses of this kind can be uncomfortable, but they rarely do any damage. Long-term stresses are another matter entirely.

Factors Causing Stress in Organisation

Life Stressors

These are personal stressors that affect the individual. Some individuals may have economic obligations towards bank or family which causes stress. The basis ten life stressors are retirement, marital reconciliation, loss of job, marriage, personal injury or illness, death of close family member, jail term, divorce and death of spouse.

Organisational Stressors

Physical Demand They are dependent on the job setting. It arises from the physical environment such as poor design of the office, high or cold temperature, humidity etc.

Task Demand These are stressors that are linked with a particular type of job or work that causes stress to the performer. *e.g.* Meeting sales targets or call centre jobs.

Role Demand The stress arises from the position in the organisation or group. Sometimes an employee is not clear about his role and there are role conflicts which lead to stress.

Interpersonal Demand They are associated with the attributes of the relationship of individuals of the organisation. This includes leadership style, personality style or pressure from the group, lack of support, racial harassment etc.

Environmental Stressors

These are stressors that are out of control of the individual.

They includes the following

Political Uncertainties An unstable political system gives stress to employees as there are unstable policies and laws.

Economic Uncertainties If a country faces recession or slow growth then the employees face job insecurity which results into stress.

Technological Advancements If the technology changes in the external environment then the employees fear loosing their jobs to machines, leading to stress.

Impact of Stress

The impact of long-term stresses can be understood by examining the body's defence against stress, a pattern known as the general adaption syndrome. **The General Adaptation Syndrome (GAS)** is a series of bodily reactions to prolonged stress.

Sely noticed that the first symptoms of almost any disease or trauma are almost identical. The body responds in the same way to any stress, be it infection, failure, embarrassment, a new job, trouble at school or a stormy romance.

During the initial alarm reaction to stress, resistance falls below normal. It rises again as bodily resources are mobilised and it remains high during the stage of resistance. Eventually, resistance falls again as the stage of exhaustion is reached. The GAS consists of three stages *i.e.* an alarm reaction, a stage of resistance and a stage of exhaustion.

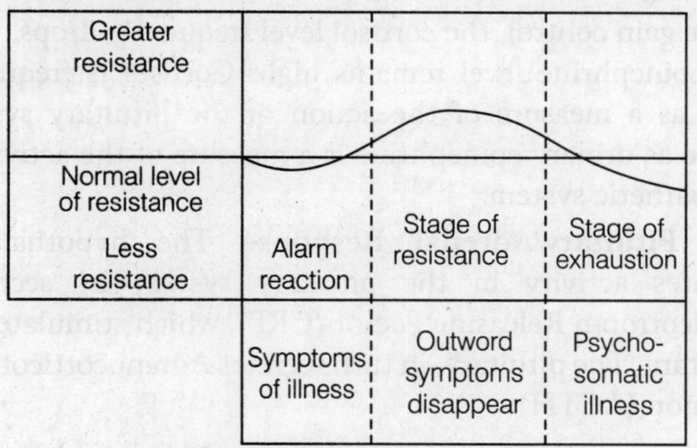

The General Adaption Syndrome

In an alarm reaction, your body mobilises its resources to cope with added stress. The pituitary gland signals the adrenal glands to produce more adrenalin, noradrenaline and cortisol.

As these stress hormones are dumped into the bloodstream, some bodily processes are speeded up and others are slowed. This allows bodily resources to be applied where they are needed.

Main effects of stress are

- Chronic stress lead to physical ailments as it reduces the immune system, upset the digestive system and nerve system.
- It causes extreme mental problems like depression, anxiety, sleep disorder, thinking and memory problems.
- It causes emotional problems related to frustration, irritability, anger, loneliness, moodiness etc.
- It also causes certain behavioural problem such as nervous habits like biting nails, neglecting/avoiding responsibilities, habitual use of alcohol, drugs, with drawing form others etc.
- It brings several other problems such as problems in marriage, difficulty in relationships, negative attitude etc.

Components of Stress

The Biological Component of Stress

This component studies the bodily reactions that occurs due to stress. Whereas the sympathetic/adrenal system takes care of arousal, the pituitary/adrenal system is more closely associated with what is traditionally called the stress reaction our fight-or-light responses. The adrenal cortex secretes two types of hormones the mineralocorticoids and the glucocorticoides.

The release of these hormones is linked to the release of other chemicals. Under stress, the sympathetic and the pituitary responses typically occur together. However, these two systems operate separately in some circumstances-generally when we attempt to gain control over stress by engaging in some kind of adaptive behaviour.

As we gain control, the cortisol level frequently drops, while the epinephrine level remains high. Cortisol is frequently used as a measure of the action of the pituitary system, where as urinary epinephrine is a measure of the activity of sympathetic system.

The Pituitary/Adrenal Response The hypothalamus initiates activity in the pituitary system by secreting Corticotropin Releasing Factor (CRF), which stimulates the pituitary. The pituitary, in turn secretes Adrenocorticotropic Hormon (ACTH).

The Learned Component of Stress

This component is related to the behavioural changes that are learned by a person in dealing with stress.

Both the nature of the stress reaction and the way a person or animal tend to respond under stress can be modified by learning. Learning to predict when a stressor will come, allow the individual to relax, when the stressor is absent. Short period of relaxation appear to help ward off the effects of stress, such as ulcers.

Habituating a response under stress seems to mobilise the body to provide the necessary physiological base for good performance. Evidence from a wide variety of sources indicates that under stress, automatic and habitual responses deteriorate. The failure to make good decisions under stress is an example of how stress disrupts performance, probably by disrupting attention.

The Cognitive Component of Stress

This refers to the adoption of cognitive methods to deal with stress. One of the most comprehensive theories about the role of cognitive factors in stress has been developed, by **Richard Lazarus** and his colleagues.

According to this theory, how an individual appraises and event plays a fundamental role in determining not only the magnitude of the stress response, but the kind of coping strategies that the individual may employ to deal with the stress.

Appraisal occurs in two stages

- **Primary Appraisal** At this stage, we determine whether a stressful event represents harm, threat or challenge. Harm refers to injury or damage that has already taken place, such as loss of a limb, loss of a job or simply loss of a self-esteem. Threat refers to something that could produce harm or loss.

  Challenge refers to the potential for growth, mastery or some form of gain. From this perspective, the origins of stress cannot be assessed by looking solely at the nature of the environmental recent that precipitates it. Rather stress involves the interaction of the individual with the environment.
- **Secondary Appraisal** After determining whether a stressful event represent loss, theat or challenge, we evaluate our coping resources and options; we ask what we can do. Generally, we have access to physical, social, psychological and material coping resources.

  Physical resources include health and energy; social resources include family and friends; psychological resources include self-esteem and problem-solving ability and material resources include money and equipment.

Sign of Stress

During the stage of resistance, bodily adjustments to stress stabilise. As the body's defences comes into balance, symptoms of the alarm reaction disappear outwardly, everything seems normal. However, this appearance of normality comes at a high cost.

The body is better able to cope with the original stressor, but its resistance to other stress is lowered. *e.g.* animals placed in extreme cold become more resistance to the cold but more susceptible to infection. It is during the stage of resistance that the first signs of psychosomatic disorders begin to appear.

Continued stress leads to the stage of exhaustion, in which the body's resource are drained and stress hormones are depleted.

Some of the typical signs or symptoms of impending exhaustion include the following

Emotional Signs Anxiety, apathy, irritability mental fatigue.

Behavioural Signs Avoidance of responsibility and relationships, extreme or self-destructive behaviour, self-neglect poor judgement.

Physical Signs Excessive worry about illness, frequent illness, exhaustion, over use of medicines, physical ailments.

Management of Stress

Stress can be managed with the help of two approaches which are as follows

Organisational Approaches to Manage Stress

Wellness Programmes and Institutional Programmes Some organisations have started a special zone for yoga or gym, sports room, which can be used by employees during non-working hours.

Redesigning Stressful Jobs By altering the methods and procedure of performing the job, rearranging work schedules.

Goal Setting When roles are defined clearly and specific goals are given to the individual, then it reduces ambiguity and the employee becomes clear and motivated.

Training By providing proper and repeated training the management can make an employee less stressed.

Removal of Rotating Shifts By providing a stable shift, the organisation will help the individual in practicing work life balance.

Increasing Employee Involvement Involvement of employee in making decisions and taking his feedback will create a sense of belonging for him.

Organisational Communication Providing a mechanism within the organisation to communicate about grievances of the employees. A grievance cell helps the individual with professional counselling and guidance in managing stress.

Health Promotion Programmes Health promotion programmes and career development programmes must be made part of the institution's programmes.

Sabbatical Leaves These are paid leaves given by the organisation to its employee to travel or study, for days and months.

Individual Approaches to Manage Stress

Exercise Physical exercises, jogging , yoga are stress busters.

Relaxation Deep breathing, hypnosis, meditation etc.

Time Management Techniques Techniques like to do list, 'pomodoro', help the individuals in managing time, thus stress is also managed.

Development of Support Groups Individuals can build their network of people who listen to their worries and problems.

Stress management encompasses a variety of techniques and more than one is typically used in any given instances.

Techniques include

- **Arousal Reduction** In arousal reduction, the person is trained in muscle relaxation. Teaching people to relax deeply and to apply these skills to real life stressors can be helpful in lowering their stress levels.
- **Cognitive Restructuring** Cognitive restructuring includes approaches such as those of Ellis and Beck. The focus is on altering peoples belief systems and improving the logical clarity of their interpretations of experience, on the assumption that people's intellectual level can affect how they feel and behave.
- **Behavioural-Skill Training** Because it is natural to feel overwhelmed if one lacks the skills in execute a challenging task, stress management often includes instruction and practice in necessary skills as well as general issues such as time management and effective prioritising.

Interpersonal Behaviour

Interpersonal behaviour relates to the actions of the human beings. The way by which people exchange their thoughts and ideas in an organisation is a way of how they react in the social world. Thus, the interpersonal behaviour shows the interaction taking place between coworkers, between the working and management and also with the customers.

Characteristics of Interpersonal Behaviour

Independent Individuals The interpersonal behaviour depends solely upon individual thinking, expectations, interpretations etc.

Communication The interpersonal behaviour of a person is communicated through verbal and non- verbal means of communication. This constitute body language, way of talking, listening skills etc.

Personal Choice Interpersonal behaviour greatly involves personal choices which gets reflected through the behaviour.

Inescapable It refers to a never ending process as people are always communicating knowingly or unknowingly. People are also interpreting the information about other people.

Social Skill Interpersonal behaviour is shown visibly within the social setup. It comes out openly which a person mixes in the society. Social skills are also learnt through the interaction.

Emotional Skill Interpersonal behaviour is highly affected by emotional quotient, emotional maturity and self-awareness. The emotional skills are also a concept developed in the environment where a child grows up. Hereditary factors also make up the emotional skill.

Types of Interpersonal Behaviour

There are three types of interpersonal behavior people normally exhibit. *They are as follows*

Aggressive

In this type of interpersonal behaviour, people express their views, thoughts or feelings openly. A person readily stands up to defend himself and behaves quite aggressively for that this kind of behaviour shown by a person may humiliate or dominate over others.

It is an outburst against something that results form part pent-up emotions like anger. It may be an over reaction at times and is subjected to hostile reactions. This happens when a person is humiliated repeatedly and rights are also violated.

Assertive

Assertive interpersonal behaviour is shown when a person stands up for his rights without showing aggression. Here, the point of resentment is conveyed in a peaceful manner without violating the rights of others.

It is an honest, direct and appropriate kind of behaviour. The feelings, thoughts and ideas are expressed respectfully. The message in conveyed to others without showing any hostility. This kind of behaviour is normally healthy.

It is effective also because here the person often gets what in wanted. This improves self confidence and relationships within the coworking space.

Non-assertiveness

This type of behaviour is generally passive and enables other people to violate a person's rights. The person showing this kind of behavior do not express wants, ideas, thoughts or feelings. These people are not able to show resistance even when others infringe upon their right.

People showing this type of interpersonal behaviour show anxiety, disappointment, guilt and shame. They feel self pity, disgusted and irritated. These type of people avoid conflicting situations, confrontation, tensions and unpleasant situations.

Interpersonal Skills

Interpersonal skills are attributes that are used to motivate employees to achieve best results. The interpersonal skills are extremely important in all modern day organisations.

The important interpersonal skills are as follows

Managing Relationships By remaining polite, respectful and cheerful a person can manage all the relationships needed at the workplace i.e relation between coworkers, with manages, with CEO.

Understanding Others Knowing about how others feel, will help to develop empathy which essential for developing interpersonal skills.

Cooperating Cooperating with coworkers and with other departments develops cooperation and collaboration which makes the tasks simpler.

Positive Attitude Having a positive attitude affects the way people look at things. It helps a person to overcome challenges with ease.

Showing Respect Showing respect by following verbal and non-verbal communication skills increases one's own respect. This also helps in gaining admiration and popularity among people.

Active Listening It refers to listening others attentively. By doing so, a person makes sure that important things are not left out and also helps in getting focussed. This can be done by maintaining eye contact, nodding and speaking in your turn.

Appropriate Contact Interpersonal skill also consist of how a person presents itself. Maintaining appropriate distance that includes the actions and the things that are done as well as the right kind of contact helps to maintain the personal space. This as one of the basic requirement of interpersonal skill needed at the workplace.

Improve Self-concept It refers to the self-image of a person. The skills, attitudes, expectations, qualifications and knowledge of a person helps him/her to develop a self image. It a person improves self concept that will feel worthy of self. This will be reflected positively in interpersonal behaviour. That person will be confident, competent and will attain a greater degree of job contentment.

Transactional Analysis

This theory was given by **Eric Berne**. TA offers a model of personality and the dynamics of self and its relationship to others. When people interact, there is social transaction in which one person respond to another.

The study of these transactions among people is called transaction analysis. This analysis can be understood by using Johari Window, that tries to evaluate concept of self with respect to others.

Ego States of Transactional Analysis (TA)

Ego states are a person's way of thinking, feeling and behaving at any time.

Berne has defined ego state as a consistent pattern of feeling and experience which is directly related to a respective consistent pattern of behaviour.

He has given three ego states which are as follows

Parent Ego State It is a state where the individual behave, feel and think in response to an unconscious imitation or mimicking of how their parents have acted in the past and how they interpreted the actions of their parents.

This is also called 'exteropsyche' state. *e.g.* An individual may yell because of frustration because they have experienced the same in their childhood.

Adult Ego State Here, the adult is directed towards an objective appraisal of reality. Here, he processes information and make predictions about various emotions that can influence his behaviour. This is also know as 'neopsyche' state.

Child Ego State Here, the individuals behave, think and feel in the same manner as they used to think in their childhood. Thus, the child is a source of intimacy, spontaneity, recreation, creation and emotions.

Thus, according to **Berner**, parental figures are either more criticising or more nurturing and childhood behaviours are either adapted or more natural, *i.e.* free. A person of any age may have any of these states in varying degrees.

Johari Window

The word Johari comes from the initials of the names of its developers **Joseph** and **Harrington Ingham**. This window is made up of four quadrants that tries to find out situations in which self-awareness is analysed. *It is as follows*

	Known to self	Not known to self
Known to others	Open	Blind
Not known to others	Hidden	Unknown

Open-self/The Area/Free Area Individual is known to self and to others. He is open minded, sharing and straight forward.

Blind-self/Blind-spot A person who is unaware about himself but others know him.

Hidden-self Characteristics known by the person about himself but not other.

Unknown-self Characteristics unknown to the person and even other do not know.

Life Position Theory-Eric Berne

Berne states that dysfunctional behaviour is the result of decisions made in childhood that were the best belief systems available to the child then, allowing them to survive and adapt to those around them, but then become a limiting life script for later life. Once a person has decided on a life position that will often remain fixed unless there is considerable effort put in to change the underlying beliefs and decisions put in about life.

The goal of transactional analysis psychotherapy is to bring into awareness, explore, challenge, and change an ineffective life script. This is based on the belief that because we were the original creators of our own script we have the power to change it.

Life Positions

There are four life positions that are as follows

- **I'm OK-You're OK** position is considered the optimal, healthy position and is generally game-free. People occupying this position will hold the belief that all people are innately worthy and valuable.

  That people are OK is a statement which describes their being or essence rather than their behaviour. This position is characterised by attitude openness and of honesty and trust. People occupying this position will be collaborative and accepting of themselves and others.

- **I'm OK-You're not OK** is occupied by those who project their difficulties onto others; they may be blaming and critical. Transactional games that reinforce this position involve a self-styled superior (the "I'm OK") who projects anger, disgust, or disdain onto a designated inferior, or scapegoat (the "You're not OK"). This position requires that there be someone to be 'worse than' in order to maintain the sense of self as ok.

- **I'm not OK-You're OK** position is depressive, it is characterised by feeling powerless and lacking in comparison with others. People occupying this position may discount their own needs in favour of others and may experience themselves as victims.

  Transactional games supporting this position include "Kick me" and "Martyr" games that support the power of others and deny one's own.

- **I'm not OK-You're not OK** is a position of hopelessness, futility and frustration. From this position life seems uninteresting and hopeless. This may result in self-destructive or violent behaviour.

Thus, the challenge of transactional analysis is to become aware of how we are attempting to make life real through our basic life position and if necessary, create a healthy alternative.

EXAM BASED QUESTIONS

1 The main dimensions which influence human behaviour in an organisation are

(a) Group, environment, organisation, gender
(b) Individual, group, organisation, environment
(c) Environment, group, individual, gender
(d) Individual, organisation, group, gender

2 Which is not an influence on behaviour?

(a) Environment
(b) Individual
(c) Group
(d) Building

3 Which is not a factor of influencing human behaviour?

(a) Ideas (b) society
(c) Perception (d) Universe

4 Which of the following is not true?

(a) Behaviour differs from one individual to other
(b) Behaviour is learnt, acquired and modified
(c) behaviour is always purposeful
(d) Behaviour is a stable concept

5 A relatively permanent change in behaviour occuring as a result of experience is……

(a) motivation (b) learning
(c) behaviour modification (d) skills

6 A dynamic organisation within the individual that determine the adjustment to the environment is

(a) personality (b) behaviour
(c) attitude (d) perception

7 Intelligence, shyness, politeness are what?

(a) Social norms that people should have
(b) Part of interpersonal behaviour
(c) Certain behavioural traits
(d) A set of positive attitudes

8 To analyse the behavioural issues in an organisation, what is not needed?

(a) Gender and ethnic difference
(b) Management process
(c) Behaviour of people
(d) Organisational context

9 Which of the following is not an individual level independent variable?

(a) Marital status (b) Gender
(c) Productivity (d) Age

10 ……… are enduring characteristics that describe on individual's behaviour.

(a) Individual dimensions
(b) Terminal values
(c) Personality traits
(d) Value systems

11 The same fire, which melts butter hardens eggs. With respect to personality development, this statement implies that

(a) all individuals react in same way to same environment
(b) all individual react differently to same environment
(c) all individual react in same way to different environment
(d) individuals do not react to environment

12 Which of the following is correct order of hierarchial model of personality?

(a) Trait, Super trait, Specific response, Habitual
(b) Super trait, Specific response, Trait, Habitual
(c) Specific response, Habitual, Trait, Super trait
(d) Habitual, Trait, Super trait, Specific response

13 Arrange the school of personalities in the order of acceptance from older days.

(a) Psychodynamic, Trait, Humanistic, Social Learning
(b) Trait, Humanistic, Psychodynamic, Social Learning
(c) Humanistic, Psychodynamic, Trait, Social Learning
(d) None of the above

14 Which one of the following statements about Type A individuals is not correct?

(a) They are aggressive
(b) They are impatient
(c) They are very sociable
(d) They worry about deadlines

15 Which one of the following is not the characteristic of Type A personality?

(a) Excessive compulsion for time keeping
(b) Meticulous analysis of problems
(c) Sleeplessness
(d) Always in a hurry

16 According to Eysenck's theory, in which of the following traits, the genetic factors explain maximum variation?

(a) Extraversion (b) Intelligence
(c) Neuroticism (d) Pyschoticism

17 Which one of the following factors is not included in the 'Big Five' dimensions of personality?

(a) Extraversion
(b) Neuroticism
(c) Agreeableness
(d) Intelligence

18 Trait approach to personality asserts that traits are

(a) adjectives describing behaviour
(b) discrete and discontinuous categories of people
(c) generalised systems which ensure consistency in behaviour of individuals
(d) psychological categories of temperament associated with specific body physique

19 **Identical twins are more similar in personality than fraternal twins even, when they are reared apart. But they are not as similar as when they are reared together. This indicates that**
(a) biological heredity determines personality
(b) social environment determines personality
(c) both heredity and environment determine personality
(d) heredity set limits, which environment cannot transcend

20 **It is found that persons behave consistently same fashion across time and situation largely due to**
(a) social pressures exerted on them
(b) their need to conform
(c) their stable personality dispositions
(d) role learning

21 **Low self-esteem can lead to a cycle of failure that is self-destructive. Which of the following is the sequence?**
(a) Low performance expectations, High anxiety, Reduced effort, Low self-esteem, Actual failure
(b) High anxiety, Reduced effort, Low performance expectations, Actual failure, Low self-esteem
(c) High anxiety, Reduced effort, Low self-esteem, Low performance expectations, Actual failure
(d) None of the above

22 **Allport suggested that each individual has a unique set of personality traits. He called these personal disposition, arrange them in order.**
(a) Cardinal, Central and Secondary
(b) Central, Secondary, Cardinal
(c) Secondary, Central, Cardinal
(d) None of the above

23 **Elsie's daughter gave her a microwave oven on her birthday. Elsie has never used a microwave and scared to use this one. Instead, she lets it kitchen and refuses to let her daughter teach how to use it. Elsie would probably score very low**
(a) agreeableness (b) neuroticism
(c) introversion (d) openness

24 **Which one of the following figures is an example of proximity principle of perceptual organisation?**
(a)
(b)
(c)
(d)

25 **A person looks at two circle. One is black and the other, is white. The retinal images are also different for the two circles, inspite of these differences, the person perceives the two circles as being identical in form. This is a case of**
(a) perception of Ganzfeld (b) transposition of form
(c) from parallax (d) law of similarity

26 **Which one of the following inferences can be drawn from the given figure?**
(a) Similar lines are grouped into one unit
(b) Lines are in different directions
(c) Proximity of lines makes it one unit
(d) Incomplete figures are seen as complete

27 **One has tendency to organise things to make a balanced or symmetrical figure that includes all parts. This is known as the law or**
(a) similarity (b) continuation
(c) closure (d) good figure

28 **Rubin is to figure ground segregation as Koffka is to**
(a) phi-phenomenon (b) perceptual organisation
(c) brightness contrast (d) perceptual constancy

29 **Which Gestalt principle is at work when a ventriloquist moves the dummy's mouth while doing the talking making it seem like the dummy is talking?**
(a) Closure (b) Similarity
(c) Contiguity (d) Continuity

30 **A reversible figure such as the Necker cube, makes use of which principle of perception?**
(a) Shape constancy
(b) Expectancy
(c) Figure-ground relationship
(d) Deep perception

31 **Television ads that are in black and white just trying to take advantage of which attention getting technique?**
(a) Loudness (b) Motion
(c) Contrast (d) Repetition

32 **Highway engineers sometimes paint stripes on freeway off-ramps to enhance the perception of depth, using the cue of**
(a) aerial perspective (b) parallax
(c) texture gradients (d) overlap

33 **The tendency to complete a figure is called**
(a) continuation (b) similarly
(c) continuity (d) closure

34 **The most basic perceptual organisation is**
(a) shape constancy (b) depth perception
(c) figure-ground (d) size constancy

35 **Seeing subjective contours in a Kaniza figure**
(a) is a uniquely human trait
(b) has no physiological basis
(c) indicates that brain damage has occurred
(d) suggests that the brain is fabricating a more likely interpretation of the figure

36 Figure and ground can be switched in
(a) shape perception (b) depth perception
(c) reversible figure (d) nonlinear figures

37 The tendency to group together objects that are the same size, shape, colour or form is known as
(a) closure (b) continuation
(c) similarity (d) nearness

38 Internal standards used to judge stimuli are referred to as
(a) adaptation level (b) context
(c) intuition (d) frames of reference

39 Although, the markings in the ceiling titles are of all different shapes and sizes, you notice that larger, spots seem to stand out against a background made up of smaller, lighter ones. Which principle of perceptual grouping explains this distinction?
(a) The principle of closure (b) The law of common fate
(c) The law of Praganan z (d) The law of similarity

40 Incidental learning refers to a situation where the subject is
(a) over-instructed (b) under-instructed
(c) properly instructed (d) not instructed

41 According to the concept of 'learning to learn', Which one of the following facilitates the maximum transfer of earning?
(a) Learner's level of motivation
(b) Learner's current perception of the task
(c) Learner's mastery of skills an principles involved in the task
(d) Repetitive practice with the task on the part of the learner. It helps in problem solving.

42 A cardinal assumption of stimulus genralisation theory of Pavlov is that
(a) locus of generalisation gradients is in the testing rather then in the training phase
(b) generalisation gradients might be the result of variations in discriminative thresholds
(c) a process that develops automatically during conditioning along with the speed of associative strength
(d) stimulus generalisation occurs due to "failure of association"

43 Freezing of response occurs in
(a) respondent conditioning
(b) instrumental conditioning
(c) viarious trial and error
(d) both respondent conditioning and trial and error

44 In instrumental conditioning,
(a) reinforcement is given irrespective of the production of an appropriate response
(b) reinforcement is given before the on set of the response
(c) appropriate response is immediately followed by reinforcement
(d) reinforcement is not given

45 Generally which one of the following CS-US relationships leads to faster conditioning?
(a) The CS is presented several minutes before the US
(b) The CS and the US are both presented simultaneously
(c) The CS is presented half a second to half a minute before the US
(d) The US is delayed for several minutes

46 Which one of the following methods is applicable in formation of habits?
(a) Reciprocal conditioning
(b) Operant conditioning
(c) Second order conditioning
(d) Differential conditioning

47 Which one of the following statements explain the incidental learning?
(a) Learning without actually trying to attain a goal.
(b) Learning in the absence of ostensible reinforcement.
(c) Learning without the knowledge of the relationship between the response and the reinforcement.
(d) Learning in the absence of changes in the perception or discriminations.

48 In Bandura's original experiments on aggression and observational learning, he found that the number of aggressive acts displayed was at its highest when observing
(a) a model act aggressively (b) a model act pleasantly
(c) a model do noting (d) All of the above

49 In Tolman's experiment, three groups of rats were taught to run a maze. The rats that were never shown food in the maze appeared not to have learned it. However, when food appeared they could find it just as quickly as rats that had always been shown food.
This demonstrates the effect of
(a) latent learning (b) observational learning
(c) operant conditioning (d) insight learning

50 The operationalised dependent variable in Tolman's experiment was
(a) the number of groups of rats
(b) whether rats were shown cheese originally
(c) the amount of electric shocks the rats were given
(d) the time it took the rats to solve the maze

51 The centrality of an attitude shows
(a) the attitudes resistance to change
(b) a person's negative or positive feelings
(c) the extent to which an attitude is part of a person's concept of self.
(d) the extent to which an attitude is related to a person's other attitudes

52 Which of the following is not true about attitudes and behaviour?
(a) Attitudes are infallible predictors of behaviour
(b) Nobody knows is there actually is a link
(c) Attitudes do not predict behaviours always
(d) Attitude may be directed towards an object

53 A way of measuring attitude is by using
(a) in-depth interviews
(b) semantic differential scales
(c) a lie detector
(d) observing people's behaviour

54 The ego-defensive function of an attitude
(a) helps a person to defend his self image.
(b) derives satisfaction form expressing central values.
(c) helps a person to adjust to his world.
(d) helps a person to organise his world.

55 If attitudes and behaviour are inconsistent, individuals will most likely
(a) change their behaviour
(b) change their attitude
(c) change either behaviour or attitude
(d) do nothing

56 The influential model of attitude change and formation of attitude is
(a) value elaboration model
(b) expectancy elaboration model
(c) elaboration likelihood model
(d) value likelihood model

57 Celebrity endorsements and objects that bring positive attitude of customer's towards a produced is classified as
(a) Peripheral cues (b) Value route
(c) Value cues (d) Central cues

58 The statement "discrimination is wrong" related to which component of attitude?
(a) Reactive (b) Behavioural
(c) Cognitive (d) Affective

59 Which component of attitude is the emotional or feeling component?
(a) Cognitive (b) Affective
(c) Evaluative (d) Behavioural

60 Which statement best describes the meaning of attitude?
(a) Attitude shows what one believes about something or someone.
(b) Attitude evaluates worth of a person, object or event or event.
(c) Attitude indicated the reaction of a person towards someone or something.
(d) Attitude measure the individual actions in varied situations.

61 Authority always flows from
(a) Superior to subordinate
(b) Subordinate to superior
(c) Both (a) and (b)
(d) None of the above

62 A common misconception about power is
(a) it is synonymous to authority
(b) it is sometimes is hidden form
(c) it is a visible phenomenon
(d) it may or may not formal

63 An employee receives orders from, and reports to only one supervisor is known as
(a) Unity of direction (b) Unity of command
(c) Line of authority (d) Centralisation

64 The power tactics frequently used either upwards or downwards is known as
(a) Coalitions (b) Sanctions
(c) Friendliness (d) Assertiveness

65 Why it is said that power exists even when you do not see it?
(a) Because people talk about it all the time.
(b) Because people like to think that someone is incharge.
(c) Because the powerful shape the needs of less powerful
(d) Because the less powerful simply concede to more powerful.

66 Power is a positive phenomenon. Why?
(a) It is how you get things done.
(b) It given mangers more control.
(c) It is a creative force that brings certain ways of thinking.
(d) It is a form of surveillance that increases effectiveness.

67 An individual's capacity to influence decisions is
(a) Control (b) Authority
(c) Power (d) Role

68 The power with a contextual power is
(a) profound knowledge about a field related to the job.
(b) being an influential member of a network.
(c) owner of important resources
(d) All of the above

69 Which source of power exists due to the personal characteristics of the power holder?
(a) Expert power (b) Legitimate power
(c) Reward power (d) Coercive power

70 The capacity to affect the behaviours of others is
(a) Power (b) Leadership
(c) Aggressiveness (d) Assertiveness

71 Who said the following, "A has power over B to the extent that he can get B to do something that B would not otherwise do"?
(a) Stephen Lukes (b) Jessery Pfeffer
(c) Robut Dahl (d) Niccolo Machiavelli

72 The power in an organisation form this list, lies with
(a) only workers
(b) only executives
(c) only management level
(d) executive, management and workers

73 Empowering workers is good for the organisation because
(a) they then work best
(b) they are better trained and productive
(c) they then make better decisions and satisfy consumer needs
(d) so that managers can have greater control

74 Which among the following is the basic source of stress?

(a) Environment
(b) Financial problems
(c) Relationship problems
(d) All of the above

75 Which among the following is a feature of negative stress?

(a) Motivation (b) Anxiety
(c) Excitement (d) None of these

76 Which of the following statements is true?

(a) Poor judgement is cognitive symptom of stress
(b) Agitation is cognitive symptom of stress
(c) Moodiness is emotional symptom of stress
(d) Irritability is physical symptom of stress

77 Which among the following is an individual strategy for dealing with stress?

(a) Learning techniques of relaxation
(b) Adopt time management skills
(c) Engaging in physical exercises
(d) All of the above

78 The management of stress is basically based on which theory?

(a) Behavioural
(b) Psychodynamic
(c) Cognitive
(d) Cognitive behavioural

79 A manger with good .... can make the work place more pleasant.

(a) knowledge (b) interpersonal skills
(c) communication (d) experience

80 Which among the following is not contributed to be improved by an organisation?

(a) Work efficiency (b) Communication
(c) Motivation (d) Interpersonal relations

81 Stereotyping affects which of the following greatly?

(a) Organisation management
(b) Interpersonal relations
(c) Organisation structure
(d) All of the above

82 Interpersonal communication at the workplace is also known as

(a) face to face public communication
(b) virtual reality
(c) mass communication
(d) dyadic communication

83 Which of Freud's parts of the personality is most likely a dictator?

(a) Id (b) Ego (c) Super ego (d) Ego ideal

84 In Freud's view of the personality, the devil would be seen as the

(a) conscience (b) id
(c) ego (d) super ego

85 Which of the following are included in the Gestalt principles of perceptual organisation?

1. Figure-ground proximity, continuity
2. Proximity, continuity, good form
3. Continuity, good form, closure
4. Good form, closure, facilitation

Select the correct answer using the codes given below

(a) 1 and 2 (b) 3 and 4
(c) 1, 2 and 3 (d) 2 and 3

86 Which one of the following pairs is correctly matched?

	Conditioning Process	Type of Conditioning
(a)	Reinforcing a spontaneously emitted response	Instrumental
(b)	Using a conditioned stimulus as an unconditioned one	Generalised
(c)	Reinforcing only one of the two simultaneously presented conditioning stimuli	Higher-order
(d)	Stimulus resembling the conditioned one eliciing the conditioned response	Differential

87 Which of the following pairs in correctly mached?

(a)	Cognitive map	Internal representation of an area
(b)	Latent learning	Remains hidden until reinforcement is provided
(c)	Rote learning	Learning by memeorisation or rules
(d)	All of the above	

88 Which of the following pairs is correctly matched?

(a)	Feedback	Information about the effect a response had
(b)	Knowledge of results	Increased feedback
(c)	Learning aids	Programmed instruction
(d)	All of the above	

89 Which of the following are the characteristic operant conditioning?

1. Stimulus-response association.
2. Law of contiguity in learning.
3. Law of effect.
4. Difference in UR an CR.

Select the correct answer using the codes given below

(a) Both 1 and 2 (b) Both 2 and 3
(c) 1, 3 and 4 (d) 2, 3 and 4

90 Which of the following are dependent variable conditioning experiment?

1. Latency of response 2. Rate of response
3. Amplitude of response 4. Direction of response

Select the correct answer using the codes given below

(a) Both 1 and 2 (b) Both 3 and 4
(c) 1, 2 and 3 (d) 2, 3 and 4

91 Consider the following statements regarding Thorndike's Law of Effect'.

1. It is only a case of law of exercise.
2. It emphasises only on situational reinforcers but does not refer to cognitive aspects of learning.
3. It cannot be applied in achievement-oriented learning.
4. It ignores, the functional effect of persons-environment interaction in learning.

Which of the statements given above is/are correct?

(a) Only 1 (b) 2, 3 and 4
(c) Both 2 and 3 (d) Both 3 and 4

92 Depending upon the task characteristic, there is a gradual transition form simple from of learning to the level of higher complex ones. These different forms are

1. Establishment of simple S-R relationships.
2. Acquiring motor and verbal skills.
3. Concept formation.
4. Problem-solving.

The correct order of learning sequence is

(a) 1, 4, 2, 3 (b) 1, 2, 3, 4
(c) 2, 4, 1, 3 (d) 2, 3, 4, 1

93 Consider the following statements about behavioural theories of learning focus on

1. stimulus and response units.
2. principle of contiguity.
3. comprehension of underlying principle.
4. organisation of stimuli.

Which of the statements statements given above are correct?

(a) Both 1 and 2 (b) Both 2 and 3
(c) Both 1 and 4 (d) Both 3 and 4

94 Teaching a rat, a very complicated response may involve the following steps.

1. Giving a closer and closer approximation for reward.
2. Rewarding simple behaviour that approximates the desired behaviour
3. Pairing a neutral stimulus with the unconditioned stimulus

The most effective sequence of these steps would be

(a) 2, 3, 1 (b) 2, 1, 3 (c) 3, 2, 1 (d) 3, 1, 2

95 Arrange the following theories in order of proposal

1. Classical Conditioning (Pavlov)
2. Social Development Theory (Vygtosky)
3. Stage Theory of Cognitive Development (Piaget)
4. Erikson's Stages of Development (Erikson)

Codes

(a) 2, 1, 3, 4 (b)1, 2, 3, 4 (c) 4, 3, 2, 1 (d) 3, 2, 4, 1

96 Arrange the following stages of child in order based on Erikson's theory of development

1. Industry *Vs* Inferiority 2. Autonomy *Vs* Shame
3. Basic Trust *Vs* Mistrust 4. Initiative *Vs* Guilt

Codes

(a) 2, 1, 3, 4 (b) 1, 2, 3, 4
(c) 4, 3, 2, 1 (d) 3, 2, 4, 1

97 Which of the following statements are true/false?

(i) Attitude is an opinion about someone, some situation or something.
(ii) Super-ego state develops at the age of 5.
(iii) Type B personality individuals are active, hard driving and competitive.
(iv) Type C personality are cooperative, unassertive and patient.

Codes

(a) (i) and (ii) are true, (iii) and (iv) are false
(b) (ii) and (iii) are true (i) and (iv) are false
(c) (i), (ii), (iii) are true and (iv) is false
(d) (i), (ii), (iv) are true and (iii) is false

98 Which of the the following statements are true/false?

(i) Skinner's model is a perfect model to understand animal behaviour.
(ii) Power is non-commutative.
(iii) Blindspot is a person who is unaware about himself but others know him well.
(iv) Open individual is known to other but not to self.

(a) (i) and (ii) are true, (iii) and (iv) are false
(b) (ii) and (iii) are true (i) and (iv) are false
(c) (i), (ii), (iii) are true and (iv) is false
(d) (i), (ii), (iv) are true and (iii) is false

99 Which of the following statements are true/false?

(i) Uender child ego state individuals think, behave and feel in the same manner as they used to think in their childhood.
(ii) Parent ego state is where the individual behave and think in response to an unconscious imitation or minicking how their parents would have acted.
(iii) Halo effect is having positive attitude towards an individual.
(iv) MBTI model is a personality assessment tool with 16 questions.

(a) (i) and (ii) are true, (iii) and (iv) are false
(b) (ii) and (iii) are true, (i) and (iv) are false
(c) (i), (ii), (iii) are true and (iv) is false
(d) (i), (ii), (iv) are true and (iii) is false

Directions (Q. Nos. 100-110) *In the question given below two statements labelled as Assertion (A) and Reason (R). In the context of the two statements, which one of following is correct?*

Codes

(a) Both (A) and (R) are true and (R) is the correct explanation of (A)
(b) Both (A) and (R) are true, but (R) is not the correct explanation of (A)
(c) (A) is true, but (R) is false
(d) (A) is false, but (R) is true

100 Assertion (A) Skinnerian radical behaviouralism no longer ciriticised or considered controveral since many new areas have since been researched.
Reason (R) Epstein (1991) carried forward Skinner radical behaviouralism and attempted to study the emergence of novel behaviours. He found the principles of multip controlling, stimulus autochaining and resurgence can explain creative behaviour.

101 Assertion (A) In classical conditioning, conditional stimulus should be immediately followed by unconditional stimulus, in instrumental conditional stimulus; in instrument conditioning the response, must be closely followed by reward.
Reason (R) Conditioning, both classical and instrumental, depends on reward.

102 Assertion (A) Human beings have the capacity for complex learning.
Reason (R) Second order conditioning follows the principle of associating a new stimulus with a natural or existing conditioned stimulus.

103 Assertion (A) People are sometimes more suscepitble to pesuasion when they are distracted by extraneous events.
Reason (R) Persuasion can be enhanced by messages that arouse strong emotions.

104 Assertion (A) Operants are emitted and not elicited.
Reason (R) The law of exercise asserts that an organism is more likely to do that task for which it has been given many more trials.

105 Assertion (A) Bandura found that children who had watched the film of an adult modeling aggressive behaviour played more aggressively then children, who had not seen the film.
Reason (R) The entire learning process appeared to take place the children's minds, without their performing any observable responses or receiving any noticeable rewards.

106 Assertion (A) Selection is part of the person-environment interaction.
Reason (R) One function of personality theory is to predict future behaviour.

107 Assertion (A) The definition of personality describes traits and mechanisms that are internal, enduring, and influence interactions with the environment.
Reason (R) A study that describes an individual life over time is an example of nomothetic research.

108 Assertion (A) A researcher who studies the self-concept probably falls most in the cognitive/experiential domain of knowledge.
Reason (R) When people fail to meet their aesthetic needs, they become sick.

109 Assertion (A) Most current personality research addresses ways, in which individuals and groups differ, not human universals.
Reason (R) Personality psychologists specialise in a particular domain, such as biological aspects of personality or how culture impacts personality.

110 Assertion (A) Personality research in often informed by personality theory.
Reason (R) Theory has several key purposes such as serves as a guide for researchers, organises known findings.

111 Match the following.

	List I		List II
A.	Gestalt psychology	1.	Muller-Lyer Illusion
B.	Arraw headed line and featherbedded line	2.	Linear motion
C.	The perception of the actual physical movement of object	3.	Whole is more then some of its part
D.	Melody	4.	Frequency of sound cauve

Codes

	A	B	C	D		A	B	C	D
(a)	2	1	4	3	(b)	1	2	3	4
(c)	3	1	2	4	(d)	1	3	4	2

112 Match the following.

	List I		List II
A.	Holway	1.	Psychophysical experiment
B.	Gilchrist	2.	Figure and round
C.	Edgar Rubin	3.	The complanar ratio hypothesis
D.	Weirtheimer	4.	Gestalt psychologist

Codes

	A	B	C	D		A	B	C	D
(a)	4	2	1	3	(b)	4	2	3	1
(c)	1	3	2	4	(d)	3	1	2	4

113 Match the following.

	List I		List II
A.	Scotopic vision	1.	Displacement of an object due to change in position of observer
B.	Induced movement	2.	Beauty is in the eye of the beholder
C.	Objective factors	3.	A right object
D.	Sensory information store	4.	Prepotency

Codes

	A	B	C	D		A	B	C	D
(a)	2	4	1	3	(b)	2	4	3	1
(c)	1	3	2	4	(d)	3	1	2	4

114 **Match the following.**

List I	List II
A. BF Skinner	1. Statistical learning theory
B. EL Thorndike	2. Systematic desensitisation
C. Estes	3. Transfer through common Elements
D. Wolpe	4. Operant conditioning

Codes

	A	B	C	D		A	B	C	D
(a)	3	4	2	1	(b)	4	3	1	2
(c)	4	3	2	1	(d)	3	4	1	2

115 **Match the following.**

List I	List II
A. CS and UCS are presented at the same time and continue till the coset of CR	1. Trace
B. CS terminates before the onset of UCS	2. Simultaneous
C. UCS precedes CS	3. Delayer
D. CS is presented first and overlaps the onset of UCS	4. Backward

Codes

	A	B	C	D		A	B	C	D
(a)	2	1	3	4	(b)	1	2	3	4
(c)	1	2	4	3	(d)	2	1	4	3

116 **Match the following.**

List I (Key phrases)	List II (Theorists)
A. Habit strength	1. E L Thorndike
B. Trial and error	2. I P Pavlov
C. Contiguity	3. C L Hull
D. Contingencies	4. B F Skinner

Codes

	A	B	C	D		A	B	C	D
(a)	3	1	2	4	(b)	1	3	2	4
(c)	3	1	4	2	(d)	1	3	4	2

117 **Match the following.**

List I (High Score Characteristic)	List II (Factor Ocean)
A. Creative, artistic, curious imaginative and non-conforming	1. Neuroticism
B. Organised, reliable neat and ambitious	2. Agreeableness (A)
C. Talkative, optimistic sociable and affectionate	3. Extraversion (E)
D. Goad natured, trusting and helpful	4. Conscientiousness (C)
E. Working, insecure ancious and temperamental	5. Openness (O)

Codes

	A	B	C	D	E		A	B	C	D	E
(a)	1	4	3	5	2	(b)	4	1	2	3	5
(c)	5	4	3	2	1	(d)	5	3	4	2	1

118 **Match the following.**

List I (Role)	List II (Players)
A. Intuitive thinkers	1. Manager
B. Intuitive feelers	2. Detectives
C. Sensation feelers	3. Pharmacists
D. Sensation thinkers	4. Engineers

Codes

	A	B	C	D		A	B	C	D
(a)	4	3	2	1	(b)	1	3	2	4
(c)	1	2	3	4	(d)	4	2	1	3

119 **Match the following.**

List I (Types of Power)	List II (Examples)
A. Coercive power	1. Legal
B. Legitimate power	2. Personal traits
C. Reward power	3. Ability
D. Referent power	4. Punishment

Codes

	A	B	C	D		A	B	C	D
(a)	1	3	4	2	(b)	4	2	1	3
(c)	4	1	3	2	(d)	4	3	2	1

120 **Match the following.**

List I (Concepts)	List II (Examples)
A. Group	1. Cognition
B. Theory of personality	2. Id
C. Perception	3. Strategic groups
D. Industrial groups	4. Conflicts

Codes

	A	B	C	D		A	B	C	D
(a)	4	2	1	3	(b)	1	2	3	4
(c)	4	3	2	1	(d)	3		2	4

121 **Match the items of List I with the items of List II and choose the correct answer from the code given below.**

List I (Type of Personality)	List II (Suitability to Job)
A. Sensation-thinking personality	1. Fit for human resource development job
B. Intuition-thinking personality	2. Fit for production and management position
C. Sensation-feeling personality	3. Fit for research and development position
D. Intuition-feeling personality	4. Fit for science and techonology field

Codes

	A	B	C	D		A	B	C	D
(a)	2	4	3	1	(b)	4	3	2	1
(c)	2	3	4	1	(d)	2	3	1	4

122 Match the below mentioned aspects with their main behavioural disciplines.

List I (Aspects)	List II (Behavioural discipline)
A. Leadership and stress management	1. Psychology
B. Group conflict management	2. Anthropology
C. Cross-cultural analysis	3. Sociology and Psychology
D. Power	4. Political Science

Codes

	A	B	C	D		A	B	C	D
(a)	4	1	2	3	(b)	2	3	1	4
(c)	1	4	2	3	(d)	4	2	3	1

123 Match the items of List I with those of List II and suggest the correct code.

List I (Behavioural Science)	List II (Contribution)
A. Anthropology	1. Attitude change
B. Psychology	2. Attitude measurement
C. Social psychology	3. Conflict
D. Sociology	4. Organisational culture

Codes

	A	B	C	D		A	B	C	D
(a)	1	2	3	4	(b)	4	2	1	3
(c)	4	2	3	1	(d)	2	4	3	1

Directions (Q. Nos. 124-128) *Read the following passage and answer the questions that follow.*

We can understand personality characteristics as types of traits. The earliest theory of personality classified people into types according to their predominant humour of body fluid. Today, most psychologists conceive of personality difference as being represented by degee, not kind. Personality traits are the factors that underlie patterns of behaviour. Presumably, these factors are biological in nature, although they may be the products of learning as well as heredity. The search for core personality traits began with Allport, who studied how everyday words are used to describe personality characteristics. Although, he never isolated a core set of traits, his work inspired others to continue the search for such traits.

Several researchers developed their theories of personality though factor anlysis, a statistical method of reducing a large amount of data to two or three themes or ideas (called factors). Cattell's analysis indicated the existence of in personality factors; Eynesck's research suggested that personality is determined by three dimensions extraversion (versus introversion), neuroticism (versus emotional stability) and psychoticism (versus self-control). Mc Crae and Costa's five-factor model, based on an analysis of words used to describe people's behavioural traits, included extraversion, neuroticism, agreeableness, openness and conscientiousness. There is strong cross-cultural agreement on the first three factors, but not on the fifth.

124 Which of the following researchers proposed biological substrates for his traits?

(a) Cattell (b) Wiggins (c) Eysenck (d) Leary

125 Which of the following of Cattell's traits is most similar to extraversion?

(a) Interpersonal warmth (b) Intelligence
(c) Emotional stability (d) Conformity

126 The five factor model is based on

(a) The lexical approach (b) the statistical approach
(c) factor analysis (d) All of these

127 According to Eysenck, introvert and extraverts are different in many respects. The most important difference is

(a) psychological health *vs* psychological disturbance
(b) subjectivity *vs* objectivity
(c) their way of viewing the world
(d) level of cortical arousal

128 The theories of Cattell and Eysenck rate

(a) high on biological determinants of personality
(b) high on teleology
(c) low on their ability to generate research
(d) high on free will *vs* determinism conformity

PREVIOUS YEARS' QUESTIONS

2018

1 The behaviour of a person under the Adult ego state under Transactional Analysis is

(a) Evaluative and judgemental
(b) Protective and critical
(c) Impulsive and emotional
(d) Rational and logical

2 Who among the following is associated with the idea that "The human personality progresses along a continuum from immaturity as an infant to maturity as an adult?"

(a) Sigmund Freud
(b) Erik Erikson
(c) Chris Argyris
(d) Daniel Levinson

3 Which of the following is/are not team building approaches?

(i) Positive Reinforcement
(ii) Johari Window
(iii) Behaviour Modification
(iv) Domain Reshuffling

Codes

(a) (i) and (iii) (b) (ii) and (iii)
(c) (iii) and (iv) (d) (i) and (iv)

4 Hans Selye's (1956) "General Adaptation Syndrome (GAS)" has been widely held as a comprehensive model to explain the stress phenomenon. This three stage model states that when an organism is confronted with a threat, the general physiological response occurs in three stages.

Which of the following stage(s) is not a part of GAS model?

(a) Intrapsychic Disorder Stage
(b) Alarm Stage
(c) Exhaustion Stage
(d) Resistance Stage

5 Which of the following statements are true/false?

(i) Organisation Behaviour (OB) has been influenced by the contingency approach and the interactional approach.
(ii) Hawthorne studies led to human relations movement.
(iii) Human relations movement's main emphasis was an economic needs *i.e.* people were more motivated by economic needs rather than social needs.
(iv) McGregor and Maslow were not the main proponents and figure heads of the human relations movement.

Codes

(a) (i), (ii) and (iii) are true, (iv) is false
(b) (iii) and (iv) are true, (i) and (ii) are false
(c) (ii) and (iv) are true, (i) and (iii) are false
(d) (i) and (ii) are true, (iii) and (iv) are false

6 Which of the following statements regarding stress related factors is/are true and false?

(i) Burnout Stress Syndrome (BOSS) is a debilirating psychological condition brought about by unrelieved work stress.
(ii) 'Good' and 'bad' stresses are also referred to as 'Distress' and 'Eustress' respectively.
(iii) It is natural and healthy to maintain optimal level of stress.
(iv) Rustout Stress Syndrome (ROSS) is indicative of stress overload.
(v) Anxiety is a state of emotional tension characterised by Apprehension, fearfulness, and psychic pain.

Codes

(a) (i), (ii) and (iv) are true, (iii) and (v) are false
(b) (ii), (iii) and (iv) are true, (i) and (v) are false
(c) (i), (iii) and (v) are true, (ii) and (iv) are false
(d) (ii), (iv) and (v) are true, (i) and (iii) are false

2017

7 Work stress is a chronic aliment caused by conditions that negatively affect one's performance and/or overall well being of the body and mind. Employers, these days, are concerned about managing stress.

Which of the following are not the typical symptoms of job related stress?

1. Insomnia
2. Lack of concentration
3. Anxiety, depression
4. Job insecurity
5. Extreme anger and mood swings
6. Family conflicts
7. Strict deadlines
8. Frustration

Codes

(a) 2 and 8 (b) 4 and 6
(c) 4 and 7 (d) 7 and 8

8 'Alarm Reaction', 'Stage of Resistance' and 'Stage of Exhaustion' are the stages of which of the following syndromes?

(a) Buggy-whip Syndrome
(b) Dissociative Identity Disorder Syndrome
(c) General Adaptation Syndrome
(d) Amoeba Syndrome

9 **In transactional analysis, if the response is by the same ego state as through which the message was received, the transaction is called**
(a) crossed transaction
(b) complementary transaction
(c) ulterior transaction
(d) feed-forward transaction

10 **"Healthy people show the behaviour of maturity, while unhealthy people tend to demonstrate child like immature behaviour". Who among the following behavioural scientists said this?**
(a) John Berry
(b) Blake and Mouton
(c) FW Tyalor
(d) Chris Argyris

11 **MBTI is the most widely used instrument for personality analysis. Which of the following statements about MBTI is/are true and false?**
(i) MBTI has 108 items.
(ii) Sixteen personality types are generated by the instrument.
(iii) MBTI has 100 items.
(iv) Sixteen personality types are based on a combination of four basic elements of psyche.
(v) MBTI was developed by a father-daughter team.
(vi) MBTI was developed by a mother-daughter team.

Codes
(a) (i), (iv) and (v) are true
(b) (ii), (iii), (iv) and (vi) are true
(c) (iii), (iv) and (v) are true
(d) (i), (ii), (v) and (vi) are true

12 **FIRO-B was developed by William Schutz in late 950s, and is based on the theory of interpersonal relations. FIRO-B stands for**
(a) Fundamental Interpersonal Response in Organisations-Behaviour
(b) Feelings in Interpersonal Relations Openness-Behaviour
(c) Fellow Interpersonal Response in Organisation-Behaviour
(d) Fundamental Interpersonal Relations Orientation-Behaviour

13 **Which of the following statements relating to 'role' is/are true and false?**
(i) The system of various roles that the individual carries and performs is 'role set'.
(ii) The system of various roles of which an individuals role is a part in 'role space'.
(iii) Self role integration, proactivity, creativity and conformation are ingredients of the role making dimension of role efficacy.
(iv) Role stress is caused by both role space conflict and role set conflict.

Codes
(a) (i) and (iii) are true, (ii) and (iv) are false
(b) (i) and (ii) are true, (iii) and (iv) are false
(c) (i) and (ii) are false, (iii) and (iv) are true
(d) (i) and (iv) are true, (ii) and (iii) are false

14 **Who has advanced 'coping styles' for role stress combining avoidance and approach to role stress with laws of control of internality and externality?**
(a) Lorsch and Lawrence
(b) Litwin and Stringer
(c) Udai Pareek
(d) TV Rao

15 **Match the following effects List I with their meanings given in List II.**

List I	List II
A. Placebo effect	1. Self fulfilled prophecy
B. Hawthorne effect	2. Rating error due to attribution to single trait
C. Pygmallion effect	3. Belief system
D. Halo effect	4. Controlled behaviour under observation

Codes

	A	B	C	D		A	B	C	D
(a)	3	4	1	2	(b)	1	2	3	4
(c)	4	3	2	1	(d)	3	4	2	1

2016

16 **Consider the following.**
1. Structural Analysis 2. Interaction Analysis
3. Life position Analysis 4. Environmental Analysis
5. Dispositional Analysis
6. Coping Behaviour Analysis

Which among the above are the components of Dr. Eric Berne's Transactional Analysis Theory?
(a) 3, 4 and 5
(b) 1, 3 and 5
(c) 1, 2 and 3
(d) 2, 3 and 5

17 **Which of the following statements about the awareness positions described below in respect of Johari Window Model of Interpersonal process are correct?**
(i) Shared and mutually held, public information, feelings, motives etc
(ii) Hidden information, motives, feelings etc. known only to the self
(iii) Unsuspected information, feelings, reactions, etc. known only to other parties
(iv) Undiscovered potentials and creative reservoir known neither to the self nor to others

Codes
(a) (i), (ii), (iii), (iv) refers to Blindspot, Dark, Closed and Arena respectively
(b) (i), (ii), (iii), (iv) refers to Arena, Closed, Blindspot and Dark respectively
(c) (i), (ii), (iii), (iv) refers to Arena, Blindspot, Dark and Closed respectively
(d) (i), (ii), (iii), (iv) refers to Blindspot, Arena, Dark and Closed respectively

2015

18 Match the following.

List I (Stress related terms)	List II (Their descriptions)
A. Coping behaviour	1. The resultant feeling caused by a sense of privation, deprivation or conflict in relation to the goal directed activities.
B. Deprivation	2. Dealing with situations of privation, deprivation, frustration and stress.
C. Frustration	3. Blocking or or interfering with goal directed activities.
D. Glow-up	4. Feeling of challenge, high job satisfaction, creativity effectiveness and better adjustment to work and life.

Codes

	A	B	C	D
(a)	2	3	1	4
(b)	3	2	4	1
(c)	1	2	3	4
(d)	4	3	2	1

19 Which of the following statements relating to 'Role Systems' is not correct?

(a) In a role set map, the occupant's role will be in the centre and all other roles in the system can be located at various points of the map
(b) The role space map of an individual can be drawn by locating the self in the centre and the various roles at varying distances from the self
(c) As the concept of the role is central to the organisation, so the concept of the self is central to the several roles of a person
(d) The role set is a pattern of inter-relationship through the distance between a role and the self which indicates the extent to which the role is integrated with the self.

20 Which of the following is/are the examples of 'Cognitive biases'?

1. Cognitive dissonance
2. Escalation of commitment
3. Ego-defence
4. Projection

Select the correct answer using the codes given below

(a) 2 and 3
(b) 1 and 4
(c) 1, 2 and 3
(d) 1, 2, 3 and 4

21 Read the statements and choose the correct answer.

I. Sigmund Freud proposed the concept of the 'structure of psyche' in terms of id, ego and superego.
II. The 'Id' does not care about reality, about the needs of an one else, only its own satisfaction.

Codes

(a) Both the statements are true
(b) Both the statements are false
(c) Statement I is true and statement II is false
(d) Statement II is true and statement I is false

22 Transactional managerial styles refer to four life positions. These life positions can be used to understand one's style of working with others. Match the following.

List I (Four life positions)	List II (Parent Regulating/Nurturing ego states)
A. I am not ok, you are not ok	1. Prescriptive/Patronising
B. I am ok, you are not ok	2. Normative/Supportive
C. I am ok, you are ok	3. Indifferent/Ingratiating
D. I am not ok, you are ok	4. Traditional/Overindulgent

Codes

	A	B	C	D
(a)	4	1	2	3
(b)	1	3	2	4
(c)	3	2	1	4
(d)	2	1	3	4

2014

23 Which of the following stages form part of General Adaptation Syndrome propounded by Hans Selye?

1. Alarm Reaction
2. Dissociative Identity Disorder
3. Stage of Exhaustion
4. Stage of Resistance

Select the correct answer using the codes given below

(a) 1, 2 and 3
(b) 1, 2 and 4
(c) 1, 3 and 4
(d) 2, 3 and 4

24 Match the following.

List I	List II
A. Cognitive bias in which one trait of a person influences overall judgement about him	1. Jargon
B. Meaningless talk or writing familiar only to a group or a profession	2. Halo effect
C. Converting the message into symbols by sender	3. Encoding
D. Manipulating information to make it appear favourable to receiver	4. Filtering

Codes

	A	B	C	D
(a)	2	1	4	3
(b)	2	4	3	1
(c)	2	1	3	4
(d)	2	3	1	4

25 The psycho-physical disposition of an individual is referred to as

(a) attitude
(b) aptitude
(c) personality
(d) perception

26 **Consider the following statements.**

1. **Monotony arises out of repetitive work.**
2. **Fatigue arises out of continuous work.**
3. **Positive stress is called eustress and negative stress is called as distress.**
4. **Morale differs from job satisfaction on the strength of it being a group behaviour.**

Which of the statements given above are correct?

(a) 1 and 2 (b) 1, 2, 3 and 4
(c) 1, 2 and 4 (d) 2, 3 and 4

27 **The term 'blind spot' in the Johari Window refers to**

(a) the 'public self' which is known to other as well as to oneself.
(b) the 'self' which is known to others, but not to oneself
(c) the 'self' which is neither known to others nor to oneself
(d) the motives, feelings etc. which are known to oneself

28 **Who developed the 'Managerial Grid' on the basis of Ohio State Study?**

(a) Rensis Likert
(b) Lewin, Lippitt and White
(c) Robert Blake and Jane S Mouton
(d) Victor Vroom and Phillip Yelton

29 **Who gave the concept of 'Life-Positions' in the context of transactional analysis?**

(a) Eric Berne
(b) Thomas A Harris
(c) Joseph Lufth and Harry Inghams
(d) Jay Galbraith

30 **When people give 'cause and effect explanation' to their behaviour, it is called**

(a) closure (b) stereotyping
(c) attribution (d) inference

ANSWERS

Exam Based Questions

Q	Ans	Q	Ans	Q	Ans	Q	Ans	Q	Ans	Q	Ans	Q	Ans	Q	Ans	Q	Ans	Q	Ans
1	(b)	2	(d)	3	(d)	4	(d)	5	(b)	6	(a)	7	(c)	8	(a)	9	(c)	10	(c)
11	(b)	12	(c)	13	(d)	14	(b)	15	(b)	16	(d)	17	(d)	18	(c)	19	(c)	20	(c)
21	(a)	22	(a)	23	(d)	24	(b)	25	(d)	26	(d)	27	(d)	28	(b)	29	(c)	30	(c)
31	(c)	32	(c)	33	(d)	34	(c)	35	(d)	36	(c)	37	(c)	38	(d)	39	(d)	40	(d)
41	(c)	42	(c)	43	(b)	44	(c)	45	(c)	46	(b)	47	(c)	48	(a)	49	(a)	50	(d)
51	(c)	52	(a)	53	(b)	54	(a)	55	(c)	56	(c)	57	(a)	58	(c)	59	(b)	60	(a)
61	(c)	62	(a)	63	(b)	64	(b)	65	(c)	66	(c)	67	(c)	68	(d)	69	(a)	70	(a)
71	(c)	72	(d)	73	(c)	74	(d)	75	(b)	76	(c)	77	(d)	78	(d)	79	(b)	80	(d)
81	(b)	82	(d)	83	(b)	84	(b)	85	(c)	86	(a)	87	(d)	88	(d)	89	(d)	90	(c)
91	(b)	92	(b)	93	(a)	94	(c)	95	(b)	96	(d)	97	(d)	98	(c)	99	(a)	100	(a)
101	(b)	102	(b)	103	(b)	104	(b)	105	(a)	106	(b)	107	(c)	108	(b)	109	(a)	110	(a)
111	(c)	112	(c)	113	(b)	114	(c)	115	(d)	116	(a)	117	(c)	118	(c)	119	(c)	120	(a)
121	(c)	122	(b)	123	(b)	124	(c)	125	(a)	126	(d)	127	(d)	128	(a)				

Previous Years' Questions

Q	Ans	Q	Ans	Q	Ans	Q	Ans	Q	Ans	Q	Ans	Q	Ans	Q	Ans	Q	Ans	Q	Ans
1	(d)	2	(c)	3	(d)	4	(a)	5	(d)	6	(c)	7	(c)	8	(c)	9	(b)	10	(d)
11	(b)	12	(d)	13	(c)	14	(c)	15	(a)	16	(c)	17	(b)	18	(a)	19	(d)	20	(d)
21	(a)	22	(a)	23	(c)	24	(c)	25	(c)	26	(b)	27	(b)	28	(c)	29	(a)	30	(c)

UNIT 5

Industrial Relations

Industrial relations have become one of the most delicate and complex problems of the modern industrial society and have played a crucial role in the emergence of this complex phenomena of 'Industrial Revolution'. It is characterised by rapid changes, industrial unrest and conflicting ideologies in the national and international spheres.

Concept of Industrial Relations

Industrial relations mean relationships that emerge out of day-to-day working and association of labour and management.

The pre-industrial revolution period was characterised by a simple process of manufacturing, involved small scale investments, had local markets and small number of persons employed. The population of world was less, industries were less, issues were less, therefore, the problems were less.

All this led to a close proximity between the managers and the labourers. Due to personal and direct relationship between the employer and the employee it was easier to secure cooperation of the latter. Any grievance or misunderstanding on the part of either party could be promptly resolved. Also, there was no interference by the state in the economic activities of the people. Under such a set up, industrial relations were simple, direct and personal.

The situations underwent a marked change with the coming of industrial revolution. Size of the business increased leading to investment of enormous financial and human resources. There emerged a new class of professional managers causing rift between ownership and management and relations between the employer and the employee became bitter and gradually antagonistic. Therefore, there was a need of new set up which required unbiased, neutral, rational and analytical approach to satisfy everybody's needs.

In this Chapter

Gone are the days when workers were hired and fired as the principle of demand and supply governed industrial relations. The employer was in commanding position and the bonded labour had to face the tortures. Today industry is not a venture of employers alone but employees also take part actively at all levels in management.

The term 'Industrial Relations' comprises of two terms, 'Industry' and 'Relations'. 'Industry' refers to "any productive activity in which an individual (or a group of individuals) is (are) engaged." By 'relations' we mean "the relationships that exist within the industry between the employer and his workmen."

It explain the relationship between employees and management which stem directly or indirectly from union-employer relationship.

Industrial relations involve the study and practice of collective bargaining, trade unionism and labour-management relations, while human resource management is a separate, largely distinct field that deals with non-union employment relationships and the personnel practices and policies of employers.

According to **Dale Yoder**, "Industrial relations is a relationship between management and employees or among employees and their organisations, that characterise and grow out of employment."

According to **RA Lester**, "Industrial relations involve attempts to have workable solutions between conflicting objectives and values, between incentive and economic security, between industrial democracy and discipline, between authority and freedom and between bargaining and cooperation."

According to **The ILO**, "Industrial relations deal with either the relationships between the state and the employers' and workers organisation or the relation between the occupational organisations themselves."

According to **Prof Dunlop**, "Industrial relations may be defined as the complex of inter-relations among workers, managers and government."

According to **Allan Flanders**, "The subject of industrial relations deals with certain regulated or institutionalised relationship in industry."

In the broad sense, industrial relations cover all such relationships that a business enterprise maintains with various sections of the society such as workers, state, customers and public who come into its contact.

In the narrow sense, it refers to all types of relationships between employer and employees, trade union and management, works and union and between workers and workers. It also includes all sorts of relationships at both formal and informal levels in the organisation.

Industrial relations, thus, include both 'industrial relations' and 'collective relations' as well as the role of the state in regulating these relations.

Such a relationship is therefore complex and multi-dimensional on economic, social, psychological, ethical, occupational, political and legal levels.

Evolution of Industrial Relations

Industrial relations have its roots in the industrial revolution which created the modern employment relationship by spawning free labour markets and large scale industrial organisations with thousands of wage workers.

Intellectually, industrial relations started emerging at the end of the 19th century as a middle ground between classical economics and Marxism, with Sidney Webb and Beatrice Webb's Industrial Democracy (1897) being the key intellectual work in the same.

Industrial relations were founded by **John R Commons** when he created the first academic industrial relations programme at the University of Wisconsin in 1920.

They were formed with a strong problem-solving orientation that rejected both the classical economists' laissez-faire solutions to labour problems and the Marxist solution of class revolution.

It is this approach that underlies the New Deal Legislations in the United States, such as the National Labour Relations Act and the Fair Labour Standards Act.

After India attained independence, there was an enactment of the Industrial Disputes Act, 1947 which provided the permanent machinery for the settlement of industrial disputes but also a system to make the awards binding and legally enforceable.

The Indian Labour Conference (ILC), a tripartite body to solve IR problems in India was also set up in the post independence period.

The major development in IR in the post independence period was the change in the government's attitude towards labour and their problems.

To handle all kinds of industrial strife, in 1981 the government issued an ordinance to ban strikes.

A new law, called the Essential Services Maintenance Act (ESMA) was also enacted, which annoyed the trade union and Baharat Band was observed as its result.

Industrial Relations in Changing Scenario

Indian industrial relations need to widen its horizon to concern itself with the larger social and national interests. The system has to curb its pre-occupation with wages, allowances and bonus.

By many accounts, industrial relations today is in crisis. In academia, its traditional positions are threatened on one side by the dominance of mainstream economics and organisational behaviour and on the other by post-modernism.

In policy making circles, the industrial relations emphasise on institutional intervention which is trumped by a neoliberal emphasise on the laissez-faire promotion of free markets. Trade unions are marginalised and kept outside the mainstream of business.

In practice, labour unions are declining and fewer companies have industrial relations functions. The number of academic programmes in industrial relations is therefore shrinking and scholars are leaving the field for other areas, especially human resource management and organisational behaviour. The strikes are losing their cutting edge and collective bargaining is being replaced by individual bargaining.

Some of the major highlights of contemporary IR are

- The institution of trade union is getting weak. In the modern sectors like IT, there are hardly any unions.
- The institution of collective bargaining has been decentralised and replaced by unit bargaining.
- Disinvestment/Privatisation and voluntary retirement schemes are almost accepted facts of industrial relations.
- Compensation patterns of time rate/piece rate wages have been replaced by performance based wages.
- Nature of jobs have been changed depending upon the mind sets of employees. Employee is allured by challenging jobs instead of secure jobs.
- Government's perspective has also changed. The establishment of 'Special Economic Zones' (SEZs) show the attitude of the government towards the emerging business scenario. In a nutshell, the government is aligning its labour policies with business imperatives.
- The attitude of judiciary is also changing; they are also sending clear messages through their awards to the unions that they mean business.

Indian industrial relation is changing and witnessing the emergence of new forces. It is the need of the hour to conduct new researches and come out with new solutions to all these issues.

Scope of Industrial Relations

The scope of industrial relations can be understood through following points

Development of Healthy Labour Management Relations To develop harmonious relationship between labour and management, it is necessary to have the existence of strong, well organised, democratic and responsible trade unions and associations which will lead to job security of employees, increased workers' participation in management, effective communication between them.

Maintenance of Industrial Peace To get rid of industrial strife and attain peace, it is necessary to set up machinery for the prevention and settlement of industrial disputes and to create implementation cell and evaluation committees which have the power to take effective measures in case of violation of norms and rules of trade unions as well as government.

Development of Industrial Democracy The term industrial democracy was first used by **Sidney** and **Beatrice Webb** in their book 'Industrial Democracy' in 1920, which was used to establish a system of worker's rights of consultation, in particular the right of collective bargaining.

To attain this, it is necessary to establish the Shop Councils and Joint Management Councils which will aim at improving the working and living conditions of employee, improving productivity, encourage suggestions from employees, assisting the administration of laws and agreement facilitating communication, creating a sense of belonging among employees.

Features of Industrial Relations

- Industrial relations are born out of employment relationship in an individual setting. Without the existence of two parties, *i.e.* labour and management, this relationship cannot exist. It is the industry which provides the environment for industrial relations.
- Industrial relations are characterised by both conflict and cooperation, so the focus of industrial relations is on the study of the attitudes, relationships, practices and procedures developed by the contending parties to resolve and minimise conflicts.
- In any industry, labour and management do not operate in isolation but in consonance with vital environmental issues like technology of the workplace, country's social, economical and political situation, nation's labour policy, attitude of trade unions, workers and employees.
- Industrial relations also comprises the procedures and practices required to elect the desired cooperative outcome from the labour as well as management.
- Industrial relations also involve the study of rules, regulations, laws, agreements, customs and traditions.

Significance of Industrial Relations

Maintenance of harmonious industrials relations is of vital importance for the survival and growth of the industrial enterprise. Good industrial relations result in increased efficiency and hence prosperity, reduced turnover and other tangible benefits to the organisation.

The significance of industrial relations can be summarised as below

Establishing Cordial Relationship in Industry Industrial relations mean settling employees' problems through collective bargaining, mutual cooperation and mutual agreement amongst the parties, *i.e.* management and employees' unions.

This helps in establishing industrial democracy in the organisation which motivates them to contribute their best to the growth and prosperity of the organisation.

Contributing to Higher Efficiency and Higher Productivity Good industrial relations lead to increased efficiency, hence higher productivity and income. This will result in economic development of the country.

Building Effective Organisational Culture Good industrial relations built in mutual cooperation and common agreed approaches motivate one to contribute one's best, resulting in higher productivity and hence income, giving more job satisfaction and boosting the morale of the workers.

Creating Group Dynamics and Synergy Good and harmonious industrial relations create a sense of belongingness and group cohesiveness among workers, and also a congenial environment resulting in less industrial unrest, grievances and disputes. This will ensure optimum use of resources, both human and materials, eliminating all types of wastage.

Discouraging the Unfair Practices of Management Industrial relations involve setting up machinery to solve problems confronted by management and employees through mutual agreement to which both these parties are bound. This results in banning of the unfair practices being used by employers or trade unions.

Promoting the Measures of Labour Welfare and Safety Industrial relations necessitate passing of certain labour laws to protect and promote the welfare of labour and safeguard interests of all the parties against unfair means or practices.

Being Instrumental to Change Good industrial relations help in improvement of cooperation, team work, performance and productivity and hence in taking full advantages of modern inventions, innovations and other scientific and technological advances. It helps the work force to adjust themselves to change easily and quickly.

Approaches to Industrial Relations

The different approaches to industrial relations are described below

1. Psychological Approach

The psychologists are of the view that industrial relations problems are deeply rooted in the perception and attitude of participants. According to psychologists, problems of industrial relations have their origin in the perceptions of the management, unions, rank and file workers. Everybody looks from their point of view.

These perceptions may be the perceptions of persons, of situations or of issues involved in the conflict. The perceptions of situations and issues differ because the same position may appear entirely different to different parties.

Mason Harie studied the behaviour of two different groups, 'Union Leaders' and 'Executives' through Thematic Application Test. Both the groups came out with entirely different interpretations of the same photograph.

The perceptions of unions and of the management of the same issues may be widely different, hence clashes may arise between the two parties. Clashes between these two groups is natural, obvious and can never be finished but efforts can be made to dilute them.

The reasons of strained industrial relations between the employers and the employees can be understood by studying differences in the perception of issues, situations and persons between the management groups and labour groups.

The organisational behaviour of inter-groups of management and workers is of crucial importance in the pattern of industrial relations. The group dynamics between the two conflicting groups in industrial relations tend to shape the behavioural pattern.

2. Sociological Approach

Every organisation is formed from people and an industry is a social world in miniature. The management goals, workers' attitude, perception of change in industry, are all in turn decided by broad social factors like the culture of the institutions, customs, structural changes, status symbols, rationality, acceptance or resistance to change, tolerance etc. Industry is, thus inseparable from the society in which it functions.

Though the main function of an industry is economic, its social consequences are also important such as urbanisation, social mobility, housing and transport problem in industrial areas, disintegration of family structure, stress and strain etc.

Sociological factors largely includes factors like value system, customs, norms, symbols, attitudes and perception of both labour and management.

As industries develop, a new industrial-cum-social pattern emerges, which provides general new relationships, institutions and behavioural pattern and new techniques of handling human resources. These do influence the development of industrial relations.

3. Human Relations Approach

The human relations school founded by **Elton Mayo** offers a coherent view of the nature of industrial conflict and harmony. Human resources are human beings. They want freedom of speech, of thought, of expression, of movement etc.

When employers treat them as inanimate objects, encroach on their expectations, conflicts and tensions arise. Human relations approach highlights the ways to improve moral, efficiency and job satisfaction.

In fact, major problems in industrial relations arise out of tension which is created because of the employer's pressures and worker's reactions, protests and resistance to these pressures through protective mechanisms in the form of workers' organisation, associations and trade unions.

Therefore, the management must realise that efforts are made to set the situation right. Services of specialists in Behavioural Sciences (namely psychologists, industrial engineers, human relations expert and personnel managers) are used to deal with such related problems. Assistance is also taken from economists, anthropologists, psychiatrists, pedagogists etc.

In resolving conflicts, understanding of human behaviour of both individual and group is a prerequisite for the employers.

Conflicts cannot be resolved unless the management learns and understands what are the basic needs of men and how they can be motivated to work effectively.

It has now been proved and recognised that much can be gained from the managers and the workers, if they understand and apply the techniques of human relations to industrial relations.

The workers are likely to attain greater job satisfaction, develop greater involvement in their work and achieve a measure of identification of their objectives with the objectives of the organisation.

This all will definitely lead to higher productivity, higher efficiency and higher effectiveness.

4. Gandhian Approach

Gandhi's approach believes that many of the evils of the modern world have come because of wrong systems not becasue of wrong individuals.

Gandhiji believed in non-violence and said, "If communism comes without any violence it would be welcomed." He gave a new perspective to protests and strikes.

He also emphasised that workmen should be regarded as equals with the shareholders and they should have therefore, every right to possess an accurate knowledge of the transaction of the mills.

He advocated voluntary arbitration and mutual settlement of disputes.

5. Socio-Ethical Approach

This approach holds that good industrial relations can be only maintained when both the labour and management realise their moral responsibility, understand each other's problems and cooperate with each other. It is not very widely accepted approach.

6. System Approach

(Actors, Context and Ideology)

It was developed by **John Dunlop** who defined industrial relations system as the one comprising of certain actors, certain contexts, an ideology which binds the industrial relations system together and a body of rules created to govern the actors at the workplace and work community.

There are three sets of independent variables the 'actors', the 'contexts' and the 'ideology' of the system. This system of industrial relations is applicable at the plant or enterprise level, national level, in totality of the economic development.

Each of them has been explained below

Actors These are the participants of the system and they include the employees/workers, employers/management and the government or specialised agencies for enactment and implementation of laws, rules and policies. Of this system, the first two had an important role to play and the third one has a role to play only in the special cases.

Context It is basically the environment in which the actors operate. It is defined in terms of technology, labor and product markets and the distribution of power. It also includes the budget in which an organisation functions.

Ideology It defines the philosophy, view-points and sentiments of the involved actors. The actors need to have a common ideology in order to arrive at a common solution. Each actor in the system will have a distinct ideology that needs to be brought in sync with the ideology of the system.

These ideologies need to be sufficiently compatible and consistent so as to permit a common set of ideas and an acceptable role for each actor.

Models and Theoretical Framework in Industrial Relations

Unitary Theory

This theory contemplates that the organisation works as a single unit. All the stakeholders work towards one common goal of the organisational development and betterment. Individual's needs take a back-seat in front of the organisational needs and goals.

In case, the stakeholders and organisational goals do not converge, it is most likely due to a poor management. In this type of approach, conflicts and strikes are viewed as destructive as these have a direct impact on the productivity and profitability of the organisation.

Pluralist Perspective

This perspective is based on the fact that each organisation is made up of management, union, and employee sub-groups. Each of them have their own bargaining powers. Trade unions play an important role in maintaining balance between the employer and employees.

According to this approach, conflicts cannot be completely done away and mediation is the key to resolve them. It also propagates that conflict is a key component for innovation and company growth. Management needs to coordinate activities among the employees instead of ordering them to comply with strict rules and regulations. All the stakeholders need to work together in order to achieve their individual as well as organisational goals.

Marxist/Radical Perspective

This perspective states that conflict among workers and leaders is the result of the capitalistic nature of society and industry. This is because the workers view the management as the leaders who are just concerned about their profits and they view themselves as the means to achieve those profits.

This mindset leads to a clash between the two parties. Conflict is therefore seen as inevitable and trade unions are a natural response of workers to their exploitation by capital. This conflict can only be resolved when the capitalistic nature of the society makes a shift to the socialistic nature.

Industrial Relations System

An industrial relations system is an integrate system of relationships between employers and employees and employers which are managed by the means of conflict and cooperation. It can also be understood as the laws dealing with the arrangements that are made between workers and employers and these laws are developed by governments.

A sound industrial relations system is the one in which relationships between management and employees (and their representatives) on the one hand and the state on the other are more harmonious and cooperative than conflicts and creates an environment conducive to economic efficiency.

Main Parts of Industrial Relations System

There are three main parties which are directly involved in industrial relations. *These are as follows*

Employers and their Organisation

Employers possess certain rights *vis-a-vis* labours. The employees are a very important variable in industrial relations. Both look at the same point differently as their interests also clash many a times.

They consider that they have provided employment to workers and therefore have the right to regulate their behaviour for getting high productivity from them.

Employees and their Organisation

Howsoever capable or rich an employer is, one needs the cooperation of employees to run the business.

The employees are very important variable in industrial relations. Workers also have right to say in business as it is their effort which makes any business profitable.

They want to exchange views with management and voice their grievances. They also want to share decision-making powers of management. No doubt, it has proved to be quite useful to get opinions from their side.

Workers generally unite to form unions against the management and get support from these unions. This strengthens them and make them powerful to present themselves in front of employers.

Government

The interference of government by making rules and laws is very necessary to resolve the conflicts between employees and employer.

The Central and State Governments influence and regulates industrial relations through laws, rules, agreements, awards of court and the like which are to improve upon working relations as well as working cultures. The government is a neutral body which has no vested interests and therefore, formulates unbiased discretionary, rational laws.

The government keeps an eye on both the trade unions and employers organisation to regulate their behaviours in the interest of the nation. It also includes third parties and labour and tribunal courts.

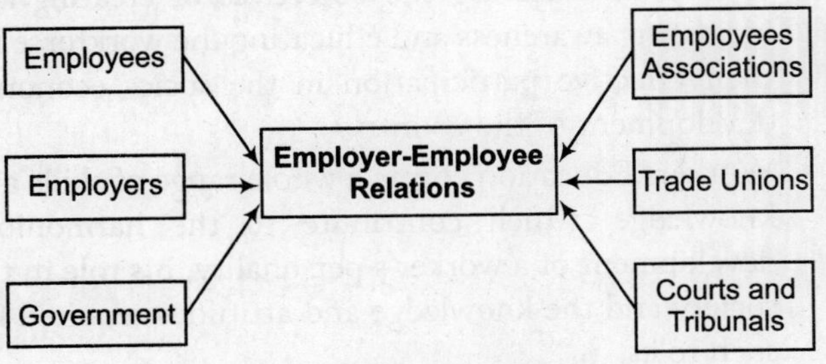

Parties to Industrial Relation

Conflict and Cooperation

Conflict and cooperation are inevitable and important components of Industrial Relations (IR). Both of them are required for the effective and efficient functioning of the organisation. There needs to be cooperation between the labour and capital.

Labour represents the workers/ employers who manage the factories, mines and other industrial establishment or services. Capital stands for the owner of the organisation. Conflict involves industrial unrest, strikes, lockouts, slowing down of work because of difference of opinion between the employer and employees. The different types of conflicts have been discussed in the further chapters.

Bi-Partitism

It is a system of IR that focuses on resolving the issues between the employer and employees. It is a consultative, and not negotiating process. *The machinery comprises two important constituents as given below*

- Work committees are constituted under the Industrial Dispute Act, 1947, in any industrial establishment in which one hundred or more workmen are employed or have been employed on any day in the preceding twelve months. It consists of equal number of representatives of employers and employees. Their mandate lies in the day-to-day functioning at the shop floor level.
- Joint Management Council (JMC) is constituted at plant level and consists of equal number of representatives of employers and employees. It shouldn't have more than 12 members. The plant should employ atleast 500 workers. The mandate of JMC lies in providing administrative welfare measures. Wages, bonus, personal problems of the workers are outside the scope of JMC.

Tri-Partitism

It is a system of Industrial Relations (IR) that involves government, employer, and worker representatives.

Some of the important Tripartite bodies in India are

1. Indian Labour Conference

- It is the apex level tripartite consultative committee in the Ministry of Labour and Employment to advise the Government on the issues concerning working class of the country.
- All the 12 Central Trade Union Organisations, Central Organisations of employers, all State Governments and Union Territories and Central Ministries/Departments concerned with the agenda items, are the members of the ILC.
- The first meeting of the Indian Labour Conference (then called Tripartite National Labour Conference) was held in 1942.
- The agenda of the ILC is finalised by the Standing Labour Committee which is again a tripartite body after detailed discussions.
- As recommended by the National Labour Conference held in 17-18th September 1982, only Trade Union Organisations, which have, a membership of more than five lakhs spread over four states and four industries are given representation in the ILC.
- It meets once a year.
- It advises the Government of India after taking into account suggestions made by the provincial government, the states and representative of the organisations of workers and employers.

2. Standing Labour Committee

- The Standing Labour Committee (SLC), a tripartite body is a precursor to the Indian Labour Conference (ILC).
- All the 12 Central Trade Union Organisations, Central Organisations of employers, all State Governments and Union Territories and Central Ministries/Departments concerned with the agenda items, are the members of the ILC and SLC.
- SLC meets as and when it is required. It has the responsibility of laying down the agenda of the ILC.
- It considers and examines such questions as may be referred to it by the central government and to render advice, taking into account the suggestions made by various governments, workers and employers.

3. Committee on Conventions

- It is a tripartite body set up in 1954 in order to work on the ILO conventions and recommendations.
- It examines the conventions and recommendations of ILO that have not been ratified by India.
- It makes suggestions for a speedy and phased implementation of ILO recommendations and conventions.

4. Industrial Committees

- These were established post the eighth session of Indian Labour Conference (ILC) and the first Industrial committee was constituted in 1947.
- They are basically related to jute, cotton, coal, mines, cement, leathers and tanneries manufacture, building and construction industry, gas and power, banking, road transport, engineering, chemical industries, metal trades.
- These provide a forum for the discussion of proposals for legislation and other matters connected with labour policy and administration.

5. Other Committees

(i) Steering Committee on Wages

- It was set up in 1956 and consists of representatives of state government, employers, workers and an economist.
- It was established to study wages, production and prices in India.

(ii) National Productivity Council (NPC)

- NPC is a national level organisation to promote productivity culture in India.
- Established by the Ministry of Industry, Government of India in 1958, it is an autonomous, multipartite, non-profit organisation with equal representation from employers' and workers' organisations and Government, apart from technical and professional institutions and other interests.
- NPC is a constituent of the Tokyo-based Asian Productivity Organisation (APO), an Inter Governmental Body, of which the Government of India is a founder member. It aims to provide solutions towards accelerating productivity, enhancing competitiveness, increasing profits, augmenting safety and reliability and ensuring better quality.

(iii) Central Boards of Workers Education

- It is an autonomous body under the Ministry of Labour and Employment, Government of India and is registered under the Societies Registration Act, 1860.
- It was started in 1958 and gets grants-in-aid from the Ministry of Labour and Employment to operate its activities.
- It aims at achieving the objectives of creating and increasing awareness and educating the workforce for their effective participation in the socio- economic development of the country.
- Workers Education covers a whole range of skills and knowledge, which contribute to the harmonious development of a worker's personality, his role in the society and the knowledge and attitudes required for such roles.

Collective Bargaining

The term collective bargaining was first used by **Beatrice Webb**. It is basically a method of negotiating the employment conditions between the employer and employees.

According to **Stevens**, "Collective bargaining is a social control technique for reflecting and transmitting the basic power relationships which underlie the conflict of interest in an industrial relations system".

According to **Flippo**, "Collective bargaining is a process in which the representatives of a labour organisation and the representatives of business organisation meet and attempt to negotiate a contract or agreement, which specifies the nature of employee-employer union relationship".

According to **Prof. Allan Flanders**, "Collective bargaining is primarily a political rather than an economic process. It is a power relationship between a trade union organisation and the management organisation. The agreement arrived at is a compromise settlement of power conflicts".

ILO convention No. 154 defines collective bargaining as all negotiations which take place between an employer, a group of employers or one or more employers' organisations, on the one hand, and one or more workers' organisations, on the other, *for*

- determining working conditions and terms of employment and/or
- regulating relations between employers and workers and/or
- regulating relations between employers or their organisations and a workers' organisation or workers' organisations.

Features of Collective Bargaining

- It is a group action in which both the employer and employees are represented by groups and not individuals.
- It is a continuous and bipartite process. The groups of employers and employees discuss, negotiate and resolve the matter without any third party intervention.
- This process involves negotiations between the parties.
- It is a complementary process as both the involved parties have something that other parties need. Employer needs the services of the employees and employees need reward and recognition by the employers.
- The process is important to improve the relations between workers and the union on the one hand and the employer on the other.

Workers' Participation in Management

The concept of workers' participation in management is considered as a mechanism, where workers have a say in the decision-making process of an enterprise.

Workers' participation in management is an essential ingredient of industrial democracy. The concept of workers' participation in management is based on 'Human Relations' approach to management which brought about new set of values to labour and management.

Workers' participation in management helps to meet the psychological needs of the workers to a greater extent. It is a human need that a worker wants to be observed, listened and get recognition in the environment where he works.

The concept of workers' participation in management crystalises the concept of industrial democracy.

According to **The International Institute for Labour Studies**, "WPM is the participation resulting from practices which increase the scope for employees' share of influence in decision-making at different Tiers of organisational hierarchy with concomitant assumption of responsibility."

It is quite obvious that when individuals are provided with opportunities to voice their opinion for expression and share in decision-making, they show much initiative and accept responsibility substantially. This participation may protect the interests of both parties, prevents exploitations and provides equity and fairness.

Workers' participation in management leads to development of a sense of involvement in their organisation, a better understanding of their role in the smooth functioning of industry. All this provides them a means of self-realisation, thereby, promoting efficiency and increased productivity. To make the participation succcessful, it is very important for both the party members to have awareness, education and conceptual skills.

Determinants of Workers' Participation in Management

There are three major factors to determine workers' participation in management. *They are as follows*

The Situational Factor It refers to the unique characteristics possessed by each enterprise such, as its size, structure, autonomy, the kind of technology adopted and legal provisions in the enterprise.

The Environment Factor It may be considered as the part of situational as the situations influence the type of authority which is responsible for the push on the part of the workers to get involved in participation in decision-making. Like stable environments do not give much scope to workers' participation in management as compared to the volatile environment.

The Human Factors It means the worker's propensity to participate and the manager's acceptance of the participation schemes.

Manager's attitude also plays a significant role in ensuring workers' participation in management. There are different kinds of leadership styles such as autocratic, democratic, participative, situational etc, which determine the acceptance of workers' participation.

Objectives of Workers' Participation in Management

The objectives of workers' participation in management can be stated through following points

- To secure full recognition of the workers to develop a sense of importance, involvement and a feeling of belongingness to enlighten workers to know better about their role in the organisation.
- To improve upon the relations between supervisors and workers.
- To provide them an environment where they can develop freely and recognise their own potential.
- To get their involvement in safety measures and environmental issues.
- To make workers conscious of their Fundamental Rights at their work place and thus bring about industrial democracy.
- To improve employee's pride, moral and integrity.

Levels of Participation

Workers' participation is possible at all the levels of management; the only difference is that of degree and nature of participation. For instance, it may be vigorous at lower level and less at top level.

There are following five levels of participation

Informative Participation It ensures that employees are able to receive information and express their views pertaining to the matters of general economic importance.

Consultative Participation Here workers are consulted on the matters of employee welfare such as work, safety and health. However, final decision always rests at the option of management and employees' views are only of advisory nature.

Associative Participation It is extension of consultative participation as management here is under moral obligation to accept and implement the unanimous decisions of employees.

Administrative Participation It ensures greater share of workers in discharge of managerial functions. Here, decision already taken by the management flows down to employees, preferably with alternatives for administration and employees have to select the best from those for implementation.

Decisive Participation Highest level of participation where decisions are jointly taken on the matters related to production, welfare etc is called decisive participation.

Forms of Workers' Participation in Management

Participation at the Board Level The workers' representatives are on the board and can take decisions related to the benefits of workers. It is the highest form of democracy. Few companies like HMT (Bengaluru), the Tatas, DCM and nationalised banks have adopted this practice.

Participation through Ownership In this way of participation, workers are encouraged to buy equity shares of the company and be the shareholders of the company. This participation makes the workers committed to the job and to the organisation.

Participation through Complete Control This way of participation ensures worker's loyalty to the organisation and was adopted in Yugoslavia. In this method, workers acquire full control of the management through elected boards.

Participation through Staff and Works Councils Staff and works councils are constituted with the representatives of employees only. They have full right in decision-making.

Participation through Councils and Committees Councils are bodies constituted by the representatives of employers and employees.

Participation through Collective Bargaining In this method, both management and workers may reach collective agreement in regard to any issue being discussed. To achieve this agreement both the parties need to bargain in good spirit.

Participation through Job Enlargement and Job Enrichment This way of participation addresses the problem of monotony and boredom. Job enlargement means expanding the job contents. Job enrichment means adding motivators to the job to make it more rewarding.

Participation through Suggestion Schemes In this way of participation, employees are encouraged to give their suggestions and best suggestion is rewarded. This provides motivation to the winner.

Participation through Quality Circles In this way of participation, a group of seven top people is formed who meet regularly and discuss, analyse and solve quality related issues. The given concept was originated in Japan in the early 1960s but now has spread all over the world. It has been tried by BHEL, Mahindra and Mahindra, Godrej, Boyce and many others in India.

Empowered Teams In this way of participation, employees/groups are empowered by living authority, power and responsibility, so that they have full control of their jobs and experience a sense of ownership. It may have negative consequences as people may misuse these given powers. The companies like Titan, Reliance, ABB, GE Plastics (India), Wipro, have empowered both frontline as well as production staff, and are enjoying positive results.

Total Quality Management This way of participation refers to passion for maintaining quality and deep commitment for the ways to improve the quality of the product. TQM is called participative because it is a formal programme involving every employee in the organisation, making each one responsible for improving quality everyday.

Financial Participation In this way of participation, the performance of an employee can be related to the performance of the organisation. Obviously when an employee will be benefitted with the profits earned by the organisation, then his commitment will be more.

Workers' Participation in Management in India

Workers' participation in management in India was given importance only after independence. Industrial Disputes Act of 1947 was the first step in this direction, which recommended for the setting up of Works Committees.

The Joint Management Councils were established in 1950, which increased the participation of labour in management. The Management Scheme 1970 gave birth to 'Board of Management'.

Since July 1975, the two-tier participation model called 'Shop Council' at the shop level and 'Joint Councils' at the enterprise level were introduced.

Based on the review and performance of previous schemes a new scheme was formulated in 1983. The new scheme of workers' participation was applicable to all central public sector enterprises, except those specifically exempted.

The scheme with equal number of representatives will operate both at shop as well as plant level. The various functions of participative forum laid down in the scheme could be modified with the consent of parties.

The scheme could not make such head way due to lack of union leaders consensus of the mode of representation and worker's tendency to discuss ultra-wired issues, *e.g.* pay scales, wages etc.

Prior to WPM Bill, 1990 all the schemes of participation were non-statutory and concentrated on particular levels. For effective and meaningful participation at all levels, a bill was introduced in Parliament on 25th May, 1990.

The bill provided for effective participation at all level by formulating schemes of participation. For electing representatives for participation, it also provides for secret ballot.

The appropriate government may also appoint inspectors to review participation schemes and the bill also has provision of punishment for those who contravene any of the provision of the Act.

The workers' participation schemes in India provide wide scope for application and upliftment of workers. But in practice, these schemes have not met with success though they are successful in some private sector units.

The factors responsible for the failure are

- The management does not encourage employees to participate in these schemes. The representatives of workers are not given due recognition by the management. They consider these schemes as concessions accorded to workers, rather than a measure of industrial democracy.
- The government agencies do not take follow up in regard of the implementation of the schemes particularly with reference to the setting up of works committees under the provisions of the ID Act, 1947.
- The attitude of trade unions towards the schemes are negative as they consider these schemes are reducing their power. Since, workers are not well educated, not aware of political matters, not socially united; cooperative participation might not be effective. Therefore, some Trade Unions boycott Joint Management Council meetings.

The success of these schemes require the fulfilment of certain conditions

- Management should appreciate the scheme and accept them in full faith.
- Trade unions have to cooperate with the schemes.
- Workers have to be educated.

Thus, workers' participation in management in India is yet to succeed. It can be done by educating the workers, creating an environment in the organisation for coordination of workers and management.

It is not easy to assess how workers' participation schemes work in general but it is important to understand the conditions under which these schemes just become a structural arrangement.

Workers' participation in management schemes would be successful when there is a transition from mere structural participation to fulfil the legal requirements towards the active participation of workers in management.

Employee Discipline

Discipline may be defined as an attitude of mind which aims at inculcating restraint, orderly behaviour and respect for and willing obedience to a recognised authority. Discipline is to work under set of rules, code, predefined norms or well defined boundaries.

In any industry, discipline is a useful tool for developing, improving and stabilising the personality of workers. Industrial discipline is essential for the smooth running of an organisation, for increasing production and productivity, for the maintenance of industrial peace and for the prosperity of the industry and the nation.

It is a process of bringing multifarious advantages to the organisation and its employees. Discipline is correlated to the organisational working. To be organised means to be disciplined and *vice-versa*.

According to **Richord D Calhoon**, "Discipline is the force that prompts an individual or a group to observe the rules, regulations and procedures which are deemed to be necessary to the attainment of an objective".

Code of discipline/conduct is the standard of expected ethical behaviour for the company's employees. The code of discipline talks about the expected behaviour such as to obey the law, conflicts of interest, preserving confidential information, no bribery etc. It is applicable to both public and private enterprises to maintain harmonious relationships.

Objectives of Discipline

- To maintain peace and harmony in industry.
- To make the employees ready on their own to accept the rules, regulations and procedures of an organisation.
- To facilitate communication at all levels.
- To develop a willing acceptance to coordinate and cooperate with each other.
- To avoid strikes/lock-outs/lay-off/work stoppage in industry.
- To give and seek direction and responsibility.
- To develop mutual trust and make the settlement machinery more active.
- To create an atmosphere of respect for human personality and human relations.
- To avoid litigation and facilitate free growth of trades unions.
- To build up an effective organisational culture where everybody respects each others' abilities and roles.
- To eliminate all forms of coercion, intimidation and violations of rules.
- To increase the participation of the employees in the organisational activities.
- To impart an element of certainty despite several changes in an organisation.

Indiscipline

The term 'indiscipline' generally means the violation of formal or informal rules and regulations in an organisation. Any amount of breaching the rules and regulations lead to misconduct/ indiscipline. It is likely to impair the reputation of employer or create unrest or chaos in the establishment.

It becomes the responsibility of management to decide as to what shall constitute acts of misconduct and to define the quantum of punishment for them.

Indiscipline means disorderliness, disobedience and insubordination.

Indiscipline, if unchecked, will affect the morale of the organisation. Hence, indiscipline is to be checked by appropriate positive means to maintain industrial peace.

Principles of Effective Discipline

Disciplinary actions have serious repercussions on the employees and on the industry and therefore must be based on certain principles in order to be fair, just and acceptable to be the employee and their unions. Therefore, in any discipline maintenance system, *certain principles are to be observed such as*

- The rules of discipline, as far as possible, should be framed in consultation with the representatives of employees for their easy implementation. The group as a whole can control an individual works much more effectively than the management's policies of imposing punishments. Informal groups are likely to exert social pressures on wrongdoers.
- The rules and regulations need to be changed at frequent and regular intervals to cope up with the psychological and environmental changes.
- The rules and regulations must be suitable enough to suit different categories of employees in the organisation, *i.e.* both the blue-collar workers and white-collar employees.
- The rules must be unbiased, indiscriminatory, impersonal, rational and uniformly enforced for their proper acceptance. In other words, all defaulters should be treated alike, depending upon the nature of their offence and past record. Any discrimination or favouritism in this regard is likely to create discontent among the employees. Further, there has to be a definite and precise provision for appeal and review of all disciplinary actions.
- The rules of discipline embodied in the standing orders, or in the company's manual, should be properly and carefully communicated to every employee preferably at the time of induction for their easy acceptance. It serves as a warning and create awareness among employees about the is do's and don'ts is of the particular organisation.
- Every kind of disciplinary action, even if it is a rebuke or a warning, should be recorded. In some of the American industries, they have what is known as the, 'pink slip system'. Pink slips are issued as warning signals to a defaulting employee. A person who has been issued with a stated number of pink slips will be liable to be laid-off or discharged, without any further explanations.
- The responsibility for maintaining employee discipline needs to be entrusted to a responsible person. It is the personnel officer who has to handle the responsibility of offering advice and assistance. In serious matters, which warrant suspension, discharge etc, the industrial relations departments have to be consulted.

- Disciplinary actions should be taken in private because its main objective is to ensure that a wrong behaviour is corrected and not that the wrongdoer is punished. If disciplinary actions are taken in the presence of other employees, it may hurt the sense of dignity of the employee and impair his social standing with his colleagues.
- A punitive action must satisfy the principle of natural justice. The punishment should be in accordance to the gravity of the offence.

Approaches to Discipline Enforcement

The different approaches to discipline include

Human Relations Approach

Under human relations approach, the employee is treated as a human being and his acts of indiscipline will be dealt from the view point of human values, aspirations, problems, needs, goals, behaviours etc. In this approach, the employee is helped to correct his deviations.

Human Resources Approach

Under the human resources approach, the employee is considered as a 'resource' and an asset to the organisation. This approach analyses the cause of indiscipline from management activities such as defects in selections, training, motivations, leadership etc. After indentifying the defects, corrective steps are carried out by the management.

Group Discipline Approach

Under the group discipline approach, group as a whole sets the standard of discipline and punishments for the deviations. In this approach, trade unions also act as agencies in maintaining discipline in work situation.

The Leadership Approach

Under the leadership approach, indisciplinary cases are dealt on the basis of legislations and court decisions. The Industrial Employment (Standing Orders) Act, 1946 to a certain extent, prescribed the correct procedure that should be followed before awarding punishment to an employee.

Code of Conduct/Discipline

The Fifteenth Indian Labour Conference discussed the question of discipline in industry.

The code embodies four parts

- **Part I** Contains the duties and responsibilities of employees, workers and the government in maintaining discipline in industry.
- **Part II** Enlists the common obligations of management and unions.
- **Part III** Deals with the obligations of management only.
- **Part IV** Relates to those of the unions only.

In addition, Annexure-A of the Code embodies the national level agreement on the criteria for the recognition of unions. A supplementary document contains the rights of recognised unions and a model grievance procedure. Thus, the Code is highly comprehensive and ethical in its approach to the industrial relations system. It came into force from June 1958.

It has been reproduced below

Part I To Maintain Discipline in Industry

(Both in Public and Private Sectors)

There has to be (a) A just recognition by employers and workers of the rights and responsibilities of either party, as defined by the laws and agreements (including bipartite and tripartite agreements arrived at all levels from time-to-time). (b) A proper and willing discharge by either party of its obligation consequent on such recognition.

Part II Common Obligations of Management and Unions

- That no unilateral actions should be taken in connection with any industrial matter and that disputes should be settled at appropriate level.
- That the existing machinery for settlement of disputes should be utilised with the utmost expedition.
- That there should be no strike or lock-out without notice.
- That affirming their faith in democratic principles, they bind themselves to settle all future differences, disputes and grievances by mutual negotiation, conciliation and voluntary arbitration.
- That neither will have recourse to (a) coercion (b) intimidation (c) victimisation (d) go-show.
- That they will avoid (a) litigation, (b) sit-down and stay-in-strikes (c) lock-outs.
- That they will promote constructive cooperation between their representatives at all levels and as between workers themselves and abide by the spirit of agreements mutually entered into.
- That they will establish upon a mutually agreed basis a Grievance Procedure which will ensure a speedy and full investigation leading to settlement.
- That they will abide by various stages in the Grievance Procedure and take no arbitrary action which would by-pass this procedure.
- That they will educate the management personnel and worker's regarding their obligations to each other.

Part III **Obligations of Management**

- Not to increase work load unless agreed upon or settled otherwise.
- Not to support or encourage the unfair labour practices such as (a) interference with the right of employees to enroll or continue as union members (b) discriminations, restraint or coercion against any employee because of recognised activity of trade unions (c) victimisation of any employee and abuse of authority in any form.
- To take prompt actions for (a) settlement of grievance (b) implementation of settlements, awards, decisions and orders.
- To display in conspicuous places in undertaking the provision of this code in local language(s).
- To distinguish between actions justifying immediate discharge and those where discharge must be preceded by a warning, reprimand, suspension or some other form of disciplinary action and to arrange that all such disciplinary action should be subjected to an appeal through normal grievance procedure.
- To take appropriate disciplinary action against its officers and members in cases where enquiries reveal that they were responsible for precipitate action by workers leading to indiscipline.
- To recognise the unions in accordance with the criteria (Annexure B) evolved at the 16th Session of the Indian Labour Conference held in May 1958.

Part IV **Obligations of Unions**

- Not to encourage any form of physical violence.
- Not to permit demonstrations which are not peaceful and not to permit rowdyism in demonstration.
- That their members will not engage or cause other employees to engage in any union activity during working hours, unless provided by law, agreement or practice.
- To discourage unfair labour practices such as (a) negligence of duty (b) careless operation (c) damage to property (d) interference with or disturbance to normal work (e) insubordination.
- To take prompt actions to implement awards, agreements, settlements and decisions.
- To display in conspicuous places in the union offices, the provision of this Code in the local language(s).
- To express disapproval and to take appropriate action against office bearers and members for indulging in action against the spirit of this Code.

The Code does not have any legal section, *but the following moral sanctions are behind it*

1. *The Central Employers' and Workers' Organisations shall take the following steps against their constituent units guilty of breach of Code*
   - To ask the unit to explain the infringement of the code.
   - To give notice to the unit to set right the infringement within a specific period.
   - To warn, and in case persistent violation of the Code.
   - Not to give countenance, in any manner, to non-members who did not observe the Code.
   - Not to give countenance, in any manner, to non-members who did not observe the Code.
2. Grave, willful and persistent breaches of the Code by any party should be widely publicised.
3. Failure to observe the Code would entail derecognition normally for a period of one year, this period may be increased or decreased by the implementing committee concerned.
4. A dispute may not ordinarily be referred for adjudication, if there is a strike or lockout without proper notice or in breach of the Code as determined by an implementation.

Grievance Handling

Grievance is a complaint by an employee against the employer. The draft Model Grievance Handling Procedure was accepted by the Labour Conference in 1958.

The different steps of grievance handling procedure are

- An aggrieved employee will approach with his grievance to the person designated by the management for this purpose. The concerned person needs to give the response within 48 hours.
- If the worker is not satisfied with the response or fails to receive the answer within 48 hours he will, either in person or accompanied by is departmental representative, present his grievance to the head of the department.
- If the worker is dissatisfied with the decision of the departmental head, he may request that his grievance be forwarded to the grievance committee.
- The grievance committee will make its recommendations to the management within 7 days of the worker's request.
- The final decision of the management shall be communicated to the worker within the stipulated period. If worker is still not satisfied, the matter may be referred to voluntary arbitration.

Disciplinary Action

Disciplinary process is the process to deal with the misconduct or irresponsible behaviour of employees towards their work. *The process involves the following steps*

Investigation It is important to conduct a basic investigation to know that if the case of misconduct or indiscipline had happened.

Issue of Charge Sheet If misconduct or the case of indiscipline is proven, a notice is issued to the alleged employees. It is a show-cause notice that gives an opportunity to the employee to put across his side of the story. The notice should explicitly mention the details of allegations against which the show-cause notice has been issued.

Suspension On the basis of severity of charges, an employee may be suspended temporarily from the work. However, according to the Industrial Employment (Standing Orders) Act, 1946, the suspended worker is to be paid subsistence allowance equal to one-half of his wages for the first ninety days of suspension and three-fourths of the wages for the remaining period of suspensions, if the delay in the completion of disciplinary proceedings is not due to the worker's own conduct.

Notice and Conduct of Enquiry In case, the worker admits all the allegations, then he is given the punishment without any further enquiry. However, if he doesn't agree to the charges, an enquiry is conducted to find the truth of the charges levied against the employee.

The enquiry conducting authority must be free from any bias and record all the evidences without any personal interest. It must be fair and just.

Awarding Punishment If the allegations are proven, it must be communicated to the suspended employee or worker in written by the management or appropriate authority. The management should decide the punishment purely on the basis of findings of the enquiry, past record of the worker and gravity of the misconduct.

Employers' Organisations in India

In India, there are number of well established employers' organisations, which represent the collective voices of private and government-owned enterprises including small, medium and large businesses. They interact with the Central and State Governments and workers' organisations to protect and promote the interests of employers.

The Council of Indian Employers is the umbrella organisation of three employers' bodies *i.e.* All India Organisation of Employers (AIOE), Employers' Federation of India (EFI) and Standing Conference of Public Enterprises (SCOPE). The Council of Indian Employers is the ILO constituent employers' organisation and is affiliated to the International Organisation of Employers (IOE).

All India Organisation of Employers (AIOE)

- The All India Organisation of Employers' (AIOE) is an allied body of the Federation of Indian Chambers of Commerce and Industry (FICCI).
- It is the oldest and apex national employers' organisation of India and is the platform for Indian Employers to raise their voice in formulating labour and social policies to promote business, trade and economy in the country.
- AIOE was set up in 1932, by eminent Indian industrialist and philanthropist of yesteryears with the objective to serve the cause of Indian enterprises by promoting sound industrial relations and better understanding between employers and workers on the mutuality of interests and provide representation to Indian employers in the tripartite set up of government to draw labour and social policies.
- Shri Kasturbhai Lalbhai was the first president of AIOE.

Employers' Federation of India (EFI)

- The Employers' Federation of India (EFI) was established in 1933, as an association of autonomous organisations of industry and was set up with the purpose of protecting, promoting and championing the interests of employers mainly in the area of human resources, industrial relations, labour problems and cognate matters.
- Employers' Federation of India plays a special role as an apex body of employers' organisations and industries on matters concerning labour, human resource management, industrial relations and other related issues.
- The Federation represents the employers' concerns and views at various tripartite fora of the Ministry of Labour, such as Standing Labour Committee, Indian Labour Conference and other industry committees and sub-committees at state and national levels.
- The Federation represents Indian employers at the international level as a member of Confederation of Asia-Pacific Employers (CAPE) and the International Organisation of Employers (IOE).

- In addition, the Federation participates in the deliberations of statutory and non-statutory bodies such as Employees State Insurance Corporation, Employees Provident Fund Organisation, Contract Labour Advisory Boards, Workers' Education Schemes and other institutions of education and science.

Standing Conference of Public Enterprises (SCOPE)

- Standing Conference of Public Enterprises (SCOPE) is an apex professional organisation representing the Central Government Public Enterprises.
- It has also some state enterprises, banks and other institutions as its members.
- SCOPE came into existence on 10th April, 1973 and was formally given recognition as an apex body of Central Public Sector Enterprises in November 1976 by a decision of the Union Cabinet.
- SCOPE looks upon its tasks as both internal and external to the public enterprises and other organisations/ corporate bodies/institutions which are its members.
- Internally, it would endeavour to assist these in such ways as would help improve their total performance.
- Externally, it would help improve its total boundary role in conveying such information and advice to the community and the government as would generally help the public enterprises and other member organisations in their respective role.

EXAM BASED QUESTIONS

1 A situation where management is unable to provide employment due to non-availability of work is called
(a) lock-out (b) lay-off
(c) termination (d) attrition

2 Reduction of Labour Force is called
(a) termination (b) retrenchment
(c) lay-off (d) rightsizing

3 The Industrial Finance Corporation of India came into existence in
(a) July 1948 (b) August 1969
(c) September 1951 (d) None of these

4 Which of the following is not a typically used procedure to reduce the total number of employees?
(a) Lay-off
(b) Terminations
(c) Downturns
(d) Early retirement inducements

5 Expansion of public sector received top priority under which industrial policy resolution?
(a) 1948 (b) 1956
(c) 1977 (d) 1980

6 Which of the following National Level Federation was established in 1921?
(a) Indian National Trade Union Congress (INTUC)
(b) All India Trade Union Congress (AITUC)
(c) Union Trade Union Congress (UTNC)
(d) Hind Mazdoor Sabha (HMS)

7 Which of the following was established by the whitely councils?
(a) Tripartite employee relations
(b) Trade unions
(c) Collective bargaining framework
(d) Employer associations

8 Which of the following not the principle of the industrial relations policy?
(a) The code of conduct (b) Labour welfare activities
(c) The code of discipline (d) All of these

9 Which of the following is not a part of industrial relations system?
(a) Government and employers
(b) Trade unions, union federations or associations
(c) Foreign companies
(d) Labour courts and tribunals

10 Which of the following methods are used in industrial relations system?
(a) Collective bargaining
(b) Discipline procedure
(c) Grievance redressal machinery
(d) All of the above

11 Which of the following is not an objective of industrial relations?
(a) To enhance economic status of worker
(b) To settle the disputes with worker's neighbour
(c) To regular production by minimising conflicts
(d) To provide an opportunity to the worker to have a say in the management decision-making

12 Which of the following are approaches to industrial relations?
(a) Sociological approach
(b) Human relations approach
(c) Gandhian approach
(d) All of the above

13 Which of the following are the major causes of the origin in industrial relations?
(a) Industrialisation
(b) Emergence of a factory system
(c) Development of a capitalist economy
(d) All of the above

14 Which of the following are the major participants of industrial relations from the following?
(a) Employers (b) Government
(c) Unions (d) All of these

15 Who gave the following definitions of industrial relations out of the following?
"Industrial relations is a relationship between management and employees or among employees and their organisations, that characterise and grow out of employment."
(a) Dale Yoder
(b) RA Lester
(c) Max Weber
(d) Frederick Taylor

16 The main issues involved in industrial relations consist of
(a) collective bargaining
(b) machinery for settlement of industrial disputes
(c) workers' participation in management
(d) All of the above

17 Which of the following measures prove to be fruitful in improving industrial relations?
(a) Strong and stable unions
(b) Workers' participation in management
(c) Mutual trust
(d) All of the above

18 Which of the following is not a principle of the industrial relations policy?
(a) The code of conduct
(b) The code of discipline
(c) Labour welfare
(d) None of the above

19 Industrial relations is a set of functional interdependence of all walks of life as it involves the issues related to

(a) economic and occupational
(b) social and psychological
(c) technological and political
(d) All of the above

20 Who of the following is not associated with the concept of industrial relations system?

(a) Frederick Taylor (b) RA Lester
(c) Dale Yoder (d) Prof Dunlop

21 Who of the following defined industrial relations as "Industrial relations may be defined as the complex of inter-relations among workers, managers and government?"

(a) Dale Yoder
(b) Prof Dunlop
(c) Frederick Taylor
(d) RA Lester

22 The scope of industrial relation does not include

(a) employer and employee relations
(b) employer and trade union
(c) employer, employee and trade union relations
(d) employer and customer relations

23 According to which of the following approaches of Industrial Relations (IR), the perceptions of situations and issues differ because the same position may appear entirely different to different parties?

(a) Psychological approach
(b) Sociological approach
(c) Human relations approach
(d) Gandhian approach

24 Human relations approach offers a coherent view of the nature of industrial conflict and harmony. Who among the following was founder of the Human relations school?

(a) FW Taylor (b) Henry Fayol
(c) Elton Mayo (d) Mary Parker Follett

25 Who among the following defined industrial relation system as the one comprising of certain actors, contexts, an ideology which binds the industrial relations system together ?

(a) FW Taylor (b) Henry Fayol
(c) Elton Mayo (d) John Dunlop

26 According to the system approach of industrial relations, which of the following is not correct?

(a) Actors include the employees, employers and the government agencies.
(b) Context is basically the environment in which the actors operate.
(c) Ideology defined the philosophy, view-points and sentiments of the involved actors.
(d) The system of Industrial Relation (IR) is applicable at only national level.

27 Who among the following studied the behaviour of two different groups 'Union leaders' and 'Executives' through Thematic Application Test (TAT)?

(a) FW Taylor
(b) Henry Fayol
(c) Manson Harie
(d) John Dunlop

28 According to the system of human relations approach, which of the following is not correct?

(a) Conflict cannot be resolved unless management learns and understands what are the basic needs of men and how they can be motivated to work effectively.
(b) The workers are likely to attain greater job satisfaction, develop greater involvement in their work and achieve a measure of identification of their objectives with the objectives of the organisation.
(c) If employers treat employees as inanimate objects, their conflicts and tensions arise.
(d) The approach advocates voluntary arbitration and mutual settlement.

29 Which of the following is not correct for the unitary theory?

(a) Conflicts and strikes are viewed as destructive as these have a direct impact on the productivity and profitability of the organisation.
(b) Individual's needs take a back-seat in front of the organisational needs and goals.
(c) All the stakeholders work towards one common goal of the organisational development and betterment.
(d) It propagates that conflict is a key component for innovation and company growth.

30 The Radical theory suggests that conflict among workers and leaders is the result of the capitalistic nature of society and industry. Which of the following is correct for Radical theory?

(a) All the stakeholders need to work together in order to achieve their individual as well as organisational goals.
(b) Management needs to coordinate activities among the employees instead of ordering them to comply with strict rules and regulations.
(c) This perspective is based on the fact that each organisation is made up of management , union, and employee sub-groups. Each of them have their own bargaining powers.
(d) Conflict is seen as inevitable and trade unions are a natural response of workers to their exploitation by capital.

31 Which of the following theory states that each organisation is made up of management , union, and employee sub-groups and each of them have their own bargaining powers?

(a) Unitary theory
(b) Radical Theory
(c) Pluralist Theory
(d) Marxist theory

32 Given below are some features of Pluralist theory. Which of the following is incorrect?
(a) Trade unions play an important role in maintaining balance between the employer and employees.
(b) Conflicts cannot be completely done away and mediation is the key to resolve them.
(c) Conflict is a key component for innovation and company growth.
(d) Conflicts and strikes are viewed as destructive.

33 The fifteenth Indian Labour Conference discussed the question of discipline in the industry and had laid down Code of Discipline. How many parts are present in Code of Discipline?
(a) Four (b) Three
(c) Seven (d) Eight

34 In which year was the draft model grievance handling procedure accepted by the Labour Conference in India?
(a) 1978 (b) 1990
(c) 1958 (d) 1989

35 The grievance handling procedure involves the establishment of grievance committee. In how many days the grievance committee will make its recommendations to the management?
(a) 4 days (b) 9 days
(c) 7 days (d) 11 days

36 If a person is suspended owing to the disciplinary action against him, what is the amount of subsistence allowance that will be paid to the workers for the first ninety days of his suspension?
(a) One-half of his wages
(b) Three-fourths of his wages
(c) Two-thirds of his wages
(d) Two-fifth of his wages

37 Which of the following is the ILO constituent employers' organisation and is affiliated to the International Organisation of Employers (IOE)?
(a) All India Organisation of Employers (AIOE)
(b) Employers' Federation of India (EFI)
(c) Standing Conference of Public Enterprises (SCOPE)
(d) Council of Indian Employers

38 The All India Organisation of Employers' (AIOE) is an allied body of the Federation of Indian Chambers of Commerce and Industry (FICCI). In which year was it established?
(a) 1931 (b) 1982 (c) 1947 (d) 1932

39 The All India Organisation of Employers' (AIOE) is the oldest and apex national employers' organisation of India. Who among the following was the first President of AIOE?
(a) Girija Swami
(b) VV Giri
(c) Sardar Vallabhbhai Patel
(d) Kasturbhai Lalbhai

40 The Employers' Federation of India (EFI) was established as an association of autonomous organisations of industry and was set up with the purpose of protecting, promoting and championing the interests of employers mainly in the area of human resources, industrial relations, labour problems and cognate matters. When was EFI established?
(a) 1998 (b) 1923 (c) 1997 (d) 1933

41 Standing Conference of Public Enterprises (SCOPE) is an apex professional organisation representing the Central Government Public Enterprises. In which year SCOPE came into existence?
(a) 1982 (b) 1973 (c) 1990 (d) 1992

42 Standing Conference of Public Enterprises (SCOPE) is an apex professional organisation representing the Central Government Public Enterprises. In which year was SCOPE formally given the recognition for the same?
(a) 1982 (b) 1973 (c) 1976 (d) 1992

43 According to the Bipartite system of the industrial relations, the work committee is formed in an industrial establishment having a minimum of how many workers?
(a) 1000 (b) 100 (c) 200 (d) 300

44 The Joint Management Council (JMC) is constituted at plant level and consists of equal number of representatives of employers and employees. What is the maximum employees in a JMC?
(a) 10 (b) 20 (c) 30 (d) 12

45 The Joint Management Council (JMC) forms an important constituent of the Bipartite system of the industrial relations. What is the minimum number of employees working in the plant in which JMC can be constituted?
(a) 500 (b) 400 (c) 300 (d) 200

46 When was the first meeting of the Indian Labour Conference (then called Tripartite National Labour Conference) held?
(a) 1942 (b) 1989 (c) 1990 (d) 1972

47 Which of the following is correct in context of a Trade Union being represented in Indian Labour Conference(ILC) ?
(a) Only Trade Union Organisations, which have, a membership of more than five lakhs spread over four states and four industries are given representation in the ILC.
(b) Only Trade Union Organisations, which have, a membership of more than four lakhs spread over four states and four industries are given representation in the ILC.

(c) Only Trade Union Organisations, which have, a membership of more than seven lakhs spread over four states and four industries are given representation in the ILC.
(d) Only Trade Union Organisations, which have, a membership of more than four lakhs spread over four states and five industries are given representation in the ILC.

48 **Committee on Conventions was set up in order to work on the ILO conventions and recommendations. In which year was it established?**
(a) 1980 (b) 1972
(c) 1999 (d) 1956

49 **Industrial Committee was established post the eighth session of Indian Labour Conference (ILC). When was the first Industrial Committee established?**
(a) 1974 (b) 1954
(c) 1994 (d) 1984

50 **Who among the following used the term 'collective bargaining' for the first time?**
(a) FW Taylor (b) Henry Fayol
(c) Elton Mayo (d) Beatrice Webb

51 **National Productivity Council (NPC) is a national level organisation to promote productivity culture in India. In which year was it established?**
(a) 1980 (b) 1958
(c) 1980 (d) 1921

52 **Which of the following is a member of Asian Productivity Organisation (APO), an Inter Governmental Body, of which the Government of India is a founder member?**
(a) Committee on Conventions
(b) Steering Committee on Wages
(c) Central Board of Workers Education
(d) National Productivity Council (NPC)

53 **Which of the following is not a feature of collective bargaining?**
(a) It is a group action in which both the employer and employees are represented by groups and not individuals.
(b) It is a continuous and tripartite process.
(c) This process involves negotiations between the parties.
(d) It is a complementary process

54 **The Central Board of Worker's Education was established under which of the following Ministries?**
(a) Ministry of Commerce and Industry
(b) Human Resource Development Ministry
(c) Ministry of Labour and Employment
(d) Ministry of Information and Broadcasting

55 **Steering Committee on wages consists of representatives of state government, employers, workers and an economist. When was the committee established?**
(a) 1972 (b) 1982 (c) 1999 (d) 1956

56 **Committee on Conventions is related to the working of which of the following international organisation?**
(a) World Trade Organisation (WTO)
(b) World Bank
(c) International Monetary Fund (IMF)
(d) International Labour Organisation (ILO)

57 **Which of the following can not categorised as the main aim of works committees?**
(a) Giving greater participation to workers
(b) Providing better opportunities outside the organisation
(c) Generating cooperative atmosphere for negotiation between parties
(d) Ensuring close interaction between labour and management

58 **By which of the following methods workers' participation can take place in management?**
(a) Staff or work councils
(b) Board level participation
(c) Joint councils and committees
(d) All of the above

59 **The main objectives of workers' participation in management, according to Gosep are**
(a) elevating the status of a worker in the society
(b) increasing the efficiency of enterprise and establishing harmonious relations
(c) for promoting solidarity among workers and tapping human talents
(d) All of the above

60 **Which of the following can be considered as the advantages of quality circles?**
(a) Employees become involved in decision-making
(b) Employees get chances of promotion
(c) Employees improve their communications and analytical skills
(d) All of the above

61 **Which of the following are the main causes of indiscipline?**
(a) Wage differentials
(b) Unreasonable work assignments
(c) Non-payment of bonus
(d) Any of the above

62 **Which of the following is not the principle of total quality management?**
(a) High quality high cost
(b) Measure the cost of quality
(c) Manage by prevention, not correction
(d) Meet the customer's requirement on time, the first time and 100% of the time

63 **Which of the following are considered to be the schemes of financial participation of workers in management?**
(a) Profit linked pay
(b) Pension fund participation
(c) Profit sharing and employees' stock option schemes
(d) All of the above

64 Which of the following are the essential prerequisites of workers' participation in management?

(a) Free flow of communication and information
(b) Mutual trust between the two parties
(c) Avoidance of participation of outside trade unions
(d) All of the above

65 Which of the following are considered to be the bottlenecks of workers' participation in management?

(a) Employers can not think beyond their knowledge and skills
(b) Role of trade unions is not satisfactory
(c) Employers are unwilling to share power with worker's representative
(d) All of the above

66 Which of the following are the basic objectives of code of discipline?

(a) Maintain peace and order in industry
(b) Avoid work stoppage in industry
(c) Promote opinions from all levels of management and employment
(d) All of the above

67 The code of discipline is based on which of the following principles?

(a) No strike or lock-out without prior notice
(b) No deliberate damage to a plant or property of the establishment
(c) Usage of existing machinery for settlement of disputes
(d) All of the above

68 In which of the following ways unions agree upon to maintain discipline in an industry?

(a) Not to engage in any form of physical duress
(b) Not to permit demonstrations which are not peaceful
(c) Not to take too much time in implementing awards, agreements, settlements and decisions
(d) All of the above

69 Which of the following is not the most important aspect of the process of collective bargaining?

(a) Negotiations (b) Confrontations
(c) Discussions (d) Compromise

70 Which of the following matters are usually brought under collective bargaining?

(a) Working conditions
(b) Labour welfare
(c) Organisational matters
(d) All of the above

71 Which of the following are the main reasons of workers' participation in management, not getting successful in India?

(a) Multiplicity of trade unions and conflicts between them
(b) Confusion and duplication of functions
(c) Lack of education and training
(d) All of the above

72 Consider the following for the sociological approach of industrial relations

1. The management goals is decided by culture of the institutions, customs.
2. The main function of an industry is economic, its social consequences are also important such as urbanisation.
3. As industries develop, a new industrial-cum-social pattern emerges, which provides general new relationships, institutions and behavioural patterns.

Which of the following is correct?

(a) Both 1 and 2 (b) Both 2 and 3
(c) Both 1 and 3 (d) All of the above

73 Consider the following for the systems approach of industrial relations

1. Context includes the budget in which an organisation functions.
2. The actors must have a different ideology in order to arrive at a final solution.
3. As industries develop, a new industrial-cum-social pattern emerges, which provides general new relationships, institutions and behavioural patterns.

Which of the following is correct?

(a) Both 1 and 2 (b) Both 2 and 3
(c) Both 1 and 3 (d) All of the above

74 Consider the following for the Marxist perspective of industrial relations

1. The workers view the management as the leaders who are just concerned about their profits.
2. Conflict is inevitable.
3. Trade unions are a natural response of workers to their exploitation by capital.

Which of the following is correct?

(a) Both 1 and 2 (b) Both 2 and 3
(c) Both 1 and 3 (d) All of the above

75 Consider the following for the joint management councils

1. These are negotiating bodies.
2. It consists of equal number of representatives of employers and employees.
3. Their mandate lies in the day-to-day functioning at the shop floor level.

Which of the following is correct?

(a) Only 2 (b) Only 3
(c) Both 1 and 3 (c) All of the above

76 Consider the following for the bipartite system of industrial relations

1. These are consultative bodies.
2. These consists of work committees and Joint Management Council (JMC).
3. They focus on providing administrative welfare measures.

Which of the following is correct?

(a) Only 2 (b) Only 3
(c) Both 1 and 2 (d) All of the above

77 Consider the following for the Indian Labour Conference

1. It is the apex level tripartite consultative committee in the Ministry of Labour and Employment to advise the Government on the issues concerning working class of the country.
2. It meets once a year.
3. It finalises the agenda for the Standing Labour Committee (SLC)

Which of the following is incorrect?

(a) Only 2 (b) Only 3
(c) Both 1 and 2 (d) All of the above

78 Which of the following statements are true/false?

(i) Joint Management Council (JMC) shouldn't have more than 12 members.
(ii) Committee on Convention is a bipartite body set up in 1954 in order to work on the ILO conventions and recommendations.
(iii) Industrial Committees were established post the first session of Indian Labour Conference (ILC)
(iv) There are 12 Central Trade Union Organisations.

(a) (i), (iv) are true and (ii), (iii) are false
(b) (i), (iii) are true and (ii), (iv) are false
(c) (ii), (iv) are true and (i), (iii) are false
(d) (iii), (iv) are true and (ii), (i) are false

79 Which of the following statements are true/false?

(i) The term collective bargaining was first used by Sidney Webb.
(ii) ILO Convention No. 154 defines collective bargaining as all negotiations which take place between an employer, a group of employers or one or more employers' organisations, on the one hand, and one or more workers' organisations.
(iii) Collective bargaining is a one-sided affair as the trade unions are too powerful to be challenged by management.
(iv) In collective bargaining the employer and employees are represented by groups and not individuals.

(a) (i), (iv) are true and (ii), (iii) are false
(b) (i), (iii) are true and (ii), (iv) are false
(c) (ii), (iv) are true and (i), (iii) are false
(d) (iii), (iv) are true and (ii), (i) are false

80 Which of the following statements are true/false?

(i) Standing Labour Committee finalises the agenda for the Indian Labour Conference (ILC).
(ii) Standing Labour Committee (SLC) is a bipartite body.
(iii) All the 12 Central Trade Union Organisations, Central Organisations of employers, all State Governments and Union Territories and Central Ministries/Departments concerned with the agenda items, are the members of the ILC and SLC.
(iv) Indian Labour Conference(ILC) is a precursor to the Standing Labour Committee (SLC).

(a) (i), (iv) are true and (ii), (iii) are false
(b) (i), (iii) are true and (ii), (iv) are false
(c) (ii), (iv) are true and (i), (iii) are false
(d) (iii), (iv) are true and (ii), (i) are false

81 Which of the following statements are true/false?

(i) According to the Radical perspective, conflict among workers and leaders is the result of the capitalistic nature of society and industry.
(ii) According to the Unitary theory, management needs to coordinate activities among the employees instead of ordering them to comply with strict rules and regulations.
(iii) Conflict and cooperation are inevitable and important components of Industrial Relations (IR).
(iv) In Unitary theory, conflicts and strikes are viewed as destructive as these have a direct impact on the productivity and profitability of the organisation.

(a) (i), (iii), (iv) are true and (ii) is false
(b) (i), (iii) are true and (ii), (iv) are false
(c) (ii), (iv) are true and (i), (iii) are false
(d) (iii), (iv) are true and (ii), (i) are false

82 Which of the following statements are true/false?

(i) Socio-Ethical approach of industrial relations is not a very acceptable approach.
(ii) Gandhian approach of Industrial Relations emphasised that workmen has every right to possess the accurate knowledge of the transaction of mills.
(iii) Sociological approach emphasises that strained industrial relations can be understood by studying the differences in the perception of issues.
(iv) The government need not intervene in the employer-employee relationship to resolve their conflicts.

(a) (i), (iv) are true and (ii), (iii) are false
(b) (i), (ii) are true and (iii), (iv) are false
(c) (ii), (iv) are true and (i), (iii) are false
(d) (iii), (iv) are true and (ii), (i) are false

83 Which of the following statements are true/ false?

(i) The Part I of Code of Discipline contains duties and responsibilities of employees, workers and the government in maintaining the discipline in the industry.
(ii) The Part II of Code of Discipline enlists the common obligations of management and unions.
(iii) The Part III of Code of Discipline deals with the obligations of management only.
(iv) The Part IV of Code of Discipline is related to unions only.

(a) (i), (ii), (iii), (iv) are true
(b) (i), (iii) are true and (ii), (iv) are false
(c) (ii), (iv) are true and (i), (iii) are false
(d) (iii), (iv) are true and (ii), (i) are false

84 Which of the following statements are true/false?

(i) The trade union should not encourage any form of demonstrations which are not peaceful.

(ii) The trade unions should take prompt actions to implement awards, agreements, settlements and decisions.

(iii) The Code of Discipline must be displayed in English in the Union's Offices.

(iv) The management must recognise trade unions in accordance with the criteria mentioned in the Annexure B of the Code of Discipline.

(a) (i), (ii) are true and (iii), (iv) are false
(b) (i), (iii) are true and (ii), (iv) are false
(c) (ii), (iv) are true and (i), (iii) are false
(d) (iii), (iv) are true and (ii), (i) are false

85 Which of the following statements are true/ false?

(i) If the person is not satisfied with the final decision of management, the matter may be referred to the voluntary arbitration.

(ii) The grievance is forwarded to the grievance committee at the first stage.

(iii) The grievance committee will make its recommendation to the management within 7 days of the worker's request.

(iv) An aggrieved employee should approach the designated person by management who needs to give response within 24 hours.

(a) (i), (ii) are true and (iii), (iv) are false
(b) (i), (iii) are true and (ii), (iv) are false
(c) (ii), (iv) are true and (i), (iii) are false
(d) (iii), (iv) are true and (ii), (i) are false

86 Which of the following statements are true/ false?

(i) The Employers' Federation of India (EFI) is an allied body of the Federation of Indian Chambers of Commerce and Industry (FICCI).

(ii) The Employer's Federation of India (EFI) is a member Confederation of Asia-Pacific Employers (CAPE) and the International Organisation of Employers (IOE).

(iii) The Employers' Federation of India (EFI) was established in 1937.

(iv) Standing Conference of Public Enterprises (SCOPE) is an apex professional organisation representing the Central Government Public Enterprises.

(a) (i), (ii) are true and (iii), (iv) are false
(b) (i), (iii) are true and (ii), (iv) are false
(c) (ii), (iv) are true and (i), (iii) are false
(d) (iii), (iv) are true and (ii), (i) are false

87 Which of the following statements are true/ false?

(i) Industrial relations are born out of employment relationship in an individual setting.

(ii) Labour and management do not operate in isolation.

(iii) To develop harmonious relationship between labour and management, it is necessary to have existence of strong well organised, democratic and responsible trade unions.

(iv) Good industrial relations lead to increased efficiency, hence higher productivity and income.

(a) (i), (ii), (iii), (iv) are true
(b) (i), (iii) are true and (ii), (iv) are false
(c) (ii), (iv) are true and (i), (iii) are false
(d) (iii), (iv) are true and (ii), (i) are false

Directions (Q. Nos. 88-98) *In the questions given below are two statements labelled as Assertion (A) and Reason (R). In the context of the two statements, which one of the following is correct?*

(a) Both (A) and (R) are correct and (R) is the correct explanation of the (A).
(b) Both (A) and (R) are correct, but (R) is not the correct explanation of (A).
(c) (A) is true, but (R) is false.
(d) (A) is false, but (R) is true.

88 **Assertion** (A) Conflicts and strikes are destructive in nature.

Reason (R) Conflicts have a direct impact on the productivity and profitability of the organisation.

89 **Assertion** (A) The employers and employees have to agree with the final decision of the Joint Management Council (JMC).

Reason (R) JMC is a consultative body

90 **Assertion** (A) National Productivity Council is a multipartite body.

Reason (R) It has equal representation from employers' and workers' organisations and Government, apart from technical and professional institutions and other interests.

91 **Assertion** (A) Employer needs the services of the employees and employees need reward and recognition by the employers.

Reason (R) Collective bargaining is a complementary process.

92 **Assertion** (A) Indian Labour Conference (ILC) advises the Government of India after taking into account suggestions made by the provincial government, the states and representative of the organisations of workers and employers.

Reason (R) The Standing Labour Committee (SLC) is a precursor to the Indian Labour Conference (ILC).

93 **Assertion** (A) Collective bargaining consists of all negotiations which take place between an employer, a group of employers or one or more employers' organisations, on the one hand, and one or more workers' organisations.

Reason (R) It is a dynamic and continuous process.

94 Assertion (A) An industrial relation system is an integrated system of relationships between employers and employees managed through conflict.

Reason (R) The central and state governments influence and regulate industrial relations through laws, rules, agreements.

95 Assertion (A) The workers' representatives are on the board and can take decisions related to the benefits of workers.

Reason (R) It ensures worker's loyalty towards the organisation.

96 Assertion (A) In consultative workers' participation in management, the workers are consulted on the matters of employee welfare and the decision of workers are final.

Reason (R) The view point of employees are advisory in nature.

97 Assertion (A) Discipline is the force that prompt the individual or a group to observe the rules, regulation and procedures which are deemed to be necessary for the attainment of an objective.

Reason (R) Code of discipline is a standard of expected ethical behaviour for the company's employees.

98 Assertion (A) The enquiry conducting authority must be free from any bias and should record all the evidence without any personal interest.

Reason (R) The worker is given punishment only after the allegations against him or her is proven.

99 Match the following.

List I	List II
A. Participation at board level	1. Making the workers shareholders
B. Participation through ownership	2. Complete control through elected boards
C. Participation through complete control	3. Only employees representation
D. Participation through staff and works councils	4. Highest level of industrial democracy

Codes

	A	B	C	D		A	B	C	D
(a)	4	1	2	3	(b)	1	2	3	4
(c)	2	1	4	3	(d)	1	4	3	2

100 Match the following.

List I	List II
A. Participation through joint council and committees	1. Bargaining between employees and workers representatives in right sprit
B. Participation through collective bargaining	2. Representatives of employee and employees
C. Participation through job enlargement and job enrichment	3. Employer's views are invited
D. Participation through suggestion schemes	4. Address the issues of toredom and other associated problems

Codes

	A	B	C	D
(a)	1	2	3	4
(b)	1	4	3	2
(c)	2	1	4	3
(d)	4	1	2	3

101 Match the following.

List I	List II
A. Participation through	1. Employees are empowered by transferring authority and responsibilities
B. Quality circles	2. Deep commitment to quality
C. Empowered teams	3. Performance of the organisation is linked to the performance of the employee
D. Financial participation	4. A group of 7 to 10 people of same area interacting regularly

Codes

	A	B	C	D		A	B	C	D
(a)	1	3	2	4	(b)	4	1	2	3
(c)	1	4	3	2	(d)	2	1	4	3

102 Match the following.

List I	List II
A. Prerequisite of workers' participation	1. Right to participate in decision-making process for workers
B. Concept of workers' participation	2. Mutual trust between employer and employee
C. Limitation of workers' participation	3. Performance of the organisation is linked to the performance of the employee
D. Industrial democracy	4. Unwillingness of employer to share power with workers

Codes

	A	B	C	D
(a)	2	3	4	1
(b)	2	4	2	1
(c)	4	3	2	1
(d)	2	1	4	3

Directions (Q. Nos. 103-107) *Read the following passage and answer the questions that follows.*

Industrial relations scholarship assumes that labour markets are not perfectly competitive and thus, in contrast to mainstream economic theory, employers typically have greater bargaining power than employees. Industrial relations scholarship also assumes that there are atleast some inherent conflicts of interest between employers and employees (for example, higher wages versus higher profits) and thus, in contrast to scholarship in human resource management and organisational behaviour, conflict is seen as a natural part of the employment relationship. Industrial relations scholars therefore frequently study the diverse institutional arrangements that characterise and shape the employment relationship from norms and power structures on the shop floor, to employee voice mechanisms in the workplace, to collective bargaining arrangements at company, regional or national level, to various levels of public policy and labour law regimes, to 'varieties of capitalism' (such as corporatism, social democracy and neoliberalism).

When labour markets are seen as imperfect and when the employment relationship includes conflicts of interest, then one cannot rely on markets or managers to always serve workers' interests and in extreme cases to prevent worker exploitation. Industrial relations scholars and practitioners therefore support institutional interventions to improve the workings of the employment relationship and to protect workers' rights. The nature of these institutional interventions, however, differ between two camps within industrial relations. The pluralist camp sees the employment relationship as a mixture of shared interests and conflicts of interests that are largely limited to the employment relationship. In the workplace, pluralists therefore champion grievance procedures, employee voice mechanisms such as works councils and labour unions, collective bargaining and labour-management partnerships. In the policy arena, pluralists advocate for minimum wage laws, occupational health and safety standards, international labour standards and other employment and labour laws and public policies. These institutional interventions are all seen as methods for balancing the employment relationship to generate not only economic efficiency, but also employee equity and voice. In contrast, the Marxist-inspired critical camp sees employer-employee conflicts of interest as sharply antagonistic and deeply embedded in the socio-political-economic system. From this perspective, the pursuit of a balanced employment relationship gives too much weight to employers' interests and instead deep-seated structural reforms are needed to change the sharply antagonistic employment relationship that is inherent within capitalism. Militant trade unions are thus frequently supported.

103 **Employers typically have greater bargaining power than employees, because**

(a) labour markets are not perfectly competitive
(b) there is greater interference from the government
(c) there is greater pressure from the employers unions
(d) None of the above

104 **Industrial relations scholars therefore frequently study the diverse institutional arrangements, because**

(a) conflict is seen as a natural part of the employment relationship
(b) there are always some inherent conflicts of interest between employers and employees
(c) Both (a) and (b)
(d) None of the above

105 **The pluralist camp sees the employment relationship as**

(a) a mixture of shared interests and conflicts of interests that are prescribed by the Government
(b) a mixture of shared interests and conflicts of interests that are beyond employment relationship
(c) a mixture of shared interests and conflicts of interests that are within employment relationship
(d) None of the above

106 **The pursuit of a balanced employment relationship gives**

(a) too much weight to employers' interests
(b) too much weight to employees' interests
(c) equal weights to both empoyers' and employees' interests
(d) None of the above

107 **For reformations of industrial relations**

(a) it is needed to change the employment relationship that is inherent within interference of the government
(b) it is needed to change the employment relationship that is inherent within socialism
(c) it is needed to change the employment relationship that is inherent within capitalism
(d) None of the above

PREVIOUS YEARS' QUESTIONS

2018

1 **Assertion (A)** In India, inequality between contracting parties in employment relationship have warranted third party intervention.

Reason (R) As a custodian of the broader social interest, the government has to ensure that the economic needs of the community are satisfied by an uninterrupted flow of goods and services.

Codes

(a) Both (A) and (R) are true and (R) is the correct explanation of (A)
(b) (A) is wrong, but (R) is correct
(c) Both (A) and (R) are true, but (R) is not the correct explanation of (A)
(d) (A) is correct, but (R) is wrong

2 A situation in which the parties to a conflict, each desire to satisfy fully the concern of all parties is known as

(a) Competing (b) Collaborating
(c) Accommodating (d) Compromising

3 The Kochan, Katz and McKersie's framework of industrial relations proposes a three-tier structure of industrial relations activities.

Match the three categories of the actvities with the respective levels where they take place, as given below

List I (Level/Tier)	List II (Category of activity)
A. Top-tier	1. Collective bargaining and personnel policy
B. Middle-tier	2. Workplace, individual and organisational relationship
C. Bottom-tier	3. Long-term strategy and policy-making

Codes

	A	B	C		A	B	C
(a)	1	3	2	(b)	1	2	3
(c)	3	1	2	(d)	2	1	3

4 Which of the following features relating to the participation of workers in management bill introduced in the year 1990 are correct?

1. This was the first comprehensive legislative effort towards promotion of workers' participation in management.
2. The Bill envisaged a two-tier system of participation in management.
3. It proposed to delete Section 3 of the Industrial Disputes Act concerning the works committee.
4. It proposed for appointment of inspectors.

Codes

(a) 1, 2 and 4 (b) 1, 2 and 3
(c) 1, 3 and 4 (d) 2, 3 and 4

5 Which of the following statements are true/false?

1. The first industrial policy resolution in India was introduced in 1948.
2. The Indian Parliament accepted the 'socialist pattern of society' as the national objective of its social and economic policy in December 1955.
3. The second industrial policy resolution in India was made in 1956.
4. Under the second industrial policy resolution, industries were classified into three categories on the basis of the role the state would play in each of them.

Codes

(a) 3 and 4 and the true and 1 and 2 are false
(b) 1, 3, 4 are true and 2 is false
(c) 1 and 2 are true and 3 and 4 are false
(d) 1, 2, 3 are true and 4 is false

6 Who proposed the three-tier structure of industrial relations activity ?

(a) John T Dunlop
(b) Kochan, Katz and McKersie
(c) JH Richardson
(d) HA Clegg

7 Which of the following theoretical perspectives implies stewardship without ownership in the context of industrial relations ?

(a) The Unitary perspective
(b) The Pluralist perspective
(c) The Radical perspective
(d) The Trusteeship perspective

8 Which among the following statements relating to the features of collective bargaining is/are correct ?

1. It is a two-way process.
2. It involves civilised confrontation.
3. It is a static process.
4. It is a complementary process.

Code

(a) 1 and 4 (b) 1, 2 and 3
(c) 1, 2 and 4 (d) 2, 3 and 4

9 **Assertion** (A) With the evoluation of industrial and employment relations in the face of rapid changes and significant advances in technology among other things, collective bargaining became an instrument of social change.

Reason (R) Shifts in the labour and product markets created pressures as well as opportunities for a new approach.

Codes
(a) (A) is incorrect and (R) is correct
(b) (A) is correct and (R) is a proper explanation of (A)
(c) (A) is correct, but (R) is incorrect
(d) (R) is not an explanation of (A)

10 Which of the following statements regarding the 'Socialist Manifesto' are true ?
1. It was drafted by Sidney and Beatrice Webb.
2. It was drafted by Karl Marx and Engels.
3. It was drafted for converting capitalist Britain into a mixed economy.
4. It was strongly opposed by the Labour Party in Britain.

Codes
(a) 1 and 2 (b) 2 and 3
(c) 1 and 3 (d) 3 and 4

11 Distributive bargaining, as described by Walton and McKersie, is also called
(a) Win-Win bargaining (b) Zero sum bargaining
(c) Composite bargaining (d) Concession bargaining

12 Which of the following statement(s) relating to the model grievance procedure is/are correct ?
1. As per the procedure, an aggrieved employee shall first present the grievance verbally (in person) to the officer designated by the management for this purpose.
2. As per the procedure, an aggrieved worker who is not satisfied with the decision of the officer at the first stage or fails to receive an answer within a stipulated period of 48 hours from the said officer, he/she shall, either in person or accompanied by his/her departmental representative, present his/her grievance to the head of the department designated by the management for the purpose of handling grievances.
3. According to the procedure, if a grievance arises out of an order given by management, the said order shall be complied with before the worker concerned invokes the procedure laid down for redressal of grievances.

Code
(a) Only 1 (b) Only 2
(c) 1 and 2 (d) All of these

13 In which of the following countries there exists a predominantly adversarial approach to industrial relations ?
(a) USA (b) Germany
(c) Sweden (d) Denmark

2017

14 Who had given the pluralist approach to industrial relations indicating 'job regulation' drawing from the theories of anomie, collective bargaining and industrial democracy?
(a) HA Clegg (b) Alan FOX
(c) R Commons (d) Allan Flanders

15 Assertion (A) Collective bargaining provides for procedural and substantial rule
Reason (R) It incorporates mechanism for dealing with interpretations and implementation of agreements as well as resolving conflicts and substantial rules concerning the substance of the agreements in both markets and managerial relationships.

Codes
(a) (A) is incorrect and (R) fails to explain (A)
(b) (A) is only partially true and therefore, (R) only partially explain (A)
(c) (A) is correct and (R) explain (A)
(d) (A) is correct and (R) is incorrect

16 Two distinct schools of thought have emerged in industrial relations. The first one, known as 'Personnel Management School', emphasised the "employers' solution" to labour problems. The second school of thought, known as 'Institutional Labour Economics School' emphasised the "workers' solution" of trade unionism and the communities' solution of protective labour legislation and social insurance to labour problems. Which of the following inferences are right relating to the broad themes of the above two schools?
1. The first school takes an 'internal' or inside-the-firm perspective on the solution of labour problems.
2. The second school favoured institutional forms of power balancing and joint governance in the employment relationship.
3. The first school takes an 'external' or outside-the-firm perspective on the solution of labour problems.
4. The second school emphasised upon building a community of interest between labour and management for which the employer has to take the initiative.

Codes
(a) 1 and 2 (b) 2 and 3
(c) 2 and 4 (d) 2, 3 and 4

17 Which of the following statement(s) relating to the Industrial Relations Policy in India is/are not true?
1. Industrial relations in India is highly regulated by state intervention.
2. Industrial Relations Policy in India tried to shift from courts to codes.
3. Tripartism was a strong policy shift in industrial relations in India.
4. Free and compulsory collective bargaining was the chief characteristic feature of Industrial Relations Policy in India.

Codes
(a) Only 1 (b) Only 2
(c) 1, 2 and 3 (d) Only 4

18 Who has propagated the bipartite, tripartite and multi-partite aspects of industrial relations with human relations as the invisible energy binding them?

(a) Sidney and Beatrice Webb (b) HA Clegg
(c) John H Richardson (d) Alan Fox

19 Associate the following conditions (List I) with the period in which they prevailed (List II).

List I		List II	
A.	Unbridled individualism, freedom contract and laissez-faire	1.	Welfarism and Post Welfarism
B.	Rise of trade unionism	2.	Political liberalism
C.	Rise of socialist and revolutionary ideas	3.	Early industrialism
D.	Rise of labour parties	4.	Marxism

Codes

	A	B	C	D		A	B	C	D
(a)	3	1	4	2	(b)	3	2	4	1
(c)	3	4	1	2	(d)	4	2	3	1

20 Match the themes of the three approaches of industrial relations under contradictions perspective approach and theme.

List I (Approach)		List II (Theme)	
A.	The Marxian approach	1.	Power struggle to control work organisations
B.	The Socialistic approach	2.	Power struggle to gain political power
C.	The Social Action approach	3.	Power struggle to improve the lot of the working class

Codes

	A	B	C		A	B	C
(a)	1	2	3	(b)	2	3	1
(c)	3	2	1	(d)	2	1	3

21 Who is/are the author(s) of the books titled, 'A History of Trade Unionism' (1897) and 'Industrial Democracy' (1902), the two early writings on industrial relations?

(a) Sidney and Beatrice Webb
(b) Alan Fox and Allan Flanders
(c) Karl Marx
(d) HA Clegg

22 Examine the following statements and identify the ones which are right and wrong.

1. Industrial relations as an activity is of recent origin.
2. Industrial relations as a field of study is of recent origin.
3. The early writings on industrial relations were mostly reflective of prevailing practices rather than theories and explanations.
4. Initially industrial relations subsumed all aspects of work, including problems and issues affecting both employers' and workers' organisations and covered only unionised employment relations.

Codes

(a) 2 and 4 are right, 1 and 3 are wrong
(b) Only 2 is right, but 1, 3 and 4 are wrong
(c) 2, 3 and 4 are right and 1 is wrong
(d) 2 and 3 are right, but 1 and 4 are wrong

23 Who has viewed collective bargaining as a process of social change?

(a) Neil W Chamberlain
(b) JH Richardson
(c) Arthur D Butler
(d) HW Davey

24 The Descending Participation, *i.e.* workers' participation in work was propounded by

(a) The Fabians (b) The Harvard Group
(c) The Oxford Group (d) The Tavistock Group

2016

25 Under which type of union security, an employee in the bargaining unit is obliged to pay dues to the union in return for the collective bargaining service which it is rendering to him, although he does not join the union?

(a) Preferential union shop (b) Closed shop
(c) Agency shop (d) Union shop

26 There exists hurdles on the way of healthy growth of collective bargaining in India. Which among the following are not the hurdles of collective bargaining?

1. Conditions of workers
2. Promotion of lasting industrial peace
3. Voluntariness in recognition of union
4. Ineffective procedure for determination of representative union
5. Provision for elaborate adjudication machineries
6. Comprehensive coverage of labour laws

Codes

(a) 1 and 2 (b) 3 and 4
(c) 5 and 6 (d) 3 and 5

27 Which of the following statements relating to the participation of workers in Management Bill, 1990 is not correct?

(a) The Bill was introduced in the Lok Sabha on the 30th May, 1990
(b) The introduction of this Bill was the first comprehensive legislative effort towards the promotion of workers' participation in management in India
(c) The Bill envisaged a three-tier system of workers' participation in management
(d) The Bill provided for the appointment of inspectors and specified penalties for violating the provisions of the Act when enacted

28 Who suggested for setting up of Joint Workers' Councils ?
(a) Bombay Committee, 1920
(b) Bengal Committee, 1920
(c) Royal Commission on Labour, 1931
(d) Government of India Act, 1935

29 Which of the following statements about Industrial Relations Systems in Multinational Corporations is true ?
1. North American MNCs attempt to make their foreign subsidiaries union free.
2. Following their tradition, Japanese MNCs set up enterprise unions at foreign subsidiaries.
3. West European MNCs believe in organised independent trade unions.
4. In general MNCs show gradations in the degree of policy of centralisation/decentralisation in the areas of industrial relations.

Codes
(a) 1, 2 and 3 (b) 2, 3 and 4
(c) 1 and 2 (d) All of these

30 Arrange the following developments in industrial relations philosophy in the order in which it occurred from the latest to the earliest.
1. Socialistic orientation
2. Kochan, Katz and McKersie's strategic choice orientation
3. Marxian orientation
4. Capitalistic orientation
5. Dunlop's system orientation

Codes
(a) 4, 1, 5, 3, 2 (b) 2, 5, 1, 3, 4
(c) 4, 3, 1, 5, 2 (d) 2, 1, 3, 5, 4

2015

31 Match the following.

	List I (Name of the acts)		List II (Also called)
A.	The National Labour Relations Act, 1935	1.	The Wagner Act
B.	The Labour Management Relations Act, 1947	2.	Taft-Hartley Act
C.	The Labour Management Reporting and Disclosure Act, 1959	3.	Landrum-Griffin Act

Codes

	A	B	C		A	B	C
(a)	1	2	3	(b)	2	1	3
(c)	3	1	2	(d)	2	3	1

32 Who has given the meaning of 'Conjunction' in industrial relations as "a state of relationship under which the parties, instead of offering their best, offer the least in the absence of which the relationship will break"?
(a) Selig Perlman (b) Neil W Chamberlain
(c) Frencis Walker (d) Ian Clegg

33 Which of the following regional groups in the internationalisation scenario is having regional associations of employers and employees as well as institutions governing their relationships?
(a) South Asian Association of Regional Cooperation (SAARC)
(b) Brazil, Russia, India, China, South Africa (BRICS)
(c) European Union (EU)
(d) Organisation of the Petroleum Exporting Countries (OPEC)

34 Which of the following statements about collective bargaining in India are true?
1. Collective bargaining is a legally sanctioned method in India.
2. Collective bargaining is not a legally sanctioned method in India.
3. Collective bargaining is partly voluntary and partly compulsory.
4. Collective agreement is binding on the parties that have signed the agreement.

Select the correct answer by using the codes given below

Codes
(a) 1 and 2
(b) 2 and 3
(c) 2 and 4
(d) 1 and 3

35 Which of the following statements is not true about Dunlop's Industrial Relations System?
(a) It consists of four basic components namely actors, ideology, rules and an environmental context
(b) In respect of rules, they can be both substantive and procedural
(c) In respect of context, it incorporates technological, economic and political contexts
(d) In respect of ideology, there is no need to have consensus between the ideology of actors

36 Which of the following studies/approaches does not come under the In-plant Theories of industrial relations?
(a) The 'Systems approach developed by John T Dunlop
(b) The Human Relations approach of Elton Mayo
(c) The Behaviouristic approach of Rensis Likert
(d) The Group Dynamics approach of Kurt Lewin, Chris Argyris and other

37 Which of the following statement(s) about disciplinary procedure is/are true?
1. A charge sheet enumerating the alleged charges shall be given to the alleged offender with a scope to give explanation within reasonable time.
2. The notice of enquiry need to contain date, time and venue.
3. If the alleged offender is not satisfied with the enquiry process; he/she cannot seek another enquiry, because it is a management prerogative to hold enquiry.

4. Under any circumstances, the enquiry cannot be held in the absence of the alleged offender.

Select the correct answer by using the codes given below

Codes

(a) 1 and 2 (b) 1 and 3
(c) 1, 2 and 4 (d) All of these

38 In which of the theoretical perspective of industrial relations it is believed that conflict is necessary, but it can be and needs to be managed and resolved?

(a) Unitarist perspective
(b) Pluralist perspective
(c) Radical perspective
(d) Trusteeship perspective

39 Who described that "industrial relations is an art, the art of living together for purposes of production (and/or services)"?

(a) John T Dunlop (b) John H Richardson
(c) M Salamon (d) A Flanders

40 Which of the following statements relating to labour-management cooperation is not correct?

(a) It does not include information sharing
(b) It includes problem sharing
(c) It includes joint consultation
(d) It includes workers' participation in management

41 Match the following.

List I		List II
A.	Works Committee	1. 1983
B.	Joint Management Councils	2. 1958
C.	Board-level participation	3. 1947
D.	Scheme of employees' participation in public sector undertakings	4. 1970

Codes

	A	B	C	D		A	B	C	D
(a)	3	2	4	1	(b)	3	4	1	2
(c)	3	1	4	2	(d)	2	4	3	1

42 Match the following.

	List I (Name)	List II (Year of Establishment)
A.	Indian Labour Conference	1. 1966
B.	Central Board for Worker's Education	2. 1942
C.	First National Commission on Labour	3. 1958
D.	All India Railwaymen's Federation	4. 1932

Codes

	A	B	C	D		A	B	C	D
(a)	1	2	3	4	(b)	4	3	2	1
(c)	2	3	1	4	(d)	3	2	4	1

43 When unions come forward for wage cuts, restriction on overtime, temporary job losses as part of collective bargaining agreements, such bargaining is called

(a) enterprise bargaining
(b) composite bargaining
(c) concession bargaining
(d) non-wage bargaining

44 Who among the following explained the prerequisite conditions of viable collective bargaining such as

1. the parties must attain a sufficient degree of organisation.
2. the parties must be ready to enter into agreements with each other.
3. the agreements must generally be observed and implemented by those to whom they apply?

Codes

(a) Allan Flanders (b) Neil W Chamberlain
(c) Robert Hoxie (d) Alan Fox

45 Which perspective on industrial relations is based on the notion that the production system is privately owned and is motivated by profit?

(a) Unitary perspective
(b) Pluralist perspective
(c) Radical perspective
(d) Trusteeship perspective

46 **Assertion** (A) The focus in industrial relations is shifting from collective to individual rights, from union to worker participation and from union to employee communication.

Reason (R) The new generation of workers (knowledge workers) expect an empowered relationship with the employer rather than protected relationship.

Codes

(a) (A) is wrong, so (R) does not explain (A)
(b) (A) is right, but (R) is wrong
(c) Both (A) and (R) are right and (R) explains (A)
(d) (A) is wrong, but (R) is right

47 Who played an instrumental role in the formulation of code of discipline?

(a) V V Giri (b) GL Nanda
(c) Khandubhai Desai (d) Ravindra Verma

48 What is not true about Industrial Relations Policy in India?

(a) Industrial Relations Policy in India is highly regulated by state intervention
(b) Industrial Relations Policy in India tried to shift from courts to codes
(c) Tripartism has been a discernible policy shift in industrial relations
(d) Free and compulsory collective bargaining has been encouraged by the relevant legislations in India

49 Government's policy relating to employment relations is mostly
(a) deregulated competitive
(b) regulated protective
(c) constrained competitive
(d) protective competitive

50 Which of the following trends is not true about the 'Industrial Relations Scenario' in India?
(a) Reduced government regulation
(b) Declining trade union density
(c) Increasing employer militancy
(d) Demand for labour reforms

51 Which of the following declared that, "There shall be unreserved acceptance of and respect for, democratic functioning of trade unions and there shall be regular and democratic elections of executive bodies and office-bearers of the trade unions"?
(a) The Code of Conduct
(b) The First National Commission on Labour
(c) The Second National Commission on Labour
(d) The Code of Discipline

52 In the first stage of the Model Grievance Procedure, an aggrieved employee may present his grievance
(a) by engaging a legal counsel
(b) through trade union
(c) through arbitrator
(d) verbally in person

53 Which segment of wages is determined by the 'escalatory clause' in collective bargaining?
(a) Basic wages (b) Incentives
(c) Dearness allowance (d) Bonus

2014

54 Which of the following is the first to recommend tripartite consultation at the national level in India?
(a) National Commission on Labour, 1969
(b) Industrial Policy Resolution, 1948
(c) Labour Investigation Committee, 1944
(d) Royal Commission on Labour, 1931

55 The British Industrial Relations Act, 1971 provided for which of the following clauses for compulsory membership of workers in unions?
1. Closed shop
2. Agency shop
3. Approved closed shop
4. Union shop

Select the correct answer by using the codes given below
Codes
(a) Both 1 and 2 (b) Both 1 and 3
(c) Both 2 and 4 (d) Both 2 and 3

56 Which of the following statements about workers' participation in management in India are true?
1. It has constitutional sanction.
2. Information sharing, problem solving, joint consultation and joint decision-making are different levels of participation.
3. It has not completely succeeded in solving the problems of mutual interest between employer and employee.
4. There is no statutory provision for institutionalising workers' participation in management excepting the Works Committee.

Select the correct answer by using the codes given below
Codes
(a) 2 and 3 (b) 3 and 4
(c) 2, 3 and 4 (d) 1, 2 and 3

57 Which of the following statements about the Marxist approach to industrial relations is not correct?
(a) It sees industrial conflict as synonymous with political and social conflicts
(b) It considers pluralism as a mere illusion
(c) It believes that capitalism cannot continue to maintain itself only by lowering the standard of living of the working class
(d) It favours transformation of trade unions into revolutionary organisations

58 Which approach to industrial relations aims to combine social stability with adaptability and freedom?
(a) Classical approach (b) Neo-classical approach
(c) Pluralistic approach (d) Social action approach

59 Who has conceptualised industrial relations as a rule making process governing both the employers and employees?
(a) Neil J Smelser (b) Arthur D Butler
(c) Neil W Chamberlain (d) John T Dunlop

60 Which of the following are the trends of industrial relations in the aftermath of the New Economic Policy?
1. Union militancy has decreased.
2. Managerial activism has increased.
3. Government intervention has reduced.
4. Free collective bargaining has substituted the third party intervention.

Select the correct answer by using the codes given below
Codes
(a) 1 and 2 (b) 2 and 4
(c) 1, 2 and 3 (d) 1, 2 and 4

61 During whose tenure as Minister of Labour, Government of India, the Indian industrial relations policy decisively shifted towards government intervention?
(a) V V Giri (b) Gulzari Lal Nanda
(c) Jagjivan Ram (d) Khandubhai Desai

62 Assertion (A) Collective bargaining is a mutual process of give and take between employer and employee.

Reason (R) Concession bargaining arises when employee plays the role of giver and employer becomes the taker.

Codes

(a) Both (A) and (R) are right and (R) explains the mutuality part in (A)

(b) Both (A) and (R) are wrong

(c) (A) is right, but (R) is wrong

(d) (A) is wrong, but (R) explains a new trend in collective bargaining

63 Which of the following is not an objective of workers' education in India?

(a) To strengthen among all sections of the working class including rural workers, a sense of patriotism, national integrity, unity, communal harmony, secularism and pride in being an Indian

(b) To equip all sections of workers including rural workers for their intelligent participation in asserting their right through strike

(c) To develop leadership among the rank and file of workers themselves

(d) To enable trade unions themselves to take over ultimately the functions of workers' education

64 The 'Socialist Manifesto' for converting capitalist economy into a mixed economy was developed by

(a) Karl Marx

(b) GDH Cole

(c) William Baveridge

(d) Sidney and Beatrice Webbs

65 Who among the following concluded that the factory was a social system and informal groups at workplace play a vital role in industrial affairs?

(a) Elton Mayo (b) Henry Fayol

(c) Blake and Mouton (d) Herzberg

66 Match the following.

	List I (Approach)		List II (Theme)
A.	Trusteeship	1.	Employers are low unto themselves, providers of job, income and social security
B.	Radical	2.	Conflict between employees is rational and inevitable
C.	Pluralist	3.	Production system is privately owned and is profit oriented
D.	Unitary	4.	Holds property on trust for others

Codes

	A	B	C	D		A	B	C	D
(a)	1	2	3	4	(b)	4	2	1	3
(c)	4	3	2	1	(d)	4	2	3	1

67 Assertion (A) The scope of industrial relations is relative to business environment.

Reason (R) It shall be universal and perpetual.

Codes

(a) (A) and (R) are true

(b) (A) is true, but (R) is false

(c) (A) is false and (R) is true

(d) (A) is true, but (R) is not the correct explanation of (A)

68 Match the following.

	List I (Approach)		List II (Propounder)
A.	Socio-Psychological approach	1.	Frank Tannenbaum
B.	Industrial Democracy approach	2.	Selig Perlmaw
C.	Scarcity Consciousness approach	3.	Sidney and Beatrice Webbs
D.	Sociological approach	4.	Robert F Hoxie

Codes

	A	B	C	D		A	B	C	D
(a)	3	1	4	2	(b)	2	3	1	4
(c)	4	3	2	1	(d)	1	2	3	4

69 Which of the following Acts was passed in USA to balance the power of employers and unions?

(a) Clayton Antitrust Act (b) Narris - Laguaradia Act

(c) Wagner Act (d) Taft - Hartley Act

70 Who used the term 'collective bargaining' first ?

(a) JH Richardson

(b) John T Dunlop

(c) Sidney and Beatrice Webbs

(d) Neil W Chamberlain

71 Which of the following statements about the role of Government in Industrial Relations in India is not true?

(a) The government continues to play a controller's role

(b) The government moved away from the controller's role to enabler's role

(c) The government is generally reticent, if not reluctant, to dole out administrative clearances for lay-offs, closures or retrenchment

(d) The government has hardly made any efforts to shift its emphasise from conflict resolution to conflict avoidance

72 Which of the following principles were taken into account while formulating the Model Grievance Procedure?

1. Conformity with the existing legislation.
2. Make the grievance handling machinery simple.
3. Make the grievance handling machinery expeditious.
4. Designating the authorities to be contacted at various levels of grievance procedure.

Codes

(a) Only 1 (b) Both 1 and 2

(c) 1, 2 and 3 (d) All of these

73 Which of the following statement(s) is/are considered as the portents for future of Industrial Relations in India?

1. The plurality of industrial relations will be seen not merely in terms of the organised and the unorganised, but also union and non-union firms.
2. Industrial relations will increasingly be driven by contextual factors.
3. Trade unions have to search for a new form and structure for maintaining voice and representation.
4. Increasingly the young, new and diverse workforce will resist joining unions.

Codes

(a) Only 1
(b) 1 and 2
(c) 1, 2 and 3
(d) All of the above

74 Which of the following have emerged as new actors in the changing industrial relations scenario?

1. Consumers
2. Community
3. Journalists
4. Environmental activists

Codes

(a) Only 1 (b) 1 and 2
(c) 1, 2 and 3 (d) All of these

75 Who is associated with the radical approach to industrial relations ?

(a) Mahatma Gandhi (b) John T Dunlop
(c) Karl Marx (d) Allan Flanders

76 According to John T Dunlop, the outputs of an Industrial Relations System include

(a) agreements, customs and traditions of the workplace and work community
(b) awards and orders of government agencies
(c) regulations and policies of the management hierarchy
(d) All of the above

ANSWERS

Exam Based Questions

1	(b)	2	(b)	3	(a)	4	(b)	5	(b)	6	(b)	7	(c)	8	(d)	9	(c)	10	(d)
11	(b)	12	(d)	13	(d)	14	(d)	15	(a)	16	(d)	17	(d)	18	(d)	19	(d)	20	(a)
21	(b)	22	(d)	23	(a)	24	(c)	25	(d)	26	(d)	27	(c)	28	(d)	29	(d)	30	(d)
31	(c)	32	(d)	33	(a)	34	(c)	35	(c)	36	(a)	37	(d)	38	(d)	39	(d)	40	(d)
41	(b)	42	(c)	43	(b)	44	(d)	45	(a)	46	(a)	47	(a)	48	(d)	49	(b)	50	(d)
51	(b)	52	(d)	53	(b)	54	(c)	55	(d)	56	(d)	57	(b)	58	(d)	59	(d)	60	(d)
61	(d)	62	(a)	63	(d)	64	(d)	65	(d)	66	(d)	67	(d)	68	(a)	69	(b)	70	(d)
71	(d)	72	(d)	73	(c)	74	(d)	75	(a)	76	(c)	77	(b)	78	(a)	79	(c)	80	(b)
81	(a)	82	(b)	83	(a)	84	(a)	85	(b)	86	(c)	87	(a)	88	(a)	89	(d)	90	(a)
91	(a)	92	(b)	93	(b)	94	(b)	95	(a)	96	(d)	97	(b)	98	(c)	99	(a)	100	(c)
101	(b)	102	(a)	103	(a)	104	(c)	105	(c)	106	(a)	107	(c)						

Previous Years' Questions

1	(a)	2	(b)	3	(c)	4	(c)	5	(b)	6	(b)	7	(d)	8	(c)	9	(b)	10	(c)
11	(b)	12	(d)	13	(a)	14	(d)	15	(d)	16	(a)	17	(d)	18	(c)	19	(a)	20	(b)
21	(a)	22	(c)	23	(c)	24	(d)	25	(c)	26	(a)	27	(a)	28	(a)	29	(d)	30	(b)
31	(a)	32	(b)	33	(c)	34	(c)	35	(d)	36	(a)	37	(c)	38	(b)	39	(b)	40	(a)
41	(a)	42	(c)	43	(c)	44	(a)	45	(c)	46	(c)	47	(b)	48	(d)	49	(b)	50	(a)
51	(a)	52	(d)	53	(c)	54	(d)	55	(d)	56	(d)	57	(c)	58	(c)	59	(d)	60	(a)
61	(d)	62	(a)	63	(a)	64	(d)	65	(a)	66	(c)	67	(b)	68	(b)	69	(d)	70	(c)
71	(b)	72	(d)	73	(d)	74	(c)	75	(c)	76	(b)								

Trade Unions

This chapter deals with the growth and evolution of trade union from the pre-independence area till date. It explains the basic concepts of trade union, its legislations and includes Trade Union Act. The chapter also throws light on the problems faced by trade union in India.

Concept of Trade Unions

Trade unionism is a worldwide movement and the major component of the modern industrial relations system. In most cases, employees' associations or trade unions seem to have emerged as 'protest movements' reacting against the employer-employee relationships and conditions created by industrialisation. Although trade unions occupy a unique position, but their role is variously interpreted and understood by different groups in the society.

According to **Frank Tannenbaum**, "The emergence of trade unionism lies in the Industrial Revolution which disrupted the older way of life and created a new society forged by the shop, the factory, the mine and the industry."

It can be said that a trade union of workers is an voluntary organisation formed by workers to protect their interests, improve their working conditions etc by collective action.

According to **Dale Yoder**, "A union is a continuing long-term association of employees, formed and maintained for the specific purpose advancing and protecting the interests of members in their working relationships."

According to **RA Lester**, "Industrial relations involve attempts to have workable solutions between conflicting objectives and values, between incentive and economic security, between discipline and industrial democracy, between authority and freedom and between bargaining and cooperation."

In this Chapter

- *Concept of Trade Unions*
- *Organisational Structure of Trade Unions*
- *Trade Unions Act, 1926*

According to **GDH Cole,** "A trade union means an association of workers in one or more professions, an association carried on mainly for the purpose of protecting and advancing the member's economic interests in connection with their daily work."

According to **Webb,** "A trade union is a continuous association of wage-earners for the purpose of maintaining and improving the conditions of their working lives."

Trade Union, Organised Labour and Labour Movement

The term **'Trade Union'** has been defined in various ways because of wide differences in the use of this term in different countries. It is a continuous association of wage-earners for the purpose of maintaining or improving the condition of their working lives.

It may be redefined as "A continuous association of wage-earners or salaried employees for maintaining the conditions of their working lives and ensuring them a better and healthier status in industry as well as in the society."

The term **'Organised Labour'** is used to distinguish workers/employees who are members of trade unions or employee association from those who are unorganised, *i.e.* who are not members of any union.

Trade unions are no more a separate entity but considered as the part of system. They serve the purpose of saving the interests of the sub-groups; there are trade unions of blue collar workers, white collar employees and also employees.

It was difficult for the individual to get his demands fulfilled, therefore, the need of trade unions arose, obviously an individual may not be able to organise and defend his interests as well as a group.

With the continuous change in technology, social and political environment and other factors; it was observed that people were more aware of their rights to bargain, organise and negotiate. This is what gave recognition to worker's unions and employer's unions.

The term **'Labour Movement'** is a broad term for the development of a collective organisation of working people, to campaign for better working condition and treatment from their employers and government through the implemention of specific laws governing labour relations.

According to **Encyclopedia of Social Sciences** labour movement is conceived as "All of the organised activity of wage-earners to better their own conditions either immediately or in the more or less distant future."

According to **GDH Cole**, "Labour movement implies, in some degree, a community of outlook. Thus, the labour movement in a country emerges from a common need to serve a common interest."

It seeks to develop amongst employees a spirit of combination, class-consciousness and solidarity of interest and generates a consciousness for self-respect.

A trade union is thus an essential basis of labour movement. The labour movement without trade unions cannot exist. Trade unions are the principal institutions in which the employees learn the lesson of self-reliance and solidarity.

Difference between Labour Movement and Trade Union Movement

Although both the terms are quite similar to each other and are used interchangeably. However, there is a slight distinction between the two.

The 'labour movement' is 'for the worker' whereas the 'trade union movement' is 'by the workers'.

This distinction needs to be noticed all the more because till the workers organised themselves into trade unions, efforts were made mainly by the social reformers to improve the working and living conditions of labour.

These efforts should be taken as forming a part of the labour movement and not that of the trade union movement.

The labour movement thus conveys a higher degree of consciousness amongst workers than conveyed by mere trade union movement.

Features of Trade Union

- A group of independent workers.
- An association formed either by employers or by workers.
- Formed on a continuous basis.
- A permanent body and not casual or temporary one.
- Basically formed to protect and promote all kinds of interests-economic, political and social of its members.
- Main focus of interest is to safeguard worker's economic issues.
- Part of management; concerned with the manpower of the enterprise.
- Includes federations of trade unions also.
- The outcome of industrial relations.
- Achieves its objectives through collective action and group effort with the tools such as negotiations and collective bargaining.
- Work towards raising the status of labours as a part of industry.

Reasons for Joining Trade Union

- One of the main reasons of workers joining a trade union is their belief to get wages compatible to the market and their understanding that individual bargaining was utterly useless for this purpose.
- Since the employee as an individual is weak, he prefers to join an organisation that gives him an opportunity to join others for the achievement of those objectives that he considers as socially desirable.
- Ensure a just and fair dealing by management.
- Through collective strength, they restrain the management from taking any such action which may be irrational, illogical, discriminatory or contrary to their general interests.
- Unions provide sufficient machinery for proper maintenance of labour-management relations.
- Employees believe that it is the only way to secure adequate protection from various types of hazards and income insecurity such as accident, injury, illness, unemployment etc; can be the reasons of hazards.
- The unions are the communication system and provide with an opportunity to share their views, ideas, feelings and frustration to the management effectively.
- The individuals join unions simply because other workers urge them to do so. They may be treated as odd man out otherwise.
- The individuals join the unions with an impression that their influence in the company management will elevate themselves and bring more career opportunities.

Objectives of Trade Union

- To represent individual workers when they have a problem.
- To improve the economic conditions of workers by ensuring better wages.
- To ensure better working conditions for the workers.
- To make an effort to provide bonus for the employees from the profit of the employer.
- To show resistance for the schemes of the management which harm employees. *e.g.* Retrenchment, automation, lay-off etc.
- To negotiate with the employers to find out the solution.
- To protect the interest of the employees by taking active participation in the management.
- To secure social welfare of the employees. Some unions provide financial help to the members when they are sick or unemployed.
- To secure organisational stability, growth and leadership.
- To run training courses for their members on employment right, health, safety and other issues.
- To provide education by offering courses on the basic skills and the courses leading to professional qualifications.
- To provide legal assistance on the issues related to employment as well as personal matters such as housing.
- To provide loans to the members and get discounts on mortgages and insurance etc.
- To provide workers an opportunity to be part of decisions related to lay-offs, retrenchment, promotion and transfer.
- To provide the workers with legal advice on employment issues.

Functions of Trade Unions

To attain or accomplish the already stated objectives, trade unions need to perform certain functions in relation to trade union members, industrial organisation, trade unions organisation and society. *These are as follows*

1. Functions related to Trade Union Members

- To save workers from all sorts of exploitation by the employers, by union leaders and by political parties.
- To protect workers from the atrocities as well as obnoxious and unfair practices of the management.
- To ensure healthy, safe and conducive working conditions.
- To pressurise management for the better compensations against the work only after making a realistic assessment of its practical implications.
- To ensure a reasonable and healthy standard of living by providing various types of social service-health, housing, educational, recreational, cooperative etc.
- To guarantee a fair and square deal and social security measures.
- To remove the dissatisfaction and redress the grievances and complaints of workers.
- To encourage workers' participation in the management of industrial organisation and trade union and to foster labour-management cooperation.
- To make the workers aware of their rights and duties.
- To stress on the significance of settling disputes through negotiation, joint consultation and voluntary arbitration.
- To raise the status of trade union members in the industrial organisation and in the society at large.

2. Functions related to Industrial Organisation

- To highlight the industrial organisation as a joint enterprise between workers and management and to promote indentity of interests.
- To promote the concept of mutual and common interests of both the workers and management.
- To increase the efficiencies and effectiveness of the organisation by laying down the norms and ensuring their adequate observance.
- To facilitate the maintenance of discipline.
- To create opportunities for workers' participation in management and to strengthen labour-management cooperation.
- To help in the removal of dissatisfaction and redressal of grievances and complaints.
- To promote cordial and amicable relations between the workers and management by settling disputes through negotiations, joint consultation and voluntary arbitration, and by avoiding litigation.
- To create favourable opinion of the management towards trade unions and improve their status in industrial organisation.
- To exert pressure on the employer to enforce legislative provision beneficial to the workers, to share the profits equitably and to keep away from various types of unfair labour practices.
- To facilitate communication with the management.
- To impose upon the management the need to adopt reformative and not punitive approach towards workers' faults.

3. Functions related to Trade Unions' Organisation

- To formulate policies and plans consistent with those of the industrial organisation and society at large.
- To improve financial position by fixing higher subscription, by realising the union dues and by organising special fund-raising campaigns.
- To preserve and strengthen trade union democracy.
- To train members to make new leaders.
- To improve the communication channel between trade union and its members.
- To reduce inter-union rivalry and encourage the creation of unified trade union movement.
- To promote unity and solidarity within the union.
- To find the solution of fractions of different unions.
- To eradicate casteism, regionalism and linguism within the trade union movement.
- To keep away from unfair labour practices.
- To continuously review the relevance of union objectives in the context of social change and to change them accordingly.
- To prepare and maintain the necessary records.
- To manage the trade union organisation on scientific lines.
- To publicise the trade union objectives and functions, to know peoples' reaction towards them and to make necessary modifications.

4. Functions related to Society

- To provide all sorts of constructive cooperation in the formulation and implementation of plans and policies concerning national development.
- To actively participate in the development of programmes of national development, *e.g.* family planning, afforestation, national integration etc.
- To launch special campaigns against the social evils of nepotism, communalism, casteism, regionalism, linguism, price rise, hoarding, black marketing, smuggling, sex, inequality, dowry, untouchability, illiteracy, corruption.
- To enable unorganised sector to organise itself.
- To create public opinion favourable to government's policies and plans, and to mobilise peoples' participation for their effective implementation.
- To create public opinion favourable to trade unions and thereby raise their status.
- To exert pressure, after realistically ascertaining its practical implications on the government to enact legislation conducive to the development of trade unions and their members.

Ancillary Functions

1. Communication

- Almost all the big unions publish a newsletter or magazine to make people aware of the union's policy or stand on certain principle issues.
- It is a good source of communication and can be made more efficient with the involvement of some professionals.
- These publications could be a source of generating money.
- The main function of communication is to make sure that the rank and file are aware of the activities of the union.

2. Welfare Activities

- Many unions perform a large number of welfare activities to improve the quality of the workers' lives.
- These welfare activities include the provision of housing, co-operative societies, banking facility etc.
- The establishment of self-employed womens' association is a part of welfare activities.
- To provide a special training to women with a kind of special skill to augment the income.

3. Education

- It helps to create awareness on the part of the workers about the environment around them.
- Although, government has worker education scheme, the trade unions have co-operated and added their own contribution to tailor it to the specific requirement of the workers.
- These educational schemes are meant to increase the workers' knowledge of his work environment and the concerned issues.
- The workers will be made more aware of his rights and responsibilities, procedures and systems existing in workers' participation.

4. Research

It is getting significant in recent times.

Some of the research activities are

- Collection and analysis of wage data including fringe and pension benefits through surveys and comparative practices. Preparation of background notes for union officials and court cases.
- Collection and analysis of macro data relating to the economy, industry sectors etc.
- Maintain contacts with other unions, research bodies and universities. To examine the current organisation structure, procedures etc.

These functions are usually carried out at the main office of the union but certainly with the support of local offices and officials.

5. Militant Functions

- It includes strikes, boycotts and gheraos.
- The functions of trade union which ultimately lead them to improving the living conditions of workers.
- Militant functions aim to ensure adequate wages, secure better conditions of work and employment, get better treatment from the employers etc.
- After the normal and peaceful measures such as collective bargaining and negotiations fail, they adopt a militant approach and put up a fight with the management in the form of go-slow, strikes, boycott and gherao etc.

6. Ministrant Functions

- These functions work with humanitarian and benevolent approach.
- There is another set of functions performed by trade unions aimed at rendering help to its members in times of need and improving their efficiency.
- These functions basically give financial support to members during strikes and lockouts.
- These activities completely depend upon the availability of funds, which the unions collect against the subscription from members, donations from outsiders and also on their competent and enlightened leadership.
- Under the fraternal functions, activities like opening schools for the children, library, reading rooms, indoor and outdoor games and other recreational activities are included.

Intra-mural Activities

These are those welfare efforts of unions which are made within the factory premises, *e.g.* improvement in working conditions, regulation of hours of work, provision of rest pauses, adequate wages, sanitation, safety etc.

Extra-mural Activities

These activities include those welfare efforts of unions which are made outside the factory premises, *e.g.* provision of educational, recreational and housing facilities to workers.

Types of Unions

Classification Based on Trade

Craft Unions Unions that represent skilled craft workers, *e.g.* journalists, weavers, teachers, engineers etc.

Industrial Unions Unions that represent all workers-skilled, semi-skilled, unskilled-employed on the basis of the kind of industry they are working in.

General Unions These represent workers from different industry and any level of skills, *e.g.* Indian National Trade Union Congress (INTUC).

White Collar Unions They represents office workers.

Employee Associations Labour organisations that represent various groups of professional and white collar employees in labour-management relations.

White collared workers are registered under the Trade Unions Act or the Societies Registration Act. It is also known as employees' union, employees' association or staff association. Such types of unions suffer from multiplicity, politicalisation and outside leadership.

Classification Based on Representation

Qualified Unions Unions having atleast 5% of membership of total employees.

Primary Unions Having membership of atleast 15% of the employees in an undertaking.

Representative Unions Having a membership of not less than 25% of the total employees as members in an undertaking.

Theories of Trade Unions

1. Revolutionary Theory

It is propounded by **Marx** and **Hegels**. According to this theory, instruments of production must belong to workers, trade unions must resort to direct action and indulge in strikes, bandhs, gheraos and even violence, if needed.

2. Industrial Democracy Theory

It was put forth by **Sidney** and **Beatrice Webb**. This theory suggests democracy is important in industry as in the government. Through unions, the workers protect themselves from the power and influence of owners. All rules and regulations are developed in order to protect the rights of the labour.

According to this theory, trade unionism is an extension of democracy from political sphere to industrial sphere. In fact, industrial democracy can only lead to real freedom of opportunity, freedom of speech and freedom of association. By industrial democracy, it is meant that workers get say in running of the industry and an important role in the decision-making in regard to day-to-day activities.

This theory believes that trade unions are the only means to achieve industrial democracy as they have the power to sought reasonable demands from the employers.

3. Business Theory

It was propounded by **Samuel Gompers**. This theory emphasised that the primary objective of the unions was to protect the economic interest of the workers. Gompers believed that unions are the collective voice of the labour in the industrial world. He proposed to have partnership with business and promotes the view of higher wages with higher profits for the betterment of the workers.

Gompers viewed unions as the labour component of a business operation, neither superior nor inferior to the management component, but an extremely essential part of the business. No business can flourish without the motivated and skilled workers, howsoever good business plan is.

4. Sociological Theory

It was propounded by **Frank Trannenbaum**. According to this theory, the emergence of unionism is spontaneous and premediated. Due to industrial revolutions, employer has started relying more on machine rather than 'man'.

Sociological theory represents a drive on the part of the workers to reestablish their identity and social life which was robbed and destroyed due to automation.

According to this theory, the workers organise themselves to reduce their loss of security.

5. Socio-Psychological Theory

It was propunded by **Robert Hoxie** in 1920. According to this theory, workers join union to meet their socio-psychological needs like physiological security, companionship, group of likely persons with similar needs and mind-sets. It means not only environmental conditions but temperamental characteristics of the workers are also important.

Thus, differences in group psychology cause different types of unions to appeal and there can be following categories of unions

Business Unionism Believes in protecting the economic interests and working conditions of the workers.

Uplift Unionism Believes in protecting the intellectual, moral and social levels of the workers.

Revolutionary Unionism believe in direct action and replacing of existing social order and installing new socialistic system.

Predatory Unionism believes in ruthless pursuit of its objectives by hook or crook without subscribing to any ideology.

Dependent Unionism rely upon the support of employers or other labour groups.

6. Change Theory

It was propounded by **Selig Perlman** in 1928.

According to **Perlman**, "Unionism is developed because of workers tendency to accomplish and control the ownership of the jobs on account of scarcity consciousness".

This kind of unionism exercises control over the opportunity by establishing certain job and then by rationing the same among its members through regulation.

Job security is the major motive behind the labour movement, and the workers are motivated more by such pragmatic goals rather than by political actions as they are more concerned about their financial positions.

7. Protest/General Theory

It was propunded by **Kerr, Dunlop** and **Myre**. According to this theory, workers' protest is inherent in industrialisation. The people involved in industrilisation play an important role in the kind of labour organisation formed.

The nature and role of such labour organisations are dependent upon the culture and environment of the country, the industrialisation process etc.

8. Sarvodaya Theory

It was propounded by **Mahatma Gandhi**. This theory is based upon the principles of truth, non-violence and trusteeship. The main function of this theory is to raise the moral and intellectual standards of labour and teach them supplementary occupations, which prove to be helpful at the time of emergency.

Evolution of Trade Unions in India

Pre 1918 Phase

This era was predominantly led by the social reformers and philanthropists and not workers. There were no trade unions and the movement was started to create an awakening among the workers about their rights. It was basically a revolt against the conditions of child labour and women workers working in various industries under appealing conditions.

The first Factory Commission was appointed in Bombay in the year 1885 and the first Factories Act, was passed in 1881. The Bombay Mill Hands Association was the first trade union of the country, and was founded by Mr. N M Lokhande in 1890.

1918-1924 Phase

This phase laid the foundation of modern trade unionism and led to the formation of a large number of trade unions. During this phase, there was the establishment of International Labour Organisation (ILO) in 1919.

India was one of the founding members of ILO. All India Trade Union Congress (AITUC) was formed in 1920. The different associations and unions formed during this phase were Ahmedabad Textile Labour Association, the Madras Labour Union (1918), Indian Seamen's Union, Calcutta Clerk's Union and All India Postal and RMS Association.

1925-1934 Phase

Trade Unions Act, 1926 and the Trade Disputes Act, 1929 were passed during this time. The National Trade Union Federation (NTUF) was established by Mr. NM Joshi and Mr. VV Giri in this era. AITUF and National Federation of Labour (NFL) merged to form the National Trade Union Federation (NTUF).

1935-1938 Phase

The Bombay Industrial Disputes Act, 1938 was passed during this era and it provided compulsory recognition of unions by the employers. There was increased awakening among the workers to their rights and change in the managerial attitude towards trade unions.

1939-1946 Phase

This was witnessed during the post-World War II phase as there were massive levels of unemployment because of the War. The Industrial Employment (Standing Orders) Act, 1946 and the Bombay Industrial Relations Act, 1946 was passed during this phase.

Since 1947

The Indian National Trade Union Congress (INTUC) was formed in 1947. The Hind Mazdoor Sabha (HMS) was formed in 1948. Eventually, a large number of trade unions came into existence. All of them have been discussed in the following sections.

Organisational Structure of Trade Unions

The Statistics on trade unions are collected annually by the Labour Bureau of the Ministry of Labour, Government of India. In India, 11 major unions are recognised as central trade union organisations and operate in many states.

These are as follows

1. Indian National Trade Union Congress (INTUC)

- It is the trade union wing of the Indian National Congress and was founded on **3rd May, 1947**.
- The first president was **Sardar Vallabhbhai Patel**.
- The first Delegates Session was held in Bombay in May, 1948.

Some of the objectives of INTUC are

- To establish an order of society that promotes overall development of worker.
- To guide and coordinate the activities of the affiliated organisations.
- To assist and coordinate the activities of the affiliated organisations.
- To assist in the formation of trade unions.
- To promote the organisation of workers of each industry on a nation-wide basis.
- To assist in the formation of Regional or Pradesh Branches or Federations.

- To secure speedy improvement of conditions of work and life and status of the workers in industry and society.
- To establish just working conditions. To raise the workers' standard of efficiency and discipline.

2. Hind Mazdoor Sabha (HMS)

- HMS was founded in **Howrah**, West Bengal on **29th December, 1948** by socialists, forward bloc followers and independent unionists.
- It was founded by Basawon Singh, Ashok Mehta, RS Ruikar, Maniben Kara, Shibnath Banerjee, RA Khedgikar, TS Ramanujam, VS Mathur, GG Mehta.
- It absorbed the Royist Indian Federation of Labour and the Hind Mazdoor Panchayat.
- HMS follows the principles and polices of the Socialist Party.

3. All India Trade Union Congress (AITUC)

- It was founded on **31st October, 1920** in **Bombay** and Lala Lajpat Rai was its first President.
- It was founded by Lala Lajpat Rai, Joseph Baptista, NM Joshi, Diwan Chaman Lall and a few others.
- It is the oldest trade union federation in the country and the founder member of the world federation of trade unions.
- AITUC adopts the policies and ideologies of Communist Party of India (CPI).

The main objectives of AITUC are

- To establish a socialist state in India.
- To socialise and nationalise the means of production, distribution and exchange as far as possible.
- To ameliorate the economic and social conditions of the working class.
- To watch, promote, safeguard and further the interests, rights and privileges of the workers in all matters relating to their employment.
- To secure and maintain for the workers the freedom of speech, the freedom of press, the freedom of association, the freedom of assembly, the right of strike and the right to work or maintenance.
- To coordinate the activities of the trade unions affiliated to the AITUC.
- To abolish political or economic advantage based on caste, creed, community, race or religion; to fight against all forms of social oppression and injustice.
- To fight against all forms of atrocities against women and harassment at place of work.

4. Bharatiya Mazdoor Sangh (BMS)

- It was founded by **Dattopant Thengadi** on **23rd July, 1955**, birthday of Lok Manya Bal Gangadhar Tilak.
- It is a non-political organisation focusing on promoting itself as a genuine trade union that strives to work for the welfare of people.
- The union works on the principle of nationalism and not on capitalism, socialism or communism.

5. All India United Trade Union Centre (AIUTUC)

- It was founded at **Kolkata 26th-27th April, 1958.**
- It is a Central Trade Union Organisation in India and the labour wing of the Socialist Unity Centre of India (Communist).
- It was formerly known as United Trade Union Centre (Lanin Sarani) or UTUC-LS.
- It is actively working in the formal and informal sector, with the most important one being agriculture.

6. Trade Union Coordination Centre (TUCC)

- The nationalist trade unions following the principles of Netaji Subhash Chandra Bose, the trade union association of independent anti imperialist movement came together and formed the Trade Union Coordination Centre (TUCC) in 1980.

Some of the major aims and objectives of TUCC are

- To watch, promote, safeguard the interests, rights, and privileges of the workers in all social, cultural, economic and political matters.
- Establish study centers/trusts to ensure training and education to its members.
- Ensure workers participation in management.
- To coordinate the activities of the trade unions affiliated to the TUCC.
- Conduct movement of collective bargaining.
- To fight against all forms of harassment on atrocities against women at their place of work.
- To bring about unity of the working class in the trade union movement.
- To work in close cooperation with the working class organisation of different countries to foster the idea of international working class unity.
- To protect the interest of the unorganised working class.
- To work for abolition of child labour.

7. Self-Employed Women's Association (SEWA)

- The Self-Employed Women's Association (SEWA) came into being in **December 1971** and it was born in 1972 as a trade union of self employed women.
- It grew out of the Textile Labour Association (TLA), India's oldest and largest union of textile workers founded in 1920 by a women, Anasuya Sarabhai.
- Mahatma Gandhi was the inspiration behind the formation of this trade union.
- It was established with the aim to assist women belonging to households of mill workers and its work was focussed largely on training and welfare activities.

8. All India Central Council of Trade Unions (AICCTU)

It is a central trade union federation in India and is politically attached to communist party of India (Marxist-Leninist) liberation.

The different federations affiliated to AICCTU are

- All India Construction Workers Federation
- Coal Mines Workers Union (CMWU)
- Municipalities
- North Central Railway Workers Union (NCRWU)
- Asha Workers Association
- Steel Workers Federation (SWF)

9. Labour Progressive Federation (LPF)

- The Labour Progressive Federation is a trade union federation in Tamil Nadu.
- It is politically attached to Dravida Munnetra Kazhagam.

10. United Trade Union Congress (UTUC)

- It was founded at an All India Labour Conference in **Calcutta** on **1st May, 1949** and the founding president was KT Shah.
- It is politically linked to the socialist party of India.

11. National Front of Indian Trade Unions – Dhanbad (NFITU-DHN)

- It is an apex body founded in the year 1969 for representation, policy making and affiliation of trade unions at the national forum.
- It achieved the status of Central Trade Union Organisation (CTUO) in the year 2008 by Government of India.
- It is affiliated to Hind Mazdoor Kisan Panchayat (HMKP). It has its presence in around 51 industries across 24 states in India.

Problems of Trade Unions in India

The different problems faced by trade unions in India are as follows

Size of the Trade Union

India predominantly has small trade unions that make them weaker in front of the management. They are not able to put forth their demands in front of management and their bargaining power is reduced considerably.

Poor Finance

As the size of trade union is small, the subscription that can be charged from the members is also small. This ultimately results in a small size of the fund that can be collected and maintained.

Politicisation

Different trade unions in India have an affiliation with different political parties. The leaders of trade unions are more focused on delivering the value to their political party instead of working for the welfare of their laborers/workers.

Internal Politics

There is a lot of internal politics prevalent in the trade unions in which the members are fighting inside and outside the trade union for the leadership and power.

Lack of Awareness

The workers have no idea about their rights and lack the basic knowledge and education they must have in order to discharge their duties well.

Miscellaneous Causes

Some other challenges include the growth of informal employment and contract workers, promoting the right to organise and bargain collectively, protection of migrant workers (both inter-state and international migrants), gender equality, lack of social security, and workers' safety and security.

Trade Union Act, 1926

This act came into force on 25th March, 1926 and helps to provide for the registration of trade unions and in certain respects to define the law relating to registered trade unions.

Definitions Under the Act (Section 2)

- In this act, **'the Appropriate Government'** means, in relation to trade unions whose objects are not confined to one state, the Central Government and in relation to other trade unions, the State Government and, unless there is anything repugnant in the subject or context.

- **'Executive'** means the body, by whatever name called, to which the management of the affairs of a trade union is entrusted.
- **'Office-bearer'**, in the case of a trade union, includes any member of the executive thereof, but does not include an auditor. [Section 2(b)]
- **'Prescribed'** means prescribed by regulations made under this Act. [Section 2(c)]
- **'Registered Office'** means that office of a trade union which is registered under this act as the head office thereof. [Section 2(d)]
- **'Registered Trade Union'** means a trade union registered under this act. [Section 2(e)]
- **'Registrar'** means
  (a) A Registrar of trade unions appointed by the appropriate Government under Section 3 and includes any Additional or Deputy Registrar of Trade Unions.
  (b) In relation to any trade union, the Registrar appointed for the State in which the head or registered office, as the case may be, of the trade union is situated. [Section 2(f)]
- **'Trade Dispute'** means any dispute between employers and workmen or between workmen and workmen, or between employers and employers which is connected with the employment or non-employment, or the terms of employment or the conditions of labour, of any person, and "workmen" means all persons employed in trade or industry whether or not in the employment of the employer with whom the trade dispute arises. [Section 2(g)]
- **'Trade Union'** means any combination, whether temporary or permanent, formed primarily for the purpose of regulating the relations between workmen and employers or between workmen and workmen or between employers and employers, or for imposing restrictive conditions on the conduct of any trade or business, and includes any federation of two or more trade unions. [Section 2(h)]

Registration of Trade Unions

Appointment of Registrars (Section 3)

The appropriate Government shall appoint a person to be the registrar of trade unions for each State. It may appoint as many additional and deputy registrars of trade unions as it thinks fit for the purpose of exercising and discharging, under the superintendence and direction of the registrar.

It will define the powers and functions of the Registrar, additional or deputy registrar under this act and specify and define the local limits.

Mode of Registration (Section 4)

Seven or more members of the trade union can apply for the registration of the trade union under this act.

The application shall become invalid if some of the applicants, but not exceeding half of the total number of persons who made the application, have ceased to be members of the trade union or have given notice in writing to the registrar dissociating themselves from the application at any time after the date of the application.

Application of Registration (Section 5)

- *The application must be accompanied with a copy of the rules of the trade union and a statement of the following particulars*
  (a) The names, occupations and addresses of the members making the application.
  (b) The name of the trade union and the address of its head office and
  (c) The titles, names, ages, addresses and occupations of the office-bearers of the trade union.
- If a trade union has been in existence for more than one year before the making of an application for its registration, it should submit a general statement of the assets and liabilities of the trade union prepared in such form and containing such particulars as may be prescribed.

Provisions to be Contained in the Rules of a Trade Union (Section 6)

A trade union shall not be entitled to registration under this act, unless the executive thereof is constituted in accordance with the provisions of this act, and the rules thereof provide for the following matters, *namely*

(a) the name of the Trade Union.
(b) the whole of the objects for which the trade union has been established.
(c) the whole of the purposes for which the general funds of the trade union shall be applicable, all of which purposes shall be purposes to which such funds are lawfully applicable under this act.
(d) the maintenance of a list of the members of the trade union and adequate facilities for the inspection thereof by the office-bearers and members of the trade union.
(e) the admission of ordinary members who shall be persons actually engaged or employed in an industry with which the trade union is connected, and also the admission of the number of honorary or temporary members as office-bearers required under Section 22 to form the executive of the trade union.
(ee) the payment of a subscription by members of the trade union which shall be not less than twenty-five naye paise per month per member.

(f) the conditions under which any member shall be entitled to any benefit assured by the rules and under which any fine or forfeiture may be imposed on the members.
(g) the manner in which the rules shall be amended, varied or rescinded.
(h) the manner in which the members of the executive and the other office-bearers of the trade union shall be appointed and removed.
(i) the safe custody of the funds of the trade union, an annual audit, in such manner as may be prescribed, of the accounts thereof, and adequate facilities for the inspection of the account books by the office-bearers and members of the trade union and
(j) the manner in which the trade union may be dissolved.

Registration (Section 8)

The registrar will register the trade union under the act after he or she is satisfied with the complete information provided by the union as per the requirements of this act.

Certificate of Registration (Section 9)

The registrar will issue a certificate in the prescribed format after the requisite formalities are done.

Cancellation of Registration (Section 10)

The trade union will be provided a previous written notice of not less than two months' specifying the ground on which it is proposed to withdraw or cancel the certificate.

The certificate can be withdrawn or cancelled by the registrar

- On the application of the trade union to be verified in such manner as may be prescribed.
- If the Registrar is satisfied that the certificate has been obtained by fraud or mistake.
- The trade union has ceased to exist or has wilfully and after notice from the Registrar contravened any provision of this act or allowed any rule to continue in force which is inconsistent with any such provision.
- Trade union has rescinded any rule providing for any matter, provision for which is required by Section 6.

Appeal (Section 11)

In case, there is a refusal of the Registrar to register a trade union or by the withdrawal or cancellation of a certificate of registration, *the person has the right to appeal in*

- Where the head office of the trade union is situated within the limits of a Presidency-town, to the High Court, or
- Where the head office is situated in any other area, to such Court, not inferior to the Court of an additional or assistant Judge of a principal Civil Court of original jurisdiction, as the appropriate Government may appoint in this behalf for that area.
- In case, the appeal is rejected by any aforementioned court, the person shall have a right of appeal to the High Court and the High Court shall, for the purpose of such appeal, have all the powers of an Appellate Court.

Incorporation of Registered Trade Unions (Section 13)

Every registered trade union shall be a body corporate by the name under which it is registered, and shall have perpetual succession and a common seal with power to acquire and hold both movable and immovable property and to contract, and shall by the said name sue and be sued.

Certain Acts not to Apply to Registered Trade Unions (Section 14)

The following acts shall not apply to any registered trade union and the registration of any such trade union under any such act shall be void. *They are*

- The Societies Registration Act, 1860
- The Cooperative Societies Act, 1912
- The Companies Act, 1956

Rights and Liabilities of Registered Trade Unions

Objects on which General Funds may be Spent (Section 15)

The general funds of a registered trade union shall not be spent on any other objects than the following, *namely*

(a) the payment of salaries, allowances and expenses to office-bearers of the trade union.
(b) the payment of expenses for the administration of the trade union, including audit of the accounts of the general funds of the trade union.
(c) the prosecution or defence of any legal proceeding to which the trade union or any member thereof is a party, when such prosecution or defence is undertaken for the purpose of securing or protecting any rights of the trade union as such or any rights arising out of the relations of any member with his employer or with a person whom the member employs.
(d) the conduct of trade disputes on behalf of the trade union or any member thereof.
(e) the compensation of members for loss arising out of trade disputes.
(f) allowances to members or their dependants on account of death, old age, sickness, accidents or unemployment of such members.
(g) the issue of, or the undertaking of liability under, policies of assurance on the lives of members, or under policies insuring members against sickness, accident or unemployment.

(h) the provision of educational, social or religious benefits for members (including the payment of the expenses of funeral or religious ceremonies for deceased members) or for the dependants of members.

(i) the upkeep of a periodical published mainly for the purpose of discussing questions affecting employers or workmen as such.

(j) the payment, in furtherance of any of the objects on which the general funds of the trade union may be spent, of contributions to any cause intended to benefit workmen in general, provided that the expenditure in respect of such contributions in any financial year shall not at any time during that year be in excess of one-fourth of the combined total of the gross income which has upto that time accrued to the general funds of the trade union during that year and of the balance at the credit of those funds at the commencement of that year and

(k) subject to any conditions contained in the notification, any other object notified by the appropriate Government in the official Gazette.

Constitution of a Separate Fund for Political Purposes (Section 16)

- A registered trade union may constitute a separate fund from which payments may be made, for the promotion of the civil and political interests of its members. The contributions will be separately levied for or made to that fund.
- No member shall be compelled to contribute to this fund.
- A member who does not contribute to the said fund shall not be excluded from any benefits of the trade union.
- *The fund will be utilised for*

(a) The payment of any expenses incurred, either directly or indirectly, by a candidate or prospective candidate for election as a member of any legislative body constituted under the Constitution or of any local authority, before, during, or after the election in connection with his candidature or election; or

(b) The holding of any meeting or the distribution of any literature or documents in support of any such candidate or prospective candidate; or

(c) The maintenance of any person who is a member of any legislative body constituted under the Constitution or of any local authority; or

(d) The registration of electors or the election of a candidate for any legislative body constituted under the Constitution or for any local authority; or

(e) The holding of political meetings of any kind, or the distribution of political literature or political documents of any kind.

Rights of Minors to Membership of Trade Unions (Section 21)

Any person who has attained the age of fifteen years may be a member of a registered trade union subject to any rules of the trade union to the contrary and may, subject as aforesaid, enjoy all the rights of a member and execute all instruments and give all acquaintances necessary to be executed or given under the rules.

Disqualifications of Office-bearers of Trade Unions (Section 21 A)

A person shall be disqualified for being chosen as, and for being, a member of the executive or any other office-bearer of a registered trade union if

- He has not attained the age of eighteen years,
- He has been convicted by a Court in India of any offence involving moral turpitude and sentenced to imprisonment, unless a period of five years has elapsed since his release.
- Any member of the executive or other office-bearer of a registered Trade Union who, before the commencement of the Indian Trade Unions (Amendment) Act, 1964 (38 of 1964), has been convicted of any offence involving moral turpitude and sentenced to imprisonment, shall on the date of such commencement cease to be such member or office-bearer unless a period of five years has elapsed since his release before that date.

Proportion of Office-bearers to be Connected with the Industry (Section 22)

- Not less than one-half of the total number of the office-bearers of every registered trade union shall be persons actually engaged or employed in an industry with which the trade union is connected.
- The appropriate Government may, by special or general order, declare that the provisions of this section shall not apply to any trade union or class of trade unions specified in the order.

Change of Name (Section 23)

Any registered trade union may, with the consent of not less than two-thirds of the total number of its members and subject to the provisions of Section 25, change its name.

Amalgamation of Trade Unions (Section 24)

Any two or more registered trade unions may become amalgamated together as one trade union with or without dissolution or division of the funds of such trade unions or either or any of them, provided that the votes of at least one-half of the members of each or every such trade union entitled to vote are recorded, and that at least sixty per cent of the votes recorded are in favour of the proposal.

Notice of Change of Name or Amalgamation (Section 25)

- In order to change the name of the trade union after amalgamation, the notice for the same must be signed by the Secretary and by seven members of the trade union and be sent to the registrar.
- The registrar of the state in which the head office of the amalgamated trade union is situated shall, if he is satisfied that the provisions of this act in respect of amalgamation have been complied with and that the trade union formed thereby is entitled to registration under Section 6, register the trade union in the manner provided in Section 8, and the amalgamation shall have effect from the date of such registration.

Dissolution (Section 27)

- When a registered trade union is dissolved, notice of the dissolution signed by seven members and by the Secretary of the trade union shall, within fourteen days of the dissolution, be sent to the registrar, and shall be registered by him if he is satisfied that the dissolution has been effected in accordance with the rules of the trade union, and the dissolution shall have effect from the date of such registration.
- Where the dissolution of a registered trade union has been registered and the rules of the trade union do not provide for the distribution of funds of the trade union on dissolution, the registrar shall divide the funds amongst the members in such manner as may be prescribed.

Returns (Section 28)

A general statement shall be sent annually to the registrar, on or before such date as may be prescribed. This will include all receipts and expenditures of every registered Trade Union during the year ending on the 31st day of December. The statement shall be prepared in such form and shall comprise such particulars as may be prescribed.

A copy of every alteration made in the rules of a registered trade union shall be sent to the registrar within fifteen days of the making of the alteration.

Regulations

Power to make Regulations (Section 29)

The appropriate Government may make regulations for the purpose of carrying into effect the provisions of this act. In particular and without prejudice to the generality of the foregoing power, such regulations may provide for all or any of the following matters, *namely*

(a) the manner in which trade unions and the rules of trade unions shall be registered and the fees payable on registration.

(b) the transfer of registration in the case of any registered trade union which has changed its head office from one state to another.

(c) the manner in which, and the qualifications of persons by whom, the accounts of registered trade unions or of any class of such unions shall be audited.

(d) the conditions subject to which inspection of documents kept by registrars shall be allowed and the fees which shall be chargeable in respect of such inspection and

(e) any matter which is to be or may be prescribed.

Publication of Regulations (Section 30)

- The power to make regulations conferred by Section 29 is subject to the condition of the regulations being made after previous publication.
- The date to be specified in accordance with Clause (3) of Section 23 of the General Clauses Act, 1897 (10 of 1897), as that after which a draft of regulations proposed to be made will be taken into consideration shall not be less than three months from the date on which the draft of the proposed regulations was published for general information.
- Regulations so made shall be published in the Official Gazette, and on such publication shall have effect as if enacted in this act.

Penalties and Procedures

Failure to Submit Returns (Section 31)

- If default is made on the part of any registered trade union in giving any notice or sending any statement or other document as required by or under any provision of this act, every office-bearer or other person bound by the rules of the trade union to give or send the same or, if there is no such office-bearer or person every member of the executive of the trade union, shall be punishable, with fine which may extend to five rupees and, in the case of a continuing default, with an additional fine which may extend to five rupees for each week after the first during which the default continues, provided that the aggregate fine shall not exceed fifty rupees.
- Any person who wilfully makes, or causes to be made, any false entry in, or any omission from, the general statement required by Section 28, or in or from any copy of rules or of alterations of rules sent to the registrar under that section, shall be punishable with fine which may extend to five hundred rupees.

Supplying False Information regarding Trade Unions (Section 32)

Any person who, with intent to deceive, gives to any member of a registered trade union or to any person intending or applying to become a member of such trade union, any document purporting to be a copy of the rules of the trade union or of any alterations to the same which he knows, or has reason to believe, is not a correct copy of such rules or alterations as are for the time being in force, or any person who, with the like intent, gives a copy of any rules of an unregistered trade union to any person on the pretence that such rules are the rules of a registered trade union, shall be punishable with fine which may extend to two hundred rupees.

Cognizance of Offences (Section 33)

- No Court inferior to that of a Presidency Magistrate or a Magistrate of the first class shall try any offence under this act.
- No Court shall take cognisance of any offence under this act, unless complaint thereof has been made by, or with the previous sanction of, the registrar or, in the case of an offence under Section 32, by the person to whom the copy was given, within six months of the date on which the offence is alleged to have been committed.

Recognition of Trade Union

Recognition means the conferring of rights on the members of the union by the management that allows the members to act as a bargaining agent during different processes of collective bargaining. They can enter into agreements with the management on behalf of its union-member. It is different from registration of the trade union and is important when there are multiple trade unions in an establishment.

Earlier, the Office of Chief Labour Commissioner (CLC) performed a recognition process as a result of which 13 Central Trade Unions/Federations of Trade Unions were recognised. *However, amendments have been brought about in the Trade Unions Act, 1926 that will facilitate*

- Recognition of trade unions at central and state level.
- Ensure true representation of workers in the tripartite bodies.
- Check on the arbitrary nomination of workers' representatives by the Government and
- Reduce litigations and industrial unrest.

Recognition of trade unions at central/state level would reduce duplicacy of such exercise by different departments. Recognised trade unions may be assigned specific roles at central or state level. *The amendments are as following*

Insertion of Section 28A It will allow the recognition of trade union at the central and state. The process of recognition will be carried out by a secret ballot process.

Amendment of Section 29 The Central and State Government will have the power to make the rules for the recognition of the respective trade unions. They will have the authority to decide the disputes and the manner in which the disputes will be resolved.

Emerging Roles of Trade Unions in India

Trade unions play an important role in voicing the concerns of the workers in front of the management. They have a major responsibility of maintaining harmonious relationship between the management and labour. However, with the changing times, the scope of activities of trade unions have also widened. *Some of them are as following*

- Trade unions have started playing an important role in the communication of information across the members of the union by publishing newspapers or magazines. This helps the members to know the stance of the union on different issues and problems.
- Many trade unions have engaged themselves in promoting the welfare activities among the union members. These include providing housing and organising cooperative societies etc. The main aim is to increase the quality of work life of the labourers.
- Some trade unions are engaging themselves in launching educational programs for the workers in order to enhance their knowledge of the issues concerning their work and workplace.
- Some of the trade unions have engaged themselves in conducting primary and secondary research in order to have sufficient data to back their demands they put across to the management.

EXAM BASED QUESTIONS

1 Which of the following is not a feature of trade unions?

(a) An association of employers, employees or independent workers
(b) A permanent body, not a casual or temporary
(c) Negotiation and collective bargaining are its tools
(d) A group of only uneducated and semi-skilled people

2 Which of the following documents are to be submitted to the registrar for the registration of a trade union?

(a) Application in Form A
(b) Minutes of the General Body Meeting
(c) Form F membership register
(d) All of the above

3 Which of the following particulars should be contained in an application for registration?

(a) The names, occupations and addresses of members making the application
(b) The name of the trade union and the address of its head office
(c) The titles, names ages, address and occupations of the office bearers of the trade union
(d) All of the above

4 Which of the following is not the main provisions to be contained in the rules of a trade union?

(a) The objects for which the trade union has been established
(b) List of the members of the trade union
(c) The manner of election of office-bearers
(d) Detailed profile of the members of the trade union

5 Where can an appeal be made on any refusal of a Registrar to register a trade union or cancellation of registration?

(a) Where the head office of the trade union is situated
(b) To High Court
(c) Either (a) or (b)
(d) None of the above

6 Which of the following acts is applied to trade unions?

(a) The Societies Registration Act, 1860
(b) The Cooperative Societies Act, 1912
(c) The Companies Act, 1956
(d) The Trade Unions Act, 1926

7 Which of the following is the main reason for disqualification of office-bearers of trade unions?

(a) If the applicant has not attained the age of eighteen years
(b) If the applicant has been convicted by a Court in India of any offence involving moral turpitude
(c) If the applicant has been sentenced to imprisonment and a period of five years has not been passed since his release
(d) All of the above

8 'Any trade union can change its name, with the consent of not less than two-thirds of the total number of its members.' This provision has been mentioned in which of the following sections of Trade Union Act?

(a) Section 25 (b) Section 13 (A)
(c) Section 25 (A) (d) Section 5

9 Which of the following is not a characteristic of trade union?

(a) Voluntary association (b) Intermediary
(c) Common goals (d) Individual actions

10 Which union is focused on making the skills of its members valuable and not easily replaceable in organisations?

(a) Industrial union (b) General union
(c) Occupational union (d) White collar union

11 A union meant to protect the interests and rights of the non-manual employees is called a

(a) white collar union (b) brown collar union
(c) blue collar union (d) None of these

12 Employees join unions to fulfil their .... needs.

(a) social (b) economic
(c) esteem (d) All of these

13 What should be the minimum number of persons required to register a trade union?

(a) Six (b) Seven
(c) Eight (d) Nine

14 Indian National Trade Union Congress was organised in

(a) 1947 (b) 1948
(c) 1962 (d) 1990

15 Which of the following trade union could be defined as 'white collar unions'?

(a) ASLEF (b) TGWU
(c) UNISON (d) EETPU

16 Which factors is the most likely to have caused as shift in power away from unions and towards management over the last decade?

(a) The existence of tacit unwritten agreements between management and unions based on 'custom and practice'
(b) The growth of 'single unionism' within the workplace
(c) The introduction of Schedule I of the Employment Relations Act of 1999
(d) The relatively healthy growth of the UK company

17 Which of the following conditions is most likely to lead to a rise in union bargaining power?

(a) Rise in union density
(b) Increased competition in the product market
(c) Relatively high elasticity of demand for labour
(d) Monopsony in the labour market

18 Which of the following organisation deals with both management and employees who do not agree on the interpretation of existing written contracts?
(a) ACAS (b) CBI
(c) NEDO (d) TUC

19 The concept of unions came into existence as a result of employees
(a) problem of communication
(b) dissatisfaction among workers
(c) longing for belongingness
(d) change in technology

20 Which of the following are the main cause of trade union movement?
(a) World War I
(b) Establishment of ILO
(c) All India Trade Union Congress
(d) All of the above

21 Trade Unions in India are associated with which of the following International Trade Union Federations?
(a) World Federation of Trade Unions (WFTU)
(b) International Confederation of Free Trade Unions (ICFTU)
(c) Both (a) and (b)
(d) Neither (a) nor (b)

22 Which of the following is not the right of registered unions?
(a) Right to employ anyone without consulting the management
(b) Right to collect membership fees with in the premises of the organisation
(c) Right to raise issues with the management
(d) Right to discuss members grievances with employer

23 'Managerial Officers' associations are registered under which of the following Act?
(a) Societies Registration Act, 1860
(b) Trade Union Act, 1926
(c) Either (a) or (b)
(d) Neither (a) nor (b)

24 Which of the following recommendations were made by National Commission on Labour in 1969?
(a) Intensification by workers education to get good internal leader
(b) The idea of one union for one plant
(c) The compulsion of registration under the Trade Union Act, 1926
(d) All of the above

25 Which of the following are considered to be the modern objectives of trade unions?
(a) Education, training and legal assistance
(b) Negotiations and collective bargaining
(c) Financial discounts and welfare benefits
(d) Both (a) and (c)

26 What per cent of membership does a trade union have to demonstrate amongst the group it is wishing to represent before it can apply to the Central Arbitration Committee (CAC)?
(a) 10% (b) 20% (c) 40% (d) 5%

27 Who is benefitted, if a local collective agreement on pay and conditions is in place?
(a) Only those employees who are members of the trade union
(b) All employees regardless of union membership
(c) All employees in that industry nationwide
(d) All employees regardless of union membership who are in the grade of work covered by the agreement

28 Apart from pay what is the second most common reason for employees to join a trade union?
(a) Group solidarity
(b) Political reasons
(c) Friendship groups
(d) Wide range of personal details

29 In organising industrial action, a union is encouraging its members to break their contractual obligation to attend work. Is this action
(a) protected by union immunity
(b) unlawful
(c) referred to as wild cat strike
(d) such that employers can see the union for loss of earnings

30 What are the types of industrial action a union is most likely to engage in?
(a) Unofficial action (b) Action short of a strike
(c) Strike action (d) Absence

31 Which of the following is not a reason for joining trade unions?
(a) Greater bargaining power
(b) Minimise discrimination
(c) Good contacts with politicians
(d) Platform for self-expression

32 Which of the following are the objectives of trade union?
(a) Wages/salaries
(b) Discipline and welfare
(c) Negotiating machinery
(d) All of the above

33 Who of the following said the following lines "Unions are not anti-capitalist organisations. They are in the least degree political. Their main aim is to increase their internal strength, to work conscientiously and to take from the employer no more than what is rightfully due to the labourers"?
(a) Robert Hoxie (b) Mahatma Gandhi
(c) Frank Tannenbaum (d) Karl Marx

34 Which of the following labour welfare measures can be put under the category of extra-mural activities?

(a) Provision of housing facilities
(b) Improvement in working conditions
(c) Provision of rest pauses
(d) Adequate wages

35 Which of the following can labour welfare measures can be put under the category of intra-mural activities?

(a) Improvement in working conditions
(b) Adequate wages
(c) Provision of rest pauses
(d) All of the above

36 Which of the following functions of trade unions is not related to society?

(a) To prepare and maintain necessary records
(b) To enable unorganised sector to organise itself
(c) To actively participate in the programmes of family planning afforestation, national integration etc
(d) To cooperate in the formulation and implementation in the policies of national development

37 Which of the following functions of trade unions are related to Trade Unions Organisation?

(a) To present and strengthen trade union democracy
(b) To improve financial position of the trade unions
(c) To curb inter-union rivalry
(d) All of the above

38 Which of the following is not a weakness of craft unions?

(a) Very easy to break as the members of the union belong to different establishment
(b) Craft union workers cannot be easily replaced
(c) Not easy to get the clear perspective of the craft unions
(d) Advancement in technology has destroyed the very basis of craft unions

39 Under which kind of trade union 'The International Wood Carvers' association and the Indian Pilots' Guild may be cited as an example?

(a) Craft Unions (b) Industrial Unions
(c) Business Union (d) General Union

40 Which of the following are the examples of industrial union?

(a) The Rashtriya Mill Mazdoor Sangh
(b) The Girni Kamgar Union at Bombay
(c) Both (a) and (b)
(d) None of the above

41 Which of the following are the merits of industrial unions?

(a) They make negotiations easy
(b) They encourage workers' solidarity
(c) New technology has removed craft distinctions so industrial unions are the only logical answer
(d) All of the above

42 In which of the following countries unions are divided on the basis of religion?

(a) France (b) Italy
(c) Belgium (d) All of these

43 Which of the following factors influenced the growth of trade unions during the period between 1919 and 1923 after World War I?

(a) Economic conditions (b) Political conditions
(c) The setting up of ILO (d) All of these

44 Which of the following acts gave fillip to our labour union movement in the period between 1924 and 1935 with the emergence of left-wing trade unions?

(a) The Mines Act of 1923
(b) Workmen's Compensation Act, 1923
(c) The Trade Unions Act, 1926
(d) All of the above

45 Who of the following cannot be said as one of the best Trade Union Leaders and Labour Organisations?

(a) NM Lokhande (b) BP Wadia
(c) Sarojini Naidu (d) Hari Harnath Shastri

46 Which of the following are the international organisations where Indian central organisations can go for affiliation?

(a) World Federation of Trade Unions in Paris
(b) International Confederation of Free Trade Unions in Brussels
(c) Both (a) and (b)
(d) None of the above

47 The All India Trade Union Congress (AITUC) was formed in......with the active support of leaders of the Indian National Congress.

(a) 1920 (b) 1921
(c) 1922 (d) 1923

48 Labour movement became a vigorous force in India after...... .

(a) World War I
(b) World War II
(c) Panipat War I
(d) Panipat War II

49 ...... the only central labour which regulates the working of the unions does not have any provision for recognition of trade unions.

(a) The Trade Union Act, 1928
(b) The Trade Union Act, 1926
(c) Workmen's Compensation Act, 1923
(d) None of the above

50 ......was established in 1971 as a result of split in the All India Trade Union Congress (AITUC).

(a) CITU (b) HMS
(c) ILO (d) None of these

51 The Indian National Trade Union Congress was organised in 1947 with active support and encouragement from the...... .
(a) employee (b) employer
(c) union (d) None of these

52 Bhartiya Mazdoor Sangh was founded on...... .
(a) 23rd July, 1955 (b) 25th July, 1955
(c) 23rd August, 1955 (d) 25th August, 1955

53 ...... is the only trade union centre which claims that it is not controlled by any of the political parties, employers/government and was founded in 1967.
(a) NFITU (b) CITU (c) BMS (d) HMS

54 ...... believes in ruthlers pursuit of its objectives by whatever means it deems fit and do not subscribe to any ideology.
(a) Predatory unionism (b) Compulsory unionism
(c) Forced unionism (d) None of these

55 According to ...... the main function of trade unions is to raise the moral and intellectual standards of labour through reformatory measures.
(a) Abraham Lincoln (b) Lenin
(c) Mahatma Gandhi (d) Bal Gangadhar Tilak

56 ...... candemned the system of private ownership and believed in replacing the existing social order.
(a) Trade union (b) Revolutionary union
(c) Productive union (d) None of these

57 Employers' associations came into existence as a result of the formation of ...... after the first world war.
(a) Hind Mazdoor Sangh
(b) Indian Labour Congress
(c) International Labour Organisation
(d) None of the above

58 According to ...... theory, in order to understand the nature of trade unionism one has consider temperamental characteristics of the workers concerned alongwith the environmental conditions.
(a) social (b) industrial
(c) religious (d) None of these

59 ...... is focussed on workers' education and has established an institute of Indian Labour in Calcutta.
(a) International Labour Organisation
(b) National Front of Indian Trade Union
(c) World Trade Organisation
(d) None of the above

60 The day-to-day operations of All India Trade Union Congress are carried out by the ...... at the National and State levels.
(a) secretariat (b) department
(c) cabinet (d) None of these

61 Negotiations and collective bargaining are the tools for ...... to accomplish the objectives.
(a) NGOs
(b) social organisation
(c) government
(d) trade union

62 At present there are ...... Central Trade Union Organisation in India.
(a) twelve (b) thirteen
(c) fourteen (d) fifteen

63 ...... represent individual workers when they have a problem and also offer legal representation.
(a) Socialism (b) Trade unionism
(c) Communalism (d) None of these

64 In ...... union representatives discuss with management the issues which affect people working in an organisation.
(a) Negotiation (b) Beater
(c) Merger (d) None of these

65 ...... unions are trade conscious rather than class conscious, they stress on immediate goals and display an instrumental orientation.
(a) Business (b) Social
(c) Religious (d) None of these

66 ...... unions are class conscious rather than trade unions.
(a) Social (b) Religious
(c) Managerial (d) None of these

67 .... exert pressure, after realistically ascertaining its practical implications, on the government to enact legislation conducive to the development of workers.
(a) Social organisation
(b) Government
(c) Trade unions
(d) International agencies

68 ...... is the term used for the workers/employees who are the members of trade unions or employee association.
(a) Unorganised labour (b) Organised labour
(c) Uneducated labour (d) None of these

69 The functions of ...... include activities like collection and analysis of wage data, preparation of notes, collection and analysis of macro data etc
(a) development (b) research
(c) improvement (d) None of these

70 ...... and ...... are the two kinds of functions in which all the functions being perfromed by trade unions can be summarised.
(a) Militant, ministrant
(b) Social reformer, social worker
(c) Government, international agencies
(d) None of the above

71 In the recent times, there has been a paradigm shift from ...... to ...... which has played a major role in the declining of trade union movement in India.

(a) collectivism, individualism (b) socialism, groupism
(c) individualism, collectivism (d) None of these

72 According to the rule of Trade Union Act, 1926, ... workers can form a union and get registered.

(a) 7 (b) 8 (c) 9 (d) 10

73 ...... organised a conference of workers in Bombay and drew up a memorandum signed by 5300 to present to the commission.

(a) MK Gandhi
(b) Bal Gangadhar Tilak
(c) Karl Marx
(d) Mr Lokhandey

74 ...... is a sort of insurance cover to members to fight against irrational, arbitrary and illegal actions of employees.

(a) Collective strength (b) Industrial strength
(c) Social strength (d) None of these

75 The first organised Trade Union in India named as ......was formed in the year 1918.

(a) Delhi labour union (b) Bombay labour union
(c) Madras labour union (d) None of these

76 Trade unions not only take care of wages/salaries of the workers but also provide valuable ...... and ...... to the workers.

(a) notice, information (b) information, advice
(c) suggestion, notice (d) None of these

77 ...... unions represent the association of officer and managers.

(a) Employees association
(b) Employers association
(c) Trade union
(d) None of the above

78 ...... are the unions which recruit workers from all types of industries and with any level or range of skills.

(a) Trade unions (b) General unions
(c) Social unions (d) None of these

79 Political and anarchist unions are the sub-types of......kind of unions.

(a) social union (b) general union
(c) revolutionary union (d) None of these

80 ...... is the result of reparation of the Marxists from the All India Trade Union Congress (AITUC).

(a) Centre for India Trade Union
(b) Madras Labour Union
(c) Hind Mazdoor Sabha
(d) None of the above

81 The basic function of trade union is

(a) to protect and promote the interest of workers
(b) acquiring the control of industry by workers
(c) imbibing sincerity and discipline in workers
(d) to provide cultural and recreational facilities

82 Which of the following aims to check inner and intra union rivalry in India?

(a) The Trade Union Act
(b) The Code of Discipline in Industry
(c) The Inner Union Code of Conduct
(d) All of the above

83 The primary sources of income for union is

(a) membership subscription
(b) donations
(c) sale of periodicals
(d) other sources

84 Consider the following for the Trade Union Act, 1926. Which of the following statement(s) is/are correct?

1. This act came into force on 25th March, 1926 and helps to provide for the registration of Trade Unions.
2. Trade Unions are defined under Section 2(h) of the Act.
3. Seven or more members of the trade union can apply for the registration of the trade union under this Act.

(a) Both 1 and 2 (b) Both 2 and 3
(c) Both 1 and 3 (d) All of the above

85 Consider the following for the fund created for political purposes under the Trade Union Act, 1926. Which of the following statement(s) is/are correct?

1. No member shall be compelled to contribute to this fund.
2. The fund will be established under the Section 21 of the Trade Union Act.
3. A member who does not contribute to the said fund shall not be excluded from any benefits of the Trade Union.

(a) Both 1 and 2 (b) Both 2 and 3
(c) Both 1 and 3 (d) All of the above

86 Consider the following for the recognition of Trade Unions in India. Which of the following statement(s) is/are correct?

1. It allows the members to act as a bargaining agent during different processes of collective bargaining.
2. It is similar as the registration of the Trade Union and is important when there are multiple trade unions in an establishment.
3. Section 28A of the Trade Union Act, 1926 will allow the recognition of Trade Union at the Central and State.

(a) Both 1 and 2 (b) Both 2 and 3
(c) Both 1 and 3 (d) All of the above

87 Consider the following for the dissolution of trade unions under the Trade Union Act, 1926. Which of the following statement(s) is/are correct?

1. When a registered Trade Union is dissolved, notice of the dissolution is signed by nine members and by the Secretary of the Trade Union.
2. The notice of dissolution must be sent within ten days to the Registrar.
3. Where the dissolution of a registered Trade Union has been registered and the rules of the Trade Union do not provide for the distribution of funds of the Trade Union on dissolution, the registrar shall divide the funds amongst the members in such manner as may be prescribed.

(a) Only 2 (b) Only 3
(c) Both 1 and 3 (d) All of the above

88 Consider the following for the Indian National Trade Union Congress (INTUC). Which of the following statement(s) is/are correct?

1. It is the trade union wing of the Indian National Congress and was founded on 3rd May, 1947.
2. The first Delegates Session was held in Bombay in May 1948.
3. The first President was Ashok Mehta.

(a) Only 2 (b) Only 3
(c) Both 1 and 2 (d) All of the above

89 Consider the following for the All India Trade Union Congress (AITUC). Which of the following statement(s) is/are correct?

1. It was founded on 31st October, 1930 in Calcutta and Lala Lajpat Rai was its first president.
2. It is the oldest trade union federations in the country and the founder member of the World Federation of Trade Unions.
3. It adopts the policies and ideologies of Communist Party of India (CPI).

(a) Only 1
(b) Only 3
(c) Both 1 and 2
(d) All of the above

90 Which of the following statements are true/false?

(i) In India, 12 major unions are recognised as central trade union organisations and operate in many states.
(ii) Bhartiya Mazdoor Sangh (BMS) adopts the policies and ideologies of Communist Party of India (CPI).
(iii) All India Trade Union Congress was founded by Dattopant Thengadi on 23rd July, 1955, birthday of Lok Manya Bal Gangadhar Tilak.
(iv) Hind Mazdoor Sabha (HMS) was founded in Howrah, West Bengal on 29th December, 1948 by socialists, forward bloc followers and independent unionists.

(a) (i), (iv) are true and (ii), (iii) are false
(b) (i), (iii) are true and (ii), (iv) are false
(c) (ii), (iv) are true and (i), (iii) are false
(d) (iii), (iv) are true and (ii), (i) are false

91 Which of the following statements are true/false?

(i) The Trade Union Coordination Center (TUCC) was established on the principles of Mahatma Gandhi.
(ii) Self-Employed Women's Association (SEWA) came into being in December 1971 and it was born in 1972 as a trade union of self employed women.
(iii) Neta Ji Subhash Chandra Bose was the inspiration behind SEWA.
(iv) All India Central Council of Trade Union (AICCTU) is politically attached to Communist Party of India (Marxist-Leninist) Liberation.

(a) (i), (iv) are true and (ii), (iii) are false
(b) (i), (iii) are true and (ii), (iv) are false
(c) (ii), (iv) are true and (i), (iii) are false
(d) (iii), (iv) are true and (ii), (i) are false

92 Which of the following statements are true/false?

(i) United Trade Union Congress was founded at an All India Labour Conference in Calcutta on 1st May, 1949 and the founding President was KT Shah.
(ii) Labour Progressive Federation (LPF) is affiliated to Hind Mazdoor Kisan Panchayat (HMKP).
(iii) SEWA grew out of the Textile Labour Association (TLA) India's oldest and largest union of textile workers founded in 1920 by a women, Anasuya Sarabhai.
(iv) HMKP has its presence in around 51 industries across 24 states in India.

(a) (i), (iv) are true and (ii), (iii) are false
(b) (i), (iii) are true and (ii), (iv) are false
(c) (ii), (iv) are true and (i), (iii) are false
(d) (iii), (iv) are true and (ii), (i) are false

93 Which of the following statements are true/false?

(i) India predominantly has small trade unions that make them weaker in front of the management.
(ii) Most of the trade unions are associated with a single ruling political party.
(iii) The workers have no idea about their rights and lack the basic knowledge and education they must have in order to discharge their duties well.
(iv) The leaders of trade unions are more focused on delivering the value to their political party instead of working for the welfare of their labourers/workers.

(a) (i), (iii) and (iv) are true and (ii) is false
(b) (i), (iii) are true and (ii), (iv) are false
(c) (ii), (iv) are true and (i), (iii) are false
(d) (iii), (iv) are true and (ii), (i) are false

94 Which of the following statements are true/false?

(i) Registered Trade Unions are registered under Section 2(e) of the Trade Union Act, 1926.
(ii) Trade Disputes are defined under Section 2(g) of the Trade Union Act, 1926.
(iii) The Application of registration of Trade Union is covered under Section 3.
(iv) The Chief Labour Commissioner will issue a certificate in the prescribed format confirming the registration of Trade Union.

(a) (i), (iv) are true and (ii), (iii) are false
(b) (i), (ii) are true and (iii), (iv) are false
(c) (ii), (iv) are true and (i), (iii) are false
(d) (iii), (iv) are true and (ii), (i) are false

95 Which of the following statements are true/false?
(i) The Societies Registration Act, 1860 shall not apply to any registered Trade Union, and the registration of any such Trade Union under any such Act shall be void.
(ii) Trade Unions may be temporary or permanent.
(iii) Workmen means all persons employed in trade or industry whether or not in the employment of the employer with whom the trade dispute arises.
(iv) Every registered Trade Union shall be a body corporate by the name under which it is registered, and shall have perpetual succession and a common seal with power to acquire and hold both movable and immovable property and to contract, and shall by the said name sue and be sued.
(a) (i), (ii), (iii) and (iv) are true
(b) (i), (iii) are true and (ii), (iv) are false
(c) (ii), (iv) are true and (i), (iii) are false
(d) (iii), (iv) are true and (ii), (i) are false

96 Which of the following statements are true/false?
(i) The Trade Union Movement was by the workers and labour movement was for the workers.
(ii) The trade unions are an outcome of industrial relations and work towards raising the status of labours.
(iii) The organised labour is not the member of any Trade Union but are the members of Employee Provident Fund Organisation (EPFO).
(iv) Trade Union movement conveys a higher degree of consciousness amongst the workers than conveyed by labour movement.
(a) (i), (ii) are true and (iii), (iv) are false
(b) (i), (iii) are true and (ii), (iv) are false
(c) (ii), (iv) are true and (i), (iii) are false
(d) (iii), (iv) are true and (ii), (i) are false

97 Which of the following statements are true/false?
(i) Trade Unions are involved in welfare activities including the provision of housing, co-operative societies, banking facility etc.
(ii) Trade Unions are involved in collecting wage data including fringe and personal benefits.
(iii) Strikes, boycotts and gheraos are militant functions of Trade Union.
(iv) Ministrant functions of Trade Unions involve providing financial support to members during strikes and lockouts.
(a) (i), (iii) are true and (ii), (iv) are false
(b) (i), (ii), (iii) and (iv) are true
(c) (ii), (iv) are true and (i), (iii) are false
(d) (iii), (iv) are true and (ii), (i) are false

98 Which of the following statements are true/false?
(i) Blue Collar Unions represent office workers.
(ii) Provision of rest pauses and adequate wages are intra-mural activities
(iii) Qualified Unions have membership of atleast 10 percent of total employees as members in an undertaking.
(iv) Representative Unions have membership of 25 percent of total employees as members in an undertaking.
(a) (i), (ii) are true and (iii), (iv) are false
(b) (i), (iii) are true and (ii), (iv) are false
(c) (ii), (iv) are true and (i), (iii) are false
(d) (iii), (iv) are true and (ii), (i) are false

99 Which of the following statements are true/false?
(i) Change theory of Trade Unions was propounded by Selig Perlman in 1928.
(ii) Industrial Democracy Theory of Trade Unions was given by Sidney and Beatrice Webb.
(iii) Protest theory of Trade Unions was given by Kerr, Dunlop and Myre.
(iv) Business theory of Trade Unions was propounded by Samuel Gompers.
(a) (i), (ii), (iii) and (iv) are true
(b) (i), (iii) are true and (ii), (iv) are false
(c) (ii), (iv) are true and (i), (iii) are false
(d) (iii), (iv) are true and (ii), (i) are false

Directions (Q. Nos. 100-107) *In the questions given below are two statements labelled as Assertion (A) and Reason (R). In the context of the two statements, which one of the following is correct?*
(a) Both (A) and (R) are correct and (R) is the correct explanation of (A)
(b) Both (A) and (R) are correct, but (R) is not the correct explanation of (A)
(c) (A) is true, but (R) is false
(d) (A) is false, but (R) is true

100 **Assertion** (A) Workers join union to meet their different socio-psychological needs like companionship, group of likely minded people.
Reason (R) Difference in group psychology cause different types of unions to appeal.

101 **Assertion** (A) In the Pre-1918 Phase, there were no Trade Unions and the movement was started to create an awakening among the workers about their rights.
Reason (R) The first Factory Commission was appointed in Bombay in the year 1885 and the first Factories Act was passed in 1881.

102 Assertion (A) Any two or more registered Trade Unions may become amalgamated together as one Trade Union with or without dissolution or division of the funds of such Trade Unions or either or any of them.

Reason (R) The votes of atleast one-half of the members of each or every such Trade Union entitled to vote are recorded, and that atleast sixty percent of the votes recorded are in favour of the proposal.

103 Assertion (A) Trade Unions have started playing an important role in the communication of information across the members.

Reason (R) Trade Unions are actively involved in publishing newspapers or magazines as this helps the members to know the stance of the union on different issues and problems.

104 Assertion (A) The central and state governments have the power to make the rules for the recognition of the respective trade unions.

Reason (R) Section 27 of the Trade Union Act, 1926 was amended to grant the power to central and state government.

105 Assertion (A) Any person who has attained the age of fifteen years may become a member of a registered Trade Union.

Reason (R) A person shall be disqualified for being chosen as, and for being, a member of the executive or any other office-bearer of a registered Trade Union if the person is not eighteen years old.

106 Assertion (A) Predatory Unionism believes in ruthless pursuit of its objectives by hook or crook without subscribing to any ideology.

Reason (R) It is important to protect intellectual, moral, and social levels of workers.

107 Assertion (A) The Trade Unions in India have a small size that makes them weaker in front of the management.

Reason (R) The bargaining power of the workers is reduced considerably.

108 Match the following.

List I	List II
A. Craft Union	1. Unions function in particular craft or industry
B. Industrial Union	2. Unions formed by a mix of industry or craft
C. General Union	3. Union of workers belonging to same occupation
D. Plant Level Union	4. Organisations of all the constituent unions in a region
E. Local Level Federation	5. Unions formed on the basis of industry
F. Regional Level Federation	6. Apex bodies at the top of the structure
G. National Federation	7. The unions function at lowest level

Codes

	A	B	C	D	E	F	G
(a)	3	5	2	7	1	4	6
(b)	2	3	4	5	6	7	1
(c)	3	4	5	6	7	1	2
(d)	3	2	1	4	6	7	5

109 Match the following.

List I	List II
A. All India Trade Union Congress (AITUC)	1. 1971
B. Indian National Trade Union Congress (INTUC)	2. 1947
C. Hind Mazdoor Sabha (HMS)	3. 1955
D. Centre of Indian Trade Union (CITU)	4. 1920
E. Bhartiya Mazdoor Sangh (BMS)	5. 1967
F. National Front of Indian Trade Union (NFITU)	6. 1948

Codes

	A	B	C	D	E	F
(a)	1	2	3	4	5	6
(b)	4	2	6	1	3	5
(c)	3	4	1	2	5	6
(d)	6	5	4	3	2	1

110 Match the following.

List I	List II
A. Business Unions	1. Without any legal, ethical ideology or code of conduct
B. Friendly or Uplift Unions	2. Bread and Butter Unions
C. Revolutionary Unions	3. Advocate non-political methods
D. Predatory Unions	4. Violent means such as strikes sabotage, boycott

Codes

	A	B	C	D
(a)	2	3	4	1
(b)	3	2	1	4
(c)	1	2	3	4
(d)	4	3	2	1

111 Match the following.

List I	List II
A. INTUC (Indian National Trade Union Congress)	1. Bhartiya Janta Party
B. BMS (Bhartiya Mazdoor Sangh)	2. CPI (Right)
C. HMS (Hind Mazdoor Sabha)	3. Socialist Party
D. AITUC (All India Trade Union Congress)	4. CPI (Marxist)
E. CITU (Centre of Indian Trade Union)	5. Congress

Codes

	A	B	C	D	E
(a)	1	2	3	4	5
(b)	5	1	3	2	4
(c)	3	2	1	4	5
(d)	5	4	3	2	1

Directions (Q. Nos. 112-116) *Read the following passage carefully and answer the questions that follows.*

In France, Germany and other European countries, socialist parties and democrats played a prominent role in forming and building up trade unions, especially from the 1870s onwards. This stood in contrast to the British experience, where moderate New Model Unions dominated the union movement from the mid 19th century and where trade unionism was stronger than the political labour movement until the formation and growth of the Labour Party in the early years of the 20th century.

Government opposition to trade unionism in the United Kingdom was a major factor in economic crisis during the 1960s and in particular the 1970s, culminating some would argue in the Winter of Discontent of late 1978 and early 1979, when a significant percentage of the nation's public sector workers went on strike. By this stage, some 1,20,00,000 workers in the United Kingdom were trade union members. However, the election of the Conservative Party led by Margaret Thatcher at the general election in May 1979, at the expense of Labour's James Callaghan, saw substantial trade union reform which saw the level of strikes fall, but also the level of trade union membership fall.

At the height of the strikes, nearly 3,00,00,000 working days were lost in Britain during 1979, but that had fallen dramatically to some 50,00,000 during 1981 as a result of the Thatcher government's union reform policies. The number of working days lost in the country due to strikes rose sharply to more than 2,50,00,000 in 1984, though most of these were miners on strike and from then on the number of working days lost in Britain due to strikes remained in the low millions.

By the end of the 1980s, membership had fallen to just over 60,00,000 little more than half the level of a decade earlier and it also counted against the Labour Party's hopes of regaining power, as its relationship with the trade unions had traditionally been seen as a strength but after the Winter of Discontent it was seen as a liability. Manufacturing, the main source of union strength in the United Kingdom, had shrunk by half during the early 1980s recession pushing unemployment from 15,00,000 to more than 30,00,000.

Earlier in the 1970s, Conservative Prime Minister, Edward Heath (elected in 1970) had attempted to reduce trade union powers due to the rising level of strikes across the country. However, he backed down with his stance against the unions following a backlash by the militant miners' union, which saw many of his own MPs turn against him. The strikes continued and heath responded by calling a snap election in February 1974. The election resulted in a hung parliament with the Tories having the most votes but labour having slightly more seats and failed attempts by Heath to form a coalition with the liberals led to the resignation of his government and the return of Harold Wilson as Prime Minister of a minority labour government, which gained a three seat majority at a second election later in the year.

112 **What was the desire of socialist parties and democrats in France and Germany?**

(a) To form and build the trade unions in order to support the socialistic views
(b) To support the British policies
(c) Both (a) and (b)
(d) None of the above

113 **What is the main factor of economic crises during 1960s in United Kingdom?**

(a) Excessive involvement of trade unions in United Kingdom was a mojar factor of economic crisis
(b) Government opposition to trade unionism in the United Kingdom was a major factor in economic crisis
(c) Government support to Trade unionism in the United Kingdom was a major factor in economic crisis during the 1960s
(d) The socialist approach in trade unionism destroyed the capitalistic structure of industry, which was a major factor in economic crisis during the 1960s

114 **According to this passage during early 1980s**

(a) the main factor of unemployment was recession
(b) the main factor of unemployment was wrong policies of government
(c) Both (a) and (b)
(d) None of the above

115 **During 1970s, Conservative Prime Minister, Edward Heath**

(a) had tried to induce extra power of trade unions due to the rising level of anti-worker policies in industries
(b) had tried to increase the power of trade unions due to the rising level of strikes across the country
(c) had tried to reduce the power of trade unions due to the rising level of strikes across the country
(d) None of the above

116 **In the election of 1974,**

(a) labour Party has got majority
(b) conservative Party has got majority
(c) there was a hung parliament
(d) None of the above

Directions (Q. Nos. 117-120) *Read the following passage carefully and answer the questions that follows.*

The Trade Union Movement in India commenced as a result of state intervention for the demand of improved working conditions. Economic reforms based on privatisation, liberalisation and austerity measures to provide favourable environment for the trade unions to engage in greater industrial disputes, but there is increasing dissension or fragmentation within the trade union movement itself. Trade union movement emerged due to the need of improved working conditions of the working class in India; there has also been a decline in trade union activities over the years. During the period from 1991 to 2000, economic reforms for liberalisation and privatisation measures were introduced by the Government of India. Privatisation refers to policies that decrease the state's role and increases the private sector's responsibility to drive the economic decisions in the market. As of 2002, the combined membership of trade unions in India is around 24,601,589, as per statistics from the Ministry of Labour. Around 11 Central Trade Union Organisations (CTUO) are documented by the Ministry of Labour in 2008.

The trade union is a continuous demand of the wage-earners for the purpose of maintaining or improving the working conditions. Political motivations and the ideologies have influenced Indian trade union movement. The twin aspects of the Indian Trade Union Movement, labours organisation for industrial bargaining and its ideological orientation were analysed with the political colour. The aspects of the trade unions were scanned in the wider background of the nationalists struggle against imperialism. There is simultaneous dissension or fragmentation within the trade union movement itself.

The initial demand for the regulations of the working conditions in the Indian factories came from the Lancashire textile capitalist lobby. They perceived that the emergence of a competitive rival in the Indian textile industry under favourable conditions would deteriorate their position. They demanded the appointment of a commission for an investigation of the factory and working conditions of the labours. The first commission was appointed in 1875, although the First Factory Act was not passed before 1881. The Act prohibited the employment of children under the age of 7. The Act also limited the working hours of children below the age of 12 years. Similar circumstances resulted in the enactment of the factory acts for the jute industry in 1909 and 1911.

The trade union movement in British India got an impetus when Bombay Mill Hands Association was formed on 24th April, 1890. The establishment of ILO, in 1919, provided a source of inspiration for the workers to become politically conscious. India's membership exerted great influence in the formation of a central organisation of workers called All India Trade Union Congress (AITUC), in 1920, for the purpose of conducting and coordinating the activities of the labour organisations.

117 What are the causes of Trade Union Movement in India?

(a) The demand of employers and industrialists
(b) The demand of workers and social activists
(c) State intervention for the demand of improved working conditions
(d) None of the above

118 How the Trade Union Movement emerged in India?

(a) Trade Union Movement emerged due to the pressure of government and international agencies
(b) Trade Union Movement emerged due to the need of improved working conditions of the working class in India
(c) Trade Union Movement emerged due to the low productivity in industrial sector in India
(d) None of the above

119 What is the effect of privatisation?

(a) The role of state has been decreased in economic decisions in the market
(b) The role of state has been increased in economic decisions in the market
(c) The role of state has been remain unchanged in economic decisions in the market
(d) None of the above

120 Which one of the following is the influencing factor for Indian Trade Union Movement?

(a) Religious thought
(b) Political motivations and the ideologies
(c) Government laws and regulations
(d) None of the above

PREVIOUS YEARS' QUESTIONS

2018

1 Assertion (A) Trade unions have to change their own attitudes and activities to sustain themselves in future.

Reason (R) Trade unions have to change their attitude from antagonism to understanding and from militancy to mutual cooperation.

Codes

(a) Both (A) and (R) are wrong
(b) (A) is correct, but (R) is wrong
(c) Both (A) and (R) are correct, but (R) is not an interpretation of (A)
(d) (A) is correct and (R) interprets (A)

2 Who among the following was the Founder President of the International Trade Union Confederation (ITUC)?

(a) Sharan Burrow
(b) Guy Ryder
(c) Jeremy Bentham
(d) Pascal Lamy

3 Arrange the following unions in a chronological order, on the basis of the years of their establishment in USA, starting from the oldest.

1. International Brotherhood of Electrical Workers, USA.
2. United Auto Workers, USA.
3. Transport Workers Union of America.

Codes

(a) 1, 2, 3 (b) 1, 3, 2
(c) 2, 1, 3 (d) 3, 1, 2

4 The Traders Union Congress, U.K. is affiliated to

(a) International Confederation of Free Trade Unions
(b) World Federation of Trade Unions
(c) International Trade Union Confederation
(d) International Federation of Christian Unions

5 Which of the following statements relating to the All India Manufacturers' Organisation are correct?

1. It was set up in 1942.
2. It was set up under the leadership of M. Vishweswarayya.
3. It was established to represent the trade and labour interests of the member firms in the medium and small sectors.

Choose the correct answer from the code given below

Codes

(a) 1 and 3
(b) 1 and 2
(c) 1, 2 and 3
(d) 2 and 3

6 Out of the following activities of trade unions, which are considered as social activities?

1. Initiating and developing workers' education scheme.
2. Running cooperatives.
3. Organising welfare and recreational activities such as mutual insurance, providing monetary and other help during periods of strikes and economic distress.

Codes

(a) 2 and 3 (b) 1 and 2
(c) 1, 2 and 3 (d) 1 and 3

7 Match the following.

List I (Type of Unions)	List II (Example)
A. Craft Unions	1. The International Woodcarvers, Association
B. Industrial Unions	2. Tata Workers' Union
C. General Unions	3. Jamshedpur Labour Union

Codes

	A	B	C		A	B	C
(a)	2	1	3	(b)	1	2	3
(c)	1	3	2	(d)	3	2	1

8 Under the provisions of the Trade Union Act, 1926, what is the maximum amount of fine to be imposed for supplying false information regarding Trade Unions?

(a) One hundred rupees
(b) Two hundred fifty rupees
(c) One hundred fifty rupees
(d) Two hundred rupees

9 The American Federation of Labour was established in the year

(a) 1885 (b) 1884 (c) 1886 (d) 1887

10 The British Trades Union Congress was formed in the year

(a) 1878 (b) 1858 (c) 1888 (d) 1868

11 Who is the present leader of the Labour Party, UK?

(a) Ed Miliband (b) Jeremy Bernard Corbyn
(c) Mary Bousted (d) Sally Hunt

12 Who among the following made significant contributions to early unions of Great Britain?

1. Francis Blake
2. Robert Owen
3. Sidney and Beatrice Webb
4. Pelloutier

Codes

(a) 1, 2 and 3 (b) 2, 3 and 4
(c) 1, 2 and 4 (d) 1, 3 and 4

13 Who is the President of the Trades Union Congress, UK for the year 2018?
(a) Mary Bousted (b) Sally Hunt
(c) Liz Snape (d) William Henry Wood

14 What is the maximum five that can be imposed on any person who supplies false information regarding a trade union under the provisions of the Trade Unions Act, 1926 ?
(a) ₹ 100 (b) ₹ 200 (c) ₹ 300 (d) ₹ 500

15 Which of the following statements relating to the system of collective bargaining in United Kingdom is true ?
1. It is covered under the Trade Unions and Labour Relations Act, 1974.
2. It is covered under the Trade Unions and Labour Relations (Consolidation) Act, 1992.
3. It is covered under the Employment Relations Act, 1999.
4. It is not covered under any legislation.

Codes
(a) 1 and 2 (b) 2 and 3
(c) Only 3 (d) Only 4

16 "An agreement between an employee and the employer stating that the employer will neither join nor participate in union activities as a condition of employment" is called
(a) Union Shop Contract
(b) Employment Contract
(c) Yellow-dog Contract
(d) Business Contract

17 Which of the following pairs is/are not correctly matched?

	List I (Organisation)		List II (Year of Formation)
A.	Trades Union Congress (England)	1.	1868
B.	Indian National Trade Union Congress	2.	1947
C.	International Confederation of Free Trade Unions	3.	1948

Codes
(a) 1 and 2 (b) 2 and 3
(c) Only 2 (d) Only 3

18 In which of the following states there exists a legislation having a provision for recognition of trade unions?
(a) Odisha (b) Karnataka
(c) Maharashtra (d) Bihar

19 Which of the following central organisations of labour was not a signatory to the Inter Union Code of Conduct, 1958 ?
(a) INTUC (b) BMS (c) HMS (d) AITUC

20 What is the maximum aggregate fine that can be imposed on a trade union for continuous default in submitting the returns under the provisions of the Trade Unions Act, 1926 ?
(a) ₹ 50 (b) ₹ 250 (c) ₹ 500 (d) ₹ 1,000

2017

21 Which one of the statements is true relating to the representation of outsiders as office bearers of any registered trade union under the Trade Unions Act, 1926 functioning other than in an unorganised sector?
(a) Not more than one-third of the total number of office bearers or five whichever is more
(b) Not more than one-third of the total number of office bearers or five whichever is less
(c) Not more than one-half of the total number of office bearers or six whichever is less
(d) Not more than one-half of the total number of office bearers

22 A dispute has arisen regarding admission of membership of a union which is a registered and recognised trade union. Few workers had filed a joint application for membership of that union. The application was not considered because the application was not in accordance with the procedure laid down by the union. Aggrieved by this, the workers filed a complaint before the Registrar of Trade Unions under Section 28 (1-A). Which one among the following is competent authority to settle the issue?
(a) Registrar of Trade Unions
(b) Industrial Tribunal
(c) High Court
(d) Civil Court of the competent jurisdiction

23 A trade union has been formed in an establishment employing five hundred employees. What is the minimum number of members it should have to apply for registering it under the Trade Unions Act 1926 ?
(a) Seven members
(b) One hundred members
(c) Fifty members
(d) Seventy members

24 **Assertion** (A) The MNCs had deeply entrenched themselves by the time unions realised the role of MNCs in spreading capitalism.
Reason (R) For a pretty long time the international trade unions did not consider the MNCs as their natural opponents.

Codes
(a) Both (A) and (R) are wrong
(b) Both (A) and (R) are right and (R) explains (A)
(c) (A) is right and (R) is wrong
(d) Both (A) and (R) are right, but (R) does not explain (A)

25 **Members of the trade union are required to pay a subscription per annum as per the provisions of the Trade Unions Act, 1926. For workers working in other unorganised sectors, excepting rural workers, the annual rate of subscription should not be less than**

(a) ₹ 1 per annum (b) ₹ 3 per annum
(c) ₹ 12 per annum (d) ₹ 24 per annum

26 **A situation, which is very serious, has arised and it warrants that the member of the trade union be financially assisted. As per the Trade Unions Act, 1926, what is the maximum quantum of benefit which a Trade Union can offer to its member out of the total gross income in the year and the balance of the credit of the preceding year**

(a) one-tenth (b) one-sixth (c) one-fourth (d) half

27 **Who regarded trade unions as "institutions for overcoming managerial dictatorship, to strengthen individual labourers and to give them some voice in the determination of the conditions under which they have to work"?**

(a) Karl Marx
(b) Mahatma Gandhi
(c) Sidney and Beatrice Webb
(d) Selig Perlman

28 **The headquarter of Trade Union International of Workers in Building, Wood and Building Materials Industries is located at**

(a) New Delhi (b) Paris (c) Kolkata (d) Helsinki

29 **Which of the following statements about the definition of 'Trade Union' as given in the Trade Unions Act, 1926 is not true?**

1. A trade union is any combination, whether temporary or permanent.
2. It regulates the relations between workmen and employer.
3. It does not regulate the relations between workmen and workmen.
4. It regulates relations between employers and employers.

Codes
(a) Only 1 (b) 1 and 2
(c) Only 3 (d) 2, 3 and 4

30 **Selig Perlman, whose views are known as 'Job Consciousness theory' of trade unionism, observed that the trade union is the outcome of pessimistic outlook of a 'manualist' worker. Which statement is not true in the context of Perlman's theory?**

(a) In order to protect one's limited job opportunity, a worker starts uniting with his/her fellow 'manualists'
(b) Emergence of trade unions mainly from 'Job Consciousness' is not tenable in all situations
(c) Genuine Trade Unions are inherently 'bread and butter' trade unions
(d) After studying the American situation, Perlman observed that during periods of expansion of economy, the American worker had the consciousness of abundance, but this phenomenon existed only for a few years. The optimism of the period of plenty was superseded by pessimism of scarcity. The moment such a situation emerged, trade unions also emerged

31 **When a union signs an agreement with management for wage revision and other benefits, in most of the cases non-members also get the benefit without either paying subscription or participating in union meetings and other struggles. Such non-members are called**

(a) parasites (b) fence sitters
(c) free riders (d) opportunists

32 **Who among the following were moderates in the context of Trade Union Movement in India?**

(a) BT Ranadive and SV Deshpande
(b) Diwan Chaman Lall and NM Joshi
(c) MN Roy and Maniben Kara
(d) HK Mehtab and Dattopant Thengadi

33 **Which of the following was formed in the year 1945?**

(a) International Federation Chemical, Energy, Mining and General Workers
(b) International Confederation of Free Trade Unions
(c) World Federation of Trade Unions
(d) International Federation of Christian Unions

34 **Which of the following is not an industrial union?**

(a) The Engineering Mazdoor Sabha
(b) The Rohtas Workers' Union
(c) The Girni Kamgar Union
(d) The Rashtriya Mill Mazdoor Sangh

35 **Which of the following Central Labour Organisations voluntarily adopted the 'Inter Union Code of Conduct' in 1958?**

(a) INTUC, AITUC, NFITU
(b) AITUC, NFL, BMS, NLO
(c) INTUC, AITUC, HMS, UTUC
(d) BMS, HMS, CITU, TUCC

36 **The inter union code of conduct aims to**

(a) Check Unfair Labour Practices
(b) Control Trade Union Rivalries
(c) Promote Labour Management Cooperation
(d) Promote Collective Bargaining in India

37 **What is the full form of 'UBC' in the context of Trade Union Movement in USA?**

(a) United Brotherhood of Carpenters
(b) Union of Building and Construction Workers
(c) Union of Buffalo Construction Inc
(d) United Brotherhood of Construction Workers

38 Who said that a trade union is a "continuous association of wage-earners for the purpose of maintaining or improving the conditions of their working lives"?

(a) GDH Cole
(b) Clyde E Dankert
(c) J Cunnison
(d) Sydney and Beatrice Webb

39 Which of the following statement(s) relating to the Wagner Act is/are not wrong?

1. It recognises an employees' right to engage in union activities.
2. It recognises employees' right to organise and bargain collectively.
3. It has a provision regarding the establishment of a National Labour Relations Board.
4. It has a provision relating to unfair labour practices by employers.

Codes

(a) Only 1 (b) 1 and 2
(c) 1, 2 and 3 (d) All of these

40 Which of the following types of trade unions groups the workers' unions horizontally, vertically or on the basis of political ideology with a view to coordinating them?

(a) Territorial Unions (b) Occupational Unions
(c) Industrial Unions (d) General Unions

2016

41 According to Sidney and Beatrice Webb, which of the following method(s) is/are employed by the trade unions to achieve their objectives?

1. Mutual Insurance
2. Protective Labour Legislation
3. Collective Bargaining

Codes

(a) Only 1 (b) 1 and 2
(c) 1, 2 and 3 (d) Only 2

42 Match the following.

List I	List II
A. Joint Consultative Board of Industry and Labour	1. 1958
B. Central Board for Workers' Education	2. 1951
C. Shop Councils and Joint Councils	3. 1977
D. Unit Councils	4. 1975

Codes

	A	B	C	D
(a)	2	1	4	3
(b)	1	2	3	4
(c)	4	3	2	1
(d)	3	1	4	2

43 The Ahmedabad Textile Labour Association is an example of

(a) Craft Union (b) Staff Union
(c) Industrial Union (d) General Union

44 **Assertion** (A) Increase in the number of wage-earners led to emergence of two sets of people in the society, the wage-earners and wage providers. Karl Marx termed these two classes, opposed to each other, as proletariat and bourgeoisie and causative factor for the emergence of trade unions.

Reason (R) After the industrial revolution, concentration of free labourers under one roof took place on a large scale. In order to resist the exploitation of employers, the labourers had no other alternative but to make a common stand.

Codes

(a) Both (A) and (R) are wrong
(b) (A) is right and (R) is wrong
(c) (A) is wrong, but (R) is right
(d) Both (A) and (R) are right and (R) explains (A)

45 Who among the following is the first Indian to become the President of the International Labour Conference?

(a) Shri Jagjivan Ram
(b) Sir Atul Chatterjee
(c) Dr. Nagendra Singh
(d) Shri Ravindra Verma

46 The first Craft Union was organised by shoemakers in Philadelphia, USA in the year

(a) 1786 (b) 1788
(c) 1792 (d) 1806

47 Read the following.

Unions demand high wages to counter inflationary pressures on the economic conditions of the working class. Higher wages enhance the purchasing power of the workers, thereby raising inflation.

Which of the following inferences are wrong?

1. Unions have the sole purpose of improving the economic conditions of workers.
2. Enhanced wages increase the purchasing power of workers.
3. Inflation and purchasing power are negatively correlated.
4. Inflation drives unions to go for demanding higher wages.

Codes

(a) 1 and 3
(b) 2 and 3
(c) 3 and 4
(d) Only 3

48 **Assertion** (A) Trade union has the potential to increase inflation.

Reason (R) Unions persistently demand upward revision of wages and thereby enhance purchasing power of labour.

Codes
(a) Both (A) and (R) are right, but (R) does not explain (A)
(b) Both (A) and (R) are wrong
(c) (A) is right and (R) explains (A)
(d) (A) is wrong and (R) is right

49 Which of the following statements relating to the trade unions under the Trade Unions Act, 1926 are not true ?

1. Every registered trade union has to submit a half yearly return to the Registrar of Trade Unions.
2. Any person who has attained the age of eighteen can become an office bearer of the trade union.
3. Retired or retrenched employees of an organisation holding an office in a trade union shall not be construed as an outsider.
4. The number of outsiders working as office bearers in registered trade union functioning other than in an unorganised section shall be limited to eight.

Codes
(a) 1 and 2 (b) 1 and 4
(c) 2 and 3 (d) 1 and 3

2015

50 Which of the following statements relating to the Trade Unions Act, 1926 are correct?

1. The act gives the definition of a trade union.
2. There is a provision in the act relating to decent work.
3. There is a provision in the act relating to the unfair labour practices.
4. There is a provision in the act relating to political fund.

Select the correct answer by using the codes given below

Codes
(a) 2 and 3 (b) 1 and 2
(c) 3 and 4 (d) 1 and 4

51 Robert Hoxie's Theory of Trade Union Movement is based on
(a) communist perspective (b) socialist perspective
(c) capitalist perspective (d) concept of trusteeship

52 The Rohtas Workers' union is an example of
(a) industrial union (b) general union
(c) craft union (d) industrial federation

53 Arrange the following central trade union organisations basing on the years of their formation starting from the oldest one AITUC, BMS, HMS and INTUC
(a) HMS, BMS, AITUC and INTUC
(b) AITUC, INTUC, HMS and BMS
(c) INTUC, HMS, AITUC and BMS
(d) BMS, INTUC, HMS and AITUC

54 In which of the following states there does not exist an enacted law for recognition of trade unions?
(a) Gujarat (b) Rajasthan
(c) Odisha (d) Maharashtra

55 Match the following.

List I (Types of Union)	List II (Examples)
A. Craft union	1. Colliery Mazdoor Sangh
B. Industrial union	2. Indian Pilots' Guild
C. General union	3. The Jamshedpur Labour Union

Codes

	A	B	C		A	B	C
(a)	3	1	2	(b)	1	2	3
(c)	2	1	3	(d)	1	3	2

56 Which of the following statements is not true about the origin of trade unions?
(a) Laissez-faire Policy was not conducive for trade union emergence
(b) Legal pronouncements did not favour the emergence of trade unions in initial stages
(c) Lack of bargaining power among the individual workers was responsible for the emergence of trade unions
(d) Governments and employers were supportive of the trade union emergence

57 In general, what would be the maximum number of outsiders as office bearers of a registered trade union functioning in the organised sector?
(a) 7 (b) 10
(c) 5 (d) 8

58 The four patterns of unionism such as business unionism, friendly or uplift unionism, revolutionary unionism and predatory unionism are given by
(a) Alan Fox (b) Robert Hoxie
(c) Allan Flanders (d) Michael Poole

59 When certain common needs of workers, such as provision of consumer items, credit/loan facilities are provided by the trade unions to their members through cooperatives, the method is called
(a) method of Direct Action
(b) method of Legal Enactment
(c) method of Mutual Insurance
(d) method of Collective Bargaining

60 **Assertion** (A) The trade unions in India are trying to strengthen themselves by mobilising membership among the unorganised workers.

Reason (R) The trade unions in the posteconomic reforms period could not oppose downsizing and outsourcing resulting conversion of many areas of formal employment into informal employment.

Codes
(a) Both (A) and (R) are right, but (R) does not explain (A)
(b) (A) is right and (R) is wrong
(c) Both (A) and (R) are wrong
(d) Both (A) and (R) are right and (R) explains (A)

2014

61 Under the provisions of the Trade Unions Act, 1926 what is the minimum subscription to be paid by the members of a trade union for rural workers?
(a) Five rupees per annum (b) One rupee per month
(c) One rupee per annum (d) Ten rupees per annum

62 Which of the following are union security measures?
1. Closed shop system
2. Union shop system
3. Maintenance membership shop
4. Open shop system
Select the correct answer by using the codes given below
Codes
(a) Only 1 (b) 1 and 2
(c) 1 and 4 (d) 1, 2 and 3

63 Match the following.

	List I		List II
A.	The Plantation Labour Act, 1951	1.	Welfare Legislation
B.	The Trade Unions Act, 1926	2.	Social Security Legislation
C.	The Payment of Gratuity Act, 1972	3.	Protective Legislation
D.	Beedi Workers Welfare Fund Act, 1976	4.	Regulative Legislation

Codes

	A	B	C	D		A	B	C	D
(a)	1	3	4	2	(b)	2	1	3	4
(c)	4	2	1	3	(d)	3	4	2	1

64 Which of the following statements about the governance of trade unions in India are wrong?
1. Trade unions are primarily member driven.
2. Trade unions are financially self-sufficient.
3. Trade unions are allowed to collect political fund.
4. Trade unions have inter-union rivalry.
Select the correct answer by using the codes given below
Codes
(a) 2 and 3 (b) 2 and 4
(c) 1 and 2 (d) 3 and 4

65 What is a 'closed shop' system?
(a) A shop closed due to non-availability of labour
(b) An impasse situation in industrial relations
(c) A situation where trade union stalls the operations of industry
(d) A business enterprise which has an agreement with the union that a worker must be a member of the union at the time of his employment and continue to do so in order to retain his job

66 Which of the following countries pioneered the establishment of an independent Labour Party by a Trade Union Congress?
(a) USA (b) Canada
(c) UK (d) Australia

67 The trade union leader who wrote the book *Amidst Dust and Fume* depicting his failure as the CEO of Durgapur Steel Plant is
(a) G Ramanujam (b) Michael John
(c) Bagaram Tulpule (d) Ravindra Verma

68 Match the following.

	List I (Definitions of Trade Union)		List II (Authors)
A.	A trade union is a continuous association of wage-earners for the purpose of maintaining or improving the conditions of their working lives	1.	GDH Cole
B.	A trade union is a continuing organisation of employees for the purpose of protecting or improving, through collective action, the economic and social status of its members	2.	Clyde E Dankert
C.	A trade union is an association of workers in one or more professions carried on mainly for the purpose of protecting and advancing the members' economic interest in connection with their daily work	3.	Sydney and Beatrice Webbs

Codes

	A	B	C		A	B	C
(a)	2	1	3	(b)	3	1	2
(c)	1	2	3	(d)	3	2	1

69 Who emphasised that the Trade Union Movement had emerged as labour's reaction to the dominance of the machine in modern society?
(a) GDH Cole
(b) Selig Perlman
(c) Karl Marx
(d) Frank Tannenbaum

70 Any union that caters to all employees working in a variety of industries under one owner located at the same place is categorised as
(a) primary union of industrial type
(b) primary union of general type
(c) primary union of craft type
(d) region-cum-industrial level union

71 Arrange the following trade union federations on the basis of their year of emergence from the earliest to the latest.
1. CITU 2. UTUC
3. AITUC 4. INTUC
5. BMS
Codes
(a) 3, 4, 2, 5, 1 (b) 1, 5, 2, 4, 3
(c) 4, 3, 2, 5, 1 (d) 3, 2, 4, 1, 5

72 Which of the following statement(s) is/are true about trade unionism in India?

1. It had moorings in the freedom struggle.
2. It had received patronage from employers.
3. It originated due to workers' demands.
4. It originated due to imperatives of tripartite representation in the ILO.

Select the correct answer by using the codes given below

Codes

(a) Only 1 (b) 1 and 2
(c) 1, 3 and 4 (d) 1, 2 and 4

73 Name the legislation which empowers Government of United Kingdom to bring settlement in an industrial dispute in the event of the parties not reaching an agreement.

(a) Trade Unions and Labour Relations Act
(b) Employment Protection Act
(c) Conciliation Act
(d) Voluntary Arbitration Act

74 The Jamshedpur Labour Union is

(a) a general union (b) an industrial union
(c) a craft union (d) an industrial federation

75 Arrange the following in a sequence according to the years of their establishment from the earliest to the latest

1. Madras Labour Union
2. Bombay Mill Hands Association
3. AITUC
4. Indian Federation of Labour

Codes

(a) 3, 4, 2, 1 (b) 1, 3, 4, 2 (c) 4, 2, 3, 1 (d) 2, 1, 3, 4

76 Which of tke following is not affected by the Trade Unions Act?

(a) Any agreement between partners as to their own business
(b) Any agreement between an employer and those employed by him as to such employment
(c) Any agreement in consideration on the sale of the goodwill of business or of instruction in any profession, trade or handicraft
(d) All of the above

77 Which one of the following is not a manifestation of inter-union rivalry?

(a) A registered union pressurising the employer to call it for negotiation on issues which are already agreed upon with the recognised union
(b) A registered union claiming itself to be the majority union and as such pressurising the employer to accord the recognition status to it
(c) Two rival groups of members emerging within a union expressing their support to two separate office bearers of the union
(d) The members of two registered unions getting engaged in a blame game while performing a job that calls for team work

78 According to Robert F Hoxie, the 'Business Unionism' is also known as

(a) friendly unionism
(b) uplift unionism
(c) predatory unionism
(d) bread and butter unionism

ANSWERS

Exam Based Questions

1	(d)	2	(d)	3	(d)	4	(d)	5	(c)	6	(d)	7	(d)	8	(a)	9	(d)	10	(c)
11	(b)	12	(d)	13	(b)	14	(a)	15	(c)	16	(b)	17	(b)	18	(a)	19	(b)	20	(d)
21	(c)	22	(a)	23	(d)	24	(d)	25	(b)	26	(a)	27	(d)	28	(d)	29	(a)	30	(b)
31	(c)	32	(d)	33	(b)	34	(a)	35	(d)	36	(a)	37	(d)	38	(b)	39	(a)	40	(c)
41	(d)	42	(d)	43	(d)	44	(d)	45	(c)	46	(d)	47	(a)	48	(b)	49	(b)	50	(a)
51	(c)	52	(a)	53	(a)	54	(a)	55	(c)	56	(b)	57	(c)	58	(a)	59	(b)	60	(a)
61	(d)	62	(a)	63	(b)	64	(a)	65	(a)	66	(a)	67	(b)	68	(b)	69	(b)	70	(a)
71	(a)	72	(a)	73	(d)	74	(a)	75	(c)	76	(b)	77	(b)	78	(b)	79	(c)	80	(a)
81	(a)	82	(d)	83	(a)	84	(d)	85	(c)	86	(c)	87	(b)	88	(c)	89	(a)	90	(a)
91	(c)	92	(b)	93	(a)	94	(b)	95	(a)	96	(a)	97	(b)	98	(c)	99	(a)	100	(a)
101	(b)	102	(a)	103	(a)	104	(c)	105	(b)	106	(c)	107	(a)	108	(a)	109	(b)	110	(a)
111	(b)	112	(a)	113	(b)	114	(a)	115	(c)	116	(c)	117	(c)	118	(b)	119	(a)	120	(b)

Previous Years' Questions

1	(c)	2	(a)	3	(b)	4	(c)	5	(d)	6	(c)	7	(b)	8	(d)	9	(c)	10	(d)
11	(b)	12	(a)	13	(b)	14	(b)	15	(d)	16	(c)	17	(d)	18	(c)	19	(b)	20	(a)
21	(b)	22	(b)	23	(c)	24	(b)	25	(b)	26	(c)	27	(c)	28	(d)	29	(c)	30	(b)
31	(c)	32	(b)	33	(c)	34	(b)	35	(c)	36	(a)	37	(a)	38	(d)	39	(d)	40	(a)
41	(c)	42	(a)	43	(c)	44	(c)	45	(b)	46	(c)	47	(d)	48	(c)	49	(b)	50	(d)
51	(c)	52	(b)	53	(b)	54	(c)	55	(c)	56	(d)	57	(c)	58	(b)	59	(c)	60	(d)
61	(c)	62	(d)	63	(d)	64	(c)	65	(d)	66	(c)	67	(c)	68	(d)	69	(d)	70	(b)
71	(a)	72	(c)	73	(c)	74	(c)	75	(c)	76	(b)	77	(d)	78	(d)				

Industrial Disputes

Industrial Disputes are one of the most important aspects of employer and employee relationship. Owing to their complex nature and intricacies involved, it is important for both to understand them. There are different laws that have provided legal backing to both employer and employees in terms of their rights and duties towards each other.

Concept of Industrial Disputes

An industrial dispute refers to any sort of disagreement or conflict that arises between employers and employees due to difference of opinions on the terms of employment.

Factors of Industrial Disputes

- Difference of opinion on rewards being offered to employees in terms of salary, wages and incentives. Non-payment, irregular payment or less payment can result in the same. Bonus is also one of the major bones of contention between the employer and employees.
- Lack of conformity of management towards the labour laws as set by the government. These can be in terms of wages offered, amenities provided, maternity leaves, paid leaves etc. Many times the amendment in labour laws done by the government are not passed on to the employees.
- Difference in opinions between management and employees over the style of working.
- Lack of proper HR and employee policies. Unethical and weak labour practices, which may be more management friendly.
- Lack of proper and responsible leadership that could handle the conflict arising between the two parties.
- A weak HR and legal department that is unable to properly implement the policies and labour laws.
- Dynamic political environment of the county. There are cases when the labour unions are supported by political parties.
- Layoffs, termination, dismissal, retrenchment and downsising.
- Lack of discipline due to weak leadership resulting in disobedience among the workers.

In this Chapter

- There may be multiple trade unions existing in an organisation. Intra and inter-union rivalry is a common practice.
- Poor grievance redressal mechanism.
- Poor working conditions that may lead to injuries and eve death in the worst case scenarios.

Forms of Disputes

Strikes

It is a situation where the workmen or employees cease or refuse to work in a collective and unified manner. Workmen or employees going on mass casual leaves also amount to strike.

When workmen or employees cease to work, the relationship of employer and employee is deemed to continue albeit in a state to belligerent suspension.

Types of Strikes

Primary Strikes These are aimed at the employers with whom the dispute exists. *These include the following types*

- **Stay-in/Sit-down/Pen-down/Tool-down Strikes** When the employees or workmen are sitting on their seats but refuse to work. They are present in the employers premises.
- **Go Slow** In this, workers do not completely stop the work but slow down their speed of working to cause losses to the employers. There is no cessation of work.
- **Stay Away Strike** In this, workmen or employees stay away from workplace and organise rallies, demonstrations.
- **Token/Protest Strike** In this, workers do not work for a short period in a day like an hour/day. This is generally done to send a warning to the employer of an impending strike, if the demands are not meant.
- **Work-to-rule Strike** In these type of strikes, 'employers' or 'workmen' are working not more than the minimum requirement as mentioned in their contracts. They are not working during intervals, weekends or extended hours, which in turn lowers down the productivity and efficiency of the organisation.
- **Hunger Strike** Under this, the workmen or employees observe fast in order to attract the attention of employer towards their grievances.
- **Wild Cat or Lightning Strike** These type of strikes happen without the permission of union. It is an unofficial strike and it is the responsibility of union to stop such a strike.

Secondary Strikes In these kind of strikes, the union protests not against the employer but against the third party that shares a good relationship with the employer. These are more popular in USA than India.

Sympathetic Strikes In these kind of strikes, workers are not having any issues with their employers. However, they are extending their support to the employees who are sitting on strike for some other cause.

Lockouts

Lockout is the counterpart of strikes. It is the weapon in the hands of employer to resist the demands of employees and make them agree their conditions. The employer decides to shut-down the workplace till his demands are met. It is different from the concept of layoff. Under layoff, the employer temporarily suspends the work in response of a strike.

Gherao

It is the confinement of managers by encircling them in order to intimidate them to accept the demands of unions. The workmen involved in Gherao are considered guilty under Section 339 or 340 of Indian Penal Code. The workmen would be liable to be arrested without warrant and punishable with simple imprisonment for a term which may be extended to one month or with a fine upto ₹ 500 or with both.

Picketing

Picketing is a form of strike and protest under which workers stand in front of the premises of employers with flash cards, banners and placards. They intend to inform people about the same and dissuade other workers to go and work in the premises. The workers who cross the picketers and still prefer to work despite the strike are known as scabs.

Boycotting

Boycotting is the disruption of normal functioning of an enterprise by the striking workers. They appeal to other employees to extend their cooperation by voluntarily boycotting the employer.

Trends of Industrial Disputes in India

The Ministry of Labour and Employment published the report Statistics on Industrial Disputes, Closures, Retrenchments and Layoffs for the year 2014. The report is published on the basis of data provided by the Labour Commissioners of the States and the Regional Labour Commissioners (Central).

The major highlights of the report were as following

- There was a decrease in the number of strikes and lockouts from the year 2014 to 2013.
- The majority of losses of mandays were seen in state sphere in comparison to the central sphere.
- The maximum disputes were in the private sector in comparison to the public sector.
- West Bengal had the highest number of disputes and the manufacturing sector witnessed the highest share of disputes.
- The major causes of industrial disputes were indiscipline followed by wage and allowances.
- Gujarat witnessed the maximum number of strikes and West Bengal had the highest number of lockouts.

Classification of Industrial Disputes According to International Labour Organisation

International Labour Organisation (ILO) classifies Industrial Disputes into two major types

Individual and Collective Disputes

A dispute is individual if it involves a single worker or a number of workers as individuals (or the application of their individual employment contracts). It becomes a collective dispute if it involves a number of workers collectively. Interests disputes, however, are necessarily collective in character.

Disputes about Rights and Interests (Economic Disputes)

This characterises the dispute settlement machinery of many countries. A rights dispute is a dispute concerning the violation of or interpretation of an existing right (or obligation) embodied in a law, collective agreement or individual contract of employment. At its core is an allegation that a worker or group of workers, have not been afforded their proper entitlement(s).

An interests dispute is one which arises from differences over the determination of future rights and obligations, and is usually the result of a failure of collective bargaining. It does not have its origins in an existing right, but in the interest of one of the parties to create such a right through its embodiment in a collective agreement and the opposition of the other party to doing so.

Prevention and Settlement of Industrial Disputes

Code of Discipline

It was introduced in the year 1958 and is applicable to both public and private sector enterprises. This lays down the guidelines for workers/employees/workmen, unions and employers. It aims to prevent dispute though negotiations without the interference of an outside agency. There is no legal liability or punishment and it involves only moral sanctions.

It is based on the following principles

- Prior and proper notice must be given before any strike or lockout.
- All the parties must be consulted before taking an action. A decision cannot be unilateral.
- There should be no deliberate damage to the employer's property.
- 'Go-slow' tactic must be avoided and acts of violations, intimidation and coercion should not be resorted.

The code is aimed at avoiding disrupting practices in the industry to stop the work and maintain discipline in the industry. It focuses on eliminating all forms of coercion and violence in the industry and promote constructive cooperation between the involved parties.

Tripartite Machinery

Tripartite body consists of representatives of the Central and State Governments, employers and workers. It was only after the 4th Labour Conference held in August 1942 that permanent tripartite collaboration machinery was set up and was known as Preliminary Labour Conference, which later came to be known as Indian Labour Conference (ILC).

These committees are advisory in nature and play a significant role in labour policy formulation. They help the aggrieved parties to mutually settle the disputes while fostering the spirit of cooperation and goodwill among them.

Some examples of such bodies are

- The Indian Labour Conference (ILC)
- The Standing Labour Committee (SLC)
- The Committee on Conventions
- The Industrial Committee

Workers' Participation in Management (WPM)

As the name implies, Workers' Participation in Management (WPM) focuses on involvement of workers by the management in the decision-making process. It helps in promoting industrial democracy and is based on 'Human Relations' approach to management. They can be involved in consultative, associative, administrative and decisive participation. *The form of workers' participation can be through anyone of the following*

- Participation at Board Level
- Participation through Ownership
- Participation through Complete Control
- Participation through Staff and Work Councils
- Participation through Council and Committees
- Participation through Collective Bargaining
- Participation through Job Enlargement and Enrichment
- Participation through Suggestion Scheme
- Participation through Quality Circles
- Empowered Teams
- Total Quality Management
- Financial Participation

Collective Bargaining

ILO Convention No 154 defines collective bargaining as all negotiations which take place between an employer, a group of employers or one or more employers' organisations, on the one hand, and one or more workers' organisations, on the other, *for*

- determining working conditions and terms of employment; and/or
- regulating relations between employers and workers; and/or
- regulating relations between employers or their organisations and a workers' organisation or workers' organisations.

In this, workers collectively bargain for their common interests and benefits. It needs to have a group of employees or trade unions and cannot be done by a single worker. It is a continuous process that involves negotiations between the employers and employees.

The best part about this process is that it is a joint decision-making process as both the workers and management arrive at an amicable solution to the problem jointly. It is a bipartite process in which employers and employee jointly negotiate voluntarily without any third party intervention.

Model Standing Orders

These are a set of rules and regulations that must be followed by the employers and employees that will help in regulating standards of their behaviour. These explicitly mention the duties and responsibilities of both employers and employees towards each other.

Works Committee

According to the Industrial Disputes Act, 1947, it is mandatory for the employer to set up a work committee in every organisation in which one hundred or more workmen are employed during the previous year.

These are consultative bodies that have members of both employer and employees. These aim at maintaining harmonious relations at workplace and sort out the differences existing between both the parties.

They should focus on

- Administration of welfare and fine funds.
- Educational and recreational activities.
- Safety and accident prevention.
- Occupational diseases and protective equipment.
- Conditions of work such as ventilation, lightening, temperature and sanitation including latrines and urinals.
- Amenities such as drinking water canteen, dining rooms, medical and health services.

Machinery for Settlement of Industrial Disputes

Conciliation

It is the process in which a third party is roped in to solve the disputes between the employers and employees. The third party helps in reconciling the differences and arriving at a mutual agreement for an amicable settlement of agreed solution. The Central and State Governments have the power to appoint conciliation officer or a board of conciliation under the Industrial Disputes Act, 1947.

The board of conciliation consists of equal representatives from the employers and employees end. The third party is the facilitator and cannot force the involved parties to accept the decision in order to arrive at a settlement. During the process of conciliation, the involved parties cannot indulge in strikes and lockouts.

Court of Inquiry

The government has the power to set up a court of inquiry in case the matter is not resolved under the conciliation method. The body is a fact-finding body that has to submit its report to the government within six months. The aim of setting up a court of inquiry is to promote the settlement of an industrial dispute.

Arbitration

Under this process, a third party is involved to settle down the disputes between the aggrieved parties. In this case, the involved parties represent their respective situations before the arbitrator or group of arbitrators. Based on the information provided to the arbitrator(s), and his/their investigation, he/they give(s) a judgement, which is a binding on both the parties. *This of two types*

Voluntary Arbitration In this, both the parties appoint a neutral arbitrator, who provides his verdict on the same. The verdict is not a legal binding. The Government of India instituted the tripartite National Arbitration Promotion Board to look into the matters of voluntary arbitration.

Compulsory Arbitration In this, the government appoints an arbitrator and refers the disputing parties to him. The judgment provided by the arbitrator is a legal binding on both the parties.

Adjudication

This is the ultimate or last step resort for the dispute resolution. In case, the conciliation process fails, the government appoints a third party to resolve the matter. Under this, the matter may be referred to the Labour Courts, Industrial Tribunal and National Tribunal. It is a three-tier system for the resolution of industrial disputes.

Differences between Arbitration and Adjudication

- Arbitration is a voluntary method, whereas adjudication is compulsory and the ultimate remedy of solving industrial disputes compulsory and the ultimate remedy of solving industrial disputes.
- In arbitration, the power to refer the dispute to an arbitrator lies with both the parties, *i.e.* employers and employee, whereas in adjudication this authority lies with the appropriate government to refer the dispute to labour courts and industrial tribunals.
- The number of arbitrators is not fixed and it can be one or more than one, whereas in adjudication the presiding officers of these bodies are appointed by the appropriate government and consist of one person only.
- Adjudicatory bodies can appoint one or two assessors having special knowledge of the subject under consideration to advice but in arbitration there is no provision of such kind.
- The awards of both the bodies arbitration and adjudication are quasi-judicial in nature with slight differences in terms of acceptability in the court.

Role of State and Central Labour Administration

The government has a proper machinery at the central, state and district level to check the proper implementation and execution of labour laws.

The Ministry of Labour and Employment is the ministry dealing with the issues of labours. The labour secretary is the overall incharge of policy formulation and administration. The organisation of the Chief Labour Commissioner (Central) also known as Central Industrial Relations Machinery is an apex organisation in the country responsible for maintaining harmonious industrial relations mainly in the sphere of Central Government.

The different departments functioning under the labour ministry are

- Directorate General of Employment and Training
- Organisation of the Chief Labour Commissioner (Central)
- Directorate General of Factory Advice Service and Labour Institute
- Directorate General of Mines Safety
- Directorate General of Labour Bureau
- Central Government Industrial Tribunals
- Offices of Labour Welfare Commissioners
- Employees' Provident Fund Organisation
- Employees' State Insurance Corporation
- Central Board for Workers Education
- VV Giri National Labour Institute
- Board of Arbitration (JCM)

The implementation of the policies in regard to the labour laws is the responsibility of the State Governments. These are subjected to control and direction of the Central Government except in the case of labour employed in railways, mines, oilfields, banking and insurance companies having branches in more than one state, major ports and Central Government Undertakings where the Central Government retains the responsibilities in labour matters including employment and training and tenders technical advice as and when necessary.

The State Governments work in coordination with their labour departments or the enforcement of laws. The commissioners of labour in the states are the operative arms and take the responsibility for the effective implementation of labour laws.

The machinery for prevention and settlement of the disputes has been shown in the following figure

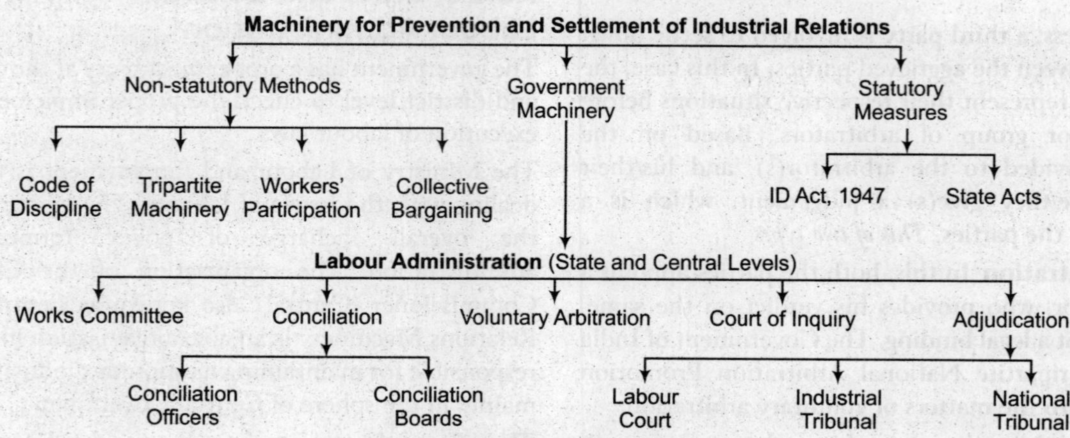

Industrial Employment (Standing Orders) Act, 1946

The act came into being on 23rd April, 1946 and is also known as Industrial Employment (Standing Orders) Act.

Applicability (Section 1)

- It extends to whole of India.
- This act is applicable to every industrial establishment wherein one hundred or more workmen are employed or were employed on any day of the preceding twelve months. However, *this act is not applicable in cases where*
  (a) Any industry to which the provisions of Chapter VII of the Bombay Industrial Relations Act, 1946, apply; or
  (b) Any industrial establishment to which the provisions of the Madhya Pradesh Industrial Employment (Standing Orders) Act, 1961 apply.

Provided that notwithstanding anything contained in the Madhya Pradesh Industrial Employment (Standing Orders) Act, 1961, the provisions of this act shall apply to all industrial establishments under the control of the Central Government.

Definitions and Interpretations (Section 2)

Appellate Authority means an authority appointed by the appropriate government by notification in the Official Gazette to exercise in such area as may be specified in the notification, the functions of an appellate authority under this act. [Section 2(a)]

Appropriate Government means in respect of industrial establishments under the control of the Central Government or a railway administration or in a major port, mine or oilfield, the Central Government and in all other cases, the State Government. [Section 2(b)]

Certifying Officer means a Labour Commissioner or a Regional Labour Commissioner and includes any other officer appointed by the appropriate government, by notification in the Official Gazette, to perform all or any of the functions of a certifying officer under this act. [Section 2(c)]

Employer means the owner of an industrial establishment to which this act for the time being applies and includes

- in a factory, any person named under [Clause (f) of Sub-section (1) of Section 7 of the Factories Act,1948], as manager of the factory;
- in any industrial establishment under the control of any department of Government in India, the authority appointed by such government in this behalf or where no authority is so appointed, the head of the department;
- in any other industrial establishment, any person responsible to the owner for the supervision and control of the industrial establishment.

Industrial Establishment means

- an industrial establishment as defined in Clause (ii) of Section 2 of the Payment of Wages Act, 1936; or
- a factory as defined in clause (m) of Section 2 of the Factories Act, 1948; or
- a railway as defined in clause (4) of Section 2 of the Indian Railway Act,1890; or
- the establishment of a person who, for the purpose of fulfilling a contract with the owner of any industrial establishment, employs workmen.

Prescribed means prescribed by rules made by the appropriate government under this act. [Section 2(f)]

Standing Orders means rules relating to matters set out in the schedule. [Section 2(g)]

Trade Union means a trade union for the time being registered under the Indian Trade Union Act, 1926. [Section 2(h)]

Wages and Workman have the meanings respectively assigned to them in Clauses (rr) and (s) of Section 2 of the Industrial Disputes Act, 1947 (14 of 1947).

Submission of Draft Standing Orders (Section 3)

- The employer shall submit to the Certifying Officer five copies of the draft standing orders proposed by him for adoption in this industrial establishment within six months from the date on which this Act becomes applicable to an industrial establishment.
- The draft shall have provisions for every matter set out in the schedule which may be applicable to the industrial establishment, and where model standing orders have been prescribed.
- The draft standing orders submitted under this section shall be accompanied by a statement giving prescribed particulars of the workmen employed in the industrial establishment including the name of the trade union, if any, to which they belong.
- A group of employers in similar industrial establishments may submit a joint draft of standing orders under this section.

Conditions for Certifications of Standing Orders (Section 4)

It shall be the function of the certifying officer or appellate authority to adjudicate upon the fairness or reasonableness of the provisions of any standing orders.

Standing orders shall be certifiable under this act, if

- provision is made therein for every matter set out in the Schedule which is applicable to the industrial establishment; and
- the standing orders are otherwise in conformity with the provisions of this Act.

Certifications of Standing Orders (Section 5)

- On receipt of the draft under Section 3, the Certifying Officer shall forward a copy thereof to the trade union together with a notice. In case, the workmen will have any objections towards the draft standing orders, he can suggest the same within fifteen days from the receipt of the notice.
- After giving the employer and the trade union or such other representatives of the workmen as may be prescribed an opportunity of being heard, the Certifying Officer shall decide whether or not any modification of or addition to the draft submitted by the employer is necessary to render the draft standing orders certifiable under this Act, and shall make an order in writing accordingly.
- The Certifying Officer shall thereupon certify the draft standing orders, after making any modifications and within seven days send copies of the certified standing orders to the employer and to the trade union or other prescribed representatives of the workmen.

Appeals (Section 6)

- Any employer, workmen, trade union or other prescribed representatives of the workmen aggrieved by the order of the certifying officer within thirty days from the date on which copies are sent, may appeal to the appellate authority.
- The decision of appellate authority shall be final. It will send the copies of the final standing order within seven days to the certifying officer, employer and to the trade union.
- In case of an appeal, they shall come into force on the expiry of seven days from the date on which copies of the order of the appellate authority are sent to the employer and trade union.

Date of Operations of Standing Orders (Section 7)

Standing orders shall come into operation on the expiry of thirty days from the date on which authenticated copies are sent to the employer and trade union by the certifying officers.

Register of Standing Orders (Section 8)

A copy of all standing orders as finally certified under this act shall be filed by the certifying officer in a register in the prescribed form maintained for the purpose and the certifying officer shall furnish a copy thereof to any person applying therefore on payment of the prescribed fee.

Posting of Standing Orders (Section 9)

The text of the standing orders as finally certified under this act shall be prominently posted by the employer in English and in the language understood by the majority of his workmen on special boards to be maintained for the purpose at or near the entrance through which the majority of the workmen enter the industrial establishment and in all departments thereof where the workmen are employed.

Duration and Maturation of Standing Orders (Section 10)

- Standing orders finally certified under this act shall not except on agreement between the employer and the workmen (or a trade union or other representative body of the workmen), be liable to modification until the expiry of six months from the date on which the standing orders or the last modifications thereof came into operation.
- An employer or workman (or a trade union or other representative body of the workmen) may apply to the Certifying Officer to have the standing orders modified, and such application shall be accompanied by five copies of the modifications proposed to be made, and where such modifications are proposed to be made by agreement between the employer and the workmen.

Payment of Subsistence Allowance (Section 10A)

- Where any workmen is suspended by the employer pending investigation or inquiry into complaints or charges of misconduct against him, *the employer shall pay to such workman subsistence allowance*
  (a) At the rate of fifty per cent of the wages which the workman was entitled to immediately preceding the date of such suspension, for the first ninety days of suspension; and
  (b) At the rate of seventy-five per cent of such wages for the remaining period of suspension if the delay in the completion of disciplinary proceedings against such workman is not directly attributable to the conduct of such workman.
- If any dispute arises regarding the subsistence allowance payable to a workman, the workman or the employer concerned may refer the dispute to the Labour Court constituted under the Industrial Disputes Act, 1947.
- The decision of the Labour Court shall be final and binding on the parties.

Powers of Certifying Officers (Section 11)

- Every certifying officer and appellate authority shall have all the powers of a civil court for the purposes of receiving evidence, administering oaths, enforcing the attendance of witnesses and compelling the discovery and production of documents and shall be deemed to be a civil court within the meaning of Sections 345 and 346 of the Code of Criminal Procedure, 1973.
- Clerical or arithmetical mistakes in any order passed by a certifying officer or appellate authority, or errors arising therein from any accidental slip or omission may, at any time, be corrected by that officer or authority or the successor in office of such officer or authority, as the case may be.

Oral Evidence in Contradiction not Admissible (Section 12)

No oral evidence having the effect of adding to or otherwise varying or contradicting standing orders as finally certified under this act shall be admitted in any court.

Penalties and Procedures (Section 13)

- An employer who fails to submit draft standing orders as required by Section 3 or who modifies his standing orders otherwise than in accordance with Section 10, shall be punishable with fine which may extend to five thousand rupees, and in the case of a continuing offence with a further fine which may extend to two hundred rupees for every day after the first during which the offence continues.
- An employer who does any act in contravention of the standing orders finally certified under this act or his industrial establishment shall be punishable with fine which may extend to one hundred rupees and in the case of a continuing offence with a further fine which may extend to twenty-five rupees for every day after the first during which the offence continues.
- No prosecution for an offence punishable under this section shall be instituted except with the previous sanction of the appropriate government.
- No court inferior to that of (a Metropolitan Magistrate or Judicial Magistrate of the second class) shall try any offence under this section.
- If any question arises as to the application or interpretation of a standing orders certified under this act, any employer or workman or a trade union or other representative body of the workmen may refer the question to anyone of the Labour Courts constituted under the Industrial Disputes Act, 1947 (14 of 1947) and specified for the disposal of such proceeding by the appropriate government by notification in the Official Gazette and the labour court to which the question is so referred shall, after giving the parties an opportunity of being heard, decide the question and such decision shall be final and binding on the parties.
- Nothing in this act shall apply to an industrial establishment in which, so far as the workmen employed therein are persons to whom the Fundamental and Supplementary Rules, Civil Services (Classification, Control and Appeal) Rules, Civil Services (Temporary Services) Rules, Revised Leave Rules, Civil Service

Regulations, Civilians in Defence Service, Classification, Control and Appeal Rules or the Indian Railway Establishment Code or any other rules or regulations that may be notified in this behalf by the appropriate government in the Official Gazette, apply.

Power to Exempt and Delegation of Power (Section 14)

The appropriate government may by notification in the Official Gazette exempt, conditionally or unconditionally, any industrial establishment or class of industrial establishments from all or any of the provisions of this act.

The appropriate government may by notification in the Official Gazette, direct that any power exercisable by it under this act or any rules made there under shall, in relation to such matters and subject to such conditions, if any, as may be specified in the direction, *be exercisable also*

- where the appropriate government is the Central Government, by such officer or authority subordinate to the Central Government or by the State Government or by such officer or authority subordinate to the State Government, as may be specified in the notification;
- where the appropriate government is a State Government, by such officer or authority subordinate to the State Government as may be specified in the notification.

Power to make Rules (Section 15)

- The appropriate government may, after previous publication, by notification in the Official Gazette, make rules to carry out the purposes of this act.
- In particular and without prejudice to the generality of the foregoing power, *such rules may*
  - (a) prescribe additional matters to be included in the schedule and the procedure to be followed;
  - (b) in modifying standing orders certified under this act in accordance with any such addition;
  - (c) set out model standing orders for the purposes of this act;
  - (d) prescribe the procedure of certifying officers and appellate authorities;
  - (e) prescribe the fee which may be charged for copies of standing orders entered in the register of standing orders; provide for any other matter which is to be or may be prescribed.

  Provided that before any rules are made under Clause (a) representatives of both employers and workmen shall be consulted by the appropriate government.

Matters to be Provided in Standing Orders under this Act

- Classification of workmen, *e.g.* whether permanent, temporary, apprentices, probationers or badlis.
- Manner of intimating to workmen periods and hours of work, holidays, pay-days and wage rates.
- Shift working.
- Attendance and late coming.
- Conditions of, procedure in applying for, and the authority which may grant, leave and holidays.
- Requirement to enter premises by certain gates and liability to search.
- Closing and re-opening of sections of the industrial establishment and temporary stoppages of work and the rights and liabilities of the employer and workmen arising there from.
- Termination of employment and the notice thereof to be given by employer and workmen.
- Suspension or dismissal for misconduct and acts or omissions which constitute misconduct.
- Means of redress for workmen against unfair treatment or wrongful exactions by the employer or his agents or servants.
- Any other matter which may be prescribed.

Industrial Disputes Act, 1947

Industrial Disputes Act, 1947 came into force on 1st April, 1947 and extends to whole of India. It enables just and equitable settlement of disputes by negotiations, conciliations, mediation, arbitration, adjudication. It denounces strikes and lockouts.

Definitions (Section 2)

Appropriate Government means any industry carried on by or under the authority of the Central Government or by a railway company or a Dock Labour Board or the Industrial Finance Corporation of India Ltd or the ESIC or the board of Trustees of the Coal Mines PF or FCI or LIC or in relation to any other industrial dispute, the State Government. [Section 2(a)]

Average Pay means the average of the wages payable to a workman

- in the case of monthly paid workman, in the three complete calendar months,

- in the case of weekly paid workman, in the four complete weeks,
- in the case of daily paid workman, in the twelve full working days.

Award means an interim or a final determination of any industrial dispute or of any question relating thereto by any Labour Court, Industrial Tribunal or National Industrial Tribunal and includes an arbitration award made under Section 10A.

Banking Company is defined in Section 5 of the Banking Companies Act, 1949, having branches or other establishments in more than one state. [Section 2BB]

Board means a Board of Conciliation constituted under this act. [Section 2C]

Conciliation Officer means a conciliation officer appointed under this act. [Section 2D]

Court means a court of inquiry constituted under this act. [Section 2F]

Employer means

- in relation to an industry carried on by or under the authority of any department of the Central Government or a State Government, the authority prescribed in this behalf or where no authority is prescribed, the head of the department; or
- in relation to an industry carried on by or on behalf of a local authority, the chief executive officer of that authority. [Section 2G]

Industry means any business, trade, undertaking, manufacture or calling of employers and includes any calling, service, employment, handicraft or industrial occupation or a vocation of workmen. [Section 2J]

Industrial Dispute means any dispute or difference between employers and employers or between employers and workmen or between workmen and workmen, which is connected with the employment or non-employment or the terms of employment or with the conditions of labour, of any person. [Section 2K]

Industrial Establishment or Undertaking means an establishment or undertaking in which any industry is carried on. Provided that where several activities are carried on in an establishment or undertaking and only one or some of such activities is or are an industry or industries, *then*

- If any unit of such establishment or undertaking carrying on any activity, being an industry, is severable from the other unit or units of such establishment or undertaking, such unit shall be deemed to be a separate industrial establishment or undertaking.
- If the predominant activity or each of the predominant activities carried on in such establishment or undertaking or any unit thereof is an industry and the other activity or each of the other activities carried on in such establishment or undertaking or unit thereof is not severable from and is, for the purpose of carrying on or aiding the carrying on of, such predominant activity or activities, the entire establishment or undertaking or, as the case may be, unit thereof shall be deemed to be an industrial establishment or undertaking.

Labour Court means a labour court constituted under Section 7. [Section 2KKB]

Layoff means the failure, refusal or inability of an employer on account of shortage of coal, power or raw materials or the accumulation of stocks or the break down of machinery [or natural calamity or for any other connected reason to give employment to a workman whose name is borne on the muster rolls of his industrial establishment and who has not been retrenched. [Section 2KKK]

Lockout means the temporary dosing of a place of employment or the suspension of work or the refusal by an employer to continue to employ any number of persons employed by him. [Section 2L]

Retrenchment means the termination by the employer of the service of a workman for any reason whatsoever, *otherwise than as a punishment inflicted by way of disciplinary action but does not include*

- Voluntary retirement of the workman; or
- Retirement of the workman on reaching the age of superannuation if the contract of employment between the employer and the workman concerned contains a stipulation in that behalf; or
- Termination of the service of the workman as a result of the non-renewal of the contract of employment between the employer and the workman concerned on its expiry or of such contract being terminated under a stipulation on that behalf contained therein; or
- Termination of the service of a workman on the ground of continued ill-health.

Settlement means a settlement arrived at in the course of conciliation proceeding and includes a written agreement between the employer and workmen arrived at otherwise than in the course of conciliation proceeding where such agreement has been signed by the parties thereto in such manner as may be prescribed and a copy thereof has been sent to an officer authorised in this behalf by the appropriate government and the conciliation officer.

Strike means a cessation of work by a body of persons employed in any industry acting in combination or a concerted refusal or a refusal, under a common understanding of any number of persons who are or have been so employed to continue to work or to accept employment. [Section 2(q)]

Tribunal means an Industrial Tribunal constituted under Section 7A and includes an Industrial Tribunal constituted before the 10th March, 1957, under this act.

Unfair Labour Practice means any of the practices specified in the Fifth Schedule.

Wages means all remuneration capable of being expressed in terms of money, which would, if the terms of employment, expressed or implied, were fulfilled, be payable to a workman in respect of his employment or of work done in such employment *and includes*

- Such allowances (including dearness allowance) as the workman is for the time being entitled to the value of any house accommodation or of supply of light, water, medical attendance or other amenity or of any service or of any confessional supply of food grains or other articles.
- Any travelling concession.
- Any commission payable on the promotion of sales or business or both.

However, it does not include

- Any bonus
- Any contribution paid or payable by the employer to any pension fund or provident fund or for the benefit of the workman under any law for the time being in force
- Any gratuity payable on the termination of his services

Workman means any person

- Including an apprentice employed in any industry to do any manual, unskilled, skilled, technical, operational, clerical or supervisory work for hire or reward, whether the terms of employment be express or implied and for the purposes of any proceeding under this act in relation to an industrial dispute, includes any such person who has been dismissed, discharged or retrenched in connection with, or as a consequence of, that dispute, or whose dismissal, discharge or retrenchment has led to that dispute.
- It does not include persons who are subject to Army Act, Air Force and Navy Act or those in police service or officer or employee of a prison.
- It does not include people who are employed in a supervisory capacity, draw wages exceeding one thousand six hundred rupees per mensem or exercises, either by the nature of the duties attached to the office or by reason of the powers vested in him, function mainly of a managerial nature.

Authorities under this Act

Works Committee (Section 3)

- These are set up to promote dialogue between employer and employee in order to have cordial relationship.
- In the case of any industrial establishment in which one hundred or more workmen are employed or have been employed on any day in the preceding twelve months, the appropriate government may by general or special order require the employer to constitute in the prescribed manner a Works Committee consisting of representatives of employers and workmen engaged in the establishment.
- The number of representatives of workmen on the committee shall not be less than the number of representatives of the employer.
- The work committees are basically advisory in nature and they do not supplement or supersede unions in collective bargaining, negotiations etc.
- The duty of the Works Committee will be to promote measures for securing and preserving amity and good relations between the employer and workmen and, to comment upon matters of their common interest or concern and endeavor to compose any material difference of opinion in respect of such matters.

Conciliation Officers (Section 4)

- These are the mediating officers appointed by the appropriate government to mediate and settle the disputes.
- A conciliation officer may be appointed for a specified area or for specified industries in a specified area or for one or more specified industries and either permanently or for a limited period.
- The conciliation officer has the power to summon any person or witness.
- He is bound to mediate where any industrial dispute exists or is apprehended or where the dispute relates to a public utility service and a notice under Section 22 has been given. He shall hold conciliation proceedings in the prescribed manner.
- The conciliation officer needs to send the report to the government within 14 days.
- If a settlement of the dispute or of any of the matters in dispute is arrived at in the course of the conciliation proceedings the conciliation officer shall send a report thereof to the appropriate government together with a memorandum of the settlement signed by the parties to the dispute.

- If no such settlement is arrived at, the conciliation officer shall, as soon as practicable after the close of the investigation, send to the appropriate government a full report setting forth the steps taken by him for ascertaining the facts and circumstances relating to the dispute and for bringing about a settlement thereof, together with a full statement of such facts and circumstances and the reasons on account of which, in his opinion, a settlement could not be arrived at.
- If the appropriate government is satisfied that there is a case for reference to a Labour Court, Tribunal or National Tribunal, it may make such reference. Where the appropriate government does not make such a reference it shall record and communicate to the parties concerned its reasons therefore.

Boards of Conciliation (Section 5)

- The appropriate government may, as occasion arises by notification in the Official Gazette constitute a Board of Conciliation for promoting the settlement of an industrial dispute.
- A Board shall consist of a chairman and two or four other members, as the appropriate government thinks fit.
- The Chairman shall be an independent person and the other members shall be persons appointed in equal numbers to represent the parties to the dispute and any person appointed to represent a party shall be appointed on the recommendation of that party.
- A Board, having the prescribed quorum, may act notwithstanding the absence of the chairman or any of its members or any vacancy in its number.
- If the board is able to arrive at a settlement, it shares its report with the appropriate government and if it is not able to arrive at any settlement, it needs to share the report mentioning the cause of failure.
- The Board gets two months for the submission of its report.
- On the basis of report, the government refers the case to a Labour Court, Industrial Tribunal, National Tribunal or for Voluntary Arbitration.

Courts of Inquiry (Section 6)

- The appropriate government may, as occasion arises by notification in the Official Gazette, constitute a Court of Inquiry for inquiring into any matter appearing to be connected with or relevant to an industrial dispute.
- A court may consist of one independent person or of such number of independent persons as the appropriate government may think fit.
- If a court consists of two or more members, one of them shall be appointed as the chairman.
- The court has six months to submit its report.

Labour Courts (Section 7)

- The appropriate government may constitute one or more labour courts for the adjudication of industrial disputes relating to any matter specified in the Second Schedule and for performing such other functions as may be assigned to them under this act.
- A labour court shall consist of one person only to be appointed by the appropriate government. A person shall not be qualified for appointment as the presiding officer of a labour court, *unless*
  (a) he is or has been, a judge of a High Court; or
  (b) he has, for a period of not less than three years, been a District Judge or an Additional District Judge; or
  (c) he has held any judicial office in India for not less than seven years; or
  (d) he has been the presiding officer of a Labour Court constituted under any Provincial Act or State Act for not less than five years.
- *The matter that falls into the jurisdiction of labour courts are mentioned in the Second Schedule and are as following*
  (a) The propriety or legality of an order passed by an employer under the standing orders.
  (b) The application and interpretation of standing orders.
  (c) Discharge or dismissal of workmen including reinstatement of or grant of relief to, workmen wrongfully dismissed.
  (d) Withdrawal of any customary concession or privilege.
  (e) Illegality or otherwise of a strike or lockout.
  (f) All matters other than those specified in the Third Schedule.

Tribunals (Section 7A)

- The appropriate government may constitute one or more Industrial Tribunals for the adjudication of industrial disputes relating to any matter, whether specified in the Second Schedule or the Third Schedule.
- A Tribunal shall consist of one person only to be appointed by the appropriate government.
- *A person shall not be qualified for appointment as the presiding officer of a Tribunal unless*
  (a) he is, or has been, a Judge of a High Court; or
  (b) he has, for a period of not less than three years, been a District Judge or an Additional District Judge.
- The appropriate government may, if it so thinks fit, appoint two persons as assessors to advise the Tribunal in the proceeding before it.

- The matters that fall within the Jurisdiction of Industrial Tribunals are covered under the Third Schedule.

These include

(a) Wages, including the period and mode of payment
(b) Compensatory and other allowances
(c) Hours of work and rest intervals
(d) Leave with wages and holidays
(e) Bonus, profit sharing, provident fund and gratuity
(f) Shift working otherwise than in accordance with standing orders
(g) Classification by grades
(h) Rules of discipline
(i) Rationalisation
(j) Retrenchment of workmen and closure of establishment
(k) Any other matter that may be prescribed

National Tribunals (Section 7B)

- The Central Government may constitute one or more National Industrial Tribunals for the adjudication of industrial disputes which, in the opinion of the Central Government, involve questions of national importance or are of such a nature that industrial establishments situated in more than one state are likely to be interested in or affected by such disputes.
- A National Tribunal shall consist of one person only to be appointed by the Central Government.
- A person shall not be qualified for appointment as the presiding officer of a National Tribunal unless he is or has been, a Judge of a High Court.
- The Central Government may, if it so thinks fit, appoint two persons as assessors to advise the National Tribunal in the proceeding before it.

Voluntary Reference of Disputes of Arbitration (Section 10A)

- The ID Act, 1947 allows settlement of dispute through the process of voluntary arbitration.
- *It is possible in the following cases*

(a) Where any industrial dispute exists or is apprehended and the employer and the workman agree to refer the dispute to arbitration, they may, at any time before the dispute has been referred under Section 10 to a Labour Court or Tribunal or National Tribunal by a written agreement, refer the dispute to arbitration and the reference shall be to such person or persons (including the presiding officer of a Labour Court or Tribunal or National Tribunal) as an arbitrator or arbitrators as may be specified in the arbitration agreement.

(b) An arbitration agreement referred to in Sub-section (1) shall be in such form and shall be signed by the parties thereto in such manner as may be prescribed.

(c) A copy of the arbitration agreement shall be forwarded to the appropriate government and the conciliation officer and the appropriate government shall, within one month from the date of the receipt of such copy, publish the same in the Official Gazette.

Protection of Workman During Pendency of Proceedings

- The period from which the conciliation/adjudication/ arbitration proceedings commences and conclude under Section 20 is called period of pandancy.
- During the proceedings of the Dispute Settlement in any form such as conciliation, adjudiction, arbitration etc, no employer has the right to alter the conditions of services.
- No employer can dismiss, punish or exploit the workman without obtaining written permission of the authority concerned.
- The employee may take action against the misconductors in accordance with the standing orders or the terms of the contract applicable to him; if the matter is not concerned to the dispute under consideration. The action taken against the employee can be in the form of dismissal of or discharge, but the employer must pay the workman wages for one month.
- There is a category of 'Protected Workman', who are given protection in the all matters, whether connected with the dispute or otherwise.
- A protected workman means a workman in an establishment, who is an officer of a registered trade union connected with the establishment, according to the rules framed under the act.
- The number of such protected workman is limited to one per cent of the total workmen employed in an establishment subject to a minimum number of five and maximum number of one hundred.
- An aggrieved workman about the provision of this act can make a complaint in writing in Form-1 direct to the Labour Court, Industrial Tribunal or National Tribunal, before whom the dispute is pending.
- The concerned authority after it receives the complaint shall try to mediate and adjudicate upon it as if it was a dispute referred to or pending before it. The authority may pass necessary order or award to change condition of service for taking disciplinary action during the proceedings of settlement of industrial disputes.

Comparison between Strikes and Lockout

- Strike is done by workman, whereas lockout is done by employer.
- Strike means cessation of work by a body of persons employed in any industry acting in combination or a concerted refusal to work or to accept employment. Lockout is just a temporary closure.
- Partial stoppage of work, hunger strike or pendown strike also falls within the definition of strike and lockout is the refusal to continue to employ the persons employed.
- Closure means the permanent closing down of a place of employment or part thereof. In the case of closure, the employer does not merely close down the place of business but finally closes. In lockout, the employer closes the place of business only not the business itself.
- No permission is required in smaller estates; where permission is required application should be submitted to the government with copy to the union atleast 90 days in advance. If no reply is received within 60 days permission can be assumed.

Illegal Strikes and Lockouts

The strike will be considered illegal under the following circumstances

In Public Utility Service

- Without giving 14 days notice.
- Commenced after 42 days of notice.
- Prior to the date indicated in the notice.
- During the pendency of proceedings.
- During the period when a settlement or award is in operation on same matters.

In Non-public Utility Service

- In breach of contract.
- During the pendency of proceedings.
- During the settlement or award is in operation.
- Both the strike and lockout will be illegal, if continued after government banning.
- If not reported for attendance, no compensation.
- If layoff is due to strike or go slow by another section of the unit, no compensation.

Penalties for Illegal Strikes and Lockouts

- Any workman who commences, continues or otherwise acts in furtherance of, a strike which is illegal under this act, shall be punishable with imprisonment for a term which may extend to one month or with fine which may extend to fifty rupees or with both.
- Any employer who commences, continues or otherwise acts in furtherance of a lockout which is illegal under this act, shall be punishable with imprisonment for a term which may extend to one month, or with fine which may extend to one thousand rupees, or with both.

Layoff

- Layoff means the failure, refusal or inability of an employer to provide employment to the workers, whose name is borne on the muster-roll of an industrial establishment, on account the shortage of resources.
- The employer is supposed to give notice of layoff workers in Form 0-1 within 7 days of such layoff. Notice of withdrawal of layoff is also to be given in Form 0-2 within 7 days of such withdraw.
- The employer of an industrial establishment employing atleast 50 but less than 100 workmen, is required to pay compensation to the workmen being laid-off. The compensation shall be payable at the rate of 50% basic wages and dearness allowance for all days of layoff, except weekly holidays.
- A worker (other than casual or badli worker) who is on the muster-roll of the establishment and who has been in continuous service under an employer for atleast one year, shall be entitled to compensation on being laid-off.
- If the employee refuses to accept alternative employment under the same employer within a radius of 5 miles the worker is not eligible for any compensation.

Retrenchment

Retrenchment means termination by the employer of the service of a workman for any reason, *excluding*

- dismissed by way of disciplinary action.
- voluntary retirement of the workman.
- retirement on reaching the age of super annuation.
- termination as a result of non-renewal of contract of employment.
- termination due to continued ill health of the workman.

Thus, termination due to reduction in volume of work or on the ground that the worker did not pass the test which would have enabled him to be confirmed or which is not in accordance with the standing orders, shall amount to retrenchment.

Retrenchment compensation is eligible for 15 days wages for evey completed year or part in excess of six months.

If at any later date the plant or process is restarted, the retrenched workmen should be given preference for reemployment and intimation given to the workmen and union and a notice should be exhibited atleast 10 days before filling up the vacancy.

Settlements

Bipartite Settlements are those which are binding only on the parties who have signed and not enforceable on others. [Section 18]

Tripartite Settlements are those which are enforceable to all parties to the dispute, all parties summoned to the conciliations, employer and his successors, on all workmen who are on roles till date as well as future employees.

Notice of Change in Employment Conditions

The IDA, 1947, stipulates that no employer will affect any change in the conditions of service in respect of matters laid down in the Fourth Schedule of the act

- without giving notice to the workman who is going to be affected by such change.
- within 21 days of giving such notice. No such prior notice is required.

The government has the power to exempt any establishment from this provision of the act, if it is considered necessary in public interest.

Unfair Labour Practices (Fifth Schedule)

On the Part of Employers and Trade Unions of Employers

- To interfere with, restrain from or coerce, workmen in the exercise of their right to organise, form, join or assist a trade union or to engage in concerted activities for the purposes of collective bargaining or other mutual aid or protection.
- Threatening workmen with discharge or dismissal, if they join a trade union.
- Threatening a lockout or closure, if a trade union is organised.
- Granting wage increase to workmen at crucial periods of trade union organisation, with a view to undermining the efforts of the trade union at organisation.
- To dominate, interfere with or contribute support, financial or otherwise, to any trade union with an employer taking an active interest in organising a trade union of his workmen and an employer showing partiality or granting favour to one of several trade unions attempting to organise his workmen or to its members, where such a trade union is not a recognised trade union.
- To establish employer sponsored trade unions of workmen.
- *To encourage or discourage membership in any trade union by discriminating against any workman by the following*
  (a) Discharging or punishing a workman, because he urged other workmen to join or organise a trade union.
  (b) Discharging or dismissing a workman for taking part in any strike (not being a strike which is deemed to be an illegal strike under this act).
  (c) Changing seniority rating or workmen because of trade union activities.
  (d) Refusing to promote workmen of higher posts on account of their trade union activities.
  (e) Giving unmerited promotions to certain workmen with a view to creating discord amongst other workmen or to undermine the strength of their trade union.
  (f) Discharging office-bearers or active members of the trade union on account of their trade union activities.
- *To discharge or dismiss workmen*
  (a) By way of victimisation.
  (b) Not in good faith, but in the colorable exercise of the employers' rights.
  (c) By falsely implicating a workman in a criminal case on false evidence or on concocted evidence.
  (d) For patently false reasons.
  (e) On untrue or trumped up allegations of absence without leave.
  (f) In utter disregard of the principles of natural justice in the conduct of domestic enquiry or with undue haste.
  (g) For misconduct of a minor technical character, without having any regard to the nature of the particular misconduct or the past record or service of the workman, thereby leading to a disproportionate punishment.
- To abolish the work of a regular nature being done by workmen, and to give such work to contractors as a measure of breaking a strike.
- To transfer a workman mala fide from one place to another, under the guise of following management policy.
- To insist upon individual workmen, who are on a legal strike to sign a good conduct bond, as a pre-condition to allowing them to resume work.
- To show favouritism or partiality to one set of workers regardless of merit.
- To employ workmen as 'badlis', casuals or temporaries and to continue them as such for years, with the object of depriving them of the status and privileges of permanent workmen.
- To discharge or discriminate against any workman for filing charges or testifying against an employer in any enquiry or proceeding relating to any industrial dispute.

- To recruit workman during a strike which is not an illegal strike.
- Failure to implement award, settlement or agreement.
- To indulge in acts of force or violence.
- To refuse to bargain collectively, in good faith with the recognised trade unions.
- Proposing or continuing a lockout deemed to be illegal under this act.

On the Part of Workmen and Trade Unions of Workmen

- To advise or actively support or instigate any strike deemed to be illegal under this act.
- *To coerce workmen in the exercise of their right to self-organisation or to join a trade union or refrain from joining any trade union*
  (a) For a trade union or its members to picketing in such a manner that non-striking workmen are physically debarred from entering the workplaces.
  (b) To indulge in acts of force or violence or to hold out threats of intimidation in connection with a strike against non-striking workmen or against managerial staff.
- For a recognised union to refuse to bargain collectively in good faith with the employer.
- To indulge in coercive activities against certification of a bargaining representative.
- To stage, encourage or instigate such forms of coercive actions as willful, 'go-slow', squatting on the work premises after working hours or 'gherao' of any of the members of the managerial or other staff.
- To stage demonstrations at the residence of the employers or the managerial staff members.
- To incite or indulge in willful damage to employer's property connected with the industry.
- To indulge in acts of force or violence or to hold out threats of intimidation against any workman with a view to prevent him from attending work.

EXAM BASED QUESTIONS

1 Which of the following is incorrect about strikes?

(a) Bonus is one of the major issues for employees going on strike
(b) Mass casual leave is a form of strike
(c) An individual ceasing to work amounts to strike
(d) The relationship of employer and employee continues in case of strikes

2 Which of the following is a cause of industrial disputes?

(a) Layoffs, termination and retrenchment
(b) Weak labour laws
(c) Dynamic political environment
(d) All of the above

3 Which of the following is correct about sit-down strike?

(a) Employees are present in the employers premises
(b) There is no cessation of work
(c) Employees stay away from workplace and organise rallies, demonstrations
(d) Workers do not work for a short period in a day like an hour/day

4 Which of the following is also known as lightning strike?

(a) Wild cat (b) Hunger strike
(c) Go-slow (d) Work-to-rule

5 In which type of strike, employees do not have issues directly with the employer?

(a) Stay in (b) Hunger strike
(c) Sympathetic strike (d) Tool down

6 Which of the following strikes happen without the permission of union?

(a) Protest strike (b) Secondary strike
(c) Lightning strike (d) Token strike

7 In which of the following strikes the employees are working not more than the minimum requirement as mentioned in their contracts?

(a) Token strike
(b) Secondary strike
(c) Sympathetic strike
(d) Work-to-rule strike

8 Which of the following is incorrect about secondary strikes?

(a) In this a third party is involved
(b) These are more common in the United States
(c) These are very common in India
(d) The union strikes against the third party

9 Under which of the following employers do not allow the employees to work until the former's conditions are met?

(a) Gherao (b) Layoff
(c) Lockout (d) Strike

10 Under which section of Indian Penal Code (IPC) has the gherao been declared illegal?

(a) 339 (b) 340
(c) 341 (d) Both (a) and (b)

11 For gherao, what is the amount of fine the workers/employees need to pay?

(a) ₹ 1,000 (b) ₹ 1,100
(c) ₹ 5,000 (d) ₹ 500

12 Which of the following is correct for lockout?

(a) It is the counterpart of layoffs
(b) This is the extreme weapon in the hands of employees
(c) The employer temporarily suspends the work
(d) The employer makes the worker agree to their demand

13 In which of the following employees stand in front of the premises of employers with flash cards, banners and playcards?

(a) Sympathetic strike (b) Boycott
(c) Picketing (d) Layoff

14 According to the International Labour Organisation (ILO), which of the following is/are covered under economic disputes?

(a) A rights dispute (b) An interest dispute
(c) Collective disputes (d) Both (a) and (b)

15 Which of the following is correct about code of discipline?

(a) It is applicable to only private sector enterprises
(b) It lays down the guidelines for employers
(c) It involves settlement of dispute through a third party intervention
(d) There is no legal liability or punishment and it involves only moral sanctions

16 Which of the following known as Preliminary Labour Conference?

(a) Industrial Committee
(b) Committee on Convention
(c) Standing Labour Committee (SLC)
(d) Indian Labour Conference (ILC)

17 Which convention of ILO defines collective bargaining?

(a) 121 (b) 154
(c) 340 (d) 341

18 Which of the following holds correct for collective bargaining?

(a) It is a tripartite process
(b) It is a joint decision-making process involving both employers and employees
(c) It can be done through a single employee as well
(d) It is an involuntary process and requires a third party intervention

19 **Which of the following is not a mandate of works committee?**
(a) Administration of welfare and fine funds
(b) Educational and recreational activities
(c) Safety and accident prevention
(d) Wages

20 **Which of the following has the power to set up the court of inquiry?**
(a) Management (b) Employee
(c) Employer (d) Government

21 **Which of the following is incorrect for conciliation?**
(a) In this a third party is roped in to solve the disputes between the employers and employees
(b) The board of conciliation consists of equal representatives from the employers and employees end
(c) The third party is the facilitator
(d) During the process of conciliation, the involved parties can indulge in strikes and lockouts

22 **How many types of arbitration are possible?**
(a) Three (b) Two
(c) Four (d) Five

23 **Which of the following is a non-statutory measure for the prevention and settlement of industrial relations?**
(a) Collective Bargaining
(b) Conciliation
(c) Court of Inquiry
(d) Adjudication

24 **Which of the following is the ultimate method of industrial dispute settlement?**
(a) Works Committee (b) Arbitration
(c) Court of Inquiry (d) Adjudication

25 **Under which section of Industrial Employment Act, 1946 is the trade union defined?**
(a) 2 (a) (b) 2 (b) (c) 2 (j) (d) 2 (h)

26 **A trade union must be registered under which of the following acts?**
(a) Factories Act, 1948
(b) Industrial Disputes Act, 1947
(c) Indian Trade Union Act, 1926
(d) Industrial Employment Act, 1946

27 **The Industrial Employment Act, 1946 is not applicable under the clauses of which of the following acts?**
(a) Bombay Industrial Relations Act, 1946
(b) Madhya Pradesh Industrial Employment (Standing Orders) Act, 1961
(c) Both (a) and (b)
(d) Industrial Act, 1947

28 **The Industrial Employment Act, 1946 will be applicable to every industrial establishment having a minimum of how many employees?**
(a) 200 (b) 100
(c) 300 (d) 400

29 **The Industrial Employment Act, 1946 is applicable to every industrial establishment wherein 100 or more workmen are employed or were employed for how many minimum months?**
(a) 9 (b) 10 (c) 11 (d) 12

30 **The employer shall submit to the certifying officer copies of the draft standing orders within how months of the applicability of Industrial Employment Act, 1946 to his establishment?**
(a) 2 (b) 4 (c) 3 (d) 6

31 **How many copies of draft standing orders need to be submitted to the certifying officer?**
(a) 4 (b) 3 (c) 7 (d) 5

32 **Which section of Industrial Employment Act, 1946 deals with conditions for specification of standing orders?**
(a) Three (b) Two (c) Four (d) Five

33 **After how many months of certification of standing of orders shall they be liable to modification?**
(a) Six (b) Two (c) Four (d) Five

34 **How much subsistence allowance is a workman entitled to for the first 90 days of his suspension?**
(a) Fifty per cent of the wages
(b) Seventy-five per cent of the wages
(c) Ninety per cent of the wages
(d) Thirty per cent of the wages

35 **How much subsistence allowance is a workman entitled to after 90 days of his suspension, if there is a delay in the completion of disciplinary proceedings against such workman?**
(a) Fifty per cent of the wages
(b) Seventy-five per cent of the wages
(c) Ninety per cent of the wages
(d) Thirty per cent of the wages

36 **The dispute regarding the subsistence allowance will be referred to which of the following?**
(a) Appropriate government
(b) Conciliation officer
(c) Labour court
(d) Top management

37 **Which section of the Industrial Employment Act, 1946 deals with the power of certifying officer?**
(a) Section 10 (b) Section 11
(c) Section 12 (d) Section 13

38 **The Industrial Employment Act, 1946 entitles the certifying officer to be a civil court under which of the following sections of Code of Criminal procedure (CrPC)?**
(a) Sections 345 and 347
(b) Sections 345 and 346
(c) Sections 343 and 344
(d) Sections 341 and 342

39 Under the Industrial Employment Act, 1946, how much penalty an employer needs to pay if the employer fails to submit draft standing orders?

(a) ₹ 4,000 (b) ₹ 7,000
(c) ₹ 8,000 (d) ₹ 5,000

40 Which of the following matters are included under standing orders?

(a) Classification of workmen
(b) Manner of intimating to workmen periods and hours of work, holidays, pay-days and wage rates
(c) Shift working
(d) All of the above

41 The text of standing orders must be published in which of the following languages?

(a) English, Hindi and regional languages
(b) Regional language and in the language understood by the majority of his workmen on special boards
(c) Hindi and in the language understood by the majority of his workmen on special boards
(d) English and in the language understood by the majority of his workmen on special boards

42 Under which section of Industrial Employment Act, 1946 is the certifying officer defined?

(a) 2(h) (b) 2(b) (c) 2(c) (d) 2(a)

43 Which of the following has been included as an industrial establishment under the Industrial Employment Act, 1946?

(a) Factory
(b) Railways
(c) Industrial establishment as defined under the Payment of Wages Act, 1936
(d) All of the above

44 Which of the following will be included under the standing orders?

(a) Suspension for misconduct
(b) Termination of employment
(c) Procedures for applying leaves
(d) All of the above

45 According to the ID Act, 1947 which of the following best defines the average pay of a monthly paid workman?

(a) Average of the wages payable to a workman in the two complete calendar months
(b) Average of the wages payable to a workman in the three complete calendar months
(c) Average of the wages payable to a workman in six complete calendar months
(d) Average of the wages payable to a workman in seven complete calendar months

46 According to the ID Act, 1947 which of the following best defines the average pay of a weekly paid workman?

(a) Average of the wages payable to a workman in the three complete weeks
(b) Average of the wages payable to a workman in four complete weeks
(c) Average of the wages payable to a workman in six complete weeks
(d) Average of the wages payable to a workman in seven complete weeks

47 According to the ID Act, 1947 which of the following best defines the average pay of a daily paid workman?

(a) Average of the wages payable to a workman in the three full working days
(b) Average of the wages payable to a workman in twelve full working days
(c) Average of the wages payable to a workman in six full working days
(d) Average of the wages payable to a workman in seven full working days

48 Which of the following best defines award under the Industrial Disputes Act, 1947?

(a) Rewards being offered to the workmen for their work
(b) Final determination of any industrial dispute that was referred to the labour court
(c) Recognition offered to the workmen for their hard work
(d) Special annual recognition given to the best performing employee

49 Which section of Industrial Disputes Act, 1947 defines an industry?

(a) 2A (b) 2J
(c) 2B (d) 2H

50 Which of the following best explains retrenchment?

(a) Voluntary retirement
(b) Termination of the service of a workman on the ground of continued ill-health
(c) Retirement of the workman
(d) Termination by the employer of the service of a workman for any reason whatsoever

51 Which of the following best explains layoff?

(a) Retrenchment of an employee
(b) Failure, refusal or inability of an employer to provide employment
(c) Refusal of the employees to work with the employer
(d) Collective bargaining

52 The labour court is constituted under which section of Industrial Disputes Act, 1947?

(a) 9 (b) 8
(c) 10 (d) 7

53 An industrial tribunal is constituted under which section of Industrial Disputes Act, 1947?

(a) 7D (b) 7B
(c) 7C (d) 7A

54 Which of the following is not included under wages?

(a) Dearness allowance
(b) Housing allowance
(c) Travelling concession
(d) Bonus

55 Who among the following is not included in the definition of workman under the Industrial Disputes Act, 1947?

(a) Police officer
(b) Employee of a prison
(c) Army, Navy and Air Force employees
(d) All of the above

56 According to the ID Act, 1947, works committee are defined under which section?

(a) 3 (b) 4 (c) 7 (d) 9

57 According to the ID Act, 1947, works committee is established in every establishment. How many minimum number of workers these establishments should have?

(a) 200 (b) 100 (c) 300 (d) 400

58 How many number of representatives should be present in the works committee from employees and employers end respectively?

(a) 2, 30 (b) Equal (c) 12,12 (d) 21, 20

59 Under the Industrial Disputes Act, 1947, which of the following is incorrect about the conciliation officer?

(a) They are the mediating officers
(b) They may be appointed either permanently or for a limited time period
(c) The conciliation officer has the power to summon any person or witness
(d) He is appointed by the employer

60 In how many days, the conciliation officer must submit the report?

(a) 12 (b) 24 (c) 30 (d) 14

61 In how many months, the Board of Conciliation need to submit its reports?

(a) 2 months (b) 3 months
(c) 7 months (d) 10 months

62 Which of the following is incorrect for the presiding officer of labour court?

(a) He is, or has been, a judge of a High Court
(b) He has, for a period of not less than three years, been a District Judge or an Additional District Judge
(c) He has held any Judicial Officer in India for not less than three years
(d) He has been the presiding officer of a labour court constituted under any Provincial Act or State Act for not less than five years

63 According to the Industrial Disputes Act, 1947, the matter that fall under the jurisdiction of labour court are mentioned in which schedule?

(a) 9 (b) 8 (c) 3 (d) 2

64 Which of the following matters are not under the jurisdiction of labour court?

(a) The application and interpretation of standing orders
(b) Discharge or dismissal of workmen including reinstatement of or grant of relief to, workmen wrongfully dismissed
(c) Withdrawal of any customary concession or privilege
(d) Wages, including the period and mode of payment

65 How many members are there in a Labour Court?

(a) 3 (b) 4 (c) 2 (d) 1

66 According to the Industrial Disputes Act, 1947, the matter that fall under the jurisdiction of tribunal are mentioned in which schedule?

(a) 8 (b) 7 (c) 2 (d) 3

67 How many members are there in the tribunal appointed by the government?

(a) 3 (b) 4 (c) 2 (d) 1

68 Which section of Industrial Disputes Act, 1947 deals with voluntary reference of disputes of arbitration?

(a) Section 10 B (b) Section 10 A
(c) Section 10 C (d) Section 10 D

69 According to the Industrial Disputes Act, 1947, the Unfair Labour Practices fall in which schedule?

(a) 2 (b) 3 (c) 4 (d) 5

70 Under the Industrial Disputes Act, 1947, the union needs to give a notice of how many days before going on strike?

(a) 12 (b) 11
(c) 19 (d) 14

71 Under the Industrial Disputes Act, 1947, the strike is considered illegal if it is commenced after how many days of giving a notice?

(a) 12 (b) 11 (c) 19 (d) 42

72 Under the Industrial Disputes Act, 1947, if any workman gets involved into illegal strike, what will be the fine charged on him?

(a) ₹ 2,000 (b) ₹ 3,000
(c) ₹ 500 (d) ₹ 50

73 Under the Industrial Disputes Act, 1947, if any employers gets involved into illegal lockout, what will be the fine charged on him?

(a) ₹ 2,000 (b) ₹ 3,000
(c) ₹ 500 (d) ₹ 1,000

74 According to the Industrial Disputes Act, 1947, the matter that fall under the jurisdiction of labour court are mentioned in which schedule?

(a) 9 (b) 8 (c) 3 (d) 2

75 According to the Industrial Disputes Act, 1947, the employer needs to give a notice period of how many days before the lockout period?

(a) 8 (b) 10
(c) 12 (d) 7

76 What percentage of the wages will be paid by the employer to the workers who are being laid-off?

(a) 30 (b) 40
(c) 20 (d) 50

77 According to the Industrial Disputes Act, 1947, in which of the following cases is the employee not eligible for any compensation?
(a) If he refuses to accept alternative employment within a radius of ten miles
(b) If he refuses to accept alternative employment within a radius of two miles
(c) If he refuses to accept alternative employment within a radius of three miles
(d) If he refuses to accept alternative employment within a radius of five miles

78 According to the Industrial Disputes Act, 1947, a worker who is being laid-off is eligible for compensation after working for minimum of how many years?
(a) 3 (b) 4 (c) 2 (d) 1

79 According to the Industrial Disputes Act, 1947, what is the minimum and maximum number of employees for which the employer needs to pay the compensation in case they are being laid-off?
(a) 100, 1000 (b) 50,100 (c) 100,200 (d) 200,300

80 Under the Industrial Disputes Act, 1947, the employer needs to give a notice of how many days before making a change in the employment conditions?
(a) 12 (b) 11 (c) 19 (d) 21

81 .... does not include any contribution paid or payable by the employer to any pension fund or provident fund or for the benefit of the workman under any law for the time being in force.
(a) Subsistence allowance
(b) Dearness allowance
(c) Gratuity
(d) Wages

82 Banking company is defined in Section .... of the Banking Companies Act, 1949, having branches or other establishments in more than one state.
(a) 9 (b) 8 (c) 3 (d) 5

83 .... means any business, trade, undertaking, manufacture or calling of employers and includes any calling, service, employment, handicraft or industrial occupation or a vocation of workmen.
(a) Employer (b) Industry
(c) Organisation (d) Establishment

84 Consider the following.
1. Retirement on reaching the age of superannuation do not fall under retrenchment.
2. It is obligatory on the part of the employer to pay retrenchment compensation at the rate of 15 days wages (for every completed year) to be calculated at the last drawn salary of an employee.
3. A notice must be put out atleast 10 days before the vacancy is filled.

Which of the following is correct?
Codes
(a) Both 1 and 2 (b) Both 2 and 3
(c) Both 1 and 3 (d) All of the above

85 Which of the following is correct in context of Industrial Disputes Act, 1947?
1. Industrial dispute is defined under Section 2(k).
2. Wages include gratuity payable on the termination of his services.
3. Workman does not include people who are employed in a supervisory capacity, draw wages exceeding one thousand six hundred rupees per mensem or exercises.
4. Works committee aim to promote measures for securing and preserving amity and good relations between the employer and workmen.

Codes
(a) 1, 3 and 4 (b) Both 2 and 3
(c) Both 1 and 3 (d) 1, 2 and 3

86 Which of the following matters are included in standing orders?
1. Closing and re-opening of sections of the industrial establishment.
2. Means of redress for workmen against unfair treatment.
3. Requirement to enter premises by certain gates and liability to search.
4. Shift working.

Codes
(a) 1, 2 and 3 (b) 2, 3 and 4
(c) Both 1 and 3 (d) All of the above

87 Which of the following is true?
1. A person qualified for a labour court should be a Judge of High Court.
2. Rules of discipline should fall within the jurisdiction of Industrial Tribunals.
3. To establish employer sponsored trade unions of workmen is an unfair labour practice of workmen.

Codes
(a) Both 2 and 3 (b) Both 1 and 3
(c) Both 1 and 2 (d) All of the above

88 Which of the following is a wrong method of dismissing a workman of his duty?
1. In the colorable exercise of the employer's rights.
2. For misconduct of a minor technical character.
3. To abolish the work of a regular nature being done by workmen.
4. For patently false reasons.

Codes
(a) 1, 2 and 3 (b) 2, 3 and 4
(c) Both 1 and 2 (d) All of the above

89 Which of the following are false in context of code of discipline?

1. The decisions must be taken unilaterally.
2. 'Go-slow' tactic must be avoided.
3. Employer needs to give a proper notice before the strikes.
4. Employees need to give a proper notice before lockouts.

Codes

(a) 1, 3 and 4 (b) 1, 2 and 3
(c) 2, 3 and 4 (d) 1, 2 and 4

90 Which of the following correctly defines 'Employer' under the Industrial Employment Act?

1. In a factory, any person named under [Clause (f) of Sub-section (1) of Section 7 of the Factories Act, 1948], as manager of the factory.
2. In any industrial establishment under the control of any department of any Government in India, the authority appointed by such government in this behalf or where no authority is so appointed, the head of the department.
3. In any other industrial establishment, any person responsible to the owner for the supervision and control of the industrial establishment.

Codes

(a) Only 1 (b) Both 2 and 3
(c) Both 1 and 3 (d) All of the above

91 Which of the following is correct for voluntary arbitration?

1. In this, both the parties appoint a neutral arbitrator, who provides his verdict on the same.
2. The judgement provided by the arbitrator is a legal binding on both the parties.
3. The Government of India instituted the Tripartite National Arbitration Promotion Board to look into the matters.

Codes

(a) Only 1
(b) Both 2 and 3
(c) Both 1 and 3
(d) All of the above

92 Consider the following for primary strikes. Which of the following statement(s) is/are correct?

1. These are aimed at the employers with whom the dispute exists.
2. In stay away strikes, workmen or employees stay away from workplace and organise rallies, demonstrations.
3. In token strikes, workers do not work for a short period in a day like an hour/day.

Codes

(a) Both 1 and 2 (b) Both 2 and 3
(c) Both 1 and 3 (d) All of the above

93 Consider the following for the layoff and lockouts. Which of the following statement(s) is/are correct?

1. Lockouts is the weapon in the hands of employer to resist the demands of employees and make them agree their conditions.
2. It is the confinement of managers by encircling them in order to intimidate them to accept the demands of unions.
3. Under 'layoff', the employer temporarily suspends the work in response of a strike.

Codes

(a) Both 1 and 2 (b) Both 2 and 3
(c) Both 1 and 3 (d) All of the above

94 Consider the following for the different types of strikes. Which of the following statement(s) is/are correct?

1. Workmen involved in Gherao are considered guilty under Section 339 or 340 of Indian Penal Code.
2. Boycotting is a form of strike and protest under which workers stand in front of the premises of employers with flash cards, banners and playcards.
3. In sympathetic strikes, workers are not having any issues with their employers.

Codes

(a) Both 1 and 2 (b) Both 2 and 3
(c) Both 1 and 3 (d) All of the above

95 Consider the following for the code of discipline. Which of the following statement(s) is/are correct?

1. Prior and proper notice must be given before any strike or lock-out.
2. 'Go-slow' tactic must be avoided and acts of violations, intimidation and coercion should not be resorted.
3. All the parties must be consulted before taking an action. A decision cannot be unilateral.

Codes

(a) Only 2 (b) Only 3
(c) Both 1 and 3 (d) All of the above

96 Consider the following statements for the conciliation process for settlement of Industrial Disputes. Which of the following statement(s) is/are correct?

1. Conciliation is the process in which a third party is roped in to solve the disputes between the employers and employees.
2. The third party can force its decisions on both the parties as a legal binding.
3. The Central and State Governments have the power to appoint conciliation officer or a board of conciliation under the Industrial Standing Order Act, 1946.

Codes
(a) Only 1
(b) Only 3
(c) Both 1 and 2
(d) All of the above

97 Consider the following statements for the process of adjudication. Which of the following statement(s) is/are correct?

1. It is a voluntary and compulsory method to resolve the disputes.
2. The power is in the hands of appropriate government to refer the dispute to Labour Court and Industrial tribunals.
3. This is the last step for the dispute resolution.

Codes
(a) Only 1
(b) Only 3
(c) Both 1 and 2
(d) All of the above

98 Which of the following statements are true/false?

(i) The labour secretary is the overall incharge of policy formulation and administration.

(ii) The implementation of the policies in regard to the labour laws is the responsibility of the Central Government.

(iii) The government has a proper machinery at the Central and State levels to check the proper implementation and execution of labour laws.

(iv) The organisation of the Chief Labour Commissioner (Central) also known as Central Industrial Relations Machinery is an apex organisation in the country responsible for maintaining harmonious industrial relations mainly in the sphere of Central Government.

(a) (i), (iv) are true and (ii), (iii) are false
(b) (i), (iii) are true and (ii), (iv) are false
(c) (ii), (iv) are true and (i), (iii) are false
(d) (iii), (iv) are true and (ii), (i) are false

99 Which of the following statements are true/false?

(i) The appropriate government under the Industrial Employment Act, 1946 is defined under the Section 2(b).

(ii) Standing orders are defined under the Industrial Employment Act, 1946 under the Section 2(g).

(iii) Certifying officer is the Labour Commissioner and is defined under Section 2(a) of the Industrial Employment Act, 1946.

(iv) Wages and workman have the meanings respectively assigned to them in clauses (c) and (d) of Section 2 of the Industrial Disputes Act, 1947.

(a) (i), (iv) are true and (ii), (iii) are false
(b) (i), (iii) are true and (ii), (iv) are false
(c) (ii), (iv) are true and (i), (iii) are false
(d) (iii), (iv) are true and (ii), (i) are false

100 Which of the following statements are true/false?

(i) The employer shall submit to the certifying Officer five copies of the draft standing orders within six months from the date on which Industrial Employment Act, 1946 becomes applicable to an industrial establishment.

(ii) The draft standing orders submitted shall be accompanied by a statement giving prescribed particulars of the organisation.

(iii) A group of employers in similar industrial establishments may submit a joint draft of standing orders.

(iv) Section 4 of the Industrial Employment Act, 1946 deals with the conditions for certifications of standing orders.

(a) (i), (iv) are true and (ii), (iii) are false
(b) (i), (iii) are true and (ii), (iv) are false
(c) (ii), (iv) are true and (i), (iii) are false
(d) (iii), (iv) are true and (ii), (i) are false

101 Which of the following statements are true/false?

(i) The Court of Inquiry will be established under the Industrial Dispute Act, 1947.

(ii) It comprises five persons.

(iii) If a court consists of two or more members, one of them shall be appointed as the Chairman.

(iv) The court has six months to submit its report.

(a) (i), (iii) and (iv) are true and (ii) is false
(b) (i), (iii) are true and (ii), (iv) are false
(c) (ii), (iv) are true and (i), (iii) are false
(d) (iii), (iv) are true and (ii), (i) are false

102 Which of the following statements are true/false?

(i) A Labor Court shall consist of one person only to be appointed by the appropriate government.

(ii) The appropriate government may constitute one or more Industrial Tribunals for the adjudication of industrial disputes relating to any matter.

(iii) Tribunal shall consist of two people only to be appointed by the appropriate government.

(iv) The matters that fall within the Jurisdiction of Industrial Tribunals are covered under the tenth schedule of the Industrial Dispute Act, 1947.

(a) (i), (iv) are true and (ii), (iii) are false
(b) (i), (ii) are true and (iii), (iv) are false
(c) (ii), (iv) are true and (ii), (iii) are false
(d) (i), (iv) are true and (iii), (ii) are false

103 Which of the following statements are true/false?

(i) The strike is illegal if it is conducted without giving a 14 days notice.

(ii) A strike is considered illegal if it is commenced after 42 days of a notice.

(iii) Workmen will be charged with a fine of fifty rupees for illegal strikes.

(iv) An employer will be fined a fine of thousand rupees for illegal lockouts.

(a) (i), (ii), (iii), (iv) are true
(b) (i), (iii) are true and (ii), (iv) are false
(c) (ii), (iv) are true and (ii), (iii) are false
(d) (iii), (iv) are true and (ii), (i) are false

104 Which of the following statements are true/false?

(i) Retrénchment does not include voluntary retirement of workman.

(ii) Retrenchment compensation becomes eligible for fifteen days wage for every completed year.

(iii) Termination as a result of non-renewal of contract of employment falls under retrenchment.

(iv) A notice should be exhibited 20 days before filling the vacancy.

(a) (i), (ii) are true and (iii), (iv) are false
(b) (i), (iii) are true and (ii), (iv) are false
(c) (ii), (iv) are true and (i), (iii) are false
(d) (iii), (iv) are true and (ii), (i) are false

105 Which of the following statements are true/false?

(i) The fifth schedule of Industrial Dispute Act, 1947 deals with unfair labour practices.

(ii) Bipartite settlements are binding only on parties who have signed the agreements and is non-enforceable on others.

(iii) The Board of Conciliation consists of two or four members and a chairman.

(iv) The Board of Conciliation needs to submit its reports within two months.

(a) (i), (iii) are true and (ii), (iv) are false
(b) (i), (ii), (iii) and (iv) are true
(c) (ii), (iv) are true and (ii), (iii) are false
(d) (iii), (iv) are true and (ii), (i) are false

106 Which of the following statements are true/false?

(i) A conciliation officer is a temporary position.

(ii) The conciliation officers need to send the report to the government within 14 days.

(iii) A conciliation officer may be appointed for a specified area and industries.

(iv) The conciliation officers are appointed by the appropriate government to mediate and settle disputes.

(a) (i), (ii) are true and (iii), (iv) are false
(b) (i), (iii) are true and (ii), (iv) are false
(c) (ii), (iii), (iv) are true and (i) is false
(d) (iii), (iv) are true and (ii), (i) are false

107 Which of the following statements are true/false?

(i) Work Committees do not supplement or supersede unions in collective bargaining.

(ii) The number of representatives of workmen on the Committee shall not be less than the number of representatives of the employer.

(iii) The Works Committee will promote measures for securing and preserving amity and good relations between the employer and workmen.

(iv) These are set up to promote dialogue between employer and employee in order to have cordial relationship.

(a) (i), (ii), (iii) and (iv) are true
(b) (i), (iii) are true and (ii), (iv) are false
(c) (ii), (iv) are true and (i), (iii) are false
(d) (iii), (iv) are true and (ii), (i) are false

Directions (Q. Nos. 108-118) *In the questions given below are two statements labelled as Assertion (A) and Reason (R). In the context of the two statements, which one of the following is correct?*

Codes

(a) Both (A) and (R) are correct and (R) is the correct explanation of (A)
(b) Both (A) and (R) are correct, but (R) is not the correct explanation of (A)
(c) (A) is correct, but (R) is incorrect
(d) (A) is incorrect, but (R) is correct

108 **Assertion** (A) The conciliating officer cannot force the involved parties to accept the decision in order to arrive at a settlement.

Reason (R) The conciliating officer is a facilitator.

109 **Assertion** (A) Tripartite body consists of representatives of the Central and State Governments, employers and workers.

Reason (R) The Indian Labour Conference (ILC) was the first tripartite body established in India.

110 **Assertion** (A) The work committee can supplement or supersede unions in collective bargaining.

Reason (R) The are advisory in nature.

111 **Assertion** (A) In the case of any industrial establishment in which one hundred or more workmen are employed or have been employed on any day in the preceding twelve months, the appropriate government may by general or special order require the employer to constitute in the prescribed manner, a Works Committee consisting of representatives of employers and workmen engaged in the establishment.

Reason (R) They provide consultation and are consulting bodies.

112 **Assertion** (A) In Work to rule strikes, 'employers' or 'workmen' are working not more than the minimum requirement as mentioned in their contracts.

Reason (R) This is done primarily to lower down the productivity and efficiency of the organisation.

113 **Assertion** (A) Picketing is a form of strike and protest under which workers stand in front of the premises of employers with flash cards, banners and placards.

Reason (R) They intend to inform people about the same and dissuade other workers to go and work in the premises.

114 **Assertion** (A) An interest dispute is one which arises from differences over the determination of future rights and obligations, and is usually the result of a failure of collective bargaining.

Reason (R) At the core of an interest dispute is an allegation that a worker, or group of workers, have not been afforded their proper entitlement.

115 **Assertion** (A) The Code of Discipline focuses on eliminating all forms of coercion and violence in the industry and promote constructive cooperation between the involved parties.

Reason (R) It promotes disrupting practices in the industry to stop the work and maintain discipline in the industry.

116 **Assertion** (A) Collective bargaining is a joint decision-making process as both the workers and management arrive at an amicable solution to the problem jointly.

Reason (R) It needs to have a group of employees or trade unions, and cannot be done by a single worker.

117 **Assertion** (A) Code of discipline explicitly mentions the duties and responsibilities of both employers and employees towards each other.

Reason (R) It is important to promote harmonious industrial relations between the employer and employees.

118 **Assertion** (A) The aim of setting up a court of inquiry is to promote the settlement of an industrial dispute.

Reason (R) The government has the power to set up court of inquiry in case the matter is not resolved under the conciliation method.

119 Match the following.

List I		List II	
A.	Gherao	1.	Unofficial Strike
B.	Tool down	2.	Confinement
C.	Wild Cat	3.	Sit down
D.	Protest Strike	4.	Token Strike

Codes

	A	B	C	D
(a)	1	3	4	2
(b)	2	3	1	4
(c)	3	1	4	2
(d)	1	3	2	4

120 Match the following.

List I		List II	
A.	Subsistence allowance	1.	Industrial Disputes Act
B.	Retrenchment	2.	Industrial Employment Act
C.	National Tribunal	3.	Section 2(s) Industrial Disputes Act
D.	Workman	4.	Section 7 (a) Industrial Disputes Act

Codes

	A	B	C	D
(a)	1	3	4	2
(b)	2	1	4	3
(c)	3	1	4	2
(d)	1	3	2	4

PREVIOUS YEARS' QUESTIONS

2018

1 Which of the following statements relating to the model standing orders are correct?

1. The model standing orders classify workers into six categories.
2. According to the model standing orders, in order to terminate the employment of a permanent monthly rated worker, the employer has to give one month's notice in writing or pay in lieu thereof.
3. The model standing orders provide a list of acts and omissions, which are to be treated as misconducts.
4. The model standing orders provide that every permanent workers shall be entitled to a service certificate at the time of dismissal, discharge or retirement from service.

Codes

(a) 1, 3, and 4 (b) 2, 3 and 4
(c) 1, 2, 3 and 4 (d) 1, 2 and 3

2 If there is a dispute regarding the subsistence allowance payable to a workman under the provisions of the Industrial Employment (Standing Orders) Act, 1946, then workman or the employer concerned may refer the dispute to

(a) The Labour Court Consitituted under the Industrial Disputes Act, 1947
(b) Industrial Tribunal Constituted under the Industrial Disputes Act, 1947
(c) The Labour Commissioner
(d) The Certifying Officer

3 In which types of strike, some of the union workers are posted at the factory gate for the purpose of watching and dissuading those who go to work?

(a) Picketing (b) Stay away strike
(c) Protest strike (d) Cat-call strike

4 Any person aggrieved by the decision of the apprenticeship advisor, relating to a dispute between an employer and an apprentice arising out of contract of apprenticeship, may perfer an appeal against the decision to which of the following under the Apprenticeship Act, 1961?

(a) The National Council to Technical Education
(b) The Apprenticeship Council
(c) The All India Council
(d) The National Council

5 Which of the following statements relating to representation of parties under the provisions of The Industrial Disputes Act, 1947 is not correct?

(a) Any of the parties can be represented by legal practioner in any conciliation proceedings.
(b) A party to a dispute may be represented by a legal practioner with the consent of the other parties in any proceeding before a labour court or tribunal.
(c) A workman who is a party to a dispute shall be represented in any proceeding under the act by any office bearer of a registered trade union of which he is a member.
(d) Any employer who is a party to a dispute shall be entitled to be represented in any proceeding under the act by an officer of an association of employers of which he is a member.

6 Which of the statements relating to the protected workman is not correct under the Industial Disputes Act, 1947?

(a) The maximum number of protected workmen is limited to one hundred.
(b) The minimum number of protected workmen is limited to ten.
(c) It shall be limited to one percent of the total number of workmen employed.
(d) It is limited to the executives or office bearers of registered trade unions connected with the establishment.

7 **Assertion (A)** Principle of compulsory arbitration leads to an authoritarian imposition of terms and conditions of employment and supresses the possible self-governance in industries.

Reason (R) In a democratic society, industrial democracy, implying collective and joint determination of the terms and conditions of employment and settlement of their disputes, should prevail without any outside interference

Codes

(a) (A) is wrong, but (R) is correct
(b) Both (A) and (R) are correct and (R) is the correct explanation of (A)
(c) Both (A) and (R) are correct, but (R) presents only one-sided view to justify (A)
(d) Is correct, but (R) is wrong

8 A strike that is conducted with a view to force an employer to recoginse or bargain with a particular trade union instead of another is known as

(a) Jurisdictional strike
(b) Political strike
(c) General strike
(d) Ordinary strike

9 Which of the following statements relating to the second industrial truce resolution are correct?

1. It was passed in 1962.
2. It emphasised that all disputes should be settled through adjudication, especially those relating to dismissal, discharge and retrenchment of workers.

3. It emphasised that all disputes should be settled by voluntary arbitration, especially those relating to dismissal, discharge and retrenchment of workers.

Choose the correct answer from the code given below

Codes

(a) 1 and 3 (b) 2 and 3
(c) 1 and 2 (d) 1, 2 and 3

10 As per the provisions of the Industrial Disputes Act, 1947, under which of the conditions a strike declared by the workmen of public utility service shall be illegal ?

(a) Resorting to strike after a lapse of fourteen days of giving a notice of strike
(b) Resorting to strike within seven days from the conclusion of conciliation proceedings pending before a conciliation officer
(c) Resorting to strike after seven days of conclusion of such proceedings pending before a Board of Conciliation
(d) Resorting to strike within two months from conclusion of such proceedings pending before a labour court

11 Which one of the following statements relating to protected workman under the Industrial Disputes Act, 1947 is not correct?

(a) A protected workman cannot be discharged or dismissed from the services during the pendency of any such proceeding in respect of an industrial dispute without the express permission in writing from the authority before which the proceeding is pending
(b) A member of the executive or other office-bearer of registered trade union can only be recognised as protected workman
(c) The number of protected workman to be recognised shall be within a range of a minimum five to a maximum one hundred
(d) Two per cent of the total workmen can be recognised protected workman

12 Which of the following authorities is not an adjudicatory body under the Industrial Disputes Act, 1947 ?

(a) Labour Court (b) Industrial Tribunal
(c) National Tribunal (d) Arbitration

13 The strikes that are intended to put pressure on the government to do something or desist from doing something are categorised as

(a) jurisdictional strikes (b) political strikes
(c) general strikes (d) quickie strikes

14 As per the Industrial Disputes Act, 1947, industrial disputes relating the subject matters covered under Second Schedule and Third Schedule are to be adjudicated upon by the Labour Court and Industrial Tribunal. But under which of the following conditions subject matter covered under the Third Schedule can be referred to the Labour Court for adjudication ?

(a) If it is not likely to affect more than one hundred workmen
(b) If the dispute has been raised by a trade union not registered under the Trade Unions Act, 1926
(c) If it is likely to affect more than one hundred workmen
(d) If the dispute has been raised by the recognised trade union

15 Which of the following is a statutory body ?

(a) Indian Labour Conference
(b) Standing Labour Committee
(c) Industrial Committee meant for Plantations
(d) Safety Committee

16 A factory has engaged two hundred fifty workers/workmen. If the employer wants to retrench any workman who has completed one year of continuous service in the establishment, then which of the conditions are to be followed by the employer under the Industrial Disputes Act, 1947?

1. It has to serve three months notice in writing in advance or pay in lieu of such notice, wage for the notice period.
2. It has to serve one month notice in writing in advance or pay in lieu of such notice, wage for the notice period.
3. Notice in the prescribed manner is served on the appropriate government.
4. Prior permission of the appropriate government has been obtained on an application made in this behalf.
5. Pay retrenchment compensation at the rate of fifteen days average pay for every completed year of continuous service or any part there of in excess of six months.

Codes

(a) 1, 3 and 5 (b) 1, 4 and 5
(c) 1 and 5 (d) All of these

17 In UK, when the parties to a dispute fail to settle their dispute through collective bargaining and having exhausted all internal procedures available to them in their establishments for settlement of disputes, can seek settlement through ....

(a) Advisory Conciliation and Arbitration Services
(b) Central Arbitration Committee
(c) House of Lords
(d) Employment Appeal Tribunals

18 A conciliation officer declares an industrial dispute to have ended in failure on 15th October, 2017 and submits the failure report to the appropriate government on 18th October. The said report is being received by the government on 29th October and the government refers the dispute to the Labour Court on 5th November, 2017. From the above information on which date it is deemed that the conciliation has been concluded ?

(a) 15th October (b) 18th October
(c) 29th October (d) 5th November

2017

19 Which one of the following acts, deals with the issue of complaints?

(a) Factories Act, 1948
(b) Payment of Wages Act, 1948
(c) Employees' Compensation Act, 1923
(d) Industrial Employment (Standing Orders) Act, 1946

20 Which of the following statements relating to the Board for Industrial and Financial Reconstruction is correct?

(a) It was established in 1986
(b) It was a non-statutory body
(c) It was located in Mumbai
(d) It was dissolved from 1st December, 2016

21 Who declared that a strike is an "inherent right of the working men for the purpose of securing justice"?

(a) Mahatma Gandhi
(b) Karl Marx
(c) Sidney and Beatrice Webb
(d) John T Dunlop

22 In which year, the Calcutta High Court held that a 'gherao' that involved wrongful restraint of a person belonging to the management was a cognisable offence?

(a) 1964 (b) 1965 (c) 1966 (d) 1967

23 Who took the initiative of setting up the Joint Consultative Board of Industry and Labour in 1951?

(a) VV Giri
(b) GL Nanda
(c) Khandubhai Desai
(d) Babu Jagjiwan Ram

24 Which of the following are true as per the provisions of the Industrial Employment (Standing Orders) Act, 1946?

1. **Draft standing orders are to be submitted by the employer to the certifying officer within six months from the date on which the act becomes applicable.**
2. **Six copies of such draft standing orders ... to be submitted to the certifying officer.**
3. **Draft standing orders are to be prepared in consultation of the workmen employed in the industrial establishment alongwith the trade unions, if any.**
4. **A statement with particulars of the workmen employed in this industrial establishment including the name of the trade unions, if any to be submitted alongwith the draft standing orders.**

Codes

(a) 1, 2 and 4 (b) 1, 3 and 4
(c) 1 and 4 (d) 2 and 3

25 A commercial establishment has employed two hundred workmen. Then which of the following provisions shall be applicable under the provisions of the Industrial Disputes Act, 1947?

1. **Setting up of Grievance Redressal Machinery**
2. **Constituting Works Committee**
3. **Provisions of Chapter V-B**
4. **Compulsory Reference of Disputes to Arbitration**

Codes

(a) 1, 2 and 3 (b) 1 and 2
(c) 2, 3 and 4 (d) All of these

26 A commercial establishment has engaged one hundred and fifty workmen. If it wants to retrench any workman who has completed one year of continuous service in the establishment, then which of the conditions are to be followed under the Industrial Disputes Act, 1947?

1. **It has to serve one month notice in writing in advance or pay in lieu of such notice, wages for the notice period.**
2. **It has to serve three months notice in writing in advance or pay in lieu of such notice, wages for the notice period.**
3. **Pay retrenchment compensation at the rate of fifteen days average pay for every completed year of continuous service or any part thereof in excess of six months.**
4. **Notice in the prescribed manner is served on the appropriate Government.**
5. **Prior permission of the appropriate government has been obtained on an application made in this behalf.**

Codes

(a) 1, 3 and 4 (b) 2, 3 and 5
(c) 2, 4 and 5 (d) 1, 3, 4 and 5

27 Which one of the following acts, explains the meaning of 'Badli Workman'?

(a) Factories Act, 1948
(b) Industrial Disputes Act, 1947
(c) Industrial Employment (Standing Orders) Act, 1946
(d) Trade Unions Act, 1926

28 The Industrial Disputes Act, 1947 empowers the appropriate government to constitute a court of inquiry to inquire into any matter appearing to be connected with or relevant to an industrial dispute. It is the duty of the court of inquiry to inquire into matters referred to it and submit its report to the appropriate government, ordinarily within which period from the commencement of its inquiry?

(a) One month
(b) Two months
(d) Four months
(d) Six months

29 **Which of the following statement(s) relating to the source of industrial disputes in the Indian context is/are correct?**

1. **Disputes relating to the implementation of labour laws and regulations fall under the category of 'disputes concerning rights'.**
2. **Disputes relating to standing orders fall under the category of 'disputes concerning rights.'**
3. **Disputes concerning collective agreements and settlements fall under the category of 'disputes concerning rights'.**

Codes

(a) Only 1 (b) 1 and 2
(c) 2 and 3 (d) All of these

30 **Under the Industrial Disputes Act, 1947, to which of the following industrial undertakings the provisions relating to layoff, retrenchment and closure provided under Chapter V-B shall be made applicable ?**

(a) Industrial establishment in which not less than one hundred workmen were employed on an average per working day for the preceding twelve months
(b) Industrial establishment in which not less than one hundred workmen were employed on an average per working day in the preceding calendar month
(c) Industrial establishment in which not less than one hundred workmen were employed on an average per working day during the preceding calendar year
(d) Industrial establishment in which not less than one hundred workmen were employed on an average for the preceding three months

31 **Which one of the following does not constitute to be a direct source of Industrial Jurisprudence in India?**

(a) The Constitution of India
(b) Legislative enactments
(c) International obligations
(d) Judicial decisions

32 **When a strike is conducted with a view to force an employer to recognise or bargain with a particular trade union instead of another, such strike is called as**

(a) political strike (b) ordinary strike
(c) protest strike (d) jurisdictional strike

33 **A workman working in an industry was demoted to a lower grade as a punishment inflicted by way of disciplinary action. If the concerned workman intends to raise an industrial dispute on it, under which of the following conditions it shall be deemed to be an industrial dispute ?**

1. **If it is supported by a union in the establishment of which he is a member.**
2. **If it is supported by a minority union of the workmen in the establishment.**
3. **If it is supported by substantial number of workmen of the establishment in the absence of a union.**

Codes

(a) Either 1 or 2 (b) Either 1 or 3
(c) Either 2 or 3 (d) 1 or 2 or 3

34 **Who among the following is/are workman under the provisions of the Industrial Disputes Act, 1947?**

1. **A person employed in a technical job draws wages of fifteen thousand rupees per month.**
2. **A person employed in a supervisory capacity draws wages of sixteen thousand rupees per month.**
3. **A person employed in a managerial or administrative capacity draws a salary of ten thousand rupees per month.**
4. **A person employed in a supervisory capacity draws wages of nine thousand rupees per month.**

Codes

(a) 1, 2 and 4 (b) 1 and 4
(c) 1 and 2 (d) 1, 3 and 4

35 **The term 'Blackleg' refers to**

(a) a worker who forcibly joins those who are on strike
(b) a worker who continues to work when his/her co-workers in the establishment are on strike
(c) a worker who wears black shoes while on duty
(d) a supervisor who breathes on the necks of his/her subordinates

36 **The bipartite consultative machinery comprises**

(a) works committees and steering committee on wages
(b) works committees and standing labour committee
(c) joint management councils and works committees
(d) joint management councils and standing labour committee

2016

37 **According to the Second National Commission on Labour, 'check-off system' must be made compulsory for members of all registered trade unions in establishments employing**

(a) 150 workers (b) 200 workers
(c) 250 workers (d) 300 workers

38 **Which of the following are ad-hoc bodies under the Industrial Disputes Act, 1947 ?**

1. **National Tribunal**
2. **Labour Court**
3. **Industrial Tribunal**
4. **Court of Inquiry**
5. **Grievance Redressal Committee**

Codes

(b) 1, 3 and 4 (b) 1, 4 and 5
(c) 4 and 5 (d) 1 and 4

39 **Which of the following is a non-statutory adhoc body?**

(a) Central Implementation and Evaluation Committee
(b) Central Committee on Labour Research
(c) Committee on Conventions
(d) Wage Board

40 With regard to the reference of industrial disputes, where State Government is the appropriate Government to different authorities, which of the following statement is false ?

(a) Refer the dispute to a Board for promoting settlement thereof
(b) Refer the dispute relating to any matter specified under Second Schedule to a Labour Court for adjudication
(c) Refer the dispute relating to any matter specified in the Second Schedule or Third Schedule to a Tribunal for adjudication
(d) Refer the dispute relating to any matter specified either in Second Schedule or Third Schedule to the National Tribunal for adjudication

41 Which of the following statements relating to the First National Commission on Labour is correct ?

(a) The Commission submitted its report in 1968
(b) The Commission recommended that it would not be desirable to make union recognition compulsory under a Central Law
(c) The Commission recommended that it would be desirable to make union recognition compulsory under a Central Law
(d) The Commission recommended that a trade union seeking recognition should have atleast 20 per cent membership of the workers of an establishment

42 As per the provisions of the Industrial Employment (Standing Orders) Act, 1946, for which of the following organisations, the Central Government is not the appropriate Government?

(a) Railways
(b) Major Ports
(c) Banks
(d) Mine and Oilfields

43 Which of the following statements relating to the court of inquiry is not correct ?

(a) The court may consist of one or more persons
(b) The court is required to submit its report within a period of three months from the commencement of inquiry
(c) The court of inquiry is an adhoc body
(d) The court of inquiry is primarily a fact-finding machinery

44 Which of the following statement(s) is/are not correct as per the provisions of the Industrial Disputes Act, 1947 ?

1. A Labour Court cannot adjudicate on disputes relating to discharge and dismissal.
2. An Industrial Tribunal can adjudicate on disputes relating to discharge and dismissal.
3. An Industrial Tribunal can adjudicate on disputes relating to hours of work and rest intervals.
4. A Labour Court cannot adjudicate on disputes relating to leave with wages and holidays.

Codes

(a) 1 (b) 1 and 3
(c) 1, 2 and 3 (d) Only 4

45 Which of the following is true relating to payment of subsistence allowance to an employee suspended pending enquiry for the first ninety days under the provisions of the Industrial Employment (Standing Orders) Act, 1946 ?

(a) Sixty per cent of the wages the workman was entitled to immediately preceding the date of suspension
(b) Seventy-five per cent of the wages the workman was entitled to immediately preceding the date of suspension
(c) Fifty per cent of the wages the workman was entitled to immediately preceding the date of suspension
(d) Thirty-three per cent of the wages the workman was entitled to immediately preceding the date of suspension

46 If there is any dispute regarding the subsistence allowance payable to a workman, then to which of the following it can be referred for a decision under the Industrial Employment (Standing Orders) Act, 1946 ?

(a) Labour Court constituted under the Industrial Disputes Act, 1947
(b) Industrial Tribunal constituted under the Industrial Disputes Act, 1947
(c) Certifying officer appointed under the Industrial Employment (Standing Orders) Act, 1946
(d) The enquiry officer conducting enquiry against the concerned workman

47 When an undertaking is closed down on account of unavoidable circumstances beyond the control of the employer, the compensation to be paid to the workmen under the Industrial Disputes Act, 1947 shall not exceed his

(a) average pay for three months
(b) average pay for four months
(c) average pay for six months
(d) average pay for five months

48 Which of the following is not true relating to prohibition of strikes in public utility services under the Industrial Disputes Act, 1947 ?

(a) Without giving to the employer notice of strike within six weeks before striking
(b) Before the expiry of the date specified in the notice of strike
(c) Within fourteen days of giving a notice of strike
(d) During the pendency of any conciliation proceedings and ten days after conclusion of such proceedings

49 The latest amendment that was made to the Industrial Disputes Act, 1947 was in the year

(a) 2008 (b) 2009
(c) 2010 (d) 2015

2015

50 Match the descriptions with the respective terms as given under the Industrial Disputes Act, 1947.

List I	List II
A. Permanent closing down of place of employment	1. Lockout
B. Failure or inability of an employer to give employment to a workman whose name is borne on the muster-rolls due to shortage of coal, power, raw materials or accumulation of stock	2. Retrenchment
C. Temporary closing of a place of employment or the suspension of work by the employer	3. Closure
D. Termination by the employer the service of a workman for any reason otherwise than as punishment	4. Layoff

Codes

	A	B	C	D		A	B	C	D
(a)	1	2	3	4	(b)	3	4	1	2
(c)	4	3	2	1	(d)	2	1	4	3

51 What is a 'wild-cat strike'?

(a) Strike perpetrated by workers with the support of the relevant union without giving notice to the employer
(b) Strike called by a group of workers on the spur of the moment without any formal notice to the employer or any consent from the relevant union
(c) Strike called by the union after resorting to a strike ballot
(d) Strike called by a union with a formal notice to the employer just a few minutes before the commencement of the strike

52 A dispute involving an individual workman relating to which of the following issues shall not be an industrial dispute without the support of a trade union or an appreciable number of workmen?

(a) Termination (b) Dismiss/Discharge
(c) Promotion (d) Retrenchment

53 The penalty prescribed under the Industrial Disputes Act, 1947 for disclosing confidential information is

(a) imprisonment for a term w' ich may extend to 1 year with a fine which may extend to ₹ 2,000 or both
(b) imprisonment for a term which may extend to 1 year with a fine which may extend to ₹ 2,000 and ₹ 500 or both
(c) imprisonment for a term which may extend to 6 months or with a fine which may extend to ₹ 1,000 or both
(d) imprisonment for a term which may extend to 6 months or with a fine which may extend to ₹ 2,000 rupees or both

54 The objects and reasons of the Industrial Disputes Bill, 1947 stated that industrial peace will be most enduring where it is founded on voluntary settlement of industrial disputes. Which of the following machineries was created for this purpose under the Industrial Disputes Act, 1947?

(a) Works committees (b) Conciliation
(c) Voluntary arbitration (d) Adjudication

55 The provision of prohibiting strikes and lockouts without 14 days notice in the public utility services provided under the Industrial Disputes Act, 1947 has been borrowed from which of the following?

(a) Report of the National Commission on Labour (first), 1969
(b) Recommendations of the Indian Labour Conference
(c) Defence of India Rules, 1942
(d) Report of the Labour Investigation Committee, 1944

56 The appropriate government either on its own motion or an application made by the employer or any workman reviews its order granting or refusing to grant permission for retrenchment of workman or refer the matter to a tribunal for adjudication. When such reference has been made, the tribunal has to pass an award within how many days from the date of such reference?

(a) 90 days (b) 60 days (c) 30 days (d) 45 days

57 Which of the following statements relating to 'Layoff' under the Industrial Disputes Act, 1947 is not correct?

(a) Layoff compensation shall be equal to 50% of the total wages and dearness allowance
(b) Layoff compensation can be paid maximum for a period of 45 days during a period of 12 months
(c) No layoff compensation can be paid if a workman laidoff refuses to accept any alternative employment in the same establishment
(d) A laidoff workman need not present himself daily for work at the establishment during the period of layoff

58 In connection with an industry and its appropriate Government, which of the following pairs is correct under the Industrial Disputes Act, 1947?

	Names of the Industries	Appropriate Governments
(a)	Rourkela Steel Plant	Government of Odisha
(b)	Durgapur Steel Plant	Government of West Bengal
(c)	Salem Steel Plant	Government of Tamil Nadu
(d)	Tata Steel	Government of Jharkhand

59 Provision relating to 'Subsistence Allowance' is covered under which of the following legislations?

(a) Minimum Wages Act, 1948
(b) Employee's Compensation Act, 1923
(c) Industrial Employment (Standing Orders) Act, 1946
(d) Employee's State Insurance Act, 1948

60 The 'Protected Workman' clause is concerned with

(a) safety provisions under the Factories Act, 1948
(b) compensation provisions under the Employee's Compensation Act, 1923
(c) sickness benefit under the Employee's State Insurance Act, 1948
(d) protection to union office-bearers from employer's punitive action under the Industrial Disputes Act, 1947

61 **Which of the following statements is not true regarding the certification of the standing orders using the Industrial Employment (Standing Orders) Act, 1946 ?**

(a) Within 6 months from the date of application of the act, the employer shall submit 5 copies of the draft standing orders ot the certifying officer

(b) There is a schedule which sets out the matters to be incorporated in the standing orders

(c) It is not mandatory to refer the draft standing orders to the unions/workmen by the certifying officer

(d) Any employer, workmen, trade union aggrieved by the order of certification issued by the certifying officer can make an appeal to the appellate authority within 30 days from the date on which copies of certification are being sent

62 **Under the provisions of the Industrial Disputes Act, 1947, what is the time period within which if no communication is received by an employer in response to his application to the appropriate Government for closing down the undertaking, then it will be deemed that permission has been granted?**

(a) 30 days (b) 45 days
(c) 60 days (d) 90 days

63 **If any money is due to a workman from an employer under a settlement or award, then for recovery of the same the concerned workman or any authorised person on his behalf may apply to which of the following authorities under the Industrial Disputes Act, 1947?**

(a) The Industrial Tribunal
(b) The Labour Court
(c) The Appropriate Government
(d) The Collector and District Magistrate

64 **Relating to layoff, which of the following statements is not correct as per the Industrial Disputes Act, 1947?**

(a) There is provision for payment of compensation for the laid-off eligible workmen

(b) Compensation for laid-off employees shall be limited to only 45 days in a period of 12 months

(c) There is no provision for providing alternative employment to the laid-off workmen

(d) A workmen has to present himself for work at the establishment at the appointed time atleast once in a day

65 **What is the time period within which the Grievance Redressal Committee constituted under the Industrial Disputes Act, 1947, has to complete its proceedings on receipt of a written application by or on behalf of the aggrieved workmen?**

(a) 15 days (b) 21 days
(c) 30 days (d) 45 days

66 **A strike that is suddenly called, generally without notice is known as**

(a) sit-in strike
(b) protest strike
(c) tools-down strike
(d) wild-cat strike

67 **The term 'court' under the Industrial Disputes Act, 1947 refers to which of the following?**

(a) Labour Court (b) Court of Inquiry
(c) High Court (d) Civil Court

2014

68 **Questions relating to the application or implementation of certified standing orders can be referred to which of the following authorities under the Industrial Employment (Standing Orders) Act, 1946?**

(a) Industrial Tribunals constituted under the Industrial Disputes Act, 1947

(b) Labour Courts constituted under the Industrial Disputes Act, 1947

(c) Chief Labour Commissioner (Central)

(d) Labour Commissioners of the States

69 **Which of the following forms of industrial conflict are not legally approved?**

1. Strike 2. Gherao
3. Lockout 4. Go-slow

Select the correct answer by using the codes given below

Codes

(a) Only 1 (b) 1 and 2
(c) 2 and 3 (d) 2 and 4

70 **Which of the following statements about a conciliation officer is not correct?**

(a) He/She has no authority to pass a final order directing the parties to a dispute to act in a particular manner

(b) He/She shall be deemed to be a public servant within the meaning of Section 21 of the Indian Penal Code

(c) The appropriate Government cannot appoint a conciliation officer for specified industries in a specified area

(d) It is mandatory for the conciliation officer to hold conciliation proceedings if a dispute relates to a public utility service and a notice has been given

71 **Industrial disputes relating to which of the following are within the jurisdiction of the Industrial tribunal?**

1. Hours of work and rest interval.
2. Withdrawal of any customary concession or privilege.
3. Rules of discipline.
4. Leave with wages and holidays.

Select the correct answer using the codes given below

Codes

(a) 1 and 4 (b) 2, 3 and 4
(c) 1, 2 and 3 (d) 1, 3 and 4

72 Discharging or dismissing workmen by way of victimisation is prohibited under which of the schedules of the Industrial Disputes Act, 1947?
(a) Schedule II (b) Schedule IV
(c) Schedule V (d) Schedule III

73 In India, strikes in contravention of the provisions of which section(s) of the Industrial Disputes Act, are illegal?
(a) Section 22 (b) Section 23
(c) Section 24 (d) All of these

74 When a conciliation proceeding relating to an industrial dispute ends without reaching a settlement, then under which of the following conditions it is deemed that conciliation proceeding has been concluded?
(a) When the conciliation officer concludes the proceedings
(b) When the conciliation officer submits the report to the appropriate government
(c) When the report of the conciliation officer is received by the appropriate government
(d) When the industrial dispute is referred to the Labour Court/Industrial Tribunal

75 Disputes that arise out of deadlocks in negotiations for a collective agreement are popularly known as
(a) grievance disputes
(b) interest disputes
(c) recognition disputes
(d) unfair labour practice disputes

76 Ordinarily which of the following principles is to be followed while retrenching workmen of one category, under the provisions of the Industrial Disputes Act, 1947?
(a) Last come first go (b) Last come last go
(c) First come first go (d) Deadwoods first go

77 **Assertion** (A) Conciliation machinery in India has been playing a positive role, but often it is not recognised and is considered as avoidable hurdle.

Reason (R) Due to the lack of professionalism and objectivity and susceptibility to political pressures, conciliation becomes ineffective.

Codes
(a) (A) is true, but (R) does not validate (A)
(b) (A) is true, but (R) is false
(c) (A) is true and (R) validates (A)
(d) Both (A) and (R) are false

78 As per latest amendment of Industrial Disputes Act, in 2010 what is the wage limit of a 'workman' to be covered under the act and what was the earlier limit?
(a) ₹ 10,000 per mensem enhanced from ₹ 1,600 per mensem
(b) ₹ 10,000 per mensem enhanced from ₹ 3,600 per mensem
(c) ₹ 5,000 per mensem enhanced from ₹ 1,600 per mensem
(d) ₹ 7,500 per mensem enhanced from ₹ 3,600 per mensem

79 According to recommendations of Second National Commission on Labour, which of the following must be regarded as 'misconduct' and not as 'industrial dispute'?
1. Go-slow 2. Work-to-rule
3. Strike 4. Lockout

Codes
(a) Only 4 (b) 1, 2 and 3
(c) 1 and 2 (d) Only 1

80 A certifying officer under the Industrial Employment (Standing Orders) Act enjoys all powers of a civil court under the Section 345 of CrPC, 1973 for purposes of
(a) receiving evidence, administering oaths, but not for enforcing the discovery or production of documents
(b) receiving evidence, administering oaths, enforcing attendance of witnesses and/or compelling discovery/production of documents
(c) receiving evidence, enforcing attendance of witnesses compelling discovery/production of documents, but not enforcing attendance of witnesses
(d) None of the above

81 The provision of Unfair Labour Practices is incorporated under which labour legislation?
(a) The Trade Unions Act
(b) The Industrial Employment (Standing Orders) Act
(c) The Industrial Disputes Act
(d) The Factories Act

82 Which of the following is a machinery for settlement of industrial disputes?
(a) National Commission on Labour
(b) Wage Board
(c) Industrial Tribunal
(d) Standing Labour Committee

83 Which of the following states pioneered the practice of setting up of 'Labour Lokadalats' for the speedy disposal of industrial disputes?
(a) Haryana (b) Gujarat (c) Maharashtra (d) Punjab

84 Which is not feature of lockout?
(a) Temporarily closing the establishment
(b) Suspending work
(c) Workers refraining from work
(d) Employer refusing to provide work to employees

85 The institutional causes of industrial disputes do not include
(a) technology and machinery (b) recognition of unions
(c) membership of unions (d) bargaining unit

86 Arrange the following in a sequence according to the years of their establishment from the earliest to latest.
1. Indian Labour Conference
2. Central Board of Worker's Education
3. Standing Conference on Public Enterprises
4. Indian National Trade Union Congress

Codes
(a) 1, 2, 3, 4 (b) 1, 4, 2, 3
(c) 4, 3, 2, 1 (d) 2, 4, 1, 3

ANSWERS

Exam Based Questions

1 *(c)*	2 *(d)*	3 *(a)*	4 *(a)*	5 *(c)*	6 *(c)*	7 *(d)*	8 *(c)*	9 *(c)*	10 *(d)*
11 *(d)*	12 *(d)*	13 *(c)*	14 *(d)*	15 *(d)*	16 *(d)*	17 *(b)*	18 *(b)*	19 *(d)*	20 *(d)*
21 *(d)*	22 *(b)*	23 *(a)*	24 *(d)*	25 *(d)*	26 *(c)*	27 *(c)*	28 *(b)*	29 *(d)*	30 *(d)*
31 *(d)*	32 *(a)*	33 *(a)*	34 *(a)*	35 *(b)*	36 *(c)*	37 *(b)*	38 *(b)*	39 *(d)*	40 *(d)*
41 *(d)*	42 *(c)*	43 *(d)*	44 *(b)*	45 *(b)*	46 *(b)*	47 *(b)*	48 *(b)*	49 *(b)*	50 *(d)*
51 *(b)*	52 *(d)*	53 *(d)*	54 *(d)*	55 *(d)*	56 *(a)*	57 *(b)*	58 *(b)*	59 *(d)*	60 *(d)*
61 *(a)*	62 *(c)*	63 *(d)*	64 *(d)*	65 *(d)*	66 *(d)*	67 *(d)*	68 *(b)*	69 *(d)*	70 *(d)*
71 *(d)*	72 *(d)*	73 *(d)*	74 *(d)*	75 *(d)*	76 *(d)*	77 *(d)*	78 *(d)*	79 *(b)*	80 *(d)*
81 *(d)*	82 *(d)*	83 *(b)*	84 *(d)*	85 *(a)*	86 *(d)*	87 *(c)*	88 *(d)*	89 *(a)*	90 *(d)*
91 *(c)*	92 *(d)*	93 *(c)*	94 *(c)*	95 *(d)*	96 *(a)*	97 *(a)*	98 *(a)*	99 *(b)*	100 *(b)*
101 *(a)*	102 *(b)*	103 *(a)*	104 *(a)*	105 *(b)*	106 *(c)*	107 *(a)*	108 *(a)*	109 *(b)*	110 *(a)*
111 *(b)*	112 *(b)*	113 *(a)*	114 *(b)*	115 *(c)*	116 *(a)*	117 *(d)*	118 *(b)*	119 *(b)*	120 *(b)*

Previous Years' Questions

1 *(c)*	2 *(a)*	3 *(a)*	4 *(b)*	5 *(a)*	6 *(b)*	7 *(c)*	8 *(a)*	9 *(a)*	10 *(c)*
11 *(d)*	12 *(d)*	13 *(b)*	14 *(a)*	15 *(d)*	16 *(b)*	17 *(a)*	18 *(c)*	19 *(d)*	20 *(d)*
21 *(a)*	22 *(d)*	23 *(b)*	24 *(c)*	25 *(b)*	26 *(a)*	27 *(c)*	28 *(d)*	29 *(d)*	30 *(a)*
31 *(c)*	32 *(d)*	33 *(d)*	34 *(b)*	35 *(b)*	36 *(c)*	37 *(d)*	38 *(d)*	39 *(d)*	40 *(d)*
41 *(c)*	42 *(c)*	43 *(b)*	44 *(a)*	45 *(b)*	46 *(a)*	47 *(a)*	48 *(d)*	49 *(c)*	50 *(b)*
51 *(b)*	52 *(c)*	53 *(c)*	54 *(a)*	55 *(c)*	56 *(c)*	57 *(d)*	58 *(d)*	59 *(c)*	60 *(d)*
61 *(c)*	62 *(c)*	63 *(c)*	64 *(c)*	65 *(c)*	66 *(d)*	67 *(b)*	68 *(b)*	69 *(d)*	70 *(c)*
71 *(d)*	72 *(c)*	73 *(d)*	74 *(c)*	75 *(b)*	76 *(a)*	77 *(c)*	78 *(a)*	79 *(c)*	80 *(b)*
81 *(c)*	82 *(c)*	83 *(d)*	84 *(c)*	85 *(d)*	86 *(c)*				

UNIT 7

Labour Legislation

Labour legislation is a holistic term to include all the laws related to employment, working conditions, wages and salaries, social security and industrial relations of the workers employed in the industry. These legislations focus on strengthening, regulating and protecting industrial relations.

Concept of Labour Legislation

In the past, the workers have been subjected to a lot of harsh and brutal treatment by the employers. Labour legislations provide a legal weapon in the hands of employee against wrong or harsh treatment rendered to him by the employer. These ensure social and economic security to the workers or labourers by providing a statutory compliance.

These establish a framework that facilitates productive individuals who work collectively to create synergistic employer-employee relationships. This in turn leads to the creation of a productive and progressive economy. India has adopted a progressive labour policy aligned with the standards of International Labour Organisation (ILO).

Importance of Labour Legislation

- These have provided statutory weapons in the hands of workers to bargain with their employers. These regulate the working conditions, payment of wages, registration of trade unions, methods of resolution of industrial disputes, certification of standing orders etc.
- These have been successful in removing the economic insecurity of the workers as an employer needs to follow the process of lay-off, retrenchment, dismissal, payment of wages and bonus as mentioned in the laws.
- With the help of labour legislations, workers are entitled to a job security. They are also liable of getting basic amenities and benefits in terms of occupational security.

In this Chapter

- Employers cannot take undue advantage of employees by making them work overtime and not providing compensation for the same. The employer needs to make sure that the basic amenities and facilities are made available to the employees as guided by different legislations.
- These are required for the economic development of the country. The premise of welfare state is embodied in the directive principles of the constitution and labour laws are important to provide protection to this section of society.
- The labour legislations provide a roadmap and framework within which employers, workers and their representatives can interact on the work-related issues. This helps in achieving and sustaining peaceful employer-employee relationships while promoting democracy at workplace.

Objectives of Labour Legislation

- Establish and facilitate social, political and economic justice to both the employer and employees.
- Provide conducive working environment while focusing on safety and welfare of the workers.
- Provide job and economic security to the workers in the times of cut-throat competition.
- Provide equal job opportunities to all irrespective of gender, caste, culture and creed.
- Promote good and harmonious relationship among employer and employees, thus leading to maintenance of industrial peace.
- Provide the rights to government to interfere in case it senses disharmony among the employer and employees.
- Provide right to employees/workmen to form union, indulge in collective bargaining and fight for their rights.

Principles of Labour Legislation

The labour legislation is based on four principles

Social Justice

As the name implies, it aims at providing justice to everyone in the society equally. This is important to ensure that poor are not exploited by rich. The profits and benefits must be equally distributed among the workers. The workers need to be provided safe and good working conditions at their workplaces. Both the employers and employees need to understand that they are two wheels of a cart and they cannot exist without each other.

Social Equality

The legislations based on this principle focus on ensuring social welfare of the workers. These laws focus on issues of wages, safety, working hours and health facilities etc. They are helpful in improving the social status of workers by improving their economic status.

National Economy

The legislations based on this principle ensure industrial peace and industrialisation of the country. Being a welfare state, India needs to formulate its laws to look after the weakest section of society and satisfy their needs while increasing their productivity. The labour legislation act as a fuel for the growth and development of the economy. The legislations need to ensure holistic development while focusing on the individual, industry and nation as a whole. The legislations need to ensure the efficiency while increasing the productivity and prosperity of workers.

International Conventions

ILO has played an important role in standardisation of labour laws across the countries. Its conventions regulate different aspects of labour laws. These convention are passed at different conferences. A country needs to ratify ILO's convention so that it becomes a law in the country. Also, the country's labour legislation needs to be guided by these convention.

Classification of Labour Legislations

It may be classified under the following heads

Laws related to Industrial Relations

- Trade Unions Act, 1926
- Industrial Employment (Standing Order) Act, 1946
- Industrial Disputes Act, 1947

Laws related to Wages

- Payment of Wages Act, 1936
- Minimum Wages Act, 1948
- Payment of Bonus Act, 1965
- Working Journalists (Fixation of Rates of Wages Act, 1958)

Law related to Working Hours, Conditions of Service and Employment

- Factories Act, 1948
- Dock Workers (Regulation of Employment) Act, 1948
- Plantation Labour Act, 1951
- Mines Act, 1952
- Working Journalists and other Newspaper Employees' (Conditions of Service and Misc. Provisions) Act, 1955

- Mines and Mineral (Development and Regulation) Act, 1957
- Merchant Shipping Act, 1955
- Motor Transport Workers Act, 1961
- Beedi and Cigar Workers (Conditions of Employment) Act, 1966
- Contract Labour (Regulation and Abolition) Act, 1970
- Sales Promotion Employees Act, 1976
- Inter-State Migrant Workmen (Regulation of Employment and Conditions of Service) Act, 1979
- Cine-Workers and Cinema Theatre Workers (Regulation of Employment) Act, 1981
- Dangerous Machines (Regulation) Act, 1983
- Dock Workers (Safety, Health and Welfare) Act, 1986
- Employment of Manual Scavengers and Construction of Dry Latrines (Prohibition) Act, 1993
- Building and Other Construction Workers (Regulation of Employment and Conditions of Service) Act, 1996
- Building and Other Construction Workers Welfare Cess Act, 1996
- Service Act, 1979
- Dock Workers (Regulation of Employment) (Inapplicability to Major Ports) Act, 1997
- Private Security Agencies (Regulation) Act, 2005

Laws related to Equality and Empowerment of Women

- Maternity Benefit Act, 1961
- Equal Remuneration Act, 1976

Laws related to Deprived and Disadvantaged Sections of the Society

- Bonded Labour System (Abolition) Act, 1976
- Child Labour (Prohibition and Regulation) Act, 1986
- Children (Pledging of Labour) Act, 1933

Laws related to Social Security

- Fatal Accidents Act, 1855
- Workmen's Compensation Act, 1923
- Employers' Liability Act, 1938
- Mica Mines Labour Welfare Fund Act, 1946
- Employees' State Insurance Act, 1948
- Employees' Provident Fund and Miscellaneous Provisions Act, 1952
- Personal Injuries (Emergency Provisions) Act, 1962
- Personal Injuries (Compensation Insurance) Act, 1963
- Payment of Gratuity Act, 1972
- Limestone and Dolomite Mines Labour Welfare Fund Act, 1972
- Beedi Workers Welfare Cess Act, 1976
- Beedi Workers Welfare Fund Act, 1976
- Iron Ore Mines, Manganese Ore Mines and Chrome Ore Mines Labour Welfare Cess Act, 1976
- Iron Ore Mines, Manganese Ore Mines and Chrome Ore Mines Labour Welfare Fund Act, 1976
- Cine Workers Welfare Cess Act, 1981
- Cine Workers Welfare Fund Act, 1981
- Unorganised Workers' Social Security Act, 2008

Prohibitive Labour Laws

- Bonded Labour System (Abolition) Act, 1976
- Child Labour (Prohibition and Regulation) Act, 1986
- The Beedi and Cigar Workers (Conditions of Employment) Act, 1966
- The Sexual Harassment at the Workplace (Prevention, Prohibition and Redressal) Act, 2013

Laws relating to Employment and Training

- Apprentices Act, 1961
- Employment Exchanges (Compulsory Notification of Vacancies) Act, 1959

Types of Legislations

Regulative

These focus on relations between the employer and employee and provide methods for settling industrial disputes. These laws lay down the rights and duties of employers and employees, also focus on relationship of workers with trade unions and *vice-versa. These include*

- The Trade Unions Act, 1926
- The Industrial Disputes Act, 1947
- Industrial Employment (Standing Orders) Act, 1946

Protective

These legislations mainly focus on protecting labour standards and improving the working conditions.

These include

- Factories Act, 1948
- The Mines Act,1952
- The Plantations Labour Act,1951
- The Motor Transport Workers Act,1961
- The Shops and Establishments Acts
- Beedi and Cigar Workers Act, 1966

Wage-Related

These legislations focus on the minimum wages that must be paid, methods and manner of their payment. *These include*

- The Payment of Wages Act,1936
- The Minimum Wages Act, 1948
- The Payment of Bonus Act, 1965
- The Equal Remuneration Act, 1976

Social Security

These legislations mainly focus on providing social security to the workers. They protect workers against risk of undue hardships and privation. *These include*

- The Workmen's Compensation Act, 1923
- The Employees' State Insurance Act, 1948
- The Coal Mines PF Act, 1948
- The Employees PF and Miscellaneous Provisions Act, 1952
- The Maternity Benefit Act, 1961
- Payment of Gratuity Act, 1972

Employee Welfare

These are the laws that have a specific aim that helps them in leading a better and good life with improved standard of living. All the laws under this category have 'welfare' in their titles. *These include*

- Limestone and Dolomite Mines Labour Welfare Fund Act, 1972
- The Mica Mines Welfare Fund Act, 1946
- The Iron Ore Mines, Manganese Ore Mines and Chrome Ore Mines Labour Welfare Cess Act, 1976
- The Cine Workers Welfare Fund Act, 1981
- Beedi Workers Welfare Fund Act, 1976

Evolution of Labour Legislation

- The history of labour legislation in India can be traced back to pre-independent India where the laws were enacted by the British to safeguard the interest of British employees.
- These laws were enacted keeping in mind the British political economy. Indian textile industry was offering tough competition to British textiles. This led to the introduction of the Factories Act in the year 1883, which aimed at making labour costlier in India. This act for the first time abolished child labour, fixed the working hours for eight hours and introduced the concept of overtime wages for work beyond eight hours.
- For the first time, Trade Dispute Act, 1929 focused on the relationship of employer and employees. This act also laid down the provisions of restraining the rights of strike and lockouts.
- However, this act was repealed in the post-independent era and Industrial Disputes Act, 1947 was brought into force. This act focused on promoting partnership between employer and employee. It clearly spelt that labour would be provided with fair wages and working conditions, in return it will have to extend its full cooperation with the employer in order to be part of strategy for National Economic Development. It also said that both employer and employees would observe a truce period of three years. This period will be free from strikes and lockouts.
- Bombay was the pioneer in the formulation of legislation on labour.
- This was followed by enactment of many laws concerning social security and regulation of labour employment.
- India has been providing for core labour standards of ILO for welfare of workers and to protect their interests.

Social Justice and Labour Legislation

Social justice aims to treat all the workers equally irrespective of their gender, caste, culture and religion. It is based on the fact that the workers can claim their share of wealth which they have helped to generate.

On one hand, globalisation has generated employment along with opportunities and on the other hand, it has led to large number of challenges for the workers. In the changing scenarios, there has been wide income disparity leading to unequal distribution of wealth among the people. Inequality not only leads to a decline in productivity but also breeds poverty, social instability and even conflict.

ILO has played a significant role in promoting social justice among the workers. It has tried to establish international standards for providing social justice and equality to the workers. The ILO declaration on social justice for a fair globalisation was signed in 2008 by the representatives of governments, employers and workers from all ILO member States.

The declaration promoted decent work through a coordinated approach for achieving four strategic objectives : employment, social protection, social dialogue and fundamental principles and rights at work. The social justice declaration is the third major statement of principles and policies adopted of the International Labour Conference. It builds on the declaration concerning the aims and purposes of the ILO (Declaration of Philadelphia) (1944) and the ILO declaration of Fundamental Principles and Rights at Work (1998).

Indian Constitution and Labour Laws

The legislations in India can be categorised as following

- Labour laws enacted by the Central Government, where the Central Government has the sole responsibility for enforcement.
- Labour laws enacted by Central Government and enforced both by Central and State Governments.
- Labour laws enacted by Central Government and enforced by the State Governments.
- Labour laws enacted and enforced by the various State Governments which apply to respective States.

Labour has been included under the concurrent list- List III in the seventh schedule of Constitution of India. A concurrent subject is a matter for which both the State and Central Government can enact laws. However, in the case of labour legislation, there is a clause which says that state cannot enact a law which is repugnant to the Center.

The following are present on the concurrent list

- Trade unions, industrial and labour disputes. These are item number 22.
- Social security and social insurance; employment and unemployment. These are item number 23.
- Welfare of labour including conditions of work, provident funds, employers' liability, workmen's compensation, invalidity and old age pensions and maternity benefits. These are item number 24.

The Union list includes the matters on which Parliament has exclusive power to legislate.

The matters that fall under the union list include the following

- Regulation of labour and safety in mines and oil-fields. These are item number 55.
- Industrial disputes concerning union employees. These are item number 61.
- Union agencies and institutions for professional, vocational or technical training. These are item number 65.

Fundamental Rights

The fundamental rights given in Chapter III of Indian Constitution deal with the relevance of the dignity of human labour and need for protecting and safeguarding the interest of labour as human being. Articles 14, 16, 19,23 and 24 of Chapter III are covered under this.

Each of these have been explained below

- Article 14 deals with equality before law. It prohibits any discrimination on grounds of religion, race, caste, sex or place of birth.
- Article 16 deals with providing equality of opportunity in matters of public employment. It clearly states that there should be equality of opportunity for all citizens in matters relating to employment or appointment to any office under the State.

  There should be no discrimination based on religion, race, caste, sex, descent, place of birth, residence or any of them in terms of employment. It also states that the government has all the rights to make laws that provide for reservation of appointments in favor of any backward class of citizens, which it feel is not adequately represented in the services.

  The article explicitly mentions that this article cannot interfere with the operation of any law that provides an appointment under which the incumbent of an office in connection with the affairs of any religious or denominational institution or any member of the governing body thereof shall be a person professing a particular religion or belonging to a particular denomination.
- Article 19 of the Indian Constitution provides for rights regarding freedom of speech and expression. It allows people to assemble peacefully without arms and to form associations and unions. It also allows people to practice any profession, or to carry on any occupation, trade or business. The government also has all the rights to enact laws that lay down professional or technical qualifications necessary for practising any profession or carrying on any occupation, trade or business.
- Article 23 of the Indian Constitution prohibits human trafficking and forced labour. It is a punishable offence.
- Article 24 of the Indian Constitution prohibits the employment of children below the age of fourteen years to be employed to work in any factory or mine or engaged in any other hazardous employment.

Directive Principles

The directive principles of Indian Constitution aim to provide the following to the citizens of the country

- Health and strength of employees, men and women.
- Prevention of child abuse.
- Citizens are not forced by economic necessity to enter avocations unsuited to their age or strength.
- Just and humane conditions of work and maternity relief.
- Secure participation of employee in the management of undertakings, establishments or other organisations engaged in any industry.

Chapter IV of the Indian Constitution deals with the directive principles of state policy. Articles 38, 39, 41, 42, 43, 43A are related with labour legislation, *which are as follows*

- Article 38 of the Indian Constitution states that the government shall promote the welfare of the people by securing and protecting as effectively as it may a social order. It should minimise the inequalities in income, and endeavor to eliminate inequalities in status, facilities and opportunities.
- Article 39 of the Indian Constitution states that men and women have equal right to an adequate means to livelihood. It also vouches for equal pay for equal work for both men and women. It prevents the exploitation of people and children at workplace by the employer.
- Article 41 provides right to work, to education and to public assistance. It states that government should provide the citizens right to work, to education and to public assistance in cases of unemployment, old age, sickness and disablement, and in other cases of undeserved want.
- Article 42 vouches for just and humane conditions of work and maternity relief.
- Article 43 states that the government should work to provide all workers, agricultural, industrial or otherwise, work, a living wage, conditions of work ensuring a decent standard of life and full enjoyment of leisure and social and cultural opportunities. It should also promote cottage industries on an individual or cooperative basis in rural areas.
- Article 43A of the Indian Constitution deals with participation of workers in management of industries.

International Labour Organisation (ILO)

The ILO is the international organisation responsible for drawing up and overseeing international labour standards.

It is the only 'tripartite' United Nations agency that brings together representatives of governments, employers and workers to jointly shape policies and programmes promoting 'decent work' for all.

The ILO was established on **19th April, 1919** by **Versailles Peace Conference** as an autonomous body associated with the League of Nations.

ILO was created as part of the Treaty of Versailles that ended World War I, to reflect the belief that universal and lasting peace can be accomplished only if it is based on social justice.

Some Important Points About ILO

- India became member of ILO in 1919, as an original signatory to the treaty of peace.
- The driving forces for ILO's creation arose from security, humanitarian, political and economic considerations.
- Underlying the ILO 's work is the importance of co-operation between governments and employers' and workers' organisations in fostering social and economic progress.
- The ILO aims to ensure that it serves the needs of working women and men by bringing together governments, employers and workers to set labour standards, develop policies and devise programmes.
- ILO is attempting to promote world-wide respect for the freedom and dignity of the working men and to create conditions in which that freedom and dignity can be more fully and effectively enjoyed.

Objectives of ILO

The objectives of the ILO are enumerated in the preamble to its constitution and in the Declaration of Philadelphia (1944) supplemented by Article 427 of the Peace Treaty of Versailles (1919). *The preamble affirms*

- Whereas universal and lasting peace can be established only if it is based upon social justice.
- Whereas conditions of labour exist involving such injustice, hardship and privation to large numbers of people as to produce unrest that the peace and harmony of the world is imperiled.
- Whereas the failure of any nation in battering the conditions of labour would reduce the economic progress of this own country.

The Declaration of Philadelphia laid down 10 objectives which the ILO was to further promote among the nations of the World. *These are*

- Full employment and raising the standards of living.
- The employment of workers in the occupation in which they can have the satisfaction of giving the fullest measure of their skill and make their contribution to the common well-being.
- The provision, as a means to the attachment of this end and under adequate guarantees for all concerned, of facilities for training and the transfer of labour including migration for employment and settlement.
- Policies in regard to wages and earnings bonus and other conditions of work calculated to ensure a just share of the fruits of progress to all and a minimum living wage to all employed and in need of protection.
- The effective recognition for the right of collective bargaining, the co-operation of management and labour in continuous improvement of protective efficiency and the collaboration of workers and employers in social and economic measures.

- The extension of social security measures to provide a basic income to all in need of such protection and comprehensive medical care.
- Adequate protection for the life and health of workers in all occupations.
- Provision for child welfare and maternity protection.
- The provision of adequate nutrition, housing and facilities for recreation and culture.
- The assurance of educational and vocational opportunity.

Principles of ILO

The Declaration of Philadelphia conference affirmed the principles of ILO namely

- Labour is not a commodity.
- Freedom of expression and cordial relationship are essential to substantial progress.
- Poverty constitutes a danger to prosperity everywhere.
- The war against want requires to be carried on with unrelenting vigor within each nation.

Structure of ILO

International Labour Conference

It sets the International labour standards and the broad policies of the ILO and meets annually in Geneva. It is often called an International Parliament of labour and the Conference is also a forum for discussion of key social and labour questions. Its role is examining of social problems and adopt conversations for ratification by the government.

Governing Body

It is the executive council of the ILO and meets three times a year in Geneva. It takes decisions on ILO policy and establishes the programme and the budget, which it then submits to the Conference for adoption. It is composed of 56 titular members (28 Governments, 14 Employers and 14 Workers) and 66 deputy members (28 Governments, 19 Employers and 19 Workers).

Ten of the titular government seats are permanently held by States of chief industrial importance (Brazil, China, France, Germany, India, Italy, Japan, the Russian Federation, the United Kingdom and the United States). The other government members are elected by the Conference every three years.

International Labour Office

It is the permanent secretariat of the International Labour Organisation. It is the focal point for International Labour Organisation's overall activities, which it prepares under the scrutiny of the governing body and under the leadership of the Director-General.

International Labour Standards-Conventions and Recommendations

- International labour standards are legal instruments drawn up by the ILO's constituents (governments, employers and workers) and setting out basic principles and rights at work.
- They are either conventions, which are legally binding international treaties that may be ratified by member states or recommendations, which serve as non-binding guidelines.
- In many cases, a convention lays down the basic principles to be implemented by ratifying countries, while a related recommendation supplements the convention by providing more detailed guidelines on how it could be applied. Recommendations can also be autonomous, *i.e.* not linked to any convention.
- Conventions and recommendations are drawn up by representatives of governments, employers and workers and are adopted at the ILO's annual International Labour Conference.
- The ILO's governing body has identified eight conventions as 'fundamental', covering subjects that are considered as fundamental principles and rights at work.

  The eight fundamental Conventions are

  (a) Freedom of Association and Protection of the Right to Organise Convention, 1948 (No. 87)
  (b) Right to Organise and Collective Bargaining Convention, 1949 (No. 98)
  (c) Forced Labour Convention, 1930 (No. 29)
  (d) Abolition of Forced Labour Convention, 1957 (No. 105)
  (e) Minimum Age Convention, 1973 (No. 138)
  (f) Worst Forms of Child Labour Convention, 1999 (No. 182)
  (g) Equal Remuneration Convention, 1951 (No. 100)
  (h) Discrimination (Employment and Occupation) Convention, 1958 (No. 111)
- The ILO's governing body has also designated four conventions as 'priority' instruments, thereby encouraging member states to ratify them because of their importance for the functioning of the international labour standards system. *The four governance conventions are*

  (a) Labour Inspection Convention, 1947 (No. 81)
  (b) Employment Policy Convention, 1964 (No. 122)
  (c) Labour Inspection (Agriculture) Convention, 1969 (No. 129)
  (d) Tripartite Consultation (International Labour Standards) Convention, 1976 (No. 144)

Impact of ILO on Indian Labour

- India is a member of the ILO since its inception and it gave great fillip to labour legislation in India.
- India has adopted many of the conventions and recommendations on international standards for improvement in labour conditions, under Article 3 of the Constitution of the ILO.
- Impact of ILO can be seen in the form of recognition of many new kinds of rights that were erstwhile not available to the labour class, but were made available post the creation of ILO.
- The guidelines issued by the ILO formed the principles on which labour legislations were drawn.
- India has been nominating non-government delegates and advisors to the ILC every year.
- ILO has so far adopted 173 conventions and 180 recommendations.
- The ILO conventions have formed the sheet anchor of Indian Labour Legislation especially after 1947, when the Indian National Government assumed office at the Centre.
- The Directive Principles of the State Policy in Articles 34, 41, 42 and 43 of the constitution lay down policy objectives in the field of labour having close resemblance and influence to the ILO constitution and the Philadelphia Charter of 1944.
- ILO adopted a series of conventions and recommendations covering hours of work, employment of women, children and young persons, weekly rest, holidays, leave with wages, night work, industrial safety, health, hygiene, social security, labour management relations, freedom of association wages and wage fixation productivity.
- The ILC wing of ILO formulates international labour standards.
- One fundamental obligation, imposed on governments by the constitution of ILO is that they must submit the instruments before the competent national or state authorities, within a maximum period of 18 months of their adoption by the conference for such action as might be considered practicable.
- After the International Labour Organisation (ILO) was formed in 1919, this Act was amended and thereafter repealed, resulting in the promulgation of the Factories Act, 1934. It makes provision for safety, health and hygiene of the workers and special provision for women and juvenile workers. It also prohibits child labour. It limits work of a child in factories, including the seasonal ones.
- Under the Mines Act, 1923, which applies to workers employed in mines, the hours of work for persons employed on surface are limited to ten per day and fifty four per week.
- The Royal Commission on labour appointed in 1929 considered the reports and suggestions of the aforesaid enquiry committee and recommended for enactment for prevention of maladies relating to payment of wages resulting in the promulgation of the Payment of Wages Act in 1936.
- The Weekly Holidays Act of 1942 prescribes one paid holiday a week for persons employed in any shop, restaurant or theatre (excepting those employed in a confidential capacity or in a position of management). The government is empowered to grant additional half-day holiday with pay in a week.
- The Industrial Disputes Act, 1947 came into being on the 1st day of April 1947. The Act provided for establishment of Industrial Tribunals by the appropriate government in British India.
- The Industrial Employment (Standing Orders) Act, 1946 came into operation for the first time requiring employers in industrial establishments employing 100 or more workmen to define the terms of employment of workmen in the form of standing orders which should be in general conformity with the model standing orders incorporated in the Act.
- The Merchant Shipping Act, 1923 provided for an agreement between a Seaman and the Master of the ship regarding terms of service.
- The ILO standards have a decisive impact on the factory, mines, social security and wage legislation in India.
- The ILO has influenced the trade union movement in India. The AITUC owes its immediate origin to it.
- India's commitment to the ILO is reflected in its adherence to the institution of tripartism as a novel method of resolving labour management conflicts.

In 2017, India ratified the two core conventions of ILO-Convention 138 regarding admission of age to employment and Convention 182 regarding worst forms of Child Labour. With ratification of these two core ILO Conventions, India has ratified 6 out of 8 core ILO Conventions, with the other 4 core ILO Conventions relating to abolition of forced labour, equal remuneration and no discrimination between men and women in employment and occupation, thus reaffirming its commitment for promoting and realising fundamental principles and right at work.

EXAM BASED QUESTIONS

1 Which of the following is incorrect about principle of social justice?
(a) The profits and benefits must be equally distributed among the workers
(b) The workers need to be provided safe and good working conditions at their workplaces
(c) Both the employers and employees need to understand that they are two wheels of a cart and they cannot exist without each other
(d) They are helpful in improving the social status of workers by improving their economic status

2 Which of the following laws is not related to Industrial Relations?
(a) Trade Unions Act, 1926
(b) Industrial Employment (Standing Order) Act, 1946
(c) Industrial Disputes Act, 1947
(d) Factories Act, 1948

3 Which of the following laws is not related to Social Security?
(a) Employees' Provident Fund and Miscellaneous Provisions Act, 1952
(b) Payment of Gratuity Act, 1972
(c) Employers' Liability Act, 1938
(d) Industrial Disputes Act, 1947

4 Which of the following is incorrect for regulative legislations?
(a) These focus on relations between the employer and employee and provide methods for settling industrial disputes
(b) These laws lay down the rights and duties of employers and employees
(c) They focus on relationship of workers with trade unions and vice
(d) These focus on improving the working conditions

5 Which of the following was the pioneer in India to formulate legislation on labour?
(a) Bombay (b) Madras (c) Delhi (d) Calcutta

6 When was the Factories Act introduced in India for the first time?
(a) 1997 (b) 1883
(c) 1999 (d) 1872

7 Which of the following is item number 22 on the concurrent list?
(a) Trade Unions
(b) Social Security
(c) Social insurance
(d) Employment and unemployment

8 Which of the following is item number 23 on the concurrent list?
(a) Trade Unions
(b) Social Security and Social insurance
(c) Industrial disputes
(d) Workmen's compensation

9 Which of the following is item number 24 on the concurrent list?
(a) Labour disputes
(b) Employment and unemployment
(c) Maternity Benefits
(d) Trade Unions

10 Which of the following is item number 55 on the union list?
(a) Employment and unemployment
(b) Union agencies and institutions for professional training
(c) Industrial disputes concerning Union employees
(d) Regulation of safety in mines and oil-fields

11 Which of the following articles of the Indian Constitution deal with providing equality of opportunity in matters of public employment?
(a) 12 (b) 11
(c) 14 (d) 16

12 Which of the following articles of the Indian Constitution allow people to practice any profession, or to carry on any occupation, trade or business?
(a) 12 (b) 11 (c) 19 (d) 16

13 Which of the following articles of the Indian Constitution prohibits human trafficking and forced labour?
(a) 12 (b) 11 (c) 23 (d) 16

14 Which of the following articles of the Indian Constitution prohibits the employment of children below the age of fourteen years to be employed?
(a) 12 (b) 11 (c) 24 (d) 32

15 Which article of the Indian Constitution states that the government shall promote the welfare of the people by securing and protecting as effectively as it may a social order?
(a) 23 (b) 22 (c) 38 (d) 39

16 Which of the following articles of the Indian Constitution clearly states that men and women have equal right to an adequate means to livelihood?
(a) 34 (b) 31
(c) 32 (d) 39

17 Which of the articles of the Indian Constitution provides right to work?
(a) 32 (b) 34
(c) 39 (d) 41

18 Which of the following articles of Indian Constitution vouches for just and humane conditions of work and maternity relief?
(a) 41 (b) 42 (c) 43 (d) 44

19 Which of the following article states that the government should work to provide all workers, agricultural, industrial or otherwise, work, a living wage?

(a) 40 (b) 42
(c) 43 (d) 44

20 Which of the following articles of the Indian Constitution deals with participation of workers in management of industries?

(a) 43A (b) 43B (c) 43C (d) 43D

21 In which year did India become a member of ILO?

(a) 1927 (b) 1947
(c) 1948 (d) 1919

22 Which of the following is incorrect for ILO?

(a) It is a bipartite body serving the needs of men and women across the world
(b) It was established by Versailles Peace Conference as an autonomous body associated with League of Nations
(c) The objectives of ILO are enumerated in the Declaration of Philadelphia
(d) It aims to promote freedom and dignity of working men and to create favourable working conditions

23 Which of the following is not a principle of ILO basis Declaration of Philadelphia?

(a) Labour is not a commodity
(b) Freedom of expression and cordial relationship are essential to the substantial progress
(c) Unemployment constitutes a danger to prosperity everywhere
(d) The war against want requires to be carried on with unrelenting vigour within each nation, and by continuous and concerted international effort in which the representatives of workers and employers, enjoying equal status with those of governments, join with them in free discussion and democratic decision with a view to the promotion of the common welfare

24 How many principle organs are there in ILO?

(a) Three (b) Four
(c) Five (d) Seven

25 Which of the following is incorrect for the International Labour Conference?

(a) It sets the International labour standards and the broad policies of the ILO
(b) It meets annually in Geneva
(c) Its role is examining of social problems and adopt conversations for ratification by the government
(d) It establishes the programme and the budget of ILO

26 Which of the following is incorrect for the governing body of ILO?

(a) It is the executive council of the ILO
(b) It takes decisions on ILO policy and establishes the programme and the budget, which it then submits to the conference for adoption
(c) It is composed of 56 titular members and 66 deputy members
(d) It meets twice a year in Geneva

27 How many governance conventions does ILO have?

(a) 6 (b) 4
(c) 3 (d) 2

28 How many core conventions does ILO have?

(a) 2 (b) 4
(c) 3 (d) 8

29 Which of the following is incorrect for the International Labour Office of ILO?

(a) It is the permanent secretariat of the ILO
(b) It is the focal point for International Labour Organisation's overall activities
(c) It works under the scrutiny of the governing body and under the leadership of the Director-General
(d) It establishes the budget of ILO

30 Which of the following is a governance convention of the ILO?

(a) Tripartite Consultation (International Labour Standards) Convention, 1976
(b) Discrimination (Employment and Occupation) Convention, 1958
(c) Minimum Age Convention, 1973
(d) Worst Forms of Child Labour Convention, 1999

31 Which of the following is incorrect for ILO's convention?

(a) The members states are not required to ratify these
(b) These are legally binding international treaties
(c) These are drawn up by representatives of governments, employers and workers
(d) These are adopted at the ILO's annual International Labour Conference

32 Which of the following is incorrect for ILO's recommendations?

(a) Recommendations can never be autonomous
(b) These are non-binding guidelines
(c) These are drawn up by representatives of governments, employers and workers
(d) These are adopted at the ILO's annual International Labour Conference

33 Which of the following is a core convention of ILO?

(a) Labour Inspection Convention, 1947
(b) Employment Policy Convention, 1964
(c) Labour Inspection (Agriculture) Convention, 1969
(d) Equal Remuneration Convention, 1951

34 How many core conventions of ILO have been ratified by India?

(a) 2 (b) 4
(c) 3 (d) 6

35 Which of the following core conventions of ILO deal with the worst forms of Child Labour?

(a) 138 (b) 100 (c) 182 (d) 98

36 Which of the following core conventions of ILO deal with the minimum age convention?

(a) 138 (b) 87
(c) 98 (d) 100

37 Which of the following core conventions of ILO has not been ratified by India?

(a) Right to Organise and Collective Bargaining Convention, 1949
(b) Abolition of Forced Labour Convention, 1957
(c) Forced Labour Convention, 1930
(d) Worst Forms of Child Labour Convention, 1999

38 The directive principles of state policy, as contained in the Constitution of India, contains Articles in corporating provisions for labour welfare. Which among the following Articles does not contain provisions for Labour Welfare?

(a) Article 38 (b) Article 39
(c) Article 40 (d) Article 41

39 Which among the following can become a member of ILO?

(a) Largest political party of a country
(b) A country
(c) A Trade Union
(d) Employers Federation

40 "Labour legislation regards the individual as a worker, whereas social legislation consider him primarily as a citizen." Who among the following made this distinction?

(a) Edwill E Witle (b) John O Hogan
(c) Jeremy Bentham (d) Francis AJ Ianni

41 Which of the following is not a publication of ILO?

(a) International Labour Review
(b) Shram Ki Duniya
(c) International Labour Statistics
(d) Indian Labour Journal

42 Which of the following conventions of the ILO relates to Freedom of Association?

(a) Convention No. 87
(b) Convention No. 100
(c) Convention No. 29
(d) Convention No. 105

43 Which of the following care conventions of the ILO has not been ratified by India?

(a) Forced Labour Convention No. 29
(b) Abolition of Forced Labour Convention No. 105
(c) Minimum Age Convention No. 138
(d) Discrimination (Employment/Occupation) No. 111

44 Which of the following statements relating to Labour Legislation is not true?

(a) It seeks to regulate the balance of power in the relationship between the employers and the government
(b) It aims to improve living conditions of the workers and their family members
(c) It has implications for promoting labour efficiency
(d) It protects minimum labour standards and improves working conditions

45 Which of the following had not been responsible for initiating enactment of Labour Legislations in India?

1. Colonial Rule
2. Adoption of Indian Constitution
3. Indian tradition/social system
4. Nationalist Movement for freedom

Codes

(a) Both 1 and 2 (b) 1, 2 and 3
(c) 1, 2 and 4 (d) All of the above

46 Which of the following statement(s) about implementation machinery of Labour Legislation is/are not true?

1. The State Government is the appropriate authority to implement Labour Legislations in the jurisdiction of the State.
2. The State Government is the appropriate implementing authority of Labour Legislation even for Central Government Organisations located in the state.
3. The State Government has no authority to implement Labour Legislations in the Central Government Organisations even though they are located in the state.
4. The Central Government can over rule the State Government in implementing Labour Legislations in any organisation irrespective of their location.

Codes

(a) Both 2 and 4 (b) Both 1 and 4
(c) 2, 3 and 4 (d) 1, 2 and 4

47 The principle of social justice regulating labour legislations which envisages the policy that "All human beings irrespective of race, creed or sex have the right to pursue both their material well-being, and their spiritual development in conditions of freedom and dignity, of economic security and equal opportunity" was propagated by

1. The Philadelphia Chapter
2. The Magna Carta
3. The Constitution of India
4. The League of Nations

Codes

(a) Only 1 (b) Both 1 and 3
(c) 1, 2 and 3 (d) 1, 3 and 4

48 Consider the following for labour legislations.

1. Labour legislations focus on strengthening, regulating and protecting industrial relations.
2. These provide a statutory compliance.
3. These are helpful in creation of a productive and progressive economy.

Which of the following is correct?

(a) Both 1 and 2 (b) Both 2 and 3
(c) Both 1 and 3 (d) All of the above

49 Which of the following is correct in context of history of Labour Legislation in India?

1. The history of labour legislation in India can be traced back to the British era to safeguard the interest of British employees.
2. Industrial Disputes Act was brought into force in the Pre-independent India.
3. Factories Act in the year 1883 aimed at making labour costlier in India.
4. Trade Disputes Act, 1929 laid down the provisions of restraining the rights of strike and lockouts.

(a) 1, 3 and 4 (b) Both 2 and 3
(c) Both 1 and 3 (d) 1, 2 and 3

50 Consider the following for the principles of labour legislations.

1. Social equity legislations focus on ensuring social welfare of the workers.
2. The principle of social justice states that the employers and employees need to understand that they are two wheels of a cart and they cannot exist without each other.
3. An ILO convention is a law in the member countries.

Which of the following is correct?

(a) Both 1 and 2 (b) Both 2 and 3
(c) Both 1 and 3 (d) All of the above

51 Consider the following for labour legislations.

1. ID Act, 1947 provides for a truce period of two years.
2. Factories Act abolished child labour for the first time.
3. Factories Act introduced the concept of overtime wages for work beyond eight hours.

Which of the following is correct?

(a) Both 1 and 2 (b) Both 2 and 3
(c) Both 1 and 3 (d) All of the above

52 Which of the following core conventions of ILO have been ratified by India?

1. Forced Labour Convention, 1930
2. Abolition of Forced Labour Convention, 1957
3. Equal Remuneration Convention, 1951
4. Freedom of Association and Protection of the Right to Organise Convention, 1948

(a) 1, 2, 3 and 4 (b) 2, 3 and 4
(c) Both 1 and 3 (d) 1, 2 and 3

53 Which of the following is true?

1. The Coal Mines PF Act, 1948 is a social security act.
2. Beedi Workers Welfare Fund Act, 1976 is an employee welfare act.
3. The Shops and Establishments Acts is a regulative act.

(a) 1, 2 and 3 (b) Both 2 and 3
(c) Both 1 and 2 (d) Both 1 and 3

54 Which of the following is true for labour legislation and Indian Constitution?

1. Articles 38, 39, 41, 42, 43B, 43C of Chapter-IV are related with labour legislation.
2. Articles 14, 16, 19,23 and 24 of Chapter III are related with labour legislation.
3. Regulation of labour and safety in mines and oil-fields are item number 55 on the concurrent list.
4. Article 43A of the Indian Constitution deals with participation of workers in management of industries.

(a) 1, 2, 3 and 4 (b) 2, 3 and 4
(c) Both 2 and 4 (d) 1, 2 and 3

55 Which of the following are true in context of ILO?

1. India is one of the founding members of ILO.
2. It has 190 member states.
3. In 1946, the ILO became a specialised agency of the United Nations.
4. It was created in 1919, as part of the Treaty of Versailles.

(a) 1, 3 and 4 (b) 1, 2 and 3
(c) 2, 3 and 4 (d) 1, 2 and 4

56 Which of the following are true in context of labour and Indian Constitution?

1. Labour is included under the concurrent list- List III in the seventh schedule of Constitution of India.
2. In the case of labour legislation, there is a clause which says that state cannot enact a law which is repugnant to the Center.
3. Security and social insurance; employment and unemployment. These are item number 23 on the list.

(a) Both 1 and 2 (b) 1, 2 and 3
(c) Both 2 and 3 (d) Both 1 and 3

57 .... of the Indian Constitution states that government should minimise the inequalities in income, and endeavor to eliminate inequalities in status, facilities and opportunities.

(a) Article 39 (b) Article 38 (c) Article 43 (d) Article 41

58 .... of the Indian Constitution vouches for equal pay for equal work for both men and women.

(a) Article 39 (b) Article 38 (c) Article 43 (d) Article 41

59 .... of the titular seats in ILO's governing body are permanently held by states of chief industrial importance.

(a) 10 (b) 19 (c) 12 (d) 11

60 .... are legally binding international treaties that may be ratified by member states.

(a) Governing recommendations
(b) Recommendations
(c) Fundamentals
(d) Conventions

61 .... of the Indian Constitution states that the government has all the rights to make laws that provide for reservation of appointments in favor of any backward class of citizens which it feel is not adequately represented in the services.

(a) Article 38 (b) Article 43
(c) Article 41 (d) Article 16

62 .... of the Indian Constitution states that government should also promote cottage industries on an individual or cooperative basis in rural areas.

(a) Article 38 (b) Article 43 (c) Article 41 (d) Article 16

63 Which of the following is true for ILO?

1. It has played an important role in standardisation of labour laws across the countries.
2. A country needs to ratify ILO's convention in order to it becoming a law in the country.
3. Its conventions regulate different aspects of labour laws and are passed at different conferences.

(a) Only 1 (b) Both 2 and 3
(c) Both 1 and 3 (d) 1, 2 and 3

64 Which of the following statements are true/false?

(i) The workers need to be provided safe and good working conditions at their workplace as a part of the principle of Social Justice.
(ii) The Workmen's Compensation Act, 1923 is a regulative legislation.
(iii) The Payment of Bonus Act is a protective legislation.
(iv) India is one of the founding members of ILO.

(a) (i), (iv) are true and (ii), (iii) are false
(b) (i), (iii) are true and (ii), (iv) are false
(c) (ii), (iv) are true and (i), (iii) are false
(d) (iii), (iv) are true and (ii), (i) are false

65 Which of the following statements are true/false?

(i) Welfare of labour is item number 21 on the concurrent list.
(ii) Labour is included in the concurrent list in the seventh schedule of the Indian constitution.
(iii) Social Security and insurance are item number 24 on the concurrent list.
(iv) Trade Union, industrial and labour disputes are item number 22 of the concurrent list.

(a) (i), (iv) are true and (ii), (iii) are false
(b) (i), (iii) are true and (ii), (iv) are false
(c) (ii), (iv) are true and (i), (iii) are false
(d) (iii), (iv) are true and (ii), (i) are false

66 Which of the following statements are true/false?

(i) Article 19 of the Indian Constitution provides or rights regarding freedom of speech and expression.
(ii) Article 14 of the Indian Constitution prohibits the employment of children below the age of fourteen years to be employed to work in any factory or mine or engaged in any other hazardous employment.
(iii) Chapter IV of the Indian Constitution deals with the directive principles of state policy.
(iv) Article 21 the Indian Constitution prohibits human trafficking and forced labour. It is a punishable offence.

(a) (i), (iv) are true and (ii), (iii) are false
(b) (i), (iii) are true and (ii), (iv) are false
(c) (ii), (iv) are true and (i), (iii) are false
(d) (iii), (iv) are true and (ii), (i) are false

67 Which of the following statements are true/false?

(i) Article 43A of the Indian constitution deals with participation of workers in management of industries.
(ii) Article 37 of the Indian constitution clearly states that men and women have equal right to an adequate means to livelihood.
(iii) Article 43 states that the government should work to provide all workers, agricultural, industrial or otherwise, work, a living wage, conditions of work ensuring a decent standard of life and full enjoyment of leisure and social and cultural opportunities.
(iv) Article 42 of the Indian constitution stands for just and humane conditions of work and maternity relief.

(a) (i), (iii), (iv) are true and (ii) is false
(b) (i), (iii) are true and (ii), (iv) are false
(c) (ii), (iv) are true and (i), (iii) are false
(d) (iii), (iv) are true and (ii), (i) are false

68 Which of the following statements are true/false?

(i) ILO was established on 19th April, 1919 by Versailles Peace Conference.
(ii) It is the only tripartite UN agency that brings together government, employers and workers to promote decent work for all.
(iii) ILO was established after World War II.
(iv) The objectives of ILO are enumerated in the Article 322 of the Peace Treaty of Versailles.

(a) (i), (iv) are true and (ii), (iii) are false
(b) (i), (ii) are true and (iii), (iv) are false
(c) (ii), (iv) are true and (i), (iii) are false
(d) (iii), (iv) are true and (ii), (i) are false

69 Which of the following statements are true/false?

(i) Governing body of ILO is the executive council of the ILO and meets three times a year in Geneva.
(ii) The governing body is composed of 56 titular members and 66 deputy members.
(iii) Ten of the titular government seats are permanently held by States of chief industrial importance.
(iv) The non-permanent government members are elected by the conference every three years.

(a) (i), (ii), (iii) and (iv) are true
(b) (i), (iii) are true and (ii), (iv) are false
(c) (ii), (iv) are true and (i), (iii) are false
(d) (iii), (iv) are true and (ii), (i) are false

70 Which of the following statements are true/false?

(i) There are eight fundamental conventions of ILO.
(ii) There are four governance conventions of ILO.
(iii) The Minimum Age Convention of ILO is No. 87 and was ratified by India in 2019.
(iv) There are seven conventions that are classified as priority instruments.

(a) (i), (ii) are true and (iii), (iv) are false
(b) (i), (iii) are true and (ii), (iv) are false
(c) (ii), (iv) are true and (i), (iii) are false
(d) (iii), (iv) are true and (ii), (i) are false

71 Which of the following statements are true/false?
(i) The International Labour Office is the permanent secretariat of the ILO.
(ii) Convention 182 regarding worst forms of Child Labour has been ratified by India.
(iii) International Labour Conference is also known as an international Parliament of labour.
(iv) International Labour Conference is a forum for discussion of key social and labour questions.
(v) Trade Unions are involved in collecting wage data including fringe and personal benefits.
(vi) Strikes, boycotts and gheraos are militant functions of trade union.
(vii) Ministrant functions of trade unions involve providing financial support to members during strikes and lockouts.
(a) (i), (iii) are true and (ii), (iv) are false
(b) (i), (ii), (iii) and (iv) are true
(c) (ii), (iv) are true and (i), (iii) are false
(d) (iii), (iv) are true and (ii), (i) are false

72 Which of the following statements are true/false?
(i) The ILO Declaration on Fundamental Principles and Rights at Work was passed in the year 1994.
(ii) The ILO Declaration on Social Justice for a Fair Globalisation was signed in 2008 by the representatives of governments, employers and workers from all ILO member States.
(iii) India has ratified 7 out of 8 core ILO conventions.
(iv) Social Justice is based on the fact that the workers can claim their share of wealth which they have helped to generate.
(a) (i), (ii) are true and (iii), (iv) are false
(b) (i), (iii) are true and (ii), (iv) are false
(c) (ii), (iv) are true and (i), (iii) are false
(d) (iii), (iv) are true and (ii), (i) are false

73 Which of the following statements are true/false?
(i) The Equal Remuneration Convention, 1951 is a fundamental convention of ILO.
(ii) Conventions are legally binding international treaties that may be ratified by member states.
(iii) Right to Organise and Collective Bargaining Convention, 1949 is a fundamental convention of ILO.
(iv) Labour Inspection Convention, 1947 is a governance convention of ILO.
(a) (i), (ii), (iii) and (iv) are true
(b) (i), (iii) are true and (ii), (iv) are false
(c) (ii), (iv) are true and (i), (iii) are false
(d) (iii), (iv) are true and (ii), (i) are false

74 Which of the following statements are true/false?
(i) The regulative legislations focus on the minimum wages that must be paid, methods and manner of their payment.
(ii) In 2017, India ratified the Conventions 138 regarding admission of age to employment.
(iii) The Mica Mines Welfare Fund Act, 1946 is a social security legislation.
(iv) The Trade Unions Act, 1926 is a protective legislation.
(a) (i), (ii), (iii) and (iv) are true
(b) (i), (iii) are true and (ii), (iv) are false
(c) (ii), (iv) are true and (i), (iii) are false
(d) (iii), (iv) are true and (ii), (i) are false

75 Which of the following statements are true/false?
(i) India ratified ILO's four fundamental conventions in 2017.
(ii) International Labour Conference meets twice a year in New York.
(iii) Recommendations of ILO are non-binding guidelines for the member countries.
(iv) The objectives of ILO are enumerated in the Declaration of Philadelphia.
(a) (i), (ii), (iii) and (iv) are true
(b) (i), (iii) are true and (ii), (iv) are false
(c) (ii), (iv) are true and (i), (iii) are false
(d) (iii), (iv) are true and (ii), (i) are false

76 Which of the following statements are true/false?
(i) The Labour legislations are based on five principles.
(ii) A country needs to ratify ILO's convention so that it becomes a law in the country.
(iii) Payment of Gratuity Act, 1972 is a an employee welfare legislation.
(iv) Regulative legislations lay down rights and duties of employer and employees, while focusing on relationship of workers with trade unions.
(a) (i), (ii), (iii) and (iv) are true
(b) (i), (iii) are true and (ii), (iv) are false
(c) (ii), (iv) are true and (i), (iii) are false
(d) (iii), (iv) are true and (ii), (i) are false

77 Which of the following statements are true/false?
(i) Regulation of labour and safety in mines and oil-fields are item number 55 of the union list.
(ii) Article 20 of the Indian Constitution allows people to practice any profession, or to carry on any occupation, trade or business.
(iii) Industrial disputes concerning Union employees are item number 61 of the union list.
(iv) Article 11 of the Indian constitution deals with equality before law and prohibits any discrimination on grounds of religion, race, caste, sex or place of birth.
(a) (i), (ii), (iii) and (iv) are true
(b) (i), (iii) are true and (ii), (iv) are false
(c) (ii), (iv) are true and (i), (iii) are false
(d) (iii), (iv) are true and (ii), (i) are false

78 Which of the following statements are true/false?
(i) Article 24 of the Indian constitution prohibits the employment of children below the age of eighteen years to be employed in any hazardous employment.
(ii) Articles 38, 39, 41, 42, 43, 43A are related with labour legislation.
(iii) Article 41 of the India Constitution prevents the exploitation of people and children at workplace by the employer.

(iv) Article 43 of the India Constitution promote cottage industries on an individual or cooperative basis in rural areas.

(a) (i), (ii), (iii) and (iv) are true
(b) (i), (iii) are true and (ii), (iv) are false
(c) (ii), (iv) are true and (i), (iii) are false
(d) (iii), (iv) are true and (ii), (i) are false

Directions (Q. Nos. 79-85) *In the following questions, the Assertion (A) and Reason (R) have been put forward. Read both the statements carefully and choose the correct alternative from the following.*

Codes

(a) (A) and (R) are true and (R) is the correct explanation of (A)
(b) (A) and (R) are true, but (R) is not the correct explanation of (A)
(c) (A) is false, but (R) is true
(d) (A) is true, but (R) is false

79 Assertion (A) Recommendations can be autonomous.

Reason (R) A related recommendation supplements the convention by providing more detailed guidelines on how it could be applied.

80 Assertion (A) The eight core conventions of ILO focus on the subjects that are considered as fundamental principles and rights at work.

Reason (R) In 2014, India ratified the two Core Conventions of ILO- Conventions 182 regarding admission of age to employment and Convention 138 regarding worst forms of Child Labour.

81 Assertion (A) Factories Act, 1883 aimed at making labour costlier in India.

Reason (R) Indian textile industry was offering tough competition to British textiles.

82 Assertion (A) The ILO declaration on Social Justice for a Fair Globalisation was signed in 2008 by the representatives of governments, employers and workers from all ILO member States.

Reason (R) ILO has played a significant role in promoting social justice among the workers.

83 Assertion (A) Based on the principle of social justice, workers can claim their share of wealth which they have helped to generate.

Reason (R) It is important to have pay parity among the workers.

84 Assertion (A) Globalisation has generated employment along with opportunities.

Reason (R) Globalisation has contributed only positively to the available employment opportunities for the workers.

85 Assertion (A) The organisations need to build their culture upon the basic principles of labour legislations.

Reason (R) Inequality not only leads to a decline in productivity but also breeds poverty, social instability and even conflict.

86 Match the following core conventions of ILO with their number.

List I	List II
A. Forced Labour Convention, 1930	1. 29
B. Abolition of Forced Labour Convention, 1957	2. 105
C. Minimum Age Convention, 1973	3. 138
D. Worst Forms of Child Labour Convention, 1999	4. 182

Codes

	A	B	C	D
(a)	1	2	3	4
(b)	2	3	1	4
(c)	3	1	4	2
(d)	1	3	2	4

87 Match the following governance conventions with their number.

List I	List II
A. Labour Inspection Convention, 1947	1. 81
B. Employment Policy Convention, 1964	2. 122
C. Labour Inspection (Agriculture) Convention, 1969	3. 144
D. Tripartite Consultation (International Labour Standards) Convention, 1976	4. 129

Codes

	A	B	C	D		A	B	C	D
(a)	1	3	4	2	(b)	2	1	4	3
(c)	3	1	4	2	(d)	1	3	2	4

88 Match the following articles and directive policies.

List I	List II
A. Equal right to an adequate means to livelihood	1. Article 42
B. Maternity relief	2. Article 39
C. Ensuring a decent standard of life and full enjoyment of leisure and social and cultural opportunities	3. Article 41
D. Right to work	4. Article 43

Codes

	A	B	C	D		A	B	C	D
(a)	1	3	4	2	(b)	2	1	4	3
(c)	3	1	4	2	(d)	1	3	2	4

89 Match the following acts with their years of enactment.

List I	List II
A. The Payment of Wages Act	1. 1948
B. The Minimum Wages Act	2. 1936
C. The Payment of Bonus Act	3. 1976
D. The Equal Remuneration Act	4. 1965

Codes

	A	B	C	D		A	B	C	D
(a)	1	3	4	2	(b)	2	1	4	3
(c)	3	1	4	2	(d)	1	3	2	4

90 Match the following acts with their years of enactment.

List I	List II
A. The Plantations Labour Act	1. 1951
B. The Factories Act	2. 1936
C. The Motor Transport Workers Act	3. 1966
D. The Beedi and Cigar Workers Act	4. 1961

Codes

	A	B	C	D		A	B	C	D
(a)	1	3	4	2	(b)	2	1	4	3
(c)	3	1	4	2	(d)	1	3	2	4

91 Match the following acts with their years of enactment.

List I	List II
A. The Sexual Harassment at the Workplace (prevention, Prohibition and Redressal) Act	1. 1976
B. The Bonded Labour System (Abolition), Act	2. 2013
C. The Fatal Accidents Act	3. 1948
D. The Employees' State Insurance Act	4. 1855

Codes

	A	B	C	D		A	B	C	D
(a)	1	3	4	2	(b)	2	1	4	3
(c)	3	1	4	2	(d)	1	3	2	4

Directions (Q. Nos. 92-96) *Read the passage and answer the questions that follow.*

International labour standards are primarily tools for governments which, in consultation with employers and workers, are seeking to draft and implement labour law and social policy in conformity with internationally accepted standards. For many states, this process begins with a decision to consider ratifying an ILO convention. Countries often go through a period of examining and, if necessary, revising their legislation and policies in order to achieve compliance with the instrument they wish to ratify. International labour standards thus serve as targets for harmonising national law and practice in a particular field; the actual ratification might come further along the path of implementing the standard. Some countries decide not to ratify a convention but bring their legislation into line with it anyway; such countries use ILO standards as models for drafting their law and policy. Still others ratify ILO conventions fairly quickly and then work to bring their national law and practice into line; the comments of the ILO's supervisory bodies and technical assistance can guide them in this process. For such countries, ratification is the first step on the path to implementing a standard.

In addition to shaping law, international labour standards can provide guidance for developing national and local policies, such as employment and work and family policies. They can also be used to improve various administrative structures such as labour administration, labour inspection, social security administration, employment services, and so on. Standards can also serve as a source of good industrial relations applied by labour dispute resolution bodies, and as models for collective agreements.

92 Which of the following is incorrect on the basis of the above passage?

(a) The first step in implementing an international labour standard is ratifying an ILO convention.
(b) International labour standards set different standards for different laws in the country.
(c) In order to implement a standard, a country needs to ratify it.
(d) Standards can also serve as a source of good industrial relations applied by labour dispute resolution bodies, and as models for collective agreements.

93 Which of the following is the first step in implementing an ILO standard?

(a) Standardisation (b) Ratification
(c) Normalisation (d) Finalisation

94 How can be international standards helpful for a country?

(a) They help to improve various administrative structures such as labour administration, labour inspection, social security administration.
(b) They provide guidance for developing national and local policies.
(c) They serve as a source of good industrial relations applied by labour dispute resolution bodies.
(d) All of the above

95 How do international standards serve as a source of good Industrial Relations?

(a) They law down the basic and universally accepted facts of Industrial Relations.
(b) They help to deregulate the working conditions.
(c) They ensure people are paid on the basis of their capabilities.
(d) It is the first step on the path to implement a standard.

96 Which of the following is correct on the basis of the above passage?

(a) The guidelines of ILO's supervisory bodies are a binding on member countries.
(b) Countries must ratify a convention to bring it into their legislation.
(c) A member country of ILO cannot do without ratifying a convention.
(d) International standards serve as models for collective agreements.

PREVIOUS YEARS' QUESTIONS

2018

1 The directive principles of state policy as contained in the Constitution of India provide for a number of articles.

Provision for just and human conditions of work and maternity relief is contained under which article of the constitution?

(a) Article 40 (b) Article 41
(c) Article 42 (d) Article 43

2 Which of the following core conventions of the International Labour Organisation has not been ratified by India?

(a) Minimum Age Convention No. 138
(b) Equal Remuneration Convention No. 100
(c) Abolition of Forced Labour Convention No. 105
(d) Freedom of Association and Right to Organise Convention No. 87

3 An order issued to public officials and public bodies to carry out their legal duties in known as

(a) Mandamus (b) Quo warranto
(c) Res judicata (d) Certiorari

4 Which one of the following authorities is a subordinate office under the ministry of labour in India?

(a) Directorate General of Mines Safety
(b) Labour Bureau
(c) Directorate General, Factory Advice Service and Labour Institutes
(d) Directorate General, Employment and Training

5 The Directive Principles of State Policy as contained in the Constitution of India provide for a number of articles.

"Securing and protecting effectively a social order in which justice shall inform all institutions of national life" is contained under which Article of the Constitution?

(a) Article 43 (A)
(b) Article 38
(c) Article 41
(d) Article 37

6 The committee of experts on welfare facilities for Industrial Workers constituted by ILO in 1963 had divided labour welfare services in two groups, intra-mural and extra-mural.

Which among the following is not an extra-mural welfare amenity?

(a) Occupational safety
(b) Social insurance measures including sports
(c) Maternity benefit
(d) Leave travel facilities

7 Which of the following conventions of the ILO was ratified by the Government of India in the year 2017?

(a) Freedom of association and right to organise (Convention No. 87)
(b) Forced labour covention (No. 29)
(c) Discrimination (Employment/Occupation) Convention (No. 111)
(d) The minimum age for admission to employment (Convention No. 138)

8 Which of the following schedules of the Constitution of India has provided the three lists namely Union list, State list and Concurrent list for making laws by the Parliament and by the legislatures of the states?

(a) Sixth Schedule
(b) Eighth Schedule
(c) Seventh Schedule
(d) Fourth Schedule

9 Match the provisions provided under the Directive Principles of State Policy given in List I with the respective Articles under which they are covered given in List II.

	List I		List II
A.	Equal pay for equal work for both men and women	1.	Article 39
B.	Participation of workers in management of industries	2.	Article 42
C.	Public assistance in cases of unemployment, old age, sickness and disablement	3.	Article 43 A
D.	Just and human conditions of work	4.	Article 41

Codes

	A	B	C	D
(a)	1	3	4	2
(b)	4	2	1	3
(c)	2	1	3	4
(d)	3	4	1	2

10 Assertion (A) Some of the earliest pieces of legislation in India appear to have been enacted to protect the interest of the employers.

Reason (R) The policy of the government was to protect the social system rather than to protect the workmen.

Codes

(a) (A) is correct, but (R) is wrong and (R) is the correct explanation of (A)
(b) (A) is correct, b[illegible] is wrong
(c) Both (A) and (R) ar[illegible] correct
(d) Both (A) and (R) are wrong

11 Which of the following countries does/do not figure in the list of Nations of Chief Industrial importance that hold permanent membership in the Governing Body of ILO ?

1. Sri Lanka 2. Russian Federation
3. Mexico 4. Brazil

Codes

(a) Only 1 (b) Only 2
(c) 1 and 2 (d) 3 and 4

12 Which one of the following is not a fundamental right under the provisions of the constitution of India ?

(a) Equality of opportunity in matters of public employment
(b) Prohibition of traffic in human beings and forced labour
(c) Prohibition of employment of children in factories etc
(d) Just and human condition of work and maternity relief

13 Which of the following statement(s) relating to the second National Commission on Labour is/are not true ?

1. The commission envisaged a system of Labour Courts, Lok Adalats and Labour Relations Commissions as the integrated adjudicatory system in labour matters.
2. The commission recommended that the Essential Services Maintenance Act should be withdrawn.
3. The commission was in favour of setting up wage boards for fixing wage rates for workers in any industry.

Codes

(a) Only 1 (b) 1 and 2
(c) Only 3 (d) All of these

14 The National Labour Relations Board (NLRB) having the responsibility to investigate Unfair Labour Practices and Complaints, was established under

(a) Industrial Disputes Act, 1947
(b) The Wagner Act, 1935
(c) Trade Unions Act, 1926
(d) The Norris-LaGuardia Act, 1932

15 Which of the following statement(s) relating to NM Lokhande is/are true ?

1. He was instrumental for the establishment of Bombay Mill Hands Association in 1896.
2. He was a philanthropic promoter of labour legislation and workers' welfare.
3. He is considered as the Father of Trade Union Movement in India.

Codes

(a) Only 1
(b) 1 and 2
(c) 2 and 3
(d) All of the above

16 **Assertion** (A) Some of the earliest piece of Labour Legislation in India appear to have been enacted to protect the interest of the employers.

Reason (R) The policy of the government was to protect the social system rather than to protect workers.

Codes

(a) (A) is correct and (R) is incorrect
(b) (A) is correct and (R) explains (A)
(c) (A) is incorrect, but (R) is correct
(d) (A) is correct, but (R) does not explain (A)

17 **Assertion** (A) It has been observed that the approach to Labour Legislations in India underwent a change after the country became independent.

Reason (R) The basic philosophy has undergone change being influenced by the concepts of social justice and welfare state.

Codes

(a) (A) is correct and (R) is incorrect
(b) (A) is correct and (R) fully explains (A)
(c) (A) is incorrect, but (R) is correct
(d) (A) is correct, but (R) does not explain (A)

18 The need for labour welfare was also emphasised by the Constitution of India. There are Articles in Indian Constitution which contain provisions for labour welfare. Which among the following Articles does not contain provision for Labour Welfare ?

(a) Article 38 (b) Article 39 (c) Article 40 (d) Article 41

19 Match the provisions given in List I with their respective Articles given in List II provided under the Constitution of India.

List I	List II
A. Right to work	1. Article 39
B. Equal pay for equal work for both men and women	2. Article 43
C. Human conditions of work	3. Article 42
D. Living wage and decent standard of life	4. Article 41

Codes

	A	B	C	D		A	B	C	D
(a)	4	1	3	2	(b)	1	2	4	3
(c)	3	4	2	1	(d)	2	3	1	4

20 "The state shall take steps, by suitable legislation or in any other way, to secure the participation of workers in the management of undertakings, establishments or other organisations engaged in any industry." The above statement was provided under

(a) Article 43(A) of Constitution (42 Amendment) Act, 1976
(b) Article 19(C) of the Indian Constitution
(c) Convention No. 11 of ILO
(d) Article 14 of the Indian Constitution

21 **Convention No. 138 of the ILO relates to**
(a) abolition of forced labour
(b) right to collective bargaining
(c) worst forms of child labour
(d) minimum age for admission to employment

2017

22 **In which year, India ratified the ILO Convention concerning the Right of Association for Agricultural Workers?**
(a) 1923 (b) 1924 (c) 1925 (d) 2017

23 **Which of the following statements relating to ILO Convention No. 182 is wrong?**
(a) The convention relates to Worst Forms of Child Labour
(b) It is one of the eight Fundamental Conventions of the ILO
(c) It was adopted in 1999 by the ILO
(d) This convention has not been ratified by India

24 **Which one of the following is not covered under Article 39 of the Indian Constitution?**
(a) Equal pay for equal work for both men and women
(b) Protection of childhood and youth against exploitation
(c) Citizens, men and women equally have the right to adequate means of livelihood
(d) Securing just and human conditions of work

25 **Which of the following labour legislations are covered under the category of Protective Labour Legislation?**
1. Minimum Wages Act, 1948
2. Motor Transport Workers Act, 1961
3. Factories Act, 1948
4. Trade Unions Act, 1926
5. Employee's Compensation Act, 1923

Codes
(a) 1 and 5 (b) 1, 3 and 5
(c) 1, 2 and 3 (d) 2, 3 and 4

26 **Which one of the following statement is true relating to the composition of the International Labour Conference?**
(a) It consists of four delegates nominated by each member state
(b) It consists of eight delegates nominated by each state
(c) It consists of six delegates nominated by each state
(d) It consists of three delegates nominated by each member state

27 **Which of the following acts in a sequence according to their years of their enactment in USA starting from the earliest to the latest?**
1. Wagner Act
2. Landrum-Griffin Act
3. Narris-LaGuaradia Act
4. Taft-Hartley Act

Codes
(a) 1, 2, 3, 4 (b) 3, 1, 4, 2
(c) 1, 3, 2, 4 (d) 2, 3, 1, 4

28 **Which of the following Articles of the Indian Constitution deals with "Securing just and humane conditions of work and maternity relief"?**
(a) Article 42 (b) Article 41 (c) Article 46 (d) Article 38

29 **Which of the following statements relating to ILO Declaration on Fundamental Principles is not correct ?**
(a) The declaration was adopted at the 86th Session of the International Labour Conference
(b) The declaration reiterates the binding nature of the ILO's Philadelphia Declaration
(c) The declaration requires compliance of Convention Nos. 88 and 89 even by those countries that have not ratified the same
(d) The declaration requires compliance of convention No. 138 even by those countries that have not ratified the same

30 **Which of the following statements characterise the objectives of labour legislation ?**
1. Improve the conditions of labour
2. To protect the rights of labour unions
3. To protect employers
4. To protect the public from possible excess on the part of organised labour

Codes
(a) 1 and 2 (b) 1, 2 and 3
(c) 1 and 3 (d) All of these

31 **Which of the following Conventions of ILO relates to the 'Right of Association' ?**
(a) Convention No. 87 (b) Convention No. 90
(c) Convention No. 121 (d) Convention No. 147

32 **In which year India became a member of the ILO?**
(a) 1919 (b) 1921 (c) 1926 (d) 1934

33 **The Constitution of India gives its citizens certain fundamental rights. Some of these fundamental rights concerns working class directly. Match the subject matter included in List I with the Articles of the Constitution of India mentioned in List II.**

	List I		List II
A.	The state shall not discriminate against any citizen on grounds only of religion, race, caste, sex, place of birth or any of them	1.	Article 19(1)
B.	There shall be equality of opportunity for all citizens in matters relating to employment or appointment to any office under the state	2.	Article 16(1)
C.	All citizens shall have the right to freedom of speech and expression and to form associations or unions and to practice any profession or to carry on any occupation, trade or business	3.	Article 15
D.	Traffic in human beings and beggar and other forms of forced labour are prohibited	4.	Article 23(1)

Codes

	A	B	C	D		A	B	C	D
(a)	3	1	4	2	(b)	3	2	1	4
(c)	4	3	2	1	(d)	4	2	3	1

2016

34 Which of the following statements are true relating to payment of equal pay for equal work both for men and women ?

1. ILO adopted equal remuneration Convention No. 100 in 1951.
2. India ratified ILO's Equal Remuneration Convention No. 100 in the year 1956.
3. Provisions relating to equal pay for equal work for both men and women are provided under Article 42 of the Indian Constitution.
4. The Equal Remuneration Ordinance was promulgated on 26th September, 1975.

Codes
(a) Both 1 and 4 are correct
(b) Both 2 and 3 are correct
(c) 1,3 and 4 are correct
(d) 1, 2 and 4 are correct

35 **Assertion** (A) All labour legislations are social in character.
Reason (R) Social legislation embraces action by government authority to eliminate objectionable elements of the socio-economic system and provide elements for which the system does not make provision.

Codes
(a) (A) is incorrect and (R) is correct
(b) Both (A) and (R) are correct and (R) explains (A)
(c) Both (A) and (R) are incorrect
(d) (A) is correct, but (R) is incorrect

36 The ILO set forth few fundamental principles at the time of its inception. These principles are embodied in the form of Charter of Freedom of Labour. These principles were again reaffirmed at its General Conference alongwith other Charter and are popularly known as Philadelphia Charter. This was done in the year

(a) 1926 (b) 1942
(c) 1944 (d) 1946

2015

37 Social dialogue include 'all types of negotiations and consultations or simple exchanges of information between/among representatives of the government, employers and workers on issues of common interest relating to economic and social policies'. This meaning was advanced by

(a) the Indian Labour Conference
(b) the Standing Labour Committee
(c) the United Nations Organisation
(d) the International Labour Organisation

38 Which of the following are the worst forms of child labour, according to the ILO?

1. All forms of slavery or pratices similar to slavery.
2. Procuring or offering a child for prostitution or pornography.
3. Using, procuring or offering of a child for illicit activities such as trafficking.
4. Work likely to harm the health, safety or morals of children.

Select the correct answer by using the codes given below
(a) 1 and 2 (b) 1 and 3
(c) 2, 3 and 4 (d) All of these

39 The General Conference of ILO, at its 26th Session held in 1944, reaffirmed the principles and adapted a declaration which is popularly known as

(a) Geneva Charter (b) Washington Charter
(c) Philadelphia Charter (d) Berne Charter

40 Which of the following comes under the 'State List' as provided under the Seventh Schedule of the Constitution of India?

(a) Relief of the disabled and unemployable
(b) Vocational and technical training of labour
(c) Social security and social insurance
(d) Welfare of labour including conditions of work

41 Which of the following is not part of the recommendations of Indian Labour Conference on 'rationalisation'?

(a) There should be a cap on recruitment
(b) There should be no retrenchment or loss of earnings of the existing employee
(c) Workers could be provided with suitable alternative jobs in the same employment or under the same employer subject to agreement between employer and the workers
(d) There should be a proper workload assessment by an export

42 What is common to Robert Owen, Titus Salt, Bournville and Port Sunlight?

(a) They were British law makers who advocated for labour welfare legislations
(b) They were British trade union leaders who demanded for improved working conditions for industrial labour
(c) They were British employers who pioneered labour welfare
(d) They were British political thinkers who conceived labour welfare as an instrument of ameliorating the evil effects of industrialisation

43 In which country the Labour Court is bifurcated into a bureau of judgement and a bureau of conciliation?

(a) Germany
(b) France
(c) Great Britan
(d) United State of America

44 Directive principles of state policy, as contained in Indian Constitution, contain various Articles, which have influenced the enactment of social and labour legislations. Match the subject matters of Directive Principles with Article Number as given in List I and List II respectively.

	List I		List II
A.	Equal pay for equal work for both men and women	1.	Article 41
B.	Right to work, to education and to public assistance in certain case	2.	A 39 (d)
C.	Provision for just and humane conditions of work and maternity relief	3.	Articlerticle 43 (A)
D.	Participation of workers in management of industries	4.	Article 42

Codes

	A	B	C	D		A	B	C	D
(a)	2	1	3	4	(b)	2	1	4	3
(c)	1	2	3	4	(d)	4	3	2	1

45 **Assertion** (A) Prior to the formation of International Labour Organisation, most of the legislations governing the working class in India were regressive in nature and aimed at serving the interest of Britishers.

Reason (R) India was a British colony.

Codes

(a) (A) is right, but (R) fails to fully justify (A)
(b) (A) is wrong and (R) is right
(c) (A) is right and (R) is wrong
(d) Both (A) and (R) are wrong

46 Under which part of the Indian Constitution, the basic foundation of labour legislations is found?

1. The Preamble
2. The Fundamental Rights
3. The Directive Principles of state policy

Select the correct answer by using the codes given below

Codes

(a) Only 3 (b) Only 1
(c) 1 and 3 (d) All of these

2014

47 Which out of the following is/are reason(s) for the low efficacy of ILO?

1. The recommendations made by ILO just advisory notes.
2. The conventions are not binding unless the member countries ratify them.
3. There is no power with ILO to instruct the member countries to adopt its recommendations and conventions.
4. The local conditions of the member countries are a constraint.

Codes

(a) 1 and 2 (b) Only 2
(c) 1, 2 and 3 (d) All of these

48 Which of the following statements about Labour Legislation in India is true ?

(a) Labour Legislation is not a part of Social Legislation
(b) Labour Legislation is influenced by the Philosophy of Laissez-faire
(c) Majority of Legislations are influenced by ILO conventions and recommendations
(d) Labour Legislation in India are largely result of trade union initiatives

49 Which of the following is the Executive Council of ILO?

(a) International Labour Conference
(b) International Labour Office
(c) International Labour Institute
(d) The Governing Body

50 Which of the following historical reasons were responsible for the enactment of the Trade Unions Act?

1. Formation of ILO
2. Emergence of Provincial Governments
3. The strike spearheaded by the Madras Labour Union in Buckingham and Carnatic Mills
4. The ascendance of labour party to the British Government as the ruling party

Codes

(a) 1 and 3 (b) 2 and 3
(c) 1, 3 and 4 (d) 2, 3 and 4

51 Which of the following conventions of the ILO has not been ratified by India ?

(a) Convention relating to forced labour
(b) Convention relating to freedom of association and right to organise
(c) Convention relating to equal remuneration
(d) Convention relating to discrimination (Employment/Occupation)

52 Which of the following factors is not responsible for growth of Social and Labour Legislation ?

(a) Early industrialisation (b) Rise of unionism
(c) Establishment of ILO (d) Ethnic association

53 Which of the following designations was suggested by the Royal Commission on Labour in its report?

(a) Welfare Officer (b) Labour Officer
(c) Personnel Officer (d) All of these

54 Which of the following is not a principle of Labour Legislation?

(a) Social Justice (b) Social Welfare
(c) National Economy (d) Control of Environment

55 Which organisation has made a declaration on Fundamental Principles and Human Rights at the workplace as one of the components of 'Decent Work' ?

(a) First National Commission on Labour
(b) Indian Labour Conference
(c) International Labour Organisation
(d) Sachar Committee on Worker's participation

56 **Match the following.**

List I (Name of the Legislation)	List II (Country in which enacted)
A. Labour Management Relations Act	1. Great Britain
B. Trade Unions and Labour Relations Act	2. USA
C. Unorganised Sertor Social Security Act	3. India

Codes

	A	B	C		A	B	C
(a)	1	3	2	(b)	1	2	3
(c)	2	1	3	(d)	2	3	1

57 **Match the following.**

List I (Committee/Commissions)	List II (Chairpersons)
A. Royal Commission on Labour	1. PB Gajendra Gadkar
B. Labour Investigation Committee	2. JH Whitley
C. First National Commission on Labour	3. Ravindra Verma
D. Second National Commission on Labour	4. WA Rege

Codes

	A	B	C	D
(a)	2	1	4	3
(b)	4	2	3	1
(c)	2	4	1	3
(d)	3	1	4	2

58 **Which one of the following is not an object of the Indian Labour Conference?**

(a) To promote uniformity in labour legislation
(b) To lay down procedure for settlement of industrial disputes
(c) To mediate between labour and management to resolve conflict
(d) To discuss all matters of all India importance between employers and employees

ANSWERS

Exam Based Questions

1 (d)	2 (d)	3 (d)	4 (d)	5 (a)	6 (b)	7 (a)	8 (b)	9 (c)	10 (d)
11 (d)	12 (c)	13 (c)	14 (c)	15 (c)	16 (d)	17 (d)	18 (b)	19 (c)	20 (a)
21 (d)	22 (a)	23 (c)	24 (a)	25 (d)	26 (d)	27 (b)	28 (d)	29 (d)	30 (a)
31 (a)	32 (a)	33 (d)	34 (d)	35 (c)	36 (a)	37 (a)	38 (c)	39 (b)	40 (a)
41 (d)	42 (a)	43 (c)	44 (a)	45 (b)	46 (a)	47 (b)	48 (d)	49 (a)	50 (a)
51 (b)	52 (d)	53 (c)	54 (c)	55 (a)	56 (b)	57 (b)	58 (a)	59 (a)	60 (d)
61 (d)	62 (b)	63 (d)	64 (a)	65 (c)	66 (b)	67 (a)	68 (b)	69 (a)	70 (a)
71 (b)	72 (c)	73 (a)	74 (c)	75 (d)	76 (c)	77 (b)	78 (c)	79 (d)	80 (d)
81 (a)	82 (a)	83 (b)	84 (d)	85 (a)	86 (a)	87 (b)	88 (b)	89 (b)	90 (b)
91 (b)	92 (b)	93 (b)	94 (d)	95 (a)	96 (d)				

Previous Years' Questions

1 (c)	2 (d)	3 (a)	4 (a)	5 (b)	6 (a)	7 (d)	8 (c)	9 (a)	10 (c)
11 (c)	12 (d)	13 (c)	14 (b)	15 (c)	16 (b)	17 (b)	18 (c)	19 (a)	20 (a)
21 (d)	22 (a)	23 (d)	24 (d)	25 (c)	26 (a)	27 (b)	28 (a)	29 (c)	30 (d)
31 (a)	32 (a)	33 (b)	34 (a)	35 (b)	36 (c)	37 (d)	38 (d)	39 (c)	40 (a)
41 (a)	42 (c)	43 (b)	44 (b)	45 (a)	46 (d)	47 (d)	48 (c)	49 (d)	50 (c)
51 (c)	52 (c)	53 (b)	54 (d)	55 (c)	56 (c)	57 (c)	58 (c)		

Labour Laws in India

This chapter deals with the important labours laws in India. The Factories and Mines Act deals with important intricacies for the employees working in factories and mines. Interstate Migrant Act lays down the legal framework for workers who migrate from one state to another. Child Labour Act is the legal mechanism to abolish child labour in India.

In this Chapter

- *The Factories Act, 1948*
- *The Mines Act, 1952*
- *The Inter-state Migrant Workmen Act, 1979*
- *The Contract Labour Act, 1970*
- *The Building and Other Construction Workers Act, 1996*
- *The Child Labour Act, 1986*

The Factories Act, 1948

The Factories Act, 1948 came into force on 1st April, 1949. It is a social legislation dealing with occupational safety, health and welfare of the workers at work place.

Applicability of the Act

- All the places where ten or more workers are working, or were working on any day of the preceding twelve months, and in any part of the place where a manufacturing process is being carried on with the aid of power, or is ordinarily so carried on.
- Places where twenty or more workers are working, or were working on any day of the preceding twelve months, and in any part of which a manufacturing process is being carried on without the aid of power, or is ordinarily so carried on.
- It does not include a mine, or a mobile unit belonging to the Armed Forces of the union, a railway running shed or a hotel, restaurant or an eating place.

Important Definitions Under the Act

- **Adult** means a person who completed 18 years of age. [Section 2(a)]
- **Adolescent** means a person between the age group of 15-18 years. The person should be more than 15 and less than 18 years of age. [Section 2(b)]
- **Calendar Year** means the period of twelve months starting from January 1 of the given year. [Section 2(bb)]
- **Child** means a person who has not completed 15 years of age. [Section 2(c)]

- **Hazardous Process** means any process or activity in relation to an industry specified in the First Schedule where, unless special care is taken, raw materials used therein or the intermediate or finished products, bye-products, wastes or effluents thereof would
  (a) cause material impairment to the health of the persons engaged in or connected therewith, or
  (b) result in the pollution of the general environment.
- **Young Person** is either a child or adolescent. [Section 2(d)]
- **Day** is a period of twenty-four hours beginning from midnight. [Section 2(e)]
- **Week** is a period of seven days beginning from the midnight of Saturday. [Section 2(t)]
- **Worker** means a person employed directly or by or through any agency (including a contractor) with or without the knowledge of the principal employer whether for remuneration or not in any manufacturing process, or in cleaning any part of the machinery or premises used for a manufacturing process, or in any other kind of work incidental to, or connected with the manufacturing process, or the subject of the manufacturing process but does not include any member of the Armed Forces of the Union. [Section 2(1)]
- **Manufacturing Process** is defined under Section 2(k) and means any process for
  (a) Making, altering, repairing, ornamenting, finishing, packing, oiling, washing, cleaning, breaking up, demolishing, or otherwise treating or adapting any article or substance with a view to its use, sale, transport, delivery or disposal.
  (b) Pumping oil, water, sewage or any other substance, or
  (c) Generating, transforming or transmitting power, or
  (d) Composing types for printing, printing by letter press, lithography, photogravure or other similar process or book binding, or
  (e) Constructing, reconstructing, repairing, refitting, finishing or breaking up ships or vessels, or
  (f) Preserving or storing any article in cold storage.
- **Factory** is defined under Section 2(m) and means any premises including the precincts thereof
  (a) Whereon ten or more workers are working, or were working on any day of the preceding twelve months, and in any part of which a manufacturing process is being carried on with the aid of power, or is ordinarily so carried on, or
  (b) Whereon twenty or more workers are working, or were working on any day of the preceding twelve months, and in any part of which a manufacturing process is being carried on without the aid of power, or is ordinarily so carried on.
- **Occupier of a Factory** means the person, who has ultimate control over the affairs of the factory. [Section 2(n)]

Inspecting Staff (Section 8 and 9)

- The State Government has the power to appoint inspecting Staff-Inspectors and Chief Inspector. It has the power to appoint as many Additional Chief Inspectors, Joint Chief Inspectors and Deputy Chief Inspectors and as many other officers as it thinks fit to assist the Chief Inspector.
- Every District Magistrate shall be an Inspector for his district.
- *The inspectors enjoy the following powers*
  (a) Enter and examine the premises, plant, machinery, factory, article or substance.
  (b) Conduct an inquiry for any accident or dangerous occurrence, resulting in bodily injury, disability.
  (c) Seize, or take copies of any register, record or other document or any portion thereof as he may consider necessary in respect of any offence under this Act, which he has reason to believe, has been committed.
  (d) Direct the occupier that any premises or any part thereof, or anything lying therein, shall be left undisturbed.
  (e) Take measurements and photographs and make such recordings as considered necessary for the purpose of any examination.

Certifying Surgeons (Section 10)

- The State Government has the power to appoint qualified medical practitioners to be certifying surgeons. *They enjoy the following powers*
  (a) Examination and certification of young persons under this Act.
  (b) Examination of persons engaged in factories in dangerous occupations or processes.
  (c) Exercise medical supervision as may be prescribed for any factory or class or description of factories.

Health of Employee

The factory needs to take the following into consideration

- **Cleanliness** Every factory needs to be kept clean and free from effluvia arising from any drain, privy or other nuisance. Dust needs to be cleaned by sweeping from floors, washrooms, staircases and passages on a daily basis. Floor of every workman needs to be cleaned at least once in every week by washing, using disinfectant. There needs to be effective drainage so that water does not accumulate.

  All doors and window frames and other wooden or metallic framework and shutters shall be kept painted or varnished and the painting or varnishing shall be carried out at least once in every period of five years. (Section 11)
- **Disposal of Wastes and Effluents** There needs to be effective arrangement for disposal and treatment of wastes and effluents due to the manufacturing process. (Section 12)
- **Ventilation and Temperature** There needs to be adequate ventilation that allows circulation of fresh air. An optimum temperature needs to be maintained inside the premises to provide good working conditions to the workers. (Section 13)
- **Dust and Fume** The factory needs to take effective measures to prevent the inhalation of dust and fumes that are injurious and offensive to health. No stationary internal combustion engine should be operated in the factory. (Section 14)
- **Artificial Humidification** The government needs to prescribe the standards of artificial humidification. (Section 15)
- **Overcrowding** There shall be no room in the factory that is overcrowded to an extent that it is injurious to the health of the workers. (Section 16)
- **Lighting** The factory needs to have adequate natural and artificial source of lighting to provide good working conditions. (Section 17)
- **Drinking Water**
  (a) The factory must have an adequate supply of wholesome drinking water and all those points must be clearly marked with 'drinking water'.
  (b) The factories that have more than 250 workers should have provisions for cooling drinking water during hot weather conditions. (Section 18)
- **Latrines and Urinals** There needs to be proper arrangement for latrine and urinals. There needs to be separate accommodations for men and women that should have adequate lighting and ventilation. (Section 19)
- **Spittoons** Each factory must have spitto[illegible] maintained in a clean and hygienic condition. Any person who shall not spit in the spittoons shall be punishable with fine not exceeding five rupees. (Section 20)

Safety of Employee

- **Fencing of Machinery** All parts of the machinery and the machinery itself needs to be kept into a well constructed closet space. All the parts must be adequately lubricated and greased so that machine works in a proper manner. (Section 21)
- **Work On or Near Machinery in Motion** It is necessary to examine the machinery and its parts. The machinery must be examined by a specially trained adult male worker wearing tight fitting clothing (which shall be supplied by the occupier), whose name has been recorded in the register prescribed in this behalf and who has been furnished with a certificate of his appointment. (Section 22)
- **Employment of Young Persons on Dangerous Machines** The factory should employ young person on a machinery after giving him adequate training under an expert supervision. (Section 23)
- **Striking Gear and Devices for Cutting-off Power** The workers need to be provided suitable striking gear or other efficient mechanical appliance to move driving belts to and from fast and loose pulleys which form part of the transmission machinery. Such gear or appliances shall be so constructed, placed and maintained as to prevent the belt from creeping back on to the fast pulley. (Section 24)
- **Self-acting Machines** No traversing part of a self-acting machine in any factory and no material carried thereon shall be allowed to run on its outward or inward traverse within a distance of 45 cms from any fixed structure which is not part of the machine. (Section 25)
- **Casing of New Machinery** Every set screw, bolt or key on any revolving shaft, spindle, wheel or pinion should be guarded in a case to prevent the machinery and keep it safe. (Section 26)
- **Prohibition of Employment of Women and Children Near Cotton-Openers** No woman or child shall be employed in any part of a factory for pressing cotton in which a cotton-opener is at work. (Section 27)
- **Hoists and Lifts** Hoists and lift should be of good mechanical construction, sound material and adequate strength. They should be properly maintained, and must be thoroughly examined by a competent person at least once in every period of six months. (Section 28)

- **Lifting Machines, Chains, Ropes and Lifting Tackles** The working gear, whether fixed or movable, of every lifting machine and every chain should be of good mechanical construction, sound material and adequate strength. They must be properly maintained. (Section 29)
- **Revolving Machinery** It is the machine in which grinding process is carried out. It should be permanently fixed at one place and effective measures must be taken in every factory to ensure that the safe working peripheral speed of every revolving vessel, cage, basket, flywheel, pulley, disc or similar appliance driven by power is not exceeded. (Section 30)
- **Pressure Plant** If in any factory, any plant or machinery or any part thereof is operated at a pressure above atmospheric pressure, effective measures shall be taken to ensure that the safe working pressure of such plant or machinery or part is not exceeded. (Section 31)
- **Floors, Stairs and Means of Access** All floors, steps, stairs, passages and gangways should be of sound construction and properly maintained and must be kept free from obstructions and substances likely to cause persons to slip, and where it is necessary to ensure safety, steps, stairs, passages and gangways shall be provided with substantial handrails. (Section 32)
- **Pits, Sumps, Opening in Floors** In every factory, every fixed vessel, sump, tank, pit or opening in the ground or in a floor which, by reason of its depth, situation, construction or contents, is or may be a source of danger, should be either securely covered or fenced. (Section 33)
- **Excessive Weights** No person shall be employed in any factory to lift, carry or move any load so heavy as to be likely to cause him injury. (Section 34)
- **Protection of Eyes** The factory needs to provide effective screens or suitable goggles for the protection of persons employed on, or in the immediate vicinity of, the manufacturing processes that can be harm. . to eyes. (Section 35)
- **Precautions against Dangerous Fumes, Gases** There needs to be effective enclosure of plant and machinery used in the process. There must be proper removal or prevention of the accumulation of such dust, gas, fume or vapour. (Section 36)
- **Precautions Regarding the use of Portable Electric Light** No portable electric light or any other electric appliance of voltage exceeding twenty-four volts shall be permitted for use inside any chamber, tank, vat, pit, pipe, flue or other confined space. (Section 36A)
- **Explosive or Inflammable Dust, Gas etc** There needs to be effective enclosure of plant and machinery used in the process. There must be proper removal or prevention of the accumulation of such dust, gas, fume or vapour. (Section 37)
- **Precautions in Case of Fire** All practicable measures need to be taken to prevent outbreak of fire and its spread, both internally and externally. There needs to be provision and maintenance safe means of escape for all persons in the event of a fire, and the necessary equipment and facilities for extinguishing fire. (Section 38)
- **Power to Require Specifications of Defective Parts or Tests of Stability** If it appears to the Inspector that any building or part of a building or any part of the ways, machinery or plant in a factory is in such a condition that it may be dangerous to human life or safety, he may serve the factory an order in writing requiring them to furnish such drawings, specifications and other particulars as may be necessary to determine whether such building, ways, machinery or plant can be used with safety.

  He can order Inspector to carry out such tests in such manner as may be specified in the order, and to inform him the results thereof. (Section 39)
- **Safety of Building and Machinery** If it appears to the Inspector that any building or part of a building or any part of the ways, machinery or plant in a factory is in such a condition that it is dangerous to human life or safety, he may serve the factory an order in writing specifying the measures which in his opinion should be adopted, and requiring them to be carried out before a specified date. (Section 40)
- **Maintenance of Buildings** If it appears to the Inspector that any building or part of a building in a factory is in such a state of disrepair as is likely to lead to conditions detrimental to the health and welfare of the workers, he may serve on the occupier or manager or both of the factory an order in writing specifying the measures which in his opinion should be taken and requiring the same to be carried out before such date as is specified in the order. (Section 40A)
- **Safety Officers** In every factory, wherein one thousand or more workers are ordinarily employed, or wherein, any manufacturing process or operation is carried on, which process or operation involves any risk of bodily injury, poisoning or disease, or any other hazard to health, to the persons employed in the factory, the occupier shall, if so required by the State Government by notification in the Official Gazette, employ such number of Safety Officers as may be specified in that notification. (Section 40B)

- **Power to Make Rules** The State Government may make rules requiring the provision in any factory or in any class or description of factories of such further devices and measures for securing safety of persons employed therein as it may deem necessary. (Section 41)

Provisions Relating to Hazardous Processes

1. Constitution of Site Appraisal Committees (Section 41-A)

- The State Government for grant of permission for the initial location of a factory involving a hazardous process or for the expansion of any such factory has the power to appoint a Site Appraisal Committee consisting of the Chief Inspector of the State who shall be its Chairman.
- The Site Appraisal Committee shall examine an application for the establishment of a factory involving hazardous process and make its recommendation to the State Government within a period of ninety days of the receipt of such applications in the prescribed form.

2. Compulsory Disclosure of Information by the Occupier (Section 41-B)

- The occupier of every factory involving a hazardous process shall disclose, in the manner prescribed, all information regarding dangers including health hazards and the measures to overcome such hazards arising from the exposure to or handling of the materials or substances in the manufacture, transportation, storage and other processes, to the workers employed in the factory, to the Chief Inspector, of the local authority within whose jurisdiction the factory is situate and the general public is in the vicinity.
- Every occupier shall, with the approval of the Chief Inspector, draw up an on-site emergency plan and detailed disaster control measures for his factory and make known to the workers employed therein and to the general public living in the vicinity of the factory, the safety measures required to be taken in the event of an accident taking place.
- The occupier of a factory involving a hazardous process shall, with the previous approval of the Chief Inspector, lay down measures for the handling, usage, transportation and storage of hazardous substances inside the factory premises and publicise them in the manner prescribed among the workers and the general public living in the vicinity.

3. Specific Responsibility of the Occupier in Relation to Hazardous Processes (Section 41-C)

Every occupier of a factory involving any hazardous process shall

- Maintain accurate and up-to-date health records or medical records of the workers in the factory who are exposed to any chemical, toxic or any other harmful substances which are manufactured, stored, handled or transported and such records shall be accessible to the workers subject to such conditions as may be prescribed.
- Appoint persons who possess qualifications and experience in handling hazardous substances and are competent to supervise such handling within the factory and to provide at the working place all the necessary facilities for protecting the workers in the manner prescribed.
- Provided that where any question arises as to the qualifications and experience of a person so appointed, the decision of the Chief Inspector shall be final.
- Provide for medical examination of every worker before such worker is assigned to a job involving the handling of, or working with, a hazardous substance.

4. Power of Central Government to Appoint Inquiry Committee (Section 41-D)

- The Central Government may, in the event of the occurrence of an extraordinary situation involving a factory engaged in a hazardous process, appoint an Inquiry Committee to inquire into the standards of health and safety observed in the factory with a view to finding out the causes of any failure or neglect in the adoption of any measures or standards prescribed for the health and safety of the workers employed in the factory or the general public affected or likely to be affected, due to such failure or neglect and for the prevention and recurrence of such extraordinary situations in future in such factory or elsewhere.
- The Committee shall consist of a Chairman and two other members and the terms of reference of the Committee and the recommendations will be only advisory in nature.

5. Emergency Standards (Section 41-E)

The Central Government has the power to direct the Director-General of Factory Advice Service and Labour Institutes or any institution specialised in matters relating to standards of safety in hazardous processes, to lay down emergency standards for enforcement of suitable standards in respect of hazardous processes.

6. Permissible Limits of Exposure of Chemical and Toxic Substances (Section 41-F)

The maximum permissible threshold limits of exposure of chemical and toxic substances in manufacturing processes whether hazardous or otherwise in any factory shall be of the value indicated in the Second Schedule.

7. Workers' Participation in Safety Management (Section 41-G)

- Every factory where a hazardous process takes place shall set-up a Safety Committee consisting of equal number of representatives of workers and management to promote cooperation between the workers and the management.
- These are required in maintaining proper safety and health at work and to review periodically the measures taken in that behalf.

8. Right of Workers to Warn About Imminent Danger (Section 41-H)

- If the workers believe there is imminent danger to their lives, they can bring same to the notice of the occupier, agent, manager or any other person who is incharge of the factory or the process concerned directly or through their representatives in the Safety Committee and simultaneously bring the same to the notice of the Inspector.
- The person in charge must take immediate action on such danger and if the people are not satisfied with the result, they can approach the nearest Inspector whose decision on the question of the existence of such imminent danger shall be final.

Welfare of Employee

Washing Facilities

- The State Government must prescribe standards of adequate and suitable facilities for washing.
- There must be separate washing areas for male and female workers. These need to clean and accessible. (Section 42)

Facilities for Storing and Drying Clothing The State Government may make rules requiring the provision therein of suitable places for keeping clothing not worn during working hours and for the drying of wet clothing. (Section 43)

Facilities for Sitting There needs to be suitable arrangements for sitting for all workers obliged to work in a standing position. (Section 44)

First-Aid Appliances

- Each factory must provide and maintain first-aid boxes or cupboards to be readily accessible during all working hours. The number of such boxes or cupboards to be provided and maintained shall not be less than one for every 150 workers ordinarily employed at anyone time in the factory.
- In every factory, wherein more than 500 workers are ordinarily employed, there shall be provided and maintained an ambulance room the prescribed size, containing the prescribed equipment and in the charge of such medical and nursing staff as may be prescribed. (Section 45)

Canteens The factory needs to maintain a canteen wherein more than two hundred and fifty workers are ordinarily employed. (Section 46)

Shelters, Rest Rooms and Lunch Rooms The factory needs to maintain adequate and suitable shelters or rest rooms and a suitable lunch room, with provision for drinking water where more than 150 workers are ordinarily employed. (Section 47)

Creches The factory needs to set-up creches where more than 30 women are employed. These rooms will be maintained for the use of children under the age of six years. (Section 48)

Welfare Officers The factory wherein 500 or more workers are ordinarily employed, the occupier shall employ in the factory such number of welfare officers as may be prescribed. (Section 49)

Working Hours of Adults

- **Weekly Hours** No adult worker should be required or allowed to work in a factory for more than 48 hours in any week. (Section 51)
- **Weekly Holidays** No adult worker shall be required or allowed to work in a factory on the first day of the week. (Section 52)
- **Compensatory Holidays** If a worker is deprived of any of the weekly holidays for which provision is made in Section 52, he shall be allowed within the month in which the holidays were due to him or within the two months immediately following that month, compensatory holidays of equal number to the holidays so lost. (Section 53)
- **Daily Hours** No adult worker shall be required or allowed to work in a factory for more than nine hours in any day. (Section 54)
- **Intervals for Rest** The periods of work of adult workers in a factory each day shall be so fixed that no period shall exceed five hours and that no worker shall work for more than five hours before he has had an interval for rest of at least half an hour. (Section 55)

- **Spread Over** The periods of work of an adult worker in a factory shall be so arranged that inclusive of his intervals for rest, they shall not spread over more than ten and a half hours in any day. (Section 56)
- **Night Shifts** Where a worker in a factory works on a shift which extends beyond midnight, a holiday for a whole day shall mean in his case a period of twenty-four consecutive hours beginning when his shift ends. (Section 57)
- **Prohibition of Overlapping Shifts** Work shall not be carried on in any factory by means of a system of shifts so arranged that more than one relay of workers is engaged in work of the same kind at the same time. (Section 58)
- **Extra Wages for Overtime** If a worker works in a factory works for more than nine hours in any day or for more than 48 hours in any week, he shall, in respect of overtime work, be entitled to wages at the rate of twice his ordinary rate of wages. (Section 59)
- **Restriction on Double Employment** No adult worker shall be required or allowed to work in any factory on any day on which he has already been working in any other factory, except in such circumstances as may be prescribed. (Section 60)
- **Notice of Periods of Work for Adults** There shall be displayed and correctly maintained in every factory, a notice of periods of work for adults, showing clearly for every day the periods during which adult workers may be required to work. (Section 61)
- **Register of Adult Workers** The manager of every factory shall maintain a register of adult workers, to be available to the Inspector at all times during working hours, or when any work is being carried on in the factory. *The register will mention*
  (a) Name of each adult worker
  (b) Nature of his work
  (c) Group in which he is included
  (d) Group works on shift (Section 62)
- **Hours of Work to Correspond with Notice Under Section 61 and Register Under Section 62** No adult worker shall be required or allowed to work in any factory otherwise than in accordance with the notice of periods of work for adults displayed in the factory and the entries made before-hand against his name in the register of adult workers of the factory. (Section 63)
- **Power to Make Exempting Rules** The Government may make rules defining the persons who hold positions of supervision or management or are employed in a confidential position in a factory. (Section 65)
- **Further Restrictions on Employment of Women** No woman shall be required or allowed to work in any factory except between the hours of 6 A.M. and 7 P.M. (Section 66)

Employment of Young Persons

- **Prohibition of Employment of Young Children** No child who has not completed his fourteenth year shall be required or allowed to work in any factory. (Section 67)
- **Non-adult Workers to Carry Tokens** A child who has completed his fourteenth year or an adolescent shall not be required or allowed to work in any factory unless he has a certificate of fitness is granted in the custody of the manager of the factory. (Section 68)
- **Certificates of Fitness** A certifying surgeon shall, on the application of any young person or his parent or guardian accompanied by a document signed by the manager of a factory that such person will be employed therein if certified to be fit for work in a factory, or on the application of the manager of the factory in which any young person wishes to work, examine such person and ascertain his fitness for work in a factory. (Section 69)
- **Effect of Certificate of Fitness Granted to Adolescent**
  (a) The surgeon will grant the certificate of fitness upon ascertaining the age of an adolescent or young person.
  (b) The certificate shall be valid only for a period of twelve months.
  (c) No female adolescent or a male adolescent who has not attained the age of seventeen years but who has been granted a certificate of fitness to work in a factory as an adult, shall be required or allowed to work in any factory except between 6 A.M. and 7 P.M. (Section 70)
- **Working Hours for Children**
  (a) No child shall be employed or permitted to work, in any factory for more than four and a half hours in any day and during the night.
  (b) Night includes a period of at least twelve consecutive hours which shall include the interval between 10 P.M. and 6 A.M.
  (c) No female child shall be required or allowed to work in any factory except between 8 A.M. and 7 P.M.
  (d) The period of work of all children employed in a factory shall be limited to two shifts which shall not overlap or spread over more than five hours each. (Section 71)

- **Notice of Period of Work for Children** There shall be displayed and correctly maintained in every factory in which children are employed showing clearly for every day the periods during which children may be required or allowed to work. (Section 72)
- **Register of Child Workers** The manager of every factory in which children are employed shall maintain a register of child workers, to be available to the Inspector at all times during working hours or when any work is being carried on in a factory. *The register will mention*
  (a) Name of each child worker
  (b) Nature of his work
  (c) Group in which he is included
  (d) Number of his certificate fitness under Section 69. (Section 73)
- **Hours of Work to Correspond with Notice Under Section 72 and Register Under Section 73** No child shall be employed in any factory otherwise than in accordance with the notice of periods of work for children displayed in the factory and the entries made beforehand against his name in the register of child workers of the factory. (Section 74)
- **Power to Make Rules**

  The State Government may make rules for
  (a) Prescribing the forms of certificates of fitness to be granted under Section 69.
  (b) Providing for the grant of duplicates in the event of loss of the original certificates and fixing the fees which may be charged for such certificates and renewals thereof and such duplicates.
  (c) Prescribing the physical standards to be attained by children and adolescents working in factories.
  (d) Regulating the procedure of certifying surgeons.
  (e) Specifying other duties which certifying surgeons may be required to perform in connection with the employment of young persons and fixing the fees which may be charged. (Section 75)
- **Certain Other Provisions of Law not Barred** The provisions of this act shall be in addition to, and not in derogation of, the provisions of the Employment of Children Act, 1938.

Leave with Wages

Application The provisions shall not apply to workers of any railway administered by the Government, who are governed by leave rules approved by the Central Government.(Section 78)

Annual Leave With Wages Every worker who has worked for a period of 240 days or more in a factory during a calendar year shall be allowed during the subsequent calendar year, leave with wages.

The number of days will be calculated as following
- If an adult, one day for every twenty days of work performed by him during the previous calendar year.
- If a child, one day for every fifteen days of work performed by him during the previous calendar year. (Section 79)

Wages During Leave Period A worker shall be entitled to wages at a rate equal to the daily average of his total full time earnings for the days on which he actually worked during the month immediately preceding his leave.

This will be exclusive of any overtime and bonus but inclusive of dearness allowance and the cash equivalent of the advantage accruing through the concessional sale to the worker of foodgrains and other articles. (Section 80)

Payment in Advance in Certain Cases A worker who has been allowed leave for not less than four days, in the case of an adult, and five days, in the case of a child shall, before his leave begins, be paid the wages due for the period of the leave allowed. (Section 81)

Mode of Recovery of Unpaid Wages Any sum required to be paid by an employer, under this act but not paid by him shall be recoverable as delayed wages under the provisions of the Payment of Wages Act, 1936. (Section 82)

General Penalty for Offences (Section 92)

- In case, there is any contravention of any of the provisions of this Act, or of any rules made there under, or of any order in writing given there under, the occupier and manager of the factory shall each be guilty of an offence and punishable with
  (a) Imprisonment for a term which may extend to two years or with fine which may extend to one lakh rupees or with both, and
  (b) If the contravention is continued after conviction, with a further fine which may extend to one thousand rupees for each day on which the contravention is so continued.
- Whoever willfully obstructs an Inspector in the exercise of any power conferred on him by or under this Act, or fails to produce on demand by an Inspector any registers or other documents in his custody kept in pursuance of this Act or of any rules made thereunder, or conceals or prevents any worker in a factory from appearing before, or being examined by, an Inspector, shall be punishable with imprisonment for a term which may extend to six months or with fine which may extend to ten thousand rupees or with both.
- Whoever publishes or discloses to any person, the results of an analysis shall be punishable with imprisonment for a term which may extend to six months or with fine which may extend to ten thousand rupees or with both.

The Mines Act, 1952

Mines Act, 1952 came into force on 1st July, 1952. It deals with regulating the health and safety of labourers working in the mines. It deals with enforcement for measures of safety and welfare of labourers working in coal, metallic, ferrous and oil mines.

If any question arises as to whether any excavation or working is a mine within the meaning of this Act, the Central Government may decide the question, and a certificate signed by a Secretary to the Central Government shall be conclusive on the point.

Important Definitions under the Act

- **Adolescent** means a person between the age group of 15-18 years. The person should be more than 15 and less than 18 years of age. [Section 2(a)]
- **Adult** means a person who completed 18 years of age. [Section 2(b)]
- **Agent** means someone who acts as the representative of the owner in respect of the management of the mine or of any part thereof. He is superior to a manager under this act. [Section 2(c)]
- **Chief Inspector** means the Chief Inspector of Mines appointed under this act. [Section 2(d)]
- **Child** means a person who has not completed 15 years of age. [Section 2(e)]
- **Day** is a period of twenty-four hours beginning from midnight. [Section 2(f)]
- **District Magistrate** means the person appointed by the Central Government to perform the duties of a District Magistrate under this Act in that town. [Section 2(g)]
- A person is said to be **'employed'** in a mine who works under appointment by or with the knowledge of the manager, whether for wages or not, in any mining operation, or in cleaning or oiling any part of any machinery used in or about the mine, or in any other kind of work whatsoever incidental to, or connected with, mining operations. [Section 2(h)]
- **Inspector** means an inspector of mines appointed under this act. It includes a District Magistrate when exercising any power or performing any duty of an Inspector which he is empowered by this act to exercise or perform. [Section 2(i)]
- **Mine** means any excavation where any operation for the purpose of searching for or obtaining minerals has been or is being carried on. *It includes*
  (a) Every shaft in the course of being sunk.
  (b) Every level and inclined plane in the course of being driven.
  (c) All shafts, levels, planes, machinery, works, tramways and sidings, whether above or below ground, in or adjacent to, and belonging to, the mine.
  (d) Any workshop situated within the precincts of the mine and under the same management and used solely for purposes connected with that mine or a number of mines under the same management.
  (e) Any power station for supplying electricity solely for the purpose of working the mine, or any group of mines. [Section 2(j)]
- **Mineral** means those substances which can be obtained from the earth by means of digging, dredging, drilling, mining or through other operations. It include mineral oils which mean natural gas and petroleum. [Section2 (jj)]
- A person working or employed in or in connection with a mine is said to be working or employed **'below ground'** if he is working or employed
  (a) In a shaft, which has been or is in the course of being sunk, or
  (b) In any excavation, which extends below superjacent ground.
- A person working or employed in or in connection with a mine is said to be working or employed **'above ground'** if he is working in an open cast working or in any other manner not specified as employed 'below ground.'

Chief Inspector and Inspectors (Sections 5, 6, 7)

The Central Government has the power to appoint a person to the post of Chief Inspector and Inspector. The Inspector of mines will be the subordinate to Chief Inspector.

The important functions are as following

- Chief Inspector has the power to authorise any Inspector to exercise the powers of the Chief Inspector.
- He may by order in writing, prohibit or restrict the exercise by any Inspector by any power conferred on Inspectors under this Act.
- The Chief Inspector has the power to declare the areas, where the Inspector can exert their power.

Power of Inspector

- They can make examination and conduct inquiry under the regulations, rules and by laws.
- They can inspect and examine any mine at any time of day or night. They need to take care that the normal functioning of mines is not disrupted.

- They can examine any inquiry into the state or condition of the mines, related to ventilation, sufficiency, working conditions, health, safety and welfare of the people employed in a mine.
- They can conduct an occupational health survey for the employees at any time during the normal working hours only after giving a written notice to the owner or the manager. The employees involved in this survey are paid overtime, if they had to spent more than the normal time in the premises.
- They can exercise the power bestowed upon them by the Central Government.

Secrecy of the Information (Section 10)

- All copies of, and extracts from, registers or other records appertaining to any mine and all other information acquired by the Chief Inspector or an Inspector will be confidential.
- These will be disclosed only when it is deemed necessary by either Chief Inspector or Inspector.

However, they can disclose information to

(a) Any Court
(b) A Mining board, Committee, or Court of inquiry
(c) An official superior or the owner, agent or manager of the mine concerned
(d) A Commissioner for workmen's compensation appointed under the Workmen's Compensation Act, 1923
(e) The Director, Indian Bureau of Mines.

- If the Chief Inspector or Inspector discloses any information to any organisation without the consent of Central Government, he/she is liable to imprisonment for a term which may extend to one year, or with fine, or with both.

Certifying Surgeon (Section 11)

- The Central Government has the power to appoint any medical practitioner as a certifying surgeon.
- *The duties of a certifying surgeon are*

(a) Examination and certification of adolescents under this Act.
(b) Examination of persons engaged in a mine in such dangerous occupations or processes.
(c) The surgeon looks into cases of illness that have occurred which due to the nature of any process carried on or other conditions of work prevailing in the mine.
(d) Examination of the adolescents to be employed in any work which is likely to cause injury to their health.

Mining Board and Committee (Section 12, 13 and 14)

The Central Government has the power to constitute mining board for any group or class of mines. They enjoy the power equivalent to the Certifying Inspector. The committee has same power as vested in the Court under Code of Civil Procedure (CrPC), while trying a suit.

It consists of

(a) A person nominated by the Central Government as the Chairman.
(b) Chief Inspector of mines.
(c) Two persons to represent the interests of miners appointed by the Central Government.
(d) Two persons to represent the interests of owners appointed by the Central Government.
(e) Two qualified mining engineers not directly employed in the mining industry appointed by the Central Government.

Functions of Committee

- It will consider proposals for making rules and regulations and make appropriate recommendations to the government.
- It can conduct enquiry into accidents or other matters as may be referred to it by the Central Government from time-to-time and make reports on it.
- It will hear and decide such appeals or objections against notices or orders passed under this Act.

Health and Safety of Workers

- There needs to be effective arrangements to provide and maintain supply of cool and wholesome drinking water at suitable points.
- There should be sufficient number of latrines and urinals separately for males and females in every mine.
- First-aid boxes and cupboards should be readily accessible to the both above and below ground workers during the working hours.
- In every mine, where more than five hundred persons are employed, ambulances and stretchers need to be readily available.

Power of Government to Appoint Court of Inquiry in Case of Accidents (Section 24)

- The Central Government may order to get a formal inquiry conducted when any accident occurs in or about a mine causing loss of life or serious bodily injury or when an accidental explosion, ignition, spontaneous heating, outbreak of fire, irruption of water, breakage of ropes, chains or other gear by which men are lowered or raised.

- This enquiry will be to understand the causes of accident.
- The Central Government will appoint any person or persons possessing legal or special knowledge to act as assessor or assessors in holding the inquiry. This person shall have all the powers of a Civil Court under the Code of Civil Procedure, 1908.

Hours and Limitation of Employment

- No person shall be allowed to work in a mine for more than six days in any one week.
- No adult employed above ground in a mine shall be required or allowed to work for more than forty-eight hours in any week or for more than nine hours in any day.
- A person will not work for more than five hours continuously before he has had an interval for rest of at least half an hour.
- No adult employed below ground in a mine, except a pump-minder, an onsetter or attendant of continuously operated machinery, shall be allowed to work for more than forty-eight hours in any week or for more than eight hours in any day.
- No person shall be allowed to work in a mine who has already been working in any other mine within the preceding twelve hours.
- No child shall be employed in any mine, nor shall any child be allowed to be present in any part of a mine which is below ground or in any open excavation in which any mining operation is being carried on.
- No woman shall be employed at anytime of the day or night in any part of a mine which is below the adjacent ground level, and no woman shall be employed in any mine above ground except between the hours of 6 A.M. and 7 P.M.
- The workers will be granted a certificate of fitness from certifying surgeon. It shall be valid only for a period of twelve months. An adolescent, who has been granted a certificate of fitness to work in a mine as an adult shall be deemed to be an adult for the purposes of this Act.
- No adolescent who has not been granted a medical certificate certifying that he is fit for work as an adult shall be employed or permitted to be employed above ground or in any workshop or power station in a mine or in any open cast workings in a mine for more than four and a half hours in any day or between the hours of 6 P.M. and 6 A.M.

Leave With Wages

- Every person employed in a mine who has completed a period of twelve months' continuous service shall be allowed, during the subsequent period of twelve months, leave with full pay or wages based on the average pay or wages for the twelve months immediately preceding the leave.
- For the leave allowed to a loader, or other person employed below ground on a piece-rate basis, he shall be paid at a rate equal to the daily average of his earnings for the month of December prior to his leave.
- For the leave allowed to a person employed in a mine who is paid by the month or week, he shall be paid at a rate equal to his normal daily wages during the week preceding his leave, and in computing such wages the cash equivalent of the advantage accruing to him through the free issue of foodgrains and any compensation in cash drawn by him shall also be taken into account.

Penalties and Procedure

- Any person who obstructs the Chief Inspector or any other Inspector shall be punishable with imprisonment for a term which may extend to three months, or with fine which may extend to five hundred rupees, or with both.
- Any person who refrains from producing the documents demanded by the Chief Inspector or any other Inspector shall be punishable with fine which may extend to three hundred rupees.
- In the case, there is any falsification of records, the person shall be punishable with imprisonment for a term which may extend to three months, or with fine which may extend to five hundred rupees.

The Inter-state Migrant Workmen (Regulation of Employment and Conditions of Service) Act, 1979

The Act aims to regulate the employment of inter-state migrant workmen and to provide for their conditions of service and for matters connected therewith.

This act is applicable to

- Every establishment in which five or more inter-state migrant workmen (whether or not in addition to other workmen) are employed or who were employed on any day of the preceding twelve months.
- To every contractor who employs or who employed five or more inter-state migrant workmen (whether or not in addition to other workmen) on any day of the preceding twelve months.

Important Definitions Under the Act

- **Appropriate Government** in relation to
  - (a) any establishment pertaining to any industry carried on by or under the authority of the Central Government or pertaining to any such controlled industry as may be specified in this behalf by the Central Government, or
  - (b) any establishment of any railway, Cantonment Board, major port, mine or oil-field, or
  - (c) any establishment of a banking or insurance company the Central Government in relation to any other establishment, the Government of the State in which that other establishment is situated.
- **Contractor** means a person who undertakes to produce a given result for the establishment, through contract labor or who supplies contract labor for any work of the establishment. He may work as an independent contractor, agent, employee or otherwise. [Section 2(b)]
- **Controlled Industry** means any industry, the control of which by the Union has been declared by any Central Act to be expedient in the public interest. [Section 2(c)]
- **Establishment** means
  - (a) Any office or department of the Government or a local authority; or
  - (b) Any place where any industry, trade, business, manufacture or occupation is carried on.
- **Inter-State Migrant Workman** means any person who is recruited by or through a contractor in one state under an agreement or other arrangement for employment in an establishment in another state. This recruitment can happen whether with or without the knowledge of the principal employer in relation to such establishment. [Section 2(e)]
- **Principal Employer** means
  - (a) In relation to any office or department of the government or a local authority, the head of that office or department.
  - (b) In a factory, the owner or occupier of the factory and where a person has been named as the manager of the factory under the Factories Act, 1948.
  - (c) In a mine, the owner or agent of the mine and where a person has been named as the manager of the mine.
  - (d) In any other establishment, any person responsible for the supervision and control of the establishment.
- **Wages** shall have the meaning assigned to it in Clause (vi) of Section 2 of the Payment of Wages Act, 1936.
- **Workman** means any person employed in or in connection with the work of any establishment to do any skilled, semi-skilled or unskilled, manual, supervisory, technical or clerical work for hire or reward, whether the terms of employment be express or implied.

  It does not include any such person
  - (i) who is employed mainly in a managerial or administration capacity; or
  - (ii) who, being employed in a supervisory capacity, draws wages exceeding five hundred rupees per mensem or exercises, either by the nature of the duties attached to the office or by reason of the powers vested in him, functions mainly of a managerial nature. [Section 2(j)]

Registration of Establishment Employing Inter-state Migrant Workmen (Section 4)

- The appropriate government has the power to appoint registering officer and confer power on him. They can define their respective limits of jurisdiction and powers under the act.
- The principal employer needs to make an application to the registering officer in the prescribed form and manner to get the registration of employment done.
- If the application is complete in all the aspects, the registering officer will issue to the principal employer of the establishment a certificate of registration in the prescribed form within one month.
- If the application is not so complete, the registering officer will return the application to the principal employer of the establishment.

- No principal employer of an establishment to which this Act applies shall employ inter-state migrant workmen in the establishment unless a certificate of registration in respect of such establishment issued under this Act is in force.

Licensing of Contractors (Section 8)

- The appropriate government has the power to appoint licensing officers and define the limits, within which a licensing officer shall exercise the jurisdiction and powers conferred on him.
- The licensing officers will grant the license to the contractor for the recruitment of workman.
- The contractor needs to make the application in the prescribed form with the details of the particulars regarding the location of the establishment, the nature of process, operation or work for which inter-state migrant workmen are to be employed.
- The licensing officer will grant the license after thorough investigations. This license will be valid for a given time frame and will have to be renewed timely.
- The licensing officer has the power to suspend, revocate and amend license in case, he finds any discrepancy.

Duties and Obligations of Contractor (Section 12)

- He needs to furnish particulars of an inter-state workman in the form as may be prescribed within fifteen days from the date of recruitment.
- To issue to every inter-state migrant workmen, a pass book affixed with a passport size photograph of the workman and indicating in Hindi and English languages and where the language of the workman is not Hindi or English, *also in the language of the workman*
    (a) The name and place of the establishment wherein the workman is employed
    (b) The period of employment
    (c) The proposed rates and modes of payment of wages
    (d) The displacement allowance payable
    (e) The return fare payable to the workman on the expiry of the period of his employment and in such contingencies as may be prescribed and in such other contingencies as may be specified in the contract of employment;
    (f) Deductions made; and
    (g) Such other particulars as may be prescribed.
- It shall be the duty of every contractor employing inter-state migrant workmen in connection with the work of an establishment to which this act applies
    (a) To ensure regular payment of wages to such workmen
    (b) To ensure equal pay for equal work irrespective of sex
    (c) To ensure suitable conditions of work to such workmen having regard to the fact that they are required to work in a state different from their own state
    (d) To provide and maintain suitable residential accommodation to such workmen during the period of their employment
    (e) To provide the prescribed medical facilities to the workmen, free of charge
    (f) To provide such protective clothing to the workmen as may be prescribed, and
    (g) In case of fatal accident or serious bodily injury to any such workman, to report to the specified authorities of both the States and also the next of kin of the workman.

Wages Welfare and Other Facilities to be Provided to Inter-state Migrant Workmen

- An inter-state migrant workman shall in no case be paid less than the wages fixed under the Minimum Wages Act, 1948.
- Wages payable to an inter-state migrant workman, under this section shall be paid in 'cash' and not in any other manner/form.
- The contractor is bound to pay every inter-state migrant workman at the time of recruitment, a displacement allowance equal to 50% of the monthly wages payable to him or seventy-five rupees, whichever is higher.
- Every inter-state migrant workman is entitled to payment of wages during the period of journeys on duty and is also entitled to journey allowance for outward and return journeys from the place of residence in his state to the place of work in the other state.
- A contractor shall be responsible for payment of wages to each inter-state migrant workman employed by him.
- Every principal employer shall nominate a representative duly authorised by him to be present at the time of disbursement of wages by the contractor and it shall be the duty of such representative to certify the amounts paid as wages in such manner as may be prescribed.
- It shall be the duty of the contractor to ensure the disbursement of wages in the presence of the authorised representative of the principal employer.
- In case, the contractor fails to make payment of wages within the prescribed period or makes short payment, then the principal employer shall be liable to make payment of the wages in full or the unpaid balance due, as the case may be, to the inter-state migrant workman

employed by the contractor and recover the amount so paid from the contractor either by deduction from any amount payable to the contractor under any contract or as a debt payable by the contractor.

Inspecting Staff

- The appropriate government has the power to appoint inspectors and define their powers and functions.
- *An inspecting officer has the powers to*
  - (a) examine any person found in any such premises or place for the purpose of determining whether such person is an inter-state migrant workman.
  - (b) require any person giving out work to any workman, to give any information, which is in his power to give, with respect to the names and addresses of the persons to, for and from whom the work is given out or received, and with respect to the payments to be made for the work.
  - (c) seize or take copies of such register, record of wages, or notices or portions thereof as he may consider relevant in respect of an offence under this act which he has reason to believe has been committed by a principal employer or contractor.

The Inter-state Migrant Workmen (Regulation of Employment and Conditions of Service) Rules, 1980

In exercise of the powers conferred by **Section 35** of the Inter-State Migrant Workmen (Regulation of Employment and Conditions of Service) Act, 1979, the Central Government made the Inter-State Migrant Workmen (Regulation of Employment and Conditions of Service) rules. It came into force on 2nd October, 1980.

Important Definitions Under the Rules

- **Appellate Officer** means an appellate officer nominated by the Central Government under Section 11.
- **Deputy Chief Labour Commission** means an officer appointed by the Central Government.
- **Inspector** means an inspector appointed by the Central Government under Section 20.
- **Licensing Officer** means an officer appointed by the Central Government under Section 7.
- **Migrant Workman** means an inter-state migrant workman as defined under Section 2.
- **Registering Officer** means a registering officer appointed by the Central Government under Section 3.
- **Specified Authority** means the authority specified by the Central Government for the purposes of Sections 12 and 16.

Manner of Making Application for Registration of Establishment (Section 3)

- In order to register an establishment, the person needs to submit an application with triplicate copies of Form I to the registering officer of the area. This must be accompanied with a Demand Draft showing details of the payment of fees. This application form can be delivered by hand or sent by post.
- Once, the officer has received the application, he needs to give an acknowledgement of the receipt.

Issue of Certificate of Registration (Section 4)

- The principal officer will be issuing a certificate of registration in Form II after the registration of establishment.
- He needs to maintain a register in Form III. This register will carry all the details of the establishment in relation to which certificates of registration are issued by him.
- In case, there are any changes in the particulars, the employer needs to update this to the registering officer within 30 days from the date of change.

Application for a License (Section 7)

- Every application by a contractor for the grant of a licence for recruiting a person must be made in triplicate in Form IV to the Licensing Officer having jurisdiction in relation to the area wherein the recruitment is made.
- Every application by a contractor for employing a migrant workman must be made in Form V to the Licensing Officer having jurisdiction in relation to the area wherein the recruitment is made.
- The application form can be delivered by hand or sent by post.
- Once, the officer has received the application, he needs to give an acknowledgement of the receipt.

Matters to be taken into Consideration for Granting or Refusing a License (Section 8)

The following points need to be taken into consideration while granting or rejecting a license

- Whether the applicant
  - (a) Is a minor, or
  - (b) Is of unsound mind and stands so declared by a competent court, or
  - (c) Is an undischarged insolvent, or
  - (d) Has been convicted at any time during the period of five years immediately preceding the date of application, of an offence which, in the opinion of the Central Government involves moral turpitude.
- Whether fees and security have been deposited by the applicant.

- Whether any order had been made in respect of the applicant and, if so, whether a period of three years has elapsed from the date of that order.

Refusal to Issue License (Section 9)

- The Licensing Officer shall investigate or cause investigation to be made to satisfy himself about the correctness of the facts and particulars furnished in such application and the eligibility of the applicant for a licensee.
- If the Licensing Officer feels that licensee should not be issued with the license, he needs to make an order rejecting the application giving the reason of the same.

Security (Section 10)

- When Licensing Officer is satisfied that any person who has applied for or who has been issued a licence should furnish security for the due performance of the conditions of the licence, he shall prepare an estimate of all the amounts needed to provide for recruitment or employment of migrant workmen on the basis of the following factors, *namely*
  (a) Wages equivalent to one wage period
  (b) Provision of medical facilities under rule 37
  (c) Provision of protective clothing under rule 38
  (d) Provision of drinking water, latrines, urinals and washing facilities under rule 39 read with rules 42 and 43
  (e) Provision of rest rooms under rule 40, wherever applicable
  (f) Provision of canteens under rule 41, wherever applicable
  (g) Provision of creche under rule 44, wherever applicable
  (h) Provision of residential accommodation under rule 45
  (i) Journey allowance under Section 15
  (j) Number of migrant workmen employed or recruited, and
  (k) Duration of work.
- The Licensing Officer must determine the amount of security to be furnished.

Forms and Terms of Conditions of Licence (Section 11)

- Every licence issued under of Section 8 shall be in Form VII.
- *The license granted or renewed will be subjected to the following conditions*
  (a) The licence shall be non-transferable.
  (b) The terms and conditions of the agreement or arrangement or the arrangement under which the migrant workman is recruited or employed.
  (c) The number of migrant workmen recruited or employed.
  (d) The number of workmen recruited or employed as migrant workmen in the establishment shall not, on any day, exceed the maximum number specified in conditions.
  (e) The rates of wages payable to the migrant workmen by the contractor shall not be less than the rates prescribed under the Minimum Wages Act, 1984, for such employment and where the rates have be end fixed by the agreement, settlement or award, not less than the rates so fixed.
  (f) Every migrant workman shall be entitled to allowances, benefits, facilities etc, as prescribed.
  (g) No female migrant workman shall be employed by any contractor before 6 A.M. or after 7 P.M.
  (h) The period for which the licence shall be valid.
- Every licence renewed under this rule 15 shall remain in force for a further period of twelve months from the date of the order of renewal.

Payment of Fees and Security Deposit (Section 20)

The payment of the various fees relating to registration, licensing and security deposits shall be made through a crossed demand draft drawn in favour of the concerned departmental officer and payable at the station at which he is stationed along with a treasury challan duly filled in dicating the relevant head of account creditable to the accounts of the concerned pay and accounts office.

Duties of the Contractor

- Every contractor needs to furnish to the specified authorities the particulars regarding recruiting and employment of migrant workmen in Form X.
- He needs to pay to the migrant workman the return fare from the place of employment to the place of residence in the home-state of the migrant workman on the expiry of the period of employment.
- In case of fatal accident or serious bodily injury to any migrant workman, the contractor shall immediately send telegrams to the specified authorities of both the states and also the next of the kins of the migrant workman intimating death or the nature of serious bodily injury sustained by the migrant workman, as the case may be, date, place and nature of accident.
- The contractor shall further send written report to the specified authorities concerned and the next of the kins of the migrant workman, under mentioned particulars by registered post within 24 hours of the occurrence of the accident.

Wages

- The rate of wages of a migrant workman in an establishment will not be less than the rate of wages paid by the principal employer to a workman in the lowest category of workmen directly employed by him in that establishment or the minimum rates of wages notified by the Central Government under the Minimum Wages Act, 1948 for the same or similar type of work performed by workmen.
- The contractor shall fix wage periods in respect of which wages shall be payable.
- No wage period shall extend one month.
- The wages of every migrant workman in an establishment by a contractor where less than 1000 workmen are employed has to be paid before seventh and in other cases before tenth every month.
- Where the employment of any migrant workman is terminated by or on behalf of the contractor, the wages earned by the migrant workman shall be paid before the expiry, the second working day from the day on which his employment is terminated.
- Wages due to every migrant workman, shall be paid to him direct or to other persons duly authorised by him in this behalf.

Medical and Other Facilities Provided to the Workmen

- The migrant worker will be entitled to the same number of holidays, hours of work including extra wages for overtime work done and other conditions of service as the regular workers.
- The contractor needs to ensure provision of suitable and adequate medical facilities for outdoor treatment to the migrant workman free of cost for treatment of any ailment from which the migrant workman or any member of his family may suffer during his employment in the establishment or to meet any preventive measure against epidemic or any virus infection.
- In the event of migrant workman or any of his family members suffering from any ailment requiring hospitalisation during his employment in the establishment, the contractor shall promptly arrange for the hospitalisation of the migrant workman or the concerned member of his family.
- The contractor shall bear entire expenses on treatment, hospital charges (including diet), if any, and travel expenses for the patient from the place of his/her residence to the hospital and back.
- Every contractor needs to provide atleast one first-aid box for one hundred and fifty workmen.
- The contractor shall provide to every migrant workman where the temperature falls below 20 degree centigrade, protective clothing consisting of one woollen coat and one woollen trousers once in two years.
- This needs to be provided by the contractor to every migrant workman before onset of winter season in the area where the establishment is located or on the 30th September. If the temperature falls below 5 degree centigrade a woollen overcoat shall also be provided to the migrant workmen once in three years.
- Sufficient quantity of wholesome drinking water, sufficient number of sanitary latrines and urinals, washing facilities for the migrant workmen should be arranged.
- The contractor needs to be provide a canteen where hundred or more employees are employed and are likely to continue their services for the next six months.
- There should be separate latrines and urinals for men and women. There should be atleast one latrine for every 25 females and 25 males.
- In every establishment, where 20 or more workmen are employed as migrant workmen and in which employment of migrant workmen is likely to continue for three months or more, there should be two rooms to be used as creche for children under the age of six years.
- The contractor needs to be provide residential accommodation to the worker. This will be in accordance with the fact that the worker is alone or with his family.

The Contract Labour (Regulation and Abolition) Act, 1970

The aim of the act is to prevent exploitation of contract labour and also to introduce better conditions at workplace for the contract labour.

This act is applicable to

- Every establishment in which twenty or more workmen are employed or were employed on any day of the preceding twelve months as contract labour.
- To every contractor who employees or who employed on any day of the preceding twelve months twenty or more workmen.

Important Definitions Under the Act

- **Appropriate Government** means
  (a) In relation to an establishment in respect of which the appropriate government under the Industrial Disputes Act, 1947, is the Central Government, the Central Government.
  (b) In relation to any other establishment, the Government of the State in which that other establishment is situated. [Section 2(a)]
- **Contract Labour** means a workman who shall be deemed to be employed as in or in connection with the work of an establishment when he is hired in or in connection with such work by or through a contractor, with or without the knowledge of the principal employer. [Section 2(b)]
- **Contractor** means a person who undertakes to produce a given result for the establishment, through contract labor or who supplies contract labor for any work of the establishment. [Section 2(c)]
- **Controlled Industry** means any industry, the control of which by the Union has been declared by any Central Act to be expedient in the public interest. [Section 2(d)]
- **Establishment** means any office or department of the government or a local authority, or any place where any industry, trade, business, manufacture or occupation is carried on. [Section 2(e)]
- **Principal Employer** means,
  (a) In relation to any office or department of the government or a local authority, the head of that office or department.
  (b) In a factory, the owner or occupier of the factory and where a person has been named as the manager of the factory under the Factories Act, 1948.
  (c) In a mine, the owner or agent of the mine and where a person has been named as the manager of the mine.
  (d) In any other establishment, any person responsible for the supervision and control of the establishment. [Section 2(f)]
- **Workman** means any person employed in or in connection with the work of any establishment to do any skilled, semi-skilled or unskilled manual, supervisory, technical or clerical work for hire or reward, whether the terms of employment be express or implied.

  It does not include
  (a) A person who is employed mainly in a managerial or administrative capacity.
  (b) A person who is being employed in a supervisory capacity draws wages exceeding five hundred rupees per mensem or exercises, either by the nature of the duties attached to the office or by reason of the powers vested in him, functions mainly of a managerial nature.
  (c) A person who is an out-worker, that is to say, a person to whom any articles or materials are given out by or on behalf of the Principal employer to be made up, cleaned, washed, altered, ornamented, finished, repaired, adapted or otherwise processed for sale for the purposes of the trade or business of the principal employer and the process is to be carried out either in the home of the out-worker or in some other premises, not being premises under the control and management of the principal employer. [Section 2(i)]

Advisory Boards

Central Advisory Boards (Section 3)

As the name implies, it will be an advisory board constituted by the Central Government. *It will consist of*

- Chairman
- Chief Labour Commissioner (Ex-officio)
- Eleven-Seventeen Central members representing Government, the railways, the coal industry, the mining industry, the contractors, the workmen.

State Advisory Boards (Section 4)

As the name implies, it will be an advisory board constituted by the State Government. *It will consist of*

- Chairman
- Labour Commissioner(Ex-officio)
- Nine-Eleven members representing State Government, industry, contractor, workmen.

Both these boards have the power to constitute committees as per the requirement.

Registration of Establishments Employing Contract Labour (Section 6)

- The appropriate government has the power to appoint registering officers and assign them powers and functions.
- Every principal employer needs make an application to the registering officer in the prescribed manner for registration of the establishment.
- If the application for registration is complete in all respects, the registering officer shall register the establishment and issue to the principal employer of the establishment a certificate of registration containing such particulars as may be prescribed.

Licensing of Contractors (Section 12)

- The appropriate government has the power to appoint Licensing Officers and assign them powers and functions.
- The application for the grant of license needs to be submitted in a prescribed format to the Licensing Officer, who on receiving the same conducts appropriate inquiry before giving the license.

Welfare and Health of Contract Labour

- A canteen needs to be provided wherein contract labour numbering 100 or more is ordinarily employed.
- Rest-rooms need to be provided, if the labour is required to take a halt at night.
- A first-aid box equipped with the prescribed contents needs to be readily accessible during all working hours at every place where contract labour is employed.
- There needs to be proper disbursement of wages in the presence of the authorised representative of the principal employer.

Inspecting Staff (Section 28)

The appropriate government has the power to appoint and define the powers of inspecting officers.

These are

- The Inspecting Officer can enter and inspect any premises or place where contract labour is employed, for the purpose of examining any register or record or notices required to be kept or exhibited by or under this.
- Examine any person whom he finds in any such premises or place and who, he has reasonable cause to believe, is a workman employed therein.
- Require any person giving out work and any workman, to give any information, which is in his power to give with respect to the names and addresses of the persons to, for and from whom the work is given out or received, and with respect to the payments to be made for the work.
- Seize to take copies of such register, record of wages or notices or portions, thereof as he may consider relevant in respect of an offence under this Act which he has reason to believe has been committed by the principal employer or contractor; and
- Exercise such other powers as may be prescribed.

Penalties and Procedures

- If anyone obstructs an Inspector in the discharge of his duties or refuses or willfully neglects to afford the Inspector any reasonable facility for making any inspection, examination, inquiry or investigation shall be punishable with imprisonment for a term which may extend to three months, or with fine which may extend to five hundred rupees, or with both.
- If anyone willfully refuses to produce on the demand of an Inspector any register or other document, he shall be punishable with imprisonment for a term which may extend to three months, or with fine which may extend to five hundred rupees, or with both.
- If any person contravenes any of the provisions of this Act or of any rules made thereunder for which no other penalty is elsewhere provided, he shall be punishable with imprisonment for a term which may extend to three months, or with fine which may extend to one thousand rupees, or with both.
- If the person committing an offence under this Act is a company, the company as well as every person incharge of, and responsible to, the company for the conduct of its business at the time of the commission of the offence shall be deemed to be guilty of the offence and shall be liable to be proceeded against and punished accordingly.

The Building and Other Construction Workers (Regulation of Employment and Conditions of Service) Act, 1996

This act came into force on the 1st March, 1996. It applies to every establishment which employs, or had employed on any day of the preceding twelve months, ten or more building workers in any building or other construction work.

This act aims to regulate the employment and conditions of service of building and other construction workers and to provide for their safety, health and welfare measures and for other matters connected therewith or incidental thereto.

Definitions Under the Act

- **Appropriate Government** means,
  (a) In relation to an establishment (which employs building workers either directly or through a contractor) in respect of which the appropriate government under the Industrial Disputes Act, 1947 (14 of 1947), is the Central Government, the Central Government.
  (b) In relation to any such establishment, being a public sector undertaking, as the Central Government may by notification specify which employs building workers either directly or through a contractor, the Central Government.

(c) In relation to any other establishment which employs building workers either directly or through a contractor, the Government of the State in which that other establishment is situated. [Section 2(a)]

- **Beneficiary** means a building workers registered under Section 12. [Section 2(b)]
- **Board** means a Building and other Construction Workers' Welfare Board constituted under Section 18. [Section 2(c)]
- **Building or Other Construction Work** means the construction, alteration, repairs, maintenance or demolition, or, in relation, to buildings, streets, roads, railways, tramways, airfields, irrigation, drainage, embankment and navigation works, flood control works (including storm water drainage works), generation, transmission and distribution of power, water works (including channels for distribution of water), oil and gas installations, electric lines, wireless, radio, television, telephone, telegraph and overseas communications, dams, canals, reservoirs, watercourses, tunnels, bridges, viaducts, aqueducts, pipelines, towers, cooling towers, transmission towers and such other work. It does not include any building or other construction work to which the provisions of the Factories Act, 1948, or the Mines Act, 1952 apply. [Section 2(d)]
- **Building Worker** means a person who is employed to do any skilled, semi-skilled or unskilled, manual, supervisory, technical or clerical work for hire or reward.

It does not include

(a) A person who is employed mainly in a managerial or administrative capacity.

(b) A person who is employed in a supervisory capacity and draws wages exceeding one thousand six hundred rupees per mensem.

- **Chief Inspector** means the Chief Inspector of Inspection of Building and Construction appointed under Section 42. [Section 2(f)]
- **Contractor** means a person who produces a given result for any establishment by the employment of building workers or who supplies building workers for any work of the establishment. [Section 2(g)]
- **Employer of an Establishment** means the owner. It means the head of the department of a building or other construction work carried on by or under the authority of any department of the Government, or local authority directly without any contractor, or with any contractor or any authority specified in this behalf. [Section 2(i)]
- **Fund** means the Building and other Construction Workers' Welfare Fund of a Board. [Section 2(k)]

Advisory Committees and Expert Committees

Central Advisory Committee (Section 3)

The Central Government has the power to constitute Central Building and Other Construction Workers' Advisory Committee. Its role will be advisory in nature.

It will consist of the following

- Chairperson to be appointed by the Central Government;
- Three members of Parliament of whom two shall be elected by the House of the People and one by the Council of States-members;
- The Director-General-member, ex officio;
- Nine to thirteen members nominated by the Central Government to represent employers,building workers, associations of architects, engineers, accident insurance institutions and any other interests which, in the opinion of the Central Government, ought to be represented on the Central Advisory Committee.

State Advisory Committee (Section 4)

The State Government has the power to constitute State Building and Other Construction Workers' Advisory Committee. *It will consist of the following*

- A Chairperson to be appointed by the State Government;
- Two members of the State Legislature to be elected from the State Legislature members;
- A member to be nominated by the Central Government;
- The Chief Inspector-member, ex-officio;
- Seven to eleven members nominated by the State Government to represent the employers, building workers, associations of architects, engineers, accident insurance institutions and any other interests.

Registration of Establishments (Section 7)

The government has the power to appoint Registering Officers (RO) and define the limits within which a registering officer shall exercise the powers conferred on him by or under this act. Every employer needs to make an application to the Registering Officer (RO) within a period of sixty days from commencement to get the establishment registered.

Registration of Building Workers as Beneficiaries (Section 12)

- Every building worker registered as a beneficiary under this act shall be entitled to the benefits provided by the Board from its fund under this Act.
- Every building worker in the age group of eighteen to sixty years who has been engaged in any building or other construction work for not less than ninety days during the preceding twelve months shall be eligible for registration as a beneficiary under this act.
- The worker needs to submit all the documents and forms alongwith a fee of fifty rupees.
- The Board shall give to every beneficiary an identity card with his photograph duly affixed thereon and with enough space for entering the details of the building or other construction work done by him.
- A building worker who has been registered as a beneficiary under this act shall cease to be as such when he attains the age of sixty years or when he is not engaged in building or other construction work for not less than ninety days in a year.
- The employer needs to maintain a register showing the details of employment of beneficiaries.

Building and Other Construction Workers' Welfare Boards

- Every State Government will constitute a state welfare board and should not exceed fifteen members in its composition.
- The Board shall include an equal number of members representing the State Government, the employers and the building workers and that atleast one member of the Board shall be a woman.
- The Board needs to appoint a secretary, who will be ·the Chief Executive Officer (CEO) of the Board.
- *The different functions of Board include*

(a) Provide immediate assistance to a beneficiary in case of accident.

(b) Make payment of pension to the beneficiaries who have completed the age of sixty years.

(c) Sanction loans and advances to a beneficiary for construction of a house not exceeding such amount and on such terms and conditions as may be prescribed.

(d) Pay such amount in connection with premia for Group Insurance Scheme of the beneficiaries as it may deem fit.

(e) Give such financial assistance for the education of children of the beneficiaries as may be prescribed.

(f) Meet such medical expenses for treatment of major ailments of a beneficiary or, such dependant, as may be prescribed.

(g) Make payment of maternity benefit to the female beneficiaries, and

(h) Make provision and improvement of such other welfare measures and facilities as may be prescribed.

Fund and It's Use

The board will have to create a Building and other Construction Workers' Welfare Fund and there shall be credited thereto

- Any grants and loans made to the Board by the Central Government under Section 23.
- All contributions made by the beneficiaries.
- All sums received by the Board from such other sources as may be decided by the Central Government.

This fund shall be used for meeting

- Expenses of the Board in the discharge of its functions.
- Salaries, allowances and other remuneration of the members, officers and other employees of the Board.
- Expenses on objects and for purposes authorised by this Act.

Hours of Work, Welfare Measures and Other Conditions of Service of Building Workers

- The government has the right to fix the number of working hours in a day, holidays and overtime wages.
- In the case of overtime, the worker will be entitled to wages at the rate of twice his ordinary rate of wages. Ordinary rate of wages mean the basic wages and allowances. It does not include any bonus.
- There needs to be proper arrangement of drinking water, latrines and urinals.
- The employer needs to provide free accommodation till the building or other construction work is in progress.
- Creche need to be built where fifty or more female workers are employed. The room will be used for the children below the age of six years of such female workers.
- The employer needs to provide and maintain in every place wherein not less than two hundred and fifty building workers are ordinarily employed, proper canteens.

Safety and Health Measures

- The government needs to constitute a Safety Committee consisting representatives of the employer and the building workers, in case, there are five hundred or more workers employed in the same.
- In case of an accident leading to injury or death, the injured person should not work for the next forty eight hours or more immediately after death.
- The appropriate government may make rules regarding the measures to be taken for the safety and health of building workers in the course of their employment and the equipment and appliances necessary to be provided to them for ensuring their safety, health and protection, during such employment.

Inspecting Staff

- The Central Government has the power to appoint the Director-General of inspection who shall be responsible for laying down the standards of inspection and shall also exercise the powers of an Inspector throughout India in relation to all the establishments for which the Central Government is the appropriate government.
- The State Government has the power to Chief Inspector of Inspection of building and construction who shall be responsible for effectively carrying out the provisions of this Act and shall also exercise the powers of an Inspector under this Act throughout the State in relation to establishments for which the State Government is the appropriate government.
- Every Inspector appointed under this section, shall be subject to the control of the Director-General or the Chief Inspector.
- *The inspectors have the following powers*
  (a) Examination of any premises or place where building or other construction work is carried on.
  (b) Examination of any person who has been employed in the building.
  (c) Seize or take copies of register, record of wages or notices or portions that are considered relevant in respect of an offence committed under this Act.

Penalties

- In case, there is contravention of safety measures, a person shall be punishable with imprisonment for a term which may extend to three months, or with fine which may extend to two thousand rupees, or with both.
- Where an employer fails to give notice of the commencement of the building or other construction work, he shall be punishable with imprisonment for a term which may extend to three months, or with fine which may extend to two thousand rupees, or with both.
- Whoever obstructs an Inspector in the discharge of his duties under this Act or refuses or wilfully neglects to afford the Inspector any reasonable facility for making any inspection, examination, inquiry or investigation authorised by or under this Act in relation to an establishment shall be punishable with imprisonment for a term which may extend to three months, or with fine which may extend to one thousand rupees, or with both.

The Child Labour (Prohibition and Regulation) Act, 1986

This act aims to prohibit the engagement of children in certain employments and to regulate the conditions of work of children in certain other employments.

Definitions Under the Act

- **Appropriate Government** means, in relation to an establishment under the control of the Central Government or a railway administration or a major port or a mine or oilfield, the Central Government, and in all other cases, the State Government. [Section 2(i)]
- **Child** means a person who has not completed his fourteenth year of age. [Section 2(ii)]
- **Day** means a period of twenty-four hours beginning at midnight. [Section 2(iii)]
- **Establishment** includes a shop, commercial establishment, workshop, farm, residential hotel, restaurant, eating-house, theatre or other place of public amusement or entertainment. [Section 2(iv)]
- **Family** means the individual, the wife or husband, as the case may be, of such individual, and their children, brother or sister of such individuals. [Section 2(v)]
- **Occupier** means the person who has the ultimate control over the affairs of the establishment or workshop. [Section 2(vi)]
- **Week** means a period of seven days beginning at midnight on Saturday night. [Section 2(ix)]
- **Workshop** means any premises wherein any industrial process is carried on, but does not include any premises to which the provisions of Section 67 of the Factories Act, 1948 apply. [Section 2(x)]

Prohibition of Employment of Children in Certain Occupations and Processes

- *No child shall be employed or permitted to work in any of the occupations given below*
  (a) Transport of passengers, goods or mails by railway.
  (b) Cinder picking, clearing of an ash pit or building operation in the railway premises.
  (c) Work in a catering establishment at a railway station, involving the movement of a vendor or any other employee of the establishment from one platform to another or into or out of a moving train.
  (d) Work relating to the construction of a railway station or with any other work where such work is done in close proximity to or between the railway lines.
  (e) A port authority within the limits of any port.
  (f) Work relating to selling of crackers and fireworks in shops with temporary licences.
  (g) Abattoirs/slaughter Houses.
- *No child shall be employed or permitted in any workshop wherein any of the following processes are conducted*
  (a) Bidi-making.
  (b) Carpet-weaving.
  (c) Cement manufacture, including bagging of cement.
  (d) Cloth printing, dyeing and weaving.
  (e) Manufacture of matches, explosives and fire-works.
  (f) Mica-cutting and splitting.
  (g) Shellac manufacture.
  (h) Soap manufacture.
  (i) Tanning.
  (j) Wool-cleaning.
  (k) Building and construction industry.
  (l) Manufacture of slate pencils (including packing).
  (m) Manufacture of products from agate.
  (n) Manufacturing processes using toxic metals and substances, such as, lead, mercury, manganese, chromium, 'cadmium, benzene, pesticides and asbestos.
  (o) Hazardous processes as defined in Section 2 (cb) and dangerous operations as defined in rules made under Section 87 of the Factories Act, 1948.
  (p) Printing as defined in Section 2(k) of the Factories Act, 1948.
  (q) Cashew and cashew nut descaling and processing.
  (r) Soldering processes in electronic industries.
- The Central Government needs to give not less than three months' notice of in case any amendment has to be made to any occupation or process to the Schedule.
- If any question arises between an Inspector and an occupier as to the age of any child, who is employed or is permitted to work by him in an establishment, the question shall, in the absence of a certificate as to the age of such child granted by the prescribed medical authority, be referred by the Inspector for decision to the prescribed medical authority.

Child Labour Technical Advisory Committee (Section 5)

- The Central Government has the power to establish the Child Labour Technical Advisory Committee, which will be advisory in nature.
- It shall have a chairman and a maximum of ten members, who will be appointed by Central Government.

Hours and Period of Work (Section 7) and Weekly Holidays (Section 8)

- No child will work for more than three hours. He will have an interval for rest for atleast one hour after that.
- No child will work more than six hours in a day including the rest interval.
- No child will be permitted or required to work between 7 P.M. and 8 A.M.
- No child will be required or permitted to work overtime.
- Every child employed in an establishment will be allowed one holiday of whole day in each week.

Maintenance of Register (Section 11)

The owner, manager or occupier needs to maintain a register with the following details

- The name and date of birth of every child so employed or permitted to work.
- Hours and periods of work of any such child and the intervals of rest to which he is entitled; and
- The nature of work of any such child.

Health and Safety (Section 13)

- The appropriate government may make rules for the health and safety of the children employed or permitted to work in any establishment or class of establishments.
- *The rules will be provided for the following matters*
  (a) Cleanliness in the place of work and its freedom from nuisance
  (b) Disposal of wastes and effluents
  (c) Ventilation and temperature
  (d) Dust and fume
  (e) Artificial humidification
  (f) Lighting

(g) Drinking water
(h) Latrine and urinals
(i) Spittoons
(j) Fencing of machinery
(k) Work at or near machinery in motion
(l) Employment of children on dangerous machines
(m) Instructions, training and supervision in relation to employment of children on dangerous machines
(n) Device for cutting-off power
(o) Self-acting machines
(p) Easing of new machinery
(q) Floor, stairs and means of access
(r) Pits, sumps, openings in floors etc.
(s) Excessive weights
(t) Protection of eyes
(u) Explosive or inflammable dust, gas etc.
(v) Precautions in case of fire
(w) Maintenance of buildings, and
(x) Safety of buildings and machinery.

Penalties (Section 14)

- Whoever employs any child or permits any child to work in contravention of the prohibited occupations and profession shall be punishable with imprisonment for a term which shall not be less than, three months but which may extend to one year or with fine which shall not be less than ten thousand rupees, but which may extend to twenty thousand rupees, or with both.
- Whoever, having been convicted under the aforementioned clause commits a like offence afterwards, he shall be punishable with imprisonment for a term which shall not be less than six months but which may extend to two years.

EXAM BASED QUESTIONS

1 According to Factories Act, 1948, who is an adult?
(a) Person who has completed the age of 18
(b) Person between the age group of 15-18 years
(c) Person above the age of 21 years
(d) Person between the age of 18-21 years

2 According to Factories Act, 1948, week is a period of seven days beginning from the midnight of which of the following days?
(a) Sunday (b) Monday
(c) Saturday (d) Tuesday

3 According to Factories Act, 1948, how many hours should an adult worker be required or allowed to work in any week?
(a) 24 hours (b) 36 hours
(c) 48 hours (d) 72 hours

4 According to Factories Act, 1948, how many hours should an adult worker be required or allowed to work in a day?
(a) 10 hours (b) 11 hours
(c) 9 hours (d) 12 hours

5 According to Factories Act, 1948, how many hours should an adult worker be allowed to work continuously in a day?
(a) 4 Hours (b) 7 Hours
(c) 9 hours (d) 5 Hours

6 According to Factories Act, 1948, a welfare officer should be appointed for how many workers?
(a) 400 (b) 700
(c) 800 (d) 500

7 According to Factories Act, 1948, what are the working hours of women?
(a) 8 A.M. and 8 P.M. (b) 8 A.M. and 7 P.M.
(c) 7 A.M. and 7 P.M. (d) 6 A.M. and 7 P.M.

8 According to Factories Act, 1948, what is the amount of overtime that can be paid to the workers?
(a) Six times of ordinary rate of wages
(b) Five times of ordinary rate of wages
(c) Thrice of ordinary rate of wages
(d) Twice of ordinary rate of wages

9 According to the Factories Act, 1948, what is the minimum age to work in a factory?
(a) 14 (b) 13
(c) 12 (d) 15

10 According to the Factories Act, 1948, what are the working hours of female children?
(a) 7 A.M. and 7 P.M.
(b) 9 A.M. and 9 P.M.
(c) 10 A.M. and 10 P.M.
(d) 8 A.M. and 7 P.M.

11 Every worker who has worked for a period of how many days or more in a factory during a calendar year shall be allowed during the subsequent calendar year, leave with wages?
(a) 240 (b) 220
(c) 210 (d) 200

12 Which section of Mines Act, 1952 defines mines?
(a) 2(i) (b) 2(j)
(c) 2(b) (d) 2(a)

13 Which section of Mines Act, 1952 defines minerals?
(a) 2(i) (b) 2(jj)
(c) 2(b) (d) 2(a)

14 According to Mines Act, 1952, what are the maximum days for which a person can work in a mine?
(a) Five (b) Four
(c) Six (d) Seven

15 According to the Mines Act, 1952, which of the following is incorrect?
(a) No person shall be allowed to work in a mine who has already been working in any other mine within the preceding twelve hours
(b) No adult employed above ground in a mine shall be required or allowed to work for more than forty-eight hours in any week
(c) No adult employed above ground in a mine shall be required or allowed to work for more than ten hours in any day
(d) A person will not work for more than five hours continuously before he has had an interval for rest of atleast half an hour

16 According to Mines Act, 1952, a person is eligible for leave with wages only after working for how many months continuously?
(a) 22 (b) 12
(c) 48 (d) 24

17 According to Mines Act, 1952, no person shall be allowed to work in a mine who has already been working in any other mine within the preceding how many hours?
(a) 24 (b) 12
(c) 48 (d) 32

18 According to Mines Act, 1952, certificate of fitness shall be valid for how many months?
(a) 12 (b) 24
(c) 48 (d) 22

19 According to Mines Act, 1952, what is the minimum time for which a person can take rest?
(a) 30 minutes (b) 40 minutes
(c) 90 minutes (d) 120 minutes

20 According to Mines Act, 1952, ambulances and stretchers need to be readily available in a mine with how many people?
(a) 900 (b) 800
(c) 1000 (d) 500

21 According to Mines Act, 1952, what will be the wages for the leave allowed to a person employed in a mine who is paid monthly or weekly?
(a) Rate thrice of his normal daily wages
(b) Rate half to his normal daily wages
(c) Rate twice to his normal daily wages
(d) Rate equal to normal daily wages

22 According to Mines Act, 1952, what will be the fine for any falsification of records?
(a) ₹ 1,000 (b) ₹ 2,000
(c) ₹ 3,000 (d) ₹ 500

23 Which section of the Inter-state Workman Act, 1979 defines inter-state workman?
(a) 2(a) (b) 2(b)
(c) 2(d) (d) 2(e)

24 The Inter-state Workman Act, 1979, is applicable in establishment in which there should be a minimum of how many inter-state employees?
(a) 5 (b) 4
(c) 7 (d) 9

25 According to Inter-state Workman Act, 1979, what is the displacement allowance to be paid to the labourer?
(a) 20% of the monthly wages payable to him
(b) 50% of the monthly wages payable to him
(c) 30% of the monthly wages payable to him
(d) 40% of the monthly wages payable to him

26 According to the Inter-state Workman Act, 1979, the contractor needs to furnish the details of inter-state workman in how many days of recruitment?
(a) 21 (b) 12
(c) 30 (d) 15

27 Which section of the Inter-state Workman Act, 1979, defines a contractor?
(a) 2(a) (b) 2(b)
(c) 2(d) (d) 2(e)

28 Which section of the Inter-state Workman Act, 1979, defines a controlled industry?
(a) 2(a) (b) 2(b)
(c) 2(d) (d) 2(c)

29 When did the Inter-state Migrant Workmen (regulation of employment and conditions of service) rules come into force?
(a) 2nd October, 1980
(b) 3rd October, 1989
(c) 7th October, 1980
(d) 10th October, 1989

30 According to the Inter-state Migrant Workman Rules, the certificate of registration will be issued in which form?
(a) Form I (b) Form III
(c) Form IV (d) Form II

31 According to the Inter-state Migrant Workman Rules, the application by a contractor for the grant of a licence for recruiting a person must be issued in which form?
(a) Form I (b) Form III
(c) Form IV (d) Form II

32 According to the Inter-state Migrant Workman Rules, the application by a contractor for the grant of a licence for employing a person must be issued in which form?
(a) Form I (b) Form III
(c) Form V (d) Form II

33 According to the Inter-state Migrant Workman Rules, the application for grant of a licence should be submitted in which form?
(a) Form I (b) Form III
(c) Form IV (d) Form VII

34 According to Inter-state Migrant Workman Rules, 1980 what are the timings under which the female migrant worker will be allowed to work?
(a) 9 A.M. to 9 P.M. (b) 8 A.M. to 8 P.M.
(c) 7 A.M. to 7 P.M. (d) 6 A.M. to 7 P.M.

35 According to Inter-state Migrant Workman Rules, 1980, a licence renewed under rule 15 shall remain in force for a further period of how many months from the date of the order of renewal?
(a) 48 (b) 12
(c) 24 (d) 36

36 According to Inter-state Migrant Workman Rules, 1980, the contractor needs to furnish to the specified authorities the particulars regarding recruiting and employment of migrant workmen in which form?
(a) Form II (b) Form III
(c) Form IV (d) Form X

37 According to Inter-state Migrant Workman Rules, 1980, what is the maximum wage period?
(a) 2 months (b) 1 month
(c) 3 months (d) 4 months

38 According to Inter-state Migrant Workman Rules, 1980, in an establishment by a contractor where less than 1000 workmen are employed the wages need to be paid by when?
(a) Before seventh of every month
(b) Before ninth of every month
(c) Before tenth of every month
(d) Before third of every month

39 **According to Inter-state Migrant Workman Rules, 1980 the contractor needs to provide one first-aid box for how many workers?**

(a) 120 (b) 110
(c) 190 (d) 150

40 **According to Inter-state Workman Rules, 1980, the contractor shall provide to every migrant workman where the temperature falls below 20 degree centigrade, protective clothing consisting of one woollen coat and one woollen trousers how many times?**

(a) Thrice in three years (b) Twice in one year
(c) Twice in two years (d) Once in two years

41 **According to Inter-state Workman Rules, 1980, a creche needs to be provided in every establishment where how many female workers are working?**

(a) 20 (b) 30
(c) 40 (d) 50

42 **According to the Inter-state Workman Rules, 1980 a canteen needs to be provided for a minimum of how many workers?**

(a) 200 (b) 300
(c) 400 (d) 100

43 **The Inter-state Workman Rules, 1980 were made by the Central Government by the power conferred to it under which section of the Inter-state Migrant Workmen (regulation of employment and conditions of service) Act, 1979?**

(a) 9 (b) 18
(c) 35 (d) 22

44 **According to the Inter-state Workman Rules, 1980, in case of an accident the contractor needs to inform the specified authorities and next of the kins of the migrant workers within how many hours?**

(a) 12 (b) 10 (c) 24 (d) 18

45 **The Contract Labour (regulation and abolition) Act, 1970 will be applicable in every establishment where how many minimum number of workers are employed as contract labour?**

(a) 30 (b) 40
(c) 20 (d) 50

46 **Which section of Contract Labour (regulation and abolition) Act, 1970 defines 'contract labour'?**

(a) 2(a) (b) 2(b)
(c) 2(c) (d) 2(d)

47 **Who is the ex-officio in the Central Advisory Board?**

(a) Chief Registering Officer
(b) Chief Labour Licensing Officer
(c) Labour Inspector
(d) Chief Labour Commissioner

48 **According to the Contract Labour (regulation and abolition) Act, 1970, what is the penalty if anyone obstructs an inspector in the discharge of his duties?**

(a) ₹ 1,000 (b) ₹ 500
(c) ₹ 200 (d) ₹ 300

49 **According to the Contract Labour (regulation and abolition) Act, 1970, what is the penalty if anyone willfully refuses to produce on the demand of an Inspector any register or other document?**

(a) ₹ 1,000 (b) ₹ 500
(c) ₹ 200 (d) ₹ 300

50 **According to the Contract Labour (regulation and abolition) Act, 1970, what is the penalty if anyone contravenes any provision of this act?**

(a) ₹ 1,000 (b) ₹ 500
(c) ₹ 200 (d) ₹ 300

51 **Which section of the Contract Labour (regulation and abolition) Act, 1970 defines a contractor?**

(a) 2(a) (b) 2(b)
(c) 2 (c) (d) 2(d)

52 **Which section of Contract Labour (regulation and abolition) Act, 1970 defines establishment?**

(a) 2(a) (b) 2(e) (c) 2(c) (d) 2(d)

53 **The Building and other Construction Workers (regulation of employment and conditions of service) Act, 1996 is applicable to an establishment with how many building workers?**

(a) 11 (b) 12
(c) 14 (d) 10

54 **Which section of Building and other Construction Workers (regulation of employment and conditions of service) Act, 1996 defines building?**

(a) 2(a) (b) 2(d)
(c) 2(c) (d) 2(e)

55 **Which section of Building and other Construction Workers (regulation of employment and conditions of service) Act, 1996 defines building worker?**

(a) 2(a) (b) 2(d) (c) 2(c) (d) 2 (e)

56 **According to the Building and other Construction Workers (regulation of employment and conditions of service) Act, 1996 every employer needs to make an application within a period of how many days from commencement to get the establishment registered?**

(a) 60 (b) 50 (c) 20 (d) 30

57 **According to the Building and other Construction Workers (regulation of employment and conditions of service) Act, 1996, what is the minimum age of a building worker to be registered as a beneficiary under this act?**

(a) 18 (b) 21 (c) 22 (d) 24

58 According to the Building and other Construction Workers (regulation of employment and conditions of service) Act, 1996, what is the minimum days a building worker must have had worked to be registered as a beneficiary under this act?
(a) 90 (b) 30 (c) 120 (d) 30

59 According to the Building and other Construction Workers (regulation of employment and conditions of service) Act, 1996 how many members constitute the State Advisory Board?
(a) 11 (b) 12
(c) 15 (d) 10

60 According to the Building and other Construction Workers (regulation of employment and conditions of service) Act, 1996, a worker ceases to be a beneficiary under this act after he attains what age?
(a) 90 (b) 50 (c) 60 (d) 70

61 According to the Building and other Construction Workers (regulation of employment and conditions of service) Act, 1996, a creche needs to be built where a minimum of how many female employees are employed?
(a) 20 (b) 30
(c) 40 (d) 50

62 According to the Building and other Construction Workers (regulation of employment and conditions of service) Act, 1996, an employer needs to maintain canteen for a minimum number of how many employees?
(a) 600 (b) 250
(c) 200 (d) 300

63 According to the Building and other Construction Workers (regulation of employment and conditions of service) Act, 1996, what is the minimum age of a building worker to be registered as a beneficiary under this act?
(a) 18 (b) 21
(c) 22 (d) 24

64 According to the Building and other Construction Workers (regulation of employment and conditions of service) Act, 1996, what should be the minimum number of employees in an establishment for which an employer needs to constitute a safety committee?
(a) 900 (b) 300 (c) 120 (d) 500

65 According to the Building and other Construction Workers (regulation of employment and conditions of service) Act, 1996, in case of an accident, the injured person should not work for how many hours?
(a) 24 hours (b) 48 hours
(c) 72 hours (d) 36 hours

66 According to the Building and other Construction Workers (regulation of employment and conditions of service) Act, 1996, what is the fine in case there is contravention of safety measures?
(a) ₹ 2,000 (b) ₹ 4,000
(c) ₹ 7,000 (d) ₹ 9,000

67 According to the Building and other Construction Workers (regulation of employment and conditions of service) Act, 1996, what is the fine if an employer fails to give notice of the commencement of the building or other construction work?
(a) ₹ 2,000 (b) ₹ 4,000
(c) ₹ 7,000 (d) ₹ 9,000

68 According to the Child Labour (Prohibition and Regulation) Act, 1986 who is a child?
(a) A person who has not completed his fourteenth year of age
(b) A person who has not completed his fifteenth year of age
(c) A person who has not completed his eighteenth year of age
(d) A person who has not completed his twelfth year of age

69 Which section of the Child Labour (prohibition and regulation) Act, 1986 defines 'child'?
(a) 2(i) (b) 2(ii)
(c) 2(iii) (d) 2(iv)

70 Which section of the Child Labour (prohibition and regulation) Act, 1986 defines 'family'?
(a) 2(i) (b) 2(ii)
(c) 2(iii) (d) 2(v)

71 According to the Child Labour (prohibition and regulation) Act, 1986, how many months notice need to be given before bringing out any amendment to the schedules dealing with any occupation or process mentioned in the schedules?
(a) 6 months (b) 2 months
(c) 10 months (d) 3 months

72 According to the Child Labour (prohibition and regulation) Act, 1986, how many members will be present in the Child Labour Technical Advisory Committee?
(a) 10 (b) 12
(c) 14 (d) 18

73 According to the Child Labour (prohibition and regulation) Act, 1986, what is the maximum continuous duration for which a child will work?
(a) 9 hours (b) 3 hours
(c) 2 hours (d) 5 hours

74 According to the Child Labour (prohibition and regulation) Act, 1986, what is the maximum duration for which a child will work in a day?
(a) 10 hours (b) 7 hours
(c) 6 hours (d) 8 hours

75 According to the Child Labour (prohibition and regulation) Act, 1986, what is the time duration for which a child will be permitted to work?

(a) 8 P.M. and 8 A.M. (b) 7 P.M. and 8 A.M.
(c) 9 P.M. and 9 A.M. (d) 7 P.M. and 7 A.M.

76 According to the Child Labour (prohibition and regulation) Act, 1986, how many holidays will be allowed to a child?

(a) 1 in a week
(b) 2 in a week
(c) 2 in a fortnight
(d) 3 in two weeks

77 According to the Child Labour (prohibition and regulation) Act, 1986, what is the rest interval a child is allowed to take?

(a) 1 hour (b) 30 minutes
(c) 40 minutes (d) 1 hour 30 minutes

78 If a worker works in a factory works for more than .... in any day, he will be eligible for overtime.

(a) 10 (b) 9
(c) 7 (d) 8

79 The period of work of all children employed in a factory shall be limited to two shifts which shall not overlap or spread over more than .... hours each.

(a) 9 (b) 8
(c) 3 (d) 5

80 According to the Factories Act, 1948, night includes a period of atleast .... consecutive hours which shall include the interval between 10 P.M. and 6 A.M.

(a) ten (b) twelve
(c) thirteen (d) fourteen

81 According to the Factories Act, 1948, the fitness certificate provided to an adolescent shall be valid only for a period of .... months.

(a) 10 (b) 11 (c) 12 (d) 13

82 If a worker works on a shift which extends beyond midnight, a holiday for a whole day shall mean in his case a period of .... consecutive hours beginning when his shift ends.

(a) 12 (b) 24
(c) 48 (d) 72

83 The certificate of fitness issued to an adolescent will fall under Section .... of the Factories Act, 1948.

(a) 30 (b) 40
(c) 20 (d) 69

84 No child shall be employed or permitted to work, in any factory for more than .... in any day and during the night.

(a) 7 hours 30 minutes (b) 4 hours 30 minutes
(c) 2 hours 30 minutes (d) 3 hours 30 minutes

85 No adult employed above ground in a mine shall be required or allowed to work for more than .... hours in any week.

(a) 40 (b) 48
(c) 32 (d) 36

86 No adult employed below ground in a mine shall be allowed to work for more than .... hours in any day.

(a) 9 (b) 8 (c) 3 (d) 5

87 No person shall be allowed to work in a mine who has already been working in any other mine within the preceding .... hours.

(a) ten (b) twelve
(c) thirteen (d) fourteen

88 No adolescent who has not been granted a medical certificate certifying that he is fit for work as an adult shall be employed above ground in any open cast workings in a mine for more than .... in any day.

(a) 3 hours 30 minutes (b) 7 hours 30 minutes
(c) 4 hours 30 minutes (d) 3 hours 30 minutes

89 The wages of every migrant workman in an establishment by a contractor where more than 1000 workmen are employed has to be paid before .... every month.

(a) seventh (b) tenth
(c) twelfth (d) eleventh

90 The migrant worker will be entitled to the .... number of holidays, hours of as the regular workers.

(a) same (b) twice
(c) half (d) thrice

91 In case, the temperature falls below 5 degree centigrade a woollen overcoat shall also be provided to the migrant workmen ....

(a) twice in two years (b) once in two years
(c) once in three years (d) thrice in three years

92 In every establishment where 20 or more workmen are employed as migrant workmen and in which employment of migrant workmen is likely to continue for three months or more, there should be .... rooms to be used as creche for children under the age of six years.

(a) 2 (b) 3 (c) 4 (d) 7

93 Consider the following for the Factories Act, 1948. Which of the following is correct?

1. The Central Government has the power to appoint qualified medical practitioners to be certifying surgeons.
2. Floor of every workman needs to be cleaned at least once in every week by washing, using disinfectant.

3. All doors and window frames and other wooden or metallic framework and shutters shall be kept painted or varnished and the painting or varnishing shall be carried out atleast once in every period of five years.

(a) Both 1 and 2 (b) Both 2 and 3
(c) Both 1 and 3 (d) All of the above

94 Which of the following is correct in the context of Factories Act, 1948?

1. The factories that have more than 150 workers should have provisions for cooling drinking water during hot weather conditions.
2. Any person who shall not spit in the spittoons shall be punishable with fine not exceeding five rupees.
3. No woman or child shall be employed in any part of a factory for pressing cotton in which a cotton-opener is at work.
4. Safety Officers need to be appointed in every factory where more than 1000 workers are working.

(a) 2, 3 and 4 (b) Both 2 and 3
(c) Both 1 and 3 (d) 1, 2 and 3

95 Which of the following is correct for the definition of 'Factory' as per the Factories Act, 1948?

1. It includes any premises whereon ten or more workers are working.
2. Manufacturing process is being carried on with the aid of power.
3. It includes any premises where 20 or more workers are working, or were working on any day of the preceding twelve months.

(a) Both 1 and 2 (b) Both 2 and 3
(c) Both 1 and 3 (d) All of the above

96 Which of the following is incorrect in the context of Factories Act, 1948?

1. No portable electric light or any other electric appliance of voltage exceeding 22 volts shall be permitted for use inside any chamber.
2. The State Government for grant of permission for the initial location of a factory involving a hazardous process or for the expansion of any such factory has the power to appoint a Site Appraisal Committee consisting.
3. The Site Appraisal Committee shall examine an application for the establishment of a factory involving hazardous process and make its recommendation to the State Government within a period of ninety days of the receipt of such applications in the prescribed form.

(a) Only 1 (b) Only 2
(c) Only 3 (d) Both 2 and 3

97 Which of the following is correct in the context of Factories Act, 1948?

1. Safety Committee consists of equal number of representatives of workers and management.
2. Every factory wherein more than 500 workers are ordinarily employed needs to maintain an ambulance room.
3. A worker is eligible for overtime if he work for more than 48 hours in any week.
4. A child who has completed his fourteenth year or an adolescent shall not be required or allowed to work in any factory unless he has a certificate of fitness is granted in the custody of the manager of the factory.

(a) 1, 2, 3 and 4 (b) 2, 3 and 4
(c) Both 1 and 3 (d) 1, 2 and 3

98 Which of the following is included in the definition of mines?

1. Every shaft in the course of being sunk.
2. Every level and inclined plane in the course of being driven.
3. All shafts, levels, planes, machinery, works, tramways and sidings, whether above or below ground, in or adjacent to, and belonging to the mine.

(a) Only 1 (b) Both 2 and 3
(c) Both 1 and 3 (d) All of the above

99 Consider the following for the definition of 'minerals' under Mines Act, 1952. Which of the following is correct?

1. It means those substances which can be obtained from the earth by means of digging, dredging, drilling, mining or through other operations.
2. It include natural gas and petroleum.
3. It is defined under Section 2(jj).

(a) Both 1 and 2 (b) Both 2 and 3
(c) Both 1 and 3 (d) All of the above

100 Which of the following is correct in context of Mines Act, 1952?

1. The Central Government has the power to appoint any medical practitioner as a certifying surgeon.
2. The State Government has the power to constitute mining board for any group or class of mines.
3. In every mine, where more than five hundred persons are employed, ambulances and stretchers need to be readily available.

(a) Both 1 and 2 (b) Both 2 and 3
(c) Both 1 and 3 (d) All of the above

101 Consider the following for the definition of workman under Inter-state Workmen Regulation Act, 1979. Which of the following is correct?

1. It includes a person who is employed mainly in a managerial or administration capacity.
2. The person may be hired for skilled, semi-skilled or unskilled, manual, supervisory, technical or clerical work.
3. He draws wages exceeding five hundred rupees per mensem or exercises.

(a) Both 1 and 2 (b) Only 2
(c) Both 1 and 3 (d) All of the above

102 Consider the following for the definition of principal employer under Inter-state Workmen Regulation Act, 1979.

1. It is the head of that office or department in any department of the government.
2. In a factory, the owner or occupier of the factory and where a person has been named as the manager of the factory under the Factories Act, 1948.
3. In a mine, the owner or agent of the mine and where a person has been named as the manager of the mine.
4. In any other establishment, any person responsible for the supervision and control of the establishment.

(a) 1, 2, 3 and 4 (b) Both 2 and 3
(c) Both 1 and 3 (d) 1, 2 and 3

103 Which of the following is correct in context of Inter-state Workmen Regulation Act, 1979?

1. The State Government will appoint licensing and Registering Officers.
2. The principal employer needs to make an application to the Registering Officer in the prescribed form and manner to get the registration of employment done.
3. The Licensing Officer will grant the license after through investigations and this license will be valid for a given time frame and will have to be renewed timely.

(a) Both 1 and 2
(b) Both 2 and 3
(c) Both 1 and 3
(d) All of the above

104 Which of the following is correct in context of Inter-state Workmen Regulation Act, 1979?

1. An inter-state migrant workman shall be paid twice than the wages fixed under the Minimum Wages Act, 1948.
2. Wages payable to an inter-state migrant workman/under this section shall be paid in 'cash' only.
3. The contractor is bound to pay every inter-state migrant workman at the time of recruitment, a displacement allowance equal to 50% of the monthly wages payable to him or ninety-five rupees.

(a) Only 2 (b) Only 3
(c) Both 1 and 3 (d) All of the above

105 Consider the following for the defmition of building worker under Building and other Construction Workers Act, 1996. Which of the following is incorrect?

1. A person who is employed in a supervisory capacity and draws wages exceeding one thousand six hundred rupees per mensem.
2. A person who is employed mainly in a managerial or administrative capacity.
3. A person who is employed to do any skilled, semi-skilled or unskilled, manual, supervisory, technical or clerical work.

(a) Both 1 and 2 (b) Only 2
(c) Both 1 and 3 (d) All of the above

106 According to the Child Labour Prohibition Act, in which of the following professions a child can be employed or permitted to work in any of the occupations?

1. Transport of passengers, goods or mails by railway.
2. Clearing of an ash pit or building operation in the railway premises.
3. A port authority within the limits of any port.

(a) Both 1 and 2
(b) Only 2
(c) Both 1 and 3
(d) All of the above

107 Which of the following statements are true/false for the Factories Act, 1948?

(i) It is applicable where twenty or more workers are working, or were working on any day of the preceding twelve months.
(ii) Adolescent is a person who completed 18 years of age.
(iii) The Central Government has the power to appoint qualified medical practitioners to be certifying surgeons.
(iv) Child is a person who has not completed 15 years of age.

(a) (i), (iv) are true and (ii), (iii) are false
(b) (i), (iii) are true and (ii), (iv) are false
(c) (ii), (iv) are true and (i), (iii) are false
(d) (iii), (iv) are true and (ii), (i) are false

108 Which of the following statements are true/false?

(i) Every factory where a hazardous process takes place shall set up a Safety Committee consisting of only representatives of workers.

(ii) The factories that have more than 250 workers should have provisions for cooling drinking water during hot weather conditions.

(iii) The factories need to set up crèches where more than 10 women are employed.

(iv) Any person who shall not spit in the spittoons shall be punishable with fine not exceeding five rupees.

(a) (i), (iv) are true and (ii), (iii) are false
(b) (i), (iii) are true and (ii), (iv) are false
(c) (ii), (iv) are true and (i), (iii) are false
(d) (iii), (iv) are true and (ii), (i) are false

109 Which of the following statements are true/false?

(i) No adult worker should be required or allowed to work in a factory for more than 48 hours in any week.

(ii) A worker will be entitled to an overtime if he works for more than 42 hours in any week.

(iii) No adult worker shall be required or allowed to work in a factory for more than nine hours in any day.

(iv) The woman shall work in the factory between the hours of 7 A.M. and 8 P.M.

(a) (i), (iv) are true and (ii), (iii) are false
(b) (i), (iii) are true and (ii), (iv) are false
(c) (ii), (iv) are true and (i), (iii) are false
(d) (iii), (iv) are true and (ii), (i) are false

110 Which of the following statements are true/false?

(i) No child shall be employed or permitted to work, in any factory for more than four and a half hours in any day and during the night.

(ii) A child who has completed his eighteenth year or an adolescent shall not be required or allowed to work in any factory unless he has a certificate of fitness is granted in the custody of the manager of the factory.

(iii) The period of work of all children employed in a factory shall be limited to two shifts which shall not overlap or spread over more than five hours each.

(iv) No female child shall be required or allowed to work in any factory except between 8 A.M. and 7 P.M.

(a) (i) , (iii), (iv) are true and (ii) is false
(b) (i), (iii) are true and (ii), (iv) are false
(c) (ii), (iv) are true and (i), (iii) are false
(d) (iii), (iv) are true and (ii), (i) are false

111 Which of the following statements are true/false?

(i) Every worker who has worked for a period of 240 days or more in a factory during a calendar year shall be allowed during the subsequent calendar year, leave with wages.

(ii) A worker who has been allowed leave for not less than four days, in the case of an adult, and five days, in the case of a child shall, before his leave begins, be paid the wages due for the period of the leave allowed.

(iii) If a worker works in a factory works for more than nine hours in any day or for more than 40 hours in any week, he shall, in respect of overtime work, be entitled to wages at the rate of twice his ordinary rate of wages.

(iv) The periods of work of an adult worker in a factory shall be so arranged that inclusive of his intervals for rest, they shall not spreadover more than eleven and a half hours in any day.

(a) (i), (iv) are true and (ii), (iii) are false
(b) (i), (ii) are true and (iii), (iv) are false
(c) (ii), (iv) are true and (i), (iii) are false
(d) (iii), (iv) are true and (ii), (i) are false

112 Which of the following statements are true/false?

(i) No person shall be allowed to work in a mine on more than six days in any one week.

(ii) No adult employed above ground in a mine shall be required or allowed to work for more than nine hours in any day.

(iii) A person will not work for more than five hours continuously before he has had an interval for rest of atleast half an hour.

(iv) No adult employed below ground in a mine shall be allowed to work for more than eight hours in any day.

(a) (i), (ii), (iii) and (iv) are true
(b) (i), (iii) are true and (ii), (iv) are false
(c) (ii), (iv) are true and (i), (iii) are false
(d) (iii), (iv) are true and (ii), (i) are false

113 Which of the following statements are true/false?

(i) The Inter-state Migrant Workmen Act, 1979 is applicable in any establishment in which five or more inter-state migrant workmen are employed.

(ii) In exercise of the powers conferred by section 35 of the Inter-state Migrant Workmen (Regulation of Employment and Conditions of Service) Act, 1979, the Central Government made the Inter-State Migrant Workmen (Regulation of Employment and Conditions of Service) rules.

(iii) An inter-state migrant workman shall be equal to the wages fixed under the Minimum Wages Act, 1948.

(iv) The principal officer issue a certificate of registration in Form III after the registration of establishment.

(a) (i), (ii) are true and (iii), (iv) are false
(b) (i), (iii) are true and (ii), (iv) are false
(c) (ii), (iv) are true and (i), (iii) are false
(d) (iii), (iv) are true and (ii), (i) are false

114 Which of the following statements are true/false?

(i) Every contractor needs to furnish to the specified authorities the particulars regarding recruiting and employment of migrant workmen in Form X.

(ii) The wages of every migrant workman in an establishment by a contractor where less than 1000 workmen are employed has to be paid before seventh and in other cases before tenth every month.

(iii) No wage period shall extend one month.

(iv) If the employment of any migrant workman is terminated by or on behalf of the contractor, the wages earned by the migrant workman shall be paid before the expiry the second working day from the day on which his employment is terminated.

(a) (i), (iii) are true and (ii), (iv) are false
(b) (i), (ii), (iii) and (iv) are true
(c) (ii), (iv) are true and (i), (iii) are false
(d) (iii), (iv) are true and (ii), (i) are false

115 Which of the following statements are true/ false?

(i) In every establishment where 40 or more workmen are employed as migrant workmen and in which employment of migrant workmen is likely to continue for three months or more, there should be two rooms to be used as crèche for children under the age of six years.
(ii) Every contractor needs to provide atleast one first-aid box for one hundred and fifty workmen.
(iii) The migrant worker will be entitled to the lesser number of holidays, hours of work including extra wages for overtime work done and other conditions of service as the regular workers.
(iv) There should be atleast one latrine for every 25 females and 25 males.

(a) (i), (ii) are true and (iii), (iv) are false
(b) (i), (iii) are true and (ii), (iv) are false
(c) (ii), (iv) are true and (i), (iii) are false
(d) (iii), (iv) are true and (ii), (i) are false

116 Which of the following statements are true/ false for the Contract Labour Act, 1970?

(i) The Chief Labour Commissioner is the ex-officio of the Central Advisory Board.
(ii) A canteen needs to be provided wherein contract labour numbering 100 or more is ordinarily employed.
(iii) Workman is defined under Section 2(i) of the Contract Labour Act, 1970.
(iv) Wages are defined under the clause (vi) of section 2 of the Payment of Wages Act, 1936.

(a) (i), (ii), (iii) and (iv) are true
(b) (i), (iii) are true and (ii), (iv) are false
(c) (ii), (iv) are true and (i), (iii) are false
(d) (iii), (iv) are true and (ii), (i) are false

117 Which of the following statements are true/ false?

(i) Ordinary rate of wages include bonus.
(ii) The central government has the power to constitute Central Building and Other Construction Workers' Advisory Committee.
(iii) Every state government will constitute a State welfare board and should not exceed ten members in its composition.
(iv) Every employer needs to make an application to the Registering Officer (RO) within a period of sixty days from commencement to get the establishment registered.

(a) (i), (ii), (iii) and (iv) are true
(b) (i), (iii) are true and (ii), (iv) are false
(c) (ii), (iv) are true and (i), (iii) are false
(d) (iii), (iv) are true and (ii), (i) are false

118 Which of the following statements are true/ false?

(i) No child will work for more than four hours.
(ii) No child will work more than seven hours in a day including the rest interval.
(iii) No child will be permitted or required to work between 7 P.M. and 8 A.M.
(iv) No child will be required or permitted to work overtime.

(a) (i), (ii), (iii) and (iv) are true
(b) (i), (iii) are true and (ii), (iv) are false
(c) (ii), (iv) are true and (i), (iii) are false
(d) (iii), (iv) are true and (ii), (i) are false

119 Which of the following statements are true/ false?

(i) Day is a period of twenty fours beginning from midnight.
(ii) A child who has completed his fourteenth year or an adolescent shall not be required or allowed to work in any factory unless he has a certificate of fitness is granted in the custody of the manager of the factory.
(iii) All doors and window frames and other wooden or metallic framework and shutters of a factory should be kept painted or varnished and the painting or varnishing shall be carried out atleast once in every period of four years.
(iv) The state government has the power to direct the Director- General of Factory Advice Service and Labour Institutes or any institution specialised in matters relating to standards of safety in hazardous processes.

(a) (i), (ii), (iii) and (iv) are true
(b) (i), (iii) are true and (ii), (iv) are false
(c) (i), (ii) are true and (iii), (iv) are false
(d) (iii), (iv) are true and (ii), (i) are false

120 Which of the following statements are true/ false?

(i) The factory needs to maintain a canteen wherein more than two hundred and fifty workers are ordinarily employed.
(ii) The Central government must prescribe standards of adequate and suitable facilities for washing.
(iii) The factory wherein 500 or more workers are ordinarily employed the occupier shall employ in the factory such number of welfare officers as may be prescribed.
(iv) The factories need to maintain adequate and suitable shelters or rest rooms and a suitable lunch room, with provision for drinking water where more than 100 workers are ordinarily employed.

(a) (i), (ii), (iii) and (iv) are true
(b) (i), (iii) are true and (ii), (iv) are false
(c) (ii), (iv) are true and (i), (iii) are false
(d) (iii), (iv) are true and (ii), (i) are false.

121 Which of the following statements are true/ false?

(i) No person shall be allowed to work in a mine who has already been working in any other mine within the preceding ten hours.
(ii) The Central government has the power to constitute mining board for any group or class of mines, who enjoy the power equivalent to the certifying inspector.
(iii) The workers will be granted a certificate of fitness from certifying surgeon and it shall be valid only for a period of twenty four months.

(iv) In every mine where more than five hundred persons are employed, ambulances and stretchers need to be readily available.

(a) (i), (ii), (iii) and (iv) are true
(b) (i), (iii) are true and (ii), (iv) are false
(c) (ii), (iv) are true and (i), (iii) are false
(d) (iii), (iv) are true and (ii), (i) are false

Directions (Q. Nos. 122-126) *In the following questions, the Assertion (A) and Reason (R) have been put forward. Read both the statements carefully and choose the correct alternative from the following.*

(a) Both (A) and (R) are correct and (R) is the correct explanation of (A)
(b) Both (A) and (R) are correct, but (R) is not the correct explanation of (A)
(c) (A) is correct, but (R) is incorrect
(d) (A) is incorrect, but (R) is correct

122 Assertion (A) **No stationary internal combustion engine should be operated in the factory.**

Reason (R) **The factory needs to take effective measures to prevent the inhalation of dust and fumes that are injurious and offensive to health.**

123 Assertion (A) **The factory needs to provide suitable goggles to its employees.**

Reason (R) **The manufacturing processes can be harmful to eyes.**

124 Assertion (A) **Safety Committee must consist of equal number of representatives of workers and management.**

Reason (R) **These are required in maintaining proper safety and health at work and to review periodically the measures taken in that behalf.**

125 Assertion (A) **No adolescent who has not been granted a medical certificate certifying that he is fit for work as an adult shall be employed or permitted to be employed above ground in mine.**

Reason (R) **An adolescent, who has been granted a certificate of fitness to work in a mine as an adult shall be deemed to be an adult for the purposes of this Act.**

126 Assertion (A) **Atleast two members of the Safety Welfare board shall be women.**

Reason (R) **This promotes equality at work place and provide a voice to the women.**

127 Match the following with their correct sections of the Factories Act, 1948.

List I		List II
A. Young Person	1.	2(k)
B. Week	2.	2(d)
C. Manufacturing Process	3.	2(f)
D. Child	4.	2(c)

	A	B	C	D		A	B	C	D
(a)	1	3	4	2	(b)	2	3	1	4
(c)	3	1	4	2	(d)	1	3	2	4

128 Match the following with their correct sections of the Mines Act, 1952.

List I		List II
A. Chief Inspector	1.	2(j)
B. Inspector	2.	2(d)
C. Mine	3.	2(i)
D. District Magistrate	4.	2(g)

	A	B	C	D		A	B	C	D
(a)	1	3	4	2	(b)	2	3	1	4
(c)	3	1	4	2	(d)	1	3	2	4

129 Match the following with their correct sections of the Contract Labour Act, 1972.

List I		List II
A. Controlled Industry	1.	2(e)
B. Principal Employer	2.	2(d)
C. Establishment	3.	2(f)
D. Control Labour	4.	2(b)

	A	B	C	D		A	B	C	D
(a)	1	3	4	2	(b)	2	3	1	4
(c)	3	1	4	2	(d)	1	3	2	4

Directions (Q. Nos. 130-134) *Read the passage and answer the questions that follow.*

Employment of children below 14 and 15 years in certain prohibited employments have been prohibited by various acts but there is no procedure laid down in any law for deciding in which employments, occupations or processes the employment of children should be banned. There is also no law to regulate the working conditions of children in most of the employments where they are not prohibited from working and are working under exploitative conditions. Accordingly it was decided to enact a comprehensive law on the subject. This Bill intended to

(i) ban the employment of children, i.e. those who have not completed their fourteenth year, in specified occupations and processes;
(ii) lay down a procedure to decide modifications to the schedule of banned occupations or processes;
(iii) regulate the conditions of work of children in employments where they are not, prohibited from working;
(iv) lay down enhanced penalties for employment of children in violation of the provisions of this act, and other acts which forbid the employment of children;
(v) to obtain uniformity in the definition of "child" in the related laws.

The Bill seeks to achieve the above objects.

The Child Labour (Prohibition and Regulation) Bill, 1986 was passed by both the Houses of Parliament received the assent of the President on 23rd December, 1986. It came on the Statute Book as The Child Labour (Prohibition and Regulation) Act, 1986. According to this act, the Central Government may, by notification in the Official Gazette, constitute an advisory committee to be called the Child Labour Technical Advisory Committee to advise the Central Government for the purpose of addition of occupations and processes to the Schedule. The Committee shall consist of a Chairman and such other members not exceeding ten, as may be appointed by the Central Government. It shall meet as often as it may consider necessary and shall have power to regulate its own procedure.

130 **Which of the following is incorrect on the basis of the above passage?**

(a) Children below the age of 14 years cannot work in specified occupations.
(b) Prior to Child Labour and Protection Act, 1986, there were no acts prohibiting the employment of children in different occupations.
(c) The Bill was passed by both houses and received President assent for the same.
(d) The act lays down a procedure to decide modifications to the schedule of banned occupations or processes.

131 **According to the Child Labour and Protection Act, 1986, what is the minimum age of a child who can work in any establishment?**

(a) Twelve (b) Fourteen
(c) Fifteen (d) Nineteen

132 **Which of the following has the power to appoint Child Labour Technical Advisory Committee?**

(a) Central Government (b) State Government
(c) Appropriate Government (d) None of these

133 **Why was there a need to enact the Child Labour and Protection Act, 1986?**

(a) Regulate the working conditions of children in most of the employments where they are not prohibited from working and are working under exploitative conditions.
(b) Lay down enhanced penalties for employment of children in violation of the provisions of this act, and other acts which forbid the employment of children.
(c) Obtain uniformity in the definition of 'child' in the related laws.
(d) All of the above

134 **Which of the following is correct for the Child Labour Technical Advisory Committee?**

(a) The appropriate government has the power to appoint the committee.
(b) The committee has no power to regulate its own procedure and it is regulated by the government.
(c) There are seven members in the committee.
(d) The recommendations of the committee are not binding on the Government.

PREVIOUS YEARS' QUESTIONS

2018

1 **Provisions relating to rehabilitation and re-employment schemes for employees are provided under which of the following legislations?**

(a) The Contract Labour (Regulation and Abolition) Act, 1970
(b) The Employees' Compensation Act, 1923
(c) The Inter-State Migrant Workmen (Regulation of Employment and Conditions of Service) Act, 1979
(d) The Employees' State Insurance Act, 1948

2 **Under the provisions of the Contract Labour (Regulation and Abolition) Act, 1970, what is the time period within which a case in to be filed for an offence punishable under the Act from the date on which the alleged commission of offence came to be knowledge of an inspector?**

(a) Six months (b) Four months
(c) Two months (d) Three months

3 **What is the maximum percent of its total expenses for the 'building and other construction workers' welfare fund during a financial year that shall be met towards salaries, allowances and other remuneration to its members and other employees?**

(a) Five percent
(b) Ten percent
(c) Six and one-fourth percent
(d) Eight percent

4 **What is the time period within which a complaint relating to an offence has to be made before a court from the date on which the alleged commission of the offence came to the knowledge of the inspector or authorised person concerned under the provisions of the Inter-State Migrant Workmen (Regulation of Employment and Conditions of Service) Act, 1979?**

(a) Two months (b) Six months
(c) One month (d) Three months

5 **Match the contents of different schedules given in List I with their respective schedules given in List II under the provisions of the Factories Act, 1948.**

List I	List II
A. Permissible levels of certain chemical substances in work environment	1. First Schedule
B. List of notifiable disease	2. Second Schedule
C. List of industries involving hazardous processes	3. Third Schedule

Codes

	A	B	C		A	B	C
(a)	2	3	1	(b)	3	1	2
(c)	1	2	3	(d)	2	1	3

6 **Match the following.**

List I (Labour Law Term)	List II (Meaning)
A. Puisne	1. Junior or subordinate
B. Ratio decidendi	2. The ground decision
C. Res judicata	3. A thing decided

Codes

	A	B	C		A	B	C
(a)	3	2	1	(b)	2	1	3
(c)	1	2	3	(d)	1	3	2

7 **The Building and Other Construction Workers (Regulation of Employment and Conditions of Service) Act, 1996 shall become applicable to an establishment engaged in building and construction work employing a minimum number of**

(a) ten building workers (b) thirty building workers
(c) twenty building workes (d) fifty building workers

8 **Under the provisions of the Bonded Labour System (Abolition) Act, 1976, what is the extent of punishment for a person, who compels any person to render any bonded labour?**

(a) Imprisonment for a maximum period of three years and also with fine which may extend to four thousand rupees
(b) Imprisonment for a maximum term of five years and also with fine which may extend to five thousand rupees
(c) Imprisonment for a maximum period of two years and also with fine which may extend to three thousand rupees
(d) Imprisonment for a maximum term of three years and also with fine which may extend to two thousand rupees

9 **An adolescent worker employed in a factory who has not attained the age of seventeen years but has been granted a certificate of fitness shall not be allowed to work between**

(a) 8 pm to 5 am (b) 8 pm to 6 am
(c) 7 pm to 6 am (d) 9 pm to 5 am

10 **Who among the following is not a contractor in relation to an establishment under the provisions of the Contract Labour (regulation and abolition) Act, 1970 ?**

(a) Any person who undertakes to produce a given result for the establishment through contract labour
(b) Any person who supplies contract labour for any work of the establishment
(c) Any person who supplies goods and articles of manufacture to such establishment
(d) Any person who works as a sub-contractor

11 **Which of the following statements relating to the Central Advisory Board under the provisions of the Contract Labour (regulation and abolition) Act, 1970 is not correct ?**

(a) Chairman to be appointed by the Central Government
(b) The Chief Labour Commissioner (Central) as an ex-officio member
(c) The Labour Commissioners of all the states as ex-officio member
(d) Such number of members, not exceeding seventeen but not less than eleven as the Central Government may nominate representing government, railways, coal industry, mining industry, the contractors, the workmen

12 **Match the authorities provided under List-I with the respective legislation under which they are covered as provided under List-II.**

List I	List II
A. The Controlling Authority	1. The Mines Act, 1952
B. The Controlling Authority	2. The Payment of Gratuity Act, 1972
C. Certifying Surgeon	3. The Contract Labour (Regulation and Abolition) Act, 1970
D. Licensing Officer	4. The Employees' Compensation Act, 1923

Codes

	A	B	C	D
(a)	2	4	1	3
(b)	1	2	3	4
(c)	3	1	4	2
(d)	4	3	2	1

13 **As per the provisions of the Building and other Construction Workers (regulation of employment and conditions of services) Act, 1996. Who among the following is the ex-officio member in the Central Advisory Committee ?**

(a) The Chief Inspector
(b) The Chief Labour Commissioner
(c) The Chairperson of the Expert Committee
(d) The Director General

14 The displacement allowance to be paid by the contractor to every inter-state migrant workman at the time of recruitment as per the Inter-state Migrant Workmen (regulation of employment and conditions of service) Act, 1979 shall be equal to

(a) fifty per cent of the monthly wages payable to him or seventy five rupees whichever is higher
(b) seventy-five per cent of the monthly wages payable to him or one hundred rupees whichever is higher
(c) sixty per cent of the monthly wages payable to him or seventy-five rupees whichever is higher
(d) fifty per cent of the monthly wages payable to him or one hundred rupees whichever is higher

15 Which one of the following is not a health provision under the Factories Act, 1948 ?

(a) Cleanliness
(b) Drinking water
(c) Latrines and Urinals
(d) First-aid appliances

2017

16 The Factories Act, 1948 came into force with effect from

(a) 1st April, 1949
(b) 1st January, 1948
(c) 1st August, 1948
(d) 1st October, 1948

17 Recently, the Government of India has enforced 'the ease of compliance to maintain registers under various Labour Laws Rules, 2017' for maintenance of combined registers provided under various labour legislations. Which of the following legislations is not covered under the above rules?

(a) Equal Remuneration Act, 1976
(b) Mines Act, 1952
(c) Factories Act, 1948
(d) Minimum Wages Act, 1948

18 Which one of the following does not find place under the Factories (Amendment) Bill 2016 initiated by the government?

(a) Enhance the limit of overtime hours to a maximum of one hundred hours per quarter under Section 64
(b) Enhance the limit of overtime hours to a maximum of one hundred twenty five hours per quarter in public interest under Section 65
(c) Empower the Central Government in addition to the State Governments to make exempting rules and exempting orders in respect of hours of work on overtime in a quarter
(d) Enhance the limit of total number of hours of work in a week including overtime to a maximum of seventy five hours

19 Which one of the following is not correct relating to working hours for children under the Factories Act, 1948?

(a) Maximum hours of work is four and half hours in any day
(b) No child shall be employed during night
(c) The hours of work including rest should be limited to a maximum spread over period of five and half hours
(d) No female child shall be allowed to work in any factory between 7 pm to 8 am

20 Which of the following facilities is to be provided by an employer employing two hundred fifty workers covered under the Factories Act, 1948?

(a) Ambulance room
(b) Canteen
(c) Shelter and rest rooms
(d) Cooling drinking water

21 An adolescent who has been given a certificate of fitness to work, has worked for 232 days during the calendar year 2016 in a factory. He has been on leave with wages for ten days during the year. How many days of leave with wages he shall be entitled to during the year 2017?

(a) Ten days (b) Twelve days
(c) Fifteen days (d) Nil

22 Under the power to make exempting orders of the Factories Act, 1948, the State Government can fix the maximum time of overtime work for any quarter is

(a) fifty hours
(b) seventy-five hours
(c) sixty hours
(d) ninety hours

23 As per the proceedings of the 46th Indian Labour Conference, 2015, the Government of India has proposed to enhance the overtime hours from the present limit of fifty hours, under the Factories Act, 1948 to

(a) seventy-five hours
(b) one hundred ten hours
(c) one hundred hours
(d) ninety hours

24 Which of the following for the first time made provisions for compulsory rest interval of half an hour each day ?

(a) Factories Act, 1911 (b) Factories Act, 1891
(c) Factories Act, 1934 (d) Factories Act, 1948

25 The maximum permissible threshold limits of exposure of chemical and toxic substances in manufacturing processes are provided under which schedule of the Factories Act, 1948 ?

(a) The First Schedule (b) The Second Schedule
(c) The Third Schedule (d) The Fourth Schedule

2016

26 There exist provisions of statutory welfare facilities under various labour legislations, match them.

List I (Provisions)	List II (Act)
A. Creche, if employing more than 30 women workers	1. The Mines Act, 1952
B. Creche, if employing 50 or more women workers	2. The Factories Act, 1948
C. Canteens, if employing 150 or more workers	3. The Motor Transport Workers Act, 1961
D. Canteens, if employing 100 or more workers	4. The Plantations Labour Act, 1951

Codes

	A	B	C	D		A	B	C	D
(a)	2	1	4	3	(b)	1	2	3	4
(c)	4	3	2	1	(d)	3	1	2	4

27 Match the provisions provided under List I with the respective legislations under which they are covered under List II.

List I	List II
A. Compulsory Insurance	1. The Payment of Gratuity Act, 1972
B. Scheduled Employment	2. The Industrial Disputes Act, 1947
C. Protected Workman	3. The Maternity Benefit Act, 1961
D. Medical Bonus	4. The Minimum Wages Act, 1948

Codes

	A	B	C	D		A	B	C	D
(a)	1	2	3	4	(b)	4	3	2	1
(b)	2	1	4	3	(d)	1	4	2	3

28 Which of the following is true relating to appointment of Site Appraisal Committee under the Factories Act, 1948 ?

(a) State Government may appoint it
(b) Both State Governments and Central Government can appoint it
(c) State Governments may appoint it in consultation with the Central Government
(d) Central Government may appoint a committee for each state in consultation with the respective State Governments

29 Which of the following is true relating to the appointment of the Chairman of the State Advisory Board constituted under the Contract Labour (regulation and abolition) Act, 1970 ?

(a) Labour Commissioner of the state is the ex-officio chairman
(b) Labour Minister of the state is the ex-officio chairman
(c) Chairman is appointed by the State Government
(d) Chairman is appointed by the State Government in consultation with the Central Government

30 Which of the following is not the prescribed hours and periods of work for a child under the Child Labour (prohibition and regulation) Act, 1986?

1. No child shall work for more than three hours before he has had an interval for rest for half an hour in any day.
2. The period of work should be so arranged that, inclusive of his rest interval, it shall not spread over more than six hours in any day.
3. No child shall be permitted to work between 8 P.M. to 7 A.M.
4. No child shall be required or permitted to ork overtime.

Codes

(a) 1 and 2 (b) 1 and 3
(c) 2 and 3 (d) 3 and 4

31 Under the provisions of the Contract Labour (regulation and abolition) Act, 1970, if any difficulty arises in giving effect to the provisions of the act, then which of the following is competent to remove the difficulty ?

(a) State Government
(b) Central Government
(c) Labour Courts established under the Industrial Disputes Act, 1947
(d) Central Advisory Board

2015

32 Institutions of workers' participation in management is/are provided under which of the following Legislations in India?

1. Industrial Disputes Act, 1947
2. Industrial Employment (standing orders) Act, 1946
3. Factories Act, 1948
4. Plantation Labour Act, 1951

Select the correct answer by using the codes given below

Codes

(a) 1, 2 and 4 (b) 1, 2 and 3
(c) Both 2 and 4 (d) 1 and 3

33 Which of the following provisions is not covered under the Contract Labour (regulation and abolition) Act, 1970?

(a) Registration of the principal employers
(b) Licensing of the contractors
(c) Abolition of contract labour
(d) Regularisation of employment of the contract labour by the principal employer

34 What is the maximum number of members to be appointed by the Central Government in addition to the chairman in constituting the Child Labour Technical Advisory Committee under the Child Labour (prohibitions and regulation) Act, 1986?

(a) 10 members
(b) 7 members
(c) 12 members
(d) 8 members

35 Which of the following statement is not correct under the provisions of the Factories Act, 1948?

(a) Cleanliness and overcrowding are covered under Chapter-III
(b) Adolescent means a person who has completed 14th year of age but not completed 18th year
(c) The occupier of the factory means the person who has ultimate control over the affairs of the factory
(d) The provision of First-Aid appliances is a welfare measure

36 Match the following.

	List I		List II
A.	Commissioner	1.	The Payment of Gratuity Act, 1972
B.	The Controlling Authority	2.	The Contract Labour (regulation and abolition) Act, 1970
C.	The Licensing Officer	3.	The Employees' Compensation Act, 1923
D.	The Certifying Surgeon	4.	The Mines Act, 1952

Codes

	A	B	C	D		A	B	C	D
(a)	1	3	4	2	(b)	3	1	2	4
(c)	2	3	1	4	(d)	4	2	3	1

37 Match the provision given in List I of the Factories Act, 1948 with the conditions relating to employment of workers given in List II.

	List I		List II
A.	Cool drinking water	1.	Five hundred or more workers
B.	Ambulance room	2.	More than one hundred and fifty workers
C.	Shelter, rest rooms and lunch rooms	3.	More than two hundred and fifty workers
D.	Welfare officer	4.	More than five hundred workers

Codes

	A	B	C	D		A	B	C	D
(a)	2	3	1	4	(b)	4	1	3	2
(c)	3	4	2	1	(d)	1	2	4	3

38 A proposal is pending pertaining to amending the present Factories Act, 1948. Which amongst the following has not been included in the proposed amendment?

(a) Changes in the present definition of factory by increasing the number of workers from ten with the aid of power and twenty without the aid of power to twenty and forty respectively
(b) Incorporation of new clause under Section 35 (A) pertaining to provisions of personal protective equipment for workers
(c) Provision for preparation of emergency plan and disaster control measures
(d) Changes in the provisions of the act relating to appointment of welfare officer

39 Which of the following statement is true relating to the purpose of constituting the Site Appraisal Committee under the Factories Act, 1948?

(a) Consider applications for grant of permission for initial location of a factory involving heavy machinery in a moving state
(b) Consider applications for grant of permission for initial location of a factory involving hazardous process
(c) Consider applications for grant of permission for initial location of a factory in an urban area
(d) Consider applications for grant of permission for initial location of a factory involving complex technology process

40 Under the provisions of the Inter-state Migrant workmen (regulation of employment and conditions of service) Act, 1979, every inter-state migrant workman is to be paid displacement allowance at the time of recruitment by the contractor an amount of

(a) 75% of the monthly wages payable to him or ₹100, whichever is higher
(b) 50% of the monthly wages payable to him or ₹75, whichever is higher
(c) 50% of the monthly wages payable to him or ₹100, whichever is lower
(d) 75% percent of the monthly wages payable to him or ₹250, whichever is lower

41 The maximum permissible limits of exposure to chemical and toxic substance in a factory involving hazardous process are provided in which schedule of the Factories Act, 1948?

(a) The First Schedule
(b) The Second Schedule
(c) The Third Schedule
(d) The Fourth Schedule

42 After receipt of an application for establishment of a factory as required under the Factories Act, 1948, in how many days the Site Appraisal Committee is required to submit its report to the State Government?

(a) 30 days (b) 60 days
(c) 90 days (d) 120 days

43 The appropriate government, under the provisions of the Contract Labour (regulation and abolition) Act, 1970 may make rules relating to canteens in which of the following areas?

1. The date by which the canteens shall be provided.
2. The number of canteens that shall be provided.
3. The foodstuffs which may be served.
4. The charges for the foodstuffs to be served.
5. The number of persons to be employed in the canteen.

Select the correct answer by using the codes given below

Codes

(a) 1, 2, 3 and 5 (b) 1, 3, 4 and 5
(c) 1, 2, 3 and 4 (d) 1, 2 and 3

44 The provisions of the Building and other Construction Workers (regulation of employment and conditions of services) Act, 1996 shall become applicable to an establishment which employs or has employed on any day of the preceding 12 months a minimum of

(a) 10 construction workers (b) 20 construction workers
(c) 30 construction workers (d) 50 construction workers

45 Under the provisions of the Factories Act, 1948, a Safety Committee is to be constituted in a factory where

(a) more than one thousand workers are employed
(b) heavy machineries are utilised
(c) hazardous substances are used
(d) complex technology is used

2014

46 Under the Factories Act, 1948, the spread over period including rest interval in a day for an adult worker should not normally exceed

(a) $10\frac{1}{2}$ hours (b) 11 hours
(c) 12 hours (d) $11\frac{1}{2}$ hours

47 The term 'wages', under the Contract Labour (regulation and abolition) Act, 1970, has the same meaning assigned to it under which of the following legislations?

(a) Payment of Wages Act, 1936
(b) Minimum Wages Act, 1948
(c) Industrial Disputes Act, 1947
(d) Industrial Employment (standing orders) Act, 1946

48 Under the provisions of the Factories Act, 1948, the total number of hours of work in a week including overtime shall not exceed

(a) 60 hours (b) 54 hours (c) 72 hours (d) 64 hours

49 As per the provisions of the Factories Act, 1948, when a worker is superannuated or dies while in-service, within how many months the wages in lieu of the leave to which he was entitled to, has to be paid from the date of such superannuation or death?

(a) 1 month (b) 3 months
(c) 4 months (d) 2 months

50 Examines the following statements about industrial accidents and safety management. Indicate the one which is not relevant?

(a) Accident proneness is a behavioural and attitudinal problem that some employees suffer from
(b) Safety consciousness is not a trainable trait
(c) Safety in industry can improve if the provisions laid down in the Factories Act, 1948 or any such relevant law are strictly followed
(d) "Accidents do not just happen but are caused" is only partly true

51 As per the Factories Act, 1948, what is the minimum number of days of leave allowed to a child worker which makes him eligible to get wages in advance for the period of leave allowed?

(a) 3 days (b) 4 days
(c) 5 days (d) 6 days

52 Which of the following statements are not true in relation to employment of contract labour in any establishment?

1. Supreme Court can abolish contract labour system in any establishment.
2. High Court can abolish contract labour and prohibit the principal employer from engaging contract labour where the government has not abolished the same.
3. An appropriate government and not the court can prohibit the employment of contract labour as per the provisions of law.
4. Neither the court nor the appropriate government can abolish the contract labour in any establishment.

Codes
(a) 1 and 2
(b) 1, 2 and 4
(c) 1, 2 and 3
(d) All of the above

53 Which of the following has the power to apply all or any of the provisions of the Factories Act to certain premises?

(a) The Chief Inspector of Factories of a State
(b) The Central Government
(c) The State Government
(d) Both (b) and (c)

54 Under the Factories Act, it is compulsory for an employer to appoint a safety officer in his factory, if the number of workers employed in factory is

(a) 400 (b) 600
(c) 800 (d) 1000

55 Which of the following are statutory consultation machineries at the central level?

1. Dock Workers' Advisory Committee
2. Central Minimum Wages Advisory Board
3. Employees State Insurance Corporation
4. Labour Welfare Advisory Committees under different Labour Fund Acts

Select the correct answer by using the codes given below

Codes
(a) 1, 2 and 4
(b) 1, 2 and 3
(c) 1, 3 and 4
(d) All of the above

56 Who was the first President of the Indian Federation of Labour established in 1941?

(a) MN Roy
(b) Jaman Das Mehta
(c) RS Ruikar
(d) Dr Rajendra Prasad

57 **Which of the following is not a modification of any existing legislation, but a proposed new legislation by the Second National Commission on Labour?**

(a) Child Labour (prohibition and egulation) Bill
(b) Labour Management Relations Bill
(c) Small Enterprises (employment relations) Act
(d) Unorganised Sector Social Security Act

58 **Under which legislation, housing is a statutory provision?**

(a) The Factories Act
(b) The Mines Act
(c) The Plantation Labour Act
(d) All of the above

59 **Who was the first President of the Indian Federation of Labour?**

(a) MN Roy (b) Jamna Das Mehta
(c) RS Ruirkar (d) V V Giri

ANSWERS

Exam Based Questions

1	(a)	2	(c)	3	(c)	4	(c)	5	(d)	6	(d)	7	(d)	8	(d)	9	(d)	10	(d)
11	(a)	12	(b)	13	(b)	14	(c)	15	(c)	16	(b)	17	(b)	18	(a)	19	(a)	20	(d)
21	(d)	22	(d)	23	(d)	24	(a)	25	(b)	26	(d)	27	(b)	28	(d)	29	(a)	30	(d)
31	(c)	32	(c)	33	(d)	34	(d)	35	(b)	36	(d)	37	(b)	38	(a)	39	(d)	40	(d)
41	(a)	42	(d)	43	(c)	44	(c)	45	(c)	46	(b)	47	(d)	48	(b)	49	(b)	50	(a)
51	(c)	52	(b)	53	(d)	54	(b)	55	(d)	56	(a)	57	(a)	58	(a)	59	(c)	60	(c)
61	(d)	62	(b)	63	(a)	64	(d)	65	(b)	66	(a)	67	(a)	68	(a)	69	(b)	70	(d)
71	(d)	72	(a)	73	(b)	74	(c)	75	(b)	76	(a)	77	(a)	78	(b)	79	(d)	80	(b)
81	(c)	82	(b)	83	(d)	84	(b)	85	(b)	86	(b)	87	(b)	88	(c)	89	(b)	90	(a)
91	(c)	92	(a)	93	(b)	94	(a)	95	(d)	96	(a)	97	(a)	98	(d)	99	(d)	100	(c)
101	(b)	102	(a)	103	(b)	104	(a)	105	(a)	106	(d)	107	(a)	108	(c)	109	(b)	110	(a)
111	(b)	112	(a)	113	(a)	114	(b)	115	(c)	116	(a)	117	(c)	118	(d)	119	(c)	120	(b)
121	(c)	122	(a)	123	(a)	124	(b)	125	(a)	126	(d)	127	(b)	128	(b)	129	(b)	130	(b)
131	(b)	132	(a)	133	(d)	134	(d)												

Previous Years' Questions

1	(d)	2	(d)	3	(a)	4	(d)	5	(a)	6	(c)	7	(a)	8	(d)	9	(c)	10	(c)
11	(c)	12	(a)	13	(d)	14	(a)	15	(a)	16	(a)	17	(c)	18	(d)	19	(c)	20	(c)
21	(b)	22	(b)	23	(c)	24	(b)	25	(b)	26	(a)	27	(d)	28	(a)	29	(c)	30	(b)
31	(b)	32	(d)	33	(d)	34	(a)	35	(b)	36	(b)	37	(c)	38	(d)	39	(d)	40	(b)
41	(b)	42	(c)	43	(c)	44	(a)	45	(c)	46	(a)	47	(a)	48	(a)	49	(d)	50	(b)
51	(c)	52	(b)	53	(c)	54	(b)	55	(d)	56	(b)	57	(c)	58	(b)	59	(b)		

UNIT 8

Wages

This chapter deals with the concept of wages and includes the important theories and wage differentials. The different methods of wage payment and legislations like Payment of Wages Act, Bonus Act, Gratuity Act etc have been covered in this chapter.

Concept of Wages

Wages are payment to labour or services of a worker, especially remuneration on hourly, daily or weekly basis or piece basis. Wage policy is a complex and sensitive area of any nation because of the status of working class, its need and relevance in the development of the country. Wages play an important role in determining the worker's morale, their motivation towards productivity, their living standard and their way of life.

An increase in wages may increase productivity but it is not definite because wage rise may induce employers to reduce the labour cost by adopting more efficient processes of production. The latest equipments and machines may raise output without increasing the number of workers. Sometimes, unnecessary high wages may even lead to closure of the enterprise. It is for sure that higher productivity is the most important means of raising real wages. With the increase in wages, the purchasing power of the worker increases, this subsequently increases the demand of such goods.

It becomes mandatory to increase the supply of consumer goods to maintain the prices of consumer goods. If both the wages and prices of consumer goods will increase side-by-side, then the living standard of the people will never improve. Thus, it can be concluded that if the wages are to be raised, arrangements are to made at the same time to increase the supply of consumer goods.

In this Chapter

- *Concept of Wages*
- *Minimum Wages Act, 1948*
- *Payment of Wages Act, 1936*
- *Payment of Bonus Act, 1965*
- *Equal Remuneration Act, 1976*
- *The Payment of Gratuity Act, 1972*
- *The Employees Provident Fund and Miscellaneous Provisions Act, 1952*

Wage Administration is a process of managing a company's compensation programme.

Wage Compensation refers to monetary payments to employees in the form of wages and salaries.

It is fixed, non-incentive kind of payment calculated on the basis of time spent by an employee on the job.

Supplementary Compensation signifies incentive payments based on the actual performance of an employee.

Essentials of a Sound Wage and Salary Structure

- **Internal Equity** Where more difficult jobs are paid more.
- **External Competitiveness** Where jobs are fairly compensated in comparison to similar jobs in labour market.
- Built-in incentives.
- Linked with productivity.
- Maintain real wages.
- Increments.
- Individual equity (where equal pay is ensured for equal work).

Types of Wages

1. Minimum Wages

- A minimum wage is the wage sufficient to provide basic amenities of life and also preserve the efficiency of the worker.
- It may be defined as the remuneration sufficient to enable an average worker to fulfil all his obligations.
- The minimum wage should also meet the requirements of the education and health of workers' family.
- It can be paid on the basis of time or piece.
- It is fixed by the government and enforced by the law and has to be revised atleast once in 5 years.
- In India, different states fix minimum wages for workers based on their skills set. VV Giri National Labour Institute Committee has recommended that the national level minimum wage for a worker should be ₹ 9,750 per month at ₹ 375 per day for 26 days.
- Minimum wages may be decided by an agreement between the management and the worker.
- Minimum Wages Act, 1948 has been enacted to regulate the minimum wages; which is applicable all over the country.
- There is a distinction between base subsistence or minimum wage and a statutory minimum wage.

These are as follows

(a) The minimum wage is a wage which should cover the physical needs of a worker and his family.

(b) The statutory minimum wage is the rate which has got to be paid to the worker irrespective of the capacity of the industry to pay. If an industrial organisation is unable to pay its workers atleast a bare minimum, it has no right to exist.

2. Fair Wage

- It is above the minimum wage but below the living wage.
- The lower level of the fair wage is the minimum wage and the upper limit is the capacity of the industry to pay.
- It is fixed, taking into account factors such as the productivity of labour, prevailing wage rates, level of national income and its distribution, the employer's capacity to pay etc.
- Fair wage works on the formula, "Equal pay for equal work".
- It can be said that wage is fair if it is equal to what the competitors are paying in the market throughout the country.
- It must be fixed only by comparison with an accepted standard wage.
- These parameters or standards are set in reference to those industries where labour is well organised and has been able to bargain well with the employers.
- Fair wage depends not only on the present economic position of the industry but also on its future prospects.
- Tribunals, awards and wage boards play major role in fair wage fixation.

3. Living Wage

- It is the highest amount of wages proposed by the government, offering basic amenities of life and satisfying the social needs of worker.
- It may be defined as the one which should enable the earner to provide for himself and his family, food, clothing, shelter, education, medical needs, social needs and security needs.
- A living wage is usually fixed; keeping in mind the general economic conditions of the country.
- The concept of living wage varies from country-to-country.

Wages and Capital Formation

- Capital formation refers to the saving and saving can only be there if we produce more than we consume.
- It is very important to save for economic development and create a competent infrastructure in the country.
- So, to form a big amount of capital, it is necessary to increase the productivity to consume and then save a little.

Principles of Wage Plan

- The wage plan must be in consonance to the productivity of the workers.
- The wage differentials should be maintained keeping in mind the job requirements, skills required, length of time required in learning, working conditions and responsibility.
- The wage plan should be structured in a way that it ensures profit to the workers, management as well as consumers.
- The wage plan should provide higher salary to the more skilled, educated and experienced people as compared to less skilled, less educated and less experienced people.
- The wage plan should be finalised considering the aspects provided by job evaluation.
- The wage plan should ensure minimum wage to protect the interest of workers and provide them with base necessities of life.
- The wage plan should be flexible in order to meet changing conditions and should not involve excessive administration cost.
- The wage plan should be streamlined with the overall national economy, the operating labour budget and firm's policy.
- The wage plan should be of such type that it increases the efficiency of the worker.

Objectives of Regulation of Wages

- To regulate and fix the quantum of wages.
- To prevent exploitation of workers.
- To prevent exploitation of women and children specifically.
- To prevent the exploitation of labour and payment of unduly low wages in those industries where workers were least organised and where employment of women workers and children predominated.
- To provide the workers minimum amount to meet even the bare necessities of life.
- To bound the employer to pay the fixed minimum wages to the employees working in a particular industry with the imposition of legal obligation.
- To mitigate the sufferings and hardships of labour in the unorganised industries or employments.
- To improve other working conditions also; apart from fixation of minimum wages.
- To fix just and fair wages for all the employees without any discrimination.
- To avoid industrial disputes and promote industrial peace.
- To control inflationary pressure as happened during the last world war.
- To maintain the purchasing power of the wage earners and thereby speeding up the pace of economic recovery.
- To pursuit the national income distribution policy and use the wage policy as an instrument of planned economic development.

Methods of Wage Payments

Time Wage System

This system is based on the fact that the workers are paid on the basis of amount of time they spend on doing the particular job. The period of time may be hours, minutes, seconds, days, weeks, months etc. Wages are paid only when the assigned task is finished. It is also known as 'day wage system'. This kind of system is possible in the cases where it is not possible to measure the production in terms of units or in any other terms or the workers are interns (under training).

Wages = Time spent by the worker × Rate of wages according to time

It is easy to calculate the wages under this method, as it provides certainty of the amount of wage payment to the employee.

Under this system of wage payment, workers do not make proper utilisation of time. This leads to killing efficiency of efficient workers.

Piece Rate System

This system is based on the fact that workers are paid the wages on the basis of quantity and quality of work performed by them. This method is useful in standard work where work can be measured easily. This system is beneficial as the efficient workers tend to work more efficiently because they will be paid accordingly.

Wages = Units of production × Rate per unit

Under this system, there is a lack of unity or mutual co-operation among the workers and there is a misuse of factors of production. Also, there is no fixed wage because the wages are dependent on the units of pieces produced.

Incentive Rate System

This system is a mixture of piece rate and time wage system of wages. Under this, the worker or employees are paid bonus for the additional work done by them over and above the fixed income. This system gives an opportunity to the workers to work to their maximum limit and ensure that they are given a basic fixed salary while ensuring that quality is maintained. However, there may be cases where workers may start ignoring quality while focusing on the production of increased quantity.

It includes following incentive plans

- **Taylor's Differential Piece Rate System** In this plan, two piece work rate, one is lower and other is higher is determined. If a worker finishes work within standard time or produces more than standard output within time, he will be given high piece rate. If the output of worker is less than standard output and does not complete his work within standard time, he is paid a low rate.

  So, this system penalises the slow worker by paying low rate because of low production, rewards on efficient worker by giving him high rate because of higher production.
- **Merrick's Differential Piece Rate System** Under this scheme, there are three piece rates.

  The basic features of this scheme are as follows

  (a) Upto 83% of the standard output, workers are paid at the ordinary piece rate.

  (b) 83% to 100% at 110% of the ordinary rate.

  (c) Above 100% at 120% of ordinary piece rate.
- **Gantt Task and Bonus Plan** This plan combines time, piece and bonus system. Here, day wages are guaranteed. Standard time for task is fixed and both time wages as well as high rate per piece are determined. A worker, who cannot finish the work within the standard time is paid on time basis. If a worker reaches the standard, he will be paid time wage plus a bonus at a fixed per cent (20%) of normal time wage. If a worker exceeds the standards, he is paid a higher piece rate.
- **Barth Variable Sharing Plan** This plan is similar to Halsey and Rowan plans because it is also based on standard time set for the completion of a job. Unlike those plans, however, it does not guarantee a time rate.

  $$\sqrt{\text{Standard hours} \times \text{Actual hours}} \times \text{Rate per hour}$$
- **Standard Hour Plan** (Halsey Plan)

  The main features of this plan are

  (a) Standard time is fixed for each job or operation.

  (b) Time rate is guaranteed and the worker receives the guaranteed wages irrespective of whether he completes the work in the time allowed or takes more time to do the same.

  (c) If the job is completed in less than the standard time, the worker is paid a bonus of 50% of time saved in addition to his normal wage.

  $$\text{Bonus} = 50\% \text{ of time saved}$$
- **Rowan Plan** Under this plan, bonus is paid on the basis of time saved. So, bonus is that proportion of the wages of time taken, which the time saved bears to the time allowed or standard time.

  $$\text{Bonus} = \frac{\text{Time saved}}{\text{Standard time or Time allowed}} \times \text{Time taken} \times \text{Hourly rate}$$

  $$\text{Total Earnings} = \text{Time taken} \times \text{Hourly rate} + \text{Bonus}$$
- **Performance Based Incentives** Here, payment is dependent on individual employee's performance. Performance is evaluated in a subjective fashion. When high achievers are rewarded, they set benchmarks for others to follow.

Wage Fixation

Wages means all remuneration, capable of being expressed in terms of money, which would, if the terms of the contract of employment, express or implied, were fulfilled, be payable, upon the regular attendance, good work or conduct or other behaviour of the person in respect of his employment or of work done in such employment,

but does not include

- The value of any house accommodation, supply of light, water, medical attendance or other amenity, or of any service excluded by general or special order of the State Government;
- Any contribution paid by the employer to any pension fund or provident fund;
- Any travelling allowance or the value of travelling concession;
- Any sum paid to the person employed to defray special expenses entailed on him by the nature of his employment; or
- Any gratuity payable on discharge.

Principles of Wage Fixation

- The basic principle of wage fixation is that it should be based on the relative contributions of different jobs and not on the bases of who the job holders are.
- To follow this principle, it becomes most important to identify the likely contributions of different jobs.
- It is done under job evaluation which provides the information about what is the worth of a job in terms of its contributions to the achievement of organisational effectiveness.

Some Anomalies in the View of Knowles and Thompson

- Payment of high wages and salaries to persons who hold jobs and positions not requiring great skill, effort and responsibility.
- Paying fresher more than what they deserve in the beginning.
- Paying higher rates to the persons whose performance does not justify the raise.
- Fixing the wages on the basis of seniority rather than ability.
- Paying differently with a wide range of differences for the same or closely related jobs and positions.
- Payment of unequal wages and salaries on the basis of race, sex, religion or political differences.

Norms for Fixation of Wages in Industry

- While computing the minimum wages, the standard working class family should be considered as consisting of four consumption units and the earnings of women, children and adolescents should be excluded.
- The minimum food requirements should be determined on the grounds of a net intake of 2700 calories as laid down by Abroad for a normal adult in India.
- Clothing needs should be established on the basis of a per capita consumption of 16.62 meters per year.
- As regards housing, the minimum wages should be determined from the standpoint of the rent corresponding to the minimum area specified under the government Industrial Housing Scheme.
- Miscellaneous expenditure on items such as fuel, lighting etc should form 20% of the total minimum wage.
- *The following institutions are involved in fixation of wages*
  - (i) Employer
  - (ii) Collective Bargaining
  - (iii) Legislation
    - (a) Payment of Wages Act
    - (b) Minimum Wages Act
    - (c) Adjudication Machinery
  - (iv) Wage Boards
  - (v) Pay Commissions

Factors Influencing Wages

1. Labour Productivity

- The economic theory connects wages to labour productivity.
- It is not always sure that increase in wages will increase productivity as the wage rise may induce employers to reduce the labour cost by adopting new ways of technology.

2. Economic Condition of Industry

- The capacity to increase the wages is a subject of argument for the owners.
- Wages add into the cost of production and results either in squeezing the profit of the owner or raising the price of goods for the consumer.
- Both the conditions do not prove to be quite beneficial for the workers.

3. Economic Condition of Nation

- The macro impact of wage increase can be viewed on inflation, competiveness etc.
- Increase in wages will increase the purchasing power of the people of that country. In this way an unbreakable chain will be formed affecting each other.

4. Supply and Demand of Labour

- The labour market conditions play an important role in determining organisational wage, structure and level.
- If the demand for certain skills and the supply are low, the result is a rise in the price to be paid for these skills.
- The other alternative is to pay higher wages if the labour supply is scarce and lower wages when it is excessive.
- To satisfy the conditions of equity, fairness at justice, a management should take these factors into consideration.

5. Market Wage Rate

- It is the most widely used criterion, where the wages are paid in accordance to what their competitors are paying.
- An organisation's compensation policies generally tend to conform to the wage rates payable by the industry and the community.
- It is observed that some companies pay on the high side of the market in order to obtain good will or to insure adequate supply of labour; while others pay lower wages as they cannot afford to and they could keep jobs adequately manned.

6. Living Wage

- Wages paid to worker should be sufficient to maintain himself and his family at a reasonable level of existence.
- However, employers do not like this principle as they want the employee to be paid based on performance rather than his personal needs.

7. Top Management's Attitude

- Top management's desire to maintain or enhance the company's prestige is a major factor in the wage policy of a number of firms.
- Top management's wage policy decisions may reflect their desires to improve or maintain morale, to attract high caliber employees, to reduce turnover and to provide a high living standard for employees.

8. Psychological and Social Factors

- Psychologically wages and success are co-related to each other.
- A person works very hard and bears lots of pressure to get better compensation.
- Sociologically and ethically, people feel that equal work should carry equal wages.
- People must feel that they are not being exploited and that no distinction is made on the basis of caste, colour, sex and religion.

9. Preserving Real Income

- The employees and the unions consider wages as an income.
- With the rise in wages, the cost of all other consumer goods raise in the same proportion or more than that; increase in wages is not of any use.
- Wages are compared to inflation in this case.
- Again it becomes necessary for the employer to pay the minimum wages and maintain comparative wage justice.

Wage Theories

1. Subsistence Theory/Brazen Law

- The given theory is based on the population theory of **Thomas Malthus.**
- Given by **David Recardo** in 1817.
- This theory is also known as **Iron Law of Wages.**
- Deals with population rather than labour.
- The theory says that each member of the society be provided enough food, clothing and shelter to continue to exist.
- This theory is based on assumption that labour, like any other commodity is purchased and sold in the market, and in the long-run, the value of labour trends to be equal to the cost of production.
- The labour cost is equal to the amount which is necessary for the maintenance of the worker and his family at the subsistence level.
- Conversely, if the wages fall below the subsistence level, some workers might decide to have fewer children, would eventually bring down the birth rate. This would result in decreased labour supply, which would ultimately be equal to the demand for it. Therefore, in the long-run, the wage rate gets adjusted at the subsistence level.

2. Wage Fund Theory

- It was given by **John Stuart Mill** in 1930.
- It assumes that the wages of an employee are paid from the fund, which presumably has been accumulated by the entrepreneur from operations of the previous years.
- According to this theory, wages are determined by the fund which has been kept for obtaining the services of labour and the number of workers seeking employment.
- It was assumed that a wage fund is fixed and does not change. Any change in the wage rate, therefore, would be due to a change in the number of workers seeking employment.
- This theory is rigid in its own way. It demonstrates that bargaining power or trade union can not raise the wage level and those efforts to discourage the accumulation of capital.
- This theory also shows that productivity of labour is determined by the level of wages.

3. Residual Claimant Theory

- This theory was given by **Francis A Walker.**
- According to this theory, wages are nothing but the residue of total revenues after deducting all other legitimate expenses such as rent, taxes, interest and profits.

4. The Marxian Theory of Surplus Value

- It was given by **Karl Marx.**
- This theory is just the inverse of **Residual Claimant Theory.**
- According to this theory, labour is the sole source of economic value and therefore labour should exercise the prime claim on revenue.
- It says that the surplus between labour cost and product cost should be paid to the labour.
- The supply of labour always tends to be kept in excess of the demand for it by a special feature of the capitalist wage system.
- The rate of surplus value, which is the ratio of surplus labour to necessary labour, is also referred as rate of exploitation under the capitalist form of production.

5. National Income Theory

- It was given by **John Maynard Keynes** in 1930.
- According to this theory, full employment is the function of National Income.
- National Income is equal to the total of consumption plus private and public investment.

6. Neo-Keynsian Distribution Theory

- According to this theory, general wage level should be maintained in the long and short-terms.
- Wages are fixed by bargaining between capitalist and the employees.
- General wages can also be determined by the entrepreneurial decisions in the short-term.

7. Consumption Theory

- This theory was given by **Ford** in 1913.
- It was formulated on the concept that more wages will lead to more consumption.
- More consumption will create more demand and therefore increase in employment will be there.

8. Investment Theory

- This theory was given by **HM Gitelman.**
- According to this theory, employees' compensation is determined by the rate of return on that employees' investment.
- Investment means education, training and experience.

9. Institutional Wage Theory

- In this theory, level of compensation is determined on empirical and quantitative bases.
- Wages are determined after having region cum industry comparison.

10. Supply and Demand Theory

- This theory was given by **Alfred Marshall.**
- In this theory, wages are determined based on demand and supply of labour.
- In this theory, Marshall explained the complexity of the economic world and tried to provide a less rigid and deterministic theory.
- According to him, the determination of wages is affected by the whole set of factors which govern demand for and supply of labour.
- The demand price of labour, however, determined by the marginal productivity of the individual worker.
- The term 'supply and labour' refers to the number of workers seeking employment, there are the works who have no alternative livelihood and join the labour market seeking employment for wages.
- Supply and labour may refer to the number of hours each worker is available for work. The supply of labour in this sense increases with any increase in the number of working hours.

11. Micro Theories

(i) The Marginal Productivity Theory

- **JB Clark** was the first one to develop this theory.
- Later on, **Marshall** made some amendments.
- According to this theory, both demand and supply together determine the factor price, which in a perfectly competitive market, is equal to the marginal revenue productivity of the factor.
- This theory assumes that there is a certain quantity of labour seeking employment and the wage rate at which this labour can secure employment in a competitive labour is equal to the addition to total production that results from employing the marginal unit of the labour force. It is also assumed that production has been carried out under the conditions of diminishing return to labour.

(ii) The Bargaining Theory

- This theory was given by **John Davidson,** an American economist.
- According to this theory, the wages and hours of work were ultimately determined by the relative bargaining strength of the employers and the workers.
- According to this theory, there is an upper limit and a lower limit on wage rates and the actual rates between these limits are determined by the bargaining power for the employers and the workers.
- The upper limit marks the highest wages, the employers would be willing to pay, whereas, the lower limit indicates the minimum wages prescribed under the strength of resistance of the workers at the subsistence.

Wage Differentials

It refers to the differences in wage rates due to the location of company, hours of work, working conditions, type of product manufactured or other factors.

Different industries have different wage structures resulting in disparities in remuneration for identical works. Wide gaps exist between wages of employees of organised sector vs unorganised sector.

A wage differential is the gap between wage rates of two similar jobs or types of workers that can occur because of a variety of circumstances.

Wage differential can be defined as the difference in wages between workers with different skills in the same industry or between those with comparable skills in different industries or localities.

Ways to Calculate

- Job analysis
- Job evaluation
- Wage survey
- Developing wage structure
- Wage administration rules
- Employee appraisal

Wage differentials among workers working in the same unit, among different units, occupations, regions and the like are common features of labour markets in various countries.

Types of Wage Differentials

Interpersonal Differentials

Such type of differentials arise because of differences in personal characteristics (age or sex) of workers who work in the same plant and the same occupation, *e.g.* age bias is becoming a significant factor in job search; the age of forty arbitrarily seems to classify employees as older workers and making if difficult to find jobs.

Differences due to sex, skills, age, knowledge, experiences in occupations which involve muscular work, women workers are employed but paid less than men workers.

Inter-Occupational Differentials

Varying requirements of skill, knowledge, demand-supply situation, different occupations require different qualifications, skills and different degrees of responsibility.

The main objectives of occupational differentials are as following

- To induce workers to undertake more demanding, 'more risky' jobs.
- To encourage workers to develop skills in anticipation of higher earnings in future.
- To perform social function by way of determining the social status of workers.

Inter-Area Differentials

Workers working in same industry and the same occupational group, but living in different geographical areas, are paid different wages because of the following reasons like cost of living, ability of employers to pay, demand and supply situation and extent of unionisation.

Inter-Firm Differentials

Such types of differentials arise when the workers in the same occupation and in the same area, but in different industries are paid different wages. Ability of employer to pay, employers' bargaining power, degree of unionisation, skill needs etc.

Inter-Sector Differentials

Such types of differentials depend upon the nature of workers' group (organised/unorganised) and level of economic development of the sector. *e.g* Agricultural workers are not able to better their living conditions, because of not having unions whereas workers in industrial sectors have their own unions to fight for them.

Inter-Religion Differentials

Such types of differentials occur on the basis of religion. India has adopted secular idealism, hence discrimination on religious ground is against the fundamental principles of the constitution.

Inter-Racial Differentials

There are some countries where racism exists. *e.g.* Black face the problem of being paid the least, hired at the last and fired first.

Inter-Sexual Differentials

The ratio of women employees is increasing day-by-day in the labour market and therefore catches serious attention. Many jobs have opened for women such as civil service, police service, plane driving etc. In India, specifically women suffer high levels of wage discrimination in the Indian market.

Few other kinds of differentials are also arising in the job market, which are as follows

- Indian Government reserves a small percentage of vacancies for the physically challenged people. There are few firms which follow and there are others, which do not.
- A new form of differential problem has arisen over the medical issue of AIDS. It has become a major issue because of non-awareness and unnecessary inhibitions about the disease.
- It is obvious that local population is preferred in the matter of employment and taking the shape of wage differentials. In this connection, the National Commission on labour has observed that, "The solution has been sought in terms of the primacy of common citizenship and geographical mobility and economic feasibility of locating industrial units, on the one hand and local aspiration on the other".

Wage Differentials and Economy Functions

Wage differentials perform important economic functions like labour productivity, attracting the people to different jobs.

Since most of the workers are mobile with a view to maximise their earnings, wage differentials reflect on variations in productivity, efficiency of management, maximum utilisation of human force etc.

Attracting efficient workers, maximisation of employee commitment, development of skills, knowledge, utilisation of human resources, maximisation of productivity can be fulfilled through wage differentials as the latter determines the direct allocation of manpower among different units, occupations and regions, so that national production can be maximised.

Thus, wage differentials provide an incentive for better allocation of human force, labour mobility among different regions.

Wage differentials play pivotal role in a planned economy in the regulation of wage and development of national wage policy by allocating the skilled human force on priority basis. Development of new skills, knowledge etc is an essential part of human resources development.

Shortage of technical and skilled personnel is not only a problem for industries but it creates bottlenecks in the attainment of planned goals. Thus, wage differentials, to certain extent, are desirable from the view point of national interest. As such they probably become an essential part of national wage policy. Complete uniform national wage policy is impracticable and undesirable.

Minimum Wages Act, 1948

This act deals with providing minimum rates of wages in certain employments. It is a welfare measure aimed at providing social justice to the workers employed in the scheduled employments. It came into force on 15th March, 1948.

Definitions Under the Act

- **Adolescent** means a person who has completed his fourteenth year of age but has not completed his eighteenth year. [Section 2(a)]
- **Adult** means a person who has completed his eighteenth year of age. [Section 2(aa)]
- **Appropriate Government** means any scheduled employment carried on by or under the authority of the Central Government or a railway administration, or in relation to a mine, oilfield or major port, or any corporation established by the Central Government, and in relation to any other scheduled employment, the State Government. [Section 2(b)]
- **Competent Authority** means the authority appointed by the appropriate government by notification in its Official Gazette to ascertain from time-to-time the cost of living index number applicable to the employees employed in the scheduled employments specified in such notification. [Section 2(c)]
- **Child** means a person who has not completed his fourteenth year of age. [Section 2(bb)]
- **Cost of Living Index Number** means the index number ascertained and declared by the competent authority to be the cost of living index number applicable to employee. This is in relation to employees in any scheduled employment in respect of which minimum rates of wages have been fixed. [Section 2(d)]
- **Employer** means any person who employs whether directly or indirectly any person in any scheduled employment in respect of which minimum rates of wages have been fixed. [Section 2(e)]
- **Schedule Employment** means an employment specified in the schedule or any process or branch of work forming part of such employment. [Section 2(g)]
- **Wages** means all remuneration in terms of money which would be payable to a person employed in respect of his employment or of work done in such employment.

  It includes house rent allowance, but does not include the value of

  (a) any house accommodation supply of light, water and medical attendance.

  (b) any contribution paid by the employer to any person fund or provident fund or under any scheme of social insurance.

  (c) any travelling allowance or the value of any travelling concession.

  (d) any sum paid to the person employed to defray special expenses entailed on him by the nature of his employment, or

  (e) any gratuity payable on discharge [Section 2(h)].
- **Employee** means any person who is employed for hire or reward to do any work skilled or unskilled manual or clerical in a scheduled employment in respect of which minimum rates of wages have been fixed. It does not include any member of the Armed Forces of the Union. [Section 2(i)]

Fixing of Minimum Rate of Wages (Section 3)

- *The appropriate government will have the power to*

  (a) Fix the minimum rates of wages payable to employees employed in an employment specified in Part I or Part II of the Schedules.

  (b) Review and revise the minimum rate of wages at fixed intervals. These fixed intervals should not exceed a period of five years.
- The appropriate government may refrain from fixing minimum rates of wages in respect of any scheduled employment in which there are in the whole state less than one thousand employees engaged in such employment. However, it can do so if the number crosses one thousand.
- *The appropriate government may fix*

  (a) **Minimum Time Rate** A minimum rate of wages for time spent by employees for the production of output.

  (b) **Minimum Piece Rate** A minimum rate based on the quantity of output employees have produced.

(c) **Guaranteed Time Rate** A minimum rate of remuneration to apply in the case of employees employed on piece work for the purpose of securing to such employees a minimum rate of wages on a time work basis.

(d) **Overtime Rate** A minimum rate to apply in substitution for the minimum rate which would otherwise be applicable in respect of overtime work done by employees.

- There will be different minimum rates of wages fixed for different scheduled employments, different classes of work in the same scheduled employment, adults, adolescents, children and apprentices and different localities.
- The minimum rates of wages may be fixed by the hour, day, month.

Minimum Rate of Wages (Section 4)

Any minimum rate of wages fixed or revised by the appropriate government in respect of scheduled employments under Section 3 will consist of

- Cost of living allowance, which will include a basic rate of wages and a special allowance at a rate to be adjusted at such intervals and in such manner that it works well in variation in the cost of living index number applicable to such workers.
- A basic rate of wages with or without the cost of living allowance and the cash value of the concessions in respect of suppliers of essential commodities at concession rates where so authorised.
- An all-inclusive rate allowing for the basic rate, the cost of living allowance and the cash value of the concessions, if any.

The cost of living allowance and the cash value of the concessions in respect of supplied of essential commodities at concession rate shall be computed by the competent authority at such intervals and in accordance with such directions as may be specified or given by the appropriate government.

Procedure for Fixing and Revising Minimum Wages (Section 5)

In order to fix minimum rates of wages, in respect of any scheduled employment for the first time under this act or in revising minimum rates of wages so fixed,

the government shall either

- Appoint as many committees and sub-committees as it considers necessary to hold enquiries and advise it in respect of such fixation or revision as the case may be.
- Publish its proposals for the information of persons likely to be affected thereby and specify a date not less than two months from the date of the notification on which the proposals will be taken into consideration.

Advisory Board (Section 7 and 8)

- The government has the power to appoint an advisory board to look into the functioning and co-coordinating work of committees and sub-committees appointed in the matter of fixing and revising minimum rates of wages.
- The Central Government has the power to appoint a Central Advisory Board for the purpose of advising the Central and State Governments in the matters of the fixation and revision of minimum rates of wages.
- The Central Advisory Board shall consist of persons to be nominated by the Central Government representing employers and employees in the scheduled employments who shall be equal in number and independent persons not exceeding one-third of its total number of members. One of the independent persons shall be appointed as the Chairman of the Board by the Central Government.

Wages in Kind (Section 11)

- Minimum wages to be paid under this act shall be paid in cash.
- The government may authorise the payment of minimum wages either wholly or partly in kind, in case where it has been the custom to pay wages wholly or partly in kind.
- The government may also make the provision for the supply of essential commodities at concessional rates.
- The cash value of wages in kind and of concessions in respect of supplies of essential commodities at concession rates shall be estimated in the prescribed manner.

Fixing Hours for Normal Working Day (Section 13)

The appropriate government has the power to

- Fix the number of hours of work which shall constitute a normal working day. These will be inclusive of one or more specified intervals.
- Provide a day of rest in a given week which shall be applicable to all the employees.
- Payment of remuneration for the working days.
- Providing for payment for work on a day of rest at a rate not less than the overtime rate.

Payment of Wage for Overtime and Less than Normal Working Hours (Section 14 -17)

- In case, an employee whose minimum rate of wages is fixed under this Act, works overtime, the employer is bound to pay the money for the extra hours devoted by the employee.
- If an employee whose minimum rate of wages has been fixed under this Act, works for a less number of hours than the requisite number of hours on a given day, he shall be entitled to receive wages in respect of work done by him on that day as if he had worked for a full normal working day.
- In case, an employee is involved in two or more classes of work, he shall be paid on the basis of time.
- If an employee is employed on piece work for which minimum time rate and not a minimum piece rate has been fixed under this Act, the employer shall pay to such employee wages at not less than the minimum time rate.

Claims (Section 20)

- The appropriate government may appoint any Commissioner for Workmen's Compensation or any officer of the Central Government exercising functions as a Labour Commissioner for any region, or any officer of the State Government not below the rank of Labour Commissioner, or any other officer with experience as a Judge of a Civil Court, or as a stipendiary Magistrate to be the authority to hear and decide for any specified area, all claims arising out of payment of less than the minimum rates of wages.
- An employee can file the claim himself or with a legal, practitioner before the designated authority. Both the employer and employees are given equal chances to be heard and based on that a final outcome is presented.

Penalties (Section 22)

Any employer who pays to any employee less than the minimum rates of wages fixed for that employee's class of work or less than the amount due to him under the provisions of this Act or contravenes any rule or order made under this Act shall be punishable with imprisonment for a term which may extend to six months or with fine which may extend to five hundred rupees or with both.

Payment of Wages Act, 1936

The Payment of Wages Act, 1936 came into force on 23rd April, 1936. *This was enacted in order to fulfil the following objective*

- Regular and timely payment of wages to the employees.
- Prevent unauthorised deductions made from wages/ salaries.
- Protect employees from the arbitrary fines being imposed on them.
- Ensure minimum wages is paid to the employees.
- Regular payment of wages to certain classes of persons employed in industries.
- Provide an effective means to address the claims arising out of illegal deduction of the wages.

Definitions Under the Act

- **Employed Person** includes the legal representative of deceased employed person.
  (a) Employer includes the legal representative of a deceased employer.
  (b) Factory means a factory as defined in clause (m) of Section 2 of the Factories Act, 1948.
- **Industrial or other Establishment** means
  (a) Tramway service or motor transport service engaged in carrying passengers or goods or both by road for hire or reward.
  (b) Air transport service other than such service belonging to or exclusively employed in the Military, Naval or Air Forces of the Union or the Civil Aviation Department of the Government of India.
  (c) Dock, wharf or jetty
  (d) Inland vessel, mechanically propelled
  (e) Mine, quarry or oil-field
  (f) Plantation
  (g) Workshop or other establishment in which articles are produced, adapted or manufactured with a view to their use transport or sale.
  (h) Establishment in which any work relating to the construction, development or maintenance of buildings roads, bridges or canals or relating to operations connected with navigation, irrigation or to the supply of water or relating to the generation, transmission and distribution of electricity or any other form of power is being carried on

(i) Any other establishment or class of establishments which the Central Government or a State Government, may having regard to the nature thereof, the need for protection of persons empolyed therein and other relevant circumstances specify, by notification in the Official Gazette.

- **Wages** means all remuneration expressed in terms of money or capable of being so expressed which would, if the terms of employment, express or implied, were fulfilled be payable to a person employed in respect of his employment or of work done in such employment.

It includes

(a) Any remuneration payable under any award or settlement between the parties or order of a court.

(b) Any remuneration to which the person employed is entitled in respect of overtime work or holidays or any leave period.

(c) Any additional remuneration payable under the terms of employment.

(d) Any sum, which by reason of the termination of employment of the person employed is payable under any law, contract or instrument which provides for the payment of such sum, whether with or without deduction, but does not provide for the time within which the payment is to be made.

(e) Any sum to which the person employed is entitled under any scheme framed under any law for the time being in force.

It does not include

(a) Any bonus which does not form part of the remuneration payable under the terms of employment or which is not payable under any award or settlement between the parties or order of a court.

(b) The value of any house-accommodation or of the supply of light, water, medical attendance or other amenity or of any service excluded from the computation of wages by a general or special order of the State Government.

(c) Any contribution paid by the employer to any pension or provident fund and the interest which may have accrued thereon.

(d) Any travelling allowance or the value of any travelling concession.

(e) Any sum paid to the employed person to defray special expenses entailed on him by the nature of his employment.

Fixation (Section 4), Time Payment of Wages (Section 5), Deductions (Section 7)

- The employer needs to fix wage period for the payment of wages and this period shall not exceed one month.
- In case of a person, who is working in any railway, factory or industrial or other establishment upon or in which less than one thousand persons are employed, the wages need to be paid by seventh of that month.
- In case of a person, who is working in any railway, factory or industrial or other establishment upon or in which more than one thousand persons are employed, the wages need to be paid by tenth of that month.
- In case, an employer terminates an employee, the wages earned by him must be paid before the expiry of the second working day from the day on which his employment is terminated.
- *The employer cannot make deductions from the wages except the following*

(a) Fines

(b) Deductions for absence from duty

(c) Deductions for damage to or loss of goods expressly entrusted to the employed person for custody or for loss of money for which he is required to account where such damage or loss is directly attributable to his neglect or default.

(d) Deductions for house-accommodation supplied by the employer or by government or any housing board set-up under any law for the time being in force (whether the government or the board is the employer or not) or any other authority engaged in the business of subsidising house-accommodation which may be specified in this behalf by the State Government.

(e) Deductions for such amenities and services supplied by the employer as the State Government or any officer specified by it in this behalf may by general or special order authorise.

(f) Deductions for recovery of advances of whatever nature (including advances for travelling allowance or conveyance allowance) and the interest due in respect thereof or for adjustment of over-payments of wages.

(g) Deductions for recovery of loans made from any fund constituted for the welfare of labour in accordance with the rules approved by the State Government and the interest due in respect thereof.

(h) Deductions for recovery of loans granted for house-building or other purposes approved by the State Government and the interest due in respect thereof.

(i) Deductions of income tax payable by the employed person.

(j) Deductions required to be made by order of a court or other authority competent to make such order.

(k) Deductions for subscriptions to, and for repayment of advances from any provident fund to which the Provident Funds Act, 1952 applies.

(l) Deductions for payments to co-operative societies approved by the State Government or any officer specified by it in this behalf or to a scheme of insurance maintained by the Indian Post Office.

(m) Deductions made with the written authorisation of the person employed for payment of any premium on his life insurance policy to the Life Insurance Corporation Act of India established under the Life Insurance Corporation, 1956 for the purchase of securities of the Government of India or of any State Government or for being deposited in any Post Office Saving Bank in furtherance of any savings scheme of any such government.

(n) Deductions made with the written authorisation of the employed person for the payment of his contribution to any fund constituted by the employer or a trade union registered under the Trade Union Act, 1926.

(o) Deductions for payment of insurance premium on Fidelity Guarantee Bonds.

(p) Deductions for recovery of losses sustained by a railway administration on account of acceptance by the employed person of counterfeit or base coins or mutilated or forged currency notes.

(q) Deductions made with the written authorisation of the employed person for contribution to the Prime Minister's National Relief Fund or to such other fund.

(r) Deductions for contributions to any insurance scheme framed by the Central Government for the benefit of its employees.

Fines (Section 8)

- No fine shall be imposed on any employed person until, he has been given an opportunity of showing cause against the fine.
- No fine shall be imposed on any employed person who is under the age of fifteen years.
- The total amount of fine which may be imposed in any one wage-period on any employed person shall not exceed an amount equal to 3% of the wages payable to him in respect of that wage-period.
- No fine imposed on any employed person shall be recovered from him by instalments or after the expiry of sixty days from the day on which it was imposed.
- If ten or more employed persons acting in concert absent themselves without due notice and without reasonable cause, deduction can be made from their salary for not more than the wages of eight days.
- In case, an employee has been making use of an accommodation, amenity or service provided by the employer, relevant deductions will be made from his wages. This shall not exceed an amount equivalent to the value of the house-accommodation amenity or service supplied.
- Recovery of an advance of money given to the employee before employment began can be made from the first payment of wages in respect of a complete wage-period.
- The employer needs to maintain a register of the employees working under him. This register needs to be preserved for a period of three years after the date of the last entry made therein.

Claims Arising from Deductions (Section 15)

- The State Government may appoint a presiding officer of any Labour Court or Industrial Tribunal constituted under the Industrial Disputes Act, 1947 or any Commissioner for Workmen's Compensation or a Judge of a Civil Court or as a Stipendiary Magistrate to be the authority to hear and decide for any specified area of all claims arising out of deductions from the wages or delay in payment of the wages of persons employed or paid in that area including all matters incidental to such claims.
- In case, there has been incorrect deductions from the wages, the employee has the right to make a claim within twelve months from the date of deduction.
- In case, there is a group of persons who have claims from the employer on the basis of same cause and during same wage period, they can submit a common application for the same.

Penalty for Offences (Section 20)

Whoever being required under this act to maintain any records or registers or to furnish any information or return,

- fails to maintain such register or record, or
- wilfully refuses or without lawful excuse neglects to furnish such information or return, or

- wilfully furnishes or causes to be furnished any information or return which he knows to be false, or
- refuses to answer or wilfully gives a false answer to any question necessary for obtaining any information required to be furnished under this act

shall for each such offence be punishable with fine which shall not be less than two hundred rupees but which may extend to one thousand rupees.

Whoever

- wilfully obstructs an Inspector in the discharge of his duties under this Act, or
- refuses or wilfully neglects to afford an Inspector any reasonable facility for making any entry inspection examination supervision or inquiry authorised by or under this Act in relation to any railway factory or industrial or other establishment, or
- wilfully refuses to produce on the demand of an Inspector any register or other document kept in pursuance of this Act, or
- prevents or attempts to prevent or does anything for which he has any reason to believe is likely to prevent any person from appearing before or being examined by an Inspector acting in pursuance of his duties under this Act,

shall be punishable with fine which shall not be less than two hundred rupees but which may extend to one thousand rupees.

Payment of Bonus Act, 1965

The act is applicable to every factory and every other establishment in which twenty or more persons are employed on any day during an accounting year. This act came into force on 25th September, 1965.

This act applies to

- every factory, and
- every other establishment, in which twenty or more persons are employed on any day during an accounting year.

Definitions Under the Act

- **Accounting Year** means
  (a) In relation to a corporation, the year ending on the day on which the books and accounts of the corporation are to be closed and balanced.
  (b) In relation to a company, the period in respect of which any profit and loss account of the company laid before it in annual general meeting is made up, whether that period is a year or not.

  In any other case, it means
  (a) The year commencing on 1st April.
  (b) If the accounts of an establishment maintained by the employer are closed and balanced on any day other than the 31st day of March, then, at the option of the employer, the year ending on the day on which its accounts are so closed and balanced. [Section 2(1)]
- **Allocable Surplus** means
  (a) 67% of the available surplus in an accounting year in context of an employer. The employer will be a company other than a banking company, which has not made the arrangements prescribed under the Income Tax Act for the declaration and payment within India of the dividends payable out of its profits in accordance with the provisions of the Income Tax Act.
  (b) In any other case, 60% of such available surplus. [Section 2(4)]
- **Appropriate Government** means
  (a) In relation to an establishment, in respect of which the appropriate government under the Industrial Disputes Act, 1947 (14 of 1947), is the Central Government, the Central Government.
  (b) In relation to any other establishment, the Government of the State in which that other establishment is situate. [Section 2(5)]
- **Available Surplus** means the available surplus computed under Section 5. [Section 2(6)]
- **Award** means an interim or a final determination of any industrial dispute or of any question relating thereto by any Labor Court, Industrial Tribunal or National Tribunal constituted under the Industrial Disputes Act, 1947, or by any other authority constituted under any corresponding law relating to investigation and settlement of industrial disputes in force in a State. [Section 2(7)]
- **Banking Company** means a banking company as defined in Section 5 of the Banking Companies Act, 1949. [Section 2(8)]
- **Company** means any company as defined in Section 3 of the Companies Act, 1956 and includes a foreign company within the meaning of Section 591 of the Companies Act, 1956. However, Companies Act, 1956 became redundant and was replaced by Companies Act, 2013. The Section 2 of Companies Act, 2013 defines company as a company incorporated under this Act or under any previous company law. [Section 2(9)]
- **Co-operative Society** means a society registered or deemed to be registered under the Cooperative Societies Act, 1912, or any other law for time being in force in any state relating to co-operative societies. [Section 2(10)]

- **Corporation** means anybody corporate established by or under any Central, Provincial or State Act but does not include a company or a co-operative society. [Section 2(11)]
- **Direct Tax** means any tax chargeable under the Income Tax Act, Super Profits Tax Act, 1963, Companies (Profits) Surtax Act, 1964 and agricultural income tax law. [Section 2(12)]
- **Employee** means any person other than an apprentice, employed on a salary or wage not exceeding 3,500 per mensem in any industry to do any skilled or unskilled manual, supervisory, managerial, administrative, technical or clerical work for hire or reward.

  There have been amendments under this act and as per the latest amendments of the Payment of Bonus (Amendment) Act, 2015, the wage ceiling for calculation of bonus has been increased from INR 3,500 to INR 7,000 per month. [Section 2(13)]
- **Employer** includes
  (a) In case of a factory, the owner or occupier of the factory, the agent of such owner or occupier, the legal representative of a deceased owner or occupier or a person who has been named as a manager of the factory.
  (b) In relation to any other establishment, the person who, or the authority which, has the ultimate control over the affairs of the establishment and these are entrusted to a manager, managing director or managing agent, such manager, managing director or managing agent. [Section 2 (14)]
- **Establishment in Public Sector** means an establishment owned, *controlled or managed by*
  (a) A government company as defined in Section 617 of the Companies Act, 1956.
  (b) A corporation in which not less than 40% of its capital is held, whether singly or taken together, by the government, the RBI or a corporation owned by the government or the RBI. [Section 2(15)]
- **Salary or Wages** means all remuneration capable of being expressed in terms of money which will be payable to an employee in respect of his employment or of work done in such employment.

  It includes dearness allowance but it does not include
  (a) Any other allowance which the employee is for the time being entitled to.
  (b) The value of any house accommodation or of supply of light, water, medical attendance or other amenity or of any service or of any concessional supply of food grains or other articles.
  (c) Any travelling concession.
  (d) Any bonus (including incentive, production and attendance bonus).
  (e) Any contribution paid or payable by the employer to any pension fund or provident fund or for the benefit of the employee under any law for the time being in force.
  (f) Any retrenchment compensation or any gratuity or other retirement benefit payable to the employee or any ex-gratia payment made to him.
  (g) Any commission payable to the employee. [Section 2(21)]

Computation of Gross Profits (Section 4) and Available Surplus (Section 5)

- For a banking company, the profit will be calculated by the method mentioned in the first schedule.
- For all the other companies, the profit will be calculated by the method mentioned in the second schedule.
- *The available surplus in respect of any accounting year shall be the gross profits for that year after deducting there from the following sums*
  (a) Any amount by way of depreciation admissible in accordance with the Income Tax Act or in accordance with the provisions of the agricultural income tax law.
  (b) Any amount by way of which the employer is entitled to deduct from his income under the Income Tax Act.
  (c) Any direct tax which the employer is liable to pay for the accounting year in respect of his income, profits and gains during that year.

Bonus

- Every employee is entitled to payment of bonus, if he has worked in the establishment for not less than thirty working days in that year.
- An employee will be disqualified from receiving the bonus, if he is dismissed from service for fraud, violent behavior while on the premises of the establishment or theft, misappropriation or sabotage of any property of the establishment.
- **Minimum Bonus** Every employer shall be bound to pay to every employee in respect of the accounting year commencing on any day in the year 1979 and in respect of every subsequent accounting year, a minimum bonus which shall be 8.33% of the salary or wages earned by the employee during the accounting year or one hundred rupees, whichever is higher, whether or not the employer has any allocable surplus in the accounting year.

- **Maximum Bonus** If the allocable surplus exceeds the amount of minimum bonus payable to the employees, the employer is bound to pay to every employee in respect of that accounting year bonus which shall be an amount in proportion to the salary or wages earned by the employee during the accounting year subject to a maximum of 20% of such salary or wage.
- In case, the salary or wages of an employee exceeds 7,000 per mense, the bonus payable to such employee shall be calculated as, if his salary or wages were 7,000 per mensem. [As per the Payment of Bonus (Amendment) Act, 2015]
- In case, an employee has not worked for all the working days in an accounting year, the minimum bonus shall be proportionately reduced.
- *An employee shall be deemed to have worked in an establishment in any accounting year on the days which*
  (a) he has been laid-off.
  (b) he has been on leave with salary or wages.
  (c) he has been absent due to temporary disablement caused by accident arising out of and in the course of his employment.
  (d) the employee has been on maternity leave with salary or wages, during the accounting year.
- If an employer has paid any puja bonus or other customary bonus to an employee, or he has paid a part of the bonus payable to an employee before the date on which such bonus becomes payable, then, the employer shall be entitled to deduct the amount of bonus so paid from the amount of bonus payable by him to the employee under this Act in respect of that accounting year and the employee shall be entitled to receive only the balance.
- Bonus will be paid in cash to the employees.
- It needs to be paid within a period of eight months from the close of the accounting year.

Penalty

In case, a person is unable to meet any requisite condition mentioned under this act, he shall be punishable with imprisonment for a term which may extend to six months, or with fine which may extend to one thousand rupees, or with both.

Equal Remuneration Act, 1976

This act aims to provide for the payment of equal remuneration to men and women workers and for the prevention of discrimination, on the ground of sex, against women in the matter of employment and for matters connected therewith.

Definitions Under the Act

- **Appropriate Government** means
  (a) In relation to any employment, carried on by or under the authority of the Central Government or a railway administration, or in relation to a banking company, a mine, oilfield or major port or any corporation established by or under a Central Act, the Central Government, and
  (b) In relation to any other employment, the State Government. [Section 2(a)]
- **Employer** has the same meaning assigned to it in Section 2(f) of the Payment of Gratuity Act, 1972. [Section 2(c)]
- **Remuneration** means the basic wage or salary, and any additional emoluments whatsoever payable to a person employed in respect of employment or work done in such employment. It may be paid either in cash or in kind. It will be paid only when the terms of the contract of employment are fulfilled. [Section 2(g)]
- **Same Work or Work of a Similar Nature** means work in respect of which the skill, effort and responsibility required are the same, when performed under similar working conditions, by a man or a woman and the differences, if any, between the skill, effort and responsibility required of a man and those required of a woman are not of practical importance in relation to the terms and conditions of employment. [Section 2(h)]
- **Worker** means a worker in any establishment or employment in respect of which this Act has come into force. [Section 2(i)]

Duties of the Employer (Section 4)

- The employer needs to pay his workers equal pay irrespective of their genders for performing the same work or work of a similar nature.

- The employer has no right to reduce the rate of remuneration of any worker.
- The employer cannot discriminate between men and women workers while recruiting them for the same work or work of a similar nature.

Powers of the Government (Section 7)

- The appropriate government has the power to set-up an Advisory Committee to provide inputs for the employment of women in establishments. Every Advisory Committee shall consist of not less than ten persons, to be nominated by the appropriate government, of which one-half shall be women.
- The appropriate government may appoint officers, not below the rank of a Labor Officer for the purpose of hearing and deciding complaints with regard to the contravention of any provision of this Act and claims arising out of non-payment of wages at equal rates to men and women workers for the same work or work of a similar nature.
- Every authority appointed by the appropriate government shall have all the powers of a Civil Court under the Code of Civil Procedure, 1908 for the purpose of taking evidence and of enforcing the attendance of witnesses and compelling the production of documents.

Penalties and Offences by Companies (Section 10 and 11)

- If an employer makes a recruitment in contravention of the provisions of this Act, or makes any payment of remuneration at unequal rates to men and women workers, for the same work or work of a similar nature, or makes any discrimination between men and women workers in contravention of the provisions of this Act, he shall be punishable with fine which shall not be less than ten thousand rupees or with imprisonment for a term which shall be not less than three months.

  The fine may extend to twenty thousand rupees and the imprisonment may extend to one year for the first offence, and may extend to two years for the second and subsequent offences.
- If any person being required so to do, omits or refuses to produce to an Inspector any register or other document or to give any information, he shall be punishable with fine which may extend to five hundred rupees.
- If an offence is committed under this Act by a company, the person in charge of the company will be considered guilty of the offence and punished accordingly.

Equal Remuneration Rules, 1976

In exercise of the powers conferred by **Section 13** of the Equal Remuneration Act, 1976, the Central Government came out with these rules.

Definitions Under Rules

- **Authority** means an authority appointed by the appropriate Government under sub-section (I) of Section 7.
- **Form** means a form appended to these rules.
- **Section** means a section of the Act.
- **Registered Trade Union** means a Trade Union registered under the Trade Unions Act, 1926.

Complaints and Claims Under this Act (Section 3)

- The claims for the complaints with regard to the contravention of any provision of this Act need to be made in triplicate in the Form A to the authority.
- A single complaint may be made by, or on behalf of, or in relation to, a group of workers, if they are employed in the same establishment and the complaint relates to the same contravention.
- Any claims related to the wages at equal rates to men and women workers for the same work or work of a similar nature shall be made in triplicate in Form B to the authority.
- A claim may be made by the worker himself or herself or by any legal practitioner, or by any official or a registered Trade Union, authorised in writing to appeal and act on his or her behalf or by any Inspector appointed under Section 9 or any other person acting with the permission of the Authority.
- The authorisation shall be in Form 'C' which shall be presented to the Authority to whom the complaint or the claim as the case may be, is made alongwith such complaint or claim and shall form part of the record.
- Every employer shall maintain a register in relation to the workers employed by him in Form 'D'.

The Payment of Gratuity Act, 1972

The Act aims to provide for a scheme for the payment of gratuity to employees engaged in factories, mines, oilfields, plantations, ports, railway companies, shops or other establishments and for matters connected therewith or incidental thereto. *This act is applicable to*

- Every factory, mine, oilfield, plantation, port and railway company.
- Every shop or establishment in which ten or more persons are employed, or were employed, on any day of the preceding twelve months;
- Such other establishments or class of establishments, in which ten or more employees are employed, or were employed or any day of the preceding twelve months.
- A shop or establishment to which this Act has become applicable shall continue to be governed by this Act notwithstanding that the number of persons employed therein at any time after it has become so applicable falls below ten.

Definitions Under the Act

- **Appropriate Government** means
  (i) In relation to an establishment
  (a) belonging to, or under the control of, the Central Government.
  (b) having branches in more than one State.
  (c) of a factory belonging to, or under the control of, the Central Government.
  (d) of a major port, mine, oilfield or railway company, the Central Government.
  (ii) In any other case, the State Government. [Section 2(a)]
- **Completed Year of Service** means continuous service for one year. [Section 2(b)]
- **Continuous Service** means uninterrupted service. This includes service which is interrupted by sickness, accident, leave, lay-off, strike or a lock-out or cessation of work not due to any fault of the employee. An employee of a seasonal establishment shall be deemed to be in continuous service, if he has actually worked for not less than seventh-five per cent of the numbers of days on which the establishment was in operation during the year. [Section 2(c)]
- **Controlling Authority** means an authority appointed by the appropriate government under Section 3. [Section 2(d)]
- **Employee** means any person employed on wages in any establishment, factory, mine, oilfield, plantation, port, railway company or shop. He can be indulged in doing any skilled, semi-skilled or unskilled, manual, supervisory, technical or clerical work. It does not include any such person who is employed in a managerial or administrative capacity, or who holds a civil post under the Central Government or a State Government or Armed Forces. [Section 2(e)]
- **Employer** means a person or authority appointed by the appropriate government for the supervision and control of employees, or where no person or authority has been so appointed, the head of the Ministry or the Department concerned. In case, the establishment belongs to any local authority, the person appointed by such authority for the supervision and control of employees or where no person has been so appointed, the chief executive officer of the local authority.

  In any other case, the persons, who, or the authority which, has the ultimate control over the affairs of the establishment, factory, mine, oilfield, plantation, port, railway company or shop, and where the said affairs are entrusted to any other person, whether called a manager, managing director or by any other name, such person. [Section 2(t)]
- **Family** consists of
  (a) In the case of a male employee, himself, his wife, his children, whether married or unmarried, his dependent parents and the widow and children of his predeceased son, if any.
  (b) In the case of a female employee, herself, her husband, her children, whether married or unmarried, her dependent parents and the dependent parents of her husband and the widow and children of her predeceased son, if any. [Section 2(h)]
- **Retirement** means termination of the service of an employee otherwise than on superannuation. [Section 2(q)]
- **Superannuation in Relation to an Employee** means
  (a) The attainment by the employee of such age as is fixed in the contract or conditions of service as the age on the attainment of which the employee shall vacate the employment; and
  (b) In any other case, the attainment by the employee of the age of fifty-eight years. [Section 2(r)]
- **Wages** means all emoluments which are earned by an employee while on duty or on leave in accordance with the terms and conditions of his employment and which are paid or are payable to him in cash. It includes dearness allowance but does not include any bonus, commission, house rent allowance, overtime wages and any other allowance. [Section 2(s)]

Payment of Gratuity (Section 2A)

- Gratuity shall be payable to an employee on the termination of his employment after he has rendered continuous service for not less than five years
  - (a) On his superannuation, or
  - (b) On his retirement or resignation, or
  - (b) On his death or disablement due to accident or disease.
- For every completed year of service in excess of six months, the employer shall pay gratuity to an employee at the rate of fifteen days' wages based on the rate of wages last drawn by the employee concerned.
- In the case of piece-rated employee, daily wages shall be computed on the average of the total wages received by him for a period of three months immediately preceding the termination of his employment.
- In the case of an employee, employed in a seasonal establishment, the employer shall pay the gratuity at the rate of seven days' wages for each season.
- The amount of gratuity payable to an employee shall not exceed three lakhs and fifty thousand rupees.
- In case of an employee, who is employed, after his disablement, on reduced wages, his wages for the period preceding his disablement shall be taken to be the wages received by him during that period, and his wages for the period subsequent to his disablement shall be taken to be the wages as so reduced.

Nomination (Section 6)

- Each employee, who has completed one year of service, shall make nomination for the purpose of receiving gratuity.
- An employee may, in his nomination, distribute the amount of gratuity payable to him under this Act amongst more than one nominee.
- If an employee has a family at the time of making a nomination, the nomination shall be made in favor of one or more members of his family, and any nomination made by such employee in favor of a person who is not a member of his family shall be void.
- If at the time of making a nomination, the employee has no family, the nomination may be made in favor of any person or persons but if the employee subsequently acquires a family, such nomination shall forthwith become invalid and the employee shall make, within such time as may be prescribed, a fresh nomination in favor of one or more members of his family.

Determination of Amount of Gratuity

- A person or any authorised person who is eligible for payment of gratuity under this Act shall send a written application to the employer for payment of such gratuity.
- As soon as gratuity becomes payable, the employer shall determine the amount of gratuity and give notice in writing to the person to whom the gratuity is payable and also to the controlling authority specifying the amount of gratuity so determined.
- If there is any dispute as to the amount of gratuity payable to an employee or as the admissibility of any claim of, the employer shall deposit with the controlling authority such amount as he admits to be payable by him as gratuity.
- The controlling authority after conducting due inquiries and after giving the parties to the dispute a reasonable opportunity of being heard, determine the amount of gratuity payable to an employee.
- In case of the result of such inquiry any amount in excess of the amount deposited by the employer is found to be payable, the controlling authority shall direct the employer to pay such amount as is in excess of the amount deposited by him.
- The controlling authority shall pay the amount deposited including the excess amount, if any, deposited by the employer, to the person entitled thereto.
- In case, the employer fails to submit the amount of gratuity within the prescribed time, the collecting authority has the power to recover the same with compound interest thereon at the rate of 9% per annum.

Penalties (Section 9)

- Whoever, for the purpose of avoiding any payment to be made by himself under this Act or enabling any other person to avoid such payment, knowingly makes or causes to be made any false statement or false representation shall be punishable with imprisonment for a term which may extend to six months, or with fine which may extend to ten thousand rupees, or with both.
- An employer who contravenes, or makes default in complying with, any of the provisions of this Act or any rule or order made thereunder shall be punishable with imprisonment for a term which may extend to one year, or with fine which may extend to twenty thousand rupees, or with both.

The Employees' Provident Fund and Miscellaneous Provisions Act, 1952

This Act provides for the institution of provident funds, pension fund and deposit linked insurance fund for employees in factories and other establishment. It came into force with effect from 4th March, 1952. *It is applicable*

- to every establishment which is a factory engaged in any industry specified in Schedule I and in which twenty or more persons are employed, and
- to any other establishment employing twenty or more persons or class of such establishments which have been mentioned by the Central Government.

Definitions Under the Act

- **Appropriate Government** means
  - (a) In relation to an establishment belonging to, or under the control of, the Central Government or in relation to, an establishment connected with a railway company, a major port, a mine or an oil-field or a controlled industry (or in relation to an establishment having departments or branches in more than one State), the Central Government; and
  - (b) In relation to any other establishment, the State Government. [Section 2(a)]
- **Authorised Officer** means the Central Provident Fund Commissioner, Additional Central Provident Fund Commissioner, Deputy Provident Fund Commissioner, Regional Provident Fund Commissioner or such other fficer as may be authorised by the Central Government. [Section 2(aa)]
- **Basic Wages** means all emoluments which are earned by an employee while on duty or on leave or on holidays with wages. *These are payable in cash but does not include*
  - (a) The cash value of any food concession.
  - (b) Any dearness allowance, house-rent allowance, overtime allowance, bonus, commission or any other similar allowance payable to the employee in respect of his employment or of work done in such employment.
  - (c) Any presents made by the employer. [Section 2(b)]
- **Contribution** means a contribution payable in respect of a member under a scheme. [Section 2(c)]
- **Controlled Industry** means any industry which is controlled by the Union and it has been declared by a Central Act to be expedient in the public interest. [Section 2(d)]
- **Employer** means
  - (a) In relation to an establishment, which is a factory, the owner or occupier of the factory, including the agent of such owner or occupier, the legal representative of a deceased owner or occupier and, where a person has been named as a manager of the factory under the Factories Act, 1948.
  - (b) In relation to any other establishment, the person who, or the authority which, has the ultimate control over the affairs of the establishment, and where the said affairs are entrusted to a manager, managing director or managing agent, such manager, managing director or managing agent.[Section 2(e)]
- **Employee** means any person who is employed for wages in any kind of work, manual or otherwise and who gets his wages directly or indirectly from the employer. It includes any person employed by or through a contractor in or in connection with the work of the establishment. [Section 2(f)]
- **Exempted Establishment** means an establishment in respect of which an exemption has been granted under Section 17 from the operation of all or any of the provisions of any scheme or the Insurance Scheme. [Section 2(fff)]
- **Factory** means any premises, including the precincts there of, in any part of which a manufacturing process is being carried on or is ordinarily so carried on, whether with the aid of power or without the aid of power. [Section 2(g)]
- **Fund** means the provident fund established under a scheme. [Section 2(h)]
- **Industry** means any industry specified in schedule I, and includes any other industry added to the Schedule by notification under Section 4. [Section 2(i)]
- **Insurance Fund** means the Deposit-linked Insurance Fund established under Section 6C. [Section 2(ia)]
- **Insurance Scheme** means the Employees' Deposit-linked Insurance Scheme framed under Sub-section (1) of Section 6C. [Section 2(ib)]
- **Manufacture or Manufacturing Process** means any process for making, altering, repairing, ornamenting, finishing, packing, oiling, washing, cleaning, breaking up, demolishing or otherwise treating or adapting any article or substance with a view to its use, sale, transport, delivery or disposal. [Section 2(ic)]
- **Member** means a member of the fund. [Section 2(j)]
- **Occupier of a Factory** means the person who has ultimate control over the affairs of the factory and, where the said affairs are entrusted to a managing agent, such agent shall be deemed to be the occupier of the factory. [Section 2(k)]

- **Pension Fund** means the Employees' Pension Fund established under Sub-section (2) of Section 6A. [Section 2(ka)]
- **Pension Scheme** means the Employees' Pension Scheme framed under Sub-section (1) of Section 6A. [Section 2(kB)]
- **Recovery Officer** means any officer of the Central Government, State Government or the Board of Trustees constituted under Section 5A, who may be authorised by the Central Government, by notification in the Official Gazette, to exercise the powers of a recovery officer under this act. [Section 2(kb)]
- **Superannuation**, in relation to an employee who is the member of the Pension Scheme, means the attainment, by the said employee, of the age of fifty-eight years. [Section 2(ll)]

Employees' Provident Funds Scheme (Section 5)

- The Central Government has the power to frame a scheme to be called the Employees' Provident Funds Scheme for the establishment of provident fund under this act for employees.
- The fund shall be administered by the Central Board constituted by the Central Government.

  It shall have the following members

  (a) A Chairman and a Vice-chairman.

  (b) The Central Provident Fund Commissioner, exofficio.

  (c) Not more than five persons appointed by the Central Government from amongst its officials.

  (d) Not more than fifteen persons representing governments of such states as the Central Government may specify in this behalf.

  (e) Ten persons representing employers of the establishments to which the scheme applies.

  (f) Ten persons representing employees in the establishments to which the scheme applies.
- The Central Board must maintain proper accounts of its income and expenditure in such manner as the Central Government may, after consultation with the Comptroller and Auditor General of India.
- The accounts of the Central Board shall be audited annually by the Comptroller and Auditor General of India and any expenditure incurred by him in connection with such audit shall be payable by the Central Board to the Comptroller and Auditor General of India.
- The Central Government has the power to constitute an Executive Committee to assist the Central Board in executing its functions properly. The Central Provident Fund Commissioner will be its ex-officio member.
- The Central Government has the power to constitute for a particular state, state board. It is basically a Board of Trustees and shall exercise such powers and perform such duties as the Central Government may assign to it from time-to-time.

Appointment of Officers (Section 5D)

- The Central Government has the power to appoint a Central Provident Fund Commissioner who shall be the Chief Executive Officer of the Central Board and shall be subject to the general control and superintendence of that Board.
- The Central Government may also appoint a Financial Adviser and Chief Accounts Officer to assist the Central Provident Fund Commissioner in the discharge of his duties.

Contributions and Matters which may be Provided for in the Scheme (Section 6)

The contribution which shall be paid by the employer to the fund shall be 10% per of the basic wages, dearness allowance and retaining allowance (if any) and the employees' contribution shall be equal to the contribution payable by the employer in respect of him.

Employees' Pension Scheme (Section 6A)

- The Central Government may frame a scheme to be called the Employees' Pension Scheme for the purpose of providing for

  (a) Superannuation pension, retiring pension or permanent total disablement pension to the employees of any establishment or class of establishments to which this act applies; and

  (b) Widow or widower's pension, children pension or orphan pension payable to the beneficiaries of such employees.
- There shall be a pension fund into which there shall be paid, from time-to-time, in respect of every employee who is a member of the Pension Scheme

  (a) Sum from the employer which shall not exceed eight and one-third per cent of the basic wages, dearness allowance and retaining allowance.

  (b) Sums from the employers of exempted establishments.

Employees' Deposit-linked Insurance Scheme (Section 6C)

- The Central Government may frame a scheme to be called the Employees' Deposit-linked Insurance Scheme for the purpose of providing life insurance benefits to the employees of any establishment or class of establishments to which this act applies.
- As soon as may be after the framing of the Insurance Scheme, a Deposit-linked Insurance Fund shall be established. Employer will be contributing regularly in this fund. The amount will not be more than 1% of the aggregate of the basic wages, dearness allowance and retaining allowance (if any).

Determination of Money Dues from the Employer (Section 7A)

- The Central Provident Fund Commissioner, any Additional Central Provident Fund Commissioner, any Deputy Provident Fund Commissioner, any Regional Provident Fund Commissioner or any Assistant Provident Fund Commissioner will have the power to decide and determine the amount due from any employer.
- The employer shall be liable to pay simple interest at the rate of 12% per annum or at such higher rate as may be specified in the scheme on any amount due from him from the date on which the amount has become so due till the date of its actual payment.

Appellate Tribunal (Section 7D)

- The Central Government has the power to constitute one or more Appellate Tribunals to be known as the Employees' Provident Funds Appellate Tribunal to exercise the powers and discharge the functions conferred on such Tribunal by this act.
- A Tribunal shall consist of one person only to be appointed by the Central Government. A person shall not be qualified for appointment as a Presiding Officer of a Tribunal unless he is or has been or is qualified to be a Judge of a High Court or a District Judge.
- The Presiding Officer of a Tribunal shall hold office for a term of five years from the date on which he enters upon his office or until he attains the age of sixty-two years.
- The Central Government shall determine the nature and categories of the officers and other employees required to assist a Tribunal in the discharge of its functions and provide the Tribunal with such officers and other employees as it may think fit.

Penalties and Offences by Companies (Section 14 and 14A)

- Whoever, for the purpose of avoiding any payment to be made by himself under this act or of enabling any other person to avoid such payment knowingly makes or causes to be made any false statement or false representation shall be punishable with imprisonment for a term which may extend to one year or with fine of five thousand rupees or with both.
- An employer who contravenes or makes default in complying with the provisions of Section 6 (contributions by employer and employees) shall be punishable with imprisonment for a term which may extend to three years.
- If the person committing offence under this act or the scheme is a company, every person, who at the time the offence was committed was in charge of and was responsible to, the company for the conduct of the business of the company, as well as the company, shall be deemed to be guilty of the offence and shall be liable to be proceeded against and punished accordingly.

EXAM BASED QUESTIONS

1 Wage boards consist of
(a) an impartial chairman
(b) two independent members
(c) two or three representative members of workers and employer
(d) All of the above

2 Which of the following is not an objective of fringe benefits?
(a) To recruit and retain the best employees
(b) To develop a sense of belongingness and loyalty
(c) To improve motivation and employee
(d) To determine training needs

3 Which of the following are the types of fringe benefits?
(a) Health and safety benefits
(b) Retirement benefits
(c) Subsidised housing, transport, food, dresses
(d) All of the above

4 Which of the following is not an essential characteristic of a sound incentive plan?
(a) Equitable, economical and flexible
(b) Simple, prompt and adequate
(c) Neat, clean and green
(d) Scientific, reasonable and logical

5 Which of the following is not time based plan from the category of individual incentive plans?
(a) Rowan plan (b) Scanlon plan
(c) Bedeaux plan (d) Emerson Efficiency plan

6 Which of the following are the output based plan from the category of individual incentive plans?
(a) Taylor's Differential Piece Rate plan
(b) Meerick's Multiple Piece Rate plan
(c) Gantt's Task and Bonus plan
(d) All of the above

7 Which of the following can not be put under the category as group incentive plans?
(a) Halsey or Weir Plan
(b) Priest Man Bonus Plan
(c) Towne's Gain Sharing
(d) Scanlon Plan

8 Who of the following propounded the surplus value theory?
(a) Karl Marx (b) David Ricardo
(c) Both (a) and (b) (d) All of these

9 Which of the following factors influence the wage and salary policy of the company?
(a) A policy to fix the wages externally competitive
(b) A policy to fix the wages internally compatible
(c) A policy that the wages should be above the industry average or below it or comparable to it
(d) All of the above

10 Which one is the first step of the process of development of pay system?
(a) Gathar wage survey information
(b) Review job description
(c) Administer individual pay adjustments
(d) Conduct job evaluation

11 Which of the following features in Indian pay system make the wage and salary system unscientific?
(a) Government subsidies to PSU's and SSI's
(b) Compulsory forms
(c) Either of them
(d) Neither of them

12 Which of the following factors are considered in the negotiations between worker's unions and management to fix up the wages?
(a) Level of skill required to complete the work
(b) Level of wages being paid in the other organisations for similar activities
(c) Paying capacity of the enterprise
(d) All of the above

13 Which of the following is not a way to calculate wage differentials?
(a) Job evaluation
(b) Recruitment
(c) Employee appraisal
(d) Wage survey

14 Which of the following is not a determinant of wage differentials?
(a) Different location of company
(b) Hours of work
(c) Worker's family background
(d) Worker's skills

15 Which of the following are the essentials of a sound wage and salary structure?
(a) Internal equity and external competitiveness
(b) Linked with productivity
(c) Increments and individual equity
(d) All of the above

16 Which of the following factor does not affect the wages?
(a) Demand and supply of labour
(b) Labour unions
(c) Population of the city
(d) Cost of living

17 Which of the following act, has not been enacted to regualte the wages?
(a) The Factories Act
(b) The Minimum Wages Act, 1948
(c) The Equal Remuneration Act, 1976
(d) The Industrial Disputes Act, 1947

18 Which of the following are the main objectives of state regulation of wages?
(a) To regulate and fix the quantum of wages
(b) To prevent exploitation of workers
(c) To eliminate the sufferings of workers
(d) All of the above

19 Who of the following gave the subsistence theory?
(a) Thomas Malthus (b) John Stuart Mill
(c) Francis A Walker (d) Karl Marx

20 JB Clark gave which of the following theory of wages?
(a) The Bargaining Theory
(b) The Marginal Productivity Theory
(c) The Marxian Theory
(d) Residual Claimant Theory

21 Who of the following said that anomalies may occur of job evaluation is not done properly?
(a) Clerk Kerr
(b) Knowles and Thompson
(c) Phelps and Karl Marx
(d) John Stuart Mill

22 Which of the following are the principles to channelise wage determination process?
(a) Labour productivity
(b) Economic condition of industry
(c) Economic condition of nation
(d) All of the above

23 Which of the following is not a norm for fixation of wages?
(a) Net intape of 2700 calories
(b) 16.62 meters per year
(c) 15.5 litres milk per year
(d) Miscellaneous 20% of total minimum wage

24 Wages paid to worker should be sufficient to maintain himself and his family at a resonable level of existence. In the above statement refers to which of the following kind of wages?
(a) Minimum wage (b) Living wage
(c) Fair wage (d) Market wage

25 'Wages add into the cost of production' keeping the above statement in view which of the following will be correct?
(a) It will result in squeezing the profit of the owner
(b) It will result in increasing the profit of the owner
(c) Either (a) or (b) may result
(d) Neither (a) nor (b) will result

26 If the cost of all other consumer goods increase in the same proportion, with the rise in wages, then which of the following statement seems relevant?
(a) Increase in wages is not of any use
(b) Increase in wages will improve the living condition
(c) Either (a) or (b)
(d) Neither (a) nor (b)

27 Which of the following anomalies may occur in case job evaluation is not properly in the view of Knowles and Thompson?
(a) Fresher may get more salary than what he deserves
(b) Potential employees may get discouraged
(c) Different payments to the same work
(d) All of the above

28 According to the efficiency wage model firms will pay the real wage that
(a) maximises worker's marginal productivity
(b) maximises the marginal productivity of capital and the marginal productivity of labour together
(c) maximises efforts in ratio of real wage
(d) minimises hiring and training costs to the firm

29 According to the efficiency wage model, during a recession, firms will not reduce real wages because
(a) unions would do on strike, reducing profitability
(b) this would reduce worker's effort and productivity
(c) the equilibrium real wage has increased
(d) profitability is more at the time of recession

30 Which of the following statement is true in relation to fixation of living wages?
(a) It is fixed, keeping in mind the general economic conditions of the country
(b) It is fixed, keeping in mind the factors such as the productivity of labour
(c) It is fixed, keeping in mind the minimum requirement of the worker
(d) It is fixed, keeping in mind the number of members in the worker's family

31 In an inflationary economy like ours to-day which of the following components of wages becomes more important?
(a) Overtime (b) Incentive
(c) Bonus (d) Dearness Allowance

32 Which of the following is not an authorised deduction under the Payment of Wags Act, 1936?
(a) Fines
(b) Income tax
(c) Contribution for LIC premium
(d) Deduction made fax payment of debt to money lender

33 Which of the following can be said to be a correct concept of wages?
(a) Wage is a reward
(b) Wage is a compensation
(c) Wage is the price of labour
(d) Wage is an incentive to work more

34 According to Minimum Wages Act, 1948, who is an adolescent?
(a) A person who has completed his sixteenth year of age but has not completed his eighteenth year
(b) A person who has completed his twelfth year of age but has not completed his eighteenth year
(c) A person who has completed his fourteenth year of age but has not completed his eighteenth year
(d) A person who has completed his thirteenth year of age but has not completed his eighteenth year

35 According to Minimum Wages Act, 1948, who is a child?
(a) A person who has not completed his fourteenth year of age
(b) A person who has not completed his thirteenth year of age
(c) A person who has not completed his twelfth year of age
(d) A person who has not completed his eighteenth year of age

36 Which section of Minimum Wages Act, 1948 defines cost of living index number?
(a) 2(d) (b) 2(b)
(c) 2(a) (d) 2(e)

37 Which section of Minimum Wages Act, 1948 defines employee?
(a) 2 (i) (b) 2 (a)
(c) 2(b) (d) 2(c)

38 Which section of Minimum Wages Act, 1948 defines employer?
(a) 2(j) (b) 2(a) (c) 2(b) (d) 2(e)

39 According to the Minimum Wages Act, 1948, what is the maximum fixed interval for reviewing and revising wages?
(a) 2 years (b) 3 years
(c) 6 months (d) 5 years

40 According to Minimum Wages Act, 1948, the minimum rate of remuneration to apply in the case of employees employed on piece work for the purpose of securing to such employees a minimum rate of wages on a time work basis is known as
(a) guaranteed time rate
(b) overtime rate
(c) minimum time rate
(d) minimum piece rate

41 What is the penalty for the employers who pay less than the minimum rates of wages fixed to its employees?
(a) ₹ 1,000 (b) ₹ 400
(c) ₹ 200 (d) ₹ 500

42 According to the Minimum Wages Act, 1948, a minimum rate based on the quantity of output workers have produced is known as
(a) guaranteed time rate
(b) overtime rate
(c) minimum time rate
(d) minimum piece rate

43 According to the Minimum Wages Act, 1948, which of the following is included in the wages?
(a) House accommodation supply of light, water and medical attendance
(b) Travelling allowance or the value of any travelling concession
(c) Gratuity
(d) House rent allowance

44 Which section of Minimum Wages Act, 1948 defines scheduled employment?
(a) 2 (g) (b) 2 (b)
(c) 2 (d) (d) 2 (a)

45 According to the Payment of Wages Act, 1936, what is the maximum wage period for the payment of wages?
(a) 2 months (b) 1 month
(c) 3 months (d) 4 months

46 According to the Payment of Wages Act, 1936, in case of an establishment that has 1000 persons, the wages need to be paid by when?
(a) Eleventh of that month
(b) Seventh of that month
(c) Tenth of that month
(d) Third of that month

47 According to the Payment of Wages Act, 1936, in case of a person who is working in any railway factory or industrial or other establishment upon or in which more than one thousand persons are employed, the wages need to be paid by when?
(a) Eleventh of that month
(b) Seventh of that month
(c) Tenth of that month
(d) Third of that month

48 According to the Payment of Wages Act, 1936, an employer terminates an employee, the wages earned by him must be paid by when?
(a) Before the expiry of the second working day from the day on which his employment is terminated
(b) Before the expiry of the fifth working day from the day on which his employment is terminated
(c) Before the expiry of the fourth working day from the day on which his employment is terminated
(d) Before the expiry of the third working day from the day on which his employment is terminated

49 According to the Payment of Wages Act, 1936, no fine shall be imposed on who among the following?
(a) Any female worker who is under the age of fifteen years
(b) Any employed person who is under the age of fifteen years
(c) Any male worker who is under the age of eighteen years
(d) Any worker who is under the age of eighteen years

50 According to the Payment of Wages Act, 1936, what is the maximum amount of fine that can be imposed on an employee?
(a) Amount equal to 2% of the wages payable to him in respect of that wage period
(b) Amount equal to 3% of the wages payable to him in respect of that wage period
(c) Amount equal to 1% of the wages payable to him in respect of that wage period
(d) Amount equal to 7% of the wages payable to him in respect of that wage period

51 According to the Payment of Wages Act, 1936, fine cannot be recovered from an employee after expiry of how many days?
(a) 60 (b) 24
(c) 48 (d) 22

52 According to the Payment of Wages Act, 1936, if ten or more employed persons acting in concert absent themselves without due notice and without reasonable cause, what is the maximum amount that can be deducted from their salary?
(a) Wages of eight days
(b) Wages of eleven days
(c) Wages of seven days
(d) Wages of ten days

53 The Payment of Wages Act, 1936, mandates the employer to preserve the register having records the employees for how many years?
(a) 2 (b) 1
(c) 4 (d) 3

54 According to the Payment of Wages Act, 1936, if there has been incorrect deductions from the wages, the employee has the right to make a claim within how much time?
(a) 9 months (b) 10 months
(c) 11 months (d) 12 months

55 According to the Payment of Wages Act, 1936, what will be the maximum fine if an employer is unable to maintain register or record?
(a) ₹ 1,000 (b) ₹ 2,000
(c) ₹ 3,000 (d) ₹ 500

56 The Payment of Bonus Act, 1965 is applicable to an establishment having a minimum of how many employees?
(a) 20 or more (b) 30 or more
(c) 40 or more (d) 10 or more

57 As per the Payment of Bonus Act, 1965, an accounting year starts from when?
(a) 1st April (b) 31st March
(c) 1st February (d) 31st January

58 According to the Payment of Bonus Act, 1965, what is the allocable surplus for any company other than a banking company?
(a) 27% (b) 67%
(c) 37% (d) 47%

59 According to the Payment of Bonus Act, 1965, what is the allocable surplus for a banking company?
(a) 20% (b) 60%
(c) 30% (d) 40%

60 What is the minimum salary or wage of an employee to be eligible for bonus?
(a) ₹ 10,000 (b) ₹ 21,000
(c) ₹ 7,000 (d) ₹ 9,000

61 According to the Payment of Bonus Act, 1965, which of the following is correct for establishment?
(a) It is an establishment owned, controlled or managed by a government company as defined in Section 617 of the Companies Act, 1956
(b) It is an establishment owned, controlled or managed by a corporation in which not less than 40% of its capital is held, whether singly or taken together, by the government, the RBI
(c) It is an establishment owned, controlled or managed by a government company, a corporation owned by the government or the RBI
(d) All of the above

62 According to the Payment of Bonus Act, 1965, which of the following is included under wages?
(a) Dearness Allowance
(b) Bonus
(c) Retrenchment compensation
(d) Gratuity

63 According to the Payment of Bonus Act, 1965, the method of calculation of profit for a banking company is mentioned in which schedule of the act?
(a) First Schedule (b) Second Schedule
(c) Third Schedule (d) Fourth Schedule

64 According to the Payment of Bonus Act, 1965, the method of calculation of profit for a company other than banking company is mentioned in which schedule of the act?
(a) First Schedule (b) Second Schedule
(c) Third Schedule (d) Fourth Schedule

65 According to the Payment of Bonus Act, 1965, what is the minimum bonus that needs to be paid to every employee?
(a) 8.33% of the salary or wages earned by the employee during the accounting year
(b) 8.1% of the salary or wages earned by the employee during the accounting year
(c) 7.33% of the salary or wages earned by the employee during the accounting year
(d) 9.33% of the salary or wages earned by the employee during the accounting year

66 According to the Payment of Bonus Act, 1965, what is the maximum bonus that can be paid to every employee?
(a) Maximum of 30% of salary or wage
(b) Maximum of 25% of salary or wage
(c) Maximum of 10% of salary or wage
(d) Maximum of 20% of salary or wage

67 According to the Payment of Bonus Act, 1965, the bonus needs to be paid within how many months from the close of the accounting year?
(a) 9 months (b) 7 months
(c) 8 months (d) 2 months

68 **According to the Payment of Bonus Act, 1965, in case the salary or wages of an employee exceeds 7000 per mensem, the bonus is calculated on what amount?**

(a) ₹ 10,000 (b) ₹ 7,000
(c) ₹ 3,500 (d) ₹ 3,000

69 **Which of the following is incorrect under the Payment of Bonus Act, 1965?**

(a) An employee shall be deemed to have worked in an establishment in any accounting year on the days which he has been laid-off
(b) Bonus will be paid in cash to the employees
(c) In case an employee has not worked for all the working days in an accounting year, the minimum bonus shall be proportionately reduced
(d) Every employee is entitled to payment of bonus if he has worked in the establishment for not less than twenty working days in that year

70 **If an employee is unable to meet any requisite condition mentioned under Payment of Bonus Act, 1965 how much penalty will be charged?**

(a) ₹ 2,000 (b) ₹ 1,000
(c) ₹ 3,000 (d) ₹ 4,000

71 **Which of the following needs to be subtracted from allocable surplus?**

(a) Any amount by way of depreciation admissible in accordance with the Income Tax Act or in accordance with the provisions of the agricultural income tax law
(b) Any amount by way of which the employer is entitled to deduct from his income under the Income Tax Act
(c) Any direct tax which the employer is liable to pay for the accounting year in respect of his income, profits and gains during that year
(d) All of the above

72 **According to Payment of Bonus Act, 1965, in which of the following cases employees will be eligible for the bonus?**

(a) Dismissed from service for fraud
(b) Violent behaviour while on the premises of the establishment or theft
(c) Misappropriation or sabotage of any property of the establishment
(d) He has been laid-off

73 **Company is defined under which section of the Companies Act, 1956?**

(a) 2 (b) 4
(c) 7 (d) 3

74 **Banking company has been defined under which section of Banking Companies Act, 1949?**

(a) 2 (b) 3
(c) 4 (d) 5

75 **According to the Payment of Bonus Act, 1965, available surplus is calculated under which of the following sections?**

(a) 2 (b) 3
(c) 4 (d) 5

76 **According to the Payment of Bonus Act, 1965 which of the following**

(a) A minimum bonus which shall be 9.33% of the salary or wages earned by the employee during the accounting year or one hundred rupees, whichever is higher
(b) Every employer shall be bound to pay to every employee in respect of the accounting year commencing on any day in the year 1978
(c) A minimum bonus which shall be 8.33% of the salary or wages earned by the employee during the accounting year or one hundred rupees, whichever is higher
(d) It will be paid only if the company has any allocable surplus in the accounting year

77 **What will be the punishment if an employer is unable to meet the requisite conditions according to the Payment of Bonus Act, 1965?**

(a) Imprisonment for a term which may extend to seven months
(b) Imprisonment for a term which may extend to four months
(c) Imprisonment for a term which may extend to six months
(d) Imprisonment for a term which may extend to three months

78 **Which of the following is true for remuneration under the Equal Remuneration Act, 1976?**

(a) It includes the basic wage or salary and any additional emoluments
(b) It may be paid either in cash or in kind
(c) It will be paid only when the terms of the contract of employment are fulfilled
(d) All of the above

79 **How many members should be present in the advisory committee set up by the government to provide inputs for the employment of women in establishments?**

(a) 20 (b) 10
(c) 12 (d) 14

80 **How many women members should be present in the advisory committee set up by the government to provide inputs for the employment of women in establishments?**

(a) 10 (b) 12
(c) 5 (d) 7

81 **What will be the fine imposed on the person who makes any discrimination between men and women workers in contravention of the Equal Remuneration Act, 1976?**

(a) ₹ 10,000 (b) ₹ 5,000
(c) ₹ 2,000 (d) ₹ 3,000

82 **What will be the fine imposed on an employer if he makes any payment of remuneration at unequal rates to men and women under the Equal Remuneration Act, 1976?**

(a) ₹ 10,000 (b) ₹ 5,000
(c) ₹ 2,000 (d) ₹ 3,000

83 **Which section of Equal Remuneration Act, 1976 empowers Central Government to make Equal Remuneration Rules, 1976?**

(a) 23 (b) 13 (c) 14 (d) 12

84 **According to the Equal Remuneration Rules, 1976, claims related to complaints with regard to the contravention of any provision of this act will be made in which of the following forms?**

(a) Form A (b) Form B
(c) Form C (d) Form D

85 **According to the Equal Remuneration Rules, 1976, claims related to the wages at equal rates to men and women workers for the same work or work of a similar nature will be made in which of the following forms?**

(a) Form A (b) Form B
(c) Form C (d) Form D

86 **According to the Equal Remuneration Rules, 1976, every employer shall maintain a register in relation to the workers employed by him in which of the following forms?**

(a) Form A (b) Form B
(c) Form C (d) Form D

87 **According to the Equal Remuneration Rules, 1976, the authorisation to the authority shall be provided under which form?**

(a) Form A (b) Form B
(c) Form C (d) Form D

88 **The Payment of Gratuity Act, 1972 is applicable to an establishment with a minimum of how many employee?**

(a) 11 (b) 12
(c) 14 (d) 10

89 **Which of the following holds true for the definition of employee under Payment of Gratuity Act, 1972?**

(a) Any person employed on wages in any establishment, factory, mine, oilfield, plantation, port, railway company or shop
(b) He can be indulged in doing any skilled, semi-skilled, or unskilled, manual, supervisory, technica[illegible] clerical work
(c) It does not include any such person who is employed in a managerial or administrative capacity
(d) All of the above

90 **Who among the following are included in family of a male member?**

(a) His wife and children
(b) His dependent parents
(c) Widow and children of his predeceased son
(d) All of the above

91 **According to the Payment of Gratuity Act, 1972, an employee attains superannuation at what age?**

(a) 60 (b) 58
(c) 70 (d) 55

92 **According to the Payment of Gratuity Act, 1972, an employee is eligible for gratuity after rendering how many years of continuous service?**

(a) 10 (b) 8 (c) 7 (d) 5

93 **For every completed year of service in excess of six months, the employer shall pay gratuity to an employee for wages based on what rate?**

(a) Rate of fifteen days
(b) Rate of ten days
(c) Rate of twenty days
(d) Rate of thirty days

94 **In the case of an employee employed in a seasonal establishment, the employer shall pay the gratuity will be paid at what rate?**

(a) Rate of seven days' wages for each season
(b) Rate of twelve days' wages for each season
(c) Rate of eleven days' wages for each season
(d) Rate of ten days' wages for each season

95 **What is the maximum amount of gratuity that can be paid to an employee?**

(a) Wages of 20 months (b) Wages of 10 months
(c) Wages of 12 months (d) Wages of 14 months

96 **An employee needs to complete how many years of service before filing for nominees under the Payment of Gratuity Act, 1972?**

(a) 1 year (b) 3 months
(c) 7 months (d) 2 years

97 **How much fine shall be imposed in case of any false statement or false representation by the employer?**

(a) ₹ 6,000 (b) ₹ 1,000
(c) ₹ 2,000 (d) ₹ 3,000

98 **In case an employer fails to submit the amount of gratuity within the prescribed time, the collecting authority has the power to recover the same at what compound interest?**

(a) 9% (b) 10%
(c) 11% (d) 12%

99 **Who among the following constitutes a family for the female employees?**

(a) Her husband and children
(b) Her dependent parents
(c) Dependent parents of her husband
(d) All of the above

100 **Which of the following is included in the wages?**

(a) Bonus
(b) Commission
(c) House Rent Allowance
(d) Dearness Allowance

101 **Under which of the following is gratuity payable?**

(a) On his superannuation, or
(b) On his retirement or resignation, or
(c) On his death or disablement due to accident or disease
(d) All of the above

102 In the case of piece rated employee, daily wages shall be computed on the average of the total wages received by him for a period of how many months immediately preceding the termination of his employment?

(a) Three months (b) Four months
(c) Five months (d) Seven months

103 The Employees' Provident Fund and Miscellaneous Provisions Act, 1952 is applicable to an establishment having a minimum of how many employees?

(a) 20 (b) 30
(c) 40 (d) 70

104 The Employees' Provident Fund and Miscellaneous Provisions Act, 1952 is applicable to an establishment mentioned in which schedule of the act?

(a) Schedule I (b) Schedule II
(c) Schedule III (d) Schedule IV

105 According to the Employees' Provident Fund and Miscellaneous Provisions Act, 1952, which of the following is incorrect in context of basic wages?

(a) All emoluments which are earned by an employee while on duty
(b) All emoluments which are earned by an employee on leave or on holidays
(c) It includes the cash value of any food concession
(d) It does not include any dearness allowance and house rent allowance

106 An exempted establishment is allowed exemption under which of the following sections?

(a) 11 (b)12 (c) 17 (d)19

107 The pension fund will be established under which section of the Employees' Provident Fund and Miscellaneous Provisions Act, 1952?

(a) 6A (b) 6B
(c) 6C (d) 6D

108 Industry means any industry established under which of the following schedules of the Employees' Provident Fund and Miscellaneous Provisions Act, 1952?

(a) Schedule I (b) Schedule II
(c) Schedule II (d) Schedule IV

109 According to the Employees' Provident Fund and Miscellaneous Provisions Act, 1952, what is the contribution of an employer?

(a) 10% (b) 14% (c) 11% (d) 13%

110 Who among the following will audit the fund established under the Employees' Provident Fund and Miscellaneous Provisions Act, 1952?

(a) Comptroller and Auditor General of India
(b) Chief Labour Commissioner
(c) Central Provident Fund Commissioner
(d) Both (a) and (b)

111 What will be the contribution of employer in the pension fund established under Employees' Provident Fund and Miscellaneous Provisions Act, 1952?

(a) Eight and one-third per cent of the basic wages, dearness allowance and retaining allowance
(b) Nine and one-third per cent of the basic wages, dearness allowance and retaining allowance
(c) Ten and one-third per cent of the basic wages, dearness allowance and retaining allowance
(d) Eleven and one-third per cent of the basic wages, dearness allowance and retaining allowance

112 What will be the contribution of employer in the insurance fund established under Employees' Provident Fund and Miscellaneous Provisions Act, 1952?

(a) 1% (b) 2%
(c) 3% (d) 4%

113 According to the Employees' Provident Fund and Miscellaneous Provisions Act, 1952, what is the contribution of an employer to the fund?

(a) 10% (b) 14%
(c) 11% (d) 13%

114 What will be the interest charged to the employer on the amount that is due?

(a) 12% (b) 14%
(c) 11% (d) 13%

115 How many members will be present in the Employees' Provident Funds Appellate Tribunal?

(a)1 (b) 2
(c) 3 (d) 4

116 .... are paid in addition to wages, salary, allowances and bonus as other benefits to the employees by the employer.

(a) TA (b) DA
(c) Fringe benefits (d) Rewards

117 .... is a managerial device of increasing a worker's productivity in the organisation.

(a) Wage Differential (b) Wage Incentive Scheme
(c) Wage Fund Theory (d) None of these

118 Individual incentive plans and group incentive plans are the two types of ....

(a) wage incentive plan (b) wage fund theory
(c) wage differentials (d) None of these

119 ...... refers to the amount produced per worker per period of time.

(a) Productivity
(b) Marginal revenue
(c) Equilibrium
(d) None of the above

120 ..... is a process of managing company compensation programme.

(a) Wage administration (b) Wage differential
(c) Wage fund theory (d) None of these

121 ...... refers to differences in wages between workers with different skills in the same industry or between those with comparable skills in different industries or localities.
(a) Wage differential (b) Wage administration
(c) Both (a) and (b) (d) None of these

122 ...... is a kind of differential which occurs when the workers in the same occupation and in the same area but in different industries are paid different wages.
(a) Intra firm differential (b) Inter firm differential
(c) Inter sector differential (d) None of these

123 ...... is the wage sufficient to provide basic amenities of life and also preserve the efficiency of the workers.
(a) Minimum wages (b) Fair wages
(c) Living wages (d) None of these

124 ...... is the rate which has got to be paid to the worker irrespective of the capacity of the industry to pay.
(a) The statutory minimum wages
(b) Fair wages
(c) Living wages
(d) None of the above

125 ...... is a wage which should cover the physical needs of workers and his family.
(a) Base subsistence/minimum wage
(b) Fair wage
(c) Living wage
(d) None of the above

126 ...... is the highest amount of wages proposed by the government, offering basic amenities of life and satisfying the social needs of a worker.
(a) Living wage (b) Fair wage
(c) Minimum wage (d) None of these

127 ...... adopted a legislation to protect workers employed in certain sweated trades such as boot-making, baking, clothing etc in 1896 for the first time.
(a) The State of Victoria (b) Calcutta Union
(c) Postal Union (d) None of these

128 In 1944, ... appointed by the Government of India was set up to investigate about the wages and earnings in industrial employments to submit a report.
(a) Wage Committee
(b) Wage Board
(c) Standing Labour Committee
(d) None of the above

129 Wage fund theory was given by ...... in 1930.
(a) John T Dunlop (b) John Stuart Mill
(c) Karl Marx (d) None of these

130 ......theory is based on the concept that more wages will lead to more consumption.
(a) Subsistance theory
(b) Wage fund theory
(c) Consumption theory
(d) None of the above

131 The demand price of labour is determined by the ...... of the individual worker.
(a) marginal revenue (b) marginal productivity
(c) Both (a) and (b) (d) None of these

132 ...... and ...... are the major legislative institutions involved in the process of wage determination.
(a) Payement of Wage Act and Minimum Wages Act
(b) Bonus Act and Minimum Wages Act
(c) Minimum Wages Act and Gratuity Act
(d) None of the above

133 ...... attitude play an important role in wage fixation and it also reflect their desire to improve or maintain morale of the workers.
(a) Top management (b) Middle management
(c) Lower management (d) None of these

134 Socially and psychologically ...... and ...... are co-related to each other.
(a) wages, success (b) salary, wages
(c) fringe benefits, salary (d) fringe benefits, success

135 Any employer who pays to any employee less than the minimum rates of wages fixed for that employee's class of work shall be punishable with imprisonment for a term which may extend to .... months.
(a) 10 (b) 6 (c) 7 (d) 8

136 The Central Advisory Board shall consist of persons to be nominated by the Central Government representing employers and employees in the scheduled employments who shall be .... in number.
(a) one-fourth (b) double
(d) half (d) equal

137 .... means all remuneration in terms of money which would be payable to a person employed in respect of his employment or of work done in such employment.
(a) Bonus (b) Wages
(c) Allowance (d) Housing Allowance

138 An employer who contravenes or makes default in complying with, the provisions of Section 6 (contributions by employer and employees) of the Employees' Provident Fund and Miscellaneous Provisions Act, 1952 shall be punishable with imprisonment for a term which may extend to ....
(a) two years (b) three years
(c) four years (d) seven years

139 An employee of a seasonal establishment shall be deemed to be in continuous service if he has actually worked for not less than .... of the numbers of days on which the establishment was in operation during the year.

(a) 70% (b) 75% (c) 80% (d) 90%

140 In case a person is unable to meet any requisite condition mentioned under Payment of Bonus Act, 1965, he shall be punishable with imprisonment for a term which may extend to .... or with fine which may extend to one thousand rupees or with both.

(a) ten months (b) twelve months
(c) six months (d) fourteen months

141 Consider the following for the Minimum Wages Act, 1948.

1. The appropriate government will have the power to fix the minimum rates of wages payable to employees employed in an employment specified in Part I or Part II of the Schedules.
2. The appropriate government will review and revise the minimum rate of wages after five years.
3. The appropriate government will fix the minimum rate of wages in any scheduled employment in which there are in the whole state less than one thousand employees engaged in such employment.

Which of the following statement given above is/are correct?

Codes

(a) Both 1 and 2
(b) Only 1
(c) Only 2
(d) All of the above

142 Which of the following is correct in context of Minimum Wages Act, 1948?

1. The minimum rate of wages will be fixed or revised by the appropriate government in respect of scheduled employments under Section 3.
2. Cost of living allowance includes basic wages.
3. The government has the power to appoint an advisory board for the matter of fixing and revising minimum rates of wages.
4. One-third members of the Central Advisory Board will be independent.

Codes

(a) 1, 2 and 3 (b) Both 2 and 3
(c) Both 1 and 3 (d) All of the above

143 Which of the following is correct for the definition of Employee as per the Minimum Wages Act,1948?

1. A person who is involved in skilled or unskilled manual or clerical work in a scheduled employment.
2. It does not include any member of the Armed Forces of the Union.
3. It is defined under Section 2(aa).

Codes

(a) Both 1 and 3
(b) Both 2 and 3
(c) Both 1 and 2
(d) All of the above

144 Which of the following is incorrect in context of Minimum Wages Act, 1948?

1. The minimum rates of wages may be fixed only by the hour.
2. There will be different minimum rates of wages fixed for different scheduled employments, different classes of work in the same scheduled employment, adults adolescents children and apprentices and different localities.
3. The appropriate government has the power to fix the number of hours of work which shall constitute a normal working day.

Codes

(a) Only 1 (b) Only 2
(c) Only 3 (d) Both 2 and 3

145 Which of the following is correct in context of Minimum Wages Act, 1948?

1. In case an employee whose minimum rate of wages is fixed under this act, works overtime, the employer is bound to pay the money for the extra hours devoted by the employee.
2. In case an employee is involved in two or more classes of work, he shall be paid on the piece basis.
3. If an employee is employed on piece work for which minimum time rate and not a minimum piece rate has been fixed under this act, the employer shall pay to such employee wages at not less than the minimum time rate.

Codes

(a) Both 1 and 3 (b) Only 2
(c) Only 3 (d) Both 1 and 2

146 Which of the following is included in the definition of industrial or other establishment?

1. Inland vessel mechanically propelled
2. Mine quarry or oilfield
3. Plantation

Codes

(a) Only 1 (b) Both 2 and 3
(c) Both 1 and 3 (d) All of the above

147 Consider the following for the definition of wages. Which of the following will not be included in Wages Act, 1936?

1. The value of any house accommodation.
2. Any contribution paid by the employer to any pension or provident fund.
3. Any remuneration payable under any award or settlement between the parties or order of a court.

Codes

(a) Both 1 and 2
(b) Both 2 and 3
(c) Both 1 and 3
(d) All of the above

148 Which of the following can be deducted from the wages as per the provisions of Wages Act, 1936?

1. Fines
2. Deductions for absence from duty
3. Deductions for house-accommodation supplied by the employer

Codes

(a) Both 1 and 2 (b) Both 2 and 3
(c) Both 1 and 3 (d) All of the above

149 In which of the following cases will be an employee eligible for bonus?

1. He has been on leave with salary or wages.
2. He has been absent due to temporary disablement caused by accident arising out of and in the course of his employment.
3. The employee has been on maternity leave with salary or wages, during the accounting year.

Which of the following statement is/are correct?

Codes

(a) Both 1 and 2
(b) Only 2
(c) Both 1 and 3
(d) All of the above

150 Consider the following for Equal Remuneration Act, 1976.

1. The employer needs to pay his workers equal pay irrespective of their genders for performing the same work or work of a similar nature.
2. Only labour officer has the right of hearing for deciding complaints with regard to claims arising out of non-payment of wages at equal rates to men and women workers for the same work or work of a similar nature.
3. The employer cannot discriminate between men and women workers while recruiting them for the same work or work of a similar nature.

Which of the following statement given above is/are correct?

Codes

(a) Only 3 (b) Both 2 and 3
(c) Both 1 and 3 (d) All of the above

151 Which of the following is correct in context of Employees' Provident Funds Appellate Tribunal?

1. Tribunal shall consist of one person only to be appointed by the Central Government.
2. A person shall not be qualified for appointment as a Presiding Officer of a Tribunal unless he is or has been or is qualified to be a Judge of a High Court or a District Judge.
3. The Presiding Officer of a Tribunal shall hold office for a term of five years.

Codes

(a) Both 1 and 3
(b) Both 2 and 3
(c) Both 1 and 2
(d) All of the above

152 Which of the following statements are true/false?

(i) The Minimum Wages Act, 1948 came into force on 15th March, 1948.
(ii) The State-Central Government has the power to appoint a central advisory board for the purpose of advising the Central and State Governments in the matters of the fixation and revision of minimum rates of wages.
(iii) The minimum rate of wages includes only cost of living allowance.
(iv) The minimum rates of wages may be fixed by the hour, day, month.

(a) (i), (iv) are true and (ii), (iii) are false
(b) (i), (iii) are true and (ii), (iv) are false
(c) (ii), (iv) are true and (i), (iii) are false
(d) (iii), (iv) are true and (ii), (i) are false

153 Which of the following statements are true/false?

(i) In case an employee whose minimum rate of wages is fixed under this Act, works overtime, the employer need not pay the money for the extra hours devoted by the employee.
(ii) If an employee whose minimum rate of wages has been fixed under this Act, works for a less number of hours than the requisite number of hours on a given day, he shall be entitled to receive wages in respect of work done by him on that day as if he had worked for a full normal working day.
(iii) In case an employee is involved in two or more classes of work, he shall be paid on the basis of pieces involved.
(iv) If an employee is employed on piece work for which minimum time rate and not a minimum piece rate has been fixed under this Act, the employer shall pay to such employee wages at not less than the minimum time rate.

(a) (i), (iv) are true and (ii), (iii) are false
(b) (i), (iii) are true and (ii), (iv) are false
(c) (ii), (iv) are true and (i), (iii) are false
(d) (iii), (iv) are true and (ii), (i) are false

154 Which of the following statements are true/false?

(i) Wages includes remuneration payable under any award or settlement between the parties or order of a court.
(ii) The employer needs to fix wage period for the payment of wages and this period shall not exceed two months.
(iii) Wages do not include travelling allowance or the value of any travelling concession.
(iv) In case of a person who is working in any railway factory or industrial or other establishment upon or in which more than one thousand persons are employed, the wages need to be paid by tenth of that month.

(a) (i), (iv) are true and (ii), (iii) are false
(b) (i), (iii) are true and (ii), (iv) are false
(c) (ii), (iv) are true and (i), (iii) are false
(d) (iii), (iv) are true and (ii), (i) are false

155 Which of the following statements are true/false?

(i) No fine shall be imposed on any employed person who is under the age of fifteen years.

(ii) The total amount of fine which may be imposed in any one wage-period on any employed person shall not exceed an amount equal to 2% of the wages payable to him in respect of that wage-period.

(iii) No fine imposed on any employed person shall be recovered from him by instalments or after the expiry of sixty days from the day on which it was imposed.

(iv) If ten or more employed persons acting in concert absent themselves without due notice and without reasonable cause, deduction can be made from their salary for not more than the wages of eight days.

(a) (i), (iii), (iv) are true and (ii) is false
(b) (i), (iii) are true and (ii), (iv) are false
(c) (ii), (iv) are true and (i), (iii) are false
(d) (iii), (iv) are true and (ii), (i) are false

156 Which of the following statements are true/false?

(i) In exercise of the powers conferred by Section 13 of the Equal Remuneration Act, 1976, the Central Government came out with the rules.

(ii) The claims for the complaints with regard to the contravention of any provision of the Equal Remuneration Act, 1976 need to be made in triplicate in the Form A to the authority.

(iii) Every employee is entitled to payment of bonus if he has worked in the establishment for not less than twenty working days in that year.

(iv) Payment of Bonus Act is applicable to ever establishment in which thirty or more persons are employed on any day during an accounting year.

(a) (i), (iv) are true and (ii), (iii) are false
(b) (i), (ii) are true and (iii), (iv) are false
(c) (ii), (iv) are true and (i), (iii) are false
(d) (iii), (iv) are true and (ii), (i) are false

157 Which of the following statements are true/false?

(i) Gratuity shall be payable to an employee on the termination of his employment after he has rendered continuous service for not less than five years.

(ii) Each employee, who has completed one year of service, shall make nomination for the purpose of receiving gratuity.

(iii) For every completed year of service in excess of six months, the employer shall pay gratuity to an employee at the rate of fifteen days' wages based on the rate of wages last drawn by the employee concerned.

(iv) An employer who contravenes, or makes default in complying with, any of the provisions of the Payment of Gratuity Act shall be punishable with imprisonment for a term which may extend to one year, or with fine which may extend to twenty thousand rupees, or with both.

(a) (i), (ii), (iii) and (iv) are true
(b) (i), (iii) are true and (ii), (iv) are false
(c) (ii), (iv) are true and (i), (iii) are false
(d) (iii), (iv) are true and (ii), (i) are false

158 Which of the following statements are true/false?

(i) Employees Provident Fund Act, 1952 is applicable to every establishment in which twenty or more persons are employed.

(ii) Basic wages means all emoluments which are earned by an employee while on duty or on leave or on holidays with wages.

(iii) Basic wages include dearness and House Rent Allowance (HRA).

(iv) Employee shall pay 10% per of the basic wages, dearness allowance and retaining allowance (if any) to Employee Provident Fund Scheme.

(a) (i), (ii) are true and (iii), (iv) are false
(b) (i), (iii) are true and (ii), (iv) are false
(c) (ii), (iv) are true and (i), (iii) are false
(d) (iii), (iv) are true and (ii), (i) are false

159 Which of the following statements are true/false?

(i) Fair wage is above the minimum wage but below the living wage.

(ii) Living wage is the highest amount of wage proposed by the government.

(iii) Different states have fixed different minimum wages based on the skill set of the employees.

(iv) Fair wage works on the formula Equal Pay for Equal work.

(a) (i), (iii) are true and (ii), (iv) are false
(b) (i), (ii), (iii) and (iv) are true
(c) (ii), (iv) are true and (i), (iii) are false
(d) (iii), (iv) are true and (ii), (i) are false

160 Which of the following statements are true/false?

(i) Wage Fund theory was given by Karl Marx.

(ii) Subsistence theory is based on the population theory of Thomas Malthus.

(iii) India has ratified 7 out of 8 core ILO conventions.

(iv) Subsistence theory was given by John Maynard Keynes.

(a) (i), (ii) are true and (iii), (iv) are false
(b) (i), (iii) are true and (ii), (iv) are false
(c) (ii), (iv) are true and (i), (iii) are false
(d) (iii), (iv) are true and (ii), (i) are false

161 Which of the following statements are true/false?

(i) The institutional wage theory states that level of compensation is determined on empirical and quantitative basis.

(ii) Consumption theory was formulated on the concept that more wages will lead to more consumption.

(iii) Investment theory states that employee's compensation is determined by the rate of return on that employee's investment.

(iv) Supply and demand theory states that wages are determined based on demand and supply of labour.

(a) (i), (ii), (iii) and (iv) are true
(b) (i), (iii) are true and (ii), (iv) are false
(c) (ii), (iv) are true and (i), (iii) are false
(d) (iii), (iv) are true and (ii), (i) are false

162 Which of the following statements are true/false?

(i) A minimum rate of wages for the time spent by employees for the production of output is minimum time rate.

(ii) Minimum piece rate is the rate based on the quantity of the output employees have produced.

(iii) The guaranteed time rate is a minimum rate of remuneration to apply in the case of employees employed on piece work for the purpose of securing to such employees a minimum rate of wages on a time work basis.

(iv) A minimum rate of remuneration to apply in the case of employees employed on piece work for the purpose of securing to such employees a minimum rate of wages on a time work basis is overtime rate.

(a) (i), (ii), (iii) and (iv) are true
(b) (i), (iii) are true and (ii), (iv) are false
(c) (ii), (iv) are true and (i), (iii) are false
(d) (iii), (iv) are true and (ii), (i) are false

163 Which of the following statements are true/false?

(i) Piece rate system is easy to calculate the wages under this method as it provides certainty of the amount of wage payment to the employee.

(ii) In time wage system, there is fixed wage because the wages are dependent on the units of pieces produced.

(iii) Time wage system is based on the fact that the workers are paid on the basis of amount of time they spend on the doing the particular job.

(iv) Piece rate system is based on the fact that workers are paid the wages on the basis of quantity and quality of work performed by them.

(a) (i), (ii), (iii) and (iv) are true
(b) (i), (iii) are true and (ii), (iv) are false
(c) (ii), (iv) are true and (i), (iii) are false
(d) (iii), (iv) are true and (ii), (i) are false

164 Which of the following statements are true/ false?

(i) Every employer shall be bound to pay to every employee in respect of the accounting year commencing on any day in the year 1979 and in respect of every subsequent accounting year, a minimum bonus which shall be 9.33% of the salary or wages earned by the employee during the accounting year or one hundred rupees, whichever is higher, whether or not the employer has any allocable surplus in the accounting year.

(ii) Bonus will be paid in cash to the employees.

(iii) If the allocable surplus exceeds the amount of minimum bonus payable to the employees, the employer is bound to pay to every employee in respect of that accounting year bonus which shall be an amount in proportion to the salary or wages earned by the employee during the accounting year subject to a maximum of 10% of such salary or wage.

(iv) Bonus needs to be paid within a period of eight months from the close of the accounting year.

(a) (i), (ii), (iii) and (iv) are true
(b) (i), (iii) are true and (ii), (iv) are false
(c) (ii), (iv) are true and (i), (iii) are false
(d) (iii), (iv) are true and (ii), (i) are false

165 Which of the following statements are true/false in context of the Employees' Provident Fund and Miscellaneous Provisions Act, 1952?

(i) Pension Fund means the Employees' Pension Fund established under Sub-section (2) of Section 6A and is defined under Section 2(ka) of the Act.

(ii) Contribution means a contribution payable in respect of a member under a scheme and is defined under Section 2(b) of the Act.

(iii) Every establishment which is a factory engaged in any industry specified in Schedule I and in which twenty or more persons are employed.

(iv) Insurance fund means the deposit-linked insurance fund established under Section 6A.

(a) (i), (ii), (iii) and (iv) are true
(b) (i), (iii) are true and (ii), (iv) are false
(c) (ii), (iv) are true and (i), (iii) are false
(d) (iii), (iv) are true and (ii), (i) are false

166 Which of the following statements are true/false?

(i) The employer needs to maintain a register of the employees working under him. This register needs to be preserved for a period of two years after the date of the last entry made therein.

(ii) In case of a person who is working in any railway factory or industrial or other establishment upon or in which more than one thousand persons are employed, the wages need to be paid by tenth of that month.

(iii) In case of a person who is working in any railway factory or industrial or other establishment upon or in which less than one thousand persons are employed, the wages need to be paid by third of that month.

(iv) In case, an employer terminates an employee, the wages earned by him must be paid before the expiry of the second working day from the day on which his employment is terminated.

(a) (i), (ii), (iii) and (iv) are true
(b) (i), (iii) are true and (ii), (iv) are false
(c) (ii), (iv) are true and (i), (iii) are false
(d) (iii), (iv) are true and (ii), (i) are false

Directions (Q. Nos. 167-170) *In the questions given below are two statements labelled as Assertion (A) and Reason (R). In the context of the two statement, which one of the following is correct ?*

Codes

(a) Both (A) and (R) correct and (R) is the correct explanation of (A)
(b) Both (A) and (R) are correct, but (R) is not the correct explanation of (A)
(c) (A) is true, but (R) is false
(d) (A) is false, but (R) is true

167 Assertion (A) The Central Government may frame a scheme to be called the Employees' Deposit linked Insurance Scheme for the purpose of providing life insurance benefits to the employees of any establishment or class of establishments to which this act applies.

Reason (R) As soon as may be after the framing of the Insurance scheme, a Deposit linked Insurance Fund shall be established.

168 Assertion (A) Continuous service means uninterrupted service.

Reason (R) This does not include service which is interrupted by sickness, accident, leave, layoff, strike or a lockout or cessation of work not due to any fault of the employee.

169 Assertion (A) Cost of living allowance will include a basic rate of wages and a special allowance at a rate to be adjusted at such intervals and in such manner that it works well in variation in the cost of living index number applicable to such workers.

Reason (R) It shall be computed by the competent authority at such intervals and in accordance with such directions as may be specified or given by the appropriate government.

170 Assertion (A) If an employee whose minimum rate of wages has been fixed under the Minimum Rate of Wages Act,. works for a less number of hours than a the requisite number of hours on a given day, he shall be entitled to receive full wages for that day.

Reason (A) It is considered that he has worked for a full normal working day.

171 Match the following with their correct sections of the Factories Act, 1948.

List I	List II
A. Adolscent	1. 2 (d)
B. Adult	2. 2 (a)
C. Cost of living index	3. 2 (aa)
D. Child	4. 2 (bb)

Codes

	A	B	C	D		A	B	C	D
(a)	1	3	4	2	(b)	2	3	1	4
(c)	3	1	4	2	(d)	1	3	2	4

172 Match the following.

List I	List II
A. Minimum wage	1. Above the minimum wage but below the living wage
B. Fair wage	2. Highest amount of wages
C. Living wage	3. Wages sufficient to have basic amenities
D. Capital formation	4. Refers to the savings in the country
E. Wage plan	5. In consonance to the productivity of the workers

Codes

	A	B	C	D	E		A	B	C	D	E
(a)	1	2	3	4	5	(b)	5	3	2	1	4
(c)	1	2	4	3	5	(d)	3	1	2	4	5

173 Match the following.

List I	List II
A. National income theory	1. Bargaining between capatalist and employees
B. Neo-Keynsian distribution theory	2. More wages will lead more consumption
C. Consumption theory	3. Wages are determined by the rate of return on the employees investment
D. Investment theory	4. Employment is the function of national income

Codes

	A	B	C	D		A	B	C	D
(a)	4	1	2	3	(b)	1	3	4	2
(c)	2	1	3	4	(d)	4	2	3	1

174 Match the following.

List I	List II
A. Subsistence theory	1. Employees are paid from fund
B. Wage fund theory	2. Deals with population rather than labour
C. Residual claiment theory	3. More wages will lead to more consumption
D. The maxima theory of surplus nature	4. Wages are residual of total revenue

Codes

	A	B	C	D		A	B	C	D
(a)	2	1	4	3	(b)	1	2	3	4
(c)	4	3	2	1	(d)	2	1	3	4

175 Match the following.

List I	List II
A. Institutional wage theory	1. Wages are determined on demand and supply of labour
B. Supply and demand theory	2. Wages determination after having comparison of region and industry
C. The marginal productivity theory	3. Wages are set between the upper and lower limit
D. The bargaining theory	4. Demand and supply inperfectly competitive market in equal to the marginal revenue productivity

Codes

	A	B	C	D		A	B	C	D
(a)	2	1	4	3	(b)	2	3	4	1
(c)	3	1	2	4	(d)	4	3	2	1

Directions (Q. Nos. 176-180) *Read the following passage and answer the questions that follow.*

Wages are the most common earnings of people. Perceived by workers, clerks, managers and employees in general, wages and salaries constitute the core element in income for the majority of active people. Similarly, many pension schemes are based on wage levels and dynamics.

By contrast, the self-employed do not receive wages, but sell directly their labour in the market. The property and enterprise owners obtain income from rents, dividends and other financial instruments' gains. The unemployed in certain countries and under constraints receive public financial support. In another perspective, wages are a major determinant of production costs.

Nominal wages are written down in contracts between the employee and the organisation. Real wages somehow correct nominal wages for prices of goods and services bought by the employee. In specific institutional settings, nominal wages may be automatically and frequently adjusted to certain inflation measures, resulting in a more or less constant real wages.

Part of the wage may be paid in nature (e.g. fringe benefits), but the core is usually paid with money. Some firms use stock options as part of the remuneration package. A part of firms' labour cost is given to the State in terms of taxes and contributions to social funds for retirement and unemployment. Thus, in many countries there exists a large discrepancy between gross and net wages.

Wage levels result from individual and collective negotiations between the employees (and their representatives) with the management (and the owners) of firms.

In public bodies, laws and negotiations decide wages. A government wanting to cut public expenditure might try to freeze or reduce public wages, whereas a stimulus-oriented policy might include increases.

Firms and organisations pay wages to employees usually depending on working time and/or on results (production made or objectives reached). Individual wage often depends on occupied position in the organisation as well as on education, cumulated experience and seniority. Wages for the same job outside the firm may serve as a conventional or mandatory reference point.

176 **What is the way of earning for self-employed people?**
(a) Through the salary given by the government
(b) Though the salary given by some organisation
(c) Through directly selling their labour in the market
(d) None of the above

177 **What is the use of taxes paid to the State Government?**
(a) Contributions to social funds for retirement and unemployment
(b) Contributions to the salary of employed in various organisation
(c) Contributions to industries in case there is deficiency in profit
(d) None of the above

178 **Which one of the following can not be a part of salary?**
(a) Fringe benefits (b) Stock option
(c) Retirement benefits (d) Fine and penalties

179 **What is the source of income for the property and enterprise owners?**
(a) Income from government aid
(b) Income from salaries and wages
(c) Income from rents, dividends and other financial instruments' gains
(d) None of the above

180 **In public enterprises, what is the deciding factor of wages?**
(a) Laws and negotiations
(b) The desire of management
(c) The desire of the employees
(d) None of the above

PREVIOUS YEARS' QUESTIONS

2018

1 An ideal wage system should fulfil certain characteristics. Which among the following is not a characteristic of an ideal wage system?
(a) It should develop harmonious relationship between parties
(b) It should be conducive to the interests of both the parties-the employer and the employees
(c) It should be capable of providing certain incentives to workers necessary to accelerate production
(d) It should be fairly complex and rigid

2 Match the provisions given under List I with the respective legislations under which they are covered as given under List II.

List I	List II
A. Subsistence allowance	1. The Payment of Gratuity Act, 1972
B. Compulsory insurance	2. The Minimum Wages Act, 1948
C. Scheduled employment	3. The Industrial Employment (Standing Orders) Act, 1946
D. Recovery officer	4. The Employees Provident Fund and Miscellaneous Provisions Act, 1952

Codes

	A	B	C	D		A	B	C	D
(a)	4	3	1	2	(b)	3	1	2	4
(c)	2	4	3	1	(d)	1	2	4	3

3 What is the minimum number of days an employee should have served in an accounting year to be entitled for receiving bonus under the Payment of Bonus Act, 1965?

(a) Ninety days (b) One hundred days
(c) Sixty days (d) Thirty days

4 Under the provisions of the Maternity Benefits Act, 1961 every woman employee who joins duty after delivery of a child shall be entitled to nursing breaks until the child attains the age of

(a) Twenty-four months (b) Twelve months
(c) Fifteen months (d) Eighteen months

5 Under the provisions of the Minimum Wages Act, 1948, what is maximum amount of fine that can be imposed on an employer of contravenation of any of the provisions of the Act?

(a) One thousand rupees
(b) Seven hundred rupees
(c) Two hundred fifty rupees
(d) Five hundred rupees

6 The first wage board in India was established for which of the following industries?

(a) Iron and steel (b) Cement
(c) Textile (d) Coal

7 Match the theories given in List I with its propounders given in List II.

List I	List II
A. Subsistence theory of wage	1. Walker
B. The wage fund theory	2. Karl Marx
C. Residual claimant theory	3. Ricardo
D. Theory of exploitation	4. J.S. Mill

Code

	A	B	C	D		A	B	C	D
(a)	1	3	2	4	(b)	1	4	2	3
(c)	3	4	1	2	(d)	3	2	1	4

8 Who among the following are eligible for appointment as presiding officers of the employees provident fund appellate tribunal?

1. A Judge of a High Court.
2. A District Judge.
3. An additional District Judge with atleast three years of experience in the grade.
4. An Officer of Indian Legal Service with five years of experience in grade III.

Codes

(a) 1, 2 and 4 (b) 1 and 2
(c) 1, 2 and 3 (d) 1, 2, 3 and 4

9 In which of the following establishments was the Equal Remuneration Act, 1976 first enforced?

(a) Mines covered under the Mines Act, 1952
(b) Plantations covered under the Plantation Labour Act, 1951
(c) Hospitals, nursing homes and dispensaries
(d) Local authorities

10 The provisions relating to 'continuous service' (Section 2-A) was inserted in the Payment of Gratuity Act, 1972 by a amendment in the year

(a) 1981 (b) 1984
(c) 1987 (d) 1980

11 Who among the following can be appointed as the authority to hear and decide any claims arising out of deductions form wages or delay in payment of wages under the Payment of Wages Act, 1936?

1. Any Commissioner for Employees Compensation Act
2. Any regional labour commissioner appointed by the Central Government
3. Any assistant labour commissioner appointed by the Central Government
4. Any assistant labour commissioner appointed by the State Government with atleast two years of experinece.
5. A Judge of a Civil Court.

Codes

(a) 2, 3, 4 and 5
(b) 1, 3, 4 and 5
(c) 1, 2, 4 and 5
(d) 1, 2, 3 and 4

12 An ideal wage system should fulfil certain characteristics. Which among the following is not a characteristic of an ideal wage system?

(a) It should develop harmonious relationship between parties
(b) It should be conducive to the interests of both the parties the employer and the employees.
(c) It should be capable of providing certain incentives to workers necessary to accelerate production
(d) It should be fairly complex and rigid

13 Assertion (A) Imperfections existing in the employment markets are the causative factor for wage differentials.

Reason (R) In developed countries, inter-industry wage differentials are narrowing.

(a) (A) is correct, but (R) is wrong
(b) Both (A) and (R) are correct and (R) is the correct explanation of (A)
(c) Both (A) and (R) are wrong
(d) Both (A) and (R) are correct, but (R) is not the correct explanation of (A)

14 As per the provisions of the Payment of Wages Act, 1936, if deductions are made for payments to cooperative societies, the maximum deductions for any wage period for any employed person shall not exceed

(a) fifty per cent
(b) sixty per cent
(c) seventy-five per cent
(d) eighty per cent

15 **Assertion** (A) In a planned economy, a certain degree of wage regulation by the state becomes inevitable as an integral part of planning itself.

Reason (R) It is socially desirable for wage earners to live on a healthy and decent plane and to participate freely in industrial government and that the state should interfere in the economic relationship of its citizens whenever these attainable ideals are not realised.

Codes

(a) (A) is correct and (R) explains (A) incorrect
(b) (A) is incorrect and (R) is correct
(c) (A) is correct and (R) is incorrect
(d) Both (A) and (R) are correct, but (R) fails to explain (A)

16 A worker working in a factory has worked for 225 days during the calendar year 2017. He has been laid-off for 20 days as per the standing order and has also availed 10 days of leave with wages during the said year. How many days of leave with wages he shall be entitled to during the calendar year 2018?

(a) Nil (b) 13 days
(c) 11 days (d) 12 days

17 Match the basic content of the theory List I with the theories List II.

	List I		List II
A.	Wages paid are equal to the productivity of the last worker hired	1.	Taussig's Theory of Wages
B.	Wages, hours and working conditions are largely a matter of relative bargaining strength of two sides	2.	Marginal Productivity Theory
C.	Wages are residue left over after the other factors of production have been paid wages	3.	The Bargaining Theory
D.	Wages equal the total product of labour of the marginal firm minus the amount discounted by the employer for advance support of the worker	4.	Residual Claimant Theory

Codes

	A	B	C	D		A	B	C	D
(a)	2	4	3	1	(b)	3	2	1	4
(c)	2	3	4	1	(d)	3	1	2	4

18 **Assertion** (A) Occupational wage differentials provide an incentive to young persons to incur the costs of training and education and encourage workers to develop skills in anticipation of higher earnings in future.

Reason (R) Occupational wage differentials perform a social function by way of determining the social status of workers.

Codes

(a) (A) is wrong and (R) is right
(b) (A) is right and (R) explains (A)
(c) (A) is right and (R) fails to explain (A)
(d) (A) is right and (R) is wrong

19 Under the provisions of the Payment of Wages Act, 1936, who among the following cannot be appointed as the authority by the appropriate government to hear and decide claims arising out of deductions from wages or delay in payment of wages and penalty for malicious or vexacious claims?

(a) Any commissioner for workmen's compensation
(b) Regional Labour Commissioner appointed by the Central Government
(c) Any Assistant Labour Commissioner appointed by the State Government
(d) Any other officer with experience as a Judge of a Civil Court or a Judicial Magistrate

20 For a person employed in a seasonal establishment, what is the rate of gratuity payable under the Payment of Gratuity Act, 1972?

(a) Fifteen day's wages for each season
(b) Seven day's wages for each season
(c) Ten day's wages for each year
(d) Ten day's wages for each season

21 An employee engaged in an industrial establishment draws wages of ₹ 20,500 per month. What is the amount of bonus to be paid to him if it is paid at the rate of 10% by the employer for an accounting year under the Payment of Bonus Act, 1965?

(a) Rupees nine thousand two hundred only
(b) Rupees eight thousand four hundred only
(c) Rupees ten thousand two hundred fifty only
(d) Rupees nine thousand six hundred only

22 As per the amendment to the Payment of Wages Act, 1936, made in 2017, the act shall apply to wages payable to an employed person drawing a monthly wage not exceeding

(a) ₹ 28,000 (b) ₹ 26,000
(c) ₹ 24,000 (d) ₹ 30,000

23 For which industry the first non-statutory Wage Board was set-up in India ?

(a) Cotton textile (b) Cement
(c) Iron and Steel (d) Coal mining

2017

24 Wages of the workers are normally, the proportionality derived from their efficiency. But the concept of efficiency of labour is itself vague such as amount of physical output, output per man hour or output per man shift. But output is not the function of man alone. There are other factors which affect the output. Which among the following is/are not the factor(s) that would affect the output directly?

1. Physical condition of work
2. Nature of machinery
3. Technical process
4. Quality of raw material
5. System of management
6. Role of fellow workers
7. Competitors in the market

Codes

(a) 1 and 5 (b) 5 and 8
(c) 6 and 7 (d) 4 and 6

25 Match the following theories of wages List I with their propagators List II.

List I	List II
A. Standard of Living theory	1. JS Mill
B. Wage Fund theory	2. JB Clark
C. Residual Claimant theory	3. Karl Marx
D. Marginal Productivity theory	4. Francis A Walker

Codes

	A	B	C	D		A	B	C	D
(a)	3	1	4	2	(b)	3	4	2	1
(c)	3	2	4	1	(d)	3	1	2	4

26 Labour is remunerated through payment of wages. There are different methods of wage payment prevalent in different industries in different countries. But the ideal wage system should fulfil certain characteristics. Which among the following is not a characteristic?

(a) It should be conducive to the interest of labour only
(b) It should be devised as to avoid industrial conflict
(c) It should be conducive to the interest of both parties employer and employee
(d) It should be fairly simple as well as flexible

27 Match the following List I with List II.

List I	List II
A. Malaviya Committee	1. Minimum wages
B. BP Adarkar Report	2. Social security for unorganised labour
C. D Aykroid's Formula	3. Labour welfare
D. Arjun Sengupta Committee	4. Employees' state insurance

Codes

	A	B	C	D		A	B	C	D
(a)	3	2	4	1	(b)	3	1	4	2
(c)	3	4	1	2	(d)	4	3	1	2

28 An employee engaged in an industrial establishment draws wages of ₹ 20,000 per month. What is the amount of bonus he shall be entitled to, if it is to be paid at the rate of 9% by the employer for an accounting year under the provisions of the Payment of Bonus Act, 1965?

(a) Rupees seven thousand five hundred sixty only
(b) Rupees eighteen thousand only
(c) Rupees eight thousand one hundred thirty only
(d) Rupees ten thousand six hundred forty only

29 A worker retires from a factory after putting in twenty years of continuous service. His last monthly wages drawn was ₹ 45,500. What is the amount of gratuity the worker is entitled to under the payment of Gratuity Act, 1972.

(a) ₹ 5,75,000 (b) ₹ 5,25,000
(c) ₹ 7,50,000 (d) ₹ 4,55,000

30 In March 2017, the Government of India in the Ministry of Labour and Employment has revised the administrative charges payable by the employers under the Employees' Provident Fund Scheme, 1952. Which one of the following statements given is correct?

(a) 0.65 per cent (zero point six five per cent) of the pay subject to a minimum of seventy five rupees per month for every non-functional establishments having no contributory member and five hundred rupees per month for other establishments
(b) 0.67 per cent (zero point six seven per cent) of the pay subject to a minimum of one hundred rupees per month for every non-functional establishment having no contributory member and five hundred rupees per month for other establishments
(c) 0.75 per cent (zero point seven five per cent) of the pay subject to a minimum of one hundred rupees per month for every non-functional establishment having no contributory member and one thousand rupees per month for other establishments
(d) 0.50 per cent (zero point five zero per cent) of the pay subject to a minimum of seventy five rupees per month for every non-functional establishment having no contributory member and one thousand rupees per month for other establishments

31 Calculate the amount of compensation to be paid to the dependants of a deceased employee, where death results from the injury, under the provisions of Employees Compensation Act, 1923. (Monthly wages drawn was ₹ 15,000 and relevant factor is 139.13).

(a) ₹ 1,20,000 (b) ₹ 4,52,400
(c) ₹ 6,50,210 (d) ₹ 5,56,520

32 Under the Minimum Wages Act, 1948, which one of the following is not a prescribed wages period for fixation of minimum rate of wages?

(a) By the hour (b) By the day
(c) By the week (d) By the month

33 Allocable surplus for a banking company under the provisions of the Payment of Bonus Act, 1965 means

(a) sixty-seven per cent of the available surplus in an accounting year
(b) sixty per cent of the available surplus in an accounting year
(c) sixty-six per cent of the available surplus in an accounting year
(d) sixty-six per cent of the available surplus in the financial year

34 An industrial establishment employing one thousand employees has to pay the wages to the employees within which period after the last day of the wage period in respect of which the wages are payable under the provisions of the Payment of Wages Act, 1936?

(a) Before the expiry of the seventh day
(b) Before the expiry of the fifth day
(c) Before the expiry of the tenth day
(d) Before the expiry of the eighth day

35 In which of the following employments the Equal Remuneration Act, 1976 was first enforced?

(a) Employments under Central and State Governments
(b) Plantations to which the Plantations Labour Act, 1951 applies
(c) Mines as defined under the Mines Act, 1952
(d) Local Authorities

36 What is the minimum period an employee should have worked in an accounting year in an establishment to become eligible for bonus under the payment of Bonus Act, 1965?

(a) Forty-five days
(b) Thirty days
(c) Sixty days
(d) Ninety days

37 Which of the following statements relating to the Constitution of the Advisory Committee under the Equal Remuneration Act, 1976 is true ?

(a) It shall consist of not less than twelve persons of which one-third shall be women
(b) It shall consist of eight persons of which one-half shall be women
(c) It shall consist of not less than ten persons nominated by the appropriate government, of which one-half shall be women
(d) It shall consist of twelve persons nominated by the Central Government of which one-third shall be women

38 Match the propounders mentioned in List I with the theories of wages mentioned in List II.

List I	List II
A. JS Mill	1. Marginal Productivity Theory
B. Walker	2. Wage Fund Theory
C. JB Clark	3. Residual Claimant Theory
D. Ricardo	4. The Subsistence Theory

Codes

	A	B	C	D
(a)	3	4	1	2
(b)	2	3	4	1
(c)	1	2	3	4
(d)	2	3	1	4

39 Under which of the following legislations the provision for payment to any trade union fee on a written authorisation from an employee has been provided ?

(a) Industrial Disputes Act, 1947
(b) Trade Unions Act, 1926
(c) Payment of Wages Act, 1936
(d) Industrial Employment (Standing Orders) Act, 1946

40 As per the Government of India notification the wage limit for employees to be covered under the Employees' State Insurance Act, 1948 is proposed to be increased to

(a) Rupees Eighteen thousand
(b) Rupees Twenty-five thousand
(c) Rupees Twenty thousand
(d) Rupees Twenty-one thousand

41 Under the Minimum Wages Act, 1948 what is the extent of representation of independent persons in the Advisory Committee ?

(a) one-half of its total members
(b) one-third of its total members
(c) one-fourth of its total members
(d) one-half of its total members subject to a maximum of light

42 Which of the following is not a best practice in High Commitment Pay ?

(a) High wage policies to attract, retain and motivate the best talent, that is based on the belief that, 'You get what you pay for'
(b) Employment security is essential to be the 'employer of choice' and it is the bed rock for high quality work and a willingness to be flexible and innovative
(c) Encourage employee ownership of the enterprise
(d) Non-egalitarian symbols and perquisites

43 Match the provisions given in List I with the legislations they are covered given in List II.

List I	List II
A. Exempted employee	1. Payment of Bonus Act, 1965
B. Compulsory Insurance	2. Factories Act, 1948
C. Right of Workers	3. Payment of Gratuity Act, 1972
D. Development Rebate	4. Employees' State Insurance Act, 1948

Codes

	A	B	C	D		A	B	C	D
(a)	4	3	2	1	(b)	1	2	3	4
(c)	2	1	4	3	(d)	3	4	1	2

44 An employee is employed in an industry on a wage of rupees eight thousand and five hundred per month, which is fixed as the minimum wage as a scheduled employment by the appropriate government. What is the amount of bonus he shall be entitled to, if it is to be paid at the minimum rate of 8.33% by the employer under the Payment of Bonus Act, 1965 ?

(a) Rupees seven thousand only
(b) Rupees nine thousand only
(c) Rupees eight thousand and five hundred only
(d) Rupees three thousand and five hundred only

2016

45 Read the following and mark your answer according to the answer code given below.

Wage incentive plans have the following objects

1. Increasing workers morale
2. Lowering unit cost
3. Lowering capital cost
4. Lowering depreciation charges

Codes

(a) 1 and 4 (b) 1 and 3
(c) 1 and 2 (d) 3 and 4

46 An employee working in an organisation draws a salary of ₹ 20,000 per month. What is the amount of bonus that he shall be paid at the minimum rate of 8.33% under the Payment of Bonus Act, 1965 ?

(a) ₹ 20,000 (b) ₹ 8,333 (c) ₹ 7,000 (d) ₹ 3,500

47 Under the provisions of the Payment of Wages Act, 1936, for which of the following organisations, the Central Government is the appropriate government ?

1. Railways and Air Transport
2. Port and Docks
3. Mines and Oilfields
4. Public Sector banks

Codes

(a) 1 and 3 (b) 2 and 4
(c) 1, 2 and 3 (d) All of these

48 What is the current wage ceiling per month for a person employed on a wage or salary to be considered as an employee under the Payment of Bonus Act, 1965?

(a) Not exceeding ten thousand rupees
(b) Not exceeding twenty-one thousand rupees
(c) Not exceeding eight thousand rupees
(d) Not exceeding eighteen thousand rupees

49 As per the provisions of the Payment of Gratuity Act, 1972, an employee working in a seasonal establishment shall be deemed to be in continuous service if he has served for not less than

(a) one hundred twenty days during the period the establishment was in operation
(b) seventy-five per cent of the number of days on which the establishment was in operation
(c) one hundred days during the period the establishment was in operation
(d) sixty-seven per cent of the number of days on which the establishment was in operation

2015

50 Under the existing provisions of the Payment of Bonus Act, 1965, a ceiling has been imposed that for the purpose of computation of bonus, the wages be considered to be ₹ 10,000 only. There exists a proposal to amend this ceiling and raise the upper wage ceiling for the purpose of calculation to

(a) ₹ 11,000 (b) ₹ 19,000 (c) ₹ 15,000 (d) ₹ 25,000

51 An employee retires from a factory after putting in 28 (twenty eight) years of service. The last wages drawn by him per month before retirement was ₹ 39,000. What is the amount of gratuity to be paid by his employer under the Payment of Gratuity Act, 1972?

(a) ₹ 5,46,000 (b) ₹ 6,16,000 (c) ₹ 5,89,000 (d) ₹ 6,30,000

52 Under the provisions of the Minimum Wages Act, 1948, in matters of fixation and revision of minimum wages, the Central Advisory Board is to advise to which of the following authority?

(a) The Central Government
(b) Various Committees Constituted under the act
(c) The Central Government and State Governments
(d) The State Governments

53 Which of the following bodies is provided under the Minimum Wages Act, 1948?

(a) Standing Labour Committee
(b) Central Council
(c) Advisory Board
(d) Executive Authority

54 Under the Payment of Bonus Act, 1965, what is the minimum number of days an employee should have served in a year in the organisation to be entitled for getting bonus?

(a) 200 and 40 days (b) 30 days
(c) 100 and 95 days (d) 100 and 20 days

55 Under the Payment of Bonus Act, 1965, for a banking company, what percentage of the available surplus shall be taken as the allocable surplus?

(a) 75% (b) 67%
(c) 50% (d) 60%

56 Consider the following statements about Hardship Allowances.

1. They compensate expatriates for exceptionally hard living and working conditions at certain locations.
2. They compensate employees for meeting difficult targets.
3. They compensate employees for working under hazardous conditions.

Which of the following statement(s) given above is/are correct?

(a) Only 1 (b) Only 2
(c) 1 and 2 (d) All of these

57 Under the provisions of the Payment of Bonus Act, 1965, the gross profit derived by an employer from an establishment in respect of any accounting year in case of a banking company shall be calculated in the manner as specified under

(a) First Schedule (b) Second Schedule
(c) Third Schedule (d) Fourth Schedule

58 What is the current maximum ceiling of wages for calculation of bonus under the Payment of Bonus Act, 1965?

(a) ₹ 5,000 (b) ₹ 7,500
(c) ₹ 10,000 (d) ₹ 12,000

59 Which of the following formulae is taken for calculating the gratuity for an employees under the Payment of Gratuity Act, 1972?

(a) Monthly rate of wages last drawn × 15 × number of years worked ÷ 26
(b) Monthly rate of wages last drawn × 26 × number of years worked ÷ 15
(c) Monthly rate of wages last drawn × 30 × number of years worked ÷ 26
(d) Monthly rate of wages last drawn × 30 × number of years worked ÷ 15

60 Match the following.

List I (Propagators)		List II (Theories of Wages)
A. David Ricardo	1.	Residual Claimant Theory
B. Francis W Walker	2.	Marginal Productivity Theory
C. Karl Marx	3.	Subsistence Theory
D. JB Clark	4.	Surplus Value Theory

Codes

	A	B	C	D		A	B	C	D
(a)	3	4	2	1	(b)	3	1	4	2
(c)	3	2	1	4	(d)	4	3	1	2

61 **Assertion** (A) Wage differentials can be attributed to the imperfections of the employment markets.

Reason (R) Inter-industry wage differentials have been narrowing in developed countries than that in developing countries.

Codes

(a) Both (A) and (R) are wrong
(b) (A) is right and (R) is wrong and so does not explain (A)
(c) (A) is wrong and (R) is right and so does not explain (A)
(d) Both (A) and (R) are right, but (R) does not explain (A)

62 The amount of gratuity payable to an employee retiring from services after completing 18 years of continuous service drawing his last wages of ₹ 39,000 per month will be

(a) ₹ 4,05,000 (b) ₹ 3,51,000
(c) ₹ 10,00,000 (d) ₹ 7,50,000

63 What is the time period within which any fine imposed on any employee shall be recovered from the day on which it was imposed?

(a) 150 days (b) 90 days (c) 100 days (d) 120 days

64 What is the minimum number of persons to be appointed in the Advisory Committee under the provisions of the Equal Remuneration Act, 1976?

(a) 5 (b) 15 (c) 10 (d) 12

65 Wage Negotiating Committees in India determine wages at

(a) plant level (b) industry level
(c) sector level (d) regional level

2014

66 Wage Boards fix wages for employees at

(a) regional level (b) plant level
(c) national level (d) industry level

67 Living wage, fair wage and minimum wage concepts were adopted by

(a) Committee on Fair Wages
(b) 15th Indian Labour Conference
(c) Wage Board
(d) Standing Labour Committee

68 Match the following under the Employers Provident Fund and Miscellancous Provisions Act, 1952.

List I (Areas of Coverage)	List II (Schedules)
A. Matters for which provisions may be made in the Pension Scheme	1. Schedule IV
B. Matters for which provisions may be made in a scheme	2. Schedule II
C. Industries covered under the provisions of the act	3. Schedule III
D. Matters to be covered under the Deposit-linked Insurance Scheme	4. Schedule I

Codes

	A	B	C	D		A	B	C	D
(a)	3	2	4	1	(b)	4	3	2	1
(c)	2	4	3	1	(d)	1	2	4	3

69 What would be the maximum representation of the independent members in the Central Advisory Board constituted under the Minimum Wages Act, 1948?

(a) One-third (b) One-half
(c) Two-third (d) One-fourth

70 **Statement** I Time wage system is suitable when workers are new and learning the jobs.

Statemment II Piece wage system is suitable where quality and workmanship are not very important.

Codes

(a) Both statements are correct
(b) Both statements are incorrect
(c) Statement I is correct, but Statement II is incorrect
(d) Statement II is correct, but Statement I is incorrect

71 Which of the following statement(s) is/are true with regard to Joint Wage Negotiation Committee?

1. It is a bipartite committee.
2. It is industry specific committee.
3. It was constituted for the first time in steel industry.
4. It is tripartite in nature.

Select the correct answer by using the codes given below

(a) Only 1 (b) 1 and 2
(c) 1, 2 and 3 (d) 2, 3 and 4

72 Which of the following Theories of Wages is called as the 'Iron Law of Wages'?

(a) Subsistence Theory
(b) The Standard of Living Theory
(c) The Wage Fund Theory
(d) The Residual Claimant Theory

73 Which of the following is not a factor that creates wage differentials?

(a) Differences due to existence of non-competing groups
(b) Non-equalising differences
(c) Differences in labour quality
(d) Labour market perfections

74 On what basis the money wage can be converted into real wages?

(a) Consumer Price Index (b) Wholesale Price Index
(c) Retail Price Index (d) Money Exchange Rate

75 Under the provisions of the Payment of Gratuity Act, 1972, employees working in a seasonal establishment and who have not been employed throughout the year, the employers shall be paid gratuity at the rate of

(a) 10 days of wages for every year
(b) 10 days of wages for every season
(c) 15 days of wages for every year
(d) 7 days of wages for every season

76 The enactment of the Equal Remuneration Act, 1976 is associated with which of the following conventions of the ILO?

(a) Convention No. 111, 1958
(b) Convention No. 100, 1951
(c) Convention No. 123, 1975
(d) Convention No. 118, 1964

77 Which of the following conditions relating to claims under the Minimum Wages Act, 1948 is not true?

(a) The authority to hear and decide for all claim cases shall be appointed by the appropriate government
(b) Any legal practitioner with a written authorisation from the concerned employee can make a claim application on behalf of the employer
(c) Any claim application shall have to be presented within 1 year from the date on which minimum wages became payable
(d) The inspector with permission of the authority appointed under the act, can make a claim application for an employee

78 What is the minimum amount of bonus payable to an adult employee during an accounting year?

(a) ₹ 1,000 (b) ₹ 100 (c) ₹ 833 (d) ₹ 750

79 What is the maximum amount of fine that can be imposed on an employee in a wage period under the payment of Wages Act, 1936 ?

(a) 3% of wage (b) 5% of wage
(c) 10% of wage (d) 8% of wage

80 Who is an 'inspector' under the Payment of Wages Act for the purposes of factories in the local limit?

(a) The Inspector appointed by the State Government in respect of such establishments
(b) The Inspector of factories appointed under the Factories Act
(c) The Inspector appointed by the Central Government for the said purpose
(d) The Inspector appointed by the appropriate government for the said purpose

81 The Minimum Wages Act in India is the outcome of recommendations of which of the following?

1. Rege Committee
2. Indian Labour Conference
3. Labour Investigation Committee
4. Royal Commission on Labour

Codes

(a) 1 and 2 (b) 1, 2 and 4
(c) 1, 2 and 3 (c) All of these

82 Chronologically arrange the years of enactments from earliest to latest of labour legislations relating to wages and remunerations given below.

1. Minimum Wages Act 2. Payment of Wages Act
3. Equal Remune... 4. P...ent of Bonus Act

Codes

(a) 1, 2, 3, 4 (b) 1, 3, 4, 2 (c) 2, 1, 4, 3 (d) 2, 1, 3, 4

83 Which of the following is not considered as 'Wage' under the provisions of Payment of Wages Act?

(a) Any sum paid to the employed person to defray special expenses entailed by him by the nature of his employment
(b) Any remuneration to which the person is entitled in respect of overtime work
(c) Any sum to which the person employed under any scheme framed under any law in force
(d) All of the above

84 Which of the following have been devoted to reduce inter-firm and inter-area wage differentials in India?

(a) Joint Negotiation Committees
(b) Wage Boards
(c) Works Committee
(d) Joint Councils

85 Under which of the following incentive plans "A worker is guaranteed a minimum wage on the time basis. Then a standard time is fixed for the completion of every work and if the worker completes the work in less time, he is given a bonus of the time actually saved in proportion to the total time"?

(a) Halsey Premium system
(b) Rowan Premium system
(c) Barth system
(d) The Emerson's Efficiency system

86 In which of the following systems, minimum wage is guaranteed, but beyond a certain efficiency level, bonus is given in addition to minimum day wages?

(a) Straight piece rate system
(b) Differential piece rate system
(c) Gantt task and bonus system
(d) Emerson's efficiency system

87 Match the following.

	List I		List II
A.	Attendance bonus paid over an unbroken series of years	1.	Pooja Bonus
B.	Biannual payment of a month's salary for a long time which has become an implied condition of service	2.	Profit-based Bonus
C.	Payment of a lumpsum amount during Pooja time	3.	Customary Bonus
D.	An amount paid being linked with dividend	4.	Contractual Bonus

Codes

	A	B	C	D
(a)	1	3	4	2
(b)	3	4	1	2
(c)	3	2	1	4
(d)	2	3	1	4

ANSWERS

Exam Based Questions

1 (d)	2 (d)	3 (d)	4 (c)	5 (c)	6 (d)	7 (a)	8 (a)	9 (d)	10 (a)
11 (c)	12 (d)	13 (b)	14 (c)	15 (d)	16 (c)	17 (a)	18 (d)	19 (a)	20 (b)
21 (b)	22 (d)	23 (b)	24 (c)	25 (a)	26 (a)	27 (d)	28 (c)	29 (b)	30 (a)
31 (d)	32 (d)	33 (c)	34 (c)	35 (a)	36 (a)	37 (a)	38 (d)	39 (d)	40 (a)
41 (d)	42 (d)	43 (d)	44 (a)	45 (b)	46 (b)	47 (c)	48 (a)	49 (b)	50 (b)
51 (a)	52 (a)	53 (d)	54 (d)	55 (a)	56 (a)	57 (a)	58 (b)	59 (b)	60 (b)
61 (d)	62 (a)	63 (a)	64 (b)	65 (a)	66 (d)	67 (c)	68 (b)	69 (d)	70 (b)
71 (d)	72 (d)	73 (d)	74 (d)	75 (d)	76 (c)	77 (c)	78 (d)	79 (b)	80 (c)
81 (a)	82 (a)	83 (b)	84 (a)	85 (b)	86 (d)	87 (c)	88 (d)	89 (d)	90 (d)
91 (b)	92 (d)	93 (a)	94 (a)	95 (a)	96 (a)	97 (b)	98 (a)	99 (d)	100 (d)
101 (d)	102 (a)	103 (a)	104 (a)	105 (c)	106 (c)	107 (a)	108 (a)	109 (a)	110 (a)
111 (a)	112 (a)	113 (a)	114 (a)	115 (a)	116 (c)	117 (b)	118 (a)	119 (a)	120 (a)
121 (a)	122 (b)	123 (a)	124 (a)	125 (a)	126 (a)	127 (a)	128 (a)	129 (b)	130 (c)
131 (b)	132 (a)	133 (a)	134 (a)	135 (b)	136 (d)	137 (b)	138 (b)	139 (b)	140 (c)
141 (b)	142 (a)	143 (c)	144 (a)	145 (a)	146 (d)	147 (a)	148 (d)	149 (d)	150 (c)
151 (d)	152 (a)	153 (c)	154 (b)	155 (a)	156 (b)	157 (a)	158 (a)	159 (b)	160 (c)
161 (a)	162 (a)	163 (d)	164 (c)	165 (b)	166 (c)	167 (b)	168 (c)	169 (b)	170 (a)
171 (b)	172 (d)	173 (a)	174 (a)	175 (a)	176 (c)	177 (a)	178 (d)	179 (c)	180 (a)

Previous Years' Questions

1 (d)	2 (b)	3 (d)	4 (c)	5 (d)	6 (c)	7 (c)	8 (b)	9 (b)	10 (b)
11 (c)	12 (d)	13 (d)	14 (c)	15 (a)	16 (c)	17 (c)	18 (b)	19 (c)	20 (b)
21 (b)	22 (c)	23 (a)	24 (c)	25 (a)	26 (a)	27 (c)	28 (c)	29 (b)	30 (a)
31 (d)	32 (c)	33 (b)	34 (c)	35 (b)	36 (b)	37 (c)	38 (d)	39 (c)	40 (d)
41 (b)	42 (d)	43 (a)	44 (c)	45 (c)	46 (c)	47 (a)	48 (b)	49 (b)	50 (b)
51 (d)	52 (c)	53 (b)	54 (b)	55 (d)	56 (a)	57 (a)	58 (c)	59 (a)	60 (b)
61 (d)	62 (a)	63 (b)	64 (c)	65 (b)	66 (d)	67 (a)	68 (a)	69 (a)	70 (a)
71 (d)	72 (a)	73 (d)	74 (a)	75 (d)	76 (b)	77 (c)	78 (b)	79 (a)	80 (b)
81 (b)	82 (b)	83 (b)	84 (d)	85 (b)	86 (d)	87 (c)			

UNIT 9

Labour Welfare

This chapter focuses on the concept of labour welfare in terms of the theories and different principles, intra and extra-mural activities. It highlights ILO's stance on the concept of social justice. It further elaborates the concept of social security in terms of social assistance and assurance.

Concept of Labour Welfare

A country's economic development is dependent upon the production of goods and services in the country. The production is a consequence of four factors of productions that include land, labour, capital and entrepreneurship. The factors of productions are the inputs required to boost the production of goods and services in order to earn profits. As labour is one of the factors of production, it is important to maintain and enhance the productivity of labour. The efficiency of labour enhances its productivity as well. This is where the concept of labour welfare comes into picture.

Labour welfare is an important dimension of industrial relations that focuses on building and improving the work life quality of the employees. The concept of labour welfare varies with time, region, industry, social values and customs, degree of industrialisation, the general socio-economic development of the people and the political ideologies prevailing at a particular time. It is also dependent on age-group, sex, socio-cultural background, marital and economic status and educational level of the workers in various industries.

Basically, the concept is focused on providing congenial working, such as proper lighting, heat control, cleanliness, low noise level, toilet and drinking-water facilities, canteen and rest rooms, health and safety measures, reasonable hours of work and holidays, and welfare services, such as housing, education, recreation, transportation and counselling.

In this Chapter

- Concept of Labour Welfare
- Social Security

In 1951, the **Planning Commission of India** observed the importance of labour welfare and stated that, "In order to get the best out of a worker in the matter of production, working conditions require to be improved to a large extent. The workers should at least have the means and facilities to keep themselves in a state of health and efficiency. This is primarily a question of adequate nutrition and suitable housing conditions. The working condition should be such as to safeguard his health and protect him against occupational hazards. The worker should also be equipped with necessary technical training and a certain level of general education."

The **International Labour Organisation** (ILO) report refers to labour welfare as, "Such services, facilities and amenities as may be established in or in the vicinity of undertakings to enable the persons employed in them to perform their work in healthy, congenial surroundings and provided with amenities conducive to good health and high morale."

The **Encyclopedia of Social Sciences** has defined labour welfare work as, "The voluntary efforts of the employers to establish, within the existing industrial system, working and sometimes living and cultural conditions of the employees beyond what is required by law, the custom of the country and the conditions of the market."

Objectives of Labour Welfare

On the basis of above definitions, one can understand that labour welfare measures should meet the following objectives

- Provide congenial and good working conditions to the employees.
- Help to improve and enhance the quality of life of the employees and their family members.
- Help in increasing the productivity and efficiency of the labour.
- Help in creating an emotional bond with the workforce.
- To promote an organisational culture that is conducive to the growth of an employee.
- To provide health, medical and maternity benefits that help the employees to take care of their health.

Scope of Labour Welfare

Labour welfare is a holistic concept that has a broad scope. It includes all the amenities and services that must be provided by the employer to its employees. These will helpful in order to enhance the productivity and efficiency of the employees that will be conducive to good health and high morale of the employees.

Labour welfare activities can be classified as the following

Statutory These are the laws created by the government to regulate the services being provided to the workers. These laws ensure minimum standards of health and safety of workers and the employers need to adhere with. Some of the examples are Factories Act, 1948, Mines Act, 1952, The Motor Transport Workers Act, 1961 etc.

Non-statutory or Voluntary These are the voluntary activities undertaken by the employers to promote the welfare of the employees. These are philanthropic in nature. These include provision of housing facilities, transportation, recreational facilities, formation of cooperative societies, children's education, and loans for purchasing scooters, cars and grains, provision of library, leave travel concessions, uniforms and gifts etc.

Mutual Labour Welfare In this, both the employer and employee work together in the direction of employee welfare. It includes the activities of trade unions which are conducive to the welfare of their members.

Types of Labour Welfare

On the basis of the location of welfare activities, labour welfare work has been classified by Dr. G.M. Broughton in two specific categories. This classification has been widely accepted by the committee of experts on welfare facilities for industrial workers constituted by ILO in 1963.

The two types are

Intra-mural

These are welfare amenities within the precincts or premises of the establishment. These include medical facilities, compensation for accidents, provision of safety measures such as fencing and covering of machines, good lay-out of the machinery and plant, sufficient lighting, first-aid appliances, fire extinguishers, activities relating to improving conditions of employment, recruitment and discipline and provision of provident fund, pension and gratuity, maternity benefits etc alongwith latrines, urinals, rest shelters, arrangements for prevention of fatigue, health service including occupational safety, administrative arrangements within a plant to look after welfare, uniforms and protective clothing and shift allowances.

Extra-mural

These are welfare amenities outside the precincts or premises of the establishment. These include cover housing accommodation, indoor and outdoor recreation facilities, amusement and sports, educational facilities for adults and children, provision of libraries and reading rooms, social insurance measures cultural activities, holiday, homes and leave travel facility, workers cooperatives including consumer' cooperative stores, fair price shops and cooperatives, thrift and credit societies, vocational training for dependents of workers, other programmes for the welfare of the women, youth and children and transport to and from the place of work.

Encyclopedia of Social Science *has classified labour welfare into three categories*

Those dealing with Immediate Working Conditions These include special provisions for adequate light, heat, ventilation, toilet facilities, accident and occupational disease prevention, lunch rooms, rest room, maximum hours, minimum wages etc.

Those concerned with less Immediate Working Condition and Group Interests These include gymnasiums, club rooms, playgrounds, gardens, dancing, music, house organs, mutual aid societies, vacation with pay, profit-sharing, stock ownership, disability and unemployment funds, pensions, savings banks, provisions for conciliation and arbitration, shop committees and workers' councils.

Those designed to Improve Community Conditions These are housing, retail stores, schools, libraries, kindergartens, lectures on domestic sciences, day nurseries, dispensary and dental service, screening of motion pictures, arranging athletic contests and picnics and summer camps.

Theories of Labour Welfare

There are eight theories that constitute the framework of labour welfare activities. *These are explained as follows*

The Police Theory

This theory is based on the assumption that employers exploit the workers using their tactics and they will not leave any such opportunity. The theory is based on the premise that a minimum standard of welfare is necessary for labourers. So, the government needs to assume the role of a policeman and enforce regulatory and legal measures upon the employer.

The employer will be punished if he doesn't comply to these measures. Based on this theory, the government enacts laws that provides minimum labour welfare amenities and services.

The Religious Theory

This theory is essentially based on the premise that man is a religious being and many acts of human beings are based on religious sentiments and beliefs. The elements of investment and atonement for the welfare of workers form the basis of this theory. Benevolent acts of welfare are treated either as investment or atonement, *i.e.*

- The benefits that are being provided by the employers are believed to be investment, that will help it reap the benefits in future. This includes provision of canteen and creche services for the employees.
- Atonement means the action of making amends for a wrong or injury. By providing amenities to the workers, the employer is doing away with the sins he did in past. This theory propagates profit sharing by the employer with his employees.

The Philanthropic Theory

This theory is essentially based on man's love for mankind. According to this theory, a company provides good working conditions, services and amenities as a gesture of kindness towards the employees.

This theory also states that it is the duty and responsibility of wealthy people to help the underprivileged people. This theory also considers that man feels happy after helping others.

Trusteeship Theory/Paternalistic Theory

This theory is based on the assumption that employees do not have the ability to take care of themselves. Thus, it is the employer who needs to take care of them. He does so by providing various benefits, services and amenities for their well-being.

The employer also establishes an enterprise in trust for the benefit of employees. It takes a paternalistic approach towards industrial production system and proprietorship of resources. This is why this theory is also known as trusteeship theory.

This theory assumes owner as the elderly person who is responsible of taking care of the complete family. So, it becomes the duty of the owner to share the wealth and profits equally with his workers. Mahatma Gandhi was a strong advocate of this theory.

The Placating Theory

This theory assumes that labour groups are becoming demanding and have become more conscious of their rights and privileges. They are becoming militant in nature. It becomes difficult for the employer or management to ignore their demands after a certain point of time. Thus, timely and periodical acts of labour welfare can appease the workers.

The Public Relation Theory

This theory states that welfare activities and facilities, are done and provided to create a good image in the eyes of workers and public. The labour welfare programs are advertisements that help the employer to create his goodwill and build healthy public relations.

Functional Theory/Efficiency Theory

Welfare work is used as a mean to ensure, preserve and develop the efficiency and productivity of labour. This theory states that the employers provide benefit to the workers to make them more efficient and productive. This theory is a reflection of contemporary support for labour welfare. It can work well, if both the parties have an identical aim in view, *i.e.* higher production.

Social Theory

This theory states that the big business houses and industrial establishments have the social responsibility and moral obligations of providing good working conditions to the employees. By doing so, they are helping in improving the workplace environment and overall condition of the society. This theory considers labour welfare as a mandate of Corporate Social Responsibility (CSR) of the organisation.

Principles of Labour Welfare

Principle of Social Responsibility Social responsibility is the obligation of industry towards the society. An industry is expected to work for the workers. It needs to build a strong image in the eyes of workers in order to expect cooperation from them. This can be done by providing secured employment, fair wages and equal opportunities for the workers.

Principle of Democratic Value It is the duty of industry to fulfill the unmet needs of the workers and it is the right of workers to decide the manner in which these needs can be met.

Principle of Adequacy of Wages The workers have right to fair wages. The labour welfare measures are in no sense substitute for wages. Both of them cannot substitute for each other.

Principle of Efficiency This principle is based on the fact that incorporating labour welfare measure is important to cultivate efficiency in the work culture. Education and training, housing, and food are the three most important aspects of labour welfare.

Principle of Co-responsibility This principle states that both employer and employees are responsible for labour welfare. Both the parties need to work towards mutually *i.e.* promoting and taking care of each other's needs and interests.

Principle of Totality Welfare The organisation needs to take care that all the labour welfare measures are uniformly accepted across all the levels of hierarchy.

Principle of Re-personalisation It is important that labour welfare measures are directed towards development of human personality. The factory must implement intra-mural and extra-mural measures for its employees. These measures must counteract baneful effects of industrial system.

Principle of Co-ordination or Integration It is based on the fact that welfare is a total concept and a coordinated approach promotes the overall development of the employee at the personal and professional fronts.

Industrial Health and Hygiene

According to OSHA, Industrial hygiene is "that science and art devoted to the anticipation, recognition, evaluation and control of those environmental factors or stresses arising in or from the workplace, which may cause sickness, impaired health and well being or significant discomfort among workers or among the citizens of the community."

In simple words, it deals with identifying, evaluating and controlling real or potential workplace environmental stressors or hazards that have an impact on the well being of workers and community members. These stressors or hazards need to be identified at initial stages only and be dealt with before they become an issue for the workers.

Industrial health is a branch of public health concerned with the health and well being of workers. Its aims are to eliminate hazards and reduce industrial fatigue in the workplace.

Types of Hazards

The different types of stressors or hazards present in the environment are

Chemical These include dust or fumes, mists, vapours and gases that are a result of chemical processes that takes place inside the industrial unit. There could be an issue due to inhalation of these vapours or these may cause allergy or irritation on skin. They can cause injury, illness, fire or even explosions.

Physical These are substances or activities that threaten the physical safety of the workers. These can cause injury, illness and death. These include excessive levels of electromagnetic and ionizing radiations, noise, irregularities in temperature, air quality.

Both non-ionizing and ionizing radiations can be dangerous. UV and laser radiations are non-ionizing in nature. Workers can be exposed to these radiations while working and these can damage cells and lead to different diseases.

Ergonomic These include improperly designed work areas with poor or excessive lightning, repetitive motions, irregularities in the processes. These categories of hazard arise because of repetitive stress or injuries caused due to different processes such as lifting, pushing, pulling etc.

The workers must be provided with proper tools and equipments to do their jobs efficiently. The processes must be designed to ensure smooth flow of work.

Psychological This includes bullying at workplace by a senior, supervisor, manger, fellow or junior employee. These also include occupational stress and sexual harassment at the workplace. It can trigger violence and have deep impact on the mental health of an employee.

An organisation can employ industrial hygienist to decipher and deal with the safety and health concerns of the workplace or an industrial unit. They will use scientific methods and risk assessment tools to evaluate the workplace and devise new ways and methodologies to control them. Once, they have an identified the hazards, they will either work to eliminate or control them.

Industrial Accidents

Industrial accidents are sudden, unexpected and unplanned mishaps that may happen at workplace. These may lead to injuries, disabilities or even death in certain cases.

The Workers' Compensation Act, 1923 lays down the guidelines and mandates for the employers to provide compensation to workers for accidents arising out of and in course of employment.

Types of Industrial Accidents

On the basis of the degree of injury, *industrial accidents can be classified into the following*

Major Accidents These are the accidents that may lead to death or permanent or prolonged disability of the involved employee or worker.

Minor Accidents These are the accidents that do not lead to any disability. These injuries can be small cuts, injuries and bruises.

Causes of Industrial Accidents

Unsafe Conditions

This is one of the biggest causes of accidents and these are conditions prevailing at the workplace. These include improper physical and atmospheric surrounding conditions of work which indirectly promote the occurrence of accidents.

Some of them could be defective plants, tools and equipments, remote location of plants, irregularly defined processes, inadequate lightning, improper ventilation, inadequate safety devices etc.

Negligence by the Workers

There could be irresponsible or negligent actions on the part of workers while doing their job. These could be mishandling or faulty handling of machines and equipments, not following the proper guidelines for completing a process, not wearing the requisite and proper clothing etc.

Miscellaneous Causes

These could be excessive noise, unhealthy working environment, slippery floors, excessive glare, dust and fume, spillage etc.

Industrial Safety

The different steps that can be taken by an employer to create a safe working environment for his employees are

- A good layout and working conditions play a major role in preventing many accidents which would have otherwise occurred. The layout needs to provide adequate working space for each employee to function. The passages need to be clear and obstruction free.
- Adequate lightning and ventilation, regulation of temperature conditions, availability of protective clothing needs to be taken care of.
- The noise level needs to be maintained at an adequate level to minimise detrimental effects such as deafness.
- Proper and regular training of employees so that there is minimum negligence on the part of employees while performing their tasks.
- The employer must conduct regular workshops to train employees deal with situation of accidents.
- Proper containers or vessels should be used for the transportation of liquid in order to prevent any spillage.
- Inflammable material must be properly marked and stored.
- Fire extinguishers must be readily available.
- The first-aid needs to be kept handy.

Occupational Disease

An 'occupational disease' is any disease contracted primarily as a result of an exposure to risk factors arising from work activity. These are chronic diseases caused due to activities or environmental factors at the workplace. These diseases can lead to costly early retirements, loss of skilled staff, absenteeism and high insurance premiums due to work related accidents and diseases.

The different causative agents include dust, allergens, mist, fumes, temperature, radiations, chemicals. They can have an impact on skin, lungs, eyes, muscles and other body organs as well.

Some of the most common types of occupational diseases are

Lung Diseases

These are the diseases that are caused due to the inhalation of certain chemical ingredient over a period of time. These include asbestosis (inflammation of lungs due to prolonged inhalation of asbestos), Chronic Obstructive Pulmonary Disease (COPD), silicosis (caused by breathing in tiny bits of silica), mesothelioma (cancer caused by the inhalation of asbestos fibers), occupational asthma and cancer.

People who are working in the construction and building, stone crushing, textiles or welding can be especially at risk of contracting a lung disease.

Farmer and other agricultural workers are prone to dust allergy and chronic bronchitis as they are indulging in handling of grain, mixing animal feedstuffs or feeding animals. The workers should wear masks to prevent the direct exposure to different allergens and chemicals.

Lead Poisoning

It is the most common type of OD that occurs due to the constant exposure to the chemical lead. It is commonly found in workers who have worked in shipbuilding, lead smelting, pottery glazing, stripping paint or plumbing industries. Prolonged exposure can lead to anaemia, seizures, infertility, kidney disease and brain damage. Besides inhalation, lead enters the body through nails as well. It is important to wash hands properly, use gloves and wear masks.

Skin Diseases

These are caused by prolonged exposure of hands and skins to different harmful chemicals and radiations. Eczema, utricaria, sunburn, dermatitis, skin cancer are the most common types. These are particularly observed in people working in catering, hairdressing, construction and printing, motor vehicle repair industry. Washing hands and wearing protective clothing can be effective ways to prevent skin diseases.

Carpel Tunnel Syndrome

It is a condition that causes pain, numbness and tingling in the hand and arm which happens due to the squeezing or compression of median nerve. It affects professional artists (sculptors, printrnakers, violinists) or any job requiring long-term repetitive motion of the wrist (jackhammer use, certain factory positions).

It is aggravated by repetitive movements, such as typing on a computer keyboard, talking on the phone (holding phone to the ear), texting or playing the piano. The work processes should be designed or redesigned in a manner in which there is a minimum movement of hand.

Computer Vision Syndrome

As the name signifies, this occurs due to focussing for long periods on computer screens. This may lead to eye strain, headaches, muscle aches, blurred vision, irritation in eyes or dry eyes. The workers can be provided with special anti-glares spectacles computer screens.

ILO's Instrument for Occupational Safety

ILO Codes of Practice set out practical guidelines for public authorities, employers, workers, enterprises and specialised occupational safety and health protection bodies. They are not legally binding instruments and are not intended to replace the provisions of national laws or regulations or accepted standards.

Codes of Practice provide guidance on safety and health at work in certain economic sectors (*e.g.* construction, opencast mines, coal mines, iron and steel industries, non-ferrous metals industries, agriculture, shipbuilding and ship repairing, forestry), on protecting workers against certain hazards (*e.g.* radiation, lasers, visual display units, chemicals, asbestos, airborne substances) and on certain safety and health measures (*e.g.* occupational safety and health management systems; ethical guidelines for workers health surveillance, recording and notification of occupational accidents and diseases, protection of workers' personal data; safety, health and working conditions in the transfer of technology to developing countries).

In 2003, the ILO adopted a global strategy to improve occupational safety and health which included the introduction of a preventive safety and health culture, the promotion and development of relevant instruments and technical assistance. It has adopted more than 40 standards specifically dealing with occupational safety and health, as well as over 40 Codes of Practice.

Some of the ILO's fundamental principles of occupational safety and health are

Occupational Safety and Health Convention, 1981 (No. 155) and its Protocol of 2002 The convention provides for the adoption of a coherent national occupational safety and health policy, as well as action to be taken by governments and within enterprises to promote occupational safety and health and to improve working conditions. This policy shall be developed by taking into consideration national conditions and practice.

The Protocol calls for the establishment and the periodic review of requirements and procedures for the recording and notification of occupational accidents and diseases, and for the publication of related annual statistics.

Occupational Health Services Convention, 1985 (No. 161) This convention provides for the establishment of enterprise level occupational health services which are entrusted with essentially preventive functions and which are responsible for advising the employer, the workers and their representatives in the enterprise on maintaining a safe and healthy working environment.

Promotional Framework for Occupational Safety and Health Convention, 2006 (No. 187) This convention aims at promoting a preventative safety and health culture and progressively achieving a safe and healthy working environment. It requires ratifying states to develop, in consultation with the most representative organisations of employers and workers, a national policy, national system and national programme on occupational safety and health.

The national policy shall be developed in accordance with the principles of Article 4 of the Occupational Safety and Health Convention, 1981 (No. 155) and the national systems and programmes shall be developed taking into account the principles set out in relevant ILO instruments.

Social Security

Concept and Scope of Social Security

ILO defines social security as the security that society furnishes through appropriate organisation against certain risks to which its members are exposed. These risks are essentially contingencies of life which the individual of small means cannot effectively provide by his own ability or foresight alone or even in private combination with his fellows.

The National Commission on Labour in India has endorsed the ILO's definition of Social Security and observed "Social security envisages that the members of a community should be protected by collective action against social risks causing undue hardship and privatisation to individuals whose prime resource can seldom be adequate to meet that."

William Beveridge has defined social security as "a means of securing an income to take the place of earnings when they are interrupted by unemployment, sickness or accident to provide for the retirement through old age, to provide against loss of support by death of another person or to meet exceptional expenditure connected with birth, death or marriage. The purpose of social security is to provide an income upto a minimum and also medical treatment to bring the interruption of earnings to an end as soon as possible."

Basically, the concept of social security is based on the fact that the society needs to provide social assurance to a person in case of a mishap over which the person has no control. Social security systems must provide for basic income in cases of unemployment, illness and injury, old age and retirement, invalidity, family responsibilities such as pregnancy and childcare and loss of the family breadwinner.

Such benefits are important not only for individual workers and their families but also for their communities as a whole. By providing health care, income security and social services, social security enhances productivity and contributes to the dignity and full realisation of the individual. Social security systems also promote gender equality through the adoption of measures to ensure that women who have children enjoy equal opportunities in the labour market.

For employers and enterprises, social security helps to maintain a stable workforce adaptable to change. Finally, by providing a safety net in case of economic crisis, social security serves as a fundamental element of social cohesion, thereby helping to ensure social peace and a positive engagement with globalisation and economic development.

Despite these advantages, only 20% of the world's population have adequate social security coverage, while more than half lack any kind of social security coverage at all.

Instruments of International Labour Organisation on Social Security

- The Social Security (minimum standards) Convention (No. 102) adopted by the ILO in 1952 lays down the minimum standard for the level of social security benefits and the conditions under which they are granted. It covers the nine principal branches of social security, namely medical care, sickness, unemployment, old age, employment injury, family, maternity, invalidity and survivors' benefits.

  To ensure that it could be applied in all national circumstances, the convention offers states the possibility of ratification by accepting atleast three of its nine branches and of subsequently accepting obligations under other branches, thereby allowing them to progressively attain all the objectives set out in the convention. India has not ratified this convention.
- The Social Protection Floors Recommendation, 2012 (No. 202) is an instrument gives guidance on introducing or maintaining social security floors and on implementing social protection floors as part of strategies to extend higher levels of social security to as many

people as possible, in accordance with the guidelines set out in ILO standards relating to social security.
- The Maintenance of Social Security Rights Convention, 1982 (No. 157) provides for certain social security rights and benefits for migrant workers, who face the problem of losing entitlements to social security benefits which they enjoyed in their country of origin.

Types of Social Security

The two most important types of social security are as follows

Social Assistance

Under this, government provides assistanceto the needy persons without any contributions from their end. The whole burden of this assistance is borne by the government. It helps the people to maintain a minimum level of living.

According to International Labour Officer, social assistance is a service or a scheme which provides benefits to persons of small means as of right in amount sufficient to meet minimum standards of need and financial from taxation. It is a voluntary help offered to the individuals by the government. *The important features of social assistance are*

- There are some conditions and legal framework in which the workers and state are bound.
- The specific target of social assurance is the poor people who are exposed to different types of risks and contingencies.
- It is a unilateral obligation which is financed wholly or for a very large measures from the government's funds.
- The beneficiaries need to fulfil certain prescribed conditions before the benefit can be granted under such scheme.

Social Assurance

Under this, employer and employees contributes to maintain a fund. The government may incentivise this scheme by providing subsidies. However, this isn't necessary. The best example of this will be the provident fund.

Some of the important features are

- Both the employers and employee contribute to this fund.
- Both the parties need to compulsorily participate in the scheme.
- The contributions are added to a special fund from which the benefits are paid.
- The contribution from employee's end is based on the earnings of the employees.
- It is helpful to maintain the minimum standard of living by the workers.

EXAM BASED QUESTIONS

1 **Which of the following is incorrect for the concept of labour welfare?**
(a) The efficiency of labour enhances its productivity as well
(b) It focuses on building and improving the work life quality of the employees
(c) This concept is the same across the different regions of the country
(d) Socio-cultural background, marital and economic status of the employees contribute to labour welfare

2 **How many factors of production are there?**
(a) Three (b) Nine
(c) Ten (d) Four

3 **Which of the following is not a factor of production?**
(a) Land (b) Labour
(c) GDP (d) Capital

4 **When did the Government of India set up Committee on Labour Welfare?**
(a) 1971 (b) 1959
(c) 1967 (d) 1969

5 **Which of the following is incorrect according to ILO's definition of labour welfare?**
(a) These amenities may be established only inside the establishment
(b) The facilities enable the persons employed in them to perform their work in healthy surroundings
(c) The services should be conducive to good health and high morale of the employees
(d) The employees must be provided healthy and congenial surroundings

6 **Which of the following is not an objective of labour welfare?**
(a) Improve and enhance the quality of life of the employees only
(b) Increasing the productivity and efficiency of the labour
(c) Promote an organisational culture that is conducive to the growth of an employee
(d) Provide health, medical and maternity benefits that help the employees to take care of their health

7 **Who among the following classified labour welfare activities on the basis of location?**
(a) Dr GM Broughton (b) Dr NR Broughton
(c) Dr TN Broughton (d) Dr AB Broughton

8 **When did ILO establish committee of experts on welfare facilities for industrial workers?**
(a) 1980 (b) 1989
(c) 1972 (d) 1963

9 **Which of the following is not an intra-mural activity?**
(a) Amusement and sports (b) Sufficient lightning
(c) First-aid appliances (d) Maternity benefits

10 **Which of the following is an intra-mural activity?**
(a) Gratuity
(b) Housing accommodation
(c) Fair price shops
(d) Vocational training for dependents of workers

11 **Which of the following is not an extra-mural activity?**
(a) Protective clothing
(b) Thrift and credit societies
(c) Transport to and from the place of work
(d) Social insurance measures

12 **Which of the following is an extra-mural activity?**
(a) Provision of libraries and reading rooms
(b) Shift allowances
(c) Pension
(d) Provision of provident fund

13 **Which of the following is not correct for labour welfare activities?**
(a) Intra-mural are welfare amenities within the precincts or premises of the establishment
(b) Extra-mural are welfare amenities outside the precincts or premises of the establishment
(c) Leave travel facility is included in the intra-mural
(d) Occupational safety is an intra-mural activity

14 **How many theories constitute the framework of labour welfare activities?**
(a) 8 (b) 9 (c) 10 (d) 11

15 **Encyclopedia of social science has classified labour welfare activities into how many types?**
(a) 2 (b) 3 (c) 4 (d) 7

16 **Which of the following labour welfare activities deal with the immediate working conditions?**
(a) Gymnasium
(b) Minimum wages
(c) Provisions for conciliation and arbitration
(d) Arranging athletic contests

17 **Which of the following labour welfare activities deal with the group interests?**
(a) Housing
(b) Disability and unemployment funds
(c) Day nursery
(d) Kindergartens

18 **Which of the following labour welfare activities are designed to improve community conditions?**
(a) Profit sharing (b) Vacations with pay
(c) Dental services (d) Stock ownership

19 **Which of the following labour welfare activities deal with less immediate working condition?**
(a) Shop committees and workers' council
(b) Screening of motion pictures
(c) Lunch rooms
(d) Rest rooms

20 Which of the following theory is based on the premise that a minimum standard of welfare is necessary?
(a) Placating theory (b) Policing theory
(c) Religious theory (d) Philanthropic theory

21 According to which of the following theories, government enforces regulatory and legal measures upon the employer?
(a) Placating theory (b) Policing theory
(c) Religious theory (d) Philanthropic theory

22 Which of the following theories is based on the assumption that employers exploit the workers using their tactics and they will not leave any such opportunity?
(a) Placating theory (b) Policing theory
(c) Trusteeship theory (d) Parenting theory

23 Which of the following theories is based on the elements of investment or atonement?
(a) Placating theory (b) Policing theory
(c) Religious theory (d) Philanthropic theory

24 Which of the following theories propagates profit sharing by the employer with his employees?
(a) Placating theory (b) Policing theory
(c) Religious theory (d) Philanthropic theory

25 Which of the following theories assume that benefits provided by the employers to the employees will help it reap the benefits in future?
(a) Placating theory (b) Policing theory
(c) Religious theory (d) Philanthropic theory

26 Which of the following theories is essentially based on man's love for mankind?
(a) Placating theory (b) Policing theory
(c) Religious theory (d) Philanthropic theory

27 Which of the following theories state that it is the duty and responsibility of wealthy people to help the underprivileged people?
(a) Placating theory (b) Policing theory
(c) Religious theory (d) Philanthropic theory

28 Which of the following theories state that a company provides good working conditions, services and amenities as a gesture of kindness towards the employees?
(a) Placating theory (b) Policing theory
(c) Religious theory (d) Philanthropic theory

29 Which of the following theories is also known as Paternalistic theory?
(a) Placating theory (b) Policing theory
(c) Religious theory (d) Trusteeship theory

30 Which of the following theories is based on the assumption that employees do not have the ability to take care of themselves?
(a) Placating theory (b) Policing theory
(c) Religious theory (d) Trusteeship theory

31 Who among the following was a strong advocate of the trusteeship theory?
(a) Netaji Subhash Chandra Bose
(b) Mahatma Gandhi
(c) Bal Gangadhar Tilak
(d) Sardar Patel

32 Which of the following theory assumes owner of an establishment as the elderly person who is responsible of taking care of the complete family?
(a) Placating theory (b) Policing theory
(c) Religious theory (d) Trusteeship theory

33 Which of the following theories state that labour groups are becoming militant in nature?
(a) Placating theory (b) Functional theory
(c) Efficiency theory (d) Trusteeship theory

34 Which of the following theory states that timely and periodical acts of labour welfare can appease the workers?
(a) Placating theory (b) Functional theory
(c) Efficiency theory (d) Trusteeship theory

35 Which theory assumes that labour welfare programs are advertisements?
(a) Placating theory (b) Public Relations theory
(c) Efficiency theory (d) Trusteeship theory

36 Which theory states that labour welfare activities are done to create a good image in the eyes of workers and public?
(a) Placating theory (b) Public Relations theory
(c) Efficiency theory (d) Trusteeship theory

37 Which theory states that the welfare work should be used to preserve and develop efficiency of labour?
(a) Placating theory (b) Functional theory
(c) Efficiency theory (d) Trusteeship theory

38 Which theory is a reflection of contemporary support for labour welfare?
(a) Placating theory (b) Functional theory
(c) Efficiency theory (d) Trusteeship theory

39 Which theory states that big business houses have moral obligations of providing good working conditions to the employees?
(a) Functional theory (b) Social theory
(c) Efficiency theory (d) Trusteeship theory

40 Which theory states that improving the condition of labour can be helpful in improving the overall condition of the society?
(a) Functional theory (b) Social theory
(c) Efficiency theory (d) Trusteeship theory

41 Which theory considers labour welfare as a mandate of Corporate Social Responsibility (CSR) of the organisation?
(a) Functional theory (b) Social theory
(c) Efficiency theory (d) Trusteeship theory

42 Which of the following is incorrect for industrial hygiene?

(a) It is the science and art devoted to the anticipation, recognition, evaluation and control of those environmental factors which may cause sickness, impaired health and well-being
(b) The stressors need to be identified at initial stages only and be dealt with before they become an issue for the workers
(c) It deals with controlling real or potential workplace environmental stressors or hazards that have an impact on the well being of workers and community members
(d) It is one of the factors of productions

43 Which of the following is not a physical hazard?

(a) Excessive noise
(b) Irregularities in temperature and pressure
(c) Dust because of an industrial process
(d) Ionizing radiations

44 Which of the following is not related to ergonomics hazard at workplace?

(a) Exposure to radiations
(b) Excessive lightning
(c) Repetitive motions
(d) Irregularities in processes

45 Which of the following hazards is basically bullying at workplace?

(a) Chemical (b) Physical
(c) Biological (d) Psychological

46 Which of the following is a physical hazard?

(a) Repetition of unwanted motions
(b) Improperly designed work areas
(c) Air quality
(d) Bullying by the supervisor

47 Mesothelioma is related to which of the following?

(a) Lead (b) Mercury
(c) Asbestos (d) Silica

48 Chronic Obstructive Pulmonary Disease (COPD) falls under which category of occupational disease?

(a) Lung Diseases (b) Skin Diseases
(c) Lead Poisoning (d) Vision Syndome

49 Carpel Tunnel syndrome is related to which of the following?

(a) Legs (b) Hand or wrist
(c) Skin (d) Brain

50 Eczema and utricaria fall under which category of disease?

(a) Lung (b) Skin
(c) Eyes (d) Brain

51 How does lead enter the body apart from inhalation?

(a) Legs (b) Nails
(c) Eyes (d) Hair

52 Which category of workers is least susceptible to lead poisoning?

(a) Ship building (b) Catering
(c) Pottery glazing (d) IT industry

53 Which category of worker is the most susceptible to Carpel Tunnel syndrome?

(a) Sculptors (b) Farmers
(c) Doctors (d) Potters

54 When did ILO adopt a global strategy to improve occupational safety and health ?

(a) 2001 (b) 1919
(c) 1990 (d) 2003

55 How many codes of practice does ILO have?

(a) Over 10 (b) Over 100
(c) Over 40 (d) Over 70

56 The Occupational Safety and Health Convention, 1981 is which convention of ILO?

(a) 110 (b) 120
(c) 140 (d) 155

57 When did ILO adopt Framework for Occupational Safety and Health Convention?

(a) 2004 (b) 2006
(c) 2009 (d) 2010

58 Which of the following provides for the adoption of a coherent national occupational safety and health policy?

(a) Codes of Practice
(b) Promotional Framework for Occupational Safety and Health Convention, 2006
(c) Occupational Health Services Convention, 1985
(d) Occupational Safety and Health Convention, 1981

59 Which of the following conventions aim at promoting a preventative safety and health culture and progressively achieving a safe and healthy working environment?

(a) Codes of Practice
(b) Promotional Framework for Occupational Safety and Health Convention, 2006
(c) Occupational Health Services Convention, 1985
(d) Occupational Safety and Health Convention, 1981

60 Which Article of Occupational Safety and Health Convention, 1981 lays down the principles for developing a national occupational safety and health policy?

(a) 4 (b) 11 (c) 10 (d) 13

61 Under which of the following recording and notification of occupational accidents and diseases should be done?

(a) Occupational Safety and Health Protocol, 2002
(b) Promotional Framework for Occupational Safety and Health Convention, 2006
(c) Occupational Health Services Convention, 1985
(d) Occupational Safety and Health Convention, 1981

62 When did ILO adopt Social Security (minimum standards) Convention?
(a) 1980 (b) 2010 (c) 1952 (d) 1919

63 Which of the following is not covered under ILO's Social Security (minimum standards) Convention?
(a) Medical care (b) Sickness
(c) Employment injury (d) Wages

64 According to ILO's Social Security (minimum standards) Convention, what are the minimum number of social security branches that need to be ratified by the country initially?
(a) 2 (b) 3 (c) 4 (d) 5

65 Who among the following will not be covered under the basic income provided as a part of social security?
(a) Old ages persons (b) Voluntary unemployed
(c) Pregnant women (d) Retired professionals

66 What percentage of the world population has an adequate social security coverage?
(a) 18 (b) 20 (c) 22 (d) 24

67 According to the Building and other Construction Workers (regulation of employment and conditions of service) Act, 1996, what should be the minimum number of employees in an establishment for which an employer needs to constitute a safety committee?
(a) 900 (b) 300 (c) 120 (d) 500

68 The Social Security (minimum standards) Convention (No. 102) adopted by the ILO in covers .... principal branches of social security.
(a) 10 (b) 9 (c) 7 (d) 8

69 .... is an example of social insurance.
(a) Salary (b) Wages
(c) Pension (d) Provident fund

70 The Maintenance of Social Security Rights Convention, 1982 (No. 157) provides for certain social security rights and benefits for ...., who face the problem of losing entitlements to social security benefits which they enjoyed in their country of origin.
(a) Voluntarily retired workers
(b) Migrant workers
(c) Unemployed workers
(d) Retired Workers

71 Sexual harassment at workplace is a .... stressor.
(a) chemical (b) physical
(c) ergonomics (d) psychological

72 Repetitive motions leading to increased time of work cycle will be a .... stressor.
(a) chemical (b) physical
(c) ergonomics (d) psychological

73 Which of the following is correct in terms of occupational disease?
1. It is contracted primarily as a result of an exposure to risk factors arising from work activity.
2. These are chronic in nature.
3. These diseases can lead to costly early retirements, loss of skilled staff.

Codes
(a) Only 1 (b) Both 2 and 3
(c) Both 1 and 3 (d) All of these

74 Consider the following for ILO's Codes of Practice.
1. These are practical guidelines for public authorities, employers, workers, enterprises, and specialised occupational safety and health protection bodies.
2. They are legally binding instruments.
3. They provide guidance on safety and health at work in certain economic sectors.

Which of the following statement given above is correct?

Codes
(a) Both 1 and 2 (b) Both 2 and 3
(c) Both 1 and 3 (d) All of these

75 Which of the following is correct in the context of Carpel Tunnel Syndrome?
1. It happens due to the squeezing or compression of median nerve of the right feet.
2. It causes pain, numbness and tingling.
3. It is aggravated by repetitive movements.

Codes
(a) Both 1 and 2 (b) Both 2 and 3
(c) Both 1 and 3 (d) All of these

76 Which of the following is correct for the concept of social security?
1. It enhances productivity and contributes to the dignity and full realisation of the individual.
2. It serves as a fundamental element of social cohesion.
3. It helps to ensure social peace and a positive engagement with globalisation and economic development.

Codes
(a) Both 1 and 2 (b) Both 2 and 3
(c) Both 1 and 3 (d) All of these

77 Which of the following is incorrect in the context of social insurance?
1. Under this, government provides assistance to the needy persons without any contributions from their end.
2. The government may incentivise this scheme by providing subsidies.

3. Under this, employer and employees contributes to maintain a fund.

Codes

(a) Only 1 (b) Only 2
(c) Only 3 (d) Both 2 and 3

78 Which of the following statements are true/ false?

(i) Dr. GM Broughton classified labour welfare activities into two categories.
(ii) Dr. GM Broughton's classification of labour activities was accepted by the committee of experts on welfare facilities for industrial workers constituted by ILO in 1971.
(iii) Fair Price shop and cooperatives are included in the extra-mural activities.
(iv) Medical facilities, compensation for accidents are included in intra-mural activities.

(a) (i), (iii), (iv) are true and (ii) is false
(b) (i), (iii) are true and (ii), (iv) are false
(c) (ii), (iv) are true and (i), (iii) are false
(d) (iii), (iv) are true and (ii), (i) are false

79 Which of the following statements are true/ false?

(i) Religious theory is based on man's love for mankind.
(ii) Police theory is based on assumption that employees exploit workers using their tactics and they will not leave any such opportunity.
(iii) Placating theory assumes that employees do not have ability to take care of themselves.
(iv) The theory of Public Relations state that welfare activities and facilities are done and provided to create a good image in the eyes of workers and public.

(a) (i), (iv) are true and (ii), (iii) are false
(b) (i), (iii) are true and (ii), (iv) are false
(c) (ii), (iv) are true and (i), (iii) are false
(d) (iii), (iv) are true and (ii), (i) are false

80 Which of the following statements are true/false?

(i) Trusteeship theory is also known as paternalistic theory.
(ii) The Philanthropic theory is based on the fact that man is a religious being.
(iii) The Functional theory is also known as efficiency theory.
(iv) Efficiency theory assumes that big business houses have the social responsibility and moral obligations of providing good working conditions.

(a) (i), (iv) are true and (ii), (iii) are false
(b) (i), (iii) are true and (ii), (iv) are false
(c) (ii), (iv) are true and (i), (iii) are false
(d) (iii), (iv) are true and (ii), (i) are false

81 Which of the following statements are true/ false?

(i) Chemical hazards include dust or fumes, mists, vapours, and gases that are a result of chemical processes that takes place inside the industrial unit.
(ii) Chemical hazards include excessive levels of electromagnetic and ionizing radiations, noise, irregularities in temperature, air quality.
(iii) Ergonomic hazards rise because of repetitive stress or injuries caused due to different processes such as lifting, pushing, pulling etc.
(iv) Psychological hazards includes bullying at workplace by a senior, supervisor, manger, fellow or junior employee.

(a) (i), (iii), (iv) are true and (ii) is false
(b) (i), (iii) are true and (ii), (iv) are false
(c) (ii), (iv) are true and (i), (iii) are false
(d) (iii), (iv) are true and (ii), (i) are false

82 Which of the following statements are true/ false?

(i) COPD (Chronic Obstructive Pulmonary Disease) is an Occupational Disease related to lungs.
(ii) Mesothelioma is cancer caused by the inhalation of asbestos fibers.
(iii) Carpel Tunnel Syndrome is a disease of eyes.
(iv) Eczema is a breathing disorder caused due to inhalation of excessive lead.

(a) (i), (iv) are true and (ii), (iii) are false
(b) (i), (ii) are true and (iii), (iv) are false
(c) (ii), (iv) are true and (i), (iii) are false
(d) (iii), (iv) are true and (ii), (i) are false

83 Which of the following statements are correct?

(i) In 2003 the ILO adopted a global strategy to improve occupational safety and health which included the introduction of a preventive safety and health culture.
(ii) It has adopted more than 40 standards specifically dealing with occupational safety and health, as well as over 40 Codes of Practice.
(iii) ILO's Codes of Practice are not legally binding instruments.
(iv) ILO's Codes of Practice are not intended to replace the provisions of national laws or regulations, or accepted standards.

(a) All are correct
(b) Only (i) and (iii) are correct
(c) Only (ii) and (iv) are correct
(d) Only (iii) and (iv) are correct

84 Which of the following statements are correct?

1. ILO's Occupational Safety and Health Convention, 1981 is convention No. 155.
2. Occupational Health Services Convention, 1985 (No. 161) provides for the establishment of enterprise-level occupational health services.
3. Promotional Framework for Occupational Safety and Health Convention, 2006 is Convention No 172.
4. The national policy shall be developed in accordance with the principles of Article 2 of the Occupational Safety and Health Convention, 1981.

(a) Only 1 and 2 are correct
(b) Only 1 and 3 are correct
(c) Only 2 and 4 are correct
(d) Only 3 and 4 are correct

85 Which of the following statements are correct?

1. Principle of adequacy of wages state that workers have right to fair wages.
2. Education and training, housing, and food are the three most important aspects of labour welfare.
3. The organisation needs to take care that all the labour welfare measures are uniformly accepted across all the levels of hierarchy.
4. It is the duty of industry to fulfill the unmet needs of the workers and it is the right of workers to decide the manner in which these needs can be met.

(a) Only 1 and 3 are correct
(b) All are correct
(c) Only 2 and 4 are correct
(d) Only 3 and 4 are correct

86 Which of the following statements are correct?

1. Labour welfare is a total concept and a coordinated approach promotes the overall development of the employee at the personal and professional fronts.
2. An industry is expected to work for the workers.
3. In social assurance, both the employers and employee contribute to this fund.
4. Social assistance is helpful to maintain the minimum standard of living by the workers.

(a) Only 1, 2 and 3 are correct
(b) Only 1 and 3 are correct
(c) Only 2 and 4 are correct
(d) Only 3 and 4 are correct

87 Which of the following statements are correct?

1. Social Insurance is a unilateral obligation which is financed wholly or for a very large measures from the government's funds.
2. The labour welfare measures can substitute for wages.
3. The Placating theory is based on the fact that employees are becoming militant in nature.
4. According to trusteeship theory, the employer establishes an enterprise in trust for the benefit of people.

(a) All are correct
(b) Only 1 and 2 are correct
(c) Only 2 and 4 are correct
(d) Only 3 and 4 are correct

Directions (Q. Nos. 88-92) *In the following questions, given below are two statements are labelled as Assertion (A) and Reason (R). In the context of the two statements, which one of the following is correct?*

Codes

(a) Both (A) and (R) are correct and (R) is the correct explanation of (A)
(b) Both (A) and (R) are correct, but (R) is not the correct explanation of (A)
(c) (A) is correct, but (R) is incorrect
(d) (A) is incorrect, but (R) is correct

88 **Assertion** (A) A country's economic development is dependent upon the production of goods and services in the country.

Reason (R) These are the important factors of productions.

89 **Assertion** (A) The workers should atleast have the means and facilities to keep themselves in a state of health and efficiency.

Reason (R) This is required to help them perform to the best of their abilities.

90 **Assertion** (A) Labour welfare is a holistic concept that has a broad scope.

Reason (R) Labour welfare policies will be helpful in order to enhance the productivity and efficiency of the employees that will be conducive to good health and high morale of the employees.

91 **Assertion** (A) Social security is furnished by society through appropriate organisation against certain risks to which its members are exposed.

Reason (R) The purpose of social security is to provide an income up to a minimum and maintain a decent standard of living.

92 **Assertion** (A) The labour groups are becoming brilliant in nature.

Reason (R) They have become demanding and have become more conscious of their rights and privileges.

93 Match the following with their correct convention number.

List I	List II
A. Occupational Safety and Health Convention, 1981	1. 161
B. Occupational Health Services Convention, 1985	2. 155
C. Promotional Framework for Occupational Safety and Health Convention, 2006	3. 187

Codes

	A	B	C		A	B	C
(a)	1	2	3	(b)	2	1	3
(c)	1	3	2	(d)	3	2	1

94 Match the following with their correct convention number.

List I	List II
A. Social Security (minimum standards) Convention	1. 202
B. Social Protection Floors Recommendation, 2012	2. 102
C. Maintenance of Social Security Rights Convention, 1982	3. 157

Codes

	A	B	C		A	B	C
(a)	1	2	3	(b)	2	1	3
(c)	1	3	2	(d)	3	2	1

Directions (Q. Nos. 95-97) *Read the passage and answer the questions that follow*

The landmark ILO declaration on social justice for a fair globalisation is a powerful reaffirmation of ILO values and ILO's key role in helping to achieve progress and social justice in the context of globalisation. The declaration promotes decent work through a coordinated approach to achieving four strategic objectives: employment, social protection, social dialogue, and fundamental principles and rights at work. The impact of the declaration, in particular the extent to which it has contributed to promoting the aims and purposes of the organisation through the integrated pursuit of the strategic objectives, was the subject of a conference review in 2016.

The International Labour Conference adopted the social justice declaration on 10th June, 2008 together with a resolution on strengthening the ILO's capacity to assist its members' efforts to reach its objectives in the context of globalisation. The social justice declaration is the third major statement of principles and policies adopted by the International Labour Conference. It builds on the declaration concerning the aims and purposes of the ILO (Declaration of Philadelphia) (1944) and the ILO Declaration on Fundamental Principles and Rights at Work (1998).

The declaration is the outcome of tripartite consultations that started in the wake of the report of the World commission on the social dimension of globalisation. By adopting this text, the governments, employers' and workers' organisations of the ILO's 187 member states commit to enhance the ILO's capacity to advance these goals through the decent work agenda. The declaration institutionalises the concept of decent work recognised since 1999, placing it at the core of the organisation's policies to reach its constitutional objectives.

The 2016 conference evaluation, undertaken eight years after the adoption of the declaration, offers a strategic opportunity for the organisation to consider the coordinated approach to the decent work objectives in a global context that has changed, particularly following the financial and economic crisis which arose after its adoption. It will be important to consider the relevance of the UN's sustainable development goals and the changing environment of international development cooperation in assessing further action that may be appropriate.

The conference evaluation is intended to address the main objectives of the social justice declaration in the context of more recent developments to reinforce the ILO's key role in helping to achieve progress and social justice in a constantly changing environment.

95 **How many strategic objectives are promoted through ILO declaration on social justice for a fair globalisation?**

(a) Two (b) Three
(c) Four (d) Five

96 **Which of the following is incorrect in the context of above passage?**

(a) The declaration is the outcome of bipartite consultations that started in the wake of the report of the world commission on the social dimension of globalisation.
(b) The International Labour Conference adopted the social justice declaration on 10th June, 2008 together with a resolution on strengthening the ILO's capacity to assist its members' efforts to reach its objectives in the context of globalisation.
(c) ILO declaration on social justice for a fair globalisation is a powerful reaffirmation of ILO values and ILO's key role in helping to achieve progress and social justice in the context of globalisation.
(d) The social justice declaration is the third major statement of principles and policies adopted by the International Labour Conference.

97 **How are Sustainable Development Goals (SDGs) important for the ILO?**

(a) They law down the basic and futuristic goals for the overall development in the dynamic environment of the world.
(b) They act as the basics for formulating the laws of a country.
(c) They ensure justice is provided to each individual irrespective of their background, gender and religion.
(d) They help in understanding the anthropology of different countries.

PREVIOUS YEARS' QUESTIONS

2018

1 Assertion (A) Labour welfare is a relative concept.

Reason (R) This is so because it is related to time and space.

Codes

(a) (A) is correct, but (R) is worng
(b) Both (A) and (R) are correct and (R) is the correct explanation of A
(c) (A) is wrong, but (R) is correct
(d) Both (A) and (R) are correct, but (R) is not the correct explanation of (A)

2 Which among the following is not an objective of labour welfare?

(a) To further the political interests of employers
(b) To combat the influence of outside agencies on employees
(c) Desire to show-off and advertise concern for labour
(d) Avoiding payment of taxes on surplus

3 What is the minimum amount of compensation payable to an employee who is permanently and totally disabled from an injury by accident arising out of and in course of employment under the Employees' Compensation Act, 1923?

(a) ₹ 1,40,000 (b) ₹ 1,20,000
(c) ₹ 1,50,000 (d) ₹ 1,60,000

4 Assertion (A) Labour welfare movement acquired new dimensions after independence.

Reason (R) It was realised the labour welfare had a positive role to play in increasing productivity and reducing industrial tensions.

Codes

(a) (A) is correct and (R) is incorrect
(b) (A) is correct and (R) is fully explains (A)
(c) (A) is incorrect and (R) is correct
(d) Both (A) and (R) are incorrect

5 Labour welfare movement has witnessed some distinctive developments. They are

1. Voluntary organisations engaged in labour welfare expanded in number and influences.
2. State through legislations tried to regulate and improve the lot of labour.
3. Some enlightened employers took the initiative to improve the working and living conditions of labour.
4. Trade Unions fought to bring about an improvement in the working conditions of labour and to raise their status socially and economically.

Arrange the developments in correct order from latest to earliest.

Codes

(a) 1, 2, 4, 3 (b) 1, 4, 3, 2
(c) 2, 3, 4, 1 (d) 2, 4, 1, 3

6 'Welfare implies welfare of man, his family and his community'. Which of the following concepts explains this ?

(a) The total concept of welfare
(b) The positive concept of welfare
(c) The social concept of welfare
(d) The relative concept of welfare

7 Match the content given in List I with the Theories of Labour Welfare given in List II.

	List I		List II
A.	Without compulsion, employers do not provide even the minimum facilities for workers	1.	The Trusteeship Theory
B.	Any good work is considered as an investment by which both the benefactor and beneficiary are rewarded	2.	The Philanthropic Theory
C.	Man is believed to have an instinctive urge by which he strives to remove the suffering of others and promote their well being	3.	The Religious Theory
D.	Employers should provide funds on an on-going basis for the well being of their employees	4.	The Police Theory

Codes

	A	B	C	D
(a)	4	3	2	1
(b)	4	2	3	1
(c)	1	4	3	2
(d)	1	3	4	2

2017

8 Assertion (A) Labour Welfare is a relative concept as it is related to time and space.

Reason (R) Welfare is growing and dynamic. The welfare potential changes as a result of which its content keeps on varying and has to keep pace with the changing times.

Codes

(a) (A) is incorrect and (R) fails to explain (A)
(b) (A) is correct and (R) fully explain (A)
(c) (A) is incorrect and (R), therefore, cannot explain (A)
(d) Both (A) and (R) are incorrect

9 Assertion (A) The aims and objectives of labour welfare have progressively changed during the last few decades.

Reason (R) It has gradually moved to the era of paternalism with philanthropic objectives from the primitive policing and placating philosophy of labour welfare.

Codes

(a) (A) is correct, but (R) fails to explain (A)
(b) (A) is correct and (R) explain (A)
(c) (A) is incorrect and (R) is correct
(d) Both (A) and (R) are incorrect

10 Labour Welfare Services were divided into two groups by the Committee of Experts on welfare facilities for Industrial Workers convened by the I.L.O. in 1963. They are within the precincts and outside the establishment.

Match the facilities given in List I with the type provided in List II.

List I	List II
A. Shift allowance	1. Outside establishment
B. Arrangements within a plant for welfare	2. Within precincts
C. Programme for the welfare of youth and children	3. Outside establishment
D. Vocational training dependants of workers	4. Within precincts

Codes

	A	B	C	D		A	B	C	D
(a)	2	1	4	3	(b)	3	2	4	1
(c)	2	4	1	3	(d)	3	2	1	4

11 Theories of Labour Welfare have been propounded after careful study and observation of the state of affairs prevalent during that particular period of time.

Which theory of labour welfare was propounded after observing "The factories and other industrial workplaces provide ample opportunities for owners and manager of capital to exploit workers in an unfair manner"?

(a) Placating theory (b) Religious theory
(c) Policing theory (d) Philanthropic theory

12 Which of the following is the correct set of contingencies identified by William Beveridge in his comprehensive social security scheme?

(a) Want, sickness, disability, squalor and idleness
(b) Want, disease, old age, squalor and unemployment
(c) Want, disease, ignorance, squalor and idleness
(d) Disease, invalidity, old age, unemployment and ignorance

13 Who was the first person to advocate an eight hours working day for workers ?

(a) Robert Owen (b) John Stuart Mill
(c) George Elliot (d) August Comte

14 Assertion (A) Welfare is a relative concept, relative in time and place.

Reason (R) Ideas of welfare differ with passage of time. Man accepted comparatively less convenient and less sumptuous conditions of existence; for Science and Technology had not made possible better amenities. Then again, meaning and content of welfare differs from country-to-country or region-to-region.

Codes

(a) (A) is correct, but (R) partially explains (A)
(b) (A) is partially correct and therefore, (R) only partially explains (A)
(c) (A) is correct and (R) explains (A)
(d) (A) is incorrect and (R) is partially correct

15 Labour Welfare Services were divided into two groups by the committee of experts on Welfare Facilities for Industrial Workers convened by ILO in 1963. These are (a) Those within the precincts of the establishment (b) Those outside the precincts of the establishment. The content of welfare activities remained the same as recommended by 1959 study team. As per the ILO classification, which one among the following is not welfare and amenities outside the precincts of the establishment?

(a) Social insurance measures including gratuity, pension and provident fund
(b) Housing facilities
(c) Recreation facility
(d) Arrangement for prevention of fatigue

16 Match the Principles of Labour Welfare mentioned in List I with the contents given in List II.

List I	List II
A. Principle of Social Responsibility of Industry	1. Concept of labour welfare must spread throughout the hierarchy of an organisation
B. Principle of Responsibility	2. Industry has an obligation towards its employees to lookafter their welfare
C. Principle of Totality of Welfare	3. Both employers and workers are responsible for labour welfare
D. Principle of Repersonalisation	4. Development of the human personality must be goal of welfare

Codes

	A	B	C	D
(a)	4	2	3	1
(b)	2	3	1	4
(c)	3	2	4	1
(d)	1	3	2	4

17 Which among the following statement is not true is relation to labour welfare ?
(a) Labour welfare is an essential part of social welfare
(b) Labour welfare work not only covers the work life of workers in the factory but also extends beyond into his life with his family and community
(c) Labour welfare is not concerned with desirable conditions of existence, biologically and socially determined
(d) Labour welfare is a relative concept, relative in time and place

18 According to William Beveridge which of the following are not part of a comprehensive social security scheme ?
1. Social assistance
2. Compulsory insurance
3. Social insurance
4. Voluntary insurance
5. Voluntary assistance

Codes
(a) 2 and 5 (c) 4 and 5
(c) 2, 4 and 5 (d) 1, 2 and 3

19 Which of the following are the characteristics/ features of 'social assistance' ?
1. It is fully financed by the state.
2. Benefits provided under the scheme is for a short duration.
3. The financial resources of social assistance scheme is for a short duration of time.
4. Social assistance is substitutive rather than supplemental to social insurance.

Codes
(a) 1, 2 and 4 (b) 2, 3 and 4
(c) 1, 2 and 3 (d) All of these

20 Labour welfare, though, is not exactly social work but any welfare is the result of social work. Social work lead to states of welfare both of individuals and groups. And, therefore, it can be derived that labour welfare is an area of social work. There exists four methods of undertaking social work. Match the subject matter given in List I with the method of social work given in List II.

List I	List II
A. Situations of layoff and retrenchment	1. Social action
B. Collective bargaining contexts	2. Community Organisation and Development
C. Housing	3. Social group work
D. Peaceful strike	4. Social case work

Codes

	A	B	C	D
(a)	1	2	3	4
(b)	4	3	2	1
(c)	2	1	4	3
(d)	4	2	3	1

21 The term 'social security' was officially first used in
(a) ILO
(b) The United States of America
(c) The USSR
(d) Germany

2016

22 **Assertion** (A) The social concept of welfare implies the welfare of man, his family and his community.

Reason (R) All the three work together or individually supplement one another, in a three-dimensional approach, each serving as ends and means.

Codes
(a) (A) is incorrect and (R) is correct
(b) (R) explains (A) properly
(c) (R) does not provide proper explanation of (A)
(d) Both (A) and (R) are incorrect

23 Match the following.

List I (Content)	List II (Principles of Labour Welfare)
A. Labour Welfare measures cannot be a substitute for wages	1. Principle of efficiency
B. Industries have an obligation towards employees to lookafter their welfare	2. Principle of re-personalisation
C. There exists relationship between welfare and efficiency	3. Principle of adequacy of wages
D. The development of human personality has to be a goal of industrial welfare	4. Principle of social responsibility of industry

Codes

	A	B	C	D		A	B	C	D
(a)	1	2	3	4	(b)	4	3	2	1
(c)	3	4	1	2	(d)	2	1	4	3

24 The conceptual framework of labour welfare is contained in various theories of labour welfare. In the names of the theories given below, pick the wrong ones
1. The Trusteeship Theory
2. The Placating Theory
3. The Need Theory
4. The Friendship Theory
5. The Public Relations Theory
6. The Functional Theory

Codes
(a) 1 and 2 (b) 3 and 4
(c) 5 and 6 (d) 2 and 5

25 Assertion (A) Labour welfare will give rise to social inequalities.

Reason (R) Workers of large undertakings having capacity of offering better welfare amenities will be better placed than those of small and medium undertakings which are not in a position to run welfare services.

Codes
(a) Both (A) and (R) are wrong
(b) (A) is right, but (R) does not explain (A)
(c) (A) is wrong and (R) attempts to justify a wrong assertion
(d) (A) is right and (R) explains the logic of (A)

2015

26 Match the following.

	List I (Philosophies)		List II (Theories of Labour Welfare)
A.	Laws are made to prescribe minimum welfare for workers, implementation of which is periodically supervised and punishment for defaulting employers is levied	1.	Religious Theory
B.	Labour welfare work is taken up in a spirit of atonement	2.	Placating Theory
C.	Labour welfare is extended in order to satisfy the appease the increasing demands of employees	3.	Public Relations Theory
D.	Labour welfare is extended to build and improve 'employer branding'	4.	Policing Theory

Codes

	A	B	C	D		A	B	C	D
(a)	2	3	1	4	(b)	4	2	3	1
(c)	4	3	1	2	(d)	4	1	2	3

27 Which of the following concepts explain that welfare implies the welfare of man, his family and his community?
(a) The total concept of welfare
(b) The social concept of welfare
(c) The positive concept of welfare
(d) The relative concept of welfare

28 Arrange the following developments in Labour Welfare Movement in the correct order from earliest to the latest.
1. Voluntary organisations engaged in labour welfare expanded in number and influences.
2. Trade unions fought to bring about an improvement in the working conditions of labour and to raise their status socially and economically.
3. Some enlightened employers took the initiative to improve the living and working conditions of labour.
4. The state tried through legislation to regulate and improve the lot of labour.

Codes
(a) 4, 3, 2, 1 (b) 3, 2, 4, 1
(c) 3, 4, 2, 1 (d) 1, 4, 3, 2

29 Assertion (A) Both proactive and reactive methods can address to the problem of accidents in companies.

Reason (R) Labour welfare provisions like good house-keeping, safety campaigns can go a long way in controlling accidents.

Codes
(a) (A) is right and (R) explains (A)
(b) (A) is not right and (R) is right
(c) Both (A) and (R) are wrong
(d) (A) is wrong and (R) tries to explain wrong (A)

30 Examine the following statements about labour welfare. Identify the one(s) that does not fit into the logical set.
1. Labour welfare has both positive and negative sides. On the positive side, it deals with the provision of opportunities which enable the worker and his family to lead a good life socially and personally.
2. On the negative side, it functions in order to neutralise the baneful effects of large scale industrialisation.
3. Labour welfare is flexible, elastic and differs from time-to-time, region-to-region, industry-to-industry and country-to-country.
4. It needs not be related to the socio-cultural background, economic status and education level of the workers.

Codes
(a) 1 and 3
(b) Only 2
(c) 2 and 4
(d) Only 4

31 Assertion (A) Labour welfare positively deals with the provision of opportunities which enable to worker and his family to lead a good life, socially and personally, as well as help him adjust to social transition in his work life, family and social life.

Reason (R) The transition and the resultant undesirable social consequences are caused by large scale industrialisation.

Codes
(a) Both (A) and (R) are wrong
(b) (A) is right, but (R) does not explain (A)
(c) Both (A) and (R) are right and (R) explains (A)
(d) (A) is wrong, but (R) is right

32 Match the following.

List I (Theories of Labour Welfare)		List II (Themes)	
A.	Police Theory	1.	Any good work is considered 'an investment' both the benefactor and the beneficiary are rewarded
B.	Placating Theory	2.	Welfare work is used as a means to secure, preserve and develop the efficiency and productivity of labour
C.	Religious Theory	3.	Labour groups are becoming demanding and militant and are conscious of their rights and privileges than even before, they need to be appeased
D.	Functional Theory	4.	Without compulsion, periodical supervision and fear of punishment, employers will not provide even the minimum welfare facilities to workers

Codes

	A	B	C	D		A	B	C	D
(a)	3	4	1	2	(b)	4	1	3	2
(c)	4	3	1	2	(d)	2	4	1	3

33 In which approach, it is considered that labour is an inevitable nuisance constantly asking for more?

(a) Philanthropic approach
(b) Citizenship approach
(c) Hard-boiled Businessman's approach
(d) Commodity approach

34 Which of the following committees/commissions has observed that "Labour welfare, by its very nature must necessarily be elastic; bearing a somewhat different interpretation in one country from another, according to the different social customs, the degree of industrialisation and the educational development of the worker"?

(a) Malaviya Committee Report on Labour Welfare
(b) The Royal Commission on Labour
(c) The Labour Investigation Committee
(d) The First National Commission on Labour

35 Which of the following statement(s) on 'labour welfare' is/are not true?

1. Labour welfare work extended to worker's and their families does not come under the areas of Corporate Social Responsibility (CSR).
2. Labour welfare measures cannot be a substitute for wages.
3. It is only employers who are responsible to extend labour welfare.
4. Self-help and empowerment are not goals of labour welfare.

Select the correct answer by using the codes given below

(a) 3 and 4 (b) Only 3
(c) 2 and 3 (d) 1 and 4

36 Which of the following is not a characteristic of labour?

(a) Labour is a factor of production
(b) Labour is a perishable commodity
(c) Labour can be separated from labourers as 'person'
(d) Labour sells his services, not himself

2014

37 Match the following.

List I (Concepts of Labour)		List II (Relevant Themes)	
A.	Commodity concept of labour	1.	Labour regarded by the employer largely as operating organisations in industry
B.	Machinery concept of labour	2.	Labour has right to be consulted in regard to the terms and conditions under which they are supposed to work
C.	Goodwill concept of labour	3.	Labour is affected by the law of supply and demand
D.	Citizenship concept of labour	4.	Paternalistic approach towards labour by the employers

Codes

	A	B	C	D		A	B	C	D
(a)	3	1	4	2	(b)	2	4	3	1
(c)	4	3	1	2	(d)	1	3	2	4

38 Which of the following is not a feature of labour market?

(a) It is essentially local in character
(b) It is not monopolistic
(c) It is less mobile compared to commodity and capital markets
(d) Monospony in the labour market is less common than monopoly

39 Which of the following is an example of 'extra-mural' labour welfare?

(a) Cooperative credit society
(b) Recreation facility
(c) Library and reading rooms
(d) Shelters and rest rooms

40 **Assertion** (A) Labour welfare is not a social work being its result but an area of social work.

Reason (R) As labour too needs the enabling help of social work professional, social work is no trespasses in the realms of labour welfare.

Codes

(a) (A) is right, (R) is wrong
(b) (A) is wrong, (R) is right
(c) Both (A) and (R) are wrong
(d) (A) is right and (R) explains (A)

ANSWERS

Exam Based Questions

1 (c)	2 (d)	3 (c)	4 (d)	5 (a)	6 (a)	7 (a)	8 (d)	9 (a)	10 (a)
11 (a)	12 (a)	13 (c)	14 (a)	15 (b)	16 (b)	17 (b)	18 (c)	19 (a)	20 (b)
21 (b)	22 (b)	23 (c)	24 (c)	25 (c)	26 (d)	27 (d)	28 (d)	29 (d)	30 (d)
31 (b)	32 (d)	33 (a)	34 (a)	35 (b)	36 (b)	37 (b)	38 (b)	39 (b)	40 (b)
41 (b)	42 (d)	43 (c)	44 (a)	45 (d)	46 (c)	47 (c)	48 (a)	49 (b)	50 (b)
51 (b)	52 (b)	53 (a)	54 (d)	55 (c)	56 (d)	57 (b)	58 (d)	59 (b)	60 (a)
61 (a)	62 (c)	63 (d)	64 (b)	65 (b)	66 (b)	67 (d)	68 (b)	69 (d)	70 (b)
71 (d)	72 (c)	73 (d)	74 (c)	75 (b)	76 (d)	77 (a)	78 (a)	79 (c)	80 (b)
81 (a)	82 (b)	83 (a)	84 (a)	85 (b)	86 (a)	87 (d)	88 (c)	89 (a)	90 (b)
91 (a)	92 (d)	93 (b)	94 (b)	95 (c)	96 (a)	97 (a)			

Previous Years' Questions

1 (b)	2 (a)	3 (a)	4 (b)	5 (b)	6 (c)	7 (a)	8 (b)	9 (b)	10 (c)
11 (c)	12 (c)	13 (a)	14 (c)	15 (d)	16 (b)	17 (c)	18 (a)	19 (c)	20 (b)
21 (b)	22 (b)	23 (c)	24 (b)	25 (d)	26 (d)	27 (b)	28 (c)	29 (a)	30 (d)
31 (c)	32 (c)	33 (c)	34 (b)	35 (a)	36 (c)	37 (a)	38 (d)	39 (b)	40 (d)

UNIT 10

CHAPTER 17

Labour Market

This chapter deals with the demand and supply of labour force while focusing on different economic systems. The Indian labour market has been explained explicitly focusing on the nature, composition and problems of labour in India.

Concept of Labour Market

A labour market is defined as a pool of all potential workers who compete for jobs. It also includes the employers who compete for workers. Labour markets are based on the supply and demand of labour in a country or a specific location where employers are able and willing to work.

Features of Labour Market

- It is a process in which a balance between supply of a particular kind of labour and demand is maintained.
- It is a market where wage rates differ for the same kind of work due to lack of perfect mobility.
- It is a long-term relationship.
- In labour market price does not change very often but remains constant for a period of time.
- It is very important to maintain the dignity of labour irrespective of his occupation and the kind of monetary award he is getting.
- Industrial revolution has brought divergent trends in the bargaining powers of employers and employees within the labour markets. Lots of associations of employers, trade unions and labour welfare schemes have come up to bargain with each other in terms of determining wages, working hours and working conditions.
- According to neo-classical economic theory, there is a market like other markets, where buyers and sellers are there in open competition with each other.

In this Chapter

- There are differences in comparison to other markets as labour is not a completely homogeneous commodity. Human beings differ from each other in terms of their skills, abilities, education, training and work experience. But, it still makes sense to analyse labour supply and demand in the aggregate.
- Different professions work in different markets. There is restrictive entry to a particular occupation by specifying the minimum qualifications and experience required.
- Labour markets are also defined spatially, given that neither employers nor workers can move to another location without incurring substantial costs. This is the reason wages may remain high in big cities. It may be termed as local labour market.

Types of Labour Market

According to Clark Kerr

Clark has given the following models of the labour market which are as follows

The Perfect Market

- In this type of market, all the buyers and sellers have freedom to make an entry or exit any time in the market area.
- There are large number of small and undifferentiated buyers and sellers in the market area.
- It is possible to regularise the market under such circumstances and mostly a single price prevails in the market.

The Neo-classical Market

- It is based on the fact that imperfections and inequality exist in the market as all the workers do not have same sort of skills.
- In spite of all these imperfections and inequalities, it is assumed that wages will tend towards equality for workers in a given skill classification.

The Natural Market

- Here workers are innocent and ignorant, therefore do not have detailed knowledge of the market.
- They have a limited knowledge and are not capable enough to analyse the advantages of the jobs they hold against the kind of the alternatives.
- They do not develop grudge against the employers, who constantly make an effort to create the greatest bargains (Hiring and firing) in the labour market.

The Institutional Market

- Usually there is free operation of the forces of demand and supply, but in the institutional market the policies of trade unions, employers and the government influence wage movements.
- In this type of market, labour market does not fix the upper and lower limits of wages but they are fixed by the institutional policies, which therefore reduces the mobility of labour.
- In the institutional markets, uniformity in a particular kind of grade of workers is found.

The Management Market

- In the management market, there is a close relationship between the wage setting and the allocation of labour.
- It is more of a hypothetical kind of marketing instead of real one.
- Institutional labour market is more popular in India where the influence of demand and supply existing in labour market is regulated by the policies of unions, employers and the government.

According to Edmund Phelps

Edmund has classified labour market in two types

Structured Labour Market

These are the markets that limit the movement of workers due to the institutional rules, policies and procedures. The hiring policies are often deciding factor in wage determination.

The main types of structured labour markets are

- The market which is for the public employees where the entry and exits can be made by legislation and administration's rules.
- The market which is known as the non-unions labour market in any big organisation, where all the rules will be made by the personnel department.
- The third type of labour market is where the rules have been formulated considering the collective bargaining agreements and the norms of trade unions.

Unstructured Labour Markets

Unstructured labour market are the ones where specified rules by any authority have not been formulated but people get the market information through established institutions.

The main types of unstructured labour markets are

- In this type of market, people have to attach themselves with any type of the organisation and show their connectivity.
- There are no unions, prescribing their rules; and workers are usually unskilled.
- Labour is paid according to the piece production rather than time production and not a huge capital have been invested in this type of labour market.

- Unstructured market is devoid of any fringe benefits and is basically for the unskilled and semi-skilled workers.

Economic Systems and Labour Market

Economic system is a manner in which the resources of country are allocated and utilised among the different entities of the economy (land, labour and capital). Labour is one of the most important factors of production in an economy. They are the ones who form the cornerstone of economic systems. Each economic system focuses on what is to be produced, its quality and quantity, for whom the production is being done.

The three types of economic systems are

- **Market Economy** As the name signifies, in this system prices are determined by the level of demand and supply in the market. Governments do not have much role to play. All the decisions related to the market economy are taken on the basis of the market factors. The government has minimalistic role that involves laying down the rules and regulations for the businesses to survive.
- **Planned Economy** In this type of economy, it is the government which all the decisions regarding the production, distribution, salaries, investment and prices are taken by the government. It is also known as a centralised economy, controlled economy or command economy.
- **Mixed Economy** It is the mixture of market and planned economy. It is an economic system in which both the private and public sector have equal roles to play. Most of the countries in the world have a mixed economic system.

Demand and Supply of Labour

In addition to making output and pricing decisions, firms must also determine how much of each input is required to the demand. Firms may choose to demand many different kinds of inputs. The two most common inputs are labour and capital.

The demand and supply of labour are determined in the labour market. The participants in the labour market are workers and firms. Workers supply labour to firms in exchange for wages. Firms demand labour from workers in exchange for wages.

There are number of factors determining the demand of labour

Wage Rates This principle works in an inverse proportion. Higher is the wage rate, lesser is the demand for labour.

Demand for Goods or Products This is directly proportional to the labour market. If the demand for the goods or product that labour produces is more, the demand for labour will also be more and *vice-versa*.

Marginal Productivity It is defined as an addition made to the total production by adding one more worker to the existing labour force. It is measured in terms of Marginal Revenue Product of Labour (MRPL), which is the additional revenue firms earn by employing one more unit of labour.

In a perfectly competitive market, the firm's marginal revenue product of labour is the value of the marginal product of labour. An employer hires the labour till the time the marginal revenue productivity of labour becomes equal to wage rate (cost of hiring of that labour).

Elasticity of Demand Demand for labour also depends upon the elasticity of demand for the product produced by the labour. If the demand for such product is elastic, the demand for labour producing such product is also likely to be elastic.

Government Schemes The government can come up with different employment schemes that will increase the demand for labour.

The Firm's Demand for Labour

The firm's demand for labour is a derived demand. It is derived from the demand for the firm's output.

If demand for the firm's output increases, the firm will demand more labour and will hire more workers. If demand for the firm's output falls, the firm will demand less labour and will reduce its workforce.

At higher wage rates the demand for labour will be less than at lower wage rates. It is because of the marginal productivity theory.

Marginal Revenue Product of Labour

When the firm knows the level of demand for its output, it determines how much labour is required to demand by looking at the marginal revenue product of labour.

The marginal revenue product of labour (or any input) is the additional revenue the firm earns by employing one more unit of labour.

The marginal revenue product of labour is related to the marginal products. In a perfectly competitive market, the firm's marginal revenue product of labour is the value of the marginal product of labour.

The Firm's Labour Demand Curve

The firm's profit maximising labour decision is depicted graphically in the graph.

When the marginal revenue product of labour is graphed, it represents **the firm's labour demand curve.**

The demand curve is downward sloping due to the law of diminishing returns; as more workers are hired, the marginal product of labour begins declining, causing the marginal revenue product of labour to fall as well.

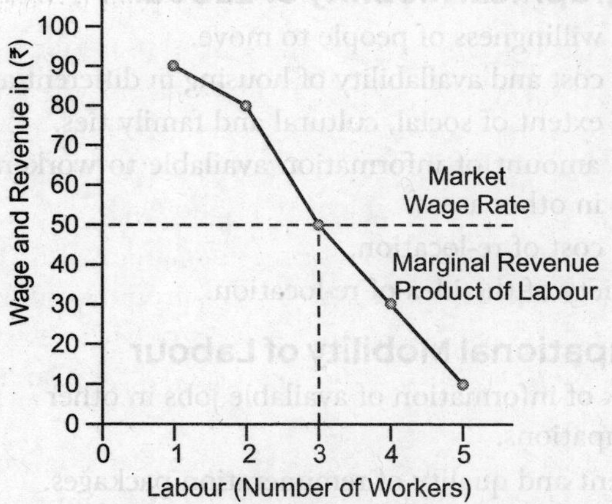

A Perfectly Competitive Firm's Profit Maximising Labour Demand Decision Curve

The intersection of the marginal revenue product curve with the market wage determines the number of workers that the firm hires, like in this case 3 workers.

Supply of Labour

The amount of people offering their labour at different wage rates. It involves opportunity cost of work leisure and the wage rate must be sufficient to overcome the opportunity cost. It is dependent on the number of available workers and number of hours they are willing to work per day per week. An individual's supply of labour is dependent on his preference for consumption or leisure goods.

Consumption goods include the goods that can be purchased with the income that an individual earns from his job or business. Leisure goods are the ones that individuals consume when they are not working. When an individual is working more (supplying more labour), an individual reduces his or her consumption of leisure goods.

The different factors affecting the supply of labour are

Population The supply of labour is dependent on the size of population. The larger is the population, there will be more supply of labour and vice-versa.

Age Composition If a country has a large percentage of working age group, *i.e.* between 18 to 40 years, the supply of labour is likely to be more.

Wage Rates This factor is directly proportional to the supply of labour. Higher is the wage rate, higher is the supply of the population.

Mobility of Labour This is one of the most important factors of supply of labour. If the labour is willing to move from one place to another according to the availability of jobs, this increases the availability and supply of labour.

Efficiency of Workers Efficiency is focusing on the qualitative output rather than focusing on the quantitative output.

An Individual's Supply of Labour

An individual's supply of labour depends on his or her preferences for two types of goods

Consumption Goods include all the goods that can be purchased with the income that an individual earns from working.

Leisure Goods are the good that individuals consume when they are not working.

By working more (supplying more labour), an individual reduces his or her consumption of leisure but is able to increase his or her purchases of consumption goods.

In choosing between leisure and consumption, the individual faces two constraints, *which are as follows*

- The individual is limited to twenty-four hours per day for work or leisure.
- The individual's income from work is limited by the market wage rate that the individual receives for his or her labour skills.

In a perfectly competitive labour market, workers like firms are wage-takers. They take the market wage rate that they receive as given.

An Individual's Labour Supply Curve

An example of an individual's labour supply curve is given in the following graph

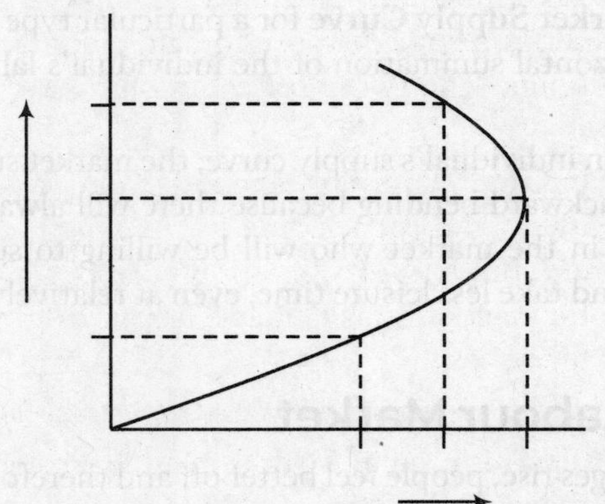

Individual's Labour Supply Curve

As wages increase, so does the **opportunity cost of leisure.**

As leisure becomes more costly, workers tend to substitute more work hours for fewer leisure hours in order to consume the relatively cheaper consumption goods, which is the **substitution effect** of a higher wage.

An **income effect** is also associated with a higher wage. A higher wage leads to higher real incomes, provided that prices of consumption goods remain constant.

As real incomes rise, individuals will demand more leisure, which is considered a **normal good** the higher an individual's income, the easier it is for that individual to take more time off from work and still maintain a high standard of living in terms of consumption goods.

The substitution effect of higher wages tends to dominate the income effect at low wage levels, while the income effect of higher wages tends to dominate the substitution effect at high wage levels.

The dominance of the income effect over the substitution effect at high wage levels is what accounts for the **backward bending shape** of the individual's labour supply curve.

Market Demand and Supply of Labour

Many different markets for labour exists *e.g.* The labour market for entry level accountants is different from the labour market for tennis pros.

The demand for labour in a particular market called the market demand for labour is the amount of labour that all the firms participating in that market will demand at different market wage levels.

The Market Demand Curve for a particular type of labour is the horizontal summation of the marginal revenue product of labour curves of every firm in the market for that type of labour.

The Market Supply of Labour is the number of workers of a particular type and skill level who are willing to supply their labour to firms at different wage levels.

The Market Supply Curve for a particular type of labour is the horizontal summation of the individual's labour supply curves.

Unlike an individual's supply curve, the market supply curve is not backward bending because there will always be some workers in the market who will be willing to supply more labour and take less leisure time, even at relatively high wage levels.

The Labour Market

- As wages rise, people feel better off and therefore, may not feel a need to work for many hours.
- As wages rise, the opportunity cost of leisure rises.
- As wages rise, the substitution effect may lead to more hours being worked.

So, the net effect depends on the relative strength of the income and substitution effects.

The elasticity of supply of labour depends upon

Geographical Mobility of Labour

- The willingness of people to move.
- The cost and availability of housing in different areas.
- The extent of social, cultural and family ties.
- The amount of information available to workers about jobs in other areas.
- The cost of re-location.
- Anxiety of the idea of re-location.

Occupational Mobility of Labour

- Lack of information of available jobs in other occupations.
- Extent and quality of remuneration packages.
- Extent of skills and qualifications to do the job.
- Anxiety at changing jobs.
- If the supply of labour is elastic, a small rise in the wage rate is sufficient to encourage more people to offer their labour. Geographical and occupational mobility are likely to be high and there is likely to be many substitutes.
- If the supply of labour is inelastic, a substantial rise in the wage rate only brings forth a small increase in the amount of people willing and able to do such work.
- The reason may be the number with those particular skills and qualifications, the time it takes to get those skills, geographical immobility etc.
- A rise in the demand for labour would force up the wage rate as there would be excess demand for labour and supply of labour.
- The wage rate will alter if there is a shift in either or both the demand and supply of labour.
- An increase in the supply of labour would lead to a fall in the wage rate as there would be an excess supply of labour.

Composition of Indian Labour Force

Labour Bureau is an attached office of the Ministry of Labour and Employment since 1946. Labour Bureau provides data for collection, compilation, analysis and dissemination of labour statistics at All India and State level on different facets of labour.

Given below are the details of Indian population working in different sectors

Sector wise changes in employment over a period of twelve months for the years 2009-2015 (in lakhs)

Sl No.	Industry/ Group	9th Jan to 9th Dec	10th Jan to 10th Dec	11th Jan to 11th Dec	12th Jan to 12th Dec	13th Jan to 13th Dec	14th Jan to 14th Dec	15th Jan to 15th Dec	Total (Sector Wise Change)
1	2	3	4	5	6	7	8	9	10
1	Textiles	3.88	1.03	0.34	1	2.86	1.41	0.72	10.56
2	Leather	– 0.25	0.41	0.21	0.03	0.44	0.07	0.08	0.27
3	Metal	0.58	0.76	1.07	0.21	0.35	0.74	0.37	3.38
4	Automobile Gems	0.55	1.27	0.47	0.09	0.16	0.25	0.08	2.71
5	Jewellery	0.78	0.22	0.28	– 0.01	0.09	0.11	0.19	1.28
6	Transport	– 0.07	0.11	0.33	0.17	0.09	0.11	0.04	0.08
7	IT/BPO	6.54	5.07	7.64	1.95	1.09	1.93	0.76	24.98
8	Handloom/ Powerloom	0.8	0.01	0.05	– 0.23	0.02	0.05	0.11	0.45
Total (Year-wise)		12.8	8.65	9.3	3.22	4.19	4.21	1.35	43.7

➡ **Note** If first Quarterly Employment Survey (QES) results covering period October 2008 to December 2008 are included, the total change in employment comes out to be 38.81 lakh persons.

Macro	**2014-15**	**2015-16**	**2016-17**
Real GDP (% change y-o-y)[1, 2]	7.5	8.0	7.1
Investment (% of GDP)	35.7	34.9	33.2
Labour Market	**2004-05**	**2009-10**	**2011-12**
Employment (million)	457.9	459.0	472.9
Unemployment (million)	11.3	9.8	10.8
Labour Force Participation Rate (%)	63.7	57.1	55.9
Male	84.0	80.6	79.8
Female	42.7	32.6	31.2
Unemployment rate (%)	2.3	2.0	2.1
Male	2.1	1.9	2.1
Female	2.6	2.3	2.3
Share of Employment in Manufacturing (%)	11.6	11.0	12.5
Male	12.0	11.1	12.2
Female	11.0	10.8	13.2
Share of Regular Wage and Salaried Workers (%)	14.4	15.7	17.9
Male	17.3	17.8	19.9
Female	8.4	10.2	12.8
Working Poverty Rate (%)			
<US$1.90 per day	35.3	28.4	17.9
>=US$1.90 & <US$ 3.10 per day	36.5	37.5	35.0
Average real daily wage index (2004-05=100)			
Rural	100.0	111.7	122.8
Urban	100.0	129.4	n.a.

Unemployment and Underemployment

Unemployment

Unemployment occurs when a person, who is actively searching for employment and is unable to find work.

The unemployment rate is a measure of the prevalence of unemployment and it is calculated as a percentage by dividing the number of unemployed individuals by all individuals currently in the labour force. There remains considerable theoretical debate regarding the causes, consequences and solutions for unemployment.

Classical economics, neo-classical economics and the Austrian School of Economics argue that market mechanisms are reliable means of resolving unemployment.

These theories argue against interventions imposed on the labour market from the outside, such as unionisation, minimum wage laws, taxes and other regulations that they claim, discourage the hiring of workers.

Keynesian economics emphasises the cyclical nature of unemployment and recommends interventions it claims will reduce unemployment during recessions.

Types of Unemployment

Structural Unemployment

It focuses on structural problems in the economy and inefficiencies inherent in labour markets including a mismatch between the supply and demand of labourers with necessary skill sets. Structural arguments emphasise causes and solutions related to disruptive technologies and globalisation.

Frictional Unemployment

It focuses on voluntary decisions to work, based on each individual's valuation of their own work and how that compares to current wage rates plus the time and effort required to find a job.

Causes and solutions for frictional unemployment often address barriers to entry and wage rates. Behavioural economists highlight individual biases in decision-making and often involve problems and solutions concerning sticky wages and efficiency wages.

Causes of Unemployment

- Physical and natural cause such as calamities
- Frequent change in season
- Influx of technological inventions
- Discrimination in the workplace
- Prospective workers outlook toward employment
- Population growth
- Lack of innovations
- Lack of opportunities

Underemployment

It refers to an employment situation that is insufficient in some important way for the worker, as compared to his expectations, *e.g.* labourers holding a part-time job despite desiring full-time work and over qualification, where the employee has education, experience or skills beyond the requirements of the job.

Underemployment has been studied in recent decades from a variety of perspectives, including economics, management, psychology and sociology. In underemployment involves a situation in which a person is working, but not satisfied. There is under-utilisation of labour.

Types of Underemployment

Involuntary Part-time Workers

A related kind of underemployment refers to 'involuntary part-time' workers. These are workers who could (and would like to) work for the standard work-week but only find part-time work. It is more prevalent during times of economic stagnation (during recessions or depressions).

Underemployment can also be used in regional planning to describe localities where economic activity rates are unusually low. This can be induced by a lack of job opportunities, training opportunities or services such as childcare and public transportation.

Such difficulties may lead residents to accept economic inactivity rather than register as unemployed or actively seek jobs because their prospects for regular employment appear so bleak. These people are often called discouraged workers and are not counted officially as being 'unemployed'.

In macroeconomics, 'underemployment' simply refers to excess unemployment. Another definition of 'underemployment' describes, it as the practice of businesses or entire economy employing workers who are not fully occupied, *i.e.* who are currently not being used to produce goods or services (in other words, employees who are not economically productive or underproductive or economically inefficient).

This may be because of legal or social restrictions on firing and layoffs or because they are overhead workers or because the work is highly seasonal.

Cyclical Underemployment

It refers to the tendency for the capacity utilisation rate of firms (and therefore of their demand for labour) to be lower at times of recession and/or depression. At such times, underemployment of workers may be tolerated and indeed may be wise business policy given the financial cost and the degradation of morale from shedding and then re-hiring staff.

Some firms do not believe in firing the workers even if they are not required at a particular point of time in the difficult economic situations; provided they have been loyal to the organisation.

In some countries, labour laws or practices (*e.g.* powerful unions) may force employers to retain excess employees. Such types of firms will have more than the needed workers to complete the given assignment.

Alternatively, paying underused overhead workers is seen as an investment in their future contributions to production. This kind of underemployment has been given as a possible reason why Airbus gained market share from Boeing. Unlike Airbus, which had more flexibility, Boeing was unable to ramp up production fast enough when prosperous times returned because the company had dismissed a great part of its personnel in lean times.

Reasons for Underemployment

Following are the common situations which can lead to underemployment

Immigrants

When highly-trained immigrants arrive in a country, their foreign credentials may not be recognised or accepted in their new country or they may have to do a lengthy or costly re-credentialing process.

As a result, when doctors or engineers from other countries immigrate, they may be unable to work in their profession, and they may have to seek menial work.

New Graduates

New graduates may also face underemployment, because even though they have completed the technical training for a given field for which there is a good job in market, they lack experience.

So, a recent graduate with a Master's degree in accounting may have to work in a low-paid job until they are able to find work in their field and get relevant experience of few years.

High Quality Skills with Low Market Demand

Underemployment may arise because of people who hold high quality skills for which there is low market place demand. While it is costly in terms of money and time to acquire academic credentials, many types of degrees, particularly those in the fine arts and classics, are valued poorly by market place; due to which they accept lower jobs, e.g. commercial pilots training is quite expensive.

Indian Labour Market

India is the sixth largest economy in the world from being the 11th in the World in 2013-14. India is the fastest growing economy of the world. The Indian labour market is divided into organised and unorganised population. Organised sector includes the people who are working with the registered organisations.

Unorganised sector includes self-employed, unlicensed or unregistered economic activity such as rural traders, handicrafts, farmers and owner manned general stores etc. It includes attached agricultural labourers, migrant workers, bonded labourers, casual and contract labours.

Characteristics/Nature of Indian Labour Market

- Indian labour market has a dual nature as it consists of organised and unorganised labour. Organised labour constitutes the formal economy and unorganised labour constitutes the informal economy.
- The Indian labour market mainly comprises three sectors namely primary (Agriculture and allied activities) secondary (Construction and manufacturing) and tertiary sector (Financial services and other services).
- India is basically an agrarian economy with the majority of its population involved in farming. However, there has been a trend of shifting of workers from agriculture to non-agriculture background.
- There is a significant migration from the rural areas to the urban areas of the country in search of better job opportunities. Migration can be seasonal or permanent. Also, it can be within the geographical boundaries of the country and outside it as well.
- The Labour Force Participation Rate (LFPR) of females in India is among the lowest in the world. According to a 2018 World Bank report, the Labour Force Participation Rate (LFPR) among females in India was 26.97. The world average stood at 48.47 percent in 2018.

New Dynamics of Labour Market in India

- Indian labour market is shifting its trends towards gainful employment, which is a situation in which employee has a steady work and payment.
- There is a remarkable shift of population working in the agriculture sector. According to the National Sample Survey Organisation and Labour Bureau's data, agricultural employment fell by 26 million and non-farm employment rose by 33 million or by more than eight million jobs a year. The labour started to make a paradigm shift from farming to construction hospitality.
- India has seen a drastic rise in the Employee Provident Fund Organisation (EPFO) membership. The membership grew from 32.6 million in 2013-14 to approx 40 million in 2018-19.
- The four sectors that contributed to non-farm jobs are trade and hospitality construction, transport, education and health.
- Job growth in transport and trade was significantly faster than average India employment growth. The construction sector added many lower productivity jobs, however, so GDP growth for the sector was lower than average national growth.

Problems of Labour In India

The major problems of labour in India have been listed below

Surplus Labour Force There is a lack of job opportunity for people in the primary, secondary and tertiary sector. Also, the population of the country has been rapidly rising leading to the addition in the existing labour force pool.

Unskilled Labour There is a lack of proper skill development training being provided to the workers because of lack of adequate vocational training institutes in the country.

Lack of Job Opportunities India has not been able to provide ample job opportunities to its educated and skilled youth as well. People are having hard time finding their desirable roles even after completing their technical education.

Informal Sector A major chunk of India's population is working in the informal sector which is highly unregulated. There is no proper training for the people working in this sector leading to decreased productivity of the employees and low value addition to the country's overall growth.

Job Security As majority of Indian population is working in the informal sector, there is a high risk associated with their jobs. They tend to witness unemployment in the form of disguised and seasonal unemployment.

Lack of Labour Reforms India needs to upgrade its labour laws in context of rapid globalisation to keep itself in accordance with the changing times.

EXAM BASED QUESTIONS

1 **Which of the following is the primary activity in the Indian economy?**

(a) Construction (b) Manufacturing
(c) Farming (d) Financial Services

2 **The LFPR of females in India is among the lowest in the world. What does LFPR stand for?**

(a) Labour Force Participating Ratio
(b) Labour Force Participating Rate
(c) Labour Force Participation Ratio
(d) Labour Force Participation Rate

3 **What was the average LFPR among females in 2018?**

(a) 36.99 (b) 36.97
(c) 26.97 (d) 16.99

4 **Which of the following is correct in context of Indian labour market?**

(a) India has proper skill development and vocational courses
(b) The Indian labour market offers jobs security to its participants
(c) There has been a trend of shifting of workers from non-agriculture to agriculture background
(d) Indian labour market has a dual nature as it consists of organised and unorganised labour

5 **In a company where demand for product demand fluctuates and despite that the company does not go for retrenchment and other downsizing practices is order to have cost savings through which of the following ways ?**

(a) Reduction in termination costs
(b) Reducing in payment needs to be made against voluntary retirement schemes
(c) Unemployment insurance
(d) All of the above

6 **Which of the following are the characteristics of unorganised labour in India?**

(a) A large number of them are below poverty line
(b) They are not educated
(c) They are migrant and dispersed all over the country
(d) All of the above

7 **Which of the following is not a medium of social security coverage?**

(a) Health insurance by way of reimbursement for major ailments
(b) House buildings assistance
(c) Life insurance coverage
(d) Unique identity card

8 **Employed persons consists of**

(a) all persons who did any work for pay or profit during the survey
(b) all persons who did atleast 15 hours of unpaid work in a family-owned enterprise operated by someone in their household
(c) all persons who are temporarily absent from their regular jobs, whether they were paid or not
(d) All of the above

9 **Which of the following is not an example of seasonal worker?**

(a) Worker working in crackers factory
(b) Worker working in beedi factory
(c) Worker working in rakhi factory
(d) Worker working in sugar factory

10 **Which of the following are the sectors of the Indian Labour Market?**

(a) Rural workers (b) Organised sector
(c) Unorganised sector (d) All of these

11 **Which of the following are the categories of labour force?**

(a) Self-employed workers and casual workers
(b) Unemployed and wage/salary earners
(c) Both (a) and (b)
(d) Neither (a) nor (b)

12 **Who of the following has given the models of the labour market?**

(a) Clark Kerr (b) Phelps
(c) Karl Marx (d) John Stuart Mill

13 **Which of the following are the determinants of supply?**

(a) Production costs (b) Price of related goods
(c) Number of suppliers (d) All of these

14 **Which of the following is not the determinant of supply?**

(a) Tables and preferences
(b) Income
(c) Number of potential consumers
(d) Number of suppliers

15 **The elasticity of labour depends upon which of the following factors?**

(a) Geographical mobility of labour
(b) Occupational mobility of labour
(c) Both (a) and (b)
(d) Neither (a) nor (b)

16 **Which of the following are the indicators to examine the labour supply in India?**

(a) Work participation rate
(b) Labour force participation rate
(c) Unemployment rate and employment status
(d) All of the above

17 **Which of the following are the situations which may lead to underemployment?**

(a) Immigrants
(b) New graduates
(c) High quality skills with low market demand
(d) All of the above

18 Which of the following is not the name of the committee set up as Labour Enquiry Committee from 1937-1946?
(a) Cawnpore Labour Enquiry Committee
(b) CP and Berar Textile Labour Enquiry Committee
(c) International Committee of the Red Cross (ICRC)
(d) UP Labour Enquiry Committee

19 The on-going industrilisation in country is contributing to which type of unemployment?
(a) Cyclical Unemployment
(b) Frictional Unemployment
(c) Seasonal Unemployment
(d) Technological Unemployment

20 The participants in the labour market are .... and ....
(a) employee, employer (b) workers, firms
(c) employee, firms (d) None of these

21 Workers .... labour to firms in exchange of ....
(a) supply, wages (b) wages, supply
(c) demand, supply (d) None of these

22 The firm's demand for labour is a .... demand.
(a) labour demand (b) firm demand
(c) Both (a) and (b) (d) Neither (a) nor (b)

23 .... is the additional revenue the firm earns by employing one more unit of labour.
(a) Marginal revenue product of labour
(b) Cost revenue
(c) Demand forecast
(d) None of the above

24 The .... is the number of workers of a particular type and skill level who are willing to supply their labour to firms at different wage levels.
(a) supply of goods and services
(b) market supply of product
(c) market supply of labour
(d) None of the above

25 .... refers to the amount produced per worker per period of time.
(a) Productivity (b) Product delivery
(c) Product manufacturing (d) None of these

26 The .... of supply of labour depends upon the geogrpahical mobility of labour.
(a) demand schedule (b) elasticity
(c) equilibrium (d) None of these

27 An increase in the supply of labour would lead to ...... in the wage rate as there would be an excess supply of labour.
(a) increase (b) decrease
(c) constant (d) None of these

28 .... function through the interaction of workers and employers.
(a) Labour market (b) Labour demand
(c) Labour marginal (d) None of these

29 The .... is calculated by multiplying the price of the end product or service by the marginal physical product of the worker.
(a) marginal revenue product
(b) market equilibrium
(c) labour demand
(d) None of the above

30 The .... is defined as the number of people currently employed divided by the adult populaton or the population of working age.
(a) wages (b) employment rate
(c) labour marginal (d) None of these

31 Health security, maternity needs, life and accident security, unemployment security, old age security, all these are the dimensions of ....
(a) social welfare (b) social legislation
(c) social security (d) None of these

32 The full form of NOAPS is ....
(a) National Old Age Pension Scheme
(b) Retirement Benefits
(c) Voluntry Retirement Scheme
(d) None of the above

33 .... refers to an employment situation that is insufficient in some important way for the workers, relative to a standard.
(a) Employment
(b) Unemployment
(c) Underemployment
(d) None of the above

34 The .... is a measure of the prevalence of unemployment and it is calculated as a percentage by dividing the number of unemployed individuals by all individuals currently in the labour force.
(a) unemployment rate (b) employment rate
(c) underemployment rate (d) None of these

35 .... increases with the long-term growth of the population; it responds to economic forces and social trends and its size changes with the seasons.
(a) The labour (b) Labour market
(c) Labour demand (d) None of these

36 ...... is the market in which the organisations compete to attract employees with the skills necessary to perform a particular job.
(a) Labour demand (b) Labour market
(c) Labour marginal (d) None of these

37 ...... are those workers who are generally employed by small entrepreneurs on daily or weekly basis on a low wage rate.
(a) Casual workers (b) Social workers
(c) Both (a) and (b) (d) Neither (a) nor (b)

38 ...... is the ratio of employed persons to the total labour force.
(a) Unemployment rate (b) Underemployment rate
(c) Employment rate (d) None of these

39 ...... are workers who are not employed according to the desired capacity and their skills are under utilised.
(a) Unemployment (b) Underemployment
(c) Employment (d) None of these

40 According to ......, the inequality exists in the market as all the workers do not acquire same sort of skills.
(a) the neo-classical market
(b) classical market
(c) labour market
(d) None of the above

41 In ......, there is a close relationship between the wage setting and the allocation of labour.
(a) labour market (b) management market
(c) Both (a) and (b) (d) None of these

42 ...... has defined and identified three types of structured labour markets.
(a) Phelps (b) Marx
(c) Kennedy (d) None of these

43 ...... are the markets where specified rules by any authority have not been formulated and established institutions spread the market information.
(a) Structured labour market
(b) Unstructured labour market
(c) Both (a) and (b)
(d) Neither (a) nor (b)

44 ...... is defined to the price quality pair where the quantity demanded is equal to the quantity supplied.
(a) Equilibrium (b) Non-equilibrium
(c) Both (a) and (b) (d) Neither (a) nor (b)

45 ...... is a situation in a market when the price is such that the quantity that consumers wish to demand in correctly balanced by quantity that firms wish to supply.
(a) Market demand (b) Market equilibrium
(c) Market supply (d) None of these

46 ...... show the relationship between the price of a good and the quantity supplied.
(a) A supply schedule (b) Demand schedule
(c) Demand and supply (d) None of these

47 ...... represents the amount of goods that buyers are willing and able to purchase at various prices.
(a) Demand schedule (b) Demand curve
(c) Demand forecast (d) None of these

48. ...... is that model of economic equilibrium where the clearance on the market of some specific goods is obtained independently from prices and quantities in other markets.
(a) Partial equilibrium (b) Equilibrium
(c) Non-equilibrium (d) None of these

49 ...... is an individual firm which takes the market wage rate as given, just as the firm in a perfectly competitive product market takes the price for its output as given.
(a) Wage differential
(b) Wage takes
(c) Both (a) and (b)
(d) Neither (a) nor (b)

50 ...... refers to a situation where the employee is not satisfied with his job in terms of economics, management, psychology and sociology.
(a) Unemployment
(b) Underemployment
(c) Employment
(d) None of the above

51 ...... refers to the practices in which employees have workers who are not fully occupied and who are not being used currently to produce goods.
(a) Over staffing (b) Layoffs
(c) Lockout (d) Strikes

52 The matter related to the fixation of minimum wages was taken up by the ...... and the ...... in 1943.
(a) international labour conference
(b) SLL and ILC
(c) royal commission on labour
(d) None of the above

53 In the ...... type of market, the policies of trade unions, employers and the government influence wage movements than free operation of the forces of demand and supply.
(a) educational
(b) institutional
(c) social
(d) economic

54 Consider the following statements for the perfect market. Which of the following statement(s) is/are correct?
1. All the buyers and sellers have freedom to make entry or exit at any time in the market.
2. There are a large number of small undifferentiated buyers.
3. A single price prevail in the market.
(a) Only 1 (b) Both 2 and 3
(c) Both 1 and 3 (d) All of these

55 Consider the following statements for the natural market. Which of the following statement(s) is/are correct?
1. Workers are innocent and ignorant.
2. The develop grudge against the employers.
3. They have limited knowledge and are not capable enough to analyse the advantages of the job.
(a) Only 1
(b) Both 2 and 3
(c) Both 1 and 3
(d) All of the above

56 Consider the following statements for the structured labour market. Which of the following statement(s) is/are correct?

1. These markets limit the movement of workers due to the institutional rules, policies, and procedures.
2. The hiring policies are often deciding factor in wage determination.
3. Edmund Phelps classified structured and unstructured labour markets.

(a) Only 1 (b) Both 2 and 3
(c) Both 1 and 3 (d) All of these

57 Consider the following statements for the unstructured labour markets. Which of the following statement(s) is/are correct?

1. They are the ones where specified rules by any authority have not been formulated.
2. People get the market information through established institutions.
3. It is devoid of any fringe benefits and is basically for the unskilled and semi-skilled workers.

(a) Only 2 (b) Only 3
(c) Both 1 and 3 (d) All of these

58 Consider the following statements for the types of unemployment. Which of the following statement(s) is/are correct?

1. Frictional unemployment focuses on structural problems in the economy and inefficiencies inherent in labour market.
2. Structural unemployment focuses on voluntary decisions to work, based on each individual's valuation of their own work.
3. The cause and solutions for frictional unemployment often address barriers to entry.

(a) Only 1 (b) Only 3
(c) Both 1 and 2 (d) All of these

59 Consider the following statements for underemployment. Which of the following statement(s) is/are incorrect?

1. It can be used in regional planning to describe localities where economic activities are low.
2. The practice of business employing workers who are not fully occupied.
3. Involuntary underemployment refers to tendency for the capacity utilisation rate of firms.

(a) Only 1 (b) Only 3
(c) Both 1 and 2 (d) All of the above

60 Which of the following statements are true/ false?

(i) The Indian labour market has a dual nature.
(ii) India is basically an industrial economy with majority of population working in industries.
(iii) There is a significant migration from the rural areas to the urban areas of the country in search of better job opportunities.
(iv) Migration is always permanent.

(a) (i), (iv) are true and (ii), (iii) are false
(b) (i), (iii) are true and (ii), (iv) are false
(c) (ii), (iv) are true and (i), (iii) are false
(d) (iii), (iv) are true and (ii), (i) are false

61 Which of the following statements are true/ false?

(i) In the market economy, the prices are determined by the level of demand and supply in the market.
(ii) Mixed economy is an economic system in which both the private and public sector have equal roles to play.
(iii) Planned economy is also known as a centralised economy, controlled economy or command economy.
(iv) In the market economy, governments do not have much role to play.

(a) (i), (ii), (iii) and (iv) are true
(b) (i), (iii) are true and (ii), (iv) are false
(c) (ii), (iv) are true and (i), (iii) are false
(d) (iii), (iv) are true and (ii), (i) are false

62 Which of the following statements are true/false?

(i) Consumption goods include all the goods that can be purchased with the income that an individual earns from working.
(ii) The individual is limited to twenty hours per day for work.
(iii) Leisure goods are the goods that individuals consume when they are not working.
(iv) The individual's income from work is limited by the market wage that individual receives for his or her labour skills.

(a) (i), (iv) are true and (ii), (iii) are false
(b) (i), (iii), (iv) are true and (ii) is false
(c) (ii), (iv) are true and (i), (iii) are false
(d) (iii), (iv) are true and (ii), (i) are false

63 Which of the following statements are true/ false?

(i) With the decrease in wages, the opportunity cost of leisure decreases.
(ii) An income effect is associated with lower wages.
(iii) The market demand curve for a particular type of labour is the horizontal summation of the marginal revenue product of labour curves of every firm in the market for that type of labour.
(iv) The market supply of labour is the number of workers of a particular type and skill level who are willing to supply their labour to firm at different wages.

(a) (i), (iii), (iv) are true and (ii) is false
(b) (i), (iii) are true and (ii), (iv) are false
(c) (ii), (iv) are true and (i), (iii) are false
(d) (iii), (iv) are true and (ii), (i) are false

64 Which of the following statements are true/ false?

(i) In institutional market, there is free operation of forces of demand and supply.
(ii) In management market, there is a close relationship between wage setting and allocation of labour.
(iii) In neo-classical markets, imperfections and inequality exists in the market.
(iv) Unstructured markets are not regulated by any authority.

(a) (i), (ii), (iii) and (iv) are true
(b) (i), (iii) are true and (ii), (iv) are false
(c) (ii), (iv) are true and (i), (iii) are false
(d) (iii), (iv) are true and (ii), (i) are false

65 Which of the following statements are true/ false?
(i) Demands for goods is directly proportional to the labour market.
(ii) Marginal productivity is the addition made to the total production by subtracting one worker from the existing labour force.
(iii) Demand for labour is dependent on the elasticity of demand for product produced by the labour.
(iv) At higher wages, the demand for labour will be higher.
(a) (i), (ii) are true and (iii), (iv) are false
(b) (i), (iii) are true and (ii), (iv) are false
(c) (ii), (iv) are true and (i), (iii) are false
(d) (iii), (iv) are true and (ii), (i) are false

Directions (Q. Nos. 66-69) *In the questions given below are two statements labelled as Assertion (A) and Reason (R). In the context of the two statements, which one of the following is correct ?*

Codes
(a) Both (A) and (R) correct and (R) is the correct explanation of (A)
(b) Both (A) and (R) are correct, but (R) is not the correct explanation of (A)
(c) (A) is true, but (R) is false
(d) (A) is false, but (R) is true

66 **Assertion** (A) India is having a surplus labour force.
Reason (R) There has been a population explosion in the country.

67 **Assertion** (A) India is an agrarian economy where the major chunk of population is dependent on the agriculture.
Reason (R) People involved in agriculture tend to become a victim of seasonal unemployment.

68 **Assertion** (A) The labour laws in India are in accordance with the global standards.
Reason (R) The labour in India started to make a paradigm shift from fanning to construction, trade, hospitality.

69 **Assertion** (A) The Labour Force Participation Rate (LFPR) of females in India is among the lowest in the world.
Reason (R) The socio-cultural norms of the country lead to lower participation of females in the workforce.

70 Match the following.

List I	List II
A. Perfect market	1. Close relationship between the wage setting and the allocation of labour
B. The Neo-classical market	2. Buyers and sellers are free to make an entry or exist any time
C. Natural market	3. Policies of trade unions, employers and the government influence wage movements
D. The Institutional market	4. Imperfections and inequality exists in the market
E. The Management market	5. Workers are innocent and ignorant

Codes

	A	B	C	D	E
(a)	1	2	4	5	3
(b)	1	2	3	4	5
(c)	2	4	5	3	1
(d)	3	2	5	4	1

71 Match the following.

List I	List II
A. Public employees market	1. Specified rules by any authority have not been formulated
B. Non-unions labour market	2. Rules and policies are well defined
C. Unions labour market	3. Market is only for the public employees
D. Unstructured labour market	4. Rules have been formulated considering collective bargaining and norms of trade unions
E. Structured labour market	5. Rules have been specified by personnel department

Codes

	A	B	C	D	E
(a)	2	3	1	4	5
(b)	3	5	4	1	2
(c)	4	2	3	1	5
(d)	5	4	3	2	1

Directions (Q. Nos. 72-76) *Read the following passage and answer the questions that follow.*

Labour market issues include employment, unemployment, participation rates and wages. In particular, in recent times, demographic changes have resulted in an increasingly ageing workforce. Labour markets provide the structure through which workers and employers interact in relation to jobs, working conditions and pay.

Labour market outcomes are influenced by the institutions and processes of collective, including the roles played by employers' organisations and trade unions.

Eurofound monitors developments in pay, working time and quality of work and employment in the EU. It reports on labour market policies and conducts research on new forms of work organisation and employment, labour flexibility and trends in job creation and labour market mobility.

In the context of an ageing population and increasing demand for care services in the EU, there is growing concern about the supply of suitably qualified care workers. Eurofound researches strategies for employment in social care to meet current demands and future needs are researched.

One area of employment that is playing an increasingly important role in European social policy is childcare. Eurofound research has taken an in-depth look at childcare for schoolchildren. It details developments in employment, demonstrates good practices in the childcare sector and takes a look at the future of the sector.

72 Which of the following is not an issue of labour market?
(a) Employment
(b) Unemployment
(c) Participation rates and wages
(d) Competition in market

73 What does the labour market provide?
(a) The structure of interaction between workers and employers in relation to jobs, working conditions and pay
(b) The structure of able management to increase the productivity of the organisation
(c) The structure of interaction between workers and employers in relation to social gathering or out of the work relations
(d) None of the above

74 Which of the following area of employment playing an increasingly important role in European social policy?
(a) Participatory management in the organisation
(b) Childcare
(c) Strikes and riots
(d) None of the above

75 Which among the following is correct ?
(a) Labour market outcomes are influenced by the institutions
(b) Labour market outcomes are influenced by the effect of the multinational companies
(c) Labour market outcomes are influenced by the effect of the government policies
(d) None of the above

76 According to this passage,
(a) there is growing concern about the supply of suitably qualified care workers
(b) there is diminishing concern about the supply of suitably qualified care workers
(c) there is no concern about the supply of suitably qualified care workers
(d) None of the above

PREVIOUS YEARS' QUESTIONS

2018

1 Which one of the following statements in correct to the 'Rajiv Gandhi Shramik Kalyan Yojana' scheme provided under the Employees' State Insurance Act, 1948?
(a) The unemployed person should have contributed to the scheme for atleast five years prior to loss of employment.
(b) The rate of unemployment allowance is at the rate of 50% of the dary wages.
(c) The minimum period of unemployment in a spell should be fifteen days for entitlement of the benefit.
(d) The allowance is payable for a maximum period of six months in one spell or different spells.

2 **Assertion** (A) Structural unemployment creates a great deal of concern and dominates the policy discussions.
Reason (R) Structural unemployment arises because of mismatch between the skills that workers are supplying and the skills that firms are demanding.
Codes
(a) (R) is wrong and therefore (A) cannot be said to be a correct assumption
(b) (A) is correct and (R) is not a proper explanation of A
(c) (A) is correct, but (R) is wrong
(d) (A) is correct and (R) explains (A)

3 Arrange the following participative schemes in a chronological order starting from the latest to the earliest.
1. The scheme which was introduced and made applicable to all central public sector enterprises.
2. The scheme that was extended to commercial and services organisation employing 100 or employees
3. The scheme which was meant for the manufacturing and mining industries employing 500 or more workers.

Codes
(a) 1, 3 and 2 (b) 1, 2 and 3
(c) 3, 2 and 1 (d) 2, 1 and 3

4 Which of the following statements relating to the recommendations of the Second National Commission on Labour are correct?
1. The commission recommended that the ITIs need to run market-driven courses, review, and if necessary, revise curriculum every 5 years to keep them contemporary.
2. The commission recommended for a skill development fund.
3. The commission recommended the some ITIs may be selected, on a pilot basis, for development into institutes of excellence.

Codes
(a) 2 and 3 (b) 1 and 2
(c) 1, 2 and 3 (d) 1 and 3

5 **Assertion** (A) Imperfections existing in the employment markets are the causative factor for wage differentials.

Reason (R) In developed countries, inter-industry wage differentials are narrowing.

Codes

(a) (A) is correct, but (R) is wrong
(b) Both (A) and (R) are correct and (R) is the correct explanation of (A)
(c) Both (A) and (R) are wrong
(d) Both (A) and (R) are correct, but (R) is not the correct explanation of (A)

6 Which among the following is not a determinant of supply of labour?

(a) Non-wage aspects of the job
(b) Number of firms
(c) Other wage rates
(d) Non-wage income

7 Indifference curves relating to supply of labour have a number of properties some of which are mentioned below

1. Indifference curves are downward slopping
2. Indifference curves are upward slopping
3. Higher indifference curves indicate lower levels of utility
4. Higher indifference curves indicate higher levels of utility
5. Indifference curves donot intersect
6. Indifference curves intersect
7. Indifference curves are concave to the origin
8. Indifference curves are convex to the origin

Which among the following properties are not true ?

Codes

(a) 1, 2, 3, 4 (b) 2, 6, 7, 8
(c) 1, 3, 5, 7 (d) 2, 3, 6, 7

8 The concept of 'invisible hand theorem' in the context of labour market was put forward by

(a) Adam Smith (b) Karl Marx
(c) JS Mill (d) Ricardo

2017

9 Supply-demand framework predicts that termination of any ambitious project depresses a particular segment of labour market. This type of prediction is an example of

(a) positive economics (b) equilibrium
(c) normative economics (d) state of saturation

2016

10 Which of the following statement is not correct?

(a) Labour market equilibrium assumes that markets adjust instantaneously
(b) Equilibrium always prevails in labour market
(c) Wages and employment change swiftly from old equilibrium level to new equilibrium level
(d) Market of highly skilled workers exhibit systematic periods of booms and busts

11 Who among the following viewed unemployment as outcome of the disorganisation of economic system ?

(a) Keynes (b) Lioneal Edie
(c) Karls Pribram (d) Fairchild

12 **Assertion** (A) Competitive labour markets can be efficient.

Reason (R) Labour market participants in search of their own selfish goals attain such conditions.

Codes

(a) (A) is right and (R) explains (A)
(b) (A) is right, but (R) does not explain (A)
(c) (A) is wrong and (R) is right
(d) Both (A) and (R) are wrong

13 Which among the following conditions will not lead to decrease in supply of labour?

(a) An increase in the wages paid in other occupations for which the worker in a particular market are qualified
(b) An increase in the income other than employment
(c) An increase in the people's preferences for work in relation to leisure
(d) A worsening of non-wage aspects of job

14 Social security provided by a 'means test' is called

(a) need based assistance
(b) social assistance
(c) social assurance
(d) mutual assistance

2015

15 The nature of demand for labour is

(a) direct demand
(b) indirect or derived demand
(c) Both (a) and (b)
(d) None of the above

16 The supply of labour for the entire economy depends upon

(a) economic factors
(b) social and political factors
(c) institutional factors
(d) all the factors combined together

17 An organisation receive 23 lakh applications for 200 posts. Which of the following interpretation(s) is/are most likely?

(a) The unemployment is high
(b) The candidates are much aware about the employment opportunities
(c) The selection process becomes complex
(d) All of the above

18 Who said "Jobs, rather than men, should wait"?

(a) Karl Marx
(b) Higgins
(c) Sir William Beveridge
(d) DR Gadgil

19 Assertion (A) There exists surplus of available workers over available, jobs but there exists shortage of skilled workforce.

Reason (R) Skill development received impetus recently.

Codes

(a) Both (A) and (R) are wrong
(b) (A) is right, but (R) does not explain (A)
(c) Both (A) and (R) are right and (R) explains (A)
(d) (A) is wrong, but (R) is right

20 Which of the following statement(s) about the 'labour market' is/are true?

1. Like a commodity market, the relationship between a buyer and a seller in a labour market is temporary.
2. There is a diversity of wage rates in a labour market even for similar nature of work.
3. Monopoly in the labour market is extremely rare.
4. Monopsony referring to the buyer's control is more in the labour market.

(a) 2, 3, 4 are true (b) 1, 2, 4 are true
(c) 1, 3, 4 are true (b) 1, 2, 3 are true

21 Competition based on cheap labour results into

1. falling employment intensity and jobless growth.
2. contracting out and out-sourcing.
3. informalisation of work and deterioration in conditions of employment.

Select the correct answer by using the codes given below

Codes

(a) 1 and 2 (b) 1 and 3
(c) 2 and 3 (d) All of these

2014

22 Which of the following statements about 'labour' is false?

(a) Labour is not a commodity
(b) Labour is perishable and does not last
(c) Labour is inseparable from labourer himself
(d) Rapid adjustment of supply of labour to its demand is possible

23 Beveridge plan is associated with

1. unemployment 2. disability
3. loss of livelihood 4. retirement benefits

Codes

(a) 2, 3 and 4 (b) 2 and 4
(c) 3 and 4 (d) All of these

24 Assertion (A) The 'hard boiled' business man's approach is that 'labour' is an inevitable nuisance constancy asking for more.

Reason (R) Unlike West, in India it was hardly realised that labour is important for the social and economic processes of an egalitarian society.

Codes

(a) (A) is false if considered by its basic philosophy and (R) validate (A)
(b) (A) is true, but (R) is false
(c) Both (A) and (R) are false
(d) (A) is true, but (R) does not validate (A)

25 Which of the following trends are currently seen in the employment front in India?

1. Increased women labour force participation.
2. Underemployment.
3. Growing employment in informal sector.
4. Increasing demand for unskilled manpower.

Codes

(a) 1, 2 and 4 (b) 1, 2 and 3
(c) 2, 3 and 4 (d) 1, 3 and 4

26 Who spearheaded the welfare movement during the early industrialisation period?

(a) Robert Owen (b) Robert Katz
(c) Andrew Ure (d) Sheebhom Rowntree

ANSWERS

Exam Based Questions

1 (c)	2 (d)	3 (c)	4 (d)	5 (d)	6 (d)	7 (d)	8 (d)	9 (b)	10 (d)
11 (c)	12 (a)	13 (d)	14 (d)	15 (c)	16 (d)	17 (d)	18 (c)	19 (d)	20 (b)
21 (a)	22 (a)	23 (a)	24 (c)	25 (a)	26 (b)	27 (b)	28 (a)	29 (a)	30 (b)
31 (c)	32 (a)	33 (c)	34 (a)	35 (a)	36 (b)	37 (a)	38 (c)	39 (b)	40 (a)
41 (b)	42 (a)	43 (b)	44 (a)	45 (b)	46 (a)	47 (a)	48 (a)	49 (b)	50 (b)
51 (a)	52 (b)	53 (b)	54 (d)	55 (c)	56 (d)	57 (d)	58 (b)	59 (c)	60 (b)
61 (a)	62 (b)	63 (d)	64 (a)	65 (b)	66 (a)	67 (b)	68 (d)	69 (a)	70 (c)
71 (b)	72 (d)	73 (a)	74 (b)	75 (a)	76 (a)				

Previous Years' Questions

1 (c)	2 (d)	3 (b)	4 (c)	5 (d)	6 (b)	7 (d)	8 (a)	9 (a)	10 (b)
11 (b)	12 (b)	13 (c)	14 (b)	15 (b)	16 (d)	17 (d)	18 (c)	19 (c)	20 (a)
21 (d)	22 (d)	23 (a)	24 (c)	25 (a)	26 (d)				

NTA UGC NET/JRF/SET

MODEL PAPERS (1-3)

HUMAN RESOURCE MANAGEMENT (Paper-2)

Model Paper-1

General Instructions

1. There are total one hundred questions in this paper. Each question carries 2 marks.
2. All questions are compulsory.

---

1 Expectancy theory of motivation is given by

(a) Herzberg (b) Vroom
(c) Porter and Lawler (d) Maslow

2 Which of the following is incorrect according to ILO's definition of labour welfare?

(a) These amenities may be established only inside the establishment
(b) The facilities enable the persons employed in them to perform their work in healthy surroundings
(c) The services should be conducive to good health and high morale of the employees
(d) The employees must be provided healthy and congenial surroundings

3 Which of the following is not an objective of labour welfare?

(a) Improve and enhance the quality of life of the employees only
(b) Increasing the productivity and efficiency of the labour
(c) Promote an organisational culture that is conducive to the growth of an employee
(d) Provide health, medical and maternity benefits that help the employees to take care of their health

4 Which of the following needs to be subtracted from allocable surplus?

(a) Any amount by way of depreciation admissible in accordance with the Income Tax or in accordance with the provisions of the agricultural Income Tax Law
(b) Any amount by way of which the employer is entitled to deduct from his income under the Income Tax Act
(c) Any direct tax which the employer is liable to pay for the accounting year in respect of his income, profits and gains during that year
(d) All of the above

5 Which of the following is correct in context of Minimum Wages Act, 1948?

1. The minimum rate of wages will be fixed or revised by the appropriate government in respect of scheduled employments under Section 3.
2. Cost of living allowance includes basic wages.
3. The government has the power to appoint an advisory board for the matter of fixing and revising minimum rates of wages.
4. One-third members of the Central Advisory Board will be independent.

Codes

(a) 1, 2 and 3 (b) Both 2 and 3
(c) Both 1 and 3 (c) All of the above

6 The matter related to the fixation of minimum wages was taken up by the ...... and the ...... in 1943.

(a) International Labour Conference, Royal Commission
(b) SLL, ILC
(c) Royal commission on Labour, State Commission
(d) None of the above

7 The elasticity of labour depends upon which of the following factors?

(a) Geographical mobility of labour
(b) Occupational mobility of labour
(c) Both (a) and (b)
(d) Neither (a) nor (b)

8 According to the Payment of Bonus Act, 1965, what is the minimum bonus that needs to be paid to every employee?
(a) 8.33% of the salary or wages earned by the employee during the accounting year
(b) 8.1% of the salary or wages earned by the employee during the accounting year
(c) 7.33% of the salary or wages earned by the employee during the accounting year
(d) 9.33% of the salary or wages earned by the employee during the accounting year

9 Who among the following was a strong advocate of the trusteeship theory?
(a) Netaji Subhash Chandra Bose
(b) Mahatma Gandhi
(c) Bal Gangadhar Tilak
(d) Sardar Patel

10 The principle of social justice regulating labour legislations which envisages the policy that "All human beings irrespective of race, creed or sex have the right to pursue both their material well-being, and their spiritual development in conditions of freedom and dignity, of economic security and equal opportunity" was propagated by
1. The Philadelphia Chapter
2. The Magna Carta
3. The Constitution of India
4. The League of Nations

Codes
(a) Only 1 (b) Both 1 and 3
(c) 1, 2 and 3 (d) 1, 3 and 4

11 Match the items given in List I with the items of List II.

List I	List II
A. Plateauing	1. A situation in which both husband and wife have distinct careers outside the home
B. Dual career couple	2. A sequence of positions occupied by a person during a cause of a life time
C. Mid career phase	3. A career stage marked by a continuous improvement in performance, levelling off in performance or the beginning of deterioration of performance
D. Career	4. A condition of stagnating in one's job

Codes

	A	B	C	D
(a)	4	1	3	2
(b)	1	2	3	4
(c)	2	1	3	4
(d)	4	3	2	1

12 Which of the following is not the name of the committee set up as Labour Enquiry Committee from 1937-1946?
(a) Cawnpore Labour Enquiry Committee
(b) CP and Berar Textile Labour Enquiry Committee
(c) International Committee of the Red Cross (ICRC)
(d) UP Labour Enquiry Committee

13 Who of the following propounded the surplus value theory?
(a) Karl Marx
(b) David Ricardo
(c) Both (a) and (b)
(d) All of the above

14 What will be the punishment if an employer is unable to meet the requisite conditions according to the Payment of Bonus Act, 1965?
(a) Imprisonment for a term which may extend to seven months
(b) Imprisonment for a term which may extend to four months
(c) Imprisonment for a term which may extend to six months
(d) Imprisonment for a term which may extend to three months

15 Which of the following matters are included in standing orders?
1. Closing and re-opening of sections of the industrial establishment.
2. Means of redress for workmen against' unfair treatment.
3. Requirement to enter premises by certain gates and liability to search.
4. Shift working.

Codes
(a) 1, 2 and 3 (b) 2, 3 and 4
(c) Both 1 and 3 (d) All of the above

16 Match the following.

List I	List II
A. National income theory	1. Bargaining between capitalist and employees
B. Neo-Keynsian distribution theory	2. More wages will lead more consumption
C. Consumption theory	3. Wages are determined by the rate of return on the employees investment
D. Investment theory	4. Employment is the function of national income

Codes

	A	B	C	D
(a)	4	1	2	3
(b)	1	3	4	2
(c)	2	1	3	4
(d)	4	2	3	1

17 According to the Mines Act, 1952, which of the following is incorrect?

(a) No person shall be allowed to work in a mine who has already been working in any other mine within the preceding twelve hours
(b) No adult employed above ground in a mine shall be required or allowed to work for more than forty-eight hours in any week
(c) No adult employed above ground in a mine shall be required or allowed to work for more than ten hours in any day
(d) A person will not work for more than five hours continuously before he has had an interval for rest of atleast half an hour

18 Who of the following said the following lines "Unions are not anti-capitalist organisations. They are in the least degree political. Their main aim is to increase their internal strength, to work conscientiously and to take from the employer no more than what is rightfully due to the labourers"?

(a) Robert Hoxie (b) Mahatma Gandhi
(c) Frank Tannenbaum (d) Karl Marx

19 Which of the following is an extra-mural activity?

(a) Provision of libraries and reading rooms
(b) Shift allowances
(c) Pension
(d) Provision of provident fund

20 Arrange the following activities in the correct sequence to describe the process of staffing.

1. Human resource planning
2. Recruitment
3. Placement and Induction
4. Selection
5. Training and Development
6. Promotion
7. Appraisal
8. Remuneration

Codes

(a) 1, 2, 3, 4, 5, 6, 7, 8
(b) 1, 2, 4, 3, 5, 7, 6, 8
(c) 2, 1, 4, 3, 5, 7, 6, 8
(d) 2, 1, 3, 4, 5, 7, 6, 8

21 Match the following.

List I	List II
A. Holway	1. Psychophysical experiment
B. Gilchrist	2. Figure and round
C. Edgar Rubin	3. The complanar ratio hypothesis
D. Weirtheimer	4. Gestalt psychologist

Codes

	A	B	C	D		A	B	C	D
(a)	4	2	1	3	(b)	4	2	3	1
(c)	1	3	2	4	(d)	3	1	2	4

22 **Assertion** (A) Workers join union to meet their different socio-psychological needs like companionship, group of likely minded people.

Reason (R) Difference in group psychology cause different types of unions to appeal.

Codes

(a) Both (A) and (R) are true and (R) is the correct explanation of (A)
(b) Both (A) and (R) are true, but (R) is not the correct explanation of (A)
(c) (A) is true, but (R) is false
(d) (A) is false, but (R) is true

23 The Industrial Employment Act, 1946 is not applicable under the clauses of which of the following acts?

(a) Bombay Industrial Relations Act, 1946
(b) Madhya Pradesh Industrial Employment (Standing Orders) Act, 1961
(c) Both (a) and (b)
(d) Industrial Act, 1947

24 Which of the following recommendations were made by National Commission on Labour in 1969?

(a) Intensification by workers education to get good internal leader
(b) The idea of one union for one plant
(c) The compulsion of registration under the Trade Union Act, 1926
(d) All of the above

25 The Industrial Employment Act, 1946 entitles the certifying officer to be a civil court under which of the following sections of Code of Criminal procedure (CrPC)?

(a) Sections 345 and 347 (b) Sections 345 and 346
(c) Sections 343 and 344 (d) Sections 341 and 342

26 Rearrange the following steps involved in the human resource planning process in proper order.

1. HR programming
2. HR demand forecast
3. Environmental scanning
4. Control and evaluation of programme
5. Surplus restricted hiring
6. HRP implementation
7. HR supply forecast
8. Organisational objectives and policies
9. Shortage recruitments and selection

Codes

(a) 1, 2, 3, 4, 5, 6, 7, 8, 9 (b) 3, 8, 2, 7, 1, 6, 4, 5, 9
(c) 8, 9, 4, 5, 2, 3, 1, 6, 7 (d) 9, 8, 7, 6, 5, 4, 3, 2, 1

27 Which of the following is item number 22 on the concurrent list?

(a) Trade unions
(b) Social security
(c) Social insurance
(d) Employment and unemployment

28 Who among the following is not included in the definition of workman under the Industrial Disputes Act, 1947?

(a) Police officer
(b) Employee of a prison
(c) Army, Navy and Air Force employees
(d) All of the above

29 Which of the following statements are true/false?

(i) Societal objectives of HRM deals with compliance with natural laws, human right laws and labour laws.
(ii) The personnel objectives entails manpower planning.
(iii) The functional objectives comprise of recruitment, selection, training, appraisal and others.

Codes

(a) (i) is true, (ii) and (iii) are false
(b) (ii) is true, (i) and (iii) are false
(c) (i) and (iii) are true, (ii) is false
(d) (iii) is true, (i) and (ii) are false

30 According to Factories Act, 1948, how many hours should an adult worker be required or allowed to work in any week?

(a) 24 hours (b) 36 hours (c) 48 hours (d) 72 hours

31 According to Factories Act, 1948, week is a period of seven days beginning from the midnight of which of the following days?

(a) Sunday (b) Monday
(c) Saturday (d) Tuesday

32 Which of the following statements are true/false?

(i) Clayton Alderfer has proposed an alternative hierarchy of needs called ERG theory of motivation.
(ii) Maslow's model comprises of growth needs.
(iii) The dual structure approach to motivation is also called Herzberg's two factor model.

Codes

(a) (i) is true, (ii) and (iii) are false
(b) (i) and (ii) are true, (iii) is false
(c) (i) and (iii) are true, (ii) is false
(d) (ii) and (iii) are true, (i) is false

33 Which of the following is correct order of hierarchial model of personality?

(a) Trait, Super trait, Specific response, Habitual
(b) Super trait, Specific response, Trait, Habitual
(c) Specific response, Habitual, Trait, Super trait
(d) Habitual, Trait, Super trait, Specific response

34 Which of the following is not a publication of ILO?

(a) International Labour Review
(b) Shram Ki Duniya
(c) International Labour Statistics
(d) Indian Labour Journal

35 **Assertion** (A) A country's economic development is dependent upon the production of goods and services in the country.

Reason (R) These are the important factors of productions.

Codes

(a) Both (A) and (R) are true and (R) is the correct explanation of (A)
(b) Both (A) and (R) are true, but (R) is not the correct explanation of (A)
(c) (A) is correct, but (R) is incorrect
(d) (A) is incorrect, but (R) is correct

36 Which of the following statement(s) is/are correct?

I Potential appraisal and performance manage- ment are HRD mechanisms.
II Personnel function is maintenance oriented while HRD is development oriented.

(a) Both are incorrect (b) I is correct, II is incorrect
(c) Both are correct (d) I is incorrect, II is correct

37 In the term ADDIE, the letter I stands for

(a) innovating (b) implementing
(c) inducting (d) None of these

38 Which of the following holds correct for collective bargaining?

(a) It is a tripartite process
(b) It is a joint decision-making process involving both employers and employees
(c) It can be done through a single employee as well
(d) It is an involuntary process and requires a third party intervention

39 Which of the following statements are the conditions required for management development?

1. The individual should be interested in developing himself.
2. The individual should know the areas of his potential development.
3. A positive emotional and professional climate should be created in the workplace for the employee to progress and review himself.
4. He should identify mechanisms of using these opportunities and get the support he needs from his superiors and the organisation.
5. The individual should have basic working knowledge.

Codes

(a) 1, 2, 3 and 4 (b) 2, 3 and 5
(c) Both 1 and 4 (d) All of the above

40 Which of the following statement(s) is/are correct?

I A job evaluation is a systematic way of determining the value/worth of a job in relation to other jobs in an organisation. It tries to make a systematic comparison between jobs to assess their relative worth for the purpose of establishing a rational pay structure.
II Compensable factor is a fundamental, compensable element of a job, which can be know-how, problem solving and accountability, knowledge, problem-solving skills and working conditions.

(a) Both statements are correct
(b) Statement I is correct and Statement II is incorrect
(c) Statement II is correct and Statement I is incorrect
(d) Both statements are incorrect

41 Which of the following acts is applied to trade unions?
(a) The Societies Registration Act, 1860
(b) The Cooperative Societies Act, 1912
(c) The Companies Act, 1956
(d) The Trade Unions Act, 1926

42 Low self-esteem can lead to a cycle of failure that is self-destructive. Which of the following is the sequence?
(a) Low performance expectations, High anxiety, Reduced effort, Low self-esteem, Actual failure
(b) High anxiety, Reduced effort, Low performance expectations, Actual failure, Low self-esteem
(c) High anxiety, Reduced effort, Low self-esteem, Low performance expectations, Actual failure
(d) None of the above

43 Which of the following are the main cause of trade union movement?
(a) World War I
(b) Establishment of ILO
(c) All India Trade Union Congress
(d) All of the above

44 The fifteenth Indian Labour Conference discussed the question of discipline in the industry and had laid down Code of Discipline. How many parts are present in Code of Discipline?
(a) Four
(b) Three
(c) Seven
(d) Eight

45 **Assertion** (A) Organisational behaviour is concerned with control processes and interactions within an organisation.

Reason (R) It deals with the behaviour or individuals and groups operating in an organisation.

Codes
(a) Both (A) and (R) are true and (R) is correct explanation of (A)
(b) Both (A) and (R) are true, but (R) is not the correct explanation of (A)
(c) (A) is correct, but (R) is incorrect
(d) (R) is correct, but (A) is incorrect

46 Given below are some features of Pluralist theory. Which of the following is incorrect?
(a) Trade unions play an important role in maintaining balance between the employer and employees
(b) Conflicts cannot be completely done away and mediation is the key to resolve them
(c) Conflict is a key component for innovation and company growth
(d) Conflicts and strikes are viewed as destructive

47 Which of the following is not correct for the unitary theory?
(a) Conflicts and strikes are viewed as destructive as these have a direct impact on the productivity and profitability of the organisation
(b) Individual's needs take a back-seat in front of the organisational needs and goals
(c) All the stakeholders work towards one common goal of the organisational development and betterment
(d) It propagates that conflict is a key component for innovation and company growth

48 Which of the following statements are true/false?
(i) The Inter-state Migrant Workmen Act, 1979 is applicable in any establishment in which five or more inter-state migrant workmen are employed.
(ii) In exercise of the powers conferred by Section 35 of the Inter-state Migrant Workmen (regulation of employment and conditions of service) Act, 1979, the Central Government made the Inter-state Migrant Workment (regulation of employment and conditions of service) rules.
(iii) An inter-state migrant workman shall be equal to the wages fixed under the Minimum Wages Act, 1948.
(iv) The principal officer issue a certificate of registration in Form III after the registration of establishment.
(a) (i), (ii) are true and (iii), (iv) are false
(b) (i), (iii) are true and (ii), (iv) are false
(c) (ii), (iv) are true and (i), (iii) are false
(d) (iii), (iv) are true and (ii), (i) are false

49 Which one of the following figures is an example of proximity principle perceptual organisation?
(a) ○○ ○○ ○○ (b) ○○ ○○ ○○
(c) ⊃○ ○○ ⊂ (d) ⊃○ ⊃○ ⊃○

50 A 'quantitative technique' in job evaluation processes is
(a) job classification
(b) alternative ranking method
(c) aligned reward strategy
(d) point method

51 Which of the following factor influence(s) employee compensation?
(a) Labour market (b) Cost of living
(c) Labour union (d) All of these

52 According to the system approach of industrial relations, which of the following factor is not correct?
(a) Actors include the employees, employers and the government agencies
(b) Context is basically the environment in which the actors operate
(c) Ideology defined the philosophy, view-points and sentiments of the involved actors
(d) The system of Industrial Relation (IR) is applicable at only national level

53 Which one of the following statements explain the incidental learning?
(a) Learning without actually trying to attain a goal
(b) Learning in the absence of ostensible reinforcement
(c) Learning without the knowledge of the relationship between the response and the reinforcement
(d) Learning in the absence of changes in the perception or discriminations

54 **Assertion** (A) One cannot be sure that the quality of appraisal is related on the basis of length of service.
Reason (R) Initial appraisal and promotion appraisal are done separately and differently since length of services is different.
Codes
(a) (R) is correct, but (A) is not correct
(b) (A) is correct, but (R) is not correct
(c) Both (A) and (R) are correct
(d) Both (A) and (R) are not correct

55 Which of the following are the main causes of indiscipline?
(a) Wage differentials
(b) Unreasonable work assignments
(c) Non-payment of bonus
(d) Any of the above

56 Behavioural factors affecting an individual consist
(a) personal attitudes
(b) behaviour patterns and work habits
(c) physical fitness
(d) None of the above

57 In which of the following ways organisations are benefitted through training and development?
(a) It leads to profitability
(b) It improves relationship between employer and employee
(c) It improves the job knowledge and skills at all levels of the organisation
(d) All of the above

58 The following is paid only at the time of employees exit after serving more than five years
(a) perquisites (b) claims (c) gratuity (d) allowances

59 An interview, in which you discuss person's career plans and plan professional development, it is said to be
(a) a satisfactory-promotable interview
(b) a satisfactory-not promotable interview
(c) an unsatisfactory-correctable interview
(d) an unsatisfactory-uncorrectable interview

60 Which of the following is not an external driver for benchmarking?
(a) Customers continually demand better quality, lower prices, shorter lead times
(b) Competitors are constantly trying to get ahead and steal markets
(c) Legislation
(d) None of the above

61 Which of the following is not a job evaluation method?
(a) Factor comparison method
(b) Point method
(c) Ranking method
(d) Assessment method

62 Hawthorne experiments were conducted under the leadership of
(a) D Bright (b) T Ford
(c) Elton Mayo (d) K Tanaka

63 To keep on track employees' performance, building block to be used is
(a) direction sharing
(b) goal alignment
(c) rewards and recognition
(d) coaching and development support

64 Consider the following statements for the types of unemployment. Which of the following statement(s) is/are correct?
1. Frictional unemployment focuses on structural problems in the economy and inefficiencies inherent in labour market.
2. Structural unemployment focuses on voluntary decisions to work, based on each individual's valuation of their own work.
3. The cause and solutions for frictional unemployment often address barriers to entry.
(a) Only 1 (b) Only 3
(c) Both 1 and 2 (d) All of these

65 Match the following governance conventions with their number.

List I	List II
A. Labour Inspection Convention, 1947	1. 81
B. Employment Policy Convention, 1964	2. 122
C. Labour Inspection (Agriculture) Convention, 1969	3. 144
D. Tripartite Consultation (International Labour Standards) Convention, 1976	4. 129

Codes

	A	B	C	D
(a)	1	3	4	2
(b)	2	1	4	3
(c)	3	1	4	2
(d)	1	3	2	4

66 Which type of information is conveyed by orientation?
(a) Training and education benefit
(b) Job location
(c) Job safety requirements
(d) General information about the daily work routine

67 Which of the followings are supporter of behaviouralist theory of organisation?
(a) A H Maslow (b) Kurt Lewis
(c) Chester Bernard (d) All of these

68 Assertion (A) Managerial roles are dynamic in nature.

Reason (R) Managerial skills define managerial roles.

Codes

(a) Both (A) and (R) are correct and (R) is the correct explanation of (A)
(b) Both (A) and (R) are correct, but (R) is not the correct explanation of (A)
(c) (A) is correct, but (R) is incorrect
(d) (A) is incorrect, but (R) is correct

69 According to Henry Fayol, which one of the following combinations of qualities are required in a manager?

(a) Physical, mental, experiene, educational and conceptual
(b) Technical, human, conceptual, mental and moral
(c) Physical, mental, moral, educational, technical and experiences
(d) Mental, moral, conceptual, educational, technical and experience

70 The organisational charts are used

(a) for giving the plan of action and the responsibilities of all employees
(b) for formulating things apart from social legitimacy
(c) for providing a picture of the organisation at a glance
(d) as manuals and statutes that define relationship between various officers

71 Why is it important to ensure that HR plans are flexible?

(a) To adapt the fast changing environments in which most organisations operate
(b) To accomodate the changes arising because of high attrition rate
(c) To ensure the availability of labour force at all times
(d) To adapt the changing skills and qualifications of all the professions

72 The following is not a type of organisational structure.

(a) Line organisation
(b) Functional organisation
(c) Line and staff organisation
(d) Flexible organisation

73 Which of the following statements are true/false?

(i) According to the Radical perspective, conflict among workers and leaders is the result of the capitalistic nature of society and industry.
(ii) According to the Unitary theory, management needs to coordinate activities among the employees instead of ordering them to comply with strict rules and regulations.
(iii) Conflict and cooperation are inevitable and important components of Industrial Relations (IR).
(iv) In Unitary theory, conflicts and strikes are viewed as destructive as these have a direct impact on the productivity and profitability of the organisation.

(a) (i), (iii), (iv) are true and (ii) is false
(b) (i), (iii) are true and (ii), (iv) are false
(c) (ii), (iv) are true and (i), (iii) are false
(d) (iii), (iv) are true and (ii), (i) are false

74 The executives working in Australian branch of United Kingdom multinational bank citizen of US are an example of

(a) Second country nationals
(b) Home country nationals
(c) Host country nationals
(d) Third country nationals

75 Match the following.

List I		List II
A.	Subsistence allowance	1. Industrial Disputes Act
B.	Retrenchment	2. Industrial Employment Act
C.	National Tribunal	3. Section 2(s) Industrial Disputes Act
D.	Workman	4. Section 7 (a) Industrial Disputes Act

Codes

	A	B	C	D		A	B	C	D
(a)	1	3	4	2	(b)	2	1	4	3
(c)	3	1	4	2	(d)	1	3	2	4

76 How can HRM help to build successful cross border alliance?

(a) Joint venture (b) Exporting ideas
(c) Spending 25% budget (d) All of these

77 Which of the following is the meaning of human resource planning?

(a) Evaluation of job
(b) Satisfaction of the employees on the job
(c) Appraising the performance of employees
(d) It is the process by which an organisation ensures that it has the right number and kind of people at the right place, at the right time

78 Why are transnational organisations becoming increasingly important?

(a) They are increasing in interdependencies
(b) Operations are facilitated by recent technical changes
(c) Increases employment of resources
(d) All of the above

79 Which test assesses an individual's achievement and motivational levels?

(a) Thurstone Temperament Survey
(b) Minnesota Multiphasic Personality
(c) Thematic Apperception Test
(d) Guilford-Zimmerman Temperament Survey

80 The key question asked while developing on IHRM policy is

(a) what cross-border training is to be given
(b) who will be the CEO of new branch
(c) when will HR policies be developed
(d) what kind of organisation is desired

81 International HRM originally consisted of three major clusters on inquiry, namely
1. the conduct of people management in internationally operating companies.
2. the international transfer of staff, focused on expatriation.
3. comparing HRM policies and practices across different countries.
4. comparing different culture with each other.

Codes
(a) 1, 2 and 3 (b) 2, 3 and 4
(c) 1, 3 and 4 (d) All of these

82 A test that seeks to predict success or failure through one's handwriting is ....
(a) polygraph (b) graphology
(c) grammatologist (d) None of these

83 Who has given the following statement of selection "Selection is the process by which candidates for employment are divided into two classes those who will be offered employment and those who will not."
(a) Yoder (b) Jucious
(c) Robbins (d) Koontz

84 Below are given four different theories
(i) Trait approach (ii) Attitude criterion
(iii) Behaviour approach (iv) Situational approach

These are indentified with
(a) administrative behaviour
(b) organisational behaviour
(c) leadership index
(d) administrative approaches.

85 The quantitative approach to management has also been referred to by which of the following names?
(a) Sales optimisation (b) Management science
(c) Managerial theory (d) Statistical reformulation

86 The purpose of any human resource information system is to
(a) replace human decision-making with computerised decision-making
(b) provide data and data summarises (statistical analysis) that are error free
(c) assist management in decision-making
(d) reduce the number of low-level support staff

87 Match the following.

	List I		List II
A.	All India Trade Union Congress (AITUC)	1.	1971
B.	Indian National Trade Union Congress (INTUC)	2.	1947
C.	Hind Mazdoor Sabha (HMS)	3.	1955
D.	Centre of Indian Trade Union (CITU)	4.	1920
E.	Bhartiya Mazdoor Sangh (BMS)	5.	1967
F.	National Front of Indian Trade Union (NFITU)	6.	1948

Codes

	A	B	C	D	E	F
(a)	1	2	3	4	5	6
(b)	4	2	6	1	3	5
(c)	3	4	1	2	5	6
(d)	6	5	4	3	2	1

88 Modern approach of HR accounting treats human resource as
(a) expenditure (b) physical assets
(c) physical liabilities (d) capital investment

89 In the view of classical theorists, an organisation is
(a) closed system
(b) open system
(c) Both (a) and (b)
(d) completely connected and influenced by its external environment

90 Simon (1960) is associated with what type of decision-making model?
(a) Programmed (b) Administrative
(c) Classical (d) Rational

91 .... are involved with efforts to improve productivity through changes in employee relations.
(a) Human resource department
(b) Cultural department
(c) Social awareness department
(d) None of the above

92 Which of the following are the characteristic operant conditioning?
1. Stimulus-response association
2. Law of contiguity in learning
3. Law of effect
4. Difference in UR and CR

Select the correct answer using the codes given below
(a) Both 1 and 2 (b) Both 2 and 3
(c) 1, 3 and 4 (d) 2, 3 and 4

93 In which of the following processes HRD is not needed?
(a) Implementing a new policy
(b) Deciding to buy the latest machinery
(c) Meeting changes in the organisational development
(d) Changing an organisation's culture

94 Match the following.

	List I		List II
A.	Participation through	1.	Employees are empowered by transferring authority and responsibilities
B.	Quality circles	2.	Deep commitment to quality
C.	Empowered teams	3.	Performance of the organisation is linked to the performance of the employee
D.	Financial participation	4.	A group of 7 to 10 people of same area interacting regularly

Codes

	A	B	C	D
(a)	1	3	2	4
(b)	4	1	2	3
(c)	1	4	3	2
(d)	2	1	4	3

95 Which among the following is a planning as well as controlling technique?

(a) Procedure (b) Method (c) Budget (d) Policy

96 Human capital comprises of which of the following?

(a) Social capital (b) Intellectual capital
(c) Organisational capital (d) All of these

97 Motivation is an element of

(a) planning function (b) organisation function
(c) direction function (d) coordination function

98 Sensitivity training is a part of

(a) in-house development (b) behaviour modeling
(c) organisational development (d) None of these

Directions (Q. Nos. 99 and 100) *Read the following passage carefully and answer the questions that follows.*

In France, Germany and other European countries, socialist parties and democrats played a prominent role in forming and building up trade unions, especially from the 1870s onwards. This stood in contrast to the British experience, where moderate New Model Unions dominates the union movement from the mid 19th century and where trade unionism was stronger than the political labour movement until the formation and growth of the Labour Party in the early years of the 20th century.

Government opposition to trade unionism in the United Kingdom was a major factor in economic crisis during the 1960s and in particular the 1970s, culminating some would argue in the Winter of Discontent of late 1978 and early 1979, when a significant percentage of the nation's public sector workers went on strike. By this stage, some 1,20,00,000 workers in the United Kingdom were trade union members. However, the election of the Conservative Party led by Margaret Thatcher at the general election in May 1979, at the expense of Labour's James Callaghan, saw substantial trade union reform which saw the level of strikes fall, but also the level of trade union membership fall.

At the height of the strikes, nearly 3,00,00,000 working days were lost in Britain during 1979, but that had fallen dramatically to some 50,00,000 during 1981 as a result of the Thatcher government's union reform policies. The number of working days lost in the country due to strikes rose sharply to more than 2,50,00,000 in 1984, though most of these were miners on strike and from then on the number of working days lost in Britain due to strikes remained in the low millions.

By the end of the 1980s, membership had fallen to just over 60,00,000 little more than half the level of a decade earlier and it also counted against the Labour Party's hopes of regaining power, as its relationship with the trade unions had traditionally been seen as a strength but after the Winter of Discontent it was seen as a liability. Manufacturing, the main source of union strength in the United Kingdom, had shrunk by half during the early 1980s recession pushing unemployment from 15,00,000 to more than 30,00,000.

Earlier in the 1970s, Conservative Prime Minster, Edward Heath (elected in 1970) had attempted to reduce trade union powers due to the rising level of strikes across the country. However, he backed down with his stance against the unions following a backlash by the militant miners' union, which saw many of his own MPs turn against him. The strikes continued and Heath responded by calling a snap election in February 1974. The election resulted in a hung Parliament with the Tories having the most votes but labour having slightly more seats and failed attempts by Heath to form a coalition with the liberals led to the resignation of his government and the return of Harold Wilson as Prime Minister of a minority labour government, which gained a three seat majority at a second election later in the year.

99 What was the desire of socialist parties and democrats in France and Germany?

(a) To form and build the trade unions in order to support the socialistic views
(b) To support the British policies
(c) Both (a) and (b)
(d) None of the above

100 What is the main factor of economic crisis during 1960s in United Kingdom?

(a) Excessive involvement of trade unions in United Kingdom was a mojar factor of economic crisis
(b) Government opposition to trade unionism in the United Kingdom was a major factor in economic crisis
(c) Government suppot to trade unionism in the United Kingdom was a major factor in economic crisis during the 1960s
(d) The socialist approach in trade unionism destroyed the capitalistic structure of industry, which was a major factor in economic crisis during the 1960s

ANSWERS

1 (c)	2 (a)	3 (a)	4 (d)	5 (a)	6 (b)	7 (c)	8 (a)	9 (b)	10 (b)
11 (a)	12 (c)	13 (a)	14 (c)	15 (d)	16 (a)	17 (c)	18 (b)	19 (a)	20 (d)
21 (c)	22 (a)	23 (c)	24 (d)	25 (b)	26 (b)	27 (a)	28 (d)	29 (c)	30 (c)
31 (c)	32 (c)	33 (c)	34 (d)	35 (c)	36 (c)	37 (b)	38 (b)	39 (a)	40 (a)
41 (d)	42 (a)	43 (d)	44 (a)	45 (b)	46 (d)	47 (d)	48 (a)	49 (b)	50 (d)
51 (d)	52 (d)	53 (c)	54 (d)	55 (d)	56 (b)	57 (d)	58 (c)	59 (a)	60 (d)
61 (d)	62 (c)	63 (c)	64 (b)	65 (b)	66 (d)	67 (c)	68 (d)	69 (c)	70 (d)
71 (a)	72 (a)	73 (a)	74 (d)	75 (b)	76 (d)	77 (d)	78 (d)	79 (c)	80 (d)
81 (a)	82 (b)	83 (a)	84 (c)	85 (b)	86 (c)	87 (b)	88 (b)	89 (a)	90 (b)
91 (a)	92 (d)	93 (b)	94 (b)	95 (c)	96 (d)	97 (c)	98 (c)	99 (a)	100 (b)

HUMAN RESOURCE MANAGEMENT (Paper-2)

Model Paper-2

General Instructions

1. There are total one hundred questions in this paper. Each question carries 2 marks.
2. All questions are compulsory.

1 Which of the factors listed below is not a reason for decision-making in organisation being a complex process?

(a) People have to make decision in a historical context
(b) Several stakeholders will have an interest in the decision
(c) Factors in the current context of the organisation affect the decision
(d) Modern information systems enable people to evaluate a range of possible outcomes

2 Which of the following statements are true/false?

(i) In India, 12 major unions are recognised as central trade union organisations and operate in many states.
(ii) Bhartiya Mazdoor Sangh (BMS) adopts the policies and ideologies of Communist Party of India (CPI).
(iii) All India Trade Union Congress was founded by Dattopant Thengadi on 23rd July, 1955, birthday of Lok Manya Bal Gangadhar Tilak.
(iv) Hindu Mazdoor Sabha (HMS) was founded in Howrah, West Bengal on 29th December, 1948 by socialists, forward bloc followers and independent unionists.

(a) (i), (iv) are true and (ii), (iii) are false
(b) (i), (iii) are true and (ii), (iv) are false
(c) (ii), (iv) are true and (i), (iii) are false
(d) (iii), (iv) are true and (ii), (i) are false

3 Which of the following functions of trade unions is not related to society?

(a) To prepare and maintain necessary records
(b) To enable unorganised sector to organise itself
(c) To actively participate in the programmes of family planning afforestation, national integration etc
(d) To cooperate in the formulation and implementation in the policies of national development

4 Which of the following statement is incorrect?

(a) Management audit signifies evaluation of the effectiveness of the management and its functional performance
(b) Ratio analysis is a synonym for cost profit volume analysis
(c) Budgetary control helps in delegation
(d) None of the above

5 Match the following.

	List I		List II
A.	Perfect market	1.	Close relationship between the wage setting and the allocation of labour
B.	The Neo-classical market	2.	Buyers and sellers are free to make an entry of exist anytime
C.	Natural market	3.	Policies of trade unions, employers and the government influence wage movements
D.	The Institutional market	4.	Imperfections and inequality exists in the market
E.	The Management market	5.	Workers are innocent and ignorant

Codes

	A	B	C	D	E
(a)	1	2	4	5	3
(b)	1	2	3	4	5
(c)	2	4	5	3	1
(d)	3	2	5	4	1

6 Which factors is the most likely to have caused as shift in power away from unions and towards management over the last decade?

(a) The existence of tacit unwritten agreements between management and unions based 'custom and practice'
(b) The growth of 'single unionism' within the workplace
(c) The introduction of Schedule I of the Employment Relations Act of 1999
(d) The relatively healthy growth of the UK company

7 Which category of worker is the most susceptible to Carpel Tunnel Syndrome?

(a) Sculptors (b) Farmers
(c) Doctors (d) Potters

8 Which of the following statements are correct with regard to FJA?

1. FJA was postulated by Sidney A Fine.
2. The foundation behind FJA is that jobs must be well defined in terms of the interaction between the task, the individuals responsible for accomplishing the task and the environment in which the task is to be performed.
3. FJA asks employees for specific examples of on-the-job behaviour that demonstrates both high and low levels of performance.
4. In FJA, the experts make judgements about the content of job.

Codes

(a) 1, 2 and 3 (b) 1, 2 and 4
(c) Both 1 and 4 (d) Both 2 and 3

9 **Assertion** (A) Conflicts and strikes are destructive in nature.

Reason (R) Conflicts have a direct impact on the productivity and profitability of the organisation.

(a) Both (A) and (R) are true and (R) is the correct explanation of the (A)
(b) Both (A) and (R) are true, but (R) is not the correct explanation of (A)
(c) (A) is true, but (R) is false
(d) (A) is false, but (R) is true

10 Labour movement became a vigorous force in India after ....

(a) World War I (b) World War II
(c) Panipat War I (d) Panipat War II

11 Which of the following statements is true?

(a) Poor judgement is cognitive symptom of stress
(b) Agitation is cognitive symptom of stress
(c) Moodiness is emotional symptom of stress
(d) Irritability is physical symptom of stress

12 According to the Child Labour (Prohibition and Regulation) Act, 1986 who is a child?

(a) A person who has not completed his fourteenth year of age
(b) A person who has not completed his fifteenth year of age
(c) A person who has not completed his eighteenth year of age
(d) A person who has not completed his twelfth year of age

13 Which of the following is included in the definition of mines?

1. Every shaft in the course of being sunk.
2. Every level and inclined plane in the course of being driven.
3. All shafts, levels, planes, machinery, works, tramways and sidings, whether above or below ground, in or adjacent to, and belonging to the mine.

(a) Only 1 (b) Both 2 and 3
(c) Both 1 and 3 (d) All of the above

14 .... is a sort of insurance cover to members to fight against irrational, arbitrary and illegal actions of employees.

(a) Collective strength (b) Industrial strength
(c) Social strength (d) None of these

15 According to the Child Labour (prohibition and regulation) Act, 1986, how many holidays will be allowed to a child?

(a) 1 in a week (b) 2 in a week
(c) 2 in a fortnight (d) 3 in two weeks

16 Which of the following is true?

1. A person qualified for a labour court should be a Judge of High Court.
2. Rules of discipline should fall within the jurisdiction of Industrial Tribunals.
3. To establish employer sponsored trade unions of workmen is an unfair labour practice of workmen.

Codes

(a) Both 2 and 3
(b) Both 1 and 3
(c) Both 1 and 2
(d) All of the above

17 One of the advantage of matrix structure is that

(a) it is easily understood by the people involved
(b) improved lateral communications
(c) product lines can be recognised as cost centres, it eases financial control
(d) top management has more time to devote to long-term strategic issues

18 Which of the following is a limitation of decentralisation?

(a) Does not aid organisation in adapting to the environment
(b) Gives managers more freedom
(c) Considerable expense for training managers
(d) Adds to burden on top management

19 An employee is rated high in performance appraisal because of 'religion', is an example of
(a) lenient/strict tendency (b) bias
(c) central tendency (d) different tendencies

20 Which one of the following statement is not true in the case of Human Resource Management?
(a) It performs developmental function
(b) Employees are motivated by salary
(c) It is proactive in nature
(d) It consists of various sub-systems

21 Which of the following is not a quantitative demand forecasting method under HRP?
(a) Regression Model
(b) Ratio and Trend Analysis
(c) Delphi Technique
(d) Bureks Smith Model

22 Hierarchy has been described as the 'scalar process' by
(a) LD White (b) Mooney and Reliey
(c) PH Appleby (d) Gullick and Urwick

23 Arrange the elements of Maslow's hierarchy of needs according to their arrangement of importance starting from the bottom of hierarchy.
(i) Need for positive self image and recognition
(ii) Needs related to security, money, workplace
(iii) Psychological needs and basic needs
(iv) Needs of realising one's potential, continued growth
(v) Needs related to love, affection, belongingness, acceptance
(a) (v), (i), (iii), (iv), (ii) (b) (iii), (v), (iv), (i), (ii)
(c) (ii), (v), (iv), (i), (iii) (d) (iii), (ii), (v), (i), (iv)

24 Which of the following are false in context of code of discipline?
1. The decisions must be taken unilaterally.
2. 'Go-slow' tactic must be avoided.
3. Employer needs to give a proper notice before the strikes.
4. Employees need to give a proper notice before lockouts.

Codes
(a) 1, 3 and 4 (b) 1, 2 and 3
(c) 2, 3 and 4 (d) 1, 2 and 4

25 The Delphi technique uses
(a) mathematical models as input to the decision-making process
(b) a panel of experts making a series of independent decisions
(c) a 'top-down' approach
(d) None of the above

26 Which of the following books provides the most comprehensive enunciation of classical theory?
(a) Principles on organisation
(b) Papers on science of administration
(c) Principle of scientific management
(d) General and industrial management

27 International organisations normally employ expatriates in the following roles, except
(a) country manager (b) technical specialist
(c) financial controller (d) union leader

28 In which type of strike, employees do not have issues directly with the employer?
(a) Stay in (b) Hunger strike
(c) Sympathetic strike (d) Tool down

29 Which of the following is incorrect for the governing body of ILO?
(a) It is the executive council of the ILO
(b) It takes decision on ILO policy and establishes the programme and the budget, which it then submits to the conference for adoption
(c) It is composed of 56 titular members and 66 deputy members
(d) It meets twice a year in Geneva

30 **Assertion** (A) HRM is becoming more competitive as there is always a dilemma between human capital and machines.
Reason (R) HRM now focus on scientific decisions in order to make efficient decision which is due to technology changes.

Codes
(a) Both (A) and (R) are true and (R) is the correct explanation of the (A)
(b) Both (A) and (R) are true, but (R) is not the correct explanation of (A)
(c) (A) is true, but (R) is false
(d) (A) is false, but (R) is true

31 Match the following 'S' with their correct explanation under Kaizen.

List I	List II
A. Sustain	1. Removing obstacles
B. Set in order	2. Keeping workstation clean
C. Sort	3. Prevention of wastage of time
D. Shine	4. Performance without being supervised

Codes

	A	B	C	D
(a)	4	3	1	2
(b)	4	3	2	1
(c)	3	4	1	2
(d)	1	3	2	4

32 Which of the following is correct about sit-down strike?
(a) Employees are present in the employers premises
(b) There is no cessation of work
(c) Employees stay away from workplace and organise rallies, demonstrations
(d) Workers do not work for a short period in a day like an hour/day

33 **The key questions to be asked when developing an international HRM policy is**

(a) who is going to coordinate the HRM functions?
(b) what type of organisation is desired?
(c) how can cross boarder training to designed?
(d) when should the HR manager begin developing HR policies?

34 **The ultimate goal of organisational development is to**

(a) structure the organisational environment so that managers and employers can use their developed skills and abilities to the fullest
(b) reduce the levels of uncertainty in managerial decision-making throughout the organisation
(c) create an internal environment which is conducive to self expression
(d) change the traditional relationship between the supervisors and subordinates

35 **Which of the following statements are correct with regard to TQM?**

(a) TQM is built around employees, their needs, aspirations and expectations
(b) Empowerment takes place when employees are properly trained, provided with all relevant results
(c) It implies lower costs, less waste and faster cycle times
(d) All of the above

36 **Who said "action research is a process of systematically collecting research data about an ongoing system relative to some objective, goal or need of that system"?**

(a) Kurt Lewin (b) D Conback
(c) Henry Fayol (d) JC Collins

37 **Match the following with their correct sections of the Factories Act, 1948.**

List I	List II
A. Adolscent	1. 2(d)
B. Adult	2. 2(a)
C. Cost of living index	3. 2(aa)
D. Child	4. 2(bb)

Codes

	A	B	C	D
(a)	1	3	4	2
(b)	2	3	1	4
(c)	3	1	4	2
(d)	1	3	2	4

38 **Hawthorne studies have proved that**

1. wherever the supervisors are employee centered, the output of the employees in high.
2. wherever the supervisors are production centered, the output of the employees is more.
3. wherever the supervisors are employee centered, the output of the employees is less.
4. wherever the supervisor are production centered, the output of the employees is less.

Codes

(a) Both 1 and 2 (b) Both 2 and 3
(c) Both 1 and 4 (d) Both 1 and 3

39 **When implementing industrial relations practices overseas, an Indian head office should ensure coordination so that**

(a) policies are the same as in India
(b) practices adhere to and reinforce strategic HRM philosophies and policies and are in harmony with the desired corporate culture
(c) all employees belong to key trade unions in the industry
(d) concessions are made in each country so that operations can run smoothly

40 **All are parts of European knowledge management framework except**

(a) develop knowledge (b) create knowledge
(c) share knowledge (d) capture knowledge

41 **Which of the following factors influence the wage and salary policy of the company?**

(a) A policy to fix the wages externally competitive
(b) A policy of fix the wages internally compatible
(c) A policy that the wages should be above the industry average or below it or comparable to it
(d) All of the above

42 **Which of the following is not the objective induction?**

(a) To orient a new employee to his work group and the organisation
(b) To train the employee how to perform his work
(c) To promote a feeling of belonging and loyalty to the organisation among new corners that increases his confidences as a result
(d) To give new employee, an information about services and facilities and provide rules, regulations and HR policies to new employees

43 **Assertion** (A) **Competency based job analysis describes jobs in terms of measurable, observable and behavioural competencies.**

Reason (R) **Re-engineering re-designs the business process in such a manner that small multi-disciplinary self-managing teams get the task done together multi-skilled competencies.**

(a) Both (A) and (R) are true and (R) is the correct explanation of the (A)
(b) Both (A) and (R) are true, but (R) is not the correct explanation of (A)
(c) (A) is true, but (R) is false
(d) (A) is false, but (R) is true

44 **Prof Robert Katz has divided managerial skills into**

(a) conceptual, analytical, technical
(b) conceptual, analytical, human relations
(c) technical, human relation, conceptual
(d) technical, analytical, social

45 Who among the following will audit the fund established under the Employees' Provident Fund and Miscellaneous Provisions Act, 1952?
(a) Comptroller and Auditor General of India
(b) Chief Labour Commissioner
(c) Central Provident Fund Commissioner
(d) Both (a) and (b)

46 Consider the following statements about behavioural theories of learning focus on
1. stimulus and response units.
2. principle of contiguity.
3. comprehension of underlying principle.
4. organisation of stimuli.

Which of the statements given above are correct?
(a) Both 1 and 2
(b) Both 2 and 3
(c) Both 1 and 4
(d) Both 3 and 4

47 Match the following.

List I (Authors)		List II (Definitions)
A. Dale Yoder	1.	The process by which management determines how the organisation should move from its current manpower position to its desired manpower position
B. Beach	2.	Training is the process by which manpower is filled for the particular jobs it is to perform
C. Flippo	3.	Training is the organised procedure by which people learn knowledge and skills for definite purpose
D. Vetter	4.	Training is the act of increasing the knowledge and skill of an employee for doing a particular job

Code

	A	B	C	D		A	B	C	D
(a)	1	2	3	4	(b)	3	1	4	2
(c)	2	3	4	1	(d)	4	2	3	1

48 The headquarters of a multinational company where it is situated is known as
(a) Host country
(b) Third country
(c) Subsidiary country
(d) Home country

49 Which of the following statements are true/ false?
(i) ILO was established on 19th April, 1919 by Versailles Peace Conference.
(ii) It is the only tripartite UN agency that brings together government, employers and workers to promote decent work for all.
(iii) ILO was established after World War II.
(iv) The objectives of ILO are enumerated in the Article 322 of the Peace Treaty of Versailles.
(a) (i), (iv) are true and (ii), (iii) are false
(b) (i), (ii) are true and (iii), (iv) are false
(c) (ii), (iv) are true and (i), (iii) are false
(d) (iii), (iv) are true and (ii), (i) are false

50 Who has given the following statement, "Management development is an attempt to Improve managerial effectiveness through a planned and deliberate learning process"?
(a) Mumford
(b) Dale
(c) Molander
(d) None of these

51 Which of the following is not a weakness of craft unions?
(a) Very easy to break as the members of the union belong to different establishment
(b) Craft union workers cannot be easily replaced
(c) Not easy to get the clear perspective of the craft unions
(d) Advancement in technology has destroyed the very basis of craft unions

52 Which of the following is true?
1. The Coal Mines PF Act, 1948 is a social security act.
2. Beedi Workers Welfare Fund Act, 1976 is an employee welfare act.
3. The Shops and Establishments Acts is a regulative Act.
(a) 1, 2 and 3
(b) Both 2 and 3
(c) Both 1 and 2
(d) Both 1 and

53 Match the following.

List I		List II
A. Staffing	1.	Helps in the reduction of uncertainty
B. Planning	2.	Optimal utilisation of resources
C. Directing	3.	Vacant positions are filled
D. Organising	4.	Integrates human efforts

Codes

	A	B	C	D		A	B	C	D
(a)	3	1	4	2	(b)	1	4	2	3
(c)	2	3	4	1	(d)	4	3	2	1

54 Which one of the following theory of organisation can be regarded as first coherent theory of organisation?
(a) Human Relation theory
(b) Scientific Management
(c) System Approach theory
(d) Classical theory

55 Which of the following was an early key management idea, pre-dating the work of FW Taylor & Max Weber?
(a) Differential pay rates
(b) Rule-by-the office
(c) Work specialisation
(d) Classical management theory

56 Performance management includes
(a) daily and weekly interactions
(b) meeting semi-annually
(c) yearly meetings
(d) never having meeting with subordinates

Directions (Q. Nos 57-59) *Read the following passage and answer the questions given at the end by picking up the appropriate answer from the given alternatives.*

In principle, a cohesive group-one whose members generally agree with one another and support one another's judgements-can do a much better job at decision-making than it could if it were non-cohesive. When cohesiveness is low or lacking entirely, compliance out of fear of recrimination is likely to be strongest. To overcome this fear, participants in the group's deliberations need to be confident that they are members in good standing and that the others will continue to value their role in the group, whether or not they agree about a particular issue under discussion. As a member of a group feel more accepted by the others, they acquire greater freedom to say what they really think, becoming less likely to use deceitful arguments or to play it safe by dancing around issues with conventional comments. Typically, then, the more cohesive a group becomes, the less its members will deliberately censor what they say out of fear of being punished socially for antagonising their fellow members. But group cohesiveness can have pitfalls as well. While the members of a highly cohesive group can feel much free to deviate from the majority, their desire for genuine concurrence on every important issue often inclines them not to use this freedom. In a highly cohesive group of decision makers, the danger is not that individuals will conceal objections they harbour regarding a proposal favoured by the majority, but that they think the proposal is a good one without attempting to carry out a critical scrutiny that could reveal grounds for strong objections. Members may then decide that any misgivings they feel are not worth pursuing that the benefit of any doubt should be given to the group consensus. In this way, they may fall victim to a syndrome known as 'groupthink'. Collective decision-making has been defined as 'a deterioration of mental efficiency, reality testing and moral judgement that results from in-group pressures. Based on analyses of major fiascos of international diplomacy and military decision-making, researchers have identified group think behaviour as a recurring pattern that involves several factors; over estimation of the groups power and morality, manifested, e.g. in an illusion of invulnerability, which creates excessive optimism; closemindedness to warnings of problems and to alternative view points and unwarranted pressures toward uniformity, including self-censorship with respect to doubts about the group's reasoning and a concomitant shared illusion of unanimity concerning group decisions. Cohesiveness of the decision-making group is an essential antecedent condition of this syndrome but not a sufficient one. So, it is important to work toward identifying the additional factors that determine whether group cohesiveness will deteriorate into group think or allow for effective decision-making.

57 Why the author does think that the cohesive group can do a much better job at decision-making than it could if it were non-cohesive?

(i) The members of a highly cohesive group can feel much free to deviate from the majority.
(ii) Individuals will not conceal objection they harbour regarding a proposal favoured by the majority.
(iii) Participants in the group's deliberations are confident that they are members in good standing and that the others will continue to value their role in the group, whether or not they agree about a particular issue under discussion.

Codes

(a) Only (i) (b) Only (ii)
(c) Both (i) and (iii) (d) (i), (ii) and (iii)

58 Which one of the following most accurately expresses the main point of the passage?

(a) Despite its value in encouraging frank discussions high cohesion can lead to a debilitating type of group decision-making called group think
(b) Group members can guard against group thinking if they have a good understanding of the critical role played by cohesion
(c) Only diplomacy and military affairs would suffer if there is tendency of group think
(d) Low cohesion is better than high cohesion resulting in group think

59 A group of closely associated colleagues has made a disastrous diplomatic decision after a series of meetings marked by disagreement over conflicting alternatives. It can be inferred from the passage that the author would most likely to say that this scenario.

(a) Provides evidence of chronic in decision, thus indicating a weak level of cohesion in general
(b) Indicates that the group's cohesiveness was coupled with some other factor to produce a group think fiasco
(c) Provides no evidence that group think played an effective role in group decision-making
(d) Provides evidence that group think can develop even in some groups that do not demonstrate an 'Illusion of Unanimity'

60 Who has (have) formulated 'Life Cycle Theory' of leadership?

(a) Reddin
(b) Fiedler
(c) Hersey and Blanchard
(d) None of the above

61 Interpersonal communication at the workplace is also known as

(a) face to face public communication
(b) virtual reality
(c) mass communication
(d) dyadic communication

62 In Likert's system approach, which of the following characteristics is not there in system?

(a) The leader does not trust the subordinates and closely supervises them
(b) The leader defines the work in great detail
(c) Fear is the main motivator
(d) There is free communication between the leader and the subordinates

63 Which of the following statement represents recent trends in HRM?

(a) HRM not only deals with humans, but also there must be a command on financial budgeting and strategic management
(b) HRM focuses on focus on scientific decisions
(c) Recentaly HRM has led emphasis on employee's health benefits
(d) Both (a) and (b)

64 Direct compensation includes which of the following?

(a) Flexible benefits
(b) Long-term incentive pay
(c) Workers' compensation
(d) Unpaid leave

65 Which of the following is not a part of industrial relations system?

(a) Government and employers
(b) Trade unions, union federations or associations
(c) Foreign companies
(d) Labour courts and tribunals

66 **Assertion** (A) Staffing promotes higher performance.

Reason (R) It enables the firm in obtaining suitable candidates for the institution.

Codes

(a) Both (A) and (R) are true and (R) is the correct explanation of the (A)
(b) Both (A) and (R) are true, but (R) is not the correct explanation of (A)
(c) Both (A) and (R) are false
(d) (A) is true, but (R) is false

67 What is group think?

(a) An approach to group decision-making that explains how decisions are made in a team
(b) An idea that shows why dictator are inevitably overthrown
(c) A model that suggests team change with time
(d) An attempt to explain why groups occasionally reach erroneous conclusions even when the prevailing data would give alternative end

68 The steps of motivation process as proposed by Keith Davis are as follows

1. Finding out objective
2. Observing the feeling of employees
3. Team spirit
4. Communication
5. Integrate personal interest with organisation's interest
6. Provide auxiliary condition

Which is the correct sequence of motivational process?

Codes

(a) 1, 2, 4, 5, 6, 3
(b) 1, 2, 3, 4, 5, 6
(c) 1, 3, 4, 6, 2, 5
(d) 6, 4, 2, 1, 5, 3

69 Which of the following statement is correct?

I Induction is designed to give new comer necessary information about the latest trends in fashion and to discuss current politcal issues.

II Induction helps to build up a two-way channel of communication between management and workers.

(a) Both statements are correct
(b) Statement I is correct and Statement II is incorrect
(c) Statement II is correct and Statement I is incorrect
(d) Both statements are incorrect

70 Under the Industrial Disputes Act, 1947, which of the following is incorrect about the conciliation officer?

(a) They are the mediating officers
(b) They may be appointed either permanently or for a limited time period
(c) The conciliation officer has the power to summon any person or witness
(d) He is appointed by the employer

71 Under the Industrial Disputes Act, 1947, the strike is considered illegal if it is commenced after how many days of giving a notice?

(a) 12
(b) 11
(c) 19
(d) 42

72 Which among the following can become a member of ILO?

(a) Largest political party of a country
(b) A country
(c) A Trade Union
(d) Employers Federation

73 Which of the following factors is not related directly to the success of expatriate assignments?

(a) The personality of expatriate employees
(b) The intentions of expatriate employees
(c) The incapability of the spouse to adjust to the new situation
(d) The nature of products produced by the company

74 The capacity to affect the behaviours of others is

(a) Power
(b) Leadership
(c) Aggressiveness
(d) Assertiveness

75 According to the Employees' Provident Fund and Miscellaneous Provisions Act, 1952, which of the following is incorrect in context of basic wages?

(a) All emoluments which are earned by an employee while on duty
(b) All emuluments which are earned by an employee on leave or on holidays

(c) It includes the cash value of any food concession
(d) It does not include any dearness allowance and house rent allowance

76 Which of the following statements are correct?

I It is the basic function of the top management to perform various activities of the organisation.

II Personnel management and HRD are included in HRM.

(a) Both statements are correct
(b) Statement I is correct and Statement II is incorrect
(c) Both statements are incorrect
(d) Statement II is correct and Statement I is incorrect

77 Match the following with their correct sections of the Contract Labour Act, 1972.

List I	List II
A. Controlled Industry	1. 2(e)
B. Principal Employer	2. 2(d)
C. Establishment	3. 2(f)
D. Control Labour	4. 2(b)

Codes

	A	B	C	D		A	B	C	D
(a)	1	3	4	2	(b)	2	3	1	4
(c)	3	1	4	2	(d)	1	3	2	4

78 Match the following.

List I	List II
1. Functional structure	A. Specialised jobs are grouped according to traditional business functions.
2. International division structure	B. Grouping each international business activity into its own division local currency.
3. Matrix division	C. Similar products are grouped under one product head.
4. Product division structure	D. Simultaneously deals with competing pressure for global integration and local responsiveness.

Codes

	A	B	C	D		A	B	C	D
(a)	1	2	3	4	(b)	1	4	2	3
(c)	1	2	4	3	(d)	1	3	4	2

79 Which of the following are the main reasons of workers' participation in management, not getting successful in India?

(a) Multiplicity of trade unions and conflicts between them
(b) Confusion and duplication of functions
(c) Lack of education and training
(d) All of the above

80 Which of the following is not an objective of wage incentive programmers?

(a) Developing ownership interest
(b) Improving employee retention
(c) Reducing labour cost
(d) Facilitating the separation of employees

81 Which one of the following is not a labour law related to wages?

(a) The Workmen's Compensation Act, 1923
(b) The Payment of Bonus Act, 1965
(c) The Payment of Wages Act, 1936
(d) The Minimum Wages Act, 1948

82 The first organised Trade Union in India named as ...... was formed in the year 1918.

(a) Delhi labour union
(b) Bombay labour union
(c) Madras labour union
(d) None of these

83 Ohio State Model suggests the following as the best leader behaviour.

(a) Low structure and low consideration
(b) High concerns both for production and people
(c) Low concern both for production and people
(d) High structure and high consideration

84 Which of the following statements are true/false?

(i) Leadership development programmes, assessment and development centres are types of potential appriaisal methods.

(ii) Top management style and personnel policies affect the HRD climate.

(iii) HRD system must try to develop a habit of the team work among human resource.

Codes

(a) (i) is true, (ii) and (iii) are false
(b) (i) and (ii) are true, (iii) is false
(c) (ii) is true, (i) and (iii) are false
(d) All are true

85 Which of the following are considered to be the bottlenecks of workers' participation in management?

(a) Employers cannot think beyond their knowledge and skills
(b) Role of trade unions is not satisfactory
(c) Employers are unwilling to share power with worker's representative
(d) All of the above

86 Which of the following conventions of the ILO relates to Freedom of Association?

(a) Convention No. 87
(b) Convention No. 100
(c) Convention No. 29
(d) Convention No. 105

87 The influential model of attitude change and formation of attitude is

(a) value elaboration model
(b) expectancy elaboration model
(c) elaboration likelihood model
(d) value likelihood model

88 Arrange the steps in manpower planning in the order in which they occur

1. identifying sources of manpower supply
2. manpower forecasting
3. determining manpower requirements
4. manpower invently
5. selection
6. recruitment
7. placement

Codes

(a) 3, 2, 4, 1, 6, 5, 7 (b) 1, 3, 2, 4, 5, 6, 7
(c) 4, 1, 2, 3, 6, 5, 7 (d) 3, 4, 1, 2, 6, 5, 7

89 Chronic Obstructive Pulmonary Disease (COPD) falls under which category of occupational disease?

(a) Lung Diseases
(b) Skin Diseases
(c) Lead Poisoning
(d) Vision Syndome

90 Which of the following statements are correct?

I It is a significant feature of human that he plans.
II A plan is a trap to capture the future.

(a) Statement I is correct, but Statement II is incorrect
(b) Statement II is correct, but Statement I is incorrect
(c) Both statements are correct
(d) Both statements are incorrect

91 In the OCTAPACE culture the letter 'C' denotes what?

(a) Climate
(b) Culture
(c) Communication
(d) Confrontation

92 Which is not normally an essential condition for an effective HRIS?

(a) Changing the HR manager
(b) Sustained enhancement of HRIS capabilities
(c) Ensuring clarity of goals related to HRIS
(d) Strengthening infrastructure and support system

93 Which of the following is considered as the first principle of management?

(a) Coordination
(b) Delegation
(c) Line, staff, auxiliary agencies
(d) Supervision

94 Which of the following is not a method of supply forecasting?

(a) Markov Analysis
(b) Replacement Chart
(c) Succession Planning
(d) Scatter Plot

95 No adolescent who has not been granted a medical certificate certifying that he is fit for work as an adult shall be employed above ground in any open cast workings in a mine for more than .... in any day.

(a) 3 hours 30 minutes (b) 7 hours 30 minutes
(c) 4 hours 30 minutes (d) 3 hours 30 minutes

96 Edward Deming argues that employee's performance is result of

(a) training communication (b) quality management
(c) own motivation (d) Both (a) and (b)

97 The Payment of Gratuity Act, 1972 is applicable to as establishment with a minimum of how many employee?

(a) 11 (b) 12 (c) 14 (d) 10

98 Which of the following is a barrier while doing human resource planning?

(a) HR information often is incompatible with the information used in strategy formulation
(b) Implementing human resource information system
(c) Managing inventories
(d) Supply forecast

99 Which section of the Contract Labour (regulation and abolition) Act, 1970 defines a contractor?

(a) 2(a) (b) 2(b) (c) 2(c) (d) 2(d)

100 Consider the following for the Minimum Wages Act, 1948.

1. The appropriate government will have the power to fix the minimum rates of wages payable to employees employed in an employment specified in Part I or Part II of the Schedules.
2. The appropriate government will review and revise the minimum rate of wages after five years.
3. The appropriate government will fix the minimum rate of wages in any scheduled employment in which there are in the whole state less than one thousand employees engaged in such employment.

Which of the following statement given above is/are correct?

Codes

(a) Both 1 and 2 (b) Only 1
(c) Only 2 (d) All of these

ANSWERS

1 (d)	2 (a)	3 (a)	4 (b)	5 (c)	6 (b)	7 (a)	8 (b)	9 (a)	10 (b)
11 (c)	12 (a)	13 (d)	14 (a)	15 (a)	16 (c)	17 (b)	18 (c)	19 (b)	20 (b)
21 (c)	22 (d)	23 (d)	24 (a)	25 (b)	26 (b)	27 (a)	28 (c)	29 (d)	30 (a)
31 (a)	32 (a)	33 (b)	34 (a)	35 (d)	36 (a)	37 (b)	38 (c)	39 (b)	40 (a)
41 (d)	42 (b)	43 (a)	44 (c)	45 (a)	46 (a)	47 (a)	48 (d)	49 (b)	50 (a)
51 (b)	52 (c)	53 (a)	54 (b)	55 (c)	56 (a)	57 (b)	58 (a)	59 (c)	60 (c)
61 (d)	62 (d)	63 (d)	64 (b)	65 (c)	66 (a)	67 (d)	68 (a)	69 (c)	70 (d)
71 (d)	72 (b)	73 (d)	74 (a)	75 (c)	76 (d)	77 (b)	78 (b)	79 (d)	80 (d)
81 (a)	82 (c)	83 (d)	84 (d)	85 (d)	86 (a)	87 (c)	88 (a)	89 (a)	90 (c)
91 (d)	92 (a)	93 (a)	94 (d)	95 (c)	96 (d)	97 (d)	98 (a)	99 (c)	100 (b)

HUMAN RESOURCE MANAGEMENT (Paper-2)

Model Paper-3

General Instructions

1. There are total one hundred questions in this paper. Each question carries 2 marks.
2. All questions are compulsory.

1 According to ......, the inequality exists in the market as all the workers do not acquire same sort of skills.

(a) the neo-classical market (b) classical market
(c) labour market (d) None of these

2 According to the efficiency wage model, firms will pay the real wage that

(a) maximises worker's marginal productivity
(b) maximises the marginal productivity of capital and the marginal productivity of labour together
(c) maximises efforts in ratio of real wage
(d) minimises hiring and training lost to firm

3 Match the following.

List I (School of Theories)	List II (Period of Development)
A. Classical Theory	1. 1890-1930
B. Behavioural Theory	2. 1930-1960
C. System Theory	3. 1965
D. Contingency Theory	4. 1960 onwards

Codes

	A	B	C	D		A	B	C	D
(a)	1	2	4	3	(b)	1	4	2	3
(c)	1	2	3	4	(d)	2	3	2	4

4 Which of the following are the characteristics of unorganised labour in India?

(a) A large number of them are below poverty line
(b) They are not educated
(c) They are migrant and dispersed all over the country
(d) All of the above

5 ...... represents the amount of goods that buyers are willing and able to purchase at various prices.

(a) Demand schedule (b) Demand curve
(c) Demand forecast (d) None of these

6 Assertion (A) People are sometimes more susceptible to persuasion when they are distracted by extraneous events.

Reason (R) Persuasion can be enhanced by messages that arouse strong emotions.

Codes

(a) Both (A) and (R) are true and (R) is the correct explanation of (A)
(b) Both (A) and (R) ar true, but (R) is not the correct explanation of (A)
(c) (A) is true, but (R) is false
(d) (A) is false, but (R) is true

7 Which of the following statements are true/false?

(i) Demands for goods is directly proportional to the labour market.
(ii) Marginal productivity is the addition made to the total production by subtracting one worker from the existing labour force.
(iii) Demand for labour is dependent on the elasticity of demand for product produced by the labour.
(iv) At higher wages, the demand for labour will be higher.

(a) (i), (ii) are true and (iii), (iv) are false
(b) (i), (iii) are true and (ii), (iv) are false
(c) (ii), (iv) are true and (i), (iii) are false
(d) (iii), (iv) are true and (ii), (i) are false

8 **Which of the following are the categories of labour force?**

(a) Self-employed workers and casual workers
(b) Unemployed and wage/salary earners
(c) Both (a) and (b)
(d) Neither (a) nor (b)

9 **The LFPR of females in India is among the lowest in the world. What does LFPR stand for?**

(a) Labour Force Participating Ratio
(b) Labour Force Participating Rate
(c) Labour Force Participating Ratio
(d) Labour Force Participation Rate

10 **Match the following.**

List I (School of Theories)	List II (Period of Development)
A. Newman & Summer	1. Organising, planning and controlling
B. Henry Fayol	2. Planning, organising commanding, coordinating and controlling
C. Luther Gullick	3. Planning, organising, staffing, directing, controlling
D. Koontz & O' Donnell	4. PODSCORB

Codes

	A	B	C	D		A	B	C	D
(a)	4	2	3	1	(b)	2	3	4	1
(c)	3	1	4	2	(d)	1	2	4	3

11 **Which of the following are the principles to channelise wage determination process?**

(a) Labour productivity
(b) Economic condition of industry
(c) Economic condition of nation
(d) All of the above

12 **What was the average LFPR among females in 2018?**

(a) 36.99 (b) 36.97 (c) 26.97 (d) 16.99

13 **Which of the following factor does not affect the wages?**

(a) Demand and supply of labour
(b) Labour unions
(c) Population of the city
(d) Cost of living

14 **Match the following.**

List I (Terms)	List II (Features)
A. Job analysis	1. Job classification
B. Wage administration	2. Merit rating
C. HRM	3. HR planning
D. Labour turnover	4. Termination

Codes

	A	B	C	D		A	B	C	D
(a)	1	3	2	4	(b)	1	2	3	4
(c)	1	4	2	3	(d)	4	2	1	3

15 **According to Mines Act, 1952, what will be the wages for the leave allowed to a person employed in a mine who is paid monthly or weekly?**

(a) Rate thrice of his normal daily wages
(b) Rate half to his normal daily wages
(c) Rate twice to his normal daily wages
(d) Rate equal to normal daily wages

16 **According to Minimum Wages Act, 1948, who is an adolescent?**

(a) A person who has completed his sixteenth year of age but has not completed his eighteenth year
(b) A person who has completed his twelfth year of age but has not completed his eighteenth year
(c) A person who has completed his fourteenth year of age but has not completed his eighteenth year
(d) A person who has completed his thirteenth year of age but has not completed his eighteenth year

17 **Match the following.**

List I (Theories)	List II (Developers)
A. X-Y Theory	1. McClelland
B. Hygiene Theory	2. F Herzberg
C. ERG Theory	3. Alderfer
D. Three Needs Theory	4. McGregor

Codes

	A	B	C	D		A	B	C	D
(a)	1	2	3	4	(b)	4	3	2	1
(c)	4	2	3	1	(d)	1	4	2	3

18 **Which organisation structure is generally followed by big steel plants?**

(a) Line organisation
(b) Functional organisation
(c) Line and staff organisation
(d) All of the above.

19 **Which of the following concepts are not associated with scientific management?**

1. Standardisation of tools 2. Unity of Direction
3. Equity 4. Scientific Selection
5. Differentiate Piece Rate Plan

Select the correct answer by using the codes given below

(a) 1, 2 and 4 (b) 2, 3 and 4
(c) Both 2 and 3 (d) 1, 4 and 3

20 **According to the Payment of Wages Act, 1936, an employer terminates an employee, the wages earned by him must be paid by when?**

(a) Before the expiry of the second working day from the day on which his employment is terminated
(b) Before the expiry of the fifth working day from the day on which him employment is terminated
(c) Before the expiry of the fourth working day from the day on which his employment is terminated
(d) Before the expiry of the third working day from the day on which his employment is terminated

21 **Which section of the Inter-state Workman Act, 1979, defines a controlled industry?**

(a) 2(a) (b) 2(b) (c) 2(d) (d) 2(c)

22 **Which of the following is incorrect about principle of social justice?**

(a) The profits and benefits must be equally distributed among the workers
(b) The workers needs to be provided safe and good working conditions at their workplaces
(c) Both the employers and employees need to understand that they are two wheels of a cart and they cannot exist without each other
(d) They are helpful in improving the social status of workers by improving their economic status

23 **According to the Inter-state Migrant Workman Rules, the application by a contractor for the grant of a licence for employing a person must be issued in which form?**

(a) Form I (b) Form III (c) Form V (d) Form II

24 **Which of the following laws is not related to Industrial Relations?**

(a) Trade Unions Act, 1926
(b) Industrial Employment (Standing Order) Act, 1946
(c) Industrial Disputes Act, 1947
(d) Factories Act, 1948

25 **According to Inter-state Workman Rules, 1980, a creche needs to be provided in every establishment where how many female workers are working?**

(a) 20 (b) 30 (c) 40 (d) 50

26 **Match the following.**

	List I		List II
A.	Achievement test	1.	Testing verbal comprehension, word fluency, memory
B.	Intelligence test	2.	Testing the knowledge about the claims
C.	Personality test	3.	Testing one's level of interest in an area
D.	Aptitude test	4.	Testing about inter-personal competence, leadership, confidence
E.	Interest test	4.	Testing the ability to do a specific job

Codes

	A	B	C	D	E
(a)	2	1	4	5	3
(b)	5	4	3	2	1
(c)	1	2	3	4	5
(d)	3	2	4	5	1

27 **Apart from pay what is the second most common reason for employees to join a trade union?**

(a) Group solidarity
(b) Political reasons
(c) Friendship groups
(d) Wide range of personal details

28 **Which of the following is not a principle of ILO basis Declaration of Philadelphia?**

(a) Labour is not a commodity
(b) Freedom of expression and cordial relationship are essential to the substantial progress
(c) Unemployment constitutes a danger to prosperity everywhere
(d) The war against want requires to be carried on with unrelenting vigour within each nation, and by continuous and concerted international effort in which the representatives of workers and employers, enjoying equal status with those of governments, join with them in free discussion and democratic decision with a view to the promotion of the common welfare

29 **Where can an appeal be made on any refusal of a Registrar to register a trade union or cancellation of Registration?**

(a) Where the head office of the trade is situated
(b) To High Court
(c) Either (a) or (b)
(d) None of the above

30 **Which of the following is not the main provisions to be contained in the rules of a trade union?**

(a) The objects for which the trade union has been established
(b) List of the members of the trade union
(c) The manner of election of office-bearers
(d) Detailed profile of the members of the trade union

31 **Which of the following points is not important for training?**

1. Reduction in supervision 2. Reduction in cost
3. Increased stability 4. Easy coordination
5. Improvement in industrial relations

Select the correct answer by using the codes given below

Codes

(a) 1, 3 and 5 (b) 1, 2 and 3
(c) All of the above (d) None of the above

32 **Which of the following is not a physical hazard?**

(a) Excessive noise
(b) Irregularities in temperature and pressure
(c) Dust because of an industrial process
(d) Ionizing rediations

33 **Under which of the following recording and notification of occupational accidents and diseases should be done?**

(a) Occupational Safety and Health Protocol, 2002
(b) Promotional Framework for Occupational Safety and Health Convention, 2006
(c) Occupational Health Services Convention, 1985
(d) Occupational Safety and Health Convention, 1981

34 **Which of the following theories state that it is the duty and responsibility of wealthy people to help the underprivileged people?**

(a) Placating theory (b) Policing theory
(c) Religious theory (d) Philanthropic theory

35 Which of the following are examples of compensable factors?

1. Technical skills, conceptual skills, inter-personal skills.
2. Experience or length of working years.
3. Efforts and initiative.
4. Responsibilities to be undertaken.
5. Supervision required.
6. Working environment in which job is to be performed.
7. Gender of the employee.

(a) 2, 3, 4, 7 (b) 1, 4, 5, 6
(c) 1, 2, 3, 4, 7 (d) 1, 2, 3, 4, 5, 6

36 Which of the following is incorrect about secondary strikes?

(a) In this a third party is involved
(b) These are more common in the United States
(c) These are very common in India
(d) The union strikes against the third party

37 According to the International Labour Organisation (ILO), which of the following is/are covered under economic disputes?

(a) A rights dispute
(b) An interest dispute
(c) Collective disputes
(d) Both (a) and (b)

38 Assertion (A) Ethnocentric approach is easily adaptable.

Reason (R) The vision, mission and objective of the parent company can be easily adopted by the subsidiaries.

Codes

(a) (A) is true, but (R) is false
(b) (A) is false, but (R) is true
(c) (R) does not subscribe to the (A)
(d) Both (A) and (R) are true and (R) validate (A)

39 In organising industrial action, a union is encouraging its members to break their contractual obligation to attend work. Is this action.

(a) protected by union immunity
(b) unlawful
(c) referred to as wild cat strike
(d) such that employers can see the union for loss of earnings

40 A union meant to protect the interests and rights of the non-manual employees is called a

(a) white collar union
(b) brown collar union
(c) blue collar union
(d) None of the above

41 Which of the following is correct for lockout?

(a) It is the counterpart of layoffs
(b) This is the extreme weapon in the hands of employees
(c) The employer temporarily suspends the work
(d) The employer makes the worker agree to their demand

42 Which among the following is the basic source of stress?

(a) Environment (b) Financial problems
(c) Relationship problems (d) All of these

43 The operationalised dependent variable in Tolman's experiment was

(a) the number of groups of rats
(b) whether rats were shown cheese originally
(c) the amount of electric shocks the rats were given
(d) the time it took the rats to solve the maze

44 Match the following articles and directive policies.

	List I		List II
A.	Equal right to an adequate means to livelihood	1.	Article 42
B.	Maternity relief	2.	Article 39
C.	Ensuring a decent standard of life and full enjoyment of leisure and social and cultural opportunities	3.	Article 41
D.	Right to work	4.	Article 43

Codes

	A	B	C	D		A	B	C	D
(a)	1	3	4	2	(b)	2	1	4	3
(c)	3	1	4	2	(d)	1	3	2	4

45 Who among the following used the term 'collective bargaining' for the first time?

(a) FW Taylor (b) Henry Fayol
(c) Elton Mayo (d) Beatrice Webb

46 Which of the following are general costs incurred in the recruitment process?

(a) Costs of material
(b) Costs of overtime and outsourcing while the vacancies remain unfilled
(c) Costs of property
(d) None of the above

47 Which of the following is not a feature of collective bargaining?

(a) It is a group action in which both the employer and employees are represented by groups and not individuals
(b) It is a continuous and tripartite process
(c) This process involves negotiations between the parties
(d) It is a complementary process

48 Arrange the school of personalities in the order of acceptance from older days.

(a) Psychodynamic, Trait, Humanistic, Social Learning
(b) Trait, Humanistic, Psychodynamic, Social Learning
(c) Humanistic, Psychodynamic, Trait, Social Learning
(d) None of the above

49 Which theory assumes that labour welfare programs are advertisements?

(a) Placating theory (b) Public Relations theory
(c) Efficiency theory (d) Trusteeship theory

50 Under which section of Industrial Employment Act, 1946 is the trade union defined?
(a) 2(a) (b) 2(b) (c) 2(j) (d) 2(h)

51 Which of the following is not true?
(a) Behaviour differs from one individual to other
(b) Behaviour is learnt, acquired and modified
(c) Behaviour is always purposeful
(d) Behaviour is a stable concept

52 Which of the following statements are true/false?
(i) Retrenchment does not include voluntary retirement of workman.
(ii) Retrenchment compensation becomes eligible for fifteen days wage for every completed year.
(iii) Termination as a result of non-renewal of contract of employment falls under retrenchment.
(iv) A notice should be exhibited 20 days before filling the vacancy.
(a) (i), (ii) are true and (iii), (iv) are false
(b) (i), (iii) are true and (ii), (iv) are false
(c) (ii), (iv) are true and (i), (iii) are false
(d) (iii), (iv) are true and (ii), (i) are false

53 Which of the following is not the advantage of delegation?
(a) It causes lack of trust in subordinates
(b) It improves managerial effectiveness
(c) It facilitates organisational growth
(d) It motivates subordinates

54 Match the following.

List I (Concepts)	List II (Examples)
A. Group	1. Cognition
B. Theory of personality	2. Id
C. Perception	3. Strategic groups
D. Industrial groups	4. Conflicts

Codes

	A	B	C	D
(a)	4	2	1	3
(b)	1	2	3	4
(c)	4	3	2	1
(d)	3	1	2	4

55 The code of discipline is based on which of the following principles?
(a) No strike or lock-out without prior notice
(b) No deliberate damage to a plant or property of the establishment
(c) Usage of existing machinery for settlement of disputes
(d) All of the above

56 Consider the following statements for the perfect market. Which of the following statement(s) is/are correct?
1. All the buyers and sellers have freedom to make entry or exit at any time in the market.
2. There are a large number of small undifferentiated buyers.
3. A single price prevail in the market.
Codes
(a) Only 1 (b) Both 2 and 3
(c) Both 1 and 3 (d) All of these

57 Match the following.

	List I		List I
A.	INTUC (Indian National Trade Union Congress)	1.	Bhartiya Janta Party
B.	BMS (Bhartiya Mazdoor Sangh)	2.	CPI (Right)
C.	HMS (Hind Mazdoor Sabha)	3.	Socialist Party
D.	AITUC (All India Trade Union Congress)	4.	CPI (Marxist)
E.	CITU (Centre of Indian Trade Union)	5.	Congress

Codes

	A	B	C	D	E
(a)	1	2	3	4	5
(b)	5	1	3	2	4
(c)	3	2	1	4	5
(d)	5	4	3	2	1

58 Committee on conventions is related to the working of which of the following international organisation?
(a) World Trade Organisation (WTO)
(b) World Bank
(c) International Monetary Fund (IMF)
(d) International Labour Organisation (ILO)

59 According to McGregor, what contributes towards the leadership?
(a) Knowledge
(b) Consistent discipline
(c) Atmosphere of approval
(d) All of the above

60 'Theory Y' states that
(a) workers prefer to be directed
(b) workers exercise self-direction and self-control
(c) workers have inherent disliking for work and will avoid it if they can
(d) workers do not work on their own

61 Which of the following statement implies motivation correctly?
(a) Exert more effort to accomplish the desired goals of the organisation
(b) Exert more efforts to accomplish the individual goals
(c) Exert more effort to accomplish the common goals of employees
(d) Exert more effort to accomplish the desired goals of the employer, employees and the government

62 Schein has identified a number of environmental, membership and dynamic factors for
(a) satisfaction of individual needs
(b) attainment of organisational goals
(c) integration of individual needs and organisational goals
(d) None of the above

63 **Kochan and Barooci's (1985) model of HRM includes which elements?**
(a) HRM/IR Systems effectiveness, extend and internal environment
(b) External environment, HRM/IR System, internal environment
(c) HRM, internal environment, HRM/IR system effectiveness
(d) External environment, HRM, HRM/IR system effectiveness

64 **Which of the following is not a feature of development?**
(a) It is an education process
(b) It is a process for a specific period of time
(c) It causes behavioural changes
(d) It leads to self-development

65 **Which of the following statements are true/false?**
(i) India predominantly has small trade unions that make them weaker in front of the management.
(ii) Most of the trade unions are associated with a single ruling political party.
(iii) The workers have no idea about their rights and lack the basic knowledge and education they must have in order to discharge their duties well.
(iv) The leaders of trade unions are more focused on delivering the value to their political party instead of working for the welfare of their labourers/workers.
(a) (i), (iii), (iv) are true and (ii) is false
(b) (i), (iii) are true and (ii), (iv) are false
(c) (ii), (iv) are true and (i), (iii) are false
(d) (iii), (iv) are true and (ii), (i) are false

66 **Why is it important to ensure that HR plans are flexible?**
(a) To adapt the fast changing environment in which most organisations operate
(b) To accommodate the changes arising because of high attrition rate
(c) To ensure the availability of labour force at all times
(d) To adapt the changing skills and qualifications of all the professions

67 **One of the major issues concerning the political impact of transnational corporations is that they**
(a) are eager to cooperate with international organisations
(b) strengthen the political independence of countries
(c) major supports of spread of democracy
(d) effectively erode state sovereignity

68 **Assertion** (A) The conciliating officer cannot force the involved parties to accept the decision in order to arrive at a settlement.
Reason (R) The conciliating officer is a facilitator.
Codes
(a) Both (A) and (R) are correct and (R) is the correct explanation of (A)
(b) Both (A) and (R) are correct, but (R) is not the correct explanation of (A)
(c) (A) is correct, but (R) is incorrect
(d) (A) is incorrect, but (R) is correct

69 **Which of the following can be referred as the best description of learning organisation?**
(a) An organisation which helps the managers to get promotions
(b) An organisation which does lots of training sessions on an adhoc basis
(c) An organisation which facilitates the learning of all its members and continuously transforms itself
(d) An organisation which encourages all its member to learn

70 **Which of the following statements is/are incorrect?**
(a) Living wage is the highest wage
(b) Minimum wage is a dynamic concept which grows in line with the growth of the national economy
(c) Fair wage is that which is above the minimum wage, but below the living wage
(d) All of the above

71 **Which one of the following represents a state of a career development cycle?**
(a) Freedom and independence
(b) Decline stage
(c) Three time frames
(d) Growth and development of employees

72 **Which of the following statement is not correct with regard to organisational analysis?**
(a) It is the analysis conducted to ascertain the progress of the company towards attainment of its objectives and goals
(b) This comprises of scanning the environment for opportunities and threats and evaluating the strengths and weakness internally
(c) It aims at improving current performance which includes specifically training new workers and those whose performance is inadequate
(d) Strategic training needs analysis describes the training workers will need to fill these jobs in the future which is done by organisational analysis

73 **Which of the following is the correct sequence of evaluating training efforts?**
(a) Reaction, Learning, Behaviour, Result
(b) Reaction, Behaviour, Learning, Result
(c) Reaction, Behaviour, Result, Learning
(d) Learning, Reaction, Behaviour, Result

74 **Minimum Wages Act, 1948 provides for setting up a tripartite body consisting of**
(a) employees
(b) union
(c) government
(d) All of these

75 **Which of the following statements are true/false?**
(i) The employer shall submit to the Certifying Officer five copies of the draft standing orders within six months from the date on which Industrial Employment Act, 1946 becomes applicable to an industrial establishment.

(ii) The draft standing orders submitted shall be accompanied by a statement giving prescribed particulars of the organisation.
(iii) A group of employers in similar industrial establishments may submit a joint draft of standing orders
(iv) Section 4 of the Industrial Employment Act, 1946 deals with the conditions for certifications of standing order.
(a) (i), (iv) are true and (ii), (iii) are false
(b) (i), (iii) are true and (ii), (iv) are false
(c) (ii), (iv) are true and (i), (iii) are false
(d) (iii), (iv) are true and (ii), (i) are false

76 Identify the odd one out.
(a) Physiological Features: Physique, height, weight, sight and endurance
(b) Personal Characteristics: Marital status, size of family and economic position
(c) Proficiency: Qualification, training and experience
(d) Competency : Mental and emotional stability, honesty, loyalty and social skills

77 Why is the classical theory of organisation known as mechanistic theory?
(a) Because it has formal declared pattern of relationship established by law
(b) Because it does not explain the dynamics of organisational behaviours
(c) Because it underestimated human factor and oversimplified human motivation
(d) Because it treats organisation as a closed system unconcerned with and uninfluenced by its external environment

78 A performance rating system is
(a) a grade or score relating to overall performance
(b) financial targets accomplished during the year
(c) attendance of the individual during the year
(d) None of the above

79 Decision-making situations can be categorised along a scale which range from
(a) certainty to risk to uncertainty to ambiguity
(b) certainty to uncertainty to risk
(e) certainty to risk to uncertainty
(d) uncertainty to certainty to risk

80 Which is not an assumption of action-research?
(a) Results enable to evaluate performance of others
(b) Researchers have basic research skills to analyse data
(c) Professionals need and want feedback on their performance
(d) People are capable of assuming responsibility for their own professional growth

81 Which of the following is not a part of basic seven quality control tools?
(a) Check sheets and pareto chart
(b) Ishikawa diagram, scatter, plot
(c) Flow diagram, histogram, control chart
(d) Correlation and regression

82 **Assertion** (A) No stationary internal combustion engine should be operated in the factory.
Reason (R) The factory needs to take effective measures to prevent the inhalation of dust and fumes that are injurious and offensive to health.
(a) Both (A) and (R) are correct and (R) is the correct explanation of (A)
(b) Both (A) and (R) are correct, but (R) is not the correct explanation of (A)
(c) (A) is correct, but (R) is incorrect
(d) (A) is incorrect, but (R) is correct

83 The greatest weakness of the informal organisation is
(a) its utter instability
(b) its behaviour can be predicted
(c) it does not change
(d) All of the above

84 Which of the following statement(s) is/are correct with TNA?
(a) It is the method of assessing the gap between training of employees and training needs
(b) It identifies the gap between present and essential levels of knowledge, skills and attitude. It makes the most of use of scarce resources
(c) It confirms that appropriate and relevant training is delivered
(d) All of the above

85 Hawthorne studies lead to the development of
(a) scientific management
(b) one best method of doing the work
(c) specialisation
(d) human relations

86 **Assertion** (A) The Central Government may frame a scheme to be called the Employees' Deposit-linked Insurance Scheme for the purpose of providing life insurance benefits to the employees of any establishment or class of establishments to which this act applies.
Reason (R) As soon as may be after the framing of the Insurance scheme, a Deposit-linked Insurance Fund shall be established.
Codes
(a) Both (A) and (R) are true and (R) is the correct explanation of (A)
(b) Both (A) and (R) are true, but (R) is not the correct explanation of (A)
(c) (A) is true, but (R) is false
(d) (A) is false, but (R) is true

87 Which of the following are the main reasons for re-designing jobs to have better quality of work life?
(a) Classical design originally gave inadequate attention to human needs
(b) The needs and aspirations of workers themselves were changing
(c) Both (a) and (b)
(d) Neither (a) nor (b)

88 **Which of the following are the decisions to be made while devising the strategies to hire?**

(a) Geographic distribution of labour markets comprising job seekers
(b) Make or buy employees
(c) Sequencing the activities in the recruitment process
(d) All of the above

89 **Which of the following statements are true about human relations theory of organisations?**

(a) It rejects formal institutionalisation
(b) It considers the informal structure more effective
(c) It assumes organisational behaviour is a complex phenomenon
(d) All of the above

90 **Which of the following is not a methods to provide work life balance?**

(a) Compressed workweek (b) Promotion
(c) Flexitime (d) Adequate leaves

91 **The final process of a job analysis is the preparation of two statements, namely,**

(a) job observation and job description
(b) job specification and job observation
(c) job description and job specification
(d) None of the above

92 **'On-the-job' training can be provided through**

(a) non-formal education (b) mobile teacher
(c) distance education (d) All of these

93 **Which of the following statements are true/false?**

(i) The term 'collective bargaining' was first used by Sidney Webb.
(ii) ILO Convention No. 154 defines collective bargaining as all negotiations which take place between an employer, a group of employers or one or more employers' organisations, on the one hand, and one or more workers' organisations.
(iii) Collective bargaining is a one-sided affair as the trade unions are too powerful to be challenged by management.
(iv) In collective bargaining, the employer and employees are represented by groups and not individuals.

(a) (i), (iv) are true and (ii), (iii) are false
(b) (i), (iii) are true and (ii), (iv) are false
(c) (ii), (iv) are true and (i), (iii) are false
(d) (iii), (iv) are true and (ii), (i) are false

94 **Which of the following statements are true/false?**

(i) In case, an employee whose minimum rate of wages is fixed under this Act, works overtime, the employer need not pay the money for the extra hours devoted by the employee.
(ii) If an employee whose minimum rate of wages has been fixed under this Act, works for a less number of hours than the requisite number of hours on a given day, he shall be entitled to receive wages in respect of work done by him on that day as if he had worked for a full normal working day.
(iii) In case, an employee is involved in two or more classes of work, he shall be paid on the basis of pieces involved.
(iv) If an employee is employed on piece work for which minimum time rate and not a minimum piece rate has been fixed under this Act, the employer shall pay to such employee wages at not less than the minimum time rate.

(a) (i), (iv) are true and (ii), (iii) are false
(b) (i), (iii) are true and (ii), (iv) are false
(c) (ii), (iv) are true and (i), (iii) are false
(d) (iii), (iv) are true and (ii), (i) are false

95 **The main difference between delegation and decentralisation are**

1. Delegation involves transfer of authority and not responsibility, where as decentralisation involves transfer of authority and responsibility.
2. Decentralisation is by the will of the superior, while delegation is done legally.
3. Distributing authority can take place at will while in decentralisation it requires a legal action.

Select the correct answer by using the codes given below

(a) Both 1 and 2 (b) Both 1 and 3
(c) Both 2 and 3 (d) All of the above

96 **Match the following with their correct convention number.**

	List I		List II
A.	Occupational Safety and Health Convention, 1981	1.	161
B.	Occupational Health Services Convention, 1985	2.	155
C.	Promotional Framework for Occupational Safety and Health Convention, 2006	3.	187

Codes

	A	B	C		A	B	C
(a)	1	2	3	(b)	2	1	3
(c)	1	3	2	(d)	3	2	1

Directions (Q. Nos. 97-99) *Read the following passage and answer the questions that follow.*

For years the managerial philosophers had called management's attention to its total responsibility. The indication of a moral oughtness was there, they stressed. As stewards for stockholders, managers had a prime to the employees, the customers, and the community -along with their well-recognised responsibility to the owners. By and large, these early pronouncements apparently fell on deaf ears. By the mid-thirties, however, heartening signs began to appear. In 1937, for example, Raymond Moley declared that while management remained legally and ethically a primary agent of the investor, its secondary responsibility to the public and labour had become relatively greater. Four years later, Roger Lapham asserted that in the narrow sense of the past, management had been considered solely responsible to its ownership - its stockholders - but there was a growing conviction that in the broader sense management's duty to its customers, to the public, and to its employees came first. By 1951, this view was well-established, and Frank Abraham's writing in the Harvard Business Review enunciated the new philosophy when he indicated that the job of management was to conduct the affairs of the enterprise in such a way as to maintain an equitable balance among the claims of the variously interested groups. In the mid-sixties and early seventies, we have again recognised changes in philosophy that reflect management's gradual assumption of its moral and social obligation of good corporate citizenship. We see it, for example, in management's assuming its social responsibility by cooperating with the federal government in withholding goods from countries if those goods would jeopardise our national security, in maintaining prices at a level consistent with a healthy economy, not raising them to a point considered critically inflationary, in training the unemployed, in cleaning up city ghettos, and in recognising and acting upon pollution problems. More examples could be cited, but the point of the broadened view taken by management of its total responsibility has been made.

97 Raymond Moley advocated management's responsibility to
- (a) owners of organisation only
- (b) owners and employees only
- (c) owners, public and labour
- (d) owners, public, labour and customers

98 Which of the following is not a part of corporate social responsibility?
- (a) Controlling prices to prevent inflation
- (b) Training of employees
- (c) Acting upon pollution related problems
- (d) Jeopardising the security of nation

99 Corporate social responsibility comprises of the following.
- (a) Moral obligations of an organisation
- (b) Social obligations of an organisation
- (c) Moral and social obligations of an organisation
- (d) None of the above

100 Which of the following is correct for the definition of 'Factory' as per the Factories Act, 1948?

1. It includes any premises whereon ten or more workers are working.
2. Manufacturing process is being carried on with the aid of power.
3. It includes any premises where 20 or more workers are working, or were working on any day of the preceding twelve months.

(a) Both 1 and 2 (b) Both 2 and 3
(c) Both 1and 3 (d) All of the above

ANSWERS

1 *(a)*	2 *(c)*	3 *(a)*	4 *(d)*	5 *(a)*	6 *(b)*	7 *(b)*	8 *(c)*	9 *(d)*	10 *(d)*
11 *(d)*	12 *(c)*	13 *(c)*	14 *(b)*	15 *(d)*	16 *(c)*	17 *(c)*	18 *(c)*	19 *(c)*	20 *(a)*
21 *(d)*	22 *(d)*	23 *(c)*	24 *(d)*	25 *(a)*	26 *(a)*	27 *(b)*	28 *(c)*	29 *(c)*	30 *(d)*
31 *(c)*	32 *(c)*	33 *(a)*	34 *(d)*	35 *(c)*	36 *(c)*	37 *(d)*	38 *(d)*	39 *(d)*	40 *(b)*
41 *(d)*	42 *(d)*	43 *(d)*	44 *(b)*	45 *(d)*	46 *(b)*	47 *(b)*	48 *(d)*	49 *(b)*	50 *(d)*
51 *(d)*	52 *(a)*	53 *(a)*	54 *(a)*	55 *(d)*	56 *(d)*	57 *(b)*	58 *(d)*	59 *(d)*	60 *(b)*
61 *(d)*	62 *(b)*	63 *(d)*	64 *(b)*	65 *(a)*	66 *(a)*	67 *(d)*	68 *(a)*	69 *(c)*	70 *(b)*
71 *(b)*	72 *(c)*	73 *(a)*	74 *(d)*	75 *(b)*	76 *(d)*	77 *(b)*	78 *(a)*	79 *(a)*	80 *(a)*
81 *(d)*	82 *(a)*	83 *(a)*	84 *(d)*	85 *(d)*	86 *(b)*	87 *(c)*	88 *(d)*	89 *(d)*	90 *(b)*
91 *(c)*	92 *(d)*	93 *(c)*	94 *(c)*	95 *(b)*	96 *(b)*	97 *(c)*	98 *(b)*	99 *(c)*	100 *(d)*